Sentencing and Penal Policy in Canada

Cases, Materials, and Commentary

SECOND EDITION

Allan Manson
Faculty of Law
Queen's University

Patrick Healy
Cour du Québec
Montréal

Gary Trotter
Superior Court
of Justice
(Ontario)

Julian Roberts
Faculty of Law
Oxford University

Dale Ives
Faculty of Law
University of Western Ontario

2008
EMOND MONTGOMERY PUBLICATIONS
TORONTO, CANADA

Emond Montgomery Publications Limited
60 Shaftesbury Avenue
Toronto ON M4T 1A3
http://www.emp.ca/lawschool

Printed in Canada.
Reprinted August 2012.

We acknowledge the financial support of the Government of Canada through the Canada Book Fund for our publishing activities.

Acquisitions and developmental editor: Peggy Buchan
Marketing manager: Christine Davidson
Sales coordinator: Jenna Williams
Copy and production editor: Nancy Ennis
Production editor: David Handelsman
Proofreader: Paula Pike

Library and Archives Canada Cataloguing in Publication

Sentencing and penal policy in Canada : cases, materials, and commentary / Allan Manson ... [et al.]. — 2nd ed.

Previous ed. written by: Allan Manson, Patrick Healy, Gary Trotter.
ISBN 978-1-55239-217-1

1. Sentences (Criminal procedure)—Canada. 2. Sentences (Criminal procedure)—Canada—Cases. 3. Alternatives to imprisonment—Canada. I. Manson, Allan II. Manson, Allan. Sentencing and penal policy in Canada.

KE9355.S45 2008   345.71'0772   C2008-901564-9
KF9685.S45 2008

Acknowledgments

This book, like others of its nature, contains extracts from published material. We have attempted to request permission from, and to acknowledge in the text, all sources of this material. We wish to make specific reference here to the authors, publishers, journals, and institutions that have been generous in giving their permission to reproduce works in this text. If we have inadvertently overlooked any acknowledgment, we offer our sincere apologies and will undertake to rectify the omission in future editions.

Bonta and Gendreau. "Re-examining the Cruel and Unusual Punishment of Prison Life," by J. Bonta and P. Gendreau, 14 *Law and Human Behaviour* 347, 1990.

Cambridge University Press. Excerpt from *Trials and Punishments*, by R.A. Duff, pp. 195-204, 1986. Reprinted with the permission of Cambridge University Press.

Canadian Criminal Justice Association. "Community Sanctions and Imprisonment: Hoping for a Miracle but Not Bothering Even to Pray for It," by A. Doob, 32 *Canadian Journal of Criminology and Criminal Justice* 415, 1990.

Canadian Criminal Justice Association. "The Renewal of Parole," by F.E. Gibson, *Canadian Journal of Criminology and Criminal Justice*, vol. 32, no. 3, pp. 487-91, July 1990.

Department of Justice Canada. "Aboriginal Peoples and Criminal Justice: Equality, Respect and the Search for Justice," Law Reform Commission of Canada, Report 34, 1991. Reproduced with the permission of the Minister of Public Works and Government Services Canada, 2008.

Department of Justice Canada. "Sentencing Reform: A Canadian Approach," Report of the Sentencing Commission, 1987. Reproduced with the permission of the Minister of Public Works and Government Services Canada, 2008.

Department of Justice Canada. "The Jury," Law Reform Commission of Canada, Report 16, 1982. Reproduced with the permission of the Minister of Public Works and Government Services Canada, 2008.

Department of Justice Canada. "Victim Impact Statements at Sentencing: Judicial Experiences and Perceptions—A Survey of Three Jurisdictions," Research and Statistics—Research Report, http://www.justice.gc.ca/eng/pi/rs/rep-rap/2006/rr06_vic3/index.html, Department of Justice, Revised 2006. Reproduced with the permission of the Minister of Public Works and Government Services Canada, 2008.

Erez. "Who's Afraid of the Big Bad Victim? Victim Impact Statements as Victim Empowerment and Enhancement of Justice," by E. Erez, *The Criminal Law Review*, 1999.

International Centre for Prison Studies. "Comparative Prison Populations," by R. Walmsley, *World Prison Population List*, 6th edition, King's College, London, 2006.

Irwin. "Mitigating Factors," by Allan Manson, from *The Law of Sentencing*, pp. 64-79, Irwin Law Books, Toronto, 2000.

Manson. "The Easy Acceptance of Long Term Confinement," by Allan Manson, 79 *Criminal Reports* (3d), 265, 1990.

National Parole Board. "Federal Full Parole Outcomes," National Parole Board, 2006. Copyright © Minister of Public Works and Government Services Canada, 2000.

Oxford University Press. Excerpt from *Censure and Sanctions*, by A. von Hirsch, pp. 9-13, Oxford, 1993. By permission of Oxford University Press Inc.

Oxford University Press. Excerpt from *Crime, Guilt and Punishment*, by C.L. Ten, Clarendon Press, Oxford, 1987. By permission of Oxford University Press Inc.

Oxford University Press. Excerpt from *Not Just Deserts—A Republican Theory of Criminal Justice*, by J. Braithwaite and P. Pettit, Oxford, 1990. By permission of Oxford University Press Inc.

Oxford University Press. Excerpt from *Punishment, Communication and Community*, by R.A. Duff, pp. 129-30, Oxford, 2003. By permission of Oxford University Press Inc.

Oxford University Press. Excerpt from *Punishment and Responsibility: Essays in the Philosophy of Law*, by H.L.A. Hart, pp. 11-19, Oxford, 1967. By permission of Oxford University Press Inc.

Purich Publishing. Excerpts from *Justice in Aboriginal Communities: Sentencing Alternatives*, by R.G. Green, Purich Publishing, 1998. By permission of Purich Publishing, Saskatoon.

Privy Council Office. "Bridging the Cultural Divide: A Report on Aboriginal People and Criminal Justice in Canada," p. 8, 1996. Reproduced with the permission of the Minister of Public Works and Government Services Canada, 2008, and Courtesy of the Privy Council Office.

Public Safety Canada. "A Work in Progress—The Corrections and Conditional Release Act—2000," from Subcommittee on Corrections and Conditional Release Act of the Standing Committee on Justice and Human Rights, 2000. Reproduced with the permission of the Minister of Public Works and Government Services Canada, 2008.

Public Safety Canada. "Recidivism Among Homicide Offenders," from Forum on Corrections Research, Correctional Service Canada, 1992. Reproduced with the permission of the Minister of Public Works and Government Services Canada, 2008.

PWGSC. "Federal Releases from Institutions," from Correctional Service of Canada, Statistical Overview, 2006. Reproduced with the permission of the Minister of Public Works and Government Services Canada, 2008.

Queen's Printer for Ontario. "Report of the Attorney General's Advisory Committee on Charge Screening, Disclosure, and Resolutions Discussions," by G.A. Martin, Department of the Attorney General for Ontario, 1993. © Queen's Printer for Ontario, 2002. Reprinted with permission.

Roberts. "Victim Impact Statements: Recent Developments and Research Findings," by J.V. Roberts, from 47 *Criminal Law Quarterly* 365, 2003.

Roberts and Jackson. "Boats Against the Current: A Note on the Effects of Imprisonment," by J.V. Roberts and M. Jackson, from 15 *Law and Human Behaviour* 557, 1991.

Saskatchewan Law Review. The following articles are reprinted with permission: (1) "Empty Promises: Parliament, the Supreme Court, and the Sentencing of Aboriginal Offenders," by P. Stenning and J. Roberts, 2001, 64 *Saskatchewan Law Review* 137; (2) Colloquy based on "Empty Promises," by Stenning and Roberts, 2001: (a) "Broken Promises: A Response to Stenning and Roberts' 'Empty Promises,'" by J. Rudin and K. Roach, 2002, *Saskatchewan Law Review* 3; (b) "Of Fairness and Faulkner," by M. Carter, 2002, *Saskatchewan Law Review* 63; (c) "On the Sentencing of Aboriginal Offenders: A Reaction to Stenning and Roberts," by Jean-Paul Brooder, 2002, *Saskatchewan Law Review* 45; (d) "Seeing and Not Seeing: Explaining Mis-Recognition in the Criminal Justice System," by Alan Cairns, 2002, *Saskatchewan Law Review* 53; (3) "The Sentencing of Aboriginal Offenders in Canada: A Rejoinder," by J.V. Roberts and P. Stenning, 2002, *Saskatchewan Law Review* 7.

Statistics Canada. (1) "Admissions to Provincial and Territorial Custody, Canada, 1978-79 to 2003-4," Corrections Canada; (2) "Adult Correctional Services, Incarceration in Canada," 1996, adapted from the Statistics Canada publication "Juristat," Catalogue 85-002, vol. 26, no. 5, released October 11, 2006, URL: http://www.statcan.ca/english/freepub/85-002-XIE/85-002-XIE2006005.pdf; (3) "Provincial Variations in Aboriginal Admissions to Custody, 1978-79 to 2003-4," Corrections Canada; (4) "The Number of Aboriginal Offenders Under Federal Jurisdiction Is Increasing," Corrections Canada, Minister of Public Works and Government Services Canada, 2008.

Taylor and Francis. Excerpts from *State Punishment: Political Principles and Community Values*, by N. Lacey. Copyright © 1988, Routledge. Reproduced by permission of Taylor and Francis Books, UK.

Tonry. "Proportionality, Parsimony, and Interchangeability of Punishments," by M. Tonry, from R. A. Duff, S. Marshall, R. Dabash, and R. Dabash, eds., *Penal Theory and Practice: Tradition and Innovation in Criminal Justice*, Manchester University Press, 1994.

University of Chicago Law School. "Reconceptualizing Punishment: Understanding the Limitations and the Use of Intermediate Sanctions," by A. Doob and V. Marinos, 2 *Chicago Law School Roundtable* 413, 1995. Reprinted with the permission of the University of Chicago Law School.

University of Chicago Press. "Proportionality in the Philosophy of Punishment," by A. von Hirsch, from *Crime and Justice: A Review of Research XVI*, pp. 55-98. Copyright © University of Chicago Press, 1992.

University of Chicago Press. Excerpt from *Punishment and Modern Society: A Study in Social Theory*, by D. Garland, pp. 204-6. Copyright © University of Chicago Press, 1990.

Preface to the Second Edition

When Gary, Patrick, and I approached our publisher with the first edition, we had been teaching sentencing courses for a number of years. We brought different perspectives to the subject but we shared the view that sentencing was an integral and challenging subject that deserved a place in every law school. Courses in criminal law and criminal procedure leave little time, if any, for sentencing issues. It was our hope that the publication of that book would encourage other teachers to engage in the sentencing discourse and offer their own courses. It was also our hope that we might promote a more informed and refined sentencing debate in academic, judicial, and policy circles.

We have had some success. There are now more sentencing courses in law schools. However, Canada still lags behind much of the western world in providing a forum for a serious debate about sentencing principles, objectives, and policies. One can look at the United Kingdom, Australia, New Zealand, and the United States and see sentencing commissions, working groups, task forces, councils, and advisory panels struggling with the hard questions of sentencing. The same is true in Europe. In Canada we have an intermittent politicized and polemical discussion that focuses on mandatory minimum sentences. With only occasional exceptions, most notably the enactment of Bill C-41 in 1995, there has been little sustained debate about sentencing principles and policy in Canada since the rejection of the report of the Canadian Sentencing Commission in 1987.

The second edition follows the same format and structure as the first. Since the first edition, however, some significant changes have occurred. The courts have been busy. A number of sentencing decisions have come from the Supreme Court of Canada that address the interpretation and application of specific provisions: for example, how s. 742.1 relates to credit for pre-sentence custody (*Fice*) and how s. 725 constrains the ability of sentencing courts to look at outstanding charges (*Angelillo*; *Larche*). In *Johnson* the Supreme Court reshaped dangerous-offender proceedings. Looking at post-conviction issues, the cases of *Sauvé v. Canada (Chief Electoral Officer)* (voting rights) and *May v. Ferndale Institution* (availability of *habeas corpus*) were landmark decisions that have received substantial attention. The recent 2008 decision in *Ferguson* dealing with mandatory minima and dismissing constitutional exemptions is also included.

Across the country, other courts have been occupied with sentencing issues and they are well represented in this edition. Teachers and students will be interested in the evolution of sentencing circles in Saskatchewan and intrigued by the debate between Justice Hill and Justice Doherty in *Hamilton and Mason*.

We have omitted the chapter on young offenders. Since the first edition, Parliament passed the *Youth Criminal Justice Act*, SC 2002, c. 1, which has been in force since April 2003. The sentencing provisions of this new Act are extensive, touching on subjects that include principles, procedure, the array of sanctions, availability of adult sentences, and the threshold to custody. The YCJA has spawned an enormous amount of litigation at every level, including the Supreme Court of Canada. There are also a number of texts that deal with it in detail, including one by Nicholas Bala. We concluded that one chapter on this growing subject would be inadequate, especially since teachers with a real interest in the subject will likely offer a course dedicated entirely to it. In view of the developing jurisprudence on the role of appellate courts in sentencing matters, we have added a chapter on sentence appeals. As well, chapter 13 is now entitled "Collateral Sentencing Orders" and includes orders in respect of the DNA databank and sex offender registry.

Other important changes relate to the authors of the second edition. We are very pleased that Professor Trotter and Professor Healy have become Mr. Justice Trotter and Mr. Justice Healy. Thankfully, their judicial responsibilities did not deter them from participating in this edition. They continue to provide high-quality scholarly work and useful insights, perhaps enhanced by their new perspectives.

We welcome Professor Dale Ives of the University of Western Ontario and Professor Julian Roberts of Oxford University. Both have been excellent, thoughtful, and diligent contributors to the second edition. Dale has expanded our capacity to deal with sanctions and procedure, while Julian has provided a much-needed criminological perspective. We are very pleased that they have joined us.

As with the first edition, each chapter was assigned to one or two authors. Then, the chapters were circulated to the other authors for comments and suggestions. In this way we hope that we are able to provide teachers and students with the benefits of the collective experiences and insights of our whole team. As before, we have included extensive notes to provide links and explanations, and to pose questions.

Before ending, I want to acknowledge the support, advice, and encouragement that we continue to receive from our good friend Bill Vancise—a.k.a. Mr. Justice Vancise of the Court of Appeal of Saskatchewan. While hundreds of Canadian judges are actively involved in the sentencing process at both trial and appellate levels, we can think of no more than a dozen who have pursued the topic with passion and intellectual tenacity. Within this group, Bill is a leader. He is extremely knowledgeable about the theory and practice of sentencing in Canada and brings a wealth of creative insights and provocative ideas. We are all indebted to him.

I also want to acknowledge the support I received from the Social Sciences and Humanities Research Council and the Faculty of Law, Queen's University for my part of this undertaking. Especially because of the cooperation of my four colleagues, it has been a thoroughly enjoyable task.

Allan Manson

Kingston, July 2008

Table of Contents

Detailed Table of Contents

Table of Cases

A page number in boldface type indicates that the text of the case or a portion thereof is reproduced. A page number in lightface type indicates that the case is merely quoted briefly or discussed by the authors. Cases mentioned within excerpts are not listed.

CHAPTER ONE

An Introduction to Punishment: Philosophy and Objectives

I. INTRODUCTION

This chapter introduces and explores the philosophical foundations of punishment. The body of literature concerning the philosophy of punishment is vast. The readings that follow provide a glimpse into this debate by illustrating some of the major theoretical themes.

The materials in this chapter consider why we have the institution of legal punishment. That is, from a philosophical perspective, how can the imposition of punishment by the state be justified? When the state intentionally inflicts an unwanted deprivation—that is, the imposition of physical and emotional pain or the loss of liberty—on its citizens, this is an act that demands a justification. A variety of philosophical justifications have been developed, but the two main philosophical traditions in this area are utilitarian and retributive.

Utilitarian or reductive theories of punishment are rooted in the work of British philosophers Jeremy Bentham and J.S. Mill. Like utilitarianism as a general moral theory, the main premise of this approach to punishment is that the infliction of pain by the state is justified only insofar as it promotes favourable consequences. In this context, the desired favourable consequence is the reduction of crime through the "mechanisms" of deterrence, denunciation, incapacitation, and/or rehabilitation.

Retributive theories of punishment, which can be traced back to the works of I. Kant and G.W.F. Hegel (and perhaps further back to biblical times), approach the problem from a completely different perspective. Punishment is imposed simply because it is *deserved* by an offender for the commission of an offence. When the state punishes an individual for the commission of an offence, the state is merely visiting on that person what he or she *deserves*.

The excerpts that are reproduced in this chapter elaborate on these philosophical traditions and consider their respective shortcomings. They provide some context for the debate. In this introductory section, the following excerpt from R.A. Duff plots the contours or boundaries of this philosophical debate. The portion of H.L.A. Hart's famous essay introduces the notion of how both philosophical traditions may operate at different levels in analyzing why we punish. Essentially, it ponders a blended or "hybrid" philosophical approach to punishment. Thereafter, separate sections are devoted to a consideration of the most influential utilitarian and retributive approaches to punishment.

R.A. Duff, *Trials and Punishments*
(Cambridge: University of Cambridge Press, 1986) (footnotes omitted)

Philosophical discussions of the meaning and justification of criminal punishment tend to move along familiar and well-worn paths. It is agreed that a system of criminal punishment stands in need of some strenuous and persuasive justification: the briefest examination of our actual penal institutions confronts us forcibly with the question of how we can justifiably subject people to such treatment; and even a more abstract or idealised account of what punishment could or should be must recognise that any punitive practice will require powerful justification. But different moral perspectives generate different accounts of why it is that punishment needs justification—of what it is about punishment that makes it morally problematic: for some it is the fact that punishment inflicts, indeed is designed to inflict, pain or suffering that most forcibly raises the issue of justification; for others it is the coercive character of punishment—the fact that it is imposed on people against their express will, thus apparently infringing their freedom and autonomy—which is most disturbing. Such different perceptions of the problem of punishment are themselves related to quite different accounts of what does or could justify a system of criminal punishment.

Consequentialists, who have been for many years the predominant party in these discussions, insist that the point of a system of criminal punishment must lie in its beneficial effects (most obviously in the reduction of harmful modes of conduct by the deterrence, reform or incapacitation of those who do or might engage in them), and its justification in the extent to which these benefits outweigh the system's costs (the harm caused by punishment; the resources needed to identify and deal with those who are to be punished). Consequentialist accounts of punishment are as diverse as the ends which consequentialists may value and which punishment may serve: but I take it to be a common and defining feature of such accounts that they require punishment to be justified by reference to benefits to which it is *contingently* related as a means to a further end. Our initial specification of the ends which we are to pursue leaves open the question of the means by which they are to be pursued, since those ends, do not of their nature require any particular method of attaining them: so we must go on to ask which methods are in fact likely to be most economically efficacious. To justify a system of punishment it is therefore not enough to show that it pursues ends which are worth pursuing, nor indeed that its benefits outweigh its costs: we must also show, by an empirical inquiry into the likely effects of actual or possible social institutions, that this way of dealing with disvalued conduct is more economically effective than other possible methods of achieving our desired ends—than, for instance, a system of "social hygiene" which regards such conduct as symptomatic of a condition which needs curative treatment rather than as an instance of criminality requiring punishment.

This contingent relation between punishment and its justifying aims generates familiar objections to such consequentialist accounts. For the whole-hearted pursuit of such aims would surely sanction the imposition of manifestly unjust punishments: the punishment of innocent scapegoats; excessively harsh punishments for relatively trivial offences; a refusal to accept excusing-conditions which should in justice be accepted.

It is at best a contingent truth that just punishments are consequentially efficient; and it may sometimes be true that unjust punishments are more efficient.

A consequentialist might respond to such objections by arguing that an adequately detailed consequentialist account, which attends to *all* the likely effects of particular kinds or systems of punishment, will not in fact have such disturbing implications; that it will come closer to an extensional equivalence which "ordinary moral views" than its critics may suppose. She may also try to provide a role for, and an explanation of, the principles of justice which her critics regard as morally significant; by arguing, for instance, that we have good consequentialist reasons to obey strict rules which forbid the punishment of the innocent or the unduly harsh punishment of the guilty. But she will still face some familiar objections; that she is relying on large and unsubstantiated empirical claims about the likely effects of different kinds of practice; that her reductive and instrumental account of the principles of justice fails to capture the sense and significance of those principles, or the role which they properly play in our moral thought; and that she "begs the institution" by assuming without adequate argument that a consequentialist concern to prevent harmful conduct will generate something like a system of criminal punishment, rather than some quite different system of social hygiene or behaviour-control. Some moral radical consequentialists have indeed taken this last route, and argued that a proper concern for the appropriate consequentialist ends should lead us to abandon punishment altogether.

An alternative response to these criticisms has been to insist that the positive justifying aims of punishment must indeed lie in its consequential benefits, but to allow that our pursuit of those aims is and should be limited by other considerations or side-constraints. Such limits may be set by our concern for ends other than, and conflicting with, those which provide the justifying aims of punishment; a concern to maximise the citizen's freedom in and control over his own life may set limits on who may be punished, and how, which are not dictated by the aim of preventing disvalued conduct: but they may also be set by an avowedly non-consequentialist concern for justice which forbids us to punish the innocent, and limits the kind or amount of punishment which may be attached to different offences. Punishment which efficiently serves its justifying aims may thus still be unjustified, if it fails to satisfy these further moral constraints—constraints which are independent of the consequential ends which punishment is to serve, and which focus on its intrinsic character.

It is here that retributivist ideas are allowed to play a part in an account of punishment. Traditional attempts to find the *positive* justification of punishment in its relation to a past offence are, their critics claim, unable to explain that justificatory relationship: insofar as they have any tolerably clear meaning they are seen to depend on an unargued and unarguable intuition that "the guilty deserve to suffer" (itself perhaps reflecting a desire for revenge which hardly deserves our moral respect); or on a covertly consequentialist appeal to some particular, and arbitrarily selected, kind of beneficial effect. But we need not therefore eliminate all notions of retribution: we can deal with them (and defuse them) by allowing that they do, once properly understood, have a role in an adequate account of punishment—though not the dominant role which their traditional proponents claimed for them. Ideas of retribution and desert are now to play an etiolated and negative role, setting constraints on our pursuit of the consequentialist goals which provide the positive justifying aim of punishment: they express independent principles of justice; or logical principles involved in the meaning of "punishment"; or subordinate principles within a Rule-Utilitarian system.

Retributivists, however, are unlikely to be satisfied with this subordinate role within a fundamentally consequentialist framework: and recent years have seen a revival of full-blooded retributivist attempts to locate the meaning of punishment, not in its contingent and instrumental contribution to some further end, but in its internal relationship to a past offence; and its justification in its intrinsic character as a response to that offence. This revival, involving both academic philosophers and more practically oriented legal theorists, has been motivated in part by the manifest failure of systems constructed or reformed along purportedly consequentialist lines to achieve their avowed ends, as well as by a more theoretical dissatisfaction with consequentialist accounts of punishment; and it has led to new attempts to explicate and defend the idea that punishment is justified as merited retribution for a past offence.

We can usefully talk of the common features, and the common logical structure, of consequentialist accounts of punishment: but can we usefully talk of retributivist accounts in this way; or has the label "retributivist" been applied to such a diversity of views and principles that it now lacks any unambiguous or unitary meaning? We must indeed distinguish retributivist accounts of the justifying purpose of punishment from those which seek only to set limits on our pursuit of consequentialist aims; and amongst the former we find a notable diversity of explanations of how it is that punishment is an appropriate response to crime. Some talk of the payment of a debt incurred by crime, or of the restoration of a balance disturbed by crime; others of the expiation, atonement, or annulment of crime; others of the denunciation of crime; and we cannot suppose that these are simply different ways of expressing the same idea. But such accounts do share what can usefully be called a retributivist perspective on punishment: for they all find the sense and the justification of punishment in its relation to a past offence.

A retributivist must explain the meaning of this justificatory relationship, and the values on which it depends. She must defend herself against the accusation that her account amounts at best to a distortion of logical or moral principles which have their proper and subordinate place within a consequentialist account of the justifying aims of punishment; and at worse to a piece of metaphysical mystery-mongering which conceals a desire for revenge or retaliation behind such opaque and unilluminating metaphors as "restoring the balance" or "annulling the crime." She must meet the claim that a coercive institution like punishment can be justified only by showing that it does some significant consequential good; and she may do this by arguing that the justification of punishment has, and need have, nothing to do with its consequences, and everything to do with its intrinsic character as a response to crime: the imposition of punishment on criminals is right independently of its consequences—even, perhaps, whatever its consequences.

The range of familiar accounts of punishment thus offers us three models for its justification. A consequentialist model justifies punishment by reference to further ends to which it is contingently and instrumentally related as a means; an intrinsicalist or retributivist model justifies it by reference to its intrinsic character as distinct form, and rather than, its consequences; and a "consequentialism with side-constraints" model seeks to combine these two modes of justification by insisting that a justified system of punishment must be an efficient method of pursuing the further ends which provide its justifying aims, whilst also satisfying the independent and intrinsicalist demands of justice.

H.L.A. Hart, "Prolegomenon to the Principles of Punishment"
in *Punishment and Responsibility: Essays in the Philosophy of Law* (Oxford: Oxford University Press, 1968), 11-19 (footnotes omitted)

I. Introductory

The main object of this paper is to provide a framework for the discussion of the mounting perplexities which now surround the institution of criminal punishment, and to show that any morally tolerable account of this institution must exhibit it as a compromise between distinct and partly conflicting principles.

General interest in the topic of punishment has never been greater than it is at present and I doubt if the public discussion of it has ever been more confused. The interest and the confusion are both in part due to relatively modern scepticism about two elements which have figured as essential parts of the traditionally opposed "theories" of punishment. On the one hand, the old Benthamite confidence in fear of the penalties threatened by the law as a powerful deterrent, has waned with the growing realization that the part played by calculation of any sort in anti-social behaviour has been exaggerated. On the other hand a cloud of doubt has settled over the keystone of "retributive" theory. Its advocates can no longer speak with the old confidence that statements of the form "This man who has broken the law could have kept it" had a univocal or agreed meaning; or where scepticism does not attach to the *meaning* of this form of statement, it has shaken the confidence that we are generally able to distinguish the cases where a statement of this form is true from those where it is not.

Yet quite apart from the uncertainty engendered by these fundamental doubts, which seem to call in question the accounts given of the efficacy, and the morality of punishment by all the old competing theories, the public utterances of those who conceive themselves to be expounding, as plain men for other plain men, orthodox or common-sense principles (untouched by modern psychological doubts) are uneasy. Their words often sound as if the authors had not fully grasped their meaning or did not intend the words to be taken quite literally. A glance at the parliamentary debates or the *Report of the Royal Commission on Capital Punishment* shows that many are now troubled by the suspicion that the view that there is just one supreme value or objective (e.g. Deterrence, Retribution or Reform) in terms of which *all* questions about the justification of punishment are to be answered, is somehow wrong; yet, from what is said on such occasions no clear account of what the different values or objectives are, or how they fit together in the justification of punishment, can be extracted.

No one expects judges or statesmen occupied in the business of sending people to the gallows or prison, or in making (or unmaking) laws which enable this to be done, to have much time for philosophical discussion of the principles which make it morally tolerable to do these things. A judicial bench is not and should not be a professorial chair. Yet what is said in public debates about punishment by those specially concerned with it as judges or legislators is important. Few are likely to be more circumspect, and if what they say seems, as it often does, unclear, one-sided and easily refutable by pointing to some aspect of things which they have overlooked, it is likely that in our inherited ways of talking or thinking about punishment there is some persistent drive towards an over-simplification of multiple issues which require separate consideration. To counter this drive what is most needed is *not* the simple admission that instead of a single value or aim (Deterrence, Retribution, Reform or any other) a plurality of different values and aims should be given as a conjunctive answer to some *single* question concerning the justification of punishment. What is needed is the realization that different principles (each of which may in a sense be called a "justification") are relevant at different points in any morally acceptable account of punishment. What we should look for are answers to a number of different questions such as: What justifies the general practice of punishment? To whom may punishment be applied? How severely may we punish? In dealing with these and other questions concerning punishment we should bear in mind that in this, as in most other social institutions, the pursuit of one aim may be qualified by or provide an opportunity, not to be missed, for the pursuit of others. Till we have developed this sense of the complexity of punishment (and this prolegomenon aims only to do this) we shall be in no fit state to assess the extent to which the whole institution has been eroded by, or needs to be adapted to, new beliefs about the human mind.

2. *Justifying Aims and Principles of Distribution*

There is, I think an analogy worth considering between the concept of punishment and that of property. In both cases we have to do with a social institution of which the centrally important form is a structure of *legal* rules, even if it would be dogmatic to deny the names of punishment or property to the similar though more rudimentary rule-regulated practices within groups such as a family, or a school, or in customary societies whose customs may lack some of the standard or salient features of law (e.g. legislation, organized sanctions, courts). In both cases we are confronted by a complex institution presenting different inter-related features calling for separate explanation; or, if the morality of the institution is challenged, for separate justification. In both cases failure to distinguish separate questions or attempting to answer them all by reference to a single principle ends in confusion. Thus in the case of property we should distinguish between the question of the *definition* of property, the question why and in what circumstances it is a *good* institution to maintain, and the questions in what ways individuals may become *entitled* to acquire property and *how much* they should be allowed to acquire. These we may call questions of *Definition*, *General Justifying Aim*, and *Distribution* with the last subdivided into question of *Title* and *Amount*. It is salutary to take some classical exposition of the idea of property, say Locke's chapter "Of Property" in the *Second Treatise*, and to observe how much darkness is spread by the use of a single notion (in this case "the labour of (a man's) body and the work of his hands") to answer all these different questions which press upon us when we reflect on the institution of property. In the case of punishment the beginning of wisdom (though by no means its end) is to distinguish similar questions and confront them separately.

(a) Definition

Here I shall simply draw upon the recent admirable work scattered through English philosophical journals and add to it only an admonition of my own against the abuse of definition in the philosophical discussion of punishment. So with Mr. Benn and Professor Flew I shall define the standard or central case of "punishment" in terms of five elements:

(i) It must involve pain or other consequences normally considered unpleasant.
(ii) It must be for an offence against legal rules.
(iii) It must be of an actual or supposed offender for his offence.
(iv) It must be intentionally administered by human beings other than the offender.
(v) It must be imposed and administered by an authority constituted by a legal system against which the offence is committed.

In calling this the standard or central case of punishment I shall relegate to the position of sub-standard or secondary cases the following among many other possibilities:

(a) Punishments for breaches of legal rules imposed or administered otherwise than by officials (decentralised sanctions).
(b) Punishments for breaches of non-legal rules or orders (punishments in a family or school).
(c) Vicarious or collective punishment of some member of a social group for actions done by others without the former's authorization, encouragement, control or permission.
(d) Punishment of persons (otherwise than under (c)) who neither are in fact nor supposed to be offenders.

The chief importance of listing these sub-standard cases is to prevent the use of what I shall call the "definitional stop" in discussions of punishment. This is an abuse of definition especially tempting when use is made of conditions (ii) and (iii) of the standard case in arguing against the utilitarian claim that the practice of punishment is justified by the beneficial consequences resulting from the observance of the laws which it secures. Here the stock "retributive" argument is: If *this* is the justification of punishment, why not apply it, when it pays to do so, to those innocent of any crime, chosen at random, or to the wife and children of the offender? And here the wrong reply is: *That*, by definition, would not be "punishment" and it is the justification of punishment which is in issue. Not only will this definitional stop fail to satisfy the advocate of "Retribution," it would prevent us from investigating the very thing which modern scepticism most calls in question: namely the rational and moral status of our preference for a system of punishment under which measures painful to individuals are to be taken against them only when they have committed an offence. Why do we prefer this to other forms of social hygiene which we might employ to prevent anti-social behaviour and which we do employ in special circumstances, sometimes with reluctance? No account of punishment can afford to dismiss this question with a definition.

(b) The Nature of an Offence

Before we reach any question of justification we must identify a preliminary question to which the answer is so simple that the question may not appear worth asking; yet it is clear that some curious "theories" of punishment gain their only plausibility from ignoring it, and others from confusing it with other questions. This question is: Why are certain kinds of action forbidden by law and so made crimes or offences? The answer is: To announce to society that these actions are not to be done and to secure that fewer of them are done. These are the common immediate aims of making any conduct a criminal offence and until we have laws made with these primary aims we shall lack the notion of a "crime" and so of a "criminal." Without recourse to the simple idea that the criminal law sets up, in its rules, standards of behaviour to encourage certain types of conduct and discourage others we cannot distinguish a punishment in the form of a fine from a tax on a course of conduct. This indeed is one grave objection to those theories of law which in the interests of simplicity or uniformity obscure the distinction between primary laws setting standards for behaviour and secondary laws specifying what officials must or may do when they are broken. Such theories insist that all legal rules are "really" directions to officials to exact "sanctions" under certain conditions, e.g. if people kill. Yet only if we keep alive the distinction (which such theories thus obscure) between the primary objective of the law in encouraging or discouraging certain kinds of behaviour, and its merely ancillary sanction or remedial steps, can we give sense to the notion of a crime or offence.

It is important however to stress the fact that in thus identifying the immediate aims of the criminal law we have not reached the stage of justification. There are indeed many forms of undesirable behaviour which it would be foolish (because ineffective or too costly) to attempt to inhibit by use of the law and some of these may be better left to educators, trades unions, churches, marriage guidance councils or other non-legal agencies. Conversely there are some forms of conduct which we believe cannot be effectively inhibited without use of the law. But it is only too plain that in fact the law may make activities criminal which it is morally important to promote and the suppression of these may be quite unjustifiable. Yet confusion between the simple immediate aim of any criminal legislation and the justification of punishment seems to be the most charitable explanation of the claim that punishment is *justified* as an "emphatic denunciation by the community of a crime." Lord Denning's dictum that this is the ultimate justification of punishment can be saved from Mr. Benn's criticism, noted above, only if it is treated as a blurred statement of the truth that the aim not of punishment, but of criminal legislation is indeed to denounce certain types of conduct as something not to be practised. Conversely the immediate aim of criminal legislation cannot be any of the things which are usually mentioned as justifying punishment: for until it is settled what conduct is to be legally denounced and discouraged we have not settled from what we are to *deter* people, or who are to be considered *criminals* from whom we are to exact *retribution*, or on whom we are to wreak *vengeance*, or whom we are to *reform*.

Even those who look upon human law as a mere instrument for enforcing "morality as such" (itself conceived as the law of God or Nature) and who at the stage of justifying punishment wish to appeal not to socially beneficial consequences but simply to the intrinsic value of inflicting suffering on wrongdoers who have disturbed by their offence the moral order, would not deny that the aim of criminal legislation is to set up types of behaviour (in this case conformity with a pre-existing moral law) as legal standards of behaviour and to secure conformity with them. No doubt in all communities certain moral offences, e.g. killing, will always be selected for suppression as crimes and it is conceivable that this may be done not to protect human beings from being killed but to save the potential murderer from sin; but it would be paradoxical to look upon the law as designed not to discourage murders at all (even conceived as sin rather than harm) but simply to extract the penalty from the murderer.

(c) General Justifying Aim

I shall not here criticize the intelligibility or consistency or adequacy of those theories that are united in denying that the practice of a system of punishment is justified by its beneficial consequences and claim instead that the main justification of the practice lies in the fact that when breach of the law involves moral guilt the application to the offender of the pain of punishment is itself a thing of value. A great variety of claims of this character, designating "Retribution" or "Expiation" or "Reprobation" as the justifying aim, fall in spite of differences under this rough general description. Though in fact I agree with Mr. Benn in thinking that these all either avoid the question of justification altogether or are in spite of their protestations disguised forms of Utilitarianism, I shall assume that Retribution, defined simply as the application of the pains of punishment to an offender who is morally guilty, may figure among the conceivable justifying aims of a system of punishment. Here I shall merely insist that it is one thing to use the word Retribution *at this point* in an account of the principle of punishment in order to designate the General Justifying Aim of the system, and quite another to use it to secure that to the question "To whom may punishment be applied?" (the question of Distribution), the answer given is "Only to an offender for an offence." Failure to distinguish Retribution as a General Justifying Aim from retribution as the simple insistence that only those who have broken the law—and voluntarily broken it—may be punished, may be traced in many writers: even perhaps in Mr. J.D. Mabbott's otherwise most illuminating essay. We shall distinguish the latter from Retribution in General Aim as "retribution in Distribution." Much confusing shadow-fighting between utilitarians and their opponents may be avoided if it is recognized that it is perfectly consistent to assert *both* that the General Justifying Aim of the practice of punishment is its beneficial consequences *and* that the pursuit of this General Aim should be qualified or restricted out of deference to principles of Distribution which require that punishment should be only of an offender for an offence. Conversely it does not in the least follow from the admission of the latter principle of retribution in Distribution that the General Justifying Aim of punishment is Retribution though of course Retribution in General Aim entails retribution in Distribution.

We shall consider later the principles of justice lying at the root of retribution in Distribution. Meanwhile it is worth observing that both the old fashioned Retributionist (in General Aim) and the most modern sceptic often make the same (and, I think, wholly mistaken) assumption that sense can only be made of the restrictive principle that punishment be applied only to an offender for an offence if the General Justifying Aim of the practice of punishment is Retribution. The sceptic consequently imputes to all systems of punishment (when they are restricted by the principle of retribution in Distribution) all the irrationality he finds in the idea of Retribution as a General Justifying Aim; conversely the advocates of the latter think the admission of retribution in Distribution is a refutation of the utilitarian claim that the social consequences of punishment are its Justifying Aim.

The most general lesson to be learnt from this extends beyond the topic of punishment. It is, that in relation to any social institution, after stating what general aim or value its maintenance fosters we should enquire whether there are any and if so what principles limiting the unqualified pursuit of that aim or value. Just because the pursuit of any single social aim always has its restrictive qualifier, our main social institutions always possess a plurality of features which can only be understood as a compromise between partly discrepant principles. This is true even of relatively minor legal institutions like that of a contract. In general this is designed to enable individuals to give effect to their wishes to create structures of legal rights and duties, and so to change, in certain ways, their legal position. Yet at the same time there is need to protect those who, in good faith, understand a verbal offer made to them to mean what it would ordinarily mean, accept it, and then act on the footing that a valid contract has been concluded. As against them, it would be unfair to allow the other party to say that the words he used in his verbal offer or the interpretation put on them did not express his real wishes or intention. Hence principles of "estoppel" or doctrines of the "objective sense" of a contract are introduced to prevent this and to qualify the principle that the law enforces contracts in order to give effect to the joint wishes of the contracting parties.

(d) Distribution

This as in the case of property has two aspects: (i) Liability (Who may be punished?) and (ii) Amount. In this section I shall chiefly be concerned with the first of these.

From the foregoing discussions two things emerge. First, though we may be clear as to what value the practice of punishment is to promote, we have still to answer as a question of Distribution "Who may be punished?" Secondly, if in answer to this question we say "only an offender for an offence" this admission of retribution in Distribution is not a principle from which anything follows as to the severity or amount of punishment; in particular it neither licenses nor requires, as Retribution in General Aim does, more severe punishments than deterrence or other utilitarian criteria would require.

The root question to be considered is, however, why we attach the moral importance which we do to retribution in Distribution. Here I shall consider the efforts made to show that restriction of punishment to offenders is a simple consequence of whatever principles (Retributive or Utilitarian) constitute the Justifying Aim of punishment.

The standard example used by philosophers to bring out the importance of retribution in Distribution is that of a wholly innocent person who has not even unintentionally done anything which the law punishes if done intentionally. It is supposed that in order to avert some social catastrophe officials of the system fabricate evidence on which he is charged, tried, convicted and sent to prison or death. Or it is supposed that without resort to any fraud more persons may be deterred from crime if wives and children of offenders were punished vicariously for their crimes. In some forms this kind of thing may be ruled out by a consistent sufficiently comprehensive utilitarianism. Certainly expedients involving fraud or faked charges might be very difficult to justify on utilitarian grounds. We can of course imagine that a negro might be sent to prison or executed on a false charge of rape in order to avoid widespread lynching of many others; but a *system* which openly empowered authorities to do this kind of thing, even if it succeeded in averting specific evils like lynching, would awaken such apprehension and insecurity that any gain from the exercise of these powers would by any utilitarian calculation be offset by the misery caused by their existence. But official resort to this kind of fraud on a particular occasion in breach of the rules and the subsequent indemnification of the officials responsible might save many lives and so be thought to yield a clear surplus of value. Certainly vicarious punishment of an offender's family might do so and legal systems have occasionally though exceptionally resorted to this. An example of it is the Roman *Lex quisquis* providing for the punishment of the children of those guilty of *majestas*. In extreme cases many might still think it right to resort to these expedients but we should do so with the sense of sacrificing an important principle. We should be conscious of choosing the lesser of two evils, and this would be inexplicable if the principle sacrificed to utility were itself only a requirement of utility.

Similarly the moral importance of the restriction of punishment to the offender cannot be explained as merely a consequence of the principle that the General Justifying Aim is Retribution for immorality involved in breaking the law. Retribution in the Distribution of punishment has a value quite independent of Retribution as Justifying Aim. This is shown by the fact that we attach importance to the restrictive principle that only offenders may be punished, even where breach of this law might not be thought immoral. Indeed even where the laws themselves are hideously immoral as in Nazi Germany, e.g. forbidding activities (helping the sick or destitute of some racial group) which might be thought morally obligatory, the absence of the principle restricting punishment to the offender would be a further *special* iniquity; whereas admission of this principle would represent some residual respect for justice shown in the administration of morally bad laws.

II. UTILITARIAN THEORIES OF PUNISHMENT

As discussed in the introduction to this chapter, utilitarian or consequentialist theories of punishment justify the imposition of punishment in terms of the benefits that it achieves. The main benefit that consequentialist theories aspire to achieve is the reduction of crime. In *An Introduction to the Principles of Morals and Legislation* (1789), Jeremy Bentham wrote:

> Pain and pleasure are the great springs of human action. When a man perceives or supposes pain to be the consequences of an act, he is acted upon in such a manner as tends, with a certain force, to withdraw him, as it were, from the commission of that act. If the apparent magnitude of that pain be greater than the apparent magnitude of the pleasure or good he expects to be the

consequence of the act, he will be absolutely prevented from performing it. The mischief which would have ensued from the act, if performed, will also by that means be prevented.

With respect to a given individual, the recurrence of an offence may be provided against in three ways:

1. By taking from him the physical power of offending.

2. By taking away the desire of offending.

3. By making him afraid of offending.

In the first case, the individual can no more commit the offence; in the second, he no longer desires to commit it; in the third, he may still wish to commit it, but he longer dares to do it. In the first case, there is a physical incapacity; in the second, a moral reformation; in the third, there is intimidation or terror of the law.

More traditionally, the language of these objectives is that punishment seeks to deter (either specifically or generally), incapacitate, or rehabilitate offenders. Moreover, punishment is said to have a denunciatory or expressive function, whereby the imposition of punishment is considered to be a symbolic reflection of society's abhorrence or abject disavowal of particular crimes.

As the readings below demonstrate, the utilitarian approach to punishment is vulnerable to attack on two levels. First, the goals that consequentialist theories seek to achieve are not met; that is, punishment is ineffective as a means of reforming offenders, deterring others, and generally reducing crime. This argument is rooted in a rather impressive body of empirical literature that bemoans the fact that social science has not been able to validate the efficacy of utilitarian claims. For a collection of a number of readings that address this issue, see Andrew von Hirsch and Andrew Ashworth, eds., *Principled Sentencing*, 2d ed. (Oxford: Hart Publishing, 1998).

The second level of attack is from a moral perspective. A theory of punishment that is founded on consequentialist notions has little regard for human dignity or autonomy in that it permits using individuals as a means to more collectivist ends. An example of this shortcoming that is popularized in the literature is the claim that a utilitarian theory of punishment authorizes the punishment of an innocent person if, in all of the circumstances, utility were to be maximized by such a practice. If this argument is valid, must we abandon our utilitarian notions *completely*, or can the point be dismissed as a fanciful complaint that occupies the most peripheral edges of an otherwise venerable philosophical tradition?

C.L. Ten, *Crime, Guilt and Punishment*
(Oxford: Clarendon Press, 1987) (footnotes omitted)

2.1. The Effects of Punishment

The utilitarian theory justifies punishment solely in terms of the good consequences produced. There are disagreements among utilitarians about the nature of the good consequences which punishment is supposed to produce. Some utilitarians may even believe that the harm done by punishment outweighs the good, and hence punishment is not justified. But many utilitarians see the main beneficial effects of punishment in terms of the *reduction of crime*, and believe that punishing offenders will have at least some, if not all, of the following good effects. First, punishment acts as a deterrent to crime. The deterrent effects can be both individual and general. Punishment deters the offender who is punished from committing similar offences in future, and it also deters potential offenders. The offender who is punished is supposed to be deterred by his experience of punishment and the threat of being punished again if he re-offends and is convicted. This is the individual deterrent effect. The general deterrent effect of punishment on potential offenders works through the threat of their being subjected to the same kind of punishment that was meted out to the convicted offender.

Secondly, punishment is supposed to have reformative or rehabilitative effects. This is confined to the offender who is punished. He is reformed in the sense that the effect of punishment is to change his values so that he will not commit similar offences in future because he believes such offences to be wrong. But if he abstains from criminal acts simply because he is afraid of being caught and punished again, then he is deterred rather than reformed and rehabilitated by punishment. So the effects of individual deterrence and rehabilitation are the same. What distinguishes them is the difference in motivation.

The third good consequence of punishment is its incapacitative effect. When an offender is serving his sentence in prison, he is taken out of general social circulation and is therefore prevented from committing a variety of offences, even though he may neither be deterred nor reformed by punishment. Of course punishment would not have an overall incapacitative effect if the offender would not have re-offended even if he were free, or if his incarceration led someone else, who would not otherwise have done so, to engage in criminal activity, perhaps as his replacement in a gang. While in prison, the offender might still commit certain offences: he might assault a fellow prisoner or a prison guard. But his opportunities are generally reduced. In some cases, however, his contacts with other prisoners would create opportunities for further involvement in crime when he is released. The incapacitative effect, though perhaps most likely in the case of imprisonment, may also be present in other forms of punishment. For example, parole may have some incapacitative effect in that although the offender is free, the fact that he is under supervision may restrict his opportunities for criminal activities.

The empirical evidence of the effects of punishment is very complex, but a brief survey will be of some use.

It looks as if the present state of our knowledge provides no basis for claiming that punishment by imprisonment reforms or rehabilitates the criminal, or that it is an individual deterrent. The position is well summed up by the Report of the Panel of the National Research Council in the United States on Research on Deterrent and Incapacitative Effects, hereafter referred to as the Panel:

> The available research on the impact of various treatment strategies both in and out of prison seems to indicate that, after controlling for initial selection differences, there are generally no statistically significant differences between the subsequent recidivism of offenders, regardless of the form of "treatment." This suggests that neither rehabilitative nor criminogenic effects operate very strongly. Therefore, at an aggregate level, these confounding effects are probably safely ignored.

By "criminogenic effects" the Panel refers to the undesirable effects of imprisonment in either increasing the criminal's propensity to commit crimes or to extend the duration of his criminal career. Such effects are the opposite of the rehabilitative effects. So the present evidence seems to suggest that in general the effect of imprisonment, or of the various programmes for rehabilitation which accompany imprisonment, is neither to make the criminal a better nor a worse person with respect to the standards of behaviour set by the criminal law.

The evidence also suggests that in general punishment has no individual deterrent effect. Daniel Nagin points out that at the observational level it is difficult to distinguish between individual (or what he calls special) deterrence and rehabilitation. He concludes that, "The figures suggest that recidivism rates cannot be affected by varying the severity of the punishment, at least within acceptable limits." But Nagin cautiously adds that the evidence is only preliminary.

In a few specific cases there is indeed some evidence of the individual deterrent effect of punishment. Thus Johannes Andenaes draws attention to a study of amateur shoplifters which shows that detection and arrest, even without prosecution, produces serious shock. There is little or no recidivism among those who are apprehended and interrogated by the store police and then set free without being formally charged. A study of drunk driving in Sweden also shows that those drivers who had been arrested estimated the risk of being arrested as many times higher than other drivers.

There is disagreement about the general deterrent effects of punishment. Johannes Andenaes believes that, "In general terms it can only be stated that general deterrence works well in some fields and works poorly or not at all in other fields." But in 1974 Gordon Tullock published an article, "Does Punishment Deter Crime?" in which he surveyed the work done by economists and sociologists. Tullock points out that economists began their work under the impression that punishment would deter crime because demand curves slope downwards showing that if the cost of a good is increased then less of it will be consumed. So if the cost of committing crime is increased by more severe punishment, then there will be fewer crimes. Sociologists, on the other hand, started out with the intention of confirming what was then the accepted view in their discipline that punishment would not deter crime. But Tullock argues that, although their starting points and assumptions were radically different, both economists and sociologists, after analysing the evidence, came to the same conclusion that punishment did indeed deter crime. After surveying their studies Tullock himself is convinced that "the empirical evidence is clear," and he states his conclusions unequivocally: "Even granting the fact that most potential criminals have only a rough idea as to the frequency and severity of punishment, multiple regression studies show that increasing the frequency or severity of the punishment does reduce the likelihood that a given crime will be committed."

However, Tullock's confidence about the clarity of the empirical evidence is not shared by the Panel. The Panel argues that although the evidence consistently establishes a negative association between crime rates and sanctions (as measured by the risks of apprehension, conviction, or imprisonment), that is higher crime rates are associated with lower sanctions and vice versa, this does not necessarily show the general deterrent effect of sanctions. The negative association may be partly or wholly explained in terms of lower sanctions being the effect rather than the cause of higher crime rates. Higher crime rates may so overburden the resources of the criminal justice system that they reduce its ability to deal with new offenders. Overburdened judges and prosecutors may use their discretion to dismiss or reduce charges, or to offer attractive plea bargains. Overcrowding of prisons may lead to a reduction in the time served in prison as more prisoners are released early on parole. The sanctions imposed on certain crimes may be reduced. So unless one can separate out the effect of higher crime rates on sanctions from the deterrent effect of sanctions on crime, one cannot interpret the evidence as establishing the presence of the general deterrent effect of punishment. The Panel's cautious assessment of the evidence is summed up in its remark that "we cannot yet assert that the evidence warrants an affirmative conclusion regarding deterrence" but the Panel adds that "the evidence certainly favours a proposition supporting deterrence more than it favours one asserting that deterrence is absent." On the other hand, the Panel believes that the evidence does not even show a significant negative association between crime rates and the severity of punishment as measured by the time served in prison, but suggests that this may partly be accounted for in terms of various distortions.

Moving from the analysis of statistics to the experimental evidence, the Panel identifies three studies which are not methodologically flawed. Of these, two show that the level of crime decreased significantly with increases in the level of sanctions, while one showed that the removal of criminal sanctions for abortions in Hawaii did not affect the incidence of abortions. So it looks as if the present experimental evidence does not permit the drawing of general conclusions. But much of the experimental evidence is consistent with the operation of deterrence, as has been noted by Nigel Walker.

Finally, we turn to the incapacitative effect of punishment. In her review of the literature for the Panel, Jacqueline Cohen suggests that disagreements about the magnitude of that effect can be attributed almost entirely to the different estimates of the average crime rate of prisoners. The estimate of the increase in crime if current prison use were reduced or eliminated has been as low as five per cent. Estimating the incapacitative effect of present prison policies is one thing. There is also the different question as to what we can expect the incapacitative effect to be if present policies are changed. Here one estimate is of a five fold decrease in crime, but Cohen points out that this can only be achieved by increasing the prison population by between 355 per cent and 567 per cent. The incapacitative effect will not be the same for all crimes. Cohen points out that using the assumptions made by the available models, the increase in prison population required to reduce violent crimes is much less than the increases needed for similar reductions in other crimes. Violent crimes can be reduced by 10 per cent with less than 30 per cent increase in prison population. This kind of consideration has led to an increasing interest in the use of selective incapacitation in which the focus of imprisonment is on certain types of offenders who are identified as having a high rate of committing crimes.

We see that the evidence is perhaps more hospitable to the claim that punishment has some general deterrent effect and some incapacitative effect than it is to the claim that it has individual deterrent effect or that it rehabilitates offenders. This will no doubt be puzzling to some, but it provides a basis for caution in responding to a high rate of recidivism. Where there is such a high rate, it shows that punishment does not deter those who are punished. But it does not show that potential offenders are not in fact deterred by punishment, or that punishment does not incapacitate.

2.2. Punishing the Innocent

Let us now assume that the beneficial consequences of punishment outweigh the suffering that it inflicts on offenders. Critics of the utilitarian theory argue that if punishment is to be justified solely in terms of its good consequences, then punishment cannot be confined to offenders. There might be situations in which punishing an innocent person would produce better consequences that alternative courses of action. The utilitarian is therefore committed to punishing the innocent person. This objection has played an important role in the rejection of the utilitarian theory.

Let us consider an example made famous in the literature by H.J. McCloskey. Suppose that in a particular town with a mixed population a man from one racial group rapes a woman from the other group. Because of existing racial tensions the crime is likely to produce racial violence with many people being injured, unless the guilty man is apprehended quickly. Suppose further that the sheriff of the town can prevent the violence by framing an innocent man who was near the scene of the crime, and who will be accepted by the community as the guilty person. Surely, it is argued, the best consequences will be produced by the sheriff's fabrication of evidence against him which will result in his conviction and severe punishment. But the critics maintain that the sheriff's act and the subsequent punishment of the innocent man are both wrong.

There are many ways in which utilitarians, or those sympathetic to them, can respond to this objection, and I shall consider some of their main arguments. First, it is argued that "punishing the innocent" is a logical contradiction because punishment implies guilt. Secondly, the premises of the objection are challenged. It is suggested that punishing the innocent man will not in fact produce the best consequences if we take into account all the consequences of such punishment including the long-term and less obvious consequences. Thirdly, it is claimed that the only situations in which punishing the innocent is optimistic are hypothetical and "fantastic" situations rather than situations which arise, or are likely to occur, in the real world. It is then argued that for a variety of reasons, utilitarians should not be worried by what they are committed to in such fantastic situations. In discussing this third response, I shall also consider the views of those utilitarians who maintain that the punishment of the innocent would indeed be justified in situations where it produces the best consequences. If "common-sense morality" or our intuition disagree, so much the worse for them.

2.3. Punishment and Guilt

In his well-known paper, "On Punishment," Anthony Quinton argues that the notion of "punishment" implies guilt in the sense that "punishment" is defined in part as the infliction of suffering on the guilty. So when suffering is inflicted on innocent people, this cannot be properly described as punishment but as something else—judicial terrorism or social surgery. If we inflict suffering on an innocent man and try to pass it off as punishment, we are guilty of lying since we make a lying imputation that he is guilty and responsible for an offence. Part of Quinton's argument seems to rest on the importance of distinguishing between, for example, typhoid carriers and criminals even though both may sometimes be treated in rather similar ways. Thus a typhoid carrier, or a person with an infectious disease, will be quarantined. He will lose his freedom in much the same way that a criminal is deprived of his freedom when he is jailed. And yet we do not call quarantine a form of punishment precisely because the disease carrier is not guilty of an offence.

It is certainly true that in the typical cases of punishment it is inflicted on a person guilty of an offence. But the crucial issue is whether we can extend the notion of punishment to the infliction of suffering on the innocent without at the same time losing the distinction between punishment and various activities like the quarantine of disease carriers and certain kinds of medical or dental treatment which are painful.

In all these cases there is the infliction of some unpleasantness or suffering, but it is only in the case of punishment that the unpleasantness is essential to what is to be done. As Wasserstrom puts it "the point of the imposition of a deprivation when it is unmistakably a punishment is that it is being imposed because it is a deprivation, because the person upon whom it is being imposed should thereby be made to suffer and in that respect be worse off than before." On the other hand, the unpleasantness experienced by those who are quarantined, or by those undergoing medical treatment, is only incidental, and not essential to what needs to be done. Advances in medical technology may lead to the replacement of painful forms of treatment by pleasant, but still effective, treatment. Medical treatment does not have to be painful at all: a sweet pill is as much a medicine as a bitter pill. Similarly, quarantine implies a degree of isolation to prevent the spread of the infection, and that in itself will be unpleasant. But it can, if resources permit, be greatly outweighed by the pleasures of the surroundings in which one is put. But punishment implies at least an overall degree of unpleasantness. So we can distinguish between punishment and quarantine without falling back on the notion that the person who is punished must be guilty, or must at least be supposed to be guilty, of an offence.

However, the truth of the matter seems to be a bit more complex than we have so far acknowledged, and Quinton's argument, though mistaken, is interesting because it gestures towards that truth. Consider the difference between a monetary fine, which is a form of punishment, and a tax which is not. Arguably both are essentially unpleasant although both may be accepted or approved of as fully justified. What then is the difference between them? In *The Concept of Law* H.L.A. Hart points out that punishment involves "an offence or breach of duty in the form of violation of a rule set up to guide the conduct of ordinary citizens." When someone is punished, he has violated a standard of conduct to which he is supposed to conform. But when he pays a tax, he has not breached any such standard of conduct. The main purpose of taxes is to raise revenue and not to set up a standard of correct conduct. Indeed the revenue-raising function of a tax would be defeated if people generally reacted to income tax by not working, or to Value Added Tax by not eating in restaurants. On the other hand, the purpose of punishment is not defeated if, as a result of it, people cease to breach the relevant standard of conduct. On the contrary, the threat of punishment is most effective when it is unnecessary to carry it out. This important difference between punishment and a tax can be blurred, as Hart acknowledges, when, for example, those running a business simply assimilate the relatively small fines for breaches of rules into the costs of the goods they produce, and pass them on to their consumers. It is also blurred in the other direction when a government imposes a tax on luxury goods partly in order to discourage their use.

A related difference between punishment and other forms of deprivation or unpleasant treatment is that punishment expresses condemnation or disapproval of the conduct punished. The person punished is blamed for what he did, and this explains the peculiar unfairness of punishing the innocent who are of course blameless.

But now, if we accept the idea that punishment involves the breach of a standard of conduct, how is this different from Quinton's point that punishment is always for an offence? The element of truth in Quinton's position is that there must be some wrong-doing or some offence for there to be punishment. But this is not to say that the person punished must be the offender. An innocent person can be punished for an offence committed by someone else. This can happen not only when the legal authority makes a mistake and punishes the wrong person, but also when it deliberately frames an innocent person.

But suppose now that my arguments fail, and Quinton's analysis of the concept of punishment is correct. It certainly does not follow that it is wrong to imprison innocent people or even to execute them. What follows is merely that we cannot *describe* these acts as *punishing* the innocent. But the real issue is a moral issue as to whether we are justified in inflicting suffering on innocent persons. Admittedly this is not exactly the same issue as whether we should *punish* the innocent which raises the additional problem of whether we may unjustly blame the blameless, but none the less it is a serious moral issue. Quinton argues that "the suffering associated with punishment *may* not be inflicted on them, firstly, as brutal and secondly, if it is represented as punishment, as involving a lie." The second objection does not hold if we do not represent the infliction of suffering on the innocent as a form of punishment. And the first objection is not one of which utilitarians can avail themselves if the brutal treatment of the innocent will in fact produce the best consequences. So the argument against the utilitarian can now be reformulated as follows: why should we confine ourselves to punishment in those cases where the infliction of suffering on the innocent will produce the best consequences?

The objection to the utilitarian position is clearly moral, and hence it cannot be evaded by appealing even to a correct definition of the notion of punishment. A proper regard for the way in which terms are used will enable us to describe correctly the moral problem which confronts us, but it cannot solve that problem for us.

2.4. The Disutility of Punishing the Innocent

The second utilitarian response to the charge that utilitarians are committed to punishing the innocent draws our attention to the less obvious bad consequences of punishing innocent persons, and argues that on balance the punishment of the innocent will always produce worse consequences than the failure to do so. For example, it is claimed that the fact that an innocent man has been punished will soon leak out, and when that happens, there will be a loss of confidence in the sheriff and widespread fear among the population that any one of them might be the next innocent victim of the sheriff's attempt to prevent similar violence in future. Furthermore, the sheriff himself will have his sensibilities blunted once the barrier against framing and punishing the innocent has been removed.

He is more likely to adopt a similar policy the next time he faces a problem of maintaining order, and on that occasion, there may be no strong utilitarian as for punishing an innocent person. It is also not certain that there will in fact be racial violence if an innocent person is not punished. On the other hand, the suffering of the innocent person who is punished is very real. The suffering of the innocent man is likely to be greater than that of the guilty. The punishment will come as a big shock to the innocent man, and he will be angered and distressed in a way that the guilty person will not be.

But at each point of this utilitarian response, the critic can counter by tightening up the description of the example under consideration. Thus the sheriff suffers from a sudden fatal illness soon after the punishment of the innocent man, and he makes no deathbed confessions. No one else knows about the fabrication of evidence and the secret is buried with the sheriff. The innocent man who is punished has no relatives or close friends, and he himself is well endowed with an unusual temperament which faces unexpected disaster with calm resignation. We must not forget the unconvicted real offender who is still free and conceivably could give the whole show away. So he dies unexpectedly when he is run over by a bus on his way to the sheriff's funeral. Now we are back where we started with an example in which the punishment of an innocent person produces the best consequences and so should be accepted by the utilitarian. ...

I have so far assumed, for the sake of argument, that it is only in fantastic situations that utilitarians are committed to punishing the innocent. But it is now time to say something about this assumption. Most utilitarians seem to make the assumption. Thus Hare writes: "The retributivists are right at the intuitive level, and the utilitarians at the critical level." But contrast this with David Richards's claim in *The Moral Criticism of Law* that the utilitarian theory of punishment "clearly seems to allow and even require the punishment of the innocent, since it is very plausible that a higher degree of criminal deterrence would be achieved by punishing the children or relatives or friends or lovers of criminals in addition to or even in place of the criminal. Primitive systems of law often do exactly this, ..." In the face of these conflicting claims, two remarks are appropriate. First, no one can claim with confidence that, on the balance of probabilities, there are no actual cases in which punishing the innocent will produce the best consequences. But secondly, the strength of our conviction, which is shared by many utilitarians, that punishing the innocent in the real world is unjustified, cannot be accounted for simply on the basis of utilitarian considerations. If we were guided by purely utilitarian considerations, we would not be entitled to be as confident as we in fact are that such punishment in the real world is wrong, and we should indeed be prepared to experiment with limited proposals for the punishment of the innocent.

Indeed we can go further and argue that in the present state of our knowledge, surveyed earlier, the evidence of the desirable effects of punishment is not always as firmly based as is often assumed, and this presents some difficulties for a purely utilitarian justification of punishment. From the utilitarian point of view punishing offenders produces bad consequences which are certain and not speculative, namely the suffering inflicted directly by punishment on offenders and indirectly on their friends and relatives. Against this, there is no equally firm evidence, in all cases where punishment is thought to be justified, of its countervailing good effects. There is some evidence of incapacitative effects although the extent of these effects varies with different types of offences, and the evidence is also consistent with there being some general deterrent effect. Again, there is good reason to think that the total abandonment of the practice of punishment would have unfortunate results. But there are specific crimes in which the utilitarian case for punishment, while not ruled out, is not particularly strong. It is then unclear what we should do in the present state of our knowledge if we were guided by purely utilitarian considerations. In fact our thinking on these matters is also guided by non-utilitarian considerations. Other things being equal, we think it better that the guilty should suffer through punishment than that there should be similar suffering by the innocent victims of crime. Again, given that the practice of punishment has some utilitarian justification, there will also be offenders who may justifiably be punished by appealing to non-utilitarian considerations. For example, if the punishment for some offences can be justified on utilitarian grounds in terms of the general deterrent effect and the incapacitative effect of such punishment, then it is unfair to allow those who have committed more serious offences to go unpunished even if in these latter cases the existing evidence is inadequate to show that punishment has similar good effects.

I do not believe that the practice of punishment would be justified if there were a decisive utilitarian case against it, or if it did not at least have some utilitarian support. But this is not to say that all desirable aspects of that practice can be justified in purely utilitarian terms.

NOTE

Another empirical problem that haunts the utilitarian tradition is the inefficacy of risk predictions concerning dangerousness or, simply, reoffending. That is, when an individual is sentenced in a manner that focuses on his or her perceived dangerousness in the future, there can be no confidence that the person has been properly identified as a dangerous individual. The social science literature generally conveys great pessimism with regard to the ability of psychiatrists and actuaries to predict dangerousness. Even more disturbing is that psychiatrists tend to overpredict dangerousness. In "Preventive Detention and Execution: The Constitutionality of Punishing Future Crimes" (1991), 15 *Law & Human Behavior* 139, Patrick Ewing provides a gloomy account of the literature:

> While there is disagreement among researchers, clinicians and legal scholars and professionals about the accuracy of predictions of dangerousness, few knowledgeable observers would disagree with the conclusion that dangerousness cannot be predicted very accurately. Some claim that predictions of dangerousness (i.e., predictions that a given individual will, at some later time, engage in violent conduct toward others) prove to be wrong ... in virtually all cases. Others suggest that the "false positive" rate for such predictions is closer to two out of three—two wrong predictions for every right one. Even the most optimistic behavioral scientists and legal commentators now seem to believe that the accuracy of predictions of dangerousness, whether made clinically or statistically, is "probably no better than one valid assessment out of two."

See, however, Webster, Harris, Rice, Cormier, and Quinsey, *The Violence Prediction Scheme: Assessing Dangerousness in High Risk Men* (Toronto: Centre of Criminology, University of Toronto, 1994), which argues for the use of actuarial prediction and provides a framework for developing an actuarial assessment. This framework can then be integrated with a clinical assessment to produce a final score that categorizes the person into one of nine groups based on probability of violent recidivism. The authors observe that clinical assessments should not alter the actuarial judgment by more than 10 percent in either direction. It seems that a number of professionals involved in the correctional field have been impressed by this model, although many, especially lawyers, are disturbed by it. Perhaps the reason for this concern is premised on one of the authors' own conclusions (at 65):

> The present VPS (violence prediction scheme) embodies within it a good deal of current knowledge and experience. No one claims that its use will guarantee "fairness," "accuracy," and "absence of bias" in each and every case.

Finally, recent reviews of the deterrence research suggest that the impact of sentencing on aggregate crime rates is modest. Increasing the severity of punishments will have little impact on the overall crime rate or on recidivism rates. Advocates of harsher sentencing regimes (including mandatory sentences of imprisonment) often assert that more severe sentencing will deter offenders and thus lower crime rates. Scholars at the Institute of Criminology, University of Cambridge, reviewed research on the relationship between sentence severity and crime rates. They conclude by drawing the following conclusion:

> The USA has had severer sentences than England in the last decade and a half, and US crime rates have generally been falling or steady while England's (at least, until recently) have been rising. But a closer analysis of the trends generally does not show substantial negative correlations between [severity] levels and crime rates. Such figures thus give scant support to recent claims that America's tougher penalties have shown demonstrably greater success in deterring crime.

A. von Hirsch, A. Bottoms, E. Burney, and P.-O. Wikstrom, *Criminal Deterrence and Sentence Severity* (Oxford: Hart Publishing, 1999).

III. RETRIBUTIVE THEORIES OF PUNISHMENT

The notion of retribution as a basis for punishment is rooted in the works of Kant and Hegel. This theory holds that punishment ought to be (or must be) imposed when it is deserved. In its purest form, retribution is reflected in the ancient *lex talionis* (that is, "an eye for an eye"). The question whether any beneficial consequences will result from the imposition of punishment is irrelevant. Indeed, an uncompromising retributivist would argue that if punishment is in fact deserved, it ought to be imposed, notwithstanding the possibility of disastrous consequences.

In the excerpts that follow (Braithwaite and Pettit and Lacey), the main features and criticisms of "classical" retributivism are explored. Classical retributivism is criticized for being intuitive or transcendental at its base and dependent on metaphor for its explanation. Retributivists attempt to justify the imposition of punishment by asserting that punishment "restores the balance," "annuls the crime," or "repays a debt to society." Do these expressions lend any force to retributivism, or do they merely restate its elemental content—that is, that the guilty *deserve* to suffer? Retributive approaches to punishment are also criticized for being nothing more than institutional revenge. Are there meaningful differences between personal revenge and a system of state punishment predicated on retributive notions?

Retributive theories of punishment have seen a revival of sorts in the last couple of decades. Some of the more positive features of retributivism have been resurrected under the banner of a "just-deserts" theory (or the "new retributivism," as it is sometimes called). Just-deserts theorists rely on retributive notions to justify proportionate sentencing. This notion should have a ring of familiarity, as the earlier excerpt from H.L.A. Hart refers to the use of retributive reasoning in the "distribution" of sanctions. Just-deserts theorists, such as Andrew von Hirsch, have invoked retributive theory to construct a sentencing regime committed to the idea of proportionality. Variations of this regime found their way into the United States when a number of states adopted determinate sentencing guidelines. The excerpts from von Hirsch and Tonry debate the value of this retributive dimension of sentencing.

J. Braithwaite and P. Pettit, *Not Just Deserts:*
A Republican Theory of Criminal Justice
(Oxford: Clarendon Press, 1990) (references omitted)

The Resurgence of Retributivism

Until the 1970s retributivism, the idea that criminals should be punished because they deserve it, was something of a dead letter in criminology; there were a few scholars in jurisprudence and philosophy who continued to dabble with retributive theories but they did so in ways that had little impact on public policy. During and since the Victorian era retributivism had become increasingly disreputable, probably unfairly, as an unscientific indulgence of emotions of revenge.

In that period a descendant of utilitarianism dominated criminal justice policy-making. This is the theory we call "preventionism." Preventionist criminologists were motivated by the search for ways of sentencing criminals that would incapacitate them from continuing to offend (as by locking them away from potential victims), that would give the healing and helping professions opportunities to rehabilitate them, and that would deter both those convicted (specific deterrence) and others who became aware of the punishment (general deterrence).

In that same period, ironically, positive criminology accumulated masses of evidence testifying to the failures of such utilitarian doctrines. All manner of rehabilitation programmes for offenders were tried without any producing consistent evidence that they reduce reoffending rates. The deterrence literature also failed to produce the expected evidence that more police, more prisons, and more certain and severe punishment made a significant difference to the crime rate. Since the literature we are referring to here is massive, and the conclusion we reach fairly uncontroversial within criminology, we will not delay the reader by reviewing it.

The evidence on incapacitation, as distinct from rehabilitation or deterrence, was not so clear. There is no doubt that we can prevent bank robbers from robbing banks by incarcerating or executing them. However, we cannot rely on incarceration to prevent assaulters or rapists from committing their type of offence; nor by such measures can we stop drug dealers from selling drugs or organized crime figures from running criminal empires. And while there is a minority of criminologists who think that if we can lock up enough of the right offenders for long enough we can have a substantial impact on the crime rate, most evidence suggests that with the best techniques available we are wrong about twice as often as we are right in predicting serious reoffending. The evidence is that we can never catch enough criminals to reduce crime substantially through incapacitation, or at least that the costs of locking up enough criminals to make a real difference to crime is beyond the fiscal capacities of even the wealthiest countries in the world. Moreover, there are questions about whether imprisonment does not actually worsen the problem in some ways: the convict often learns new illegal skills in "schools for crime" and criminal groups may recruit new members to fill the gap while colleagues are incarcerated.

The flight to retributivism was not only fuelled by the realization that utilitarian and preventionist criminology had failed to deliver on its promises. There was also growing documentation of the injustices perpetrated in the name of preventionist criminal justice. Indeterminate sentences, on the grounds of rehabilitation or incapacitation, allowed offenders to be locked up until they were "safe" to be returned to the community. Many offenders were locked up for extremely long periods for minor crimes; others got very short terms for serious crimes, thanks to their acting skills in feigning rehabilitation. This disparity was often the product of genuine but misguided utilitarian beliefs that certain minor offenders could be prevented from a downward spiral into more serious crime if only psychologists had long enough to work on their rehabilitation. But it also happened that rehabilitation and incapacitation were used to excuse locking up indefinitely some minor offenders who were regarded as subversive or insolent. At the other extreme, bribes were sometimes paid to secure the early release of serious offenders, ostensibly on grounds of their remarkable rehabilitation.

These indeed were good reasons for the retributivists to reject utilitarianism and preventionism. Furthermore, the new retributivists rightly accused preventionists of denying the human dignity of offenders by treating them as determined creatures whose behaviour could not be accounted for by their own choices to break the law. Preventionists tended to back off from blaming offenders; instead of holding them responsible for their wrongdoing, they sought to manipulate them by curing their sickness (rehabilitation), changing the reward–cost calculations that determined their offending (deterrence), and keeping them away from criminal opportunities (incapacitation). The retributivists were struck by the injustice, not to mention the futility, of this. So they called for punishment of offenders in proportion to their desert; mostly this meant in proportion to the harmfulness and blameworthiness of their actions. Criminals should get what they deserve—no more, no less.

By and large, then, the new retributivists who gained the ascendency in the punishment debate during the 1970s were responding to what they correctly identified as the failures, the excesses, the injustices, and the denigration of human agency of utilitarianism and preventionism. The retributivists, we will argue, were moved by the right reasons but took the wrong turn. In particular, they turned too sharply away from the positive, caring strands in the utilitarian and preventionist traditions. Tony Bottoms made the point well when he remarked: "The rehabilitative ethic, and perhaps still more the liberal reformism which preceded it, was an ethic of coercive caring, but at least there was caring."

Why the Debate Matters

For most of its history criminology has played a significant role in legitimating state intrusions into the lives and liberties of citizens. In the 1990s it is now playing this role again, thanks in part to the revival of retributivism. Yet in the 1960s and 1970s mainstream criminology began to delegitimate punitive crime control and intrusive police powers. It did this because by then criminology had shown that increased investment in deterrence, rehabilitation, and incapacitation made little or no difference to the crime rate and cost the taxpayer a fortune. The conventional wisdom of criminology was that imprisonment was a discredited institution and the less we had of it the better, that police were necessary but that attempts to give them more powers and resources should be resisted because it could not be demonstrated that doing this would reduce crime.

In some crucial respects criminologists still play this role. In Australia, for example, public opinion polls consistently show a community where those who support capital punishment outnumber those who oppose it. Most expert criminological opinion sits on the side of the opponents, from time to time trotting out evidence in public debates that where capital punishment has been reintroduced crime rates have not fallen. If expert opinion shifted to support for the view that crime could be reduced by capital punishment, the balance in the debate would probably tip, and the noose return.

But this is a vestige of the 1960s and 1970s when mainstream criminology was more consistently delegitimating of punishment. Instead of continuing to contribute to a healthy scepticism about the rationality of punishment, many of the brightest and best criminologists have now begun to cast around for alternative justifications for maintaining punishment as the pre-eminent response to crime. Retributivism serves them well, for the community can be assured that it matters not whether acts of punishment protect them from crime; we do right when we punish because we give people their just deserts. Even scholars who are anything but law and order conservatives have caught the enthusiasm: There is a feeling of a Kantian imperative behind the word "deserts." Certain things are simply wrong and ought to be punished. And this we do believe.

It follows from the theory we defend, which we will summarize in a moment, that it is good when societies feel uncomfortable about punishment, when people see punishment as a necessary evil rather than a good in itself. Just as it is healthy for citizens to be uncomfortable rather than morally smug about the rightness of killing others in war, so too with punishing criminals. Wilkins reminds us that: "if freedom is to be protected, it must be protected at its frontiers," by which he means that if we are to respect freedom, we must be particularly watchful for the freedom of those who seem least deserving of our concern. A society which feels morally comfortable about sending thousands of terrified young men and women to institutions in which they are bashed, raped, and brutalized, stripped of human dignity, denied freedom of speech and movement, has a doubtful commitment to freedom. A theory which assures us that any human being can deserve these things is subversive of that commitment.

In contending that the new retributivism has provided this assurance, we are not accusing its adherents of necessarily wanting to increase the oppressiveness of the criminal justice system. A good number of the new retributivists, especially some of the more influential among them, are liberals, even radicals, and they see the punishments deserved as much less than those currently administered by criminal justice systems. But liberal versions of just deserts inevitably reduce, in the realities of table-thumping politics, to a strategy of "getting tough."

When you play the game of criminal justice on the field of retribution, you play it on the home ground of conservative law-and-order politicians. You give full rein to those who play to the sense of normality of the majority, urging them to tyrannize the minority. Once all the players agree that retribution, or giving people what they deserve, is the rationale for punishment, the genteel visions of liberal retributivists count for nought. Some of the left retributivists now concede that they may have been co-opted into playing on the conservatives' home ground. Complicated notions like the balancing of benefits and burdens which can underpin liberal egalitarian versions of retributivism are quickly discarded by law-and-order politicians who find that their press releases are most likely to get a run by appealing to simple-minded vengeance. The long-term effect of the new retributivism in criminal justice theory will be to make the community feel more comfortable with punishment, encouraging prisons which are even more overcrowded and more brutal than at present.

None of this proves that retributivism is wrong or inadequate as a theory. It is perhaps just another illustration of Thorsten Sellin's dictum on criminal justice reform that "beautiful theories have a way of turning into ugly practices." All we have wanted to show in this section is that the debate is one that matters. Whether for good or ill, whether in the way they would have wanted or not, the new retributivists have certainly changed both the punishment debate and criminal justice policy. The long list of American states that have shifted to "flat," "determinate," or "presumptive" sentencing codes since the mid-1970s—Illinois, California, Connecticut, Colorado, Alaska, Arizona, Maine, Indiana, Minnesota, and others—is sufficient testimony to that.

N. Lacey, *State Punishment: Political Principles and Community Values*
(London: Routledge, 1988) (footnotes omitted)

Backward-Looking Justifications

The central case of an exclusively backward-looking justification is that of classical retributivism in its strong form. I take this theory to be making the claim that the state has both a right and a duty to punish, in the sense of inflicting unpleasant consequences upon an offender in response to her offence to the extent that, and by reason of that fact that, she deserves that punishment. Desert thus operates as both a necessary and a sufficient condition for justified punishment. Theories which present desert as a necessary but not a sufficient condition will be considered as mixed theories. Thus the key notion employed by backward-looking theories is that of desert. Some writers treat desert as an axiomatic or self-evident moral principle, assuming that it needs no further explanation. Others, however (the present writer included), whilst acknowledging the place of desert in our moral intuitions and reactive attitudes, find the concept puzzling when they attempt further to analyze its normative appeal, at least in the context of punishment. Indeed, it has been argued that the apparent irreducibility of the notion gives rise to suspicions that the claim that X ought to be punished because she deserves to be punished merely amounts to the claim that X ought to be punished because she ought to be punished. If the intuition is not shared, it seems impossible to push the argument further—so this is hardly a helpful contribution to the complex debate about the justifiability of punishment. Thus many writers have acknowledged the necessity of further unpacking the notion of desert, and we need to examine some of these attempts in order to fairly evaluate the adequacy of backward-looking justifications of punishment.

The Lex Talionis

Perhaps the crudest yet the most fundamental attempt is represented by the ancient lex talionis: an eye for any eye, a life for a life, and so on. This principle, if it merits the name, certainly has the attraction of simplicity: unfortunately this is all that can be said for it. Two devastating objections eliminate it from the list of possible candidates as adequate explications of the desert principle. Most obviously, in terms of the question of how much punishment is inflicted, it supplies clear practical guidance as to the proper measure only in a selective number of cases. The penalty for murder or mutilation may seem clear, but what punishment ought to be inflicted for fraud, perjury or blackmail? The indeterminancy of the principle in these cases ought to make us wary of the status of its apparent clarity in others. And any subtler reinterpretation, such as the argument that murderers simply lose their right not to be killed, or thieves not to be stolen from, hardly generates a morally adequate or even clear set of prescriptions for a criminal justice system. Secondly, and more importantly, this principle fails to capture one of the greatest strengths of the retributivist tradition: that is, its accommodation of a strong principle of responsibility generating limitations on who may properly be punished. It is generally claimed that no punishment is deserved unless the offence is committed by an agent who is responsible in the sense of having a certain degree of knowledge of relevant circumstances and capacity for control of her actions. [As for the] significance and meaning of the principle of responsibility ... for the moment it is sufficient to recall that our moral response appears to differ enormously according to whether a killing is intentional or accidental; a wounding deliberate or negligent. This commonly acknowledged moral distinction between responsibility based merely on causation—strict liability—and that based on "mental elements"—such as intent or recklessness—is ignored by the lex talionis, which directs the same response in each case. Added to the fact that the lex talionis offers no real arguments about why we should punish in the first place, these defects make it clear that we shall have to look further afield for an adequate explanation of the principle of desert central to the retributivist tradition.

The Culpability Principle

A more promising account explicates the idea of desert in terms of culpability, using this notion not only to identify the justifying reasons for punishment and those who may properly be punished, but also to fix the proper measure of punishment, in terms of a relationship of commensurability or proportionality between the offence and the punishment inflicted. Culpability is generally explained as a function of the gravity of the harm caused (such as death, injury or damage to property) combined with the degree of responsibility (intent, recklessness, negligence or mere inadvertence) of the actor. But the notion of culpability also enshrines, as indeed it must if it is to count as a justifying argument for punishment, a moral judgment about the wrongfulness of the behaviour in question. Cuplability, in other words, is equated with blameworthiness, and blameworthiness is equated in turn with punishment-worthiness. This does seem to reflect an important aspect of our entrenched habits and attitudes of praising and blaming, and in a more accurate way than does the lex talionis. However, as a normative theory of punishment, this approach too has its difficulties. Some of these, which I shall call internal criticisms, take the form of problems thrown up by the argument from culpability on its own terms: if we were to accept the principle, what would its implications be? Others, which I shall call external criticisms, cast doubt more fundamentally on the adequacy of the principle itself: does it offer an adequate explication of the content and normative force of arguments from desert? Both kinds of difficulty will have to be addressed in order to give a fair appraisal of the culpability principle. ...

Finally, and most importantly, however, serious external criticisms can be made of the culpability principle's account of why it is that we should punish. For it is not clear that the move from a judgment of blameworthiness to one of punishment-worthiness should be made so lightly. Even though our desert-based reactive attitudes may be firmly held, surely we should reflect carefully and seek further reasons before we take the additional step of deliberately acting in a harmful way against a particular individual on the basis of them? A judgment that someone has behaved wrongly does not involve or justify the further judgment that they should be punished. Ultimately, the culpability principle seems to give us no explanation of why we should think it right to punish offenders merely by reason of their past culpable actions. By what means does such an argument, if argument it is, distinguish itself from a principle of vengeance? By what moral alchemy does the prima facie wrong of punishment following on the wrong of the offence create a morally preferable situation? Why should an offence alone generate a moral reason for punitive action? None of these issues is demystified by the culpability principle.

Forfeiture of Rights, Unfair Advantages and the Restoration of a Moral Equilibrium

Given what has been said of the failure of these first two models of desert theory to generate a satisfactory justification of punishment, it makes sense to attempt further to explicate the desert principle within the context of some wider, compatible, background political philosophy. Thus the other attempts I shall consider explore the links between the concept of desert and those of justice, fairness and equality. The concepts of justice and fairness have indeed been central to the desert tradition, and it is thus with these that I shall begin.

The first of the more sophisticated versions of the desert principle which I shall consider may conveniently be labeled the forfeiture of rights view. On this view, the meaning of the claim that an offender deserves to be punished is explained within the context of the existence of a legal system which generates reciprocal political obligations upon citizens to obey its norms. Thus by virtue of a voluntarily committed offence an individual violates here obligations not only to the state but also to all other citizens, and the state is justified in depriving her of her civil rights. The thesis can be put in an extreme and a moderate form. In its extreme form it claims that an offender forfeits all her civil rights by virtue of any voluntarily committed offence. This seems on the face of it to be an implausible claim, generating as it does no limit on the amount or type of justifiable punishment and thus abandoning the proportionality principle central to the retributive tradition. A more plausible version is that which argues that the offender only forfeits a set of rights equivalent to these which she has violated: once the proportionate set of rights has been forfeited, the offender can re-enter political society on fair terms with the law-abiding.

Thus on the moderate view a full set of political rights is due to a citizen so long as she meets her political and legal obligations. This argument does generate a clear principle identifying who may be punished, but doubts remain about just what the argument amounts to as a set of positive justifying reasons for punishment. *Why* should an offender forfeit any civil rights? What does the argument add to the blank, mysterious claim that she deserves it? A further refinement argues that a voluntary offence is taken to show that the offender in a sense chose or willed her own punishment, or at least consented to it, where she was responsible for the offence, aware of its normative consequences, and acting within a fair system of rules. The punishment therefore respects the autonomy of the agent, treating her as an end in herself rather than as a means to some diffused social good. Again, this argument has some appeal as a claim about who should be punished, but as an account of why they should be punished it is inadequate: it can hardly be claimed that offenders consent to their disadvantaging punitive treatment in anything like the strong sense of consent which we generally take to be necessary to justify harsh treatment of one person by another. We can easily imagine an offender who meets the conditions of the principle yet who states in committing her offence that she does not consent to any punishment: the only way in which such an offender can be brought within the ambit of the principle is through some form of social contract argument. I shall consider the difficulties with this approach in commenting on the second sophisticated version of the desert principle, which raises a similar issue. Before moving on, however, it is worth raising the question of whether in any case the consent argument for punishment could count as a genuinely desert-based principle. In attempting to unpack that idea, we seem to have moved a considerable distance from our unreconstructed starting point.

The second version may be called the unfair advantage view. Again, we are to imagine a background system of reciprocal political obligations, and we are invited to take the view that the essence of a voluntary offence is the taking by the offender of an unfair advantage: in failing to restrain herself, the offender has had the advantage of fulfilling choices forbidden to others. The purpose and justification of punishment is, in effect, to remove that unfair advantage and to restore the "moral equilibrium" or relationships of justice that existed prior to the offence. On one extreme version of the view, until punishment is inflicted, all members of society are in some way implicated in the moral disequilibrium created by the crime, which they have failed to redress. It is presumably this type of thought which prompts Kant to say that even on the dissolution of society all murderers held in the jails ought to be executed. There is perhaps a connection between such views about the value to be attached to the restoration of the oral equilibrium and the argument that punishment "reaffirms the right"—both in terms of the rightness of the standards breached by the offence and in terms of the pre-existing relationships of justice between the members of political society. Here at last we have not only an argument about who may properly be punished, but also a positive claim about the reasons for that punishment—although reasons which, as I shall argue, are at such a high level of abstraction that their contribution to de-mystification of the desert principle is limited.

These two versions of desert theory have the important advantage over those so far considered of locating principles of punishment in their proper context—that is, within a general set of political principles. Indeed, these views are probably best understood within the social contract tradition in political philosophy, which asks us to imagine some hypothetical initial agreement upon a certain system of rules and methods of enforcement which can and must then fairly be administered by means of imposition of the agreed sanctions. But these views are not without their practical and theoretical difficulties. In the first place, neither of them gives very clear practical guidance about the fair measure of punishment in particular cases. What actual punishment would forfeit a set of rights equivalent to those violated by a rapist, a petty thief, a reckless driver? What sanction would be sufficient to remove the unfair advantage gained by the provoked manslaughterer, the tax evader or the burglar? As in the case of the law of the talion and the culpability principle, resort to arguments from conventionality agreed, customary or consequence-based penalty scales seem hard to avoid. Secondly, real difficulties have been raised about the social contract tradition itself; in what sense can a *fictitious* agreement generate obligations for real people? This subject will have to be taken up in detail in later chapters. Furthermore, these views are dependent for their force, as we have already noted, on the existence of a fair set of rules. This is not fatal in itself, but the criteria which dictate that there is indeed a just equilibrium which can be restored are not generated by the forfeiture of rights or unfair advantage principles alone. The views do presuppose an independent account of what counts as an unfair advantage and a just equilibrium.

Finally, it seems legitimate to ask whether the metaphorical ideas of restoring relationships of justice or moral equilibria outweigh the obvious disvalues attached to the suffering and other costs of punishment. Do these theories really ignore such cost completely? If not, what weight do they accord them? In what real sense does punishment "restore the right"? Do these theories really remove the mystery attaching to the original, simple desert principle, or are they, too, a form of moral alchemy? Or, in trying to avoid the mystery, do they not collapse into versions of utilitarian or other consequentialist justification? Is the real reason for punishment underlying these theories the need to uphold a just and effective legal system, to prevent private vengeance, to remove feelings of unfairness on the parts of victims? Can any account of punishment which ignores these factors generate a satisfactory justification? And if so many questions crucial to the justification of punishment can only be answered by looking beyond the desert principle, how strong a claim can that principle make to constitute *the* justification of punishment?

Let us turn finally to a version of the desert principle which explores its links with a principle of equality. On this view, to punish someone who deserves punishment is to act in accordance with a principle of equal treatment: treat like cases alike, and different ones differently. Through her voluntary offence, the offender has singled herself out from other citizens: offenders and non-offenders ought to be treated differently. But this will not do as a theory of desert, let alone as a theory of punishment. First of all, it is too minimal: on this basis alone it might justify treating the offender better than the non-offender, so long as this was done consistently. In addition, the principle generates no answer to the question of how much we ought to punish. Finally, the principle tells us nothing about why an offence makes the offender relevantly different in a way which justifies punitive treatment. Not every type of voluntary differentiating action, even one affecting others, justifies a punitive response. Thus the principle of equal treatment cannot explain the principle of desert, although it may form an important part of that principle.

Retributive Theory

We are now in a position to evaluate the question of whether any of the arguments we have considered as possible explications of the idea of desert makes sense of the puzzle of the justification of punishment. This can best be done by means of a summary of the answers generated by those arguments to the three questions originally imposed. First of all, why should we punish? It is really in answering this fundamental question that the arguments associated with desert are at their most deficient. Even the more sophisticated versions barely rise above the level of metaphor, and leave us with the suspicion that the idea of desert cannot be distinguished from a principle of vengeance or the unappealing assertion that two wrongs somehow make a right. Within the context of a general set of political principles, arguments such as that from unfair tax advantage can answer this question, but when such a supplementation is made, it is no longer clear that what we have is a desert theory at all, rather than a consequence-based account. In addition, the possibility of a background system which is not universally just complicates the force of the claim that punishment aims to restore a moral equilibrium. Moreover, why should we necessarily give absolute priority to the demands of this narrow retributive conception of justice as opposed to those of mercy, forgiveness and humanity?

Secondly, how much ought we to punish? This is the question to which the idea of desert promises us a clear and determinate answer, yet on analysis it fails to fulfill that promise. Without supplementation by either conventionally agreed scales of punishment or arguments from consequences, arguments from desert tell us very little about what punishments we ought to inflict. Thirdly, many of the arguments closely associated with the retributive tradition do generate a determinate answer to the question of whom we should punish: we should only punish those who have responsibly committed offences. It is perhaps in this area that the tradition really does encompass a principle which will be fundamental to the justification of punishment, and one which is indeed reflected in our differing response to the accidental, the negligent and the deliberate offence. Yet it is not clear why these arguments need employ the concept of desert: they can be developed perfectly adequately in terms of responsibility, fairness and other arguments from distributive as opposed to retributive justice, as we shall see. And in the absence of any adequate explanation of what the desert principle amounts to, let alone of a desert-based answer to the central question of why we should punish, the responsibility principle in any case only operates as a limiting one which would have to be combined with some other arguments to generate a justification of punishment. In addition, with respect to the broader aspect of the third question, that is, what kinds of actions ought to be punished, the principles we have considered have to be supplemented by a set of general, consistent yet independent political principles in order to give any complete guidance.

Negatively, then, the retributive tradition seems accurately to reflect our considered judgment about excuses, justifications and mitigating principles: it can tell us why not to punish certain categories of person; but it fails to tell us why we should punish any persons, and in what sorts of circumstances. In addition, consistent adherence to the main purported arguments from desert would issue in a criminal justice system in some respects radically more extensive, in others greatly less so, than those generally acknowledged to be acceptable. This last factor is of course not decisive, but we may use our intuitions where they are reflected in the shape of current systems as at least pointers to the need for modification of possible theories.

A. von Hirsch, "Proportionality in the Philosophy of Punishment"
in M. Tonry, ed., *Crime and Justice—A Review of Research, XVI*
(Chicago: University of Chicago Press, 1992) (references omitted)

The last two decades have witnessed continuing debate over the rationales for allocating sanctions among convicted offenders. Various guiding theories or strategies have been put forward: "just deserts," "limiting retributivism," "selective incapacitation." The choice among them is sometimes treated as a matter of deciding allegiances: one adheres to "just deserts" or not, just as one decides to be a Democrat or a Red Sox fan or not. If one opts for just deserts, then one must worry about the scaling of penalties. If one does not, then perhaps one can disregard such issues.

Such a perspective is, I think, misleading. Sanctioning rationales differ from one another largely in the emphasis they give the principle of proportionality that is, the requirement that sanctions be proportionate in their severity to the seriousness of offenses. A desert rationale is one that gives the principle a dominant role. Other viewpoints permit proportionality to be trumped, to a greater or a lesser degree, by ulterior concerns such as those of crime control. ...

B. Desert Theories

Traditional retributive theories, such as Kant's, were sketchy. While contending that justice calls for deserved punishments, they seldom explored the grounds of penal desert claims: namely, *why* wrongdoers deserve punishment. Recently, philosophers have been looking for explanations. The two leading accounts today are, respectively, the "benefits and burdens" theory and "expressive" desert theories.

1. *Benefits and Burdens.* The benefits and burdens theory originated in the writings of two contemporary philosophers, Herbert Morris and Jeffrie Murphy. Both have recently questioned the theory, but a number of other philosophers continue to support it.

The theory offers a retrospectively oriented account of why offenders should be made to suffer punishment. The account focuses on the law as a jointly beneficial enterprise: it requires each person to desist from predatory conduct; by desisting, the person not only benefits others but is benefited by their reciprocal self-restraint. The person who victimizes others while still benefiting from their self-restraint thus obtains an unjust advantage. Punishment's function is to impose an offsetting disadvantage.

The theory has some attractions. It goes beyond fuzzy notions of "paying back" wrongdoing or "righting" the moral balance. It points to a particular unwarranted advantage the wrongdoer obtains: namely, that of benefiting from others' self-restraint while not reciprocally restraining himself. The rationale for the penalty is retrospective in focus, as a desert-oriented account should be: to offset, through punishment, the unjustly obtained benefit.

The theory has difficulties, however. One problem is that it requires a heroic belief in the justice of the underlying social arrangements. Unless it is true that our social and political systems succeed in providing mutual support for all members, including criminal offenders, then the offender has not necessarily benefited from others' law-abiding behavior.

The theory also becomes awkward when one uses it to try to decide the quantum of punishments. One difficulty is assessing benefits and burdens. The theory cannot focus on literal benefits the offender obtains as some of the worst assaultive crimes can be quite unprofitable whereas other (apparently less serious) theft crimes may provide the offender with a considerable profit. What thus must matter, instead, is the additional degree of freedom the offender has unfairly appropriated. But notions of degrees of freedom are unhelpful in making comparisons among crimes. It is one thing to say the armed robber or burglar permits himself actions that others refrain from taking and thereby unfairly obtains a liberty that others have relinquished in their (and his) mutual interest. It is different, and far more obscure, to say the robber deserves more punishment than the burglar because, somehow, he has arrogated to himself a greater degree of unwarranted freedom than the burglar has.

The theory would also seem to distort the way the gravity of crimes is assessed. R.A. Duff has pointed out the artificiality of treating victimizing crimes, such as armed robbery, in terms of the "freedom-of-action" advantage the robber gains over uninvolved third parties, rather than in terms of the intrusion into the interests or rights of actual or potential victims. Perhaps, tax evasion can be explained in terms of unjustified advantage: the tax evader refuses to pay his or her own tax, yet benefits from others' payments through the services he or she receives. Tax evasion, however, is scarcely the paradigm criminal offense, and it is straining to try to assess the heinousness of common offences such as robbery in similar fashion.

2. *"Expressive" Theories.* "Expressive" theories are those that base desert claims on the censuring aspects of punishment. Punishing someone consists of doing something painful or unpleasant to him, because he has committed a wrong, under circumstances and in a manner that conveys disapprobation of the offender for his wrong. Treating the offender as a wrongdoer, Richard Wasserstrom has pointed out, is central to the idea of punishment. The difference between a tax and a fine, for example, does not rest in the kind of material deprivation imposed: it is money, in both cases. It con-

sists, rather, in the fact that with a fine the money is taken in a manner that conveys disapproval or censure; whereas with a tax no disapproval is implied.

A sanction that treats conduct as wrong that is, not a "neutral" sanction has two important moral functions that, arguably, are not reducible to crime prevention. One is to recognize the importance of the rights that have been infringed. Joel Feinberg has argued that the censure in punishment conveys to victims and potential victims that the state recognizes they are wronged by criminal conduct, that rights to which they are properly entitled have been infringed.

The other role of censure, discussed by R.A. Duff, is to address the wrongdoer as a moral agent, by appealing to his or her sense of right or wrong. This, Duff suggests, is not just a preventive strategy. While it is hoped that the actor will reconsider his actions and desist from wrongdoing in the future, the censure is not merely a means of changing his behavior otherwise, there would be no point in censuring actors who are repentant already (since they need no blame to make the effort to desist) or who are seemingly incorrigible (since they will not change despite the censure). Any human actor, the theory suggests, is a moral agent, capable (unless clearly incompetent) of evaluating others' assessment of their conduct. The repentant actor has his own assessment of the conduct confirmed through the disapproval of others; the defiant actor is made to understand and feel others' disapproval, even if he refuses to desist. Such communication of judgement and feeling, Duff argues, is what moral discourse among rational agents is about. What a purely "neutral" sanction not embodying blame would deny even if no less effective in preventing crime is precisely that essential status of the person as a moral agent. A neutral sanction would treat potential offenders much as beasts in a circus as beings that must be restrained, intimidated, or conditioned into submission because they are incapable of understanding that harmful conduct is wrong.

Such censure-oriented desert theories have some potential advantages. They are less dependent on the supposition that the underlying social system is wholly just: an actor with cause for complaint against the social system may still be to blame, for example, if he knowingly injures those who have done him no wrong. Moreover, the theory is more easily squared with notions of proportionality. If punishment is seen as an expression of blame for reprehensible conduct, then the quantum of punishment should depend on how reprehensible the conduct is. The punishment for typical victimizing crimes would depend on how much harm the conduct does, and how culpable the actor is for the harm and no longer on how much extra freedom of action the actor has arrogated to himself vis-à-vis third parties. ...

V. The Desert Model

A desert model is a sentencing scheme that observes the proportionality principle: punishments are scaled according to the seriousness of crimes. While speaking of a "desert model" might suggest a unique scale, that is not the intent. A variety of scales of differing overall severity and differing sanctions might satisfy the requirements of this model. It is the core elements of a desert model that are sketched here. Fuller accounts of the model and its rationale are available elsewhere, as are discussions of the use of the model in scaling noncustodial sanctions.

A. Ordinal Proportionality

Ordinal proportionality is the requirement that penalties be scaled according to the comparative seriousness of crimes. Two main sub-requirements are involved. First, parity. The proportionality principle permits differences in severity of punishments only to the extent these differences reflect variations in the degree of blameworthiness of the conduct. Accordingly, when offenders have been convicted of crimes of similar seriousness, they deserve punishment of similar severity unless special circumstances (i.e., of aggravation of mitigation) can be identified that render the offense, in the particular context, more or less deserving of blame than would normally be the case. Second, rank ordering. Punishing one crime more than another expresses more disapproval for the former crime, so that it is justified only if that crime is more serious. Punishments thus are to be ordered on a penalty scale so that their relative severity reflects the seriousness rankings of the crimes involved. This restricts the extent to which the arrangement of penalties on the scale can be varied internally for crime preventive purposes. Imposing exemplary penalties for a given type of offense to halt a recent upswing in its incidence, for example, would throw the ranking of offenses out of kilter unless other penalties are adjusted accordingly. ...

B. Scale Anchoring and Cardinal Proportionality

Cardinal proportionality requires that a reasonable proportion be maintained between overall levels of punitiveness and the gravity of the criminal conduct. The scale should not, for example, be so inflated that even lesser criminal conduct is penalized with substantial deprivations.

Since cardinal proportionality places only broad and imprecise constraints on how much the penalty scale can be escalated or deflated, substantial leeway remains for locating the scale's anchoring points. What other factors would be relevant?

The penal traditions of the jurisdiction would be a starting point. Since the censure expressed through punishment is a convention, it, like any other convention, will be influenced by tradition. Normative considerations, however, may justify altering this convention. One such consideration is the goal of reducing the suffering visited on offenders.

Should crime prevention also be considered in setting the anchoring points? Certain preventive strategies would alter the comparative rankings of punishments and thus infringe ordinal proportionality. Selective incapacitation, for example, calls for the unequal punishment of offenders convicted of similar offenses on the basis of predictive criteria that do not reflect the seriousness of the criminal conduct.

Other preventive strategies, however, would not necessarily be open to this objection. Consider general deterrence. Were the penalties for particular offense categories to be set by reference to those penalties' expected deterrent effects, it would infringe ordinal proportionality, as it would no longer be the seriousness of crimes that determined the ordering of sanctions. Suppose, instead, that deterrence were used differently: penalties might be ordered according to the crimes' seriousness on the scale, with the scale's overall magnitude being decided (in part) by its expected net impact on crime. Were the requisite empirical knowledge available (which it is not today), it might be possible to compare the overall deterrent impacts of alternative scale magnitudes.

That information could then be used to help anchor the scale, without disturbing the ordering of penalties. Moreover, this approach would not necessarily lead to increases in severity. Penalties might be cut back below their historical levels, on grounds that no significant loss of deterrence would occur.

• • •

A desert-based scheme is necessarily somewhat confining in its requirement that offense seriousness, and not a variety of possible other considerations, should decide comparative punishment. Its confining character makes it easier to scale penalties in a coherent fashion, but it also limits the possibilities of achieving various other goals or objectives. Moreover, the proportionality principle rests on a particular value that of equity. Other values of various sorts might be thought to override equity considerations, in at least some situations. Hence, we need to consider the "hybrid" models: those that, to a lesser or greater extent, allow departures from ordinal desert requirements in order to achieve other purposes. ...

There is also the question of the degree of guidance a theory provides for the scaling of penalties. The proportionality principle, we have seen, offers no unique solutions, particularly because of the leeway it allows in the setting of a scale's anchoring points. However, the principle does offer considerable structure (although not unique solutions) for the comparative ordering of penalties. If proportionality is dislodged from this central, organizing role, it may not be easy to develop alternative (e.g., prevention-based) rationales that can provide much guidance. While a considerable body of theory exists concerning the principle of proportionality, lacunae remain. More thought needs to be given to the following topics, among others.

The Criteria for Gauging the Seriousness of Crimes, Particularly the Harm Dimension of Seriousness. A "living-standard" conception of harm may be a start, but it requires further scrutiny and elaboration.

Spacing. Proportionality calls not only for penalties ranked according to the gravity of crimes but also for spacing among penalties that reflects degrees of difference in crime seriousness. The spacing question, however, has received little attention.

Anchoring the Scale. If penalties are graded according to offense seriousness and the scale as a whole is not inflated or deflated unduly, the requirements of ordinal and cardinal proportionality have been satisfied, and one must look elsewhere for grounds for anchoring the scale. What these grounds might be remains largely to be explored.

There are also a number of practical issues needing further thought. One concerns back-up sanctions. Under any punishment theory emphasizing proportionality, non-custodial sanctions (rather than the severe penalty of imprisonment) should be employed for crimes other than serious ones. Using such sanctions raises the question of what should befall defendants if they violate the terms of the penalty or example, if they refuse to pay a fine or complete a stint of community service. How much added punitive bite may the back-up sanction legitimately entail?

M. Tonry, "Proportionality, Parsimony, and Interchangeability of Punishments"

in R.A. Duff, S. Marshall, R. Dobash, and R. Dobash, eds., *Penal Theory and Practice: Tradition and Innovation in Criminal Justice* (Manchester: Manchester University Press, 1994) (references omitted)

Critique of Principle of Proportionality

Efforts to apply philosophers' distinctions to policy-makers' decisions necessarily raise different concerns than do disagreements among philosophers. Current initiatives to increase use of "non-custodial" penalties in the United Kingdom and "intermediate" sanctions in the United States necessarily require translation of theorists' distinctions into practitioners' realities.

It is at this point of translation that the case for strong proportionality conditions breaks down. There are at least five major difficulties. First, strong proportionality conditions require objectification of categories of offenders and offenses that are over-simplified and overinclusive. Second, proportionality arguments are often premised on objective legal measures of desert, typically current and past crimes, other than on the subjective degree of moral culpability expressed by the offender, under particular circumstances and conditions. Third, strong proportionality conditions run head-on into "just deserts in an unjust society." Fourth, strong proportionality conditions violate notions of parsimony by requiring imposition of unnecessarily severe punishments in individual cases in order to assure formal equivalence of suffering. Fifth, strong proportionality conditions presuppose that imposition of offenders' deserved punishments is an overriding moral imperative rather than one of several competing ethical considerations.

The Illusion of "Like-Situated Offenders"

If recent efforts in the United Kingdom and the United States to increase use of intermediate sanctions are to succeed, the appropriateness of different punishments for "like-situated offenders" must be recognised.

"Like-situated offender" is nested in quotation marks to express the artificiality of notions of like-situated offenders, comparable crimes, and generic punishments. A strong proportionality-in-punishment argument insists on equal treatment of like-situated offenders and proportionately different treatment of differently situated offenders. A fundamental difficulty is that this assumes that offenders can conveniently and justly be placed into a manageable number of more-or-less dessert categories and that standard punishments can be prescribed for each category. Unfortunately, neither side of the desert–punishment equation lends itself to standardization.

Neither offenders nor punishments come in standard cases. The practice of dividing offenders and punishments into generic categories produces much unnecessary suffering and provides only illusory proportionality. A look at Minnesota's sentencing guidelines shows why. ...

Problems of objectification of crimes, offenders, and punishments are especially stark in a numerical guidelines system. In systems that feature written policy guidelines, they lurk beneath the surface. The Minnesota illustration is generally relevant to

analysis of proportionality in punishment, however, because it makes real world implications of strong proportionality conditions starkly apparent. If proportionality is an,
or the, overriding principle in the distribution of punishment in practice, then the imperfections of objectification that I describe are presumably regrettable but acceptable
costs to be paid for a principled punishment system. If they appear unacceptable, the
problem may be that the principle of proportionality offers less helpful guidance than
its proponents urge.

Objective Measure of Responsibility

Von Hirsch's proportionality argument relies on objective measures of penal deserved-
ness. This is curious. Desert theories, especially blaming theories, are premised on notions of individual blameworthiness, which seem inexorably linked to particularised
judgments about moral responsibility. Objective measures of harm are seldom sufficient for conviction in the criminal law: that is why doctrines of competency, *mens rea*,
and affirmative defense exist and why doctrines like strict liability and felony-murder
are disfavored. If individualised moral judgments are germane to conviction, it is not
obvious why they are not also germane to punishment.

If punishment is principally about blaming, surely it is relevant whether the offender
was mentally impaired, socially disadvantaged, a reluctant participant, or moved by
humane motives. Surely it is morally relevant, whatever the path to conviction, what
the offender did, with what *mens rea*, and under what circumstances. Surely it is morally relevant whether a particular punishment will be more intensely experienced by
one person than by another. In other words, the three subjective considerations that
Minnesota's guidelines ignore—what did he really do, what will the conditions of his
sanction really be, will he suffer more intensely than others—are relevant to moral
judgments of blameworthiness and proportionate punishments. Nigel Walker expresses
this when he observes: "Retributive reasoning would lead instead to a 'personal price
list' which would take into account not only gradations of harm but offenders' culpability and sensibility."

The failure of von Hirsch's arguments to take account of individualised differences
in culpability and individual effects of punishment looks strange when we recall that
von Hirsch's is a retributive theory. Utilitarian theories reject interpersonal comparisons
of utility, as Lionel Robbins' classic essay explains, either on measurement grounds
(variable intensity of satisfactions, utility monsters, and so on), or on normative
grounds (no individual's satisfactions *should* count for more). However, utilitarian
theories are concerned with general policies and aggregate social measures and not with
fine-tuned moral judgments.

An Unjust Society

Punishment schemes that attach high value to proportionality necessarily ignore the
differing material conditions of life, including poverty, social disadvantage, and bias,
in which human personalities and characters take form. The substantive criminal law
rejects motive for intention and in the English-speaking countries allows no formal ex-
cusing or mitigating defense of social disadvantage. Yet in both the United Kingdom

and the United States, most common law offenders are products of disadvantaged and deprived backgrounds and in both countries vastly disproportionate numbers of alleged, convicted, and imprisoned offenders are members of racial and ethnic minorities. The likelihood, for example, that a black American male is in prison today is eight times greater than that a white American male is in prison.

The problem of "just deserts in an unjust world" is a fundamental problem for a strong proportionality constraint. Whether retributive theories are rationalised in terms of benefits and burdens, or equilibrium, or blaming, or condemnation, or penance, they must presume equal opportunities for all to participate in society. when some are disabled from full participation by discrimination, disability, or exclusion, by denial of access to public goods, by the burdens of social and economic disadvantage, it is difficult to claim that they enjoy the benefits of autonomy that produce obligation. To take just one example, proponents of benefits and burdens theories are hard pressed to explain how a person who is denied society's benefits deserves to be burdened by social obligation. ...

Parsimony

Proponents of strong proportionality conditions necessarily prefer equality over minimization of suffering. For nearly two decades in the United States, Andrew von Hirsch and Norval Morris have been disagreeing over the role of parsimony in punishment. Von Hirsch has argued for strong desert limits on punishment and high priority to pursuit of equality and proportionality in punishment. Morris has argued that desert is a limiting, not a defining, principle of punishment and that policy should prescribe imposition of the least severe "not undeserved" sanction that meets legitimate policy ends. Within these outer bounds of "not undeserved" punishments Morris has consistently argued for observance of a principle of parsimony.

To some extent Morris and von Hirsch have argued past each other. Morris argues that a desert approach is unnecessarily harsh and von Hirsch responds by noting that he personally favors relatively modest punishments and, in any case, desert schemes are not inherently more severe than other schemes. In turn, von Hirsch argues that Morris's "not undeserved" proportionality constraints are vague, the breadth of allowable ranges of sentencing discretion is never specified, and Morris responds by noting that absolute measures of deserved punishment are unknowable and that his aim is to minimise imposition of penal suffering within bounds that any given community finds tolerable.

The problem is that they start from different major premises—von Hirsch's is the "principle of proportionality," Morris's the "principle of parsimony." The difference between them can be seen by imagining a comprehensive punishment scheme, perhaps resembling Minnesota's. Imagine that policy makers have conscientiously classified all offenders into ten categories and, using von Hirsch's ordinal/cardinal magnitude and anchoring points approach, have decided that all offenses at level VII deserve twenty-three-to twenty-five-month prison terms. Imagine further that reliable public opinion surveys have shown that 90 per cent of the general public would find a restrictive non-custodial punishment, "not unduly lenient" and a 36-month prison term "not unduly severe" for level VII offenses.

· · ·

Sorting Out Principles

Disagreements about just punishments, like disagreements about the death penalty or abortion, are often in the end disagreements about powerful intuitions or deeply embedded values. It may be that differences in view between those who give primacy to proportionality and those who give primacy to parsimony cannot be bridged.

The burden of persuasion should rest, however, it seems to me on those who reject Isaiah Berlin's observations that "not all good things are compatible, still less all the ideals of mankind" and that "the necessity of choosing between absolute claims is then an inescapable characteristic of the human condition."

Punishment raises at least two important conflicts between ideals—between the principles of proportionality and parsimony, between the quests for criminal justice and social justice. ...

If we were single-mindedly devoted to equal opportunity, then, we should view equalization of life chances as an overriding goal of social policy. However, Fishkin argues, efforts to equalize life chances run head on into another powerful principle, that the value of autonomy in a private sphere of liberty encompasses a principle of family autonomy, of non-intrusion by the state into the family's sphere of private liberty.

In other words, equal opportunity and family autonomy conflict fundamentally. Full respect for equal opportunity would involve intrusion into the family that would widely be seen as objectionably intrusive. Full respect for family autonomy would widely be seen as cruel disregard for children's basic needs.

And so it may be with punishment. Principles of proportionality and parsimony may simply conflict, with resolutions between them necessarily partial and provisional.

IV. COMMUNICATIVE DIMENSIONS OF LEGAL PUNISHMENT

Two important theories of punishment emphasize the communicative nature of sentencing. In the first, Andrew von Hirsch elaborates upon his censure-based account of legal punishment. In the second, an alternative perspective that is also communicative in nature is described by R.A. Duff. Duff's theory shares some commonalities with von Hirsch's theory, but it is also conceptually distinct. According to Duff, punishment should be understood as a kind of secular penance that seeks to communicate censure of the offender, but also (and here is where his theory differs from that of von Hirsch) to persuade the offender to repent, reform, and seek reconciliation with the victim and the community. From this description it can be seen that Duff's penitential theory is more ambitious than the communicative theory advocated by von Hirsch, according to which the expression of censure is sufficient (along with the prudential disincentive to reoffend).

A. von Hirsch, *Censure and Sanctions*
(Oxford: Oxford University Press, 1996), at 9-13 (footnotes omitted)

2. *Censure-Based Justifications for Punishment*

Reprobative accounts of the institution of the criminal sanction are those that focus on that institution's condemnatory features, that is, its role as conveying censure or blame. The penal sanction clearly does convey blame. Punishing someone consists of visiting a deprivation (hard treatment) on him, because he supposedly has committed a wrong, in a manner that expresses disapprobation of the person for his conduct. Treating the offender as a wrongdoer, Richard Wasserstrom has pointed out, is central to the idea of punishment. The difference between a tax and a fine does not rest in the kind of material deprivation (money in both cases). It consists, rather in the fact that the fine conveys disapproval or censure, whereas the tax does not.

An account of the criminal sanction which emphasizes its reprobative function has the attraction of being more comprehensible, for blaming is something we do in everyday moral judgements. A censure-based account is also easier to link to proportionality: if punishment conveys blame, it would seem logical that the quantum of punishment should bear a reasonable relation to the degree of blameworthiness of the criminal conduct.

Why the Censure?

That punishment conveys blame or reprobation is, as just mentioned, evident enough. But why *should* there be a reprobative response to the core conduct with which the criminal law deals? Without an answer to that question, legal punishment might arguably be replaced by some other institution that has no blaming implications—a response akin to a tax meant to discourage certain behaviour.

P.F. Strawson provides the most straightforward account. The capacity to respond to wrongdoing by reprobation or censure, he says, is simply part of a morality that holds people accountable for their conduct. When a person commits a misdeed, others judge him adversely, because his conduct was reprehensible. Censure consists of the expression of that judgement, plus its accompanying sentiment of disapproval. It is addressed to the actor because he or she is the person responsible. One would withhold the expression of blame only if there were special reasons for not confronting the actor: for example, doubts about one's standing to challenge him.

While Strawson's account seems correct as far as it goes—blaming *does* seem part of holding people accountable for their actions—it may be possible to go a bit further and specify some of the positive moral functions of blaming.

Censure addresses the victim. He or she has not only bee injured, but *wronged* through someone's culpable act. it thus would not suffice just to acknowledge that the injury has occurred or convey sympathy (as would be appropriate when someone has been hurt by a natural catastrophe). Censure, by directing disapprobation at the person responsible, acknowledges that the victim's hurt occurred through another's fault.

Censure also addresses the act's perpetrator. He is conveyed a certain message concerning his wrongful conduct, namely that he culpably as injured someone, and is disapproved of for having done so. Some kind of moral response is expected on his part—

an expression of concern, and acknowledgement of wrongdoing, or an effort at better self-restraint. A reaction of indifference would, if the censure is justified, itself be grounds for criticizing him.

Censure gives the actor the opportunity for so responding, but it is not a technique for evoking specified sentiments. Were inducing penitent reflection the chief aim, as R.A. Duff has claimed, there would be no point in censuring actors who are either re-pentant or defiant. The repentant actor understands and regrets his wrongdoing already; the defiant actor will not accept the judgement of disapproval which the censure ex-presses. Yet we would not wish to exempt from blame either the repentant or the seem-ingly incorrigible actor. Both remain moral agents, capable of understanding others' assessment of their conduct—and censure conveys that assessment. The repentant actor finds his self-evaluation confirmed through the disapproval of others; the defiant actor is made to feel and understand the disapproval of others, whatever he himself may think of his conduct. Such communication of judgement and feeling is the essence of moral discourse among rational agents.

Were the primary aim that of producing actual changes in the actor's moral attitudes, moreover, the condemnor would ordinarily seek information about his personality and outlook, so as better to foster the requisite attitudinal changes. But blaming, in ordinary life as well as in more formal contexts, does not involve such enquiries. One ascribes wrongdoing to the actor and conveys the disapprobation—limiting enquiry about the actor to questions of his capacity for choice. The condemnor's role is not that of the mentor or priest.

The criminal law gives the censure it expresses yet another role: that of addressing third parties, and providing them with reason for desistence. Unlike blame in everyday contexts, the criminal sanction announces in advance that specified categories of con-duct are punishable. Because the prescribed sanction is one which expresses blame, this conveys the message that the conduct is reprehensible, and should be eschewed. It is not necessarily a matter of inculcating that the conduct is wrong, for those addressed (or many of them) may well understand that already. Rather the censure embodied in the prescribed sanction serves to *appeal* to people's sense of the conduct's wrongful-ness, as a reason for desistence.

This normative message expressed in penal statutes is not reducible, as penal utili-tarians might suppose, to a mere inducement to compliance—one utilized because the citizenry could be more responsive to moral appeals than bare threats. If persons are called upon to desist because the conduct is wrong, there ought to be good reasons for supposing that it *is* wrong; and the message expressed through the penalty about its de-gree of wrongfulness ought to reflect how reprehensible the conduct indeed is. This point will be elaborated upon in the next chapter, where penal censure is contrasted with instrumentalist strategies of "shaming."

The foregoing account explains why predatory conduct should not be dealt with through neutral sanctions that convey no disapproval. Such sanctions—even if they were no less effective in discouraging the behaviour—deny the status of the person as an agent capable of moral understanding. A neutral sanction would treat offenders or potential offenders much as tigers might be treated in a circus, as beings that have to be restrained, intimidated, or conditioned into compliance because they are incapable of understanding why biting people (or other tigers) is wrong. A condemnatory sanction treats the actor as a *person* who is capable of such understanding.

A committed utilitarian might insist that treating the actor as a person in this fashion can only be warranted on instrumental grounds. Nigel Walker takes this view: if "… the message which expresses blame need have not utility," he asserts, "where lies the moral necessity?" This, however, is reductionist. Treating the actor as someone capable of choice, rather than as a tiger, is a matter of acknowledging his dignity as a human being. Is this acknowledgement warranted only if it leads to beneficial social consequences? Those consequences would not necessarily be those of crime prevention—for, as just noted, it might be possible to devise a "neutral" sanction (one designed to visit material deprivation but convey no blame) that prevents crime at least as well. Might society somehow have better cohesion if actors are treated as being responsible (and hence subject to censure) for their actions? Making such a claim would involved trying to re-duce ethical judgments to difficult-to-confirm predictions about social structure. While one can have some confidence in the moral judgement that offenders should be treated as agents capable of choice, it will be difficult to verify that so treating them will lead to a more smoothly running society.

Why the Hard Treatment?

It is still necessary to address punishment's other constitutive element: deprivation or hard treatment. Some desert theorists (John Kleinig and Igor Primoratz, for example) assert that notions of censure can account also for the hard treatment. They argue that censure (at least in certain social contexts) cannot be expressed adequately in purely verbal or symbolic terms; that hard treatment is needed to show that the disapprobation is meant seriously. For example, an academic department does not show disapproval of a serious lapse by a colleague merely through a verbal admonition; to convey the requisite disapproval, some curtailment of privileges is called for. This justification has plausibility outside legal contexts, where the deprivations involved are modest enough to serve chiefly to underline the intended disapproval. However, I doubt that the argument sustains the criminal sanction.

The criminal law seems to have preventive features in its very design. When the State criminalizes conduct, it issues a legal threat; such conduct is proscribed, and vio-lation will result in the imposition of specified sanctions. The threat appears to b e ex-plicitly aimed at discouraging the proscribed conduct. Criminal sanctions also seem too onerous to serve just to give credibility to the censure. Even were penalties substantially scaled down from what they are today, some of them still could involved significant deprivations of liberty or property. In the absence of a preventive purpose, it is hard to conceive of such intrusions as having the sole function of showing that the State's dis-approval is seriously intended.

This reasoning led me to suggest, in a 1985 volume, a bifurcated account of punish-ment. The penal law, I said, performs two interlocking functions. By threatening un-pleasant consequences, it seeks to discourage criminal behaviour. Through the censure expressed by such sanctions, the law registers disapprobation of the behaviour. Citizens are thus provided with moral and not just prudential reasons for desistence.

However, the two elements in my account, reprobation and prevention, remained uneasily matched. Whereas the censuring element appeals to the person's moral agency, does not the preventive element play merely on his fear of unpleasant consequences? If the person is capable of being moved by moral appeal, why the threat? If not capable and thus in need of the threat, it appears that he is being treated like a tiger. A clarification of the preventive function—and its relation to the censuring function—is needed.

The preventive function of the sanction should be seen, I think, as supplying a prudential reason that is tied to, and supplements, the normative reason conveyed by penal censure. The criminal law, through the censure embodied in its prescribed sanctions, conveys that the conduct is wrong, and a moral agent thus is given grounds for desistence. He may (given human fallibility) be tempted nevertheless. What the prudential disincentive can do is to provide him a further reason—a prudential one—for resisting the temptation. Indeed, an agent who has accepted the sanction's message that he ought not offend, and who recognizes his susceptibility to temptation, could favour the existence of such a prudential disincentive, as an aid to carrying out what he himself recognizes as the proper course of conduct.

A certain conception of human nature, of which I spoke in the previous chapter, underlies this idea of the preventive function as a supplementary prudential disincentive. Persons are assumed to be moral agents, capable of taking seriously the message conveyed through the sanction, that the conduct is reprehensible. They are fallible, nevertheless, and thus face temptation. The function of the disincentive is to provide a prudential reasons for resisting the temptation. The account would make no sense were human beings much better or worse; an angel would require no appeals to prudence, and a brute could not be appealed to through censure.

R.A. Duff, *Punishment, Communication, and Community*
(Oxford: Oxford University Press, 2001), at 129-30

On my account, criminal punishment should be conceived of as a communicative enterprise that aims to communicate to offenders the censure they deserve for their crimes, and thus to bring them to repent their crimes, to reform themselves, and to reconcile themselves with those they have wronged. This account, I claim, provides a morally plausible rationale for penal hard treatment as part of this communicative enterprise— as a secular penance, which itself serves the aims of repentance, reform, and reconciliation. It does justice to the central retributivist concern that punishment must focus on and be justified by its relationship to the crime for which it is imposed. It also does justice to the consequentialist concern that punishment must be justified by some good that it aims to achieve, and to the abolitionist concern that we should aim not to "deliver pain" to offenders but to achieve such goods as restoration, reparation, or reconciliation. But it does justice to such concerns by revising or reinterpreting them.

In relation to retributivism, it explains the meaning of the idea that the guilty deserve to suffer, but it does so partly by insisting that punishment cannot be purely backward-looking. It must also aim to achieve some future good. In relation to consequentialism, it identifies the goods that punishment should aim to achieve, but insists that punishment is not to be justified as a contingently efficient instrumental means to those ends. It is justified as a method that is intrinsically appropriate to those ends, once they are properly understood. From this it also follows that punishment can be justified as a proper attempt to pursue those ends even when we have good reason to believe that it will fail to achieve them.

In relation to abolitionism (and accounts of "restorative" justice, of mediation, and of probation that portray their aims as essentially non-punitive), it agrees that we should aim at such ends as restoration and reconciliation, but insists that in the kinds of cases that properly concern the criminal justice system, what makes these reparative aims necessary is the fact that a wrong has been committed and the restoration and reconciliation are then properly achieved precisely by punishment—understood not as mere pain delivery but as a secular penance.

Punishment as thus conceived is consistent with, indeed expressive of, the defining values of a liberal political community. It addresses offenders, not as outlaws who have forfeited their standing as citizens, but as full members of the normative political community; it is inclusionary rather than exclusionary. It treats them as citizens who are both bound and protected by the central liberal values of autonomy, freedom and privacy. It holds them answerable, as responsible moral agents, for the public wrongs they commit. But it also respects their own autonomy (since it seeks to persuade rather than merely coerce), their freedom (since it constitutes a legitimate response to their wrongdoing and leaves them free to remain unpersuaded), and their privacy (since it addresses only those aspects of their lives and actions that properly fall within the public sphere).

V. TRANSCENDING THE PHILOSOPHICAL DEBATE

In the introduction to this chapter, we sounded the warning that the philosophical debate framed here for consideration might be unsatisfying in certain respects. David Garland and Peter Young (in "Towards a Social Analysis of Penalty," in Garland and Young, eds., *The Power to Punish: Contemporary Penality and Social Analysis* (Aldershot: Gower Publishing, 1983), explain the shortcomings of this debate in the following way:

> But the important point for our purposes is that within all of these philosophical tests, "punishment" is presented and discussed as a singular, unitary phenomenon. The actual practices, institutions and sanctions are disregarded as mere empirical "accidents" and manifestations—the object of the analysis is seen as "punishment itself." A whole tradition of philosophical writing and debate conspires to present "punishment" as something we can talk of and refer to in the singular, whilst disregarding the plurality and complexity of its empirical supports. Indeed, the fact that we continue to talk of the realm of penal sanctions in the singular term "punishment" (and not "corrections" or social defence) not only signifies the influence of penal philosophy in shaping our attitudes to the phenomenon, but also indicates which strand of philosophical argument has prevailed in British culture.

A. Garland's Penality

In his more recent work, David Garland has attempted to construct an original social theory of punishment. Garland examines and critiques the major sociological paradigms of punishment (including Marx, Weber, Durkheim, and Foucault) and finds each lacking in a similar way: none of these theories focuses beyond a particular cultural trait or characteristic of modern society. In the excerpt below, Garland describes how cultural mentalities and sensibilities influence the shape of penal institutions and how punishment, as a social artifact, in turn contributes to the formation of culture.

In his important work "Punishment and Modern Society: A Study in Social Theory" (Chicago: University of Chicago Press, 1990), Garland provides a thoughtful critique of much of the earlier theoretical work on punishment and then offers his view that sentencing is a cultural artifact. What he calls "penality," both influences, and is influenced by, the prevailing culture. He argues:

> The suggestion that will be pursued [here] is that penal practices, discourses, and institutions play an active part in the generative process through which shared meaning, value, and ultimately culture are produced and reproduced in society. Punishment, among other things, is a communicative and didactic institution. Through the media of its practices and declarations it puts into effect and into cultural circulation some of the categories and distinctions through which we give meaning to our world.
>
> Values, conceptions, sensibilities, and social meanings—culture, in short—do not just exist in the form of a natural atmosphere which envelopes social action and makes it meaningful. Rather, they are actively created and recreated by our social practices and institutions and punishment plays its part in this generative and regenerative process. Punishment is one of the many institutions which helps construct and support the social world by producing the shared categories and authoritative classifications through which individuals understand each other and themselves. In its own way, penal practice provides an organizing cultural framework whose declarations and actions serve as an interpretative grid through which people evaluate conduct and make moral sense of their experience. Penality thus acts as a regulatory social mechanism in two distinct respects: it regulates conduct directly through the physical medium of social action, but it also regulates meaning, thought, attitude and hence conduct through the rather different medium of signification. ...
>
> The suggestion which I wish to make here, and to explore in the pages that follow, is that penality communicates meaning not just about crime and punishment but also about power, authority, legitimacy, normality, morality, personhood, social relations, and a host of other tangential matters. Penal signs and symbols are one part of an authoritative, institutional discourse which seeks to organize our moral and political understanding and to educate our sentiments and sensibilities. They provide a continuous, repetitive set of instructions as to how we should think about good and evil, normal and pathological, legitimate and illegitimate, order and disorder. Through their judgments, condemnations, and classifications they teach us (and persuade us) how to judge, what to condemn, and how to classify, and they supply a set of languages, idioms, and vocabularies with which to do so. These signifying practices also tell us where to locate social authority, how to preserve order and community, where to look for social dangers, and how to feel about these matters, while the evocative effect of penal symbols sets off chains of reference and association in our minds, linking the business of punishment

into questions of politics, morality, and social order. In short, the practices, institutions, and discourses of penality all *signify*, and the meanings which are conveyed thereby tend to outrun the immediacies of crime and punishment and "speak of" broader and more extended issues. Penality is thus a cultural text or perhaps better, a cultural performance which communicates with a variety of social audiences and conveys an extended range of meanings. No doubt it is "read" and understood in very different ways by different social groups and the data we have on this crucial issue of "reception" (as the literary critics call it) are woefully inadequate. But if we are to understand the social effects of punishment then we are obliged to trace this positive capacity to produce meaning and create "normality" as well as its more negative capacity to suppress and silence deviance.

B. Limiting Retributivism and the American Law Institute

Relying on the work of Norval Morris (*The Future of Imprisonment* (University of Chicago Press: Chicago, 1974)), the sentencing discourse in the United States has spawned another approach, now known as "limiting retributivism." This takes some utilitarian concerns and caps them with proportionality. Limiting retributivists argue that a sentence cannot be imposed which is out of proportion to the particular offence and that attention must always be paid to what the sentence is intended to achieve. That is, restraint or "the principle of parsimony," as Morris called it, must operate to ensure that the least intrusive sentence is imposed. While this recognizes the importance of proportionality, it stands in stark contrast to von Hirsch and Ashworth, who argue that individual desert should determine the sentence, generally without regard to consequential effects. While Morris would agree (at 75) that it is unjust to impose "punishment in excess of what is felt by the community to be the maximum suffering justly related to the harm the criminal has inflicted," he would add that judges must be able to choose and pursue legitimate sentencing objectives within the limit of what the community finds acceptable.

Pragmatism has influenced the evolution of limiting retributivism, which now accepts that judicial discretion needs to be constrained to a greater extent than simply providing an upper limit. Recent accounts accept a greater role for proportionality and less room for judicial discretion. As a result, proportionality now also imposes a lower limit, thereby establishing a band or range of acceptable punishment.

The American Law Institute (ALI) (Model Penal Code: Sentencing, Discussion Draft 2003) has embarked on the project of developing a new model sentencing code that will follow this general approach (at 65-66):

> One goal of a revised Model code should be to encourage the introduction of generally applicable rules and principles to the sanctioning process to the extent such governance is feasible, reserving room for individualized discretion in cases where good reasons can be cited for a more qualitative mode of decision-making.

The ALI discussions and reports start with Norval Morris and limiting retributivism by acknowledging the importance of proportionality in sentencing, but also expressing concern that proportionality cannot provide sufficiently precise guidance. Despite its endorsement of limiting retributivism in general, the ALI's notion of penal parsimony is different from that advocated by Norval Morris. Section 1.02(2) of the current ALI draft makes proportionality the first general principle of sentencing, followed by their version of penal parsimony, which requires judges "to render sentences no more severe than necessary to achieve the applicable purposes from subsections (a)(i) [to impose roughly proportionate sentences] and (a)(ii) [to serve goals of deterrence, rehabilitation, incapacitation, and restoration]" (at 129). The ALI concludes (at 40-41) that the relative ordering of desert and instrumentalism could depend on the degree of seriousness of an offence. That is, priorities as between sentencing objectives can vary with the gravity of an offence.

In crafting its new model, the ALI makes a number of important choices, many of which reflect pragmatic considerations spawned by the recent American experience and developed by leading limiting retributivism advocates, particularly Michael Tonry. Essentially, among other related elements, it decides that a sentencing system must:

- pursue the "elusive commodity" of a high degree of uniformity in sentences;
- apply its principles on a system-wide basis;
- include some power to provide, or at least address, resources;
- deal with "racial and ethnic over-representations"; and
- provide better information about itself and its effectiveness.

. . .

The ALI's current draft leaves some important questions to judicial discretion. Section 1.02(2)(b)(i) states that a sentencing system should look "to preserve substantial judicial discretion to individualize sentences within a framework of recommended penalties." It defines a range of severity within which a sentence must fall but permits judges to pursue specific objectives within that range (so long as they do so with restraint). As well, it encourages the use of intermediate sanctions. Significantly, the draft currently adds nine procedural and normative factors to the sentencing matrix, including individualization, the elimination of discrimination, the prevention of unjustified racial overrepresentation in sentenced groups, and the encouragement of intermediate punishments. This permits judges to impose proportional sentences while still maintaining judicial concern for the human aspects of the sentencing system and preserving the courts' ability to respond where warranted by the circumstances of the case. Perhaps the breadth of these considerations leaves the ALI open to the criticism that Andrew Ashworth calls "cafeteria-style" sentencing. That is, as in Canada, judges are free to choose among principles largely according to their own predilections.

As we have said, much of the ALI approach is pragmatic. This may be attributable to recent American experiences, including the expanding and highly racialized jail population. As well, it needs to be remembered that the ALI wants to create a model that is likely to be adopted. Hence, in many respects, its work represents not only pragmatism but also compromises. An important but controversial aspect of the ALI approach is its advocacy of the role of a "sentencing commission" to construct the guidelines that would be provided to judges. This is a response to a two-pronged argument: the judiciary needs guidance, but it lacks the institutional competence to do the empirical and policy analysis that fair and proportionate guidelines require. While some sentencing commissions in the United States (Minnesota, for example) have been applauded for their work, other schemes, including the federal one, have been heavily criticized for their rigidity and punitive nature. Recognizing the potential pitfalls, the ALI draft details the constitution, structure, mandate, and resources that an effective commission requires.

NOTE

It is important to recognize that the initial focus of this introductory chapter was on punishment and the traditional debate between retributivist and utilitarian justifications for punishment. When we moved into the more recent period, we observed how contemporary thinkers have wrestled with issues that go beyond any general justifications and attempt to provide theoretical explanations for how punishments ought to be allocated across a range of offences. In other words, the debate has shifted from punishment to the more pragmatic institution of sentencing and its distribution of punishments. The next chapter continues in this direction but moves from theory to the set of concepts and methodologies that Canadian judges have used to decide which sentencing option should be used in a particular case.

FURTHER READING

Ashworth, A. *Sentencing and Criminal Justice*, 4th ed. (Cambridge: Cambridge University Press, 2005).

Canadian Sentencing Commission (Hon. O. Archambault, Chair). *Sentencing Reform—A Canadian Approach: Report of the Canadian Sentencing Commission* (Ottawa: Supply and Services Canada, 1987).

von Hirsch, A. *Censure and Sanctions* (Oxford: Oxford University Press, 1993).

von Hirsch, A., and A. Ashworth, eds. *Principled Sentencing*, 2d ed. (Oxford: Hart Publishing, 1998).

von Hirsch, A., and A. Ashworth. *Proportionate Sentencing* (Oxford: Oxford University Press, 2005).

Simmons, A.J., M. Cohen, J. Cohen, and C. Beitz, eds. *Punishment—A Philosophy and Public Affairs Reader* (Princeton: Princeton University Press, 1995).

Tonry, M. *Reform and Punishment: The Future of Sentencing* (Cullompton, UK: Willan Publishing, 2002).

Tonry, M., and R. Frase, eds. *Sentencing and Sanctions in Western Countries* (New York: Oxford University Press, 2001).

Walker, N. *Why Punish?* (Oxford: Oxford University Press, 1991).

CHAPTER TWO

Judicial Methodology and the Legislative Context

I. INTRODUCTION

The previous chapter illustrates the historical divergence of philosophical views about punishment. The vigorous debate is understandable given that it encompasses not only the controversial subject of punishment but also fundamental questions about the relationship between the state and its citizens. Punishment is, after all, about the application of coercive force. Of course, punishment and sentencing are not synonymous or congruent concepts. Sentencing involves considerations and objectives that are not purely punitive.

This chapter examines the positive law of sentencing as stated by Parliament and applied by the courts. It traces the evolution of judicial attitudes in Canada toward sentencing and the changing statutory framework, especially the reform in 1996 of Part XXIII in the *Criminal Code*, RSC 1985, c. C-46 (as am.). The statutory statement of principles and purposes is set out later in this chapter.

We have three purposes. First, we try to identify the aims of sentencing as they are formally recognized in Canada. Second, we look at the methodological guidance that is provided to judges who must make sentencing decisions. We consider whether there is any more consistency or coherence in the Canadian law on sentencing than there is in debates concerning the philosophical dimensions of the subject. In practical terms, is there sufficient guidance to sentencing judges so that the function of sentencing can be considered a principled exercise that produces acceptable results?

The third purpose of this chapter relates to issues of sentencing efficacy. Aside from controversies about the premises of sentencing, there is also considerable debate about the effectiveness of particular sentences and sentencing objectives. While this subject takes up much space in the media, it is really the domain of modern criminology, which is concerned not only with theoretical aspects of sentencing, but empirical assessments of the administration of criminal justice. This chapter begins to explore the question of whether judges ought to be attuned to these questions and, if so, how current research can be integrated into judicial methodology.

II. THE ROLE OF JUDICIAL DISCRETION

The question of judicial discretion is at the heart of understanding sentencing in Canada. Until 1996, the *Criminal Code* did not provide any guidance as to the objectives of sentencing or its relevant principles. Judges filled in the conceptual blanks as part of a discretionary exercise. Over the years, many jurists have asserted that the chief aim of sentencing was the protection of society. However, even this simple statement has produced various interpretations, uncertainty, and contradiction, given the conflicting views about how protection is best achieved. More recently, we see that our Code designates the concept of proportionality as a "fundamental" principle of sentencing. Some suggest that it is *the* "fundamental" principle. If proportionality is clearly understood and consistently applied, it would indeed produce greater uniformity. But is uniformity the only goal of a sentencing system? What about utilitarian and restorative objectives? What about individualization? The scope for debate and disagreement has produced a degree of disparity in sentencing. Perhaps some degree of disparity is healthy. However, from a systemic perspective, there is a very strong argument that there must be principles that shape judicial discretion to ensure that examples of disparity are justifiable and clearly explained.

The problem for the judiciary starts with the recognition that phrases such as "a proper and just sentence," "a fit sentence," or "an appropriate sentence" do not lead inevitably to a specific result. Without providing a clear decision-making template, two reasonable people could reach different conclusions about what is a fit sentence in a given case with neither being self-evidently wrong. Moreover, if sentencing is an individualized exercise, as our Supreme Court has regularly pronounced, it requires flexibility to ensure a result that is fit for the offender and for the administration of criminal justice. In Canada, the historical record suggests that the best mechanism for ensuring this result is the trained use of judicial discretion. Parliament has rarely prescribed sentences that must be imposed following a finding of guilt. Recently, there is a trend in this direction that arises in certain visceral high-profile situations. As a result, one observes a growing number of situations in which Parliament has declared penalties that must be imposed, usually a mandatory minimum term of imprisonment. Still, the majority of offences, as set out in the *Criminal Code*, only stipulate a maximum term of imprisonment and allow for a range of alternatives to imprisonment.

Although the reform of 1996 (discussed later in this chapter) refined the debate, judicial discretion continues to play the central role in Canadian sentencing, and its importance is acknowledged in the *Criminal Code* in much the same form as it appeared in the 1892 legislation:

> 718.3(1) Where an enactment prescribes different degrees or kinds of punishment in respect of an offence, the *punishment to be imposed is, subject to the limitations prescribed in the enactment, in the discretion of the court that convicts a person who commits the offence.*
>
> (2) Where an enactment prescribes punishment in respect of an offence, the punishment to be imposed is, subject to the limitations prescribed in the enactment, in the discretion of the court that convicts a person who commits the offence, but no punishment is a minimum punishment unless it is declared to be a minimum punishment. [Emphasis added.]

The breadth of the discretion recognized in the law of sentencing should be immediately apparent. Judges not only are empowered to determine what is a fit sentence in the individual case, but also have a discretion to determine the proper aims of sentencing decisions in the general run of cases. Wherever there is such discretion, there is also the possibility of disparity in approach and in result.

A. The Amalgam or "Wise Blending" of Values

Whether by design or default, Canadian courts historically adopted an approach that allowed judges to recognize and weigh various aims of sentencing, including rehabilitation, incapacitation, retribution, denunciation, and deterrence. In *R v. Lyons* (1987), 61 CR (3d) 1 (SCC), a dangerous offender case, La Forest J said (at 24):

> In a rational system of sentencing, the respective importance of prevention, deterrence, retribution and rehabilitation will vary according to the nature of the crime and the circumstances of the offence.

This approach has made individualization the key perspective for judicial decision making.

R v. Willaert
(1953), 105 CCC 172 (Ont. CA)

MACKAY JA: The appellant was tried at Sarnia on September 16, 17, 18, 19 and 22, 1952, before Barlow J and a jury, on an indictment charging that he on May 2, 1952, committed rape on one Shirley Post, and was found guilty. The learned trial Judge sentenced the appellant to imprisonment for life. This application is taken for leave to appeal against the length of sentence.

By s. 299 of the *Cr. Code*, a person guilty of rape may be sentenced "to suffer death or to imprisonment for life, and to be whipped." ...

A useful statement of the policy of the law as administered in England is set forth in 9 Hals., 2nd ed., pp. 254-5, para. 362: "The policy of the law is, as regards most crimes, to fix a maximum penalty, which is intended only for the worst cases, and to leave to the discretion of the judge to determine to what extent in a particular case the punishment awarded should approach to or recede from the maximum limit. The exercise of this discretion is a matter of prudence and not of law."

There is little in the record itself to mitigate the gravity of the crime; nevertheless, in measuring sentence, every circumstance should be taken into consideration, and in the exercise of judicial discretion regard should be had to: the age of the prisoner; his past and present condition of life; the nature of the crime; whether the prisoner previously had a good character; whether it is a first offence; whether he has a family dependent upon him, the temptation; whether the crime was deliberate or committed on momentary impulse; the penalty provided by the Code or statute; whether the offence is one for which under the code the offender is liable to corporal punishment and, if so, whether corporal punishment should be imposed.

I am respectfully of opinion that there are three principles of criminal justice requiring earnest consideration in the determination of punishment, *viz.*, deterrence, reformation and retribution.

The governing principle of deterrence is, within reason and common sense, that the emotion of fear should be brought into play so that the offender may be made afraid to offend again and also so that others who may have contemplated offending will be restrained by the same controlling emotion. Society must be reasonably assured that the punishment meted out to one will not actually encourage others, and when some form of crime has become widespread the element of deterrence must look more to the restraining of others than to the actual offender before the Court.

Reformation is the most hopeful element in the question of punishment in most cases, and it is in that direction that the efforts of those concerned with criminal justice will be more and more directed. But reformation, too, has its distinct limitations. It has been found in England that many who have passed through all the stages of binding over to keep the peace, probation, approved school, Borstal institution, and prison, have yet become habitual criminals. They appear to be beyond all human reformative agencies.

The underlying and governing idea in the desire for retribution is in no way an eye for an eye or a tooth for a tooth, but rather that the community is anxious to express its repudiation of the crime committed and to establish and assert the welfare of the community against the evil in its midst. Thus, the infliction of punishment becomes a source of security to all and "is elevated to the first rank of benefits, when it is regarded not as an act of wrath or vengeance against a guilty or unfortunate individual who has given way to mischievous inclinations, but as an indispensable sacrifice to the common safety": See Bentham, Rationale of Punishment, p. 20, quoted at p. 255 of Halsbury *loc. cit.*

I am respectfully of opinion that the true function of criminal law in regard to punishment is in a wise blending of the deterrent and reformative, with retribution not entirely disregarded, and with a constant appreciation that the matter concerns not merely the Court and the offender but also the public and society as a going concern. Punishment is, therefore, an art—a very difficult art—essentially practical, and directly related to the existing needs of society. A punishment appropriate today might have been quite unacceptable 200 years ago and probably would be absurd 200 years hence. It is therefore impossible to lay down hard and fast and permanent rules.

. . .

The tendency in recent years has been to impose more moderate sentences. At one time it was commonly assumed that the only purpose of punishment was to punish, but today its function is conceived in very different terms. It may be to try to reclaim the offender for society, to induce and stimulate habits of regularity and reliability even to compensate partially for an education that ended prematurely, and generally to try to awaken in the mind of the vicious and irresponsible a sense of the obligations of life and citizenship. Such moderation in sentence may not be warranted in the case of confirmed criminals but in that of the first offender an effort at reclamation is surely the part of wisdom and prudence in judicial discretion.

NOTE

The general principle stated in *Willaert* remains good law in the sense that it provides a fair explanation of the Canadian approach: a proper sentence requires a wise blending of penal aims to be "fit" for the offence and the offender. Some of the more specific claims made by Mackay JA have been eclipsed by later developments.

However, the characterization of sentencing and punishment as an art is astonishing. In what other area of law can one find resort to such an unprincipled explanation of the judicial role? Perhaps this was simply a reflection of an inability to provide a clearer explanation. Certainly it could not have been an assertion of some special talent bestowed on judges at the moment of their appointment. For many decades, *Willaert* was often cited as the leading example of the role of judicial discretion, which included not only the issue of specific options that might be considered but a determination of what are "fit" or appropriate aims of sentencing in a given case. The scope of discretion, in both senses, might be constrained by the guidance of appellate courts or, in some instances, by legislative directive. Indeed, the evolution of sentencing policy requires guidance on a number of fronts. The *Willaert* approach provided an open and flexible template for sentencing judges, leaving their discretion dramatically unconstrained.

One person's flexibility is another person's vagueness and lack of clarity. The "amalgam" or "wise blending" approach was discussed by Cole and Manson in *Release from Imprisonment: The Law of Sentencing, Parole, and Judicial Review* (Toronto: Carswell, 1990), at 16-17:

> While this blending of penal objectives permeates the sentencing process and provides both systemic and individual justifications, it generates its own inevitable tensions due to the inherent contradictory nature of some objectives. At the same time, it hides the uncomfortable observation that precision and consistency may be unattainable goals.
>
> Added to this calculus we see judicial recognition of particular factors which highlight the influence of one or another of the principles of sentencing. Cases involving youthful offenders, mentally ill offenders or recidivists, and cases arising from violence against children, women or racial minorities have provoked judges to emphasize particular principles. Thus, notwithstanding the general acceptance of the amalgam approach, the existence of some distinctive features highlights the significance of protection of the public, rehabilitation, deterrence or denunciation in direct response to the category of case.

The amalgam approach allowed judges to determine sentences by referring to an array of different considerations. It asserts no priority among the aims of sentencing, although the courts of the various provinces have developed some rules of practice under the guidance of the Court of Appeal. The amalgam approach does not prevent the courts of different provinces from adopting different approaches, nor does it prevent judges within a single court from disagreeing. Is this a healthy example of the common law in action, or is it a recipe for unjustified disparity?

An interesting example of a conflict in perspective within a court can be seen in *R v. McGinn* (1989), 75 Sask. R 161 (CA), where the majority allowed a Crown appeal against a non-custodial sentence for possession for the purposes of trafficking that arose from the seizure of one-quarter of an ounce of marijuana. It imposed in its place a six-month period of incarceration. Vancise JA, in dissent, supported the trial judge's conclusion that a period of probation and a $300 fine was appropriate. At the heart of the opinion of Vancise JA was his view that the efficacy of general deterrence had been overemphasized for many offences where a non-custodial alternative was both reasonable and justifiable. In the classroom this kind of policy debate seems healthy. However, the courtroom is a different story. The fundamental nature of the debate in *R v. McGinn* shows how the scope of judicial discretion can easily produce disparate results. Aside from disparity of outcome, the court's ability to explain its decision is dependent on a controversial matter of sentencing policy. Is this fair?

Is it simply an inevitable by-product of a system implemented by people who necessarily will bring different backgrounds and perspectives to their judicial task?

III. JUDGES SEARCH FOR A PRINCIPLED APPROACH

Over time, the amalgam approach has made protection of society, deterrence, denunciation, rehabilitation, and reparation the major objectives of sentencing. These objectives are sometimes referred to as the principles of sentencing, but that is an erroneous characterization. Principles are substantive rules that shape how judicial discretion is applied to choices between these objectives and to the various sentencing options that the *Criminal Code* provides. For many years, one could find no real discussion of principles and objectives by the Canadian judiciary. While this was a by-product of the amalgam approach, it must have struck many thoughtful and conscientious judges as unsatisfactory. Those who recognized that sentencing was a serious matter were left with little guidance from Parliament and little discussion of central tenets by their judicial colleagues.

Judicial attitudes toward sentencing objectives and the applicable principles have not always been consistent, and certainly have not been static. Currently, the most important principles are proportionality, parity, and restraint. However, it is not until the late 1980s that one starts to see helpful examples of judges struggling with hard sentencing questions dealing with the application of principles and the scope of sentencing objectives. The following cases are efforts by judges to grapple with undeveloped principles and conflicting objectives. When reading them, try to assess whether the decision reflects a change in judicial attitude and, if so, consider what may have motivated it. Also, take note of the variety of sources on which the decisions rely. The individual pronouncements may not be the last word on the subject but they are important elements in an evolutionary process.

A. Rehabilitation, Protection, and Denunciation

R v. Preston
(1990), 79 CR (3d) 61 (BCCA)

WOOD JA: The Crown applies for leave to appeal, and if leave is granted, appeals from the sentences imposed with respect to each of three convictions recorded against the respondent for possession of the narcotic diacetylmorphine (heroin). In each case the passing of sentence was suspended for a period of two years, and the respondent was ordered to be released on the terms and conditions contained in three separate probation orders.

. . .

II

The respondent is now 41 years old. She has been a heroin addict for over 20 years. In that time she has made a number of unsuccessful attempts to overcome her addiction. As a result of her lack of skills and education, her addiction, and poor health brought on by the self-abuse associated with that addiction, she has not worked for most of that time. She has been on social assistance continuously since 1974.

Up to the time of the matters now before the court, she has amassed at total record of 23 convictions, including eight for narcotics offences, four of which were for trafficking in heroin, five soliciting or other prostitution related convictions, and an assortment of escape, unlawfully at large, failing to appear and breach of probation convictions. Apart from concurrent sentences of two years less one day on three counts of trafficking in heroin, imposed in 1976, her longest sentences have been 18 months on a charge of confinement, also in 1976, and 18 months for another heroin trafficking conviction in 1985. All other sentences imposed upon her have been for 90 days or less.

• • •

While conceding that the prospect of full and complete rehabilitation was not assured, counsel for the respondent pointed out to the trial judge that whatever hope there was would be destroyed by a term of imprisonment. Counsel for the Crown, stressing the importance of deterrence and the protection of the public, submitted that in light of the nature of the offence and her previous criminal record the respondent ought to be sentenced to a term of imprisonment.

The trial judge gave lengthy reasons for making the orders he did. He was clearly aware of the many decisions of this court, which have either upheld or imposed substantial periods of imprisonment for similar offences committed by similar offenders. In the end he took the view that he ought to order a disposition of these charges which would encourage what he saw as a genuine motivation for rehabilitation on the part of the respondent.

• • •

There is no doubt that heroin addicts present as poor candidates for rehabilitation, if such is measured only in terms of the number who successfully overcome their addiction. Little in the way of reliable statistics is available, but what information there is suggests that it is unrealistic to talk of a "cure" for heroin addiction. Success is measured by the extent to which the addiction is controlled, often by substitute drugs which can be legally prescribed. Some of these substitutes, like methadone, are themselves highly addictive, but their pharmacological properties are such that the addict can, if willing, maintain a relatively normal and even useful lifestyle, free from the need to commit crimes to support the craving for heroin.

• • •

The role of incarceration in this cycle not only fails to achieve its ultimate goal which is the protection of society, but it also costs society a great deal of money, which might better be spent elsewhere. Statistics Canada reports that during the 1988/1989 fiscal year the cost of maintaining a prisoner in a custodial facility averaged $46,282 in a federal penitentiary and $36,708 in a provincial jail.

The object of the entire criminal justice system, of course, is the protection of society, and I say at once that if incarceration is the only way of protecting society from a particular offender then, transitory and expensive though it may be, that form of protection must be invoked. But where, as in this case, the danger to society results from the potential of the addict to commit offences to support her habit, and it appears to the court that there is a reasonable chance that she may succeed in an attempt to control her addiction, then it becomes necessary to consider the ultimate benefit to society if that chance becomes a reality.

. . .

With respect, that benefit seems obvious. If the chance for rehabilitation becomes a reality, society will be permanently protected from the danger which she otherwise presents in the fashion described above. As well, the cost associated with her frequent incarceration will be avoided.

. . .

What then is the proper approach for the court to take when sentencing in a case such as this? When the benefit to be derived to society as a whole, as a result of the successful rehabilitation of a heroin addict, is balanced against the ultimate futility of the short-term protection which the community enjoys from a sentence of incarceration, I believe it is right to conclude that the principle of deterrence should yield to any reasonable chance of rehabilitation which may show itself to the court imposing sentence. To give the offender a chance to successfully overcome his or her addiction, in such circumstances, is to risk little more than the possibility of failure, with the result that the cycle of addiction leading to crime leading to incarceration will resume, something that is inevitable, in any event, if the chance is not taken. On the other hand, as has already been pointed out, if the effort succeeds the result is fundamentally worthwhile to society as a whole.

I am not persuaded that the trial judge erred in principle in this case when he considered the rehabilitation of the respondent to be of greater importance than any deterrent value that a sentence of incarceration might have. Indeed, I am of the view that he was right in the approach that he took.

Underlying much of the argument of counsel for the Crown was the suggestion that to approve the disposition of the trial judge in this case would be to "decriminalize" heroin. Nothing could be further from the truth. A court would only be justified in giving more weight to the possibility of rehabilitation, rather than deterrence, where there is a reasonable basis for believing that the motivation for such change is genuine and there is a reasonable possibility that it will succeed. There will undoubtedly be many cases in which no such prospect exists, and in such cases it would be an error in principle to allow the factor of deterrence to be overshadowed by the illusion of rehabilitation. I have every confidence in the ability of the trial judges in this province to successfully separate fact from fiction in such matters.

. . .

It is also worth noting that the report of the Canadian Sentencing Commission (the "Archambault" Commission), *Sentencing Reform: A Canadian Approach* (1987), recommends that possession of a narcotic carry a maximum sentence of six months, together with an unqualified presumption that such sentence be served in the community, rather than in a custodial facility. While the recommendations of the commission do not have the force of law, and cannot therefore be said, in that sense, to represent the will of either Parliament or the people, they are nonetheless the end product of a process which included over two years of extensive public hearings held all across the country. In making its recommendations the commission recognized and took into account the fact that one of the goals of sentencing is to preserve the authority of, and to promote respect for, the law through the public's perception that the commission of offences will be met by the imposition of just sanctions.

To the extent that this goal must be considered by the court when imposing sentence, it may be, and often is, referred to as a "factor" of sentencing. In *R v. Pettigrew*, [1990] BCWLD 1260, BCCA, Vancouver No. CA011983, 12th April 1990 [now reported 56 CCC (3d) 390], Taylor JA referred to it, at p. 5 [394 (CCC)], as:

> ... the elusive "fifth factor" of the sentencing system—the imposition of punishment, so as [sic] to speak, "for its own sake," rather than for isolation of the offender, rehabilitation, deterrence of the offender or deterrence of others.

As Taylor JA pointed out, this factor has been given different labels over the years, as its role in the rationale of sentencing has undergone at least the perception, if not the reality, of change. Retribution was one of its earlier titles. This court rejected retribution per se as a legitimate goal of sentencing in *R v. Hinch*, 62 WWR 205, 2 CRNS 350, [1968] 3 CCC 39. Denunciation has been used as a descriptive term for this factor as well. This court has from time to time upheld or imposed sentences designed to express society's abhorrence of the crime committed. Another, more recent, perception is that the punishment imposed ought to represent "just deserts" for the crime committed, thus suggesting a proportionality between the moral blameworthiness of the offender and the sanction imposed.

...

In light of everything that has been said so far about the benefit to society if the respondent succeeds in her efforts to control her addiction to heroin, I am of the view that a sentence of imprisonment could not be justified or imposed in this case on the basis of the so-called fifth factor of sentencing.

It is important to recognize that, in the case of most offences, apart from setting the maximum punishment which can be imposed upon conviction, Parliament has consistently and deliberately avoided any involvement in setting the "policy" to be applied in matters of sentencing. Thus all policy in the law of sentencing is judge-made and it is quite incorrect to say that any change in such policy ought to be left for Parliament.

It is the courts, including this court, in decisions such as those cited above, and others, which have set the policy here being re-examined, namely that as a general rule an addicted substance abuser, who is a repeat offender and who has an extensive record, must be sentenced to jail as a consequence of a conviction for possession of a prohibited narcotic. It can hardly be suggested that we are not free to re-examine that policy from time to time. Indeed, I believe it is our duty to do so.

B. Proportionality, Culpability, and Driving Offences Causing Death or Bodily Harm

R v. Sweeney, below, was one in a series of cases involving penitentiary sentences for driving offences where bodily harm or death had resulted. The BC Court of Appeal decided to hear a group of cases together so that it could assess whether the level of sentencing had been creeping upward and, if so, whether the increased penalties were justified or not. Wood JA considers the relative weight that should, in his view, be given to the different aims in sentencing decisions. However, there is another point that runs through the opinion—that is, the principle of proportionality, in the sense that a fit sentence must reflect the blameworthiness of the offender as it is defined by the substantive criminal law.

R v. Sweeney
(1992), 11 CR (4th) 1 (BCCA) (footnotes omitted)

WOOD JA (concurring in the result) (McEACHERN CJBC concurring): These appeals presented the court with a rare opportunity to undertake a thorough re-examination of the principles governing the imposition of sanctions in our criminal justice system. We sat five judges so that we could embark upon that exercise free from the constraints imposed by previous decisions. I believe that it is important, not only for the guidance of trial judges, but also for the information of the public, that such an opportunity not be missed.

II

While the proper role of this court on a sentence appeal is to determine the fitness of the sentence imposed in the court below according to the application of recognized legal principles, we do not perform that function in a legal vacuum devoid of any understanding of the realities of life to which our decisions must be applied. In order to understand the approach which I have taken on these appeals, it is necessary to consider some of those realities which cannot be ignored while en route to a principled determination of the fitness of the sentences imposed below.

I start with the fact that the drinking driver is an enormous social problem. The numbers alone tell us that. Every year over 10,000 convictions are recorded in this province for drinking/driving offences. The experts agree that these numbers represent only a fraction of the number of such offences actually committed. While only a small number of those who are caught have caused death or bodily harm, it is beyond dispute that in most cases that is more the result of good luck than it is an accurate reflection of the risk or danger created by such an offender.

Words alone cannot adequately describe the havoc caused by the drinking driver who is not caught in time. Beyond acknowledging the tragic and utterly futile human loss which lies in the scattered wake of such an offender's path, it is impossible to measure the consequences of his crime other than through the heartache and suffering of the surviving victims.

Yet notwithstanding our alarm over the death and destruction caused on our highways by drinking drivers, we are reluctant, as a society, to impose an absolute prohibition on drinking and driving. By setting the legal blood alcohol limit at 80 mg of alcohol in 100 ml of blood, rather than at zero, we do, in fact, permit some drinking and driving, and because the social use of alcohol is so widespread, we therefore accept the certainty that many of those who drink will also drive. Thus as a society we have clearly opted to accept the risk that there will be those who drink more than the law permits and then drive, either because they do not care, because they think they will not be caught or because they are chronic alcohol abusers whose illness destroys both the ability to know when the line has been crossed and the fear of getting caught.

. . .

Ordinary, reasonable and fair-minded people expect that any punishment meted out under criminal law will bear some direct proportionality to the moral culpability of the offence for which it is imposed. For reasons which I will explain more fully later, the moral culpability of the offence of impaired driving simpliciter is the same as that of the same offence, committed by the same individual, which causes either death or bodily harm to an innocent victim, irrespective of whether the latter offence is characterized as impaired, dangerous or criminally negligent driving. That is because, apart from the personal circumstances relating to that offender, the moral culpability of both offences lies in the intention to drive a motor vehicle after having voluntarily consumed more alcohol than the law permits, together with a reckless disregard for the foreseeable consequences of such driving.

. . .

(a) Parliamentary Direction: The 1985 Amendments

. . .

The 1985 amendments, which did away with the offence of criminal negligence in the operation of a motor vehicle, increased the range of charges that can now be laid in a drinking/driving case resulting in either death or bodily harm. ...

The stated purpose of this Parliamentary initiative was to enhance the role of the criminal justice system in the war against the drinking driver. Thus it is important to note that the maximum sentences set for the offences created to address that specific problem, i.e., impaired driving causing death and impaired driving causing bodily harm, were 14 years and 10 years respectively.

. . .

Much has been written in recent years about the purpose of sentencing. In February of 1987 the Canadian Sentencing Commission, under the chair of Judge J.R. Omer Archambault, published its report entitled *Sentencing Reform: A Canadian Approach* (Ottawa: Supply and Services, 1987). That study was devoted to recommending legislative initiatives designed to correct perceived inadequacies in the existing sentencing process. While it would not be proper for the courts to implement specific legislative proposals, particularly when Parliament has chosen not to do so, the report nonetheless contains much information and learned discussion which is of assistance when searching for a principled judicial approach to sentencing within the existing legislative framework. Although I do not accept all of the commission's conclusions, much of what I have to say in this part of my reasons borrows heavily from the theoretical content and the informational material contained in its report.

At p. 153 of that report, the commission suggested the following "Fundamental Purpose of Sentencing":

"It is further recognized and declared that in a free and democratic society peace and security can only be enjoyed through the due application of the principles of fundamental justice. In furtherance of the overall purpose of the criminal law of maintaining a just,

peaceful and safe society, the fundamental purpose of sentencing is to preserve the authority of and promote respect for the law through the imposition of just sanctions."

This philosophical statement, which I adopt, finds a more practical equivalent in the
simple proposition that the purpose of sentencing is to enhance the protection of society. That purpose is achieved if the imposition of legal sanctions discourages both convicted offenders from re-offending and those who have yet to offend from doing so at
all. Overlying and influencing the ability of the legal sanction or sentencing process to
achieve this purpose, however, is the extent to which that process enjoys the acceptance
and respect of the community at large.

A number of factors govern the community's acceptance of the sentencing process.
There is a prevailing belief that sentences should reflect, and be proportionate to, both
"the gravity of the offence and the degree of responsibility of the offender." In my view,
the gravity of the offence and the degree of responsibility of the offender are determined
by the moral culpability of the offender's conduct.

As a society, we long ago opted for a system of criminal justice in which the moral
culpability of an offence is determined by the state of mind which accompanies the offender's unlawful act. Thus the consequences of an unlawful act when either intended,
or foreseen and recklessly disregarded, aggravate its moral culpability. But consequences which are neither intended nor foreseen and recklessly ignored cannot aggravate the moral culpability of an unlawful act, except and to the extent that Parliament
so decrees.

As I noted earlier, for the same offence committed by the same offender, the moral
culpability of the offence of impaired driving simpliciter is the same as that of impaired
driving causing either death or bodily harm. That is because in both cases the mental
element of the crime consists of the intention to drive with a reckless disregard for
foreseeable consequences. The fact that death or bodily harm does or does not result
when any such offence is committed is more likely to be due to chance than to any circumstance of foreseeability, for such consequences are always foreseeable whenever a
person impaired by alcohol gets behind the wheel of a car and drives.

The degree of moral culpability will, of course, vary from offender to offender according to a number of factors which will be discussed later in these reasons, all of
which relate in some way to that person's state of mind. But, except to the extent that
Parliament has made the consequences of impaired driving part of the actus reus of the
offences under consideration, I do not accept that the moral culpability of an impaired
driver who unintentionally, albeit recklessly, causes either death or bodily harm is
greater than it would otherwise have been if he had been caught before such tragic consequences occurred.

· · ·

Another factor which enhances community acceptance of the sentencing process is
the extent to which it reflects consistency in the ultimate sanctions imposed upon like
offenders for similar offences. However, while consistent treatment of like cases is an
important goal in a principled approach to sentencing, the principle of accountability
requires that the aggravating and mitigating circumstances peculiar to each offence and
each offender be taken into account. Therefore, each sentence must, to some extent, be

tailor-made for the circumstances peculiar to its own case. Any adherence to the principle of consistency which denies such legitimate variation would necessarily result in the imposition of arbitrary sanctions.

The respect which the community at large has for the sentencing process will also depend on the extent to which the specific goals of any sanction imposed can be seen to serve the ultimate purpose of sentencing. Those goals have traditionally been described as (i) general deterrence, (ii) specific deterrence, (iii) isolation, and (iv) rehabilitation. In recent years some cases and literature on the subject have suggested a fifth, which has come to be known as "denunciation." The Archambault Commission suggested a sixth called "just deserts." Each of these goals must be examined more closely, with particular reference to the offences under consideration in these appeals.

· · ·

In its report, at p. 136, the Archambault Commission noted:

"With regard to general deterrence, the overall assessment of the deterrent effects of criminal sanctions ranges from an attitude of great caution in expressing an opinion to outright scepticism."

One of the many studies referred to by the commission dealt specifically with the deterrent effect of long sentences on the rate of drinking/driving offences: A.C. Donelson, *Impaired Driving Report No. 4: Alcohol and Road Accidents in Canada—Issues Related to Future Strategies and Priorities* (Ottawa: Department of Justice, 1985). The author asserts that

"law-based, punitive measures alone cannot produce large, sustained reductions in the magnitude of the problem." ...

In a follow-up study in 1989, after analyzing the statistical data and other materials available, the same author concluded that the persistence of serious drinking/driving offences as a social and criminal justice problem is due largely to the significant number of drivers with serious alcohol abuse problems. These, Donelson concludes, are the persons least likely to be deterred by the threat of arrest or punishment.

Counsel presented a considerable amount of published research material at the hearing of these appeals, most of it dedicated to an examination of the drinking and driving problem specifically. It is impossible to summarize all of that material in detail. Suffice it to say that none of it supports the argument that the imposition of severe sanctions, specifically, lengthy sentences of imprisonment, will produce a proportionate general deterrent effect on potential drinking/driving offenders.

What is clear from this material is that more education, greater enforcement, more media coverage and longer licence suspensions represent the best hopes for lessening the incidence of drinking and driving offences.

In considering this difficult subject, of course, it must be kept in mind that we are dealing with a theory, the ultimate proof or disproof of which probably lies beyond human ingenuity, for we are not likely ever to know with certainty who has, or who has not, been deterred by the imposition of a specific legal sanction. That being the case, we must not ignore any reasonable possibility that a particular sanction will deter a potential offender. But the key word in that precaution is "reasonable" and, when considering the general deterrent effect of sentences of imprisonment in respect of drinking/driving offences causing death or bodily harm, the material presented on this appeal establishes that it would be unreasonable to conclude that a sentence of five or six years' imprisonment will deter where one or two years will not.

. . .

While it is easier, from a historical vantage, to determine whether any particular sanction has been successful in persuading an individual not to re-offend, there are also reasonable limits to the specific deterrent effect which can be expected from a sentence of imprisonment in connection with the offences under discussion. In many cases, of course, imprisonment will not be necessary to ensure that the individual does not re-offend. But in those cases where the court finds that such a sanction is necessary to meet the goal of specific deterrence, it would be unreasonable, in the absence of any cogent evidence to the contrary, to conclude that the specific deterrent value of a sentence of imprisonment will be any greater than its overall general deterrent effect. Any person who would not likely be deterred by such a sentence falls into the category of offender for whom an isolative sentence must be considered.

Isolation is achieved primarily by a sentence of imprisonment. It is justified as a "goal" of sentencing by the simple proposition that so long as an offender is separated from society, he or she cannot re-offend. In terms of the protection of society, it is the option of last resort. Even as such, it suffers from the ultimate weakness that if the fundamental requirement of proportionality is observed, the individual concerned must eventually be released from jail. Experience teaches us that most people emerge from prison a worse threat to society than when they entered. Thus care and restraint must be exercised when imposing a sentence of imprisonment even when the goal is to isolate the offender.

In relation to the offences under consideration, of course, the chronic alcohol abuser, whose inability to refrain from driving a motor vehicle while intoxicated is demonstrated by a number of previous convictions for drinking/driving-related offences, presents as a candidate for an isolative sentence unless the court is persuaded that rehabilitative treatment can and will be undertaken with a reasonable prospect of success. Even in such cases, however, the fundamental requirement of proportionality must be observed.

. . .

It has long been recognized that rehabilitation, as a goal of the sentencing process, cannot be achieved through the imposition of custodial sentences. That does not mean that rehabilitation should be regarded as a less important goal of sentencing. Indeed, in my view it is self-evident that rehabilitation remains the only certain way of permanently protecting society from a specific offender.

Thus if the rehabilitation of a specific offender remains a reasonable possibility, that is a circumstance which requires the sentencing court to consider seriously a non-custodial form of disposition. In some cases, even those involving serious criminal offences, where the chances of rehabilitation are significant, or its benefits to society substantial, the importance of imposing a rehabilitative non-custodial form of sentence may outweigh the perceived general deterrent advantages of a custodial sentence. If so, a court should not hesitate to impose the former, for in such circumstances the requirements of accountability and proportionality can be met with carefully crafted terms and conditions which both restrict the individual's freedom and enhance supervision of the rehabilitative process.

I have previously noted that while minimum penalties are provided in the *Criminal Code* for simple impaired driving and its related offences, Parliament has so far seen fit not to impose any such requirement on drinking and driving offences which result in death or bodily harm. Thus it clearly remains open to a court to impose a non-custodial sentence upon conviction for offences of this sort where the circumstances in favour of such a disposition are sufficiently compelling to overcome the need for a sentence of imprisonment, which would otherwise be required to meet the other goals of sentencing.

· · ·

(v) Denunciation

This court first gave formal recognition to the denunciation as a goal of sentencing in *R v. Oliver*, [1977] 5 WWR 344, a case in which a lawyer was convicted of converting trust funds to his own benefit with the intent of defrauding his clients. Chief Justice Farris, speaking for the court, said at p. 346 of the report:

> Courts do not impose sentences in response to public clamour, nor in a spirit of revenge. On the other hand, justice is not administered in a vacuum. Sentences imposed by courts for criminal conduct by and large must have the support of concerned and thinking citizens. If they do not have such support, the system will fail. There are cases, as Lord Denning has said, where the punishment inflicted for grave crimes should reflect the revulsion felt by the majority of citizens for them. In his view, the objects of punishment are not simply deterrent or reformative. The ultimate justification of punishment is the emphatic denunciation by the community of a crime.

· · ·

As pointed out in the report of the Archambault Commission, the notion of denunciation as a goal of sentencing is one associated with the retributive theory of sentencing as declared in *R v. Hinch*, supra. That means that denunciation as a goal of sentencing must be strictly limited to ensuring that sentences imposed for criminal convictions are proportionate to the moral culpability of the offender's unlawful act.

· · ·

For the reasons to which I have already referred I do not accept that the consequences of the offences under discussion can be an aggravating circumstance except to the extent that Parliament has mandated by including those consequences as part of the actus reus of the offence. Thus, for example, I do not accept the proposition ... that the offence of the impaired driver who has caused the death of one innocent victim is any less culpable than it would be if he had instead caused the death of two or three innocent victims.

While on the subject of the important principle of proportionality between any sentence imposed and the moral culpability of the offence for which it is imposed, a special note of caution is necessary in those cases where the proper application of the sentencing goals indicates that imprisonment is necessary. In those cases it is important to ensure that the court's consideration of such a sentence be removed from the abstract realm of numbers to the reality of what those numbers mean when they refer to years of real-life experience in one of our jails. Numbers such as 2, 3, 4 and 5, are low numbers, particularly when viewed through the eyes of a society which has been ravaged by inflationary pressures of one kind or another for over 50 years. But when they refer to, and define the years of, a sentence of imprisonment, they represent a very significant deprivation of freedom for the offender, during which all semblance of a normal lifestyle is withdrawn, dignity and self-esteem are suppressed, and little, if any, chance for reformation exists.

(vi) Just Deserts

Notwithstanding the efforts of the authors of the Archambault Commission report to distinguish this "goal" of sentencing from that of retribution, I am of the view that from a practical as opposed to a theoretical viewpoint, they are indistinguishable. Accordingly, I am of the view that it has no place in a principled approach to sentencing.

NOTE

Of course, judge-made sentencing policy is not static. Nor does it always satisfy other members of even the same bench. It can be refined as new dimensions of an issue come forward. For example, Mr. Justice Wood concluded in *Sweeney*, and also in *Preston*, that rehabilitation cannot be achieved through incarceration. However, a different panel of the BC Court of Appeal decided in *R v. Robitaille*, [1993] BCJ No. 1404 (BCCA), released May 19, 1993, that rehabilitative concerns must give way when protection of the public demands a lengthy custodial sentence. The accused challenged a sentence of seven years for armed robbery and two years, consecutive, for use of a firearm while committing an indictable offence. Noting the relevance in not discouraging "any effort he may be making to rehabilitate himself by the imposition of a sentence that may be seen by him to be a dead weight on his future life," the appeal was dismissed on the basis that this was trumped by the "sentencing goal of protection of the public." Does a decision such as this conflict with the approach taken by Wood JA in *Preston* and *Sweeney*?

C. Retribution and Denunciation in Relation to Serious Offences Against the Person

Although trial judges are the primary instruments of sentencing, there are many sentence appeals each year to provincial and territorial appellate courts. These courts have an opportunity to make a substantial impact on judicial thinking about sentencing. For example, we look later at the efforts of the Alberta Court of Appeal to affect the results of sentencing by imposing a new methodology of sentencing—the starting point.

But the saga of sentencing does not end with provincial or territorial appellate courts. The Supreme Court of Canada has jurisdiction to entertain sentence appeals with leave: see *R v. Gardiner* (1982), 68 CCC (2d) 477 (SCC). The court rarely grants leave on legal issues in sentencing cases, but recently there have been a significant number of sentencing cases heard in the Supreme Court. Some of these decisions have had dramatic effects. For example, the Supreme Court has articulated a standard of deference to determine the threshold for appellate intervention. In a series of cases (see *R v. M.(C.A.)* and *R v. McDonnell*, below, and *R v. Shropshire* (1996), 43 CR (4th) 269), the court held that an appellate court should vary a sentence only if the original sentence involved an error of law or the application of wrong principles or if the sentence was demonstrably unfit. We will return to the issue of deference and appellate review in a later chapter. For now, the issue to consider in the following case is retribution and its role in sentencing.

R v. M.(C.A.)
(1996), 46 CR (4th) 269 (SCC)

[The Crown appealed a decision of the BC Court of Appeal that had reduced a 25-year sentence to a sentence of 18 years and 8 months. The accused had pleaded guilty to numerous counts of sexual assault, incest, assault with a weapon, and other offences, establishing a pattern of sexual, emotional, and physical abuse inflicted on his children over a period of years. The trial judge described the offences "as egregious as any" he had ever seen in the courts, transcending "the parameters of the worst case." None of the offences carried a maximum penalty of life imprisonment. In the Court of Appeal, the accused's counsel successfully argued that where a life sentence cannot be imposed, the maximum fixed-term sentence available to a sentencing judge is 20 years. Part of the argument relied on the parole eligibility rules under the *Corrections and Conditional Release Act*, which allow a person serving life as a maximum sentence to be eligible for parole after serving seven years, but a person serving a fixed sentence to be eligible after serving one-third of his or her sentence. The Supreme Court reversed. Speaking for a unanimous court, the decision of Lamer CJC is interesting in a number of respects. Our focus is on his discussion of the distinction between legitimate retributive goals and vengeance.]

LAMER CJC: ... In my view, within the broad statutory maximum and minimum penalties defined for particular offences under the Code, trial judges enjoy a wide ambit of discretion under s. 717 in selecting a "just and appropriate" fixed-term sentence which adequately promotes the traditional goals of sentencing, subject only to the fundamental principle that the global sentence imposed reflect the overall culpability of the offender and the circumstances of the offence. As such, I decline to delineate any prefixed outer boundary to the sentencing discretion of a trial judge, whether at 20 years, or even at 25 years as suggested by Seaton JA in dissent at the Court of Appeal. Similarly, I see no reason why numerical sentences in Canada ought to be de facto limited at 20 years as a matter of judicial habit or convention. Whether a fixed-term sentence beyond 20 years is imposed as a sentence for a single offence where life imprisonment is available but not imposed, or as a cumulative sentence for multiple offences where life imprisonment is not available, there is no a priori ceiling on fixed-term sentences under the Code.

The bastion which protects Canadians from unduly harsh fixed-term sentences is not found in the mechanics of the *Corrections Act* but rather in the good sense of our nation's trial judges. For many of the lesser crimes presently before our courts, a single or cumulative sentence beyond 20 years would undoubtedly be grossly excessive, and probably cruel and unusual. In other circumstances, such a stern sentence would be both fitting and appropriate. In our system of justice, the ultimate protection against excessive criminal punishment lies within a sentencing judge's overriding duty to fashion a "just and appropriate" punishment which is proportional to the overall culpability of the offender.

However, in the process of determining a just and appropriate fixed-term sentence of imprisonment, the sentencing judge should be mindful of the age of the offender in applying the relevant principles of sentencing. After a certain point, the utilitarian and normative goals of sentencing will eventually begin to exhaust themselves once a contemplated sentence starts to surpass any reasonable estimation of the offender's remaining natural life span. Accordingly, in exercising his or her specialized discretion under the Code, a sentencing judge should generally refrain from imposing a fixed-term sentence which so greatly exceeds an offender's expected remaining life span that the traditional goals of sentencing, even general deterrence and denunciation, have all but depleted their functional value. But with that consideration in mind, the governing principle remains the same: Canadian courts enjoy a broad discretion in imposing numerical sentences for single or multiple offences, subject only to the broad statutory parameters of the Code and the fundamental principle of our criminal law that global sentences be "just and appropriate."

Pursuant to the foregoing discussion, I conclude that the British Columbia Court of Appeal erred in applying as a principle of sentencing that fixed-term sentences under the *Criminal Code* ought to be capped at 20 years, absent special circumstances.

. . .

B. Did the Court of Appeal Err in Holding that Retribution Is Not a Legitimate Principle of Sentencing?

As a second and independent ground of appeal, the Crown argues that the Court of Appeal erred in law by relying on the proposition that "retribution is not a legitimate goal of sentencing" (p. 116) in reducing the sentence imposed by Filmer Prov. Ct. J to 18 years and 8 months. In my reading of the judgment of the Court of Appeal below, I find little evidence that the passing remarks of Wood JA in relation to the legitimacy of retribution played a significant role in his conclusion that the respondent's sentence ought to be reduced to 18 years and 8 months' imprisonment. It should be noted that Rowles JA, in her concurring reasons, did not even discuss retribution as a principle of sentencing. Similarly, there is no evidence that Filmer Prov. Ct. J placed any explicit reliance on the objective of "retribution" in initially rendering his stern sentence. Accordingly, whether or not Wood JA erred as a strict matter of law in his discussion of the philosophical merits of retribution as a principle of sentencing, I conclude that Wood JA's discussion of retribution was not a decisive element in the majority of the Court of Appeal's conclusion that the sentence of the respondent ought to be reduced to below 19 years. Therefore, I am persuaded that the remarks of Wood JA in relation to retribution did not constitute a reversible error. However, given the continued judicial debate over this issue, particularly in recent judgments of the BC Court of Appeal (see, e.g., *R v. Hicks* (1995), 56 BCAC 259, at para. 14 (rejecting retribution); *R v. Eneas*, [1994] BCJ No. 262, at paras. 45 and 46 (endorsing retribution); *R v. M.(D.E.S.)* (1993), 80 CCC (3d) 371, at p. 376 (rejecting retribution); *R v. Hoyt*, [1992] BCJ No. 2315 [reported at 17 CR (4th) 338], at paras. 21 and 22 (rejecting retribution); *R v. Pettigrew* (1990), 56 CCC (3d) 390, at pp. 394-95 (endorsing retribution)), it would be prudent for this Court to clarify briefly the existing state of Canadian law in this important area.

It has been recognized by this Court that retribution is an accepted, and indeed important, principle of sentencing in our criminal law. As La Forest J acknowledged in discussing the constitutionality of the dangerous offender provisions of the *Criminal Code* in *R v. L.(T.P.)*, (sub nom. *R v. L.*) [1987] 2 SCR 309, at p. 329:

> In a rational system of sentencing, the respective importance of prevention, deterrence, retribution and rehabilitation will vary according to the nature of the crime and the circumstances of the offender. No one would suggest that any of these functional considerations should be excluded from the legitimate purview of legislative or judicial decisions regarding sentencing.

This Court has since re-endorsed this passage on a number of occasions as a proper articulation of some of the guiding principles of sentencing in a number of subsequent cases. See *Luxton*, supra, at p. 721; *Goltz*, supra, at p. 503; and *Shropshire*, supra, at para. 23.

The Canadian Sentencing Commission in its 1987 Report on Sentencing Reform also endorsed retribution as a legitimate and relevant consideration in the sentencing process. While the Commission noted that strict retributivist theory on its own fails to provide a general justification for the imposition of criminal sanctions, the Commission argued that retribution, in conjunction with other utilitarian justifications of punishment (i.e., deterrence and rehabilitation), contributes to a more coherent theory of punishment (supra, at pp. 141-42, 143-45). More specifically, the Commission argued that a theory of retribution centred on "just deserts" or "just sanctions" provides a helpful organizing principle for the imposition of criminal sanctions (at p. 143). Indeed, as the Commission noted, retribution frequently operates as a principle of restraint, as utilitarian principles alone may direct individualized punishments which unfairly exceed the culpability of the offender. As the Report stated at pp. 133-34:

> The ethical foundation of retributivism lies in the following principle: it is immoral to treat one person as a resource for others. From this principle it follows that the only legitimate ground for punishing a person is the blameworthiness of his or her conduct. It also follows that sanctions must be strictly proportionate to the culpability of a person and to the seriousness of the offence for which that person has been convicted. ... According to these principles, all exemplary sentences (i.e. the imposition of a harsher sanction on an individual offender so that he or she may be made an example to the community) are unjustified, because they imply that an offender's plight may be used as a means or as a resource to deter potential offenders.

See, similarly, B.P. Archibald, *Crime and Punishment: The Constitutional Requirements for Sentencing Reform in Canada* (August 1988), at p. 18. With these considerations in mind, the Commission explicitly defined the fundamental purpose of sentencing with reference to the normative goal of imposing "just sanctions." As the Commission cast the guiding purpose of criminal sentencing, at p. 153:

> In furtherance of the overall purpose of the criminal law of maintaining a just, peaceful and safe society, the fundamental purpose of sentencing is to preserve the authority of and promote respect for the law through the imposition of just sanctions.

A majority of this Court has since expressed approval of this passage as an accurate statement of the essential goals of sentencing. See *R v. Jones*, [1994] 2 SCR 229, at p. 291 (although I dissented on the merits of the case).

Retribution, as an objective of sentencing, represents nothing less than the hallowed principle that criminal punishment, in addition to advancing utilitarian considerations related to deterrence and rehabilitation, should also be imposed to sanction the moral culpability of the offender. In my view, retribution is integrally woven into the existing principles of sentencing in Canadian law through the fundamental requirement that a sentence imposed be "just and appropriate" under the circumstances. Indeed, it is my profound belief that retribution represents an important unifying principle of our penal law by offering an essential conceptual link between the attribution of criminal liability and the imposition of criminal sanctions. With regard to the attribution of criminal liability, I have repeatedly held that it is a principle of "fundamental justice" under s. 7 of the Charter that criminal liability may only be imposed if an accused possesses a minimum "culpable mental state" in respect of the ingredients of the alleged offence. See *R v. Martineau*, [1990] 2 SCR 633, at p. 645. See, similarly, *Motor Vehicle Act* (British Columbia), supra; *R v. Vaillancourt*, [1987] 2 SCR 636. It is this mental state which gives rise to the "moral blameworthiness" which justifies the state in imposing the stigma and punishment associated with a criminal sentence. See *Martineau*, at p. 646. I submit that it is this same element of "moral blameworthiness" which animates the determination of the appropriate quantum of punishment for a convicted offender as a "just sanction." As I noted in *Martineau* in discussing the sentencing scheme for manslaughter under the Code, it is a recognized principle of our justice system that "punishment be meted out with regard to the level of moral blameworthiness of the offender" (p. 647). See the similar observations of W.E.B. Code in "Proportionate Blameworthiness and the Rule against Constructive Sentencing" (1992), 11 CR (4th) 40, at pp. 41-42.

However, the meaning of retribution is deserving of some clarification. The legitimacy of retribution as a principle of sentencing has often been questioned as a result of its unfortunate association with "vengeance" in common parlance. See, e.g., *R v. Hinch*, supra, at pp. 43-44; *R v. Calder* (1956), 114 CCC 155 (Man. CA), at p. 161. But it should be clear from my foregoing discussion that retribution bears little relation to vengeance, and I attribute much of the criticism of retribution as a principle to this confusion. As both academic and judicial commentators have noted, vengeance has no role to play in a civilized system of sentencing. See Ruby, *Sentencing*, supra, at p. 13. Vengeance, as I understand it, represents an uncalibrated act of harm upon another, frequently motivated by emotion and anger, as a reprisal for harm inflicted upon oneself by that person. Retribution in a criminal context, by contrast, represents an objective, reasoned and measured determination of an appropriate punishment which properly reflects the moral culpability of the offender, having regard to the intentional risk-taking of the offender, the consequential harm caused by the offender, and the normative character of the offender's conduct. Furthermore, unlike vengeance, retribution incorporates a principle of restraint; retribution requires the imposition of a just and appropriate punishment, and nothing more. As R. Cross has noted in *The English Sentencing System* (2nd ed. 1975), at p. 121: "The retributivist insists that the punishment must not be disproportionate to the offender's deserts."

Retribution, as well, should be conceptually distinguished from its legitimate sibling, denunciation. Retribution requires that a judicial sentence properly reflect the moral blameworthiness of that particular offender. The objective of denunciation mandates that a sentence should also communicate society's condemnation of that particular offender's conduct. In short, a sentence with a denunciatory element represents a symbolic, collective statement that the offender's conduct should be punished for encroaching on our society's basic code of values as enshrined within our substantive criminal law. As Lord Justice Lawton stated in *R v. Sargeant* (1974), 60 Cr. App. Rep. 74 (CA), at p. 77: "society, through the courts, must show its abhorrence of particular types of crime, and the only way in which the courts can show this is by the sentences they pass." The relevance of both retribution and denunciation as goals of sentencing underscores that our criminal justice system is not simply a vast system of negative penalties designed to prevent objectively harmful conduct by increasing the cost the offender must bear in committing an enumerated offence. Our criminal law is also a system of values. A sentence which expresses denunciation is simply the means by which these values are communicated. In short, in addition to attaching negative consequences to undesirable behaviour, judicial sentences should also be imposed in a manner which positively instills the basic set of communal values shared by all Canadians as expressed by the *Criminal Code*.

As a closing note to this discussion, it is important to stress that neither retribution nor denunciation alone provides an exhaustive justification for the imposition of criminal sanctions. Rather, in our system of justice, normative and utilitarian considerations operate in conjunction with one another to provide a coherent justification for criminal punishment. As Gonthier J emphasized in *Goltz*, supra, at p. 502, the goals of the penal sanction are both "broad and varied." Accordingly, the meaning of retribution must be considered in conjunction with the other legitimate objectives of sentencing, which include (but are not limited to) deterrence, denunciation, rehabilitation and the protection of society. Indeed, it is difficult to perfectly separate these inter-related principles. And as La Forest J emphasized in *L.(T.P.)*, the relative weight and importance of these multiple factors will frequently vary depending on the nature of the crime and the circumstances of the offender. In the final analysis, the overarching duty of a sentencing judge is to draw upon all the legitimate principles of sentencing to determine a "just and appropriate" sentence which reflects the gravity of the offence committed and the moral blameworthiness of the offender.

· · ·

With the greatest respect, I believe the Court of Appeal erred in this instance by engaging in an overly interventionist mode of appellate review of the "fitness" of sentence which transcended the standard of deference we articulated in *Shropshire*. Notwithstanding the existence of some empirical studies which question the general deterrent effect of sentencing, it was open for the sentencing judge to reasonably conclude that the particular blend of sentencing goals, ranging from specific and general deterrence, denunciation and rehabilitation to the protection of society, required a sentence of 25 years in this instance. Moreover, on the facts, the sentencing judge was entitled to find that an overall term of imprisonment of 25 years represented a "just sanction" for the crimes of the respondent.

The respondent committed a vile pattern of physical and sexual abuse against the very children he was entrusted to protect. The degree of violence exhibited in these crimes was disturbingly high, and the respondent's children will undoubtedly be scarred for life. The psychiatrist and psychologist who examined the respondent agree that he faces dim prospects of rehabilitation. Without doubt, the respondent deserves a severe sentence which expresses the society's revulsion at his crimes.

After taking into account all the circumstances of the offence, the trial judge sentenced the respondent to 25 years' imprisonment. In imposing that term of imprisonment, Filmer Prov. Ct. J was at liberty to incorporate credit for time served in custody pursuant to s. 721(3) of the Code, but chose not to. I see no reason to believe that the sentencing order of Filmer Prov. Ct. J was demonstrably unfit.

D. General Deterrence and Drug Offences

There are many factors that influence judicial attitudes toward sentencing: legislative amendments, perceptions of public opinion, empirical evidence, and the results of official studies. In *R v. McLeod*, below, Vancise JA brings a fresh consideration of the efficacy of general deterrence to the decision to incarcerate in a case involving a 31-year-old offender with a lengthy record who had been convicted of trafficking in 50 tablets of Xanax, contrary to s. 31 of the *Food and Drugs Act*, RSC 1985, c. F-27, as it then existed. The trial judge had placed the offender on intensive probation for two years, including an initial period of electronic monitoring for six months. The judge had been impressed by the progress made by the offender during the 13 months on bail between the charge and the sentencing, especially with respect to his alcohol- and drug-abuse problems and his educational upgrading. For the majority of the Court of Appeal, Vancise JA dismissed the Crown appeal.

R v. McLeod
(1993), 81 CCC (3d) 83 (Sask. CA)

VANCISE JA: ... The issue here is whether the Provincial Court judge erred in imposing the alternate sentence of intensive probation of two years, with a term which requires that the accused be confined to his residence for the first six months and that his whereabouts for that period of confinement be electronically monitored, instead of a custodial sentence. It is not necessary for me to repeat what I said in *R v. McGinn* (1989), 49 CCC (3d) 137, 75 Sask. R 161, 7 WCB (2d) 338, concerning the historical development and purpose of custodial sentences. Suffice it to say, imprisonment began as an alternative to harsher punishment and with the hope that hard work served in isolation would reform the offender. The concept has not been an overwhelming success.

A number of inquiries (the latest being in 1987) have examined the use of incarceration as a sanction when sentencing offenders. They all say, without exception, that the use of incarceration has failed and should be used with restraint. As the Ouimet Report noted, the object of the Canadian judicial system is to protect society from crime in a manner commanding public support while avoiding needless injury to the offender. The Ouimet Report proposed that incarceration be used with restraint and proposed the following all-encompassing sentencing policy:

> ... segregate the dangerous, deter and retrain the rationally motivated professional criminal, deal as constructively as possible with every offender as the circumstances of the case permit, release the harmless, imprison the casual offender not committed to a criminal career only where no other disposition is appropriate. In every disposition, the possibility of rehabilitation should be taken into account.

The committee concluded that, in so far as minor offences are concerned, all noncarceral options should be exhausted before there is recourse to incarceration. No one, or at least few, would disagree with lengthy prison terms for violent offences. I agree with the committee that a strong case can be made for alternate forms of sentences for offenders who do not pose a threat of physical violence or harm or endanger the safety of others. In determining whether a custodial term should be imposed it is necessary to examine a number of concepts which are inherent in the sentencing process. One must examine, first, the definition and purpose of sentencing; secondly, the principles or factors which determine what constitutes a fit sentence; thirdly, the effectiveness of custodial sentences as deterrence; fourthly, the role of appellate courts in developing sentencing guidelines, fifthly, alternate sanctions, and finally, public confidence in the administration of justice which includes disparity in sentences.

Prior to embarking on such an examination it is worth repeating that sentencing does and must take place within a framework of principles wherein the courts seek to impose a fit sentence having regard to the offence and the offender. As noted, the real problem is not enumerating the factors or stating the principles but rather, the emphasis to be accorded to the factors (about which I will have more to say) in each case.

The Definition and Purpose of Sentencing

The Law Reform Commission of Canada defines sentencing as:

> Sentencing is used to refer to that process in which the court or officials, having inquired into an alleged offence, give a reasoned statement making clear what values are at stake and what is involved in the offence. As the sentence is carried out, it may be necessary from time to time, as in probation, to change or amend conditions relating to the sentence.

There are two distinct elements in sentencing: punishment, and the determination or expression of the sanction. As Culliton CJS noted in *R v. Morrissette* (1970), 1 CCC (2d) 307 at pp. 309-10, 12 CRNS 392, 75 WWR 644 (Sask. CA):

> Both trial and appellate Judges must be ever mindful of the fact that the principal purpose of the criminal process, of which sentencing is an important element, is the protection of society.

From time to time, Courts have reviewed the principles to be considered in the determination of proper sentences. This Court recently did so in *R v. Kissick* (1969), 70 WWR 365. As has been stated many times, the factors to be considered are:

(1) punishment;
(2) deterrence;
(3) protection of the public; and
(4) the reformation and rehabilitation of the offender.

The real problem arises in deciding the factor to be emphasized in a particular case. Of necessity, the circumstances surrounding the commission of an offence differ in each case so that even for the same offence sentences may justifiably show a wide variation.

Fit Sentences

It is therefore within this broad framework that a Provincial Court of Appeal must deal with appeals in respect of sentencing in an effort to give guidelines which will as much as possible permit the courts to achieve uniformity of sentencing. One must, however, recognize that uniformity is the ideal and that its achievement is impossible given the need to consider the individual circumstances of accused persons. The appellate court must, when discrepancies occur, ensure that the disparate sentences for similar offences can be distinguished and rationalized.

Effectiveness of Custodial Sentences as Deterrence

General deterrence has been defined as the "inhibiting effect of sanctions." Deterrence is but one of a number of factors in determining a fit sentence. It has, as Culliton CJS stated in *Morrissette*, at p. 310, two aspects, general and specific. It must be considered from an objective point of view if the purpose is to deter others. If the purpose is to deter the accused then greater consideration must be given to the individual, his record, attitude and possibility of rehabilitation and reformation. If both general and specific deterrence are important then all factors must be weighed and a sentence fixed which properly balances the two.

Having said that, one must ask whether general deterrence is effective in reducing the crime rate because it is this factor on which the Crown relies, above all others, for the imposition of a carceral sentence. The appellant Crown contends that general deterrence is necessary to control and reduce crime in seeking to justify a custodial sentence.

There is no empirical evidence that general deterrence as it relates to length of sentences is effective in reducing the crime rate. There is no evidence that higher sentences are effective in reducing the crime rate.

A study done for the US National Academy of Science stated:

In summary ... we cannot yet assert that the evidence warrants an affirmative conclusion regarding deterrence. We believe scientific caution must be exercised in interpreting the limited validity of the available evidence and the number of competing explanations for the results. Our reluctance to draw stronger conclusions does not imply support for a position that deterrence does not exist, since the evidence certainly favors a proposition supporting deterrence more than it favors one asserting that deterrence is absent. The major challenge for future research is to estimate the magnitude of the effects of different sanctions on various crime types, an issue on which none of the evidence available thus far provides very useful guidance.

Daniel Nagin makes the same point concisely in a separate study made for the US panel:

> ... despite the intensity of the research effort, the empirical evidence is still not sufficient for providing a rigorous confirmation of the existence of a deterrent effect. Perhaps more important, the evidence is woefully inadequate for providing a good estimate of the magnitude of whatever effect may exist.
>
> Policy makers in the criminal justice system are done a disservice if they are left with the impression that the empirical evidence, which they themselves are frequently unable to evaluate, strongly supports the deterrence hypothesis.

Professor Cousineau, after reviewing the research on this issue for the Canadian Sentencing Commission (1984), stated:

> Drawing upon some nine bodies of research addressing the deterrence question, we contend that there is little or no evidence to sustain an empirically justified belief in the deterrent efficacy of legal sanctions. However, to go beyond a review of this literature and set out several arguments which document the mitigation of deterrent oriented legal sanctions [sic].
>
> Our thesis, however, is not confined to deterrence oriented legal sanctions. We suggest that many factors mitigate the effects of any legal sanctions intended to produce specific uniform outcomes.

That is not say that deterrence is not, as Culliton CJS noted, a factor to be taken into account. The research referred to emphasizes that there is no evidence to indicate that the level of sentence is effective in reducing the crime rate and that its importance has been overstated. The best evidence in support of general deterrence is that the likelihood of apprehension is important in reducing the crime rate. That seems to suggest that society would be better served by directing more resources towards prevention and rehabilitation rather than building prisons to house people who are not in any way deterred by longer sentences.

It would appear that general deterrence has a limited effect on criminal activity. To conclude that longer sentences have a greater deterrent effect than shorter sentences one must demonstrate that:

1. the public is aware of the sentence (a somewhat dubious proposition);
2. the offender will perceive the likelihood of apprehension (a dubious proposition);
3. the offender, being aware of the likelihood of apprehension, would commit the offence for the lower penalty, say one month, but not for the higher penalty, say six months (a very dubious proposition).

Viewed in this way, is it any wonder that increases in penalties have had little effect on the crime rate. If upward variations are not effective are there other things that can be done? With an abundance of evidence available to demonstrate that carceral sentences do not curb the crime rate should alternatives not be examined? I believe the answer to both questions is yes. I believe that the answer lies with the greater use of alternate sanctions, sanctions that are somewhere between probation and incarceration. I propose to deal with some of those alternatives.

Role of Appellate Courts in Developing Guidelines

The right to appellate review of sentences was introduced in Canada in 1921, but no consistent principles of sentencing have resulted from such right of review. The role of the appellate court is to "[state] the principles underlying the imposition of sentences so that at least a uniformity of approach [to the imposition of sentences] may be achieved": *R v. Morrissette*, at p. 311. There are, however, no absolutes in the matter of sentences and while, as Culliton CJS stated in *Morrissette*, there can be no such thing as a uniform sentence, the court has an obligation to ensure that the disparities between sentences can be rationalized.

Within this broad mandate, should the appellate courts, in the absence of specific legislative directives, not be examining the fundamental issue of when non-carceral sentences ought to be used? Put another way, should the appellate courts not, in a principled way, identify those offences which ought not to attract a custodial sentence and provide guidelines to the trial courts. I believe that they should and I believe that such an approach is consistent with the role of an appellate court. It is consistent with the approach described by Culliton CJS in *Morrissette*, where after dealing with the principles of sentencing he stated (at pp. 309-10):

> There is as well, as there should be, a constant changing of approach to the problem of sentencing. This changing attitude, in my opinion, was properly expressed by Ernest A. Cote, QC, who, in an address to the John Howard Society of Alberta, said:
>
>> "Perhaps the principal difference between criminal justice in the past and today is that the concepts of retribution, deterrence, and denunciation of evil are slowly being abandoned and gradually being replaced by what are considered to be realistic, social science concepts."
>
> Such a changing attitude requires, from time to time, a review and reappraisal of both the elements underlying an appropriate sentence and the emphasis to be placed on thereon.

Given that there are no legislative guidelines, it is for the appellate courts to develop and articulate guidelines. There have been a number of suggestions from the Canadian Sentencing Commission and parliamentary committees but no legislation has been enacted. Parliament attempted to establish principles with respect to the use of incarceration in the *Criminal Law Reform Act*, 1984 (Bill C-19), which died on the order paper. That Act sought to limit incarceration to cases where the protection of the public was necessary and where it was necessary to punish an offender because of non-compliance with an order or sentence imposed by the court. In other words, restraint was urged. As long ago as 1975 in *R v. Wood* (1975), 26 CCC (2d) 100, [1976] 2 WWR 135, the Alberta Court of Appeal stated (at p. 107): "... offences which require a prison sentence ...

grow fewer and fewer as more humane and varied types of punishment are developed."
Unfortunately, some 18 years later, we are still not using those forms of punishment to
advantage and are still sending people to prison when an alternate sanction would be
more effective.

In my opinion, a strong case can be made out for developing guidelines for the use
of alternate forms of sentencing for the majority of non-violent crimes. I say this, notwithstanding the presumption that seems to exist that incarceration is the norm and that
non-carceral sentences are exceptions to the norm. The custodial presumption has been
expressed in a number of ways but it is usually expressed under the guise of a public
interest requirement for certain offences. Professor Alan Young, in his research entitled:
The Role of an Appellate Court in Developing Sentencing Guidelines, which was prepared for the Canadian Sentencing Commission (1984), noted that an examination of
the list of offences caught by the custodial presumption reveals that it encompasses almost every offence except obscenity, gambling and some property offences that are
neither repetitive nor involve a breach of trust. Those offences caught by the presumption include theft by a person in a position of trust, drug trafficking, crimes of violence,
perjury and related offences against the administration of justice, repetitive break and
enters, extortion and sophisticated commercial crime. An offender has a difficult task
in displacing the presumption of incarceration and in most cases the presumption is dis-
placed by factors peculiar to the accused and not by an overriding principle.

The fundamental question to be answered here is whether incarceration is an appropriate sanction. The courts must determine whether the offence is one which requires
that the public be protected and that the offender be removed from society in order to
ensure that protection. In deciding whether a non-custodial sentence should be imposed, the court should take into account the following factors:

(a) whether the accused's conduct caused or threatened serious harm to another person
or his property;
(b) whether the act was planned or the resultant harm was planned;
(c) the conduct of the offender during the commission of the offence;
(d) whether the victim's conduct facilitated the commission of the offence;
(e) the likelihood of reoffending;
(f) the possibility of the offender responding positively to probationary treatment;
and
(g) the record of the offender.

This list is not exhaustive but contains a number of factors which I believe should
be considered in deciding whether or not a non-custodial sentence should be imposed.
There are certain categories of offences which, prima facie, require incarceration, for
example, trafficking in heroin or cocaine. The presumption of incarceration should remain when dealing with hard drugs where the social costs and the potential for enormous profit in the retailing and wholesaling of the drug exists. Offences such as possession, possession for the purpose of trafficking and even trafficking in small amounts
of drugs ought not to attract the presumption of incarceration. Trafficking in and possession of commercial quantities as retailer, wholesaler, importer or courier should
carry the presumption of incarceration.

NOTE

The views of the Supreme Court of Canada on the role of retribution and the meaning of denunciation are a guide for all sentencing courts. The remarks in *R. v. M.(C.A.)* are conceptual and do not dictate particular sentencing results as much as they add content to the sentencing analysis. Although the views expressed in *Sweeney* and *McLeod* come from provincial appellate courts, do you not find the arguments compelling? Are there counterarguments worthy of attention? Later, we discuss the 1996 amendments. Keep these cases in mind and consider whether the insertion of a statement of purpose, objectives, and principles into the *Criminal Code* has affected the impact or legitimacy of the views expressed.

IV. DISPARITY AND THE DESIRE FOR UNIFORMITY OF APPROACH

Is uniformity of outcomes required in a sentencing system? Certainly the concept of parity as between similar offenders and similar offences has been around for a long time, and seems to be a natural attribute of the rule of law. This is particularly so when one considers the effects of some crimes on their victims and the consequences in human terms of some punishments on those on whom they are inflicted. But in a principled system, it is not disparity but unjustified disparity that cannot be condoned. Offences are committed in myriad ways, by various offenders producing an array of consequences. Canadian courts constantly remind us that sentencing is an individualized process. In *R. v. M.(C.A.)*, Lamer CJC said (at para. 92):

> It has been repeatedly stressed that there is no such thing as a uniform sentence for a particular crime ... . Sentencing is an inherently individualized process, and the search for a single appropriate sentence for a similar offender and a similar crime will frequently be a fruitless exercise of academic abstraction. As well, sentences for a particular offence should be expected to vary to some degree across various communities and regions in this country, as the "just and appropriate" mix of accepted sentencing goals will depend on the needs and current conditions of and in the particular community where the crime occurred.

Still, parity should produce a high degree of consistency but the Canadian Sentencing Commission in its 1987 report (at 77) found "considerable unwarranted variation in sentencing." But without an overarching coherent theory with clearly articulated principles, uniformity may be difficult to produce. Without guidance, the scope of judicial discretion in sentencing matters places the sentencer in a difficult position. Clearly there are diverse views and controversies about issues as fundamental as the underlying philosophy of sentencing, the efficacy of various sentences, and the legitimacy of certain factors such as public opinion. One would hope that a principled approach could be developed so that the intrusive impact of sentences is not left entirely to the predilections of a particular judge or the extent to which a judge is able to rise above public uproar. But, so far, we have not been able to discern a clear and easily applicable set of principles with the unequivocal support of either philosophers or jurists.

Andrew Ashworth has observed that there are three techniques available to avoid unjustified disparity: (1) legislating a clear statement of purpose and principles; (2) legislating sentencing guidelines for specific categories of offences; or (3) encouraging guidelines judgments from appellate courts (see A. Ashworth, "Three Techniques for Reducing Sentence

Disparity," in von Hirsch and Ashworth, eds., *Principled Sentencing* (Boston: Northeastern University Press, 1992), at 282. In 1996, Parliament responded with a statutory statement of purposes and principles of sentencing. Later in this chapter, we will consider whether this approach has been successful in providing a principled approach. Other jurisdictions have looked to sentencing commissions to provide stipulated prescriptive guidelines for sentencing judges with greater or lesser opportunities to deviate from the norm. Appellate courts have been delegated as the tool for inducing principled uniformity in some jurisdictions through the encouragement of guideline judgments. In *McLeod*, above, Vancise JA argued that it is the role of the appellate courts to "develop and articulate guidelines."

In Canadian law, the attraction of "individualization" means that a measure of disparity is inherent. Many practitioners claim that this element of disparity is the strongest virtue of a system that seeks to ensure the protection of society through fit sentences. They argue that a sentence cannot be fit unless it can be justified as an appropriate response to the individual offence and the individual offender that acknowledges the unique character of each case. The prospect of disparity obviously undermines uniformity, but it can also affect certainty, predictability, and the appearance of fairness. Perhaps it is right that the priority of principles and objectives in sentencing should vary, or at least evolve, over time. It may also be right that the principles of sentencing in Canada should vary from place to place, or at least from jurisdiction to jurisdiction, given recognized differences. These are controversial questions. Assuming that a strong argument for reduction of unjustified disparity can be made, which institution and which technique ought to be used to achieve it?

In considering this issue, imagine a spectrum of approaches. At each end of that spectrum are positions that can, for convenience only, be described as "subjective" and "objective." The essential characteristic of "subjective" sentencing is the individualized decision, determined entirely at the discretion of the judge. As we move along the spectrum, we find a growing set of principles, each building on its predecessors, that are established by statute and the authoritative decisions of appellate courts. Finally, at the end of the spectrum is the truly "objective" approach to the sentencing decision, which eliminates or suppresses the exercise of judicial discretion by stipulating the appropriate penalty. This conceptual spectrum allows for various models of sentencing that lie somewhere between a purely subjective and purely objective model. The imperfections of purely subjective or purely objective models of sentencing are immediately apparent. Both would be unjust—the former because discretion would be unconstrained by principle and the latter because principle could not bend to ensure that justice is done in the individual case.

It can be argued that a natural and useful tendency of a system that emphasizes the need for individualized sentencing is to construct a range of sentencing options that are considered appropriate for the offence and the offender. Ideally, this range emerges over time. But how many cases are required before one can say what constitutes the "usual range"? While the individualized approach to sentencing and the "wise blending" of principles have applied in Canada for a considerable time, the appellate courts of some provinces have attempted to introduce a greater measure of objectivity in sentencing decisions so as to enhance consistency and reduce disparity. The crux of these initiatives is to identify a "starting point" for sentences in a given class of offences.

The decision that follows illustrates the starting-point approach to sentencing as developed by the Alberta Court of Appeal and later followed in other provinces, at least with respect to sexual assault cases. When you read it, consider whether this approach is consistent with the "amalgam" or "wise blending" of sentencing principles discussed earlier. Also ask yourself whether there are any aspects of sentencing usually considered relevant that are deleted or truncated by this methodology.

R v. Sandercock
(1985), 22 CCC (3d) 79 (Alta. CA)

KERANS JA: This is a Crown appeal from a sentence of three years on a charge of sexual assault. Judgment was reserved to consider the general idea of the starting-point approach to sentencing, as well as the appropriate starting-point for a major sexual assault and, of course, to consider the fitness of the sentence under review. All members of the court were consulted about the first two issues and we are authorized to say that the conclusions in these reasons were approved by a majority of all of the judges of the court, as well as this panel, and are to be considered as a guideline.

I

We first re-affirm the commitment of this court to the "starting-point approach" to sentencing. This approach, first expressed by this court in *R v. Johnas et al.* (1982), 2 CCC (3d) 490, 32 CR (3d) 1, 41 AR 183, has been criticized as a euphemism for a mandated minimal sentence. Also, Crown counsel often make that suggestion. These interpretations misunderstand that approach. On the contrary, it does not arbitrarily confine the discretion of the sentencing court. Rather, it offers a rational structure for its exercise, and a structure which is just because it guards against both disparity and inflexibility.

At the risk of stressing the obvious, we will consider these twin difficulties (disparity and inflexibility) in detail. On the one hand, appellate guidance offered cannot be so vague as to permit unjustified disparity of sentences. The discretion of sentencing judges is wide, but is not unfettered. Each sentence must, in the words of the *Criminal Code*, be "fit," and a significantly disparate sentence is not a fit sentence unless there is a reason for the disparity. Justice requires that two offenders in identical life circumstances who commit identical crimes should receive identical sentences. Such a twinning is rare, but the sentence process must be such that the reason for any apparent disparity is clear.

On the other hand, the guidance offered should not be too rigid. A fixed guideline, or tariff (or, indeed, even an "approved range"), fails to take into account the immense variety of circumstances which can be found in different cases involving a conviction for the same offence. Even putting aside the offender's circumstances, those who advocate some form of fixed sentences fail to appreciate that the definitions of the crimes in the *Criminal Code* contain only certain key elements required for guilt. For example, the definition of robbery requires only the taking of the property of another accompanied by an act of violence. The elements for guilt are the same whether the offence involves an elaborate bank hold-up or, literally, taking candy from a baby. The category of "robbery" is simply too broad for any meaningful sentence regime. The manifest object of the *Criminal Code* is that the sentencing process will adjust for the other important factors, whether aggravating or mitigating. This is why the sentencing judge is given a wide scope of terms of possible sentences.

The crime of sexual assault, like the crime of robbery, is so broadly defined that it encompasses all manner of crimes, some serious, some not so serious. A rational sentencing structure segregates them into meaningful categories. The minimal and maximal sentences permitted by law remain possible, although to be sure the former is unlikely for the serious categories and the latter for the less serious.

The sentencing process now adopted by this court is to state atypical categories with precision, and to acknowledge at the same time that each actual case presents differences from the archetypical case. These differences might mitigate or aggravate. Nevertheless, the idea of a typical case affords a starting-point for sentencing because one can state a precise sentence for that precise category. An actual sentence in a real case will vary upwards or downwards from that depending upon the balance of the factors present in the actual case. Many archetypes already exist, of which "bank hold-up" is a good example. What cannot always be found in the cases is a precise definition of such typical cases, and this imprecision can lead to confusion. Nor can a precise starting-point always be found.

This, then, is the starting-point approach: first, a categorization of a crime into "typical cases," second, a starting sentence for each typical case, third, the refinement of the sentence to the very specific circumstances of the actual case.

This court has a duty to offer guidance in the form of a statement of typical cases and starting-points. Sentencing courts, in turn, are asked to acknowledge the starting-point and then summarize the relevant factors before passing sentence. We thus have not the injustice of uniform sentences but the justice of a uniform approach. Dangerous rigidity is avoided because there are no arbitrary end-points. Nor is there real disparity, because all sentences of the same genre start at the same point and differences are rationally explained.

This is the sentencing policy adopted by this court.

II

The second issue is to describe a fit starting-point for offences under s. 246.1 of the *Criminal Code*.

The crime of sexual assault covers the huge spectrum of cases from a stolen kiss to the worst forms of human degradation: see *R v. Taylor* (1985), 19 CCC (3d) 156, 44 CR (3d) 263, 36 Alta. LR (2d) 275. The first step, as with robbery, is to describe some "typical" cases. Several will probably appear, and a starting-point be found. There is no magic in this; it is simply a description of the basic elements of a meaningful category of crimes which fall within the broadly defined code offence: see, for example, *R v. R.P.T.* (1983), 7 CCC (3d) 109, [1983] 5 WWR 558, 46 AR 87.

Sometimes, the crime is not serious: see, for example, *R v. Croft* (1979), Alta. D 7505-02. It is not, however, the purpose of these reasons to deal with minor sexual assaults.

One archetypical case of sexual assault is where a person, by violence or threat of violence, forces an adult victim to submit to sexual activity of a sort or intensity such that a reasonable person would know beforehand that the victim likely would suffer lasting emotional or psychological injury, whether or not physical injury occurs. The injury might come from the sexual aspect of the situation or from the violence used or from any combination of the two. This category, which we would describe as major sexual assault, includes not only what we suspect will continue to be called rape, but obviously also many cases of attempted rape, *fellatio, cunnilingus*, and buggery where the foreseeable major harm which we later describe more fully is present.

The paramount sentencing factors for a major sexual assault must be deterrence and what has been called denunciation. In *R v. Wood* (1975), 26 CCC (2d) 100 at p. 107, [1976] 2 WWR 135 at p. 143 McDermid JA adopts these words from a Law Reform Commission paper to explain the denunciatory effect of sentencing:

> Assuming that one of the purposes of the criminal law is the protection of certain core values in society, is it not an important function of sentencing and dispositions to assist in making clear what those values are? The educative effect of the sentencing process cannot be lost sight of. Through the sentence the courts may influence the behavior of others by confirming for them that their law abiding conduct is approved and that it is still worthwhile to resist temptation.

The key, then, to a major sexual assault is the evident blameworthiness of the offender, which was described by Laycraft JA (as he then was) in *R v. Fait* (1982), 68 CCC (2d) 367, 20 Alta. LR (2d) 90 *sub nom. R v. F.*, 37 AR 273, as [at p. 374] "... contemptuous disregard for the feelings and personal integrity of the victim." It is sometimes said that we live in a sexually permissive era, the age of the liberated libido. Many believe that gratification of sexual desire by almost any means is not only normal but "healthy." This attitude unsurprisingly has led to some confusion, and the belief by some that society also permits the use of others as objects for sexual gratification. It does not, and denunciatory sentences are needed to reinforce the point.

The other aspect which creates a major sexual assault is the effect on the victim. Notwithstanding statements in some authorities to the contrary, the tradition is to assume, in the case of a rape for example, that the victim has suffered notable psychological or emotional harm aside entirely from any physical injury. Of course, once this assumption is brought into question, the Crown must prove it. Nevertheless, harm generally is inferred from the very nature of the assault. This harm includes not just the haunting fear of another attack, the painful struggle with a feeling that somehow the victim is to blame, and the sense of violation or outrage, but also a lingering sense of powerlessness. What we mean by his last is that, while we all are aware in an intellectual way about the fragility of normal existence, to experience a sudden and real threat to one's well-being, a threat so intense that one must beg to be spared, tends to destroy that sense of personal security which modern society strives to offer and humanity so obviously wants. It matters little in this respect whether that threat comes from a robber, a rapist, or any swaggering bully.

The starting-point to sentencing for a major sexual assault is three years, assuming a mature accused with previous good character and no criminal record. On the other hand, we emphasize that the typical case just described does not include a major aggravating factor which is present sufficiently often that it could almost be called a secondary category: this is where the attack is planned and deliberate, whether the offender has stalked his victim or chosen her at random: see, by way of example, *R v. Cardinal* (1983), Alta. D 7515-01 [summarized 9 WCB 118]. ...

Before turning to the facts of the appeal before us, we propose to discuss the last step in this sentencing approach, a consideration of the many aggravating and mitigating factors which often arise and which must be weighed in fixing a fit sentence in a specific case.

• • •

In the circumstances of this case, it could be said that the victim was imprudent as to her own safety. This does not, however, offer the slightest mitigation. Nor is the drunkenness of the accused relevant except in support of the argument that the attack was spontaneous. Nor can Sandercock claim that he previously had good character, nor that he spared the victim the added pain of offering testimony. In the circumstances, any claim of remorse rings hollowly. The most that can be said for him is that he did offer a plea of guilty and thereby waived some of his constitutional rights in deference to the expeditious administration of justice.

In my view, on a balance of all the factors here, I would allow the Crown leave to appeal, allow the appeal, and substitute a sentence of four and one-half years for the sentence of three years imposed by the learned trial judge.

NOTE

Subsequently, the Alberta Court of Appeal extended the starting-point or tariff approach to sentencing by applying it to a number of offences. In *R v. S.(W.B.)* (1992), 73 CCC (3d) 530 (Alta. CA), the court established a starting point of four years for sexual offences against children in the context of a trust or "near-trust" relationship. Similarly, in *R v. Brown et al.* (1992), 73 CCC (3d) 242 (Alta. CA), a starting point for interspousal assaults was established and subsequently confirmed in *R v. Ollenberger* (1994), 29 CR (4th) 166 (Alta. CA). With respect to manslaughter, however, the variety of ways in which the offence can be committed persuaded the Alberta Court of Appeal that it was not amenable to the starting-point approach (see *R v. Tallman* (1989), 68 CR (3d) 367). The Manitoba Court of Appeal has applied the starting-point analysis to this type of case. In *R v. C.D.* (1991), 75 Man. R (2d) 14 (CA) and *R v. M.F.D.* (1991), 75 Man. R (2d) 21 (CA), the court established a four- to five-year starting point for sexual assaults perpetrated by family members where the victim is a young child and the sexual abuse extends over a period of time. The Nova Scotia Court of Appeal has also adopted the starting-point approach in a number of different types of cases (see *R v. Owen* (1982), 50 NSR (2d) 696 (CA) and *R v. Boutilier* (1985), 66 NSR (2d) 310 (CA)).

The Court of Appeal for Ontario refused to follow the starting-point approach established in *Johnas* and *Sandercock*. In *R v. Glassford* (1988), 42 CCC (3d) 259 (Ont. CA), a case involving a sexual assault on a woman, the court reiterated this position (at 265):

As in the past, this court declines to follow and apply the judgment in *Sandercock*. A review of the other cases cited reveals that primarily each case must be decided on its own facts. Further, the cases reflect a trend in recent years towards longer sentences for offences of this character.

However, consider the judgment of the Court of Appeal for Ontario in the following case, *R v. Joseph B.* (1990), 36 OAC 307, in which Blair JA concluded (at 308):

> The decisions of provincial appellate courts establish that, except in unusual circumstances, a penitentiary sentence is called for in all cases of sexual abuse of children to whom the convicted person stands in loco parentis if the abuse involves sexual intercourse. Such sentences reflect society's denunciation of this abhorrent conduct and the breach of trust reposed on parents or guardians of children. Both counsel agreed that the usual range of sentences for this type of offence is from three to five years. The length of sentence within the range of three to five years depends on a number of factors. These include the age of the victim, the duration and frequency of the sexual assaults, the criminal record of the offender, the effects on the victim and the presence or absence of collateral violence or remorse.

Does this case not establish a stratified tariff of sorts? The Alberta Court of Appeal in *R v. S.(W.B.)*, above, made the following observations about the *Joseph B.* case (at 551):

> The view we take of the matter is consistent with that expressed by the Ontario Court of Appeal in *R v. B.(J.)* and by this court in *R v. Jankovik*. To state that the "usual range" of sentence in cases of sexual abuse of children by a person who stands in loco parentis in cases of sexual intercourse will be three to five years (as the Ontario Court of Appeal said) is not far different from saying that the starting point is four to five years.

Now, more than 15 years after *Joseph B.*, the same range is recognized by the Ontario Court of Appeal, with expanded room for sentences at the top end. In *R v. Noftall* (2004), 181 CCC (3d) 470, the court said:

> Subsequent decisions of this court have affirmed this range. See *R v. M.(D.)* (1999), 136 CCC (3d) 412, *R v. H.(D.A.)* (2003), 171 CCC (3d) 309, and *R v. B.L.* (2000), 138 OAC 383.
>
> [57] Here, two aggravating factors put the sentence at the high end of the range: the appellant had a lengthy criminal record; and the complainant suffered traumatic psychological scars, in part because of the sexual assaults and in part because the appellant terrorized the C. household.
>
> [58] Additional aggravating factors may entitle a court to impose a sentence exceeding the usual range. In *R v. B.(J.)* itself this court upheld a sentence of eight years where the accused had sexually abused his stepdaughter for eight years, despite an intervening conviction for attempted rape, and where the acts of intercourse were accompanied by threats of punishment if the victim did not comply. In *R v. B.L.* this court upheld a sentence of six and a half years where the incest lasted seven years and twice resulted in the victim becoming pregnant.

These sexual assault cases raise an important question: from a methodological perspective, is a "usual range" the same as a starting point? Is the starting-point approach radically different from or inconsistent with the idea of an appropriate range? Does it do more than define a starting point within a range and compel trial judges to have good reasons for departing from the starting point? See the approach to manslaughter sentencing in *R v. Devaney* (2006), 213 CCC (3d) 264 (Ont. CA).

Whether the starting-point approach provides an improvement in sentencing methodology is contentious. The appropriate starting point must be stated for a defined class of offences but, as the Alberta Court of Appeal makes clear, a "class of offences" is not a broad abstraction but a comparatively narrow category, such as break-and-enter committed by youthful offenders in an urban setting. In *Sandercock* and *Ollenberger*, the court noted that the classes of sexual assault and domestic assault, respectively, must be significantly subdivided before it can determine a suitable starting point. Some of these subdivisions are concerned with characteristics pertaining to the mode of committing the offence while others are concerned with characteristics of offenders. These subdivisions assume that the Court of Appeal is competent to make decisions that distinguish not only in degree but in kind between different classes of offences. Unless it can be shown that the appellate courts have this experience and competence, it is far from evident that the starting-point approach is an improvement over the more flexible "range" approach.

The issue of institutional competence has a number of other dimensions. At present, appellate courts do not have resources to conduct empirical research and may not, without help, have resources to critically assess research that exists. Still, starting points were a creative idea. It is difficult to know in retrospect whether the goal was to induce greater uniformity, provide a more clearly explicable methodology, or, even, to encourage a harsher sentencing regime.

In 1997, the Supreme Court of Canada heard an appeal in a starting-point case from Alberta, where the trial judge had imposed 2 sentences of 12 months each, to be served concurrently, for sexual assaults on a 16-year-old foster child and a 14-year-old babysitter. The Alberta Court of Appeal, applying *Sandercock*, held that the judge erred in not characterizing the offences as major sexual assaults and raised the sentences to 4 years and 1 year consecutive. On appeal to the Supreme Court of Canada, a majority of 5 to 4 reversed the Court of Appeal decision and restored the original sentence. When reading the following extracts, consider the controversy between legality and sentencing policy and between individualization and reducing disparity, and whether either judge takes into account issues of institutional competence.

R v. McDonnell
(1997), 6 CR (5th) 231 (SCC)

SOPINKA J (Lamer CJC, Cory, Iacobucci, and Major JJ concurring): ... The respondent submitted that the sentencing judge in the present case failed to consider relevant factors and that the sentence was demonstrably unfit. Moreover, both the respondent and the Court of Appeal appear to have treated the failure of the sentencing judge to characterize the offence as a major sexual assault as an error in principle. I will discuss these contentions in turn.

B. Relevant Factors and Demonstrable Unfitness

[18] *Sandercock*, supra, established in Alberta the notion of a "major sexual assault," which carried with it a presumptive sentence ("starting point") of three years. *Sandercock* stated at p. 84 that the key to a major sexual assault is the "evident blameworthiness of the offender" as reflected in the extent to which the offender's actions demonstrated a "contemptuous disregard for the feelings and personal integrity of the

victim." The Court of Appeal held in the present case that the sentencing judge erred in failing to find that the first offence amounted to a major sexual assault.

[19] In concluding that the sentencing judge had mischaracterized the nature of the assault which was the subject of the first offence, the Court of Appeal relied on several factors. First, the court stated (at p. 173):

> One salient fact cannot be overlooked. This was not, despite the defence suggestion, a case of "fondling." It was a case of penile penetration of the vagina. The fact that McDonnell only succeeded in partially penetrating the complainant's vagina with his penis because of the complainant's efforts to resist him does not make this any less a major sexual assault. Partial penetration will suffice. Accordingly, this assault falls squarely within what is described in *Sandercock* as one of the archetypical cases of major sexual assault.

Second, the court did not accept the submission of the defence, which the court stated (at p. 173) the "trial judge appears to have implicitly accepted," that the first offence could not constitute major sexual assault because of the absence of psychological harm. The court held that non-consensual intercourse leads to a very high likelihood of trauma, which likelihood is one of the indicia of a major sexual assault according to *Sandercock*. In any event, the court concluded based on viva voce evidence and the victim impact statement that the complainant in the first case did suffer psychological harm. On the basis of these factors, the court concluded that the first offence was a major sexual assault and that the sentence ordered by the sentencing judge was insufficient.

[20] In my view, the Court of Appeal fails to point to a relevant factor not considered by the sentencing judge that would give rise to appellate review of the sentence. The first factor emphasized by the Court of Appeal, partial penetration, was explicitly cited by the sentencing judge. She stated:

> The assault, while reprehensible, was an isolated one, and it was a situation of far more than fondling as the accused attempted penetration. However, in that case, there was no involvement of violence nor of threats. It did not involve oral sex nor anal intercourse, and there was only partial penetration.

Clearly, the sentencing judge did consider penetration as a factor in reaching a sentence. Thus, consideration of this factor fails to give grounds to alter the sentence.

[21] The second factor alluded to by the Court of Appeal, psychological trauma, was also considered by the sentencing judge. The judge stated:

> It was a traumatic experience for the victim, but she was already 16 years old and was having other problems which may have contributed to her subsequent state of mind.

The judge later stated:

> In sentencing Terry McDonnell, I take into account his strong family support, the strong community support, his remorse and his desire to quit drinking, but also the trauma suffered by the victim at a time when she was already troubled, and the fact that FACS doesn't see counselling as being of any use to prevent re-offending, for Mr. McDonnell might simply re-offend if drunk again.

It is clear, in my view, that the sentencing judge did not fail to consider the trauma to the complainant in the first assault.

[22] Finally, the Court of Appeal stated (at p. 175) that it was "perverse" for the sentencing judge to treat the other personal problems the first complainant had been having around the time of the assault as a mitigating factor. I disagree with this characterization of the sentencing judge's views in the matter. It appears to me that in the first statement above the sentencing judge noted the problems the complainant had been having as a partial explanation of her personal problems after the assault; that is, not all her problems after the assault were attributable to the assault. The second statement by the sentencing judge indicates that while there were mitigating factors, the complainant's personal problems actually made the assault more serious. The Court of Appeal did not interpret the judge correctly, in my view, in reaching its conclusion that the sentencing judge had misused the evidence of the problems that the first complainant had been having.

[23] The respondent's submission that the judge failed to consider relevant factors in my view cannot succeed with respect to the first offence. The respondent also submits that the sentence imposed was demonstrably unfit. The sentence originally imposed for the first offence was one year, whereas the Court of Appeal imposed a four-year sentence. The "starting point" as set out in *Sandercock* for a major sexual assault was three years. These differences in themselves provide me no basis to conclude that the judge's sentence originally passed was demonstrably unfit.

[24] *Sandercock* does not purport to create a rigid tariff. At pp. 82-83 the Alberta Court of Appeal stated:

> … the [sentencing] guidance offered should not be too rigid. A fixed guideline, or tariff (or, indeed, even an "approved range"), fails to take into account the immense variety of circumstances which can be found in different cases involving a conviction for the same offence. Even putting aside the offender's circumstances, those who advocate some form of fixed sentences fail to appreciate that the definitions of the crimes in the *Criminal Code* contain only certain key elements required for guilt. … The manifest object of the *Criminal Code* is that the sentencing process will adjust for the other important factors, whether aggravating or mitigating. This is why the sentencing judge is given a wide scope of terms of possible sentences.

Indeed, for reasons which follow, I conclude that it would be inappropriate to do so. Faithful to this instruction, the sentencing judge took into account all relevant mitigating and aggravating circumstances and arrived at what she considered was an appropriate sentence. Accordingly, the sentence's departure from the Court of Appeal's view of the appropriate starting point does not in itself imply that the sentence was demonstrably unfit.

[25] Moreover, I note that in a case not dissimilar to the present case, the Alberta Court of Appeal imposed a custodial sentence of one year. In *R v. A.B.C.* (1991), 120 AR 106, the accused had sexually assaulted his sedated 16-year-old daughter, fondling her breasts and vagina and possibly penetrating her vagina with his penis. The Court of Appeal vacated the two-year suspended sentence and imposed a custodial sentence of one year. The respondent submitted in oral argument, and my colleague McLachlin J appears to have accepted this submission, that *A.B.C.* was decided on the basis of procedural delays and other particular facts and should not affect the present analysis. On the contrary, to the extent that the particular facts in *A.B.C.* determined the sentence in

that case, it may also be equally argued that the particular facts of the present case determined the one-year sentence meted out by the sentencing judge for a sexual assault similar in nature to that in *A.B.C.* It is difficult to conclude that a sentence of one year in the present case, given the similarities to *A.B.C.*, was demonstrably unfit. While this sentence is at the bottom of the scale, this does not make it demonstrably unfit. I note that in both *Shropshire* and *M.(C.A.)*, two recent, unanimous decisions, this Court refused on the basis of deference to reduce sentences that were clearly at the high end of the spectrum.

[26] In summary, with respect to the first assault, the trial judge did not fail to consider relevant factors, nor was the sentence demonstrably unfit.

[27] With respect to the second offence, the same conclusion applies: the judge did not ignore the factors raised by the Court of Appeal, nor is there any indication that the sentence was demonstrably unfit. The sentencing judge did, as the Court of Appeal acknowledged (at p. 176), consider the trauma to the complainant, stating:

> Regarding the charges of assault against [the second complainant], the victim in this case has been traumatized, but the acts of the accused were very much in the "less grave" category. Mr. McDonnell is a man of otherwise good character and is a strong member of his community. He has always maintained employment and supported his family. An additional lengthy consecutive custodial sentence to the custodial sentence imposed on the first charge would only seek to destroy the accused and his family and is not necessary to deter others from committing such an offence.
>
> I will thus sentence him to six months in jail concurrent to the first sentence, plus probation for the same period of time.

Neither the Court of Appeal nor the respondent points out a factor ignored by the sentencing judge in reaching her conclusion of a sentence of six months for the second offence. Nor is there any reason given by either the respondent or the Court of Appeal to conclude that a six-month sentence was demonstrably unfit. The Court of Appeal simply disagreed with the sentence ordered and substituted its own opinion for that of the sentencing judge.

[28] My colleague McLachlin J disagrees with this analysis and states that the sentences imposed by the sentencing judge were outside the acceptable range. While the above analysis generally addresses her reasoning, I add here that I disagree with her conclusion that a variety of past cases reveals that the sentence in the present case was demonstrably unfit. McLachlin J provides at para. 110 a lengthy list of cases which she contends support the conclusion that a sentence under two years in the present case was inappropriate. While I will not review each case upon which she relies, I will note that, in my view, many of the cases provided are inappropriate cases to consider in the present context. For example, in *R v. S.G.O.R.* (1991), 113 AR 36 (CA), aside from other sexual offences involved in the case, the accused raped his daughter over 20 times from when she was four years old until she was 12. In *R v. S.(W.B.); R v. P.(M.)* (1992), 73 CCC (3d) 530 (Alta. CA), the accused S. engaged repeatedly in anal intercourse with his six-year-old stepdaughter and his stepson, who was initially in grade three, over a period of two years. The accused P. committed both anal and vaginal rape of a seven-year-old child, physically beating her head and body. *R v. Spence* (1992), 78 CCC (3d) 451 (Alta. CA), involved an accused raping his 15-year-old cousin and physically beat-

ing and threatening her. *R v. Nicholson* (1993), 145 AR 262 (CA), involved 20 to 30 acts of intercourse starting when the complainant was 12 years old; associated with this abuse, the accused, amongst other things, discharged a rifle in the direction of the complainant as she attempted to escape his residence. Other cases cited by McLachlin J involved children much younger than the complainants in the present case, such as *R v. Lapatak* (1995), 169 AR 385 (CA), which involved a three-year-old victim.

[29] In my view, many of the cases cited by McLachlin J involved offences considerably more serious than the present case. While any sexual offence is serious, particularly on young people, the violence of the offences, the repetition of the offences, and the extreme youth of the victims in the cases cited above clearly distinguish them from the present case. Indeed, contrary to supporting McLachlin J's position, in my view the variable circumstances in the cases she cites highlight the importance of individualized sentencing. In any event, in my respectful view, the sentences in the cases she cites do not lead to the conclusion that the sentences in the present case were demonstrably unfit. The sentences in the present case, while low, were not demonstrably unfit.

C. Error in Principle

[30] While I have concluded that the sentencing judge did not ignore factors and that the sentences were not demonstrably unfit, according to *M.(C.A.)* and *Shropshire*, appellate review of a sentence is also appropriate if the sentencing judge committed an error in principle. Both the Court of Appeal and the respondent appear to treat the alleged departure from *Sandercock* as an error in principle. For example, the Court of Appeal found and the respondent submitted that the first assault was a "major sexual assault" in contradiction to the finding of the sentencing judge. The Court of Appeal stated (at pp. 172-73):

> We have concluded that the trial judge erred in finding that this was not a major sexual assault. This court made it clear in *R v. Sandercock* … , that the key to a major sexual assault is the "evident blameworthiness of the offender" as reflected in the extent to which the offender's actions demonstrated a "contemptuous disregard for the feelings and personal integrity of the victim." Here, McDonnell's actions in the first case clearly fall within the category of a major sexual assault.

The court then treated the error as one which justified alteration of the sentence, which implicitly treated the failure to find the major sexual assault as an error in principle. The Court of Appeal concluded that the sentencing judge wrongly declined to find a major sexual assault in part on the basis of what the court viewed as a misapprehension of the requirements for a major sexual assault. The court stated that the sentencing judge appeared to accept the argument of the defence that there was no significant psychological harm in the first case, and therefore there was no major sexual assault. The court stated (at p. 173) that while actual psychological harm may generally be presumed from non-consensual intercourse, it is not the actual harm, but the high likelihood of harm from the nature of the assault that gives rise to a major sexual assault.

[31] I disagree with the Court of Appeal that the sentencing judge accepted the argument of the defence that there was no psychological harm. As noted above, the

sentencing judge specifically found psychological harm to the complainants in both cases. In my view, even if the sentencing judge required proof of such harm before finding a major sexual assault, the sentencing judge appeared to find such harm so any "error" in this regard did not affect the outcome.

[32] In any event, in my view it can never be an error in principle in itself to fail to place a particular offence within a judicially created category of assault for the purposes of sentencing. There are two main reasons for this conclusion. First, *Shropshire* and *M.(C.A.)*, two recent and unanimous decisions of this Court, clearly deference should be shown to a lower court's sentencing decision. If an appellate court could simply create reviewable principles by creating categories of offences, deference is diminished in a manner that is inconsistent with *Shropshire* and *M.(C.A.)*. In order to circumvent deference and to enable appellate review of a particular sentence, a court may simply create a category of offence and a "starting point" for that offence, and treat as an error in principle any deviation in sentencing from the category so created. Indeed, that is what the Court of Appeal in Alberta has done in the present case. If the categories are defined narrowly, and deviations from the categorization are generally reversed, the discretion that should be left in the hands of the trial and sentencing judges is shifted considerably to the appellate courts.

[33] Second, there is no legal basis for the judicial creation of a category of offence within a statutory offence for the purposes of sentencing. As has been true since *Frey v. Fedoruk*, [1950] SCR 517, it is not for judges to create criminal offences, but rather for the legislature to enact such offences. By creating a species of sexual assault known as a "major sexual assault," and by basing sentencing decisions on such a categorization, the Alberta Court of Appeal has effectively created an offence, at least for the purposes of sentencing, contrary to the spirit if not the letter of Frey.

[34] The danger of courts encroaching into the realm of Parliament by creating offences is illustrated by the present case. The Court of Appeal appeared to base its conclusion that the first assault was a "major sexual assault" on the likelihood of psychological harm and indeed on the existence of actual harm. The court thus concluded that the sentence should be based on the existence of such harm. There is, however, a specific offence that deals with sexual assault causing bodily harm within the *Criminal Code*, namely s. 272(c). I note that *R v. McCraw*, [1991] 3 SCR 72, established that psychological harm from a sexual assault may be considered bodily harm. Given Parliament's intention to treat sexual assaults causing bodily harm under s. 272(c), it is particularly inappropriate to create a "major sexual assault," which is based at least in part on the existence of harm to the complainant pursuant to s. 271. While the Court of Appeal at times appeared to rely simply on the likelihood of harm in the present case, in *Sandercock* itself, actual harm was contemplated. *Sandercock* stated at p. 85, "[t]he other aspect which creates a major sexual assault is the effect on the victim." In my view, if the prosecution is to be based on the harm to the victim, the accused should be charged under the appropriate section, s. 272(c). It is not for the courts to establish a subset of offence within s. 271 that is based on harm.

[35] There is a further problem with the treatment of harm by the Court of Appeal in the present case in that it appeared at times to establish a presumption of psychological harm from a sexual assault. Admittedly, at other times the Court discussed the

likelihood of psychological harm from an offence as illustrating the seriousness of the offence, rather than actual harm itself. To illustrate this ambiguity, consider the following passage (at p. 173):

> The first point we wish to make is that we cannot envision a situation where nonconsensual intercourse—vaginal, anal or oral—would not fall into the major sexual assault category. ... In addition, in each case, there also exists a very real likelihood of psychological harm. Therefore, what must be understood is that it is not necessary that the Crown prove the existence of this kind of harm as a condition precedent to the courts classifying a sexual assault as a major one. Psychological harm is presumed in the absence of evidence to the contrary.

The court later stated (at p. 174):

> To put the matter another way, the offender is being sentenced on the basis of a major sexual assault, not because any specific psychological consequences have flowed from the attack but rather because of the nature of the attack and the fact that it poses the very real likelihood of long-term emotional or psychological harm. The fact that no such harm may materialize, a fact one could not possibly know until the victim's life had been lived in its entirety, is not a mitigating factor. However, that said, this does not mean that the consequences of the sexual assault are irrelevant. The degree of seriousness of the actions may be measured against the likely long-term consequences of the prohibited act. In other words, where the psychological harm has been severe, that may well be an aggravating factor. Of course, where harm beyond that which would be normally presumed is claimed in a case, the Crown must lead evidence to substantiate it.

[36] These passages are somewhat unclear. At one point it appears that the court presumes that psychological harm would result from a sexual assault, while at another point it appears that the court is not presuming psychological harm, but rather is simply noting, correctly in my view, the likelihood of psychological harm resulting from the actions of the accused. *McCraw*, supra, established that a threat to commit sexual assault amounted to a threat to commit assault causing bodily harm because of the high likelihood of psychological harm resulting from a sexual assault, a likelihood recognized by the Court of Appeal in the present case. Such a likelihood does not, however, establish a legal presumption of harm in cases involving an actual assault, as opposed to a threat. If harm is an element of the offence, the Crown must prove its existence beyond a reasonable doubt.

[37] To the extent that the Court of Appeal held that the Crown need not prove psychological harm in some instances, but rather such harm may be presumed, it was in error. As stated above, if the Crown wishes to rely upon the existence of psychological harm, in my view the Crown should charge under the section set out in the Code that contemplates harm, s. 272(c), and prove the offence. If an element of the offence, bodily (psychological) harm, is presumed, the Crown is improperly relieved of part of the burden of proof, which is contrary to the presumption of innocence. Accepting that harm may be an aggravating factor under s. 271, *R v. Gardiner*, [1982] 2 SCR 368, held that each aggravating factor in a sentencing hearing must be proved beyond a reasonable doubt. Such an approach is confirmed by Parliament in the new s. 724(3)(e) of the

Criminal Code (as amended by SC 1995, c. 22, s. 6). If psychological harm may be presumed, the burden of proving harm as an aggravating factor is improperly lifted from the Crown and shifted to the accused to disprove harm.

[38] In the present case, a presumption of harm is unnecessary. The sentencing judge found as a fact that each complainant in the present case was traumatized. The sentence was reached after considering the harm that resulted from the offences. Thus, the Court of Appeal's discussion of the presumption of harm was, in my view, both erroneous and unnecessary; harm existed and was considered in setting the sentence.

[39] The Court of Appeal appeared to make two other suggestions of errors in principle by the trial judge. I note that the respondent did not specifically raise these alleged errors in written argument before this Court, but raised them specifically only in oral argument. One error alleged by the Court of Appeal was that the trial judge improperly relied on *R v. R.P.T.* (1983), 7 CCC (3d) 109 (Alta. CA). The court stated that, notwithstanding that the principles it set out were revisited in *R v. S.(W.B.)*; *R v. P.(M.)*, supra, *R.P.T.* was factually inapplicable because in the present case there was no family that might be restored. In my view, the court erred in finding that the trial judge relied on *R.P.T.* with respect to the restoration of the family. *R.P.T.* held at p. 114 that even where there is a family to restore, if the sexual assault by a person in loco parentis on a family member were serious, "[t]he only solution, however imperfect ... must be to graft a rehabilitative sentence to a denunciatory sentence." If the assault were less serious and if there were a family to restore, a lesser sentence may be imposed; indeed, if the circumstances were "less significant" (p. 115), a suspended sentence may be appropriate.

[40] In the present case, the sentencing judge stated that while she was cognizant of *R.P.T.*, "this is not a case where simple rehabilitation will suffice." She stated that a rehabilitative sentence must be grafted to a denunciatory sentence. She thus apparently relied on the aspect of *R.P.T.* which held that despite the existence of a family, both a denunciatory and a rehabilitative sentence are required where the assault is serious. Contrary to the position of the Court of Appeal, she did not rely on the aspect of *R.P.T.* which stated that restoration of the family should be a mitigating consideration in cases where the assault is less serious. Given that the sentencing judge did not follow *R.P.T.* to rely on family restoration to mitigate the sentence, the Court of Appeal failed to point out an error in principle by the sentencing judge with respect to *R.P.T.*

[41] Another error suggested by the Court of Appeal was that the sentencing judge improperly relied upon the passage of time "between the first and second offence (and sentencing)" (p. 177). The sentencing judge did not in any way rely upon the passage of time between the first offence and the second offence. Neither did the sentencing judge rely upon the passage of time between the first offence and sentencing per se, but rather the judge stated that "the time elapsed since the offence has relevance in relation to the relative effect of this on both the accused and the victim." I presume that the sentencing judge was referring to effect of the actions on the accused since the offence, which included, for example, remorse and a desire to quit drinking, and to the effect of the actions on the victim since the offence, which included the psychological harm that the victim had displayed since the offence. These factors may be relevant considerations and the sentencing judge did not err in principle in referring to them.

[42] I note that my colleague McLachlin J states that she agrees that failing to characterize the offence into a particular, judicially created category of assault is not an error in principle which would justify appellate review. However, I am concerned that while she states she does not view it as such an error, she effectively treats it, if not as an error in principle, then otherwise as an error giving rise to appellate review. She states at para. 109:

> As indicated earlier, the "starting point" is not a principle of law, but rather a tool to determine the proper range of sentence for a certain type of offence. Failure to allude to the appropriate starting point or range is not an error of principle as that term is used in *M.(C.A.)*, supra. If the trial judge fails to refer to the appropriate starting point or range but in the end imposes a sentence within the acceptable range of sentence for the offence as adjusted for the particular circumstances of the offender, a court of appeal should not interfere. On the other hand, if the sentence falls outside the appropriate range, the court of appeal must interfere: *Shropshire, supra.*

This statement, combined with her emphasis on starting points in her analysis of demonstrable unfitness in the present case, suggests to me that McLachlin J in effect treats the failure to characterize an assault properly as an error permitting appellate intervention on sentencing. That is, the failure to characterize the assault properly is not an error in principle, but if the sentence reached as a result of that error is not very similar or identical to the sentence that would have been reached had the mischaracterization not occurred, appellate courts may intervene. In my view, this effectively states that while appellate courts must permit sentencing judges to err in characterizing the offence, appellate courts may intervene, notwithstanding deference, if the trial judge's mischaracterization affected significantly the sentence ordered. Given that different views of the nature of the assault would almost inevitably lead to different sentences, in my view, mischaracterization is treated by McLachlin J as an error which will often lead to appellate intervention. In my view, as stated, mischaracterization of the offence according to judicially created categories is not an error in principle, nor should it be treated as one. In my respectful opinion, McLachlin J takes an overly permissive approach to appellate intervention that is inconsistent with both *Shropshire* and *M.(C.A.)*.

[43] I add that I do not disagree with McLachlin J that appellate courts may set out starting-point sentences as guides to lower courts. Moreover, the starting point may well be a factor to consider in determining whether a sentence is demonstrably unfit. If there is a wide disparity between the starting point for the offence and the sentence imposed, then, assuming that the Court of Appeal has set a reasonable starting point, the starting point certainly suggests, but is not determinative of, unfitness. In my view, however, the approach taken by McLachlin J in the present case places too great an emphasis on the effect of deviation from the starting point. Unless there otherwise is a reason under *Shropshire* or *M.(C.A.)* to interfere with the sentence, a sentence cannot be altered on appeal, notwithstanding deviation from a starting point. Deviation from a starting point may be a factor in considering demonstrable unfitness, but does not have the significance McLachlin J gives it.

. . .

McLACHLIN J dissenting (La Forest, L'Heureux-Dubé, and Gonthier JJ concurring):

· · ·

[57] My difficulty with the position of the appellant and the reasons of Sopinka J stems mainly from a different understanding of the nature and effect of the "starting-point" approach to sentencing. It is therefore necessary to set out my conception of that approach at the outset.

[58] The starting-point approach to sentencing involves two steps. First, the judge determines the range of sentence for a typical case. Using that range as a starting point, a trial judge then adjusts the sentence upward or downward on the basis of factors relating to the particular offence and offender: *R v. Hessam* (1983), 43 AR 247 (CA), *R v. Sandercock* (1985), 22 CCC (3d) 79 (Alta. CA). This approach is distinguished from the tariff approach to sentencing which takes no account of the individual circumstances of the offender: C.C. Ruby, *Sentencing* (4th ed. 1994), at p. 479. The tariff approach looks only at the nature of the offence. In contrast, the starting-point approach mandates consideration of specific aggravating and mitigating factors directly relevant to the individual accused. In this way, the starting-point approach combines general considerations relating to the crime committed with personalized considerations relating to the particular offender and the unique circumstances of the assault.

[59] The first step on the starting-point approach consists of determining the appropriate range of sentence for an offence of this type in a typical case, assuming an offender of good character with no criminal record. In the case of sexual assault, the judge looks at the manner in which the assault was committed (e.g., by violence or threats or trickery), the nature of the sexual activity, and, most importantly, whether or not this sort of offence is likely to cause lasting emotional or psychological injury. The "key ... to a major sexual assault is the evident blameworthiness of the offender," the "contemptuous disregard for the feelings and personal integrity of the victim": *Sandercock*, supra, at p. 84. The inquiry at this stage, to repeat, is generalized and objective. The task of the judge at this stage is to determine the blameworthiness of an offender who commits the type of offence at issue in a typical case. Because the inquiry at this point is general, it proceeds on certain assumptions. The issue, on harm, is not whether actual trauma occurred, but whether this sort of criminal act would be likely to cause lasting emotional or psychological trauma. As to the offender, it is assumed that the offender is of good character and has no criminal record. See *Sandercock*, supra.

[60] The exercise of choosing a starting point in this way resembles the long-standing practice of setting a range of sentence as a tool to arrive at a just and appropriate sentence that reflects both the crime and the individual circumstances of the offence and the offender. As Ruby, supra, at p. 482, notes, "[i]t certainly is not a new method of sentencing." The starting point may be viewed as the mid-point in the traditional range of sentences for a particular sort of crime.

[61] The choice of a starting point is only—as the phrase makes clear—a starting point. Based as it is on assumptions as to the harm likely to flow from a typical case of the type of criminal act and the good character of the accused, it could not in fairness or principle serve as a final indication of the appropriate sentence in a particular case. As noted in *Sandercock*, supra, every case has its own unique characteristics, and every offender his or her own unique history. The goals of sentencing—deterrence, retribu-

tion and rehabilitation—play out differently depending on the peculiar concatenation of circumstances presented in each case. In short, the sentence must be individualized to the particular crime and the particular offender before the court. Having determined a starting point, the judge must go on to consider these factors and their effect on the appropriate sentence. The factors peculiar to the particular case and offender before the court may mitigate, resulting in a lower sentence than the typical case reflected by the starting point. Or they may exacerbate, resulting in a higher sentence than would prevail in the typical case.

(2) Why Was the Starting-Point Approach Developed?

[62] The starting-point approach was developed as a way of incorporating into the sentencing process the dual perspectives of the seriousness of the offence and the need to consider the individual circumstances of the offender. It represents a restatement of the long-standing practice of sentencing judges of beginning by considering the range of sentence that has been posed for similar criminal acts followed by consideration of factors peculiar to the case and offender before them.

[63] Despite the common practice of first determining a range and then individualizing the sentence, the jurisprudence dealing with the proper approach to sentencing is not as clear as might be desired. Professor A. Young, *The Role of an Appellate Court in Developing Sentencing Guidelines* (1988), a report written for the Canadian Sentencing Commission, offers a useful history of sentencing theory in Canada and the failure of the courts to adequately meet the challenge of devising a principled and consistent approach to sentencing.

[64] Appellate review of sentences was initiated only in 1921, explaining the absence of long-standing principles to guide trial judges. Prior to 1921, trial judges gave the sentence they saw fit and that was the end of the matter. Nor, in the years after 1921, were the courts instrumental "in designing relevant sentencing principles to assist lower-courts. ... Only in recent years have the appellate courts begun to express dissatisfaction with the impressionistic nature of sentencing decisions" (Young, supra, at p. 6). The maxim "Let the punishment fit the crime" might rule on Gilbert and Sullivan's stage, but in the courts the theme was "that the punishment should fit the offender" (Young, at p. 8). Precedents and theory played little part in the sentencing process. "In a sentencing model based upon the primacy of the individual there is little need for precedents that can extend beyond the characteristics of the offender in any given case" (Young, at p. 8). The Saskatchewan Court of Appeal (*R v. Natanson* (1927), 49 CCC 89) put the conventional wisdom this way (at p. 90):

> It would be impossible, and if possible it would be undesirable to lay down any general rule as to the punishment to be inflicted for any particular class of offence. Every case must be dealt with on its own facts and circumstance[s].

Similarly, in *R v. Connor and Hall* (1957), 118 CCC 237, the Ontario Court of Appeal opined (at p. 238):

> It serves little useful purpose and affords little assistance to the Court to know what sentences have been imposed in other countries or jurisdictions or by other Courts.

[65] The traditional notion that sentencing is primarily a matter of impression for the sentencing judge and only secondarily a matter of principle began to be questioned by the courts in the mid-60s. Behind the challenge lay increasing recognition that some measure of uniformity was essential in a sentencing process that not only was just, but was perceived to be just. In *R v. Baldhead*, [1966] 4 CCC 183 (Sask. CA), it was held that a sentence could be reviewed if it represented "a marked departure from the sentences customarily imposed in the same jurisdiction for the same or similar crimes" (p. 187).

[66] *Baldhead* did no more than confer judicial respectability on an emerging general consensus that the law should award similar sentences for similar crimes, subject to adjustment for factors peculiar to each case. Sentences may properly vary somewhat from case to case to reflect factors peculiar to the particular act and offender on trial. But it affronts common-sense notions of justice if people who have committed the same criminal act receive wildly disparate sentences. It is neither fair nor just that one person languish in prison years after another, who committed a similar act, is released to liberty. *Baldhead* expressed the growing view that a measure of uniformity, tempered but not obliterated by considerations particular to each case, must stand as a fundamental goal of sentencing law.

[67] Many courts since *Baldhead* have embraced the objective of uniformity as a factor to be considered in sentencing. However, the relationship between the goal of sentencing uniformity and the goal of reflecting in a sentence the circumstances of the particular case and offender remained largely ill-defined up until the jurisprudence advocating a starting-point approach. Alongside decisions advocating the need for a measure of uniformity, stand other decisions evincing reluctance to commit it to principle. As Young, supra, puts it: "The courts have not wholly embraced the notion of uniformity for fear that broad, general principles will fail to take into account the unique characteristics of every offender" (pp. 9-10). By contrast, the starting-point approach represents an attempt to marry in one sentencing principle the values of uniformity and individualization.

[68] It was no accident that the starting-point approach was eventually applied in the context of the crime of sexual assault. The wide spectrum of conduct embraced by the crime of "sexual assault" and the disparate views different judges may take with respect to the gravity of particular types of sexual assaults give rise to wide variations in sentences for offences that seem quite similar. See P. Marshall, "Sexual Assault, The Charter and Sentencing Reform" (1988), 63 CR (3d) 216. Depending on where a particular judge placed a particular type of sexual assault on the spectrum of severity and the seriousness with which he or she regarded that assault, a sentence might be high or low or anywhere in between. The disparities between sentences threatened to go beyond the legitimate area of divergence represented by the individual circumstances of a particular offender and offence, to a more generalized divergence based on judicial views of the seriousness of the offence. This called for judicial action. As the Manitoba Court of Appeal put it in *R v. Jourdain and Kudyba* (1958), 121 CCC 82, at p. 87:

> It is the duty not only of this Court but of all the Courts of the Province and the Crown to do whatever is possible to bring about uniformity and equalization of sentences for crimes of the same or similar gravity.

The response of courts, charged as they were with maintaining reasonable uniformity of sentences, was to introduce the concept of the "starting point."

(3) In What Jurisdictions Has the Starting-Point Approach Been Adopted?

[69] The Courts of Appeal for Alberta, Nova Scotia (*R v. Zong* (1986), 173 APR 432), Manitoba (*R v. Muswagon* (1993), 88 Man. R (2d) 319), British Columbia (*R v. Post* (1996), 72 BCAC 312) and Saskatchewan (*R v. Jackson* (1993), 87 CCC (3d) 56) have applied the starting-point approach to sentencing to deal with marked disparities in sentences for certain crimes. The Ontario Court of Appeal in *R v. Glassford* (1988), 27 OAC 194 explicitly rejected the starting-point approach to sentencing articulated in *Sandercock*, supra. However, that same court has recently adopted the approach in narcotics cases. See *R v. Cunningham* (1996), 104 CCC (3d) 542.

[70] In addition to the Canadian examples, the English Court of Appeal also appears to have adopted this approach. In *R v. Edwards*; *R v. Brandy*, the English Court of Appeal, Criminal Division, suggested that "[a]n appropriate level of sentencing for serious dwelling house burglary where the house was unoccupied was three years on a conviction, with variations either way to reflect the particular circumstances of the case" (*The Times*, July 1, 1996). In fact, it appears that the starting-point concept is not of recent origin in England. Cross, *The English Sentencing System* (2nd ed. 1975), states at p. 148:

> The statement of 1900 is contained in a Memorandum produced by Lord Alveston (the then Lord Chief Justice) in an effort to get agreement among the Queen's Bench Judges about the normal punishment of offences. It was sent to the Home Office and no further action appears to have been taken on it; but it is now printed as Appendix 5 of *Enforcing the Law* by Professor Jackson of Cambridge. The Memorandum states that it is not possible to do more than recommend "a range of punishments within certain limits" and throughout it speaks of periods such as three to five years penal servitude as the "correct range."

When dealing with rape, for instance, the Memorandum mentions five to seven years penal servitude as giving:

> a reasonable range of punishment to be increased if there are accompanying circumstances of aggravation, such, for example, as rape by a gang or by a parent or master, or with brutal violence, and to be reduced if there are extenuating circumstances.

[71] The Australian courts appear to follow a similar approach. In *R v. Jabaltjari* (1989), 46 A Crim. R 47, the Court of Criminal Appeal (Northern Territory) did not interfere with the trial judge's approach described as follows: "Having fixed on the objective sentence his Honour then made appropriate adjustments downward to give effect to the mitigating circumstances personal to the respondent" (p. 64). Although the approach is referred to by the Court as the "tariff" approach, it seems to be identical to the starting-point approach.

NOTE

The practical result of the majority's decision in this case is to restore the concurrent sentences of 12 months' imprisonment. Do you think this is appropriate or "fit" for these offences? Does the majority decision signal the end of starting points, or does it merely reduce them to guides for sentencing judges? See the decision in *R v. Waldner* (1998), 15 CR (5th) 159 (Alta. CA) per Berger JA at 169, where he distills the following principles from *McDonnell*:

1. Appellate courts may set out starting points as guides to lower courts;

2. The starting point set by a Court of Appeal must be reasonable;

3. If the starting point is reasonable, it may be a factor to consider in determining whether a sentence is demonstrably unfit;

4. A wide disparity between the starting point and the sentence imposed suggests unfitness; it is not determinative of unfitness;

5. Unless there is a reason under Shropshire or M.(C.A.) to interfere with the sentence, a sentence cannot be altered on appeal, notwithstanding deviation from a starting point.

Subsequently, in dealing with an array of cocaine trafficking cases in *R v. Rahime* (2001), 156 CCC (3d) 341, a unanimous Alberta Court of Appeal said:

For over twenty years, beginning with the decision in *R v. Maskell* [(1981), 58 CCC (2d) 408 (Alta. CA)], this Court has offered guidance to sentencing judges in cocaine trafficking cases by establishing a starting point of three years incarceration in cases of a commercial operation on something more than a minimal scale.

It is worth repeating that the guidance given is simply a starting point. It is implicit in that concept that the sentencing judge may depart from the starting point by increasing or decreasing the severity of the sentence depending upon the sentencing judge's assessment of the aggravating and mitigating circumstances presented by the offender and the offence.

At an early stage in its formulation of this guidance, this Court in *R v. Getty* (1990), 104 AR 180 at 187 expressly recognized the importance of aggravating and mitigating factors by referring to its earlier decision in *R v. Simoneau* (1988), 84 AR 155 (CA) at para. 24:

[24] Simoneau stands for the proposition that from the Maskell starting point of three years, a lesser sentence may be justified on a weighing of the mitigating and aggravating circumstances. A statement to the like effect is made by Laycraft CJA, in *Ness* [(1987), 77 AR 319 (CA)]. *R v. Goodman* (1989), 96 AR 313 (CA), and *R v. Thompson* (1989), 50 CCC (3d) 126; 98 AR 348 (CA) are recognitions of this principle. It is a general principle applied in all guideline cases setting a starting point for sentences as for instance robbery, sexual offences, etc.

The application of this proposition has resulted in this Court imposing sentences below the three year starting point and, indeed, below two years incarceration.

So it looks like starting points are alive and well, perhaps in the guise of guidelines, but alive and well all the same. See also *R v. Beaudry* (2000), 5 WWR 724 (Alta. CA); *R v. M.G.B.*,

[2007] AJ No. 745 (Alta. CA) (QL); *R v. Law*, [2007] AJ No. 644 (QL). To assess the health of starting points in other provinces see *R v. J.L.S.*, [2006] 10 WWR 642 (Sask. CA); *R v. Bratzer* (2001), 198 NSR (2d) 303 (NSCA); *R v. R.W.T.*, [2006] MJ No. 291 (QL).

V. THE 1996 AMENDMENTS AND THE INTRODUCTION OF LEGISLATIVE GUIDANCE

In 1996, the *Criminal Code* was amended to provide a legislative statement of the aims of sentencing in Canadian law. The absence of such a statement until that date underscores the importance of judicial decision-making as the primary source of guidance. For many years, however, it had been argued that Canadian law needed a statutory statement of the aims of sentencing. This point was made forcefully in the studies of several committees and commissions working under the authority of the government or Parliament, including the Ouimet committee, the Law Reform Commission of Canada, and the Royal Commission on Sentencing. The same idea was endorsed by a standing committee of the House of Commons (see *Taking Responsibility*, Report of the House of Commons Standing Committee on Justice and Solicitor General on Its Review of Sentencing, Conditional Release, and Related Aspects of Corrections (Ottawa: 1988)).

The government of Canada introduced legislation in 1984 that would have included a statutory statement of aims in sentencing, but this bill died. Another attempt was made with Bill C-41 in 1994, which was passed by Parliament in 1995 as SC 1995, c. 22. It came into force on September 3, 1996. This legislation was heralded by the minister of justice as initiating a major reform of the law of sentencing in Canada.

An important aspect of Bill C-41 is the statement of the "Purpose and Principles of Sentencing" in s. 718. This provision was the subject of considerable controversy during consultations respecting the bill:

> 718. The fundamental purpose of sentencing is to contribute, along with crime prevention initiatives, to respect for the law and the maintenance of a just, peaceful and safe society by imposing just sanctions that have one or more of the following objectives:
>
> (a) to denounce unlawful conduct;
>
> (b) to deter the offender and other persons from committing offences;
>
> (c) to separate offenders from society, where necessary;
>
> (d) to assist in rehabilitating offenders;
>
> (e) to provide reparations for harm done to victims or to the community; and
>
> (f) to promote a sense of responsibility in offenders, and acknowledgment of the harm done to victims and to the community.
>
> 718.1 A sentence must be proportionate to the gravity of the offence and the degree of responsibility of the offender.

To what extent does the statement of principles in s. 718 respond to the issues raised in this chapter? Is it possible to discern in s. 718 any statement of the priority that should be given among the principles identified? Will it resolve the weaknesses of the amalgam approach, or does it merely codify that approach and all of its problems?

Some commentators have already identified some deficiencies in s. 718. In "Statutory Sentencing Reform: The Purpose and Principles of Sentencing" (1995), 37 *Crim. LQ* 220,

Julian Roberts and Andrew von Hirsch state that s. 718 is not sufficiently detailed to provide prescriptive guidance for judges. They favour the implementation of specific sentencing guidelines. They write:

> The challenge to drafters of a statement of sentencing purpose and principle is to reconcile diverse and frequently conflicting sentencing aims. The task is not impossible, and nor does it necessarily mean promoting a single sentencing purpose at the expense of all the others. Multi-purpose statements can still offer guidance and affect sentencing practices at the trial court level but they must specify the conditions under which certain aims are favoured over others. This section of the article will also necessitate some discussion of the utility of sentencing guidelines, for guidelines are the means by which a statement of purpose effects changes in sentencing practices. *The statement of purpose is the compass and guidelines the road map. Without the guidelines, judges know roughly where they are going but not necessarily how to get there. Without the statement judges would be following instructions in the absence of a clear sense of over-all direction.* [Emphasis added.]

In addition to the statement of purpose and objectives, the following statement of principle is stated in the legislation:

> 718.2 A court that imposes a sentence shall also take into consideration the following principles:
>
>   (a) a sentence should be increased or reduced to account for any relevant aggravating or mitigating circumstances relating to the offence or the offender, and, without limiting the generality of the foregoing,
>
>   (i) evidence that the offence was motivated by bias, prejudice or hate based on race, national or ethnic origin, language, colour, religion, sex, age, mental or physical disability, sexual orientation or any other similar factor,
>
>   (ii) evidence that the offender, in committing the offence, abused the offender's spouse or child,
>
>   (iii) evidence that the offender, in committing the offence, abused a position of trust or authority in relation to the victim, or
>
>   (iv) evidence that the offence was committed for the benefit of, at the direction of or in association with a criminal organization
>
>   shall be deemed to be aggravating circumstances;
>
>   (b) a sentence should be similar to sentences imposed on similar offenders for similar offences committed in similar circumstances;
>
>   (c) where consecutive sentences are imposed, the combined sentence should not be unduly long or harsh;
>
>   (d) an offender should not be deprived of liberty, if less restrictive sanctions may be appropriate in the circumstances; and
>
>   (e) all available sanctions other than imprisonment that are reasonable in the circumstances should be considered for all offenders, with particular attention to the circumstances of aboriginal offenders.

What does this statement achieve? Does it effectively entrench the principle of restraint? If so, what is the relationship between restraint and proportionality referred to in s. 718.1?

By the end of the 1990s, two appeals were heard by the Supreme Court that addressed the effect of the 1996 amendments. *R v. Gladue*, below, dealt specifically with the application of s. 718.2(e), and *R v. Proulx*, below, involved the interpretation of s. 742.1, the conditional sentence provision. For further discussion of *Proulx*, see chapter 12, Conditional Sentence of Imprisonment.

R v. Gladue
[1999] 1 SCR 688

[The offender had pleaded guilty to manslaughter in the stabbing death of her husband. The trial judge sentenced her to three years' imprisonment. He remarked that although she was an Aboriginal person, s. 718.2(e) could not apply because she did not reside in an Aboriginal community. On appeal, the BC Court of Appeal disagreed with this narrow application of s. 718.2(e), but the majority (Rowles JA dissenting) did not vary the sentence. Gladue appealed to the Supreme Court. Notwithstanding the court's important examination of overincarceration in Canada, particularly in relation to the sentencing of Aboriginal offenders (a topic discussed in detail in chapter 16, Aboriginal Offenders), it dismissed the appeal. In this regard, it must be noted that the offender was on day parole by the time the case was heard. In the course of dealing with s. 718.2(e), the court considered the 1996 amendments in general to provide a context for its decision.]

CORY and IACOBUCCI JJ: ... The interpretation of s. 718.2(e) must begin by considering its words in context. Although this appeal is ultimately concerned only with the meaning of the phrase "with particular attention to the circumstances of aboriginal offenders," that phrase takes on meaning from the other words of s. 718.2(e), from the purpose and principles of sentencing set out in ss. 718-718.2, and from the overall scheme of Part XXIII.

The respondent observed that some caution is in order in construing s. 718.2(e), insofar as it would be inappropriate to prejudge the many other important issues which may be raised by the reforms but which are not specifically at issue here. However, it would be equally inappropriate to construe s. 718.2(e) in a vacuum, without considering the surrounding text which gives the provision its depth of meaning. To the extent that the broader scheme of Part XXIII informs the proper construction to be given to s. 718.2(e), it will be necessary to draw at least some general conclusions about the new sentencing regime.

A core issue in this appeal is whether s. 718.2(e) should be understood as being remedial in nature, or whether s. 718.2(e), along with the other provisions of ss. 718 through 718.2, are simply a codification of existing sentencing principles. The respondent, although acknowledging that s. 718.2(e) was likely designed to encourage sentencing judges to experiment to some degree with alternatives to incarceration and to be sensitive to principles of restorative justice, at the same time favours the view that ss. 718-718.2 are largely a restatement of existing law. Alternatively, the appellant argues strongly that s. 718.2(e)'s specific reference to aboriginal offenders can have no purpose unless it effects a change in the law. The appellant advances the view that s. 718.2(e) is in fact an "affirmative action" provision justified under s. 15(2) of the *Canadian Charter of Rights and Freedoms*.

Section 12 of the Interpretation Act deems the purpose of the enactment of the new Part XXIII of the *Criminal Code* to be remedial in nature, and requires that all of the provisions of Part XXIII, including s. 718.2(e), be given a fair, large and liberal construction and interpretation in order to attain that remedial objective. However, the existence of s. 12 does not answer the essential question of what the remedial purpose of s. 718.2(e) is. One view is that the remedial purpose of ss. 718, 718.1 and 718.2 taken together was precisely to codify the purpose and existing principles of sentencing to provide more systematic guidance to sentencing judges in individual cases. Codification, under this view, is remedial in and of itself because it simplifies and adds structure to trial level sentencing decisions: see, e.g., *McDonald* [(1997), 113 CCC (3d) 418 (Sask. CA), at pp. 460-64], per Sherstobitoff JA.

In our view, s. 718.2(e) is more than simply a re-affirmation of existing sentencing principles. The remedial component of the provision consists not only in the fact that it codifies a principle of sentencing, but, far more importantly, in its direction to sentencing judges to undertake the process of sentencing aboriginal offenders differently, in order to endeavour to achieve a truly fit and proper sentence in the particular case. It should be said that the words of s. 718.2(e) do not alter the fundamental duty of the sentencing judge to impose a sentence that is fit for the offence and the offender. For example, as we will discuss below, it will generally be the case as a practical matter that particularly violent and serious offences will result in imprisonment for aboriginal offenders as often as for non-aboriginal offenders. What s. 718.2(e) does alter is the method of analysis which each sentencing judge must use in determining the nature of a fit sentence for an aboriginal offender. In our view, the scheme of Part XXIII of the *Criminal Code*, the context underlying the enactment of s. 718.2(e) and the legislative history of the provision, all support an interpretation of s. 718.2(e) as having this important remedial purpose.

In his submissions before this Court, counsel for the appellant expressed the fear that s. 718.2(e) might come to be interpreted and applied in a manner which would have no real effect upon the day-to-day practice of sentencing aboriginal offenders in Canada. In light of the tragic history of the treatment of aboriginal peoples within the Canadian criminal justice system, we do not consider this fear to be unreasonable. In our view, s. 718.2(e) creates a judicial duty to give its remedial purpose real force.

Let us consider now the wording of s. 718.2(e) and its place within the overall scheme of Part XXIII of the *Criminal Code*.

Section 718.2(e) directs a court, in imposing a sentence, to consider all available sanctions other than imprisonment that are reasonable in the circumstances for all offenders, "with particular attention to the circumstances of aboriginal offenders." The broad role of the provision is clear. As a general principle, s. 718.2(e) applies to all offenders, and states that imprisonment should be the penal sanction of last resort. Prison is to be used only where no other sanction or combination of sanctions is appropriate to the offence and the offender.

The next question is the meaning to be attributed to the words "with particular attention to the circumstances of aboriginal offenders." The phrase cannot be an instruction for judges to pay "more" attention when sentencing aboriginal offenders. It would be unreasonable to assume that Parliament intended sentencing judges to prefer certain categories of offenders over others. Neither can the phrase be merely an instruction to a sentencing judge to consider the circumstances of aboriginal offenders just as she or he would consider the circumstances of any other offender. There would be no point in adding a special reference to aboriginal offenders if this was the case. Rather, the logical meaning to be derived from the special reference to the circumstances of aboriginal offenders, juxtaposed as it is against a general direction to consider "the circumstances" for all offenders, is that sentencing judges should pay particular attention to the circumstances of aboriginal offenders because those circumstances are unique, and different from those of non-aboriginal offenders. The fact that the reference to aboriginal offenders is contained in s. 718.2(e), in particular, dealing with restraint in the use of imprisonment, suggests that there is something different about aboriginal offenders which may specifically make imprisonment a less appropriate or less useful sanction.

The wording of s. 718.2(e) on its face, then, requires both consideration of alternatives to the use of imprisonment as a penal sanction generally, which amounts to a restraint in the resort to imprisonment as a sentence, and recognition by the sentencing judge of the unique circumstances of aboriginal offenders. The respondent argued before this Court that this statutory wording does not truly effect a change in the law, as some courts have in the past taken the unique circumstances of an aboriginal offender into account in determining sentence. The respondent cited some of the recent jurisprudence dealing with sentencing circles, as well as the decision of the Court of Appeal for Ontario in *R v. Fireman* (1971), 4 CCC (2d) 82, in support of the view that s. 718.2(e) should be seen simply as a codification of the state of the case law regarding the sentencing of aboriginal offenders before Part XXIII came into force in 1996. In a similar vein, it was observed by Sherstobitoff JA in *McDonald*, supra, at pp. 463-64, that it has always been a principle of sentencing that courts should consider all available sanctions other than imprisonment that are reasonable in the circumstances. Thus the general principle of restraint expressed in s. 718.2(e) with respect to all offenders might equally be seen as a codification of existing law.

With respect for the contrary view, we do not interpret s. 718.2(e) as expressing only a restatement of existing law, either with respect to the general principle of restraint in the use of prison or with respect to the specific direction regarding aboriginal offenders. One cannot interpret the words of s. 718.2(e) simply by looking to past cases to see if they contain similar statements of principle. The enactment of the new Part XXIII was a watershed, marking the first codification and significant reform of sentencing principles in the history of Canadian criminal law. Each of the provisions of Part XXIII, including s. 718.2(e), must be interpreted in its total context, taking into account its surrounding provisions.

It is true that there is ample jurisprudence supporting the principle that prison should be used as a sanction of last resort. It is equally true, though, that the sentencing amendments which came into force in 1996 as the new Part XXIII have changed the range of available penal sanctions in a significant way. The availability of the conditional sentence of imprisonment, in particular, alters the sentencing landscape in a manner which gives an entirely new meaning to the principle that imprisonment should be resorted to only where no other sentencing option is reasonable in the circumstances. The creation of the conditional sentence suggests, on its face, a desire to lessen the use of incarceration. The general principle expressed in s. 718.2(e) must be construed and applied in this light.

Further support for the view that s. 718.2(e)'s expression of the principle of restraint in sentencing is remedial, rather than simply a codification, is provided by the articulation of the purpose of sentencing in s. 718.

Traditionally, Canadian sentencing jurisprudence has focussed primarily upon achieving the aims of separation, specific and general deterrence, denunciation and rehabilitation. Sentencing, like the criminal trial process itself, has often been understood as a conflict between the interests of the state (as expressed through the aims of separation, deterrence and denunciation) and the interests of the individual offender (as expressed through the aim of rehabilitation). Indeed, rehabilitation itself is a relative latecomer to the sentencing analysis, which formerly favoured the interests of the state almost entirely.

. . .

Clearly, s. 718 is, in part, a restatement of the basic sentencing aims, which are listed in paras. (a) through (d). What are new, though, are paras. (e) and (f), which along with para. (d) focus upon the restorative goals of repairing the harms suffered by individual victims and by the community as a whole, promoting a sense of responsibility and an acknowledgment of the harm caused on the part of the offender, and attempting to rehabilitate or heal the offender. The concept of restorative justice which underpins paras. (d), (e), and (f) is briefly discussed below, but as a general matter restorative justice involves some form of restitution and reintegration into the community. The need for offenders to take responsibility for their actions is central to the sentencing process: D. Kwochka, "Aboriginal Injustice: Making Room for a Restorative Paradigm" (1996), 60 *Sask. L Rev.* 153 at p. 165. Restorative sentencing goals do not usually correlate with the use of prison as a sanction. In our view, Parliament's choice to include (e) and (f) alongside the traditional sentencing goals must be understood as evidencing an intention to expand the parameters of the sentencing analysis for all offenders. The principle of restraint expressed in s. 718.2(e) will necessarily be informed by this reorientation.

Just as the context of Part XXIII supports the view that s. 718.2(e) has a remedial purpose for all offenders, the scheme of Part XXIII also supports the view that s. 718.2(e) has a particular remedial role for aboriginal peoples. The respondent is correct to point out that there is jurisprudence which predates the enactment of s. 718.2(e) in which aboriginal offenders have been sentenced differently in light of their unique circumstances. However, the existence of such jurisprudence is not, on its own, especially probative of the issue of whether s. 718.2(e) has a remedial role. There is also sentencing jurisprudence which holds, for example, that a court must consider the unique circumstances of offenders who are battered spouses, or who are mentally disabled. Although the validity of the principles expressed in this latter jurisprudence is unchallenged by the 1996 sentencing reforms, one does not find reference to these principles in Part XXIII. If Part XXIII were indeed a codification of principles regarding the appropriate method of sentencing different categories of offenders, one would expect to find such references. The wording of s. 718.2(e), viewed in light of the absence of similar stipulations in the remainder of Part XXIII, reveals that Parliament has chosen to single out aboriginal offenders for particular attention.

C. Legislative History

Support for the foregoing understanding of s. 718.2(e) as having the remedial purpose of restricting the use of prison for all offenders, and as having a particular remedial role with respect to aboriginal peoples, is provided by statements made by the Minister of Justice and others at the time that what was then Bill C-41 was before Parliament. Although these statements are clearly not decisive as to the meaning and purpose of s. 718.2(e), they are nonetheless helpful, particularly insofar as they corroborate and do not contradict the meaning and purpose to be derived upon a reading of the words of the provision in the context of Part XXIII as a whole: *Rizzo & Rizzo Shoes* ... [[1998] 1 SCR 27], at paras. 31 and 35.

For instance, in introducing second reading of Bill C-41 on September 20, 1994 (House of Commons Debates, vol. IV, 1st sess., 35th Parl., at pp. 5871 and 5873), Minister of Justice Allan Rock made the following statements regarding the remedial purpose of the bill:

> Through this bill, Parliament provides the courts with clear guidelines ... .
>
> The bill also defines various sentencing principles, for instance that the sentence must be proportionate to the gravity of the offence and the offender's degree of responsibility. When appropriate, alternatives must be contemplated, especially in the case of Native offenders. ...
>
> A general principle that runs throughout Bill C-41 is that jails should be reserved for those who should be there. Alternatives should be put in place for those who commit offences but who do not need or merit incarceration. ...
>
> Jails and prisons will be there for those who need them, for those who should be punished in that way or separated from society. ... [T]his bill creates an environment which encourages community sanctions and the rehabilitation of offenders together with reparation to victims and promoting in criminals a sense of accountability for what they have done. It is not simply by being more harsh that we will achieve more effective criminal justice. We must use our scarce resources wisely.

The Minister's statements were echoed by other Members of Parliament and by Senators during the debate over the bill: see, e.g., House of Commons Debates, vol. V, 1st sess., 35th Parl., September 22, 1994, at p. 6028 (M.P. M. Bodnar); Debates of the Senate, vol. 135, No. 99, 1st sess., 35th Parl., June 21, 1995, at p. 1871 (Sen. D.J. Jessiman).

In his subsequent testimony before the House of Commons Standing Committee on Justice and Legal Affairs (Minutes of Proceedings and Evidence, Issue No. 62, November 17, 1994, at p. 62:15), the Minister of Justice addressed the specific role the government hoped would be played by s. 718.2(e):

[T]he reason we referred specifically there to aboriginal persons is that they are sadly overrepresented in the prison populations of Canada. I think it was the Manitoba justice inquiry that found that although aboriginal persons make up only 12% of the population of Manitoba, they comprise over 50% of the prison inmates. Nationally aboriginal persons represent about 2% of Canada's population, but they represent 10.6% of persons in prison. Obviously there's a problem here.

What we're trying to do, particularly having regard to the initiatives in the aboriginal communities to achieve community justice, is to encourage courts to look at alternatives where it's consistent with the protection of the public—alternatives to jail—and not simply resort to that easy answer in every case.

It can be seen, therefore, that the government position when Bill C-41 was under consideration was that the new Part XXIII was to be remedial in nature. The proposed enactment was directed, in particular, at reducing the use of prison as a sanction, at expanding the use of restorative justice principles in sentencing, and at engaging in both of these objectives with a sensitivity to aboriginal community justice initiatives when sentencing aboriginal offenders.

D. The Context of the Enactment of Section 718.2(e)

Further guidance as to the scope and content of Parliament's remedial purpose in enacting s. 718.2(e) may be derived from the social context surrounding the enactment of the provision. On this point, it is worth noting that, although there is quite a wide divergence between the positions of the appellant and the respondent as to how s. 718.2(e) should be applied in practice, there is general agreement between them, and indeed between the parties and all interveners, regarding the mischief in response to which s. 718.2(e) was enacted.

The parties and interveners agree that the purpose of s. 718.2(e) is to respond to the problem of overincarceration in Canada, and to respond, in particular, to the more acute problem of the disproportionate incarceration of aboriginal peoples. They also agree that one of the roles of s. 718.2(e), and of various other provisions in Part XXIII, is to encourage sentencing judges to apply principles of restorative justice alongside or in the place of other, more traditional sentencing principles when making sentencing determinations. As the respondent states in its factum before this Court, s. 718.2(e) "provides the necessary flexibility and authority for sentencing judges to resort to the restorative model of justice in sentencing aboriginal offenders and to reduce the imposition of jail sentences where to do so would not sacrifice the traditional goals of sentencing."

The fact that the parties and interveners are in general agreement among themselves regarding the purpose of s. 718.2(e) is not determinative of the issue as a matter of statutory construction. However, as we have suggested, on the above points of agreement the parties and interveners are correct. A review of the problem of overincarceration in Canada, and of its peculiarly devastating impact upon Canada's aboriginal peoples, provides additional insight into the purpose and proper application of this new provision.

(1) The Problem of Overincarceration in Canada

Canada is a world leader in many fields, particularly in the areas of progressive social policy and human rights. Unfortunately, our country is also distinguished as being a world leader in putting people in prison. Although the United States has by far the highest rate of incarceration among industrialized democracies, at over 600 inmates per 100,000 population, Canada's rate of approximately 130 inmates per 100,000 population places it second or third highest: see First Report on Progress for Federal/Provincial/Territorial Ministers Responsible for Justice, Corrections Population Growth (1997), Annex B, at p. 1; Bulletin of US Bureau of Justice Statistics, "Prison and Jail Inmates at Midyear 1998" (1999); The Sentencing Project, Americans Behind Bars: US and International Use of Incarceration, 1995 (1997), at p. 1. Moreover, the rate at which Canadian courts have been imprisoning offenders has risen sharply in recent years, although there has been a slight decline of late: see Statistics Canada, Infomat: A Weekly Review (February 27, 1998), at p. 5. This record of incarceration rates obviously cannot instill a sense of pride.

The systematic use of the sanction of imprisonment in Canada may be dated to the building of the Kingston Penitentiary in 1835. The penitentiary sentence was itself originally conceived as an alternative to the harsher penalties of death, flogging, or imprisonment in a local jail. Sentencing reformers advocated the use of penitentiary imprisonment as having effects which were not only deterrent, denunciatory and preventive, but also rehabilitative, with long hours spent in contemplation and hard work contributing to the betterment of the offender: see Law Reform Commission of Canada, Working Paper 11, *Imprisonment and Release* (1975), at p. 5.

Notwithstanding its idealistic origins, imprisonment quickly came to be condemned as harsh and ineffective, not only in relation to its purported rehabilitative goals, but also in relation to its broader public goals. The history of Canadian commentary regarding the use and effectiveness of imprisonment as a sanction was recently well summarized by Vancise JA, dissenting in the Saskatchewan Court of Appeal in *McDonald*, supra, at pp. 429-30:

> A number of inquiries and commissions have been held in this country to examine, among other things, the effectiveness of the use of incarceration in sentencing. There has been at least one commission or inquiry into the use of imprisonment for each decade in this century since 1914. ...
>
> An examination of the recommendations of these reports reveals one constant theme: imprisonment should be avoided if possible and should be reserved for the most serious offences, particularly those involving violence. They all recommend restraint in the use of incarceration and recognize that incarceration has failed to reduce the crime rate and should be used with caution and moderation. Imprisonment has failed to satisfy a basic function of the Canadian judicial system which was described in the Report of the Canadian Committee on Corrections entitled: "Toward Unity: Criminal Justice and Corrections" (1969) as "to protect society from crime in a manner commanding public support while avoiding needless injury to the offender."

In a similar vein, in 1987, the Canadian Sentencing Commission wrote in its report entitled *Sentencing Reform: A Canadian Approach*, at pp. xxiii-xxiv:

> Canada does not imprison as high a portion of its population as does the United States. However, we do imprison more people than most other western democracies. The *Criminal Code* displays an apparent bias toward the use of incarceration since for most offences the penalty indicated is expressed in terms of a maximum term of imprisonment. A number of difficulties arise if imprisonment is perceived to be the preferred sanction for most offences. Perhaps most significant is that although we regularly impose this most onerous and expensive sanction, it accomplishes very little apart from separating offenders from society for a period of time. In the past few decades many groups and federally appointed committees and commissions given the responsibility of studying various aspects of the criminal justice system have argued that imprisonment should be used only as a last resort and/or that it should be reserved for those convicted of only the most serious offences. However, although much has been said, little has been done to move us in this direction.
>
> • • •

With equal force, in *Taking Responsibility* (1988), at p. 75, the Standing Committee on Justice and Solicitor General stated:

> It is now generally recognized that imprisonment has not been effective in rehabilitating or reforming offenders, has not been shown to be a strong deterrent, and has achieved only temporary public protection and uneven retribution, as the lengths of prison sentences handed down vary for the same type of crime.
>
> Since imprisonment generally offers the public protection from criminal behaviour for only a limited time, rehabilitation of the offender is of great importance. However, prisons have not generally been effective in reforming their inmates, as the high incidence of recidivism among prison populations shows.
>
> The use of imprisonment as a main response to a wide variety of offences against the law is not a tenable approach in practical terms. Most offenders are neither violent nor dangerous. Their behaviour is not likely to be improved by the prison experience. In addition, their growing numbers in jails and penitentiaries entail serious problems of expense and administration, and possibly increased future risks to society. Moreover, modern technology may now permit the monitoring in the community of some offenders who previously might have been incarcerated for incapacitation or denunciation purposes. Alternatives to imprisonment and intermediate sanctions, therefore, are increasingly viewed as necessary developments.

The Committee proposed that alternative forms of sentencing should be considered for those offenders who did not endanger the safety of others. It was put in this way, at pp. 50 and 54:

> [O]ne of the primary foci of such alternatives must be on techniques which contribute to offenders accepting responsibility for their criminal conduct and, through their subsequent behaviour, demonstrating efforts to restore the victim to the position he or she was in prior to the offence and/or providing a meaningful apology. [E]xcept where to do so would place the community at undue risk, the "correction" of the offender should take place in the community and imprisonment should be used with restraint.

Thus, it may be seen that although imprisonment is intended to serve the traditional sentencing goals of separation, deterrence, denunciation, and rehabilitation, there is widespread consensus that imprisonment has not been successful in achieving some of these goals. Overincarceration is a long-standing problem that has been many times publicly acknowledged but never addressed in a systematic manner by Parliament. In recent years, compared to other countries, sentences of imprisonment in Canada have increased at an alarming rate. The 1996 sentencing reforms embodied in Part XXIII, and s. 718.2(e) in particular, must be understood as a reaction to the overuse of prison as a sanction, and must accordingly be given appropriate force as remedial provisions.

R v. Proulx
(2000), 140 CCC (3d) 449 (SCC)

[Along with a number of companion cases, the Supreme Court in *Proulx* articulated its view of the new conditional sentence. This concept is discussed in detail in chapter 11, Imprisonment. Before dealing with that sanction, Lamer CJC for a unanimous court addressed some comments about the thrust of the 1996 amendments.]

LAMER CJ: ... Parliament has sought to give increased prominence to the principle of restraint in the use of prison as a sanction through the enactment of s. 718.2(d) and (e). Section 718.2(d) provides that "an offender should not be deprived of liberty, if less restrictive sanctions may be appropriate in the circumstances," while s. 718.2(e) provides that "all available sanctions other than imprisonment that are reasonable in the circumstances should be considered for all offenders, with particular attention to the circumstances of aboriginal offenders." Further evidence of Parliament's desire to lower the rate of incarceration comes from other provisions of Bill C-41: s. 718(c) qualifies the sentencing objective of separating offenders from society with the words "where necessary," thereby indicating that caution be exercised in sentencing offenders to prison; s. 734(2) imposes a duty on judges to undertake a means inquiry before imposing a fine, so as to decrease the number of offenders who are incarcerated for defaulting on payment of their fines; and of course, s. 742.1, which introduces the conditional sentence. In *Gladue*, at para. 40, the Court held that "the creation of the conditional sentence suggests, on its face, a desire to lessen the use of incarceration."

(2) Expanding the Use of Restorative Justice Principles in Sentencing

Restorative justice is concerned with the restoration of the parties that are affected by the commission of an offence. Crime generally affects at least three parties: the victim, the community, and the offender. A restorative justice approach seeks to remedy the adverse effects of crime in a manner that addresses the needs of all parties involved. This is accomplished, in part, through the rehabilitation of the offender, reparations to the victim and to the community, and the promotion of a sense of responsibility in the offender and acknowledgment of the harm done to victims and to the community.

Canadian sentencing jurisprudence has traditionally focussed on the aims of denunciation, deterrence, separation, and rehabilitation, with rehabilitation a relative latecomer to the sentencing analysis: see *Gladue*, at para. 42. With the introduction of Bill C-41, however, Parliament has placed new emphasis upon the goals of restorative justice. Section 718 sets out the fundamental purpose of sentencing, as well as the various sentencing objectives that should be vindicated when sanctions are imposed.

QUESTIONS

What do you think will be the impact of these general comments about restorative justice? In what practical circumstances can you envisage the conceptual analysis in *Gladue* and *Proulx* playing an important role in future cases?

An example of the entrenched principle of restraint successfully butting its head against methodology can be seen in *R v. Cody*, [2007] PEIJ No. 20 (PEISCAD) (QL), in which the Crown argued for a minimum penitentiary term as a starting point for a category of trafficking. The court concluded:

> The Crown urges the Court to impose a minimum two-year term of incarceration in a penitentiary as "general range" of sentence in cases where offenders are small street level traffickers. I am unable to agree it is within the appellate power of the court and consistent with its jurisdiction to develop policy in relation to sentencing, to set a range in the sense that the Crown urges us in this case. Essentially, the Crown is asking the Court to establish a starting point sentence for small street level traffickers at a minimum federal penitentiary term of two years. Not only would this remove from consideration the option of a conditional sentence, but it would also detract from the individualized process of sentencing which is guided by the most fundamental principle of sentencing in s. 718.1 of the *Criminal Code*. A sentence must be proportionate to the gravity of the offence and the degree of responsibility of the offender.
>
> This court has previously rejected a starting point approach to a sentence that has incarceration as the starting point. In *R v. Drake* (1997), 151 Nfld. & PEIR 220 (PEISCAD) at para. 5 Mitchell J stated:
>
>> Another problem with a sentencing approach that has incarceration as a starting point is its inconsistency with two of the principles the sentencing court is mandated to consider by s. 718.2 of the *Criminal Code* which became law on September 3, 1996. Subsections 718.2(d) and (e) direct as a matter of principle that an offender should not be deprived of his liberty if less restrictive sanctions may be appropriate and that all available sanctions other than imprisonment that are reasonable should be considered for all offenders. Thus, Parliament has now directed sentencing courts to use incarceration only as a last resort and not a starting point.

VI. RESTATING THE JUDICIAL METHODOLOGY

The period since the 1996 *Criminal Code* amendments has seen a number of important changes to the Canadian sentencing system. One would be hard-pressed to find anyone arguing that sentencing is an art. However, it is still common and still understandable to hear trial judges say that sentencing is the most difficult part of their job. This would suggest that, in many respects, the statutory statement of purpose and principles has not completely filled the methodological deficiency. In 2004, the Ontario Court of Appeal heard a sentence appeal in two cocaine importing cases. Extracted below, *R v. Hamilton; R v. Mason* dealt with a number of important evidentiary issues that went to the heart of the sentencing judge's role. These are discussed in chapter 4, Facts of the Offence for Sentencing. For now, we want to examine the part of Doherty JA's decision that sets out in clear language the modern methodological view—that is, the sequence of issues and relevant factors that a sentencing judge must consider to come to a fit and appropriate sentence. Note that Doherty JA is one of the leading criminal law judges in Canada. The excerpt below is a good example of what many jurists and practitioners would consider to be the current, principled approach to sentencing. As you read the excerpt, imagine you are a trial judge with a hard sentencing problem that could make the difference between custody and a community-based sentence. Will this discussion help you make a decision ? Will you be confident that your decision is fair and just?

R v. Hamilton and Mason
(2004), 186 CCC (3d) 129 (Ont. CA) (footnotes omitted)

[In two prosecutions for importing cocaine, the Crown submitted that the sentences to be imposed needed to be consistent with the range of penitentiary sentences already stipulated by the Ontario Court of Appeal in "drug mule" cases. Counsel for the offenders argued, on a variety of bases, that a sentence of less than two years was appropriate such that conditional sentences should be considered. The trial judge heard expert opinion evidence from Professor Anthony Doob, which in essence concluded that, for these offences, a harsher sentence would not produce a general deterrent effect. The judge also considered a mountain of data that he had uncovered and that he considered relevant to the sentencing of the two black, single mothers convicted of importing cocaine. He gave both accused conditional sentences and the Crown appealed.]

DOHERTY JA (for the court):

I

[1] The imposition of a fit sentence can be as difficult a task as any faced by a trial judge. That task is particularly difficult where otherwise decent, law-abiding persons commit very serious crimes in circumstances that justifiably attract understanding and empathy. These two cases fall within that category of cases.

[2] As difficult as the determination of a fit sentence can be, that process has a narrow focus. It aims at imposing a sentence that reflects the circumstances of the specific offence and the attributes of the specific offender. Sentencing is not based on group characteristics, but on the facts relating to the specific offence and specific offender as revealed by the evidence adduced in the proceedings. A sentencing proceeding is also not the forum in which to right perceived societal wrongs, allocate responsibility for criminal conduct as between the offender and society, or "make up" for perceived social injustices by the imposition of sentences that do not reflect the seriousness of the crime.

[3] In the two sentences under appeal, the trial judge lost that narrow focus. He expanded the sentencing proceedings to include broad societal issues that were not raised by the parties. A proceeding that was intended to determine fit sentences for two specific offenders who committed two specific crimes became an inquiry by the trial judge into much broader and more complex issues. In conducting this inquiry, the trial judge stepped outside of the proper role of a judge on sentencing and ultimately imposed sentences that were inconsistent with the statutory principles of sentencing and binding authorities from this court.

II

Overview

[4] The respondents were caught trying to smuggle cocaine they had swallowed into Canada from Jamaica. Each pleaded guilty to one count of importing cocaine. The charges were unrelated, but as the respondents proposed to rely on the same expert evidence, the charges proceeded by way of a joint sentencing hearing.

[5] At trial, counsel for the respondents indicated they would seek conditional sentences relying on Dr. Doob's expert opinion evidence to the effect that general deterrence had little or no value in sentencing offenders like the respondents, and on the respondents' positive antecedents. The Crown, relying on cases from this court to the effect that cocaine importers—even if they are classified as couriers—should usually receive substantial jail terms, sought sentences of between two and three years.

[6] After a lengthy hearing, the trial judge, in thoughtful and detailed reasons, concluded that the respondents should receive conditional sentences. He rested his conclusion that conditional sentences were appropriate primarily on his finding that the respondents, because of their race, gender, and poverty, were particularly vulnerable targets to those who sought out individuals to act as cocaine couriers. He made these findings based on material he had produced during the hearing and his own experiences as a judge. Ms. Hamilton received a conditional sentence of twenty months on terms that provided for partial house arrest in the first year of the sentence and a curfew for the remainder of the sentence. Ms. Mason received a conditional sentence of two years less a day on terms that provided for partial house arrest in the first fifteen months of the sentence and a curfew for the rest of the sentence.

[7] The Crown appealed. I agree with Crown counsel's submission that the trial judge effectively took over the sentencing proceedings, and in doing so went beyond the role assigned to a trial judge in such proceedings. I am also satisfied that the sentences imposed reflect errors in principle. While I would not hold that sentences of less than two years were inappropriate in all of the circumstances, I would hold that the trial judge fell into reversible error in imposing conditional sentences. On a proper application of the relevant principles of sentencing and the authorities of this court, these offences merited substantial prison terms, despite the mitigating effect of the respondents' personal circumstances.

. . .

The Analytical Framework

[87] Sentencing is a very human process. Most attempts to describe the proper judicial approach to sentencing are as close to the actual process as a paint-by-numbers landscape is to the real thing. I begin by recognizing, as did the trial judge, that the fixing of a fit sentence is the product of the combined effects of the circumstances of the specific offence with the unique attributes of the specific offender: *R v. Currie* (1997), 115 CCC (3d) 205 at 219 (SCC); *R v. Gladue*, [1999] 1 SCR 688 at para. 80; *R v. Proulx, supra*, at 485-86; *R v. Borde* (2003), 172 CCC (3d) 225 at 238 (Ont. CA).

[88] The case-specific nature of the sentencing inquiry is reflected in the proportionality requirement, described as the fundamental principle of sentencing in s. 718.1 of the *Criminal Code*:

1. A sentence must be proportionate to the gravity of the offence and the degree of responsibility of the offender.

[89] The proportionality requirement, long a touchstone of Canadian sentencing law (see *R v. Wilmott*, [1967] 1 CCC 171 at 178-79 (Ont. CA)), accepts the "just deserts" rationale for state-imposed punishment. Whatever other ends a sentence may hope to achieve, it must first and foremost fit the specific crime and the specific offender: Andrew Ashworth, *Sentencing and Criminal Justice*, 2nd ed. (London: Butterworths, 1995) at 70.

[90] The "gravity of the offence" refers to the seriousness of the offence in a generic sense as reflected by the potential penalty imposed by Parliament and any specific features of the commission of the crime which may tend to increase or decrease the harm or risk of harm to the community occasioned by the offence. For example, in drug importation cases, the nature and quantity of the drug involved will impact on the gravity of the offence. Some of the factors which increase the gravity of the offence are set out in s. 718.2(a).

[91] The "degree of responsibility of the offender" refers to the offender's culpability as reflected in the essential substantive elements of the offence—especially the fault component—and any specific aspects of the offender's conduct or background that tend to increase or decrease the offender's personal responsibility for the crime. In drug importation cases, the offender's role in the importation scheme will be an important consideration in assessing the offender's personal responsibility.

[92] In *R v. Priest* (1996), 110 CCC (3d) 289 at 297-98 (Ont. CA), Rosenberg JA described the proportionality requirement in this way:

2. The principle of proportionality is rooted in notions of fairness and justice. For the sentencing court to do justice to the particular offender, the sentence imposed must reflect the seriousness of the offence, the degree of culpability of the offender, and the harm occasioned by the offence. The court must have regard to the aggravating and mitigating factors in the particular case. Careful adherence to the proportionality principle ensures that this offender is not unjustly dealt with for the sake of the common good.

[93] Fixing a sentence that is consistent with s. 718.1 is particularly difficult where the gravity of the offence points strongly in one sentencing direction and the culpability of the individual offender points strongly in a very different sentencing direction. The sentencing judge must fashion a disposition from among the limited options available which take both sides of the proportionality inquiry into account. As indicated in *Priest, supra*, factors which may accentuate the gravity of the crime cannot blind the trial judge to factors mitigating personal responsibility. Equally, factors mitigating personal responsibility cannot justify a disposition that unduly minimizes the seriousness of the crime committed.

[94] In some circumstances, one side of the proportionality inquiry will figure more prominently in the ultimate disposition than the other. For example, where a young first offender is being sentenced for a number of relatively serious property offences, the sentence imposed will tend to emphasize the features which mitigate the offender's personal culpability rather than those which highlight the gravity of the crimes: *R v. Priest, supra*. If, however, that same young offender commits a crime involving serious personal injury to the victim, the "gravity of the offence" component of the proportionality inquiry will be given prominence in determining the ultimate disposition.

[95] Proportionality is the fundamental principle of sentencing, but it is not the only principle to be considered. Parity, totality, and restraint are also principles which must be engaged when determining the appropriate sentence: *Criminal Code*, ss. 718.2(b)-(e). The restraint principle is of particular importance where incarceration is a potential disposition. That principle is reflected in ss. 178.2(d) and (e):

3. (d) an offender should not be deprived of liberty, if less restrictive sanctions may be appropriate in the circumstances; and

4. (e) all available sanctions other than imprisonment that are reasonable in the circumstances should be considered for all offenders, with particular attention to the circumstances of aboriginal offenders.

[96] The express inclusion of restraint as a principle of sentencing is one of the most significant features of the 1996 *Criminal Code* amendments statutizing sentencing principles for the first time. As Professor Manson explains:

5. Restraint means that prison is the sanction of last resort … . Restraint also means that when considering other sanctions, the sentencing court should seek the least intrusive sentence and the least quantum which will achieve the overall purpose of being an appropriate and just sanction.

[97] Counsel on the appeal addressed at some length the potential application of s. 718.2(e) to groups, like blacks, who it is alleged have also been the victims of discrimination in the justice system and the community at large.

[98] There can be no doubt that s. 718.2(e) applies to all offenders. Imprisonment is appropriate only when there is no other reasonable sanction. The closing words of the section recognize that restraint in the use of imprisonment is a particularly important principle with respect to the sentencing of aboriginal offenders. The restraint principle takes on added importance because the historical mistreatment of aboriginals by the criminal justice system as reflected in the highly disproportionate number of aboriginals

sentenced to imprisonment, taken with aboriginal cultural views as to the purpose of punishment, can combine to make imprisonment ineffective in achieving the purpose or objectives of sentencing where the offender is an aboriginal: *R v. Wells* [[2000] 1 SCR 207], at p. 385. The restraint principle is applied with particular force where the offender is an aboriginal not to somehow try to make up for historical mistreatment of aboriginals, but because imprisonment may be less effective than other dispositions in achieving the goals of sentencing where the offender is aboriginal.

[99] Parliament has chosen to identify aboriginals as a group with respect to whom the restraint principle applies with particular force. If it is shown that the historical mistreatment and cultural views of another group combine to make imprisonment ineffective in achieving the goals of sentencing, it has been suggested that a court may consider those factors in applying the restraint principle in sentencing individuals from that group: see *R v. Borde, supra*, at p. 236. There was no evidence in the mass of material adduced in these proceedings to suggest that poor black women share a cultural perspective with respect to punishment that is akin to the aboriginal perspective.

[100] In any event, proportionality remains the fundamental principle of sentencing. Section 718.2(e) cannot justify a sentence which deprecates the seriousness of the offence. Where the offence is sufficiently serious, imprisonment will be the only reasonable response regardless of the ethnic or cultural background of the offender: *R v. Wells, supra*, at p. 386.

[101] In addition to complying with the principles of sentencing, sentences must promote one or more of the objectives identified in s. 718:

6. (a) to denounce unlawful conduct;
7. (b) to deter the offender and other persons from committing offences;
8. (c) to separate offenders from society, where necessary;
9. (d) to assist in rehabilitating offenders;
10. (e) to provide reparations for harm done to victims or to the community; and
11. (f) to promote a sense of responsibility in offenders, and acknowledgement of the harm done to victims and to the community.

[102] The relevance and relative importance of each of the objectives identified in s. 718 will vary according to the nature of the crime and the circumstances of the offender: *R v. Lyons*, [1987] 2 SCR 309 at 329; *R v. Morrisey* (2000), 148 CCC (3d) 1 at 23 (SCC).

[103] If the offence is particularly serious in that it causes or threatens significant harm to an individual or segment of the community, the objectives of denunciation and general deterrence will usually dominate the other objectives identified in s. 718. Prior to the introduction of the conditional sentence, where the objectives of deterrence and denunciation dominated, imprisonment was almost inevitable.

[104] The importation of dangerous drugs like cocaine and others found in Schedule I of the *Controlled Drugs and Substances Act*, SC 1996, c. 19 has always been considered among the most serious crimes known to Canadian law: *Sentencing Reform: A Canadian Approach*. Report of the Canadian Sentencing Commission, Ottawa Ministry of Supply and Services (1987), p. 205. The immense direct and indirect social and economic harm done throughout the Canadian community by cocaine is well known:

Pushpanathan v. Canada (Minister of Citizenship and Immigration) (1998), 160 DLR (4th) 193 at 235-37 (SCC), *per* Cory J, in dissent on another issue; *R v. Smith* (1987), 34 CCC (3d) 97 at 123-24 (SCC). The use and sale of cocaine kills and harms both directly and indirectly. The direct adverse health effects on those who use the drug are enormous and disastrous. Cocaine sale and use is closely and strongly associated with violent crime. Cocaine importation begets a multiplicity of violent acts. Viewed in isolation from the conduct which inevitably follows the importation of cocaine, the act itself is not a violent one in the strict sense. It cannot, however, be disassociated from its inevitable consequences. Unlike the trial judge (para. 224), I characterize cocaine importation as both a violent and serious offence: see *R v. Pearson* (1992), 77 CCC (3d) 124 at 143-44 (SCC).

[105] Cocaine is not indigenous to Canada. Without the cocaine importer, whatever his or her motive or involvement, there would be no cocaine problem. Both before and after the amendments to the sentencing provisions in Part XXIII of the *Criminal Code* and the introduction of the sentencing provision (s. 10) into the *Controlled Drugs and Substances Act*, SC 1996, c. 19, this court has emphasized the gravity of the crime and, therefore, the need to stress denunciation and deterrence in sentencing all drug importers, even vulnerable first offenders. In *Cunningham, supra*, at pp. 546-47, the court, in fixing a range of six to eight years for couriers who smuggle large amounts of cocaine into Canada, said:

> 12. We recognize as well that the suggested range will often require the imposition of a severe penalty for first offenders. *We are not insensitive to this concern, mindful as we must be that in many instances, couriers tend to be weak and vulnerable, thereby becoming easy prey for those who engage in drug trafficking on a commercial basis.*
>
> 13. *Sympathetic though we are to the plight of many couriers, such concerns must give way to the need to protect society from the untold grief and misery occasioned by the illicit use of hard drugs.* [Emphasis added.]

[106] This court has repeatedly reiterated the approach set out in *Cunningham*, e.g. see *R v. H.(C.N.)* (2002), 170 CCC (3d) 253 (Ont. CA); *R v. Wilson*, [2003] OJ No. 144 (CA).

[107] Because the sentencing of drug couriers presents one of the more difficult, and unfortunately more common, situations in which the gravity of the offence and the personal responsibility of the offender suggest different dispositions, this court has set out different ranges of sentences to assist trial judges in fixing appropriate sentences in individual cases. The ranges established by this court in *Madden* and *Cunningham* do not have direct application to this case. However, the factors justifying the fixing of those ranges have equal application here. I think it would be helpful to set a sentencing range for the importation of amounts of cocaine below "the one kilogram more or less" range identified in *Madden*.

...

[110] My conclusion that sentences at or near two years are within the appropriate range for the importation of the amounts of cocaine in issue on these appeals is consistent with the range described by Durno J in *R v. Bennett* (31 July 2003), Brampton

5889/02 (Ont. Sup. Ct.). It is also consistent with the length of the sentences imposed by the trial judge on these respondents.

[111] Fixing the range of sentences for a particular offence, of course, does not determine the sentence to be imposed on a particular offender. The range is in large measure a reflection of the "objective seriousness" of the crime: *R v. H.(C.N.)*, *supra*, at p. 266. Once the range is identified, the sentencing judge must consider specific aggravating and mitigating factors. The mitigating factors may be so significant as to take the case below the otherwise appropriate range. For example, in *R v. H.(C.N.)*, the offender's cooperation with the authorities and his belief that he was importing marijuana and not cocaine, along with other more common mitigating factors, justified a sentence that was well below the range of sentence established for the importation of very substantial amounts of cocaine.

NOTE

Does this methodology provide a "principled approach"? Can this methodology be easily transposed to other circumstances and other offences? Does it fit with the "individualized" approach advocated by the Supreme Court of Canada in cases like *Proulx*, [2001] 1 SCR 61, where Lamer CJ said that "sentencing is an individualized process, in which the trial judge has considerable discretion in fashioning a fit sentence"?

Let us imagine a serious and experienced trial judge faced with this problem. A 22-year-old offender has just pleaded guilty to trafficking in 2006 in crystal methamphetamine. The offender is a landed immigrant with a pregnant spouse. He was arrested while in the process of selling more than a kilogram of what was represented to be crystal meth to an undercover officer for $60,000. (The substance turned out to be a crystalline water softener.) In 2005, Parliament moved methamphetamine from Schedule III to Schedule I of the *Controlled Drugs and Substances Act* (CDSA), thereby placing it in the same category as heroin and cocaine and subjecting someone convicted of trafficking to a maximum penalty of life imprisonment. Notwithstanding Doherty JA's efforts to explain the current "principled approach" to sentencing, look at the myriad unanswered questions:

- Do pre-2005 methamphetamine cases have any bearing on proportionality?
- Is gravity affected by the fact that the substance was not really crystal meth?
- If the "usual range" will be helpful in determining proportionality, where does one find it given that the heroin cases are different from the cocaine cases and there are no post-2005 crystal meth cases?
- What about the individual factors—for example, no record, a pregnant spouse, and a vulnerable immigration status?

See the valiant effort of MacDonnell J in *R v. Villanueva* (2007), 46 CR (6th) 129 (Ont. CJ) as he struggles with this very difficult sentencing problem. Surely, our judges are entitled to more guidance than what is now available.

CHAPTER THREE

Aggravating and Mitigating Factors

I. INTRODUCTION

The Canadian approach to sentencing requires the judge to impose a sentence that reflects relevant objectives and principles, and emphasizes any that, in the circumstances, are predominant. Section 718.2(e) of the *Criminal Code*, RSC 1985, c. C-46, as amended, requires the judge to consider all available sanctions that are reasonable. These two exercises may point to a specific sanction or subset of available sanctions. Moreover, it may suggest a quantum band for specific sanctions. The ultimate decision, however, is refined by factors that are more discriminating than the broadly conceived objectives and principles. Traditionally, judges have recognized sets of factors that affect the gravity of the offence and the court's perception of the offender's culpability and then have applied them to make the ultimate decisions about which sanction to impose and its quantum. Depending on the nature of the consequential effect, these are known as either mitigating or aggravating factors.

Section 718.2(a) now entrenches the common law by requiring judges to increase or reduce a sentence by taking into account aggravating or mitigating circumstances, relevant to the offence or the offender. The Code lists a few examples of aggravating circumstances, some of which were clearly encompassed by the common law and others that were being applied in some cases but were also, to some extent, controversial. There are no examples of mitigating factors in the Code. This asymmetry is puzzling, as is the selection of factors now placed on a statutory footing. Why did Parliament select these aggravating factors and not others? Was there a perception that courts were paying insufficient attention to these factors? No evidence was offered to justify the decision. Some of the codified aggravating factors are relatively obvious, in which case one wonders why the legislature believed it necessary to direct judges in this respect. Finally, it is unclear why Parliament declined to provide guidance about the role of previous convictions at sentencing, a factor that affects large numbers of sentencing decisions and that remains open to multiple interpretations.

Virtually every written or oral decision includes some characterization of the relevant aggravating and mitigating factors. Over the years, the common law has recognized dozens of factors that can have a mitigating or aggravating effect. Yet, these factors are rarely examined and courts seem to accept their aggravating or mitigating effect without much debate. Of course, some are self-evident, but others are not so clear. There can be legitimate controversies about their relation to the sentencing function.

Mitigating and aggravating factors represent a truly enigmatic aspect of the sentencing process in that they are always present, rarely discussed, and there is no coherent theory of mitigation and aggravation outside those cases that affect the gravity of an offence or the culpability of the offender. It would be worthwhile to pursue the issue of a principled approach to mitigation and aggravation for the following reasons:

- All aspects of sentencing decisions need to be principled to avoid arbitrariness.
- Only principled decisions can generate reasons that are essential to a legal decision-making process.
- Only principled decisions can be properly communicated to the offender and the public.
- Understanding the rationale for a mitigating or aggravating factor can lead to the recognition of other factors that, although seemingly distinct, strike the same sentencing chord.
- Principles will help determine the proper extent of mitigation and aggravation.

It is also important to use mitigating and aggravating factors in an appropriate way to ensure proportionality in sentencing. As noted earlier, the sentencing reforms of 1996 designated proportionality as the fundamental principle of sentencing. If a particular factor is given excessive weight at sentencing, or if an extra-legal factor is incorporated into the sentencing decision, will this not undermine proportionality?

For the most part, the underlying premises that explain the applicability of an aggravating or mitigating factor seem to relate to one of two considerations:

1. The gravity of the offence as defined by the offender's culpability and the consequential harm that was caused.
2. The ways in which character and conduct seem to relate to applicable objectives of sentencing.

The first category is self-evident while the second is extremely elastic, often contentious, and devoid of a sound theoretical underpinning. It includes the ever-expanding categories of pro-social and anti-social conduct that courts accept as being relevant to making sentencing choices.

R v. Sandercock (discussed in chapter 2, Judicial Methodology and the Legislative Context, as it relates to starting points) contains one of the rare examples of a discussion, albeit brief, of some of the relevant and irrelevant factors that were apparent in the case. Read the following excerpt and consider whether you agree with the court's assessment of what should or should not be taken into account.

R v. Sandercock
(1985), 22 CCC (3d) 79 (Alta. CA)

KERANS JA: ... Before turning to the facts of the appeal before us, we propose to discuss the last step in this sentencing approach, a consideration of the many aggravating and mitigating factors which often arise and which must be weighed in fixing a fit sentence in a specific case.

In recent years, great emphasis has been put on a prompt guilty plea as a special and major mitigating factor. It used to be said that this was relevant only to show remorse. Aside entirely from any remorse, however, an accused should receive substantial recognition either for sparing the victim the need to testify or to wait to testify, or for waiving some of his constitutional rights in deference to expeditious justice.

Many other mitigating and aggravating factors are often present. It is impossible to offer a complete catalogue. We can, however, mention some. (We cite reports of actual cases at this point simply to illustrate that the sentence can increase markedly when aggravating factors shift the balance.) Some involve protracted forcible confinement or kidnapping: *R v. Craig* (1975), 28 CCC (2d) 311; others include repeated assaults or other acts of degradation: *R v. Beauregard* (1982), 38 AR 350; others, further acts of horror or degradation: *R v. Sweitzer*, [1982] 5 WWR 552, 26 AR 208; others, the invasion of the sanctity of the home: see *R v. Henry* (1983), 44 AR 242; others, the display or use of a weapon: *R v. Sinitoski*, [1983] 6 WWR 247, 27 Alta. LR (2d) 141, 46 AR 206; others, several offenders acting together: *R v. Brown and Murphy* (1982), 41 AR 69; others, more than one victim: *R v. Brandon*, November 8, 1983, Edmonton 16807. It is even possible for almost all these factors to be present in one case: see *R v. Graham* (1984), Alta. D 7515-01. Mitigating factors often present include remorse, immaturity, and the global effect of several sentences for several matters.

Most actual cases show a mix of aggravating and mitigating factors. The sentencing process involves noting and weighing each and settling upon a sentence which reflects that balancing. As a result, the presence of most of the mitigating factors just mentioned and the absence of any aggravating factor might lead to a sentence of less than penitentiary time: see, for example, *R v. Harper* (1982), Alta. D 7515-02 [summarized 8 WCB 281]; *R v. Clay* (1984), Alta. D 7517-04 [reported 35 Alta. LR (2d) 20]; *R v. Frand* (unreported October 8, 1980, Edmonton 13108); or the recent case of *R v. Kergan* (unreported as yet, published August 9, 1985) [since reported 21 CCC (3d) 549, 62 AR 161]. It is unthinkable, however, that a substantial jail sentence would not be imposed in the face of the blameworthiness and harm I have described, in other words, so long as the offence remains within the category of "major sexual assault." At the other end of the scale, the presence of certain aggravating factors now justify the laying of a charge under ss. 246.2 or 246.3 of the *Criminal Code* or additional charges such as breaking and entering, kidnapping, forcible confinement, or attempted murder. Such charges, which might well have been considered redundant for a crime which carries a maximum penalty of life imprisonment, will no doubt now be seen more often. As the majority for this court said in *Kergan* and *R v. Daychief* (published the same day) [summarized 14 WCB 449] nothing in the recent statutory changes justifies the view that Parliament now views any particular sexual assault as less serious than it once did. The recent legislative changes, however, also now require that if the accused is a dangerous offender, an application for preventive detention must be made by the Crown under s. 687 of the *Criminal Code*: see *R v. Hastings*. In the past, this court has imposed life sentences on rapists who will re-offend: see, for example, *R v. Leech* (1972), 10 CCC (2d) 149, 21 CRNS 1, [1973] 1 WWR 744, and *R v. Brandon* (unreported) November 8, 1983, Edmonton, No. 16807.

We will conclude by reference to factors sometimes offered in mitigation but which are often suspect: those cases where the offender says he was drunk, or the victim of cultural conflict, or where the victim was allegedly negligent as to his or her own safety, or provoked the assault, or where the victim is of bad character.

Drunkenness generally should not be a mitigating factor. Nevertheless, the fact that an assault is totally spontaneous can offer mitigation, and sometimes drunkenness is a factor in determining whether the attack is spontaneous or whether the likely consequences were fully appreciated.

The circumstances in life of the victim, if known to the offender, can affect the assessment of the foreseeable pain to the victim: see, for example, *R v. Ricketts* (unreported, May 31, 1985, Calgary Appeal No. 17000) [since reported 61 AR 175]. Ricketts, in breach of his earlier agreement with a prostitute to pay her for an act of fellatio, suddenly demanded it free at knife-point. Her sense of outrage and fear should not be minimized, but I am sure that she would agree that the foreseeable risk of psychological shock to her was not as great as would be, say, a similar threat to somebody who had led a sheltered life: see *R v. Marsh* (unreported February 4, 1980, 12641). In this limited sense, the life-circumstances, or "character," of the victim might be relevant to sentencing. This is because these factors alter the level of reasonably foreseeable harm, which is the test, and not because grave consequences chanced to happen. In general terms, an accused is punished for blameworthiness and not for the actual consequences of the crime, although these are not to be disregarded: see *R v. Jacobs* (1982), 70 CCC (2d) 569, 16 MVR 15, 39 AR 391.

Provocation of the offender by the victim is an obvious mitigating factor. More difficult to decide is whether, in a given case, there has been provocation. It is surely not provocation, for example, simply to be a woman, or to be attractive, or to be prettily attired. Sexual arousal is not the same thing as the arousal of a desire to seek sexual satisfaction by violence to another, and provocation of the first is not necessarily provocation of the second.

Negligence of the victim as to his or her own safety is generally not relevant. The blameworthiness of the offender is not in the least diminished because the victim imprudently provides the offender with an opportunity for crime, nor does it necessarily follow that such imprudence lessens the likely pain, outrage and indignity which then visits the victim.

II. THE MENU OF RELEVANT MITIGATING FACTORS

The case law dealing with aggravating and mitigating factors is vast. Many of the commonly accepted factors are discussed in Allan Manson's *The Law of Sentencing*. When you are reviewing the factors included in the following excerpt, consider whether and how they relate to the objectives of sentencing in s. 718.

A. Manson, "Mitigating Factors"
in *The Law of Sentencing* (Toronto: Irwin, 2000), 131-48 (footnotes omitted)

First offender: The status of being a first offender is a significant mitigating factor. The fact that the offender has not been found guilty by the criminal process before generates a number of favourable inferences, with rehabilitative prospects always at the forefront of consideration. First, being a first offender suggests that the conviction itself constitutes a punishment. It is assumed that the offender will respond positively to the deterrent effects of the process of arrest, charging, finding of guilt and imposition of sanction. This discounts any special need for individual deterrence and suggests that a lenient response is in order. Being a first offender is also consistent with demonstrating good character prior to the offence. Although it does not guarantee a non-custodial sentence, there is both a presumption against custody and a significant reducing effect if custody is mandated.

. . .

Prior good character: Good character evidence during a trial when responsibility is at stake is usually limited to reputation in the community. For sentencing purposes, character is much broader and will often include achievements and opinions attributed to relatives, friends, associates and acquaintances. It is usually directed to showing that the offence is out of character. In this way, evidence of conduct which shows values antithetical to those which ordinarily underlie the particular offence will be helpful. Accordingly, evidence of honesty and generosity will be relevant to a crime of dishonesty. Similarly, evidence of compassion will be relevant to a crime of violence.

Claims of prior good character are often misconceived. For example, it is often confused with a claim about standing in the community. While this is often put forward, it has a nebulous and questionable basis as a mitigating factor, more suited to showing re-integrative potential. For some offences, evidence of a person's pro-social community commitment through volunteer work is not mitigating when the offence arises from those activities. Assaulting children involved in the volunteer activity is an obvious example. In general, courts have found that good character claims are inappropriate when dealing with offences committed in the dark corners of people's lives. With respect to sexual offences, the Supreme Court has recognized that they are usually perpetrated in private, out of sight and knowledge of friends and associates. Accordingly, evidence of good community reputation has little probative value. While this conclusion was directed to the use of character evidence at trial, it applies equally to sentencing issues.

Guilty plea and remorse: The reason that a guilty plea is usually considered to be a mitigating factor is because it implies remorse and an acknowledgement of responsibility by the offender. The extent of the mitigating value is affected by the timing of the guilty plea: the earlier, the better. This is especially true if one intends to include consideration for the victims as an added element. Avoiding the need to have a victim testify is a legitimate dimension of remorse but gets little credence if a guilty plea is entered only after hearing the witness at preliminary hearing. Convenience to the court by saving its time is not a reason for mitigation. While this is a systemic benefit, it would be wrong to give the impression that foregoing the constitutional right to plead not guilty will garner credit simply because it makes the judge's life easier. The court is a public institution exercising an important public function and a guilty plea must reflect more than time-saving to support mitigation. In this sense, it ought to be communicated as an acceptance of responsibility.

Of course, a guilty plea is not the only way to show remorse. Sincere apologies and other efforts at reparation can convey a stronger message than simply the guilty plea.

Moreover, remorse can be indicated even after a trial. The right to compel the Crown to prove its case does not entirely remove the opportunity to show remorse although it may diminish it.

Evidence of impairment: Impairment of judgment can be a mitigating circumstance. Sentencing ought to respond proportionately to culpability; intended consequences should be treated more severely than those caused negligently. This is a principle of fundamental justice. Accordingly, evidence that an accused was suffering from impaired judgment can be very significant.

Within the criminal law generally, voluntary intoxication has been the subject of variable and inconsistent treatment. In the 19th century, it was not considered a factor that could mitigate fault but, in this century, it became an accepted defence to a crime of specific intent. During the same period, it was accepted as a mitigating factor on sentencing. However, this has changed. Kerans JA has said:

> Drunkenness generally should not be a mitigating factor. Nevertheless, the fact that an assault is totally spontaneous can offer mitigation, and sometimes drunkenness is a factor in determining whether the attack is spontaneous or whether the likely consequences were fully appreciated.

This puts intoxication in its proper place as a factor that can distinguish between a planned offence and one generated spontaneously with little regard for consequences. Moreover, with respect to crimes of violence where there is a history of drunken violence, intoxication is an aggravating circumstance.

However, there are other situations where emotional, physical and psychological impairment can mitigate culpability because they affect judgment. Cool and deliberate choices are more culpable than those clouded by depression, medication, and extraordinary stress. Gambling addiction has been recognized as a mitigating background factor especially with respect to thefts and frauds. In *R v. Horvath*, a former bank manager was convicted of thefts totaling almost $200,000 from her employer and fraud in the amount of $35,000 from another financial institution. She was a 36 year old married woman with a child. She had become pathologically addicted to video lottery terminals and would leave work at the end of the day to gamble until late at night. She lost money and incurred huge debts. Then, she started stealing from her employer using an elaborate scheme involving fictitious and actual accounts. The trial judge heard expert evidence about her gambling addiction and her efforts to deal with it, and sentenced her to a conditional sentence of two years less a day in duration. The Crown appealed arguing that the amount stolen and the breach of trust required a custodial sentence. For the court, Bayda CJS dismissed the appeal. He said:

> Perhaps the factor that carries most weight in assessing the gravity of the offences in the particular case is the one that generated those offences. The offences were the products of a distorted mind—a mind seriously diseased by a disorder now recognized by the medical community as a mental disorder. The acts committed at the command of that mind were not acts of free choice in the same sense as are the acts of free choice of a normal mind. A pathological gambler does not have the same power of control over his or her acts as one

who does not suffer from that complex disease. Accordingly, where those acts constitute criminal offences, the moral culpability—moral blameworthiness—and responsibility are not of the same order as they would be in those cases where the mind is not so affected.

Horvath highlights the ability of an addiction to reduce culpability to warrant a conditional sentence even in a case aggravated by a breach of trust. Of course, this mitigating effect of a gambling addiction has its limits. The offender in *Horvath* had no prior record and was making serious efforts to address her problem. In cases where there is a prior record, courts have not been so sympathetic to the gambling addiction factor.

While many courts have followed the *Horvath* approach to proven gambling addictions for breach of trust thefts and even for robbery, the Alberta Court of Appeal has rejected conditional sentences in cases of substantial thefts from employers. It has held that the proven gambling addiction did not constitute an exceptional circumstance that warranted a conditional sentence. This view does not seem to give proper weight to the basis for using a gambling addiction in mitigation. The gambling addiction does not serve as an excuse but it does diminish culpability if it has affected the offender to the point where there is little or no free will, as described in *Horvath*. Then, blameworthiness has been substantially reduced and this should be reflected in the sentence.

Employment record: A good employment record is always a mitigating factor although its impact may be diminished or even superceded by the nature of the offence. The reason why courts respond favourably to a good work record is because it demonstrates pro-social responsibility and conformity to community norms which are the antithesis of crime. Accordingly, the offender is considered to be more redeemable with more promising rehabilitative prospects particularly if the record is consistent over a long period of time. However, courts should be careful not to turn the absence of a good work record into an aggravating factor. Many offenders, especially those with little training and education, have diminished opportunities for work. Moreover, many offences are committed in places with high unemployment. In these situations, offenders should not be prejudiced. However, lawyers should consider finding out about community volunteer work or even a pattern of assistance to family and friends. These facts can serve the same mitigating purpose.

Collateral or indirect consequences: As a result of the commission of an offence, the offender may suffer physical, emotional, social or financial consequences. While not punishment in the true sense of pains or burdens imposed by the state after a finding of guilt, they are often considered in mitigation. However, careful distinctions need to be made.

When an offender suffers physical injury as a result of an offence, this may be relevant for sentencing purposes especially if there will be long-lasting effects. This kind of consequence may bear on a number of sentencing goals like individual and general deterrence. Certainly, this is the result when an offender is seriously injured after a driving offence. Given the general familiarity with automobiles as part of modern life, the direct conduct/consequence image plays a communicative role consistent with traditional sentencing objectives. This is not the case when the personal injury arises from uncommon conduct that is purely criminal such as might occur during a robbery.

The loss of employment or professional qualifications will often be raised as relevant collateral consequences. However, there is a distinction between situations where the specific criminal act results in disqualification from a profession or employment, and those situations where employment is lost as a result of personal or community response that stigmatizes the offender. The latter should be taken into account because it flows from the criminal process while disqualification is a more difficult issue. Careful distinctions are required. Some mitigation may be available if the disqualification arises from an offence which is not centrally related to professional responsibility. For example, there is a difference between a surgeon who is struck off the professional roll for criminal negligence causing death after performing surgery while intoxicated, and a physician who commits an offence of dishonesty in his billing practice. The former receives no sympathy for losing a profession which his conduct shows he was ill-suited to perform while the loss of livelihood for the latter is not directly related to professional qualities. Another example is a police officer who is convicted of an offence related to policing. A conviction for assaulting a prisoner will likely end a career and should not generate any mitigation when being sentenced for the assault. An off-duty offence may also end a law enforcement career but this factor would be viewed in a different light depending on the nature of the offence.

The mitigating effect of indirect consequences must be considered in relation both to future re-integration and to the nature of the offence. Burdens and hardships can flow from a conviction which are relevant because they make the rehabilitative path harder to travel. Here, one can include loss of financial or social support. People lose jobs, families are disrupted, sources of assistance disappear. Notwithstanding a need for denunciation, there are indirect consequences which arise from stigmatization and they cannot be isolated from the sentencing matrix if they will have bearing on the offender's ability to live productively in the community. The mitigation will depend on the weighing of these obstacles against the degree of denunciation appropriate to the offence.

Some indirect consequences are so inevitably linked to an offence that they seem to be part of the punishment and cannot be considered mitigating. Some realism has to be brought to the analysis. For example, losing a year in school is a relevant mitigating indirect consequence when it is put in the context of a short custodial sentence but if the exclusion from school arises from an assault on a teacher, it has no mitigating effect. The point is simply that indirect consequences must be viewed in the light of the offence itself. Where the consequence is so directly linked to the nature of an offence as to be almost inevitable, its role as a mitigating factor is greatly diminished.

Post-offence rehabilitative efforts: Progress in dealing with personal problems, and efforts to improve or repair one's social situation are always given mitigating credit. There may be concerns that such efforts are self-serving but they warrant credit because they show both recognition of personal difficulties and a commitment to remedying them. Of course, one needs to show sincerity and motivation which can usually be done through material from a treatment programme, job, family or friends. At the sentencing stage, some credit will be given for rehabilitative plans but it is always preferable if an offender is already participating and achieving some degree of progress than simply explaining the plan for the future. Regrettably, not all communities have appropriate resources available locally. Moreover, not all treatment facilities are available at public expense. Accordingly, there is a real opportunity for the privileged offender to gain an advantage over the non-privileged. This does not diminish the mitigating effect of an offender's sincere rehabilitative efforts. However, it does mean that courts should be sensitive to these resource difficulties and be prepared to credit time and energy spent looking for appropriate resources and attempting to qualify for them as important factors. These efforts are a first step to reform since they reflect introspection and a commitment to change. The extent of the mitigating effect of post-offence efforts will depend on sincerity, actual progress and relevance to the offence. In cases of drug and alcohol abuse where the offence is closely linked to the addiction, courts should be cautious about imposing a sentence which may disrupt the rehabilitative progress. More to the point, the absence of progress is not as critical as the fact that efforts at treatment show some interest in change. It is an accepted part of dealing with drug addiction that hard-core addicts will fail a number of times along the road to recovery.

Unrelated meritorious conduct: Some courts have accepted the mitigating effect of acts of charity or bravery unrelated to the offence. The basis is that such conduct suggests something positive about the offender which should enhance the court's view of rehabilitative prospects. Also, this conduct is the kind of community involvement which one wants to encourage. This is sometimes referred to as "moral credit." Examples are saving a child from drowning or attempting to rescue people trapped in a fire. Such conduct can have taken place before or after the offence.

Acts of reparation or compensation: Reflecting the common law, two of the potential objectives of a sentence are now described in s. 718(e) and (f) as:

(e) to provide reparations for harm done to victims or to the community; and

(f) to promote a sense of responsibility in offenders, and acknowledgment of the harm done to victims and to the community.

For the same reasons that a sentence may be directed to these ends, an offender is entitled to some mitigating credit for acts of reparation or compensation done prior to sentencing. It may be impossible to know whether an act is purely self-interested or really reflects remorse and a concern to rectify harm done. Absent contradictory evidence, the benefit of any doubt should always go to the offender. Obviously, some harm is more easily rectified and some offenders are in a better position to take steps to repair damage. Still, these are steps which should be encouraged. While lawyers may want to encourage the repair of a broken window, they should exercise some caution in advising offenders. A victim may harbour some residual fear of the offender. In the absence of an organized and responsible attempt at reconciliation, damage should be repaired by a third party and not the offender personally.

Provocation and duress: Any situations which reduce the degree of culpability or moral blameworthiness present relevant mitigating circumstances. The defence of duress or compulsion is limited by s. 17 of the Code both in terms of qualifying offences and factual pre-conditions. Accordingly, there will be situations where there is evidence of compulsion but no defence to the charge. Because it can be considered less blame-worthy to act under threat than of one's own initiative, these situations can mitigate a sentence. The common case is a drug courier who argues that a threat was made to en-courage his or her participation. If there is no defence of duress, there may still be facts that support its use for sentencing purposes.

Acts or words which provoke a violent response are in the same category. In cases of murder, provocation under s. 232 reduces the offence to manslaughter. For all other forms of assault, provocation is not a partial defence but can provide mitigation on sentencing. Again, the premise is straight-forward. Punching someone is an assault but it is a less blameworthy assault if it was provoked by an insult, threat, violent gesture or other form of offensive or wrongful conduct. At some point, the response is so dis-proportionate to the provocation that the provocation becomes irrelevant. Conversely, the provocation may have been so severe and the retaliation so slight that the mitigating effect produces a discharge.

In *R v. Stone*, the offender was convicted of manslaughter after being charged with the murder of his wife. Evidence of provocation had been placed before the jury. In im-posing a sentence of seven years for manslaughter, the trial judge took into account the provocation evidence. On appeal, it was argued by the Crown that this constituted a double counting since the provocation evidence had already resulted in mitigating the offence from murder to manslaughter. For the court, Bastarache J rejected this argument and commented:

> In reaching a sentence which accurately reflects a particular offender's moral culpability, the sentencing judge must consider all of the circumstances of the offence, including whether it involved provocation. Indeed ... to ignore the defence of provocation accepted by the jury and the evidence upon which that defence was based, would be to ignore pro-bative evidence of an offender's mental state at the time of the killing.

Accordingly, provocation was relevant in determining the level of moral culpability. At the same time, the fact that the killing occurred in the context of a spousal relationship was a relevant aggravating factor.

Delay in prosecution: Before discussing delay by authorities, it is necessary to say something about delays by victims in coming forward. It is not uncommon to find a case on a docket alleging an offence that was committed decades before, usually a seri-ous charge involving physical or sexual abuse of the victim when the victim was a child. Regardless of the attitude at the time of the offence towards assaults on children, these are matters which are taken very seriously today. Often these offences involve a breach of trust which is now recognized in the Code as an aggravating factor and a cus-todial sentence of some length is usually sought for denunciatory and deterrent pur-poses. But what about the delay in bringing the charges forward? By itself, the interven-ing period does not mean very much and will not be considered as a mitigating factor. However, delay may present corollaries which can be mitigating. They are often raised in the context of submissions for a conditional sentence. For example, a lengthy period with no repetition of offending is an important mitigating factor. This, of course, is en-hanced to some extent by evidence of productive social integration in terms of employment and family life during that period. The extent of its influence is affected by the gravity of the offence and is diminished by a lack of remorse or denial that the offence was a serious matter. The age of the offender can play a role. On the one hand, through the passage of time, the offender may have become elderly. While this is not mitigating, it may be accompanied by ill-health or infirmity which ought to be considered because of the inherent hardships of incarceration. From a different perspective, the offences may have been committed when the offender was very young and exemplary conduct during adulthood will be a serious mitigating factor. These examples demonstrate how the passage of time may produce changes that are relevant mitigating factors. While the ability of the justice system to reach back into time for the subject matter of prosecutions may cause some to grimace, we do not have limitations on prosecutions and there is no automatic benefit that accrues to offenders because of the passage of time.

There are Charter issues arising from delay. A prosecution may have moved slowly but not slow enough to constitute a violation of s. 11(b) and support a stay. Some courts have held that excessive delay which can be attributed to either the police or the prosecution may be a mitigating factor even if it was insufficient to produce a s. 11(b) breach. To some extent, this question is enmeshed in the debate about whether a Charter breach that does not produce a stay as a remedy can be resurrected at the sentencing stage in mitigation. However, given the recognition that any prosecution produces burdens and stress, and impinges on liberty, it is not necessary to engage in that controversy to argue that a deliberate or unnecessary expansion of the period during which these factors operate is akin to added punishment. Accordingly, it is appropriate to give it a mitigating effect.

The second issue is whether delay in sentencing can produce a s. 11(b) breach which leads to a stay rather than simply a mitigating consideration. The Supreme Court has concluded that s. 11(b) includes the right to be sentenced within a reasonable time. McLachlin J, as she then was, noted the potential adverse effects of living in "suspense" pending sentencing, and held:

> Delay in sentencing extends the time during which these constraints on an individual's liberty are imposed. While the sentencing judge may take these into account, there is no guarantee that this will occur. It follows that delay in sentencing may prejudice the accused's liberty interest.

For the purpose of s. 11(b), she applied the usual tests and concluded that, in the absence of any indicia of prejudice, the bulk of the delay occasioned by judicial illness could not be considered unreasonable. Accordingly, stays were not warranted. What is significant, however, is the recognition that delay can be an appropriate mitigating factor since it extends the ordinary impact of a sentence. Regardless of a s. 11(b) claim, one can argue that any delay that is deliberate, unnecessary or unreasonable ought to be a mitigating factor.

While pre-charge delay has no bearing on an accused's s. 11(b) rights to a speedy trial, some courts have taken deliberate delay into account in mitigation of sentence. The basis flows from the proposition that it is in everyone's interests, including the offender's, to proceed expeditiously to determine responsibility and impose a fair sanction. This kind of claim usually occurs when an offender is already serving a sentence of imprisonment and needs to resolve an outstanding charge before proceeding with release plans. From the offender's perspective, the authorities should not be able to arbitrarily postpone release by sitting on a warrant or evidence. Given the recognized interest in sentencing within a reasonable time, an example of deliberate or negligent delay which may prolong a term of imprisonment should generate mitigating consideration, including the possibility of a concurrent sentence even if otherwise not warranted.

Gap in criminal record and the intermediate recidivist: These are related factors which serve to place an offender's record into a context which has bearing on rehabilitative prospects. By definition, a recidivist is someone with a long record of previous convictions. A significant gap in that record, especially one that occurs just prior to the instant offence, indicates an ability to conform to legal norms for a substantial period of time. Notwithstanding the cynical view that a charge-free period does not mean a crime-free period, a significant gap shows a rehabilitative potential. Of course, the effect of the gap is relative but it would be enhanced if it included a period of good employment or responsible domestic relations. How the mitigation is applied depends on the nature of the offence. Where it can legitimately be concluded that imprisonment is the only reasonable alternative, a significant gap should be an important argument against an automatic escalation of the duration of imprisonment.

The "intermediate recidivist" is a category described by D.A. Thomas which includes an offender with a record who has arguably reached a point in life where a corner can be turned. For example, there may be a recent record of constructive employment with good prospects, a new domestic relationship, long-awaited success in dealing with an addiction or other personal difficulty, or a combination of these kinds of significant and potentially reformative life events. Notwithstanding the record, and depending on the nature of the instant offence, a court should give very serious consideration to a non-custodial sanction that will enhance the prospect of solid rehabilitation rather than frustrate it. One vehicle which may be particularly well-suited to this category of offender is the conditional sentence ... . There may be serious factual issues about the extent to which these significant life events have occurred, but courts are equipped to deal with issues of disputed fact and credibility. While sincerity may be a hard issue, courts should not be shy to address it.

A good example of the intermediate recidivist, although that label was not used, can be found in the case of *R v. McLeod*, an offender with a long criminal record and a long-standing problem with prescription drugs. At the age of 30, facing another drug offence and a charge of breach of probation, he experienced a number of positive changes. He returned to school and finished grades 11 and 12 before entering a college program. He attended church and AA, and did volunteer work at his school. The trial judge imposed a non-custodial sentence consisting of a two year probation period with electronic monitoring for the first six months. The Crown appealed seeking a term of imprisonment in light of the offences and the offender's record. Vancise JA wrote a lengthy decision supporting the non-custodial sentence. Recognizing the apparent change in the offender's life, he held that a fit sentence is one that is neither excessive nor inadequate judged on the merits of the particular case taking into account the circumstances of the offence and the characteristics of the offence. In his view, intensive probation supervision aided by a period of electronic monitoring was a sufficient and appropriate sanction.

Test case: Legislative provisions which have novel or ambiguous dimensions can generate good faith attempts to test their scope. With respect to non-violent crimes, an effort to create a test case for adjudicative purposes can result in a mitigated sentence. Of course, just being one of the first individuals prosecuted is not the same as an offence which was the product of a will to test the legislation. However, given the costs, rigours and uncertainties of protracted litigation, there can be a mitigating effect for an accused who decides to carry a case forward even if this decision arose after the charge.

• • •

Mistaken belief in the nature of a prohibited substance: Currently, substantive criminal law has produced some complicated and sometimes contradictory ruling about when a mistaken belief can exonerate. For example, with drug offences, knowledge of the general nature of a substance as an illicit drug is sufficient for culpability even if the offender believes the substance was a less serious drug. There is still a controversy over whether the offence committed is the factually completed offence or an attempt at the intended offence. For sentencing purposes, it is important to remember the central role of culpability as measured by blameworthiness. As a result, the offender's mental state should be the focus of sentencing attention. While the factual context cannot be ignored, a belief that a less serious offence was in progress is a mitigating factor. Accordingly, a belief that a transaction involved only a substance held out to be heroin should be distinguished between knowledge that a substance was heroin. The Ontario Court of Appeal reached a different conclusion in an importing case where the offender believed the substance involved to be marijuana but, in fact, it was cocaine. Finlayson JA concluded that the offender should be sentenced on the basis of participation in cocaine importing. This is inconsistent with the principle of fundamental justice that recognizes greater blameworthiness in intended consequences compared to those which are negligently produced. Some mitigating distinction should be drawn to reflect the mistaken belief. Even if it has no impact on criminal responsibility, it does reflect a reduced level of blameworthiness. More recently, in *R v. Sagoe* the same court considered a situation where the offender had been convicted of possession of heroin for the purposes of trafficking. She maintained that she did not know that the substance was heroin. The court, in reducing the sentence from two years to six months, commented:

> The trial judge appears to have thought that it was irrelevant that the appellant was wilfully blind to the nature of the narcotic involved, as opposed to having knowledge that it was heroin. This is not correct. Although the appellant had to be sentenced as being in possession of heroin for the purpose of trafficking, the fact that she did not know it was heroin was a mitigating factor.

Combined with her passive role in the offence and the absence of any personal benefit, the original two year sentence was reduced to six months. This case reflects recognition that the proper basis for assessing culpability for sentencing purposes is the factual context known to the offender.

NOTE

Without much effort, one could add other factors to Manson's mitigation list. For example, what about assistance to police authorities? In the drug case *R v. John Doe*, below, Hill J discussed what has come to be known as the "informer's discount."

R v. John Doe
(2000), 142 CCC (3d) 330 (Ont. SC)

HILL J: ...

[19] An alleged offender's willingness to co-operate in the investigation or prosecution of others, or the extent to which he or she has already done so, is relevant to both the public interest in continuing a prosecution of the accused or, if immunity is not granted, to plea agreements respecting the appropriate sentence: *Report of the Attorney-General's Advisory Committee on Charge Screening, Disclosure and Resolution Discussions* (the Martin Committee Report) (1993) (chaired by the Honourable G.A. Martin, QC), at pages 100, 303.

[20] The recognition of sentencing consideration co-operation with the authorities has a long tradition in the Province of Ontario: *R v. Alfs* (1974), 17 CLQ 247 (Ont. CA); Recommendation 38(b) (xiv), vol. 1, at pp. 235-6 of the *Report of the Royal Commission on the Donald Marshall Jr. Prosecution*, as approved by the Martin Committee Report at pp. 99-100; *Report to the Attorney General of Ontario on Certain Matters Relating to Karla Homolka* (1996), the Honourable P. Galligan, QC at pp. 64-70.

[21] While assistance given the authorities may serve to mitigate sentence, no additional penalty, of course, should be imposed for a failure to do so: *R v. Rosen* (1976), 18 CLQ 402 (Ont. CA); *R v. Phillips* (1974), 24 CRNS 305 (PEISC) at pp. 308-9, per Nicholson J (as he then was).

[22] The consideration in sentencing for a police informer's assistance has been described as being more a matter of expediency than principle ... .

[23] The entirely utilitarian objectives of uncovering serious criminality and apprehending dangerous individuals means that, in appropriate cases, an offender may justifiably receive a less severe punishment than the objective facts of his or her own offence deserves. While this pragmatic approach may be a high price for information, in the right circumstances, society is prepared to pay such a price.

[24] The recognition of informer assistance in sentencing is not limited to the offender manifesting contrition. Whatever the informer's motive, including pure self-interest, the assistance may be deserving of leniency.

[25] The government, and indeed accused persons, must recognize that a sentencing court, at the end of the day, is obliged to punish an offender, including an accused/informer, for his or her crime. There are limits to judicial leniency. Informer assistance to the police may be taken into account as a factor, even a substantial factor, in determining a just and fit disposition for the crime committed by the offender but the sentencing court is not the appropriate vehicle for granting immunity or awarding sentences that in effect amount to no sentence at all.

[26] For a number of years, in England, in large-scale informant sentencing proceedings described as "supergrass cases," the accused who informs or "grasses" respecting another criminal has generally received substantial credit for the assistance. The encouragement for informers to come forward benefits society and the accused/informer. There are several public policy reasons for a reduction of the punishment otherwise proportionate to the informer's own crime(s) [at 339]:

(1) The authorities can apprehend serious criminals including upper-level offenders in criminal organizations: *R v. Debbag and Izzet* [(1991), 12 Cr. App. R (S) 733 (CA)], at p. 736; *R v. Lowe* (1977), 66 Cr. App. R 122 (CA) at p. 125.

(2) The police are able to seize contraband or to prevent the distribution of drugs: *R v. Debbag and Izzet, supra,* at p. 736; *R v. Preston and McAleny* (1987), 9 Cr. App. R (S) 155 (CA) at pp. 156-7.

(3) The speedy preferring of information is encouraged by those who have it as part and parcel of their acceptance of responsibility for the matters with which they are charged: *R v. Debbag and Izzet, supra,* at p. 736; *R v. Salameh* (1991), 55 A Crim. R 384 (CCA New South Wales) at p. 388.

(4) The known availability of a sentence reduction for meaningful assistance to the police encourages other informers to come forward: *R v. Rose and Sapiano* (1980), 2 Cr. App. R (S) 239 (CA) at p. 242; *R v. Sinfield* [(1981), 3 Cr. App. R (S) 258 (CA)], at p. 259.

(5) The spectre of substantial sentencing leniency for informer assistance encourages criminals to have less confidence in each other: *R v. Salameh, supra,* at p. 387.

(6) A sentence for an offender who has helped the police may be one of intense severity in prison on account of such matters as fear of reprisals or removal to a prison far from family: *R v. Davies* (1979), 68 Cr. App. R 319 (CA) at p. 322; *R v. Perrier* [(1990), 59 A Crim. R 164 (CCA Victoria)], at pp. 169-170, 172; *R v. Cartwright* (1989), 17 NSWLR 243 (CCA) at p. 250; *R v. Heaney and Others,* [1992] 2 VR 531 (CCA) at pp. 559-560; *R v. Harris* (1992), 59 SASR 300 (SC in banco) at p. 302.

(7) Time spent in jail may, of necessity, have to be in solitary confinement or protective custody for the informer prisoner's protection: *R v. Davies, supra,* at p. 322; *R v. Lowe, supra,* at p. 126; *R v. Sinfield, supra,* at p. 259; *R v. Cartwright, supra,* at p. 247, 255; *R v. Harris, supra,* at p. 302; *R v. Salameh, supra,* at p. 388.

(8) In some cases, the accused/informer's family may be at risk of vengeance from the criminal element: *R v. Salameh, supra,* at p. 388; *R v. Harris, supra,* at p. 302.

(9) Where the informer's identity is known, as in the instance where he or she provides testimony against others, the risks to the informer and family may subsist after release: *R v. Sehitoglu and Ozakan,* [1998] 1 Cr. App. R (S) 89 (CA) at pp. 94-5; *R v. Davies, supra,* at p. 322; *R v. King* [(1985), 7 Cr. App. R (S) 227 (CA)], at p. 230; *R v. Rose and Sapiano, supra,* at p. 243; *R v. Sivan and Others* (1988), 10 Cr. App. R (S) 282 (CA) at p. 287; *R v. Sinfield, supra,* at 259; *R v. Salameh, supra,* at p. 388.

(10) Where an informer's identity is known, that person's days of living by crime are probably at an end: *R v. King, supra*, at p. 230; *R v. Sinfield, supra*, at p. 259.

Are there other kinds of assistance or cooperation that might also qualify for some mitigation?

Can you think of any other situations or characteristics that ought to mitigate a sentence? Explain why. What about a supportive family? On what basis could this factor mitigate? What about mental disorder? Is it a mitigating factor? Can the victim's conduct ever be a mitigating factor? What about police misconduct during the investigation stage that, while proven, does not give rise to a Charter remedy like a stay or exclusion of evidence?

Although s. 718.2(a) establishes the role for "relevant" mitigating factors, we have no coherent theory of mitigation. Instead, we have the vague reminder that sentencing is an individualized process.

III. STATUTORY AGGRAVATING FACTORS

A. Criminal Code, Section 718.2

718.2 A court that imposes a sentence shall also take into consideration the following principles:

(a) a sentence should be increased or reduced to account for any relevant aggravating or mitigating circumstances relating to the offence or the offender, and, without limiting the generality of the foregoing,

(i) evidence that the offence was motivated by bias, prejudice or hate based on race, national or ethnic origin, language, colour, religion, sex, age, mental or physical disability, sexual orientation or any other similar factor,

(ii) evidence that the offender, in committing the offence, abused the offender's spouse or child,

(iii) evidence that the offender, in committing the offence, abused a position of trust or authority in relation to the victim,

(iv) evidence that the offence was committed for the benefit of, at the direction of or in association with a criminal organization, or

(v) evidence that the offence was a terrorism offence

shall be deemed to be aggravating circumstances.

NOTE

Clearly, ss. 718.2(a)(i)-(iii) were recognized by the common law before statutory entrenchment. Their inclusion in the Code emphasizes the aggravating role that these factors play. Underlying these provisions are two unifying themes: the promotion of equality and the recognition of power imbalances as an aggravating context. The gravity of an offence is increased when it manifests a rejection of equal respect or an abuse of power against a vulnerable individual, or when it is motivated by a wrongful assertion of power. For an example of the role of s. 718.2(a)(i), see *R v. Miloszewski*, [1999] BCJ No. 2710 (QL) (Prov. Ct.), where sentences of 12 to 15 years were imposed on relatively young offenders for manslaughter. A caretaker at a Sikh temple had been brutally beaten to death. This case demonstrates the potential of aggravating factors to increase the severity of the sentence. Sentences for manslaughter are typically in the range of 5 to 8 years.

As a result of an amendment in 2003, the Code now also provides the following factors, some aggravating and some potentially mitigating, which are applicable when sentencing an "organization":

> 718.21 A court that imposes a sentence on an organization shall also take into consideration the following factors:
>
>   (a) any advantage realized by the organization as a result of the offence;
>
>   (b) the degree of planning involved in carrying out the offence and the duration and complexity of the offence;
>
>   (c) whether the organization has attempted to conceal its assets, or convert them, in order to show that it is not able to pay a fine or make restitution;
>
>   (d) the impact that the sentence would have on the economic viability of the organization and the continued employment of its employees;
>
>   (e) the cost to public authorities of the investigation and prosecution of the offence;
>
>   (f) any regulatory penalty imposed on the organization or one of its representatives in respect of the conduct that formed the basis of the offence;
>
>   (g) whether the organization was—or any of its representatives who were involved in the commission of the offence were—convicted of a similar offence or sanctioned by a regulatory body for similar conduct;
>
>   (h) any penalty imposed by the organization on a representative for their role in the commission of the offence;
>
>   (i) any restitution that the organization is ordered to make or any amount that the organization has paid to a victim of the offence; and
>
>   (j) any measures that the organization has taken to reduce the likelihood of it committing a subsequent offence.

An organization is defined in s. 2 as

>   (a) a public body, body corporate, society, company, firm, partnership, trade union or municipality, or
>
>   (b) an association of persons that
>   (i) is created for a common purpose,
>   (ii) has an operational structure, and
>   (iii) holds itself out to the public as an association of persons.

B. Controlled Drugs and Substances Act

This statute, enacted in 1996 by SC 1996, c. 19 to replace the *Narcotic Control Act*, contains its own statement of purpose and a list of applicable aggravating factors:

> 10(1) Without restricting the generality of the *Criminal Code*, the fundamental purpose of any sentence for an offence under this Part is to contribute to the respect for the law and the

maintenance of a just, peaceful and safe society while encouraging rehabilitation, and treatment in appropriate circumstances, of offenders and acknowledging the harm done to victims and to the community.

(2) If a person is convicted of a designated substance offence, the court imposing sentence on the person shall consider any relevant aggravating factors including that the person

(a) in relation to the commission of the offence,

(i) carried, used or threatened to use a weapon,

(ii) used or threatened to use violence,

(iii) trafficked in a substance included in Schedule I, II, III or IV or possessed such a substance for the purpose of trafficking, in or near a school, on or near school grounds or in or near any other public place usually frequented by persons under the age of eighteen years, or

(iv) trafficked in a substance included in Schedule I, II, III or IV, or possessed such a substance for the purpose of trafficking, to a person under the age of eighteen years;

(b) was previously convicted of a designated substance offence; or

(c) used the services of a person under the age of eighteen years to commit, or involved such a person in the commission of, a designated substance offence.

(3) If, under subsection (1), the court is satisfied of the existence of one or more of the aggravating factors enumerated in paragraphs (2)(a) to (c), but decides not to sentence the person to imprisonment, the court shall give reasons for that decision.

IV. JUDICIALLY RECOGNIZED AGGRAVATING FACTORS

As with mitigating factors, there are numerous references in the case law to factors that are considered to be aggravating. Most of these bear on the gravity of the offence: the extent of harm caused, number of victims, use of weapons, infliction of brutal injury, etc. They are, for the most part, self-evident. They describe characteristics that necessarily place an offence at the more serious end of the gravity spectrum. There is ample case law that accepts the following list of aggravating factors as being relevant to sentencing:

- previous convictions,
- actual or threatened violence or use of weapon,
- cruelty or brutality,
- substantial physical injuries or psychological harm,
- offence committed while subjected to judicially imposed conditions,
- multiple victims or multiple incidents,
- group or gang activity,
- impeding victim's access to the justice system,
- substantial economic loss,
- planning and organization,
- vulnerability of victim, and
- deliberate risk taking.

Consider this list and try to explain exactly why the particular circumstance or characteristic should be aggravating. How does it increase culpability or make the offender more blameworthy? Should there be any limits on the applicability of any of these factors? Are there other factors that you would consider aggravating? If so, can you articulate why they warrant a more severe penalty? What about personal characteristics? Are there any that you consider aggravating? Why?

V. FACTORS NOT TO BE TREATED AS AGGRAVATING

There are also some factors that, at first blush, may appear relevant to sentencing but on closer analysis cannot be logically or fairly linked to the proper set of considerations that should bear on the sentencing function. Courts of appeal have identified a small number of factors that sentencing judges should not consider to be aggravating. The fact that the offender pleaded not guilty should not be used to aggravate the sanction. Otherwise, an accused is being penalized for exercising the constitutional right to be presumed innocent until the Crown has proven the case beyond a reasonable doubt. Similarly, courts of appeal have held that the conduct of the defence at trial should not be held against an offender: see *R v. Kozy* (1990), 80 CR (3d) 59 (Ont. CA).

A harder question to resolve concerns the absence of evidence of remorse. Although a guilty plea and other indicia of remorse are considered to be mitigating factors, does this mean that an absence of remorse is an aggravating factor? If it did, it would mean that anyone who did not accept guilt at the time of sentencing would be subjected to an increased sentence. Given that convictions are subject to appeal, and convicted persons are entitled to continue to deny guilt, should an absence of evidence of remorse be treated as a neutral factor? Of course, this does not include conduct that demonstrates callousness or actual absence of remorse. If every mitigating factor has a reciprocal aggravating factor, itself a contentious proposition, then callousness is the reciprocal of remorse.

A similar issue arises with respect to cooperation with authorities. Evidence of assistance is often considered to be mitigating. What about the converse—that is, a situation where the authorities want information and the offender refuses to assist? Remember that the law does not require confessions and it does not compel an accused person to divulge information about accomplices.

In *R v. Wristen* (1999), 47 OR (3d) 66 (Ont. CA), a second-degree murder case, the Ontario Court of Appeal said:

> The appellant was not legally obliged to assist the police. He was entitled to exercise his right to silence and require the prosecution to prove the case against him beyond a reasonable doubt. Exercising this right is not an aggravating consideration on sentence.

However, after accepting that principle, the court upheld the increase in parole eligibility to 17 years even though the trial judge was influenced by the convicted man's efforts to conceal the killing of his wife. It held that it was proper that the judge consider the efforts to hide the offence and the refusal to provide any information about the location of the body. The defence was that the woman had just disappeared and that the husband was not responsible for her death. This position was maintained throughout the appeal. Given the accused's denial of responsibility, can he be expected to disclose the location of the body? Is this different from a situation where the failure to cooperate with authorities can be characterized as callous disregard for the survivors or a victim, which is legitimately aggravating?

VI. SPECIAL ISSUES

A. Assessing Relevant Factors in Cases of Sexual Abuse

One of the difficult areas of sentencing arises when there are convictions for sexual abuse of children. Such cases often involve a panoply of aggravating factors: extensive harm, multiple victims, abuse of position of trust. Many cases, however, are the result of old offences. What is the impact of the passage of time? Does it produce a mitigating effect if there has been no repetition of offending? Does it mitigate only if conduct has been exemplary? What is the relevance of indicia of good character in business or civic circumstances?

R v. Gordon M.
(1992), 11 OR (3d) 225 (CA)

ABELLA JA: This is an appeal by the Crown from a suspended sentence and one year's probation following a guilty plea by Gordon M., the respondent in this appeal, to twelve charges of indecently assaulting his two daughters. The charges relate to assaults which occurred from 1973 until 1979, starting when the girls were eleven or twelve years old. They stopped, as did the marriage, when the oldest daughter in 1980 disclosed the assaults to her mother. The incidents involved extensive touching, digital penetration and cunnilingus. The Crown submits that the trial judge, Misener J, erred in failing to apply principles of general deterrence and denunciation when he imposed a non-custodial sentence.

The trial judge characterized the conduct as "an extremely serious breach of trust"; "systematic," "gross," and "outrageous" misconduct; and a "serious ... and a continuing trauma" to the daughters.

The trial judge rejected the application of specific deterrence because the respondent needed no further personal deterrence, having acknowledged, apologized for, and medically treated his former behaviour, and having remarried in 1988. Nor, for the same reasons, was the principle of rehabilitation of any relevance to the respondent, there being no indication that the possibility of recidivism or anti-social conduct existed. The trial judge then considered whether the principle of general deterrence applied, and concluded that it did not. In his words:

> I have the greatest difficulty understanding sexual assault in the context of the family. I wish I knew more about it, I wish I knew why it occurs. But I'm pretty certain of one thing, I'm pretty certain that the concept of general deterrence as I've just defined it has no part to play in fashioning a sentence for those who sexually assault members of their family. Or, to be specific about it, for cases such as this. I cannot believe, indeed, I think it very insulting to the human race for me to say that there is a given body of fathers out there who are going to weigh the penalty and decide whether or not they will abuse their daughters or their children. I just can't believe that that concept expressed in such basic terms as I've just expressed it—and that's how it should be expressed, it seems to me—I just can't believe that concept has any significance, any part, any relevance at all to this type of case. ...
>
> I simply cannot believe that in all the circumstances of this case the right thing to do is to send [the respondent] to jail.

In the end, of course, the sentence must attempt to blend a particular accused with the gravity of his or her offence. Aggravating and mitigating circumstances are weighed, with the objective of arriving at a disposition which is, to the extent that such a thing is humanly achievable, let alone universally accepted as such, reasonable and just in all the circumstances.

Looking at the circumstances in the respondent's case, the trial judge, in my view, placed inappropriate reliance on several factors he characterized as mitigating.

He identified the following as mitigating factors:

a)   the respondent was 51 years of age;
b)   he was a well-respected, successful and accomplished businessman;
c)   the respondent had the respect of the community;
d)   there was a breakdown in intimacy and sexual relations between the respondent and his first wife which, in part, was a cause of the misconduct;
e)   there were no threats or violence involved;
f)   the respondent "fully disclosed" his misconduct to all concerned in 1980;
g)   he sought treatment after the initial disclosure and was successful in his rehabilitation; and
h)   the respondent "fully and generously" supported his wife and children until 1988.

While aspects of character are of varying relevance in sentencing depending on the offence (see *R v. R.S.* (1985), 19 CCC (3d) 115 (Ont. CA), at p. 127, per Lacourcière JA), I have difficulty seeing how someone who is accomplished and successful in business is entitled to any more consideration from a court for an offence of this kind, than someone with less business acumen or fewer resources.

Nor is it clear to me why the breakdown of "the sexual part" of the relationship between the respondent and his wife, for whatever reason is in any way relevant to his having abused his daughters. It suggests either that the daughters were understandable substitutes in the same home, or that the wife was in some way morally culpable for the father assaulting their daughters, both completely untenable suggestions.

Nor do I accept that the absence of tangible violence makes the offence less worthy of censure, since in my view "the offence of sexual assault is an inherently violent crime": *R v. Khan*, a decision of the Ontario Court (General Division), released June 5, 1991, per Moldaver J at p. 4. There is no doubt, however, that there are escalating degrees of violence and that these degrees are undoubtedly relevant as aggravating factors where they exist.

Nor, in my view, do threats have to be articulated for a situation such as this to be deemed threatening. The dimensional harm of this offence when it occurs between parent and child is in its exploitation of the trust the child is entitled to place in a person upon whom she is dependent. While the conduct may often be explained by reference either to personal or social pathologies, it cannot ever be, or be seen to be, excused. The child is always, by virtue of the power imbalance inherent in his or her status as a child, in a more vulnerable position than the parent. In *Norberg v. Wynrib*, a decision of the Supreme Court of Canada, released June 18, 1992 [now reported [1992] 2 SCR 226; 92 DLR (4th) 449], La Forest J at p. 23 cites with approval the observations of one writer who refers to relationships where there is the capacity to "dominate and influence" as "power dependency" relationships [at 255 SCR; 463 DLR]:

> Professor Coleman outlines a number of situations which she calls "power dependency" relationships; see Coleman, "Sex in Power Dependency Relationships: Taking Unfair Advantage of the 'Fair' Sex," 53 Alb. L Rev. 95. Included in these relationships are parent–child, psychotherapist–patient, physician–patient, clergy–penitent, professor–student, attorney–client, and employer–employee. She asserts that "consent" to a sexual relationship in such relationships is inherently suspect.

(See also the opinion in *Norberg* of McLachlin J, who discusses such power imbalances and the duty they create at pp. 6-8 [at 271-74 SCR; 486-88 DLR].)

If consent is inherently suspect in these relationships, then while degrees of violence or threats may undoubtedly be considered as more or less aggravating factors in sentencing, it does not necessarily follow that their absence operates to reduce the seriousness of the offence. The status of parent–child, the dependency and vulnerability which flow from that status, and the trust the child is entitled to presume, all underscore that the relationship between parents and their children is a fiduciary one. The trust is offended no less when exploited in what appears otherwise to be a warm relationship between father and daughter, where the love a child feels for her father may generate acquiescence on her part without his subjecting her to additional physical or verbal victimization. It may even be seen, as it was by these two victims, as a greater and more traumatic invasion of their trust when it comes from a loved parent whom they are anxious to please.

I agree that the respondent acknowledged and apologized for his assaults, but only after his older daughter disclosed them to her mother. His "fully and generously" complying with his legal obligation to pay financial support to his wife and children after the disclosure resulted in their separation is, it seems to me, a neutral factor, as is his age in this case.

But while a custodial term is clearly warranted in this case, there are some mitigating factors which should be considered. From the evidence, the trial judge correctly concluded that neither specific deterrence nor rehabilitation applied. The respondent, after acknowledging the assaults, immediately sought and successfully completed counselling and therapeutic psychiatric care when his daughters disclosed his behaviour. He has consistently shown genuine remorse for his conduct. He has, according to a medical report filed with the court at sentencing, completely rehabilitated himself. The high regard and respect he enjoyed in his community have undoubtedly been irrevocably and profoundly impaired. And finally, it has been well over a year between the suspension of the respondent's sentence in May 1991, and the imposition of this custodial term on appeal.

The factors the trial judge accepted as aggravating are the following:

a) exploitation of the vulnerability of children;
b) "extremely serious" breach of parental trust or duty;
c) two victims;
d) number of offences, which the learned sentencing judge described as "gross" or "outrageous" systematic misconduct;
e) nature of the misconduct; and
f) victim impact.

Having identified them, however, he none the less found them to be worthy of less consideration than the factors he identified as mitigating. In my view, his emphasis was misplaced.

In erroneously concluding that general deterrence has no application in cases of this kind, the trial judge relied exclusively on whether there was any value of imprisonment for the particular accused, rather than taking into account any potential impact on the public perception of a father indecently assaulting two daughters over a six-year period. This court rejected that approach in *R v. Palmer* (1985), 7 OAC 348 (CA), where MacKinnon AJCO said, at p. 350:

> The learned trial judge seemed to have only the welfare and rehabilitation of the accused in mind when he imposed the sentence he did. While it is a consideration and an important consideration, it is obviously not the only consideration. The sexual abuse of a child by one *in loco parentis* is a very serious crime. It is a gross abuse of trust and power which society does not tolerate. It warrants, absent quite exceptional circumstances, a denunciatory sentence which reflects society's revulsion at this type of conduct and at the same time has regard to the possibility of rehabilitation of the offender. It is not unusual that such offenders have steady work; that it is their first brush with the criminal law; and that they express remorse when their activities are discovered. There is also an aspect of general deterrence to such a sentence which should not be ignored.

Counsel for the respondent conceded before this court that the principle of general deterrence is not only applicable but paramount in cases involving the personal sexual abuse of children. But he submits that the mitigating circumstances in this case are sufficiently exceptional that no custodial term is required. I disagree both with the proposition that the mitigating circumstances are exceptional and with the submission that a custodial term is not justified in this case.

In *R v. Clayton* (1982), 69 CCC (2d) 81 (Ont. CA), at p. 83, Cory JA stated:

> Incest is a serious crime. Although performed without violence, it may well leave lasting scars. The crime is one which often has terrible consequences for the victim. It constitutes a breach of the greatest trust that can be bestowed on a man, the trust of his children. ... It is appropriate that in most cases of incest involving young children that a term of imprisonment should be imposed.

More recently, this court confirmed that view in *R v. Fraser* (1987), 20 OAC 78 (CA). Lacourcière JA, in language directly apposite to this case, stated at p. 80:

> We are, nonetheless, all of the view that the sentence imposed failed totally to reflect the gravity of the offence and society's abhorrence with the conduct of the respondent. This court has on many previous occasions set out the principles which should be applied in determining the sentence in these and similar cases. Those principles establish that, in the absence of exceptional circumstances, the imposition of a suspended sentence in such cases is inappropriate. Sexual abuse of children cannot be tolerated and must be denounced so that society will be made aware of the court's revulsion for such conduct which, in this case, involved a serious breach of trust.
>
> General deterrence was not referred to in the reasons for sentence and does not seem to have been considered. The trial judge emphasized the voluntary interruption of the

sexual activity as well as the rehabilitation of the offender. In our view, however, the extremely serious nature of the offence which, in itself continued over a lengthy period of time, requires a substantial period of incarceration in a reformatory. ...

In the circumstances, I would grant leave to appeal, allow the appeal, and vary the sentence to a term of 12 months. But for the mitigating factors, a heavier penalty would clearly have been justified. I can see no basis for ordering a term of probation.

NOTE

While the discussion of mitigating and aggravating factors in *Gordon M.* continues to be illustrative, two historical facts should be noted. First, the case occurred before the advent of conditonal sentences (see chapter 12, Conditional Sentence of Imprisonment). Second, there has been a marked increase in sentencing norms for sexual offences against children since the early 1990s.

In *R v. R.S.H.*, [2005] BCJ No. 1393, Wedge J convicted a man who had no prior record of a series of sexual assaults by a person in a position of authority on a child who was aged seven and eight at the time of the assaults. The offences were described as follows:

At trial, the victim testified that the accused assaulted her on several occasions when her family was living in Houston. She also testified that he assaulted her when she and her family visited the accused in Kamloops, and when the accused visited her family ... . From the child's evidence, I concluded that the accused used his hand and his penis in attempts to masturbate her. She described the accused rubbing her genital area "for a long, long, long, long, time" with his penis and his hand.

Wedge J offered the following synopsis of the principles relating to the sentences for sexual assaults of children in the extract below.

R v. R.S.H.
[2005] BCJ No. 1393 (QL)

WEDGE J: ...

[38] The Supreme Court of Canada has, in several recent decisions, observed that the principle of denunciation is of particular importance in cases of offences committed against young children by adults in positions of authority: see *R v. W.(L.F.)* (2000), 140 CCC (3d) 539, 2000 SCC 6 per L'Heureux-Dubé J at para. 29; *R v. S.(R.N.)* (2000), 140 CCC (3d) 553, 2000 SCC 7.

[39] In *R v. S.(R.N.)*, which involved the sexual abuse of a child, the Court set aside as "clearly unfit" a nine-month conditional sentence imposed on appeal from a sentence by the trial judge of nine months incarceration. At para. 19, Lamer CJC said:

In conducting its re-sentencing, the Court of Appeal should have recognized that the relatively lenient nine-month term imposed by [the trial judge] was the result of his taking into account the precarious health of the [accused] at the time of sentencing, his marital difficulties and the social stigma he had already suffered, as the sentencing judge would have been inclined to agree with the Crown's submission that a term of incarceration in the range of 18 to 24 months was warranted. By imposing a conditional sentence of only nine months, the Court of Appeal transformed what was already a lenient sentence into an unfit sentence.

[40] The Court went on to explain why it had not overturned a conditional sentence in its earlier decision in *R v. W.(L.F.)*. In that case, there were three distinguishing factors. First, the conditional sentence that had been imposed was significantly longer. Second, the offender had been arguably rehabilitated. Third, the conditional sentence was imposed by the trial judge, and was accordingly entitled to considerable deference. Had the Court not been bound to give such deference to the trial judge's sentence, it might well have imposed a term of incarceration.

[41] The comments of the Ontario Court of Appeal in *R v. D.(D.)* (2002), 163 CCC (3d) 471, 58 OR (3d) 788 are particularly relevant to the discussion here. The Court held that in cases of sexual offences against children, the principles of denunciation and deterrence must be the primary considerations. At paras. 34-36, the Court explained why that is so:

> Adult sexual predators who would put the lives of innocent children at risk to satisfy their deviant sexual needs must know that they will pay a heavy price. In cases such as this, absent exceptional circumstances, the objectives of sentencing proclaimed by Parliament in s. 718(a), (b) and (c) of the *Criminal Code*, commonly referred to as denunciation, general and specific deterrence, and the need to separate offenders from society, must take precedence over the other recognized objectives of sentencing.
>
> We as a society owe it to our children to protect them from the harm caused by offenders like the appellant. Our children are at once our most valued and our most vulnerable assets. Throughout their formative years, they are manifestly incapable of defending themselves against predators like the appellant and as such, they make easy prey. People like the appellant know this only too well and they exploit it to achieve their selfish ends, heedless of the dire consequences that can and often do follow.
>
> In this respect, while there may have been a time, years ago, when offenders like the appellant could take refuge in the fact that little was known about the nature or extent of the damage caused by sexual abuse, that time has long since passed. Today, that excuse no long holds sway. The horrific consequences of child sexual abuse are only too well known.

[42] The Ontario Court of Appeal reiterated its view as to the approach that ought to be taken in cases involving sexual offences against children in *R v. D.R.* (2003), 169 OAC 55 at para. 8:

> While sentences imposed by sentencing judges attract considerable deference from this court, on the facts of this case, we conclude that the governing principles of denunciation and deterrence, both specific and general, cannot be satisfied by a conditional sentence. This court has repeatedly indicated that a conditional sentence should rarely be imposed in cases involving the sexual touching of children by adults, particularly where, as here, the sexual violation is of a vulnerable victim by a person in a position of trust.

[43] Those comments by the Ontario Court of Appeal were cited with approval in the recent decision of Romilly J of this Court in *R v. R.E.M.*, [2005] BCJ No. 1191, 2005 BCSC 698. Mr. Justice Romilly also said the following at para. 29 of his decision:

> Children are among our society's most vulnerable members. They are easily victimized, particularly by their relatives. Relatives of children have ready and often unlimited access to them because of the position of trust they hold. It is my view that general deterrence and denunciation must be prime considerations in imposing a sentence upon those who sexually abuse children.

[44] Again, at para. 32, Romilly J said:

> It is my view that a clear message must be sent to every person in a position of trust in relation to a child that sexual contact with them will not be tolerated in this society and that it will result in lengthy periods of imprisonment being imposed.

[45] A similar observation was made by our Court of Appeal in *R v. J.A.F.* (1998), 50 BCLR (3d) 312, 109 BCAC 229, which involved sexual abuse of a child by a person in a position of trust. On the issue of sentencing principles in such a case, Hall JA said at para. 24:

> It is essential for the protection of young and vulnerable children that instances of [sexual] misconduct of this sort should attract sentences which will tend to deter such activity. In my judgment, it will be the extremely rare case in which it would be appropriate for anything but a sentence of incarceration to be imposed when conduct of the sort disclosed in this case occurs.

[46] The Court of Appeal in *J.A.F.* also emphasized the weight that must be given to the principles of deterrence and denunciation where the offence involves a breach of trust. Also important, said Hall JA at para. 19, is the oft-forgotten role of retribution:

> In the course of giving reasons for judgment in a relatively recent case in this Court Madam Justice Ryan made some comments that I think are worth repeating. I refer to the case of *R v. Johnson* (1996), 84 BCAC 261 at p. 268:
>
>> In analyzing the place that retribution has in the sentencing process, the court compared it to the concept of denunciation. The Chief Justice said this (at pp. 558-559):
>>
>>> Retribution requires that a judicial sentence properly reflect the moral blameworthiness of that particular offender. The objective of denunciation mandates that a sentence should also communicate society's condemnation of that particular offender's conduct. In short, a sentence with a denunciatory element represents a symbolic, collective statement that the offender's conduct should be punished for encroaching on our society's basic code of values as enshrined within our substantive criminal law ... . The relevance of both retribution and denunciation as goals of sentencing underscores that our criminal justice system is not simply a vast system of negative penalties designed to prevent objectively harmful conduct by increasing the cost the offender must bear in committing an enumerated offence. Our criminal law is also a system

of values. A sentence which expresses denunciation is simply the means by
which these values are communicated. In short, in addition to attaching
negative consequences to undesirable behaviour, judicial sentences should
also be imposed in a manner which positively instills the basic set of communal values shared by all Canadians as expressed by the Criminal Code.

Wedge J sentenced the accused to 20 months' imprisonment followed by 2 years' probation. This sentence was affirmed on appeal: see *R v. Hall*, [2005] BCJ No. 2590 (QL). In
that brief judgment, Southin JA added the comment (at para. 7):

The appellant in this case has no previous criminal record. He is a man now, I think, in his early
50s. It is quite probable that putting him in prison will do him no good and the possibility that
putting him in prison will deter others from committing these crimes is at least a doubtful one
in my opinion. But though that being so, that is not what Parliament has said and it is not what
the authorities say. The authorities do express the proposition that these sentences have both a
deterrent and a denunciatory effect and we are obliged to apply that proposition in this Court.

What does this comment suggest about deterrence and denunciation as appropriate sentencing goals in this situation? Is this kind of judicial frankness refreshing, dangerous, or
superfluous?

B. Social Disadvantage

There is little doubt that much crime can be traced back to histories of poverty, abuse, and
family dysfunction. Some people can rise above the limiting and even crippling circumstances of their impoverished backgrounds; many cannot. In a wealthy country like Canada,
young people are the products not only of their family environments but also of the community's schools and hospitals, and sometimes of other public entities like children's aid
agencies and social institutions that intervene in the lives of dysfunctional families. Can a
disadvantaged background be excluded from the sentencing matrix?

In *R v. George*, a dangerous offender case, the BC Court of Appeal had to consider the
"pattern of aggressive behaviour" test in s. 753(a)(ii). In doing so, it observed:

The dangerous offender provisions may fall more heavily on the poor and disadvantaged
members of our society if their childhood conduct is counted against them. This appellant had
to face school as an aboriginal foster child living in a non-aboriginal culture with an IQ at or
near the retarded level. It is understandable that any child with this background would get into
a lot of trouble by lashing out aggressively when challenged by his or her environment.

In *R v. Borde*, Rosenberg JA said:

The appellant's fundamental submission is that because of the similarity between the plight of
Aboriginal Canadians and African-Canadians, the court should adopt a similar form of analysis
for the purposes of sentencing. Further, he submits that the background of the appellant exhibits many of the same factors often found in the background of Aboriginal offenders including
poverty, family dislocation, chaotic child rearing and alcoholism. I accept that there are some

similarities and that the background and systemic factors facing African-Canadians, where they are shown to have played a part in the offence, might be taken into account in imposing sentence. However, for the following reasons, the evidence is not relevant in this case.

One can construct a number of arguments that support the recognition of social disadvantage as a mitigating factor:

1. *Sentencing as a moral exercise:* R.A. Duff, the Scottish legal philosopher from Stirling University, has argued that when a community has denied to some people full membership in that community it loses its moral standing to sentence them. Therefore it needs to take into account their social disadvantage when sentencing them: see R.A. Duff, *Punishment, Communication, and Community* (Oxford: Oxford University Press, 2001). This argument derives from his earlier work, where he describes sentencing as a form of moral exercise that is communicative in nature where the sentence communicates censure to the offender and the community. Duff's view, along with other claims, was subjected to a careful critique by von Hirsch and Ashworth in *Proportionate Sentencing: Exploring the Principles* (Oxford: Oxford University Press, 2005), at 62-74. Their major concern seems to be that if one agrees with Duff then the factor goes beyond mere mitigation. If a community lacks standing to sentence, then it compels an exemption from sentencing rather than mitigation.

2. *Fairness:* A related argument concerns the pressures on socially disadvantaged defendants. Regardless of whether society is responsible for the disadvantage, it may be unfair to expect the same level of compliance with the law from people who are greatly disadvantaged. Compliance is much easier for well-placed individuals than for impoverished ones. Should a court mitigate punishment on these grounds?

3. *Substantive equality jurisprudence under s. 15:* Charter equality jurisprudence has expounded the view that difference matters in the pursuit of equality. Accordingly, material differences need to be taken into account to achieve equal treatment. This means that in a case like *Hamilton and Mason*, discussed in chapter 2, race and gender are relevant in respect of the offenders, but also in relation to the findings made by the trial judge about drug couriers and the city of Brampton. In that case, Hill J at trial found (at para. 180):

On the evidentiary record, I am satisfied that in Brampton:

(1) black persons, men and women, are charged with cocaine importation in numbers disproportionate to their percentage in the general population;

(2) black women, more often than not single mothers, are charged and sentenced to penitentiary sentences for cocaine importation in numbers disproportionate to their percentage in the general population.

4. *Sentencing viewed from an instrumental or functional perspective:* Sentencing creates a traditional inquiry that produces individualized findings about the offender including matters like work record, school achievements, family support, and prior criminal record. For some people, because of a background of social disadvantage in respect of a particular family or community, this is an illusory inquiry. The court is then deprived of essential

information in a way that also deprives the offender of a fair sentencing hearing. Accordingly, some accommodation must be made to bring the case within an acceptable framework that is at least comparable to the sentencing matrix available for other offenders. This bears some similarity to the "fairness" argument made above.

Do you find any of these arguments persuasive?

C. Mercy

The issue of mercy and its relation to sentencing is a difficult one. We have chosen to deal with it separately because it touches on many aspects of mitigation that can produce leniency, but it also generates arguments that, as a discrete concept, it ought to remain outside the judicial sentencing process. Most people would accept with little difficulty the claim that there must be some residual concept or principle that does not relate to a specific sentencing objective but that permits a compassionate response. However, aside from the hard questions about scope and applicability, there are harder fundamental questions. Does mercy operate outside the justice system, within the justice system, or a bit of both, depending on what you consider is encompassed by the rubric?

For some time, there has been a healthy philosophical debate about this issue. However, lawyers have tended to assume that there are some matters that speak solely to compassion and mercy, which judges can consider, and the post-sentence arena known as the pardon or clemency process can pick up what's left.

Austin Sarat and Nasser Hussain published an interesting array of articles on this topic entitled *Forgiveness, Mercy and Clemency* (Stanford: Stanford University Press, 2007). From that collection, the following excerpt from Carol Streiker's thoughtful article "Tempering or Tampering: Mercy and the Administration of Criminal Justice" conveys the tone of the philosophical debate while also raising considerations that the sentencing system needs to consider (at 20):

> The first and openly normative question immediately implicates a host of related inquiries. What is the relationship between mercy and justice? Does justice require the imposition of deserved punishment? Is mercy related or opposed or indifferent to the moral desert of an offender? Does mercy describe merely an act, or does it describe something about the state of mind of the mercy giver? Or something about the relationship between the mercy giver and receiver? What is the relationship between mercy and the constellation of emotions or attitudes we call pity, empathy, compassion and forgiveness. Is mercy opposed to reason? Can the exercise of mercy be evaluated? How, if at all, can whatever view of mercy we choose to embrace guide us to its proper application? In short, is mercy a good normative lens, among others, through which to judge the exercise of discretion within our sentencing system?
>
> The second, more institutional question comes with its own host of corollaries. Is mercy appropriate for the public spheres at all? If so, is it possible to realize institutionally? Which institutional actors would be best suited to promote any particular vision of mercy? Should prosecutors think of themselves as open to appeals for mercy in the exercise of their charging discretion? What about juries? Should their power to render acquittals that are unreviewable be recognized as a proper locus for the power of mercy? Should sentencing judges consider

appeals for mercy, or are such appeals more properly directed toward those with the powers of executive clemency and pardon? Can legislatures be merciful? Or is mercy necessarily individual, perhaps the province only of discrete victims of crime? Under this last view, should the legal system have any role in fostering conditions for reconciliation between victims and offenders? By attempting to carve out and protect a power of mercy within our criminal justice system, do we inevitably increase the problems of arbitrariness and bias beyond what we would endorse without such a commitment.

These extremely perceptive questions cover the landscape of contemporary sentencing issues. The answers that you might explore are affected dramatically by your own views on such controversial issues as the appropriate theoretical basis for sentencing, the proper role of judicial discretion and judges, the importance of forgiveness and redemption as aspects of human inter-relationships, how reasons for sentencing decisions can satisfy the diverse range of audiences for whom they are intended, and whether a sentencing system should be self-conscious about the impact of its outcomes in racial, class, and gender terms.

Assume that a jury has returned a verdict of guilty against a business person who allegedly defrauded the shareholders of a public company of millions of dollars. Four weeks prior to his sentencing, his entire family, his spouse and three teenaged children, are killed in a multi-vehicle highway collision. Surely, at the sentencing hearing, every defence counsel in the world would raise this tragic fact. Would any prosecutor object on the ground of relevance? But what is the relevance of the four deaths? Can the judge take them into account to mitigate the sentence? Notwithstanding the offender's suffering, this suffering was not imposed by the state nor did it flow from the offence or the prosecution. Would you respond differently if the offence had caused physical rather than financial harm? In that case, how important are the victims' views—that is, whether they speak of forgiveness or retribution?

It is not coincidental that the residual pardoning power in Commonwealth jurisdictions can be traced to what was known as the "Royal Prerogative of Mercy." Justice may have been administered by the courts but mercy came from the sovereign. Is this dichotomy too simplistic, too stark, and just anachronistic?

In driving offences resulting in death or serious harm the victim is often a passenger in the offender's vehicle. Imagine that the offender is convicted of impaired driving causing death and the deceased victim is his son or best friend. The loss of this individual constitutes an "immanent punishment," the severity of which far exceeds any legal sanction. Should the court take this circumstance into account at sentencing? A custodial sentence is the norm for this offence. Should a sentencing court impose a lesser, non-custodial sentence in such cases? Is the concept of proportionality blind to such considerations? Aside from the issue of proportional sentencing, counsel for the defendant may argue that, from a utilitarian persective, a non-custodial sanction is justified. The fatal consequences of the crime are unlikely to leave the offender and this suggests that an individual deterrent sentence is unnecessary. Is this an appropriate application for the exercise of mercy on the ground of compassion?

PROBLEMS

Consider the following problems and identify the factors that you believe should be mitigating and those that are aggravating. Justify your selection by reference to the purpose and principles of sentencing, or some consideration that may be considered external to the sentencing process, such as mercy.

1. Green was convicted of three counts of assault causing bodily harm that occurred in 1977 and 1978. In 1975, Green and his spouse adopted the two young daughters of Green's spouse's sister. The two girls, Helen and Doris, were five and seven at the time. Their parents had been killed in an automobile collision. For the next 10 years, the girls led terrible lives within the Green household. Essentially, they were family slaves performing all the washing, cleaning, and meal preparation for the Greens and their three sons. Their days were marked with abuse. Helen was so damaged by the experience that it took her 10 years to move from kindergarten to grade 6. She left school in grade 7 and ran away.

The offences consisted of: (1) Helen being beaten with the cord from the iron; (2) Helen being struck with a broom handle; and (3) Doris being punched and kicked, resulting in a broken nose and bruises. While there was a suggestion that Green would often walk into the bathroom when the girls were naked, Green denied these events and any voyeuristic or other illicit purpose.

Green is now 63 years old. He owned a successful hardware store in a small town from 1974 to his retirement in 1994. He was a hockey coach, a member of the Rotary, and a supporter of local charities. In 1986 he was selected as Man of the Year for his work on the new hospital wing. Although it is not well known, Green has had an alcohol problem all his adult life. When Doris first advised Green in 1994 that she had talked to the police about these events, he sought psychiatric help and began attending AA. Green's counsel has advised the court that the beatings occurred when Green was drunk. He has a previous record of two common assaults, one in 1954 and one in 1956 for which he received a $25 and $50 fine, respectively. In 1988, he was convicted of impaired driving.

After the preliminary inquiry, Green wrote a lengthy letter of apology to both Helen and Doris. Doris does not want to see Green go to jail, but wants the community "to know Green for the cruel man he is." Helen, who has had a very difficult life, has written that "Green should pay for the harm he has caused. Only a long jail term will be sufficient." Green pleaded guilty at trial.

2. Smith has been convicted of two counts of fraud that occurred in 1979, and one in 1981. Each offence involved $10,000. The victims were Mrs. Wilson and Mrs. Stein. In 1979, Smith was involved in a large land-development project. He had been promised substantial financing from ABC Investments Inc. and was very optimistic that everyone who participated in his project would earn a lot of money. To raise the small amount not covered by ABC, he started to sell units at $10,000 each. In 1979, he approached Mrs. Wilson and Mrs. Stein, two of his clients. They were both widows in their late 60s. When they expressed concern about the risk, Smith told them that the investments were insured and that the principal could always be recovered. He sold them each one unit for $10,000. Although Smith believed the investment was safe because of ABC's backing, there was no insurance.

That was a lie. In 1980, the president of ABC died before providing the capital. Smith approached Mrs. Wilson in 1981 and sold her another unit, repeating that the investment was insured. The project failed in 1983 and all funds were lost.

Mrs. Stein died in 1986. She had been living on her old-age pension and the $10,000 was her entire life savings. When Mrs. Stein's daughter learned of the fraud, she told the police that, because of the investment, her mother had to discontinue her July vacations to Lake Simcoe, where she had been going for the past 15 years to escape the city heat. She said, "Smith should be in jail for robbing my mother." Mrs. Wilson was still alive and was a wealthy woman. She advised that the $20,000 meant nothing to her. Smith had been a "good lad, always ready with a joke to warm a dull day" and she did not want to see him hurt.

Smith entered guilty pleas shortly after the preliminary inquiry. He voluntarily sent payments of $2,000 each to Mrs. Wilson and to Mrs. Stein's daughter. He explained that, at the time of the offence, he had many projects on the go and many debts. He was shocked that the project failed and never intended to harm anyone. At the time he was drinking heavily, but in 1985 sought help for his alcohol problem.

Smith is now 58 years old. He had been a good father to his four children. He had a career as a lawyer and financial adviser, which was sometimes successful but was now over. After the charges, he resigned from the Law Society and now works as the night manager of a hotel. Smith had been involved with his community throughout his life. He volunteered with local sports leagues and gave to local charities. Now, his counsel argued, "his good deeds were forgotten and his reputation was ruined."

In 1969, before he entered law school, Smith was charged with trafficking in narcotics and conspiracy to traffick along with a number of other people. The serious charges were withdrawn when a major prosecution witness disappeared. Smith pleaded guilty to possession of a narcotic (marijuana) and was fined $500. In 1982, his name was publicly linked to various municipal politicians by journalists who tried to show that Smith had been extending various gifts to them. No charges were laid but two politicians resigned their offices.

3. Ferris has pleaded guilty to assaulting his estranged spouse. They had agreed to meet to discuss financial arrangements for their two children. While having a cup of coffee, his spouse told him she needed more money. Ferris said that he would talk to his lawyer but that business had been bad. (He was an electrician who had become an electrical contractor.) As they were leaving the coffee shop an altercation took place. According to Frank, he removed his wallet to pay the bill and she grabbed for the wallet saying, "Do you still carry wads of money?" Her account was that she asked to see his wallet and did not make a grab for it. Frank grabbed her by the shoulders and threw her down.

Ferris is 38 years old with no prior record. He was charged with assaulting an employee in 1997, but the charge was withdrawn when the employee did not attend for his trial.

Since the assault, he attempted to persuade his spouse not to proceed with the charges but she refused. He threatened to stop making his maintenance payments but, in fact, has continued them at an increased level. A few weeks ago, he jumped into a creek to rescue an infant who had fallen in. This kind of heroic behaviour is not new. He received a civic medal for rescuing a man from a burning car in 1996.

Although he and his wife are separated, he has continued his relationship with his children. He went to a psychologist for anger-management counselling once. Since the offence, he has been charged with another assault arising from an argument over a parking space. (It is alleged that he jumped from his truck and punched a driver who had taken a space that he was waiting for.)

4. Harry had a great time at university in the late 1960s. One "down" episode was when he was arrested for possessing an ounce of marijuana. At the time, some judges were participating in a mini-version of the war on drugs. As a result, he was sentenced in 1968 to 30 days in jail. While judicial attitudes toward possession of marijuana ameliorated substantially, the same could not be said for trafficking. In 1972, Harry was convicted of possession for the purposes of trafficking when a parcel containing two kilograms of marijuana was seized after being delivered to his home. For this offence, he was sentenced to 12 months' imprisonment.

After his release from prison, Harry completed his B.Comm. degree and obtained an MBA at a prestigious business school. He redirected his entrepreneurial skills and ambitions and started to work for a stock brokerage firm. By 1990, he had made a fortune. He and his wife decided to retire to the country. They purchased a huge farm and built a new home on the property. It was a huge house on a hill with dozens of windows looking out over a lush valley. They kept horses, sheep, and llamas. They grew their own vegetables and even used a windmill to generate electricity.

In June 2007, the local RCMP drug squad executed a search warrant on an expensive downtown condominium apartment in Toronto. After seizing a few pounds of marijuana, the Mounties began interrogating the occupier of the premises trying to obtain information. The man named Harry as his source of supply. (Harry denies knowing this man or ever having met him.) Armed with a search warrant, the RCMP officers travelled to Harry's farm where they found four huge underground rooms devoted entirely to growing marijuana. They contained hundreds of plants of all sizes, at various stages of development. Specialized areas were set aside for drying and packing. Sergeant Turnbull, a Mountie with 25 years' experience, said: "This is the most sophisticated grow operation I have ever seen." He estimated that the plants could be translated into a value of $100,000 on the street. Harry and his wife were charged with "production" contrary to s. 7(2)(b) of the *Controlled Drugs and Substances Act*. It was agreed that Harry would plead guilty and the charge against his wife would be withdrawn.

Harry is now 59 years old. Other than a conviction for mischief to property ($500 fine) arising from a political demonstration in 1995, his record consists of the two drug convictions in 1968 and 1972. Harry has been self-supporting since his retirement. Along with his wife, Anne, he has been active in the life of their rural community. They were the prime movers in starting a food bank and are directors of the annual arts festival. Harry is an active volunteer with various environmental groups and has turned a large portion of his acreage to solar power collection so that he can do his bit to fight global warming. Harry and Anne have recently adopted two young orphans, three and eight years old, from a third-world country. At the moment, the children only speak French. Harry is bilingual, but Anne is a unilingual Anglophone.

Harry's counsel submitted that a conditional sentence was an appropriate disposition, especially given his child-care obligations and his commitment to pro-social activities. The prosecutor submitted that a deterrent sentence was needed, especially given the planning, profit potential, and sheer size of the operation. He suggested two to three years' imprisonment. When asked if he had anything to say, Harry commented:

> Marijuana is a natural substance which is helpful to many sick and disabled people. Our goal was to ensure access to this beneficial plant. I stand before this court as a victim of narrow-minded and oppressive governmental policies. Thank you, Your Honour, for permitting me to express my views.

Identify the relevant mitigating and aggravating factors.

FURTHER READING

Ashworth, A. "Aggravation and Mitigation," in *Sentencing and Criminal Justice*, 4th ed. (Cambridge: Cambridge University Press, 2005), chapter 5.

Walker, N. "Aggravation, Mitigation, and Mercy," in *Criminal Justice* (London: Blackstone Press, 1999).

CHAPTER FOUR

Facts of the Offence for Sentencing

I. INTRODUCTION

The sentencing hearing follows a finding of guilt. That finding might be the result of a trial in which the trier of fact has found that the guilt of the accused has been proved beyond reasonable doubt. Alternatively, and this covers most cases, a finding of guilt is made after the accused enters a plea of guilty. In either case, once there is a finding of guilt, the trial judge must consider and pronounce sentence. However, this cannot be done unless the judge has factual information about the offender and the offence. This chapter primarily considers the manner in which facts about the commission of an offence are put in evidence at the time of sentence, but it also considers more broadly the manner in which disputed facts are put in evidence at the sentencing hearing.[1]

Where a finding of guilt is made following a guilty plea, there has been no trial of the general issue. The plea is a formal admission of the averments in the information or indictment.[2] These averments typically disclose little more than the name of the offender, the offence, and the event to which it relates. Thus it is incumbent on the court to inquire into the facts concerning the offence and the offender. Where there has been a trial, most relevant facts will have emerged in evidence already, although there might yet be information relevant to sentence that has not been adduced. Further difficulties can arise in cases of trial by jury. The trial judge, of course, is bound to impose a sentence that is consistent with the jury's verdict. The verdict typically leaves no doubt about the relevant findings, but there are cases where the findings underlying the verdict are ambiguous or unclear. Apart from facts essential to the verdict, there are often other facts disclosed by the evidence that will be material for purposes of sentencing.

II. THE SENTENCING HEARING

A judge who is properly seized of jurisdiction to record a finding of guilt is compelled to pronounce sentence and until then there is no final judgment in the matter.[3] Although this

---

[1]   With respect to fact finding concerning the offender and the victim, see chapter 5, Sources of Information Relating to the Offender.

[2]   Guilty pleas are discussed in chapter 7, Plea Discussions and Joint Submissions.

[3]   See Criminal Code, RSC 1985, c. C-46, as amended, s. 720, reproduced later in this chapter.

principle applies in all cases, sentencing hearings can take different forms. There are many high-volume courts where the disposition of cases, including sentencing hearings that follow guilty pleas, appears almost perfunctory. Pleas are recorded at speed; sentences are pronounced quickly and with a minimum of reflection. So, too, in straightforward cases, where the parties have nothing to add following the production of evidence at trial, the judge will often proceed directly to sentence unless counsel seek a postponement in order to prepare submissions. In other cases, at the request of counsel or the judge, a future date might be set for a sentencing hearing in which the parties may present evidence and submissions that are relevant to an appropriate disposition.

A conviction is not perfected until and unless there has been both a recorded finding of guilt and the pronouncement of a lawful sentence. The Code provides basic principles of law and procedure, but sentencing practice also varies from jurisdiction to jurisdiction. The significance of this point is not merely formal or technical. A finding of guilt is a necessary condition for the imposition of a sentence but, excepting mandatory minimum sentences, the finding does not of itself determine a sentence, let alone a fit sentence, for the offence or the offender. The determination of a sentence is an integral but distinct aspect of judgment in criminal cases. In this aspect of adjudication, the law requires judges to respond to the offender's wrongdoing in a manner that reflects accepted principles of sentencing.

III. THE FACTUAL BASIS OF SENTENCING

In *R v. Gobin*, below, Huband JA summarized the standard procedure for submissions on sentence and noted that it is the same whether there has been a finding of guilt after trial or on a guilty plea.

R v. Gobin
(1993), 85 CCC (3d) 481 (Man. CA)

HUBAND JA: ...

[2] Usually Crown counsel and defence counsel will agree on the factual circumstances relating to the commission of the offence. Those will be outlined to the Court, and counsel will make their submissions on that factual foundation.

[3] Where there is no firm agreement, Crown counsel is entitled to put forth the prosecution's understanding of the facts. It is open to defence counsel to make a submission based upon a different and less aggravated version of facts, so long as it is consistent with the wording of the indictment to which the plea of guilty has been entered.

[4] If the Crown wishes to contest the accused's version, evidence must be tendered to support the more aggravated scenario. The accused can, of course, then elect to produce evidence to support his version.

[5] If the Crown does not call evidence to support the more aggravated circumstances, then the accused's description of events is to be accepted, unless there is some manifest reason why that interpretation of the facts is contrived or erroneous.

. . .

[7] The question raised on this appeal is whether those same principles hold when the accused is found guilty after a trial rather than by entering a plea.

. . .

[21] The fact that the Crown was put to the task of proving the case against the accused does not change the basic rules. If a plea of guilty had been entered, Crown counsel would have been in a position to recount the circumstances much as they were revealed in the testimony of witnesses, and defence counsel would have been entitled to make his submission.

To determine an appropriate sentence the court must have relevant information. If this is not found in the evidence at trial or in an agreed statement of facts by the parties, additional evidence must be produced. Such evidence will be produced by the parties if they wish, but the judge may also request that parties produce evidence for purposes of sentencing. There might be no dispute between the parties regarding the evidence, but often there is. While the evidence for sentencing cannot contradict the facts that support the finding of guilt, it will have a decisive effect on the severity of the sentence.

R v. Gardiner
[1982] 2 SCR 368

[Gardiner pleaded guilty to a charge of assault causing bodily harm to his wife. At the sentencing hearing, Gardiner's testimony conflicted with that of the victim as to the circumstances of the offence. The trial judge accepted the evidence of the victim and held that the standard of proof was that of a balance of probabilities.]

DICKSON J (Martland, Ritchie and Chouinard JJ concurring):

. . .

In *Principles of Sentencing*, 2nd ed. (1970), Professor D.A. Thomas speaks at pp. 366-7 of an "evolving body of principle designed to ensure that the version of the facts adopted for the purpose of sentence is supported by evidence and reached according to appropriate procedural standards." One of those evolving principles, lying at the heart of this appeal, concerns the standard of proof to be applied for establishing aggravating facts that, while not affecting guilt or innocence, do have a critical effect on the length of sentence.

. . .

The Burden of Proof

A. Introduction

The question now to be addressed is this: What burden of proof must the Crown sustain in advancing contested aggravating facts in a sentencing proceeding, for the purpose of supporting a lengthier sentence; is the standard that of the criminal law, proof beyond a reasonable doubt, or that of the civil law, proof on a balance of probabilities?

The Crown [appellant] argues for the acceptance of a lesser onus of proof at sentencing than the traditional criminal onus of beyond a reasonable doubt, which applies at trial to the determination of guilt.

Relying heavily on American authorities, the Crown suggests that there is a sharp demarcation between the trial process and the sentencing process. Once a plea or finding of guilty is entered, the presumption of innocence no longer operates and the necessity of the full panoply of procedural protection for the accused ceases. Sentencing is a discretionary and highly subjective exercise on the part of the trial judge. The primary concern at a sentencing hearing is the availability of accurate information upon which the trial judge can rely in determining an appropriate sentence in the particular circumstances of the offender. For this reason the strict rules on the admissibility of evidence are relaxed. The trial judge is no longer confined to the narrow issue of guilt but is engaged in the difficult task of fitting the punishment to the person convicted. To require that the Crown prove contested issues beyond a reasonable doubt would be to complicate and extend sentencing hearings and convert the sentencing process into a second trial, with a resultant loss of economy.

In the event that the essentially civil onus of preponderance of evidence is rejected, the Crown proposes, in the alternative, an "intermediate" standard of "clear and convincing" evidence to apply to sentencing hearings.

The respondent [accused], on the other hand, argues for the application of the reasonable doubt standard to sentencing hearings. The "bifurcation" between trial and sentencing, proposed by the Crown, the respondent finds artificial and against the authorities. From the offender's point of view, sentencing is the most critical part of the whole trial process, it is the "gist of the proceeding," and the standard of proof required with respect to controverted facts should not be relaxed at this point. To do so is prejudicial to the accused. Administrative efficiency is insufficient justification for so radical a departure from the traditional criminal onus of beyond a reasonable doubt.

· · ·

[Dickson J then reviewed authorities in Canada, England, the United States, and elsewhere.]

· · ·

F. The Principles

Sentencing is part of a fact-finding, decision-making process of the criminal law. Sir James Fitzjames Stephen, writing in 1863 [in "The Punishment of Convicts," *Cornhill Magazine* 189], said (quoted in Olah, "Sentencing: The Last Frontier of the Criminal Law" (1980), 16 CR (3d) 97, at p. 98) that: "the sentence is the gist of the proceeding. It is to the trial what the bullet is to the powder." The statement is equally true today.

One of the hardest tasks confronting a trial judge is sentencing. The stakes are high for society and for the individual. Sentencing is the critical stage of the criminal justice system, and it is manifest that the judge should not be denied an opportunity to obtain relevant information by the imposition of all the restrictive evidential rules common to a trial. Yet the obtaining and weighing of such evidence should be fair. A substantial liberty interest of the offender is involved and the information obtained should be accurate and reliable.

It is a commonplace that the strict rules which govern at trial do not apply at a sentencing hearing and it would be undesirable to have the formalities and technicalities characteristic of the normal adversary proceeding prevail. The hearsay rule does not govern the sentencing hearing. Hearsay evidence may be accepted where found to be credible and trustworthy. The judge traditionally has had wide latitude as to the sources and types of evidence upon which to base his sentence. He must have the fullest possible information concerning the background of the accused if he is to fit the sentence to the offender rather than to the crime.

It is well to recall in any discussion of sentencing procedures that the vast majority of offenders plead guilty. Canadian figures are not readily available but American statistics suggest that about 85 *percent* of the criminal defendants plead guilty or *nolo contendere*. The sentencing judge therefore must get his facts after plea. Sentencing is, in respect of most offenders, the only significant decision the criminal justice system is called upon to make.

It should also be recalled that a plea of guilty, in itself, carries with it an admission of the essential legal ingredients of the offence admitted by the plea, and no more. Beyond that, any facts relied upon by the Crown in aggravation must be established by the Crown. If undisputed, the procedure can be very informal. If the facts are contested, the issue should be resolved by ordinary legal principles governing criminal proceedings, including resolving relevant doubt in favour of the offender.

To my mind, the facts which justify the sanction are no less important than the facts which justify the conviction: both should be subject to the same burden of proof. Crime and punishment are inextricably linked. "It would appear well established that the sentencing process is merely a phase of the trial process.": Olah, at p. 107. Upon conviction the accused is not abruptly deprived of all procedural rights existing at trial: he has a right to counsel, a right to call evidence and cross-examine prosecution witnesses, a right to give evidence himself and to address the court.

· · ·

In my view, both the informality of the sentencing procedure as to the admissibility of evidence and the wide discretion given to the trial judge in imposing sentence are factors militating *in favour of* the retention of the criminal standard of proof beyond a reasonable doubt at sentencing. Olah at p. 121:

> [B]ecause the sentencing process poses the ultimate jeopardy to an individual enmeshed in the criminal process, it is just and reasonable that he be granted the protection of the reasonable doubt rule at this vital juncture of the process.

The rationale of the argument of the Crown for the acceptance of a lesser standard of proof is administrative efficiency. In my view, however, the administrative efficiency argument is not sufficient to overcome such a basic tenet suffusing our entire criminal justice system as the standard of proof beyond a reasonable doubt. I am by no means convinced that, if the standard of proof were lowered, conservation of judicial resources would be enhanced. In the event of a serious dispute as to facts, it would be in the interests of the accused to plead not guilty in order to benefit at trial from the higher standard of reasonable doubt. This would be not only destructive of judicial economy but at the same time prejudicial to whatever mitigating effect might have come from a guilty plea, as evidence of remorse.

[Dickson J then rejected a lesser standard than proof beyond a reasonable doubt in respect of aggravating facts.]

Appeal dismissed.

NOTE

Few sentencing cases involve a formal evidentiary hearing. More often, the trial judge will proceed informally to hear submissions on sentence once a finding of guilt has been made. The following case considers what should be done when conflicts arise as to the factual basis of a sentence and no evidence has been called on the points in dispute.

R v. Poorman
(1991), 6 CR (4th) 364 (Sask. CA)

VANCISE JA: The appellant was charged with assault causing bodily harm, entered a plea of guilty and was sentenced to 9 months consecutive to any sentence currently being served.

He appeals, contending that the sentence was excessive in the circumstances.

During the oral sentencing presentation by the Crown and defence, the trial Judge was presented with conflicting statements of the circumstances surrounding the offence: the circumstances alleged by the Crown which, if accepted, must be considered as aggravating; and the circumstances alleged by the defence which, if accepted, would be mitigating. No sentencing hearing was held to resolve this apparent conflict.

Thus, this Court is once again called upon to comment upon and set out the procedure to be followed by trial judges during oral informal sentencing submissions when confronted with conflicting submissions, material, or assertions surrounding the commission of the offence or the personal circumstances of the accused. The issue encompasses not only the procedures to follow but the power of the trial judge to resolve conflicting assertions and facts which do not go to guilt or innocence but which have or could have a critical effect on the length of the sentence.

Facts

Mr. Poorman and the victim, Mr. Elaschuk, were serving prisoners in the Regina Correctional Centre at the time of the offence. On the day in question, Mr. Poorman was in a common area of the Correctional Centre watching television when Mr. Elaschuk and some other inmates entered the area. The Crown prosecutor contends that Mr. Poorman got up from his chair, walked to where he, the victim, and his friends were seated, and for no reason and without any warning or provocation struck the victim in the face, breaking his glasses and inflicting a 1-inch-long wound which bled profusely. As noted, both counsel gave conflicting versions of the circumstances surrounding the events which took place. In order to appreciate the degree of conflict between the two versions, it is necessary to set out specifically the submissions made by both sides.

The Crown, after narrating the facts in the previous paragraph, stated that Mr. Elaschuk then asked the appellant why he hit him and continued with the following submission:

> What he describes following that is the Accused grabbing him and holding what the victim called a knife, a butter knife that they use in their eating routine, holding this thing into his back and forcing him from the common area into a cell, delivering to him a Kleenex, or having someone deliver Kleenex or toilet paper or something like that to him, telling him "close up the bleeding and don't say anything of this to the guards or—" He threatened to stick him with the knife. And stated that, you know, that he had done this before and he'd be prepared to do it again.
>
> . . .

There had been no communication between these persons even as acquainted residents in the unit, and the victim has testified that there was no oral or gesturing provocation whatever to this. There appears to have been no reason for this.

He submitted:

> In sentencing, the Court is asked to consider the particular circumstances as between victim and Accused here being, in essence, strangers, the absence of anything provocative on the part of the victim orally or in gesture, the apparent absence of any reason for the—the assault, the potential danger that could have resulted from the location of the assault, the location of the injury from the assault. It's fortunate that he is not injured more so from the blow in the glasses that were worn. I believe the glasses were filed in exhibit at Preliminary Hearing and should be here at Court.
>
> The Court is also asked to consider significant, very significant, the setting in which this occurs; at the correctional centre as—between inmates.

The appellant's counsel also made oral submissions. The relevant portion is as follows:

> MS. MALONEY: First of all, My Lord, with respect to the circumstances of the offence I wish to emphasize that this assault is a single blow, minor injuries. There were no stitches or anything of that sort required, no effect on this person's eyesight or anything of that nature, and that Mr. Poorman was acting alone. He had not ganged upon this person, so to speak, by means of acting in concert with anyone else.
>
> Mr. Poorman has maintained from the outset that there was never any knife involved, never any weapon of any sort involved. What he does indicate is that there is some background to this assault, to this single blow that he administered to the complainant in the area where they were all watching television.
>
> My client indicates that there was some provocation, or at least some—

> THE COURT: Now, whoa.

MS. MALONEY: ... some situation that resulted in him being angry.

THE COURT: I'm wondering, then, whether—are you so questioning the facts given to me by the Crown that perhaps we should vacate the not guilty plea.

MS. MALONEY: No, My Lord.

THE COURT: Excuse me, the guilty plea.

MS. MALONEY: It's not my intention to dispute that Mr. Poorman is guilty of an assault causing bodily harm in this situation. There is some background, though, that should have some bearing. I would suggest, in terms of trying to afford the Court some understanding—

THE COURT: Okay.

MS. MALONEY: ... of the context in which to place its sentencing.

My client indicates that the complainant had made an advance to him by touching him in a way that Mr. Poorman perceived as a sexual touching and as a result he flared up in anger and struck the person the single blow. It was impulsive and in some anger, certainly. But the situation was not prolonged. As I indicated it was a single striking motion.

The Crown replied to the issue of the knife and the provocation as follows:

If I may respond to some of my friend's comments, My Lord, before filing the record. Concerning the knife, I don't think anything significant turns on the Crown's submission concerning the knife aspect of this, and my friend's response is that that is not the item for sentencing before the Court, that aspect is—was stayed this morning, *there is that dimension to the story, though, and it is in opposition. There is issue on the fact there.*

Concerning the item of provocation that my friend raises there is issue in that regard. The Crown represents there was nothing provocative said or done prior to this. If that causes the Court a distress in considering sentence the victim is present and prepared to testify, as is the Accused present and able to testify if he chooses. [Emphasis added]

The Crown prosecutor went on to state on issue of provocation:

I invite the Court to hear evidence on the issue of provocation (inaudible—not near microphone). If it is not a matter of distress to the Court in sentencing then certainly the Crown will not proffer the evidence.

There was an adjournment, and when the proceedings resumed, and before sentencing, the appellant, in response to an invitation from the trial Judge to speak, again raised the issue of provocation in these terms:

Yes, Your Honour. Yes, I do. This assault wasn't (inaudible—not near microphone) mention a few facts about what I told that evolved around the assault. (Inaudible—not near microphone) time the assault happened we were sitting around the TV area and the victim was sitting behind me talking to somebody and they were talking about the use of jails (inaudible—not near microphone) and I turned around and told them "You guys want to keep it down." And I got up and I walked away and then (inaudible—not near microphone) I was leaving he touched me. That's when I blew up, you know. And that's what— that's what provoked me.

Thus there is a clear contradiction on two issues: (a) the presence of a knife; and (b) provocation. The trial Judge was invited to order a hearing on the issue of provocation but declined. It is not clear from the transcript whether he declined because he had resolved the issue contrary to the interests of the appellant or whether he considered it was not relevant in the circumstances.

Disposition

There are two questions raised here: (1) the power of the trial judge to resolve conflicting oral submissions on informal sentencing presentations; and (2) the procedure to be followed in informal sentencing hearings. Dickson J (as he then was) considered the standard of proof which is applicable on a sentencing hearing in *R v. Gardiner*, [1982] 2 SCR 368, 30 CR (3d) 289, 140 DLR (3d) 612, 68 CCC (2d) 477, 43 NR 361. In that case, he was dealing with a formal sentencing hearing and considered the onus and standard of proof.

. . .

The Court was not required to consider the procedure where there is a conflict between the Crown and the defence version of facts which are not crucial for the determination of guilt or innocence in an informal sentencing hearing. Bayda CJS considered the issue at length in *Canada (Attorney General) v. Boulet* (*sub nom. R v. Boulet*) (1990), 78 CR (3d) 309, 58 CCC (3d) 178, 85 Sask. R 93 (CA) (in dissent on other issues). The other two members of the panel disagreed with the result reached by the Chief Justice respecting the fitness of the sentence under appeal and specifically stated that they found it unnecessary to consider the principles stated by him respecting the rules, power of the trial judge to resolve questions of dispute, and the procedure to be followed in a sentencing hearing. In this case, it is not necessary to consider the issue in as detailed a fashion as did the Chief Justice, but it is useful to refer to some of the cases and comments that he referred to. The Chief Justice referred to the English cases of *R v. Newton* (1982), 77 Cr. App. R 13; and *Williams v. R* (1984), 77 Cr. App. R 329 (Div. Ct.) which set out the law of England as it relates to the powers of a trial judge to resolve conflicting versions of fact made during an informal sentencing hearing.

In *Newton*, the Lord Chief Justice of England set out the choices available to a trial in similar circumstances. Two of the three choices he commented upon are relevant in Canada. He stated at p. 15:

> The second method which would be adopted by the judge in these circumstances is himself to hear the evidence on one side and another, and come to his own conclusion, acting so to speak as his own jury on the issue which is the root of the problem.

The third option he described as follows:

> The third possibility in these circumstances is for him to hear no evidence but to listen to the submissions of counsel and then come to a conclusion. But if he does that, then ... where there is a substantial conflict between the two sides, he must come down on the side of the defendant. In other words where there has been a substantial conflict, the version of the defendant must so far as possible be accepted.

Thus in this case, if the trial Judge was of the opinion that the matter should have been resolved, his choice was to "so far as possible accept" the version of the accused and sentence him on that version of the facts, or, if he was not of the opinion that he could resolve the matter on that basis, he would hear the sworn evidence, resolve the dispute, and then sentence the accused. In *Williams*, supra, the Crown made certain statements not proved by evidence nor admitted by the accused, and the accused declined an invitation to have the disputed issues tried. The Crown submitted that because the accused had failed to call evidence as was suggested by the Crown, the version of the Crown should be accepted. Lord Justice Goff, in dealing with the procedures suggested by the Crown, said the following:

> [I]n my judgment, following the principles stated by the Lord Chief Justice in *Newton* ... the Court had really only two courses open to it, assuming, as I do, that there has been a sharp divergence or substantial conflict: either to listen to submissions on both sides and proceed on the basis that the version the defendant should, as far as possible, be accepted or, if the court was not prepared to do that, then to hear evidence. It may be that such evidence, when called, will be very slight; it may be that it will be the subject of cross-examination and no evidence will be called in contradiction. But even so, given the sharp divergence or substantial conflict and given the fact that the court is not prepared to proceed on the basis that the defendant's version is substantially correct, the Court must, it seems to me, hear the evidence before forming its own view in respect of the matter which is in dispute.
>
> As did Bayda CJS, we adopt these principles and hold that where there is a divergence of opinion or conflict of evidence not proven, the trial judge must not accept the Crown's version of the unproven facts as related at an informal hearing. If there is substantial conflict he must either: (1) hold a formal sentencing hearing at which time the Crown must prove the facts alleged on the criminal standard of proof, that is, beyond a reasonable doubt; or, (2) "so far as possible," accept the accused's version of the facts stated at the informal hearing, at which there is no evidence.
>
> In this case, there were two disputed issues surrounding the circumstances of the offence which do not bear on the guilt or innocence of the appellant but which could affect the length of the sentence: the possession of the knife by the appellant at the time of the commission of the offence and the threat to use it if the victim "ratted"; and, whether the appellant was provoked as a result of the overtures of a homosexual nature which he alleges were made by the victim before he, the appellant, smacked him in the face.
>
> The trial Judge, in sentencing the appellant to 9 months imprisonment consecutive to any other sentence he is currently serving, did not accept the version of the facts of the appellant. In our view, in circumstances such as this he should have ordered a sentencing hearing, at which point the Crown could call evidence on the disputed facts and appellant could call evidence or at the very least cross-examine the witnesses proffered by the Crown.
>
> The sentence of 9 months consecutive is therefore set aside and the matter is remitted to the trial Judge for the holding of a sentencing hearing to determine the proper sentence to be imposed.

NOTE

The courts have repeatedly stressed that the determination of a fit sentence requires the production of adequate information about the offender and the offence. See, for example, *Gardiner*, above; *R v. Jones*, [1994] 2 SCR 229, at 398; and *R v. Lévesque*, [2000] 2 SCR 487, para. 30. This requirement is reflected in the reforms of 1996. Part XXIII of the *Criminal Code* codifies in part the procedure that should be followed to establish the factual basis for sentencing. Sections 720 to 726.2 of the Code (as amended by SC 1995, c. 22) read as follows:

. . .

720. A court shall, as soon as practicable after an offender has been found guilty, conduct proceedings to determine the appropriate sentence to be imposed.

. . .

723(1) Before determining the sentence, a court shall give the prosecutor and the offender an opportunity to make submissions with respect to any facts relevant to the sentence to be imposed.

(2) The court shall hear any relevant evidence presented by the prosecutor or the offender.

(3) The court may, on its own motion, after hearing argument from the prosecutor and the offender, require the production of evidence that would assist it in determining the appropriate sentence.

(4) Where it is necessary in the interests of justice, the court may, after consulting the parties, compel the appearance of any person who is a compellable witness to assist the court in determining the appropriate sentence.

(5) Hearsay evidence is admissible at sentencing proceedings, but the court may, if the court considers it to be in the interests of justice, compel a person to testify where the person

(a) has personal knowledge of the matter;

(b) is reasonably available; and

(c) is a compellable witness.

724(1) In determining a sentence, a court may accept as proved any information disclosed at the trial or at the sentencing proceedings and any facts agreed on by the prosecutor and the offender.

(2) Where the court is composed of a judge and jury, the court

(a) shall accept as proven all facts, express or implied, that are essential to the jury's verdict of guilty; and

(b) may find any other relevant fact that was disclosed by evidence at the trial to be proven, or hear evidence presented by either party with respect to that fact.

(3) Where there is a dispute with respect to any fact that is relevant to the determination of a sentence,

(a) the court shall request that evidence be adduced as to the existence of the fact unless the court is satisfied that sufficient evidence was adduced at the trial;

(b) the party wishing to rely on a relevant fact, including a fact contained in a presentence report, has the burden of proving it;

(c) either party may cross-examine any witness called by the other party;

(d) subject to paragraph (e), the court must be satisfied on a balance of probabilities of the existence of the disputed fact before relying on it in determining the sentence; and

(e) the prosecutor must establish, by proof beyond a reasonable doubt, the existence of any aggravating fact or any previous conviction by the offender.

• • •

726.1 In determining the sentence, a court shall consider any relevant information placed before it, including any representations or submissions made by or on behalf of the prosecutor or the offender.

726.2 When imposing a sentence, a court shall state the terms of the sentence imposed, and the reasons for it, and enter those terms and reasons into the record of the proceedings.

These provisions restate the conclusions of the Supreme Court in *Gardiner* in general terms. There are, however, some ambiguities in these provisions that merit attention. For example, what is meant by the requirement that disputed but non-aggravating facts need only be proved to a balance of probabilities? If it means that disputed mitigating facts must be proved by the offender on a balance of probabilities, does this not diminish the principle that underlies *Gardiner*? It may be argued that *Gardiner* was concerned specifically with aggravating factors but that the court's observations concerning the application of the higher criminal standard addressed all situations. Moreover, in *R v. Pearson*, [1992] 3 SCR 665, Lamer CJC suggested that the Crown's obligation was a principle of fundamental justice within the meaning of s. 7 of the *Canadian Charter of Rights and Freedoms*, part I of the *Constitution Act, 1982*, RSC 1985, app. II, no. 44. Does this mean that the validity of s. 724(3)(d) is open to challenge as being inconsistent with principles of fundamental justice? Also at the core of these considerations is a concern about the nature and scope of the presumption of innocence following a finding of guilt. While that finding establishes the offender's liability, the sentencing decision must reflect the offender's culpability in the commission of the offence.

As noted in *Gardiner*, the courts have long held that the strict rules of admissibility at trial do not apply in the sentencing hearing. There is some analogy, therefore, to principles that apply in bail hearings. Section 723(5) expressly allows the judge to receive and consider hearsay, thus relaxing an exclusionary principle that has greater force at trial. Section 726.1 allows the court to consider "any relevant information that is placed before it." Information in this context is a broader concept than evidence that is admissible under strict rules of admissibility at trial. Although the range of information that may be considered at the sentencing hearing is broad, it is not without constraint.[4] A heightened degree of reliability and persuasiveness is necessary, obviously, where aggravating factors are in dispute. Furthermore, no degree of reliability or persuasiveness would entitle a judge to consider information that tends only to support conclusions expressly rejected in determining the finding of guilt. Finally, the requirement to give reasons (s. 726.2) will also force judges to

---

[4] In *R v. Hunter* (1997), 11 CR (5th) 156 (Alta. QB), the court noted, too, that the power to compel the production of information in a sentencing hearing requires some "logical nexus" between what is ordered and issues that are properly before the sentencing judge.

note the factual considerations that are the basis for sentencing decisions. Indeed, this might be one of the most important effects of this requirement.

The Code and the cases address distinctions that affect the factual basis for sentencing. Was the trial before a jury, or before a judge alone? Are the facts for sentencing disputed, and, if so, are the facts aggravating or mitigating?

R v. Brown
[1991] 2 SCR 518

STEVENSON J: The accused appeals, by leave, a sentence of 12 months' imprisonment for dangerous driving imposed at trial and affirmed on appeal by a divided Court of Appeal [reported (1990), 75 CR (3d) 76; 23 MVR (2d) 89; 53 CCC (3d) 521; 81 Sask. R 295]. The issue is whether the trial Judge and the majority of the Court of Appeal erred in considering the consequences of death and bodily injury when the jury had acquitted the accused of dangerous driving causing death and bodily injury.

The accused was the driver of a motor vehicle involved in a collision with another motor vehicle. As a result of the collision, two passengers in the other vehicle died and two others were injured.

The accused was initially charged with two counts of causing death by criminal negligence. This was reduced by the preliminary inquiry Judge to dangerous driving causing death. Shortly before the trial, a new indictment was filed, adding two additional counts of dangerous driving causing bodily injury.

At the trial, the Crown argued that the accused was speeding and had driven through a red light, that this manner of driving was dangerous, and that the dangerous driving had caused the collision and resulted in death and injuries. The defence argued that the appellant was not exceeding the speed limit by an excessive amount, nor did he disobey the traffic light. Moreover, the defence urged that the manner of the appellant's driving was not causally connected to the collision or the deaths or the injuries.

The jury found the accused not guilty of causing death or bodily injury by dangerous driving but guilty of the included offences of dangerous driving, simpliciter.

On sentencing, the trial Judge noted that deterrence was the element that was most significant in this case and then turned to various relevant facts. The appellant's traffic infractions, he said, "do reflect some disregard for the rules to be obeyed in driving a vehicle." He then commented that:

> Now in this case, under the jury, they found you guilty of dangerous driving alone. And it's probably fortunate for you that they did. But the facts still are that two people died as the result—or following that collision. And two others suffer injuries that they are still being treated for today.

Included in the case on appeal was a letter or report written by the trial Judge to the Court of Appeal, which contains the following statement:

Nothing is clearer than the death and injuries to the four victims arose directly from that collision. It was a flagrant example of dangerous driving taking all the circumstances into account.

Before the Court of Appeal, the accused argued that the sentence was excessive for dangerous driving, simpliciter. The majority of the Court of Appeal noted that, "If the [accused] is correct, the sentence here does not bear an acceptable comparison [to other cases]."

In the Court of Appeal, the majority upheld the trial Judge's sentence. In the course of his majority judgment Wakeling JA said:

> The appellant suggests that the trial judge's right is restricted severely because if he goes too far he is basing the sentence on facts which must have been rejected by the jury, otherwise the lesser verdict of dangerous driving would not have been rendered. The Crown says the trial judge not only can but has a duty to consider all of the evidence in order to determine a proper sentence, which evidence includes the fact the accused is at least partly to blame for a serious accident which took two lives. If the appellant is correct, the sentence here does not bear an acceptable comparison to such cases. ... If the Crown is correct, then the sentence is not exceptional when compared to cases in which the consequences are similar to those involved in this case.

In dissent, Tallis JA noted the Judge's obligation to respect the jury verdict, which expressly rejected any causal connection between the way he was driving and the deaths and injuries, and concluded the sentence should have been reduced to 6 months' imprisonment.

The majority referred to an apparent divergence between English and Australian courts on the position to be taken regarding findings of fact by a sentencer when the determination of guilt has been made by a jury. Clayton C. Ruby, *Sentencing*, 3d ed. (Toronto: Butterworths, 1987), at pp. 61-62; D.A. Thomas, *Principles of Sentencing*, 2d ed. (London: Heinemann, 1979), at p. 367; and *Tremblay v. R* (1969), 7 CRNS 315 (Que. CA), were cited.

The divergence to which the majority of the Court of Appeal referred centres on the question of whether the judge is bound to assume that the jury took the most lenient view of the facts which would support the verdict. That issue does not arise here because the only factual question relates to the consequences, and on that factual question the jury's decision is not in doubt. Thomas makes it clear that subject to the jury's express and implied factual findings, the judge must make the necessary sentencing findings. He or she must, of course, make those findings in keeping with the law relating to the finding of facts on sentencing set out in *R v. Gardiner*, [1982] 2 SCR 368, 30 CR (3d) 289, 140 DLR (3d) 612, 68 CCC (2d) 477, 43 NR 361, which establishes that while all credible and trustworthy evidence may be accepted, disputed facts relied upon by the Crown in aggravation must be established beyond a reasonable doubt.

In *Tremblay*, supra, the trial Judge, in sentencing for a manslaughter conviction, expressed his opinion that the accused was guilty of deliberate murder. The majority of the Court of Appeal decided not to interfere with the sentence on the basis that rid of references or expressions of opinion to give the accused's acts the character of murder, the acts were sufficiently grave to justify the sentence (a maximum). The dissenting Judge found that the sentence was not fit and that it was influenced by the conclusion that the acts were murder. The majority thus found the sentence was "fit," untainted by impermissible considerations.

Before us, the parties were agreed that there is no relevant difference between the English and Australian positions. In its factum filed here, the Crown set out the English position, again quoting Thomas from an article, "Establishing a Factual Basis for Sentencing" [1970] Crim. LR 80, at p. 82, where he says:

> [T]he Court of Appeal has developed the principle that where the factual implication of the jury's verdict is clear, the sentencer is bound to accept it and a sentence which is excessive in the light of the facts implied in the verdict will be reduced. ... This principle can only apply however where the factual implication of the jury's verdict is clear; where ... the factual implication is ambiguous, the court has held that the sentencer should not attempt to follow the logical process of the jury, but may come to his own independent determination of the relevant facts.

This statement reflects the correct principle, namely, that the sentencer is bound by the express and implied factual implications of the jury's verdict. There are other authorities to the same effect: *R v. Speid* (1985), 46 CR (3d) 22, 9 OAC 237, 20 CCC (3d) 534 (CA) at p. 47 [CR]; Kevin Boyle and M.J. Aiken, *Sentencing Law and Practice* (London: Sweet & Maxwell, 1985), at pp. 225, 227 and 229; Richard George Fox and Arie Freiberg, *Sentencing: State & Federal Law in Victoria* (Melbourne: Oxford University Press, 1985), at p. 48; Eric Stockdale and Keith Devlin, *Sentencing* (London: Waterloo, 1987), at p. 62.

The Crown, here, took a different position, namely, that the "narrow question" was whether the jury's verdict was ambiguous, leaving the sentencing Judge free to make an independent determination. The argument is that the Judge did not adequately describe the test for causation set out in *R v. Smithers*, [1978] 1 SCR 506, 40 CRNS 79, 15 NR 287, 34 CCC (2d) 427, 75 DLR (3d) 321; *R v. Pinske* (1988), 6 MVR (2d) 19, 30 BCLR (2d) 114 (CA), affirmed orally by this Court, [1989] 2 SCR 979, 18 MVR (2d) xxxiv, 100 NR 399, 40 BCLR (2d) 1515. Counsel for the Crown analyzed the jury charge and argued that questions that were asked by the jury indicated that it may not have been properly instructed or that it had misunderstood the law on causation. Those are arguments against the jury's acquittal on the more serious charges and, if correct, would found an appeal of the acquittal. The Crown did not appeal the acquittals for dangerous driving causing death and bodily injury and must accept the verdicts.

The findings of dangerous driving, simpliciter, in the face of the more serious charges leaves no room for speculation. The jury has negated the factor of causation. This verdict was unambiguous and the trial Judge was bound by it. So was the Court of Appeal.

Since Parliament has chosen to make dangerous driving a consequence-related crime, the consequence of death or bodily injury must be taken to be excluded under a determination of guilt of dangerous driving, simpliciter. The Crown, here, conceded that had the accused entered a guilty plea to dangerous driving, simpliciter, it could not argue a more serious sentence based upon these consequences: *R v. Doerksen* (1990),

19 MVR (2d) 16, 62 Man. R (2d) 259, 53 CCC (3d) 509 (CA). There is, in my view, no valid distinction between the two situations.

It follows that the appeal must be allowed. The appellant invites us to substitute an appropriate sentence. The determination of a fit sentence for an offence is generally to be determined by the provincial appellate courts. In my view, Tallis JA has fully considered the matter and determined the fit sentence in Saskatchewan in the circumstances of this offence. I would adopt his conclusion and impose a sentence of 6 months' imprisonment and affirm the driving prohibition of 3 years imposed at trial.

Appeal allowed.

NOTE

At issue in *Brown* was whether the trial judge imposed sentence on an improper factual basis. The Supreme Court leaves no doubt that it is an error of law for the trial judge to take into consideration factors that were specifically rejected by the jury in reaching their verdict. But a more frequent issue in jury trials arises when the jury's findings cannot be identified precisely. In such circumstances, the trial judge must make his or her own findings of fact for the purpose of sentencing. These matters are now partly covered in s. 724 of the *Criminal Code*.

R v. Lawrence
(1987), 58 CR (3d) 71 (Ont. HC)

CAMPBELL J: The jury had a choice of two different bases of manslaughter. The first basis was that the accused shook the child to death. The second basis was that McLeod shook the child to death and he was criminally negligent in failing to prevent her. ... I must therefore determine the findings of fact upon which the accused must be sentenced.

I am satisfied, beyond a reasonable doubt, that Lawrence shook the little girl to death. McLeod testified that he picked up the little girl or knelt or crouched beside her and grabbed her about 9:30 a.m. on 7th March 1986, because she was crying. McLeod testified that he shook her back and forth violently for minutes, despite the baby's crying, despite McLeod's pleas to stop, despite McLeod's threats to call the police and despite her warnings that something would happen to the baby if Lawrence did not stop shaking her. McLeod said that Lawrence shook and shook and kept shaking until the little girl went limp, "like a rag doll," her head flopping back and forth, her feet dragging back and forth across the floor. The baby lapsed into a final and fatal coma, from which she never emerged. She died in hospital some two or three days later, after being on life support machines for some time.

Lawrence testified that he was in the next room within earshot, heard nothing unusual, then was called in, to find the baby in the fatal coma. His testimony that he heard no noise from the next room while Jade Wilson suddenly and silently went into her fatal coma, with no crying from her and no noise from McLeod, is not worthy of belief and does not give rise to a reasonable doubt, in light of the testimony of the sustained and savage violence that was necessary to kill the little girl.

There is evidence, independent of McLeod, of admissions by Lawrence that he shook the child. Even more importantly, there is a powerful body of medical evidence about the cause of death. That evidence, which I accept, is consistent only with McLeod's evidence and is completely inconsistent with the evidence of Lawrence. The medical evidence of the degree of force necessary to cause the fatal injuries, together with the respective versions of McLeod and Lawrence, other pieces of evidence and all the surrounding circumstances, satisfies me beyond a reasonable doubt that the prisoner before the bar, Lawrence, killed the child in essentially the manner described by McLeod.

Dr. Gregory Wilson, the pathologist who conducted the post mortem examination at the Hospital for Sick Children, testified that the cause of death was "shaken child syndrome," in this case a violent shaking that made the brain move back and forth within the bony vault of the skull, causing fatal injuries to the brain. ... He said that the brain injuries which he saw were even more severe than the injuries of a child thrown 40 feet to 50 feet from a car onto concrete. He said the least number of shakes he could give credit to is 50 or 60 shakes, and it could have been 200 or more.

While Dr. Jaffe questioned those conclusions or opinions of Dr. Wilson, the evidence of Dr. Smith, another eminently qualified pathologist, was very definite about the kind of force used. He described as "tremendous" the force that must have been used to kill the little girl. ... [He] used the comparison of children who had fallen from a three-story building. ... He said it would more likely take minutes than seconds to administer the amount of shaking that was required to kill the child. ... He thought that there would be 25 or 30 shakes, probably more than that, and more likely much more than that. ... He testified as to how much violent and repeated directed energy would be required to deliver the fatal shaking.

I conclude, on this evidence, that the shaking administered by Lawrence to the little girl was violent and sustained and pitiless. The extreme violence of the attack on the child is difficult to visualize, let alone to understand. It is only after some reflection on the evidence of Dr. Wilson and Dr. Smith, together with the evidence of McLeod, that one can develop a picture of the prolonged and unremitting savagery of that attack.

This was not the first time that the accused had attacked the little girl. Her body was covered with bruises. McLeod testified as to a systematic series of assaults by the prisoner on the child over a period of some weeks before the culminating and final assault. There were various bruises on the child's arms, corresponding bruises on the left and right side of her abdomen, bruises on the buttocks, bruises on the tops and very significant bruises on the bottom of both feet. There was an abrasion on the big toe of the right foot and an abrasion on the child's hand. There were two head injuries, reflecting a subdural haemorrhage about three weeks old and a subarachnoid haemorrhage about one week old.

I cannot be satisfied on all of the evidence that all of these previous injuries were caused by Lawrence. I am, however, satisfied, beyond a reasonable doubt, that a significant number of them are his work, including the bite mark on the toe and the hand, the bruises on the arms and chest and abdomen, where he held the child at various times while assaulting her, and particularly the bruises on the soles of the feet, caused by his repeated and forceful pounding of the child on the floor on a number of separate occasions when she would not, at his direction, remain quiet or when she would not stay in the corner for hours at a time, as he directed.

For a comment on *Lawrence*, see R.J. Delisle, "Annotation to Lawrence" (1987), 58 CR (3d) 71.

R v. Craig
(2003), 177 CCC (3d) 321 (Ont. CA)

LASKIN JA:

A. Introduction

The appellant, Steven Craig, was convicted by a jury of manslaughter in the death of his lover. The trial judge sentenced him to ten years' imprisonment. Craig appeals his sentence. He submits that the trial judge made the following four errors justifying appellate intervention:

1. Although the basis for the jury's verdict was unclear, the trial judge did not give the appellant the benefit of the doubt;
2. He relied on a statement of the appellant that he had already ruled inadmissible at trial;
3. He failed to take into account several mitigating factors; and
4. He failed to give the appellant any credit for pre-trial custody.

The Crown acknowledges that the appellant was entitled to credit for seven months' pre-trial custody, but submits that otherwise the trial judge did not err and imposed a fit sentence.

B. Agreed Facts About the Offence and the Appellant's Statement

The appellant and the Crown filed an agreed statement of facts.

The appellant met the victim, James Detzler, while both were serving sentences in the Kingston Penitentiary. In prison they developed a sexual relationship. After Detzler was released they maintained their relationship by sexually explicit correspondence.

On May 6, 1997, the appellant was released on parole. He moved to Toronto and rented a bachelor apartment. On May 28, Detzler visited him in his apartment. By the end of the evening Detzler was dead. The pathologist who performed the post mortem testified that the cause of death was drowning associated with blunt force injury. In the doctor's opinion, Detzler's injury could not have been caused by a single punch, but more likely resulted from the sustained application of force.

Two days after Detzler's death, the appellant went to the office of his lawyer, who got in touch with the police and told them where the body was located. The police picked up the appellant and took him to the police station. At the station the appellant gave three statements.

In his first statement, which was inculpatory, he said that he and Detzler were drinking and that Detzler made sexual advances to him. The appellant rejected the advances and they got into a fight. The appellant felt "pissed off" because Detzler had been "coming on" to him. He "freaked out" and began hitting Detzler with his fists. He kept hitting him for ten or twenty minutes, then he grabbed Detzler's clothes and purse and threw them into the incinerator.

The appellant said that he left his apartment after locking the door behind him and breaking the key inside the lock. He maintained that when he left Detzler was in the kitchen and conscious, as far as he knew, though he was bruised and in "not very good" condition. The appellant "couldn't say" how Detzler ended up being found in the bathroom. He said that he told his lawyer he had done something accidentally.

After he gave his first statement the appellant was charged with second degree murder. He was advised of his right to speak to counsel and immediately asked to telephone his lawyer. The police telephoned his lawyer's office and left a message. However, instead of waiting for the lawyer to return the call, the police took the appellant into a video room and obtained a second, lengthier and even more inculpatory statement. The trial judge later ruled this statement inadmissible on the ground that the appellant had not waived his right to counsel.

In the second statement the appellant said that Detzler had arrived at his apartment between 9:30 and 10:00 p.m. After talking for a while Detzler asked to be handcuffed. The appellant obliged by handcuffing Detzler behind his back. Detzler then wanted to have anal intercourse. The appellant refused and began hitting Detzler because Detzler was "bugging" him and he got "fed up with it."

For between five and twenty minutes the appellant used his closed fist to hit Detzler on his lower back, on his shoulder blades, around his neck and on the back of his neck. Detzler fell into the bathtub, which had water in it because the appellant was going to soak his blistered feet. The appellant slammed the bathroom door and went to another room of the apartment, leaving Detzler leaning over in the water.

About five minutes later the appellant went back to the bathroom to see if Detzler was all right. He saw that Detzler's head was further down in the water and that he was not moving. The appellant removed the handcuffs and noticed that Detzler's arms were limp. He didn't think of getting him any medical help because he was "pissed off." However, he felt scared because he thought that he had killed him. He threw Detzler's clothing down the incinerator and left the apartment, locking the door behind him and breaking the key in the lock so that no one could enter.

The next morning the appellant got rid of the shirt he was wearing during the incident so that it could not be traced. After walking the streets, he "felt [his] conscience following [him] around," so he went to his lawyer and told him what had happened.

After the appellant gave his second statement he was charged with first degree murder under s. 231(5) of the *Criminal Code*. The prosecution alleged that he forcibly confined or sexually assaulted Detzler while murdering him.

The appellant then gave a third, brief statement to the police in which he said that on the evening of May 28 he had been drinking four or five beers but was not drunk. He also said that Detzler did not drink or "do drugs."

At trial, the appellant pleaded not guilty to the charge of first degree murder but guilty to the included offence of manslaughter. The trial judge ruled that the appellant's first and third statements were admissible, but excluded his second statement. At the end of the Crown's case the trial judge directed a verdict of acquittal on the first degree murder charge because the prosecution had not presented any evidence that Detzler was either forcibly confined or sexually assaulted during the alleged murder.

The jury was given two competing theories of what occurred. The Crown contended that the appellant strangled or choked Detzler and that he either intended to cause Detzler's death or intended to cause him bodily harm that he knew was likely to cause his death and was reckless whether death ensued. Under the Crown's theory the appellant was guilty of second degree murder.

The defence acknowledged that the appellant assaulted Detzler and that the assault had led to his death. The defence contended that Detzler sustained his neck injuries by blows administered before he fell into the bathtub and that, therefore, the killing was not intentional. Under the defence's theory the appellant was guilty of unlawful act manslaughter. The jury returned a verdict of manslaughter.

In sentencing the appellant to ten years' imprisonment, the trial judge concluded that "this homicide cannot under any view of the evidence be described as accidental ... . It is a homicide which is at the higher end of the scale."

C. Is Appellate Interference With the Sentence Justified?

Despite the deference accorded to sentencing decisions, in my view this court is justified in interfering with the appellant's sentence, largely for the four reasons he gives. I will discuss them briefly.

(i) Benefit of the Doubt When the Basis of the Jury's Verdict Is Unclear

The appellant submits that the trial judge erred by failing to apply the principle that a sentencing judge must give an accused the benefit of any doubt about the basis of a jury's verdict. I agree with this submission.

In *R v. Brown*, 1991 CanLII 73 (SCC), [1991] 2 SCR 518, the Supreme Court held that a sentencing judge is bound by the express and implied factual implications of a jury's verdict. Parliament codified the Supreme Court's holding by enacting s. 724 of the *Criminal Code*, which states:

[The court then quotes s. 724.]

Thus, in this case, following s. 724(2)(a), the trial judge had to accept the necessary implication from the jury's manslaughter verdict that the appellant did not have the specific intent to kill Detzler. He had to sentence him for unlawful act manslaughter, where the unlawful act was the assault.

Beyond the appellant's assault of Detzler, however, the basis on which the jury arrived at a verdict of manslaughter is unclear. Although s. 724(3) requires disputed facts to be proven before the sentencing judge may rely on them, the Code does not address cases of factual ambiguity such as this one.

In such cases, the accused is entitled to the benefit of any doubt about the basis of the jury's verdict. This principle was set out by Finlayson JA in *R v. Cooney* 1995 CanLII 707 (ONCA), (1995), 98 CCC (3d) 196 at 204 (Ont. CA):

> My own view is that, consistent with *R v. Gardiner*, supra, and the proposition that the normal burden of proof still rests on the Crown when dealing with disputed facts, the sentencing judge is obliged to give to the convicted accused the benefit of the doubt regarding the basis on which he was convicted by the jury.

See also *R v. Poorman* 1991 CanLII 2759 (SKCA), (1991), 66 CCC (3d) 82 at 89 (Sask. CA).

Although the trial judge is not bound to accept the most lenient view of the facts, or the accused's characterization of the facts, any doubt about the basis of the verdict must be resolved in the accused's favour. I am not persuaded that the trial judge applied this principle.

In sentencing the appellant, the trial judge rejected the idea that Detzler's death was "accidental." In his words:

> On all of the evidence it is clear to me that this homicide cannot under any view of the evidence be described as accidental. The injuries that were suffered by the victim were substantial—very serious injuries caused by the accused. The most significant of those injuries were those to the neck structures which were described as having been caused by a sustained application of pressure to the throat and voice box of the victim consistent with strangulation.
>
> The cause of death was described and was not in any way seriously challenged as death by, in effect, drowning, that is, the ingestion of water consistent with the deceased being alive and having his head put under water.

I am not sure what the trial judge meant by his use of the word "accidental." He could not have meant that the killing of Detzler was intentional. Yet, in this passage, the trial judge seems to have concluded that the appellant strangled his victim. Although I suppose it is possible the jury convicted the appellant of manslaughter on the basis that he strangled Detzler and put his head underwater but did not intend to kill him, this harsh inference from the evidence was not the only one available to the trial judge. It is also possible that the assault, including the neck injuries consistent with strangulation, caused Detzler to fall into the bathtub, where he later drowned. In this sense, his death could be described—as his defence counsel contended—as "accidental." Nonetheless, the appellant would still be guilty of manslaughter because the death was objectively foreseeable.

In seemingly rejecting this possible characterization of what occurred the trial judge did not give the appellant the benefit of the doubt about the basis of the jury's verdict. Had he given the appellant the benefit of the doubt about when Detzler sustained his neck injuries, he likely would not have imposed a sentence at the higher end of the range for manslaughter. The trial judge's failure to apply the principle in *Cooney* justifies appellate review.

(ii) Reliance on an Inadmissible Statement

The trial judge ruled the appellant's second statement—in which he confessed to hand-cuffing Detzler—inadmissible because it was obtained in breach of s. 10(b) of the Charter. Having ruled the statement inadmissible at trial, the trial judge was not entitled to rely on the contents of the statement in sentencing the appellant. This much the Crown acknowledges. See s. 724(2)(b) of the *Criminal Code*; and *R v. Gardiner*, 1982 CanLII 30 (SCC), [1982] 2 SCR 368.

What the parties disagree about is whether the trial judge did rely on the statement. The appellant says that he did and points to this troubling passage at the beginning of the reasons for sentence:

> The jury was deprived of cogent evidence in this case by reason of a ruling made by me for the exclusion of evidence of a statement which had been obtained from the accused in viola-tion of his rights under the Charter of Rights. It was a statement which was voluntary in the classic sense and would otherwise have been part of the evidence before the jury. The jury if they had had that evidence would have had a somewhat larger and somewhat more com-plete picture of at least what the accused had said about the commission of the offence.
>
> In assessing the penalty that is appropriate in this case I must, of course, be bound by the verdict of the jury and must impose a sentence which is a fit sentence for the offence of manslaughter. I am, however, at liberty to take into account all of the evidence and make my own assessment of the facts of the case and my own view as to what it was that caused the death of the victim.

In support of his submission the appellant emphasizes the juxtaposition of the judge's statement that "[t]he jury was deprived of cogent evidence in this case by reason of a ruling made by me for the exclusion of ... a statement" with his assertion that "I am, however, at liberty to take into account all of the evidence." The appellant also emphasizes that the evidence of handcuffing could well—in the trial judge's mind—have justified a sentence for manslaughter at the "higher end of the scale."

The Crown, however, argues that the trial judge commented on the exclusion of the second statement solely to explain why the jury convicted the appellant of manslaugh-ter instead of second degree murder. The Crown observes that in his reasons for sen-tence the trial judge did not refer to the handcuffing of Detzler and that he would have done so had he actually relied on the excluded statement.

I do not think that the absence of any reference to the handcuffing in the reasons for sentence adequately answers the appellant's submission. Other than a brief reference to the pathologist's evidence and to the seriousness of Detzler's injuries, the trial judge did not discuss or make findings on how the death occurred. Instead, he emphasized how little was known:

> Whatever it was that really transpired that night we may never know. Clearly what Mr. Craig told to the police was only part of the story. We have not heard the exact details as to what it was that caused the assault on Mr. Detzler which eventually ended in his death.

It thus seems to me that the trial judge's reasons are unclear about whether he used the excluded statement to sentence the appellant. Both the appellant and this court are left to wonder whether he improperly took the contents of this statement into account.

This lack of clarity in the trial judge's reasons about whether he used such an important piece of evidence justifies appellate review of the sentence. As Binnie J observed in *R v. Sheppard*, 2002 SCC 26 (CanLII), [2002] 1 SCR 869 at para. 46:

> These cases make it clear, I think, that the duty to give reasons, where it exists, arises out of the circumstances of a particular case. Where it is plain from the record why an accused has been convicted or acquitted, and the absence or inadequacy of reasons provides no significant impediment to the exercise of the right of appeal, the appeal court will not on that account intervene. On the other hand, where the path taken by the trial judge through confused or conflicting evidence is not at all apparent, or there are difficult issues of law that need to be confronted but which the trial judge has circumnavigated without explanation, or *where (as here) there are conflicting theories for why the trial judge might have decided as he or she did, at least some of which would clearly constitute reversible error*, the appeal court may in some cases consider itself unable to give effect to the statutory right of appeal. *In such a case, one or other of the parties may question the correctness of the result, but will wrongly have been deprived by the absence or inadequacy of reasons of the opportunity to have the trial verdict properly scrutinized on appeal.* In such a case, even if the record discloses evidence that on one view could support a reasonable verdict, the deficiencies in the reasons may amount to an error of law and justify appellate intervention. [Emphasis added.]

I therefore hold that this lack of clarity about the use of the second statement is another justification for reviewing the fitness of the sentence.

(iii) Mitigating Factors Not Considered

The trial judge did take into account the appellant's plea of guilty to manslaughter. In his reasons he said, "The accused has in some measure accepted responsibility and offered a plea of guilty to manslaughter." But the trial judge did not take into account another important mitigating consideration: the appellant turned himself in to the police and confessed to his crime. Where, as in this case, an accused implicates himself to help solve a crime he spares the public the cost of an investigation and shows that he has accepted some responsibility for his actions. He is entitled to some credit for having done so.

· · ·

D. What Is a Fit Sentence?

Once this court is justified in interfering with the sentence imposed by the trial judge, it is entitled to impose a sentence that it considers fit. See *R v. Rezaie* 1996 CanLII 1241 (ONCA), (1996), 31 OR (3d) 713 (CA).

I would reduce the ten-year sentence. Giving the appellant the benefit of the doubt, I assume that the trial judge derived the lengthy sentence in part from excluded evidence and an unnecessarily harsh interpretation of the facts underlying the jury's verdict.

[The court reviewed several mitigating and aggravating factors and concluded that a sentence of seven years is appropriate.]

NOTE

The question of consequences is a recurring issue in sentencing. This was addressed in chapter 2, Judicial Methodology and the Legislative Context, in the context of assessing culpability for driving offences that cause death or bodily harm (see *R v. Sweeney*). Another example of a related issue arose in *R v. Petrovic* (1984), 41 CR (3d) 275 (Ont. CA) (leave to appeal refused), where the appellant was convicted of assault causing bodily harm and sentenced to five years' imprisonment. After being abused and assaulted, Petrovic's spouse took her life by jumping from the balcony of their apartment. For the court, Lacourcière JA made the following observations (at 290-91):

> It was not part of the Crown's case that the appellant drove his wife to commit suicide. If that had been the case, the charge laid would have involved culpable homicide. The severity of a five-year sentence which the Crown concedes has to be reviewed, was no doubt considerably influenced by this factor. The appellant's punishment was increased for an intent which was not alleged against him and which he did not possess. In fact, the appellant was found guilty of assault causing bodily harm. The conduct causing injury to the victim was callous and not an isolated impulsive act but part of a long-standing pattern of physical abuse. However, the circumstances of the assault do not support an inference that the appellant intended or even contemplated the tragic result of his wife's death. To paraphrase the language of Chief Justice Trainor, delivering the judgment of the Prince Edward Island Supreme Court in *R v. Griffin* (1975), 23 CCC (2d) 11 at p. 15, 7 Nfld. & PEIR 139, it would appear that the learned trial judge gave undue weight to the actual result of the assault rather than to the probable result.
>
> The appellant is a first offender. He is 35 years of age and trained as a musician in Yugoslavia. He has since formed a new relationship, and married again on 16th March 1984. At the time of the sentence hearing, the Crown's position was that an early parole for purposes of deportation be recommended. The learned trial judge made this recommendation.
>
> Mr. Ruby's submission is that the appellant should be treated as a first offender and released on the basis of "time served" which is the equivalent of four and a half months. This would not, in my view, give sufficient weight to the necessity of general deterrence in cases involving callous and repeated acts of violence against a vulnerable victim belonging to a class requiring this court's protection. However, the sentence of five years was disproportionate to the gravity of the offence.
>
> I would allow the appeal from sentence and substitute a sentence of two years in the penitentiary.

See also the annotation to *Petrovic* by Price at (1984), 41 CR (3d) 276-78.

In *R v. Tempelaar*, [1995] 1 SCR 760, the accused was charged with sexual assault. The complainant testified as to the nature of the assault. The accused called no evidence and the trial judge instructed the jury that any of three stages in the complainant's version of events could constitute the offence charged, namely (1) the accused's touching of the victim's breast, (2) his touching of her crotch, and (3) his act of non-consensual intercourse with the victim. After deliberating for approximately two hours, the jury returned a verdict of guilty. After the jury was excused, the accused's counsel expressed concern that the verdict was unclear for the purposes of sentencing. As a result, the judge held the jury back, and after consultation with counsel, asked the jury to determine whether their verdict was based on the sexual touching or on the unwanted act of intercourse. About 15 minutes later, the jury returned and asked the judge whether the court required "a unanimous decision on each of the three separate incidents." The judge replied that they should be unanimous with regard to each of the incidents. In response to a further question from the jury, the judge told them to determine whether or not the accused had penetrated the victim.

One hour later, the judge informed the jury that he had erred in asking them to particularize their verdict, and he discharged them. The trial judge sentenced the accused to 30 months' imprisonment. The Ontario Court of Appeal dismissed the accused's appeal against conviction and sentence, holding that, on the authority of their decision in *R v. Tuckey* (1977), 34 CCC (2d) 572 (Ont. CA), "the trial judge was entitled to make up his own mind on disputed questions of fact which were relevant to sentence."

On further appeal to the Supreme Court, the accused argued that his right to the benefit of a trial by jury guaranteed by s. 11(f) of the Charter, as well as his right to be presumed innocent under s. 11(d), had been compromised when the trial judge failed to pass sentence on the basis of the least aggravating set of facts that would support a finding of guilt. He argued that when the Crown exercised its discretion to rely on alternative bases of liability, he should have been entitled, as a matter of principle, to be sentenced on the basis of the least aggravating theory of liability unless the Crown had particularized its theories in separate counts. The court summarily rejected the appeal:

> LAMER CJC (orally): We find no reason to depart from the law as regards sentencing as it now stands, and has for many years. The appeal is accordingly dismissed.

For examples of how this line of cases is applied, see *R v. Cooney* (1995), 98 CCC (3d) 196 (Ont. CA); *R v. Gauthier (No. 2)* (1996), 108 CCC (3d) 231 (BCCA); *R v. Holder* (1998), 21 CR (5th) 277 (Ont. Gen. Div.); and *R v. Englehart* (1998), 124 CCC (3d) 505 (NBCA). See also Downes, "Findings of Fact for Sentencing in Jury Trials" (1995), 37 CR (4th) 93. In *R v. Braun* (1995), 95 CCC (3d) 443, the Manitoba Court of Appeal ruled that a person who has been found guilty after a trial in which he did not testify cannot later testify at the sentencing hearing in a manner that contradicts the clear findings of the jury.

IV. SELF-INCRIMINATION AND SILENCE AT THE SENTENCING HEARING

Because the sentencing process begins only after a finding of guilt has been registered, does this mean that the presumption of innocence is not applicable? We have seen that with respect to factors raised to aggravate the sentence, the Crown must prove them beyond a reasonable doubt if they are contested. (This is subject to the judge's ability in a jury trial to make findings of fact so long as they are consistent with the verdict.) Accordingly, allegations are not sufficient; there must be a satisfactory factual foundation for the sentencing process even though the accused has been found guilty. What about silence? It is now clear that for purposes of determining criminal responsibility, the accused's silence cannot be considered (see *R v. Noble*, [1997] 1 SCR 874). Can the absence of an explanation for the conduct that comprises the offence be considered and used as an aggravating factor?

R v. Shropshire
[1995] 4 SCR 227

[The accused pleaded guilty to second-degree murder after shooting the deceased in the chest three times. He offered no explanation for the killing. The trial judge sentenced him to life imprisonment and set the parole ineligibility period at 12 years. On appeal, the BC Court of Appeal reduced the period to 10 years on the basis that, *inter alia*, there were no unusual circumstances to warrant an increase beyond the minimum of 10 years. The Supreme Court of Canada reversed and restored the 12-year period. Iacobucci J spoke for the court.]

IACOBUCCI J: ... I do not see any error on the part of the trial judge. He adverted to the fact that the respondent had pleaded guilty and was only 23 years old. He recognized that the Crown was not seeking a period of parole ineligibility beyond the minimum. Nevertheless, in a legitimate exercise of his discretionary power, and after correctly reviewing the factors set out in s. 744, he imposed a 12-year period of parole ineligibility. He referred to the following factors as specifically justifying the 12-year period of parole ineligibility:

   (a) [T]he circumstances of the killing were strange in that they provided no real answer to why it took place, and the respondent was unwilling or unable to explain his actions;

• • •

Factor (a), however, presents some difficulty. The respondent raises the question whether the trial judge erred in interpreting the respondent's silence in such a manner as to justify extending the period of parole ineligibility.

In response, I would affirm the analysis of Goldie JA in the court below and would hold that this silence is readily assimilable within the "circumstances surrounding the offence" criterion. The crux of Goldie JA's comments is that, in the absence of any explanation for a random and seemingly senseless killing, the trial judge was correct in sentencing the respondent in light of his refusal to offer an explanation. It was found that his refusal was deliberate and in and of itself unusual. After all, the respondent, a drug dealer with previous convictions for robbery and armed robbery, shot the victim Buffam in cold blood without provocation of any kind.

It is not for the trial judge to speculate what the respondent might have said to mitigate the severity of the offence. I quite agree with Goldie JA that the right to silence, which is fully operative in the investigative and prosecutorial stages of the criminal process, wanes in importance in the post-conviction phase when sentencing is at issue. However, in so agreeing, I emphasize that the respondent pleaded guilty; I leave for future consideration the question of drawing a negative inference from the silence of the accused when he or she has pleaded not guilty and wishes to appeal the conviction. In the case at bar, the trial judge even went so far as to invite the accused to suggest why he may have committed the offence, but no response was forthcoming. As held by Goldie JA, the respondent "cannot expect to be rewarded for remaining silent in the circumstances." The court and the public clearly have an interest in knowing why a human life was taken by an offender.

Goldie JA's comments and the decision of the trial judge on the "silence" issue are fully consonant with the position taken by the Ontario Court of Appeal. In *R v. Able* [(1993), 65 OAC 37 (CA)], the Court of Appeal increased two co-accused's periods of parole ineligibility. At p. 39 it was held:

> No explanation has been forthcoming from either of the appellants with respect to the reason for the killing ... [which] can be best described as a callous, brutal, pointless, execution-style killing of a helpless victim.

I conclude that in certain circumstances, such as those presented in this case, it is proper to take into account the absence of an explanation of attenuating factors.

The respondent suggests that Goldie JA's comments and the decision of the trial judge contravene the pronouncements of this court in *R v. Gardiner*, [1982] 2 SCR 368. I recognize that, in *Gardiner*, this court extended certain procedural rights to sentencing proceedings. However, these were limited to the right to counsel, the right to call evidence, the right to cross-examine and the right to address the court. There is no mention made of the creation in its identical form of a substantive right such as the right to silence.

At the sentencing stage, the Crown has already proved beyond a reasonable doubt that the accused has committed the crime for which he or she stood charged or, as in this appeal, the accused has pleaded guilty to the offence; if the accused then seeks to receive the least severe sentence commensurate with his or her conviction (*i.e.* for second degree murder, life imprisonment with eligibility for parole after 10 years have elapsed) it is incumbent upon the accused to play a somewhat active role in the process. I note that the right to silence is a manifestation of the presumption of innocence: *R v. Broyles*, [1991] 3 SCR 595; *R v. Hebert*, [1990] 2 SCR 151; *R v. Chambers*, [1990] 2 SCR 1293. The presumption of innocence flows to those "charged with an offence" or suspected of having committed one; once an individual has been convicted of an offence he or she is no longer simply "charged."

Appeal allowed; parole ineligibility set at twelve years.

NOTE

Can these comments be reconciled with *Gardiner* and *Noble*? Is the court converting an absence of evidence into an aggravating factor?

Once there is a finding of guilt, it is true that the presumption of innocence is spent to the extent that the prosecution is relieved of further obligation to prove the offence beyond reasonable doubt. If the burden and standard of proof are all that is meant by the presumption of innocence, it would seem to follow that there is no scope for its application in the sentencing hearing. But this might be an unduly hasty conclusion because there is a meaningful way in which the presumption of innocence can apply in sentencing. It is clear that the prosecutor must prove disputed facts beyond a reasonable doubt if those facts are aggravating. Thus the higher standard of proof is required to establish heightened culpability.

The rationale for this standard might not flow directly from the presumption of innocence, but it serves a purpose that is entirely consistent with that principle.[5] Similarly, the conclusion in *Brown*, above, can be explained in an analogous fashion. The court concluded that the accused could not properly be sentenced with reference to elements of culpability that were rejected by the jury. What is this at the sentencing stage if not some vestigial protection of the principle against self-incrimination?

For general discussions of *Shropshire*, see Trotter, "Murder, Sentencing, and the Supreme Court of Canada" (1996), 43 CR (4th) 288, and Norris, "Sentencing for Second-Degree Murder" (1996), 1 *Can. Crim. LR* 199.

V. FACTS RELATING TO OTHER OFFENCES

Another issue addressed by the Code, at least in part, concerns the extent to which the sentencing judge may take into account facts relating to the commission of another offence by the accused, whether charged or not. The matter is of great importance, obviously, because a fit sentence can only be one that is fit for the offence of which the offender was found guilty. In *R v. Edwards* (2001), 155 CCC (3d) 473 (Ont. CA), after a careful review of the jurisprudence, Rosenberg JA concluded that apart from the provisions of s. 725 the sentencing judge has a discretion to admit and consider evidence of previous uncharged conduct by the accused in the assessment of his background and character. The interpretation of s. 725 and the views expressed in *Edwards* have been considered by the Supreme Court of Canada.

R v. Larche
[2006] 2 SCR 762

FISH J:

I

Offenders are punished in Canada only in respect of crimes for which they have been specifically charged and of which they have been validly convicted.

To this general rule, there is only one true exception: In sentencing an offender, the judge may consider any uncharged offences *that form part of the circumstances of the offence.*

The trial judge in this case applied s. 725(1)(c) of the *Criminal Code*, RSC 1985, c. C-46, over the objections of Crown counsel, and the decisive question is whether he was entitled to do so. I agree with the courts below that he was.

. . .

II

The respondent Jean-Paul Larche participated in a criminal operation that exported cannabis from the Eastern Townships of Quebec across the American border and repa-

---

[5]   See *R v. Pearson* (1992), 17 CR (4th) 1, at 54-55 (SCC), per Lamer CJC.

triated the proceeds to Canada. For that, Mr. Larche and others were arrested and charged in Canada in June 2002. Less than one month later, they were indicted in the United States in connection with the same operation.

Mr. Larche was indicted in Canada on two counts, the first for having conspired to produce, possess, and traffic in cannabis, and to possess the proceeds; the second for having committed drug-related offences under the direction of a criminal organization or for its profit.

Both counts were drafted as if the underlying criminal enterprise, which was plainly transnational in scope, ended right at the US–Canadian border. [This was done to facilitate an anticipated extradition request from the United States government for conspiracy to distribute marijuana, during essentially the same period, in that country.]

Mr. Larche pleaded guilty to both counts ... .

. . .

Defence counsel ... urged the trial judge—over the Crown's objections—to apply s. 725(1)(c) of the *Criminal Code* in determining the sentence. The Crown's own submissions on sentence, he argued, established that the prerequisites of that provision were satisfied. Mr. Larche had participated in the Cusson gang's operations both in Canada and in the United States. His participation in these crimes constituted "facts forming part of the circumstances of the offence[s]" for which he was to be sentenced, within the meaning of s. 725(1)(c). And, again in the words of s. 725(1)(c), these facts "could constitute the basis for a separate charge."

Sansfaçon JCQ agreed and, applying s. 725(2) of the *Criminal Code*, he noted three "facts"—or uncharged offences—on the indictment:

1. [translation] Between December 2001 and July 2002, Jean-Paul Larche participated on 3 (three) occasions in the exportation of marihuana from Quebec to Massachusetts on behalf of the criminal organization headed by Marc-André Cusson.
2. Between December 2001 and July 2002, Jean-Paul Larche on several occasions brought back from the United States money derived from the sale of marihuana, in total between $500,000 and $600,000 in US currency, on behalf of the criminal organization headed by Marc-André Cusson.
3. On May 31, 2002, in the state of Vermont, Jean-Paul Larche had in his possession $110,000 in US currency (Yankee Barn Home incident in New Hampshire) derived from the sale of marihuana on behalf of the criminal organization headed by Marc-André Cusson.

The first two notes describe what might reasonably be characterized as the missing half of the single criminal enterprise that was the true substratum of the indictment. As earlier explained, it had been "carved out" of the offences charged to accommodate an anticipated request for Mr. Larche's extradition to the United States. Both notes relate to facts over which Canadian courts have jurisdiction and I agree with the Court of Appeal that Sansfaçon JCQ was entitled to consider those facts in determining the sentence. He was then required by s. 725(2) to enter them on the indictment, as he in fact did.

Like the Court of Appeal, however, I believe s. 725(1)(c) only applies to uncharged offences over which Canadian courts have territorial jurisdiction. The third note, by its plain terms, does not satisfy this requirement. It concerns an event that occurred entirely in Vermont. This alone is sufficient to dismiss Mr. Larche's cross-appeal, which seeks to revive that note.

III

. . .

The Crown contends that s. 725 is a codification of pre-existing common law principles, particularly those set out in *R v. Garcia*, [1970] 3 CCC 124 (Ont. CA). This is true of s. 725(1)(*a*) and (*b*), and to some extent of para. (*b*.1). But the rest of s. 725—including s. 725(1)(*c*) and s. 725(2), which concern us here—is new law.

Under *Garcia*, facts capable of supporting separate charges could be considered in determining the sentence *only if they were covered by other pending charges*. *R v. Robinson* (1979), 49 CCC (2d) 464 (Ont. CA), also cited by the Crown, is to the same effect. Section 725(1)(*b*) and, albeit in a more structured way, para. (*b*.1) thus express in statutory form the practice recognized by *Garcia* and *Robinson*. See *R v. Howlett* 2002 CanLII 45068 (ONCA), (2002), 163 OAC 48 (CA), at para. 13.

Section 725(1)(*c*), on the other hand, allows the court to take into consideration facts that *could* constitute the basis for a separate charge that *has not*—or at least not yet—been laid.

. . .

As Cory and Iacobucci JJ emphasized in *R v. Gladue*, 1999 CanLII 679 (SCC), [1999] 1 SCR 688, at para. 39:

> One cannot interpret the words of s. 718.2(e) simply by looking to past cases to see if they contain similar statements of principle. The enactment of the new Part XXIII was a watershed, marking the first codification and significant reform of sentencing principles in the history of Canadian criminal law. Each of the provisions of Part XXIII, including s. 718.2(e), must be interpreted in its total context, taking into account its surrounding provisions.

This cautionary injunction applies here. ... Section 725(1)(*c*) and s. 725(2) are best understood not by looking to past cases but by considering their plain terms, their evident purpose, and their relationship not only to the rest of s. 725 but also to other provisions of Part XXIII of the *Criminal Code* and to the scheme of the *Criminal Code* as a whole.

I mentioned earlier that the decisive question on this appeal is whether s. 725(1)(*c*) can be applied without the Crown's consent, as in this case. To that question, the plain words of s. 725 command an affirmative answer. Parliament has provided that trial judges cannot apply paras. (*b*) and (*b*.1) without the consent of both the Crown and the offender. No such requirement appears in para. (*c*). This could not have been a legislative oversight. Had Parliament intended to require the consent of either the Crown or the accused in order for trial judges to apply s. 725(1)(*c*), it would have said so, as it did in the two immediately preceding paragraphs of the same subsection of the *Code*.

This view of the matter is entirely consistent with the purpose of the provision. Read together, s. 725(1)(*c*) and s. 725(2) serve two main purposes.

First, s. 725(1)(*c*) dispels any uncertainty whether a sentencing judge can take into account as aggravating factors other uncharged offences that satisfy its requirements.

Second, s. 725(2) then protects the accused from being punished twice for the same offence: incrementally, as an aggravating circumstance in relation to the offence charged, and then for a second time should a separate charge subsequently be laid in respect of the same facts. This protection is essential, since the usual safeguards would not apply: The accused, if later charged with offences considered by the trial judge under s. 725(1)(c), could neither plead *autrefois convict* nor, unless charged with what is found to be "the same delict," invoke the rule against multiple convictions set out in *Kienapple v. The Queen*, [1975] 1 SCR 729.

I stated at the outset that s. 725(1)(c) was the only true exception to the rule that offenders are punished in Canada only in respect of crimes for which they have been specifically charged and of which they have been validly convicted. I do not consider subs. (1)(b) and (b.1) to be true exceptions to that rule because they both relate to *separately charged offences* for which offenders may be punished only (1) *with their consent* and (2) if they *agree to plead guilty* (para. (b)) or, "*agre[e] with the facts asserted*" and "*acknowledg[e] having committed the offence*" (para. (b.1)).

As we have seen, s. 725(1)(c) permits a court, in determining the sentence, to consider any fact that forms part of the circumstances of the offence even if it could form the basis for a separate charge. These uncharged but proven offences, if they are considered at all, will invariably be treated as "aggravating circumstances" within the meaning of s. 718.2(a) and related provisions of the *Criminal Code*. It is true, of course, that not all aggravating circumstances, or factors, are crimes in themselves. The offender's previous convictions, for example, and the vulnerability of the victim due to infirmity or age, are not offences in themselves. But, like uncharged offences that may be considered under s. 725(1)(c), they are aggravating as opposed to mitigating circumstances because they warrant *more severe*—not *more lenient*—sentences.

This typical effect of s. 725(1)(c) is well illustrated by the Crown's position in this case: The Crown urged the trial judge to sentence Mr. Larche to six years' imprisonment, less time served, *if he applied s. 725(1)(c)*, or three to four years' imprisonment *if he did not*.

On appeal, the three-year sentence imposed by the trial judge was increased to six years due to the requirement in s. 467.14 of the *Criminal Code* that sentences for crimes committed under the direction or for the benefit of criminal organizations be served consecutively. Consistent with its position that s. 725 should not apply and with its submissions at trial, the Crown recommended in the Court of Appeal a total sentence of three years in all—two years on the first count, and one year, consecutive, on the second. That recommendation was reiterated in this Court.

The Crown's position in this regard should not be mistaken for compassion or leniency. It was driven by the Crown's attempt to ensure that Mr. Larche could later be extradited to the United States to face trial there for the corresponding half of his crimes committed in that country. That would expose Mr. Larche, upon conviction, to a mandatory minimum sentence of five years' and a maximum of forty years' imprisonment. The Crown's suggestion that a total sentence of three years be imposed on the Canadian charges, if s. 725(1)(c) were not applied, must be understood in that light.

IV

As appears from the plain wording of both provisions, s. 725(1)(*c*) and s. 725(2), read together, are at once discretionary and mandatory. Discretionary, because courts *may*—not *must*—consider the facts that could support other charges; mandatory, because if they do, they *must*—not *may*—note on the record that they have done so.

In my view, the discretion afforded judges by s. 725(1)(*c*) is not trumped by s. 718.2, which enumerates principles of sentencing that courts "shall ... take into consideration." One of these principles, set out in s. 718.2(*a*), is that "a sentence should be increased or reduced to account for any relevant aggravating or mitigating circumstances." Though framed in mandatory terms—"shall" and "should"—s. 718.2 must be read in its entire context and in its grammatical and ordinary sense harmoniously with the scheme of the Act, the object of the Act, and the intention of Parliament: see *65302 British Columbia Ltd. v. Canada*, 1999 CanLII 639 (SCC), [1999] 3 SCR 804, at para. 50.

I turn first to the context of s. 718.2. It is part of a detailed, intricate and comprehensive sentencing scheme introduced by Parliament, as I have already mentioned, in 1995. The "Fundamental purpose of sentencing" and its objectives are set out in s. 718. Under the heading "Fundamental principle," s. 718.1 then provides that "[a] sentence must be proportionate to the gravity of the offence and the degree of responsibility of the offender." In this context and under the heading "Other sentencing principles," s. 718.2 then states:

> 718.2 A court that imposes a sentence shall also take into consideration the following principles:
>
> (a) a sentence should be increased or reduced to account for any relevant aggravating or mitigating circumstances relating to the offence or the offender, and, without limiting the generality of the foregoing ... .

Taking this principle into consideration does not require the court to apply it without regard to the other principles of sentencing set out in the *Code* or in binding decisions of the courts. Nor does it override s. 725.

V

It was argued before us that there is an implicit requirement of consent of either the accused, or the Crown—or both—before s. 725(1)(*c*) can apply.

The Crown submits that it would be [translation] "absurd" and would violate prosecutorial discretion to hold that s. 725(1)(*c*) allows the accused to [translation] "unilaterally" avoid extradition or escape a more severe sentence resulting from the Crown's decision to segment charges. It follows, says the Crown, that s. 725(1)(*c*) cannot be applied without the Crown's consent.

This submission fails because s. 725(1)(*c*) is not subject to "unilateral" application by *either* of the parties. Its application remains at all times subject to the sentencing judge's discretion.

It is true that prosecutorial discretion in the laying of charges will not lightly be interfered with by the courts. But proceedings cannot be delayed abusively to increase punishment: *R v. Parisien* (1971), 3 CCC (2d) 433 (BCCA), particularly at p. 437. Nor can offences be artificially fractioned in the pursuit of a like objective.

In the present case, the Court of Appeal held that s. 725(1)(*c*) can only be applied with the consent of the accused. Applying its previous decision in *R v. Pearson*, [2001] RJQ 69, ... the court stated:

> [translation] If s. 725(1)(c) can be applied only with the consent of the accused, it must therefore be because this provision permits the court to consider facts *extrinsic* to the offence to which *the accused has pleaded guilty*. Given the right of every accused person to be presumed innocent, it cannot be that the provision permits the court to consider facts not strictly within the framework of the offence for which the accused is to be punished unless the accused has been tried for [the other] offence. [Emphasis in original; para. 25.]

This position flows from a legitimate concern that an accused's conviction or plea of guilt on one charge could be hijacked for the purpose of punishing that accused for unanticipated accusations of wrongdoing. An indictment must be sufficiently precise factually for the accused to grasp the reproached circumstances or "transaction," and sufficiently precise legally to permit the accused to know which charge he or she must answer among the various charges that might characterize the act: *R v. G.R.*, 2005 SCC 45 (CanLII), [2005] 2 SCR 371, 2005 SCC 45.

However, with respect for the contrary view, this concern does not justify reading in the requirement of the accused's consent where the legislator has declined to provide for it. On the contrary, in s. 724(3)(*e*), the legislator has specifically provided a procedure for considering aggravating facts over the accused's objection.

Section 724(3)(*e*) provides that "[w]here there is a dispute with respect to any fact that is relevant to the determination of a sentence, ... the prosecutor must establish, by proof beyond a reasonable doubt, the existence of any aggravating fact." As I have already said, the facts relevant to the determination of a sentence in accordance with s. 725(1)(*c*) would normally be aggravating facts. A dispute arises when the accused refuses to recognize the veracity of such facts, or, to put it another way, does not consent to the application of s. 725(1)(*c*). This procedure appears to me to contemplate the application of s. 725(1)(*c*) without the accused's consent.

The requirement in s. 724 of proof beyond a reasonable doubt is imperative in light of the presumption of innocence, which applies to *all* alleged offences. The finality of s. 725(1)(*c*) is to increase punishment on the basis of an uncharged offence. Where the offender disputes his guilt of that offence, the presumption of innocence applies.

In addition to the requirement of proof beyond a reasonable doubt, the legislator has provided two other safeguards in s. 725(1)(*c*). Applied with vigour, these three safeguards are together adequate to address the important concerns expressed by the Quebec Court of Appeal in *Pearson* and again in the present case.

First, as Rosenberg JA observed in *R v. Edwards* 2001 CanLII 24105 (ONCA), (2001), 54 OR (3d) 737 (CA), "the occasions on which [s. 725(1)(*c*)] may be invoked are carefully circumscribed by the requirement that the facts form part of the circumstances of the predicate offence" (para. 35). Unrelated offences, which the offender would not expect to be confronted with, are excluded. Second, judges can be relied on, in the exercise of their discretion under s. 725(1)(c), to decline to consider uncharged offences if this would result in unfairness to the accused—or for that matter, to the Crown, for example in taking the Crown by surprise so as to foreclose prematurely the laying of additional charges.

Section 725(1)(c) has three components, which may be broken down this way: "In determining the sentence, a court ... [1] may consider any facts [2] forming part of the circumstances of the offence [3] that could constitute the basis for a separate charge." The use of the word "may" signifies that the provision is discretionary, as I have already mentioned. The requirements of "forming part of the circumstances of the offence" and the necessity that these facts be capable of constituting "the basis for a separate charge" are two necessary preconditions for the exercise of that discretion.

I begin by considering the requirement that the facts form part of the circumstances of the offence. Parliament has made plain the need to establish a nexus or "connexity" between the uncharged criminal conduct and the offence for which the offender has been convicted.

Care must also be taken, in applying s. 725 over the accused's objection, to ensure that the sentencing hearing is not transformed into a "trial within a trial." This is relevant to a court's exercise of discretion, once the threshold requirements of s. 725(1)(c) have been met, especially given the need for the accused to anticipate the extent of their jeopardy and the right to jury trial for certain offences. But the need to avoid a series of "spin-off" trials at the sentencing stage is, at best, of marginal value in determining whether an uncharged offence forms part of the circumstances of the offence for which the accused must be sentenced.

In my view, whether facts form part of the circumstances of the offence must ultimately be resolved on a case-by-case basis. Broadly speaking, however, there do appear to me to be two general categories of cases where a sufficient connection may be said to exist. These two categories, as we shall see, are not hermetic or mutually exclusive, and will often overlap.

The first would be connexity either in time or place, or both. This flows from the ideal animating s. 725(1)(c): In principle, a single transaction should be subject to a single determination of guilt and a single sentence that takes into account all of the circumstances. In its application, this principle is subject, of course, to the constraints fixed by Parliament in the governing provisions of the *Criminal Code*, including, notably, s. 725.

· · ·

In *Edwards*, Rosenberg JA refers to the concept of *res gestae* as applied in *R v. Gourgon* (1981), 58 CCC (2d) 193 (BCCA). The notion of *res gestae*—or "things done" (*Black's Law Dictionary* (8th ed. 2004), at p. 1335)—relates to a close spatial and temporal connection, and may therefore be helpful in this context.

In *R v. Paré*, 1987 CanLII 1 (SCC), [1987] 2 SCR 618, this Court considered whether culpable homicide perpetrated "while committing" an indecent assault had to be "exactly coincidental" with the underlying assault, or merely form part of the same sequence of events or transaction. Wilson J, for a unanimous court, adopted the transactional definition (see pp. 632 and 634).

Both *res gestae* and the phrase "while committing" are narrower than the expression "facts forming part of the circumstances of the offence" employed in s. 725(1)(*c*). The "circumstances" of an offence are more than the immediate transaction in the course of which it transpires. Thus, in addition to encompassing the facts of a single transaction, s. 725(1)(*c*) also applies, in my view, to the broader category of related facts that inform the court about the "circumstances" of the offence more generally.

"Facts" (or uncharged offences) of this sort that have occurred in various locations or at different times cannot properly be said to form part of the transaction covered by the charge for which the offender is to be sentenced. Recourse to s. 725(1)(*c*) may nevertheless be had where the facts in question bear so close a connection to the offence charged that they form part of the circumstances surrounding its commission. In determining whether they satisfy this requirement of connexity, the court should give appropriate weight to their proximity in time and to their probative worth as evidence of system or of an unbroken pattern of criminal conduct.

In this case, Sansfaçon JCQ made plain in his reasons that it was of the very essence of the enterprise that cannabis would be exported and sold in the United States and that the proceeds would be repatriated to Canada. From the perspective of both object and *modus operandi*, this enterprise did not stop at the border. Its constituent elements were seamlessly connected and, considered globally, the offences charged were in fact committed partly north and partly south of the border. Accordingly, I am satisfied that the facts set out in all three notes "form[ed] part of the circumstances of the offence" and therefore met the requirement of connexity.

The second requirement of s. 725(1)(*c*) is that the facts "could constitute the basis for a separate charge." The question is whether that means a separate charge *in Canada*. I believe that it does. To hold otherwise would permit Canadian courts, through the indirect mechanism of s. 725, to punish for crimes *entirely* committed abroad and thus to arrogate unto themselves an extraterritorial jurisdiction not vested in them by Parliament.

This jurisdictional requirement is particularly relevant to the third note entered by the trial judge. It relates to an uncharged offence that was committed entirely in the United States and, in particular, to an incident that occurred in Vermont on May 31, 2002. Acting on information provided by the RCMP, the American Drug Enforcement Administration ("DEA") began on that day to follow Mr. Larche as he headed towards the Canadian border with US$110,000 in cash. Mr. Larche sensed that he was under police surveillance. In the apparent hope of later recuperating the money, he deposited it precipitously as a down payment on a "Yankee Barn" home. The DEA, however, was by then not far behind—and "beat him to the draw."

The test for territorial jurisdiction according to *Libman v. The Queen*, 1985 CanLII 51 (SCC) [1985] 2 SCR 178, is a "real and substantial connection" to Canada (*United States of America v. Lépine*, 1994 CanLII 116 (SCC), [1994] 1 SCR 286). Facts that form "part of the circumstances of the offence" may *often*—but will not *always*—have a real and substantial connection to Canada. The two phrases are neither synonymous nor co-extensive, though the inquiries they mandate may sometimes overlap. Thus, my earlier conclusion that the third note forms part of the circumstances of the offence does not necessarily mean that it also has the required "real and substantial connection" to Canada.

A real and substantial connection has been found to be absent in more compelling cases than this one. For example, in *R v. B.(O.)* 1997 CanLII 949 (ONCA), (1997), 116 CCC (3d) 189 (Ont. CA), a Canadian trucker sexually assaulted his 13-year-old Canadian granddaughter in his Canadian registered vehicle while travelling through the US en route back to Canada. It was held that Canadian courts did not have jurisdiction.

While on the day of the "Yankee Barn" home incident Mr. Larche intended to operate in the same fashion as usual, fate intervened and he never made it back to Canada with the money. The event took place entirely in the United States. I agree with the Court of Appeal that Canadian courts therefore have no jurisdiction over it, and I would dismiss the cross-appeal formed by Mr. Larche in that regard.

On the facts of this case, considering the criminal enterprise as a whole, a real and substantial connection to Canada *did* exist, however, for the facts contained in the first two notes. These facts are analogous to the foreign component of a transnational fraud headquartered in Canada, over which Canadian courts have jurisdiction according to *Libman*.

• • •

Crown appeal and cross-appeal dismissed.

R v. Angelillo
[2006] 2 SCR 728

CHARRON J:

1. Introduction

During sentencing, is it appropriate for the court to consider evidence of facts tending to establish the commission of another offence in respect of which the offender has been charged but not convicted? If such evidence is admissible in principle, is it in the interests of justice in the instant case to allow the Crown to introduce this fresh evidence on appeal?

After pleading guilty to a charge of theft, Gennaro Angelillo was sentenced to a term of imprisonment of two years less a day to be served in the community, subject to his complying with certain conditions that are not in issue in this appeal. At the time of sentencing, Crown counsel was unaware that Mr. Angelillo was under police investigation once again for incidents that had occurred after his guilty plea and that later led to new charges. Relying on that evidence, the Crown introduced three motions in the Quebec Court of Appeal in which it sought leave to introduce fresh evidence, leave to appeal the sentence and a stay of sentence. The Court of Appeal dismissed the motion to introduce fresh evidence, because in its view [translation] "[t]his evidence is not relevant" and because "[t]o accept what the prosecution is proposing would mean accepting that the respondent can be punished more severely for committing an offence of which he might be found not guilty" ([2004] QJ No. 11670 (QL), at paras. 6 and 14). The court also dismissed the other two motions. The Crown has appealed to this Court.

• • •

The Crown submits that the Court of Appeal erred in holding that evidence of facts tending to establish the commission of another offence is irrelevant to the determination of the appropriate sentence, regardless of the purpose being pursued, unless the offence in question resulted in a conviction. The Crown wishes to produce this fresh evidence not to prove that the other offence was committed, but for the sole purpose of establishing Mr. Angelillo's character—a distinction that was accepted by the Ontario Court of Appeal in *R v. Edwards* 2001 CanLII 24105 (ONCA), (2001), 155 CCC (3d) 473, but rejected by the Court of Appeal in the case at bar. In light of the sentencing submissions, and more particularly of the pre-sentence report, according to which Mr. Angelillo [translation] "has done some soul-searching, which seems to be sincere, about his inappropriate behaviour" and his "time in court [has] had a major deterrent effect," the Crown contends that the fresh evidence easily meets the requirement of relevance.

Although I have concluded that the fresh evidence is relevant and I recognize that, in principle, evidence of facts tending to establish the commission of another offence of which the offender has not been convicted can in certain cases be admitted to enable the court to determine a just and appropriate sentence, I would, for the reasons that follow, dismiss the appeal. Since the fresh evidence constitutes the basis for outstanding charges against Mr. Angelillo for which he has not yet stood trial, it can be admitted only in the context of the procedure provided for in s. 725(1)(*b*) or (*b*.1) *Cr. C*. The conditions for that procedure include a requirement that the offender's consent be obtained. Furthermore, I feel that the Crown has not shown due diligence. Accordingly, the Court of Appeal's decision not to admit the fresh evidence is affirmed and the appeal is dismissed.

. . .

... I feel that it may be helpful to make a few general comments regarding the relevance of evidence of acts that have resulted neither in charges nor in convictions, since the Court of Appeal seems to have rejected out of hand the reasoning of Rosenberg JA of the Ontario Court of Appeal in *Edwards*. The court stated in particular that it did not see the distinction Rosenberg JA had drawn in saying that evidence of such acts cannot be adduced for the purpose of obtaining a disproportionate sentence against the offender for the offence in question or of punishing the offender for an offence of which he or she has not been convicted, but that such evidence can be adduced to shed light on the offender's background and character. In my view, Rosenberg JA was correct in drawing that distinction, and it is an important one. I will therefore begin by discussing certain general principles relating to the admissibility of extrinsic evidence for sentencing purposes before commenting on the relevance of the evidence the Crown wished to adduce in the case at bar.

3.2 Presumption of Innocence and Sentencing

Every accused person has the right to be presumed innocent. This fundamental right is not only set out in s. 6 *Cr. C*, but is also guaranteed by s. 11(d) of the *Canadian Charter of Rights and Freedoms*. However, the presumption of innocence is not irrebuttable. At the sentencing stage, it has obviously been rebutted with respect to the offence of which the accused has been convicted. There is therefore no question that, in determining the just and appropriate sentence, the judge can consider the underlying facts of the offence that has been proved. Moreover, sentencing is an individualized process in which the court must take into account not only the circumstances of the offence, but also the specific circumstances of the offender. I would like to note at the outset that the requirements for admissibility and the standard of proof to be applied in establishing all the relevant circumstances for sentencing purposes are issues that have already been considered by this Court, and that they are not in any way new principles.

• • •

3.3 Sentencing Principles

The principles of sentencing are now codified in ss. 718 to 718.2 *Cr. C.* These provisions confirm that sentencing is an individualized process in which the court must take into account not only the circumstances of the offence, but also the specific circumstances of the offender (see *Gladue*; *Proulx*, at para. 82). Thus, the objectives of sentencing cannot be fully achieved unless the information needed to assess the circumstances, character and reputation of the accused is before the court. The court must therefore consider facts extrinsic to the offence, and the proof of those facts often requires the admission of additional evidence.

Since the offender must be punished only for the offence in issue, the court will generally not admit evidence of other offences that have not been proved. In the present case, the Court of Appeal rightly referred to the following comment by LeBel JA in *R v. Pelletier* (1989), 52 CCC (3d) 340, at p. 346:

> [translation] While the accused's character may be shown, and his previous criminal record established, the sentencing process must not become the occasion for indirectly punishing the accused for offences which have not been established by the normal means of proof and procedure, or that one did not wish to bring.

There are many provisions of the *Criminal Code* under which evidence that is, by nature, capable of showing that the offender has committed another offence can be admitted at the sentencing hearing. First, evidence of any prior convictions may be adduced. The admissibility of such extrinsic evidence does not generally pose any problems. For example, s. 721(3)(*b*) provides that, unless otherwise specified by the court, any pre-sentence report must contain the history of prior convictions. There is no doubt that the court may take prior convictions into account in determining the appropriate sentence. In taking them into account, however, the court must not punish the offender again. The fundamental principle of proportionality requires that the sentence be proportionate to the gravity of the offence and the degree of responsibility of the offender; a prior conviction cannot, therefore, justify a disproportionate sentence. This principle, which is set out in s. 718.1 *Cr. C,* assures repeat offenders the right not to be "punished … again," as guaranteed in s. 11(*h*) of the *Charter.* The sentence imposed on a repeat offender may well be more severe, but this is not contrary to the offender's right not to be punished again. From the standpoint of proportionality, the sentence imposed in such a case is merely a reflection of the individualized sentencing process.

• • •

Since the fresh evidence in the present case has resulted in new charges against Mr. Angelillo, s. 725(1)(*b*) or (*b*.1) could have been invoked in respect of those charges, but neither of these provisions could be applied without Mr. Angelillo's consent. On the other hand, s. 725(1)(*c*)—under which a court may consider facts forming part of the circumstances of the offence that have not resulted in charges—does not require the offender's consent. The scope of that provision is discussed in *R v. Larche*, 2006 SCC 56 (CanLII), [2006] 2 SCR 762, 2006 SCC 56. I will simply note, for the purposes of my analysis, that s. 725(1)(*c*) would have been inapplicable even if new charges had not been laid against Mr. Angelillo, because the facts alleged in the fresh evidence did not "[form] part of the circumstances of the offence" within the meaning of that provision. When the conditions set out in s. 725 are met, the consideration of other offences does not violate the offender's rights. In such cases, as specified by Parliament, the court must note on the information or indictment any charges or facts considered in determining the sentence, and s. 725(2) provides that "no further proceedings may be taken with respect to any offence described in those charges or disclosed by those facts."

Third, if none of the paragraphs of s. 725(1) are applicable, the evidence in the instant case may be the type of extrinsic evidence that was in issue in *Edwards*. As Rosenberg JA recognized, there may be situations in which evidence that relates to one of the sentencing objectives or principles set out in the *Criminal Code* shows that the offender has committed another offence but *never been charged with or convicted of it*. Such facts may nevertheless be relevant and must not automatically be excluded in every case. As is often the case, the admissibility of the evidence will depend on the purpose for which its admission is sought. For example, let us assume that—as happens too often, unfortunately—a man is convicted of assaulting his spouse. The fact that he abused his spouse in committing the offence is an aggravating circumstance under s. 718.2(*a*)(ii). Section 718 requires the court to determine the appropriate sentence that will, among other things, denounce unlawful conduct, deter the offender from reoffending, separate the offender from society where necessary, and promote a sense of responsibility in the offender and acknowledgment of the harm he or she has done. It is therefore important for the court to obtain all relevant information. This is why several provisions of the *Criminal Code* authorize the admission of evidence at the sentencing hearing.

. . .

I now return to my example of the man who has assaulted his spouse. The extrinsic evidence could establish that this was an isolated incident for which the offender has expressed remorse and that the offender has demonstrated an ability to change his behaviour to prevent any risk of re-offending. However, the evidence could also show, on the contrary, that it was a common occurrence in the couple's relationship and one that could well occur each time the offender is intoxicated or frustrated. In the latter case, the offender would not be able to argue that facts extrinsic to the offence that demonstrate his violent character are irrelevant, on the basis that this evidence may show that he has committed other assaults in respect of which he has been neither charged nor convicted. These facts are relevant and, in my opinion, are admissible in principle because they relate to the sentencing objectives and principles that are expressly set out in the *Criminal Code*. The offender cannot invoke the presumption of innocence to *exclude* character evidence, since that presumption has in fact been rebutted with respect to the offence of which he has been convicted.

I cannot agree with Fish J, who would admit no evidence of acts tending to establish the commission of another offence in respect of which the offender has not been charged, except in the context of s. 725(1)(*c*). Under that provision, as is explained in *Larche*, the court may consider any facts *forming part of the circumstances of the offence* that could constitute the basis for a separate charge. I concede that there may be cases in which such facts are also relevant to the offender's character or reputation. But it is not always easy to tie evidence of reputation or character to a separate offence. Nor does such evidence always form part of the circumstances of the offence—sometimes it only forms part of the circumstances of the offender. With respect, if Fish J were right, a pre-sentence report setting out facts demonstrating that the offender has a violent character, is a drug addict, has no respect for the court's authority or has not learned his or her lesson could violate the presumption of innocence, since such facts could very well tend to establish the commission of various offences, including assault, possession of narcotics and breach of recognizance. I do not believe this to be the effect of the presumption of innocence. The presumption does not constitute a general exclusionary rule of evidence that precludes the admission of all extrinsic evidence relevant to sentencing for the offence in issue on the basis that it might establish the commission of another offence. This does not mean that the offender has no procedural protection where extrinsic evidence is concerned. There are a number of other principles that assure the offender's right to a fair trial. I will explain this.

If the extrinsic evidence is contested, the prosecution must prove it. Since the facts in question will doubtless be aggravating facts, they must be proved beyond a reasonable doubt (s. 724(3)(*e*)). The court can sentence the offender only for the offence of which he or she has been convicted, and the sentence must be proportionate to the gravity of that offence. In addition, the judge can and must exclude otherwise relevant evidence if its prejudicial effect outweighs its probative value such that the offender's right to a fair trial is jeopardized. Finally, the court must draw a distinction between considering facts establishing the commission of an uncharged offence for the purpose of punishing the accused *for that other offence*, and considering them to establish the offender's character and reputation or risk of re-offending for the purpose of determining the appropriate sentence for *the offence of which he or she has been convicted*. In my example, the sentence imposed on a violent offender may well be more restrictive than the sentence imposed on an offender who has committed an isolated act, but this is in no way contrary to the presumption of innocence. The sentence may also be more restrictive in the case of a repeat offender if the Crown presents evidence of the offender's criminal record, but this does not violate the offender's right, guaranteed by s. 11(*h*) of the *Charter*, not to be "punished ... again." In both cases, again from the standpoint of proportionality, the more severe sentence is merely a reflection of the individualized sentencing process.

Finally, Fish J fears that the Crown could easily, and even in good faith, avoid the application of s. 725 by withdrawing or postponing a new charge for the sole purpose of introducing evidence of subsequent acts as aggravating facts in order to obtain a more severe sentence (para. 59). In my view, there is no real danger that this would happen. It must be recalled, as Fish J himself mentions in *Larche*, at para. 39, that "proceedings cannot be delayed abusively to increase punishment: *R v. Parisien* (1971), 3 CCC (2d) 433 (BCCA)." In *Parisien*, the Court of Appeal reduced the sentence because of the Crown's actions.

• • •

For these reasons, the Court of Appeal's decision not to admit the fresh evidence is affirmed and the appeal is dismissed.

FISH J (Binnie J concurring):

I

I agree with Justice Charron that the appeal should be dismissed. I agree as well with the reasons on which her conclusion rests.

With respect, however, I do not share my colleague's view that sentencing courts may consider uncharged *and unrelated* offences. Parliament has addressed the issue in s. 725(1)(*c*) of the *Criminal Code*, RSC 1985, and c. C-46. In virtue of that provision, sentencing courts may consider uncharged offences only if they are related to the offence charged—that is to say, only if they consist in "facts forming part of the circumstances [of the crime for which the accused is to be sentenced]." And Parliament has taken care to protect offenders from being twice punished in this regard: Offences considered by the sentencing court pursuant to s. 725(1)(*c*) cannot form the basis of further proceedings against the offender.

Justice Charron would permit sentencing courts to consider uncharged offences even if they are unrelated, and she would remove for these unrelated offences the protection that Parliament has expressly provided for related offences. Moreover, as we shall see, this proposal rests on the doubtful proposition that evidence of an aggravating factor—other offences—is not introduced for purposes of punishment although it will almost invariably have that effect.

• • •

III

Parliament put in place barely a decade ago a comprehensive set of statutory provisions on sentencing. As Justice Charron mentions, these provisions together form "a true penological code" (para. 21). And as part of that "code," Parliament has set out in s. 725 the requirements for considering, in the determination of a sentence, other offences for which the offender has been neither tried nor convicted.

Charged but untried offences, as in this case, cannot be considered unless they meet the requirements of s. 725(1)(b) or (b.1). As my colleague explains, those conditions have not been met and it is for that reason that they could not be considered in determining Mr. Angelillo's sentence—even if the Crown had proceeded with diligence.

The facts underlying these charged offences are no less relevant to Mr. Angelillo's "background and character" than they would be if charges had not been laid. My colleague nonetheless finds, and I agree of course, that evidence of those facts could not be admitted because it failed to satisfy the requirements for its admission established by Parliament in s. 725(1)(b) and (b.1) of the Criminal Code. Yet she would admit that evidence if the charges had not—or not yet—been laid. As mentioned at the outset I do not share that view.

In any event, Parliament has provided in s. 725(1)(c) that *uncharged* offences may only be considered if they are based on "facts forming part of the circumstances of the offence" for which the offender is to be sentenced. For the sake of brevity, I refer to these offences as "connected" or "related" offences.

In *R v. Larche*, 2006 SCC 56 (CanLII), [2006] 2 SCR 762, 2006 SCC 56, released concurrently, I have dealt in some detail with this requirement of connexity. The criteria set out there should in large measure allay the understandable concerns mentioned by Justice Charron with respect to cases of domestic abuse, where a history of similar incidents that have never given rise to charges would nonetheless form "part of the circumstances of the offence" within the meaning of s. 725(1)(c): *Larche*, at paras. 54-55.

Parliament has decided that not all evidence relevant to the background and character of the offender may be considered by the sentencing judge. The rule proposed by Justice Charron would give a court the discretionary power to consider uncharged offences that do *not* form part of the circumstances of the offence. This would in practice override the inherent restriction of s. 725(1)(c) and render it entirely superfluous.

The rule proposed by Justice Charron would also lack the statutory procedural safeguards that Parliament has provided with regard to s. 725 of the *Criminal Code*. Section 725(2) prohibits the subsequent prosecution of uncharged offences considered by a court in determining the sentence under s. 725(1)(c). These uncharged offences, once considered, must be noted on the information or indictment. This protects the accused from double punishment, unless the conviction for the offence of which the offender has been found guilty is set aside or quashed on appeal.

It is true, as my colleague mentions, that previous convictions may properly be taken into account in determining the sentence for a subsequent offence. Here, however, the question was whether the sentencing court could consider *subsequent offences* for which the respondent *had not been convicted*. My colleague would answer that question in the affirmative, but for the fact that charges had already been laid. In her view, a sentencing court may consider unrelated and uncharged offences, previous or subsequent, under the rubric "background and character"—or, more accurately perhaps in this case, "*future* background and character." With respect, I do not agree.

In the case of previous convictions, the book has been closed—no further proceedings may be instituted. In the present case, proceedings not only can be, but in fact *were*, instituted.

My colleague's proposal would permit subsequent prosecution of uncharged offences that have already led to a stiffer penalty for a charged offence. And, where the uncharged offence relates to facts that occurred after those for which the offender has been charged and convicted, a "feedback loop" would almost invariably operate. The offender would then be more severely punished on the first offence because he or she later committed a second offence. Once that second offence has been made the subject of a charge, the offender would likely be punished more severely on this new charge *because of the earlier offence for which the offender has already received a stiffer sentence on account of the second offence which was not yet then charged.*

In this context, I note in passing that *R v. Edwards* 2001 CanLII 24105 (ONCA), (2001), 155 CCC (3d) 473 (Ont. CA), and *Lees v. The Queen*, [1979] 2 SCR 749, upon which my colleague relies, are both readily distinguishable from the present matter. In *Edwards*, the contentious facts related in part to an offence that was said to have been committed 18 years earlier in Jamaica and no charge could therefore be laid in Canada. The other contentious facts related to evidence of a "pattern of violence," a matter I have already considered above (para. 50). In *Lees*, no charge had been laid either, and it was "even doubtful whether there was a possible offence" (McIntyre J, at p. 754).

• • •

Justice Charron disagrees only with respect to *uncharged* offences, which are in her view admissible if they go to "background and character," whether or not they comply with s. 725(1)(*c*) of the *Criminal Code*. In her opinion, as I understand it, if the uncharged offences go to background and character *and comply* with s. 725(1)(*c*), they cannot form the basis of further proceedings; but if they go to background and character *and do not comply* with s. 725(1)(*c*), the offender may subsequently be charged and punished for those previously considered offences. In short, as mentioned earlier, Justice Charron would permit sentencing courts to consider uncharged offences even if they are unrelated, and she would remove for these unrelated offences the protection that Parliament has expressly provided for related offences.

• • •

In this light, I am unable to agree that evidence of uncharged offences, an acknowledged aggravating factor, can be admitted on the ground that it goes to "background and character" *but not to punishment*. Offenders whose sentences are increased on account of this aggravating factor—uncharged offences—will be forgiven for thinking that it has caused them to be more severely punished.

H.L.A. Hart put this aspect of the matter admirably almost a half-century ago. Dealing then with the putative distinction between considerations of "background and character" and "punishment" in the determination of sentences—in the context of what had since at least 1908 been characterized in central Europe as "double-track" penology—Professor Hart stated:

> [T]he "double-track" system has been elaborated in ways which may seem to us somewhat metaphysical: punishment which is to be "guilt-adequate," i.e. orientated towards the criminal act, is carefully distinguished from mere "measures" orientated to the criminal's character and the needs of society. The recent German Penal Code preserves this distinction though it is regretted as artificial by many. Certainly the prisoner who after serving a three-year sentence is told that his punishment is over but that a seven-year period of preventive detention awaits him and that this is a "measure" of social protection, not a punishment, might think he was being tormented by a barren piece of conceptualism—though he might not express himself in that way.

(Punishment and the Elimination of Responsibility (1962), at p. 12.)

Nor would the prisoner be much moved by my colleague's explanation that a more severe sentence for a charged offence is not punishment for the uncharged offence that is the reason for its increased severity.

. . .

IV

It is not my position, as my colleague suggests (at para. 31), that offenders can invoke the presumption of innocence to exclude evidence of unrelated and uncharged offences. Nor is there any need for them to do so: In my respectful view, that evidence is inadmissible for the reasons set out above. I think it nonetheless useful to add a brief word on Justice Charron's suggestion that the offender cannot invoke the presumption of innocence to exclude the evidence of untried offences because "that presumption has in fact been rebutted with respect to the offence of which he has been convicted" (para. 30 (emphasis added)).

It is true of course, as Justice Charron mentions, that the presumption of innocence is overcome by a conviction—but only by a conviction *for the offence charged*. A finding of guilt on charges that have been tried has no bearing on the offender's presumed innocence regarding offences that were never charged or admitted.

The court was unanimous in *Larche*, and unanimous in the result in *Angelillo*, but there remain divided views on the extent to which the judge may consider evidence of other conduct when deciding on sentence. One division relates to the admissibility—for any purpose—of evidence of conduct that is unrelated to the offence for sentence. Another point is whether territorial jurisdiction is a constraining factor.

VI. JUDICIAL NOTICE OF RELEVANT FACTS

To what extent may a judge take judicial notice of facts relevant to sentencing? This question arose incidentally in *Gladue* and has also been posed in several other cases. It is a question that affects fact finding not only in relation to the particular offender but also in relation to the nature and incidence of the offence. At least part of the answer would seem to be obvious. If the facts in question are in dispute between the parties, they must be proved by affirmative evidence. If there is no direct dispute on the facts between the parties, might it be argued nonetheless that the principle of judicial notice is inapplicable to facts that are contentious in themselves—that is, facts that are a matter of dispute?

R v. Gladue
[1999] 1 SCR 688

[This case is considered more fully in chapter 16, Aboriginal Offenders. The Supreme Court of Canada considered a wide range of issues relevant to the determination of a fit sentence for an Aboriginal offender. Reference to judicial notice was made toward the end of the opinion of Cory and Iacobucci JJ.]

CORY and IACOBUCCI JJ: ... The foregoing discussion of guidelines for the sentencing judge has spoken of that which a judge must do when sentencing an aboriginal offender. This element of duty is a critical component of s. 718.2(e). The provision expressly provides that a court that imposes a sentence *should* consider all available sanctions other than imprisonment that are reasonable in the circumstances, and *should* pay particular attention to the circumstances of aboriginal offenders. There is no discretion as to whether to consider the unique situation of the aboriginal offender; the only discretion concerns the determination of a just and appropriate sentence.

How then is the consideration of s. 718.2(e) to proceed in the daily functioning of the courts? The manner in which the sentencing judge will carry out his or her statutory duty may vary from case to case. In all instances it will be necessary for the judge to take judicial notice of the systemic or background factors and the approach to sentencing which is relevant to aboriginal offenders. However, for each particular offence and offender it may be that some evidence will be required in order to assist the sentencing judge in arriving at a fit sentence. Where a particular offender does not wish such evidence to be adduced, the right to have particular attention paid to his or her circumstances as an aboriginal offender may be waived. Where there is no such waiver, it will be extremely helpful to the sentencing judge for counsel on both sides to adduce relevant evidence. Indeed, it is to be expected that counsel will fulfil their role and assist the sentencing judge in this way.

However, even where counsel do not adduce this evidence, where for example the offender is unrepresented, it is incumbent upon the sentencing judge to attempt to acquire information regarding the circumstances of the offender as an aboriginal person. Whether the offender resides in a rural area, on a reserve or in an urban centre the sentencing judge must be made aware of alternatives to incarceration that exist whether inside or outside the aboriginal community of the particular offender. The alternatives existing in metropolitan areas must, as a matter of course, also be explored. Clearly the presence of an aboriginal offender will require special attention in pre-sentence reports. Beyond the use of the pre-sentence report, the sentencing judge may and should in appropriate circumstances and where practicable request that witnesses be called who may testify as to reasonable alternatives.

Similarly, where a sentencing judge at the trial level has not engaged in the duty imposed by s. 718.2(e) as fully as required, it is incumbent upon a court of appeal in considering an appeal against sentence on this basis to consider any fresh evidence which is relevant and admissible on sentencing. In the same vein, it should be noted that, although s. 718.2(e) does not impose a statutory duty upon the sentencing judge to provide reasons, it will be much easier for a reviewing court to determine whether and how attention was paid to the circumstances of the offender as an aboriginal person if at least brief reasons are given.

NOTE

The allusion to judicial notice is not developed further in *Gladue*. In this context, it means clearly that judges should take judicial notice of facts relating to systemic and background characteristics of Aboriginal communities. It obviously does not mean that the sentencing of Aboriginal offenders alone would raise this concern about judicial notice because there might be many other sentencing contexts in which systemic or background factors would be material. The extent to which judicial notice should be permitted with respect to such issues is a matter that requires caution. Is it possible, for example, for a judge to take judicial notice of the incidence or prevalence of a certain type of offence within a community? For these purposes, what are the differences among evidence, notice, and mere anecdote or hearsay?

R v. Laliberte
(2000), 31 CR (5th) 1 (Sask. CA) (footnotes omitted)

[The accused, an Aboriginal woman, pleaded guilty to two counts of trafficking in a controlled substance and two counts of possession of the proceeds of trafficking. She was sentenced to a conditional sentence of 12 months' imprisonment, including 4 months of electronically monitored house arrest, two years' probation, and restitution in the amount of $120. The Crown sought leave to appeal. It was granted, and the appeal was dismissed. The opinion of Vancise JA is more fully reproduced in chapter 16. In the course of his judgment, Vancise JA refers to the question of judicial notice.]

VANCISE JA:

. . .

[60] The sentencing judge must also be provided with general information concerning systemic poverty, alcohol and substance abuse, cultural and racial bias in the community at large. As well, the sentencing judge must receive information concerning the particular circumstances surrounding the offence.

[61] The Supreme Court suggested [in *Gladue*] that to accomplish the sentencing task, it would be necessary for the sentencing judge to "take judicial notice of the systemic or background factors and the approach to sentencing which is relevant to aboriginal offenders." [[1999] 1 SCR 688, 731-32 (para. 83).] This raises an evidentiary issue which is problematic. Surely in the context of this judgment Justices Cory and Iacobucci are not suggesting that the systemic or background factors are so "notorious" in general as to be capable of proof without evidence or that they can be verified by resort to reports of indisputable accuracy and applied to the particular facts.

[62] The systemic cultural and background factors to which Justices Cory and Iacobucci refer are set out in great detail in *Gladue*. All the factors described are conclusions of fact taken from texts, articles, studies, or commissions of inquiry on aboriginal problems, including the *Report of the Aboriginal Justice Inquiry of Manitoba*, and *The Justice System and Aboriginal People*. Those factors were described as:

Years of dislocation and economic development have translated, for many aboriginal peoples, into low incomes, high unemployment, lack of opportunities and options, lack or irrelevance of education, substance abuse, loneliness, and community fragmentation. These and other factors contribute to a higher incidence of crime and incarceration.

It will be necessary for the sentencing judge to take into account those factors which have been demonstrated as having caused or contributed to the aboriginal offender being before the court.

[63] The issue of how to deal with discrimination of aboriginal peoples was examined by the Supreme Court in *R v. Williams* [[1998] 1 SCR 1128] in the context of a challenge for cause, where the issue was widespread bias or prejudice in the community which had the potential to impact on the impartiality of a jury. McLachlin J concluded *on the evidence* of that case that there was widespread bias against aboriginal peoples in Canada and there is evidence that this widespread racism has translated into systemic discrimination in the criminal justice system [at para. 58]. McLachlin J did not take judicial notice of that fact.

[64] In *Williams*, the accused called witnesses and tendered evidence to establish widespread prejudice and bias in the community against aboriginal people. This evidence demonstrated there was a reasonable possibility of bias or a realistic potential of racial bias or prejudice on the part of jurors in the context of challenge for cause in the selection of a jury. McLachlin J stated it might not be necessary to duplicate that effort in future cases to establish racial prejudice in the community because the potential for racial prejudice could be demonstrated either by evidence or by judicial notice or by proving facts capable of immediate and accurate verification.

[65] In *R v. Fleury* [[1999] 3 WWR 62 (Sask. QB)] Barclay J considered whether widespread bias or prejudice existed in Saskatchewan which might impact on the impartiality of a jury in the context of a challenge for cause. Again, after hearing evidence from an expert in the field and examining reports of commissions of inquiries, he concluded on the evidence that there was systemic racism sufficient to permit the accused to challenge jurors for cause.

[66] Klebuc J in *R v. Carratt* [[1999] SJ No. 626 (QB)] refused to take judicial notice of racial bias in the context of a sentencing hearing held to determine whether to impose a conditional sentence on an aboriginal offender. He was unwilling to accept the finding made by Barclay J in *Fleury* that systemic racism exists in Saskatchewan. He found he could not make such a finding in the absence of evidence on that issue in the particular community where the offence occurred. He was unable to determine on the evidence before him whether anti-aboriginal racism existed and had materially affected the particular offender's ability to obtain employment for example, and was the cause of the offender being before the Court.

[67] Klebuc J was satisfied on the evidence of Professor Quigley of the Faculty of Law of the University of Saskatchewan, that aboriginal peoples suffered from poverty, substance abuse and racism and were overrepresented in the prison population. At the end of the day, however, he was unable to find that those factors were the cause of the particular aboriginal offender's criminal conduct and he refused to impose a community-based sentence. I agree generally with the approach he used in attempting to comply with the directives in *Gladue*.

[68] The evidentiary question is thus reduced to: are the systemic or background matters so "notorious" that a sentencing judge can take judicial notice of them without

further evidence when deciding whether to apply a restorative approach to sentencing so as to make the system more relevant to aboriginal peoples?

[69] Justices Cory and Iacobucci seem to have provided at least a partial answer to that evidentiary question by stating, immediately after their comments on judicial notice, that it will probably be necessary for some evidence to be adduced to assist the sentencing judge to decide these issues. In my opinion, evidence will be required on the "*Gladue* sentencing hearing" to establish the systemic factors referred to by the Supreme Court as well as to demonstrate how those factors have contributed to the offender being before the court and how those factors should influence the type of sentence to be imposed on the particular aboriginal offender. No operation of the principle of judicial notice will provide enough specific relevant evidence about the particular systemic or background factors which exist in the offender's community. Nor will it provide specific evidence as to how those factors have affected the particular aboriginal offender and whether they resulted in him being before the Court. It will be necessary for the accused to call some evidence to assist the sentencing judge in determining whether, in the particular community where the offender resides, there are systemic or other background factors which have had an influence on how this particular offender came before the court with the result that there will be a different approach to sentencing and the kind of sentence to be imposed.

If the Supreme Court intended in *Gladue* to approve the use of official reports or social science data as sources of information, further clarification will be required on this point because, as Vancise JA observes in *Laliberte*, the statement by Cory and Iacobucci JJ concerning judicial notice is broad and problematic. For example, what about the personal experience of the judge, a matter that raised controversy when it was considered (in another context) in *R v. R.D.S.*, [1997] 3 SCR 484? No one expects a judge to dissociate herself from her entire experience as a citizen, a lawyer, or a judge, but personal experience is not always reliable—and might be positively unreliable—as a basis for making decisions on sentence. A judge should be able to rely on her knowledge of local sentencing practices or treatment options, but this should also be expressed in open court and put on the record so that the parties know the basis of the decision. The statutory requirement that the sentencing judge provide reasons for her decision is consistent with this.

Judicial notice dispenses with the need for proof of relevant facts, and it is problematic, to say the least, where those facts are complex and contentious. The personal experience of the judge as a source of relevant factual information is also problematic, either because it might be unreliable or because it might induce the judge to ignore relevant evidence. Some issues require a firm evidentiary foundation before they can affect a sentencing decision. One way of accomplishing this is to produce expert evidence, as was done in *Laliberte*. An issue that illustrates the need for firm evidence is the prevalence or incidence of an offence in the local community. Reliance on such information for stronger sentences is controversial because it is a form of exemplary justice. Nonetheless, a marked increase in the incidence of an offence or the recognition of a substantial rate of occurrence has been accepted by the courts as a relevant aggravating factor. But a judge cannot rely on her personal experience or observations concerning the court's recent cases as a basis for this decision.

See, for example, *R v. Priest* (1996), 110 CCC (3d) 289, 293 (Ont. CA). Moreover, courts have demanded solid evidence and not just anecdotal accounts from local police officers. See, for example, *R v. Petrovic* (1984), 41 CR (3d) 275 (Ont. CA) and *R v. Edwards* (1996), 105 CCC (3d) 21 (Ont. CA).

In *R v. Spence*, [2005] 3 SCR 458, the Supreme Court held that the permissible scope of judicial notice may vary according to the nature of the issue in question and that stricter standards should be applied where the fact in issue is determinative of an issue before the court. This decision signalled a caution against expansive use of judicial notice and provides another good reason to be wary of judicial notice in sentencing decisions. For other comments, see Vancise & Healy, "Judicial Notice in Sentencing" (2002), 65 *Sask. L Rev.* 97.

VII. LIMITS OF FACT FINDING

There is a distinction between evidence and argument but, taken together, these are the materials that constitute the record of the case before adjudication. There are principles governing the presentation of acceptable evidence and argument. Related to these principles are others concerned with the respective roles of parties, advocates, and judges.

The distinction between evidence and argument is sometimes obscure. For example, suppose a research report is published in a peer-reviewed journal by a criminologist. The publication includes empirical data and an analysis of that data, and concludes that a legislated increase in the sentencing regime for a specific offence produced a significant reduction in the subsequent occurrence of that offence. In other words, the new article tends to show that deterrence works. Relying on this article, a prosecutor argues that, in the face of increasing prevalence of the same offence, the sentencing judge should raise the "usual range" substantially to pursue the goals of protection and crime reduction through deterrence.

If the criminologist is not called, qualified, and examined, any assertion in the essay that is offered for the truth of its contents would appear to be a farrago of expert opinion and hearsay. What if the article is not cited by a party at all but is raised by the trial judge? What if the essay is not cited by anyone at trial but appears for the first time in an appellate factum? What if it is not argued on appeal by the parties but is cited by the appellate court in its judgment?

The criminologist's essay, including the empirical data and the conclusions, is only one example in an array of matter between evidence and argument that could variously be characterized as hearsay, opinion, literature, or anecdote. Some of this might well be credible and trustworthy, but much of the time it does not easily fit with the orthodox views on evidence and argument. Moreover, it can be extremely dangerous and open to exaggeration and manipulation. Academic views, data, and interpretation can be refuted. See the wonderful controversy involving a challenge to a position on crime reduction taken by Steven Levitt of "Freakonomics" fame, "The Case of Critics Who Missed the Point: A Reply to Webster et al."; Webster, Doob, and Zimring, "Proposition 8 and Crime Rates in California: The Case of the Disappearing Deterrent"; and other related commentary in (2006), *Criminology and Public Policy* 413-78.

In the interests of having the fullest range of information relevant to sentence, perhaps there should be some relaxation of orthodox views. But it is terrain that is fraught with difficulty, as the next case illustrates.

R v. Hamilton and Mason
(2004), 186 CCC (3d) 129 (Ont. CA)

DOHERTY JA:

I

The imposition of a fit sentence can be as difficult a task as any faced by a trial judge. That task is particularly difficult where otherwise decent, law-abiding persons commit very serious crimes in circumstances that justifiably attract understanding and empathy. These two cases fall within that category of cases.

As difficult as the determination of a fit sentence can be, that process has a narrow focus. It aims at imposing a sentence that reflects the circumstances of the *specific* offence and the attributes of the *specific* offender. Sentencing is not based on group characteristics, but on the facts relating to the *specific* offence and *specific* offender as revealed by the evidence adduced in the proceedings. A sentencing proceeding is also not the forum in which to right perceived societal wrongs, allocate responsibility for criminal conduct as between the offender and society, or "make up" for perceived social injustices by the imposition of sentences that do not reflect the seriousness of the crime.

In the two sentences under appeal, the trial judge lost that narrow focus. He expanded the sentencing proceedings to include broad societal issues that were not raised by the parties. A proceeding that was intended to determine fit sentences for two *specific* offenders who committed two *specific* crimes became an inquiry by the trial judge into much broader and more complex issues. In conducting this inquiry, the trial judge stepped outside of the proper role of a judge on sentencing and ultimately imposed sentences that were inconsistent with the statutory principles of sentencing and binding authorities from this court.

II

Overview

The respondents were caught trying to smuggle cocaine they had swallowed into Canada from Jamaica. Each pleaded guilty to one count of importing cocaine. The charges were unrelated, but as the respondents proposed to rely on the same expert evidence, the charges proceeded by way of a joint sentencing hearing.

At trial, counsel for the respondents indicated they would seek conditional sentences relying on Dr. Doob's expert opinion evidence to the effect that general deterrence had little or no value in sentencing offenders like the respondents, and on the respondents' positive antecedents. The Crown, relying on cases from this court to the effect that cocaine importers—even if they are classified as couriers—should usually receive substantial jail terms, sought sentences of between two and three years.

After a lengthy hearing, the trial judge, in thoughtful and detailed reasons, concluded that the respondents should receive conditional sentences. He rested his conclusion that conditional sentences were appropriate primarily on his finding that the respondents, because of their race, gender, and poverty, were particularly vulnerable targets to those who sought out individuals to act as cocaine couriers. He made these findings based on material he had produced during the hearing and his own experiences as a judge. Ms. Hamilton received a conditional sentence of twenty months on terms that provided for partial house arrest in the first year of the sentence and a curfew for the remainder of the sentence. Ms. Mason received a conditional sentence of two years less a day on terms that provided for partial house arrest in the first fifteen months of the sentence and a curfew for the rest of the sentence.

The Crown appealed. I agree with Crown counsel's submission that the trial judge effectively took over the sentencing proceedings, and in doing so went beyond the role assigned to a trial judge in such proceedings. I am also satisfied that the sentences imposed reflect errors in principle. While I would not hold that sentences of less than two years were inappropriate in all of the circumstances, I would hold that the trial judge fell into reversible error in imposing conditional sentences. On a proper application of the relevant principles of sentencing and the authorities of this court, these offences merited substantial prison terms, despite the mitigating effect of the respondents' personal circumstances.

III

The Reasons for Sentence

As will be discussed in more detail below, the sentencing proceedings evolved over several months into an inquiry into a variety of issues, most of which were introduced and pursued by the trial judge. Although all of the issues canvassed during the proceedings were dealt with in the reasons for judgment, not all were ultimately germane to the sentences imposed by the trial judge. For example, the trial judge concluded that Dr. Doob's evidence could play no role in his determination of the appropriate sentence (paras. 165-69). I do not propose to review those parts of the reasons that do not figure in the ultimate dispositions.

The trial judge's decision to impose conditional sentences can be traced through four stages. First, he held (paras. 178, 220) that the sentencing guidelines set down in *R v. Madden* (1996), 104 CCC (3d) 548 (Ont. CA) and *R v. Cunningham* 1996 CanLII 1311 (ONCA), (1996), 104 CCC (3d) 542 (Ont. CA) providing for sentences in the range of three to five years for the importation of cocaine in amounts of "one kilogram more or less," did not have direct application since the amounts of cocaine imported by the respondents were significantly less than one kilogram. ...

Second, the trial judge held, based on materials he had produced and his own experience presiding in a court that dealt with many cases involving cocaine importation from Jamaica, that the respondents were the victims of systemic racial and gender bias. These biases contributed to the respondents' impoverished circumstances and made them particularly vulnerable to those who sought out persons to courier cocaine to Canada from Jamaica. The trial judge concluded that the systemic racial and gender bias played a role in the commission of the offences and should mitigate the sentence imposed. He said at para. 224:

> Since cocaine importation by a courier is not a violent and serious offence, as that expression is used in the *Wells* and *Borde* cases, the question naturally arises as to whether

systemic and background factors relating to the commission of this offence can more generously serve to mitigate the sentence to be imposed. *In my view, systemic and background factors, identified in this case … should logically be relevant to mitigate the penal consequences for cocaine importers conscripted as couriers.* [Emphasis added.]

Third, after considering the systemic and background factors and other mitigating factors relevant to each respondent, the trial judge concluded that sentences in the upper reformatory range were appropriate (para. 231).

Fourth, in deciding that the respondents should receive conditional sentences under s. 742.1, the trial judge again said at para. 234:

> Neither Pre-sentence report rejected community supervision as a potential aspect of any sentence imposed. Systemic and background factors relating to the offender's involvement in these crimes militate toward serious consideration of imprisonment to be served conditionally. In all of the circumstances, the sanction of a conditional term of imprisonment does not violate the principles of sections 718 to 718.2 of the *Criminal Code*.

The trial judge justified the imposition of conditional sentences on an alternative basis. After observing that the case law could be read as limiting the availability of conditional sentences for convicted cocaine importers to "exceptional circumstances," the trial judge held that such circumstances existed in these cases, indicating at para. 234:

> [I]n the highly unusual circumstances of the excessive delay between plea and sentencing and the test case features of these cases, the terms of imprisonment ought to be served conditionally.

. . .

V

The Arguments on Appeal

The Crown challenges the manner in which the sentencing proceedings were conducted and the fitness of the sentences imposed.

Crown counsel acknowledges that the trial judge has a broad discretion in the conduct of sentencing proceedings. He alleges, however, that the trial judge lost his appearance of impartiality by raising various issues on his own initiative, directing the Crown to locate and produce evidence on those issues, producing his own evidence on some of those issues, and eventually imposing sentences based in large measure on findings that were the product of the material produced by the trial judge and his personal experiences. It is the Crown's contention that, while no doubt well-intentioned, the trial judge effectively took on the combined role of advocate, witness, and judge, thereby losing the appearance of a neutral arbiter.

Insofar as the fitness of the sentences is concerned, the Crown submits that stripped to the essentials, the respondents received conditional sentences because they were poor, black, and female. He submits that none of these factors diminish the seriousness of the offence or justify a conditional sentence. Counsel further argues that the imposition of conditional sentences based on the race and gender of the respondents will only reinforce the prevailing wisdom among drug overlords that young black women make ideal drug couriers, thereby perpetuating and exacerbating the vulnerability of the very group the trial judge sought to assist.

Crown counsel advances several specific alleged errors in principle in support of his submission that the sentences are unfit. He contends that:

- the trial judge made findings of fact pertaining to the respondents' involvement in the crimes that had no basis in the evidence;
- there was no evidence to support the finding that systemic racism or gender bias played a role in the commission of the offence;
- the trial judge improperly used evidence of systemic racial and gender bias to lower the respondents' sentences below sentences which could properly reflect the seriousness of the offences;

. . .

The respondents submit that there was nothing wrong with the way in which the trial judge conducted the sentencing hearing. They contend that a trial judge's obligation to impose a fit sentence may require the judge to go beyond the case as presented by counsel. The respondents submit that through the trial judge's initiative, several important issues, all of which were relevant to the imposition of a fit sentence, were raised and addressed in the course of these proceedings. They rely on s. 723(3) of the *Criminal Code*, which specifically permits a trial judge to raise matters on his or her own initiative at sentencing.

The respondents further contend that the trial judge took pains to raise the issues in a way that would ensure that all parties had a full and fair opportunity to respond to those issues. Counsel argue that it was much better for the trial judge to make counsel aware of the relevant material available to him before using that material, rather than simply relying on it without giving counsel any chance to address its merits. The respondents submit that there is nothing in the conduct of the proceedings or in the nature of the material produced by the trial judge that suggests he had formed firm, unalterable views on the issues he raised with counsel.

The respondents also observe, accurately, that the Crown did not object to the manner in which the proceedings were conducted, but instead fully participated in those proceedings. They strongly contend that as the Crown did not object at trial, it cannot raise these objections on appeal.

With respect to the fitness of sentence, the respondents begin with a submission that the length of the sentences imposed by the trial judge—slightly less than two years—is within the appropriate range having regard to the amounts of cocaine imported by Ms. Mason and Ms. Hamilton. The respondents next argue that the trial judge properly took into consideration the personal mitigating factors. The respondents further submit that the trial judge was obliged to factor his own experience into the assessment of the evidence before him and to place that evidence in its proper social context. In these circumstances, the systemic racial and gender bias suffered by the respondents was properly viewed as a relevant mitigating circumstance. The respondents further submit that if they are correct in arguing that sentences of less than two years were within the appropriate range, the circumstances of these offenders fully justify conditional sentences. Counsel quite properly remind this court that the trial judge's weighing of the various relevant factors must be accorded deference in this court unless it can be said to be unreasonable.

. . .

VI

The Conduct of the Proceedings

(a) How the Proceedings Unfolded

Ms. Hamilton and Ms. Mason entered guilty pleas on March 6 and April 16, 2002, respectively. The proceedings were adjourned for the preparation of pre-sentence reports and to allow the respondents to obtain expert evidence directed at the efficacy of general deterrence as a principle of sentencing in cases like these.

The defence retained Dr. Doob, a respected criminologist. His report was provided to the Crown shortly before July 29, 2002. On July 29th, the Crown requested a brief adjournment to consider its position in light of Dr. Doob's report. On that same day, the trial judge, purporting to act under s. 723(3) of the *Criminal Code*, advised the Crown that he wanted the Crown to produce evidence on what the trial judge referred to as the "certainty of detection." In exchanges with Crown counsel, it became clear that the trial judge was concerned about a number of issues. These included:

- the steps, if any, taken by the Government of Canada to reduce the incidence of drug smuggling from Jamaica;
- the extent to which the Government of Canada used its power to regulate and license air carriers to encourage those carriers to take steps to curtail illicit drug importation;
- Canada's treaty obligations and any protocol obligations applicable to the interdiction of drug smuggling; and
- steps taken at airports in Jamaica and Pearson International Airport to combat drug importation.

During his dialogue with Crown counsel, the trial judge said:

> I'm not at all clear, in my mind, what, if anything, Canada has done to the licensing and regulatory scheme for landing rights for airplanes, international flights, in order to make the point with air carriers that we do have illicit narcotic laws that exist and we expect partnership and enforcement.

The trial judge also expressed concern that the airlines could be seen as being "wilfully blind" to the importation of cocaine from Jamaica.

The trial judge candidly acknowledged that his inquiry into the "certainty of detection" issues as part of the sentencing process was "admittedly a new way of looking at the world."

. . .

Some time before November 12th, the Crown produced material in response to the "certainty of detection" issues raised by the trial judge.

A few days before November 12th, the proceedings took a dramatic turn. The trial judge, through his secretary, sent counsel about 700 pages of material garnered from his own researches. The material consisted of reports from various governmental agencies in different countries, statistical information relating to the Canadian population at large and the prison population, law reform material from various countries, and newspaper articles. The material related to [four] broad areas:

- the extent of cocaine use and the harm caused by its use;
- the "certainty of detection" issues earlier identified by the trial judge and, in particular, "high tech" steps taken in other jurisdictions to combat drug importation through international airports;
- statistical information and various reports relating to rates of imprisonment generally, rates of imprisonment broken down by gender and race, and rates of imprisonment for drug-related offences; and
- reports relating to racial and gender discrimination in and out of jail.

On November 12th, the trial judge advised counsel that he had decided to produce this material when it became apparent to him that information of the kind contained in his material was "not coming from either side." There had been no suggestion by any party to the proceedings that race or gender had any relevance to the determination of fit sentences for the respondents before the trial judge distributed his material.

The trial judge invited submissions on the admissibility of the material he had produced. Crown counsel indicated that he was "a bit surprised" when he received the material as, in his view, it substantially broadened the scope of the sentencing hearing. Crown counsel observed that the material introduced "a racial issue" into the sentencing proceedings for the first time.

A lengthy discussion ensued between the Crown and the trial judge. After acknowledging that the defence had not raised race, the trial judge said:

> But clearly as a trial judge in this port of entry, Brampton, responsible for the Pearson International Airport, I think it is fair to say that having done this for almost nine years, that I have been struck by the number of single mothers, black women who have appeared before me over that time period. *And it leads me to wonder whether this is a group that is targeted for courier conscription by the overseers, whether in fact, compared to other narcotics offences or other offences generally, females, female blacks, form a disproportionate group within the population of people sentenced for cocaine importing.* Where that takes me I'm not sure, but we should know in sentencing, it seems to me, whether there is a disproportionate effect on any particular group by a sentencing policy. [Emphasis added.]

The trial judge made it clear that he was not suggesting that the respondents' arrests or prosecutions were racially motivated or otherwise tainted by racial or gender bias. The trial judge was, however, concerned that the substantial jail sentences routinely imposed for cocaine importation had a disproportionate effect on a disadvantaged group, namely poor black single mothers, because drug overseers selected their couriers from that disadvantaged group. The trial judge referred to race and gender as part of the "contextual perspective" he was obliged to take on sentencing.

Ultimately, Crown counsel indicated that he wished some time to consider his position on the issue of race as raised by the trial judge. Counsel added:

> I'm not suggesting that it is not appropriate for a court to consider that, it's just that I didn't direct my mind to it and it may significantly add to the amount of time I require to re-focus my attention on that issue. ...

The sentencing proceedings continued on November 12th, 13th, and 14th. Dr. Doob testified on November 12th and November 13th. On November 14th, the Crown called three witnesses, one from Air Canada and two from Canada Customs, to address some of the "certainty of detection" issues raised by the trial judge. Two of these witnesses were questioned at length by the trial judge.

The sentencing proceedings recommenced on December 19, 2002, and continued on January 20 and January 22, 2003. During these proceedings, the trial judge produced approximately 300 additional pages of material relating to the issues he had raised during the sentencing proceedings. The Crown called one more witness to address some of the "certainty of detection" issues and also filed certain material dealing with those issues as well as the race/gender issues raised by the trial judge. Throughout this part of the proceedings, the trial judge continued to request additional information from the Crown and the Crown continued to attempt to respond to those requests. In the end, the Crown was unable to produce all of the statistical information that the trial judge had requested.

At no stage of the proceedings did the Crown object to the trial judge raising the issues that he raised, or object to the trial judge taking into account the material the trial judge had produced.

The trial judge rendered judgment on February 20, 2003. His reasons made extensive reference to the material he produced and tracked the concerns he expressed when he introduced the issues of race and gender bias into the proceedings.

(b) Did the Trial Judge Go Too Far?

I will first address the respondents' argument that this court should not reach the merits of this ground of appeal. ...

... Crown counsel contends that the trial judge, in overstepping his role, fundamentally altered the nature of the proceedings. Counsel contends that the trial judge turned the proceedings from one designed to determine a fit sentence for individual offenders, to one designed to enquire into a variety of societal problems which, the trial judge, through his experience, had come to associate with the sentencing of black women who courier drugs into Canada from Jamaica. Crown counsel contends that this fundamental alteration of the essential purpose of the proceeding in and of itself invalidates the result.

... I think there is merit to ... the Crown's submission. The nature of the proceedings was fundamentally changed and this change contributed to the errors in principle reflected in the sentences imposed.

Having read and reread the transcripts, I must conclude that the trial judge does appear to have assumed the combined role of advocate, witness, and judge. No doubt, the trial judge's extensive experience in sentencing cocaine couriers had left him with genuine and legitimate concerns about the effectiveness and fairness of sentencing practices as applied to single poor black women who couriered cocaine into Canada for relatively little gain. The trial judge unilaterally decided to use these proceedings to raise, explore, and address various issues which he believed negatively impacted on the effectiveness and fairness of current sentencing practices as they related to some cocaine importers. Through his personal experience and personal research, the trial judge became the prime source of information in respect of those issues. The trial judge also became the driving force pursuing those issues during the proceedings.

No one suggests that a trial judge is obliged to remain passive during the sentencing phase of the criminal process. Trial judges can, and sometimes must, assume an active role in the course of a sentencing proceeding. Section 723(3) of the *Criminal Code* provides that a court may, on its own motion, require the production of evidence that "would assist in the determination of the appropriate sentence." Quite apart from that statutory power, the case law has long recognized that where a trial judge is required by law to consider a factor in determining the appropriate sentence and counsel has not provided the information necessary to properly consider that factor, the court can, on its own initiative, make the necessary inquiries and obtain the necessary evidence: *R v. Wells* 2000 SCC 10 (CanLII), (2000), 141 CCC (3d) 368 at 390-91 (SCC); *R v. Gladue*, 1999 CanLII 679 (SCC), [1999] 1 SCR 688 at paras. 84-85.

Recognition that a trial judge can go beyond the issues and evidence produced by the parties on sentencing where necessary to ensure the imposition of a fit sentence does not mean that the trial judge's power is without limits or that it will be routinely exercised. In considering both the limits of the power and the limits of the exercise of the power, it is wise to bear in mind that the criminal process, including the sentencing phase, is basically adversarial. Usually, the parties are the active participants in the process and the judge serves as a neutral, passive arbiter. Generally speaking, it is left to the parties to choose the issues, stake out their positions, and decide what evidence to present in support of those positions. The trial judge's role is to listen, clarify where necessary, and ultimately evaluate the merits of the competing cases presented by the parties.

The trial judge's role as the arbiter of the respective merits of competing positions developed and put before the trial judge by the parties best ensures judicial impartiality and the appearance of judicial impartiality. Human nature is such that it is always easier to objectively assess the merits of someone else's argument. The relatively passive role assigned to the trial judge also recognizes that judges, by virtue of their very neutrality, are not in a position to make informed decisions as to which issues should be raised, or the evidence that should be led. Judicial intrusion into counsel's role can cause unwarranted delay and bring unnecessary prolixity to the proceedings.

Judges must be very careful before introducing issues into the sentencing proceeding. Where an issue may or may not be germane to the determination of the appropriate sentence, the trial judge should not inject that issue into the proceedings without first determining from counsel their positions as to the relevance of that issue. If counsel takes the position that the issue is relevant, then it should be left to counsel to produce whatever evidence or material he or she deems appropriate, although the trial judge may certainly make counsel aware of materials known to the trial judge which are germane to the issue. If counsel takes the position that the issue raised by the trial judge is not relevant on sentencing, it will be a rare case where the trial judge will pursue that issue.

It is also important that the trial judge limit the scope of his or her intervention into the role traditionally left to counsel. The trial judge should frame any issue that he or she introduces as precisely as possible and relate it to the case before the court. This will avoid turning the sentencing hearing into a de facto commission of inquiry.

The manner in which the proceedings were conducted created at least four problems. First, by assuming the multi-faceted role of advocate, witness, and judge, the trial judge put the appearance of impartiality at risk, if not actually compromising that appearance. For example, the trial judge introduced the issues of race and gender bias into the proceedings, and then, through the material he produced and the questions he addressed to Crown counsel, the trial judge appeared to drive the inquiry into those matters towards certain results. Those results are reflected in his reasons. Looking at the entirety of the proceedings, there is a risk that a reasonable observer could conclude that the trial judge's findings as to the significance of race and gender bias in fixing the appropriate sentences had been made before he directed an inquiry into those issues. At the very least, the conduct of the proceedings produced a dynamic in which the trial judge became the Crown's adversary on the issues introduced by the trial judge.

Although the appearance of impartiality was put at risk by the conduct of these proceedings, the trial judge did take steps to try and preserve the appearance of fairness. He gave counsel clear indications of his concerns and any tentative opinions he had formed. He also provided the material to counsel to which he planned to refer in considering the issues he had raised. This procedure was much fairer to the parties and much more likely to produce an accurate result than had the trial judge simply referred to the material without giving counsel any notice: *R v. Paul* 1998 CanLII 12246 (NBCA), (1998), 124 CCC (3d) 1 (NBCA); *Cronk v. Canadian General Insurance Co.* 1995 CanLII 814 (ONCA), (1995), 25 OR (3d) 505 at 518 (CA); Ian Binnie, "Judicial Notice: How Much Is Too Much?" in *Law Society of Upper Canada, Special Lectures 2003: The Law of Evidence* (Toronto: Irwin Law, 2004) 543 at 564-65. Much of the material produced by the trial judge was not suggestive of any particular answer to the questions raised by the trial judge in the course of the proceedings. The scrupulous fairness with which the trial judge conducted the proceedings went some way towards overcoming the potentially adverse effects of the extraordinary role he assumed in the conduct of the proceedings.

The second problem arising from the trial judge's approach is that it produced a fundamental disconnect between the case on sentencing presented by counsel for the respondents and the case of the paradigmatic cocaine courier constructed by the trial judge. From the time he first introduced race and gender into the proceedings, the trial judge spoke in terms of poor black single women who were "targeted" and "conscripted" by drug overseers to act as couriers. The trial judge referred to these couriers as "virtue-tested" by drug overseers and as living "in the despair of poverty." The trial judge also described these couriers as using the small compensation they received from the drug overseers to pay rent, feed children, and support a subsistence-level existence.

Counsel for the respondents chose to provide next to no information about the respondents' involvement in these crimes. Ms. Hamilton indicated she acted out of financial need. Ms. Mason offered no explanation. There was no evidence that these respondents were conscripted, virtue-tested, or paid minimal compensation, nor was there evidence that such compensation was used to pay for the necessaries of life. The reasons for sentence indicate to me that the trial judge based his sentences more on his concept of the typical drug courier than on the evidence pertaining to these two individuals.

A third problem with the trial judge's conduct of the proceedings is that it created a real risk of inaccurate fact-finding. The trial judge introduced a veritable blizzard of raw statistical information. He also produced various forms of opinion on a wide variety of topics. None of this material was analyzed or tested in any way.

It is difficult to know what to make of the statistical data without the assistance of evidence from a properly qualified witness. For example, the trial judge made extensive reference to statistics dealing with the incarceration of black women in Canadian penitentiaries. As I understand his analysis, he concluded that since the percentage of black women in the penitentiary was approximately three times higher than the percentage of black women in the general population, black women were over-represented in the prison population. He inferred from that conclusion support for his further conclusion that sentencing practices as applied to those who imported cocaine from Jamaica reflected systemic social, racial, and gender bias against poor black women.

It is not clear to me what connection, if any, there is between the number of black women in the penitentiary and the relevance, if any, of race or gender to sentencing principles as applied to the crime of cocaine importation. Furthermore, it is not apparent to me that any inference can be drawn from a single statistic indicating that black women make up six per cent of the female penitentiary population and only about two per cent of the general population. That statistic would have to be considered in the context of other statistical information indicating that the percentage of black women in the penitentiary has dropped dramatically over the last eight years (by almost a third), as has the actual number of black women in the penitentiary system. These decreases have occurred despite significant increases in the general black population and significant increases in the overall female penitentiary population. These statistical trends could suggest that current sentencing practices are well on their way to eliminating any over-representation of black females in the penitentiary.

Even the one statistical feature highlighted by the trial judge is of questionable value. The population giving rise to the trial judge's conclusion that black females are over-represented in the penitentiary population is a very small one. As of January 2003, there were twenty-five black women in the penitentiary out of a total population of almost 350,000 black women in Canada. That means that .007 per cent of the female black population in Canada is in the penitentiary. The validity of any inferences drawn from such small numbers must be open to question.

Similarly, the trial judge compared the number of black women appearing before him charged with cocaine importation with the number of black women he saw in his local shopping mall to support his conclusion that black women were over-represented in the population of persons charged with cocaine importation. Absent some expert evidence, I do not think the trial judge could make any informed decision as to the significance of that personal observation in determining the relevance, if any, of race or gender to sentencing practices as applied to cocaine importation.

The trial judge acknowledged that there were other reasons which could explain the over-representation of black women among couriers bringing cocaine into Canada from

Jamaica. The population of Jamaica is largely a black population. It seems sensible that those seeking couriers would seek out individuals with some connection to Jamaica and some "innocent" explanation to offer to the authorities for travel to and from Jamaica. Absent any evidence, the trial judge could not make an informed choice from among the various possible explanations for this over-representation.

I do not think the meaning of the statistics introduced by the trial judge or the inferences that could be properly drawn from them is self-evident. There were real risks that these statistics could be misunderstood and misused absent proper expert evidence. Instead of being treated with the caution that all statistics deserve, these statistics—probably because they were introduced by the trial judge—took on a strong aura of reliability and were treated as if they were self-explanatory.

A fourth difficulty with the way the trial judge conducted these proceedings is evident from his introduction of the "certainty of detection" issues. These issues consumed a good deal of time and effort. In the end, quite properly, they played virtually no role in determining the appropriate sentence. The trial judge summarized the evidence at length (paras. 27-51), but then made only two brief references to it. He referred to the evidence when rejecting the respondents' argument that general deterrence should be discounted as a principle of sentencing (paras. 154-56) and he referred to it in rejecting the Crown's argument that a conditional sentence would deprecate the gravity of the offence of importing cocaine (para. 228). With respect, I see no connection between the "certainty of detection" issues and the question of whether a conditional sentence would deprecate the gravity of the offence.

In the end, the inquiry into the "certainty of detection" issues produced little, if anything, of assistance in the determination of the appropriate sentences. This is not surprising. The complexity of those issues could not be properly identified and explored in a sentencing hearing. A sentencing hearing is not the appropriate forum in which to inquire into Canada's compliance with various treaty obligations. The inquiry into the "certainty of detection" issues did, however, lengthen and complicate the proceedings. The inquiry into these issues also contributed to the impression that the trial judge had decided to conduct an inquiry into matters that concerned him rather than conduct a sentencing hearing to determine the appropriate sentence for these two respondents.

. . .

(c) The Errors in Principle

(i) The Findings of Fact

The trial judge concluded that conditional sentences were appropriate largely because the personal responsibility of the respondents for their crimes was significantly diminished by the effects of systemic racial and gender bias. In the trial judge's view, society had to take its share of the responsibility for the respondents' crimes (paras. 188, 221). On the trial judge's approach, society assumed its share of responsibility for the respondents' conduct through a mitigation of the penalty imposed on the respondents.

The trial judge made several findings of fact which were specific to the respondents' involvement in their offences. He relied on these findings to support his conclusion that their personal culpability was significantly reduced. He found as a fact that:

- the respondents were "conscripted" by the "drug distribution hierarchy" to participate in their crimes (para. 198);
- the involvement of the respondents was the result of "virtue-testing" by "drug operation overseers" (para. 195);
- the respondents were paid relatively minimal amounts and used those amounts to provide the bare necessities for their families (para. 191); and
- the respondents' children would be "effectively orphaned" if the respondents were incarcerated (para. 198).

Although the rules of evidence are substantially broadened on the sentencing inquiry, factual findings that are germane to the determination of the appropriate sentence and are not properly the subject of judicial notice must be supported by the evidence. There was no evidence to support the findings of fact outlined immediately above.

The respondents chose not to offer any explanation for, or description of, their involvement in the crimes, apart from Ms. Hamilton's indication that she acted out of financial need. The trial judge had no information as to how the respondents came to be involved in this scheme, what their prior association or relationship was with the individuals who may have hired them, when or where the importation plans were formed, what amount of compensation was paid to the respondents, or how the respondents proposed to use that compensation. He also had no information concerning the care of the children if the respondents went to jail. All of this information was uniquely within the knowledge of the respondents. If the respondents were conscripted—that is, compelled to engage in this activity—they could have said so. If they agreed to be involved in the crimes only after repeated requests, they could have said so, just as they could have provided other details concerning their involvement in the scheme and the compensation they received. Similarly, if the effect of the respondents' imprisonment on the children was as drastic as the trial judge held it to be, I would have expected the respondents to have led evidence to that effect.

The Crown's concession that the respondents were couriers did not constitute an admission that they possessed every characteristic that the trial judge ascribed to couriers. Nor do I accept the contention that requiring the respondents to lead the kind of evidence described above works any hardship on them. This kind of evidence has been given in other cases: *e.g.* see *R v. Bennett, supra.* Safety concerns arising out of implicating others in the scheme can be addressed if and when they arise. In any event, concerns about the potential safety of the offender should he or she provide certain evidence, do not justify assumptions that have no basis in the evidence.

The trial judge did not purport to base the findings of fact outlined above on any material that actually related to these respondents. Instead, he relied on his experiences in sentencing other individuals who couriered cocaine from Jamaica. He applied those generalizations to these respondents (paras. 179-83, 191-98). In doing so, he relied on *R v. S.(R.D.)* 1997 CanLII 324 (SCC), (1997), 118 CCC (3d) 353 (SCC). I read that authority as prohibiting the very kind of fact-finding made by the trial judge.

· · ·

R v. S.(R.D.) draws a distinction between findings of fact based exclusively on personal judicial experience and judicial perceptions of applicable social context, and findings of fact based on evidence viewed through the lens of personal judicial experience and social context. The latter is proper; the former is not.

The proper use of personal experience and social context can be demonstrated by reference to Ms. Hamilton's evidence concerning the motive for her crime. She testified that she acted out of dire financial need. The fact that a crime was committed for financial gain can, in some circumstances, mitigate personal responsibility, and, in different circumstances, it can increase personal responsibility. The trial judge was required to determine what weight should be given on sentencing to Ms. Hamilton's admitted financial motive for committing the crime. In making that assessment, he was entitled to put her statement as to her motive in its proper context by recognizing, based on his experiences and the operative social context, that individuals in the circumstances of Ms. Hamilton often find themselves in very real financial need for reasons that include societal factors, like racial and gender bias, over which those individuals have no control. Used in this way, the tools of personal judicial experience and social context help illuminate the evidence. This use can be contrasted with the trial judge's use of his experience in other cases to make the specific finding of fact that these respondents were conscripted—that is, compelled by drug overseers to engage in this criminal activity—when there was no evidence as to how the respondents came to be involved.

The limits on judicial fact-finding based on prior judicial experience and social context are necessary for at least two reasons. First, fact-finding based on a judge's personal experience can interfere with the effective operation of the adversary process. It is difficult, if not impossible, to know, much less explore or challenge, a trial judge's perceptions based on prior judicial experiences or his or her appreciation of the social issues which form part of the context of the proceedings. Second, fact-finding based on generalities developed out of personal past experience can amount to fact-finding based on stereotyping. That risk is evident in this case. The trial judge appears to have viewed all poor black single women who import cocaine into Canada from Jamaica as essentially sharing the same characteristics. These characteristics describe individuals who, because of their difficult circumstances, have virtually no control over their own lives and turn to crime because they are unable to otherwise provide for their children. While this may be an apt description of some of the individuals who turn to cocaine importing, it is stereotyping to assume that all single black women who import cocaine into Canada fit this description.

(ii) The Relevance of Systemic Racial and Gender Bias

The trial judge took findings of fact for which I have found there was no evidence and combined them with what he described as the "systemic and background factors" of the respondents to mitigate the length of their sentences (para. 224) and to justify conditional sentences (para. 234). The phrase "systemic and background factors" referred to the trial judge's findings that the respondents were the subjects of societal racial and gender bias. The combined impact of the trial judge's specific findings of fact and his use of racial and gender bias is evident in para. 224:

> In my view, systemic and background factors, identified in this case ... should logically be relevant to mitigate the penal consequences for cocaine importers conscripted as couriers.

In making his findings with respect to the "systemic and background factors," the trial judge relied on his personal observations in sentencing cocaine couriers and conclusions drawn from the material he produced during the sentencing inquiry. He reasoned that institutional racism and gender bias contributed to the respondents' poverty and their inability to escape that poverty through legitimate means. He further held that those circumstances made the respondents ideal targets for those seeking individuals willing to take the risk of bringing cocaine into Canada for relatively minimal compensation. Finally, the trial judge held that single black women were over-represented among those who acted as cocaine couriers. This line of reasoning led him to hold at para. 193:

> The cocaine importation proscription has a differential impact on African Canadians in large measure because of social and economic inequalities.

I can accept the trial judge's observation that in his jurisdiction black women make up a higher percentage of the population charged with cocaine importation from Jamaica than do black women in the general Canadian population. At trial, Crown counsel conceded this kind of over-representation. I also have no difficulty accepting the self-evident observation that individuals in difficult economic circumstances with few prospects for improvement make ideal targets for criminals seeking individuals willing to bring cocaine into Canada from Jamaica for relatively little compensation. Nor do I think that anyone can take issue with the general assertion that racial and gender bias can contribute to the economic plight of individuals like the respondents. That is, of course, not to say that racial and gender bias must be taken as accounting for the poverty of all single black women who find themselves in the same position as the respondents. Each case must be assessed individually on the basis of the material placed before the sentencing court.

However, it is the criminal drug overseer who chooses couriers from among those whose economic condition makes them possible candidates. To the extent that economic circumstances makes one a potential courier, the pool of potential couriers is obviously large and not limited to blacks or women. If black women are over-represented among those who courier drugs into Canada from Jamaica, it must be because the criminal drug overseers choose individuals fitting that description in a disproportionate number. There was no suggestion in the material adduced before the trial judge that black females are over-represented among those hired to courier drugs from places other than Jamaica, or among those hired to smuggle other forms of contraband into Canada. This suggests to me that the obvious explanation for the over-representation of black females among cocaine couriers is the correct explanation. Jamaica is a predominantly black country. Presumably, those selecting couriers are more likely to select individuals with some connection to Jamaica and some plausible, innocent explanation to offer for their trip to Jamaica because experience tells them that these individuals have a better chance of avoiding detection than would other individuals whose economic circumstances would make them equally willing to take the chance. The direct cause of over-representation of black women among drug couriers is found in the selection processes of those who hire them.

The fact that an offender is a member of a group that has historically been subject to systemic racial and gender bias does not in and of itself justify any mitigation of sentence. Lower sentences predicated on nothing more than membership in a disadvantaged group further neither the principles of sentencing, nor the goals of equality.

A sentencing judge is, however, required to take into account all factors that are germane to the gravity of the offence and the personal culpability of the offender. That inquiry can encompass systemic racial and gender bias. As the court explained in *R v. Borde*, *supra*, at p. 236:

> However, the principles that are generally applicable to all offenders, including African-Canadians, are sufficiently broad and flexible to enable a sentencing court in appropriate cases to consider both the systemic and background factors that may have played a role in the commission of the offence. ...

Reference to factors that may "have played a role in the commission of the offence" encompasses a broad range of potential considerations. Those factors include any explanation for the offender's commission of the crime. If racial and gender bias suffered by the offender helps explain why the offender committed the crime, then those factors can be said to have "played a role in the commission of the offence."

It is explicit in the case of Ms. Hamilton and implicit in the case of Ms. Mason that their impoverished circumstances and poor economic prospects played an important role in their decision to commit these crimes. The reason for their desperate financial circumstances was relevant on sentencing. On the evidence, the respondents were not poor because they did not want to work, were irresponsible or because they had led a lifestyle beyond their means. The respondents were in dire economic circumstances for two main reasons. First, they assumed the responsibilities of parenthood at a very early age thereby substantially limiting their economic and educational prospects. Second, at an almost equally young age, they were burdened with the full responsibility for raising young children when the fathers of their children abandoned them.

The respondents did not try to forge any evidentiary connection between institutional racial and gender inequality and their particular circumstances. There was no attempt to bring the generalizations set out in the material relied on by the trial judge home to the lives of these respondents. Absent that kind of evidence, the trial judge could not find that the respondents' difficult economic circumstances were the direct result of systemic racial and gender bias. In any event, I do not think it is particularly helpful or necessary to try to attribute the respondents' economic circumstances to systemic societal racial or gender bias. What is important for the purpose of sentencing is that the respondents' very difficult economic circumstances, the underlying causes of their crimes, are very real and are to a large extent the product of circumstances that are either beyond their control, or for which they cannot be faulted.

As indicated earlier, an offender's explanation for a crime committed for money can enhance or mitigate personal culpability. The respondents' explanation for their crimes, heard by a judicial ear attuned to the realities of the lives of persons like the respondents, warranted some mitigation of the respondents' personal culpability.

How should the respondents' dire economic circumstances be taken into consideration? Clearly, they do not affect the seriousness of the offence. The crime of importing cocaine is no less serious because the importer did it for reasons which attract empathy and mitigate personal culpability. Because factors which go to explain the reason for the offender's commission of the crime do not reduce the seriousness of the crime, those factors must be given less weight in cases like these where the seriousness of the offence is the pre-eminent consideration on sentencing. The same factors could be given more weight in cases involving less serious crimes where the personal responsibility of the offender takes on more significance.

Even where the crime committed is very serious, however, factors going to personal culpability for the crime must still be considered. For the reasons outlined above, the circumstances which led the respondents to commit these crimes entitle them to some mitigation. It must, however, be stressed that consideration of the circumstances which led an offender to commit a crime is only part of the overall assessment that must be made in determining personal culpability for the purposes of imposing a sentence which complies with the proportionality principle. Our criminal law rejects a determinist theory of crime. The respondents had a choice to make and they made that choice knowing full well the harm that the choice could cause to the community. The economic circumstances of the respondents made their choice more understandable than it would have been in other circumstances, but it remains an informed choice to commit a very serious crime. The blunt fact is that a wide variety of societal ills—including, in some cases, racial and gender bias—are part of the causal soup that leads some individuals to commit crimes. If those ills are given prominence in assessing personal culpability, an individual's responsibility for his or her own actions will be lost.

There is nothing unique or new in the approach to sentencing outlined above. Trial judges have always entertained submissions to the effect that an offender is basically a good person whose crime is the product of a combination of circumstances, some of which are beyond the offender's control or responsibility. Put in the language of proportionality, these arguments are directed at lessening the personal culpability of the individual offender. If the trial judge accepts such arguments, the sentence imposed will be less onerous than it would have been but for those arguments. As Durno J put it in *R v. Bennett, supra*, a case very much like these cases, at pp. 14-15:

> The offender's background is always a relevant factor on sentencing. A sentence must be appropriate for both the offence and the offender. A person with a disadvantaged background, who has been subjected to systemic prejudices or racism, or was exposed to physical, sexual or emotional abuse, may receive a lower sentence than someone from a stable and peaceful background, where the offence is in some way linked to the background or systemic factors. The relevant factors in one person's background will be case specific. A single factor will rarely be determinative.

Evidence of the respondents' economic circumstances and the causes of those circumstances were potentially relevant to sentencing in a second way. One of the purposes of sentencing is to get at the root causes of the criminal activity and where possible eliminate that cause. If the cause of criminal activity can be addressed in probation terms relating to things such as job training, the fact that the offender's economic circumstances are the result of factors beyond his or her control would offer support for the claim that the sentence should be tailored to include probationary terms which address the underlying causes of the criminal activity. In cases involving serious crimes like this one, those terms would usually follow some period of imprisonment. Counsel for Ms. Hamilton suggested the kind of probation terms I have outlined above. None were imposed.

For the reasons set out above, the trial judge erred in holding that systemic racial and gender bias justified conditional sentences. Those factors provided part of the context for the respondents' explanation for their commission of the crimes. That explanation could not detract from the seriousness of the crimes, the principal reason the proportionality principle usually requires incarceration of drug importers.

The trial judge's imposition of conditional sentences is also inconsistent with existing jurisprudence, holding that conditional sentences will seldom be available for drug importation. If the trial judge accurately identified the prototypical drug courier, then on his analysis conditional sentences must become the norm for those caught couriering cocaine into Canada from Jamaica. That approach undermines the seriousness of the crimes and the harm done by those crimes to Canadian society, and it is in direct conflict with decisions from this court that were binding on the trial judge.

· · ·

VIII

The Appropriate Sentence

Where a trial judge commits an error in principle, the sentence imposed is no longer entitled to deference and it falls to the appellate court to impose the sentence it thinks fit: *R v. Rezaie* 1996 CanLII 1241 (ONCA), (1996), 112 CCC (3d) 97 at 103 (Ont. CA). Applying the analysis described earlier in these reasons, and bearing in mind the gravity of these offences and the circumstances tending to mitigate the personal culpability of the respondents, I think a term of imprisonment of twenty months would have been an appropriate sentence for Ms. Hamilton and a term of imprisonment of two years less a day would have been an appropriate sentence for Ms. Mason.

· · ·

I would grant leave to appeal and dismiss the appeals.

PROBLEMS

1. The accused has been found guilty of five counts of fraud on the government, including fraud on the scheme for social assistance and fraud on a program for the creation of jobs. The facts disclose that these fraudulent activities occurred over a period of seven years and the amounts gained, in total, exceeded $85,000. At trial, the accused raised a defence of necessity that was based on the theory that there was no other source of income for the accused and the accused's child. The defence was expressly rejected by the judge, who said that even if the accused was experiencing extremely hard times, there could still be no defence of necessity in law.

At the sentencing hearing, the accused intends to again raise the issue of necessitous circumstances—that is, having no source of income.

The prosecution intends to adduce evidence of a previous conviction of trafficking in marijuana that was recorded some 15 years ago. It intends to show the existence of an outstanding support order that the accused has done nothing to enforce. The prosecution also wishes to put in evidence the fact that the accused faces a pending charge of possession of stolen goods. Finally, the prosecution seeks to prove that despite the absence of a regular and legitimate income, the accused's standard of living is relatively high, not least because she lives with others who have been charged with unrelated, but similar, offences of fraud.

What difference would it make if the finding of guilt were based on a plea of guilty?

2. Small was charged with two counts of sexual assault, both allegedly committed during the summer of 1988 when he was the manager of a resort hotel in Muskoka. The Crown's disclosure indicates that the two victims will say:

Count 1: V was a 17-year-old maid at the hotel. One morning, Small walked into a room where she was cleaning. He spoke with her for a while and offered her a better job if she was "friendlier" to him. She quickly left the room. The next day, he followed her into a room and locked the door. He began talking about how difficult it was to get employment that summer and what a shame it would be if she lost her job. He started rubbing her arm and then grabbed her toward him. She fought with him and he threatened her if she didn't "shut up." After the rape, he avoided her and never spoke to her again.

Count 2: B was a 15-year-old babysitter hired to look after Small's young son while he and his wife worked. He returned to his apartment one day when his son was asleep. He and B had a cup of tea together. After the tea, Small began asking questions about B's boyfriends and the level of sexual activity among her peers. B was uncomfortable with the conversation and started to leave. Small grabbed her shoulders and threw her onto a sofa. He pinned her down and tried to removed her shirt, but she screamed. This woke up his son and Small ran out of the apartment.

a. Assume that the Crown elects to proceed summarily, and Small enters guilty pleas. When the facts, as above, are read in, Small's counsel says:

The essential elements of the offence of sexual assault are admitted with respect to both counts. However, the accused does not admit that the interaction in count one included sexual intercourse. Also, the involvement in count two did not extend beyond touching.

b. Assume that the Crown elects to proceed by indictment and Small elects trial by judge and jury. At his trial, V and B testify as above. On the witness stand, Small denies count one. He says that he and V had a consensual sexual relationship that continued all summer. With respect to B and count two, he testified that one day she sat beside him on a sofa when his son was asleep. She started asking him about V and made some suggestive comments to him. He interpreted these as a "come on," and he touched her breast. When she backed away, he jumped from the sofa. He never went close to her again. The jury found him guilty on both counts.

How should the judge determine the factual basis for sentencing in (a) and (b)?

CHAPTER FIVE

Sources of Information Relating to the Offender

Because of the relaxed rules of evidence at a sentencing hearing, an offender may participate in the process in a number of ways. Witnesses, such as family members, friends, or employers, may be called to give evidence about the offender's character and employment record. The offender's counsel may submit expert evidence from a physician, psychiatrist, or psychologist to offer an explanation for the offender's conduct or place it in a behavioural context. Information from these latter sources is usually tendered by way of written reports or letters.

There are two codified aspects of the sentencing hearing that bear directly on the offender's participation:

1. s. 726 gives the offender the right to speak personally at the hearing; and
2. s. 721 empowers the court to order a pre-sentence report (PSR).

Both of these provisions generate some interesting questions about the manner in which information from and about the offender enters the sentencing process.

I. THE RIGHT TO SPEAK TO SENTENCE

By virtue of s. 726 of the *Criminal Code*, RSC 1985, c. C-46, as amended, the offender is given the opportunity to address the judge before sentence is imposed. This section provides as follows:

> 726. Before determining the sentence to be imposed, the court shall ask whether the offender, if present, has anything to say.

This section was placed in the Code in 1996, but must be considered within the context of the Code's sentencing scheme. Section 723 secures the right of an offender and the prosecutor to make submissions on the issue of sentence and to adduce "any relevant evidence." This is consistent with the long-held recognition of the need to provide some degree of fairness at the sentencing hearing. What, then, is the role of s. 726? Does it confer a further, personal right on the offender to address the court? When an offender is represented by counsel, should any remedy flow from a failure to observe s. 726 if counsel has made sentencing submissions?

The predecessor provision, s. 668, provided as follows:

> 668. Where a jury finds an accused guilty … the judge presiding at the trial shall ask the accused whether he has anything to say before sentence is passed on him, but an omission to comply with this section does not affect the validity of the proceedings.

Note that the current Code provision does not include the caution that an omission does not affect validity. Different views were expressed on the consequences of this saving provision. In *R v. Schofield* (1976), 36 CRNS 135 (NBCA), Bugold JA concluded that it was a denial of the right to a fair trial to impose sentence without giving the offender an opportunity to make submissions as to sentence and the sentence could not therefore stand. In contrast, in *R v. Dennison* (1990), 80 CR (3d) 78 (NBCA), Ryan JA (Ayles JA concurring) agreed that the failure to give an offender the opportunity to speak was a denial of the right to a fair trial, but he adopted a narrower view of the effect of the provision by distinguishing between deliberate and inadvertent denials of the opportunity to speak. He concluded that the saving provision applied to inadvertent denials of the opportunity to speak, which could therefore be remedied by giving the offender the opportunity to speak on appeal. In contrast, deliberate denials violated the offender's s. 7 Charter rights, and therefore justified a Charter remedy in the form of a meaningful yet proportionate reduction in sentence. Hoyt JA dissented on the basis that neither type of omission constituted a Charter breach and that both types of omissions could therefore be remedied by granting leave to appeal and by allowing the offender to speak to sentence on the appeal. Moreover, where counsel had spoken to sentence on the offender's behalf, there was no violation of the s. 7 of the Charter.

In *R v. Glykis* (1995), 41 CR (4th) 311 (Ont. CA), the Court of Appeal for Ontario rejected the argument that a breach of the Charter should mitigate the sentence. However, in its subsequent decision in *R v. Leaver* (1996), 3 CR (5th) 138 (Ont. CA), the court affirmed the trial judge's sentencing decision that took into account trial delay insufficient to justify a violation of s. 11(b). The court stated that

> the sentence imposed by the trial judge reflected an appropriate mitigation of sentence in the circumstances of this case.

Appeal courts in other provinces have also debated whether a breach of the Charter should mitigate an offender's sentence: see, for example, *R v. Carpenter* (2002), 165 CCC (3d) 159 (BCCA); *R v. Collins* (1999), 133 CCC (3d) 8 (Nfld. CA). For an analysis of this issue, see A. Manson, "Charter Violations in Mitigation of Sentence" (1995), 41 CR (4th) 318.

The following case was decided under the current legislation. Does the Manitoba Court of Appeal (particularly Philp JA in his concurring reasons) go too far in limiting the right contained in s. 726?

R v. Senek
(1998), 130 CCC (3d) 473 (Man. CA)

LYON JA (Monnin JA concurring): The appellant pled guilty to a count of break, enter and theft of commercial premises and was sentenced by Swail PJ to nine months in jail. He appeals from this sentence on the principal ground that the trial judge erred in failing, before passing sentence, to ask the appellant if he had anything to say on his own behalf pursuant to s. 726 of the *Criminal Code* (the Code).

The facts in brief are that on April 29, 1996, the appellant and a co-accused formulated a plan to break into the Riverboat Restaurant in Selkirk. They gained entry through the roof of the mall by prying off a hot water tank ventilation door and then entered the business premises. Once inside, they broke into a kiosk that held a small safe which they also broke open and from which [they] stole $3,000 in one dollar coins. For the next three days the appellant and a friend went to Winnipeg, stayed at a local hotel, and spent the money buying clothing, drinking and eating in restaurants.

· · ·

At trial, counsel for the Crown, after relating the facts of the charge, suggested a sentence of 9 to 12 months in jail. Thereafter Mr. Sawchuk, counsel for the accused, made a lengthy submission (9½ pages in the 20-page transcript of the proceedings) urging the court that any sentence imposed be a conditional one.

At the conclusion of counsel's address, the trial judge proceeded immediately to thank counsel and to deal with the question of [the appropriate] sentence ... . He did not ask the offender if he had anything to say as required by s. 726 of the Code, which states as follows:

Offenders May Speak to Sentence

726. Before determining the sentence to be imposed, the court shall ask whether the offender, if present, has anything to say.

· · ·

Defence counsel submits that the sentencing hearing was invalidated by this error and asks this Court to vacate the trial judge's sentence and substitute for it a 9-month sentence to be served conditionally. Counsel relies primarily on *R v. Dennison* (1990), 80 CR (3d) 78, 60 CCC (3d) 342 (NBCA). *Dennison* was decided under the predecessor of this section (formerly s. 668) which contained a proviso that the failure to give the accused an opportunity to make a statement before sentencing did not affect the validity of the proceedings. That proviso was removed by amendment in 1995.

In *Dennison*, both Crown and defence counsel addressed the court with respect to sentence following the appellant's conviction by a jury on a charge of attempted murder. Ryan JA, for the majority, said (at p. 84) that the trial judge made "... a conscious decision ... to take away this right of the accused to be heard ... ." It was not a matter of inadvertence but was a (at pp. 84-85):

... [D]eliberate act of denial of a codified right relating to imprisonment. ...

It is not enough, in the case of an advertent act by the judge, to give an accused an automatic leave to appeal and ask him what he would have or might have said. ... The consequences of inadvertence and advertence should not be identical.

In the result, the majority of the court reduced the sentence from 12 years to 9 years. It is to be noted, of course, that *Dennison* is clearly distinguishable from the case at bar in that the trial judge here merely proceeded inadvertently to pass sentence after an extended plea by defence counsel for a conditional sentence.

Significantly in *Dennison*, Hoyt JA (as he then was) in his dissenting opinion noted that Ryan JA in his reasons had indicated that the majority was following a practice which had developed in the New Brunswick court of granting leave and reducing the original sentence. Hoyt JA submitted that the New Brunswick practice differed from that adopted in other provinces and in the Supreme Court, citing authorities where the courts had fashioned a remedy for failure to permit an accused to speak before sentence. He also stated (at p. 80), in support of his dissent, "… that omission, whether accidental or deliberate, does not amount to a violation of the accused's Canadian Charter of Rights and Freedoms rights."

A more recent example of this approach is found in *R v. Gorrill* (1995), 139 NSR (2d) 191 (CA), where the accused was convicted by a jury of infanticide. The trial judge inadvertently failed to ask the accused if she wished to speak to sentence. The Nova Scotia Court of Appeal held that the failure was overcome by permitting the accused to submit a written statement. Pugsley JA, speaking for the unanimous court, said (at p. 204):

> The failure of the trial judge to comply with s. 668 (supra) was inadvertent. The failure has been remedied by the acceptance of the written statement prepared by LG [the accused] (*R v. Lowry*, [1974] SCR 195). This was not a case where there was a conscious decision by a trial judge to take away the right of the accused to be heard before sentence and, accordingly, a violation of LG's Charter rights resulted (*R v. Dennison* (1991), 109 NBR (2d) 388; 273 APR 388; 60 CCC (3d) 342 (CA)). *It is also pertinent that the representations to the trial judge from LG's counsel respecting sentence were thorough and covered all of the issues, lasting the best part of one hour.* [My emphasis.]
>
> • • •

In *Lowry and Lepper v. The Queen*, [1974] SCR 195, 6 CCC (2d) 531, the appellants were acquitted at trial of assaulting peace officers in the execution of their duty. The Crown appealed and the Manitoba Court of Appeal allowed the appeal, set aside the acquittals, entered convictions and sentenced the appellants to six months' imprisonment. The appellants were not present at the hearing of the appeal and had no opportunity to make submissions in respect of sentence. They appealed to the Supreme Court of Canada which held that the appeal should be dismissed on the merits, but the case should be remitted to the Court of Appeal for re-sentencing after receiving any submissions which the appellants wished to make or have made on their behalf with respect to sentence.

In the course of his judgment, Martland J said (at p. 199):

> The next question which arises is as to the power of the Court of Appeal to impose sentence without having given to the appellants an opportunity to make, or to have made on their behalf, any submission on this matter.

After determining that the imposition of sentence should be remitted to the Court of Appeal, Martland J continued (at p. 204):

> ... [A]fter the appellants have been given the opportunity to make submissions to that Court on that matter.
>
> In the result, I would dismiss this appeal on the merits, but remit the case to the Court of Appeal to pass sentence, after receiving any submissions which the appellants wish to make, or to have made on their behalf, with respect to that matter.

In the case at bar, it is worthwhile to note that no objection was made by defence counsel to the trial judge's failure to ask the accused if he had anything to say. Indeed the record discloses that there was no comment or objection before or after sentencing about this oversight on the part of the trial judge. Similarly, on the hearing of the appeal, counsel for the accused admitted that the 9-month sentence was within the appropriate range but should have been a conditional one. The only error the trial judge made was his failure to ask the accused if he had anything to say, a matter that was not raised until the notice of appeal was filed.

In summary, on the hearing of the appeal, no affidavit evidence was submitted on behalf of the accused, nor was there any indication by the accused or his counsel that he had anything to say either to the trial court or to the appellate court beyond what his counsel had said *in extenso* at trial and on appeal. Practice indicates that an accused sometimes wishes to correct the record given by the Crown or to supplement or correct his counsel's submissions. There was no indication of such a desire by the appellant either at trial or on appeal. The appellant was well represented by counsel both at trial and on appeal who, on both occasions, set forth his argument thoroughly and at length. In the words of Martland J in *Lowry*, counsel's submissions which the appellant had "made on his behalf" constituted the accused's best hope for the conditional sentence he sought.

This pure, inadvertent oversight by the trial judge resulted in no disadvantage or unfairness to the accused, nor did the trial judge's error constitute a substantial wrong or miscarriage of justice. In my opinion, it was simply a procedural oversight which had no bearing either on the trial judge's sentence or on our determination of the fitness of that sentence on appeal. At best, this ground of appeal could aptly be described as an afterthought advanced in support of an appeal which otherwise was without merit.

Accordingly, I would dismiss the appeal.

PHILP JA: I am in complete agreement with the analysis and disposition of this appeal by my colleague, Justice Lyon. The accused was represented by counsel at his sentencing hearing and on his appeal in this Court. Complete and thorough submissions were made on his behalf in mitigation of his sentence. The omission of the sentencing judge to ask the accused whether he had anything to say had no effect on the validity of the proceedings.

In my view, s. 726 of the *Criminal Code* should not be interpreted so as to accord to a convicted person the right to address the court personally at his sentencing hearing when his counsel has made a submission on his behalf in mitigation of sentence.

The legislative history of s. 726 suggests that the origins of the provision have long since been obscured and forgotten. Originally, the provision applied only to jury trials. It had no application to offenders who were tried for indictable offences without a jury.

And until the 1953-54 re-enactment of the *Criminal Code*, SC 1953-54, c. 51, the provision was directed to whether the accused had "anything to say why sentence should not be passed upon him according to law." The provision had nothing to do with the mitigation of the sentence that was to be passed.

The provision may well be a vestige of the "benefit of clergy" privilege that existed into the 19th century and which "operated greatly to mitigate the extreme rigor of the criminal laws." (See *Black's Law Dictionary* (6th ed. 1990), at pp. 158-59.) The privilege did not mitigate the sentence to be imposed, but rather, its application exempted the person claiming the privilege after his conviction from the punishment of death.

Appeal dismissed.

NOTE

Philp JA might be right that the "origins of the provision have long since been obscured and forgotten" in Canada, but this is not the case in the United States. The right to speak to one's sentencer, historically known as the right of allocution, has been traced back to the period in England when capital penalties were common and an accused person had no ability to give evidence.[1] Not surprisingly, the issue has been given new life south of the border with the proliferation of capital punishment and the use of juries within the capital phase of sentencing. It has been argued that the ancient right of allocution permits the prisoner to seek leniency by speaking directly to the jury without cross-examination. Some circuit courts of appeal have held allocution to be a constitutional[2] right. The US Supreme Court has not yet directly addressed this issue. In *Green v. United States*, 365 US 301 (1961), a case that did not deal with capital punishment, the Supreme Court was unanimous in accepting the proposition that an offender should be entitled to speak to the sentencing judge even if represented by counsel who has made a sentencing submission. Frankfurter J noted that even "the most persuasive counsel may not be able to speak for a defendant as the defendant might, with halting eloquence, speak for himself." However, in *Hill v. United States*, 368 US 424 (1962), at 428, the Supreme Court concluded that the sentencing judge's failure to give an offender who was represented by counsel the opportunity to speak on his own behalf was "neither a jurisdictional nor constitutional" error, and, therefore, the denial of the right could not be collaterally attacked through a *habeas corpus* application.

If s. 726 creates an entitlement, is there a difference between an inadvertent failure to ask whether the offender has anything to say and a deliberate refusal to hear from an offender, as occurred in *Dennison*, above?

What is defence counsel's role in safeguarding the offender's entitlement to speak? See Smith JA in *R v. MacMillan*, [2003] BCJ No. 1479 (QL) (CA):

The appellant was represented at the trial by experienced counsel who ... did [not] advise the trial judge that the appellant wished to address the Court. After hearing submissions on sentence,

---

1   See *Green v. United States*, 365 US 301 (1961) and P. Barrett, "Allocution" (1944), 9 *Missouri L Rev.* 115.

2   See, for example, *Badman v. Estelle*, 957 F2d 1253 (9th Cir. 1992) and *United States v. Moree*, 928 F2d 654 (5th Cir. 1991).

the trial judge reserved overnight and pronounced sentence the next day. Nothing was said at that time ... about any desire on the part of the appellant to make a statement. If the appellant had something to say to the trial judge, his counsel would have or should have so advised the judge.

Another issue that arises when an offender chooses to speak is whether the remarks must be given under oath and the accused can be cross-examined. This proposal, of course, is inconsistent with the right of allocution. But if the offender's comments are given informally, is there any limit on the subject matter? Surely, the offender cannot attempt to relitigate guilt or rebut factual evidence adduced in the usual manner, but must restrict the comments to personal attitudes, beliefs, or commitments that have some bearing on the sentencing.[3]

II. PRE-SENTENCE REPORTS

Pre-sentence reports are provided for in s. 721 of the *Criminal Code* as follows:

721(1) Subject to regulations made under subsection (2), where an accused, other than an organization, pleads guilty to or is found guilty of an offence, a probation officer shall, if required to do so by a court, prepare and file with the court a report in writing relating to the accused for the purpose of assisting the court in imposing a sentence or in determining whether the accused should be discharged pursuant to section 730.

(2) The lieutenant governor in council of a province may make regulations respecting the types of offences for which a court may require a report, and respecting the content and form of the report.

(3) Unless otherwise specified by the court, the report must, wherever possible, contain information on the following matters:

(a) the offender's age, maturity, character, behaviour, attitude and willingness to make amends;

(b) subject to section 119(2) of the *Youth Criminal Justice Act*, the history of previous dispositions under the *Young Offenders Act*, chapter Y-1 of the Revised Statutes of Canada, 1985, the history of previous sentences under the *Youth Criminal Justice Act*, and of previous findings of guilt under this Act and any other Act of Parliament;

(c) the history of any alternative measures used to deal with the offender, and the offender's response to those measures; and

(d) any matter required, by any regulation made under subsection (2), to be included in the report.

(4) The report must also contain information on any other matter required by the court, after hearing argument from the prosecutor and the offender, to be included in the report, subject to any contrary regulation made under subsection (2).

(5) The clerk of the court shall provide a copy of the report, as soon as practicable after filing, to the offender or counsel for the offender, as directed by the court, and to the prosecutor.

---

3   See *R v. Braun* (1995), 95 CCC (3d) 443 (Man. CA). See also *R v. Izzard*, [1999] NSJ No. 18 (CA) for an example of the difficulties that a judge can get into if the conversation with an offender moves into factual issues about the offence.

The cases that follow were decided under the predecessor provisions, which did not include any indication of what a PSR should contain. However, these cases illustrate what courts considered appropriate in terms of the content of a PSR. It is important to realize that although counsel may make submissions to the sentencing judge on the issue whether a PSR ought to be prepared, it is a matter that falls within the (unreviewable) discretion of the sentencing judge. Accordingly, in some circumstances, ordering a PSR coerces the offender and his or her family to participate in the sentencing process. This is why it is important to ensure that only appropriate information finds its way into these reports.

R v. Dolbec and *R v. Arsenault* illustrate the problem of unnecessary and prejudicial information appearing in a PSR.

R v. Dolbec
[1963] 2 CCC 87 (BCCA)

BIRD JA: Dolbec and one Olson were involved in the theft of a motor car over the value of $50 on July 29, 1962, for which offence Dolbec was charged and convicted on July 30, 1962, on a plea of guilty entered before Magistrate J.J. Lye at Port Coquitlam, British Columbia. He was then remanded for sentence to August 7, 1962.

Meantime a pre-sentence report required by the learned Magistrate was prepared by an officer of the Provincial Probation Branch which was considered by the Magistrate prior to the imposition of the sentence.

It is apparent ... that the learned Magistrate in imposing a sentence of nine months' imprisonment on this 19-year-old youth, whose record showed no prior convictions, was strongly influenced in determining sentence by the information furnished in the pre-sentence report.

Regrettably that report was not furnished to the appellant before sentence was imposed, nor was he given any information relative to the contents of the report which was highly prejudicial to the appellant. Dolbec was not represented by counsel either at the time of his conviction or sentence.

It is evident from examination of the report that the Probation Officer had formed a poor opinion of the appellant based to a substantial degree upon information received from other persons, none of whom are named therein, nor does the report otherwise disclose the source of any such information or the grounds for the officer's belief in its validity. The Probation Officer closes the report with the following comment and recommendation:

Comment

Subject is a 19 year old single male presently facing sentence on a charge of car theft. He is intelligent and seeks to blame his accomplice. Although chronologically he is 19, emotionally he is much less—he has never grown up, shows a marked degree of immaturity and irresponsibility. Locally he is described as a smart alec, lippy punk who frequents all the questionable cafes and hangouts. His earnings come from the pool cue and part time work at Fraser Mills (he has lost the latter source of income). Exacerbating the above is his love of alcohol and it is suggested that has a greater hold on him than he is prepared to admit.

This is the first criminal offence on his record but he is certainly heading for serious trouble. An extremely doubtful candidate for probation because of his irresponsibility and also that placing him on Probation would bring pressures to bear that he probably couldn't stand thereby forcing him into a worse situation than at present. He has been getting away with so much for so long that Probation to him would probably mean he had once again "beat the rap." The strong point in this whole situation is the family rallying to keep closer tabs on him but unfortunately there seems no motivation from within himself to lead a different life. Institutionalization would assist him in forming definite living habits and may exercise a stabilizing influence on a lad who has been drifting from some time.

On the hearing of the appeal counsel for the appellant filed affidavits of Dolbec, as well as of the principal of the High School attended by him in 1961, and of his parish priest.

The appellant in his affidavit questions the factual accuracy of the probation report in many respects. He deposes further to the following

(a) The Magistrate did not ask me if I had anything to say before sentence or suggest that I was permitted to say anything.

(b) The Magistrate was incorrect in stating in his report that my brother-in-law was in Court and addressed the Magistrate regarding probation. In fact my brother, Roger Dolbec was in Court as well as my sister Theresa O'Bray and neither were asked whether they had anything to say on my behalf nor did either of them address the Magistrate before sentence was passed upon me. My sister Theresa informs me she did have a conversation with the Magistrate after the sentence was imposed.

The appellant's school principal in his affidavit deposed in substance as follows: The appellant

(a) was keenly interested in his studies, was an intelligent student who showed maturity beyond the majority of students in his class.

(b) I found Dolbec pleasant, cheerful and cooperative. He was one of the best and most pleasant students of his class.

(c) I found him to be no discipline problem and his manners and cooperation were better than the majority of his fellow students.

The parish priest, Father A. Frechette, in his affidavit, deposes to the fact that he has known the appellant for some nine years. "He was a very good student." "I found him helpful and cooperative. He has constantly attended church and to the best of my recollection the first time he missed Sunday service was when the said charge of theft was laid against him."

In my judgment this appeal from sentence must be allowed for the following reasons:

1. The appellant was seriously prejudiced by the fact that the Magistrate took into account when sentence was imposed the contents of the probation report, no part of which was communicated to the appellant and of which he had no knowledge and, consequently, no opportunity to refute factual statements contained therein which he now says were untrue.

In *R v. Benson & Stevenson* (1951), 100 CCC 247, 13 CR 1, 3 WWR (NS) 29, the late Chief Justice Sloan, speaking for this court, laid down the following principles in respect of the use to be made of pre-sentence reports, and I quote from the [WWR] headnote which is fully supported by the text of the reasons:

> In so far as a pre-sentence report from a probation officer contains factual allegations prejudicial to the prisoner it cannot be placed in a higher or different category than a pre-sentence statement made by a police officer and the same principles must be applied to both. Therefore a convicted man ought to be informed of the substance of a probation officer's report, in so far as it is detrimental to him, so that he may have an opportunity to agree therewith or deny it if he chooses so to do. If the report contains prejudicial observations which the court considers relevant and likely to influence the sentence and this material is denied by the prisoner then proof of it, if required, should be given in open court when its accuracy may be tested by cross-examination. Alternatively, if the court does not consider it of sufficient importance to justify formal proof then such matters should be ignored as factors influencing sentence.
>
> • • •
>
> 2. The prejudicial comments contained in the probation report as to the character and conduct of the appellant are so greatly at variance with the depositions made by the appellant's high school principal in 1961, and by his parish priest, as to arouse a doubt of the validity of the information obtained by the Probation Officer.

• • •

For the foregoing reasons the appeal from sentence is allowed and the sentence imposed below set aside. There will be substituted a direction that upon entering a recognizance ... to keep the peace and be of good behaviour during the term of one year from the date of the judgment ... the appellant shall be released on probation, the recognizance to incorporate the usual terms.

R v. Arsenault
(1981), 21 CR (3d) 269 (PEISC)

MacDONALD J: The appellant applies for leave to appeal against the sentence imposed on the respondent and, if this is granted, appeals the decision of Carruthers C Prov. J. I would grant leave to appeal.

The facts are not in dispute. The respondent, who is 19 years of age, has no criminal record. On 22nd March 1980 he entered a liquor store and was told that because he was drunk he would not be served. He continued on into the store, picked up a case of beer and presented himself at the checkout counter, where the beer was taken from him by a store employee. Upon this occurring the respondent became very abusive, using coarse and foul language toward a female cashier. Mr. Arthur Clarke, a man standing behind him in the checkout line-up, told him to watch his language. The respondent, who was wearing a cast on his arm, swung with the arm bearing the cast and struck Mr. Clarke in the face. As a result of the blow Mr. Clarke, who was 70 years of age, fell and broke his hip and had to have two teeth removed. The respondent was charged pursuant to s. 245(2)(a) [en. 1974-75-76, c. 93, s. 22] of the *Criminal Code*, RSC 1970, c. C-34, with the indictable offence of assault.

On the above facts the trial judge fined the respondent $500 or, in default, sentenced him to 45 days' imprisonment, and placed him on probation for 18 months. In addition he was required to abstain from alcohol and obtain treatment for his alcohol problem if so required by his probation officer.

...

I wish to make a short comment on the contents of the pre-sentence report that was prepared in this matter. In *R v. Bartkow* (1978), 24 NSR (2d) 518, 1 CR (3d) S-36, 35 APR 518 (CA), MacKeigan CJNS at p. 522 stated:

> I wish those who prepare such reports would realize that it is no part of their job to give any information, whether inculpatory or exculpatory, respecting offences which the accused committed, especially ones for which he has not been convicted. Their function is to supply a picture of the accused as a person in society—his background, family, education, employment record, his physical and mental health, his associates and social activities, and his potentialities and motivations. Their function is not to supply evidence of criminal offences or details of a criminal record or to tell the court what sentence should be imposed.

This court has never made any comment on the contents of a pre-sentence report. However, I have noted that over the past few years an increasing amount of information, some of which was of the sort disapproved of in *R v. Bartkow*, has found its way into reports submitted to this court. In the present case the report contains information relating to the respondent in the following manner:

(1) Extensive reference is made to the respondent's becoming involved in fights at various branches of the Royal Canadian Legion. As these altercations involve offences for which the respondent has not been convicted, there should be no reference to them. Neither should the appellant have directly referred to them in an attempt to show the respondent as an aggressive and violent person.

(2) The probation officer gave his opinion concerning the respondent's conduct, stating it was "uncalled for."

(3) The report dealt extensively with the injuries sustained by Mr. Clarke. Information of this nature should be submitted to the court only by counsel.

(4) The report dealt with the matter of restitution to Mr. Clarke.

(5) A great number of facts concerning the commission of the offence are related in the report.

(6) The report mentions Mr. Clarke's sentiments concerning the assault and his hope that there should be "a fair measure of justice."

The report should not have dealt with any of these listed items. It is not enough to say that neither the respondent nor his counsel objected to the contents of the pre-sentence report. The report dealt with matters which the court should not have been made aware of; or, if they were properly admissible, they were not presented in the correct manner. Again, I wish to emphasize that I attach no blame to the probation officer who prepared the report in question as he merely was following a practice that has evolved over the years. This practice should now be discontinued.

NOTE

In several recent cases courts have reiterated the restricted nature of PSRs and the importance of probation officers remaining within that mandate. See, for example, the comments of Ryan JA in *R v. Donovan* (2004), 188 CCC (3d) 193 (NBCA):

> A particularly disturbing aspect of the pre-sentence report is an unjustifiable negative implication of a failure by [the accused] to co-operate with the interviewing probation officer. She, inappropriately, commenced her interview with an attempt to question the accused about his involvement in the offence. He consulted his lawyer and was advised, correctly, not to answer questions relating to the commission of the offence. Such incursions are outside the bounds of the report. The design of the report is governed by the wording of s. 721 of the Code and any direction provided by the sentencing judge. It is not to be used as an investigative arm of law enforcement, nor can it be used as a fact-finding excursion for the inquisitive or the misinformed.

In *R v. Wharry*, [2007] AJ No. 753 (QB) the court emphasized the need to keep distinct the respective roles of the police, the Crown, and probation:

> This pre-sentence report is unfortunately flawed. It strikes me that Ms. Dryden became preoccupied with the publicity and profile of the case and some of its more sensational aspects, including the alleged association with gang activities. It was not for this probation officer to be investigating or buttressing the Crown's contention about whether or not Mr. Wharry has been associated with a gang. Rather, it was her job to explore the personal circumstances of Mr. Wharry, features of his background that might explain his conduct, features of his character that might assist the Court with the job of prognosticating what this man's future might hold.
>
> The second aspect of the process undertaken by Ms. Dryden that is troublesome is the communications she had with the Crown Prosecutor that were not shared with the defence. Further, at the behest of the Crown, she interviewed two police officers to deal with the subject of alleged gang association. Such a hotly contested and disputed subject matter requires evidence, not conveyance of information from police officers on that subject through a pre-sentence report.
>
>   • • •
>
> ... I would add that, as in any criminal or associated proceeding, due process is of the utmost importance. In my view, it is inappropriate for a probation officer preparing a pre-sentence report to have communications with the Crown without affording the defence the opportunity to be privy to those communications. The preparation of pre-sentence reports is intended to provide neutral observations for the assistance of the court concerning the subject matters listed in s. 721(3) of the *Criminal Code*. Probation officers and the probation services are not an arm of the Crown, to be used as a vehicle for the Crown to explore unanswered questions about the offence or other alleged illegal activity in which the offender is said to have been involved. Such information received through the report is untested hearsay, although in this case one of the police officers interviewed did testify at the sentencing hearing. In addition, there is the risk that the probation officer will be swayed in the legitimate areas of her inquiry by the observations of the police officers or others as to unproved allegations. I accept, however, that the Crown acted with the best of intentions in this case.
>
> For all these reasons, I have no choice but to disregard the contents of the pre-sentence report concerning the motivations of Mr. Wharry and his alleged illegal associations.

See also *R v. Green*, [2006] OJ No. 3925 (Prov. Ct.), per Trotter J:

Probation officers, who usually prepare pre-sentence reports, are dependent upon others in the criminal justice system to provide them with the offence-specific information they require to prepare pre-sentence reports. Ideally, probation officers should rely on the same facts presented to or found by the sentencing judge. However, the ideal is not always possible, such that probation officers sometimes depend on the police for this information. This institutional dependency puts a premium on accurate reporting to probation officers by the police officers involved in individual cases.

The following two cases present a different problem. In these cases, exculpatory information from the offenders found its way into their PSRs. What use should sentencing judges make of this type of information? Should it make any difference if the offender testified at trial?

R v. Rudyk
(1975), 1 CR (3d) 26 (NSCA)

MacKEIGAN CJNS: The Crown has appealed herein from the sentences imposed on the respondent by His Honour Judge P.J.T. O'Hearn in the County Court Judge's Criminal Court District No. 1 at Halifax following conviction of the respondent on two charges [of unlawfully stealing money while armed with an offensive weapon, a knife, contrary to s. 303 of the *Criminal Code*.]

. . .

The learned trial judge sentenced the respondent to 14 days' imprisonment to be served intermittently and, in addition, to pay a $500 fine (or 60 days in default of payment), together with a period of probation of one year.

. . .

Leave to appeal should be granted.

The respondent Rudyk was originally charged with both offences jointly with one Nelson Michael Lawlor. Following a preliminary inquiry in May 1974, both were committed for trial. On 10th October 1974 Lawlor pleaded guilty to both offences before O'Hearn Co. Ct. J who, on 25th October 1974, sentenced him to four years' imprisonment on each count, to run concurrently.

Rudyk was tried on both charges jointly before O'Hearn Co. Ct. J. After most of the Crown's case had been presented Rudyk changed his plea to guilty and, after an adjournment for a pre-sentence report, was sentenced by O'Hearn Co. Ct. J on 25th January 1975.

The facts disclosed by the Crown evidence are as follows. At about 11:40 p.m. on 30th April 1974 Rudyk, accompanied by Lawlor, parked his car in front of Richard's Grocery, a small corner shop in south-end Halifax. Lawlor entered the shop and, at knife-point, robbed the female clerk of over $200. Rudyk meanwhile got out of the car, stood near the trunk and glanced several times at a witness who was parked across the street. Lawlor ran from the shop and shouted, "Let's go!" Both men jumped in the car and drove away.

Driving directly to the scene of the second crime, a small shop in north-end Halifax, Rudyk stopped and Lawlor entered the shop at about 11:55 p.m. Holding a knife to the shopkeeper's stomach, he robbed him of about $93. Afterward Rudyk's car, a bright yellow Toyota, was seen driving away.

Only a few minutes later the car containing the pair was stopped on the approaches to the Angus L. Macdonald Bridge. Rudyk, the driver, had about $240 of the stolen money in his jacket. Lawlor, in the passenger's seat, had the rest of the money in his possession.

Neither Lawlor nor Rudyk gave evidence. Rudyk also did not testify at the time of sentencing.

The pre-sentence report, however, contained a version of the events quite different from that recounted above, one which, if true, would make one wonder why Rudyk pleaded guilty. I set it forth in full:

> He had been drinking with a friend, his girlfriend, and the friend's wife. His friend suggested the two of them go for a drive. Along the way, the friend told the accused to stop the car, whereupon he entered a store and came running back to the car and stuffed something into the accused's pockets. The accused drove on and was again asked to stop for cigarettes at another store. The friend entered this store, and re-entering the car, told the accused to get moving. Shortly afterward, they were apprehended by the police.
>
> The accused stated that it was the police who had informed him that a knife had been used in the robberies, and that when he later searched for the knife in the glove compartment of his car, it was missing. He stated that ordinarily when he drinks, he gives his car keys to a reliable person, or else takes a taxi home. He described his condition as one of inebriation for he had few recollections of the offence, apart from what the co-accused and the police had informed him.

The probation officer who prepared the report stated that the Halifax police inspector who had investigated the crimes said that "although the accused had been drinking, he was fully aware of what he was doing at the time."

The respondent was 24 years old at the time of the offence. He has a good family and employment background and no criminal record. He has been employed in the navy for over five years. All his superior officers spoke very well of him. He had performed his work satisfactorily and had never been in trouble.

The learned trial judge in imposing sentence said:

> ... I am not satisfied that it was your initiative, but I think that at some point in the thing you understood what was going on and went along with it, through, probably through weakness more than anything else and possibly because of intoxication. In other words, I don't accept the theory that you were the initiator of it, or the prime mover and I don't necessarily accept the theory that you knew how it was being done ... So, I am giving you the benefit of considerable amount of doubt.

In this report to this court, he said:

> On the day fixed for sentencing I heard counsel for the Crown and for the accused and did not accept the theory of the prosecution that the accused was more aware of the offences

than he pretended to be because of the evidence I had heard and *because of the contents of the pre-sentence report*. (The italics are mine.)

He said further that he imposed the sentence he did:

As there appeared to be a very real prospect of public benefit from the rehabilitation of the accused in this case and as his participation appeared to be relatively minor.

I respectfully think that the learned judge should not have been influenced, as he obviously was, by the story which Rudyk told the probation officer. That self-serving story was not given to the court by Rudyk himself, when he could have been cross-examined by the Crown. It was inconsistent with the guilty plea. It strains one's credulity. It is quite conceivable that Rudyk had no prior knowledge that Lawlor was going to rob the first store. But how could he, after having $200 placed in his jacket following Lawlor's hasty departure from the first store, have believed that Lawlor's visit to the second store was an innocent search for cigarettes?

I would here urge that a pre-sentence report be confined to its very necessary and salutary role of portraying the background, character and circumstances of the person convicted. It should not, however, contain the investigator's impressions of the facts relating to the offence charged, whether based on information received from the accused, the police or other witnesses, and whether favourable or unfavourable to the accused. And if the report contains such information the trial judge should disregard it in considering sentence.

In the present case, putting aside the pre-sentence report, I can find nothing in the evidence before the learned trial judge to support the theory that the respondent did not know what was going on and was thus an innocent dupe who was, at worst, party after the fact.

· · ·

These facts make it impossible to reconcile the sentence imposed on the respondent with the four years' imprisonment meted out to his companion Lawlor.

· · ·

Having regard to all the circumstances, and giving the respondent the benefit of all doubts that the evidence permits, I would allow the Crown's appeal and vary the sentence imposed on the respondent to one of two years' imprisonment in a federal institution on each charge, to run concurrently, without probation. Any time already served by him will, of course, be credited to him and the fine imposed, if paid, will be refunded to him.

R v. Urbanovich and Brown
(1985), 19 CCC (3d) 43 (Man. CA)

MATAS JA:

• • •

Tracie Marie Urbanovich and Robin Harold Brown have appealed from conviction and sentence on a joint charge of causing the death by criminal negligence of Lee Anna Brown, between March 1st and May 29, 1981 (*Criminal Code*, s. 203). Each appellant was sentenced to seven years' incarceration. (I will refer to the parties as the appellants or the accused.)

The appellants had been living together for some time prior to January, 1981, and continued their relationship during the material time. The victim was the appellants' four-month-old daughter.

• • •

The trial was held before Lockwood Co. Ct. J (as he then was) sitting without a jury. The appellants were separately represented. They did not testify but their lengthy voluntary statements were admitted in evidence.

• • •

Lockwood Co. Ct. J reviewed the evidence of ... [the doctors and nurses who treated the child at the Children's Hospital, and Mr. Brown's sister]. He mentioned the evidence of [Ms. Urbanovich's] mother and said that [at 171] "In the light of the medical evidence little weight should be attached" to her evidence.

Lockwood Co. Ct. J relied on the definition of criminal negligence in s. 202 of the *Code* and the provisions of s. 197 prescribing the duty to provide necessaries of life, which would include medical treatment: *R v. Popen* (1981), 60 CCC (2d) 232 at p. 240 (Ont. CA). Lockwood Co. Ct. J found that the infant sustained a series of serious injuries caused by the acts of Mr. Brown and that the inference to be drawn from all the evidence is that the child was a victim of deliberately applied trauma. ... [He] held as well that Mr. Brown was liable for depriving the child of the opportunity of receiving proper medical treatment.

Lockwood Co. Ct. J held that Ms. Urbanovich was not directly responsible for the injuries to the infant but that she failed to take reasonable steps to protect the infant from the violence which caused the injuries. ... [He also] held Ms. Urbanovich had deprived the infant of necessary medical attention. ...

The proceedings were adjourned to September 28, 1983, for submissions on sentence. In the meantime, separate pre-sentence reports for each appellant were prepared and a psychiatric assessment was prepared in respect of Mr. Brown by Dr. I.J. Kowalchuk. The learned trial judge made extensive references to the pre-sentence reports in giving his reasons for imposition of the sentence. At the conclusion of his remarks, Lockwood Co. Ct. J said [24 Man. R (2d) 189 at pp. 191-92]:

> At trial I drew the inference from the evidence that "the child was a victim of deliberately applied trauma." However, the new evidence introduced at the sentencing hearing, by way of pre-sentence reports, bears out what Dr. Ferguson said [at the trial] about the acts not being "committed." He testified:

I have never stated that I felt that these were committed acts, but I nevertheless feel that the onus on individuals as parents is grave to protect children and to admit to a string of events of this nature resulting in a child's death, to me, is a very serious matter.

It now seems clear from this further evidence that the acts of the accused Brown were probably not consciously deliberate, but rather took place when his mind was besotted by the effects of the consumption of alcohol, or drugs, or both. Seen in this light, the acts were not any less criminal. They do however, fall into a different category for the purposes of determining sentence. Deliberate acts of violence over a period of time resulting in death, in my view, should attract a higher range of sentence than acts which are not deliberate in the strict sense of the word.

In my view, Lockwood Co. Ct. J was right in convicting the appellants. The evidence at the trial amply supported the convictions. But, in my opinion, Lockwood Co. Ct. J erred in the way he treated the material presented at the sentencing hearing.

· · ·

Pre-Sentence Reports

· · ·

In *Criminal Pleadings and Practice in Canada* (1983), Eugene Ewaschuk QC (now Ewaschuk J) summarized the principles applicable to the contents of a [pre-sentence] report, at p. 497, as follows:

A pre-sentence report should be confined to the background, character and circumstances of the accused but not the accused's nor the investigator's version of the facts relating to the offence.

In Nadin-Davis, *Sentencing in Canada* (1982), pp. 524-5, reference is made to *Bernier v. The Queen* (1978), 5 CR (3d) S-1, which cited with approval a statement of MacKeigan CJNS in *R v. Bartkow* (1978), 1 CR (3d) S-36, 24 NSR (2d) 518, 35 APR 518 (NSSCAD). At p. 525 the following comment appears:

The decision is typical of a growing trend across the country to confine the ambit of reports to personal, family, educational and employment information and similar matters. The emphasis, reading between the lines, appears to be on factual rather than opinion evidence.

To the same effect is the comment in Ruby on *Sentencing*, 2nd ed. (1980), p. 254, where the learned author says:

It is quite often the case, especially when probation is a possible part of a sentence, that the trial judge will call for a presentence report in order to assist him in assessing the proper sentence. In *R v. Rudyk* (1975), 11 NSR (2d) 541 at p. 544 (CA)), the probation officer prepared a report which elicited from the accused his version of the facts of the case. As it turned out that version contradicted the guilty plea. The Court of Appeal said:

I would here urge that a presentence report be confined to its very necessary and salutary role of portraying the background, character and circumstances of the person convicted. It should not, however, contain the investigator's impressions of the facts relating to the offence charged, whether based on information received from the accused, the police, or other witnesses, and whether favourable or unfavourable to the accused. And if the report contains such information the trial judge should disregard it in considering sentence.

The reasoning involved was that any story given to the probation officer may well be self-serving, and in any event was not subject to cross-examination by counsel for the Crown. The proper place for the facts of the offence to be investigated is in open court.

In the pre-sentence report with respect to Mr. Brown, the author of the report began by saying: "In view of the evidence presented at this trial, the circumstances of this offence will not be mentioned here." However, under the heading of "Attitude Towards This Offence," Mr. Brown is quoted as referring to the "accidents" and to his criticism of the medical authorities for not being diligent enough in their examination, observation and treatment. Mr. Brown also denied any assaults. Later in the report, under the heading "Children," Mr. Brown is quoted extensively on his consumption of drugs and alcohol and on a description of several incidents involving the infant.

With respect to Ms. Urbanovich, the author of the pre-sentence report also said that since evidence was presented to the court on the circumstances of the offence it would not be presented in the report. Under the heading "Attitude Toward Offence," Ms. Urbanovich is quoted as maintaining innocence and as being critical of the pediatrician. She also referred to the consumption of alcohol and/or marijuana and referred to having been present on at least "four accidents that Brown had with the baby." Ms. Urbanovich is quoted as repeating her innocence. Throughout the report references are found to the kind of care the infant was receiving by the parents.

In my respectful opinion, none of this evidence was admissible in so far as the conviction was concerned and should have been disregarded by the learned trial judge.

. . .

I agree that a trial judge is not *functus officio* until the completion of the sentencing process and that it would have been open to Lockwood Co. Ct. J, had he felt it necessary, to permit the reopening of the trial for the calling of further evidence by the defence. What was not open to him was to consider self-serving statements by the accused as affecting the conclusions he arrived at after hearing the evidence called by the Crown and the submissions of counsel on conviction.

I think we would be opening the door to a very difficult procedure if we were to permit persons accused of crime to await the conclusion of all the evidence, decide not to give evidence as it is their right to do, and to provide information helpful to themselves, with respect to the conviction, through the medium of a pre-sentence report.

R v. Hildebrandt elaborates further on the proper content of a PSR by examining the treatment of disputed facts in the report, the use (and abuse) of risk assessments, and the relevance of general victim-impact information.

R v. Hildebrandt
(2005), 198 CCC (3d) 546 (Sask. Prov. Ct.)

WHELAN PROV. CT. J:

Introduction and Issues

Mr. Hildebrandt plead guilty to charges ... [of possession of child pornography contrary to s. 163.1 of the *Criminal Code*].

The Crown sought a conditional sentence of 18 months duration and defence counsel asked the court to impose a conditional sentence followed by probation. This sentencing became protracted for a variety of reasons, including; a dispute over the facts, the content of the pre-sentence report and a request for a psychological assessment. I undertook to provide my reasons for sentence subsequent to imposition of sentence on April 7, 2005.

These reasons address the following issues:

1. Having regard to the content of the pre-sentence report:

    a. How should the author of a pre-sentence report address disputed facts?
    b. What weight, if any, should be given to the risk assessments contained in the pre-sentence report and the opinion of the probation officer concerning risk?
    c. What, if any, general information pertaining to victim impact is appropriately contained in the pre-sentence report?

            ...

Facts Surrounding the Offences

The defendant took his computer in for repairs. A technician found pornographic images and text involving children under 12 years of age. Shortly after this discovery, the defendant called the technician to tell him not to look at the CD as the contents were private. The defendant initially admitted to the police that he knew the images and text were on his computer but maintained that he didn't know they were illegal. He subsequently gave a written statement admitting that he possessed the material which formed the basis of the counts for which he was sentenced.

The defendant insisted that he didn't intend to download images involving children. He believed that he was downloading adult pornography involving adult females. He observed pictures of nude female children whom he believed to be under age 10. He said that once he appreciated the nature of the pictures, he knew that he should get rid of them and in the course of doing so, his computer crashed.

The defendant offered several reasons for his belief that the downloaded written material was not illegal, including that they were fiction and were obtained on the internet. He said that he believed that stories which involved children who were 14 years of age or older were legal. He also said he believed that as the stories were fictional, they were legal. He knew that he had 30 to 40 such stories stored on his computer. There were two stories in particular, "Teens for free" and "Asians for free," according to counsel, that formed the basis of the second charge. The court was advised that he attempted to write a story that offended s. 163.1.

He admitted to being aroused by stories involving sex between fathers and teenage daughters and brothers and teenage sisters. He used these stories as masturbatory fantasies. He spoke of being aroused by teens, aged 14 years and up. The pornographic material was for Mr. Hildebrandt's own use. There was no evidence of distribution.

The Crown filed with the court 20 of the images seized from the defendant's computer, with a view to illustrating the behaviour complained of. Of these, all but 1 were nude poses. There was some doubt in my mind about the age of some of the persons featured and indeed whether they offended the Code section as there was no apparent sexual activity, but clearly there were several images of pre-pubescent children. There were many images in which genitalia were depicted. Two of the images were very explicit; one included a male partner in a pose of what appeared to be partial penetration of a young girl. There were no signs of distress in any of the images.

Background Information

Pre-Sentence Report

Mr. Hildebrandt is single. He had no prior criminal record. He is a long-term resident of the city and has maintained his current residence for 10 years. His longest intimate relationship lasted about one year and ended in 1982. His father was described as an evangelical Mennonite minister and a staunch disciplinarian who meted out punishment which was abusive in nature.

He has been fairly open about these offences with his pastor, who offered some insight into the defendant's personality. He described him as an unusual fellow whom others may find difficult to interact with and understand. He lacks social skills and this impacts upon his ability to form and maintain relationships and contributes to his social isolation. His faith has been a source of grounding. The pastor expressed concern about the defendant's idleness but believed him capable of personal change.

The defendant obtained grade 12 and a bachelors degree ... from Briarcrest Bible College. He was in the military for seven years and for a time was stationed overseas. Since 1993 he has been dependent upon social assistance and has been designated as unemployable due to medical issues.

He was assessed as a suitable candidate for supervision and sexual offender programming in the community.

Psychological Assessment

Mr. Hildebrandt was referred by the Court for a psychological risk assessment pertaining to suitability for treatment and risk for re-offending.

Dr. D. Helmer assessed the defendant. He reported that Mr. Hildebrandt suffered a stroke in November 2004. He wrote:

Formulation

Mr. Hildebrandt does not show significant cognitive or motor deterioration from his stroke of November 2004. He presents with schizoid personality features and is likely to remain fairly isolated socially. He has no criminal history. Mr. Hildebrandt is somewhat vague about what he finds stimulating sexually. Since he doesn't have any significant cognitive deficits, he would likely benefit from community programming, assuming his level of affective involvement is sufficient. This profile suggests that Mr. Hildebrandt is likely a low risk to the community and can be managed through community programming.

Recommendations
1. Mr. Hildebrandt has not suffered cognitively to any significant extent as a result of his stroke. Cognitively, he is functional enough to benefit from community programming.
2. Because of the distancing and avoidance of affect, one key issue for psychological intervention will be to generate sufficient affect to make the intervention viable.
3. Phallometric testing may be an option to pursue pertaining to ascertaining what Mr. Hildebrandt finds sexually stimulating.
4. As long as he doesn't personally own a computer the chances of relapse are likely low in this case.

· · ·

Reasoning

· · ·

I inquired of the Crown whether there were specific policies in place concerning the content of the pre-sentence report. The Crown agreed to pass on this request for information to the probation officer but no further information was provided. I am unaware of any provincial regulations in this regard and from the foregoing it would seem that no provincial regulations affecting the preparation of the adult pre-sentence report are intended. I have been provided with a policy paper pertaining to same, having conveyed my request to the preparer of the paper, K. Bell. This paper prepared by Saskatchewan Justice Corrections Division Policy, revised August 1, 2000, entitled: *Format and guide for the preparation of pre-sentence reports*, is authorized by the Director of Community Operations. This Policy provides in part:

Principles
• The content of the Pre-Sentence Report will be based on a risk/needs assessment of the offender's criminogenic factors and will identify effective intervention strategies to reduce and manage the risk presented by the offender.
• The Pre-Sentence Report will be shared with the offender in compliance with the law and the guiding principle of duty to act fairly.

Standards
1.0 General
    1.1 A Pre-Sentence Report will be completed and provided to the court in compliance with Section 721 (1 to 4) of the *Criminal Code of Canada*. ...
    1.2 The probation officer is impartial and only completes a Pre-Sentence Report at the request of the court.
    1.3 The Pre-Sentence Report recognizes that the court has determined the facts of the offence and does not reinvestigate the offence.

2.0 Report Content
    2.1 The Pre-Sentence Report will make reference only to offences where a conviction was registered.
    2.2 The Probation Officer is responsible for ensuring the Pre-Sentence Report is accurate, objective, and comprehensive, free of bias or hearsay, and free of inadequate or unverified information that is not disclosed in the Pre-Sentence Report.
    2.3 In family violence cases, including child sexual abuse, patterns of previous behaviour can be recorded in the Pre-Sentence Report when this information is confirmed by the offender, or confirmed by third party information.
    2.4 Pre-Sentence Report information regarding sexual offences or family violence must be provided by a probation officer who has completed the Sex Offender Training Module or the Family Violence Training Module, or through consultation with persons who have expertise in these areas.

• • •

5.0 Report Format
    5.1 The Pre-Sentence Report will be in accordance with Appendix "A."

Appendix "A" provides in part:

• • •

Criminal Involvement

• • •

The impact on the victim of the present offence will be noted in this section ... . When preparing the Pre-sentence Report, the probation officer will contact the victim as outlined in the VICTIM CONTACT PROTOCOL.

• • •

This section will also address the offender's attitude. It looks at the offender's acceptance of responsibility for the offence(s) and willingness to change and accept help. Attitude is assessed by examining the offender's view, opinion and explanations of the offending behaviour. ...

Criminogenic Risk Assessment
This section will include information pertaining to:

• Primary RISK ASSESSMENT evaluation
• Secondary RISK ASSESSMENT evaluation

This section will address the findings of the OFFENDER RISK ASSESSMENT & MANAGEMENT SYSTEM (ORAMS) primary and secondary assessments, and dimensions thereof, and will substantiate them by emphasizing significant factors included in the body of the report. No new information should be included in this section. Information used to complete the RISK ASSESSMENT MUST be verified as per the OFFENDER RISK/NEED ASSESSMENT MANUAL. It is important to distinguish between a summary of the information in the body of the report and a professional assessment of the information. It is the latter that will be included here.

1. Having Regard to the Content of the Pre-Sentence Report

a. How Should the Author of a Pre-Sentence Report Address Disputed Facts?

Disputed facts should ideally be resolved by counsel, preferably before the plea is recorded and in any event before the sentencing hearing. As a matter of experience, factual disputes often first make their appearance in the pre-sentence report.

In this case a factual dispute was addressed by the author of the pre-sentence report. This is an excerpt from the report under Criminal Involvement:

> ... Daniel denies he intended to download images of child abuse and claims he believed he was downloading pornography involving adult females, which he had done numerous times before. He admits he observed pictures of nude female children, whom he estimated to be under the age of ten, but that once he realized the content of these pictures he knew he had to get rid of them. ... As he was doing so he states his computer crashed. Daniel could not recall where he downloaded these pictures from but maintains he was seeking adult pornography at the time.
>
> *... Daniel possesses a variety of cognitive distortions that he used to justify his behavior. While he denies intending to download images of child abuse, his position is discredited and contradicted by the content of the pornographic stories he admits to downloading* (emphasis added).

In *Criminal Pleadings & Practice in Canada*, Second Edition Volume 2, The Honourable Mr. Justice E.G. Ewaschuk, Canada Law Book, Aurora, Ontario discussed the reporting of facts in the pre-sentence report:

> *18:3720 Contents of Report*
>
> • • •
>
> A pre-sentence report should be confined to the background, character and circumstances of the accused but not the accused's, nor the investigator's version of the facts relating to the offence [citations omitted].

In the judgment of Chief Justice Bayda, in *R v. Boulet* (1990), 58 CCC (3d) 178 (Sask. CA), there is a discussion concerning the admissibility of facts reported by a probation officer in a report. In his reasoning, Justice Bayda addressed the question from the standpoint of onus and the flexible informal evidentiary approach upon sentencing. This judgment was not concerned with the situation when the probation officer addresses the facts in a way which is problematic. He stated [at 193]:

> I mentioned that the accused's version of the disputed facts was contained in a pre-sentence report. There was some suggestion on the part of the prosecution that this form of evidence about the facts of the offence was not admissible at the sentencing hearing and should have been ignored by the sentencing judge. In my respectful view, the submission, if that is what it was, should be found untenable. The report was requested by, prepared for, and filed at the request of the judge pursuant to s. 735 of the Code. That section reads as follows:
>
> > Sec. 735(1) Where an accused, other than a corporation, pleads guilty to or is found guilty of an offence, a probation officer shall, if required to do so by a court,

prepare and file with the court a report in writing relating to the accused for the purpose of assisting the court in imposing sentence or in determining whether the accused should be discharged pursuant to section 736.

(2) Where a report is filed with the court under subsection (1), the clerk of the court shall forthwith cause a copy of the report to be provided to the accused or his counsel and to the prosecutor.

As a document properly filed, the pre-sentence report forms part of the court record. This Court in *R v. G.O.M.* (1989), 51 CCC (3d) 171 in considering a pre-disposition report filed pursuant to s. 14 of the *Young Offenders Act*, RSC 1985 c. Y-1, which became part of the record of the case pursuant to s. 14(4) of that Act, found that the version by the accused youth of the facts of the offence, which was incorporated in the report, was "before the judge." That was the only evidence before the judge of the youth's version of the circumstances of the offence. This Court found that it was sufficient evidence to form the base for an order directing that the guilty plea by the youth should not have been accepted by the judge and should now be expunged. For the purposes of deciding whether the accused's version of the facts of an offence is "before the judge" I can see no difference in logic or principle between that version appearing in a predisposition report filed pursuant to s. 14 of the *Young Offenders Act* and a presentence report filed pursuant to s. 735 of the *Criminal Code*.

My conclusion in this respect is buttressed by the words of Dickson J in *Gardiner* which I now repeat (p. 414):

> It is a commonplace that the strict rules which govern at trial do not apply at a sentencing hearing and it would be undesirable to have the formalities and technicalities characteristic of the normal adversary proceeding prevail. The hearsay rule does not govern the sentencing hearing. Hearsay evidence may be accepted where found to be credible and trustworthy. The judge traditionally has had wide latitude as to the sources and types of evidence upon which to base his sentence."

...

R v. Morelli (1977), 37 CCC (2d) 392 (Ont. Prov. Ct.), which is referenced at 18:3730 in Ewaschuk, addresses the contrary problem; when the report contains information which the accused denies, as follows:

18:3730 Challenge of report's contents
When the accused denies or challenges the validity of a statement in the pre-sentence report which the sentencing judge considers relevant, the judge must disregard the statement unless the Crown leads evidence proving its validity beyond a reasonable doubt.

The difficulty with the information contained in the pre-sentence report is that the probation officer presented the defendant's version in such a way that it suggested a denial of responsibility, disputed the defendant's version, and presented argument in so doing. While having regard to the decision of Bayda CJA in *R v. Boulet, supra*, it may be appropriate, even helpful, to outline a version of the facts that differs from that of the Crown, especially where it is a denial of responsibility. By presenting argument, the probation officer entered into the realm of advocacy; this function must remain reserved for counsel. The approach taken by the probation officer was not in keeping with the *Format and guide for the preparation of pre-sentence reports*, excerpted above, at 1.2 and 1.3, which provides that the probation officer is to be impartial and is not to reinvestigate the facts. Further, pursuant to 2.2 the probation officer is directed to ensure that the report is objective and free of bias.

On an instructive note, it is important, when facts contained in the pre-sentence report are challenged, that the record be corrected. In their article, Using Pre-Sentence Reports to Evaluate and Respond to Risk, Vol 47 *Criminal Law Quarterly* 302, Justice David P. Cole and Glenn Angus discussed the potential for misleading and inaccurate information in a pre-sentence report to be conveyed to the authorities who deal with the offender post-sentence and wrote at page 350:

7. Post-Sentence Uses of the PSR

If no objection is taken to the facts contained in the PSR, or if any factual disputes are resolved in favour of what has been written in it, obviously future users—the probation service, penal and parole authorities—may rely on it as valid. However, where the sentencer accepts as accurate some other version of any of the facts relevant to the sentence contained in the PSR, there are several points that need to be considered about whether or when these officials will obtain this information so that they will be in a position to make informed decisions about how to address the offender's potential for future offending.

It is my view, based on the foregoing, that the author of a pre-sentence report may, in the event of a guilty plea, outline the accused's account of the offence. This is in keeping with *R v. Boulet, supra*. However, this should not be done after a trial where the trial judge will have made findings of fact. While the offender's attitude may be relevant, there is no purpose in providing an account which has the potential to conflict with the trial judge's findings. It is the responsibility of the author of the report to inform him/herself about whether or not the offender plead guilty or was found guilty after a trial. Where the probation officer reports the offender's version of the facts after a guilty plea, he or she must refrain from being argumentative about the facts and must maintain a position of neutrality.

b. What Weight If Any Should Be Given to the Risk Assessments Contained in the Pre-Sentence Report and the Opinion of the Probation Officer Concerning Risk?

The author of the pre-sentence report apparently administered three separate risk assessments: the Offender Risk Assessment Management System (ORAMS), the Static 99, and the Stable 2000 Risk Assessment.

The ORAMS was described as an "actuarial based assessment with a primary scale for predicting general recidivism and a secondary scale for sexual offending." The latter scale has not been validated by research. With respect to the general recidivism scale, Mr. Hildebrandt was assessed as a low risk to re-offend. The author did not report the results of the secondary scale.

The Static 99 was described as an instrument "designed to assist in the prediction of sexual recidivism for sexual offenders." Mr. Hildebrandt's score placed him in the moderate-low risk category for sexual recidivism. No information regarding validation was provided. With respect to this score the probation officer stated: "It is concluded that this Static 99 score under represents Daniel's risk at this time." This statement was not elaborated upon.

The Stable 2000 Risk Assessment was described as follows:

> The focus of this assessment is on more dynamic risk factors including significant social influences, intimacy deficits, sexual self-regulation, attitudes, cooperation with supervision and general self-regulation. While these factors are amenable to change, without intervention, they tend to remain relatively constant.

The author then discussed in some detail these several factors and concluded:

> ... Out of a possible twelve, Daniel scored 7 which places him in the medium risk category. This risk assessment tool is empirically informed and in the process of being validated. It provides very useful information as it pertains to not only determining risk level but also the factors that contribute to this level of risk. This information is practically utilized in the development of intervention strategies.

In their article, Using Pre-Sentence Reports to Evaluate and Respond to Risk, Vol 47 *Criminal Law Quarterly* 302, Justice David P. Cole and Glenn Angus discussed the use of risk assessment tools in the sentencing process in the context of the validity and reliability of the tools and the *Mohan* test (*R v. Mohan* (1994), 29 CR (4th) 243, 89 CCC (3d) 402, [1994] 2 SCR 9.) At page 314:

> Although the case law will no doubt continue to emerge, it seems reasonably safe to assume that the validity and reliability of some of the major offender assessment tools either have or very soon will pass the *R v. Mohan* test. Thus, it becomes important for criminal justice professionals to understand the circumstances and the context in which these instruments are already being used in the PSR process.

The authors discussed three dangers regarding the use of the risk assessment tools, including the practice of probation officers providing their personal opinions in what amounts to a risk assessment override. They state beginning at page 315:

> All of the literature on assessment tools emphasizes that the assessor must have "seasoned judgment [to arrive at] a balanced decision-making model." If the assessment tool is used as a file organizer in concert with other verified file information, and if it is completed by a properly trained person, we would suggest that it may be an appropriate diagnostic instrument. However there are at least three dangers.
>
> The first is that the instrument may be completed by an insufficiently trained person, without complete and accurate background documentation. In the present context, we question whether a probation officer, however well motivated, can be said to have been appropriately trained to use these complex tools properly, on the basis of a brief in-service training. Most psychologists, for example, advocate for tools to be used as part of measures or batteries that are culture-fair and updated for norms and statistical properties.
>
> A second problem that is beginning to emerge is that results achieved on one or more assessment instruments are sometimes "overridden" by Minister policy .... In *R v. Clarke*, ... the writer of the PSR administered a risk assessment instrument being used by correctional and probation authorities in that province. She concluded as follows:

Utilizing the Primary Risk Assessment, Mr. Clarke presents as a low-medium risk to reoffend. However, given the serious nature of the assault, the risk would be overridden and the defendant would be supervised as a high risk offender. The factors which would impact upon the risk include two prior convictions, his age and sex. As well, Mr. Clarke's attitude is such that he is not receptive to assistance and not motivated to change because he maintains the incident was one of self-defence ... . He expresses no empathy for his victim in this case.

• • •

Finally, as discussed in section 6 of this article, there can be little doubt that probation officers sometimes try to affect the sentence imposed through what is—or is not—included in the PSR. Consciously or not, any assessor can affect the outcome of the assessment by the manner in which the "fields" are completed. This points up the need for ongoing checks of what is referred to in the literature as "inter-rater reliability"—trying to ensure that responses are properly and consistently recorded [footnotes omitted].

• • •

I was not content to accept the information and opinion in the pre-sentence report with respect to risk to re-offend and ordered a psychological assessment with a view to receiving a qualified assessment of risk for sexual offending and cognitive ability. These were my concerns:

- the author conducted 3 distinct risk assessments, and in doing so reported different outcomes, and used different terminology. Without explanation the author did not report the outcome with respect to the secondary scale for sexual offending in the ORAMS.

- the author appeared to have applied a personal override with respect to the outcome on the Static 99, without adequate explanation.

- Uneven information regarding validation was provided. It appeared that only the primary scale for predicting general recidivism in the ORAMS has been validated.

- I had no information regarding the training or qualifications of the probation officer to administer these risk assessments. There was no evidence that a supervisor or other qualified person had reviewed the risk assessment information provided.

- The author's misguided approach with respect to:

    – the victim impact information taken from an internet website, discussed below, and
    – handling of an apparent dispute as to the facts, referred to above.

- The risk assessment aspect of the pre-sentence report appeared to makes reference to information not contained in the facts before the court. In particular, under the heading of sexual self regulation, item c) it states: "Daniel's offending behavior, which occurred over a substantial period of time is a clear indication of deviant sexual interests." The court's information is that the offences occurred between

September 1, 2002 and October 7, 2002. While it may be a matter of perception, I would not regard this as a substantial period of time in this context.

With respect to the risk assessment tool itself, authors Cole and Angus, *supra* at pages 321 to 322, questioned the objectivity of the tool when areas of the risk assessment call for clinical assessment by persons who may not be sufficiently qualified. The Stable 2000 Risk Assessment, referenced in the pre-sentence report, contains categories described as: intimacy deficits, sexual self regulation, and attitudes tolerant of sexual assault. Greater examination of the three risk assessments used may or may not respond to questions about qualifications. It has been this court's practice in the past to request a psychological assessment when addressing the risk to re-offend sexually where the nature of the offence and the circumstances of the offender suggest that such care be taken.

c. What If Any General Information Pertaining to Victim Impact Is Appropriately Contained in the Pre-Sentence Report?

The report included information taken from the internet which has been reproduced in part:

Victim Impact

Renold and Creighton (2003) observed that this was an under-researched and neglected area. Such information as is available is from small scale clinical and survivor studies. The impact of a child's involvement in child pornography is difficult to distinguish from that of the other forms of sexual exploitation they were undergoing when the pictures were taken. Studies have looked at children involved in sex rings, prostitution and intra and extra-familial sexual and ritual abuse. Whilst many of the short- and long-term symptoms are similar to those associated with other forms of sexual exploitation some seem to be exacerbated by involvement in child pornography. Feelings of powerlessness, shame and fear of disclosure were heightened (Silbert, 1989; Itzin, 1996; Hunt & Baird, 1990).

. . .

Whether or not expert evidence regarding the impact of child pornography upon the victim will be introduced is best left to counsel in an advocacy setting. The author of the pre-sentence report was not presented as an expert witness, nor was the author of the article that was referred to in the report. There was no suggestion by counsel that such information met the criteria of necessity. Rather, counsel provided me with several reported decisions which discuss the impact of child pornography on the children featured [citations omitted].

. . .

The information provided did not come within the framework of a victim impact statement; it did not pertain to impact on an individual victim. While the author was likely motivated by a genuine desire to inform the court, it was not appropriate that the pre-sentence report reproduce such information. It was not in keeping with the requirement that the pre-sentence report be impartial and objective and did not meet the *Mohan* test for the admission of expert evidence, most particularly the requirement of necessity.

Even having regard to the more flexible approach regarding the reception of information for sentencing, the admission of expert evidence should be determined by the court upon application by counsel, after argument. The sentencing hearing has great potential in its impact upon the defendant and the court must be careful that information filed with the court be scrutinized for relevance, necessity, and reliability or that the source meets with appropriate qualifications. Further, it is important that pre-sentence reports not present information, under the authority of a court order, which would not otherwise be accepted in sentencing submissions, without the exercise of judicial consideration.

I do not know whether the author of the pre-sentence report was following policy set by the Department of Corrections and Public Safety with respect to the risk assessment material included in the report. I obtained and referred to general policy information regarding the preparation of pre-sentence reports. My comments are not intended to be personally critical of the author, whom I know to have considerable experience as a probation officer. I do not question his personal integrity or commitment to his work. However, I felt that the issues that arose were of sufficient importance that I should elaborate upon my comments expressed in open court. On one occasion, the probation officer attended court and offered to give testimony about the report. Unfortunately the matter had been adjourned to an exceptionally busy docket and the expectation was that we were dealing with a routine adjournment at that time. It was suggested that he return on the adjourned date but he did not and hence the court did not have the benefit of his remarks, nor did he have the benefit of the court's reasoning.

Before leaving this discussion about the content of the pre-sentence report, I might add that I considered a number of options, including; rejecting the report entirely, amending or deleting those portions that were offensive, and reordering the report. I resolved rather to provide my written reasons following sentence in the interests of a more expedient approach to time and resources. I felt that it would not be possible to amend or delete some offending portions of the report, given the presentation of background information in the context of the risk assessments. I did not wish to reject the report outright and order a new pre-sentence report as I felt that there was some useful information in the report and I saw no use in ordering a new one. In *R v. Purchase*, [1992] NSJ No. 582 (QL), 22 WCB (2d) 479 (NSSC), the court considered a rather extreme example of an unsuitable report. It was rejected and a new pre-sentence report was ordered After hearing argument and considering a number of authorities, the court remarked:

> [12] Writers of PSR's would do well to remember the purpose of a pre-sentence report. It is a public document written to assist the presiding Justice in the imposition of a fit and proper sentence. It is of no assistance if it cannot be relied upon. ...
>
> [13] It should present a fair and objective view of the individual and his or her standing in the community. However well meaning this author's intentions, a PSR should not contain references which might leave the impression that its purpose is to buttress a conviction or result in a greater sentence.

PROBLEM

Bill Carver has been charged with theft over $5,000 and 10 counts of fraud under $5,000. In a separate prosecution, he was charged with possession of cocaine, which was found in his home when he was arrested on the other charges. The federal Crown proceeded with the cocaine charge, but it was dismissed when the certificate of analysis proved defective (the reference number did not correspond to the reference on the seized substance). Carver entered guilty pleas to the theft and fraud counts.

Carver is a 38-year-old man, self-employed in the insurance and financial services business. The charges arise from events that occurred over a two-month period. First, Carver did not remit approximately $6,800 in premiums to the Mutual of Yamaha Insurance Company but converted it to his own use. Second, he offered 10 customers the opportunity to buy investment units in a fictitious "dot.com" company for $3,000 each and obtained a total of $30,000 from the 10 victims. None of the money has been recovered. Other than these offences, he has a record consisting of a single fraud conviction that dates back to 1984.

Carver's counsel has described him as a hard-working family man who suffers from a compulsive gambling addiction. His addiction overcame him and, in a period of weakness, he committed the offences. Counsel advises that he has started going to Gambler's Anonymous meetings. He submitted that a conditional sentence with house arrest and compulsory treatment was an appropriate response.

Crown counsel disputes this characterization. She submits that Carver used the money for gambling and cocaine, but that he suffers from no psychiatric disorder. He just lives an exorbitant life that includes trips to Las Vegas, high stakes poker, and cocaine. (The evidence of cocaine use comes from the drugs seized upon arrest and the PSR below.) She submits that a six-month jail sentence is appropriate.

The trial judge obtained a PSR, which contains the following comments:

> I have spoken with the fraud victims who were all either business clients or acquaintances of Carver. One of the victims advised that she works in a bar that Carver frequents and that it is common knowledge that he is a heavy cocaine user. Another victim, a 74-year-old retired factory worker who lives on a pension, said that the money taken from him was his only savings. Almost all of the victims feel betrayed and asked me to advise the court that a period of incarceration is required. The author agrees with this view. I have taken the file information and applied the IJMIU risk assessment scale to Carver. (A brochure describing the IJMIU and its validity prepared by its developers is attached.) He got a score of 75+, which puts him in the category of moderate to high risk to re-offend.

On the date of the sentencing, one of the victims, Colin Collins, comes to court. Crown Counsel advises that

> Mr. Collins wants to make an oral victim impact statement. He has not prepared anything in writing, but wants to explain to the judge exactly how he felt when he learned that his trusted financial adviser had defrauded him. He also wants to describe the effect of the loss of the money.

1. Are there any problems with the PSR?
2. What is the consequence of the dispute over whether Carver suffers from a disorder? Can the court order a psychiatric assessment to resolve the dispute and, if so, what is the authority for it?
3. Can the court consider the cocaine use?
4. Should the court hear from Mr. Collins?
5. How should the court handle the victim impact information in the report?

CHAPTER SIX

Victim Participation in the Sentencing Process

I. INTRODUCTION AND BACKGROUND

The role of the victim in the sentencing process has always been controversial and, until recently, somewhat uncertain. Controversy and uncertainty still characterize the role of the victim at other critical junctures of the criminal process as victims' rights continue to crystallize.[1] The sentencing process is the only juncture in the criminal prosecution where the participation of victims is formalized. Section 722 of the *Criminal Code*, RSC 1985, c. C-46, as amended, allows for the introduction of victim impact statements (VISs) at the sentencing hearing. Victim impact statement regimes now exist in almost all common law jurisdictions, and VISs have been the subject of a considerable volume of scholarship and commentary.

This chapter addresses the modern approach to victim participation in the sentencing process in Anglo-Canadian law. However, it is necessary to step back and consider historical developments in this area. The participatory rights of victims in the sentencing process have not always been so accommodating. Criminal prosecutions evolved from a system of "blood feuds" in which wrongful acts that we now characterize as "criminal" were considered merely "tortious." This gave considerable power to the aggrieved person (and/or his or her family) to control the process that brought redress. Apparently, this "golden age" of the victim lasted into medieval times.[2] In the 13th century, when certain wrongs were considered a breach of or an affront to the King's Peace, the victim started to fade from the forefront of the legal process. The law relating to the redress of criminal wrongs was arrogated by the state.[3]

Until very recently, the criminal justice system was reluctant to afford the victim any formal rights of participation in the sentencing process. *R v. Antler* (1982), 29 CR (3d) 283 (BCSC) and *R v. Robinson* (1983), 38 CR (3d) 255 (Ont. HC) exemplify the early judicial approach to VISs in Canada. In *Antler*, McLachlin J (as she then was) held that it was for

---

[1]   See, generally, Kent Roach, *Due Process and Victims' Rights—The New Law and Politics of Criminal Justice* (Toronto: University of Toronto Press, 1999).

[2]   Alan Young, "Two Scales of Justice—A Reply" (1993), 35 *Crim. LQ* 355, at 364-67.

[3]   Sociologist Nils Christie argues that the historical record of criminal prosecutions is an example of the state "stealing the conflict" from the real parties—that is, the wronged and the wrongdoer. See N. Christie, "Conflicts as Property" (1975), 17 *Brit. J Crim.* 1.

Parliament, not the courts, to grant victims the right to make representations at an offender's sentencing. In *Robinson*, the court concluded that the views of the victim were not relevant to establishing a fair and just sentence. Research suggested that victims of crime were "re-victimized" because they were disempowered by the criminal process.[4] As a result, victims felt alienated from the criminal justice system. This alienation sometimes manifested itself in the victim's lack of confidence in the process and his or her withdrawal of cooperation with criminal justice officials.[5]

The organization of the so-called victims' rights movement and the use made of this movement by law-and-order crime-control politics[6] have generated a renewed interest in the role of victims in the criminal process. The enactment of legislation permitting the introduction of VISs is one concrete reform in this area. The enactment of various victims' bills of rights (mentioned below in section III, Looking to the Future) is another result of this movement.

The chapter begins with three extracts, each dealing with the role of the victim at sentencing. In the first extract, Edna Erez provides a context for the discussion of the use of VISs in Canada. The next two extracts deal with research into the VIS regime in Canada and the perceptions and experiences of judges in four provinces. Further information on the use of VISs in Canada and other common law jurisdictions can be found in the selected readings provided at the end of the chapter.

E. Erez, "Who's Afraid of the Big Bad Victim? Victim Impact Statements as Victim Empowerment *and* Enhancement of Justice"
[1999] *Crim. LR* 545 (footnotes omitted)

Victim-oriented reforms have been adopted in numerous countries with different legal systems. Many jurisdictions have passed legislation providing for restitution from the offender, compensation from the state and various services to victims who have been impacted by a crime. Whereas most of these reforms have been accepted and welcomed, the reform providing victims with a voice, most commonly in the form of victim impact statements (VIS), has been very controversial. As recently as last summer, Andrew Ashworth, in a conference on "Integrating the Victim Perspective in Criminal

---

[4] See the *Canadian Federal–Provincial Task Force on Justice for Victims of Crime Report* (Ottawa: Solicitor General, 1983), at 60.

[5] See Alan Young, supra note 2, at 375. See also Edna Erez, "Victim Participation in Sentencing: Rhetoric and Reality" (1990), 18 *J Crim. J* 19.

[6] See, generally, Roach, supra note 1. See also Leslie Sebba, *Third Parties—Victims and the Criminal Justice System* (Columbus: Ohio State University Press, 1996), who reminds us that the study of social movements like the victims' rights movement is complex. Nevertheless, Sebba notes seven sociolegal/historical developments that are relevant to the renewed interest in victims: (1) the rise of victimology as a subdiscipline of criminology; (2) the results of victimization surveys in many countries; (3) the rise of "law-and-order" politics; (4) the role of feminist and other grassroots movements; (5) the alignment of the victim movement with political and social radicalism; (6) the resurgence of just-deserts theory in the current dialogue on the philosophy of punishment; and (7) the development of "informalist" approaches to punishment that attempt to reconcile the victim with the offender (at 2-10).

Justice," warned against two dangers inherent in current practices of victim integration in criminal justice: "victims in the service of severity" and "victims in the service of offenders." According to Ashworth, the movement to incorporate victim perspectives has sometimes coincided with the movement toward greater penal severity. Ashworth echoes concerns, raised previously by others, that the use of victim impact statements in criminal justice decision making may cause increases in sentence severity. He further claims that submission of victim impact statements (VIS) to the court may be detrimental to procedural and substantive justice, as well as to the victims who provide input. Using victims to accomplish the goal of harsher sentences, according to Ashworth, amounts to "victim prostitution."

This line of thinking is a continuation and expansion of Ashworth's earlier article on victim impact statements ["Victim Impact Statements and Sentencing," [1993] *Crim. LR* 498] in which he offered several legally based arguments against the use of victim impact statements in court. In this earlier article, Ashworth also examined the available social science evidence on the effect of VIS on criminal procedure, sentencing, and victims, and concluded, for a variety of reasons discussed below, that VIS is not a desirable practice to adopt.

This article is a response to the objections to the use of VIS in criminal justice and to concerns about the presumed detrimental effects of incorporating victim perspectives as expressed in Ashworth's earlier and more recent writing. It examines the arguments against the use of VIS in court and presents recent research findings on the effects of VIS on substantive and procedural justice, and on victims. The article then discusses the policy implications of recent research for victims' perspectives in adversarial legal systems, and concludes with a call for reconsidering the usefulness of VIS for criminal justice.

Definition and Practices of Victim Input

Victim impact statements address the effects of the crime on the victim, in terms of the victim's perceptions and expressions of the emotional, physical or economic harm he or she sustained as a result of the crime. The information for the VIS is collected, depending on the country, by justice agents such as the police (in Canada, Australia and New Zealand), or by probation officers, victim assistance or prosecution staff (in the USA). There is an agreement that the preparation of VIS should preferably be conducted by an agency that is not associated with offenders' information, such as a probation department. In a minority of jurisdictions victims prepare the statements themselves, without the assistance of any agency assigned to the task.

There is also a consensus that victim statements should ideally be contemporaneous, that is, describe the physical and emotional status of the victim at the time of sentencing. VIS, therefore, need to be updated prior to sentencing, usually by the agency responsible for the initial preparation of the VIS.

Cynicism and Research: The Use of VIS in Sentencing

The major arguments raised by Ashworth against the use of victim impact statements in sentencing revolve around three distinct issues: preservation of defendants' rights, or guarding against the erosion of the adversarial legal system, the question of sentencing for unforeseen results, and the difficulties of raising expectations. A separate issue (relevant only for those endorsing the VIS as a tool designed to better inform the court about victim harm) is whether the VIS should be read only by the prosecutor when he or she prepares the case for prosecution, or whether the VIS should be tendered to the court and available to the judge.

Procedural Issues, Sentencing Aims, and Defendant Rights

Most commentators and practitioners view the provision of victim impact information as important and generally consider victim input on the harm they suffered a step toward improving criminal justice procedures and goals. However, some observers are concerned about the potential of VIS negatively to affect defendant rights in adversarial legal systems. They also highlight the presumed incongruence between the concept of VIS, which implies a restitutive model of justice, and the conventional approach to justice. Under the restitutive model, calls for punishment that satisfies or restores the victim are inconsistent with conventional visions of justice, which view crime as a violation against the State, not a specific victim. Critics also view VIS as undermining consistent and "proportionate" treatment of offenders, and the penological system which views the "public interest" as the only justification for increased severity of penalties. Lastly, the practice of victim input could provide victims with an opportunity to subject offenders to "unfounded or excessive allegations, made from the relative security of VIS."

Research suggests that the concerns expressed by opponents of the VIS concerning possible erosion of adversarial criminal justice principles, rights of defendants and imposition of harsher sentences have not materialised. Studies conducted in the USA and in Australia comparing sentencing outcomes of cases with and without VIS, and research in Australia on sentencing trends and comparison of sentence outcomes before and after the VIS reform, suggest that sentence severity has not increased following the passage of VIS legislation. Nor has the VIS affected sentencing patterns or outcomes in the majority of the cases. The findings of qualitative research shed a better light on these "no difference" aggregate patterns. For instance, based on in-depth interview data of legal professionals in Australia, judges and prosecutors (and some defence lawyers) recognised that the information available from the VIS shed new light in a few cases, and assisted in imposing a more commensurate sentence. Although they stated that VIS were sometimes redundant or the harm was inferentially available from other documents in the file, they also described in detail a few cases they tried in which the content of VIS caused them to rethink the penalty they had in mind prior to reading the VIS. In this minority of cases in which VIS made a difference, the data revealed that the sentence was as likely to be more lenient as it was to be more severe than initially thought. For example, if the offence was perpetrated in an unusually cruel manner, or with disregard to special vulnerability of the victim, then the sentence was likely to be higher. The practitioners likewise provided instances of cases they tried where the VIS led to the imposition of a more lenient sentence than would have been indicated. For example, cases in which the victim's statement disclosed that the victim had made a complete recovery or in circumstances where certain injury had been mistakenly attributed to the crime. These kinds of qualitative findings provide a more textured account of the apparent pattern of "no difference" findings in quantitative studies of sentencing outcomes: some changes in outcomes do occur, but they are hidden as in the aggregate they offset each other. Without victim input, sentences might well have been too high or too low. In other words, contrary to the suggestions of Ashworth and others, it seems that VIS make an important contribution to proportionality rather than to severity of sentencing.

The concern that victims would use the VIS as an opportunity to subject offenders to unfounded accusations has also not materialised. In most jurisdictions currently practising VIS, victims do not prepare their own statement but it is filtered or "edited" by the specific agency responsible for the preparation of VIS. Moreover, "retelling" victims' stories often "sterilizes" them to such an extent that judges noted that the VIS was mild compared to what would have been expected in the light of the offence involved. VIS therefore turns out to be an understatement rather than an overstatement of the harm sustained in the particular offence. The recent pilot project in England confirms that victim statements tend to understate the impact of offences, and that the VIS scheme does not encourage exaggeration, inflammatory input or vindictiveness.

Concern that defendants would challenge the content of VIS thereby subjecting victims to unpleasant cross-examination on their statements has also not materialised. Legal professionals have stated that challenges to VIS in court are quite rare. According to these professionals, there are strategic disincentives militating against calling victims to the witness stand and cross-examining them on the content of their statements. There was an agreement among the legal professionals that a good defence attorney would not challenge the VIS directly and would not call victims to be cross-examined because of the adverse effects it may have on the sentence. Decision makers who hear and observe victims testifying about the impact of the crime on them may be affected by the testimony and therefore more inclined, according to the legal professionals, to impose a harsher sentence. In this respect, the concern about protecting victims from unnecessary and possibly degrading questioning regarding the content of their VIS (as distinguished from cross-examining victims about their testimony in the trial) seems to be unwarranted.

The Optimal Procedure for Bringing the VIS to the Court's Attention

There is a disagreement about whether VIS should be presented directly to the court. Some suggest that VIS should only assist prosecutors in the preparation of the case, and should not be available for the court to read. The rationale is that prosecutors represent both the victim and "the public interest," and they are charged with preparing and presenting the case. The recent report by JUSTICE, as well as a position paper by Victim Support, recommend that victims only provide details of the relevant harm they suffered to the prosecution, for preparation of the case. Prosecutors then will present the harm to the court, using their discretion as to what and how it should be presented.

This strategy, however, warrants closer examination in the light of the research on the effects of "retelling" on the content of the resulting story. This "construction of stories" or "retelling" of facts for legal consumption is often affected by various resource considerations and by the priorities of the collecting agency. When information is mediated through justice agents, there is a higher likelihood of loss or distortion of critical details. Also, research suggests that stories are often constructed to suit the goals and objectives of the mediating agency.

The Effects of VIS on Victims

Another argument against the use of VIS in sentencing is that it has harmful effects on victims. Some argued that VIS subject victims to pressures, and that victims may feel burdened by the responsibility for deciding the penalty.

This argument is empirically inaccurate, and does not represent the majority of victims who get involved in criminal justice proceedings. The cumulative knowledge acquired from research in various jurisdictions, in countries with different legal systems, suggests that victims often benefit from participation and input. With proper safeguards, the overall experience of providing input can be positive and empowering. Research conducted in the United States and Australia on victims of various crimes, where a VIS is relevant (i.e. a personal harm or loss was suffered by a specific victim), suggests that victims are interested in having a voice. These studies indicate that by and large victims do not feel burdened by being heard, nor do they feel pressured by knowing that their input has been conveyed to decision makers. The English victim statements pilot project confirms this finding. In fact, victims in continental legal systems who served as a party to the prosecution (as continental legal procedures allow) were highly satisfied with this role in the proceedings, and their level of satisfaction with justice was positively correlated with the amount of their participation. The literature on procedural justice provides theoretical explanations for these findings. According to procedural justice theories, litigants' satisfaction with justice and sense of fairness of the outcome is more affected by the procedures in which decisions were made rather than by the outcomes. Proceedings which provide victims with a voice or "process control" enhance their satisfaction with justice and sense of fair treatment.

Research in adversarial legal systems also suggests that the majority of victims of personal crimes wished to participate and provide input, even when they thought their input was ignored or did not affect the outcome of their case. Victims have multiple motives for providing input, and having a voice serves several functions for them. For some, input restores the unequal balance between themselves and the offender, particularly in cases in which the victim did not have an opportunity to testify or be heard because they were resolved by a plea. Others wanted "to communicate the impact of the offense to the offender." For the majority of the victims, filling out a VIS was a forum to formally express the crime impact on them, a civil duty they considered important for reaching a just sentence.

Providing input for VIS also helps victims to cope with the victimisation and the criminal justice experience. Many victims who filled out VIS claimed that they felt relieved or satisfied after providing the information. The recent English pilot project found that for the majority of the victims filing the statement was a worthwhile therapeutic experience, and the cathartic effect of recording the impact of the offence had been an end in itself. In-depth interviews of rape victims in the United States about their reasons for participation in criminal justice provide textured insights into the psychological, internally oriented benefits for victims' voices. Over half of the victims felt that input will assist with achieving substantive justice, and almost three quarters sought procedural justice. Through participation and input, victims wanted to engage the criminal justice process and, in the words of Nils Christie, to assert "ownership of the conflict" which they felt was misappropriated from them in the name of the state. Others wanted to reduce the power imbalance they felt with the defendant, resolve the emotional aspects of the rape, achieve emotional recovery, or achieve formal closure. This was particularly true for victims who never had the chance to be involved in the justice process because of a plea. Many victims also wanted to remind judges of the fact that behind the crime is a real person who is a victim.

The literature in the growing field of therapeutic jurisprudence provides support to the proposition that having a voice may improve victims' mental condition and welfare. Scholars in this area have discussed in length the therapeutic advantages of having a voice, and the harmful effects that feeling silenced and external to the process may have on victims.

Research further suggests that the overwhelming majority of the victims want their VIS to be used in sentencing, and many of them seek to influence the sentence imposed on the offender via the input. Although some of those who thought their input was ignored showed a lower level of satisfaction with justice because of raised expectations, this issue need not be used as an argument against the proposition that VIS can increase victim satisfaction with justice. First, the potential problem of heightening victim expectations can be resolved by explaining to victims that the VIS is only *one* of the factors judges use to determine the type and severity of penalties. As Ashworth recognises, research has shown that victims who receive explanations of the proceedings throughout the process tend to be satisfied with the outcome. Further, explanations may enhance victim satisfaction even when the outcome does not reflect victims' conception of a deserved sentence. There is no reason to suspect that explanations about the multiple factors that affect sentencing decisions will not be effective in preventing heightened expectations. One of the major aims of the victim movement, and the driving force behind it, was to help victims overcome their sense of powerlessness and reduce their feelings that the system is uncaring. Properly administered VIS schemes may be an effective way of achieving this objective, as well as creating realistic expectations.

Victims can also receive indirect benefits from providing input. A major source of satisfaction for victims is when judges pay attention to their input by citing victims' own phrases from impact statements in judicial sentencing comments. Victims feel gratified when their sense of harm is validated in judges' remarks. Victim advocates in Australia as well as in the United States indicate that victims who have heard or read sentencing comments in which judges quote their impact statements in sentencing remarks often say, "I could not believe the judge has actually listened to what I had to say."

Research also confirms that judges are sometimes unaware of victim suffering and injuries resulting from crime, because the information did not find its way into the file, either intentionally (due to bargaining considerations, or because of priorities of agencies charged with receiving the information and preparing the statements) or accidentally (due to agents underestimating the importance of the information, lack of resources to do the job, or mere incompetence or laziness). In the past, judges and other legal professionals had little opportunity to receive direct detailed input from victims and become acquainted with short and long-term effects of various crimes. Research shows that legal professionals who have been exposed to VIS have commented on how uninformed they were about the extent, variety and longevity of various victimisations, and how much they have learned from VIS about the impact of crime on victims from properly prepared VIS.

Sentencing, Unforeseen Results, and the "Normal" Victim

One of the major challenges in criminal justice sentencing is forming a fair and accurate picture of crime and its consequences to guide decision makers in their difficult task. As I have argued elsewhere, being regularly exposed to victim input may provide a more balanced notion of the "normal" victim and the boundaries of harm and injury in criminal victimisation. The prosecution has its priorities and constraints in addressing the task of prosecuting offenders. More often than not, its organisational interests are in opposition to those of the victim, and they may not be interested in disclosing the full scope of the crime impact. Research also suggests that judges employ several justifications in discarding victim input, including its subjective or emotional nature, or its alleged unreliability due to victims' motives to lie or exaggerate. To resist victims' input because, for instance, it is subjective (the most common reason judges offer for objecting to VIS) is to suggest that there is an objective way to measure harm, or to experience loss, damage and injury. Yet, harm is perceived and experienced differently, according to victims' demographic and personal attributes as well as their prior experiences. Research about the relativity of harm questions the notion of the "normal" victim, and highlights legal professionals' resistance to consider victim input which differs from their own assessment of "appropriate" level of suffering and hence a "believable VIS." As feminists have shown in the context of rape and sexual harassment, the subjectivity of harm (or for that matter any personal experience) cannot be transformed to, or be judged by, "objective" measures without doing injustice to the experience and the person reporting it. Many recent legislative acts include what has been defined in the past as "merely" subjective experience. Research has also documented that harm descriptions which legal professionals have considered exaggerated or unbelievable are indeed common experiences which those acquainted with crime's impact on victims view as within the range of "normal" reactions to victimisation.

Conclusion

The purpose of instituting VIS was to provide victims a voice, not to restructure sentencing priorities. The legislation concerning victim input was not intended to substitute harm for culpability, nor to consider harm as the overriding criterion in sentencing. Providing victims with a voice has not only many therapeutic advantages and related fairness considerations, it also ensures that sentencing judges become aware of the extent of harm suffered by victims. Incorporation of victim statements also enhances sentence proportionality rather than harshness. Although it might be argued that the number of cases in which VIS make a difference in the outcome (i.e. result in either lower or higher penalty) is relatively low, to the individuals involved, and to the justice system as it whole, this makes all the difference.

To institute a meaningful reform in the area of victim participation, it is important to win the co-operation of all parties involved: prosecutors, judges and defence attorneys. These players have various professional and organisational incentives to oppose the introduction of victim input in proceedings. To date, legal professionals have had ample substantive and procedural reasons to excuse or justify their reluctance to comply with the VIS reform. The purpose of this paper was to expose these unsubstantiated justifications, and to oppose the use of research findings, which are taken out of context, to buttress what is essentially a political stand against victim integration in criminal justice.

In the light of recent evidence which challenges the traditional legal arguments against the VIS, it is time to re-evaluate the legal profession's approach to the concept and practice of victim input. Researchers in this area have pointed out that the problem of VIS has not been the instrument itself or its effect on proceedings, defendants and victims, but rather the hostile environment in which VIS has been implemented. Comparativists encourage us to increase appropriate legal transplants and decrease inappropriate ones. There is sufficient evidence at this point to suggest that VIS (among other victim-oriented reforms) is an appropriate transplant. VIS can hardly be considered a form of "victim prostitution" which "ought to be exposed and opposed." Rather, it needs to be redefined and viewed as a useful vehicle to enhance justice in adversarial criminal justice systems while it simultaneously helps and empowers victims. To approach victims in a paternalistic manner, and ignore victims' wishes to be heard, is to continue past approaches to victims as the "forgotten persons" of the system, and perpetuate the time-honoured tradition of treating victims as invisible. The social science evidence clearly suggests that we have no reason to fear, and every reason to include, victims in the criminal justice process.

J.V. Roberts, "Victim Impact Statements: Recent Developments and Research Findings"
(2003), 47 *Crim. LQ* 365 (edited; footnotes omitted)

Purposes Ascribed to Victim Impact Statements at Sentencing

Almost every scholarly article and research report begins with some discussion of the purpose that a victim impact statement is designed to serve. Many consist of anodyne statements that lack clarity while others fail to do full justice to the concept of victim impact, or reflect a deep mistrust of the whole notion of victim involvement in sentencing. VIS have been described as a "sop" to victims, a political reform designed to placate victims without actually influencing the sentencing process, and a form of therapy for victims: the system provides the victim with an opportunity to ventilate their feelings, and then business of the courts carries on.

The following purposes and benefits have been ascribed to Victim Impact Statements:

- to provide crown counsel with information about the offence;
- to provide sentencing judges with information about the seriousness of the crime, and, to a lesser extent, the culpability of the offender. This should help

the court impose a sentence which is consistent with the principles of sentencing;

- to provide the court with a direct source of information about the victim's needs which may assist in the determination of more appropriate reparative sanctions;
- to provide the court with information about the appropriate conditions which might be imposed on the offender;
- to provide the victim with a public forum in which to make a statement reflecting their suffering;
- to provide the court with an opportunity to recognize the wrong committed against an individual victim;
- to provide the victim with the opportunity to communicate the effects of the crime to the offender;
- to allow victims to participate in sentencing, albeit in a non-determinative fashion; [and]
- to promote the idea that although crimes are committed against the state, and the judicial process involves a bipartite proceeding, crimes are committed against individual citizens.

From these primary purposes, proponents of the use of VIS hope:

- to increase victim satisfaction with the judicial process, in particular sentencing, and conversely to decrease the sense of alienation felt by many victims as they pass through the criminal justice system;
- to increase awareness among offenders of the harm they cause;
- to increase awareness among criminal justice professionals of the effects of criminal victimization;
- to increase public confidence in the administration of justice, particularly with respect to sentencing;
- to promote the possibility of reconciliation between the offender and the victim by encouraging offender empathy; [and]
- to provide victims with some sense of closure with respect to the crime, and thereby facilitate psychological healing.

Victim Impact Statements and the Codified Purpose and Principles of Sentencing

The link between many of the traditional sentencing purposes such as rehabilitation and deterrence and victim impact statements is certainly tenuous or non-existent; knowing more about the impact of the crime will not help the court devise a more effective deterrent sentence. However, retributive theories of sentencing are concerned with the limited input of victims at sentencing, at least with regard to the seriousness of the offence. Crime seriousness is the primary (but not exclusive) determinant of sentence severity under a desert-based rationale. Some commentators argue that the danger with the use of VIS is that they carry the potential to render the sentencing process more punitive. Thus Kent Roach describes them as a "symbolic and punitive reform." There has been apprehension that, nursing personal animus as a result of the crime, and adhering to unrealistic expectations of the sentencing process, victims may demand sentences well outside the normal range. When these demands remain unfulfilled, disappointment and resentment of the criminal justice system will surely follow.

Codified Purpose of Sentencing

Section 718 of the *Code* describes the purpose of sentencing, and contains two clear references to the role of the victim. This section articulates the fundamental purpose of sentencing, and identifies a number of sentencing objectives, including deterrence, denunciation, incapacitation and rehabilitation. These include most of the traditional goals of sentencing. However, the last two sentencing objectives in section 718 make specific reference to crime victims. One of these objectives relates to reparation, and the second has a particular significance for victim impact. According to section 718(f), one of the statutory sentencing objectives is: "*to promote a sense of responsibility in offenders, and acknowledgment of harm done to victims and to the community.*"

A clear way of acknowledging the harm to the victim is for the judge to cite the victim impact information communicated to the court by means of a VIS, or through submissions from the Crown. And further, promoting a sense of responsibility in offenders may well begin by sensitising them to the harm that they have inflicted, and the VIS may prove a useful conduit for this information. While judges may not cite victim impact in the absence of the victim, it is worth recalling that the offender is always present.

Codified Principles of Sentencing

Sections 718-718.2 of the *Code* identify a fundamental purpose of sentencing, a fundamental principle, as well as a series of subordinate principles. Section 718.1 articulates the "fundamental" principle in sentencing, namely proportionality. This principle is derived from retributive theories of punishment, specifically the just deserts version articulated by von Hirsch. Desert-based theories are essentially communicative theories of sentencing. A message of disapprobation is conveyed to the offender, and the severity of the sentence represents the measure of legal censure. But the communication is not restricted to a single message conveyed by a legal authority to an offender.

The sentence also carries a communication for the victim of the crime. The imposition of a sanction constitutes official recognition that this individual has been wronged. By permitting a victim to submit a statement of impact, the sentencing process introduces another possible communication: between the victim and the offender. The VIS thus plays a central role within communicative sentencing. Duff makes this point in his recent monograph on the subject: "criminal punishment ... is a mode of communication ... . It seeks to induce remorse in the offender." Remorse is more likely to emerge during a sentencing hearing in which the victim addresses the impact of the crime, rather than a prosecutor. No relationship exists between the prosecution and the offender. However, one has been established between the offender and the victim. In addition, for many crimes of violence, a relationship between the two parties will have pre-dated the commission of the crime.

The VIS provides the most appropriate vehicle by which to convey information about the impact of the crime. Indeed, a number of judgments have acknowledged as much. Crown submissions on the seriousness of the crime made prior to sentencing deprive the victim of the direct communication to the court, and the offender. This results in an interpretation being filtered through a professional's experience, one that may not always correspond with the view of the victim.

The VIS therefore represents a means by which to communicate a message to the offender. Confronting the offender with the consequences of his or her actions, and accompanying the message by the censure of the court (the sentence) is essential if the sentencing process is to achieve its codified goals. In fact, the VIS is a communication directed at two audiences: the sentencing judge and the offender. To date, almost all the emphasis in the scholarly literature has been upon the former. The case law to date as well as much of the research has represented VIS almost exclusively as a source of information for the court. In *Gabriel* for example, Hill J identifies four principal purposes of VIS. Three of these relate to the sentencing judge while the fourth relates to promoting the image of the administration of justice. None of these purposes involves communication between the parties giving rise to the criminal proceeding in the first place: victim and offender. The VIS offers a vehicle for communication from the victim to the offender, and from the judge to the victim and the offender.

Encouraging these forms of communication should not transform the sentencing hearing into a tripartite proceeding, nor should it undermine the central assumption of the adversarial system that a crime is committed against the state and not a private party. One of the few judgments that relate the VIS to the offender is written by Bagnall J in *R v. Redhead* where the judgment notes that: "the words of the victim of a crime might well serve to educate the offender as to the effects of his or her criminal behaviour."

The importance of the message to the offender should not be under-estimated. Hearing from the victim involves a completely different communicative dynamic from hearing about the impact of the crime through the sentencing submissions of the prosecutor. The adversarial system creates an antagonistic dynamic between the accused or offender and the prosecutor; this dynamic may well undermine the effectiveness of the communication. Hearing from the victim may also serve as a salutary reminder to the offender of the consequences of his actions. This should not be interpreted as a means of humiliating the offender, or an attempt at public debasement. Nor is it a message of intimidation associated with a deterrent sentence. Rather, it is a message of *sensitization*; an appeal from one individual to another: the victim sensitizes the offender to the effects of his or her conduct on other people.

At this point I review research relating to a series of questions arising from the use of victim impact statements.

How Often Are VIS Submitted?

Several commentators have noted that a major problem with VIS programs is that few victims actually submit an impact statement. This may be the case, but it is unclear what an appropriate or acceptable participation rate would be. It is unrealistic to expect all crime victims to submit an impact statement. It is the prerogative of the victim to decide whether or not to submit a statement, and many victims may have sound reasons for not participating in the sentencing process in this way. Evaluating whether the participation rate is high or low inevitably leads to a consideration of the reasons why many victims elect not to submit a statement. If a victim decides not to submit a VIS for personal reasons unrelated to the crime, or because they have sufficient faith that the prosecutor will faithfully represent the impact of the crime, it is hard to consider their "non-participation" a failure of the criminal justice system. On the other hand, if victims decide not to submit an impact statement because they have little faith that it will be used, because they have been warned that it will not be considered by the judge, or because they fear that submission of a VIS will have a negative impact on them personally, then remedial action is necessary.

The completion rates in the Department of Justice VIS research conducted in the 1980s generated an overall completion rate of 23%. It would be wrong to infer that the remainder of the samples of victims refused to participate, as the failure to contact the victim was twice as likely to be the cause of non-completion than refusal on the part of the victim. This research was conducted over a decade ago, and it is probable that participation rates are higher now, as a result of the legislative amendments and the existence of provincial victim assistance programs. Nevertheless, the inescapable conclusion is that for one reason or another, only a minority of crime victims elect to submit a statement of impact, and far fewer are actually present in court at the sentencing hearing. This result is consistent with research in other jurisdictions. Alexander and Lord cite a participation rate of one victim in four, and rates appear to be lower still in Australia and England and Wales.

Which Factors Influence the Victim's Decision to Submit an Impact Statement?

The Canadian research identified three principal reasons cited by victims for submitting a statement: (a) to ensure that justice was done; (b) because it "seemed like a good idea and was their civic duty," and (c) to "communicate the impact of the crime to the offender." It is also clear that part of the low rate of participation arises from the fact that many victims of property crimes see little benefit, and no need, to submit an impact statement. This explains the fact that the refusal rate with respect to submitting a VIS was twice as high for property crimes as personal injury offences in one of the site studies conducted by the Department of Justice in 1990. In her study of VIS, Muir reports that the most common reason given by victims for not submitting were (i) they did not perceive the VIS to be important, (ii) the incident was too trivial to justify a VIS, and (iii) the victims had forgotten about the VIS. She adds that: "The notion that revenge or desire to bring about harsher sentences is the main motivating factor for victim participation was not supported by the data." Campbell Research Associates found that the most frequently cited reason for completing a VIS was to influence sentencing.

Findings with respect to this issue vary across jurisdictions. Hoyle et al. found that the majority of the victims in their study in England and Wales explained that they had submitted a VIS for expressive reasons (i.e., to communicate a message of impact). Slightly over half cited an instrumental reason, namely the desire to influence the outcome of the sentencing hearing. In the survey of crime victims in South Australia, Erez, Roeger and Morgan report that the main reason that victims cited for providing information for a VIS was to ensure that justice was done (cited by over two-thirds of the respondents). The other reasons cited included communicating the impact of the crime to the offender, and in order to discharge a civic duty.

Many victims who submit a VIS, it would appear, expect the VIS to have an impact on sentencing outcomes. This suggests that even if they do not overtly seek to influence judges, victims expect their statement to have some effect. Either way, disappointment may arise if the victim perceives the statement to have had no impact on the sentence imposed. Since in both jurisdictions the victim's statement is incorporated in the same way, namely to inform the court but not to influence the sentence, the discrepancy in victims' expectations may be explained by the nature of information provided by criminal justice professionals.

Do VIS Influence Sentencing Practices?

Much of the research in the area has addressed the question of whether the introduction of victim impact statements changes sentencing practices. The answer is critical to advocates and critics alike: many of the former argue that if VIS do not affect sentencing practices, victims will become disillusioned by the process. Critics respond that if sentencing practices do change as a result of the introduction of VIS, the principle of parity in sentencing will be undermined. Indeed, apprehension of the effect of VIS on sentencing patterns drives much of the opposition toward the role of the victim in sentencing. VIS are therefore criticized from both directions: if they affect the sentence of the court, they will be criticized for undermining equity in sentencing; if they have no impact, they will be faulted for having raised (and then subsequently dashed) victims' expectations.

Tests of the "impact" hypothesis have been conducted in many jurisdictions, and these have generally found little effect on sentencing patterns. Erez, Roeger and Morgan report the results of an analysis of aggregate sentencing patterns in South Australia before and after the introduction of victim impact statements (in 1989). The results are crystal clear: sentencing patterns did not become more severe in the post-reform phase. The researchers also concluded that the introduction of the VIS did not have any significant impact on the length of sentences of imprisonment. Fears that the arrival of victim impact statements would result in harsher sentencing were therefore groundless. The same pattern has emerged from Canadian research. Muir examined the impact of VIS on sentencing outcomes on her study in Calgary and summarizes the results in the following way: "It must be concluded from this [analysis] that the availability of victim impact statements did not have any important or noticeable impact on sentences handed down by the courts." A similar pattern of findings emerged from other sites in this research. The finding of no impact on sentencing patterns has been replicated in many other studies.

Interviews with legal professionals confirm the findings from empirical research. Erez, Roeger and Morgan note that there is agreement among the legal professionals in South Australia that victim input has not increased sentence severity. This conclusion also applies to surveys of criminal justice professionals in other jurisdictions. Finally, with respect to the question of impact on sentencing patterns, it is perhaps not surprising that there is little evidence of change, in light of the fact that in Canada (as elsewhere), there is no specific direction to judges; they are simply asked to "consider" the victim's statement, which could mean anything, and is probably interpreted by judges in a protean fashion.

Other factors also militate against victim impact statements having the kind of impact on sentencing outcomes that can be detected by an aggregate analysis. First, most sentencing hearings follow a guilty plea. Often the plea is itself the result of negotiations between counsel, and these discussions may well have resulted in agreement to place a joint submission before the court. Plea negotiations of this kind impair the ability of the system in at least two ways. First, the case is most likely to proceed expeditiously to a sentencing hearing. Second, the Crown will not have the time or the resources to contact the victim. It is unclear, at present, what effect the statutory requirement that the court solicit the Crown with respect to whether the victim has been apprised of her right to submit a VIS has had in cases such as these.

How Well Do Victims Understand the Role of VIS in Sentencing?

A near universal issue concerns the gap between what victims expect, and the use actually made of VIS at sentencing. Many victims expect the content of their statements to influence the nature and severity of the sanction imposed. It is perhaps not an unreasonable expectation in light of the wording in s. 722, which, it will be recalled, states that: "For the purpose of *determining the sentence* to be imposed on an offender or whether the offender should be discharged pursuant to section 730 in respect of any offence, *the court shall consider* any statement that may have been prepared in accordance with subsection (2) of a victim of the offence judges" (emphasis added). A report on focus groups conducted with victims in Toronto makes the point clearly: "When the concept of [VIS] was first presented to victims, they all believed that it would affect the sentence given." This result is consistent with the findings from the Department of Justice research conducted shortly after the 1988 legislation was proclaimed.

Once again, some VIS forms may contribute to confusion among victims. The Victim Impact Statement information guide used in Ontario states that "[t]he Victim Impact Statement *may* be used during the sentencing hearing" (emphasis added), and, more curiously, "[t]he judge will decide whether or not to consider the victim impact statement when determining the sentence." Small wonder, then, that in the research on victims conducted by Meredith and Paquette "participants were unclear as to whether or not judges are required to actually read the statements that they had prepared at all."

In addition to holding misperceptions about the true purpose of a VIS, many victims are simply confused: Campbell Research Associates report that approximately one-quarter of the victims in their study did not know the purpose of the statements. This study was conducted in 1989, but it is unlikely that victims have a much clearer perception of the purpose of VIS in 2002. The fact that many victims want to influence sentencing is hardly surprising; indeed it is a natural reaction, reflecting widespread public confusion over the role of the victim in the sentencing process, and indeed the true nature of a criminal proceeding under the adversarial system. But victims may well accept the role currently assigned to them if it is explained thoroughly, with sensitivity, and by the right authority.

A clear danger associated with VIS concerns the problem of unfulfilled expectations. If victims expect their statement to affect sentence outcome, and then perceive (correctly, in light of the research findings described earlier) that their input had no discernible impact, what is their reaction likely to be? This question has been addressed in a number of studies, and the result is predictable. Erez and Tontodonato for example, report that victims who expected to influence the outcome but who thought their input had not affected the sentence were less satisfied. It is also worth noting that this negative reaction generalized to the criminal justice system as a whole; victims who had expected their statement to affect sentencing held more negative opinions of the system. Herein lies the danger of arousing, and then failing to fulfill, expectations among crime victims. In this way, a reform designed to promote victim satisfaction may actually result in lower levels of satisfaction. This finding points to the importance of clarifying for victims the true nature and purpose of a VIS.

Do VIS Improve Victim Satisfaction with the Sentencing Process?

If submitting a VIS has no positive, or even a negative effect on victim satisfaction levels, one of the principal justifications for encouraging victims to submit a statement vanishes. Researchers have accordingly attempted to ascertain whether submitting a VIS increases victim satisfaction. In the early Canadian work there were no significant differences in satisfaction levels of victims who had submitted or had not submitted a VIS. Unfortunately, that research had an important design flaw: there is no way of knowing about the influence of other pre-court differences between the groups (in addition to whether they submitted a VIS). What is needed is a pre-post design of people who choose to submit a statement.

Research in other jurisdictions that has avoided this methodological problem has generally found little increase in satisfaction levels of victims who have submitted a VIS. Davis and Smith conducted an experiment in which participants were assigned at random to either participate or not participate in a victim impact program. The results revealed that the victim impact statements had no effects on a number of different measures. The use of random assignment permits clear causal inferences to be drawn. Davis and Smith concluded that victim impact statements constituted an "unfulfilled promise" to crime victims.

Recent empirical research on victim impact statements in Canada consisted of focus groups involving victims. The findings suggest that completing a victim impact statement was perceived to have some benefits for the victim. Perhaps the best measure of whether victims perceive any utility to the VIS lies in their response to the question "Would you complete this form again in the future, knowing what you know now?" Most respondents in the focus group research reported that they would go through the process again. This finding is consistent with the research conducted in the 1980s. Thus Campbell Research Associates report that almost all the victims who had completed a VIS would be willing to submit a statement if they were victimized again. There is clearly variation with respect to this issue, however. Respondents participating in the

Toronto focus group in this research took a very negative view, responding that they would not participate again. They cited the lack of impact on sentencing patterns, and the experience of being cross-examined as the factors responsible for their resolve to not participate in the future. This outcome underlines the fact that local variation exists with respect to the nature of victims' experiences.

J.V. Roberts and A. Edgar, *Victim Impact Statements at Sentencing:*
Judicial Experiences and Perceptions—A Survey of Three Jurisdictions
(Ottawa: Department of Justice Canada, 2006) (edited)

Since their introduction in 1988, victim impact statements (VIS) have generated considerable controversy. This is true in Canada as well as other jurisdictions. To this point however, there has been an almost complete absence of information about the attitudes and experiences of the most important criminal justice professional with respect to sentencing: judges. The present research explored judicial perceptions and experiences in four provinces: Ontario, British Columbia, Alberta and Manitoba.

Most Judges Sentence a Large Number of Offenders Every Month

The caseload in Canada's criminal courts creates a large number of sentencing hearings. Respondents were asked how many sentencing hearings they conducted each month, and the averages were: BC: 55; Alberta: 33; Manitoba: 38. The aggregate average for the three jurisdictions was 42 sentencing hearings per month, considerably lower than the average number reported by judges in Ontario (71). These statistics have important implications for the sentencing process, and in particular for the question of victim input: judges are under great pressure to get through a large number of cases.

Victim Impact Statements (VIS) Are Submitted in Only a Small Percentage of Cases

One of the problems identified in the research literature is confirmed in this survey of judges: victim impact statements appear in only a small percentage of cases being sentenced. In BC, judges reported that a VIS had been submitted in 8% of cases, compared to 11% in Manitoba and 13% in Alberta. These statistics are comparable to the responses from Ontario in 2002 when on average judges reported seeing a VIS in 11% of cases.

Many Judges Report an Increase in the Number of VIS Submitted

Judges in all four jurisdictions reported an increase in the number of VIS submitted in recent years. This is particularly true in Manitoba where 41% of the respondents reported seeing a moderate or significant increase in the number of VIS.

Judges Report Having Difficulty in Determining Whether the Victim Has Been
Apprised of His or Her Right to Submit an Impact Statement

It is sometimes challenging for a judge to know whether a victim impact statement has been submitted. Respondents were asked about this particular issue. Almost half (42%) the respondents in all jurisdictions stated that it was "difficult in most cases." This pattern of responses suggests that it is frequently difficult to ascertain whether the victim has been provided with the opportunity to submit a victim impact statement.

Judges Often Have to Proceed to Sentencing Without Knowing
Whether the Victim Has Been Apprised of the Right to Submit a VIS

Judges often have to proceed to sentence the offender without knowing whether a victim impact statement has been prepared. The results of the survey revealed considerable variability regarding whether judges have to proceed to sentence the offender without knowing the status of the victim impact statement. The percentage that responded that they often proceeded without this information varied from 35% in Manitoba to 70% in British Columbia. Across the three 2006 surveys almost two-thirds of judges stated that they often had to proceed without knowing the status of the victim impact statement.

Only Rarely Do Victims Elect to Make an Oral Presentation of
the Impact Statement

How often do victims elect to make an oral presentation of their victim impact statement? It seems to be a quite rare occurrence in all jurisdictions. The most frequent response across all jurisdictions was "very occasionally." Approximately three-quarters of respondents held this view. In British Columbia 24% of the sample stated that the victim had never expressed an interest in delivering the statement orally whereas in Alberta only 5% gave this response.

Most Judges Report No Change in the Number of Victims Wishing to Make an
Oral Presentation of Their Victim Impact Statements

Judges were asked whether they had perceived any increase since 1999 in the number of victims who expressed a desire to deliver their statements orally. Considerable variation emerged across jurisdictions. Thus in British Columbia 69% of respondents reported no change in the number of victims expressing a desire to deliver statements orally whereas in Manitoba fewer than one quarter held this view. Manitoba judges were significantly more likely to report seeing an increase in requests for an oral delivery of the statement.

Victims Seldom Cross-Examined on Contents of Their
Victim Impact Statements

Some victims have been cross-examined on the contents of their victim impact statements. This can be stressful for the victim, as several victims have affirmed. It is unclear how often this practice occurs. Responses to the survey suggest that it is a relatively rare occurrence: 97% stated that it never or almost never took place. This is consistent with findings from the survey conducted in Ontario, where 84% of respondents stated that cross-examination of the victim never or almost never took place.

Most Judges Perceive Victim Impact Statements to Contain Information That Is in General Useful, as well as Relevant, to Sentencing

Judges were asked: "*In general, are victim impact statements useful?*" The response options were that the statements were useful "in all cases," "in most cases," "in some cases" and "in just a few cases." Consistent with the responses from Ontario, judges in the three other jurisdictions clearly found victim impact statements to be useful. Combining the first two response categories it can be seen that 62% of judges in British Columbia reported that VIS were useful in most or all cases. The percentage was slightly lower in Manitoba (59%) and lowest in Alberta (35%). Over all three jurisdictions 50% of judges held this view. Only 19% of judges believed that VIS are useful in "just a few cases." This pattern of results suggests that contrary to some commentators, judges do in fact find victim impact statements useful.

The second question relating to this issue asked judges whether they found VIS useful in terms of providing information relevant to the principles of sentencing. Again, the general reaction was affirmative although there was considerable inter-jurisdictional variability. The response was particularly positive in Manitoba where almost half (47%) of judges stated that they found VIS to contain information relevant to sentencing principles often, almost always or always. This response was made by fewer judges in British Columbia (36%) and far fewer in Alberta (12%). Over the three jurisdictions, approximately three quarters of judges reported finding relevant information; only one-quarter of the total sample stated that VIS never contained information relevant to the principles of sentencing.

Perceptions of Judges Consistent with Those of Crown Counsel

It is worth noting that a similar trend emerged from the survey of Crown counsel conducted in Ontario. In that survey, approximately one-third of respondents indicated that in most cases, or almost every case, the VIS contained new or different information relevant to sentencing (see Cole, 2003). Similarly, when asked whether victim impact statements were useful to the court, approximately two-thirds of the Crown counsel responded, "yes, in most cases." No respondents in that survey indicated that victim impact statements were never or almost never useful to the court at sentencing.

VIS Constitute a Unique Source of Information Relevant to Sentencing

It may be argued that the information contained in the victim impact statement is useful, but redundant, in the sense that it has already emerged at trial or from the Crown submissions at sentencing. To address this question the survey posed the following question: "*How often do victim impact statements contain information relevant to sentencing that did not emerge during the trial or in the Crown's sentencing submissions?*" As with a number of other questions, the most positive response came from the Manitoba judges where 29% stated that VIS often represented a unique source of information. In British Columbia only 17% held this view, and not one respondent in Alberta held it. The aggregated response was more positive than negative. Across the three jurisdictions 47% stated that VIS often or sometimes contained useful information unavailable from other sources; only 21% responded that VIS almost never contained such information. These trends parallel those emerging from the survey of Ontario judges. Taken together the responses to these inter-related questions suggest that from the judicial perspective—which is surely the most important—the victim impact statement represents a useful source of information relevant to sentencing.

The VIS Often Contains the Victim's Recommendations Regarding Sentence

The survey asked judges how often, in their experience, victim impact statements contain the victims' wishes regarding the sentence that should be imposed. The pattern of responses varied according to the respondent's jurisdiction. Only 12% of judges in Manitoba stated that the victim's wishes regarding sentencing were often, always or almost always present. The proportion of judges responding in this way was significantly somewhat higher in Alberta (19%), and much higher in British Columbia (37%). It was highest of all in Ontario where almost half the sample (43%) in 2002 reported seeing victim "submissions" on sentencing often, almost always or always. Across the three new jurisdictions 24% stated that sentence recommendations were often, almost always or always present. Only one quarter (25%) stated that victim sentence recommendations were never or almost never present. These responses demonstrate the need to better inform victims about the true purpose of the victim impact statements, and to guide them regarding the kinds of information that should not be included in their statement.

Judges Often Refer to the Victim Impact Statement or Its Contents

Consistent with the trend for judges to be sensitive to the issue, we found that most judges reported that they almost always or often referred to the victim impact statements in their reasons for sentence. This trend was most noticeable in British Columbia where over half (53%) almost always referred to VIS or victim impact in reasons for sentence. The percentages reporting this were considerably lower in Manitoba (35%) and Alberta (29%). Across the three jurisdictions, 39% of respondents almost always referred to victim impact when giving reasons for sentence. Overall, only 5% stated that they never referred to victim impact statements.

If the Victim Is Present at Sentencing Judges Often
Address Him or Her Directly

Most sentencing hearings take place in the absence of the victim. However, when they are present, it is clearly of assistance to be addressed by the court. The last question on the survey was the following: "*Do you ever address the victim directly in delivering oral reasons for sentence?*" Results indicated that judges are certainly alive to this issue: almost two-thirds (63%) of all respondents stated that they sometimes or often addressed the victim directly. Sixteen percent never or almost never addressed the victim, and 21% stated that they did so "only occasionally."

Many Judges Believe That VIS Increase Victim Satisfaction

One purpose of the VIS is to promote victim satisfaction with the sentencing process. Respondents were next asked whether in their experience victims who submitted an impact statement appeared more satisfied. Before reviewing the findings it is worth noting that a substantial proportion of respondents expressed the view that they were unable to respond to the question. The trends were consistent across jurisdictions: judges were more likely to hold the view that submitting a victim impact statement promoted victim satisfaction.

Overall, in the three jurisdictions approximately one third of respondents (32%) held the view that victims who submitted a statement were often or always more satisfied. Alberta judges held the most positive views. Thus, 39% of respondents in that province believed that victims who submitted a statement often or always seemed more satisfied. In the other two provinces the proportions of respondents holding this view were slightly lower (26% and 27%).

Conclusion

As a result of the surveys conducted in four jurisdictions we now have a much more informed view of the utility of victim impact statements. It was encouraging to note that while variability emerged across the jurisdictions in response to some questions, there was generally considerable consensus—particularly regarding the most important issues concerning the victim impact statement regime. We would end this report on the perceptions of judges in four jurisdictions by concluding that despite a number of criticisms victim impact statements perform a useful function in the sentencing process in Canada.

II. THE CURRENT LEGAL FRAMEWORK

The first formal statutory provision for the admission of VISs was enacted by *An Act to Amend the Criminal Code (Victims of Crime)*, RSC 1985, c. 23 (4th Supp.), s. 7 (passed in 1988). This provision has been amended from time to time[7] and now appears as s. 722 of the *Criminal Code*, set out below. It is important that s. 722 be read and interpreted in its proper statutory context in conjunction with the purposes and principles of sentencing in ss. 718 to 718.2 of the *Criminal Code*. In particular, "providing reparations for harm done

---

[7] The section was re-enacted in Bill C-41, *An Act to Amend the Criminal Code (Sentencing)*, SC 1995, c. 22 and amended by *An Act to Amend the Criminal Code (Victims of Crime)*, SC 1999, c. 25, ss. 17 and 18, and the *Modernization of Benefits and Obligations Act*, SC 2000, c. 12, s. 95(d). These Acts made changes throughout the *Criminal Code* to recognize victims explicitly and to extend various Code provisions to common law partners. An example of these types of changes is seen in the bail provisions. Victims may also provide impact statements for disposition hearings for individuals found not criminally responsible for an offence and for parole hearings for convicted offenders. See *Criminal Code*, ss. 672.5(14) to (16) and s. 745.63.

to victims or to the community" (s. 718(d)) and promoting "a sense of responsibility in offenders … and acknowledgment of the harm done to victims and to the community" (s. 718(e)) are identified as objectives of the sentencing function.[8]

The current version of s. 722 of the *Criminal Code* provides as follows:

> 722(1) For the purpose of determining the sentence to be imposed on an offender or whether the offender should be discharged pursuant to section 730 in respect of any offence, the court shall consider any statement that may have been prepared in accordance with subsection (2) of a victim of the offence describing the harm done to, or loss suffered by, the victim arising from the commission of the offence.
>
> (2) A statement referred to in subsection (1) must be
>
> (a) prepared in writing in the form and in accordance with the procedures established by a program designated for that purpose by the Lieutenant Governor in Council of the province in which the court is exercising its jurisdiction; and
>
> (b) filed with the court.
>
> (2.1) The court shall, on the request of a victim, permit the victim to read a statement prepared and filed in accordance with subsection (2), or to present the statement in any other manner that the court considers appropriate.
>
> (3) Whether or not a statement has been prepared and filed in accordance with subsection (2), the court may consider any other evidence concerning any victim of the offence for the purpose of determining the sentence to be imposed on the offender or whether the offender should be discharged under section 730.
>
> (4) For the purpose of this section and section 722.2, "victim," in relation to an offence,
>
> (a) means a person to whom harm was done or who suffered physical or emotional loss as a result of the commission of the offence, and
>
> (b) where the person described in paragraph (a) is dead, ill or otherwise incapable of making a statement referred to in subsection (1), includes the spouse or common law partner or any relative of that person, anyone who has in law or fact the custody of that person or is responsible for the care or support of that person or any dependant of that person.
>
> 722.1 The clerk of the court shall provide a copy of a statement referred to in subsection 722(1), as soon as practicable after a finding of guilty, to the offender or counsel for the offender, and to the prosecutor.
>
> 722.2(1) As soon as practicable after a finding of guilt and in any event before imposing sentence, the court shall inquire of the prosecutor or a victim of the offence, or any person representing a victim of the offence, whether the victim or victims have been advised of the opportunity to prepare a statement referred to in subsection 722(1).
>
> (2) On application of the prosecutor or a victim or on its own motion, the court may adjourn the proceedings to permit the victim to prepare a statement referred to in subsection 722(1) or to present evidence in accordance with subsection 722(3), if the court is satisfied that the adjournment would not interfere with the proper administration of justice.

---

8   See the discussion of these issues in chapter 2, Judicial Methodology and the Legislative Context. Note, as well, that s. 718.2 identifies certain victim features or characteristics that are relevant for sentencing purposes.

Following the enactment of this legislation, the courts grappled with the question of who is a victim within the meaning of this provision. The restrictive approach to the role of victims is perpetuated in *Curtis*, a case that interpreted the original version of the provision (s. 735). Note that the original version of the legislation referred to "*the* person to whom harm is done or who suffers physical or emotional loss as a result of the commission of the offence." The amended and broader version of the section (see s. 722(4) above, amended by SC 1999, c. 25, s. 17(3)) contemplates a wider class of persons affected by a crime.

R v. Curtis
(1992), 69 CCC (3d) 385 (NBCA)

STRATTON CJNB: The appellant, Randolph Hayward Curtis, raises [the following issue] on this appeal: (1) Did the trial judge err in admitting into evidence a victim impact statement from a person who, it is alleged, was not a victim as defined in s. 735(1.4) of the *Criminal Code* ... ?

The Facts

Mr. Curtis pleaded guilty to the offence of assault causing bodily harm to Mr. George MacMullin contrary to s. 267(1)(b) of the Code. ... The Crown agrees that the assault occurred as the result of the breakdown of Mr. Curtis' marriage and the resulting frustration which he experienced.

On November 25, 1982, Mr. Curtis married Kimberley Ann Wilson. They have one child, Kathleen Ann Curtis, who was born July 31, 1988. On March 9, 1990, the parties separated.

...

In March, 1991, Mrs. Curtis commenced divorce proceedings. Mr. Curtis, however, continued to hope for reconciliation. Shortly after the commencement of the divorce proceedings, Mrs. Curtis began seeing the victim of the assault, Mr. George MacMullin, Mrs. Curtis advised her husband that this was not a romantic relationship. In any event, Mr. Curtis approached Mr. MacMullin and requested that he have no involvement with his wife until after the divorce hearing which was scheduled for June 26, 1991.

On Sunday morning, May 26, 1991, Mr. Curtis went to his wife's residence and in the parking-lot of her apartment he met Mrs. Curtis, his daughter Kathleen and Mr. MacMullin. All of them, including Mr. Curtis, were on their way to church. Mr. Curtis voiced his objection to his daughter going to church with Mr. MacMullin. Mr. Curtis followed the MacMullin vehicle from Mrs. Curtis' residence to the church. After the parties had parked their vehicles, Mr. Curtis approached Mr. MacMullin and threatened him. Mr. Curtis then proceeded to punch and kick Mr. MacMullin a number of times. All of this happened in front of the church and in the presence of a number of witnesses including Mrs. Curtis and the daughter Kathleen.

As a result of the assault, Mr. MacMullin suffered serious injuries including a broken nose, a fractured jaw and two broken ribs. Mr. MacMullin was hospitalized for a period of time and required surgery to repair the fractures.

... At the sentencing hearing, the judge received into evidence ... a victim impact statement from Mr. MacMullin. Over the objection of counsel for Mr. Curtis, the judge also accepted into evidence a victim impact statement from Mrs. Curtis on behalf of herself and her daughter, Kathleen. In her statement, Mrs. Curtis relates her recollection of the assault and its effect upon her and her daughter and her future relationship with the victim's mother. It is the acceptance of Mrs. Curtis' statement which is raised as one of the two issues in this appeal.

The Legislation

Section 735(1.1) to (1.4) of the *Criminal Code* authorizes the preparation and reception of victim impact statements. Section 735(1.1) permits a sentencing court to consider a statement made by a victim of an offence which describes the harm done to or the loss suffered by the victim arising from the commission of the offence.

• • •

The Judgment at Trial

• • •

In dismissing Mr. Curtis' contention that Mrs. Curtis was not a "victim" within the meaning of s. 735(1.4) of the Code, the judge said:

> As far as the Victim Impact statement itself is concerned, victims as defined under the Code are certainly defined very broadly. And my understanding of what I've heard today is that the wife, still a wife I believe, of Randolph Hayward Curtis and the girlfriend of the victim in this matter, George MacMullin, certainly suffered emotional harm. She was there when it happened. I understand again just briefly of what has been said that the daughter was also there when this assault took place. Chances are that the daughter as well suffered emotionally, emotional harm from that.
>
> And again on the broad definition of a victim under the Code I hold that in this case the wife of Randolph Hayward Curtis and the now girlfriend of the victim George Mac-Mullin would be entitled to present to the Court a Victim Impact Statement. ...

• • •

The Victim Impact Statement

• • •

Discussion

1(a) Who Is a "Victim"?

[T]he trial judge concluded that the word "victim" as used in ss. 735(1.1) to (1.4) of the Code should be given a broad meaning so as to include persons other than the person that one might call the direct victim. I have looked, unsuccessfully, for assistance in the case-law. While there are many cases in which victim impact statements are mentioned, in no case did I find a court that considered directly the meaning of the word "victim."

A survey of the reported decisions shows, however, that in general it is the direct victim whose statement is introduced and used.

There have, however, been a number of exceptions to the general rule of receiving only the statements of "direct" victims. Impact statements have been received from an aunt (*R v. H.(A.)* (1991), 65 CCC (3d) 116, 13 WCB (2d) 49 (BCCA)); a mother (*R v. Melville*, New Westminster Registry, No. X019013, January 13, 1989); a maternal grandmother (*R v. McMurrer* (1990), 84 Nfld. & PEIR 248, 10 WCB (2d) 381 (SC); reversed on appeal, PEI CA, No. AD-0230, January 28, 1991 [reported 89 Nfld. & PEIR 36, 12 WCB (2d) 168]; leave to appeal to SCC refused, No. 22378, June 20, 1991); the members of families of the victim (*R v. Poole*, Ont. Dist. Ct. Thunder Bay District, No. 1216-88 [summarized 7 WCB (2d) 51]; *R v. Lecaine* (1990), 105 AR 261 (Alta. CA), and *R v. Black* (1990), 110 NBR (2d 208, 11 WCB (2d) 324); "many people," referring to people in the community (*R v. Sousa*, BCCA, Vancouver Registry, No. CA 12625, September 27, 1991 [summarized 14 WCB (2d) 111]), and from a series of physicians and psychiatrists who had worked with the victim: *R v. S.(C.C.)* (1990), 81 Nfld. & PEIR 81, 9 WCB (2d) 558 (SC). In *R v. McMurrer*, the case involving the statement from the maternal grandmother, the court mentioned that there was "no indication that the statement complied with s. 735(1.4)(*b*); however, the accused did not object to it." One court did say that it had concerns with respect to the introduction of the statements in general: *R v. K.(S.A.)*, BCCA, Vancouver Registry, No. CA011597, November 5, 1990 [summarized 11 WCB (2d) 484]. An Ontario court manifested "critical scepticism about unsworn testimony": see *R v. Scott*, Ont. Ct. (Gen. Div.), Hamilton, No. 1183/90, January 4, 1991 [summarized 13 WCB (2d) 394].

It is to be observed that the definition of "victim" contained in s. 735(1.4)(a) refers to "*the* person" to whom harm is done or who suffers loss. In my opinion, the use of the definite article in the definition section restricts the meaning of the word "victim" to the "direct" victim of the offence.

In addition to the use of the definite article in para. (a) of s. 735(1.4), support for a restricted meaning of the word "victim" can be found in para. (b) of s. 735(1.4) which permits certain other persons to submit a victim impact statement where "the person" referred to in para. (a) is dead, ill or otherwise incapable of making a statement. From this it would seem to follow that if the direct victim is not dead, ill or otherwise incapable, these other persons would not be allowed to submit a victim impact statement. Moreover, one of these other persons is a victim's spouse. If it was intended to allow anybody affected by an offence to submit a victim impact statement, surely one such person would be the spouse of the direct victim. Yet it appears that she or he is excluded unless the "victim" is incapacitated.

Furthermore, it is to be noted that s. 735(1.2) of the Code directs that a victim impact statement shall be prepared in accordance with procedures established by the Lieutenant-Governor in Council of the province in which the court is exercising jurisdiction. On August 23, 1990, the Lieutenant-Governor in Council of New Brunswick by OC 90-721, designated a program for the preparation and submission of victim impact statements in the province. The designated program refers specifically and repeatedly to victim impact statements describing the harm done to, or the loss suffered by, "*the* victim of a criminal offence." The program also directs that a statement should state only the effect on "*the* victim of the crime for which the offender could be sentenced." Additionally, the "guiding principles" of the program refer to "the direct victim of the offence." Thus, in my opinion, the words used in the approved program for New Brunswick support the conclusion that a restricted meaning should be given to the word "victim" under the existing legislation.

While an argument can perhaps be made that the definition of "victim" in s. 735(1.4)(a) could be read to include not only the direct victim of an offence but also a person who suffers physical or emotional loss as the result of the commission of an offence, I am not persuaded that this would be a proper reading of the legislative intent as expressed in the definition. In this respect, it is to be noted that prior to the amendment of s. 735, the Code did not allow for the introduction of victim impact statements. If Parliament had intended to permit courts to receive statements from anyone other than a direct victim, it is my opinion it could more clearly have made provision for the reception into evidence of multiple victim impact statements.

In summary, it is my opinion that even though there appears to be a tendency to relax the rules of evidence with respect to the introduction of evidence at the sentencing hearing (see, for example, the decision of the Supreme Court of Canada in *R v. Albright* (1987), 37 CCC (3d) 105, 45 DLR (4th) 11, [1987] 2 SCR 383), of the legislation in question here, given their plain and ordinary meaning, do not permit the introduction of victim impact statements except from the direct victim. If, however, the direct victim is dead, ill or otherwise incapable of making a statement, others may be permitted to do so pursuant to s. 735(1.4)(b). In the result, I have concluded that Mrs. Curtis' statement should not have been admitted into evidence.

Phillips addresses the same issue raised in *Curtis*, but reaches a different conclusion. Phillips was convicted of second-degree murder in the killing of a police officer. The Crown tendered victim impact statements from the deceased's fiancée, his partner on the force, and a representative of a local police–community association. The latter statement spoke of the impact that the death had on the small community where he lived and served. This decision was also decided before the 1999 amendments to s. 722. The revised version of the provision, s. 722(4), undoubtedly supports the *Phillips* approach.

R v. Phillips
(1995), 26 OR (3d) 522 (Gen. Div.)

McISAAC J: With the greatest of respect to the New Brunswick Court of Appeal [in *Curtis*], I am unable to accept this interpretation which I find would unreasonably limit the ambit of this provision in the *Criminal Code*. I do so for two reasons. They both relate to the application of the *Interpretation Act*, RSC 1985, c. I-21.

First, s. 33(2) of that Act states that words in the singular include the plural. Accordingly, there is no reason to restrict the definition of "victim" in s. 735(1.4)(a) to the singular. I find nothing in para. (b) thereof to lead me to the conclusion that it was in any way intended to, or in fact, has the effect of limiting the definition of "victim" in para. (a).

This proposition would appear to be directly contrary to the legislative intent of the amendment which was adopted by the House of Commons Legislative Committee prior to the third reading of Bill C-89. See "Two Scales of Justice: The Victim as Adversary" (1993), 35 *CLQ* 334, an article by Mr. Steven Skurka, at p. 344 (footnote 27):

> It would appear that s. 735(1.4)(b) was adopted by the legislative committee without much, if any, discussion prior to the third reading of Bill C-89. The proposer of the amendment was moved by a particular case in British Columbia where a court had refused to accept a victim impact statement from a member of the family of a deceased victim even though other members of the family suffered from that particular crime: Commons Debates, 3rd Reading, May 3, 1988, at p. 15086.

My second concern related to the *Interpretation Act* involves s. 12 thereof which states:

> 12. Every enactment is deemed remedial, and shall be given such fair, large and liberal construction and interpretation as best ensures the attainment of its object.

As I read *R v. Curtis*, supra, Stratton CJNB was unable to find any case-law to support the submission advocating a broad interpretation of "victim" that was made by the Crown in that case: see pp. 390-91. However, the Supreme Court of Canada subsequently had occasion to assess the interplay of the principle of broad and liberal interpretation as provided for by s. 12 of the *Interpretation Act* with the rule of strict interpretation of penal statutes: see *R v. Hasselwander*, [1993] 2 SCR 398, 81 CCC (3d) 471. In [this case,] the Supreme Court of Canada rejected an interpretation based on the principle of strict interpretation of a penal statute for a broad and remedial interpretation based on social policy grounds [because the strict interpretation would have frustrated the obvious intent of Parliament in enacting the provision].

Applying that approach to the issue at bar, I have to consider the policy that motivated Parliament to permit consideration of a VIS and then apply those principles to the definition of "victim" in s. 735(1.4). In *R v. Nelson*, Stuart TCJ of the Yukon Territorial Court, unreported, April 13, 1992, outlined the purpose of this 1988 amendment (quoted in "Two Scales of Justice: A Reply" (1993), 35 *CLQ* 355, an article by Professor Alan N. Young at pp. 362-63):

> The victim impact statement accords the victim an opportunity to ensure that their concerns are incorporated in the sentencing process without being exposed to the trauma of testifying ... Sentencing, among its many objectives, aspires to impose a sentence that the victim will regard as just. Ensuring that their concerns are heard creates the basis for victims to accept and believe in the fairness of the process ... . Finally, without the victim's impact, the seriousness of the crime cannot be fully appreciated. What may be viewed from the bench as trivial, may in fact be serious, and conversely what may be generally regarded as a serious crime may not be if the full story was before the court ... Victim impact statements can help offenders appreciate the ramifications of their conduct on others and thereby add an awareness essential to promote and sustain genuine contrition and the will to change their behaviour.

...

[T]hese comments reflect the virtual flood of victims' rights initiatives that have been undertaken in the common law jurisdictions in the last decade: see pp. 359-61 of Professor Young's article, supra. As well, they confirm the fact that retribution continues to be a valid consideration in the sentencing process: see *R v. Lyons*, [1987] 2 SCR 309 at p. 329, 32 CRR 41 ... .

• • •

... My experience has not been that victims wish to monopolize the sentencing process; they merely want to be able to participate in it in a meaningful way.

The provision of the three contested VIS herein will assist me in lifting the character of P.C. Nystedt from the status of a "faceless human cipher." I see no potential for them to distort the sentencing hearing into an exclusive process to rectify the purely private interests of their authors. They will merely provide a balance to the anticipated evidence that will be advanced on behalf of the offender in mitigation of sentence. Accordingly, both sides will be afforded a hearing that reflects the principles of fundamental justice: see *R v. Cunningham*, [1993] 2 SCR 143, 14 CRR (2d) 234. I am persuaded that the definition of "victim" in s. 735(1.4) should be given a broad and liberal interpretation.

V. Conclusion

For these reasons, I am compelled to the conclusion that I should not follow the judgment of the New Brunswick Court of Appeal in *R v. Curtis*, supra. Based upon rules of judicial comity, I do so reluctantly. Accordingly, the VIS of PC Mike Landry, Joanne McPhee and Ms. Presley will be admitted and considered in this sentencing hearing.

Statements admissible.

The following judgment in *Gabriel* looks at the role of VISs from a functional perspective within the sentencing process. Hill J focuses on the content of VISs and how they relate to the aims and principles of sentencing in ss. 718 to 718.2 of the *Criminal Code*.

R v. Gabriel
(1999), 26 CR (5th) 364 (Ont. Ct. (Gen. Div.))

HILL J: On May 31st, 1999, Raymond Gabriel was sentenced to a term of imprisonment of 2 years less 1 day following his guilty plea to the charge of criminal negligence causing death. This disposition was imposed allowing the offender a 7-month credit for pre-sentence custody. In addition, Mr. Gabriel was made the subject of a 2-year probationary term with special conditions and a 5-year driving prohibition.

During the sentencing hearing, counsel acknowledged a general lack of direction or guidance respecting victim impact statements in particular relating to the permissible limits of content subject matter.

• • •

The Victim Impact Statements

The victim impact statements filed in the *Gabriel* case included documents authored by the deceased's parents, grandparents, aunts, uncles, cousins, fiancé, and employer. As well, some statements were filed by authors whose relation to the victim could not be determined. As well, a statement was filed by the stepmother of Ms. Hunt's best friend.

As one would expect, given the number of statements, there existed considerable repetition in content within the population of documents filed.

Almost without exception, the victim impact statements were titled "Auto Accident by Raymond Gabriel Killing Samantha Hunt."

Some of the victim impact statements were in the form of letters. The majority of the statements, however, were set out in a form entitled, Victim Impact Statement, with the following subtitles:

(1) My Name
(2) Address
(3) Phone Number
(4) Relationship to Samantha Hunt
(5) Description of Impact (including emotional, psychological, social and financial loss)
(6) Date; Signature.

Some of the statements appended photographs of the deceased or poetry.

More than half of the victim impact statements contained references to one or more of the following topics:

(1) the facts of the offence,
(2) the character of the offender,
(3) the punishment Mr. Gabriel deserved.

. . .

Analysis

Victim Impact Statements

Prior to codification, there existed mixed judicial reaction to the admissibility of victim impact statements. However, the trend was toward acceptance of evidence, at least from the direct victim of the offence. In *Swietlinski v. Attorney-General of Ontario* (1994), 92 CCC (3d) 449 (SCC) at 465, Lamer CJC observed: "It is well known that the victim's testimony is admissible at a hearing on sentencing ... ."

As a general rule, in criminal cases, harm cannot be presumed. As an aggravating feature of sentencing, loss or harm is to be established by the prosecution: *McDonnell v. The Queen* (1997), 114 CCC (3d) 436 (SCC) at para. 22-38 per Sopinka J; *Criminal Code*, s. 724(3).

Assessment of the harm caused by a crime has long been an important concern of the law of sentencing and evidence of specific harm relates to assessment of an offender's moral culpability and blameworthiness: *Payne v. Tennessee*, 501 US 808 (1991) at 2605-6, 2608 per Rehnquist CJ.

The victim impact statement regime was first introduced into the *Criminal Code* in 1988 (section 735). The sentencing court was afforded a discretion as to whether it would consider any tendered victim impact statements.

· · ·

Accordingly, the following essential features should exist in order for a victim impact statement (the statement) to be admissible:

(1) the statement is to be prepared in writing,

(2) the statement is to be in the form and in accordance with procedures established by a program designated for that purpose by the province,

(3) the statement is to be authored by a person meeting the definition of "victim" (s. 722(4) of the Code),

(4) the statement is to describe the harm done to, or loss suffered by, the victim arising from the commission of the offence,

(5) the statement is to be filed with the court,

(6) the clerk of the court is to provide a copy of the statement to the prosecution and the defence (s. 722.1 of the Code).

Where a statement is admissible, it "shall" be considered by the sentencing court acting under Part XXIII of the *Criminal Code*.

Section 722(3) of the Code affords the sentencing court a discretion to consider other evidence concerning the victim of an offence beyond that contained in a victim impact statement.

The victim impact statement serves a number of purposes, including:

(1) *Nature of the Offence* The court receives relevant evidence as to the effect or impact of the crime from the person(s) able to give direct evidence on the point. The evidence is not filtered through a third party reporter. The evidence is relevant to the seriousness of the offence which in turn assists the court in imposing proportionate punishment (s. 718.1 of the Code).

(2) *Victim Reparation* Sections 718(e) and (f) recognize that a just sanction by the court should have amongst its objectives reparation for harm done to victims and the promotion of acknowledgement by the offender of harm done to a victim. Resort to the best evidence on the subject of victim loss, the victim himself or herself, not only assures an accurate measure of any necessary compensation but also serves to bring home to the offender the consequences of the criminal behaviour.

(3) *Repute of the Administration of Criminal Justice* Victim participation in the trial process serves to improve the victim's perception of the legitimacy of the process. The satisfaction of being heard, in the sense of a direct submission to the court, enhances respect for the justice system on the part of the harmed individual, and over time, the community itself. Incidental to the victim impact statement process is the ability of the victim to secure a sense of regaining control over his or her life and the alleviation of the frustration of detachment which can arise where the victim perceives that he or she is ignored and uninvolved in the process.

(4) *Parity of Identity* A significant concern of the sentencing hearing is finding a disposition tailored to the individual offender in an effort to ensure long range protection of the public. As a consequence, much becomes known about the accused as a person. In this process, there is a danger of the victim being reduced to obscurity—an intolerable departure from respect for the personal integrity of the victim. The victim was a special and unique person as well—information revealing the individuality of the victim and the impact of the crime on the victim's survivors achieves a measure of balance in understanding the consequences of the crime in the context of the victim's personal circumstances, or those of survivors.

The victim impact statement is not, however, the exclusive answer to the civilized treatment of victims within the criminal process. Communication with victims of crime by prosecutorial authorities, victim/offender reconciliation projects, and community support initiatives for victims, are as, or more, essential.

Victim impact statements contribute significantly to a just sentencing process. Sentencing is a reasoned, not an arbitrary, exercise. Context remains important. It is to be remembered that there is a civil justice system to address actionable wrongs between individual citizens. The criminal court is "not a social agency" (*R v. M.(E.)* (1992), 76 CCC (3d) 159 (Ont. CA) at 164 per Finlayson JA, in dissent in the result).

Without, in any fashion, diminishing the significant contribution of victim impact statements to providing victims a voice in the criminal process, it must be remembered that a criminal trial, including the sentencing phase, is not a tripartite proceeding. A convicted offender has committed a crime—an act against society as a whole. It is the public interest, not a private interest, which is to be served in sentencing.

The historic lack of legislative codification, and a similar silence in Bill C-79—*An Act to Amend the Criminal Code (Victims of Crime)* [now SC 1995, c. 22], as to the procedural circumstances of the introduction of a victim impact statement tends to foster a victim's expectations that he or she is a party to the proceeding and not a witness. Who is responsible for identifying the victim of the crime? What searches ought to be made to provide notice to all victims of the crime? Is there judicial authority to limit the number of statements filed, or which may be read under the pending amendments? It is implicit that a victim statement constitutes evidence to be considered in arriving at a fit and just sentence. Accordingly, is the statement, where written, or if read in court, under oath? subject to cross-examination? subject, to the introduction of extrinsic contradictory evidence adduced by the offender? In the court's exercise of its supervisory jurisdiction to ensure a fair trial and to control its own proceedings, can the court edit an impact statement in terms of inflammatory, overly prejudicial or irrelevant content? Should the court not be able to intercede to halt what is in effect a mini-trial within the sentencing hearing designed to supplement the record in parallel civil proceedings between victim and offender?

The dangers of a runaway model for victim participation in the sentencing process can, in the long run, serve to defeat the very objectives of victim input.

Retribution remains an important sentencing objective in sanctioning the moral culpability of the offender: *The Queen v. M.(CA)* (1996), 105 CCC (3d) 327 (SCC) at 365-369 per Lamer CJC. Vengeance, however, has no place in a humane sentencing regime: *The Queen v. M.(CA)*, supra at 368-370; *R v. Sweeney* (1992), 71 CCC (3d) 82 (BCCA) at 95 per Wood JA; *R v. Lauzon* (1940), 74 CCC 37 (Que. CA) at 52 per Walsh JA.

• • •

Accordingly, the victim impact statement regime should not be structured so as to foster or encourage any element of personal revenge on the part of a victim. This is a very real danger. In "Two Scales of Justice: The Victim as Adversary" (1993), 35 *CLQ* 334, Steven Skurka observed at pages 340 and 341:

> By asking a victim to express his comments and concerns without any further guidance, invariably this category will be used by many victims to vent their feelings about such matters as the nature of the crime, the offender, the failings of the criminal justice system and the appropriate sentence to be imposed on the offender. ...

Equally, it cannot be denied that many victims, perceiving themselves as real adversaries, will use such an opportunity as a platform for revenge against the accused. ...

There must be guidelines to ensure that victim statements "only contain relevant information": *Swietlinski v. Attorney-General of Ontario*, supra at 465. The guidelines need to limit the statements to what the Code authorizes: *R v. Barling*, [1995] BCJ No. 2225 (CA) at para. 9 per McEachern CJBC.

In Ontario, under the prior discretionary scheme, it was recognized that it was proper to consider a victim impact statement in sentencing: *R v. W.(H.W.)*, [1992] OJ No. 2407 (CA) at 2 per curiam. Concern was expressed that undue reliance not be placed upon such material: *R v. Smith*, [1994] OJ No. 3899 (CA) at para. 1 per Lacourcière JA. Improper statement contents have led to partial consideration of submitted victim impact materials: *R v. Barling*, supra at para. 7-9; *R v. Ohlenschlager*, [1994] AJ No. 510 (CA) at para. 3 per MacKenzie JA.

Impact statements should describe "the harm done to, or loss suffered by, the victim arising from the commission of the offence." The statements should not contain criticisms of the offender, assertions as to the facts of the offence, or recommendations as to the severity of punishment.

Criticism of the offender tilts the adversary system and risks the appearance of revenge motivation.

Attempts to state, or presumably to restate, the facts of the offence usurp the role of the prosecutor and risk inconsistency with, or expansion of, prior trial testimony, or facts read in, and agreed to, on the guilty plea appearance. Such was the case in *R v. McAnespie* (1993), 82 CCC (3d) 527 (Ont. CA) (reversed (1994), 86 CCC (3d) 191 (SCC)) where additional disclosure by the complainant, relating to the offence, was made by the complainant in her victim impact statement.

The Attorney General represents the public interest in the prosecution of crime.

Recommendations as to penalty must be avoided, absent exceptional circumstances, i.e. a court-authorized request, an aboriginal sentencing circle, or as an aspect of a prosecutorial submission that the victim seeks leniency for the offender which might not otherwise reasonably be expected in the circumstances. The freedom to call for extraordinary sentences, beyond the limits of appellate tolerance, unjustifiably raises victim expectations, promotes an appearance of court-acceptance of vengeful submissions, and propels the system away from necessary restraint in punishing by loss of liberty (s. 718.2(d) of the Code; *Gladue v. The Queen*, supra at paras. 40, 41, 57, 93). It has been suggested that frequently the victim's limited knowledge of available sentencing options may lead the victim to rely on more severe options: H.C. Rubel, "Victim Participation in Sentencing Proceedings" (1985-86), 28 *CLQ* 226 at 240-241. The independent neutrality of the judiciary requires that the court not react to public opinion as to the severity of sentences: *R v. Porter* (1976), 33 CCC (2d) 215 (Ont. CA) at 220 per Arnup JA.

Some mention is necessary as to circumstances where the written impact statement can be presented orally. In Mr. Gabriel's sentencing hearing, leave was given to two of the "victims" to read their victim impact statements in the courtroom. There is a discretion to do so: *R v. Selig* (1994), 134 NSR (2d) 385 (CA) at 391 per Roscoe JA. There is, however, at present, no statutory or constitutional obligation to permit this: *R v. Coelho* (1995), 41 CR (4th) 324 (BCSC) at 327-330 per Saunders J. Indeed, it is not infrequent, in this courthouse, that a victim has emotionally disintegrated while reading his or her statement or has improvised beyond the four corners of the statement directing accusations and personal invectives toward the offender. In yet other instances of victim allocution, disturbances have erupted in the public area of the courtroom. However, a sensible exercise of discretion is warranted, having regard to the totality of the circumstances, including the health and stability of the victim, the nature of the crime(s) committed, concerns as to control of the courtroom, and the number of statements filed.

The statute does not directly speak to the mechanism by which a victim impact statement is filed. Since s. 722.1 of the Code refers to the clerk of the court providing a copy of a filed victim impact statement to the "prosecutor," there is some parallel to the pre-sentence report which is submitted directly to the court with copies to the parties. The tradition has generally been that Crown counsel tenders the victim impact statement(s) on the sentencing hearing as opposed to direct line access to the court for a victim. Regardless of whether the prosecution office, or the personnel administering the program designated by the Province of Ontario (under s. 722(2)(a) of the Code), is principally involved with the victim(s), there should be some pre-filing gatekeeper function exercised in terms of ensuring that victim impact statements comply with the *Criminal Code* requirements. In this way, victim disappointment will be avoided.

The Ontario Program

Section 722(2) of the Code requires that, to be admissible, a victim impact statement "must be prepared in writing in the form and in accordance with the procedures established by a program designated for that purpose" by the province.

In Ontario, the designated program is the Victim Witness Assistance Program (VWAP) of the Ministry of the Attorney General.

By virtue of this approach, the written victim impact statement is not itself a prescribed form—it is the program (responsible for designing the form) which is designated.

The established form in Ontario mandated by the VWAP is appended to these reasons together with the government-generated Information for Victims instruction sheet provided to victims.

The February, 1994 form, apparently still in use, is not the form employed by any of the "victims" in the *Gabriel* case. I will return to this observation in due course.

The VWAP documentation is disturbing in several respects, including:

(1) The form requests information relating to physical injuries and to financial impact resulting from the crime. No reference is made to emotional loss (s. 722(4)(a)) or to other forms of harm done to the victim (ss. 722(1), 722(4)(1)) i.e. psychological or social impacts or effects.

(2) The form invites, through broad and open-ended titlage (Personal Reaction; Other Comments), statements by the victim relating to the offender, the facts of the offence, and the suggested punishment. Despite the admonition in the information circular: "Please avoid recommending a sentence," the form is cast in very broad terms. I agree with Steven Skurka's observations ("Two Scales of Justice: The Victim as Adversary," supra at pages 340-341) that this type of unfocused direction leads to improper material in victim impact statements.

(3) The accompanying information sheet, also of 1994 origin, states:

> The judge will decide whether or not to consider the Victim Impact Statement when determining the sentence.

While this statement was a correct description of the 1994 legislation, specifically s. 735(1.1) of the Code ("... the court may consider a statement ..."), the amendment proclaimed September 3, 1996 (SC 1995, c. 22), s. 722(1), assures judicial consideration of an otherwise admissible victim impact statement ("... the court shall consider any statement ...").

In some instances, along with the victim impact statement form, a victim may receive a two-page document entitled, Victim Impact Statement: An Information Guide, also appended to these reasons. For those who receive this additional material, the following advice is provided:

> Please remember that the Victim Impact Statement is about you, not the accused. Please avoid vengeful comments; instead, concentrate on providing a description of the impact of the crime on your life. Suggestions about the penalty are not helpful since it is entirely up to the judge to make that decision. You may, however, wish to express any concerns you have about probation conditions. For example, it may be important for you to say whether you do or don't want contact with the accused.

It would appear that many of the victims in this case were not provided, or failed to abide by, this direction.

As to the non-compliance in the *Gabriel* case with use of the very form utilized by the VWAP, s. 722(2)(a) speaks in mandatory terms requiring the designated program form to be the one filed with the court—in this instance, the established form which, apart from accompanying informational supplements, invites the inadmissible contents encountered in the sentencing hearing. This point was not argued by the defence. Accordingly, whether on the basis of substantial compliance with the designated form, waiver, or receipt through the vehicle of s. 722(3) of the Code, the statements are admissible subject to excision of some of their contents.

Application of Principles to This Case

Much can be said for an interpretation of "victim" in s. 722 of the Code which limits the production of a victim impact statement to the direct victim of the crime: see *R v. Curtis* (1992), 69 CCC (3d) 385 (NS CA) at 391-393 per Stratton JA. Similarly, a restrictive view is warranted regarding s. 722(4)(b) of the Code where a victim impact statement is received in a case where the crime has caused death.

In this case, statements were filed beyond the category of "spouse" or "relative" as "victim" is defined in s. 722(4)(b) of the Code. "Victim" is likely to be interpreted in the plural: *Interpretation Act*, RSC 1985, c. I-21, s. 33(2); *R v. Phillips* (1996), 26 OR (3d) 522 (Gen. Div.). Assuming that more than one relative of the deceased is authorized to file a victim impact statement pursuant to s. 722(4)(b) of the Code, it does not assist the court to have 20 relatives do so. I note that in at least one case the court considered a joint victim impact statement: *R v. F.(R.)*, [1994] OJ No. 2101 (CA) at para. 3 per curiam. While some discretion exists, by virtue of section 722(3) of the Code, to expand the receivable scope of victim impact statements, the number filed here far surpassed what was helpful to the court.

In a case of a crime resulting in death, human experience, logic and common sense surely go some distance to presuming the existence of profound grief, loss and despair. It has been observed that "the criminal law does not value one life over another" (*R v. M.(E.)*, supra at 164 per Finlayson JA) and that "A consideration of the measure of loss of a human life is not only a demeaning process but also leads to a potentially egregious weighing of the worth of an individual's life" (S. Skurka, "Two Scales of Justice: The Victim as Adversary," supra at page 343).

Also, with respect to the statements, authors, either unidentified in their connection to the deceased, or remote in connection, are not of assistance.

Statements purporting to refer to the facts of the offence were inaccurate.

Statements speaking of the offender were not informed views of the background circumstances of the offender.

Suggested penalties were made without regard to the "worst offence/worst offender" sentencing principle.

A number of statements promoted eye-for-an-eye retributive justice only, without regard to other overarching principles and objectives of sentencing.

The labelling of the impact statements as involving a "killing" is inflammatory and jeopardizes the desired restraint of the sentencing hearing.

In a couple of instances, the offender's crime was wrongfully equated to "murder." A similar problem arose in *R v. Lecaine*, [1990] AJ No. 360 (CA) drawing disapproval from the court. Stevenson JA (as he then was) stated at page 2:

> Those statements feelingly portray the grief of the mother and brother of the victim at the loss of the victim. One cannot help but have very great sympathy for these people, for their loss. We point out, however, that these statements show an understandable misapprehension of the function of the criminal law in the punishment process. The mother says that her son's life was worth "a twelve month sentence to his murderer." This accused was not his murderer. The brother says "Thou shall not kill." This accused was not a killer in the sense of being a murderer. Murder is intentional killing and this accused was not convicted of intentional killing.

In the end result, the court considered only the contents of victim impact statements which described the harm done to, or loss suffered by, the identifiable victims in this case.

NOTES

1. Given the wording of s. 722 and the comments of Hill J, what do you think about the following excerpts from actual VISs filed in *Gabriel*?

Raymond Gabriel made choices on the night of July 1st that have serious consequences. His mockery of the law resulted in Samantha's death. We have a judicial system in place in Canada that states there are now consequences that he must pay for disobeying the law and taking someone's life. I expect that system to work as the court determines Raymond's consequence. He has taken every future choice that should have existed for Samantha and me and the rest of her family and friends as far as our relationship with her. …

It terrifies me to think that Raymond Gabriel may be back on the streets in short time and be in a position to cause more harm to other innocent people in this or some other manner. Based on his prior offences, it's obvious he shuns the law. So if his punishment is deemed to be removal of his license, he's the type that would drive anyway without one. I have worked hard all my life and I've paid my taxes faithfully—I contribute financially into this country in order that among other things, I and my family can be protected. The judicial system exists to protect those who honour it, not those who shun it. Let's not make a mockery of our system and Samantha's life by not allowing Raymond to pay the true debt he owes. …

I trust that you will show Raymond Gabriel the same regard that he showed for our dear Samantha.

I am distressed that in spite of a huge publicity campaign against drinking & driving that there are still criminals that ignore these laws. To be so intoxicated and consciously decide to drive a motor vehicle is the same as pointing a loaded gun at a crowd and firing. I would request that a maximum sentence be imposed to help deter others from considering such actions. I do not feel safe on the roads with drivers like this on the road. …

Those who breach the law are irresponsible and don't deserve the privilege of driving. I abhor the fact that so much leniency is shown for alcohol abusers. Everyone who was with this man or who served him drinks is responsible for Sam's death. At every family get together we've missed her, at Christmas, her birthday, mother's day. Please help stop this type of crime happening to another family. …

Your Honourable Judge, as a distraught family member, as a concerned teacher and as a law abiding member of our society, I implore that you will use your authority to uphold the law and send an indisputable message to Mr. Gabriel and others who choose to drink and drive that with every choice comes a proper consequence and equally important—that the worth of a soul is great! …

No sentence for Mr. Gabriel can bring Samantha back to us—this we know. But we want to know that the forces of justice in Canada are prepared to make a strong statement. We pray that Canada will declare that it is NOT prepared to allow itself to become a place where decent human lives are fair game, to be destroyed by careless and criminally irresponsible people, with no fear of consequence. If Mr. Gabriel is not punished to the maximum allowed by the law, it will demonstrate that the suffering he has caused—suffering which will continue for many years—means nothing. It will show that Canada does not care about the fate of its brightest and most promising asset—its youth! ...

The lesson, that the crime he has committed will not be tolerated in a decent society, must be fully impressed upon him with a just, and adequately severe sentence.

2. Clearly, a VIS must be relevant to issues that are properly before the court and should not cross into extraneous areas. This includes limiting the statement to the offence actually before the sentencing court. See *R v. Talbot*, [1995] OJ No. 4304 (Gen. Div.). However, the demarcation lines are not easy to draw and maintain given the personal nature of the victim's input. There can be particular problems related to the oral presentation of a VIS. Although it is relatively easy to vet the contents of a prepared written statement in advance, must the victim be warned not to stray beyond its wording? What if the victim engages in impromptu additions? How should the judge intervene? For an example of the personal and visceral kinds of comments that victims may deliver when given an opportunity to make an oral statement, see *R v. K.L.*, [1999] OJ No. 5085 (QL) (SCJ), per Kurisko J, where one of the victims launched into a personal attack on the offender.

3. In *Gabriel*, Hill J noted that the 1999 amendments, specifically the new s. 722(2.1), would "remove the court's ability to prevent a victim reading an impact statement." Is this correct? Certainly, the amendments are directed at giving victims a greater role in the decisions about whether and how to present a VIS. But do they have the effect of entirely precluding the judge's discretion to rule that a written statement is the proper manner of presentation? Hill J identified some reasons why a victim should, in specific cases, present a written rather than an oral VIS. Principally, the reasons relate to the health and stability of the victim and the need to ensure security in the courtroom. Can a judge no longer respond to these concerns by requiring a written VIS only? Has s. 722(2.1) elevated the victim's status to almost that of a party? Surely, all Code provisions must be interpreted in the manner that best preserves the integrity and fairness of the judicial process. Does s. 722(2.1) go too far? For a response to these issues, see *R v. Sparks* (2007), 251 NSR (2d) 181 (Prov. Ct.).

4. In *Gabriel*, Hill J held that VISs should not contain sentence recommendations "absent exceptional circumstances, i.e. a court-authorized request, an Aboriginal sentencing circle, or as an aspect of a prosecutorial submission that the victim seeks leniency for the offender which might not otherwise reasonably be expected in the circumstances." In *R v. Proulx*, [2000] 1 SCR 61, the Supreme Court of Canada held that "[i]n determining whether restorative objectives can be satisfied ... the judge should consider ... the victim's wishes as revealed by the victim impact statement." In what other circumstances might a court seek a victim's views on the sentence? Is it appropriate to consider a victim's plea for leniency? See *R v. Tkachuk* (2001), 159 CCC (3d) 434 (Alta. CA); *R v. R.G.* (2003), 232 Nfld. & PEIR 273 (CA).

5. Section 722(4)(b) states that "victim" includes spouses, common law partners, relatives, and custodians. Given the use of the term "includes," exactly how broad is the definition of "victim"? Does it include anyone who observed or reacted to the crime? Is it restricted to those listed in the definition? See *Gabriel*; *R v. Hames*, [2000] AJ No. 1538 (QB); and *R v. McDonough* (2006), 209 CCC (3d) 547 (Ont. SCJ).

6. In *Gabriel*, Hill J indicated that 20 VISs were far too many. What is the danger in accepting a multiplicity of statements? How many VISs should a court accept? If too many

statements are filed, how does a sentencing judge select which statements to consider? See *R v. Roberts* (2001), 289 AR 127 (QB); *R v. McDonough*, above.

7. What happens if a sentencing judge imposes a sentence without inquiring whether a victim has been advised of the opportunity to make a VIS and therefore fails to comply with s. 722.2? See *R v. Tellier* (2000), 261 AR 360 (CA).

8. In *R v. Geddes* (2006), 201 Man. R (2d) 34 (CA), the Manitoba Court of Appeal rejected a victim's application for intervenor status in a sentence appeal. The court noted both the lack of jurisprudence granting such a right to private individuals and Crown counsel's role as representative of the public interest.

In *Jackson*, the Ontario Court of Appeal commented further on the proper content of a VIS, the procedure to be followed in placing victim impact evidence before the court, and the relationship between sections 722(2), 722(3), and 723(3).

R v. Jackson
(2002), 163 CCC (3d) 451 (Ont. CA)

SHARPE JA: A uniformed police officer attempted to stop the appellant for riding double on a bicycle. The appellant jogged away, then turned and fired a .357 calibre handgun in the direction of the officer. A second shot was also fired. The police officer took cover behind a car. There were bystanders in the vicinity but no one was injured.

[T]he appellant was convicted of discharging a firearm with intent to endanger the life of the police officer, possession of an unregistered restricted firearm, carrying a weapon for a purpose dangerous to the public peace, and discharging a firearm with intent to prevent arrest.

· · ·

Sentence Appeal

After both Crown counsel and the appellant's counsel had made their submissions with respect to sentencing, Crown counsel stated: "Your Honour, I have just been advised that P.C. MacDonald would like to address the court." Counsel for the appellant objected. The trial judge permitted P.C. MacDonald to be sworn and to make a statement.

In his statement, P.C. MacDonald explained to the trial judge that he was concerned about the increasing risk to police officers from the use of handguns and firearms. P.C. MacDonald complained that the hands of the police are "increasingly more and more tied down by regulations and rules and bureaucratic red tape." He indicated that, in his opinion, the appellant had deliberately lured P.C. MacDonald to follow him "for the sole purpose" of shooting him. He explained his belief that although the appellant could easily have escaped, the appellant had deliberately "egged" him on.

Defence counsel interrupted to renew his objection. He pointed out that no victim impact statement had been filed, nor had the defence been given any notice of P.C. MacDonald's intention to make a statement. The trial judge ruled that the officer should not be permitted to continue.

As required by s. 726 of the *Criminal Code*, the trial judge gave the appellant an opportunity to make a statement before being sentenced. The appellant reiterated his concerns regarding police racism but stated that he was sorry for what he had done and that he had learned a great deal from the 14 months he had spent in pre-trial detention.

In the trial judge's reasons for sentence, he began as follows:

> The sad fact is that this case has done absolutely nothing to contribute to the resolution of one of the most serious chronic social problems in our community. If anything it has exacerbated the problem. The comments that have been made by the accused, the comments that have been made by the victim, Police Constable MacDonald, fortify the grave concern that we should all have about the problem that continues to fester and does not seem to be adequately addressed by persons who should be in a position of responsibility to address those issues before the conflicts flare up. It is somehow left to the Court, the last post to deal with the problems after the event, to decree some sort of just resolution to an ongoing problem that does nothing more than to bring more and more of these tragic events to this level.

> ...

In my view, the trial judge erred in permitting P.C. MacDonald to make his statement during the sentence proceedings.

Section 722 of the *Criminal Code* provides that a court shall consider a victim impact statement filed by a victim. As a victim, P.C. MacDonald was entitled to file a victim impact statement. However, he did not do so and did not offer any reason to explain why he had not followed the procedure under the *Criminal Code*, which was intended to afford him the opportunity of conveying to the trial judge the impact of the offence on him.

P.C. MacDonald's statement was inappropriate from both a procedural and a substantive perspective. From a procedural perspective, the statement did not follow the *Criminal Code* provisions concerning the filing of a victim impact statement, and the sentencing procedure mandated by the *Criminal Code* does not provide for or contemplate the making of the kind of statement at issue here. Further, the defence had no notice or warning of what the officer intended to say. Indeed, it appears that even Crown counsel was unaware of P.C. MacDonald's intention to make a statement and of what P.C. MacDonald intended to say. Crown counsel, therefore, was not equipped to ensure that P.C. MacDonald would at least confine his remarks to what is permitted in a victim impact statement. In these circumstances, I find it surprising that Crown counsel would ask the trial judge to hear P.C. MacDonald, particularly at such a critical point in the proceedings. In my view, Crown counsel had a responsibility to ensure that the proposed content of the statement was admissible. While I do not wish to be taken as endorsing the appellant's concerns regarding racist attitudes among the police, it does seem to me that given those concerns and the strong feelings they provoked, it was particularly inappropriate for Crown counsel to allow P.C. MacDonald to make a statement just as the trial judge was about to impose the sentence.

From a substantive perspective, P.C. MacDonald's statement exceeded the limits of what is permitted in a victim impact statement. Section 722 provides that a victim impact statement may describe "the harm done to, or loss suffered by, the victim arising from the commission of the offence." However, P.C. MacDonald's statement went well beyond this permissible scope of a victim impact statement. P.C. MacDonald gave evidence regarding the causes and incidence of crime, the use of firearms and the facts of the offences alleged against the appellant. Even assuming that any Crown evidence along these lines was admissible, the evidence should have been led earlier in the sentencing proceedings to afford the appellant the opportunity to test, meet or answer it with evidence or submissions.

I do not accept the respondent's submission that a statement of this kind falls within the contemplation of the *Criminal Code* provisions relating to victim impact statements. At the time of sentencing, s. 722(3) provided as follows:

> 722(3) A statement of a victim of an offence prepared and filed in accordance with subsection (2) *does not prevent the court from considering any other evidence concerning any victim of the offence for the purpose of determining the sentence to be imposed on the offender* or whether the offender should be discharged pursuant to section 730. (Emphasis added)

The respondent also relies on s. 723(2), which required the court to hear "any relevant evidence" on sentencing, and on s. 723(3), which provided as follows:

> 723(3) The court may, on its own motion, *after hearing argument from the prosecutor and the offender*, require the production of *evidence that would assist it in determining the appropriate sentence*. (Emphasis added.)

In my view, these provisions do not assist the respondent. I do not read s. 722(3) as giving the prosecution or the victim the option of either providing a victim impact statement or making a statement to the court immediately before a sentence is passed. The references to filing a victim impact statement in accordance with s. 722(2) and to "any other evidence" indicate to me that s. 722(3) is subsidiary to s. 722(2) and that it merely supplements the normal procedure with respect to victim impact statements. Section 722(3) does not allow for an alternate method of placing victim impact evidence before the court. With respect to s. 723(2), I do not read this provision as requiring a court to consider evidence tendered in a manner that fails to respect directly applicable *Criminal Code* provisions governing its admissibility. Finally, I fail to see how s. 723(3) has any relevance to the present case as the court clearly did not require the production of further evidence on its own motion.

By enacting the victim impact provisions as part of the sentencing process, Parliament has indicated the importance of giving due regard to the views and concerns of victims and to the need to treat victims with courtesy, dignity and respect. I can certainly understand why P.C. MacDonald felt as strongly as he did about this serious crime, which had endangered his life. However, it is important that the procedures contemplated by the *Criminal Code* for victim impact evidence be followed. In my view, the *Criminal Code* does not allow a victim, especially one who has not given a victim impact statement, to make his own plea for a stiff sentence after all of the evidence has been called and after both counsel have made their submissions. By asking the court to follow this unusual procedure, Crown counsel and P.C. MacDonald brought about a situation that created an appearance of unfairness at one of the most critical moments in the process.

· · ·

In my respectful view, the trial judge's error in permitting P.C. MacDonald to make his statement was compounded when the trial judge made explicit reference to certain impermissible aspects of that statement in his reasons. In view of these errors, it is open to this court to review the sentence imposed by the trial judge.

· · ·

Disposition

In my view, a total sentence in the range of seven years rather than ten years is appropriate. In view of the appellant's 14 months of pre-trial custody, I would vary the sentence of seven years for discharging a firearm with intent to endanger life to a sentence of four years and eight months. I would not interfere with the concurrent sentences imposed for the other offences.

NOTE

In *Jackson*, the Ontario Court of Appeal indicated that the Crown is responsible for ensuring that a VIS complies with the Code requirements. Other appellate courts have expressed similar views: see *R v. Labrash*, [2006] BCJ No. 1768 (CA). Ideally, the Crown should therefore review the statement before it is submitted to the court, delete any inadmissible content, and explain to the victim why that information is being excluded. If this is not possible because of the late preparation or delivery of the statement, Crown counsel should request that the court disregard or ignore the improper information. For a discussion of these issues, see *R v. McDonough*, above, and *R v. Unger* (2007), 292 Sask. R 191 (Prov. Ct.).

III. LOOKING TO THE FUTURE

As noted at the beginning of the chapter, the sentencing process is the only juncture in the criminal process where the role of victims has been articulated. The preceding case excerpts demonstrate that the courts still adhere to the traditional dualistic models of criminal justice that do not afford a great role for victims. Nevertheless, Parliament has sought to amplify the voices of victims by amending s. 722 to permit greater knowledge of the rights they have in the process. It seems likely that the next locus of debate will revolve around how the courts interpret s. 722(2.1), which requires a court to permit a victim to read a VIS or present it "in any other manner the court considers appropriate." This right of allocution, which exists in many US jurisdictions, may have a serious, and perhaps undesirable, effect on the tone and mood of Canadian sentencing hearings.

Not all reforms in the name of victims' rights have come from Parliament. As noted in the introduction to this chapter, most provinces and territories have proclaimed victims' bills of rights. These pieces of legislation are largely declaratory and informational. First and foremost, they declare the importance of victims to the criminal process. The rights of victims are also part of Parliament's amendments to the *Criminal Code* in SC 1999, c. 25. This legislation contains the following preamble:

Preamble

Whereas the Parliament of Canada continues to be gravely concerned about the incidence of crime in Canada and its impact on society, particularly on persons who are the victims of offences;

Whereas the Parliament of Canada recognizes that the co-operation of victims of and witnesses to offences is essential to the investigation and prosecution of offences, and wishes to encourage the reporting of offences, and to provide for the prosecution of offences within a framework of laws that are consistent with the principles of fundamental justice;

Whereas the Parliament of Canada recognizes and is committed to ensuring that all persons have the full protection of the rights guaranteed by the *Canadian Charter of Rights and Freedoms* and, in the event of a conflict between the rights of accused persons and victims of and witnesses to offences, that those rights are accommodated and reconciled to the greatest extent possible;

Whereas the Parliament of Canada supports the principle that victims of and witnesses to offences should be treated with courtesy, compassion and respect by the criminal justice system, and should suffer the least amount of inconvenience necessary as a result of their involvement in the criminal justice system;

Whereas the Parliament of Canada, while recognizing that the Crown is responsible for the prosecution of offences, is of the opinion that the views and concerns of the victims should be considered in accordance with prevailing criminal law and procedure, particularly with respect to decisions that may have an impact on their safety, security or privacy;

Whereas the Parliament of Canada wishes to encourage and facilitate the provision of information to victims of and witnesses to offences regarding the criminal justice system and their role in it, and regarding specific decisions that have an impact on them;

Whereas the Parliament of Canada wishes to encourage and facilitate the participation in the criminal justice system of victims of and witnesses to offences in accordance with prevailing criminal law and procedure;

And whereas the Parliament of Canada acknowledges the fundamental importance of an open justice system that treats all persons who come before it with dignity and respect;

Provincial bills of rights also entitle victims to information from police and prosecutors at each stage of the criminal process. However, there is no formal mechanism by which these rights may be enforced against those who fail to measure up to the requirements of the statute.[9] These bills also contain provisions that are relevant to civil litigation.

Because they are provincial enactments, these bills have no *direct* bearing on the participatory rights of victims in criminal proceedings. However, they provide a rich context of

---

[9]　See, for example, the note about two limiting provisions in Ontario's *Victims' Bill of Rights*, 1995 (SO 1995, c. 6, as am.). Section 2(1) establishes the basic rights of victims. Section 2(2) provides that the principles set out in s. 2(1) are "subject to the availability of resources and information, what is reasonable in the circumstances of the case, what is consistent with the law and the public interest and what is necessary to ensure that the resolution of criminal proceedings is not delayed." Section 2(5) provides that "no new cause of action, right of appeal, claim or other remedy exists in law because of this section or anything done or omitted to be done under this section."

victim empowerment in which s. 722 must be interpreted. Thus, these types of enactments and other societal recognition of victims' rights may well have considerable *indirect* impact on the criminal process. Indeed, they may lend legitimacy to the evolution of criminal justice models from dualistic paradigms (accused versus the state) to more encompassing models that recognize broader victims' interests.

The legitimate needs of victims who have suffered physical injury, personal loss, or financial loss likely extend beyond the criminal justice system, which has a narrower focus and limited resources and is circumscribed by the limits of federal jurisdiction. The practical operation of schemes for the compensation, counselling, and rehabilitation of victims is best dealt with by agencies designed specifically for those purposes. These agencies are often under provincial and territorial jurisdiction. Provincial and territorial statutes that address the role of victims are typically drafted in broad terms that, at least symbolically, champion the rights of victims. The preamble reproduced above is a good example of this approach. However, it is important to ask what resources and/or concrete ameliorative steps, if any, accompany the grand claims made by provincial and territorial legislation bearing upon victims' rights.

IV. FURTHER READING

Ashworth, A. "Victim Impact Statements and Sentencing" [1988] *Crim. LR* 498-509.

Meredith, C., and C. Paquette. *Summary Report on Victim Impact Statement Focus Groups* (Ottawa: Policy Centre for Victim Issues, Department of Justice Canada, 2001).

Roach, K. "Crime Victims and Sentencing," in D. Stuart, R. Delisle, and A. Manson, eds., *Towards a Clear and Just Criminal Law: A Criminal Reports Forum* (Toronto: Carswell, 1999).

Roberts, J.V. "Victim Impact Statements and the Sentencing Process: Enhancing Communication in the Courtroom" (2003), 47 *Crim. LQ* 365-96.

Roberts, J.V., and A. Edgar. *Victim Impact Statements at Sentencing: Judicial Experiences and Perceptions* (Ottawa: Department of Justice Canada, 2006).

Sanders, A., C. Hoyle, R. Morgan, and E. Cape. "Victim Impact Statements: Don't Work, Can't Work" [2001] *Crim. LR* 447-58.

CHAPTER SEVEN

Plea Discussions and Joint Submissions

I. INTRODUCTION

The preceding chapters on procedure and evidence portray the sentencing process as primarily adversarial in nature. Indeed, it is when matters are in dispute in the criminal justice process that the parties must resort to the rules of evidence and procedure. However, at the sentencing stage, there may be little dispute between the prosecutor and the offender. Although estimates vary, it is beyond dispute that the overwhelming majority of cases are resolved by a guilty plea.[1] Often, guilty pleas follow discussion between the prosecutor and defence counsel about what sentence ought to be imposed. This same process can occur when sentencing follows a finding of guilt at trial.

The practice of plea bargaining continues to be the subject of great controversy both in the legal profession and in the public at large.[2] Every aspect of the practice was considered in the *Report of the Attorney General's Advisory Committee on Charge Screening, Disclosure, and Resolution Discussions* (Toronto: Queen's Printer for Ontario, 1993), chaired by the Honourable G.A. Martin ("the Martin Report"). This chapter does not retrace the contours of this elaborate debate. Instead, we take as our starting point the Martin Report's statement in recommendation 46 (at 281):

> 46. The Committee is of the opinion that resolution discussions are an essential part of the criminal justice system in Ontario, and, when properly conducted, benefit not only the accused, but also victims, witnesses, counsel, and the administration of justice.

This chapter focuses on the extent to which prior arrangements made by counsel can constrain the discretion of the sentencing judge in his or her approach to the sentencing function. As we shall see, the boundaries of these constraints are often elucidated in situations where the sentencing judge rejects the arrangements presented by counsel. It then falls to the appellate courts to unravel what happened and decide whether the judge should have taken the joint submission more seriously.

---

[1]   See Report of the Canadian Sentencing Commission, *Sentencing Reform: A Canadian Approach* (Ottawa: The Commission, 1987), at 406.

[2]   See S.A. Cohen and A.N. Doob, "Public Attitudes to Plea Bargaining" (1989-90), 32 *Crim. LQ* 85.

II. THE JOINT SUBMISSION

A. Definitions

Discussions surrounding joint submissions are often encumbered by problems of nomenclature. It is therefore important to define relevant terms.

Plea bargains may take many forms. A joint submission is really just one method of plea bargaining.[3] The Canadian Sentencing Commission defines a plea bargain as "any agreement by the accused to plead guilty in return for the promise of some benefit."[4] A plea bargain or plea arrangement may take the form of the Crown's withdrawal of one or more charges in exchange for the accused's guilty plea to one or more charges.[5] There need be no further agreement about the type or quantum of punishment that ought to follow. Similarly, a plea bargain may involve a plea of not guilty to the charge as laid, but a plea of guilty to a lesser and included offence. A good example of this type of arrangement is when an accused person who is charged with murder enters a plea of guilty to the lesser and included offence of manslaughter.

These two aspects of the plea-bargaining process are engaged largely without the sentencing judge's input—that is, these types of arrangements are conceived of and driven by counsel, and do not depend on the assent of the sentencing judge.[6] There is little that a sentencing judge can do to upset this type of "charge-bargaining" arrangement. This is not to say, however, that these types of arrangements ought to be shrouded in secrecy. On the contrary, the public interest is better served by the public disclosure of any agreement in open court.[7]

---

[3]   See S. Verdun-Jones and A. Hatch, *Plea Bargaining and Sentencing Guidelines* (Ottawa: Canadian Sentencing Commission, 1985), 3, where the authors list 13 forms of plea bargaining. These are reproduced in the Report of the Canadian Sentencing Commission, supra note 1, at 404-5.

[4]   Ibid., at 404.

[5]   The plea of guilty may be taken into account as a mitigating factor: see *R v. Johnston and Tremayne*, [1970] 4 CCC 64 (Ont. CA). See *R v. Fegan* (1993), 80 CCC (3d) 356 (Ont. CA), where Finlayson JA (at 8), in discussing the guilty plea, made the following statement: "It is considered by the sentencing judge as an expression of remorse. By expressing finality to the conviction process, it invites leniency in the sentencing portion of the trial." However, this is not always the case. See *Report of the Attorney General's Advisory Committee on Charge Screening, Disclosure, and Resolution Discussions* (Toronto: Queen's Printer for Ontario) ("the Martin Report"), at 310, which emphasizes that the earlier the guilty plea is entered, the greater the mitigation that may be enjoyed. This principle is exemplified in *R v. Pitkeathly* (1994), 29 CR (4th) 182 (Ont. CA).

[6]   See s. 606(4) of the *Criminal Code*, RSC 1985, c. C-46, as amended. It is recognized that the trial judge is granted the discretion to reject a plea to a lesser offence if the facts do not support such a reduction, although the Court of Appeal for Ontario in *R v. Naraindeen* (1990), 80 CR (3d) 66 (Ont. CA) suggests that some deference ought to be afforded to prosecutorial discretion in this context. The potential for a clash between judicial and prosecutorial discretion may be avoided if, instead of relying on s. 606(4) to facilitate a plea to a lesser offence, the prosecutor has a new information laid (or a new indictment drafted) to charge the specific offence for which the guilty plea is offered.

[7]   See the Martin Report, supra note 5, at 315-17, where the virtues of openness and accountability of this aspect of the process are discussed. This view is also shared by the Canadian Sentencing Commission, supra note 1, at 422-23. Of course, there will be exceptions to openness where the exigencies of unique circumstances dictate.

The joint submission may be a subset of the broader category of plea bargains or may follow a finding of guilt. There is no magic in the term "joint submission." It simply reflects a process whereby both counsel advocate the same disposition for the offender. Such an arrangement may be attached to other arrangements like those discussed above, or it may be the only aspect of the case on which counsel agree. However, it is unique in that it takes effect only on the assent of the sentencing judge. The following discussion of joint submissions focuses mainly on the judicial role. When reviewing the material in this chapter, consider the following issues: What is the test for rejecting a joint submission? How much must the sentencing judge know about the basis for the joint submission? If a sentencing judge is considering rejecting a joint submission, what procedure should be followed? If the sentencing judge decides to reject a joint submission, what are the offender's options (if any)?

B. The Treatment of the Joint Submission: Sentencing Judge Not Bound

The practice of Canadian courts has been somewhat inconsistent in dealing with the treatment of joint submissions. On the one hand, the courts have recognized the value of plea arrangements and demonstrated concern for the consequences that would accrue if judges were to give them little consideration. On the other hand, it is vital to preserve judicial independence and integrity by allowing sentencing judges to refuse to accede to a joint submission when circumstances dictate.

Appeal courts have therefore held that while sentencing judges are not bound by a joint submission, they should depart from them only in specific circumstances. However, appeal courts have used different terminology in setting down the exact test that sentencing judges must apply in deciding whether to reject a joint submission. The following case considers whether this differing terminology reflects different standards, or merely different ways of expressing the same standard.

R v. Douglas
(2002), 162 CCC (3d) 37 (Que. CA)

FISH JA: We are concerned in this case with a plea agreement negotiated by experienced Crown counsel in consultation with the police officers in charge of the investigation.

The main elements of the agreement—manifestly interdependent—were joint submissions on sentence in exchange for pleas of guilty in two related files.

Pursuant to the agreement, the appellant pleaded guilty, in the first file, to armed robbery and illegal confinement, and the parties jointly recommended concurrent sentences of four years' imprisonment on each count. The trial judge found that four years was "unreasonable" and imposed five instead.

In the second file, the appellant pleaded guilty to conspiracy and, as agreed, Crown counsel suggested a concurrent one-year sentence. The trial judge imposed a one-year consecutive term, or the equivalent of six-years concurrent.

With commendable integrity and candour, Crown counsel now urges us to allow the prisoner's appeal.

For the reasons that follow, I would do so.

. . .

III

Canadian appellate courts have expressed in different ways the standard for determining when trial judges may properly reject joint submissions on sentence accompanied by negotiated admissions of guilt.

Whatever the language used, the standard is meant to be an exacting one. Appellate courts, increasingly in recent years, have stated time and again that trial judges should not reject jointly proposed sentences unless they are "unreasonable," "contrary to the public interest," "unfit," or "would bring the administration of justice into disrepute."

The Ontario Court of Appeal has enunciated the applicable standard in terms proposed by the *Report of the Attorney General's Advisory Committee on Charge Screening, Disclosure and Resolution Discussions*, chaired by The Honourable G. Arthur Martin ("Martin Report").

The policy purposes underlying the Court's approach and its choice of terminology are well explained in the Martin Report. These are the particularly relevant passages:

. . .

The Committee recognizes that an important, sometimes the most important, factor in counsel's ability to conclude resolution agreements, thereby deriving the benefits that such agreements bring, is that of certainty. Accused persons are ... prepared to waive their right to a trial far more readily if the outcome of such a waiver is certain, than they are for the purely speculative possibility that the outcome will bear some resemblance to what counsel have agreed to. And likewise, from the perspective of Crown counsel, agreed upon resolutions that have a stronger, rather than weaker sense of certainty to them are more desirable because there is less risk that what Crown counsel concludes is an appropriate resolution of the case in the public interest will be undercut.

. . .

While the presiding judge cannot have his or her sentencing discretion removed by the fact of there being a joint submission, it is none the less appropriate ... for the sentencing judge to have regard to the interest of certainty in resolution discussions when faced with a joint submission. Accordingly, where there is no reason in the public interest or in the need to preserve the repute of the administration of justice to depart from a joint submission, a sentencing judge should ... give effect to the need for certainty in agreed upon resolutions by accepting the joint submission of counsel.

. . .

These considerations are reflected in *Cerasuolo* [(2001), 151 CCC (3d) 445 (Ont. CA)], where Finlayson JA, speaking for a unanimous Court, observed:

This court has repeatedly held that trial judges should not reject joint submissions unless the joint submission is contrary to the public interest and the sentence would bring the administration of justice into disrepute: e.g. *R v. Dorsey* (1999), 123 OAC 342 at 345. This is a high threshold and is intended to foster confidence in an accused, who has given up his right to a trial, that the joint submission he obtained in return for a plea of guilty will be respected by the sentencing judge.

The Crown and the defence bar have cooperated in fostering an atmosphere where the parties are encouraged to discuss the issues in a criminal trial with a view to shortening the trial process. This includes bringing issues to a final resolution through plea bargaining. This laudable initiative cannot succeed unless the accused has some assurance that the trial judge will in most instances honour agreements entered into by the Crown. While we cannot overemphasize that these agreements are not to fetter the independent evaluation of sentences proposed, there is no interference with the judicial independence of the sentencing judge in requiring him or her to explain in what way a particular joint submission is contrary to the public interest and would bring the administration of justice into disrepute.

Commenting on these observations and likewise speaking for the Court, Prowse JA, of the British Columbia Court of Appeal, stated in *Bezdan* [[2001] BCJ No. 808 (CA)]:

I am in general agreement with the sentiments expressed in the second paragraph of the passage quoted. It is apparent that the administration of criminal justice requires cooperation between counsel and that the court should not be too quick to look behind a plea-bargain struck between competent counsel unless there is good reason to do so. In those instances in which the sentencing judge is not prepared to give effect to the proposal, I also agree that it would be appropriate for that judge to give his or her reasons for departing from the "bargain." I would not go so far as to say that a sentencing judge can only depart from the sentence suggested in the joint submission if he or she is satisfied that the proposal is contrary to the public interest, or that the sentence proposed would bring the administration of justice into disrepute. It is not clear to me that these two circumstances cover all situations in which a sentencing judge might conclude that the sentence proposed was "unfit."

A similar threshold appears to have been established in Alberta. Speaking for a unanimous court in *C.(G.W.)* [(2000), 150 CCC (3d) 513 (Alta. CA)], Berger JA explained:

The obligation of a trial judge to give serious consideration to a joint sentencing submission stems from an attempt to maintain a proper balance between respect for the plea bargain and the sentencing court's role in the administration of justice. The certainty that is required to induce accused persons to waive their rights to a trial can only be achieved in an atmosphere where the courts do not lightly interfere with a negotiated disposition that falls within or is very close to the appropriate range for a given offence. "The bargaining process is undermined if the resulting compromise recommendation is too readily rejected by the sentencing judge." *R v. Pashe* (1995), 100 Man. R (2d) 61 (Man. CA) at para. 11.

Joint submissions, however, should be accepted by the trial judge unless they are unfit: *R v. Sinclair*, [1996] AJ No. 464 (QL) (Alta. CA) at para. 4, online: QL (AJ), or unreasonable: *R v. Hudson*, [1995] AJ No. 797 (QL) (Alta. CA) at para. 1, online: QL (AJ). In *R v. Dorsey* (1999), 123 OAC 342, the Ontario Court of Appeal held at p. 345 that "a joint submission should be departed from only where the trial judge considers the joint submission to be contrary to the public interest and ... if accepted, would bring the administration of justice into disrepute." That view accords with the position of the Manitoba Court of Appeal in *R v. Pashe*, *supra*, at para. 12, that "while a sentencing judge has an overriding discretion to reject a joint recommendation, *there must be good reason to do so*, particularly ... where the joint recommendation is made by experienced counsel." [Emphasis added by Berger JA.]

The approach adopted by the Manitoba Court of Appeal in *Pashe*, cited with approval in *C.(G.W.)*, was again implemented by that Court in *Chartrand* [(1998), 131 CCC (3d) 122 (Man. CA)], where Kroft JA, delivering the unanimous judgment, put the matter this way:

> A sentencing judge is not bound to accept the recommendation, but it should not be rejected unless there is good cause for so doing. This case does not fall into that category.
>
> Notwithstanding the discretion of the trial judge, and even though the sentence imposed might not be so high as to be declared unreasonable, where a joint submission has been made between competent counsel which is not so unfit that it demands rejection, then that recommendation should not be ignored.

> • • •

Finally, in *Dubuc* [(1998), 131 CCC (3d) 250 (Que. CA)], again a unanimous judgment, this Court, too, cited and applied *Pashe, supra*.

In my view, a reasonable joint submission cannot be said to "bring the administration of justice into disrepute." An unreasonable joint submission, on the other hand, is surely "contrary to the public interest." Accordingly, though it is purposively framed in striking and evocative terms, I do not believe that the Ontario standard departs substantially from the test of reasonableness articulated by other courts, including our own. Their shared conceptual foundation is that the interests of justice are well served by the acceptance of a joint submission on sentence accompanied by a negotiated plea of guilty—provided, of course, that the sentence jointly proposed falls within the acceptable range and the plea is warranted by the facts admitted.

> • • •

In the present case, the Crown and the defence jointly urged the trial judge to impose carefully negotiated sentences of four years' imprisonment in one file and one year, concurrent, in the other. The trial judge considered that the four year sentence was "unreasonable," in part because that was the minimum sentence permitted by law and did not adequately take into account the aggravating factors present in this case. Instead, the judge imposed a sentence of five years.

With respect, moreover, I find it difficult to conclude, as the trial judge did, that a five-year sentence was reasonable, but the proposed four-year sentence was not.

Appellate courts in the other provinces and territories have used the same or similar terms in articulating the standard for rejecting a joint submission. See, for example, *R v. Guignard* (2005), 195 CCC (3d) 145 (NBCA); *R v. Druken* (2006), 215 CCC (3d) 394 (Nfld. CA); and *R v. Cromwell* (2005), 202 CCC (3d) 310 (NSCA).

What factors should a sentencing judge consider in deciding whether to reject a joint submission? How much information should counsel present to the sentencing judge when putting forward a joint submission? What procedure should sentencing judges follow if they are considering rejecting a joint submission? The following two cases address these issues.

R v. Sinclair
(2004), 185 CCC (3d) 569 (Man. CA)

STEEL JA: This case raises once more the difficult question of when it is appropriate for a court to deviate from a joint recommendation as to sentence.

The accused pled guilty to a charge of assault causing bodily harm. The assault was completely unprovoked. There was a joint submission by counsel that since the accused had already spent an equivalent of between 10 and 12 months in custody (assuming double credit), he should now be released with a sentence of time served. In addition, a period of probation with conditions was suggested. The sentencing judge was clearly troubled by the unprovoked nature of the assault. He asked the accused for some sort of reason given the fact that the victim was unknown to him and had said nothing to him as he was passing. The accused had no explanation.

After considering the matter and the fact that he had been presented with a joint recommendation from experienced counsel, he declined to follow that submission. Instead, considering the accused's criminal record, including several convictions for violent offences, the completely unprovoked nature of the assault and the need for specific and general deterrence, he sentenced the accused to an additional three months in custody, which, taking pre-sentencing detention into account, constituted an effective sentence of 15 months, with no order of probation. This court dismissed the accused's appeal as to sentence, with reasons to follow. These are those reasons.

. . .

When deciding whether to depart from a joint recommendation, a court should consider the following factors.

There is a continuum in the spectrum of plea bargaining and joint submissions as to sentence. In some cases, the Crown's case has some flaw or weakness and the accused agrees to give up his or her right to a trial and to plead guilty in exchange for some consideration. This consideration may take the form of a reduction in the original charge, withdrawal of other charges or an agreement to jointly recommend a more lenient sentence than would be likely after a guilty verdict at trial. Evidence always varies in strength and there is always uncertainty in the trial process. In other cases, plea negotiations have become accepted as a means to expedite the administration of criminal justice. That is the case here, where the accused's decision to forego his right to a trial must be considered within the context of a backlog in trial dates and the months already spent in pre-trial detention. The clearer the *quid pro quo*, the more weight should be given an appropriate joint submission by the sentencing judge. See *R v. Broekaert (D.D.)* (2003), 170 Man. R (2d) 229, 2003 MBCA 10, at para. 29, and *Booh* [(2003), 170 Man. R (2d) 249, 2003 MBCA 16], at para. 11.

Recognizing that cases fall at various places in the continuum, the essence of the plea bargain or joint submission should be placed on the record in open court. The judge must have a solid factual basis on which to make an independent, reasoned decision. If a trial judge is not given or fails to inquire into the circumstances underlying a joint sentencing submission, then he or she will be hard pressed to determine whether there is good cause to reject that joint submission.

. . .

If the joint submission is as a result of, for example, an evidentiary gap in the Crown's case or the absence of an essential witness, this is information that should be provided to the court by counsel, and particularly Crown counsel.

. . .

In this case, Crown counsel indicated he was recommending a sentence of time served since the "Crown's recommendation is still that the time having spent in custody is appropriate in the circumstances considering the nature of the offence, considering any exigencies in, in the Crown's case. And I make reference to that only in respect of having spoken to the complainant this morning." Defence counsel, in his submission, elaborated on that point by adding that the police were not able to identify the accused and the complainant told the Crown attorney something different than in his statement given to police on the day in question.

The sentencing judge did give serious consideration to the joint submission. However, he also considered several other factors upon which he placed considerable weight in his reasons. The "exigencies" of the case referred to by both counsel when speaking in favour of the joint submission were mitigated by the fact that the accused had made, what the judge considered, a clear admission of guilt to the police. The offender had a record of prior involvement that included elements of violence. He had ended up in custody as a result of continued involvement. The accused had initially been released after six days in custody, but was arrested again as a result of a breach of recognizance. He spent another 26 days in custody, was released again, breached again and then remained in custody until his sentencing since his bail was revoked. Perhaps most troubling to the judge was the fact that the offence was totally unprovoked, and when questioned, the accused showed "a complete lack of care, a complete lack of concern, a total disinterest."

Consequently, the sentencing judge concluded that the proposed sentence was unreasonably low and that to send the proper "message to those in the community" for purposes of denunciation and deterrence, the circumstances required more than a sentence of time served. In so rejecting the joint submission, he articulated clear and cogent reasons. There should be deference to the exercise of the sentencing judge's discretion in these circumstances.

R v. C.(G.W.)
(2000), 150 CCC (3d) 513 (Alta. CA)

BERGER JA: The Appellant is a 32 year old aboriginal male. On November 15, 1999, he pleaded guilty to two counts of sexual assault in connection with events which took place between January 1983 and December 1985 when he was between the ages of 14 and 17. The offences, which included numerous incidents of sexual impropriety, were visited upon two children aged 6 to 9 and 9 to 12 respectively, who were in the care of the Appellant in his parents' home.

The learned sentencing judge received a joint submission urging a period of probation subject to strict conditions. That submission was rejected for reasons set out below. The Appellant was sentenced to one year of closed custody plus 18 months probation on each count to be served concurrently.

In rejecting the joint submission, the learned sentencing judge reasoned as follows:

> With the greatest of respect to two lawyers, whom I both respect, the sentence that is proposed, or the disposition that is proposed does not take into account adequately the principles of general deterrence, individual deterrence, the principles enunciated in Section 718 of the *Criminal Code*, the need for rehabilitation of this accused, and more importantly, the interests of the victims.
>
>   ...
>
> I am mindful of the [Saddle Lake Youth Justice Committee's] recommendations insofar as the best interests of this accused, that a probation period of two years would be appropriate. I am also mindful of the other side of the coin, being the position of the victims, that general deterrence—or deterrence, both general and individual, is of primary consideration here.

This Court has made clear on more than one occasion that a joint submission need not be followed as long as it is given "serious consideration," particularly where there is a guilty plea. *R v. Wood* (1989), 43 CCC (3d) 570 (Ont. CA). Where a trial judge "demonstrated a thorough appreciation of the relevant facts, their significance, and of the proper sentencing principles" appellate intervention on the basis of reviewable error in rejection of a joint sentencing submission will not likely be warranted. *R v. Beaulieu* (1997), 118 Man. R (2d) 148 (Man. CA) at para. 8, and *R v. L.(S.M.)*, [1998] AJ No. 1442, 40 WCB 449 (Alta. QB).

But "serious consideration" cannot occur in a factual vacuum. In my opinion, no "thorough appreciation of the relevant facts" can occur in the absence of a careful and diligent inquiry of counsel as to the circumstances underlying a joint sentencing submission. Given the high level of deference afforded to sentencing judges in the exercise of their discretion to reject joint submissions, the need for a thorough inquiry takes on even greater significance. Yet, in the case at bar, the learned trial judge did not inquire into the circumstances which formed the basis of the joint sentencing submission.

In *R v. Morissette*, [1996] OJ No. 3071 (Ont. CA) at para. 1, the trial judge had rejected a joint submission as to sentence without giving reasons for doing so, and had imposed a higher sentence than that recommended jointly by counsel. The majority of the Court were of the view "that without hearing the basis upon which the joint submission was made, it cannot be said that there were compelling reasons to reject it. In the absence of such reasons, it should have been accepted." More recently, in *R v. Quinn*, [1999] OJ No. 2706 (Ont. CA), Doherty JA, speaking for the Court, held that "the trial judge erred in principle in departing from a joint submission without calling upon the Crown to explain the basis upon which the final submission was arrived at." In neither case did the Ontario Court of Appeal expand upon the articulated principle.

The Manitoba Court of Appeal also appears to have touched upon the issue in *R v. Sherlock* (1998), 131 Man. R (2d) 143 (CA), Kroft JA made the following observations regarding plea bargaining and joint submissions (at para. 32):

> I fully accept that the efficient administration of justice requires that there be an element of negotiation between counsel for the Crown and counsel for the accused relating to the

entry of pleas and the recommendation of sentence. The negotiations, or bargaining, will often go on over a substantial period of time. On other occasions, legitimate pragmatism will require that arrangements be made at the courtroom door. *In either case, it is important to trial judges and courts of appeal that the nature of the bargain be clearly presented on the record. Without that assistance, no court can adequately assess the extent to which it should be constrained by the joint recommendation of counsel.*

In the past, Courts have been inclined to acknowledge that, in the face of a joint submission, they must be mindful that the prosecution possesses a much more intimate understanding of the case at bar than the Court itself. In *R v. Maheu*, [1992] AQ No. 21 (Que. CA), the Quebec Court of Appeal commented as follows:

But, it is also clear that serious consideration should be given by the court to recommendations of Crown counsel, particularly where the facts outlined, following a guilty plea, are sparse. The Court then has to recognize that Crown counsel is more familiar than itself with the extenuating or aggravating circumstances of the offence which may not be fully disclosed in the summary of facts: see *R v. Fleury* (1971), 23 CRNS 164 (Que. CA).

With respect, no one should have a more intimate understanding of the case at bar than the Court itself. The facts that guide the sentence disposition ought not to be "sparse." Crown counsel, at the end of the day, ought not to be more familiar with the extenuating or aggravating circumstances of the offence than the sentencing judge. The facts of the case ought to be fully disclosed. Those facts must surely include the circumstances underlying the joint sentencing submission (subject, of course, to any claim of privilege).

Joint submissions are often the result of [what is] commonly referred to as a "plea bargain." The plea bargain may have been struck because of an evidentiary gap in the Crown's case. The absence of Crown witnesses may have influenced the plea bargain and the resulting joint submission. On the other hand, the plea bargain may well have been the result of an appreciation by the accused of the futility of running a trial. The inevitability of a finding of guilt may well have resonated. If the latter consideration motivated the plea bargain, the credit for the guilty plea would, surely, not be as great as if the guilty plea truly represented an acknowledgement of wrong doing and an expression of remorse. It is essential that the sentencing judge determine what facts or factors motivated the plea and gave rise to the joint submission. The sentencing disposition may vary accordingly. It follows that the failure to so inquire prior to rejecting a joint submission may well constitute reversible error.

In addition to the foregoing, the procedure followed by the sentencing judge in rejecting the joint submission in this case is a matter of concern. Once a sentencing judge concludes that he might not accede to a joint submission, fundamental fairness dictates that an opportunity be afforded to counsel to make further submissions in an attempt to address the sentencing judge's concerns before the sentence is imposed. In this case, lengthy submissions were made by both counsel in support of a probationary term which evoked no expressions of concern by the sentencing judge. He then retired to consider the disposition of the case. It was only upon his return to the courtroom, and in the course of giving reasons for rejecting the joint submission, that counsel had any indication of concern on his part. As a result, they were afforded no opportunity to address that concern. Indeed, had the sentencing judge made his concern known to counsel in a timely fashion, the foundation upon which the joint submission rested might well have been laid. I do not suggest that any particular procedure is de rigueur; I say only that the principle of *audi alteram partem* should be followed.

Conclusion

For all of these reasons, the appeal must be allowed.

... [T]his Court, like the trial judge, has no information as to the factual foundation that gave rise to the joint submission. Accordingly, counsel are directed to provide the Court, within 21 days of the release of this judgment, with advice in writing (letter form will do) as to the facts or factors underlying the joint submission. The Court will then be in a position to impose an appropriate sentence in accordance with s. 687(1)(a) of the *Criminal Code*.

For further guidance on the information to be provided to the sentencing judge, see *R v. Tkachuk* (2001), 159 CCC (3d) 434 (Alta. CA), which indicates that counsel: (1) should fully disclose the facts of the case, including the aggravating and mitigating factors; (2) if the proposed sentence is not obviously within the accepted range of sentence for that offence, explain to the court the reasons for departing from a sentence within that range; and (3) normally need not and should not disclose their negotiating positions and the substance of their discussions leading to the agreement as these are private.

Section 726.2 of the *Criminal Code* requires sentencing judges to provide reasons for sentence. When sentencing judges reject a joint submission, must they explain their reasons for rejecting it or is it sufficient to simply explain the reasons for the sentence that is ultimately imposed on the offender? This issue is considered in the following case.

R v. Haufe
[2007] OJ No. 2644 (CA)

THE COURT: The appellant, Oliver Haufe, seeks leave to appeal the sentence imposed by Justice B.J. Frazer following the appellant's guilty plea for robbery. The sentence imposed was 18 months in custody (in addition to credit given for 48 days spent in pre-trial detention) followed by two years probation.

The robbery occurred on December 29, 1995. It was a home robbery in which two intruders were surprised by the returning home owner. An altercation followed and the home owner was beaten, injured and taken to hospital. A fingerprint left at the scene led to the arrest of the appellant more than ten years later on April 1, 2006.

The appellant's principal ground of appeal is that the trial judge erred by rejecting the joint submission for sentence of counsel (namely, six months in custody) and imposing a sentence that tripled the proposed sentence (18 months).

The sentencing judge did warn defence counsel that he was considering the imposition of a sentence higher than the joint submission. He also afforded defence counsel an opportunity to make further submissions after he issued his warning. However, in our view, the sentencing judge did not comply with the legal principles that apply to the rejection of a joint submission relating to sentence. In the leading case, *R v. Cerasuolo* (2001), 151 CCC (3d) 445 at 447-8 (Ont. CA), Finlayson JA stated:

> This court has repeatedly held that trial judges should not reject joint submissions *unless the joint submission is contrary to the public interest and the sentence would bring the administration of justice into disrepute*: e.g. *R v. Dorsey* (1999), 123 OAC 342 at 345. *This is a high threshold and is intended to foster confidence in an accused, who has given up his right to a trial, that the joint submission he obtained in return for a plea of guilty will be respected by the sentencing judge.*
>
> The Crown and the defence bar have cooperated in fostering an atmosphere where the parties are encouraged to discuss the issues in a criminal trial with a view to shortening the trial process. This includes bringing issues to a final resolution through plea bargaining. *This laudable initiative cannot succeed unless the accused has some assurance that the trial judge will in most instances honour agreements entered into by the Crown.* While we cannot overemphasize that these agreements are not to fetter the independent evaluation of the sentences proposed, *there is no interference with the judicial independence of the sentencing judge in requiring him or her to explain in what way a particular joint submission is contrary to the public interest and would bring the administration of justice into disrepute.* [Emphasis added (by the court).]

With respect, the sentencing judge's reasons in this case do not meet the requirements of *Cerasuolo*. The sentencing judge said nothing about the joint submission that counsel placed before him. This was particularly regrettable given that the Crown position on sentence had been the subject of a litigation conference in the Crown office which led to a formal letter to defence counsel setting out the Crown position. In these circumstances, the sentencing judge's silence about the joint submission does not "explain in what way a particular joint submission is contrary to the public interest and would bring the administration of justice into disrepute."

Finally, in our view, it cannot be said that the sentence proposed in the joint submission (six months) was so clearly unreasonable as to make the imposition of an 18 month sentence more or less self-evident. The sentencing judge himself identified several factors—the fact that the offence was committed in 1995, the guilty plea, and the appellant's good conduct including employment, overcoming addiction, and non-commission of crimes in the two years before being sentenced for the 1995 robbery. In our view, these factors called out for an explanation of why the sentencing judge rejected the joint submission and imposed a custodial sentence three times higher than the joint submission.

Leave to appeal sentence is granted, the appeal is allowed and a custodial sentence of six months is imposed. The other components of the sentence (credit for pre-trial custody and probation) are affirmed.

NOTE

1. Can offenders withdraw their guilty plea if it becomes apparent during the presentation of submissions that the sentencing judge will not accede to a joint submission? See *R v. Rubenstein* (1987), 41 CCC (3d) 91 (Ont. CA):

> The power of the trial Judge to impose a sentence cannot be limited to a joint submission, and the joint submission cannot be the basis upon which to escape the sentencing judge when it appears that he chooses to reject the joint submission. As Judge Draper observed, an accused who could thus withdraw his plea could simply keep doing so until he found a trial judge who would accept a joint submission. A plea of guilty in the same way as a finding of guilt after trial exposes an accused to a proper sentence to be determined by the trial judge. ... To permit an accused to withdraw his plea when the sentence does not suit him puts the court in the unseemly position of bargaining with the accused.

2. In the light of the ability of sentencing judges to reject joint submissions, is there an obligation on defence counsel before entering a guilty plea to inform the accused that the court is not bound to accept a joint submission? What if the accused is unrepresented? See *R v. Grimsson* (1997), 100 BCAC 253 (CA); *R v. Samms* (1993), 107 Nfld. & PEIR 172 (Nfld. CA).

3. How important is the contingency of a guilty plea in determining whether a joint submission is enforceable on appeal? Is there a qualitative difference between a joint submission that essentially induces a guilty plea and one that does not? Is one entitled to more deference than the other? In addition to the cases excerpted above see *R v. Dubuc* (1998), 131 CCC (3d) 250 (Que. CA); *R v. Neale*, [2000] BCJ No. 668 (CA).

4. When co-accused are being sentenced in separate proceedings, what weight, if any, should the sentencing judge give to the sentence imposed on another co-accused if that sentence was the result of a joint submission? See *R v. Christie* (2004), 189 CCC (3d) 274 (Alta. CA).

5. Joint submissions usually occur in the context of a guilty plea, but sometimes Crown and defence counsel may make a joint submission as to the appropriate sentence after a contested trial. In such circumstances, does a sentencing judge have broader latitude to reject the submission?

6. If a joint submission is "obviously" unfit, is a sentencing judge still required to give reasons for rejecting the joint submission? On an appeal, what are the consequences, if any, of failing to do so?

7. Entirely apart from joint submissions, some appellate courts have suggested that sentencing judges should not normally exceed the sentence sought by the Crown, particularly if the sentence proposed by the Crown might have influenced the accused to plead guilty. See *R v. Farizeh* (1994), 78 OAC 399 (CA); *R v. Brown* (2000), 277 AR 178 (CA).

III. SENTENCE APPEALS AND JOINT SUBMISSIONS

Appellate review of sentencing decisions is a complex aspect of the law. Although it has inspired a great deal of activity over the last number of years, we leave the nuances of this area to chapter 17, Appeals.[8] For now, we examine only the impact of joint submissions in the appellate sphere. As discussed in previous chapters, the sentencing judge at first instance is granted substantial discretion in determining an appropriate sentence. The power of the courts of appeal to review sentencing decisions is found in s. 687 of the *Criminal Code*. This section provides as follows:

> 687(1) Where an appeal is taken against sentence, the court of appeal shall, unless the sentence is one fixed by law, consider the fitness of sentence appealed against, and may on such evidence, if any, as it thinks fit to require or to receive,
>
> > (a) vary the sentence within the limits prescribed by law for the accused was convicted;
>
> or
>
> > (b) dismiss the appeal.

Although this appellate power appears to be quite broad on its face, recent cases from the Supreme Court of Canada have narrowed the scope of review considerably. The Supreme Court has sent a clear message that the decisions of sentencing judges must be approached with great deference. Today courts of appeal may intervene only if there was an error in principle or if the sentence imposed at first instance was "demonstrably unfit" or "clearly unreasonable." See *R v. Shropshire*, [1995] 4 SCR 227, 102 CCC (3d) 193; *R v. M.(C.A.)*, [1996] 1 SCR 500, 46 CR (4th) 269; and *R v. McDonnell*, [1997] 1 SCR 948, 114 CCC (3d) 436.

A. Appeals by the Offender

The appropriateness of a joint submission can arise in two situations when the offender launches an appeal. First, the offender may appeal on the basis that the sentencing judge erred in failing to abide by a joint submission. The principles that apply to this situation are set out in the first part of this chapter. The other, and less common, situation is where the sentencing judge imposes a sentence in accordance with the joint submission, but, on appeal, the offender disavows the joint submission and contends that the sentence is unfit. In the cases that follow, consider whether the approach of the appeal court respects the interests that are said to be recognized by joint submissions.

R v. Wood
(1988), 43 CCC (3d) 570 (Ont. CA)

LACOURCIÈRE JA: ... Following the committal of the accused for trial for first degree murder, Crown counsel ... indicated that a plea of guilty to manslaughter would be acceptable if a joint submission for a sentence of 14 years was agreed upon. At trial,

---

8   See, generally, A. Manson, "The Supreme Court Intervenes in Sentencing" (1996), 43 CR (4th) 306 and G. Trotter, "Appellate Review of Sentencing Decisions," in J.V. Roberts and D.P. Cole, eds., *Making Sense of Sentencing* (Toronto: University of Toronto Press, 1999).

counsel for the appellant, who had considerable experience in criminal matters, partici-pated in this joint submission. [The trial judge accepted the joint submission. However, he also made a recommendation that the appellant not be released on parole until at least one-half of his sentence had been served. The appellant appealed.]

• • •

While the Crown generally will not be a allowed to repudiate a position taken at trial where the accused has relied on his position before entering a guilty plea, Crown coun-sel has no authority to bind the Attorney-General in the exercise of his discretion to ap-peal. The ultimate responsibility to determine the fitness of sentence is on the Court of Appeal … . Certainly the accused is given greater latitude than the Crown on an appeal of this kind in that he is generally not bound to the same extent by the submissions of his counsel as to sentence.

• • •

In the present case, the learned trial judge indicated his awareness of the case-law with respect to joint submissions and, in agreeing with the joint submission, he said:

> The problem for any trial judge in sentencing is to decide on the fitness of the sentence to be imposed and I am always prepared to consider the recommendations of counsel as to their views on the range of sentence, particularly when their observations fall within the range which is normally imposed for offences of this kind, but there is a duty on the judge to ignore such recommendations if, in his view, they are improper, because a sentence is a matter of public interest and should be consistent with the gravity of the offence and the relevant facts and all the cogent surrounding circumstances. I may say that I am in accord with the sentence proposed of 14 years. I think it falls within the reasonable range for a crime of this nature and the circumstances under which it was committed.

However, in analyzing the competing principles to be considered in determining the fitness of sentence, we believe that the learned trial judge over-emphasized the inci-dence of violent crimes in the community and the need for general deterrence for the protection of society. In doing so, in our view, he failed to give sufficient weight to the appellant's obvious remorse and to his incipient rehabilitation. In addition, no reference was made on the available record, or in the reasons for sentence, to the 16-month period of pre-trial incarceration.

The facts disclose a spontaneous stabbing following a family quarrel in circum-stances where both the appellant and the victim had ingested alcohol and drugs. There was room for doubt as to the requisite intent for murder. In our view, it was appropriate for Crown counsel to consent to the plea of manslaughter. But, in our view, the Crown overreached in attaching a condition of a joint submission to a sentence which was far in excess of the usual range of sentences for manslaughter in the circumstances of the present case. The condition placed the accused, as well as experienced defence counsel, in a difficult position and to some extent may have hampered the trial judge. It would have been preferable to submit an appropriate range of sentence and to let the trial judge determine the sentence.

• • •

Having regard to the gravity of the offence, the mitigating circumstances, the appel-lant's pre-trial custody, his sincere remorse and his exemplary institutional record and notwithstanding the joint submission at trial, we think an appropriate and fit sentence would be eight years. The trial judge's recommendation to the Parole Board should be disregarded, but the s. 98 order for a period of 10 years will stand.

R v. Sriskantharajah
(1994), 90 CCC (3d) 559 (Ont. CA)

FINLAYSON JA: The appellant pleaded not guilty to an indictment containing two counts of murder in the first degree of her two young daughters. After the trial commenced, she changed her plea to guilty of manslaughter on both counts. [In accordance with a joint submission], [t]he trial judge ... sentenced her to six years on each count to be served concurrently. [The appellant appealed.]

There are very strong mitigating circumstances in favour of the appellant, as found by the trial judge. [The offender was severely and chronically depressed, virtually abandoned by her husband (who otherwise abused her), and left to raise her two young children (one of whom had been brain damaged) in a country where she did not speak the language of the dominant culture.]

It was conceded that there is no danger of the appellant re-offending and she is not a risk to society. As counsel for the Crown put it, she is a greater risk to herself than to anyone else.

The court received fresh evidence which supports counsel for the appellant's submission that the cultural and linguistic isolation of the appellant, a Tamil from Sri Lanka, would be alleviated to some extent if she could be incarcerated in Toronto where she would be in contact with Parkdale Community Legal Services, the South Asian Women's Centre, and the Elizabeth Fry Society of Toronto, all of which have agreed to co-operate in a program directed to teaching her English and assisting her in re-integrating into the community. These facilities are not available to the same extent in the Kingston Prison for Women.

This court has stated repeatedly that it will not lightly interfere with a sentence imposed following a joint recommendation, but I do not agree with the submission of the Crown that the burden rests upon the appellant to demonstrate that the sentence imposed would bring the administration of justice into disrepute. In this case, it is worth noting that the sentence imposed amounts really to 10 years, which was reduced by the trial judge to six years in order to give the appellant credit for two years of pre-trial custody. I note also that the trial judge stated that in ordinary circumstances he would have considered the recommend range of sentence (10 to 12 years) to be markedly excessive.

In support of her contention that this court must be satisfied that the sentence imposed by the trial judge would bring the administration of justice into disrepute, counsel for the Crown referred the court to the *Report of the Attorney General's Advisory Committee on Charge Screening, Disclosure and Resolution Discussions* (chaired by the Honourable G. Arthur Martin, QC) and particularly to p. 329 where it is stated:

> The sentencing judge will not ... have committed any error in principle in accepting a joint submission ... provided he or she arrives at the independent conclusion, based upon an

adequate record, that the sentence proposed does not bring the administration of justice into disrepute and is otherwise not contrary to the public interest. Indeed, this recommendation embodies the essence of the sentencing judge's obligations in passing sentence. In so recommending, the Committee has endeavoured to define the discretion of the sentencing judge in sufficiently broad terms to ensure that the sentence imposed is ultimately just, but at the same time accorded the parties as much assurance as can be had that their agreed-upon resolutions will find favour with the Court. In this way, it is hoped that the justice system and the community as a whole can profit to the greatest extent possible from the benefits of resolution discussions.

· · ·

I acknowledge the appropriateness of this recommendation, especially as an admonition against imposing sentences that are too lenient, but, as stated in the excerpt, the sentence must be in the public interest, embracing a variety of concerns. Certainly, there can be no suggestion that review of these arrangements by this court is not to be exercised in an appropriate case. Deference to this court in these matters appears to be accepted by the Martin Report (at p. 332):

> Appellate review is essential to ensure that sentences imposed following resolution discussions are, at all times, within an appropriate range. Permitting Crown counsel in the appellate courts to take a position that need not necessarily accord with the position taken by the Crown at trial, permits the Crown to assist the appellate courts as fully as possible in discharging their duty to ensure that the trial courts have resolved cases in a manner that is fit and just.
>
> The Committee notes that the rule permitting Crown appeals from joint submissions is complemented by a similar rule benefitting an accused. Indeed, the Ontario Court of Appeal has stated in *R v. Wood* that:
>
>> Certainly the accused is given greater latitude than the Crown on an appeal of this kind in that he is generally not bound to the same extent by the submissions of his counsel as to sentence.
>
> The Court went on to observe that, ultimately, the fitness of the sentence imposed, not the positions of the parties, is the dominant consideration.

This case is exceptional. The appellant was diagnosed at the Clarke Institute of Psychiatry as suffering from a major depression combined with a mixed personality disorder. This depression significantly impacted upon the appellant's judgment. Her perception of life, its reality and future prospects were negatively or fatalistically skewed by this depression. Suicide became the only logical solution to her problems. In the circumstances of this crime and this particular accused, a plea bargain made eminent sense and was in the best interest of justice. However, the sentence recommended in the joint submission was simply too long.

A non-penitentiary sentence is justified where, as here, the case demonstrates that the offence arose from the compulsion of mental illness, the offender poses little or no risk to the community, there is no significant risk of re-offence and an appropriate treatment and rehabilitation is available.

· · ·

Accordingly, leave to appeal is granted, the appeal is allowed and the sentence is reduced to a reformatory term of two years less one day to be followed by a period of probation for three years. In addition to the usual terms of probation, such as an undertaking to be of good peace and be of good behaviour, it is recommended that the appellant seek and continue to receive treatment and counselling as recommended by her probation officer. The order prohibiting the appellant from possessing any firearm, ammunition or explosive for life pursuant to s. 100 of the *Criminal Code* ... is undisturbed.

NOTES

1. In *Wood*, was it fair for Lacourcière JA to conclude that the joint submission "may have hampered" the trial judge? Should the Court of Appeal have so easily disregarded the opinion (reflected in the agreement to the joint submission) of very experienced defence counsel as to Wood's chances of being convicted of second-degree murder?

2. In *Sriskantharajah*, what was the precise basis on which the Court of Appeal intervened in this case? Given the more deferential standard of review signalled by the Supreme Court of Canada in the *Shropshire* line of cases, would *Sriskantharajah* be decided differently today? See *R v. Ranger*, [2006] OJ No. 1271 (SCJ).

3. It is fair to say that the overwhelming majority of joint submissions are accepted by sentencing judges and left undisturbed by courts of appeal. The decisions reproduced in this chapter are therefore atypical. Still, these are the cases that find their way into the law reports and attract considerable attention. What effect do cases like those discussed above have on plea bargaining in general?

4. Another issue that sometimes arises in appeals against sentence by the offender (where the trial judge imposes a sentence in excess of the joint submission) is whether the Crown is duty-bound to maintain the "agreement" on appeal. The range of possible answers to this question is apparent in the discussion of the limits on the Crown in the next section.

B. Appeals by the Crown

Cases involving joint submissions may sometimes result in an appeal by the Crown. Situations where the sentencing judge disregards a joint submission and imposes a more *lenient* sentence are straightforward and would seem to call into play the principles reflected in the cases cited above.[9] However, what principles apply when the sentencing judge accepts the

---

[9]   In *H.(C.N.)*, [2002] OJ No. 1112 (QL) (CJ); aff'd. (2002), 170 CCC (3d) 253 (CA), the Court of Appeal for Ontario discussed whether a different test applies when a sentencing judge undercuts, rather than jumps, a joint submission:

> With respect to the [latter], the Martin Committee recommendation has become the law in Ontario: see *R v. Cerasuolo* (2001), 151 CCC (3d) 445 (Ont. CA). To my knowledge the Court of Appeal has not specifically adopted the same rule with respect to undercutting a joint submission. It may be that distinguishing factors—such as the reduced need on the part of the Crown for a predictable sentence outcome, the fact that the Crown does not, like an accused, give up anything when a plea is entered, and the need to do individual justice for each accused—would justify a less stringent test for undercutting. Certainly the Court of Appeal has always been willing to reduce a sentence that it considers excessive, notwithstanding that it was imposed pursuant to a joint submission.

joint submission, but the Crown appeals in any event? The Court of Appeal for Ontario addressed this issue in *R v. Dubien*.

R v. Dubien
(1982), 67 CCC (2d) 341 (Ont. CA)

MacKINNON ACJO: This is an application by the Crown for leave to appeal and, if leave be granted, an appeal from a sentence imposed of five years after a plea of guilty to a charge of rape.

The application for leave to appeal is strenuously opposed on the ground that the Crown is "estopped" from appealing as, it is argued, the respondent relied on the position taken by Crown counsel at the trial and changed his plea to guilty on the basis of that "position."

The parties presented an agreed statement of facts to this court as to what was discussed between counsel at the trial and in the trial judge's chambers. These facts are as follows.

[Dubien was charged with raping a 14-year-old girl. During the trial, a discussion about a possible plea occurred in chambers between defence counsel, the Crown, and the trial judge. The defence offered to plead guilty to attempted rape because the Crown had stated that if the accused was found guilty of rape at the conclusion of trial, it would seek to have the accused declared a dangerous offender. The trial judge indicated that he would sentence the accused to 4 to 5 years in prison on a guilty plea to attempted rape. The Crown would not accept a plea to attempted rape, but indicated that if the accused pleaded guilty to rape and acknowledged a need for psychiatric assistance, the Crown would abandon the dangerous offender application and seek a sentence of 7 to 10 years. The trial judge indicated that given the slight degree of penetration an appropriate sentence for a guilty plea to either rape or attempted rape was 5 years. Crown counsel maintained his position. However, he also indicated that a term of 5 years was not so lenient as likely to be appealed; if it was imposed he would not recommend an appeal to the Crown law office and, in his view, absent such a recommendation, no appeal would be brought. At the same time, Crown counsel stated, and the accused understood, that he had no power to bind the attorney general on matters of appeal and that it was ultimately for the attorney general to decide whether to appeal. After discussion with the accused, defence counsel indicated that the accused would plead guilty to rape in the expectation of a sentence of 5 years and a recommendation that the sentence would be served in a psychiatric hospital.]

The Ontario Court of Appeal held that the trial judge had not acted improperly in questioning the joint submission, but did not decide what test "should apply where he or she is of the view that the proposed sentence is excessive" because the accused had withdrawn from the joint submission without objection from the Crown. In contrast, the Saskatchewan Court of Appeal's decision in *R v. Webster* (2001), 207 Sask. R 257 (CA) suggests that the same principles apply in both situations.

When the matter resumed before the trial judge, Crown counsel argued that the sentence for the offence to which the respondent had now pleaded guilty should be a penitentiary term of from seven to ten years. When the trial judge imposed a five-year penitentiary term, Crown counsel did not recommend an appeal nor had he, of course, proceeded with an application to have the respondent declared a dangerous offender. [The matter, however, came to the attention of the office of the Attorney General independently and the application for leave to appeal resulted.]

Counsel for the respondent argues that the whole system of "plea bargaining" will collapse if leave to appeal is given. It was an *in terrorem* submission that has little relevance to the facts of this case. The Attorney General's hands cannot be tied because counsel for the respondent failed to give his client a complete exposition of the Crown's position, namely, that Crown counsel could not and was not purporting to bind the Attorney General's exercise of his authority to decide whether an appeal should or should not be taken from the sentence imposed in the instant case.

On reviewing the material filed on the appeal one cannot help feeling that even if counsel had fully explained to the respondent the Crown's position as to the rights and duties of the Attorney General, it would have made no difference to his decision to plead guilty. He had succeeded in having the threat of an application to have him declared a dangerous offender withdrawn and he knew that he was going to receive a five year sentence whether he pleaded guilty to rape or attempted rape and he knew that counsel for the Crown would not recommend an appeal no matter how upset he was at that sentence. When the trial was completed with the sentencing there was no repudiation by Crown counsel of any of his "undertakings" to which he attached the caveat already noted.

Counsel for the respondent submitted that to grant the Attorney General leave to appeal would bring the whole administration of justice into question and destroy the necessary trust which must exist between the Crown and defence counsel. I do not agree. Of course discussions between counsel can be appropriate and helpful in certain cases and I can think of many situations where there is an "understanding," based on many relevant factors and experience, between counsel, which the Attorney General would not seek to repudiate. But that is not this case. Counsel for the Crown made it quite clear that the Attorney General could still exercise his discretion in the matter of an appeal, and that he (Crown counsel) was "upset" (to use the terminology of the respondent in his affidavit) about the proposed sentence of five years, even though he would not recommend an appeal if such a sentence were imposed. Even if he had not "conditioned" his understanding, counsel for the Crown could not take away the discretion vested in the Attorney General to determine whether an appeal should or should not be taken or the obligation imposed on this court to consider the fitness of the sentence when the matter is before us.

With great deference to the very experienced and able trial judge, I am of the view that it is not advisable for a judge to take any active part in discussions as to sentence before a plea has been taken, nor to encourage indirectly a plea of guilty by indicating what his sentence will be. It was apparent in the instant case that the sentence was going to be the same whether the respondent changed his plea or not, and there was no suggestion or implication so far as the trial judge was concerned, that the sentence would be lighter if the respondent changed his plea to guilty. A trial judge can only determine what a just sentence should be after he has heard all relevant evidence in open court on that subject and listened to the submissions of counsel.

One would expect that if there was essential agreement between counsel in their submissions as to the "usual" sentence, that would carry weight, and the Crown's position at trial would be a circumstance for an appeal court to consider in considering the fitness of the sentence appealed against: *R v. Wood* (1975), 26 CCC (2d) 100 (Alta. CA). In *R v. Turner*, [1970] 2 QB 321 at p. 327, Lord Parker CJ stated that the only exception to the rule that the judge should never indicate the sentence he has in mind to impose is where it may be helpful to indicate, "whether the accused pleads guilty or not guilty, the sentence will or will not take a particular form, e.g., a probation order or a fine, or a custodial sentence."

It seems to me that the failure of the Attorney General to raise the question of the fitness of the sentence under the circumstances of this case would be more likely to bring the administration of justice into disrepute than otherwise. There was an error, in my view, in the sentence imposed of such a nature as to require the Attorney General, in the discharge of his duty, to appeal that sentence to ensure that the administration of justice is fairly and properly carried out. The appeal, as I have stated, is not a repudiation of the Crown's qualified position at trial. I would grant leave to appeal.

In *Dubien*, the Court of Appeal allowed the appeal and substituted a sentence of nine years' imprisonment. In a sense, the court was not required to address squarely the issue of the Crown repudiating an agreement. Had Crown counsel in Dubien recommended an appeal to the attorney general, how might this have altered the court's response? Is it a relevant consideration that the position of Crown counsel at trial "induced" or "encouraged" a plea of guilty? If it did not, should a court of appeal feel less constrained to assess the fitness of sentence? See *R v. Agozzino*, [1970] 1 CCC 380 (Ont. CA); *Attorney General of Canada v. Roy* (1972), 18 CRNS 89 (Que. QB); and *R v. Cusack* (1978), 41 CCC (2d) 289 (NSCA).

Consider whether the position expressed in the following excerpt from the Martin Report strikes a fair balance in this area.

Report of the Attorney General's Advisory Committee on Charge Screening, Disclosure, and Resolution Discussions
(Honourable G.A. Martin, QC, Chair) (Toronto: Queen's Printer for Ontario, 1993)

59. The Committee observes that Crown counsel at trial cannot bind the Attorney General's discretion to appeal. The Committee recommends that where Crown counsel at trial agrees to a joint submission which the sentencing judge accepts, the Attorney General should appeal only where the sentence is so wrong as to bring the administration of justice into disrepute.

While it is clear that neither Crown nor defence counsel on appeal is bound in law by the position of the Crown at trial, the Committee recognizes that such a rule has great potential to undermine the finality of resolution agreements. This in turn may reduce the tendency for resolution agreements to be pursued, thereby diminishing the advantages which they offer, as discussed above. There is an important need for certainty in resolution agreement outcomes that appellate counsel must respect, in the same manner as a sentencing judge should respect the need for certainty when imposing sentence following a joint submission. Accordingly, the Committee has recommended that where Crown counsel at trial has agreed to a joint submission which the sentencing judge has accepted, that sentence should be appealed by the Crown only where the sentence is so wrong as to bring the administration of justice into disrepute. Much like the balance struck in the Committee's recommendation with respect to sentencing on a joint submission at the trial level, the Committee is of the view that this recommendation strikes the appropriate balance at the appellate level between ensuring resolution agreement outcomes are final, and preserving the role of the Attorney General's appellate counsel in ensuring the due administration of criminal justice. The Committee also observes that in may be undesirable for an accused person to appeal as a matter of course from a sentence imposed that is in accordance with a joint submission.

It is important to note that, while the present recommendation is similar in some respects to the recommendation concerning sentencing on a joint submission at trial, it does have a significant difference. The Committee has recommended that the sentencing judge may depart from a joint submission if the sentence proposed would bring the administration of justice into disrepute or if the sentence is not in the public interest. However, the Committee has recommended that the Crown should appeal from an accepted joint submission only if the sentence imposed would bring the administration of justice into disrepute. Thus, in the Committee's view, the circumstances in which it is appropriate for the Crown to appeal against a joint submission sentence are more limited than the circumstances in which it is appropriate for the sentencing judge to depart from a joint submission. The Crown's right to appeal from a joint submission sentence should not be exercised simply to seek minor adjustments or refinements to a sentence. Rather, the Crown should appeal only where the sentence imposed pursuant to a joint submission represents an error so grave as to bring the administration of justice into disrepute.

There are few common law jurisdictions that accord the Crown rights of appeal as broad as those found in the *Criminal Code*. The Committee's recommendation with respect to launching Crown appeals following a sentence imposed in accordance with a joint submission is therefore consistent with traditional notions of restraint which should invariably accompany the exercise of the Crown's right of appeal. Such restraint recognizes the importance for preserving, to the greatest extent possible, the finality of resolution agreements entered into by the Crown. It also recognizes that both the joint submission itself and the fact that it was accepted by the sentencing judge as not being contrary to the public interest, must be accorded due weight by appellate Crown counsel considering an appeal.

This chapter has addressed several aspects of plea bargaining in the sentencing process. There are, however, many other aspects of plea bargaining worthy of discussion, especially those that are practical in nature. Some issues that have not been addressed relate to matters such as the trial judge's role in resolution discussions, the prospect of counsel approaching trial judges in chambers to discuss a proposed resolution, and a lawyer's duty to another lawyer when disavowing a plea bargain entered into by previous counsel. Local plea-bargaining practices vary so significantly that it is not possible to fully canvass these issues here, nor does the case law reflect the range of practices that exist across and within jurisdictions.

The Martin Report is a good place to start any assessment of the procedural aspects of plea bargaining and joint submissions. For cases dealing with judicial involvement in plea bargaining and resolution discussions, see *R v. Wood* (1975), 26 CCC (2d) 100 (Alta. CA); *R v. Dubien*, above; *R v. White* (1982), 39 Nfld. & PEIR 196 (Nfld. CA); and *R v. O'Quinn* (2002), 59 OR (3d) 321 (CA). For a general discussion of the scope of the Crown's discretion and the circumstances in which the Crown is entitled to repudiate a plea agreement, see *R v. M.(R.N-Z.)* (2006), 213 CCC (3d) 107 (Ont. SCJ).

CHAPTER EIGHT

Absolute and Conditional Discharges

I. INTRODUCTION

The sentencing options that are available to a judge are set out in Part XXIII of the *Criminal Code*, RSC 1985, c. C-46, as amended. They range from a discharge, which is considered to be the least intrusive option, to imprisonment, the most serious and restrictive sanction available under Canadian law. This chapter and subsequent chapters discuss the various options that a court may impose as a sanction for wrongdoing.

Typically, the imposition of a sentencing option or sanction is dependent upon a conviction being entered against an offender. However, in certain circumstances, the *Criminal Code* permits a judge to provide relief against the full opprobrium of a criminal conviction by allowing for an absolute or a conditional discharge. These sanctions are best understood by considering the registration of a conviction as a two-stage process. While a conviction is generally considered to be synonymous with the finding of guilt by a judge or jury, it is more accurate to say that a conviction is perfected when a finding of guilt and sentence are formally recorded. (See *R v. McInnis* (1973), 23 CRNS 152, at 156-63 (Ont. CA); *R v. Senior* (1996), 181 AR 1 (CA); aff'd. (1997), 116 CCC (3d) 152, at 158-59; and *R v. Pearson* (1998), 130 CCC (3d) 297 (SCC).) It is only *after* a finding of guilt that the judge considers whether a *conviction* (as opposed to a discharge) ought to be imposed. In other words, in appropriate circumstances, it is open to a judge to sanction an offender with a discharge, whether absolute or conditional, and not record a conviction. As illustrated below, a conditional discharge involves a term of probation.

The immediate effect of a discharge, whether it is absolute and immediate in its effect or conditional and thus delayed during the probationary term, is that there is no criminal record of conviction and sentence against the accused under the *Criminal Records Act*, RSC 1985, c. C-47, as amended. This is a matter of great importance to the offender because there are disabilities that may follow the recording of a criminal conviction, including difficulties with employment, travel, immigration, or other significant personal matters. As will be seen below, a discharge may be granted in the discretion of the court only if this disposition is in the best interests of the offender and is not contrary to the public interest.

II. THE STATUTORY CRITERIA

There are certain restrictions on when a discharge is available, some of which are fixed. For example, a discharge cannot be imposed on a corporation. Discharges are not available if the offence is punishable by a minimum penalty or carries a maximum penalty of more than 14 years. In all other cases, the availability of a discharge is determined by a balancing of the best interests of the offender and the public, as required by s. 730 of the Code, which provides as follows:

730(1) Where an accused, other than a corporation, pleads guilty to or is found guilty of an offence, other than an offence for which a minimum punishment is prescribed by law or an offence punishable by imprisonment for fourteen years or for life, the court before which the accused appears may, if it considers it to be in the best interests of the accused and not contrary to the public interest, instead of convicting the accused, by order direct that the accused be discharged absolutely or on the conditions prescribed in a probation order made under subsection 731(2).

(2) Subject to Part XVI, where an accused who has not been taken into custody or who has been released from custody under or by virtue of any provision of Part XVI pleads guilty of or is found guilty of an offence but is not convicted, the appearance notice, promise to appear, summons, undertaking or recognizance issued to or given or entered into by the accused continues in force, subject to its terms, until a disposition in respect of the accused is made under subsection (1) unless, at the time the accused pleads guilty or is found guilty, the court, judge or justice orders that the accused be taken into custody pending such a disposition.

(3) Where a court directs under subsection (1) that an offender be discharged of an offence, the offender shall be deemed not to have been convicted of the offence except that

(a) the offender may appeal from the determination of guilt as if it were a conviction in respect of the offence;

(b) the Attorney General and, in the case of summary conviction proceedings, the informant or the informant's agent may appeal from the decision of the court not to convict the offender of the offence as if that decision were a judgment or verdict of acquittal of the offender or a dismissal of the information against the offender; and

(c) the offender may plead autrefois convict in respect of any subsequent charge relating to the offence.

(4) Where an offender who is bound by the conditions of a probation order made at a time when the offender was directed to be discharged under this section is convicted of an offence, including an offence under section 733.1, the court that made the probation order may, in addition to or in lieu of exercising its authority under subsection 732.2(5), at any time when it may take action under that subsection, revoke the discharge, convict the offender of the offence to which the discharge relates and impose any sentence that could have been imposed if the offender had been convicted at the time of discharge, and no appeal lies from a conviction under this subsection where an appeal was taken from the order directing that the offender be discharged.

III. APPLYING THE CRITERIA

The following cases illustrate how the courts determine whether to grant a discharge. A discharge must be either absolute or conditional, not some combination of the two. As the cases below illustrate, the decision is largely discretionary in nature, constrained only by the balancing of the best interests of the accused and the public interest. There is no guidance in s. 730, or in the relevant cases, on the issue of when it is appropriate to grant an absolute discharge instead of a conditional discharge, which involves a period of probation. It is clear that certain conditions of probation are improper in this context. The Code does not authorize the payment of a fine as one of the conditions of a conditional discharge (see *R v. Carroll* (1995), 38 CR (4th) 238 (BCCA). However, a restitution order may be imposed along with a discharge, whether it is absolute or conditional (see *R v. Roberts* (2004), 190 CCC (3d) 505 (Sask. CA)). As discussed in chapter 10, Monetary Sanctions: Fines and Restitution, a fine may be imposed only after the entering of a conviction, whereas a restitution order may be imposed when the offender is convicted or discharged under s. 730.

R v. Fallofield
(1973), 22 CRNS 342 (BCCA)

FARRIS CJBC: The two questions in this appeal are:

1. Did the Provincial Court Judge err in refusing to grant an absolute or a conditional discharge; and
2. If the answer is yes, has this Court the power to make such an order?

In my opinion, the answer to both questions is yes.

The appellant pleaded guilty to a charge of being in unlawful possession of some pieces of carpet of a total value of less than $200, knowing the same to have been obtained by theft. The appellant is a corporal in the Canadian Armed Forces, aged 26, married, and with no previous record. He and his two co-accused were employed by the Fairfield Moving & Storage Company in Victoria. Apparently the appellant was supplementing his income by what is commonly known as "moonlighting."

In September last, the three men were delivering refrigerators to a new apartment building and took from the premises some left-over pieces of carpeting. The accused had five pieces of carpeting of a value of $33.07. The co-accused likewise had small quantities of carpet.

The police officer who investigated the matter said that, when he attended at the residence of the accused, the accused turned over the five pieces of carpet and stated that he thought they were scraps. The officer also testified that he found the accused to be friendly and co-operative and would agree that "rather than being a thief, was more simply a foolish individual, getting involved in something slightly more serious than a foolish prank but not really a thief at nature."

A warrant officer from the Canadian Armed Forces was called and testified that "Corporal Fallofield is one of the best men we have. He is a very good worker—a very conscientious man." He further testified that this conviction "could very possibly affect his future career in the Navy."

At the hearing in the Court below, counsel for the appellant applied under the *Criminal Code*, RSC 1970, c. C-34, s. 662.1(1) [en. 1972, c. 13, s. 57] for a conditional discharge. This section reads as follows:

> 662.1(1) Where an accused, other than a corporation, pleads guilty to or is found guilty of an offence, other than an offence for which a minimum punishment is prescribed by law or an offence punishable, in the proceedings commenced against him, by imprisonment for fourteen years or for life or by death, the court before which he appears may, if it considers it to be in the best interests of the accused and not contrary to the public interest, instead of convicting the accused, by order direct that the accused be discharged absolutely or upon the conditions prescribed in a probation order.

The trial judge declined to grant the discharge, convicted the appellant, and sentenced him to a fine of $100, or in default, 30 days in prison. It is from this disposition of the matter that the present appeal is brought.

The basis of the trial Judge's refusal to grant the discharge was that he did not think that "this was a case of strict liability or that it is a case where the offence being committed was entirely completely unintentional or unavoidable." In doing so, he relied on an extract from Devlin on *Sentencing in Magistrates' Courts* which has reference to the provisions of the English legislation.

In my respectful opinion, the trial Judge proceeded upon a wrong principle. There is nothing in the language of the section that so limits its application. In *Mark Fishing Co. v. United Fishermen and Allied Workers Union* (1968), 64 WWR 530, 68 DLR 92d) 41 (BCCA), beginning at p. 543, there is a review of a number of cases, the gist of which may be gathered from one of the expressions quoted [p. 545]: "a discretion which is unfettered by law must not be fettered by judicial interpretation of it." To the same effect, in *Ebrahimi v. Westbourne Galleries Ltd.*, [1973] AC 360—where the case turned on the application of a clause in the *Companies Act* that authorizes a court to wind up a company "if the court is of the opinion that it is just and equitable that the company should be wound up." Lord Reid, with whose judgment other learned Law Lords agreed, said at p. 374H:

> There are two other restrictive interpretations which I mention to reject. First, there has been a tendency to create categories or headings under which cases must be brought if the clause is to apply. This is wrong. Illustrations may be used, but general words should remain general and not be reduced to the sum of particular instances.

Nevertheless, it is useful to review the manner in which the Courts have dealt with cases arising under this section in the less than two years since its enactment. In *R v. Derkson* (1972), 20 CRNS 129, 9 CCC (2d) 97, where the accused pleaded guilty to a charge of possession of cannabis resin, the Provincial Court refused to grant an order of absolute or conditional discharge, notwithstanding that counsel for the Crown stated "that the Crown will in future adopt a more tolerant posture in these cases," namely, where the accused had no previous convictions and was of good character and reputation. The

Judge held that the discharge provisions should never be applied routinely to any criminal offence.

In *R v. Stafrace* (1972), 10 CCC (2d) 181, the Court of Appeal of Ontario considered that where the appellant had been convicted of theft of two boxes of potato chips, having a value of approximately $10, the property of his employer, it was a proper case for the exercise of the power but that the Court of Appeal had no jurisdiction to grant the discharge.

In *R v. Campbell*, 21 CRNS 273, [1973] 2 WWR 246, 10 CCC (2d) 26 (Alta.), the District Court Judge granted an absolute discharge where the accused was charged with taking part in an immoral performance, after having been told that a judge had recently held—wrongly, as was later decided on appeal—that taking part in a similar performance was not an offence.

In *R v. Sanchez-Pino*, [1973] 2 OR 314, 11 CCC (2d) 53, the Court of Appeal considered that a conditional or absolute discharge should not be granted in a shoplifting case, although they agreed that their decision did not mean that shoplifting could never be an offence in respect of which s. 662.1(1) can apply.

In *R v. Millen* (1973), 21 CRNS 225, 11 CCC (2d) 70 (NS), the accused was granted an absolute discharge where he had pleaded guilty to a charge under s. 236 of the Code of driving with more than 80 milligrams of alcohol in 100 millilitres of blood.

In *R v. Christman*, [1973] 3 WWR 475, 11 CCC (2d) 245, a conditional discharge was granted by the Alberta Appellate Division in respect of a charge of theft under s. 294(b) [am. 1972, c. 13, s. 23] of the Code.

In *R v. Hampton*, an unreported judgment of this Court dated 13th February 1973, an absolute discharge was granted in respect of a charge of shoplifting, on the ground that there was "good reason for thinking that it will be in the public interest to grant a discharge."

In *R v. Barrett*, an unreported judgment of the Court of Appeal for the Yukon Territory delivered on 2nd March 1973, the accused was found guilty of theft by conversion; instead of being convicted, he was granted a conditional discharge. On appeal this disposition was set aside, a conviction was entered and a term of imprisonment was imposed, the Court being of the opinion that the magistrate had overlooked that he could grant a discharge only if he was of the opinion that so to do was not contrary to the public interest.

In *R v. Tifenbach*, an unreported judgment of this Court dated 18th May 1973, absolute or conditional discharge was refused where the accused had been found guilty on two counts of indecent assault on a male person.

From this review of the authorities and my own view of the meaning of s. 662.1, I draw the following conclusions; subject, of course, to what I have said above as to the exercise of discretion.

(1) The section may be used in respect of *any* offence other than an offence for which a minimum punishment is prescribed by law or the offence is punishable by imprisonment for 14 years or for life or by death.

(2) The section contemplates the commission of an offence. There is nothing in the language that limits it to a technical or trivial violation.

(3) Of the two conditions precedent to the exercise of the jurisdiction, the first is that the court must consider that it is in the best interests of the accused that he should be discharged either absolutely or upon condition. If it is not in the best interests of the accused, that, of course, is the end of the matter. If it is decided that it is in the best interests of the accused, then that brings the next consideration into operation.

(4) The second condition precedent is that the court must consider that a grant of discharge is not contrary to the public interest.

(5) Generally, the first condition would presuppose that the accused is a person of good character, without previous conviction, that it is not necessary to enter a conviction against him in order to deter him from future offences or to rehabilitate him, and that the entry of a conviction against him may have significant adverse repercussions.

(6) In the context of the second condition the public interest in the deterrence of others, while it must be given due weight, does not preclude the judicious use of the discharge provisions.

(7) The powers given by s. 662.1 should not be exercised as an alternative to probation or suspended sentence.

(8) Section 662.1 should not be applied routinely to any particular offence. This may result in an apparent lack of uniformity in the application of the discharge provisions. This lack will be more apparent than real and will stem from the differences in the circumstances of cases.

Applying these conclusions, this is a case where it is appropriate to grant an absolute discharge. It is clear that it is in the best interests of the accused that such a discharge be granted. I cannot see that such a grant is contrary to the public interest. I find it difficult to believe that the deterrence of others will be in any way diminished by the failure to render a conviction against this accused.

Accordingly, if this Court has the power so to do I would grant a discharge and I see no point in imposing conditions.

• • •

In *R v. Stafrace* (supra), the Ontario Court of Appeal held that the power conferred upon a judge of first instance by s. 662.1 of the *Criminal Code* to order an accused discharged is to be exercised "instead of" entering the conviction and if a conviction is entered there is no power as far as an appellate court is concerned to enter a discharge unless the conviction can be vacated upon proper grounds. Thus, if the accused proceeds on an appeal from sentence alone there is no jurisdiction to grant a discharge.

In a later case of *R v. Sanchez-Pino* (supra), the Ontario Court of Appeal held that, if the Court of Appeal considered that the trial judge erred in law in entering a conviction instead of granting an order for discharge, this would enable the Court of Appeal to quash the conviction and order a new trial. At such a new trial the trial judge would then consider whether he should make an order for discharge or enter a conviction.

In *R v. Christman* (supra), the Appellate Division of the Supreme Court of Alberta reached a different conclusion. Delivering the judgment of the Court, Clement JA said in part:

> I have no doubt that the determination by the trial court whether or not it will make an order for discharge is a disposition under subs. (1) of s. 662.1 ... .
>
> Since it is the "disposition" that is in appeal as a matter of sentence, this Court is empowered to vary the disposition within the limits prescribed by law. Those limits range from an unfavourable exercise of the discretion (as in the present case), to an order directing an unconditional discharge. If the disposition by the trial court is varied on such an appeal against sentence, the judgment of the Court of Appeal has the same force and effect as a disposition duly made by the trial court. The consequence is that the conviction recorded against the accused must be expunged, since by statute an order directing a discharge is made *instead* of making a conviction, and in its place the order directing a discharge is recorded and, by virtue of s. 614(2), must have the same effect as if made by the trial court prior to formal conviction.
>
> I regret that the foregoing views are at variance with those expressed by the Court of Appeal of Ontario in *R v. Stafrace* (supra). Our divergence appears to arise largely because of the effect above given to the statutory definition of "sentence."

With respect, I agree with the views of the Alberta Court of Appeal and think that they are to be preferred to the views expressed in the decisions of the Ontario Court of Appeal. The line of reasoning that commends itself to me is briefly as follows. Under s. 601 the word "sentence" in Part XVIII of the Code includes a disposition made under s. 662.1(1). A determination by a trial court before which an accused pleads guilty or by which an accused is found guilty whether or not it will make an order for discharge is such a disposition. Section 603(1)(b) confers a right of appeal against a sentence and so against such a disposition. Under s. 614(1) the Court of Appeal may vary a sentence and, applying the reasoning above, may substitute for the decision to convict the accused instead of discharging him an order directing that he be discharged.

Accordingly, it is my opinion that this Court has the power to grant a discharge. The order I would make would be to allow the appeal from sentence, to quash the conviction and to order that the appellant be discharged absolutely.

Appeal allowed; absolute discharge ordered.

R v. McInnis
(1973), 23 CRNS 152 (Ont. CA)

MARTIN JA: This is an appeal by the appellant from her conviction by His Honour Provincial Court Judge R.T. Bennett on two charges of theft and from the sentence imposed, namely, suspended sentence and probation for two years.

The appeal was initially from sentence only but the Court, on the hearing of the appeal, granted leave to the appellant to amend the notice of appeal to include an appeal from conviction as well as sentence in order that the broad questions raised by the appeal might be considered fully.

The questions raised by the appeal are:

(a) Whether the Court of Appeal is empowered to direct that an accused who has been convicted by the trial Court be discharged absolutely or upon conditions pursuant to s. 662.1(1) of the *Criminal Code.*

(b) Whether, if the Court is empowered under the above circumstances to direct that the accused be discharged absolutely or upon conditions, it is appropriate in the present case to direct an absolute or conditional discharge.

· · ·

The manifest purpose of the legislation is to enable a Court before which an accused pleads guilty to an offence or which finds an accused guilty of an offence, to make a disposition of the case, in appropriate circumstances, which will avoid ascribing a criminal record to the accused.

· · ·

In my view, s. 662.1(1) of the *Criminal Code* which provides that, in the circumstances envisaged therein, the Court may, *instead of convicting the accused*, direct that he be discharged absolutely or upon conditions simply means that notwithstanding the plea of guilty or the finding of guilt, the Court may, instead of passing judgment, that is sentence, and recording a conviction, direct that he be discharged either absolutely or conditionally. Where the Court directs that the accused be discharged, the accused is by the section deemed not to have been convicted. It is to be observed that in many cases the finding of guilt followed by the imposition of sentence constitutes the only record of the registering of a conviction.

· · ·

Turning now from the jurisdictional question to the merits of the appeal, I am of the view that the case is a proper one for the application of s. 662.1. The appellant was 16 years of age at the time of the commission of the offences. Both offences were committed on the same day and involved the theft by appellant and her co-accused of two sweaters from one store and another sweater from a second store. The offences were committed during a brief period when the appellant had left the family home because of a dispute with her parents. The pre-sentence report indicates that emotional stress and possibly undesirable influences may have brought about the conduct in question. The appellant at the time of the commission of the offences was, as she still is, a high school student in Grade 11. Both her academic and attendance records are satisfactory and the pre-sentence report is a favourable one.

I would dismiss the appeal from conviction, allow the appeal from sentence and in the place of the sentence imposed by the trial judge, would direct that the appellant, pursuant to s. 662.1, be discharged upon the same conditions as those set out in the probation order.

Appeal allowed.

R v. Bram
(1982), 30 CR (3d) 398 (Alta. CA)

LAYCRAFT JA: In this case the accused was convicted after trial of the offence of offering money to an employee of Edmonton Telephones to release to him the addresses and telephone numbers of persons with silent numbers. He was employed as a "skip tracer," that is, one whose job it is to trace persons who have changed their addresses for the purposes of avoiding payment of sums due on credit accounts. The accused was granted an absolute discharge and the Crown now appeals that disposition. The Crown does not seek incarceration or, indeed, any other particular sentence. It merely argues that on his conviction for this offence the accused should be left with a criminal record.

The accused is a survivor of the holocaust of World War II, in which many millions of his co-religionists were murdered. He is the only member of a family of 12 persons who survived the European death camps. At some time after World War II he arrived in Canada, where he married and raised a family. He has been an exemplary citizen and at 58 years of age has never been convicted of any offence other than the present one. In the material filed with us a wide range of citizens speak highly of him. He is described as an upright man and a citizen of exceptional quality. It is apparent that he did not for a time realize that he was doing wrong in the commission of this offence. He seemed to feel that in tracing persons who deliberately avoid obligations such conduct is permissible, though he now does realize that he was doing wrong.

Section 662.1 [en. SC 1972, c. 13, s. 57; am. SC 1974-75-76, c. 93, s. 80] of the *Criminal Code*, RSC 1970, c. C-34, authorizes an absolute discharge when, in the words of the section, the court "considers it to be in the best interest of the accused and not contrary to the public interest."

The tests for the application of this section were extensively reviewed by this court in *R v. MacFarlane*, 3 Alta. LR (2d) 341, [1976] WWD 74, in which a number of factors were listed particularizing the general words of the section. The case points out that, apart from those cases in which there is need to deter the accused himself from further offences, the absolute discharge will in almost every case be in the interests of the accused. There is no such need in the present case, and the contest is therefore whether an absolute discharge would or would not be in the public interest.

R v. MacFarlane states that the jurisdiction to grant an absolute discharge should be used sparingly in the interests of preserving the general deterrence principle of criminal sentencing. Nevertheless that is not to say that it is only in the case of trivial or unintentional offences that absolute discharges should be granted. This point is expressed in Nadin-Davis on *Sentencing in Canada* (1982), at p. 479 in these terms:

> While frugality is in order in the application of discharges, the Courts have repeatedly emphasized the wide range of possible candidates and offences. In *Fallofield* [*R v. Fallofield*, 22 CRNS 342, [1973] 6 WWR 472, 13 CCC (2d) 450 (BCCA)] it was held that s. 662.1 is not limited in application to cases of strict liability, or cases where the offence was completely unintentional or unavoidable. Extending this principle, the Ontario court in *Vicente* [*R v. Vicente* (1975), 18 Cr. LQ 292 (Ont. CA)] has added that the granting of

discharges should not be confined to trivial matters. In appropriate circumstances, a discharge may be granted in a case which is not trivial.

The author also notes that the seriousness of the offence is naturally a pertinent consideration, and cites the *MacFarlane* decision, supra, for this proposition.

In this case, applying the principles enunciated in *R v. MacFarlane*, we conclude that we will not interfere with the absolute discharge granted by the learned trial judge. The offence is not prevalent in the community, as the Crown readily conceded. The accused had little to gain directly from it, since his income was determined on an hourly basis and not as a percentage of recovery of unpaid accounts. For this accused in relation to this offence we see no need for deterrence, nor do we perceive that the public interest requires that persons dealing with him in the future be able to determine that the offence was committed. He has been an excellent citizen of his adopted country, of whom it may be said with a high degree of confidence that he will not offend again. That conclusion was apparently reached also by the learned trial judge, who observed him giving evidence for upwards of 1½ hours. No adequate grounds have been shown to us to interfere with the disposition by the trial judge. Accordingly the Crown is refused leave to appeal.

Leave to appeal refused.

The possibility of deportation is sometimes relied on as a factor in favour of mitigation of sentence. In *R v. Critton* [2002], OJ No. 2594 (SCJ), the court stated, at para. 77: "The jurisprudence is not entirely uniform as to the legal significance of an accused's pending deportation." More recently, in *R v. Hamilton* (2004), 186 CCC (3d) 129 (Ont. CA), the court recognized no more than a discretion to take the possibility of deportation into account in fashioning an appropriate sentence. The immigration status of an offender is regularly offered in support of a discharge, rather than conviction. Sometimes, a conviction, as opposed to a mere finding of guilt, is said to have dramatic consequences for the purpose of immigration.

R v. Shokohi-Manesh
(1992), 69 CCC (3d) 286 (BCCA)

TAYLOR JA: Subject to leave being granted Mehran Shokohi-Manesh appeals the suspended sentence with two years probation which was imposed on him two years ago for possession of a stolen cellular telephone.

The appellant, who is now 23, arrived in the country as a refugee some three years ago from Iran. He had at the time of trial been working part-time as a waiter while studying at Douglas College and was awaiting the processing of his application for landed immigrant status as a refugee. No previous record was alleged at his trial but Crown counsel opposed the granting of a discharge on the grounds that the property involved was of considerable value, that the accused had not assisted the police and the court, and that he showed no remorse. Crown counsel suggested that a fine should properly be imposed. The sentencing judge accepted that a discharge was not appropriate, and instead suspended sentence and imposed a two-year probation order in the standard terms requiring that the appellant report as directed to a probation officer.

The consequences for the appellant's hopes of obtaining refugee status in Canada of the refusal of a discharge were not gone into before the trial judge. Before us it was explained that the entry of a conviction on the present charge absolutely prevents consideration of the appellant's application. It is solely for this reason that he now seeks leave to appeal.

The circumstances of the offence were these. The appellant was arrested when he returned to a cellular telephone store to pick up a cellular telephone which he had taken there in order to have it "renumbered" so that he could make use of it. The manager of the store was suspicious that the phone might have been stolen and reported the matter to the police. Officers were waiting at the store when the appellant came back.

The manager testified that the appellant said the phone had been given to him by an uncle who had left the country. When questioned by the police, however, the appellant said he found it abandoned in a public phone booth late at night two or three months earlier and had taken it to a department store in an effort to locate the owner. At his trial the appellant repeated the account of finding the telephone and said that he kept it hoping that he would get a reward for its return. The judge accepted that the crime was in effect one of theft after finding, that is to say that the appellant did indeed find the telephone outside the restaurant, as he said, and that he proceeded thereafter to convert it to his own use.

After the probation order had been in effect for one year the appellant's probation officer reported to the court favourably on his conduct. The officer wrote:

> In my opinion Mehran's offence is an isolated one for him and is not part of an ongoing pattern of criminal activity. His offence is really part of "the second year syndrome," which many newcomers to Canada experience. It is characterized by loneliness, homesickness, depression, confusion and sometimes by a foolish illegal act.
>
> All in all he has cooperated with the probation order to his benefit, and I feel the order has now served its purpose.

The sentencing judge accepted this recommendation and vacated the probation order.

It is, in effect, urged on us by Mr. Goldberg on behalf of the appellant that had the information now available been before the sentencing judge the judge might have taken a different view of the appropriateness of granting a discharge. The appellant is a first offender. It appears that despite his unfortunate lapse in the face of temptation he has come to be regarded by a skilled probation officer as a person of good character. Plainly, it would be in his best interests that the bar which the conviction creates to his prospects of receiving landed status should be removed. The remaining question under s. 736(1) is whether the granting of a discharge would be contrary to the public interest. Obviously, this is a dispensation to be used judiciously by the courts.

The fact that an accused person's immigration status will be adversely affected by a conviction does not in itself justify the granting of a discharge: see *R v. Melo* (1975), 26 CC (2d) 510, 310 CRNS 328 (Ont. CA). Clearly, the granting of a discharge will not in itself ensure that the appellant's application before the immigration authorities will in fact be approved. But I think the fact that here a refusal of a discharge would absolutely bar him from consideration for refugee status admission is a consideration that, in this particular case, can properly be given weight without offending the public interest.

Because of his age and because he has been steadily employed at all times while in Canada, because he has satisfied the probation authorities that the adverse impression created at his trial is not in fact warranted, because his crime in the end result did not cause loss to anyone, because of the nature of his apology and the rescission of the punishment imposed on him, I am of the view that this is a case in which it would not be contrary to the public interest that the relief sought be granted.

I would grant leave to appeal. I would allow the appeal against sentence and substitute for the penalty imposed an unconditional discharge.

Appeal allowed and sentence varied.

Since *R v. Shokohi-Manesh*, the following provisions of the *Immigration and Refugee Protection Act*, SC 2001, c. 27 have been enacted:

36(1) A permanent resident or a foreign national is inadmissible on grounds of serious criminality for

(a) having been convicted in Canada of an offence under an Act of Parliament punishable by a maximum term of imprisonment of at least 10 years, or of an offence under an Act of Parliament for which a term of imprisonment of more than six months has been imposed;

(b) having been convicted of an offence outside Canada that, if committed in Canada, would constitute an offence under an Act of Parliament punishable by a maximum term of imprisonment of at least 10 years; or

(c) committing an act outside Canada that is an offence in the place where it was committed and that, if committed in Canada, would constitute an offence under an Act of Parliament punishable by a maximum term of imprisonment of at least 10 years.

(2) A foreign national is inadmissible on grounds of criminality for

(a) having been convicted in Canada of an offence under an Act of Parliament punishable by way of indictment, or of two offences under any Act of Parliament not arising out of a single occurrence;

(b) having been convicted outside Canada of an offence that, if committed in Canada, would constitute an indictable offence under an Act of Parliament, or of two offences not arising out of a single occurrence that, if committed in Canada, would constitute offences under an Act of Parliament;

(c) committing an act outside Canada that is an offence in the place where it was committed and that, if committed in Canada, would constitute an indictable offence under an Act of Parliament; or

(d) committing, on entering Canada, an offence under an Act of Parliament prescribed by regulations.

(3) The following provisions govern subsections (1) and (2):

(a) an offence that may be prosecuted either summarily or by way of indictment is deemed to be an indictable offence, even if it has been prosecuted summarily;

(b) inadmissibility under subsections (1) and (2) may not be based on a conviction in respect of which a pardon has been granted and has not ceased to have effect or been revoked under the *Criminal Records Act*, or in respect of which there has been a final determination of an acquittal;

(c) the matters referred to in paragraphs (1)(b) and (c) and (2)(b) and (c) do not constitute inadmissibility in respect of a permanent resident or foreign national who, after the prescribed period, satisfies the Minister that they have been rehabilitated or who is a member of a prescribed class that is deemed to have been rehabilitated;

(d) a determination of whether a permanent resident has committed an act described in paragraph (1)(c) must be based on a balance of probabilities; and

(e) inadmissibility under subsections (1) and (2) may not be based on an offence designated as a contravention under the *Contraventions Act* or an offence under the *Young Offenders Act*.

For thoughtful applications of these provisions, see *R v. Morovati*, [2007] OJ No. 111 (CJ) and *R v. Kadotchnikov*, [2002] SJ No. 112 (Prov. Ct.).

As the following case illustrates, some courts have discouraged the use of discharges in cases where general deterrence must be emphasized.

R v. Roberts
(2005), 190 CCC (3d) 504 (Sask. CA)

THE COURT (orally): [1] Mr. Roberts was convicted, after trial, of fraud exceeding five thousand dollars, contrary to s. 380(1)(a) of the *Criminal Code*.

[2] Mr. Roberts wrote a cheque for $11,000.00 on his personal bank account in February of 2001, knowing that the account lacked sufficient funds. He deposited the cheque into his CIBC Visa account and the next day withdrew the $11,000.00 in cash. About five days later, he repeated the same process, this time depositing and withdrawing $13,000.00. CIBC Visa lost the entire $24,000.00.

[3] Mr. Roberts was 28 years old at the time of sentencing. He was married and had two young children. At sentencing, his debt load was $402,000.00 and there were some 37 different creditors interested in his affairs. Mr. Roberts had no criminal record and a pre-sentence report suggested that he was a low risk to re-offend.

[4] The learned Provincial Court judge granted a conditional discharge with a probation order of one year and a requirement of 200 hours of community service work. He also made a restitution order in the amount of $24,000.00. He explained his decision as follows:

Having heard comments from counsel for the Crown and counsel for the defence, and having heard the evidence; having perused the pre-sentence report in its brevity; taking into consideration the fact that this man has no previous involvement with the system; taking further into consideration the fact that this was a rather intricate kiting system that this man was involved in, there'll be a conditional discharge, one year, usual terms and conditions, plus 200 hours of community service work.

[5] In this Court, the Crown took issue with the discharge and asked that a 12 month conditional sentence be imposed with a condition of 200 hours of community service work.

[6] In our view, leave to appeal should be granted and the Crown's appeal should be allowed.

· · ·

[8] In *R v. Elsharawy* (1997), 119 CCC (3d) 565, at pp. 566-67, the Court of Appeal for Newfoundland commented as follows on the prerequisites to a valid discharge:

> [3] For the Court to exercise its discretion to grant a discharge under s. 730 of the Criminal Code, the Court must consider that that type of disposition is: (i) in the best interests of the accused: and (ii) not contrary to the public interest. The first condition presupposes that the accused is a person of good character, usually without previous conviction or discharge, that he does not require personal deterrence or rehabilitation and that a criminal conviction may have significant adverse repercussions. The second condition involves a consideration of the principle of general deterrence with attention being paid to the gravity of the offence, its incidence in the community, public attitudes towards it and public confidence in the effective enforcement of the criminal law. See *R v. Fallofield* (1973), 13 CCC (2d) 450 (BCCA), and *R v. Waters* (1990), 54 CCC (3d) 40 (Sask. QB).

[9] We are of the view that the learned Provincial Court judge failed to give proper consideration to the public interest criterion in s. 730(1). First, the sentence imposed did not properly reflect the principle of general deterrence. A conditional discharge would do little to discourage others in Mr. Roberts' situation from undertaking similar sorts of criminal activity. See: *R v. Wileniec (S.)* (2003), 238 Sask. R 214 (CA).

[10] Second, the sentence imposed did not reflect the gravity of the offence. This was a serious fraud accomplished by virtue of what the Provincial Court judge called "a rather intricate kiting system." It involved a total of $24,000.00 which amount was lost by CIBC Visa.

[11] Third, public confidence in the criminal justice system would be undermined if there was no conviction on the facts at hand. This offence was significant and should attract a criminal record.

[12] In the result, leave to appeal is granted and a twelve month conditional sentence is substituted in place of the conditional discharge. We prescribe the compulsory conditions set out in s. 742.3(1) of the *Criminal Code* and a further condition that Mr. Roberts perform 200 hours of community service work, with credit to be given in that regard for any such work performed to date pursuant to the probation order made by the sentencing judge. The restitution order will remain in place.

Appeal allowed.

See also *R v. Collier* (2006), 212 CCC (3d) 1 (NBCA), in which discharges imposed by the trial judge were overturned on appeal on two counts of trafficking in small amounts of marijuana. Discharges have also been refused in cases involving hockey violence (see *R v. Aussem*, [1997] OJ No. 5582 (Ont. Prov. Ct.)) and in cases of violent behaviour of parents at their children's hockey games (see *R v. Bebis*, [1989] OJ No. 1620 (Dist. Ct.) and *R v. Musselman*, [1999] OJ No. 4666 (SCJ)). In *R v. Batshaw* (2004), 186 CCC (3d) 473 (Man. CA), a conditional discharge was overturned in a case involving possession of child pornography as the Court of Appeal held that a discharge did not sufficiently emphasize the principle of denunciation.

The general approach in *Fallofield* and *McInnis* has been followed in subsequent cases, but the specific criteria for granting a discharge, whether conditional or absolute, cannot easily be enumerated. It is clear that in the absence of a prescribed minimum or maximum of more than 14 years, a discharge is a viable option for all offences. The courts have said repeatedly that discharges should not be routinely granted and should not be routinely refused for any class of offence or offender. For example, the courts have not precluded discharges in cases of sexual assault (see *R v. Moreau* (1992), 76 CCC (3d) 181 (Que. CA) and *R v. Rozon*, [1999] RJQ 805 (SC)).

Courts have held that an offender who has previously been discharged is not for this reason alone ineligible for a discharge on a subsequent offence (*R v. Elsharawy* (1997), 119 CCC (3d) 565 (Nfld. CA); *R v. Tan* (1974), 74 CCC (2d) 184 (BCCA); and *R v. Drew* (1978), 45 CCC (2d) 212 (BCCA)). Recurring themes in decisions concerning discharges are the possibility that a criminal conviction would place the offender in a position of disproportionate adversity or difficulty. For further illustrations see, for example, *R v. Mullin* (1990), 56 CCC (3d) 476 (PEICA); *R v. Cyr*, [1992] RL 13 (Que. CA); *R v. Burke* (1996), 108 CCC (3d) 260 (Nfld. CA); *Elsharawy*, above; and *Rozon*, above.

With respect to employment, there are instances in which the nature of the offence, because of the offender's area of employment, militates against a discharge. There are numerous cases involving discharges and police officers. See *R v. Carson* (2004), 185 CCC (3d) 541 (Ont. CA), in which the accused, a police officer, assaulted a police officer with whom he was involved in a relationship. The Court of Appeal allowed his appeal against sentence and imposed a conditional discharge partly because the offence was unrelated to the accused's professional duties. However, the situation may be different when the offending act has a meaningful connection to the officer's professional duties. In *R v. Blackburn* (2004), 186 CCC (3d) 51 (Ont. CA), the accused was an off-duty police officer who was convicted of dangerous driving arising out of a "road rage" incident. During this incident, the officer intimidated the complainant by flashing his police badge. The Court of Appeal held that a discharge was inappropriate, partly because the accused's use of his badge constituted a "clear abuse of [his] position of authority and trust as a police officer." See also *R v. LeBlanc* (2003), 180 CCC (3d) 265 (NBCA) in which a discharge was overturned in a case where a police officer committed theft during an investigation of a residential fire. In these types of cases, is the question for the judge whether the consequence can be characterized as unfair or disproportionate to culpability?

NOTE

The *Criminal Records Act*, RSC 1985, c. C-47, deals with the duration of the record of the discharge. Section 6.1(1) provides that "no record of a discharge" shall be disclosed to any person, nor shall the existence of the record or the fact of the discharge be disclosed to any person if more than one year has passed since the offender was discharged absolutely or more than three years have passed "since the offender was discharged on the conditions prescribed in a probation order." Moreover, pursuant to s. 6.1(2), the commissioner of the Royal Canadian Mounted Police, who is responsible for the custody of criminal records kept in an automated retrieval system known as CPIC, must purge the record of a discharge from the system after the relevant period has expired.

CHAPTER NINE

Probation

I. INTRODUCTION

Community-based sanctions occupy a crucial position in the Canadian sentencing scheme. Unless they receive an absolute discharge, most first offenders can realistically expect to receive a sentence that includes probation. Probation may be imposed on its own or in combination with a term of imprisonment (real or conditional) or a fine, but not both. It is a sanction that is restorative and rehabilitative in focus, as emphasized by the Supreme Court of Canada in *R v. Proulx* (2000), 30 CR (5th) 1 (discussed in chapter 12, Conditional Sentence of Imprisonment).

When probation was first introduced into Canadian law (SC 1889, c. 44), it was restricted to young first offenders and relatively minor offences. Moreover, it required the offender to enter into a recognizance sometimes with sureties. Initially, there was no supervision or reporting but simply a requirement to keep the peace and be of good behaviour. In 1921, the *Criminal Code* was amended to permit forms of supervision that led eventually to an official probation service for adults. Legislation authorizing the appointment of probation officers was enacted in Ontario in 1922 and in British Columbia in 1946. See Hamai, Ville, Harris, Hough, and Zvekic, *Probation Around the World: A Comparative Study* (London: Routledge, 1995), 36. In Jaffary, "Probation for the Adult Offender" (1969), 27 *Can. Bar Rev.* 1020, at 1036, the author speculated that there were fewer than 20 probation officers in Canada at the time and that their qualifications fell far below those recommended by the Archambault commission in 1938.

After major revision of the *Criminal Code* in 1955, two basic kinds of probation were available to sentencing judges. First, a court was allowed to order an offender to enter into a recognizance for up to two years, with or without sureties, and "to keep the peace and be of good behaviour." Such an order could be made in addition to a sentence for an indictable offence or "in addition to or in lieu of sentence" in summary conviction matters. The underlying intention seemed to be that sureties might be useful to encourage lawful behaviour. (See the notes following s. 637 in *Martin's Criminal Code*, 1955, which include a quotation from *Greaves' Consolidated Acts* explaining the English predecessor legislation.) The second form of probation empowered a court to suspend the passing of sentence and order the accused to enter into a recognizance that could include reporting conditions, conditions requiring restitution or reparation, or "such further conditions as [the court] considers desirable." Here, the person responsible for supervision could return the offender to court and, in cases of breach, the offender could be re-sentenced.

These were the provisions applicable at the time of the review conducted by the Canadian Committee on Corrections. In the committee's 1969 report, *Towards Unity*, known commonly as the Ouimet report, an entire chapter was dedicated to probation. In general, the committee supported expanded use of community sanctions. It described probation as providing

[o]ne of the most effective means of giving expression to one of the fundamental principles on which this report is based—that, whenever feasible, efforts to rehabilitate an offender should take place in the community.

The report was critical because the only remedy for non-compliance was for the Crown to apply for forfeiture of the indebtedness created by the recognizance. Moreover, it questioned the utility of attaching probation to a sentence of imprisonment because of the degree of prediction involved. However, the report noted a "substantial rate of success" with probation and advocated expanded use of it. The committee recommended using probation orders rather than recognizances with mandatory conditions that the offender keep the peace and be of good behaviour, appear in court when required, be under the supervision of a probation officer, and report periodically to that officer. It also recommended that the Code be amended to permit discretionary conditions "to fit the needs of the individual case." The report added the following comment:

Conditions in a probation order should be kept to a minimum. Particularly, conditions that interfere with aspects of a probationer's life that have nothing to do with his offence should be avoided.

It can readily be seen that the committee viewed probation as a rehabilitative tool that ought not to be encumbered by extraneous prohibitions.

Not all of the Ouimet report recommendations dealing with probation were adopted by Parliament. Probation continued to be available in addition to terms of imprisonment so long as the term did not exceed two years. Parliament did replace the recognizance with a probation order and a list of mandatory and discretionary conditions. (See SC 1968-69, c. 38, s. 75.) It also created a separate offence for breach of probation.

For further discussion of probation, see Clayton C. Ruby, *Sentencing* (Markham, ON: Butterworths, 2000), chapter 9; Allan Manson, *The Law of Sentencing* (Toronto, ON: Irwin, 2001), 219 to 245; and Barnett, "Probation Orders Under the Criminal Code" (1977), 38 CRNS 165. See also the Report of the Canadian Sentencing Commission, *Sentencing Reform* (1987), chapter 12, and the Report of the Standing Committee of the House of Commons on Justice and the Solicitor General, *Taking Responsibility* (1988) ("the Daubney report"), chapter 7.

When thinking about the role of probation, consider Professor Doob's views on alternatives to imprisonment in the following excerpt.

A. Doob, "Community Sanctions and Imprisonment: Hoping for a Miracle but Not Bothering Even to Pray for It"
(1990), 32 *Canadian Journal of Criminology* 415 (footnotes omitted)

. . .

Our thinking and sometimes our laws reflect a presumption in favour of imprisonment. Our penalty structure for criminal offences is uniformly stated in terms of the maximum sentence of imprisonment that can be imposed. Other sanctions, then, become "alternatives." This is not true of the *Young Offenders Act* where a number of different dispositions are listed (in s. 20(1) of the Act), the final one being custody. The problem is that even our language tends to encourage us to think first of imprisonment, and then of "alternatives."

It was in part for these reasons that the Canadian Sentencing Commission, in its 1987 report, used the term "community sanctions" instead of the more common terms such as "non-custodial" or "non-carceral" sanctions or "alternatives" to imprisonment. The Commission wanted to get away from the dichotomy between custody and all other sanctions, and wished to emphasize that it does not view imprisonment as the pivotal sanction with all other possible sentences being measured against it.

The linguistic distinction between the term "alternatives" and some term like "community sanctions" which emphasizes the independent status of the sanction is important beyond the symbolic point that it makes. It leads one to ask the obvious and critical question: if we have "community sanctions," when should they be imposed?

This in turn forces us to ask a series of other questions including the following:

How should sentences—community sanctions included—be allocated?
What purpose or purposes should sentencing serve?
What principles should govern the determination of sentences?
What kinds of offenders convicted of what kinds of offences should normally receive community sanctions?

An Example of an Attempt to Increase the Use of Community Sanctions: The Report of the Canadian Sentencing Commission

The formal Declaration of Purpose and Principles of Sentencing proposed by the Canadian Sentencing Commission need not be reproduced here (See Canada 1987: 152-155). For the purposes of this paper, it is sufficient to consider the following aspects of it:

a) The paramount principle determining the sentence is that the sanction be proportionate to the gravity of the offence and the degree of responsibility of the offender for the offence.
b) There is a presumption in favour of the least onerous sanction.
c) Imprisonment is to be imposed only for specific purposes.

The implications of this policy are important. First of all, since the severity of the sentence is supposed to be proportionate to the seriousness of the offence, it follows that the less serious offences—in particular the very common but less serious property offences—should predominately receive less severe sentences. Given that the Commission also endorsed the principle of restraint in the use of imprisonment, this statement could be operationalized as meaning that there should be an increased use of community sanctions.

But a statement of purpose and principles is not enough. It may tell judges what principles to follow and may give judges a fairly good idea for a particular case of the appropriate levels of sanction *in relation to* other cases. But on its own, such a statement does not tell the judge explicitly what kinds of sanctions should be imposed for particular kinds of cases. Thus a "proportionality" model such as that recommended by the Canadian Sentencing Commission is neither harsh nor lenient on its own: without further elaboration, it does not imply either an increased use of community sanctions nor an increased use of imprisonment. Principles are necessary, but they do not provide sufficient guidelines for the sentencing judge.

The Canadian Sentencing Commission went one step further in suggesting that explicit policy be made. It recommended that guidelines—created by a Commission, but assented to by Parliament—be made part of our sentencing law. Guidelines, under its recommendations, could consist of two separate parts. For all offences, there would be an explicit presumption of custody or community sanction. If the presumptive disposition were a sentence of imprisonment, the guidelines would indicate the presumptive range. If it were not, then, a community sanction would be imposed. Furthermore, the Commission recommended that specific guidance—presumably in the form of guidelines—be developed for the use of community sanctions. As von Hirsch, Wasik, and Greene (1989) have noted, explicit guidance for community sanction can be given that is consistent with an over-riding sentencing rationale.

Conclusion

In the context of the theme of this paper, then, community sanctions should not be "alternatives," but should become sanctions in their own right. More importantly, they should be sanctions that would be described in appropriate legislation as appropriate for certain kinds of cases. In other words, they wouldn't be add-ons to the system, but would be, presumptively, the correct sanction for many offences.

According to the Canadian Sentencing Commission, community sanctions should often be used instead of imprisonment and should be designated as the appropriate sentence for many common offences. Many very common property offences (for which a sizable number of offenders are currently imprisoned) would have, as the presumptive sentence, a community sanction. It is expected that, if the Canadian Sentencing Commission recommendations were implemented, the number of people incarcerated would drop because of the increased use of community sanctions.

Clearly, however, there can be no guarantee of success. There is a good deal of evidence that the criminal justice system is quite resistant to change. Changes cannot be made at one level of the system—in this case in the law governing sentencing—with an assurance that the changes would be implemented exactly as intended. It was for that reason, among others, that the Canadian Sentencing Commission recommended that a permanent sentencing commission be created. It could have as one of its major responsibilities the monitoring of sentencing to ensure that desired changes occurred. It would be able to recommend—and implement—changes quickly to eliminate unanticipated problems should they occur.

In Canada it would appear that a number of conditions must be met to be confident that there will be increased use of community sanctions, or "alternatives." These would include:

The presence of well-run community sanctions;
A policy that endorses the use of them;

Legal and administrative procedures that put community sanctions on an equal footing with imprisonment as sentencing choices;

Guidance to decision makers on the appropriate use of community sanctions.

Obviously it is possible to have successful "alternatives" without the policy changes I have suggested just as it might happen, to use the analogy I made earlier, that adding a third type of wine to a menu will shift customers away from the wines in short supply. However, if we want to ensure success, we probably have to work a little harder to achieve the changes we want. Those who believe in the effectiveness of prayer might try that. But Parliamentary action would seem to be a more sure bet.

II. THE STATUTORY FRAMEWORK

The statutory provisions governing probation (*Criminal Code*, RSC 1985, c. C-46, as amended by SC 1995, c. 22) are reproduced below. When reading them, consider the following questions: When *must* and when *may* a sentencing judge impose a probation order? Can a probation order be combined with other sentencing options and, if so, which ones?

731(1) Where a person is convicted of an offence, a court may, having regard to the age and character of the offender, the commission,

(a) if no minimum punishment is prescribed by law, suspend the passing of sentence and direct that the offender be released on the conditions prescribed in a probation order; or

(b) in addition to fining or sentencing the offender to imprisonment for a term not exceeding two years, direct that the offender comply with the conditions prescribed in a probation order.

(2) A court may also make a probation order where it discharges an accused under subsection 730(1).

731.1(1) Before making a probation order, the court shall consider whether section 109 or 110 is applicable.

(2) For greater certainty, a condition of a probation order referred to in paragraph 732.1(3)(d) does not affect the operation of section 109 or 110.

• • •

732.1(2) The court shall prescribe, as conditions of a probation order, that the offender do all of the following:

(a) keep the peace and be of good behaviour;

(b) appear before the court when required to do so by the court; and

(c) notify the court or the probation officer in advance of any change of name or address, and promptly notify the court or the probation officer of any change of employment or occupation.

(3) The court may prescribe, as additional conditions of a probation order, that the offender do one or more of the following:

(a) report to a probation officer

(i) within two working days, or such longer period as the court directs, after the making of the probation order, and

(ii) thereafter, when required by the probation officer and in the manner directed by the probation officer;

(b remain within the jurisdiction of the court unless written permission to go outside that jurisdiction is obtained from the court or the probation officer;

(c) abstain from

(i) the consumption of alcohol or other intoxicating substances, or

(ii) the consumption of drugs except in accordance with a medical prescription;

(d) abstain from owning, possessing or carrying a weapon;

(e) provide for the support or care of dependants;

(f) perform up to 240 hours of community service over a period not exceeding eighteen months;

(g) if the offender agrees, and subject to the program director's acceptance of the offender, participate actively in a treatment program approved by the province;

(g.1) where the lieutenant governor in council of the province in which the probation order is made has established a program for curative treatment in relation to the consumption of alcohol or drugs, attend at a treatment facility, designated by the lieutenant governor in council of the province, for assessment and curative treatment in relation to the consumption by the offender of alcohol or drugs that is recommended pursuant to the program;

(g.2) where the lieutenant governor in council of the province in which the probation order is made has established a program governing the use of an alcohol ignition interlock device by an offender and if the offender agrees to participate in the program, comply with the program; and

(h) comply with such other reasonable conditions as the court considers desirable, subject to any regulations made under subsection 738(2), for protecting society and for facilitating the offender's successful reintegration into the community.

(3.1) The court may prescribe, as additional conditions of a probation order made in respect of an organization, that the offender do one or more of the following:

(a) make restitution to a person for any loss or damage that they suffered as a result of the offence;

(b) establish policies, standards and procedures to reduce the likelihood of the organization committing a further offence;

(c) communicate those policies, standards and procedures to its representatives;

(d) report to the court on the implementation of those policies, standards and procedures;

(e) identify the senior officer who is responsible for compliance with those policies, standards and procedures;

(f) provide, in the manner specified by the court, the following information to the public, namely,

(i) the offence with which the organization was convicted;

(ii) the sentence imposed by the court, and

(iii) any measures that the organization is taking – including any policies, standards and procedures established under paragraph (b) – to reduce the likelihood of it committing a subsequent offence; and

(g) comply with any other reasonable conditions that the court considers desirable to prevent the organization from committing subsequent offences or to remedy the harm caused by the offence.

(3.2) Before making an order under paragraph (3.1)(b), a court shall consider whether it would be more appropriate for another regulatory body to supervise the development and implementation of the policies, standards and procedures referred to in that paragraph.

(4) A probation order may be in Form 46, and the court that makes the probation order shall specify therein the period for which it is to remain in force.

(5) A court that makes a probation order shall

(a) cause to be given to the offender

(i) a copy of the order,

(ii) an explanation of the substance of subsections 732.2(3) and (5) and section 733.1, and

(iii) an explanation of the procedure for applying under subsection 732.2(3) for a change to the optional conditions; and

(b) take reasonable measures to ensure that the offender understands the order and the explanations given to the offender under paragraph (a).

732.2(1) A probation order comes into force

(a) on the date on which the order is made;

(b) where the offender is sentenced to imprisonment under paragraph 731(1)(b) or was previously sentenced to imprisonment for another offence, as soon as the offender is released from prison or, if released from prison on conditional release, at the expiration of the sentence of imprisonment; or

(c) where the offender is under a conditional sentence, at the expiration of the conditional sentence.

(2) Subject to subsection (5),

(a) where an offender who is bound by a probation order is convicted of an offence, including an offence under section 733.1, or is imprisoned under paragraph 731(1)(b) in default of payment of a fine, the order continues in force except in so far as the sentence renders it impossible for the offender for the time being to comply with the order; and

(b) no probation order shall continue in force for more than three years after the date on which the order came into force.

(3) A court that makes a probation order may at any time, on application by the offender, the probation officer or the prosecutor, require the offender to appear before it and, after hearing the offender and one or both of the probation officer and the prosecutor,

(a) make any changes to the optional conditions that in the opinion of the court are rendered desirable by a change in the circumstances since those conditions were prescribed,

(b) relieve the offender, either absolutely or on such terms or for such period as the court deems desirable, of compliance with any optional condition, or

(c) decrease the period for which the probation order is to remain in force,

and the court shall thereupon endorse the probation order accordingly and, if it changes the optional conditions, inform the offender of its action and give the offender a copy of the order so endorsed.

(4) All the functions of the court under subsection (3) may be exercised in chambers.

(5) Where an offender who is bound by a probation order is convicted of an offence, including an offence under section 733.1, and

(a) the time within which an appeal may be taken against that conviction has expired and the offender has not taken an appeal,

(b) the offender has taken an appeal against that conviction and the appeal has been dismissed, or

(c) the offender has given written notice to the court that convicted the offender that the offender elects not to appeal the conviction or has abandoned the appeal, as the case may be,

in addition to any punishment that may be imposed for that offence, the court that made the probation order may, on application by the prosecutor, require the offender to appear before it and, after hearing the prosecutor and the offender,

(d) where the probation order was made under paragraph 731(1)(a), revoke the order and impose any sentence that could have been imposed if the passing of sentence had not been suspended, or

(e) make such changes to the optional conditions as the court deems desirable, or extend the period for which the order is to remain in force for such period, not exceeding one year, as the court deems desirable, and the court shall thereupon endorse the probation order accordingly and, if it changes the optional conditions or extends the period for which the order is to remain in force, inform the offender of its action and give the offender a copy of the order so endorsed.

(6) The provisions of Parts XVI and XVIII with respect to compelling the appearance of an accused before a justice apply, with such modifications as the circumstances require, to proceedings under subsections (3) and (5).

733.1(1) An offender who is bound by a probation order and who, without reasonable excuse, fails or refuses to comply with that order is guilty of

(a) an indictable offence and is liable to imprisonment for a term not exceeding two years; or

(b) an offence punishable on summary conviction and is liable to imprisonment for a term not exceeding eighteen months, or to a fine not exceeding two thousand dollars, or both.

III. A TERM NOT EXCEEDING TWO YEARS

A probation order cannot be added to a term of imprisonment that exceeds two years (see s. 731(1)(b)). Over the years, this has proven to be a complicated issue. It has given rise to the following questions: Does this include a sentence arising only from the current proceedings? Does it apply when the offender is serving a term made up of more than one element that exceeds two years in the aggregate? Is the amount of time an accused person spends in pre-trial custody included in the calculation?

R v. Young
(1980), 27 CR (3d) 85 (BCCA)

LAMBERT JA: This is an application for leave to appeal against sentence imposed upon four counts in an indictment following guilty pleas on those four counts.

The four offences occurred on three separate days. Three of the counts related to the offence of buggery, under s. 155 of the *Criminal Code*, RSC 1970, c. C-34, for which the maximum sentence is 14 years.

The other count related to the offence of an indecent assault under s. 156 of the Code. The maximum sentence is 10 years.

• • •

Counsel for the appellant urges us to consider a sentence of two years on the first count of buggery, two years consecutive on the second count of buggery, one year concurrent for the third count of buggery, as well as the two years concurrent for indecent assault, and then to impose, consecutive to the second two year consecutive term for buggery, a term of three years' probation.

Thus at the conclusion of a total of four years' imprisonment there would be imposed three years' probation.

It was urged upon us that a sentence in those terms would be consistent with the provisions of s. 663(1)(b) of the *Criminal Code* and s. 664(2)(b) provides that no probation order shall continue in force for more than three years.

• • •

In my opinion, it is contrary to the intent of the Code and to the intent of Parliament when s. 663(1)(b) was enacted to contemplate imposing a period of probation following consecutive sentences which total more than two years, even if none of those sentences is in itself longer than two years.

• • •

Appeal dismissed.

What if the offender is serving a *remanet* from a previous sentence as a result of the revocation of parole or statutory release? See *R v. Currie* (1982), 27 CR (3d) 118 (Ont. CA), which held that the aggregate includes a *remanet*.

What if the offender receives a probation order in addition to a sentence of less than two years but subsequently receives another sentence that brings the aggregate above the two-year limit? See *R v. Miller* (1987), 36 CCC (3d) 100 (Ont. CA), *R v. Hendrix* (1999), 137 CCC (3d) 445 (Nfld. CA), *R v. Cuthbert* (2004), 191 CCC (3d) 560 (Ont. CJ) and *R v. Amyotee* (2005), 192 CCC (3d) 412 (BCCA), which held that the subsequent sentence renders the probation period illegal.

R v. Goeujon
(2006), 209 CCC (3d) 61 (BCCA)

RYAN JA: [1] The appellant, Paul Kennedy Gerard Goeujon, was convicted of assault and uttering a death threat on December 9, 2005, after a trial before a judge sitting alone. After spending seven and one-half months in pre-sentence custody, the appellant was sentenced to 15 months imprisonment to be followed by a period of probation for 18 months. Mr. Goeujon appeals both the fitness of the term of imprisonment and the legality of the probation order.

• • •

The Legality of the Probation Order

• • •

[26] Thus probation is only available if the term of imprisonment imposed is two years or less.

[27] Section 719(3) provides:

719(3) In determining the sentence to be imposed on a person convicted of an offence, a court may take into account any time spent in custody by the person as a result of the offence.

[28] The appellant says that the probation order is illegal in his case because his total punishment for this offence must be viewed as 30 months incarceration. To reach this conclusion he adds the credit given to him for the time he spent in custody before sentencing to the actual sentence he received—seven and one-half months in prison credited as 15 months plus the 15-month sentence.

[29] The appellant's position turns on whether time spent in pre-sentence custody should be part of the calculation of the term of imprisonment for the purposes of interpreting s. 731(1)(b). The appellant submits that the Supreme Court of Canada's analysis of the effect of pre-sentence custody on the availability of a conditional sentence set out in *R v. Fice*, 2005 SCC 32, 196 CCC (3d) 97, should apply in this case. In other words, that the phrase "imprisonment for a term not exceeding two years" found in s. 731(1)(b) must include a consideration of credit for time spent in pre-sentence custody.

[30] The appellant contends that if probation continues to be available where an offender is effectively sentenced to a term over two years after the calculation of pre-sentence custody, it would contradict the purposes of sections of other parts of the *Criminal Code*. Specifically, the appellant submits that such an approach would render meaningless the interpretation of s. 742.1(a) made by the Supreme Court of Canada in the *Fice* case. I will return to *Fice* presently.

[31] The Crown submits that the probation order imposed in this case is legal according to the plain meaning of s. 731(1)(b). The Crown's position is that the words "sentencing the offender to imprisonment for a term not exceeding two years" refer to the actual sentence imposed by a sentencing judge at the time of sentencing, irrespective of time which may have been served in pre-sentence custody.

[32] The Crown submits that probation orders are available for all types of offences and offenders, provided that the offence does not have a minimum punishment pre-

scribed by law and that the term of imprisonment does not exceed two years. It is clearly possible, the Crown says, that a probation order can in fact follow a penitentiary term. The Crown submits that this defeats the appellant's submission that Parliament did not intend for probation orders to attach to federal terms of imprisonment.

[33] The Crown therefore submits that Parliament did not intend to restrict probation to less serious offences and less serious offenders. Rather, the purpose of probation is rehabilitation. An offender who has committed a serious offence, has spent a significant period of time in pre-trial custody, and may warrant a further period of incarceration can still benefit from a probation order.

[34] Professor Allan Manson in his text, *The Law of Sentencing* (Irwin Law, 2001), suggests that the purpose of the two-year rule in s. 731(1)(b) is this:

> ... The two-year limitation on imprisonment has been subject to extensive judicial interpretation. Perhaps reflecting the Ouimet concern that adding probation onto imprisonment was unsound, courts have interpreted the phrase "for a term not exceeding two years" to render probation illegal when attached to terms which, in the aggregate, add up to more than two years. The intention attributed to Parliament was that the utility of community-based probation was limited to persons who had served terms of no more than two years. Prisoners released from longer sentences would be subject to supervision by federal parole officers. As a result of this analysis, it is the length of incarceration that is important and not how it was constructed.

[35] While conceding that this analysis fails to explain why Parliament set the limit for terms of imprisonment at two years, rather than two years less one day, the Crown supports the intention attributed to Parliament by Professor Manson. I agree. It may be assumed that most offenders sentenced to a combination of imprisonment and probation will serve their custodial sentence in provincial institutions. In the federal system, an offender is on parole until warrant expiry. In the provincial system, offenders who do not apply for or are not granted parole are simply released on their statutory release date, having served two-thirds of their sentence. For such offenders, a probation order will be the only means of supervision in the community.

[36] The issue raised by the appellant was litigated in the Ontario Court of Appeal. In *R v. Fazekas*, [2001] OJ No. 4128 (QL), 51 WCB (2d) 440 (CA), in imposing sentence the trial judge said this at para. 4:

> I am of the view that a penitentiary sentence of 36 months, followed by a probationary term, would be appropriate. Because sir, you have served the equivalent of 24 months, you are sentenced to a further 12 months in custody. This will be followed by a term of probation for three years. ...

[37] Mr. Fazekas argued that three years probation on top of a "sentence of three years" was illegal. The Ontario Court of Appeal rejected the argument saying:

> [5] Mr. Fazekas argues that the three years probation on top of his sentence of three years is illegal. The sentence imposed, however, though awkwardly phrased, was for one year in addition to time served, plus three years probation. The time served was from May 12, 2000 to May 22, 2001, a period of about 12.5 months for which the Trial Judge gave

credit of 24 months. The "time served" is not part of the sentence. The sentence in issue was for twelve months or one year plus three years probation. There is nothing unlawful or illegal about that sentence.

[38] A similar conclusion was reached by the Manitoba Court of Appeal in *R v. Duczminski*, 2003 MBCA 96:

> [2] [The Appellant] argues that the imposition of a probation order to follow a term of imprisonment of two years is illegal because of the time he had spent in pre-trial custody. We find no merit in this submission. The pre-trial custody the accused had spent was taken into account by the sentencing judge in fixing the term of imprisonment. However, the sentence that she imposed does not exceed a term of two years so as to preclude an order for probation pursuant to s. 731(1)(b) of the *Criminal Code*.

[39] The Crown also points to the decision of this court in *R v. Robinson*, [1997] BCJ No. 2829 (QL), 121 CCC (3d) 240 (CA), where an appeal was allowed from a life sentence imposed after the appellant pleaded guilty to manslaughter. The court determined that 12 years was a fit sentence, and gave credit for nine years in pre-sentence custody. Therefore, the remaining time to be served was three years from the date of sentencing. At the appellant's request, the court reduced the custodial sentence to two years so that it could add a three-year probation period and therefore provide a maximum period of supervision following the appellant's release from prison. [at 71]

[40] These cases were decided before Fice. The question raised by this appeal is whether the reasoning in that case should apply to the section in question in the case at bar.

[41] The question in *Fice* was whether pre-sentence custody should affect a sentencing judge's determination of the availability of a conditional sentence. I have reproduced s. 719(3) earlier in these reasons. ...

[42] Mr. Justice Bastarache, writing for the majority in Fice, held that s. 742.1 required a sentencing judge to make a preliminary determination of the appropriate range of available sentencing in determining whether to impose a conditional sentence. The court reasoned that the object of the requirement is to exclude categories of offenders from the conditional sentence regime on the basis of the range of sentence that would apply to them. Thus, it was fitting that the total punishment (pre- and post-sentence custody) imposed would determine whether a conditional sentence was available to a particular offender.

[43] In reaching this conclusion Mr. Justice Bastarache emphasized that the appeal before the court dealt only with the availability of a conditional sentence and the unique concerns that s. 742.1(a) attracts. The effect of pre-sentence custody on other sentencing measures, including a probation order, was specifically not in issue. ...

[44] Recently, the Ontario Court of Appeal in *R v. J.L.*, [2005] OJ No. 2787 (QL), 66 WCB (2d) 54, held that *Fice* ought not to change the manner in which pre-sentence custody is analyzed in relation to s. 731(1)(b) of the Code.

• • •

[47] In my view the analysis in *Fice* is, in any event, distinguishable from the analysis which is applicable in the context of probation orders. The analysis in *Fice* fol-

lows the purposive interpretation given to s. 742.1(a) in *R v. Proulx*, 2000 SCC 5, 140 CCC (3d) 449, and is unique to conditional sentences which serve different objectives than probation orders.

[48] In *Fice*, Mr. Justice Bastarache found that a conditional sentence cannot become available to an offender "who otherwise deserves a penitentiary term" (para. 4), and that Parliament, in enacting the conditional sentence regime, intended only to capture conduct serious enough to attract a sentence of incarceration but not so severe as to warrant a penitentiary term (para. 17). The availability of a conditional sentence is dependent upon the gravity of the offence and the degree of responsibility of the offender. Time spent in pre-sentence custody does not change those factors (para. 24). Therefore, time spent in pre-sentence custody should not function as a mitigating factor that can affect the range of sentence and the availability of a conditional sentence (para. 22).

[49] The availability of a probation order depends on different factors. Probation is not intended to punish the offender so much as to rehabilitate the offender. Regardless of the gravity of the offence and the degree of responsibility of the offender, it may be that a particular offender who has spent time in pre-sentence custody and deserves a sentence of imprisonment of two years may still benefit from the rehabilitative aspects of probation.

[50] Probation orders may also be particularly useful for offenders who have served time in pre-sentence custody. The reason that many judges give double credit for time served in pre-sentence custody is that it is often served in difficult conditions in which rehabilitative programs are not available: see *R v. Rezaie* (1996), 112 CCC (3d) 97 (Ont. CA) at 104. An offender who has served time in pre-sentence custody, without access to programs, would benefit from the imposition of probation upon release, whether such release takes place immediately at the time of sentencing or following a further sentence of imprisonment not exceeding two years.

[51] The present case provides a good example of that point … .

[52] Finally, if probation orders are not available in circumstances like the present case, sentencing judges may find it necessary to impose a longer period of imprisonment, which would be an unfortunate result.

[53] I would not accede to the appellant's argument that time credited for pre-sentence custody ought to be included in determining the duration of a sentence for purposes of s. 731(1).

Appeal dismissed.

IV. WHEN DOES THE PROBATION PERIOD BEGIN?

When probation is part of a suspended sentence, it usually starts immediately. However, if the period of probation follows a term of imprisonment, when does it begin? This is tricky because federal prisoners can be released on parole or statutory release subject to conditions, supervision, and the possibility of re-commitment if revoked. But a provincial prisoner who is released due to earned remission is released free and clear. Before the 1996 amendments, this was a real controversy: see *R v. Constant* (1978), 40 CCC (2d) 329 (Man. CA). Now, s. 732.2(1)(b) distinguishes between the two kinds of confinement and provides that the period probation begins "as soon as the offender is released from prison or, if released from prison on conditional release, at the expiration of the sentence of imprisonment." Parole, whether provincial or federal, and statutory release all qualify as conditional release.

V. OPTIONAL CONDITIONS

What kinds of conditions can be attached to a probation order? Some of the optional conditions are clear; others are vague. Sometimes the vagueness relates to how an order should be structured or monitored. Appellate courts have occasionally stuck out conditions as being too vague: see *R v. Timmins* (2006), 211 CCC (3d) 333 (BCCA) and *R v. Kirton* (2007), 219 CCC (3d) 485 (Man. CA). Vagueness also pervades the kinds of sanctions that may be encompassed. For example, there is a residual subcategory, s. 732.1(3)(h) that is now defined as "such other reasonable conditions as the court considers desirable ... for protecting society and for facilitating the offender's successful reintegration into the community."

In this part, we explore some of the more contentious optional conditions. The following cases, while dealing with the definitions of available conditions as they were worded before 1996, provide insights into the interpretive issues that arise from the optional condition categories. In evaluating the propriety of these conditions in general, and as applied, remember that conditions that are imposed need not be related to the offences that were committed by the offender so long as they are otherwise linked to the needs of the offender: see *R. v. Traverse* (2006), 205 CCC (3d) 33 (Man. CA).

A. Driving Prohibitions

R v. Ziatas
(1973), 13 CCC (2d) 287 (Ont. CA)

MARTIN JA: This is an application for leave to appeal and an appeal by the accused from the sentence imposed upon him by Provincial Judge Foster upon conviction of the accused on his plea of guilty to a charge of assault with intent to resist arrest contrary to s. 246(2)(b) of the *Criminal Code*.

The Provincial Judge imposed a fine of $150 and placed the appellant on probation for a term of one year. One of the conditions of the probation order was that the appellant should not operate a motor vehicle for the period of one year. Counsel for the appellant contended that, since s. 238 [am. 1972, c. 13, s. 18] of the *Criminal Code* expressly empowers a Court that convicts an offender of any of the offences enumerated in the section, to prohibit the offender from driving a motor vehicle for the period specified in the section, and since the offence of which the appellant was convicted is not one of the enumerated offences, the Court had no power to require as a condition of the probation order that the accused not operate a motor vehicle during the period of probation. Without deciding whether or not the Provincial Judge had jurisdiction to impose this condition as a term of the probation order, we are all of the view that he proceeded upon a wrong principle, inasmuch as he imposed this term of the probation order as an additional punishment to be imposed upon the accused, whereas his only power, if he had any jurisdiction to impose the condition under s. 663(2) of the *Criminal Code*, was to impose such reasonable conditions as he considered desirable for securing the good conduct of the accused and for preventing the repetition by him of the same offence or the commission of other offences.

In the circumstances the appeal is allowed and the condition that the accused not operate a motor vehicle during his term of probation is struck out of the probation order and the appeal is allowed to give effect to this variation.

Appeal allowed.

The ruling in *Ziatas* with respect to the residual subcategory has been followed in a number of cases. See *R v. Caja and Billings* (1977), 36 CCC (2d) 401 (Ont. CA); *R v. Lavender* (1981), 59 CCC (2d) 551 (BCCA); and *R v. L.* (1986), 50 CR (3d) 398 (Alta. CA).

B. Community Service

An important term that is often included in probation orders is a provision that the accused person devote a certain amount of time to "community service." Until 1996, there was no specific authorization to impose this type of term. Courts used the residual subcategory as the authorization for community-service orders.

R v. Tanner
(1983), 36 CR (3d) 64 (Man. Prov. Ct.)

ALLEN PROV. J: The information in this case charges that:

> Dennis Nelson Tanner, at the City of Winnipeg (in Manitoba) between the 16th day of December AD 1981 and the 28th day of August in the year of Our Lord one thousand nine hundred and eighty-two, while bound by a probation order made by Judge H. Collerman on the 25th day of June 1981, in Provincial Judges Court (Criminal Division), Public Safety Building, Winnipeg, did unlawfully and wilfully fail to comply with such order to wit: to carry out ninety-six hours of community work free of charge, terms, location and type of work to be arranged by Manitoba Probation Services, and failing to carry out ninety-six hours of community work as arranged by Manitoba Probation Service.

From the representations made to me, I understand, although it is not clearly stated, that the essential ingredients of the offence are admitted for the purpose of my deciding a preliminary question raised by accused's counsel. I do not understand that he is precluded from advancing evidence or argument should the first question raised be decided contrary to submissions.

From the information quoted above, it can be seen that the learned trial judge specified that the accused perform 96 hours of community service work free of charge but left the terms, location, and type of work to be arranged by the Manitoba Probation

Service. This, it is argued, is an unauthorized delegation by the learned trial judge of his judicial function; therefore, the order is void *ab initio*, and there is no basis for the present charge against the accused.

. . .

On the authorities cited herein and referred to by other courts, I believe my opening comment relative to the power to delegate one's judicial function is well founded. Equally, since the decision of the Supreme Court of Canada in *R v. Sterner*, [1982] 1 SCR 173, 64 CCC (2d) 160, 14 Sask. R 79, 40 NR 423, it is established that judges can delegate administrative functions.

The task in each case is to determine whether the delegation is of a judicial or administrative function. In determining that, regard must be had to the object of the legislation under which we act, what we wish to achieve, and the practicalities of the situation. Parliament has not legislated in a vacuum and programs providing for supervised probation, community service, and other means of punishing, rehabilitating, and deterring an accused person were created under a perceived need and after much study and consideration. The purpose of probation, community service and programs of like nature is to avoid, in appropriate cases, the imposition of terms of incarceration on those who, with assistance of whatever type may be necessary, may be rehabilitated and adequately punished without incarceration. The effort is made, through the type of programs described, to solve and alleviate anti-social behaviour, upgrade skills and education, and appraise and treat a variety of problems such as drug abuse, alcoholism and even a lack of social skills. The need for such programs can be, and under our laws must be, discovered by the court, with the assistance of persons and agencies available for that purpose, and it is the court that must prescribe the nature of the program to be followed by an accused person who is placed on probation in order to achieve the desired result. That I see as part of the judicial function.

But I cannot see that the day-to-day supervision of probationers is to be considered part of the judicial function. While as judges we may be able to identify the need for a program, few, if any of us, have the training or experience to oversee such programs on a day-to-day basis; we are dependent more and more on those who are probation officers, representatives of the Alcoholism Foundation, Alcoholics Anonymous, X-Kalay, the Salvation Army, and many other groups dedicated to assisting those who require these skills. It is the workers in these fields who have the necessary knowledge, skill and training to adapt the program of rehabilitation to the needs of the subject. The programs may require revision from time to time during the period of probation to adapt to the progress, or lack of it, by the subject. Efforts at first considered appropriate may have to give way to other methods that prove more appropriate. To have to specify in detail how a particular program should be carried out may be impossible for a judge at the time of sentencing.

At the risk of being over-zealous in making my point, let me give an example. Assume, as is often the case, that the accused is one who requires counselling. To assure that counselling, he is placed on probation with directions to report to the probation officer. Must we specify the time, place, frequency and method of reporting? If we do so, the result could be that the accused does not get the counselling required and the probation officer is unable to fulfil his assigned task properly. In another instance, the accused may respond rapidly and the need for counselling diminishes and eventually disappears well before the time of the expiration of the probation. Should the requirement to report be such that the already busy time of our social workers be utilized unnecessarily? Should the accused be imposed upon to comply with the conditions which, in this case, are no longer necessary or appropriate? The answer to these rhetorical questions is, in my opinion, no. I say this not only because I think it is the only workable answer (need and convenience do not change the law), but because, once the objective is recognized and prescribed by the court, surely the day-to-day application of the court order is administrative. Once a court has ordered, say, counselling, the manner, place, time and frequency of such counselling is surely a manner of carrying out, i.e., administering, the court's order.

This approach is, in my opinion, recognized by the legislation. So far as probation officers are concerned, they are, by virtue of s. 4(1)(a) of the *Manitoba Corrections Act*, CCSM, c. C230, officers of the court. The *Criminal Code* has, at least by implication, recognized probation officers and others as necessary adjuncts of the court: see ss. 662 [re-en. 1972, c. 13, s. 57] and 663(2) of the Code. I repeat, Parliament was not acting in a vacuum but, in providing for probation and conditions of probation, recognized the need of the court for the assistance of those usually more fitted to carry out the administrative part of probation.

I realize that community service is somewhat different from other conditions of probation in that there is an element of punishment involved. It is a program designed to impress upon offenders that they must pay to an extent for their transgressions; it also recognizes that imprisonment is not necessary. The difficulty in a judge dictating the details of such service at the time of sentencing, particularly where the period of probation is lengthy, is mind-boggling. I repeat, difficulty is not the determining factor, but surely, once the need for community service is recognized by the court, the details of the nature of that work and time and place of performance are but administrative details.

· · ·

Under the circumstances, I am of the view that the order of Collerman Prov. J is a valid order.

R v. Richards
(1979), 11 CR (3d) 193 (Ont. CA)

HOWLAND CJO: The Attorney General of Canada applies for leave to appeal and, if leave be granted, appeals from the sentence imposed upon the respondent by Graburn Co. Ct. J on 24th October 1978, following a conviction entered the previous day on the respondent's plea of guilty to the offence of possession of diacetylmorphine (heroin), contrary to s. 3(1) of the *Narcotic Control Act*, RSC 1970, c. N-1. Although initially arraigned on an indictment charging him with the possession of heroin for the purpose of trafficking, the respondent pleaded guilty to the included offence of simple possession of heroin. This plea was accepted by the trial judge, with the concurrence of Crown counsel.

The learned trial judge suspended the passing of sentence and released the respondent on the following statutory and special conditions contained in a probation order to be in force for one year, namely:

(1) to keep the peace and be of good behaviour, and come and receive judgment when called upon;

(2) within the next 24 hours to report to a probation officer;

(3) to continue treatment for heroin addiction with Dr. Stevens at Stevens Psychiatric Centre in New York City and at such other places as she directs when elsewhere than in New York;

(4) to report to the probation officer in Toronto during the week of 7th May 1979 and 24th September 1979 and to file up-to-date reports from the Stevens Psychiatric Centre in New York City and reports from such other psychiatric facilities as Dr. Stevens or the probation officer considers necessary; and

(5) within the first six months of the probation, after making the necessary arrangements through the probation officer and with officials of the Canadian National Institute for the Blind ("CNIB") here in Toronto, either personally or with a group of musicians of choice, to the blind young people associated with the Canadian National Institute for the Blind.

This probation order was subsequently varied by Graburn Co. Ct. J on 23rd April 1979, following an application by counsel for the Crown on 4th April 1979 to vary the probation order so as to postpone the benefit performance originally ordered.

The variation which was made ordered the respondent to report to his probation officer during the week of 23rd April 1979 instead of during the week of 7th May 1979, and further provided for two benefit performances at the Oshawa Civic Centre, Oshawa, instead of the one performance at the CNIB Bayview Auditorium, Toronto.

The facts leading to the charge, so far as material, are these. On 27th February 1977 officers of the Ontario Provincial Police and the RCMP went to the Harbour Castle Hotel in Toronto to execute a warrant for the arrest of Anita Pallenberg, described as the "common law wife" of the respondent. In the course of the search of a bedroom in which the respondent was sleeping the officers found paraphernalia suitable for the administration of heroin. These items contained traces of heroin. The officers also found in the top drawer of a dresser a leather pouch, inside of which was a clear plastic bag containing a white powder; which on analysis proved to be 22 grams of heroin of 32 per cent purity.

The respondent remained asleep during the search, which lasted about half an hour. He was then awakened, arrested and charged with being in possession of heroin for the purpose of trafficking.

The respondent is a musician and is a leading member of the Rolling Stones, a well-known "rock and roll" band. The respondent gave a statement to the police in which he admitted that the heroin was his. He indicated to the police that he had been a heavy user for four years and that he had purchased a large quantity of the drug to satisfy his habit for the five to six weeks that he was going to be in Canada. (It was conceded by the Crown that the heroin was purchased in Canada.) He also told the police that he had tried to "kick" the habit several times, but that he was on tour and did not have time to complete his treatment programmes.

The normal purity of "street heroin" is between 10 and 20 per cent. Using 15 per cent as the average, the 22 grams of heroin seized were said to be equal to 44 grams of "street heroin." An extremely heavy user would use ten capsules a day. The heroin seized was said to have a wholesale value of $2,000 to $3,000. It is conceded, however, that the quantity found in the possession of the respondent is not inconsistent with the amount required by the respondent for his personal consumption during his Canadian tour.

The following facts derived from the submission of counsel, and the reports filed with the consent of both counsel on the proceedings with respect to sentence are not in dispute. The respondent is a British citizen and at the time of the imposition of sentence was 34 years of age. He received his early education at Dartford, Kent. He then attended an art school, where he studied graphic design and while there learned to play the guitar. The group known as the Rolling Stones was formed in 1962, and has been giving performances and making recordings since that time. In 1967 the respondent began to use drugs, and in 1969 he commenced to inject himself with heroin subcutaneously. Counsel for the respondent at trial attributed the respondent's experimentation with drugs to exhaustion following a grueling schedule. Be that as it may, the respondent's use of drugs developed to the point where he was using large amounts of heroin daily. The respondent, prior to his arrest on the present charge, had made several attempts to cure his addiction. His first attempt, early in 1972, was apparently successful, but the treatment did not result in a permanent cure. The respondent also took treatment in Switzerland later in the year 1972. He was convicted in London, England, in November 1973 of the possession of heroin, for which a fine of £50 was imposed. We are informed that the conviction resulted from traces of heroin found on spoons and a syringe, and that the quantity of heroin involved was not substantial. The appellant continued to use heroin, and in 1974 was again treated unsuccessfully in Switzerland.

The respondent, following his arrest on the present charge, again sought treatment, and in the month of May 1977 he came under the care of Dr. Anita Stevens in New York City. Crown counsel at the trial filed two reports from Dr. Stevens, and defence counsel filed a number of reports from her, the latest of which was dated 21st October 1978. The reports disclosed that the respondent was receiving from Dr. Stevens psychiatric treatment for his drug addiction, on a regular basis; further, that he was receiving psychotherapy to assist him in overcoming the underlying reasons for his previous use of drugs; that he had made remarkable progress; and that he was strongly motivated to overcome his addiction. Regular laboratory tests showed that he was free from drugs and, in particular, free from heroin. In her report dated 21st October 1978 Dr. Stevens recommended that the respondent continue to receive psychotherapy without interruption for a further period of 6 to 12 months. Dr. Stevens' assessment and recommendation was supported by a letter from Dr. Lewis R. Wolberg, Clinical Professor of Psychiatry at New York University Medical School.

On the hearing of the appeal, we received additional material, including a post-sentence report dated 12th June 1979, from the respondent's probation officer, to whom Dr. Stevens has been providing periodic reports. The post-sentence report verifies that the respondent has complied with the terms of the probation order with respect to treatment, that he has remained free from drugs and that he has continued to be strongly motivated to rid himself of his previous drug dependency.

The two concerts provided for in the amended probation order were held in April 1979. 2700 blind persons and their escorts attended the concerts and were admitted without charge. Tickets were sold to the general public. The respondent and the supporting musicians received no payment for their services. In addition, the respondent and Mick Jagger, the lead singer of the group, paid their own expenses. The CNIB received a net amount of $39,000 after the payment of all its expenses in connection with the concerts.

• • •

The statistics to which reference has been made do not, of course, disclose the circumstances of the offence or the offender in those cases where a non-custodial sentence was imposed for possession of heroin, and undue weight should not be given to them. The high percentage of cases in which non-custodial sentences were imposed is nonetheless a fact of some significance, which the learned trial judge was entitled to take into account. Whether a non-custodial sentence is an appropriate disposition following a conviction of an addict for simple possession of heroin must of necessity depend on all the circumstances. There can be little doubt that the cure of heroin addiction is, at best, difficult, and that the offender must be strongly motivated to overcome his addiction if there is to be any chance of success. Past experience with respect to the offender may show that the offender is not likely to respond to community-based treatment, or the circumstances may be such as to require the temporary removal of the offender from his environment and to indicate that he can be assisted only in a correctional facility. In those circumstances, a custodial sentence is appropriate.

• • •

In *R v. Shaw* (1977), 36 CRNS 358, this court, although of the view that the trial judge had erred in not imposing a custodial sentence, declined to interfere with the sentence imposed, where the positive rehabilitation program in progress was proving effective, being of the opinion that the public interest would be best served by permitting the sentence imposed upon the respondents to stand.

We wish to make it clear that the appeal was pursued and brought on as expeditiously as the circumstances permitted, and no blame attaches to anyone in that respect. We are nonetheless of the view that at this stage of the proceedings, when the terms of the probation order with respect to treatment have been virtually completed and the prescribed community service has been performed, we ought not to vary the sentence unless we are satisfied that it is so manifestly wrong that we are required in the interest of justice to intervene.

We have not been so satisfied. To impose a custodial sentence now would impose a hardship greatly in excess of that which would have resulted from a custodial sentence in the first instance: see *R v. Bartkow* (1978), 1 CR (3d) S-36 (NSCA): and *R v. Binder*, Ont. CA, 3rd May 1979 (not yet reported).

There are two subsidiary grounds of appeal which may be dealt with quite briefly. The appellant contends that the trial judge erred in suspending the passing of sentence and releasing the respondent on probation, since, in the absence of international arrangement, the terms of the order could not be supervised or enforced. The learned trial judge was of the view that in the special circumstances the terms of the order were capable of enforcement. Even if initially it was an error in principle to make a probation order with respect to a non-resident of Canada—a question which we do not find it necessary to decide—the respondent has voluntarily complied with the terms of the order. Accordingly, we would not give effect to this ground of appeal.

Mr. Scollin also contended that the type of community service directed to be performed was wholly inappropriate—that the giving of a concert by the respondent is not seen as punishment. With respect to the desirability, in general, of imposing a requirement in a probation order that an offender perform community services, we reiterate the views of this court expressed by Dubin JA in *R v. Shaw*, supra. He said at p. 362:

> During the appeal some concern was expressed as to the validity of that term in each probation order which required both of the respondents to perform community services. The trial judge was anxious that both these two young men make amends in a positive way for the damage that they had done, not only to society, but to their own peer groups. In my opinion s. 663(2)(h) of the *Criminal Code* authorizes the imposition of such a term ... .
>
> Not only do I think that the provisions in the probation orders relating to this matter are valid, but in appropriate cases should be more extensively used.

In general, it is appropriate to require an offender to perform community services of the type that he is fitted to perform. In the present case, the service performed by the respondent benefitted substantially the CNIB. In the case of another offender not possessing the advantages of the respondent, a lesser service within the abilities of the offender may count as an equivalent.

Although we are strongly of the view that the probation order should also have contained a term that, in addition to performing the concerts, the respondent should engage in a programme to point out the disastrous consequences that the drug addict faces and actively to discourage the use of drugs, we do not consider it would now be appropriate or practical to impose new terms.

Appeal dismissed.

C. Treatment

Psychiatric treatment as a condition of probation has been controversial, especially since the *Canadian Charter of Rights and Freedoms*, Part I of the *Constitution Act, 1982*, RSC 1985, app. II, no. 44, came into force. Consider the different approaches in the two following decisions.

R v. Rogers
(1990), 61 CCC (3d) 481 (BCCA)

ANDERSON JA: This is an appeal from a sentence imposed on May 22, 1990, by McGivern Prov. Ct. J, wherein he ordered that the appellant be placed on probation for a period of 15 months. The probation order reads, in part, as follows:

WHEREAS on May 22nd, 1990, at Vancouver, BC Donald Rogers, hereinafter called the offender, pleaded guilty to, or was tried under the *Criminal Code* and was convicted or found guilty, as the case may be, upon the charge that

On the 9th day of April, 1990, in the City of Vancouver, Province of British Columbia, did have in his possession a weapon to wit: a knife, for a purpose dangerous to the public peace, contrary to Section 87 of the *Criminal Code* of Canada.

Pursuant to Section 606(4) CCC, with the consent of the prosecutor, the accused pleads not guilty to the offence charged, but guilty to the offence of possession of a concealed weapon, and find the accused not guilty of the offence charged but guilty of the offence of possession of a concealed weapon.

AND WHEREAS on May 22nd, 1990, the Court adjudged that the offender be imprisoned in the Province of British Columbia, for the term of one (1) day, and, in addition thereto, that the said offender comply with the conditions hereinafter prescribed:

Now, therefore, the said offender shall, for the period of fifteen (15) months from the date of expiration of his sentence of imprisonment, comply with the following conditions, namely that the said offender shall keep the peace and be of good behaviour and appear before the Court when required to do so by the court, and, in addition,

> 1. You will report today to a Probation Officer at 275 E Cordova St., Vancouver, BC and then report to the Inter Ministerial Project at 219 Main St., Vancouver, BC. After that you will have to go back to the Inter Ministerial Project Office whenever they tell you to, at least once a month.
>
> 2. *You will, under their direction, seek and take whatever psychiatric assessment or treatment that can be arranged for you, and you shall do that as you are directed by the Inter Ministerial Project Office.*
>
> 3. As directed by the Inter Ministerial Project Office you shall report to the Forensic Psychiatric Outpatient Clinic on West Broadway, Vancouver, BC.
>
> 4. You will not have any knives in your pocket; on your possession in a public place, except while eating in a restaurant.
>
> (Emphasis added.)

On April 9, 1990, the appellant was arrested on a charge of possession of a knife for a purpose dangerous to the public peace.

The circumstances of the offence were described by counsel for the Crown as follows:

> Your Honour, the circumstances here, it was April 9th, 1990, at approximately three twenty in the afternoon. A witness sees the accused cross Hornby and approaches a woman who's standing on the corner. Apparently there's quite a few peoples standing on the corner.
>
> He is holding what appears to be a kitchen knife in his right hand. He is described as poking it, one of the people, one of these women who was standing there. The woman moves. There's no contact. The light changes and people start crossing the street. The accused then picks the knife up, puts it over his head and does really nothing with it. He then puts the knife back into his pocket.

. . .

The appellant appeared in court on April 11, 1990, and was remanded at that time for 30 days in order that a psychiatric assessment be obtained.

...

From the above assessment, the following facts may be gleaned:

(1) The appellant has been suffering from a chronic mental illness, schizophrenia, since 1982 or earlier.

(2) Since his admission to hospital, the appellant has received medication and his mental condition has greatly improved.

(3) Prior to his discharge from hospital, Dr. Levy discussed with the appellant the possibility of a "long acting," intramuscular injection but this was refused.

(4) The appellant has a past history of non-compliance with medication programs and, therefore, his future prognosis is poor.

We were informed by counsel for the appellant that he is now under the care of a private physician and that he is now, by consent, taking medication as prescribed by his physician.

The order made by McGivern Prov. Ct. J was made pursuant to s. 737(2)(h) of the *Criminal Code* reading as follows:

> (h) comply with such other reasonable conditions as the court considers desirable for securing the good conduct of the accused and for preventing a repetition by him of the same offence or the commission of other offences.

Counsel for the appellant submits that, in the circumstances of this case, a probation order compelling an accused person to "seek and take whatever psychiatric assessment or treatment that can be arranged for you" is contrary to s. 7 of the *Canadian Charter of Rights and Freedoms*.

He made reference to several reports of the Law Reform Commission of Canada in his factum as follows:

> The Law Reform Commission of Canada has considered the issue of treatment in relation to the criminal law in a number of publications. As far back as 1975, the Law Reform Commission in its working Paper number 14, "THE CRIMINAL PROCESS AND MENTAL DISORDER" [1975], indicated that probation orders which contained conditions of psychiatric treatment should only be made where the offender consents. See page 45 of the aforesaid report:
>
> > Probation orders with conditions of psychiatric treatment should be made only where: (1) the offender understands the kind of program to be followed, (2) he consents to the program and, (3) the psychiatric or counselling services have agreed to accept the offender for treatment.
>
> See also Working Paper 26, "MEDICAL TREATMENT AND CRIMINAL LAW" [1980], p. 73, where the following recommendations are contained:
>
> > (10) that the right of a competent adult to refuse treatment be specifically recognized by the *Criminal Code*;

(11) that treatment shall not be administered against an individual's refusal, unless there is a finding of incompetence or an exception recognized in law.

He also relied upon the judgment of the Supreme Court of Canada in *Reference re s. 94(2) of Motor Vehicle Act* (1985), 23 CCC (3d) 289.

I agree with the submissions made by counsel for the appellant. In my opinion, a probation order which compels an accused person to take psychiatric treatment or medication is an unreasonable restraint upon the liberty and security of the accused person. It is contrary to the fundamental principles of justice and, save in exceptional circumstances, cannot be saved by s. 1 of the Charter. Exceptional circumstances are not present here.

While, as counsel for the Crown has stated, it is unlikely that an accused person would be subjected to unusual or dangerous medication or treatment, that risk always exists. In my opinion, it is the protection of the public which is the principal support for an order compelling the compulsory taking of treatment or medication. That is insufficient to save the order under s. 1 of the Charter. Other less drastic means are available to accomplish that purpose.

The fact that the probation order in this case is invalid, as being contrary to the Charter, does not solve the problem confronting the court. While the rehabilitation of the appellant is important, the court must consider the risks involved in permitting the appellant to be at liberty on probation. In other cases, where the trial judge finds as a fact that an accused person is suffering from schizophrenia or a like illness and refuses to consent to prescribed treatment or medication, it might very well be that the trial judge would not consider probation. The risk to society might be too great and only incarceration may afford the necessary protection.

I do not think it is possible to say that a particular form of probation order will be appropriate for all cases. The sentence to be imposed on each offender must be based on the general principles of sentencing which include a consideration of the circumstances of the offence and of the offender. The result is that different conditions may be imposed in probation orders depending on the circumstances of each case. To the extent possible, the conditions should be designed to ensure the protection of the public. However, they should not compel an offender to undergo medical treatment including the compulsory taking of medication. It is with those considerations in mind that now consider the conditions numbered one to four in the probation order in the case at bar.

In this case the appellant has a history of non-compliance with prescribed treatment and medication. However, he has now consented to, and is taking, treatment and medication under the care of a private physician. If he continues to take the advice of his physician and takes medication as prescribed, the risk of unlawful behaviour on the part of the appellant will be greatly reduced.

Having regard to the above, I would supplant conditions numbered one to four in the probation order with the following provisions:

1. You will take reasonable steps to maintain yourself in such condition that:

    (a) your chronic schizophrenia will not likely cause you to conduct yourself in a manner dangerous to yourself or anyone else; and

    (b) it is not likely you will commit further offences.

2. You will forthwith report to a Probation Officer at 275 E Cordova St., Vancouver, BC and thereafter, if directed to do so, you will forthwith report to the Inter Ministerial project at 219 Main St., Vancouver, BC.

3. You will thereafter attend as directed from time to time at the Inter Ministerial project for the purpose of receiving such medical counselling and treatment as may be recommended except that you shall not be required to submit to any treatment or medication to which you do not consent.

4. If you do not consent to the form of medical treatment or medication which is prescribed or recommended, you shall forthwith report to your Probation Officer and thereafter report daily to your Probation Officer. If directed to do so by your Probation Officer, you shall report to the Inter Ministerial Project at 219 Main Street, Vancouver, BC for the purpose of being monitored with respect to a possible breach of Condition 1 above.

5. You shall provide your treating physician with a copy of this order and the name, address and telephone number of your Probation Officer. You shall instruct your treating physician that if you fail to take medication as prescribed by him or fail to keep any appointments made with him, he is to advise your Probation Officer immediately of any such failures.

6. Except when eating in a restaurant you will not have any knife in your possession.

Appeal allowed.

For a similar ruling, see *R v. Kieling* (1991), 64 CCC (3d) 124 (Sask. CA), where the court deleted a term of probation that required the offender to "take prescribed medication." The offender had a long history of persistently harassing entertainer Anne Murray and her family.

D. Electronic Monitoring

The use of electronic monitoring technology is sometimes considered as a mechanism to achieve compliance with conditions imposed as part of bail, a probation order or a conditional sentence. It is usually associated with the objective of effecting the "house arrest" of the offender or monitoring compliance with other conditions, such as curfews. In some Canadian jurisdictions, it has become an important aspect of conditional sentences.

    Electronic monitoring has been administered on a small scale in England and in some parts of Canada. See Nellis, "The Electronic Monitoring of Offenders in England and Wales" (1991), 31 *Brit. J Criminology* 165 and Mainprize, "Electronic Monitoring in Corrections: Assessing Cost Effectiveness and the Potential for Widening the Net of Social Control" (1992), 34 *Can. J Criminology* 161.

R v. Erdmann
(1991), 64 CCC (3d) 188 (Sask. CA)

WAKELING JA: The respondent pleaded guilty to two charges of trafficking in *cannabis* resin (hashish), and one charge of possession of hashish for the purpose of trafficking. It is not a case of an isolated incident, but rather a situation where the appellant acknowledges she is a user and has been trafficking for some time but thought it was safe to do so if she restricted her customers to her circle of friends and fellow users. The possession charge did not relate to a relatively trifling quantity, rather, it amounted to one-half pound, for which a price of $2,000 was being considered.

The respondent is 22 years of age and has one child which she has placed with her mother for care and upbringing. She lives common law with a man who is also a user. At the time of the offence, she was employed part time at Sears, working approximately 30 hours per week.

The trial judge felt a sentence of nine months was justified, applying the reasoning of such cases as *R v. McGinn* (1989), 49 CCC (3d) 137, 75 Sask. R 161, 7 WCB (2d) 338, emanating from this court. He, however, concluded that this was a suitable occasion to utilize an electronic monitoring device and therefore ordered a suspended sentence with six months of electronic monitoring and probation for one year.

The principal issue on this appeal was whether the use of an electronic monitoring device was appropriate in this case.

A Crown employee was present in court to answer questions regarding that program and she indicated the electronic monitoring device was being used effectively in a number of cases. When questioned about the criteria which was employed to determine which of the many convicted persons should serve their sentence in this fashion, she responded that it largely depended on the temperamental suitability of the party. In this case, Erdmann was considered a suitable candidate and this had been largely confirmed by reason of the fact she had been successfully monitored for approximately three months.

A program summary was provided and that document described the target group in this way:

> Though a wide range of offenders are eligible for consideration of this sanction, the project's primary emphasis will be on native and female offenders as well as those individuals that normally would receive a sentence of incarceration with probation to follow.
>
> The selection of cases must be done on an individualized basis and will require careful screening of the offenders. In identifying these cases, Corrections will be looking for people that rate at the very high end of the offenders classification system and are clearly candidates for incarceration.

This same issue regarding the use of an electronic monitoring device came before this court fairly recently when on a conviction for dangerous driving the trial judge imposed a sentence of 18 months' probation plus the application of the electronic monitoring program for approximately five months: *R v. Pearman*, delivered November 5, 1990 [since reported 26 MVR (2d) 1; 11 WCB (2d) 430].

In *Pearman*, it was decided that the monitoring device did not provide a suitable penalty and a term of six months should have been imposed. The concern was expressed by the court in the following manner [at 3-4 (MVR)]:

> We note at the outset that the respondent was charged with dangerous driving, a serious offence which resulted in serious injury and damage to the victim. In our opinion, a suspended sentence and imposition of terms under the intensive probation supervision/electronic monitoring program was inappropriate in the circumstances of the case. The sentence failed to take into account the factor of deterrence and public confidence in the administration of justice. This Court recently stated in *R v. Powell* (1989), 19 MVR (2d) 36, 52 CCC (3d) 403, 81 Sask. R 301 [at 43 (MVR)]:
>
> > [I]n a crime of this nature, the factor of deterrence must be given adequate consideration. If the sentence adequately emphasizes community disapproval of such conduct by branding it reprehensible, one can hope that it will have a moral and educative effect on the attitude of the public. Not only will the offender refrain from repeating such conduct, but perhaps some other members of the public will appreciate the seriousness of such conduct.
>
> In our opinion, a sentence of 6 months' imprisonment is the minimum imprisonment that should have been imposed in these circumstances.

We are obviously proceeding through the early stages of the electronic monitoring program. It is impossible to say how effective it may become and the extent of its application. It would be unfortunate for this court to set firm and absolute standards for the application of the program in its developmental stage, but at the same time it is quite appropriate to be somewhat cautious in our approach to its implementation. This is particularly so when others have incurred the penalty of institutional incarceration and no special circumstances have been shown to exist for the application of the program in this case, other than the fact the respondent is a temperamentally suitable candidate.

This court has shown its concern about the harmful social consequences of the drug trade and the need to have special concern for the concept of general deterrence in order that everyone may be aware there is no easy way to experiment with the profits available from the sale of drugs. It is not sufficiently clear that the use of this program, in circumstances such as exist here, will adequately continue that message. This concern is consistent with that expressed in *R v. Pearman*.

In the circumstances, this appeal is allowed. A sentence of nine months would ordinarily have been the minimum we would have imposed, but as a period of three months has already been spent with the program, the sentence is set at six months. The question of equivalency was discussed, and Crown counsel seemed generally to accept that it was reasonable to allow a month for a month, and we see no reason in this case to provide otherwise.

The above represents, in a general way, the oral judgment delivered after the hearing. However, upon further reflection, the panel expresses its concern that if the courts are to play the dominant role in determining when this form of punishment is to be

adopted, as may well be necessary and appropriate, then more help must be provided
to the courts to enable the formulation of appropriate general criteria and the application
of that criteria. A decision as to the suitability of this form of punishment cannot be adequately made without some form of report, such as a pre-sentence report, outlining the
basis upon which the recommendation is being made. Obviously, only a small percentage of those convicted of an offence are offered the opportunity of participating in this
program. That selection must therefore, in fairness, be carefully made and should not
be the result of a haphazard process. On the basis of what was before us, we cannot be
assured of much more than the temperamental suitability of the respondent.

Appeal allowed.

E. Random Drug Testing

The following decision addresses the propriety of random drug testing as a means of enforcing compliance with a probation order. The accused was convicted of breaking and entering
with intent to commit sexual assault. A psychological assessment of the accused revealed
that drug use was a problem and recommended that the accused be subject to random urinalysis. While the Crown did not request such a condition, and the accused did not consent,
the trial judge included a condition that required the accused to submit to urinalysis, blood
test, or breathalyser test on the demand of a police officer or a probation officer. The condition
specified that a positive reading would constitute a breach of the condition. The Court of Appeal ((2004), 192 CCC (3d) 176 (BCCA)) deleted the part of the condition that provided that
a positive test amounted to a breach of probation. A majority of the Court found that there was
legal authority for the testing, but that it violated s. 8 of the Charter in the circumstances.

R v. Shoker
(2006), 212 CCC (3d) 417 (SCC)

CHARRON J (McLachlin CJC, Binnie, Fish, and Abella JJ, concurring): [1] This appeal raises the question whether a sentencing judge may require a probationer to provide, on demand by the probation officer, samples of breath, urine or blood for analysis
to determine compliance with an abstention term of the probation order. ...

[2] The Crown appeals to this Court and seeks to reinstate the enforcement condition. At issue is whether ss. 732.1(3)(c) and 732.1(3)(h) of the *Criminal Code*, RSC
1985, c. C-46, authorize the enforcement condition and, if permissible, whether the
condition must be predicated by reasonable and probable grounds to suspect a violation
of an abstention condition.

[3] For the reasons that follow, I would dismiss the appeal. A sentencing judge has
a broad jurisdiction in determining appropriate conditions of probation. However, there
is no authority under the *Criminal Code* to authorize a search and seizure of bodily
substances as part of a probation order. In light of the fact that the impugned condition
must be quashed for lack of jurisdiction, it is neither necessary nor advisable for this
Court to answer the constitutional question. It is Parliament's role to determine appro-

priate standards and safeguards governing the collection of bodily samples for enforcement purposes.

The Facts and Proceedings Below

. . .

[6] The trial judge sentenced Mr. Shoker to 20 months' incarceration to be followed by a two-year period of probation subject to a number of conditions. The Crown did not ask that the order of probation include any condition for treatment or testing of bodily substances and the offender did not consent to those conditions. The following two conditions were later challenged by Mr. Shoker on his appeal before the British Columbia Court of Appeal:

> CONDITION 7: You shall attend for such treatment and counselling as directed by the Probation Officer and successfully complete any such programs to which you are referred.

. . .

> CONDITION 9: Abstain absolutely from the consumption and possession of alcohol and non prescription narcotics and to submit to a urinalysis, blood test or breathalyzer test upon the demand/request of a Peace Officer or Probation Officer to determine compliance with this condition. Any positive reading will be a breach of this condition.

. . .

Analysis

. . .

Probation has traditionally been viewed as a rehabilitative sentencing tool: *R v. Proulx*, [2000] 1 SCR 61, 2000 SCC 5, at paras. 31-33. The probationer remains free to live in the community but certain restraints on his freedom are imposed for the purpose of facilitating his rehabilitation and protecting society. An offender who is bound by a probation order and who, without reasonable excuse, fails or refuses to comply with that order is guilty of an offence under s. 733.1 punishable by up to two years' imprisonment.

. . .

[13] Before discussing the issue that arises in this case, I wish to make a few general comments about the power to impose optional conditions under s. 732.1(3). The residual power under s. 732.1(3)(h) speaks of "other reasonable conditions" imposed "for protecting society and for facilitating the offender's successful reintegration into the community." Such language is instructive, not only in respect of conditions crafted under this residual power, but in respect of the optional conditions listed under s. 732.1(3): before a condition can be imposed, it must be "reasonable" in the circumstances and must be ordered for the purpose of protecting society and facilitating the particular offender's successful reintegration into the community. Reasonable conditions will generally be linked to the particular offence but need not be. What is required is a nexus between the offender, the protection of the community and his reintegration into the community. See, for example, *R v. Kootenay* (2000), 150 CCC (3d) 311 (Alta. CA), and *R v. Traverse* (2006), 205 CCC (3d) 33 (Man. CA), where appellate courts have upheld

conditions requiring abstinence from alcohol or drugs even though these played no part in the commission of the offence for which the offender was sentenced. On the other hand, conditions of probation imposed to punish rather than rehabilitate the offender have been struck out: *R v. Ziatas* (1973), 13 CCC (2d) 287 (Ont. CA); *R v. Caja* (1977), 36 CCC (2d) 401 (Ont. CA); *R v. Lavender* (1981), 59 CCC (2d) 551 (BCCA); *R v. L.* (1986), 50 C.R. (3d) 398 (Alta. CA). In contrast, punitive conditions may be imposed pursuant to s. 742.3(2)(f) as part of a conditional sentence: *Proulx*, at para. 34.

[14] The residual power to craft individualized conditions of probation is very broad. It constitutes an important sentencing tool. The purpose and principles of sentencing set out in ss. 718 to 718.2 of the *Criminal Code* make it clear that sentencing is an individualized process that must take into account both the circumstances of the offence and of the offender. It would be impossible for Parliament to spell out every possible condition of probation that can meet these sentence objectives. The sentencing judge is well placed to craft conditions that are tailored to the particular offender to assist in his rehabilitation and protect society. However, the residual power to impose individualized conditions is not unlimited. The sentencing judge cannot impose conditions that would contravene federal or provincial legislation or the Charter. Further, inasmuch as the wording of the residual provision can inform the sentencing judge's exercise of discretion in imposing one of the listed optional conditions as I have described, the listed conditions in turn can assist in interpreting the scope of "other reasonable conditions" that can be crafted under s. 732.1(3)(h). As we shall see, none of the listed conditions is aimed at facilitating the investigation of suspected breaches of probation. I will come back to this point later.

[15] The underlying purpose for imposing conditions of probation also serves to define the role of the probation officer. The intervener the Attorney General of Canada aptly describes the probation officer's functions in its factum (at para. 21):

> It is in the nature of a probation officer's duties to act as an officer of the court, to assist the probationer in his rehabilitation, and to monitor compliance with the conditions of probation imposed by the sentencing court. The supervising probation officer simultaneously performs two distinct functions, rehabilitation and enforcement. The twin goals of probation—rehabilitation of the offender and protection of society—require and justify supervision in order to ensure that the probationer in fact observes his conditions. This supervised control is a restraint on the probationer's freedom.
>
> The supervisory function of the probation officer in ensuring compliance with the conditions and the manner in which this function must be performed becomes of central importance in this case when we consider the full implications of enforcing an abstention order by requiring bodily samples. The determinative question is whether the supervisory power to demand samples of bodily substances for enforcement purposes may be conferred upon the probation officer by the court as a discretionary exercise of discretion or whether it must be authorized by statute.

The Impugned Condition

[16] For ease of reference, I repeat the terms of Condition 9:

> CONDITION 9: Abstain absolutely from the consumption and possession of alcohol and non prescription narcotics and to submit to a urinalysis, blood test or breathalyzer test upon the demand/request of a Peace Officer or Probation Officer to determine compliance with this condition. Any positive reading will be a breach of this condition.

[17] As indicated earlier, the sentencing judge did not have the jurisdiction to pre-determine that any positive reading would constitute a breach of probation. Therefore, the last sentence of Condition 9 was properly deleted by the Court of Appeal. The first part of the condition is also not in issue. The abstention condition is expressly authorized under s. 732.1(3)(c) and, given Mr. Shoker's particular circumstances, it is entirely reasonable to impose this condition to facilitate his rehabilitation and to protect society. The prohibition against the possession of alcohol and non-prescription drugs, imposed pursuant to the s. 732.1(3)(h) residual power, is also not in dispute. What remains at issue is the requirement that bodily samples be provided on demand.

[18] The impugned condition is challenged essentially on Charter grounds. In reviewing a sentencing judge's exercise of discretion on Charter grounds, an appellate court should first consider whether the sentencing judge acted within his statutory jurisdiction. If a sentence is illegal on the basis that it is unauthorized under the governing legislation, it must be struck down and the constitutional issue does not arise. I will therefore consider whether the requirement to provide bodily samples as a condition of probation falls within the scope of s. 732.1.

Requiring Bodily Samples and Section 732.1 of the Criminal Code

[19] The Crown submits that s. 732.1(3)(c) abstention conditions are highly desirable for the rehabilitation of the offender and the protection of the public and that the sentencing objectives of such abstention terms can only be achieved if there is also an effective mechanism to enforce them. Therefore, the Crown argues that ss. 732.1(3)(c) and 732.1(3)(h), read together, authorize the imposition of random sampling of an offender's bodily substances to ensure compliance with the abstention condition. Mr. Shoker argues that the power to impose enforcement terms to the abstention condition neither flows implicitly from s. 732.1(3)(c) nor does it fall within the scope of s. 732.1(3)(h) "reasonable conditions." If Parliament had intended to authorize the seizure of bodily samples, he argues, it would have expressly so stated as it has done in other existing legislative schemes.

[20] I will deal firstly with s.732.1(3)(c). With respect to Hall JA's opinion to the contrary, the jurisdiction to impose enforcement terms cannot simply flow from the power to impose an abstention condition. The effect of including a s. 732.1(3)(c) abstention condition in a probation order is to define a criminal offence, the commission of which is punishable under s. 733.1. Enforcement powers are not implicit from the simple creation of an offence. For example, it cannot reasonably be contended that the prohibition against impaired driving under s. 253 implicitly includes the enforcement scheme for demanding bodily samples contained in ss. 254 to 258. Yet, in essence, that

is the argument here. The Crown submits that the enforcement scheme should be implied as necessary to give effect to a s. 732.1(3)(c) abstention condition. I do not accept this argument. Breach of probation is a criminal offence under the *Criminal Code* and, as such, it is subject to the usual investigatory techniques and manner of proof as any other offence. Hence, the probationer who is found consuming alcohol with his friends in a drinking establishment can be prosecuted based on the evidence of witnesses to the event. Likewise, the probationer who exhibits signs of alcohol or drug impairment can be prosecuted and the offence can be proven by testimonial evidence much in the same way as an offence for impaired driving. The power to demand bodily samples and the resulting analyses would undoubtedly assist in the enforcement of a s. 732.1(3)(c) condition, but it cannot on that basis simply be implied.

[21] The authority to impose enforcement terms, if any, must be found rather in the residual clause. As indicated earlier, s. 732.1(3)(h) gives the sentencing judge a broad power to craft other reasonable conditions designed to protect society and facilitate the offender's successful reintegration into the community. Hall JA was of the view that the authority could not be found under s. 732.1(3)(h) because Parliament has specifically addressed alcohol and drugs in s. 732.1(3)(c). The fact that Parliament has specifically addressed alcohol and drugs under s. 732.1(3)(c)—and also in ss. 732.1(3)(g.1) and 732.1(3)(g.2)—is certainly a relevant factor but, in my respectful view, it does not preclude the imposition of "other" alcohol and drug-related "reasonable conditions" under the residual clause. Any number of additional conditions aimed at ensuring that the probationer comply with the abstention condition can be imposed. Indeed, the prescription against the possession of alcohol and drug found in Condition 9 is one example. Similarly, a sentencing judge could prescribe that the offender not enter any premises where alcohol is sold or served; that he not associate with his favourite drinking buddies; or that he obey a curfew. All these conditions could be imposed to ensure better compliance with the abstention condition and thereby facilitate the offender's rehabilitation and protect society. Absent peculiar circumstances, it could not seriously be contended that any such condition would be unreasonable. LeBel J, in his concurring reasons, expressed concerns that a narrow interpretation of the residual clause would cast doubt on a number of useful monitoring methods, more particularly the use of electronic monitoring. The legality of electronic monitoring under s. 732.1(3)(h) is not before us and, hence, this Court is not deciding this issue. We are concerned here only with the compelled seizure of bodily samples as an enforcement mechanism. It is also noteworthy that in each case referred to by LeBel J, the probationer's consent was required for participation in the Saskatchewan electronic monitoring program. Further, the Saskatchewan Court of Appeal in *R v. McLeod* (1993), 81 CCC (3d) 83, at p. 99, also made it clear that "the constitutionality of this form of sanction was not argued or considered during argument."

[22] On the face of it, s. 732.1(3)(h) therefore appears wide enough to permit enforcement terms such as the one imposed in this case since, it is argued, submitting to testing would also ensure better compliance with the abstention condition. However, the residual provision must be read in context. Since it provides for "other" reasonable conditions, the listed conditions under ss. 732.1(3)(a) to 732.1(3)(g.2) can assist in de-

lineating the scope of the residual provision. It is noteworthy that the fulfilment of any of the listed conditions can have no incriminating consequence for the probationer. In addition, when the condition may pose a risk, such as participating in a treatment program, the consent of the offender is required before the condition can be imposed. Section 732.1(3)(h) speaks of "other reasonable conditions." It is reasonable to infer that additional conditions imposed under the residual power would be of the same kind as the listed conditions. However, conditions intended to facilitate the gathering of evidence for enforcement purposes do not simply monitor the probationer's behaviour and, as such, are of a different kind and, because of their potential effect, absent the probationer's consent to such conditions, raise constitutional concerns. For example, could Mr. Shoker be compelled, as a condition of his probation, to make his home available for inspection on demand to better monitor the prescription against the possession of alcohol or drugs? Such a condition in effect would subject him to a different standard than that provided by Parliament for the issuance of a search warrant. In my view, it could not reasonably be argued that the sentencing judge would have the jurisdiction to override this scheme under the authority of the open-ended language of s. 732.1(3)(h). It would be up to Parliament, if it saw fit, to enact any such scheme.

[23] The sentencing judge's jurisdiction can be no greater in respect of the seizure of bodily samples. The seizure of bodily samples is highly intrusive and, as this Court has often reaffirmed, it is subject to stringent standards and safeguards to meet constitutional requirements. Significantly, in *R v. Borden*, [1994] 3 SCR 145, this Court held that where there is no statutory authorization for the seizure of bodily samples, consent must be obtained if the seizure is to be lawful. In *R v. Stillman*, [1997] 1 SCR 607, Cory J, speaking for the majority, held that the seizure of bodily samples such as hair, buccal swabs and dental impressions, was not authorized by the common law power to search incident to arrest. The principle was again reaffirmed in *R v. Golden*, [2001] 3 SCR 679, 2001 SCC 83. Again here, it is my view that such statutory authorization cannot be read in the general language of s. 732.1(3)(h). In the various circumstances where Parliament has chosen to authorize the collection of bodily samples, it has not only used clear language; it has also included in the legislation, or through regulations, a number of standards and safeguards: see for example, the collection of DNA samples for investigative purposes or, on conviction, for inclusion in the DNA databank (ss. 487.04 to 487.091 of the *Criminal Code*); the collection of breath and blood samples during the investigation of impaired driving offences (ss. 253 to 261 of the *Criminal Code*); and the collection of urine samples from federal inmates and parolees (ss. 54 to 57 of the *Corrections and Conditional Release Act*, SC 1992, c. 20, and ss. 60 to 72 of the *Corrections and Conditional Release Regulations*, SOR/92-620).

• • •

[25] The establishment of these standards and safeguards cannot be left to the discretion of the sentencing judge in individual cases. There is no question that a probationer has a lowered expectation of privacy. However, it is up to Parliament, not the courts, to balance the probationers' Charter rights as against society's interest in effectively monitoring their conduct. Since the purpose of s. 8 is preventative, the following principle in *Hunter v. Southam Inc.*, [1984] 2 SCR 145, at p. 169, is particularly apposite here:

While the courts are guardians of the Constitution and of individuals' rights under it, it is the legislature's responsibility to enact legislation that embodies appropriate safeguards to comply with the Constitution's requirements. It should not fall to the courts to fill in the details that will render legislative lacunae constitutional.

In this case, the Crown argues that reasonable and probable grounds are not required for the search and seizure of bodily substances from probationers and that the seizure of blood samples is also reasonable. Hall JA disagreed. He would have deleted the requirement to provide blood samples as too intrusive and conditioned the requirement to provide urine and breath samples upon the establishment of reasonable and probable grounds. Those are precisely the kinds of policy decisions for Parliament to make having regard to the limitations contained in the Charter. Parliament has specifically addressed the issue of alcohol and intoxicating substances in ss. 732.1(3)(c), 732.1(3)(g.1) and 732.1(3)(g.2) but it has not provided for a scheme for the collection of bodily samples as it has done in respect of parolees. Such a scheme cannot be judicially enacted on the ground that the court may find it desirable in an individual case. In addition to the constitutional concerns raised by the collection of bodily samples, the establishment of such a scheme requires the expenditure of resources and usually the cooperation of the provinces. This reality is exemplified in this case where the funding for urinalysis has been discontinued in British Columbia rendering the probation condition moot. This is yet another reason why the matter is one for Parliament.

[26] For these reasons, I would conclude that there is no statutory authority for requiring Mr. Shoker to submit bodily samples. In the absence of a legislative scheme authorizing the seizure of bodily samples, the enforcement of abstention conditions must be done in accordance with existing investigatory tools. The majority of the Court of Appeal was therefore correct in deleting that part of Condition 9 following the words "non prescription narcotics." I would dismiss the appeal.

LeBEL J (Bastarache J, concurring): [27] I have read the reasons of my colleague Charron J Although I agree with her that the appeal should be dismissed, I reach this result on a different basis. In my opinion, there is statutory authority for the kind of order made by the sentencing judge. But the terms of the order were open to review under s. 8 of the *Canadian Charter of Rights and Freedoms*. As they did not meet the requirements of s. 8, the appeal should fail.

• • •

[36] With respect for those who hold other views, under very well-established rules of statutory interpretation, the *Criminal Code* grants the sentencing judge the authority to include monitoring procedures in probation orders. To hold otherwise might well cause unforeseen and undesirable effects, as the inflexibility of such an interpretative approach would likely require Parliament to attempt to foresee a wide range of individual situations and to address them in minute detail. A drafting technique such as this would hardly be consistent with the canons of sound legal drafting, even if it were feasible.

[37] Moreover, a narrow interpretation of the residual clause would cast doubt on a number of useful monitoring methods, which sentencing judges appear to be resorting to with increasing frequency. For example, it might prevent the use of electronic moni-

toring, which allows probation officers or public authorities to make sure that conditions relating to house arrest or curfews are complied with. I note that a number of judges have found such conditions to be valid:

> The conclusion is that section 732.1(3)(h) allows orders which restrict a defendant's lifestyle, such as curfews, orders that he or she not frequent specified places, or associate with specified persons, or orders that a defendant be confined on electronic monitoring.
>
> • • •
>
> The terms of probation can control the defendant's lifestyle. For example, a defendant might be ... ordered to wear an electronic monitoring device ... .
>
> • • •
>
> Thus, curfews, house arrest (with or without electronic monitoring), bed checks ... etc., can all be appropriate "other conditions." It does not matter whether one sees them as rehabilitative measures, control measures, or punishment. What counts is not the label but an intent that the condition should further public protection or the acceptance of the defendant in the community, and some reasonable grounds for belief that it will have a tendency to effect those purposes.

(T.W. Ferris, *Sentencing: Practical Approaches* (2005), at pp. 79, 116 and 216–17)

Ferris reports that the courts in the following cases held that electronic monitoring is lawful under s. 732.1(3)(h) : *R v. Carlson* (1996), 141 Sask. R 168 (CA); *R v. Curtis* (1996), 144 Sask. R 156 (CA); *R v. McLeod* (1992), 109 Sask. R 8 (CA).

[38] The range of possible conditions is broad. The purpose of such conditions is often to control aspects of the lifestyle of an accused to ensure that the goals of probation—protection of society and reintegration into the community—are achieved.

[39] We should not assume that such a discretion would be abused by sentencing judges or exercised in an unconstitutional manner in the absence of a detailed statutory framework. In another context—a case concerning an exercise of discretion by an administrative authority—this Court asserted that it should not rely on assumptions of prospective breaches of the Charter:

> I do not think there is any constitutional rule that requires Parliament to deal with Customs' treatment of constitutionally protected expressive material by legislation (as the appellants contend) rather than by way of regulation (as Parliament contemplated in s. 164(1)(j)) or even by ministerial directive or departmental practice. Parliament is entitled to proceed on the basis that its enactments "will be applied constitutionally" by the public service.
>
> • • •
>
> [I]t is in the nature of government work that the power of the state is exercised and the Charter rights of the citizen may therefore be engaged. While there is evidence of actual abuse here, there is the potential for abuse in many areas, and a rule requiring Parliament to enact in each case special procedures for the protection of Charter rights would be unnecessarily rigid.

(*Little Sisters Book and Art Emporium v. Canada (Minister of Justice)*, [2000] 2 SCR 1120, 2000 SCC 69, at paras. 71 and 137)

[40] Any challenge in the instant case should have related to the reasonableness of the order under s. 8 of the Charter. The authority to impose the monitoring conditions exists. It remains to be seen whether the conditions meet the standards of the Charter (see Ruby, at para. 10.63).

[41] Before I move on to some brief comments on the application of s. 8 in the context of the case at bar, I must add that I agree with Charron J that the part of the order that would, in essence, turn a positive test into a breach of the conditions set out in the order is contrary to the principles of criminal law. Guilt must be proved in the usual manner, that is, beyond a reasonable doubt, and the accused is entitled to the protection of the law of criminal evidence and criminal procedure.

Application of Section 8

[42] Section 8 raises difficulties in respect of parts of the order. I agree that the part compelling the accused to undergo blood tests would be far too intrusive and would breach s. 8 absent a statutory framework consistent with the standards of the Charter.

[43] Although it may very well be a more efficient way to monitor compliance, random drug testing at the probation officer's discretion could become highly arbitrary. Courts would have difficulty defining a proper framework to supplement the silence of the Code. This is a situation where Parliament would be in a better position to address the issue. Its solution would then be open to review by the courts under s. 8 and s. 1 of the Charter.

[44] For these reasons, I agree with my colleague that the appeal should be dismissed.

Appeal dismissed.

F. Banishment

R v. Rowe
(2006), 212 CCC (3d) 254 (Ont. CA)

SHARPE JA: [1] The appellant was convicted of one count of criminal harassment of his former common-law partner contrary to s. 264(2)(b) of the *Criminal Code*. This was his third offence involving the same victim. He was sentenced to thirty days concurrent to an existing sentence. He was also sentenced to three years probation, also concurrent with an existing probation order. The sentencing judge imposed the following probation condition: "Forthwith or in any event within two weeks of release leave the province of Ontario immediately."

[2] The appellant appeals both conviction and sentence. I see no merit in the conviction appeal. In my view, the reasons of the trial judge provide an adequate explanation of the basis for rejecting the appellant's evidence and for entering a conviction.

[3] The appellant submits that the trial judge erred in law by imposing a term of probation that amounts to banishment. In his reasons for sentence, the sentencing judge stated that he did not consider this "to be an injudicious exile" because the appellant

had stated that he wanted to end his relationship with the victim and that upon release he intended to leave the jurisdiction and return to the Maritimes. The sentencing judge added that this was a serious offence and that the appellant's "continuation within a community such as Napanee/Kingston area, in Ontario, will cause [the victim and her children] to be constantly in fear of his presence." The sentencing judge added that it would be open to the appellant to apply to vary the condition if he received employment in some other part of Ontario.

[4] The appellant submits that banishment from Ontario cannot be justified as a condition of the probation order under s. 732.1(3) (h) … .

[5] As the *Criminal Code* specifies that conditions of probation should facilitate "the offender's successful reintegration into the community," banishment remains the exception rather than the rule. It has been said on more than one occasion that banishment orders "should not be encouraged": see *R v. Malboeuf* (1982), 68 CCC (2d) 544 (Sask. CA) at 547; *R v. Williams*, [1997] BCJ No. 2101 (QL) at para. 9, 36 WCB (2d) 79 (BCCA). As a member of the Manitoba Court of Appeal, Dickson JA frowned on the practice of banishment in *R v. Fuller*, [1969] 3 CCC 348 at 351:

> In Canada communities are interdependent and relations between them should be marked by mutual respect and understanding. A practice whereby one community seeks to rid itself of undesirables by foisting them off on other communities violates this basic concept of consideration for the rights of others and should not be tolerated.

[6] On the other hand, orders banishing an offender from a specific community have been made against estranged spouses with a view to protecting the victim or to assisting with the offender's rehabilitation: see e.g. *R v. Stack*, [1998] BCJ No. 1492 (QL), 39 WCB (2d) 79 (BCCA); *R v. Peyton*, [1996] N.J. No. 120 (QL), 30 WCB (2d) 561 (Nfld. SC).

[7] Plainly, the larger the ambit of the banishment, the more difficult the order will be to justify. In *R v. Brooks*, [2005] OJ No. 105 (QL), this court upheld a probation term excluding the appellant from Muskoka, but, at para. 1, the court stated that it did so "given the appellant's avowed intention to leave that area as a step in his rehabilitative process." Banishment from an entire province is an extreme measure that could be justified only in exceptional circumstances, even in cases of domestic violence. The only case I have been able to uncover that upholds banishment from a province is *R v. Banks*, [1991] BCJ No. 424 (QL), 12 WCB (2d) 279, where the British Columbia Court of Appeal upheld such an order specifically on the ground that the appellant had proposed and consented to the condition. On the other hand, in a case similar to the one at bar, *R v. Stulac* (1983), 63 N.S.R. (2d) 357, at para. 5, the Nova Scotia Court of Appeal struck down a condition requiring an offender who had committed an offence against his domestic partner to leave the province for the term of his probation as "unnecessary to accomplish the purpose of keeping the appellant away from the victim."

[8] In my view, the probation term requiring the appellant to leave Ontario upon his release from prison cannot be justified as a reasonable measure for the protection of society. Moreover, banishment from the province far exceeds what is required to protect the victim. I note that the offence in the present case involved communications by telephone and mail. Banishment to another province will not effectively protect the victim

from repetitions of that conduct and less drastic restrictions will protect the victim from other forms of harassment. Banishment from the province would be contrary to the second factor mentioned in s. 732.1(3)(h), "facilitating the offender's successful reintegration into the community." As neither of the factors specified in s. 732.1(3)(h) are present, the term cannot be justified as a reasonable condition and must be set aside.

[9] As this issue can be decided on the wording of s. 732.1(3)(h), it is not necessary for me to consider whether the order also constituted a violation of the appellant's mobility rights under s. 6(2) of the *Canadian Charter of Rights and Freedoms* and I leave that question for another day.

. . .

Conviction appeal dismissed; sentence appeal allowed.

While the court analyzed the propriety of the banishment condition solely on the basis of s. 732.1(3)(h) of the *Criminal Code*, are there other provisions that might be applicable in the circumstances? For further discussion of this type of probationary condition, see Allan Manson, *Sentencing*, above, at 234-39.

VI. BREACH OF PROBATION

Some attention has been paid to the meaning of breaching the peace for the purposes of a probation order. In *R v. Grey* (1993), 19 CR (4th) 363 (Ont. Prov. Div.), it was held that a failure to keep the peace required at least an apprehended breach of municipal, provincial, or federal law and not some lesser standard of disruption. This was also the view of the Newfoundland Court of Appeal in *R v. D.R.* (1999), 138 CCC (3d) 405. In *R v. Greco* (2001), 159 CCC (3d) 146 (Ont. CA), the court upheld a ruling that an offender who breaches the peace abroad can still be tried for breach of probation in Canada. The court rejected the suggestion that keeping the peace was restricted to the Queen's peace in Canada. For comparison of procedures on breach of probation and breach of a conditional sentence, see chapter 12.

When probation accompanies a suspended sentence, theoretically it is the passing of sentence that is suspended. Accordingly, s. 732.2(5) of the Code provides a framework for dealing with a prisoner who, while bound by a probation order, is convicted of another offence, including the offence of non-compliance with a probation order. This can include imposing "any sentence that could have been imposed if the passing of sentence had not been suspended." This procedure is rarely used in most jurisdictions. It is also skeletal in the sense that it is triggered "on application of the prosecutor." Fairness requires more.

R v. Tuckey
(1977), 34 CCC (2d) 572 (Ont. CA)

DUBIN JA: On June 26, 1974, the appellant was given a suspended sentence and placed on probation for a period of three years by His Honour Judge Street, after pleading guilty to a charge of theft. On February 12, 1976, while in custody with respect to other matters, he was brought before the trial Judge. He was given no notice as to the nature of the proceedings which were to be held on that day.

. . .

Although the present *Criminal Code* does not require the formalities of an information and is silent as to procedure, I am satisfied that the basic principles of natural justice must prevail; one of which principles relevant here is that no man shall be condemned unless he has been given prior notice of the allegations against him and a fair opportunity to make full answer and defence.

In a proceeding under s. 664(4), although there is no longer a requirement for an information on oath, the minimum requirement surely must be that the accused before being brought before the tribunal should be given reasonable notice in writing of the Crown's intention to take such proceedings, which notice should clearly articulate the nature of the proceedings, the grounds upon which the Crown intends to rely in support of its application, the nature of the order sought, and the hearing date. Section 664(5) provides for the procedure which may be followed in bringing the accused before the Court.

In the instant case no such notice was given. The appellant had no opportunity to defend himself. Section 664(4) gives the Court that made the probation order a broad discretion as to the appropriate order to be made on an application brought pursuant to that section. The inquiry is not limited to proof of the violation of any condition in the probation order. It follows that the trial Judge had no right in the circumstances of this case to refuse the appellant his request for an adjournment to obtain counsel. It is to be noted that the appellant's ultimate acquiescence that the proceedings should continue was given *in terrorem*.

. . .

The appellant had pleaded guilty to a charge of theft. He had a prior criminal record, but the trial Judge originally thought it appropriate to suspend the passing of sentence and make an order for three years' probation. The appellant breached his probation, and an application under s. 664(4) was in order. By his conduct the appellant had forfeited his right to leniency. The function of the trial Judge was then to impose a sentence proportionate to the offence which the appellant had committed. The sentence of 30 months was not proportionate to that offence, even when it was imposed upon a person who was not entitled to leniency.

Appeal allowed.

NOTE

The revocation of a suspended sentence discussed in *Tuckey* is now found in s. 732.2(5). This revocation and re-sentencing process, while available, is rare. The usual response in cases of probation breach or new offences is to commence a prosecution under s. 733.1. This is a hybrid offence, which, on indictment, can lead to a sentence of up to two years, or a maximum of 18 months on summary conviction.

CHAPTER TEN

Monetary Sanctions: Fines and Restitution

I. INTRODUCTION

In this chapter, we consider the use of those forms of intermediate sanctions that involve orders to pay money. A fine is a sanction that uses a monetary burden as a punitive measure. Fines are paid to the state. A fine can be imposed on its own or in conjunction with other sanctions. Although the imposition of a fine raises important procedural issues, it also raises fundamental questions about quantum. The amount of the monetary burden imposed depends on the financial resources and income-earning abilities of the offender.

Restitution refers to a monetary order intended to compensate for certain kinds of loss occasioned by the offence. These amounts are paid to the victims. Restitution orders are typically imposed in addition to other sanctions. As with the imposition of fines, the courts are often concerned with ensuring that any restitution order made does not exceed the offender's financial capabilities.

In reviewing the cases and materials below, consider the different penological aims of these two sanctions. In determining whether either of these sanctions should be imposed, and the amount that is appropriate, have the courts properly distinguished between fines and restitution orders? Do ss. 718 to 718.2 of the *Criminal Code*, RSC 1985, c. C-46, as amended, lend any assistance to this analysis?

II. THE FINE

A. The Public Attitude to Fines

Before examining the relevant statutory provisions, it will be useful to consider how the Canadian public views fines as a sanction. It appears that most Canadians do not believe that a monetary penalty is "punishment."

A. Doob and V. Marinos, "Reconceptualizing Punishment:
Understanding the Limitations on the Use of Intermediate Sanctions"
(1995), 2 *University of Chicago Law School Roundtable* 413 (footnotes omitted)

The Limits on the Use of the Fine: A Case Study of the
Limits on Interchangeability

Canada makes heavy use of fines. In fact, fines are the most heavily used disposition in Canadian Criminal Courts. The Canadian Sentencing Commission ... recommended increased use of fines and suggested that a day or unit fine system be developed. Interestingly, however, the Canadian Sentencing Commission never addressed itself to the purposes that fines might or might not be able to serve at sentencing. In particular, it did not explore directly the limits on the use of intermediate punishments generally or the fine in particular. ... [It] saw all punishments as more or less qualitatively similar. This view of the simplicity of punishments was consistent with some very specific Canadian data on the community service order that had been carried out a few years earlier.

In a national public opinion poll, Canadian adults were asked what they thought the most appropriate sentence was for a first-time offender convicted of breaking and entering a private home and stealing property worth $250. They were given various traditional choices: probation, fines, imprisonment, or some combination. Twenty-nine percent chose imprisonment. When these respondents were asked whether instead of imprisonment, they would favor a community service order, almost everyone (90 percent) indicated they would favor it at least sometimes. Forty-one percent would prefer the community service order in all or most cases. An additional 36 percent would want it for "some" cases, with 14 percent favoring it "only in very rare cases."

We and others interpreted these findings to mean that Canadians, in general, support the use of intermediate punishments instead of imprisonment. Perhaps we were partially correct. However, it may simply be wrong that one can automatically substitute any convenient intermediate punishment such as a fine or community service for imprisonment when looking for a way to avoid using prison. Even if true, presumably there are limits: the size of the penalty has to be appropriate, and of course, ... the penalty must be imposed, and not just pronounced.

Some data recently collected by one of the authors of this Article suggest that the world is not so simple. In this study, a heterogeneous sample of people in Toronto answered a series of questions about fines. A number of conceptually separate sub-studies were embedded in the survey questionnaire. First, respondents were asked to think about a sentence handed down for a minor shoplifting charge. The sentence was described, for different groups of respondents, as being either a fine of two hundred dollars or four hundred dollars, or a prison sentence of four or eight days. The respondents viewed imprisonment as considerably more effective than fines in "expressing society's disapproval for the harm that was caused." At least as interesting is that the size of the penalty (within the rather constrained limits used in this experiment) did not make any difference in the perceived denunciatory value of the penalty. However, for both fines and imprisonment, those who had the sentence described to them as involving the higher penalty rated this penalty as being more severe. The results, then, do not appear to be a product of simple differences in perceived severity; if they had been, the results of the denunciatory value of the punishment would be parallel to those of the severity of the punishment.

In the experiment, harsher penalties were seen as being more severe, but imprisonment was seen as having a greater denunciatory value than fines. There appears to be something "special" about imprisonment that fines do not possess. Nevertheless, most of the respondents favored the use of a fine as a punishment for the offense. About 19 percent of the respondents saw a fine or imprisonment as being equally appropriate; about two-thirds of those who differentiated between fines and imprisonment favored the fine. Although the two types of penalties have different denunciatory values in the eyes of the respondents, denunciation cannot be too important, since respondents favor the use of the punishment that is not as able to "express society's disapproval for the harm that was caused."

Respondents were additionally asked whether they thought that "first time offenders who have committed the following offenses [should be given] a fine instead of imprisonment." If they thought that a fine was appropriate, they were to indicate the dollar value of the fine that they would recommend. Respondents could set the fine, then, at any amount they thought appropriate. In terms of severity, the sky was the limit.

The data ... demonstrate the limited acceptability of the fine. Even when respondents could set a fine of any size, they were generally unwilling to substitute a fine for imprisonment for minor violent offenses. They were, however, willing to suggest a fine as a substitute for imprisonment for most property offenses, even when the value of the property taken is relatively high. Imprisonment can, of course, be used to incapacitate an offender. Hence it is theoretically possible that respondents may have preferred imprisonment for those convicted of violent offenses in order to accomplish this goal. It is unlikely, however, that in the case of "touching a woman in a sexual manner without consent" incapacitation would be seen as an important goal.

There is a final piece of evidence showing that fines had a meaning different from imprisonment. Respondents answered a series of questions in which they were asked to imagine that a particular sentence of imprisonment (expressed in months) was appropriate. They were asked whether they would find a fine of so many months of take-home income as an appropriate substitute. Half of the respondents were told what the cost of imprisonment would be. The critical issue here was whether respondents were affected in their decision by having the cost of imprisonment made salient. It turns out, once again, that the results were offense-specific. For the theft that was described, but not for minor assaults, mentioning the cost of imprisonment led the respondent to favor a fine. Despite being presented with the cost of imprisonment, fines were still viewed as being more appropriate for minor property offenses rather than minor instances of violence.

B. Criminal Code, Sections 734 to 737

The following sections of the *Criminal Code* are concerned with the applicability of the fine. They incorporate substantial amendments made to the sentencing provisions in 1996. Although s. 734, the main section relating to fines, is quite straightforward, the provisions become complex in their response to defaults after an offender has been ordered to pay a fine.

734(1) Subject to subsection (2), a court that convicts a person, other than an organization, of an offence may fine the offender by making an order under section 734.1

(a) if the punishment for the offence does not include a minimum term of imprisonment, in addition to or in lieu of any other sanction that the court is authorized to impose; or

(b) if the punishment for the offence includes a minimum term of imprisonment, in addition to any other sanction that the court is required or authorized to impose.

(2) Except when the punishment for an offence includes a minimum fine or a fine is imposed in lieu of a forfeiture order, a court may fine an offender under this section only if the court is satisfied that the offender is able to pay the fine or discharge it under section 736.

(3) For the purposes of this section and sections 734.1 to 737, a person is in default of payment of a fine if the fine has not been paid in full by the time set out in the order made under section 734.1.

(4) Where an offender is fined under this section, a term of imprisonment, determined in accordance with subsection (5), shall be deemed to be imposed in default of payment of the fine.

(5) The length, in days, of the term of imprisonment referred to in subsection (4) is the lesser of

(a) a fraction, rounded down to the nearest whole number, of which

(i) the numerator is the unpaid amount of the fine plus the costs and charges of committing and conveying the defaulter to prison, calculated in accordance with regulations made under subsection (7), and

(ii) the denominator is equal to eight times the provincial minimum hourly wage, at the time of default, in the province in which the fine was imposed, and

(b) the maximum term of imprisonment, expressed in days, that the court could itself impose on conviction.

(6) All or any part of a fine imposed under this section may be taken out of moneys found in the possession of the offender at the time of the arrest of the offender if the court making the order, on being satisfied that ownership of or right to possession of those moneys is not disputed by claimants other than the offender, so directs.

(7) The lieutenant governor in council of a province may make regulations respecting the calculation of the costs and charges referred to in subparagraph (5)(a)(i) and in paragraph 734.8(1)(b).

(8) This section and sections 734.1 to 734.8 and 736 apply to a fine imposed under any Act of Parliament, except that subsections (4) and (5) do not apply if the term of imprisonment in default of payment of the fine provided for in that Act or regulations is

(a) calculated by a different method; or

(b) specified, either as a minimum or a maximum.

734.1 A court that fines an offender under section 734 shall do so by making an order that clearly sets out

(a) the amount of the fine;

(b) the manner in which the fine is to be paid;

(c) the time or times by which the fine, or any portion thereof, must be paid; and

(d) such other terms respecting the payment of the fine as the court deems appropriate.

734.2 A court that makes an order under section 734.1 shall

 (a) cause to be given to the offender

  (i) a copy of the order,

  (ii) an explanation of the substance of sections 734 to 734.8 and 736,

  (iii) an explanation of available programs referred to in section 736 and of the procedure for applying for admission to such programs, and

  (iv) an explanation of the procedure for applying under section 734.3 for a change in the terms of the order; and

 (b) take reasonable measures to ensure that the offender understands the order and the explanations given to the offender under paragraph (a).

734.3 A court that makes an order under section 734.1, or a person designated either by name or by title of office by that court, may, on application by or on behalf of the offender, subject to any rules made by the court under section 482 or 482.1, change any term of the order except the amount of the fine, and any reference in this section and sections 734, 734.1, 734.2 and 734.6 to an order shall be read as including a reference to the order as changed under this section.

. . .

734.5 If an offender is in default of payment of a fine,

 (a) where the proceeds of the fine belong to Her Majesty in right of a province by virtue of subsection 734.4(1), the person responsible, by or under an Act of the legislature of the province, for issuing, renewing or suspending a licence, permit or other similar instrument in relation to the offender may refuse to issue or renew or may suspend the licence, permit or other instrument until the fine is paid in full, proof of which lies on the offender; or

 (b) where the proceeds of the fine belong to Her Majesty in right of Canada by virtue of subsection 734.4(2), the person responsible, by or under an Act of Parliament, for issuing or renewing a licence, permit or other similar instrument in relation to the offender may refuse to issue or renew the licence, permit or other instrument until the fine is paid in full, proof of which lies on the offender.

734.6(1) Where

 (a) an offender is in default of payment of a fine, or

 (b) a forfeiture imposed by law is not paid as required by the order imposing it,

then, in addition to any other method provided by law for recovering the fine or forfeiture,

 (c) the Attorney General of the province to whom the proceeds of the fine or forfeiture belong, or

 (d) the Attorney General of Canada, where the proceeds of the fine or forfeiture belong to Her Majesty in right of Canada,

may, by filing the order, enter as a judgment the amount of the fine or forfeiture, and costs, if any, in any civil court in Canada that has jurisdiction to enter a judgment for that amount.

(2) An order that is entered as a judgment under this section is enforceable in the same manner as if it were a judgment obtained by the Attorney General of the province or the Attorney General of Canada, as the case may be, in civil proceedings.

734.7(1) Where time has been allowed for payment of a fine, the court shall not issue a warrant of committal in default of payment of the fine

(a) until the expiration of the time allowed for payment of the fine in full; and

(b) unless the court is satisfied

(i) that the mechanisms provided by sections 734.5 and 734.6 are not appropriate in the circumstances, or

(ii) that the offender has, without reasonable excuse, refused to pay the fine or discharge it under section 736.

(2) Where no time has been allowed for payment of a fine and a warrant committing the offender to prison for default of payment of the fine is issued, the court shall state in the warrant the reason for immediate committal.

(2.1) The period of imprisonment in default of payment of the fine shall be specified in a warrant of committal referred to in subsection (1) or (2).

• • •

(4) The imprisonment of an offender for default of payment of a fine terminates the operation of sections 734.5 and 734.6 in relation to that fine.

• • •

735(1) An organization that is convicted of an offence is liable, in lieu of any imprisonment that is prescribed as punishment for that offence, to be fined in an amount, except where otherwise provided by law,

(a) that is in the discretion of the court, where the offence is an indictable offence; or

(b) not exceeding one hundred thousand dollars, where the offence is a summary conviction offence.

(1.1) A court that imposes a fine under subsection (1) or under any other Act of Parliament shall make an order that clearly sets out

(a) the amount of the fine;

(b) the manner in which the fine is to be paid;

(c) the time or times by which the fine, or any portion of it, must be paid; and

(d) such other terms respecting the payment of the fine that the court deems appropriate.

(2) Section 734.6 applies, with any modifications that are required, when an organization fails to pay the fine in accordance with the terms of the order.

736(1) An offender who is fined under section 734 may, whether or not the offender is serving a term of imprisonment imposed in default of payment of the fine, discharge the fine in whole or in part by earning credits for work performed during a period not greater than two years in a program established for that purpose by the lieutenant governor in council

(a) of the province in which the fine was imposed, or

(b) of the province in which the offender resides, where an appropriate agreement is in effect between the government of that province and the government of the province in which the fine was imposed,

if the offender is admissible to such a program.

(2) A program referred to in subsection (1) shall determine the rate at which credits are earned and may provide for the manner of crediting any amounts earned against the fine and any other matters necessary for or incidental to carrying out the program.

(3) Credits earned for work performed as provided by subsection (1) shall, for the purposes of this Act, be deemed to be payment in respect of a fine.

(4) Where, by virtue of subsection 734.4(2), the proceeds of a fine belong to Her Majesty in right of Canada, an offender may discharge the fine in whole or in part in a fine option program of a province pursuant to subsection (1), where an appropriate agreement is in effect between the government of the province and the Government of Canada.

737(1) Subject to subsection (5), an offender who is convicted or discharged under section 730 of an offence under this Act or the *Controlled Drugs and Substances Act* shall pay a victim surcharge, in addition to any other punishment imposed on the offender.

(2) Subject to subsection (3), the amount of the victim surcharge in respect of an offence is

    (a) 15 per cent of any fine that is imposed on the offender for the offence; or

    (b) if no fine is imposed on the offender for the offence,

        (i) $50 in the case of an offence punishable by summary conviction, and

        (ii) $100 in the case of an offence punishable by indictment.

(3) The court may order an offender to pay a victim surcharge in an amount exceeding that set out in subsection (2) if the court considers it appropriate in the circumstances and is satisfied that the offender is able to pay the higher amount.

(4) The victim surcharge imposed in respect of an offence is payable at the time at which the fine imposed for the offence is payable, and when no fine is imposed, within the time established by the lieutenant governor in council of the province in which the surcharge is imposed for payment of any such surcharge

(5) When the offender establishes to the satisfaction of the court that undue hardship to the offender or the dependants of the offender would result from payment of the victim surcharge, the court may, on application of the offender, make an order exempting the offender from the application of subsection (1).

(6) When the court makes an order under subsection (5), the court shall state its reasons in the record of the proceedings.

(7) A victim surcharge imposed under subsection (1) shall be applied for the purposes of providing such assistance to victims of offences as the lieutenant governor in council of the province in which the surcharge is imposed may direct from time to time.

(8) The court shall cause to be given to the offender a written notice setting out

    (a) the amount of the victim surcharge;

    (b) the manner in which the victim surcharge is to be paid;

    (c) the time by which the victim surcharge must be paid; and

    (d) the procedure for applying for a change in any terms referred to in paragraphs (b) and (c) in accordance with section 734.3.

(9) Subsections 734(3) to (7) and sections 734.3, 734.5, 734.7 and 734.8 apply, with any modifications that the circumstances require, in respect of a victim surcharge imposed under subsection (1) and, in particular,

    (a) a reference in any of those provisions to "fine," other than in subsection 734.8(5), must be read as if it were a reference to a "victim surcharge"; and

    (b) the notice provided under subsection (8) is deemed to be an order made under section 734.1.

(10) For greater certainty, the program referred to in section 736 for the discharge of a fine may not be used in respect of a victim surcharge.

C. The 1996 Amendments to the Fine Provisions

The new statutory provisions have addressed a number of situations that presented problems in the past. One anachronism required that a fine could be imposed for a sentence punishable by more than five years' imprisonment *only* if it was imposed *in addition to* a term of imprisonment. To satisfy this peculiar requirement, the courts were forced to impose ludicrous one-day prison sentences. This charade saw the offender enter into custody, only to be released moments later. Now, s. 734(1) authorizes the use of a fine for any offence, either in addition to or in lieu of another punishment.

Another controversial issue was whether courts had to inquire into an offender's means to pay before imposing a fine. In *R v. Snider* (1977), 37 CCC (2d) 189 (Ont. CA), Martin JA concluded that an inquiry was mandatory, holding that a sentencing judge "should only impose a fine that is within the offender's ability to pay, bearing in mind of course, the possibility that he may extend the time for payment." This approach is now codified in s. 734(2). The importance of considering the financial means of the offender is apparent in the light of enforcement provisions. Fines that are beyond the means of an offender may turn into *de facto* prison terms due to the enforcement mechanism of imprisonment in default. It is therefore critical that, at the "front end" of the process, when the fine is actually imposed, it does not exceed the means of the offender. Even small fines may be beyond the means of some people.

Until 1996, ordering imprisonment in default of payment of a fine was discretionary but such orders were commonly made and large numbers of Canadians were incarcerated for non-payment of fines. The extent of such imprisonment raised the anachronistic spectre of "debtor's prison." Yet, surely incarceration should be a response to the offender's criminal conduct, not to his or her financial status.

The 1996 amendments dramatically changed the mechanism for dealing with fine defaults. First, s. 734(5) provides a formula for calculating the extent of imprisonment in default that, pursuant to s. 734(4), is "deemed to be imposed." Does this mean that a judge has no discretion to refuse to add default time? Second, pursuant to s. 734.7(1), a court cannot issue a warrant for committal unless it is satisfied that the alternative collection steps provided for in the Code are not appropriate or the offender has, "without reasonable excuse," refused to pay the fine or participate in a fine option program. Do these sections allow an offender who simply cannot afford to pay a fine to be imprisoned for default of payment?

In *R v. Wu*, the Supreme Court of Canada considered these issues in the context of deciding whether a conditional sentence could be imposed on an impecunious offender in default of payment of a mandatory minimum fine. We will consider conditional sentences in detail in chapter 12, Conditional Sentence of Imprisonment. For now, we focus on the court's reasons for rejecting the use of a conditional sentence in such circumstances and its comments on the process that must be followed before a court can order an offender imprisoned for default of payment of a fine.

R v. Wu
[2003] 3 SCR 530

BINNIE J: [1] In this appeal we are asked to consider whether a conditional sentence was validly imposed on the respondent offender for possession of contraband cigarettes. The offender might otherwise have been sent to jail for 30 days for non-payment of a mandatory $9,600 fine. In the trial judge's view, jail was not appropriate for this offender. On the other hand, the offender simply had no means to pay the fine. The trial judge thought a conditional sentence to be served by the offender in his home offered a way to avoid jail. I agree with the trial judge's initial conclusion that this was not an appropriate case for jail. I disagree with his sentencing solution. The *Criminal Code*, RSC 1985, c. C-46, properly interpreted, offered the sentencing judge a range of alternative solutions for this offender but a conditional sentence was not amongst them.

[2] Debtors' prison for impoverished people is a Dickensian concept that in civilized countries has largely been abolished. Imprisonment for civil debt was abolished in Ontario by the end of the 19th century. In its 1996 sentencing reforms, Parliament decreed that jail should be reserved for those whose conduct deserves to put them there. Here, the trial judge thought a fit sentence would be a suspended sentence with probation, but this was not possible under the Act. Yet debtors' prison "in the community," which is what a conditional sentence amounts to, is repugnant in the case of an individual who is undeserving of jail yet who simply cannot pay.

[3] ... [T]he purpose of imposing imprisonment in default of payment is to give serious encouragement to offenders with the means to pay a fine to make payment. Genuine inability to pay a fine is not a proper basis for imprisonment. A conditional sentence is a form of imprisonment. Therefore, a conditional sentence is not an appropriate sentence to impose on an offender simply because he or she has no means to pay a fine. Nothing in the Code authorises a conditional sentence to be used for collection purposes. Unless, in the terms of s. 734.7(1), the Crown can establish that a defaulter has "without reasonable excuse, refused to pay," a warrant of committal should not be issued.

[4] The conditions precedent to the imposition of a conditional sentence were accordingly not met. The sentencing judge commented that "hard cases make bad law and this is a hard case." In my view, with respect, it also made bad law. I would allow the appeal.

I. Facts

[5] The respondent, Yu Wu, was convicted of possession of 300 cartons of contraband cigarettes. The *Excise Act*, RSC 1985, c. E-14, s. 240(1.1)(a)(i), carried a minimum penalty of $0.16 per cigarette, which amounted to $9,600. ...

. . .

III. Analysis

[16] The principles of sentencing include Parliament's direction that "an offender should not be deprived of liberty, if less restrictive sanctions may be appropriate in the circumstances," and "all available sanctions *other than imprisonment* that are reasonable in the circumstances should be considered for all offenders" (s. 718.2(d) and (e) of the Code (emphasis added)).

[17] Applying these principles, the trial judge concluded very firmly that the respondent should not go to jail for what was seen as a relatively minor role in this cigarette smuggling operation. The respondent did not bring the goods across the border. He had no previous record for such an offence. He was no danger to the community. He was the sole support for his teenage daughter. Yet, in default of payment of a mandatory minimum $9,600 fine, which the judge believed the respondent had no ability to pay, he felt obliged to consider a significant period of incarceration. ... The judge found he retained a discretion [as to the length of the default period] and would have sentenced the respondent to 30 days in jail in default of payment were a conditional sentence not an available option.

[The statutory formula in s. 734(5) of the Code for calculating default periods of imprisonment does not apply to the *Excise Act*. Under that formula, the period of default would have been 174 days.]

[18] That said, the trial judge concluded that a conditional sentence *was* available ... . [The trial judge therefore fined the accused $9,600 without time to pay and in default of payment immediately sentenced the accused to a conditional sentence of 75 days to be served in the community.]

• • •

[19] ... [T]he Crown argues that the trial judge made an error of law in concluding that a conditional sentence was an available option. I agree.

[20] The Crown has a very practical interest in the subject matter of this appeal. Imprisonment terminates the Crown's power to pursue civil enforcement remedies to collect the money (s. 734.7(4) of the Code). Some individuals with savings in the bank might prefer spending 75 days under house arrest rather than paying $9,600. In this case, however, the evidence is that the respondent's poverty left him with no choice in the matter.

A. The Mandatory Minimum Fine

[21] Parliament is quite specific about the range of penalties in s. 240 of the *Excise Act*:

240(1) Subject to subsections (2) and (3), *every person who sells or offers for sale or has in the person's possession any manufactured tobacco* or cigars, whether manufactured in or imported into Canada, not put up in packages and stamped with tobacco stamps or cigar stamps in accordance with this Act and the ministerial regulations

• • •

(b) is guilty of an offence punishable on summary conviction and liable to

(i) a fine of not less than the amount determined under subsection (1.1) and not more than the lesser of $500,000 and the amount determined under subsection (1.2), or

(ii) both the fine described in subparagraph (i) and imprisonment for a term not exceeding two years.

[Emphasis added.]

[22] The trial judge could, in a proper case, have concluded that a fit sentence would include both the mandatory minimum fine *and* a period of imprisonment. He emphatically decided that imprisonment was not a fit punishment. Indeed, as stated, his preference would have been to impose no more than a suspended sentence with probation. Yet in *Proulx* [[2000] 1 SCR 611, 40 CCC (3d) 449] itself, Lamer CJ stated, at para. 55:

At one end of the range, Parliament denied the possibility of a conditional sentence for offenders who should receive a penitentiary term. At the other end, Parliament intended to ensure that offenders who were entitled to a more lenient community measure—*such as a suspended sentence with probation*—did *not* receive a conditional sentence, a harsher sanction in this legislative scheme. [Emphasis added.]

[23] A mandatory minimum fine of $9,600 imposed irrespective of the offender's means to pay is a legislated exception to the usual sentencing principles. Even before the 1996 sentencing reforms, the correct rule was that a fine should be assessed having regard to "the offender's ability to pay" (*R v. Snider* (1977), 37 CCC (2d) 189 (Ont. CA), at p. 190). It was quite open to Parliament to impose a minimum fine, but Parliament's amendments did not require that inability to pay should necessarily land the offender in jail. Indeed, the 1996 amendments show that Parliament did not intend to send the impoverished to jail by reason only of their inability to pay.

B. Availability of Conditional Sentences

. . .

[24] The conditional sentencing regime [which was added by the 1996 sentencing reforms] is dealt with in s. 742.1 of the Code which provides as follows:

742.1 Where a person is convicted of an offence, except an offence that is punishable by a minimum term of imprisonment, and the court

(a) imposes a sentence of imprisonment of less than two years, and

(b) is satisfied that serving the sentence in the community would not endanger the safety of the community and would be consistent with the fundamental purpose and principles of sentencing set out in sections 718 to 718.2,

the court may, for the purpose of supervising the offender's behaviour in the community, *order that the offender serve the sentence in the community*, subject to the offender's complying with the conditions of a conditional sentence order made under section 742.3.

[25] In *Proulx, supra*, it was held that the requirement that the court impose "a sentence of imprisonment of less than two years" was intended to identify the type of offenders who could be entitled to a conditional sentence (para. 55). Specifically, Parliament

did not intend conditional sentences to be "probation under a different name" (para. 28). A conditional sentence is a sentence of imprisonment, albeit the sentence is served in the community. It is imprisonment without incarceration. Only when the sentencing judge has rejected other sentencing options, such as a conditional discharge, a suspended sentence, probation or a fine, and has concluded that a term of imprisonment of less than two years is required by the gravity of the offence and the degree of responsibility of the offender, does a conditional sentence arise for consideration. At that point, the question is where the term of imprisonment is to be served, in a penal institution or, under punitive conditions, in the community. "It is this punitive aspect that distinguishes the conditional sentence from probation" (*Proulx*, *supra*, at para. 22).

[26] The trial judge's explicit finding that this was a proper case for a suspended sentence and probation, and that imprisonment was *not* warranted, puts this case outside the scope of a conditional sentence. As stated in *Proulx*, at para. 37: "Sentencing judges should always be mindful of the fact that conditional sentences are only to be imposed on offenders who would otherwise have been sent to jail" for the offence that gave rise to the conviction.

[27] The statutory conditions precedent to a conditional sentence were not met in two important respects:

(i)   The trial judge, with the best of intentions, stood the *Proulx* reasoning on its head. He was searching for a mechanism to deal with an offence that in his view did *not* warrant imprisonment at all. He thought justice would be served by keeping the respondent, if at all possible, *out* of jail entirely. But the conditional sentencing regime is predicated on a finding in a particular case that jail for less than two years would be a fit sentence. The effect of the trial judge's approach would be to widen the net of the conditional sentencing regime to imprison in their homes offenders under punitive conditions purely on the basis of their inability to pay a fine. Net widening is repugnant to the conditional sentence regime: *Proulx*, *supra*, at para. 56. What is more, if the punitive conditions are breached, the offender would face the prospect of serving the balance of the sentence in an institution without possibility of parole (*Proulx*, at paras. 42-44), thereby adding further to the high rates of incarceration that the 1996 sentencing reforms were designed to alleviate.

(ii) Conditional sentences are presented in s. 742.1 of the Code as a sentencing option, if the conditions precedent are met, for the *original* offence, as Doherty JA emphasized in the present case. The distinction between sentencing provisions and enforcement of sentences is of long standing: *Regimbald v. Chong Chow* (1925), 38 Que. KB 440, at p. 445. Section 240 of the *Excise Act* permits the sentencing judge to send an offender to jail on summary conviction for up to two years. The trial judge rejected jail as a fit punishment for this offence. Jail only entered his calculation as a default provision for non-payment. As such, jail was triggered by the default, not the offence. No default, no jail. The decision of the judge to collapse the sentencing hearing into a default of payment hearing was done for administrative convenience, apparently, but it did not eliminate the fact that legally there was a shifting of gears from sentence to default to consideration of the appropriate sentence for default to committal. The conditional sentence is a creature of statute and nowhere in s. 742.1 or elsewhere in the Code is it suggested that conditional sentences are available to enforce unpaid fines.

C. The Trial Judge's Dilemma

[28] The trial judge's dilemma was that he was required by the *Excise Act* to impose a *minimum* fine of $9,600, rising to a *maximum* of $14,400 based on a mechanical formula applied to the quantity of contraband cigarettes found in the offender's possession. The trial judge did not dispute the logic of the minimum mandatory fine because in his view contraband is a serious problem in the community. His concern was the perceived inevitability of incarceration that would arise from enforcement action consequent on the respondent's inability to pay.

[29] The error in the trial judge's approach, with respect, was his conclusion that, in the case of this respondent, the only alternative to a conditional sentence was actual jail time.

[30] As a matter of law, there was nothing inevitable about incarceration in the event the respondent was simply unable to pay the $9,600 fine by reason of his poverty.

D. No Time Given for Payment

[31] As stated, the trial judge gave the respondent no time to pay. This was in accordance with a request from the defence, which sought to lay the basis for a conditional sentence. But it was an error. If it is clear that the offender does not have the means to pay immediately, he or she should be given time to pay: see *R v. Andrews*, [1974] 2 WWR 481 (BCSC), and *R v. Brooks*, [1988] NSJ No. 94 (QL) (CA). The time should be what is reasonable in all the circumstances: *R v. Beaton* (1984), 49 Nfld. & PEIR 15 (PEICA), and *R v. Tessier* (1957), 21 WWR 331 (Man. Co. Ct.). In *Attorney General of Canada v. Radigan* (1976), 33 CRNS 358, the Quebec Court of Appeal allowed the offender to pay a fine of $5,000 through semi-annual instalments of $625. The courts have considerable flexibility to respond to the particular facts of an offender's situation. It is wrong to assume, as was done in this case, that the circumstances of the offender at the date of the sentencing will necessarily continue into the future.

[32] Here, the trial judge issued a committal order forthwith. The Code provides that "[w]here no time has been allowed for payment of a fine and a warrant committing the offender to prison for default of payment of the fine is issued, the court shall state in the warrant the reason for immediate committal" (s. 734.7(2)). This language suggests that only in exceptional circumstances that call for judicial explanation should an immediate committal order be made. Here there were no exceptional circumstances. The reason given was simply that the respondent was on welfare and lacked the ability to pay.

[33] An offender's inability to pay is precisely the reason why time is allowed, not a reason why it should be altogether denied: *R v. Natrall* (1972), 9 CCC (2d) 390 (BCCA), at p. 397; *R v. Zink* (1992), 13 BCAC 241. It is true that the fine could not have been paid immediately, and perhaps never in full, but the mandatory minimum fine

scheme imposed by Parliament was effectively nullified by immediately shifting the penalty from the respondent's financial interest to his liberty interest. Parliament clearly intended that an economic punishment be imposed for an economic offence. The Crown in its factum says that tobacco smuggling results in an estimated $1 billion loss in tax revenue per year. As noted, committal of an offender for default of payment terminated the operation of all other enforcement mechanisms to collect the fine (s. 734.7(4)). It is often difficult to predict with certainty whether an offender will in future acquire the means to pay the fine, whether through his or her own labour, or perhaps a windfall.

E. Imprisonment for Debt

[34] The trial judge of course put his finger on a serious problem. Debtors' prison, a dreadful institution excoriated by Charles Dickens in *Little Dorrit*, is no longer with us. But according to the most recent report from Statistics Canada, 17 percent of all people in custody in provincial or territorial institutions in 2000-2001 were jailed for default on unpaid fines, i.e., at least one of the causes for their committal arose from a fine default: see Canadian Centre for Justice Statistics, *Adult Correctional Services in Canada, 2000-2001* (2002), at Table 7. The numbers are fairly steady, if in slight decline, from 20 percent in 1998-1999 to 19 percent in 1999-2000.

[35] A similar picture was presented by the National Council of Welfare in its report *Justice and the Poor* (2000), at p. 76. The Council says that in 1989-1990, fine default "played a major role" in the imprisonment of women, especially of Aboriginal women in the Prairie provinces. At the time, 47 percent of female prisoners in Saskatchewan were admitted for fine default. On a provincial basis, the Council noted of the Quebec system, at pp. 76-77, for example:

> A 1994 Quebec survey found that 35 percent of the imprisoned defaulters had been fined for offences under the Criminal Code or other federal criminal laws (average fine of $262 or, in case of default, average of 26 days in prison), 10 percent for both federal and provincial offences (average $1,366 or 50 days), and 55 percent for violations of provincial laws (average $342 or 13 days) or municipal bylaws (average $116 or 8 days). The vast majority (65 percent) of the fines had been issued for driving/traffic offences, mostly under provincial laws (45 percent). The rest of the fines were for thefts and other property offences under the Criminal Code (5 percent), violations of drug laws and other federal statutes (3 percent), assaults and other offences against the person (2 percent), illegal hunting, poaching and other violations of provincial laws (2 percent), failure to appear in court and other Criminal Code violations (15 percent) as well as unspecified municipal offences (8 percent).

[36] It is curious that, while a force behind the 1996 sentencing reforms to the Code was a reaction to the overuse of prison as a sanction (*R v. Gladue*, [1999] 1 SCR 688, at para. 57), prison as an enforcement mechanism for unpaid fines remains at such a high level. In its 1987 report, the Canadian Sentencing Commission had observed that "[t]he imposition of a 'semi-automatic' prison term for fine default has been the subject of relentless criticism in the sentencing literature. There is statistical evidence to support the conclusion that the imprisonment of fine defaulters without reference to their

ability to pay discriminates against impoverished offenders": *Sentencing Reform: A Canadian Approach—Report of the Canadian Sentencing Commission* (1987), at p. 380. The Commission recommended that "a quasi-automatic prison term not be imposed for fine default and that offenders only be incarcerated for *wilful* breach of a community sanction" (p. 381), meaning probation or fines (p. 347). In its 1996 sentencing reforms, Parliament took these views into account.

[37] I do not overlook the corollary problem that poverty should not become a shield against any punishment at all. Otherwise, smugglers will simply be encouraged to redouble their efforts to recruit impoverished people as runners. Nor is it suggested that jail is never a fit sentence for people in the respondent's position. In this case, however, we are confronted with a specific finding by the sentencing judge, not unreasonable in the circumstances, that jail was not a fit sentence for *this* offender.

[38] It is one thing if the judge forms the view that jail is a fit sentence, albeit one from which the offender can extricate him[self] or herself by payment of a fine. It is another thing altogether where the judge, as here, concludes that jail time is *not* appropriate.

F. Encouragement to Pay

[39] The appellant Crown states in its factum on the present appeal, "[t]he purpose of a term of imprisonment in default is to encourage fine payment; it is not punishment for an offence." "Encouragement" presupposes the offender has the wherewithal to somehow organize payment. If, as the collection lawyers say, you cannot get blood from a stone, no amount of "encouragement" is going to cause the stone to bleed.

[40] The Crown's submission finds an echo in late 18th century England. A leading scholarly study of the King's Bench debtors' prison points out that what creditors wanted

> was, above all, the power to *threaten* imprisonment. A debtor who was brought to court, even if he could put up bail, received a forceful reminder of his perilous situation. Court appearance might well induce a debtor with resources to re-order his priorities and settle outstanding claims. Even a debtor without resources might find himself able, under the shadow of the law, to dredge up sufficient funds from friends and relatives. [Emphasis in original.]

(J. Innes, "The King's Bench Prison in the Later Eighteenth Century: Law, Authority and Order in a London Debtors' Prison," in J. Brewer and J. Styles, eds., *An Ungovernable People: The English and Their Law in the Seventeenth and Eighteenth Centuries* ([London: Hutchinson's,] 1980), 250, at p. 254)

[41] Debtors' prison was used to enforce civil debts. In this case, we are dealing with debts owed to the Crown. One of the ideas underlying the 1996 sentencing reforms is that it was no more appropriate to use jail as a general collection agency for debts owed to the Crown than it is for debts owed to ordinary citizens.

[42] It is true, of course, that some of those serving jail time in default of payment even today are doing so for reasons of personal preference, a matter of choice, as documented in a recent study for the British Home Office: R. Elliott and J. Airs, *New Measures*

for Fine Defaulters, Persistent Petty Offenders and Others: The Reports of the Crime (Sentence) Act 1997 Pilots (2000), at pp. 32-35, 44 and 68-69.

[43] However, the illusory nature of the "choice" between fine or imprisonment in many situations was noted by Kelly J in *R v. Hebb* (1989), 69 CR (3d) 1 (NSSC (TD)), at p. 13:

> It is irrefutable that it is irrational to imprison an offender who does not have the capacity to pay on the basis that imprisonment will force him or her to pay. If the sentencing court chooses a fine as the appropriate sentence, it is obviously discarding imprisonment as being unnecessary under the particular circumstances. However, default provisions may be appropriate in circumstances where the offender may *choose* not to pay, presumably on principle, and would elect to spend time incarcerated rather than make a payment to the state. For the impecunious offenders, however, imprisonment in default of payment of a fine is not an alternative punishment—*he or she does not have any real choice in the matter*. At least this is the situation until fine option programs or related programs are in place. In effect, imprisonment of the poor in default of payment of a fine becomes a punishment that would not otherwise be imposed except for the economic limitations of the convicted person. [[Emphasis] added.]

[44] It was to address some of these weaknesses in the sentencing options that the Minister of Justice subsequently introduced Bill C-41, proclaimed in force on September 3, 1996.

G. No Constitutional Question Raised

[45] Both the respondent and the intervener Charter Committee on Poverty Issues expressed the view that a Charter challenge *ought* to have been taken against the mandatory fine provision of the *Excise Act*. In particular, the Charter Committee on Poverty Issues contended that the law operates unequally as between the rich and the poor. A similar Charter challenge was made and rejected in *R v. Zachary*, [1996] RJQ 2484 (CA), and *R v. MacFarlane* (1997), 121 CCC (3d) 211 (PEICA). In the absence of a successful Charter challenge, we take the law as Parliament has passed it. This was accepted by the trial judge who rightly felt he had no option but to impose a $9,600 fine.

H. The 1996 Sentencing Reforms

[46] The 1996 amendments made a number of important clarifications in this area of the law.

[47] Firstly, Parliament rejected in general the notion that a fine should be set without regard to an offender's ability to pay. A means inquiry is now a condition precedent to the imposition of a fine except where otherwise provided by law. Section 734(2) of the Code now provides:

> 734. ...
>
> (2) Except when the punishment for an offence includes a minimum fine or a fine is imposed in lieu of a forfeiture order, a court may fine an offender under this section only if the court is satisfied that the offender is able to pay the fine or discharge it under section 736.

In this case, of course, Parliament did impose a minimum fine which, in his present circumstances, the respondent was unable to pay.

[48] Secondly, in s. 734(2), Parliament cross-referenced s. 736 which introduced into the Code recognition of provincial "fine option programs" in which, assuming such a plan exists and the offender is eligible for it, the fine may be discharged "in whole or in part by earning credits for work performed during a period not greater than two years."

[49] Thirdly, Parliament provided that a defaulting offender should not be sent to jail unless he or she has "without reasonable excuse, refused to pay the fine or discharge it under s. 736" (see s. 734.7(1) of the Code).

[50] The Court of Appeal expressed concern that a fine that is not backed up with the threat of jail might be seen as a "hollow" sentence. The 1996 amendments make it clear, however, that while impoverished offenders are not to be jailed simply because of an inability to pay, they are nevertheless subject to available collection methods short of jail, including an obligation to work off their debts where a fine option program is in place. Moreover, the sentencing judge can certainly impose a fine plus a period of jail in default of payment to encourage payment. The problem here was that the sentencing judge moved directly from imposition to committal without passing through the intermediate stages of default and a s. 734.7(1) committal hearing.

[51] If no "fine option program" is in place and the offender defaults, the Crown has a number of civil remedies, including refusal to "issue or renew or may suspend [any] licence, permit or other instrument until the fine is paid in full" (s. 734.5 of the Code), or the criminal court order may be filed as a judgment in a court of civil jurisdiction, with all the usual civil law collection remedies (s. 734.6). A third option is committal to jail for default, but, as will be seen, this option is fenced in with important restrictions.

(i) The Lack of a Functioning Fine Option Program in Ontario

[52] The trial judge in this case made it clear that if a fine option program had been available in Ontario, he would have enrolled the respondent to work off the debt over a period of time through community service. "[I]f there was a regime in this province permitting offenders to work off the fines," he said, "this entire discussion would be obviated."

[53] All provinces and territories have a fine option program in place except for British Columbia, Newfoundland and Labrador, Nunavut and Ontario. Of these four jurisdictions, Newfoundland and Labrador has enabling legislation in place to allow the program, but has not promulgated a regulation to create the program: see *Provincial Offences Act*, SNL 1995, c. P-31.1, s. 38. Nunavut is in the process of drafting legislation to create a program. British Columbia does not at present have a statute that allows for the creation of such a program.

[54] Ontario has a regulation in place that establishes such a program in designated areas, but, as part of budget cuts, it has dismantled the administrative apparatus required to support it. Specifically, the Fine Option Program, RRO 1990, Reg. 948, made pursuant to the *Provincial Offences Act*, RSO 1990, c. P.33, contemplated a fine option program in Ontario, but while the regulation has never been repealed, the administrative apparatus essential to administer the program was eliminated in 1994: see O. Reg. 925/93.

(ii) Licence Suspension and Revocation

[55] Enforcement options available to the Crown include the suspension or revocation of licences and permits held by the respondent. In the present case, the fine was imposed under the federal *Excise Act*. There is no evidence of what federal permits or licences, if any, were held by the respondent. It is possible that he possessed a Canadian passport.

[56] In most cases, revocation or suspension of permits is a potent collection tool, especially where the fine is owed to the provincial Crown. Anyone who has tried to renew a driving licence despite an unpaid fine is familiar with the procedure. While suspension or revocation do not themselves produce payment of the fine, they put pressure on the offender to find the money. This remedy is frequently resorted to. It appears that in 2002 there were 95,909 driving permits in Ontario suspended as a result of default in the payment of fines: Ontario, Ministry of Transportation, *Driver Control Statistics* (2003). Apart from driving licences, suspension or revocation would be available provincially in respect of registration of vehicles, taxicab licences, hunting permits, work permits, timber cutting permits, mineral exploration licences, building permits and the full range of activities touched by the apparatus of the regulatory state.

[57] It may be that suspension of federal permits and licences would not have produced any significant payment in the respondent's case, but nevertheless, where applicable, it would be a punishment less restrictive of his liberty than house arrest.

(iii) Civil Enforcement

[58] Governments use collection agencies. If there is money to be found, these people are nothing if not persistent.

[59] Under s. 734.6, the Crown can register the unpaid sentence as a civil judgment. Providing the civil judgment is renewed at appropriate intervals, it carries on indefinitely. The fact the respondent was impoverished on the day of his sentencing does not mean he will be ever thus.

(iv) Committal Proceedings

[60] Under the Code, a fine default is not punishable by committal *unless* the other statutory remedies, including licence suspensions and civil proceedings, are "not appropriate in the circumstances," or "the offender has, *without reasonable excuse, refused* to pay the fine or discharge it under section 736 [fine options program]" (emphasis added). Section 734.7(1) of the Code provides:

> 734.7(1) [Warrant of committal] Where time has been allowed for payment of a fine, the court shall not issue a warrant of committal in default of payment of the fine
>> (a) until the expiration of the time allowed for payment of the fine in full; and
>> (b) unless the court is satisfied
>>> (i) that the mechanisms provided by sections 734.5 and 734.6 are not appropriate in the circumstances, or
>>> (ii) that the offender has, without reasonable excuse, refused to pay the fine or discharge it under section 736.

[61] Where the offender's "reasonable excuse" under subpara. (ii) for failure to pay a fine is poverty, the question is whether it is nevertheless open to a court to jail him or her under subpara. (i) because the self-same poverty makes it "not appropriate," i.e., futile, to resort to civil collection methods or permit suspensions. In my view, such a reading of s. 734.7, despite the drafter's use of the word "or" at the end of s. 734.7(1)(b)(i), would be absurd.

[62] Courts have not infrequently read "or" as "and" where the legislative context so requires: *Clergue v. H.H. Vivian and Co.* (1909), 41 SCR 607, *Re International Woodworkers of America, Local 2-306 and Miramichi Forest Products Ltd.* (1971), 21 DLR (3d) 239 (NBCA), and *Sullivan and Driedger on the Construction of Statutes* (4th ed. 2002), at pp. 66-69. See also, on this specific point, A. Manson, *The Law of Sentencing* (2001), at p. 249.

[63] If poverty were to be upheld as a stand-alone justification for a committal court to find collection methods other than jail "not appropriate," then the "without reasonable excuse" limitation in s. 734.7(1)(b)(ii) would afford poor people no protection at all. Yet it was the concern about overuse of jail for poor people for unpaid fines that was an important impetus behind the 1996 sentencing reforms.

[64] Use of the word "refused" in s. 734.7(1)(b)(ii) indicates a parliamentary expectation that the offender's particular circumstances allow him or her a choice. In this case, at least at the date of the sentencing, the respondent had no choice.

[65] The Crown, in its factum, fully accepted that committal proceedings are governed by the principle in s. 734.7(1)(b)(ii) that "the offender has, *without reasonable excuse, refused* to pay the fine or discharge [the debt]" (emphasis added). For example, the Crown argues:

By operation of the warrant of committal provisions in s. 734.7 of the *Criminal Code*, there must be a judicial determination that an offender has "without reasonable excuse, refused to pay the fine" before he or she is ordered into custody.

• • •

While the "slamming of the jail door" is the incentive to make offenders with means pay their fines, *no one will go to jail for their genuine inability to pay.*

• • •

However, as will be discussed below, where a sentencing judge chooses to impose a default term of imprisonment, the warrant of committal provision in s. 734.7 of the *Criminal Code* operates to ensure that only those who *wilfully* evade payment will be incarcerated.

• • •

If the judge was satisfied that the Respondent was not *wilfully* evading the payment of the fine, there would be no basis for issuing a warrant of committal and the Respondent would not go to jail. [Emphasis in original.]

[66] Parliament has imposed a mandatory minimum fine in s. 240 of the *Excise Act*, but it has with equal authority provided in s. 734.7(1) of the *Code* that the offender should not go to jail for failure to pay it unless it is shown that he or she has "without reasonable excuse, refused to pay." That was not the position of the respondent when

he was sentenced. He ought not to have been sentenced to serve a "term of imprisonment" in an institution *or* in the community.

III. The Proper Order

[67] In my view, the trial judge ought to have proceeded with his initial instinct to impose the mandatory minimum fine of $9,600 plus a reasonable time to pay and 30 days in default. If, as the trial judge expected, the respondent went into default despite the Crown's resort to available remedies short of committal, the Crown would then have had the choice whether to proceed further or not.

[68] If, as the trial judge anticipated, the respondent had continued simply to be unable to pay, the Crown, on its own acknowledgement to this Court, would not have sought such a committal.

[69] If, on the other hand, the respondent had come into money to pay all or part of the debt, he should quite properly have been required to do so.

IV. Disposition

[70] The appeal is allowed. As the respondent has served his conditional sentence, which would bar all further collection procedures under s. 734.7(4) of the *Code*, the Crown ought not to take any further collection procedures as a result of the conditional sentence's being set aside. A stay is therefore entered against any further collection procedures. As the appeal was brought by the Crown as a test case, the respondent should have his costs in this Court.

[Deschamps J dissented. Applying a "purposive sentencing approach," she concluded that because a court could impose a period of imprisonment in default of payment of the mandatory minimum fine, it could equally impose a conditional sentence in default of payment of that fine.]

In *Wu* the offender was being sentenced under the *Excise Act*, which gives courts a discretion whether to impose a period of imprisonment in default of payment of a fine. Does such discretion exist under the *Criminal Code*? See ss. 734(4) and (5). If not, what impact does this have on the court's analysis? For a discussion of this point, see Tim Quigley, "Annotation: *R v. Wu*" (2003), 16 CR (6th) 291.

For further consideration of the use of imprisonment in default of payment of a fine, see MacDougall, "Hebb: Imprisonment in Default of Fine Payment and Section 7 of the Charter" (1989), 69 CR (3d) 23; Jobson and Atkins, "Imprisonment in Default and Fundamental Justice" (1986), 28 *Crim. LQ* 251; and Kimball, "In the Matter of Judicial Discretion and the Imposition of Default Orders" (1989-90), 32 *Crim. LQ* 467.

D. Victim Surcharge

The victim surcharge in the *Criminal Code* is a mechanism to fund services for victims of crimes. It must be imposed on a convicted or discharged offender unless it would cause undue hardship to the offender or the offender's dependants. Is this a proper exercise of Parliament's criminal law power? In the case below, the court considers both the nature and constitutionality of the surcharge.

R v. Crowell
(1992), 76 CCC (3d) 413 (NSCA)

FREEMAN JA: The issue in this appeal is whether the victim fine surcharge that courts are required to impose under s. 727.9 of the *Criminal Code* is constitutional.

• • •

Judge Hughes Randall of the Provincial Court refused to order a victim fine surcharge when he fined the respondent $500 for driving with an unlawful blood-alcohol level. He stated:

> A fine is one form of punishment that may be imposed in a lot of cases but the amount of the fine is to be paid ... is [sic] within the range of either a minimum or a maximum and not a percentage like this surcharge. I see no difference between this charge and what the federal government imposes by legislation as a percentage surcharge for income tax purposes in any given year through the federal budget. It is not the function of the courts to collect a surcharge on behalf of the government to support a particular program; therefore, I do not intend to access the victim fine surcharge because in my opinion it is a form of taxation.

The Crown has appealed, asserting that the surcharge is another penalty within the jurisdiction of the federal government to legislate punishment for criminal offences.

• • •

Sentencing is not a science but an art, practised, often with great skill, by judges in courts of criminal jurisdiction. The overriding concern is protection of the public, which is achieved through a careful balancing of factors relating to deterrence and reform. The judge must bring a wide array of considerations into an intensely personal focus upon the particular offender before the bench in relation to the offence for which he has been convicted. On its face the surcharge intrudes into the sentencing process of the courts by imposing a consideration unrelated to the particular offence or the offender. In cases in which a fine is the appropriate penalty, a carefully crafted fine is theoretically a precise monetary expression of the numerous factors which a judge must balance. The addition of a victim fine surcharge skews the result, not primarily to punish the offender but to raise money for a program administered by the province.

• • •

The victim fine surcharge is a new concept in restitution: general rather than specific restitution made by an offender not to his or her own victim but to victims of crime generally by creating a fund to provide them with certain services. It is a statutorily imposed deterrent with perhaps a secondary relevance to reformation; its role as a deterrent is incidental to its fund-raising purpose.

It is not surprising that the victim fine surcharge should be regarded with suspicion by judges in criminal courts; it is an intrusion into the art of sentencing unrelated to the peculiar requirements for the protection of the public with respect to the characteristics of the individual offender before the court. Thus it is a limitation on both the discretion and the independence of the sentencing judge.

Nevertheless, it is a limitation within the criminal law-making powers of Parliament, which fetters judicial discretion in sentencing in various ways, for example, by prescribing both minimum and maximum sentences and by such mandatory provisions as firearms prohibitions. ...

· · ·

The victim fine surcharge is like a tax for the purpose of raising a revenue, but unlike a tax in that it is also a further expression of public reprobation at the time of sentencing. In an important aspect it is penal in its application and its consequences. In its fundraising aspect it represents an effort to rectify the harm done by criminal activity, a public purpose wholly related to the field of criminal law. Its identification with criminal law interests is so strong I would characterize it as a valid exercise of the federal criminal law-making power even if it were structurally indistinguishable from a tax. The purpose will govern.

It is not necessary to go so far; it may be structurally distinguished from a tax as well: it is not compulsory. The judge imposing it has discretion as to the percentage of the fine it is to represent, and it can be avoided on grounds of hardship.

... [V]ictims of crime are a federal concern under s. 91(27) and it is not a delegation of powers, but a delegation of an administrative function, to transfer the funds collected directly to the provinces for appropriate programs.

· · ·

The victim fine surcharge is therefore neither a true tax nor a true fine, but rather a unique penalty in the nature of a general kind of restitution. As such it is penal in its pith and substance and therefore constitutional as a proper matter for parliamentary legislation under s. 91(27) of the *Constitution Act, 1867*. It must be taken into account by criminal court judges in crafting the sentences they impose.

The appeal is allowed and the matter is remitted to the Provincial Court for the disposition of victim fine surcharge issues. Appeal allowed.

III. RESTITUTION

Before the 1996 amendments, the *Criminal Code* addressed the issue of making an offender reimburse his or her victims through two mechanisms. First, the Code contained a provision that permitted sentencing judges to make "compensation orders" in favour of named victims that could be enforced against the offender in the same way as a civil judgment. Second, the Code authorized the inclusion of "restitution orders" as a term of probation, which were enforceable, like any other term of probation, with the threat of a criminal charge under s. 733.1.

In 1996 a discrete form of restitution order replaced the earlier provisions. The current scheme is set out in ss. 738 to 741.2 of the *Criminal Code*. These provisions answer a number of the technical issues that plagued the earlier scheme. Many cases dealing with the prior mechanisms of compensation and restitution therefore have little relevance today except to show the legislative history and explain why some provisions have been enacted. In considering the current sections and the applicable cases, keep in mind the following two purposes of sentencing as stated in s. 718 of the Code:

(e) to provide reparations for harm done to victims or to the community; and

(f) to promote a sense of responsibility in offenders, and acknowledgement of the harm done to victims and to the community.

A. Criminal Code, Sections 738 to 741.2

738(1) Where an offender is convicted or discharged under section 730 of an offence, the court imposing sentence on or discharging the offender may, on application of the Attorney General or on its own motion, in addition to any other measure imposed on the offender, order that the offender make restitution to another person as follows:

(a) in the case of damage to, or the loss or destruction of, the property of any person as a result of the commission of the offence or the arrest or attempted arrest of the offender, by paying to the person an amount not exceeding the replacement value of the property as of the date the order is imposed, less the value of any part of the property that is returned to that person as of the date it is returned, where the amount is readily ascertainable;

(b) in the case of bodily or psychological harm to any person as a result of the commission of the offence or the arrest or attempted arrest of the offender, by paying to the person an amount not exceeding all pecuniary damages incurred as a result of the harm, including loss of income or support, if the amount is readily ascertainable; and

(c) in the case of bodily harm or threat of bodily harm to the offender's spouse or common-law partner or child, or any other person, as a result of the commission of the offence or the arrest or attempted arrest of the offender, where the spouse or common-law partner, child or other person was a member of the offender's household at the relevant time, by paying to the person in question, independently of any amount ordered to be paid under paragraphs (a) and (b), an amount not exceeding actual and reasonable expenses incurred by that person, as a result of moving out of the offender's household, for temporary housing, food, child care and transportation, where the amount is readily ascertainable.

(2) The lieutenant governor in council of a province may make regulations precluding the inclusion of provisions on enforcement of restitution orders as an optional condition of a probation order or of a conditional sentence order.

739. Where an offender is convicted or discharged under section 730 of an offence and

(a) any property obtained as a result of the commission of the offence has been conveyed or transferred for valuable consideration to a person acting in good faith and without notice, or

(b) the offender has borrowed money on the security of that property from a person acting in good faith and without notice,

the court may, where that property has been returned to the lawful owner or the person who had lawful possession of that property at the time the offence was committed, order the offender to pay as restitution to the person referred to in paragraph (a) or (b) an amount not exceeding the amount of consideration for that property or the total amount outstanding in respect of the loan, as the case may be.

740. Where the court finds it applicable and appropriate in the circumstances of a case to make, in relation to an offender, an order of restitution under section 738 or 739, and

(a) an order of forfeiture under this or any other Act of Parliament may be made in respect of property that is the same as property in respect of which the order of restitution may be made, or

(b) the court is considering ordering the offender to pay a fine and it appears to the court that the offender would not have the means or ability to comply with both the order of restitution and the order to pay the fine,

the court shall first make the order of restitution and shall then consider whether and to what extent an order of forfeiture or an order to pay a fine is appropriate in the circumstances.

741(1) Where an amount that is ordered to be paid under sections 732.1, 738, 739 or 742.3, is not paid without delay, the person to whom the amount was ordered to be paid may, by filing the order, enter as a judgment the amount ordered to be paid in any civil court in Canada that has jurisdiction to enter a judgment for that amount, and that judgment is enforceable against the offender in the same manner as if it were a judgment rendered against the offender in that court in civil proceedings.

(2) All or any part of an amount that is ordered to be paid under section 738 or 739 may be taken out of moneys found in the possession of the offender at the time of the arrest of the offender if the court making the order, on being satisfied that ownership of or right to possession of those moneys is not disputed by claimants other than the offender, so directs.

741.1 Where a court makes an order of restitution under section 738 or 739, it shall cause notice of the content of the order, or a copy of the order, to be given to the person to whom the restitution is ordered to be paid.

741.2 A civil remedy for an act or omission is not affected by reason only that an order for restitution under section 738 or 739 has been made in respect of that act or omission.

B. The Constitutionality of Restitution

It has been argued that the inclusion of restitution provisions in the *Criminal Code* is improper because reparation between offender and victim is a matter for the civil litigation process. The Supreme Court of Canada addressed this issue in *R v. Zelensky*. Although *Zelensky* was decided under the prior provisions, it is still relevant to the current legislative scheme. It explains the proper place and scope of restitution sanctions within the criminal law sphere.

R v. Zelensky
[1978] 2 SCR 940

LASKIN CJC: This appeal ... challenges the majority judgment of the Manitoba Court of Appeal ... which invalidated s. 653 of the *Criminal Code* and held also, and in any event, that [the trial judge] erred in law in making an order for compensation under that provision and in directing restitution of stolen property under s. 655. The order for compensation and for restitution was a composite order made at the time the respondent

Anne Zelensky was sentenced to imprisonment and to a term of probation after pleading guilty to theft and was in pursuance of an application for such relief made by T. Eaton Company Limited, the victim of the theft.

The validity of s. 655 was not impeached before the Manitoba Court of Appeal or before this court ... and, in my view, it must stand as a severable order validly made under s. 655, whatever be the disposition as to the order for compensation under s. 653 and as to the validity of this last-mentioned provision.

...

Sections 653, 654 and 655 have been in the *Criminal Code* in similar but not exact formulation since the Code's enactment in 1892: see ss. 836, 837, 838. The original of the present s. 653, namely s. 836, provided for compensation not exceeding $1,000 upon the application of the person aggrieved, the amount to be deemed a judgment debt owing by the accused and enforceable in the same way as an order for costs under s. 832, which provided, *inter alia*, for satisfaction in whole or in part out of money belonging to and taken from the accused on his arrest.

The provision for compensation was not then tied expressly to the sentencing process as is now the case under s. 653. Under the original of the present s. 654, namely, s. 837, where property involved in the offence was sold to a *bona fide* purchaser and restored to the true owner, the purchaser could apply for compensation out of money of the accused taken from him on his apprehension. The present s. 654 clearly goes farther in providing for an order for a money payment, subject to the Court being able to direct that all or part of the compensation to the purchaser be paid out of money in the possession of the accused at the time of his arrest and which is indisputably his. Neither in [s.] 836 [nor in s.] 837 was there any such express provision as now exists in ss. 653 and 654 for filing the order for compensation, with effect as a judgment enforceable as if it was a judgment in civil proceedings.

The principle of restitution under the present s. 655 is carried forward from the original s. 838, but the present provision is more explicit (if, indeed, the original provision covers the point at all) that an order will not be made if there is a dispute as to ownership of the property involved by claimants other than the accused. No such issue arose in the present case and, as I have already said, the order for restitution must stand.

It appears to me that ss. 653, 654 and 655, historically and currently, reflect a scheme of criminal law administration under which property, taken or destroyed or damaged in the commission of a crime, is brought into account following the disposition of culpability, and may be ordered by the criminal Court to be returned to the victimized owner if it is under the control of the Court and its ownership is not in dispute or that reparation be made by the offender, either in whole or in part out of money found in his possession when arrested if it is indisputably his and otherwise under an order for compensation, where the property has been destroyed or damaged.

I think s. 655(2) gives particular emphasis to the scheme in providing for an order of restitution, even if the accused has been acquitted, where the property involved in the commission of an offence is under the control of the Court. The integrity of the scheme is seen in s. 654, already mentioned, which enables the criminal Court to tidy up a situation where stolen property has been sold to a *bona fide* purchaser and it is available for restoration to the victimized owner, the Court authorized upon such restitution to inflict upon the offender a liability to pay to the innocent purchaser what he gave for the goods.

· · ·

Apart from the question of enforcement under s. 666(1) (which may be contrasted with the enforcement open under s. 653 by filing the compensation order in a superior Court with effect as a judgment thereof), I see no difference in principle between a provision for reparation in a probation order, as an additional term of what is in effect a sentence, and a direction for compensation or reparation by an order under s. 653 which, if made at all, must be made at the time sentence is imposed. I find little to choose, except on the side of formality, in the requirement of s. 653 that the compensation order must be based on an application by the person aggrieved rather than be made by the Court *suo motu* as is apparently, but only apparently, the position under s. 663(2)(e).

· · ·

There is, moreover, another important aspect of s. 653 that must be kept in mind. The court's power to make a concurrent order for compensation as part of the sentencing process is discretionary. I am of the view that in exercising that discretion the Court should have regard to whether the aggrieved person is invoking s. 653 to emphasize the sanctions against the offender as well as to benefit himself. A relevant consideration would be whether civil proceedings have been taken and, if so, whether they are being pursued.

There are other factors that enter into the exercise of the discretion, such as the means of the offender, and whether the criminal Court will be involved in a long process of assessment of the loss, although I do not read s. 653 as requiring exact measurement. A plea of guilty will, obviously, make the Court's task easier where it is asked to make an order of compensation, but there is no reason why an attempt to secure agreement on the amount of loss should not be made where the conviction follows a plea of not guilty. It is probable, of course, that the likelihood of an appeal will militate against agreement but I would add that I do not regard it as a function of the criminal Court to force agreement to enable it to make an order for compensation. What all of this comes to is that I agree ... that, constitutionality apart, an order for compensation should only be made with restraint and with caution.

The present case is one in which restraint and caution should have been exercised in a refusal to make a compensation order. The aggrieved company instituted civil proceedings, for the recovery of money and merchandise stolen from it by the offenders, a day before criminal charges were brought against them. It continued with the civil proceedings, taking steps in connection therewith while the criminal proceedings were in progress, and even after the offenders had pleaded guilty to theft. The aggrieved company then decided to seek a compensation order under s. 653 and a dispute arose with respect to the amount of the loss, particularly in relation to the money that was allegedly stolen. So far as appears, the civil proceedings were maintained while the application for a compensation order was pursued. The civil proceedings were justified because of the desire to get a garnishment order. In all the circumstances, I would not interfere with that part of the judgment of the majority of the Manitoba Court of Appeal holding that the order for compensation should not have been made.

I wish to dwell further on the course of proceedings in this case in order to provide some guidance to trial Judges on the proper application of s. 653 and in order to make clear that s. 653 is not to be used *in terrorem* as a substitute for or a reinforcement for civil proceedings. Its validity is based, as I have already said, on its association with the sentencing process, and its administration in particular cases must be limited by that consideration.

What emerges from the facts here is that the T. Eaton Company sought to use the criminal process as a more expeditious means of recovering the money lost by the fraudulent activities of the accused. Its co-operation with the Crown during the early course of the criminal proceedings is understandable, but at the same time it was pursuing a civil remedy against the accused, and the civil proceedings had reached the stage of discovery when the accused came up for sentencing by the criminal Court. Eaton's then joined in the criminal proceedings as an "aggrieved person," and it became evident immediately that the amount of the loss suffered by it was in dispute. The dispute was not resolved, as it would have been under the procedures available in a civil Court, and the order for compensation made in the criminal proceedings was somewhat arbitrary as to amount.

Section 653 does not spell out any procedure for resolving a dispute as to quantum; its process is, *ex facie*, summary but I do not think that it precludes an inquiry by the trial Judge to establish the amount of compensation, so long as this can be done expeditiously and without turning the sentencing proceedings into the equivalent of a civil trial or into a reference in a civil proceeding. What is important is to contain s. 653 within its valid character as part of the sentencing process and thus avoid the allegation of intrusion into provincial legislative authority in relation to property and civil rights in the Province. Although ... the Courts have recognized the wide scope of the federal power in relation to criminal law and criminal procedure, and although there is now a broad range of powers in a sentencing Court to deal with offenders, it none the less remains true that the criminal law cannot be used to disguise an encroachment upon provincial legislative authority ... .

It must be obvious, therefore, that s. 653 is not the platform upon which to unravel involved commercial transactions in order to provide monetary redress to those entitled thereto as against an accused. The latter, too, may have a proper interest in insisting that civil proceedings be taken against him so that he may avail himself of the procedures for discovery and production of documents, as well as of a proper trial of issues which go to the merit of monetary claims against him. Again, the criminal Court cannot be expected to nor should it act under s. 653 if it would be required to interpret written documents in order to arrive at a sum of money sought through an order of compensation. So too, it would be improper to invoke s. 653 if the effect of provincial legislation would have to be considered in order to determine what order should be made. Indeed, any serious contest on legal or factual issues, or on whether the person alleging himself to be aggrieved is so in fact, should signal a denial of recourse to an order under s. 653.

The following case of *R v. Yates* outlines the considerations that a sentencing court should take into account in deciding whether to make a restitution order against an offender. In reading this decision, consider the following questions: What must be shown in order to make a restitution order against an offender? Who bears the burden of proof? What is the relevance, if any, of related civil proceedings? To what extent, if any, must the court consider the offender's ability to pay? How is ability to pay to be assessed? Must the court allow time to pay? How is a restitution order enforced against an offender?

R v. Yates
(2002), 169 CCC (3d) 506 (BCCA)

PROWSE JA: [1] ... Ms. Yates [was found] guilty of one count of defrauding the Ministry of Human Resources (the "Ministry") of a sum of money in excess of $5,000.

[She falsely stated that she was not in a common law relationship with the man with whom she shared a home during the relevant period, and further misrepresented that she was making one-half of the mortgage payments on the home.]

Mrs. Yates was given a two-year suspended sentence ... [and] ordered to pay restitution to the Ministry in the amount of $13,124, pursuant to s. 738(1) of the *Criminal Code*, RSC 1985, c. C-46 (the "Code"). This was the amount the Crown estimated Ms. Yates had obtained by way of overpayment from the Ministry for the period January 5, 1994 to March 30, 1997.

[2] Ms. Yates ... submits that the sentencing judge erred in imposing a restitution order without regard to her limited income.

· · ·

[4] Ms. Yates ... provided this Court with a lengthy letter and several attachments setting out the unfortunate circumstances leading to the charge against her. It appears from this information, and from a pre-sentence and medical report provided to the sentencing judge, that she suffered from serious health, emotional and financial difficulties during the relevant period. She finally sought counselling and was advised to obtain financial assistance to enable her to free herself from the deteriorating and abusive relationship which was the source of much of her unhappiness. In seeking that assistance, she made the misrepresentations which ultimately led to her being charged with fraud.

[5] Before turning to the appropriateness of the particular order for restitution in this case, I find it useful to review the basic principles relevant to the imposition of restitution orders, including the relevant provisions of the Code and some of the relevant authorities.

· · ·

[7] The authorities establish that restitution orders give effect to many of the principles of sentencing including denunciation, specific and general deterrence and rehabilitation. Further, ss. 718(e) and (f) of the Code refer to two objectives of sentencing particularly applicable to restitution orders, namely:

(e) to provide reparations for harm done to victims or to the community; and

(f) to promote a sense of responsibility in offenders, and acknowledgment of the harm done to victims and to the community.

[8] One of the leading authorities dealing with restitution orders (then called "compensation orders"), which arose in the context of a constitutional challenge to [s. 653,] a predecessor to s. 738 of the Code, is *R v. Zelensky*, [1978] 2 SCR 940. ...

[9] In *Zelensky*, the majority of the Supreme Court of Canada upheld the constitutionality of s. 653 as a valid part of the sentencing process. In reaching that conclusion, the majority discussed the nature of compensation orders and the circumstances in which they should be imposed. At p. 961 of the decision, Chief Justice Laskin, speaking for the majority, stated:

> There is, moreover, another important aspect of s. 653 that must be kept in mind. *The Court's power to make a concurrent order for compensation as part of the sentencing process is discretionary.* I am of the view that in exercising that discretion the Court should have regard to whether the aggrieved person is invoking s. 653 to emphasize the sanctions against the offender as well as to benefit himself. A relevant consideration would be whether civil proceedings have been taken and, if so, whether they are being pursued. *There are other factors that enter into the exercise of the discretion, such as the means of the offender*, and whether the criminal court will be involved in a long process of assessment of the loss, although I do not read s. 653 as requiring exact measurement.

[Emphasis added.]

[10] Chief Justice Laskin went on to say that orders for compensation should be made "with restraint and caution."

[11] *Zelensky* and numerous other authorities dealing with restitution orders were considered by the Manitoba Court of Appeal in *R v. Siemens* (1999), 136 CCC (3d) 353 (Man. CA). There, Mr. Justice Huband, speaking for the Court of Appeal, summarized many of the principles governing the imposition of restitution orders (at para. 8 of the decision):

> From the wording of s. 738(1)(a) and its predecessor, the old s. 725(1), it is obvious that it is discretionary as to whether the court orders restitution or not. There is case law concerning both the old s. 725(1) and the present s. 738(1)(a) which forms a useful guide as to how that discretion should be exercised.
>
> (1) The constitutional justification for a provision in the Code permitting restitution orders is that restitution is a part of the punishment. Where punishment is exacted in the form of a restitution order, there should be a corresponding reduction in other forms of punishment which might be imposed. In some cases, a restitution order will be a significant factor, while in others it will be trivial, depending on the circumstances, but it must be included as a factor in the totality of the punishment imposed.
>
> (2) *The means of the offender are to be considered as an important factor in determining whether restitution should be ordered.* That factor was specifically mentioned

by Laskin CJC, who wrote for the majority of the Supreme Court of Canada in *R v. Zelensky* ... .

In the subsequent decision of the Ontario Court of Appeal in R v. Scherer (1984), 16 CCC (3d) 30, Martin JA, speaking for the appeal panel, agreed that the means of the offender is a factor to be considered, but that it is not a controlling factor in every case. Martin JA went on to note at pp. 37-38:

> It may be that in some cases it would be inappropriate and undesirable to make a compensation order in an amount that it is unrealistic to think the accused could ever discharge.

(3) The impact of a restitution order upon the chances of rehabilitation of the accused either pro or con, is a factor to be considered. In *R v. Spellacy (R.A.)* (1995), 131 Nfld. & PEIR 127, at para. 79, the Court of Appeal of Newfoundland approbated a passage from *Sentencing in Canada* (1982), by R. Paul Nadin-Davis, which contained the following passage at p. 497:

> A compensation order which would ruin the accused financially, thus impairing his chances of rehabilitation, should not be imposed ... .

(4) The shorter the sentence, the more likely it will be that a restitution order will be appropriate. Where the amount is manageable, there is every reason to impose an order of restitution when a sentence either does not involve imprisonment or is so short that it does not affect the offender's employment or the sentence can be served conditionally. Conversely, as an incarceratory sentence becomes longer, the futility of an order of restitution will become increasingly apparent.

(5) An order of restitution need not be for the full amount of the loss. As an example, in *R v. Ali (K.N.M.)* (1997), 98 BCAC 239, a restitution order of $42,500 was reduced by the British Columbia Court of Appeal to $10,000 to better reflect the accused's capacity to meet the obligation which the order imposed.

(6) Difficulties in determining the amount of the victim's loss will militate against a restitution order since it would be unwise for a criminal court to become involved in the determination of damages.

[Emphasis added.]

Huband JA referred to other considerations in relation to restitution orders which are not relevant to this discussion.

[These were: (1) an order of restitution must not be made as a mechanical afterthought to an incarceratory sentence; (2) where there is a plea bargain that does not include restitution, a court should be slow to make an order of restitution unless it is for a very modest sum; (3) the existence of multiple victims with differing entitlements to whatever monies are paid by way of restitution militates against a restitution order; and (4) the existence of multiple participants in the crimes militates against a restitution order enforceable against one accused but not against the others.]

[12] It is apparent from several of the authorities relating to restitution orders that, while ability to pay restitution is a factor which should be taken into account by the sentencing judge, it is not the predominant factor in certain types of cases. For example, in *R v. Fitzgibbon*, [1990] 1 SCR 1005, a lawyer misappropriated funds entrusted to him and subsequently declared bankruptcy. The Law Society reimbursed his clients out of its compensation fund and then sought a compensation order against the lawyer in the criminal proceedings. The Supreme Court of Canada upheld the imposition of a compensation order even though the lawyer's means at the time of sentencing were minimal. The court concluded in that case that "the claims of the victims of the fraudulent acts should be paramount."

[13] The Ontario Court of Appeal came to the same conclusion in *R v. Scherer* (1984), 42 CR (3d) 376 (leave to appeal to SCC refused (1984), 16 CCC (3d) 30), which also involved a solicitor who had misappropriated client funds.

[14] A similar result was reached by this Court in *R v. Moscone*, [1985] BCJ No. 1755, with respect to a bank manager who defrauded his employer of substantial sums of money. On appeal, counsel for the accused submitted that a compensation order should not have been made since the accused did not have the means to pay it. Mr. Justice Taggart, speaking for the majority, upheld the compensation order. In so doing, he stated (at para. 25):

> Unquestionably, means of the offender and his ability to meet the provisions of the compensation order, is something that a trial judge ought to consider. The trial judge is faced with the necessity to balance the requirements of the law in imposing a sentence that will meet the circumstances of the offender and the circumstances of the offence. In circumstances such as these, where a person in a position of trust has abused that position, this court has consistently required the imposition of substantial periods of incarceration. The question whether a compensation order should be made brings into question the ability of the offender to comply with the order. It will often be a matter of some delicacy for the trial judge to decide whether in the circumstances of the case such an order should be made.

(By way of comparison, see *R v. Biegus* (1999), 141 CCC (3d) 245 (Ont. CA), where the Court of Appeal reduced a restitution order made against a security officer employed by the bank who had stolen substantial moneys from it on the basis the sentencing judge knew the accused would be unable to pay it.)

[15] Future ability to pay is also an important factor in determining whether a restitution order is appropriate. In *R v. Hoyt* (1992), 77 CCC (3d) 289 (BCCA), Mr. Justice Wood, speaking for the majority, discussed the importance of the offender's future ability to pay compensation at paras. 34-5 of the decision:

> While recognizing that the offender's means to pay cannot be ignored, the key to a fair use of such orders will lie in taking a broad approach to what constitutes such means. In any such inquiry, the offender's future ability to earn will be at least as important, if not more so, than his or her present means to pay.
>
> Where the future ability to pay a compensation order does exist, and the crime itself is one for which such an order is appropriate, as at least part of the overall sanction which the court must impose, care must be taken to ensure that the deterrent and denunciatory effects

of such an order are taken into account when measuring the other components of the sentence imposed. To add a compensation order to a sentence of imprisonment which would by itself be a fit sanction for the offence in question, would result in excessive punishment.

[16] The relevance of ability to pay restitution at the time of sentencing was also the subject of comment by this Court in *R v. Brown* (1999), 130 BCAC 250. There, Madam Justice Ryan, speaking for the Court, stated (at para. 10) that:

> It is common ground that ability to pay *at the time of sentence* is not a central consideration when imposing an order of restitution (by analogy to the old compensation order cases: *R v. Scherer* (1984), 16 CCC (3d) 30 (Ont. CA); *R v. Moscone* (October 2, 1985), Vancouver CA004383, [1985] BCJ No. 1755 (BCCA); *R v. Fitzgibbon*, [1990] 1 SCR 1005, 55 CCC (3d) 449).

[Emphasis added.]

[17] Thus, when determining whether a restitution order is appropriate, the court must consider, amongst other things, both the present and future ability of the accused to pay restitution. Further, where the circumstances of the offence are particularly egregious (for example, where a breach of trust is involved) a restitution order may be made even where there does not appear to be any likelihood of repayment. In those cases, the ability of the accused to pay may be relegated to a relatively minor consideration in the overall sentencing process.

[18] Before leaving this point, I note that counsel for the Crown placed particular reliance on the decision of this Court in *R v. Marcelino* (1998), 107 BCAC 43, as authority for the proposition that it is always appropriate for a court to make a restitution order where the amount owing is certain since the victim could obtain a civil remedy for that amount in any event. There, this Court upheld a conditional sentence and restitution order made against an accused who had defrauded the Ministry by failing to declare employment income. There was no discussion of the means of the accused or the basis upon which she was seeking to set the restitution order aside.

[19] In my view, the *Marcelino* decision (a brief oral judgment which does not refer to any authorities) does not purport to stand for the broad proposition suggested by the Crown. I would interpret the decision as providing that where a restitution order is otherwise appropriate, and particularly where the amount owing is certain, no useful purpose would be served by refusing to make such an order.

[20] In summary, I am satisfied that the principles set forth in *Siemens* (and elaborated upon by the other authorities to which I have referred) fairly encapsulate, without purporting to exhaust, the relevant principles which sentencing judges should bear in mind when considering the imposition of a restitution order under s. 738 of the Code. With reference to the issue on this appeal, the present or future ability of the accused to pay restitution are relevant considerations, but the weight to be given to those considerations will vary according to the specific circumstances of the offence and of the offender.

[21] I now turn, briefly, to the standard of review to be applied by an appellant court when reviewing orders for restitution. I am satisfied that the standard of review for such orders is the same standard which applies in reviewing sentences generally. In *R v. Devgan* (1999), 136 CCC (3d) 238 (leave to appeal to the SCC refused, [1999] SCCA

No. 518), Mr. Justice Labrosse, speaking for the court, set forth the standard at para. 28 of his reasons:

> I appreciate that a reviewing court should not lightly interfere with the exercise of discretion necessarily involved in imposing a sentence. As made clear by the Supreme Court of Canada in *R v. Shropshire* (1995), 102 CCC (3d) 193 (SCC), the appropriate standard of review in this context is one of reasonableness. This court should therefore only interfere with the trial judge's exercise of discretion in granting the compensation orders under s. 725(1) if the trial judge applied wrong principles or if the sentence was excessive or inadequate. See, also, *R v. M.(C.A.)* (1996), 105 CCC (3d) 327 (SCC).

[22] In this case, the sentencing judge imposed an order of restitution in the amount requested by the Crown, which amount was not seriously in dispute. He provided no reasons for that aspect of his decision. As earlier stated, the issue is whether he exercised his discretion in accordance with the principles governing the imposition of restitution orders to which I have referred, and, in particular, whether he considered Ms. Yates's ability to pay in making his order.

[23] At the sentencing hearing, defence counsel submitted that the sentencing judge should not make a restitution order on the basis that Ms. Yates had no ability to pay it. ...

[24] Following defence counsel's submission, the sentencing judge asked to be directed to the provision of the Code governing restitution orders. After a short adjournment, he returned and imposed a two-year suspended sentence, including a provision that Ms. Yates complete 200 hours of community service. He then imposed the restitution order. In so doing, he did not make any reference to Ms. Yates's financial circumstances, or otherwise comment on the basis upon which he determined that such an order was appropriate.

[25] It appears from the transcript that counsel did not provide the sentencing judge with any authorities governing the imposition of restitution orders. We were advised by Crown counsel on appeal that restitution orders are imposed as a matter of course in the lower courts in cases involving welfare fraud. To the extent that submission was offered as a basis for upholding this order, I simply observe that the fact such orders may be being made as a matter of course does not justify their imposition unless they are made in accordance with the principles to which I have referred.

[26] In this case, it is apparent that Ms. Yates's income, standing alone, was a factor weighing against a restitution order. At the time of sentencing, she had income of $801 per month arising from a disability pension and income from a boarder, out of which she had to make mortgage payments of $600 per month. That left her with only $201 per month from which to pay all of her other living expenses. I find Crown counsel's submission that Ms. Yates could make modest monthly payments on the restitution order from this $201 completely unrealistic.

[27] Further, there was no reasonable prospect of Ms. Yates having additional income in the future from which to pay such an order given the fact that she was 58 years of age and on a disability pension arising from her various health problems. (Nor did this case involve a breach of trust in the sense discussed in such cases as *Fitzgibbon* and *Scherer, supra*, which involved persons in positions of responsibility and power taking advantage of their position for personal gain.)

[28] In determining whether a restitution order is appropriate, however, it is not simply the income of the accused which must be examined. Their overall financial circumstances must be taken into account, including any assets owned by them. In this case, the evidence disclosed that Ms. Yates had an interest in a residence. No reference was made to this asset by either defence counsel or Crown counsel at the time of sentencing, which took place five months after Ms. Yates was convicted. According to documents filed at trial and referred to by Crown counsel on this appeal, Ms. Yates equity in this home at the time of trial and sentencing would appear to have been in the range of $100,000.

[29] Is there any justification for excluding Ms. Yates's equity in her home as a relevant consideration in determining whether a restitution order was appropriate in this case? Unfortunately, the Court was not provided with any authority which would assist in answering that question. The only authority which has come to my attention in that regard is *R v. Heath* (1984), 6 Cr. App. R (S) 397 (CA). The brief report of that case indicates that the accused was convicted of three offences of theft and one of handling of goods valued at over 20,000 pounds. He was sentenced to two years' imprisonment and ordered to pay 5,000 pounds restitution. It was apparent that the accused had no means to pay the restitution except through the sale of his home. On appeal, the English Court of Appeal quashed the restitution order on the basis "that it was wrong in principle to make a compensation order which would inevitably mean the sale of the appellant's house, as he was going to prison and would have no means to earn anything to pay the amount ordered."

[30] The legislation governing the imposition of compensation orders in England differs from ours and, without the benefit of submissions, I am reluctant to rely on authorities from that jurisdiction. In the result, I am not persuaded that the *Heath* decision provides a convincing basis for disregarding Ms. Yates's equity in her home in determining whether a restitution order was appropriate.

[31] Because of the absence of reasons, I am unable to say whether the sentencing judge considered Ms. Yates's home as a relevant factor in imposing a restitution order. Given Ms. Yates's limited income, however, it seems likely that he had her equity in the property in mind when he made the order. The evidence before him at trial indicated that her equity in the home was substantially more than that required to satisfy the restitution order.

[32] In fact, Ms. Yates acknowledged in the materials she filed on this appeal that she would be able to make restitution in a lesser amount than that ordered if the Ministry were to remove its charge against her property (arising from the restitution order) to permit her to remortgage the property or otherwise use it as collateral to raise funds. In my view, this Court should not engage in what amounts to a negotiation between Ms. Yates and the Ministry as to how she will satisfy the judgment it holds against her arising from the restitution order. The only question this Court must address on this appeal is whether the sentencing judge erred in his imposition of a restitution order, or in the amount of the restitution order, and, if so, what order should be substituted to accord with the principles to which I have referred.

[33] In the result, I am satisfied that the sentencing judge was entitled to take Ms. Yates's equity in her home into account in determining whether to impose a restitution

order. Where an accused's equity in his or her home is minimal, or where an accused is supporting children or other dependants in the home, a restitution order which effectively forces a sale of the home may give rise to an error in principle, but that is not this case. Here, Ms. Yates has significant equity in her home and has indicated in the materials she has filed that she has some ability to utilize that equity to satisfy the restitution order. It is not unlikely that she and the Ministry will find a way to enable her to satisfy the compensation order without losing her home. As earlier stated, that is a matter for them to resolve, not for this Court to resolve on a sentence appeal.

[34] In conclusion, I am satisfied that there was a foundation upon which the sentencing judge could make an order for restitution in this case in the full amount which Ms. Yates was found to have wrongfully obtained from the Ministry.

[35] I would, therefore, grant leave to appeal, but dismiss the appeal.

Additional difficulties arise when restitution orders are sought in cases with multiple victims with different claims to restitution and/or where multiple offenders were involved in the commission of the offence. The following case illustrates some of the complexities that arise in cases involving multiple offenders.

R v. Biegus
(1999), 141 CCC (3d) 245 (Ont. CA)

[The accused, Biegus, committed a series of 7 thefts against the Royal Bank of Canada. All of the thefts were committed with Hornett, who was the ringleader, and on one occasion with a third man, Vance. Hornett and a fourth man, Dobson, also committed 4 other thefts. All 4 offenders pleaded guilty, but the accused did so in separate proceedings. The accused, who cooperated fully with the police, was sentenced to 2 years' imprisonment less a day and ordered to pay the bank restitution in the amount of approximately $639,000, which represented the total loss from the 7 thefts that the accused participated in, less $14,000 that had already been repaid by the accused. In a separate proceedings, relating to all 11 thefts, Hornett was sentenced to 4 years and ordered to pay restitution totalling approximately $863,000, comprising an order in favour of the bank and another in favour of the bank's insurer. This amount represented the entire unrecovered portion of the bank's total loss. Approximately $453,000 of this amount, which related only to the 7 thefts that the accused had been involved in, had been repaid to the bank by its insurer. Dobson, who was involved in 4 thefts with Hornett but not with the accused, received a sentence of 2 years and was ordered to pay restitution of approximately $210,000 to the bank. Vance, who was involved in only 1 theft and was very cooperative with the police, received a conditional sentence of 60 days. The restitution orders were each joint and several, so that if the bank recovered from one of the offenders, that recovery accrues to the others' benefit and the principle of subrogation also applies.]

FELDMAN JA: ...

The Effect of Ordering Restitution of the Full Amount Stolen
Against Each of the Three Perpetrators

In this case, the effect of the restitution orders against Hornett, Dobson and Biegus works a potential unfairness to Biegus in the event that the Bank or its insurer may be able to recover any portion of the loss from Hornett.

First, on the facts presented by the Crown on the appeal $453,387.70 of the $638,534 for which the appellant is responsible has been repaid to the Bank by its insurer. Nevertheless, the appellant was ordered to pay the full amount as restitution to the Royal Bank, although at the sentencing hearing, counsel did attempt to explain the insurance involvement to the court. No issue was raised on appeal as to the propriety of the order made, and as such, I make no comment on it. However, one potential problem for the appellant is that to the extent that payment may be made by Hornett on the American Home judgment, there is no mechanism by which such payment will be treated as credit to the appellant on his judgment in favour of the Bank.

Second, because of the fact that Biegus and Dobson were involved in entirely separate thefts, neither is entitled to any credit on his judgment for a payment by the other to the Bank. However, if Hornett makes any payment, there is no mechanism for determining which thefts are to be credited and therefore whose judgment is to be reduced, Dobson's or the appellant's. Because these orders were made as restitution orders in separate criminal proceedings, instead of through the civil process where the issues of the mechanics of orderly and fair recovery could be fully canvassed and the appropriate orders or directions made, the result is that these issues have not been addressed or provided for.

In *Devgan* and *Siemens*, the courts both reiterated the long-standing principle that restitution orders are to made cautiously and with restraint and are intended to be applied where the circumstances are relatively simple and straightforward in terms of the amount to be ordered and the effect of the order. In *Siemens*, at p. 357 the court stated as the final principle that "The fact that there were multiple participants in the crimes … is a factor which militates against a restitution order enforceable against one accused, but not against the others." This case is a variation on that fact situation, and suggests a variation on that principle: Where there are multiple perpetrators, the order must ensure not only the proper recovery for the victim, but also not work an unfairness as between the perpetrators that would not result if the matter had been left to the civil courts.

Although there is no bar which prevents a court from making an order against each co-accused for the full amount of the victim's loss if the circumstances justify such an order, because of the various complications resulting from the orders made in the separate proceedings on the guilty pleas of Hornett and Dobson, it was not appropriate for the sentencing judge in this case to make a restitution order against the appellant for the full amount stolen. However, in another case it may be possible to reconcile orders made against co-accused or in separate proceedings in a way that would not have the potential to work unfairness to any of the parties.

The issue then becomes the appropriate amount of the restitution order in this case. In all the circumstances, the amount of the order should be limited to the amount that the appellant acknowledged he received from the robbery and for which he could not seek indemnity from Hornett, nor claim credit for any amount paid by Hornett. There is no suggestion on this record that this amount is inaccurate.

Such an order would not preclude the Bank from continuing with the civil proceedings against the appellant for the higher amount if it so chose ... . It would also make the restitution order a fair one within the principles which are applicable for the imposition of such orders.

Conclusion

. . .

I would therefore grant leave to appeal sentence in respect of the restitution order, allow the appeal, set aside the restitution order in favour of the Royal Bank in the amount of $638,534, and impose an order in favour of the Royal Bank in the amount of $264,000.

NOTES

1. Section 741.2 specifically states that the fact that a restitution order has been made under the *Criminal Code* does not itself affect the victim's ability to obtain a civil judgment for the harm caused and losses suffered as a result of the offence. What about the converse situation? That is, if the victim has already obtained a civil judgment against the offender, does the doctrine of *res judicata* apply to bar an order for restitution under the *Criminal Code*? In *R v. Devgan* (1999), 136 CCC (3d) 238 (Ont. CA), which was decided under the prior legislation, the Ontario Court of Appeal concluded that it did not:

> The position of the appellant cannot succeed ... . Just as s. 725 does not purport to interfere with any right of civil recourse, neither can a civil judgment purport to usurp the power given to a sentencing judge under s. 725(1). Compensation orders are discretionary, both as to whether an order should be made and as to amount. At most, the existence of a civil judgment is but a factor for the sentencing judge to consider in exercising this discretion.

If a restitution order is made in such a situation, can it include legal fees and disbursements incurred by the complainant in obtaining the civil judgment? What about prejudgment interest? See *Devgan*, above. Where both restitution orders and civil judgments are in place, civil courts have the ability to prevent double recovery by requiring a proper accounting of all sums recovered from the offender.

2. In *Devgan*, the Ontario Court of Appeal summarized the considerations that apply to the making of a compensation (now restitution) order. Many of these considerations were discussed in *Yates*, above. The court also identified several considerations dealing with the impact of related civil actions. It emphasized that restitution orders are not the appropriate mechanism to unravel complicated commercial transactions and they should therefore be granted only when the loss is readily calculable. A court should not make a restitution order if this would require the court to interpret written documents or consider the effect of provincial legislation in order to determine the amount of money to be paid or if there is a serious contest on legal or factual issues. In short, restitutions orders are not a substitute for civil proceedings.

3. In *R v. Fitzgibbon*, [1990] 1 SCR 1005, which involved fraud by a lawyer, the court held under the prior legislation that the Law Society of Upper Canada qualified as an aggrieved person because its compensation fund had made payments to the clients who had been defrauded. Could an order in favour of the Law Society still be made under the current provisions?

4. Although it seems self-evident that the means of the offender ought to be relevant to the *quantum* of a fine imposed on an offender, should it be relevant to the application of the restitution provisions? If the amount of the restitution order is easily quantifiable, why should a court refrain from making a restitution order if the offender demonstrates that he is unable to pay? Inability to pay is no answer to a civil action for damages. Why should it be relevant in the criminal law sphere? In *Biegus*, above, the court offered the following rationale for taking ability to pay into account:

> A restitution order made by a sentencing court survives any bankruptcy of the accused: *Bankruptcy and Insolvency Act*, RSC 1985, c. B-3, s. 178(1)(a). Therefore, it is there for life. It is not intended to be such a burden that it may affect the prospects for rehabilitation of the accused. That is why ability to pay is one of the factors which the court must consider.

5. Before the 1996 amendments the probation provisions contained a discrete optional condition dealing with restitution, which was commonly used to sequence payments over time. This provision was repealed and not replaced with one that deals expressly with sequenced payments. For discussion of this issue, see Manson, *The Law of Sentencing* (Toronto: Irwin Law, 2001), at 254-55.

PROBLEM

Assume that you are a trial judge. You have just convicted an offender on a charge of "fraud over $5,000" where the loss totalled $9,000. You have decided that a conditional sentence of 18 months is the appropriate disposition but you also want to order restitution. The offender works as an engineer and can make periodic payments. Can you order that he pay $500 per month? How would you make this order? What if you decide that the appropriate disposition is a suspended sentence and a probation period of 18 months? Could you use the probation order to include a schedule for payment of the restitution?

CHAPTER ELEVEN

Imprisonment

I. INTRODUCTION

Imprisonment is available as a penalty for all offences. The *Criminal Code*, RSC 1985, c. C-46, as amended, stipulates the maximum period of imprisonment that may be imposed. Only rarely does it provide for minimum penalties (see the discussion of minimum penalties below). Sentences of less than two years are served in provincial or territorial institutions (see s. 743.1(3)), while sentences that extend for two years or more, either by themselves or in the aggregate with other sentences, are served in federal penitentiaries (see ss. 743.1(1) and (5)). The structure and decision-making processes of the federal penitentiary system are determined by the *Corrections and Conditional Release Act*, SC 1992, c. 20, which replaced both the *Penitentiary Act* and the *Parole Act*. Each province and territory has its own enabling legislation. Later, in chapter 19, Prisoners and the Review of Penitentiary and Parole Decision Making, we discuss judicial review of internal prison and parole decisions.

The use of incarceration in Canada is striking. The Supreme Court has concluded that it is overused as a sentencing option. In *R v. Gladue*, the court said (at para. 58):

> Thus, it may be seen that although imprisonment is intended to serve the traditional sentencing goals of separation, deterrence, denunciation, and rehabilitation, there is widespread consensus that imprisonment has not been successful in achieving some of these goals. Over-incarceration is a long-standing problem that has been many times publicly acknowledged but never addressed in a systematic manner by Parliament. In recent years, compared to other countries, sentences of imprisonment in Canada have increased at an alarming rate. The 1996 sentencing reforms embodied in Part XXIII, and s. 718.2(e) in particular, must be understood as a reaction to the overuse of prison as a sanction, and must accordingly be given appropriate force as remedial provisions.

This statement, however, cannot be viewed in the abstract. It needs to be put in context. How does one understand a concept like "over-incarceration" without some yardsticks with which to measure the use of incarceration. First, let us look at hard data, which can be compared over time to provide an historical perspective. In the 2004-05 fiscal year, incarceration in Canada looked like the data in table 11.1. The data reveal two important trends. First, since 1996 (a significant date given the enactment of Bill C-41 on September 3, 1996), there has been a marked decrease in the total number of prisoners in Canada. The number of sentenced prisoners has been significantly reduced, from 28,189 in 1996-97 to 22,131 in 2004-05. Arguably, this may be a result, at least in part, of the introduction of conditional sentences in 1996. Second, and a matter of great concern, is the dramatic rise

Table 11.1   Incarceration in Canada, 2004-05

	1996-97	2004-5
Federal prisoners	14,143	12, 301
Provincial/territorial prisoners		
• Sentenced	14,046	9,830
• Remand.	5,737	9,640
• Other.	240	346
Total	34,166	32,117

Source: Based on Statistics Canada, Adult Correctional Services, October 11, 2006 and 1996.

in the number of remand prisoners to the point where their population is roughly the same as that of provincial and territorial sentenced prisoners.

Another way to think about the use of incarceration is by comparison to other sanctions. However, this is deceptive, because the analysis will be fruitful only in a sample where multiple options are available at the same time for the same offence. Otherwise, gross numbers are unhelpful. Looking at fines, however, as was noted in chapter 10, Monetary Sanctions: Fines and Restitution, Doob and Marinos have concluded that Canadians do not view a fine as a sufficiently serious response to many crimes. This suggests that we have embedded in our national psyche the notion that anything less than jail is a lenient, and perhaps too lenient, response to crime. If a crime is serious, it must lead to jail. Otherwise, we are denigrating its seriousness. This attitude may suggest that jail is a preferred sanction, but, in fact, jail is ordered in only a small minority of cases and the substantial majority of jail sentences are extremely short—less than 30 days. The point is that when gravity is emphasized at the sentencing stage, in the public perception, non-custodial options suffer as not having a punitive bite.

Another common comparison is with the international scene, where data are available based on the rate of incarceration per 100,000 population (see table 11.2).

International imprisonment statistics can be deceiving, and comparisons should be made carefully. First, it is important to ensure that similar data are compared. Admissions—the number of people received in custody during a period—should not be confused with an average count—the average population over a period. Second, when looking at count or population data, it is essential to segregate sentenced offenders from the total population, which, in many systems, will include remand prisoners awaiting trial. Table 11.2 provides an incarceration ratio.

Again, it is useful to look at historical trends. Recently, it has been argued that the rate of incarceration in Canada has been relatively constant (see Doob and Webster) over the past decades. Other countries have shown dramatic increases in the use of imprisonment. In 1997, the rate for the United States was calculated at 445 sentenced prisoners per 100,000 US residents: see A. Blumstein and A.J. Beck, "Population Growth in US Prisons, 1980-1996," in Tonry and Petersilia (1999), 26 *Crime and Justice* 17-61, at 18. By 2003, it had risen to 714. The website "World Prison Brief" puts the total number of incarcerated people in the United States in 2007 at 2,193,798. This is a direct effect of such penal strategies as the "war on drugs" and "three strikes, you're out." Some countries, like Finland, have shown substantial decreases in the post-World-War-II years, while the Netherlands' substantial decline was followed by a marked increase starting with a political move in 1985 to harsher penalties.

Table 11.2   Comparative Prison Populations

Country	Year of survey	Prison population rate per 100,000 population
United States	2003	714
Russia	2005	532
New Zealand	2004	168
England and Wales	2005	142
Netherlands	2004	123
Australia	2004	117
Canada	2003	116
Italy	2004	98
Turkey	2004	95
France	2004	91
Belgium	2004	88
Ireland	2004	85
Greece	2004	82
Switzerland	2004	81
Sweden	2003	75
Finland	2004	71
Denmark	2004	70
Croatia	2004	68
Norway	2004	65
Slovenia	2004	56
Cyprus	2004	50
Iceland	2004	39

Source: R. Walmsley, *World Prison Population List*, 6th ed. (London: International Centre for Prison Studies, King's College London, 2006).

II. THE EFFECTS OF INCARCERATION

The literature in this area is complex and vast. Imprisonment serves the twin purposes of incapacitation and separation. Certainly, incarceration provides a dramatic restriction in liberty during the period of incarceration, but whether this promotes any other anticipated goals of sentencing is controversial. Imprisonment not only separates the prisoner from the community but also places control over the environment and the daily routines of his or her life into the hands of the correctional system. Thus, the impact of imprisonment must be measured both in terms of its duration and its personal effects. Supporters of imprisonment assume that its rigours will produce deterrence. Also, it is expected that there may be some degree of rehabilitation. This, of course, is a function of the extent that the system provides programming directed at education, vocational training, or problems like substance abuse.

It cannot be assumed without confirming evidence that any system or institution in which a particular prisoner will eventually be confined actually provides relevant programming.

There are, of course, intrinsic negative consequences. Communities, families, and employment situations change over time and a prisoner does not simply return to fill the place that he previously vacated. The mere separation of the offender from his or her family and friends is often the source of both economic and emotional repercussions. Moreover, depending on the quality of the correctional system and the way in which it is manifested in a particular institution, imprisonment can produce serious negative effects: see the discussion of health risks, violence, mental health, institutionalization, and other negative effects in N. Walker and N. Padfield, *Sentencing: Theory, Law and Practice*, 2d ed. (London: Butterworths, 1996), 153-63.

One Canadian study dealing with violence in prisons concluded that a male prisoner runs a 14 times greater risk of being a victim of homicide in prison than does a man of comparable age living in the community: see F.J. Porporino and P. Doherty, *An Historical Analysis of Victims of Homicide in Canadian Penitentiaries* (Ottawa: Solicitor General Canada, 1985); also see A. Bottoms, "Interpersonal Violence and Social Order in Prisons" and A. Liebling, "Suicide and Prison Coping" (1999), 26 *Crime and Justice Review* at 205-82 and 283-360 respectively.

The following materials illustrate an ongoing debate about the potential consequences of long-term confinement. This debate is especially significant given the growing number of prisoners serving life sentences as a result of both the aggregate of people with long periods of parole ineligibility and an apparent lengthening of sentences for some offences. Combined with the claim that imprisonment is inefficacious in achieving sentencing objectives, this body of literature ought to be significant from a law reform perspective. However, substantive debate has too often been replaced by the politics of law and order.

J. Bonta and P. Gendreau, "Re-examining the Cruel and Unusual Punishment of Prison Life"
(1990), 14 *Law and Human Behavior* 347 (references omitted)

Historically, prisons have been described as barren landscapes devoid of even the most basic elements of humanity and detrimental to the humanity of the offender. Perhaps one of the best known descriptions of the inhumanity of prison is Cohen and Taylor's description of long-term inmates in a British maximum security prison. Such notions about prison life have been pervasive whether from the perspective of investigative journalists or academics writing for basic criminology texts.

Mitford (1973), in her very effective polemical style, painted a scathing indictment of prisons. Not only does imprisonment strip offenders of civil liberties, but also prison reforms are nothing but rhetoric and rehabilitation initiatives are despotic. Goffman (1961) also has been equally harsh in his assessment of the prison as a "total institution."

Careful empirical evaluations, however, have failed to uncover these pervasive negative effects of incarceration that so many have assumed. Mitford (1973) and Cohen and Taylor (1972) did not provide empirical evidence for psychological or behavioral deterioration. We need to be reminded that even Goffman (1961) did not collect data directly from prisons. His conclusions were based upon a review of the prison literature combined with data gathered from "asylums." Furthermore, earlier reviews of empirical studies also failed to uncover the widespread harm that is presumed inherent to prisons.

For some, the quantitative data, gathered as much as possible under conditions of objectivity, must not be believed. The failure of such data to confirm popular expectations has led to a number of responses. One is an increased dependence upon a phenomenological approach, or, at the very least, a shift from quantitative psychology to a process that examines prison existence in a qualitative and interpretive manner.

Another expression of disbelief in the data comes from critics who have argued that the failure to find damaging effects of incarceration has been due to the "false reality" of the researchers concerned. This false reality has apparently been ascribed to the fact that government researchers have vested interests in reporting results uncritical of the penal establishment.

A final concern, in this case emanating from researchers who have not yet embraced phenomenology, has been that much of the research has reached a "dead end." Historically, incarceration research examined informal social organizations within prisons and did not speak persuasively to the actual effects of imprisonment itself. In addition, the methodological problems in much of the early work were considerable and a number of researchers have been rather critical of the early simplistic approaches to imprisonment research. That is, much of the early research was guided by the "all or none" views of the deprivation and the early importation theorists. Thus, the complex nature of incarceration was not addressed.

In the past, most prisons were maximum security, and psychoeducational programming was minimal. Daily prison life featured 20-hour lock-up for a few and highly regimentized and monotonous work duties for the rest. Until recently, approaching the examination of prison life from a uniform perspective made eminently good sense. Now, however, the realities of prison life are far different. It is now appropriate to reexamine the effects of incarceration with special attention to the specific conditions of confinement. Although prisons may appear similar on the surface, closer examination finds them varying widely in security, living conditions, and the degree of programming.

Prison overcrowding, almost unknown in the early 1970s, is now very evident. Today, both very long-term and short-term periods of incarceration have dramatically increased. The number of offenders incarcerated is over 700,000. Current government crime control strategies, in the United States at least, will likely ensure that imprisonment will be the preferred option for the time being. In addition, one of the most extreme forms of prison life, solitary confinement, is still frequently employed.

Thus, research examining the effects of prison life is critically important. More knowledge must be generated and analyses of prison life must take into account the deprivation and importation literature, while also recognizing the great variety of structures and experiences that incarceration currently includes.

Selection and Organization of Studies

This review focuses on quantitative studies about effects of imprisonment. Qualitative or phenomenological studies were not included. To be included in the review, a study was required to employ objective measures of the variables of interest and to evaluate the relationship between them by means of statistical tests.

Thus, the majority of studies were of a correlational or quasiexperimental nature. The only truly experimental studies (i.e., random assignment) were found in the solitary confinement literature. Some studies appeared to straddle both the quantitative and qualitative camps. In these instances, we made a judgment call and only included them for discussion where appropriate.

The studies were identified with the aid of a computer search of the prison adjustment and penal literature. Other reviews and a review of recent criminological journals identified additional studies.

We viewed imprisonment as an independent variable and the behavioral and psychological observations of inmates as dependent variables. This organization appeared to work well with the studies dealing with specific conditions of confinement (e.g., solitary confinement). There is, on the other hand, a voluminous and frequently reviewed literature that has the independent variable, imprisonment, less clearly defined and investigates dependent variables, such as attitude and self-esteem changes. These later studies were not included in the present review.

Finally, a further comment on the dependent variables in the review is in order. Our interest was on the evaluation of assumed negative effects due to incarceration, and, therefore, we reviewed topics that were most likely to evidence such effects. We did not review the literature on rehabilitation and educational programs in prisons because their stated purpose is to actively promote positive behaviors. In general, *negative effects* were behaviors that threatened the physical welfare of the offender (e.g., aggressive behavior, suicide) and indicators of physiological stress levels (e.g., elevated blood pressure) and psychological distress (e.g., depression).

We examined specific aspects of confinement, namely, crowding, long-term imprisonment, solitary confinement, short-term detention, and death row. We make one departure from this format and provide a commentary on the health risks associated with imprisonment, which follows from our discussion of prison crowding. In our review of the prison crowding literature, we were able to use meta-analytic techniques because there were both an identifiable theoretical perspective and sufficient studies that could be subjected to analysis. With respect to the other aspects of confinement, either there were too few studies (e.g., death row) or they consistently failed to show negative consequences (e.g., solitary confinement), or, as in the case of long-term confinement, the cross-sectional methodology with multiple groups did not make the data amenable to meta-analytic techniques.

Crowding

Crowding is invariably perceived negatively. It is seen by many correctional managers as *the* major barrier to humane housing of offenders despite an estimated 170,000 additional new beds since 1980. This population explosion has prompted court interventions, sentencing reforms, and innovative classification systems intended to reduce prison populations.

Researchers view crowding as a complex phenomenon. Stokols (1972) distinguished *density*, a physical condition, from *crowding*, a psychological condition involving the individual's perception of constraints imposed by limited space. Loo (1973) further differentiated physical density into *spatial density* (number of people constant but the available space varies) and *social density* (space is constant but the number of people vary). For example, prison renovations might reduce the amount of space available to a number of inmates (spatial density), but the effects of this spatial rearrangement on the inmates may differ from the effects of a sudden influx of new inmates into the institution (social density).

Despite these distinctions, corrections research has been inconsistent in the use of the concepts of crowding and spatial and social density. Studies have described crowding as both an independent and dependent variable, and the distinction between social and spatial density has infrequently been noted.

Most researchers agree that crowding describes a psychological response to high population density which is often viewed as stressful. Although high population density is a necessary condition for crowding, it is not a sufficient condition, and other variables may be required to produce the perception of crowding. Sundstrom (1978) described crowding as a sequential process resulting form an interaction of person variables, high population density, correlates of high density (e.g., increased noise levels), and situational variables (e.g. duration of exposure).

Following Sundstrom's model, we would expect that the behaviors observed under high population densities would vary in intensity and variety with length of exposure. For example, under brief exposure we may see elevated blood pressure, followed by reports of anxiety as exposure increases, and ending with violent behavioral outbursts under prolonged exposures. To test this hypothesis, a longitudinal design is required, and, to the best of our knowledge, there is only one study that has approximated this goal. Indirect support of the model may be gathered from comparisons of the relative strength of the relationships between population density and a variety of outcomes. That is, we would expect that reports of physiological and psychological stress would be relatively easy to come by and that the findings would be robust, whereas observations of violent behavior would be more infrequent and equivocal.

To explore this model, we undertook both a qualitative and quantitative review of the prison crowd in literature. Studies that provided sufficient statistical information on the relationship between population density and the dependent variable were subject to a meta-analysis. The dependent variable was arranged into three categories: physiological, psychological, and behavioral. Some studies reported more than one measure within a category. In these situations, we gave priority to systolic blood pressure for the physiological category, a paper-and-pencil measure of perceived crowding described by Paulus (1988) for the psychological category, and misconduct for the behavioral category. These measures were the most frequently used. We would have liked to categorize the measures of crowding into aggregate, social, and spatial density, but to have done so would have drastically reduced our samples in each cell.

The strength of the relationship, or effect size, was measured by Cohen (1977) and calculated using the statistical conversion formulas described by Glass, McGaw, and Smith (1981). In our analysis, d indicated the size of the difference in standard units between crowded and noncrowded conditions. Standardizing the measures (d) allowed us to compare results from different studies. For studies that reported nonsignificant results, d was set at zero. ...

... [P]hysiological and psychological stress responses (Outcomes A and B) were very likely under crowded prison conditions. The majority of studies employing such measures found significant results. The one inconsistent finding was the *inverse* relationship between crowding and blood pressure ($d = -.70$) reported by McCain, Cox, and Paulus (1980). This may have been a spurious result because there was no relationship between blood pressure and crowding for the institution in question for the previous year (1978). If this size effect is removed from the calculation of the mean, then we obtain a mean of $d = .51$ for Outcome A, which is quite consistent with the model. In the case of behavioral acting-out, the strength of the relationship diminished to the point of being relatively insignificant as the studies ranged in effect size from $-.90$ to $+.87$.

While the results outlined under Outcomes A and B seem straightforward, some clarification is required. That is, although physiological stress in response to population density was the rule, reports of psychological stress concomitant with physiological stress were not always observed and, for the most part, rarely studied. When the two were observed together, the relationship was usually dependent upon other variables. In 1973, Paulus, McCain, and Cox reported (no data were presented) that social density was related to a physiological measure of stress (palmer sweat) but not to a subjective appraisal of feeling crowded. However, in a subsequent study, which considered length of exposure, there was an increased perception of feeling crowded for inmates in dormitories (high social density) but not for inmates in cells (low social density). Other studies have noted the moderating effect of length of exposure on physiological and psychological measures of stress.

In the one longitudinal study reported in the literature, Ostfield and his colleagues (1987) followed 128 inmates through their incarceration to release and postrelease. Physiological and psychological measures were taken at regular intervals and controls were introduced for other confounding variables such as weight and criminal history. They found changes in blood pressure associated with population density but no statistically significant changes for anxiety, hostility, and depression.

These studies, nevertheless, suggested a positive relationship between social density and physiological indicators of stress and subjective reports of discomfort. Indications of physiological stress appear as immediate consequences to high social density, and it is possible that with increased exposure to such a situation other cumulative consequences such as psychological distress may follow.

It is important, however, from a policy perspective, to evaluate whether or not population density is related to severe, disruptive behavior that may jeopardize the physical safety of the inmates. The findings ... do not support an overall relationship between crowding and disruptive inmate behavior.

Megargee (1977) was the first to empirically study the relationship between crowding and reported disciplinary infractions. He collected data over a 3-year span at a medium security prison for youthful offenders (aged 18 to 25). Spatial density was more highly correlated with institutional misconduct than was social density, but social interaction factors (e.g., friendship ties) may have played an important role. Density, without distinction to spatial or social density, and disciplinary infractions are, according to some investigators, positively related, but no such association was found by others.

From our appraisal of the empirical literature we cannot conclude that high population density is always associated with aggressive behavior. Most researchers agree that other variables play important moderating roles. One important moderator variable is age of the inmates. The relationship between misconduct and population density has been more pronounced in institutions housing young offenders. Even in studies that failed to uncover a general positive relationship, the introduction of age as a moderator showed a correlation between population density and misconduct. In the Ekland-Olson et al. study (1983), when institutions with a relatively young population (median age of 27) were selected for analysis, a highly significant correlation was found ($r = .58$ or a $d = 1.43$). The authors concluded that age is a much better predictor of disciplinary infractions than prison size.

Only one study discounts the importance of age. Gaes and McGuire (1985) assessed a variety of predictors along with age and under these conditions age became relatively less important. The authors observed that most studies of overcrowding and misconduct typically assess few variables and may overestimate the importance of any one variable.

Interpreting the behavioral consequences of prison overcrowding is further confounded by the use of aggregate level data. ... [A]lmost all the studies under Outcome C are aggregate level data. The problem with this level of analysis is that many other factors (e.g., age, release policies) may play more important roles than population density. Clayton and Carr (1987) have shown that aggregate data analysis overestimates the relationship between crowding and behavior (a point already made in the preceding paragraph). In their study investigating the relationship between prison overcrowding and recidivism (2 years postrelease), age was the critical variable. The only other study that used recidivism as an outcome measure was by Farringotn and Nuttall (1980), and they found a significant relationship between crowding and postrelease recidivism. However, Gaes (1983) has suggested that other extraneous variables (e.g., age, staff–inmate ratios) could better account for the results.

Although age has consistently been identified as an important moderating variable, explanations of why this is so have not been carefully researched. Are the young simply impulsive, lack coping skills, and more easily susceptible to stress? MacKenzie (1987) found oppositional or "assertive" attitudes and fear of victimization rather than coping ability as most relevant to misconducts. Clearly further research on this issue is desirable.

The identification of person variables as moderators in the experience of prison crowding raises the enduring issue of importation versus deprivation. That is, are the behaviors observed in prison reflective of behavioral patterns that were present prior to incarceration or a response to the deprivation of liberties imposed by confinement? As Freedman (1975) wrote, "crowding has neither good nor bad effects but rather serves to intensify the individual's typical reactions to a situation." Thus, the disciplinary infractions observed in crowded prisons may be the result of either high population densities or a continuation of behaviors that existed before incarceration, or both. As Ruback and Innes (1988) have remarked, there are no studies that have partitioned inmates with violent histories from nonviolent inmates. This is very important because it is usually the maximum security settings that are crowded, and they are also the settings most likely to house violent inmates. The possibility of an interaction can be seen in Smith's (1982) account of how assertive inmates became more aggressive and the passive inmates more submissive under crowded conditions.

There are other factors, besides person variables, that may influence aggressive behavior in crowded prisons. For instance, crowded prisons may be poorly managed. Although prison populations may fluctuate widely, corresponding changes in the number of supervisory staff, counselors, and programs rarely occur. When the population is large, there are fewer correctional staff to monitor behavior and provide inmates with the opportunities to learn adaptive coping skills. The management of prisons and prison systems may account for some inmate disturbances. A case in point is the occurrence of sudden changes in the population membership. Porporino and Dudley (1984), in reviewing evidence from 24 Canadian penitentiaries, found high inmate turnover more important than population density in the prediction of inmate disruptions. The authors speculated that inmates are required to deal with newly arrived inmates more frequently and this may be extremely stressful. For example, in the 1980 New Mexico prison riot, the inmate population was not at its peak but there was a sudden influx of new inmates in the months preceding the riot.

Another factor appears to be the chronicity of the situation. That is, as sentence length or exposure to crowded situations increase so does the risk for misconduct. This is a tentative conclusion because of other confounding factors such as age and type of institution.

In summary, crowded prisons may produce physiological and psychological stress among many inmates. More disruptive effects, however, depend upon moderating person variables such as age, institutional parameters (e.g., sudden shifts in the inmate membership), and the chronicity of the situation. In addition, aggressive behavior may be a cumulative effect of high population densities. More research into the parameters that govern this effect is required.

Two theoretical models have been advanced in an effort to explain the inmate's response to prison overcrowding. The social-interaction demand model favored by Paulus and his colleagues assumes that social interactions interfere with goal attainment and increase uncertainty and cognitive load. That is, it is the nature of the social interactions that may produce negative effects and high population densities are important only to the degree that they affect social interactions. The second model is based on a cognitive social-learning model.

This latter model places greater emphasis on individual differences (person variables) and stresses two processes: attribution and learned coping behavior. Increases in population density produce changes not only in social interactions but also changes in noise level, temperature, etc., and these in turn produce physiological arousal. When inmates attribute this arousal to violation of their personal space rather than some other factor they then report feeling crowded. Once the attribution is made, existing coping behaviours are activated with the goal to reduce arousal and feelings of crowding.

Except for MacKenzie's (1987) findings, penal researchers have found that coping behavior plays a significant role in the inmates' response to incarceration and that inmates vary in the effectiveness of their coping behaviors. Clements (1979) has suggested that coping behavior may be influential in the inmates' adaptation to prison overcrowding, although some of these behaviors, such as assault and suicide, are clearly not adaptive. Unfortunately, poor coping skills are all too prevalent among inmate populations and this is reflected in their disruptive behavioral responses to high population densities. However, other behaviors can alleviate crowding-induced arousal and at the same time be adaptive. For example, class-room attendance and psychological interventions have been shown to decrease feelings of being crowded. Besides searching for ways to control the prison population growth we can also develop programs to teach individual inmates more effective skills to cope with high prison populations.

Health Risks

As we have seen with the prison crowding literature, it is not uncommon to observe physiological and psychological distress associated with high population densities. Such outcomes are also commonly associated with stress and physical disorders. In fact, many studies of prison overcrowding will use illness complaints as a dependent measure. Thus, we now turn our attention to a related topic and ask ourselves if imprisonment threatens the health of the confined.

Most of the research has dealt with the identification and description of illnesses reported by prisoners. Available data fail to clearly indicate whether inmates display more or less health risks than the general population. When threats to health come from suicide and self-mutilation, then inmates are clearly at risk. Though it is widely believed that the risk of homicide is greater within prison than in the community, the evidence is mixed. In Canadian penitentiaries, the homicide rates are close to 20 times that of similar aged males in Canadian society. In the United States, deaths due to homicide are actually less likely within prison. With respect to self-injurious behavior, the results are more consistent. Inmate suicides for a 20-year period in the United States were at a rate of 17.5 per 100,000 inmates in contrast to 11 per 100,000 people in the general population. Self-mutilations are at an even higher rate.

When one examines the incidence of physical illnesses, the findings are less conclusive. One of the classic studies comes from Jones (1976) who surveyed the health risks of Tennessee prisoners and compared them where possible to probationers and data existing on the general adult male US population. The patterns of results are rather complex but, by and large, a variety of health problems, injuries, and selected symptoms of psychological distress were higher for certain classes of inmates than probationers, parolees, and, where data existed, for the general population.

In contrast to Jones (1976), a number of other researchers have failed to find deleterious effects on health. Goldsmith (1972) followed 50 inmates over a 2-month period and found no major health problems as assessed by physical examinations. On a larger inmate sample ($N = 491$), Derro (1978) found that only 12% of the symptoms reported on admission related to a significant illness. This is an important point because many studies "count" health care contacts without differentiating the nature of the contact. Inmates may seek the aid of health care professionals for reasons other than a physical illness.

Two studies also reported a significantly lower incidence of hypertension among inmates compared to the general population. Culpepper and Froom (1980) found the incidence of hypertension among a prison population at 6%. In another study, the incidence of hypertension among 1,300 inmates was 4.5%. We remind the reader, however, that this finding relates to the effects of incarceration in general and not to specific conditions such as prison crowding where the results are different (Gaes, 1985).

One of the problems with the interpretation of the above data has been that there is so little use of adequate control groups especially with respect to age and race. Also, Baird (1977) found that many prisoners with physical complaints were displaying a variety of health risks well *before* incarceration. As a case in point, Bentz and Noel (1983) found that upon entering prison, inmates were reporting a higher incidence of psychiatric disorder than a sample of a rural population in North Carolina. This finding is also of interest in light of Gibbs' (1987) claim that incarceration aggravates psychological symptomatology (we will say more about this in the discussion on short-term detention).

A final consideration is that many prisons may actually be conductive to good health. In a number of cases, illness complaints have either decreased with time served or remained unchanged. In most prisons, inmates have regular and nutritious diets, access to recreational exercise, and opportunity to sleep. Furthermore, offenders can obtain fairly immediate health care. Because of this last possibility, health risks could easily be overreported in prisons with extensive health services and thus bias some of the research findings.

In summary, the current findings recall Glueck and Glueck's (1950) comparison of 500 delinquents with 500 nondelinquents: In training school, the boys were generally healthy and physically fit, whereas in the community, as a result of their adventurous lifestyles, they were prone to more serious accidents. More than 35 years later, Ruback and Innes (1988) make this same observation based upon information from adult inmates. Thus, as far as physical health is concerned, imprisonment may have the fortuitous benefit of isolating the offender from a highly risky lifestyle in the community.

Long-Term Incarceration

In 1984 there were approximately 1,500 offenders serving life sentences in Canadian prisons and with recent legislation defining minimum sentences (25 years) without parole for first and second degree murder, those numbers are expected to increase significantly. Similar trends have also been noted in the United States, where mandatory and lengthy prison terms have been widely implemented. What happens to these people as a result of such lengthy sentences? Most of the research has focused upon time spans not longer than 2 or 3 years, and our knowledge regarding offenders serving sentences of 5, 10, or more years is less adequate.

Using cross-sectional designs, Heskin and his colleagues measured inmates' performances on cognitive tests, personality measures, and attitudinal scales. Four groups of prisoners, all sentenced to at least 10 years, were studied. The average time served was 2.5 years for the first group of inmates, 4.9 years for the second group, 6.9 years for the third, and 11.3 for the last group. No differences were found among the groups in intellectual performance, although there was a decline in perceptual motor speed on the cognitive tasks. On the personality and attitudinal tests, there were increases in hostility and social introversion and decreases in self-evaluations and evaluations of work and father.

Subsequently, Bolton, Smith, Heskin, and Banister (1976) retested 154 of the original 175 inmates in the Heskin research (average retest interval was 2 years). Their findings showed no evidence of psychological deterioration. In fact, verbal intelligence improved over time and hostility decreased. The findings with respect to hostility are in contrast to the cross-sectional studies, but, as the authors noted, there was a significant drop-out rate. Furthermore, the initial testing occurred during a period of institutional tensions, which may have produced artificially high hostility scores.

Sapsford (1978) administered a psychometric test battery to 60 prisoners sentenced to life imprisonment. The prisoners formed three groups: (1) reception (newly received), (2) middle (6th year of sentence), and (3) hard core (average sentence served was 21.4 years). Some matching was attempted but it is not clear the extent to which the procedure was successful. From the results, only three inmates could be described as having failed to cope with their sentence. The only deteriorating effects observed were increases in dependency upon staff for direction and social introversion. In fact, depression and anxiety were lower for inmates serving longer sentences.

Reed's (1978) geriatric prisoner research also has relevance to the issue. His aged prisoners (mean age of 60 years), with an average sentence served of 23 years, reported fewer life problems than their peers in the outside community. Furthermore, they reported active interests and feelings younger than their age.

Similarly, Richards (1978) also failed to note negative differences between British prisoners who had served at least 8 years of their sentences and inmates who had served more than 10 years. The two groups were matched on age at sentencing and type of offense. The inmates were asked to rate the frequency and severity of 20 different problems that may be initiated by incarceration (e.g., missing social life, sexual frustration). The results showed no differences in the perception of problems by the two groups, and there was agreement by the inmates that coping could be best accomplished by relying on "myself."

Utilizing Richard's (1978) problem-ranking task, Flanagan (1980a) assessed American inmates who had served at least 5 years and compared his results to those reported by Richards (1978). He found that the American inmates perceived similar problems to those reported by the British prisoners in that they also did not perceive the problems as particularly threatening to their mental health. Furthermore, they preferred to cope with their sentences on their own rather than seek the aid of others. In another study, Flanagan (1980b) compared misconduct rates of 701 short-term prisoners (less than 5 years) and 765 long-term inmates. Even after controlling for age, the misconduct rate among the long-term inmates was approximately half that of the short-term offenders.

Rasch (1981) assessed lifers who had served 3, 8.5, and 13.5 years and found no deterioration in health, psychiatric symptoms, or intellect. The results of MMP1 testing documented decreased pathology over time, replicating Sapsford's (1980) findings. Another German study, cited by Wormith (1984a), apparently found similar results. Moreover, when long-term inmates (20 years) displayed pathology, such behaviors were apparent long before incarceration

A series of studies conducted by Wormith (1984, 1986) observed a differential impact from long-term incarceration. In the first study, 269 inmates who had served from 1 month to 10 years were administered a psychometric test battery. Once again those inmates who had served the most time displayed significantly less deviance. This relationship remained even after the introduction of controls for sentence length, age upon admission, and race. Improvement over time was also noted on attitudinal measures and nonpathological personality characteristics. Finally, changes in intelligence did not vary with length of incarceration.

The second study by Wormith (1986) consisted of a random sample of 634 male prisoners stratified according to sentence length and time served. Long-term inmates (8 years to life), compared to short-term inmates, demonstrated better adjustment on measures of self-reports of emotions and attitudes (e.g., anger) and institution discipline. On measures of criminal sentiments, long-term offenders displayed a U-shaped function while short-term offenders became more antisocial. As expected, long-term inmates had deteriorating community relationships over time but made more use of institutional programs (e.g., education), which was likely important for a successful adaptation to prison life.

MacKenzie and Goodstein (1985) reported findings similar to those described by Wormith (1984, 1986). Long-term inmates (more than 6 years served) found the earlier portion of their sentences more stressful, but with time they learned to cope effectively. Of particular interest was their differentiation of two subgroups of long-term offenders. Using prison experience as a discriminating factor, they identified two groups, inmates with minimal prison experience (lifers) and inmates with extensive prison experience (habituals). Both groups showed the same adjustment patterns, contrary to the expectation that habituals would evidence disruptive behaviors. Similar findings with respect to female offenders have also been reported by MacKenzie, Robinson, and Campbell (1989). In fact, long-term inmates were more bothered by boredom and lack of activities than by anxiety.

Most of the above studies have been cross-sectional. A publication by Zamble and Porporino (1990) on how inmates cope with prison assumes importance for two reasons. First, it is longitudinal. Of their sample ($N = 133$), 30% were serving sentences of more than 10 years. They were assessed within 1 month of admission and 1½ years later, Zamble and Porporino found no *overall* indication of deterioration of coping skills over time, even for inmates serving their first incarceration. As well, there was no increase in identification with "criminal others" and their "view of the world" did not change. The authors surmise that as prisons, by and large, constrain behavior and do little to encourage changes in behavior one way or the other, inmates typically undergo a "behavioral deep freeze." The outside-world behaviors that led the offender into trouble prior to imprisonment remain until release.

Secondly, it is important to emphasize that Zamble and Porporino do not in the least deny the fact that individual differences are meaningful. They reported that how some inmates coped with incarceration correlated with postprison recidivism. For example, some of the significant factors were changes in perceptions of prison life, degree and type of socialization with incarcerated peers, planning for the future, and motivation regarding work and educational goals. We will return to this point later.

In summary, from the available evidence and on the dimensions measured, there is little to support the conclusion that long-term imprisonment necessarily has detrimental effects. As a caution, however, Flanagan (1982) claims that lifers may change upon other dimensions that have yet to be objectively measured. For example, family separation issues and vocational skill training needs present unique difficulties for long-term inmates. Unfortunately, cross-sectional designs and, until recently, small subject populations have been characteristic of these studies.

Solitary Confinement

Solitary confinement is "the most individually destructive, psychologically crippling and socially alienating experience that could conceivably exist within the borders of the country." So wrote Jackson (1983) in his scathing denouncement of the use of solitary confinement for prisoners. The commonly accepted definition of prison solitary confinement is maximum security lock-up, usually for punitive reasons. Sensory stimulation is very limited. The inmate may have a book to read and access to a half hour of "recreation" (alone). Conditions of prison solitary should not be confused with other forms of protective segregation where admission is usually voluntary, and the inmate has access to programming, TV, and so forth. No doubt, if any prison experience is evidence of cruel and unusual punishment, then surely that experience is prison solitary.

In contrast to the popular notions of solitary's negative effects, there exists an extensive experimental literature on the effects of placing people (usually volunteer college students) in solitary, or conditions of sensory deprivation, which has been ignored in the penology literature. It should be noted that the conditions in some of the sensory deprivation experiments are more severe than that found in prison solitary. In fact, this literature has much relevance to prison solitary confinement. Considerable research has also been undertaken with prisoners, themselves, and many of these studies are, methodologically, the most rigorous of all the prison studies. Therefore, conclusions drawn from this source are especially informative.

Experimental studies have found few detrimental effects for subjects placed in solitary confinement for periods up to 10 days. All but one of these studies employed random assignment and most employed a double blind assessment of dependent variables. Perceptual and motor abilities were not impaired, physiological levels of stress were lower than for the control groups, and various attitudes toward the environment and the self did not worsen. Individual differences have also been observed. Experience with prison life, conceptual ability, anxiety, diurnal adrenal levels, and EEG patterns were related to some of the results reported, although it should be noted that results are based upon very small sample sizes. Some of the experimental studies even reported beneficial results. In certain respects, the prison literature is quite consistent with the experimental sensory deprivation laboratory data.

In contrast to the studies that used volunteer subjects, Weinberg (1967) looked at 20 inmates who were involuntarily placed for 5 days in solitary confinement. Using measures such as cognitive and personality tests, language usage, and time estimation, he, too, found no deleterious effects. Suedfeld, Ramirez, and Baker-Brown (1982), also studying inmates involuntarily in solitary confinement, also failed to find detrimental effects. Their data were collected from five prisons in Canada and the United States, and they found that, in general, inmates found the first 72 hours the most difficult but after that they adjusted quite well. The authors reached this conclusion: "Our data lend no support to the claim that solitary confinement ... is overwhelmingly aversive, stressful, or damaging to the inmates."

In contrast, Cormiet and Williams (1966) and Grassian (1983) recorded signs of pathology for inmates incarcerated in solitary for periods up to a year. No objective measures or control groups were used. In the former study, most of the inmates exhibited substantial pathology prior to solitary. In the second study, all subjects were involved in a class action suit against their keepers at the time of the interview, and the author actively encouraged more disclosure when the inmates were not forthcoming with reports of distress. Similarly, the experimental literature on sensory deprivation demonstrates that once controls for set and expectancies are introduced, bizarre experiences, under even the most severe conditions (immobilization and sensory deprivation for 14 days, were minimal for the majority of subjects.

The real culprit may not necessarily be the condition of solitary per se but the manner in which inmates have been treated. There is evidence suggesting that this is the basis for most inmate complaints. Jackson (1983) himself acceded to this fact. When inmates are dealt with capriciously by management or individual custodial officers, psychological stress can be created even in the most humane of prison environments. Therefore, solitary confinement may not be cruel and unusual punishment under the humane and time-limited conditions investigated in experimental studies or in correctional jurisdictions that have well-defined and effectively administered ethical guidelines for its use.

We must emphasize that this is *not* an argument for employing solitary and certainly not for the absurdly lengthy periods as documented by Jackson (1983). Gendreau and Bonta (1984) have outlined several research issues that urgently need to be addressed. Some of these are studies investigating individual tolerance of solitary confinement, its possible deterrent effect, and a compelling need to find alternatives to humanely restrain those who are a danger to themselves and others while incarcerated. With rare exceptions, the necessary research has not been conducted.

Short-Term Detention

In 1972, nearly 4,000 jails in the United States processed 1 million male and female offenders per year. The offenders were charged with a variety of crimes and approximately 75% of them were awaiting trial. Despite the extensive use of jails, little is known about the effects of short-term detention. Perhaps this is the area that requires most attention, as it is the initial adjustment phases that are important in assessing the impact of incarceration. For example, 50% of suicides occur in the first 24 hours of imprisonment.

A common belief is that waiting for trial and sentencing produces a considerable amount of anxiety. More specifically, anxiety increases as the trial and sentencing dates approach and then decreases after sentencing when the uncertainty surrounding trial has passed.

A study by Dyer is difficult to evaluate because of the lack of information provided. Dyer administered an anxiety scale to adolescent females and found a decrease in anxiety over time in detention. However, no information regarding the number of subjects, the setting, and the interval between tests was provided. Oleski (1977) administered the same scale to 60 male inmates (ages 18 to 26) in a Boston city jail. All were awaiting trial and all had limited prior prison experience. The tests were administered 1 week after admission and again 8 weeks later. Anxiety levels were found to be higher at posttest.

Bonta and Nackivell (1980) administered the same anxiety scale used in the previous studies to four groups of inmates selected without age and court status limitations. Group 1 inmates were remanded into custody and sentenced by the time they were retested; Group 2 were still awaiting sentencing. Group 3 inmates entered the jail already sentenced, and Group 4 was a control group for the effects of testing. The test was administered within 1 week of reception and again 3 to 4 weeks later. No changes in anxiety over time or after sentencing were observed.

Gibbs (1987) assessed psychopathology among 339 jail inmates. The inmates were asked to rate symptoms prior to incarceration, 72 hours into confinement, and again 5 days later. He found symptoms to increase between preincarceration and 72 hours of imprisonment and interpreted this finding as showing that detention per se affects symptoms. However, the interpretation is not entirely convincing. First of all, symptomatology prior to incarceration was based upon the inmates' recollections of their difficulties before detention and thus subject to memory and reporting biases. Second, at the 5-day retest, symptoms actually diminished, and third, the finding that those without prior hospitalizations did worse was a puzzling finding and not consistent with the prison as stress model.

There is another intriguing, albeit tangential, aspect to the short-term detention literature, and that is the use of short-term detention as a deterrent. Three common strategies are "Scared Straight," "boot camp," and shock probation programs. The assumption is that prison life is aversive in some form or other and that exposure to it will decrease the probability of future criminal behavior, particularly for impressionable young offenders.

The classic evaluation of "Scared Straight" by Finckenauer and Storti (1978) found only one of nine attitudinal measures significantly changed for juveniles as a result of brief exposure to hardened prisoners and no reduction in recidivism. Other variations on the original program have also found no overall deterrent effect, although some individual differences were noted. Similarly, there is now general consensus that shock probation (i.e., short prison terms prior to probation) has also failed to demonstrate significant deterrent effects. There is even one report suggesting that shock probation for a subgroup of probationers increased recidivism!

Some jurisdictions have received media attention by employing quasimilitary, boot camp regimes for offenders. In the only evaluation with a follow-up that we are aware of—although more will be forthcoming in the near future—juveniles taking part in such a program did not have reduced reconviction rates compared to nonparticipatory youths. Curiously, older adolescents reported an easier time in the program compared to their previous experiences with incarceration.

· · ·

Summary and Conclusion

When it comes to scholarly inquiry in the field of criminal justice, a pernicious tendency has been to invoke rhetoric over reality and affirm ideology over respect for empirical evidence. We have witnessed this sad state of affairs in the debates over the effectiveness of rehabilitation, personality and crime, and the relationship between social class and criminal behavior.

If we are to make progress in understanding what it is our prisons do to inmates, then we must respect the available evidence. We do not discount the importance of phenomenology in assessing prison life; this line of inquiry does provide valuable insight. But, if we stray too far from the epistemic values that are crucial to a vigorous social science then we run the risk of making disastrous policy decisions. Therefore, if we are to have a more constructive agenda we must face the fact that simplistic notions of the "pains of imprisonment" simply will not be instructive and will mitigate against the inmate's well-being.

The facts are that long-term imprisonment and specific conditions of confinement such as solitary, under limiting and humane conditions, fail to show any sort of profound detrimental effects. The crowding literature indicates that moderating variables play a crucial role. The health risks to inmates appear minimal. Unfortunately prisons, in a way, may minimize some stress by removing the need to make daily decisions that are important for community living.

If we approach prison life with sensitivity, however, we will foster a much more realistic and proactive research and policy agenda. Our literature review revealed considerable support for this notion. We repeatedly found that interactions between certain types of individual differences and situational components explained a meaningful percentage of the variance. To illustrate, we found that age, changes in the prison population, and the chronicity of the situation had profound influences on the responses of inmates to high population density. There also appear to be some cognitive and biological individual differences that may influence adjustment to solitary confinement.

In regard to the above, it is important that the assessment of environments reach the same level of methodological sophistication as the assessment of individuals. There have been some promising developments toward that end. Wenk and Moos (1972) have developed the correctional Institutions Environment Scale; Toch (1977), the Prison Preference Profile; and Wright (1985), the Prison Environment Inventory. These are initial steps and it is hoped that research along these lines will continue.

Our final comments are in regard to theory development. To date, the incarceration literature has been very much influenced by a "pains of imprisonment" model. This model views imprisonment as psychologically harmful. However, the empirical data we reviewed question the validity of the view that imprisonment is *universally* painful. Solitary confinement, under limiting and humane conditions, long-term imprisonment, and short-term detention fail to show detrimental effects. From a physical health standpoint, inmates appear more healthy than their community counterparts. We have little data on the effects of death row, and the crowding literature indicates that moderating variables play a crucial role.

On a brighter note, the stress model does provide a positive agenda for ameliorative action. In the long-term incarceration literature, researchers have found that some inmates cope successfully with prison but others do not and that the type of coping is modestly related to future recidivism. Furthermore, on the basis of their analysis, if emotional distress is reported by inmates, it is more often early on in their incarceration. It is at this point that they may be receptive to treatment. The implications for the timing of prison-based treatment programs is obvious. The crucial point is that on the basis of this evidence, we can now develop a variety of cognitive-behavioral and/or skills training programs that could assist prisoners in dealing with their experiences in the most constructive manner possible. There is accumulating and persuasive evidence, moreover, that certain types of offender programming strategies in prison can reduce subsequent recidivism. This proactive agenda, we wish to emphasize, was not forthcoming from those who viewed prisons as invariably destructive. Unfortunately, their recommendations were for almost total deinstitutionalization, which is not only an extreme view, but also one that is totally unpalatable given North American cultural values and the current sociopolitical reality.

In our view, a social learning perspective provides a more comprehensive explanation of the evidence. Social learning theory examines behavior (attitudes, motor actions, emotions) as a function of the rewards and punishments operating in a prison environment. There is an explicit acceptance of personal variables moderating the responsivity to imprisonment. Several questions emerge from this perspective: *Who* perceives prisons as stressful? *What* aspect of imprisonment shapes behavior? And *how* do individuals respond to imprisonment? Answers to these questions would provide insight into the individuals who do not perceive their environments as stressful while imprisoned and what aspects of imprisonment attenuate the prison experience. In addition, this perspective would clarify the links between emotions, attitudes, and behavior.

From this review, we also see a clear research agenda. Further efforts to understand the effects of prison overcrowding should focus on individual levels of analysis along with multiple measures of the three outcome variables (emotions, attitudes, and behavior). Longitudinal designs should be the rule. The inherent difficulties in interpreting aggregate level data appear only to confuse our understanding of the impact of crowded conditions on the individual. We need to know under what conditions an individual feels crowded, becomes emotionally distressed, and copes with this distress in a maladaptive manner. For example, Ruback, Carr, and Hopper (1986) suggested that perceived control is a possible mediator. The solution to prison overcrowding is not to embark on a prohibitively expensive prison construction program but rather to alter the rate of intake and release. One way of accomplishing this task is to increase community correctional treatment programs that would allow the diversion of inmates away from prisons. Despite the reluctance of many correctional administrators to develop such programs, there appears to be considerable public support not only for community treatment initiatives but for rehabilitation in general.

The application of longitudinal designs using data collected at the individual level is also needed in the other areas we have discussed. This is especially so with long-term imprisonment and health risks where the data suggest that if anything, the prison system may actually prevent deterioration. However, only longitudinal designs will allow us to make such a conclusion with any high degree of certainty. If future research leads us to the same conclusion, then the next step would be to identify the system contingencies that support such an environment, for certainly we can learn something positive from this type of result. Finally, and remarkably, we know so little about the psychological impact of a system that houses over a million individuals: the jails. Here, almost any type of reasoned research would be a step in the right direction.

All of the above is easier said than done. The host of issues that need to be researched seem infinite. The methodological complexities in examining both person and situation interaction are pronounced. But, it appears to us to be a positive agenda in order to gain knowledge addressing a vital question.

J.V. Roberts and M. Jackson, "Boats Against the Current:
A Note on the Effects of Imprisonment"
(1991), 15 *Law and Human Behavior* 557 (footnotes and references omitted)

In their review of research on the effects of imprisonment, Bonta and Gendreau (1990) draw the rather startling conclusions that "long-term imprisonment and specific conditions of confinement such as solitary, under limiting and humane conditions, fail to show any sort of profound detrimental effects" and "many prisons may actually be conducive to good health." In light of our experience, both direct and indirect (through research as well as the sworn testimony of witnesses), we have difficulty sharing this upbeat assessment of the effects of incarceration. We feel imprisonment should be used with far more restraint than at the present, and before rejecting the view that imprisonment is intrinsically destructive, we would require evidence more compelling than that generated by contemporary social science research.

The authors assume that a sentence of custody is more punitive than, but in other ways no different from, other sanctions. In our opinion, this view fails to take into account the phenomenology of the prison as it has evolved in western society. Incarceration has acquired a significance that exceeds description as mere punishment. This is not to say that the effects of imprisonment are impervious to scientific investigation, but simply that the experience of incarceration might not be adequately captured by the usual social science dependent variables. Can the effects of an experience such as living on death row really be captured by psychiatric interviews or the MMPI? Bonta and Gendreau state: "From the *available evidence and on the dimensions measured* there is little to support the conclusion that long-term imprisonment necessarily has detrimental effects" (emphasis added). Our point is that the available evidence does not permit one to draw a conclusion that flies in the face of centuries of human experience.

Post-Release Consequences of Imprisonment

The research reviewed focused exclusively on inmates. This eliminates from consideration consequences of imprisonment that await the inmate upon emerging from prison. These consequences have been well documented: some are psychological (including self-perceptions, self-esteem, and so on), some are related to the workplace (the absence of job skills resulting from protracted incarceration), but perhaps the most pernicious effects concern the reactions of others.

The stigmatizing effect of a prison record has, of course, long been recognized. In 1859, the report of the Board of Prison Inspectors noted that an inmate is released "with the stamp of the prison upon him" and that this fact has important consequences for the individual. The fact that an individual has served time is fraught with implication. A Harris poll in the US in 1968 found that many people would feel uneasy working with ex-inmates; a Canadian survey found that people are more at ease in the presence of an ex-mental patient than an ex-inmate. The social reaction to an individual who has spent time in prison can be as damaging as the direct effects of incarcerations. Bonta and Gendreau's review is curiously silent regarding this kind of effect.

One of us recently represented a man released from prison after serving 37 years under an indeterminate sentence. He was released on the grounds that his continued imprisonment constituted cruel and unusual punishment. From the evidence presented to the courts, this man, measured by Bonta and Gendreau's objective indices of negative effects of imprisonment—"behaviors which threaten the physical welfare of the offender (e.g., aggressive behavior, suicide) ... psychological stress levels (e.g., elevated blood pressure) and psychological stress (e.g., depression)"—is in better shape after imprisonment. According to the Bonta and Gendreau approach to the scientific measurement of long-term imprisonment, there is therefore nothing cruel or unusual about 37 years in prison.

It would be a salutary exercise in scientific humility for Bonta and Gendreau to put aside their "objective measures" and to consider the effects of such a period of imprisonment in the manner in which it was described by the Supreme Court of Canada. In the words of Mr. Justice Cory: "The period of incarceration has been long indeed. ... During his incarceration, governments have changed, wars have begun and ended and a generation has grown to maturity." Understanding the negative impact of 37 years of imprisonment on Mr. Steele requires an acknowledgment that he finds himself separated by an unbridgeable gap of social experience from his peers in the free community. The generation of free men and women with whom he lost contact 37 years earlier are now thinking about retirement. For his part, Mr. Steele has to think about starting a new life. While his peers reap the rewards associated with parenthood (and grandparenthood), he must confront the isolation accumulated over 37 years of separation from society. Bonta and Gendreau would argue that this is to confuse rhetoric with science. We would argue that their approach substitutes a spurious objectivity for the human dimension of punishment as it is experienced by prisoners.

Suicide: What Exactly Are the Risks?

The suicide data from Canada are far more chilling than suggested by Bonta and Gendreau. Burtch and Ericson (1979) cite rates for specific Canadian institutions that range from 164 to 528 per 100,000. In fact, the picture is bleaker still, for almost all comparisons to date between suicide rates for inmates and populations outside prison have failed to correct for critical demographic differences. Frequently the comparison is between inmates and the general public (as in Bonta and Gendreau's review). The comparison is clearly inappropriate; the two populations are still not comparable in terms of their a priori suicide risk. In the US, the modal suicide profile is of a white male, over 65, living in the western States and belonging to the upper social strata. Dunne, McIntosh, and Dunne-Maxim (1987) note that suicide rates are "directly proportional to age level." They also note the "extremely low rate for blacks." The average penitentiary inmate is young (relative to the general population), from a lower-class, urban background. As well, a disproportionate percentage are black. In short, a priori suicide rates for incarcerated men are much lower than the rates for the population at large. Thus when Coggan and Walker (1982) note that the suicide rate in British prisons is 11 times the national rate, this comparison *under*estimates considerably the risk created by prisons. (Suicide in British prisons is approaching epidemic proportions: Almost 200 inmates have killed themselves within the last 4 years—*Guardian Weekly*, 1991). An additional issue is that estimates of suicide risk due to incarceration are based upon suicides committed during imprisonment; no one has studied suicide in ex-inmate populations. Imprisonment increases the likelihood of social isolation, divorce, unemployment, and many other factors that elevate the individual's suicide risk. In addition, suicide is not a phenomenon that touches 17.5 individuals but to which the remainder are impervious: For every successful suicide there are many times more attempted suicides. And yet, Bonta and Gendreau can conclude that "the health risks to inmates [due to imprisonment] appear minimal."

Solitary Confinement: Rhetoric and Reality

Bonta and Gendreau maintain that the extensive experimental literature on the effects of placing people (usually volunteer students) in solitary or conditions of sensory deprivation is being ignored in the penology literature. They argue that "in fact, this literature has much relevance to prison solitary confinement." Suedfeld, who has written extensively in this area using the same conceptual framework as Bonta and Gendreau, argues exactly the opposite. In his most recent article, after rejecting the comparability of the experience of political prisoners (or prisoners of war) to that of convicts who have been placed in solitary, he states:

> *Even less appropriate* is the comparison between the SC (solitary confinement) condition and field or laboratory experiments on isolation and stimulus reduction. ... Significant differences between the conditions are the duration of the confinement, the amount of movement allowed inside the confinement area ... the perceived benevolence of the people in charge, and the purpose for which the individual is undergoing the experience. Furthermore, experimental subjects—unlike SC prisoners—can end their participation at will. Some of these differences may make SC less severe than the laboratory technique while others may do the opposite; their combination makes a complex pattern that *ensures non-comparability.* (emphasis added)

Bonta and Gendreau cite their own research using volunteers in solitary for periods of up to 10 days. Suedfeld et al. (1982) noted that "this literature has several major flaws" including the use of measures that lack ecological validity, brief periods of isolation, and inmate volunteer subjects.

Bonta and Gendreau, in referring to the Suedfeld et al. (1982) study, cite their conclusion in the following way: "Our data lend no support to the claim that solitary confinement is overwhelmingly aversive, stressful, or damaging to the inmates." Noticeably absent from Bonta and Gendreau's citation are the important qualifications and disclaimers made by Suedfeld et al. Thus, Suedfeld et al. pointedly noted that one of the shortcomings of their study was that "the sample is truncated. *Individuals who are completely unable to adapt to SC and become psychotic or committed suicide were obviously not included*" (emphasis added). Suedfeld et al. also acknowledge that

> there is a rather extensive autobiographical, anecdotal, and clinical literature indicating that many prisoners find long periods of SC intolerable and that for some inmates even short periods of relatively mild SC may be very stressful. *It should be clear that our data do not in any way contradict this literature, and that we do not deny its validity.* (emphasis added)

Our point here is that Bonta and Gendreau seriously overstate what their kind of empirical research can tell us about the effects of solitary confinement.

Our other major point regarding solitary confinement addresses a different issue altogether. The authors lament what they refer to as "the pernicious tendency to invoke rhetoric over reality"; yet their own conclusions reflect a disregard for the reality they admire, and they embrace the very rhetoric they disdain. They conclude that "the real culprit may not necessarily be the condition of solitary *per se* but the manner in which inmates have been treated."

Research on the Canadian federal correctional regime regarding administrative segregation reveals that over the last 20-year period there have been extensive changes in federal administrative policy and rules. The official "rhetoric" for the use of administrative segregation speaks of Bonta and Gendreau's "well-defined and effectively administered ethical guidelines for its use." The reality as reflected in these studies of what actually happens in Canadian prisons is that administrative segregation continues to be applied in an arbitrary manner that violates fundamental principles of justice. By defining empirical research in such a way as to exclude studies such as those cited here, Bonta and Gendreau reduce the horizon of empirical research relevant to the evaluation of solitary confinement to studies that are, in effect, quite irrelevant to the real-life experience of prisoners.

The Ideology of Imprisonment

Bonta and Gendreau reject the relevance of ideology to criminal justice research and policy making. They thus fail to acknowledge the extent to which a certain ideology has achieved a constitutional and legal foundation that has direct implications for the resolution of criminal justice policy questions. The report of the Fraser Commission on Prostitution and Pornography in Canada is an important case in point. Advocates of the decriminalization of pornography argued that the research in the area had failed to demonstrate the necessary causal link between increased availability of pornographic material and sexual violence toward women. Such a failure was, so the argument went, fatal to using the criminal law to prohibit material that was entitled to constitutional protection as freedom of expression. The Commission, while accepting that the evidence failed to meet the threshold of proving a causal link, nevertheless concluded that this did not resolve the issue. Referring to the ideology of equality and the manner in which this was now entrenched in Section 15 of the *Canadian Charter of Rights and Freedoms*, the Fraser Commission found compelling the argument that some pornographic material, by virtue of the way in which it portrays and demeans the common humanity and dignity of women, violates the ideology of equality and of Section 15 of the *Canadian Charter of Rights and Freedoms*.

One can and should make an analogy between this principal (rather than pernicious) application of ideology and the practice of imprisonment and the question of whether it is destructive to the psychological and emotional well-being of prisoners. No one, including Bonta and Gendreau, will argue that imprisonment does not involve a major assault on a prisoner's privacy. Bonta and Gendreau, however, maintain that it is a matter of scientific inquiry to measure the extent to which imprisonment has negative physiological, psychological, and behavioral effects. To them, without such objective measurements, no negative conclusions about the pains of imprisonment should be drawn. We maintain that this is misconceived.

Policy Implications

The policy implications that we fear will be drawn from a review of this nature is that incarceration should continue to serve as the primary response to crime. This will then impede the movement to reduce our dependence upon correctional institutions, a dependence that has been denounced by every major commission of inquiry in Canada from 1849 (the Brown Commission) to 1987 (the Canadian Sentencing Commission).

The ethos of criminal justice in the 20th century can be characterized as a movement away from punishment *per se* and toward a position that incarceration is at best a necessary evil. This movement is reflected in the conditions under which sentences of imprisonment are served. We have abandoned special diets, hard labor, corporal punishment, and other privations of mind and body. As well, we have introduced intermittent sentences, educational and employment-related programs, conjugal visits, and other such innovations that either render prison life more like life in the community or otherwise reduce the impact of prison upon the individual. Guiding this transformation is the recognition that the practice of imprisonment in contemporary society is frequently a disgrace while the underlying principle is an admission of failure, a holdover from earlier times. Articles that question the negative consequences of prison hearken back to an earlier era and can only be, in F. Scott Fitzgerald's words, "boats against the current, borne back ceaselessly into the past."

NOTE

This debate is still alive and well in 2008. For a recent review of studies dealing specifically with solitary confinement, see Peter Scharff Smith, "The Effects of Solitary Confinement on Prison Inmates: A Brief History and Review of the Literature" (2006), 34 *Crime and Justice Review* 441 (University of Chicago Press). This article surveys the research and concludes that "solitary confinement can have serious psychological, psychiatric and sometimes physiological effects on many prison inmates." It also contains an interesting account of the Scandinavian practice of using solitary confinement for a significant subset of remand prisoners.

Another interesting element to this controversy arises from a "meta-analysis" study conducted by Gendreau, Goggin, and Cullen (see "The Effects of Prison Sentences on Recidivism," *User Report 1999-24* (Ottawa: Solicitor General Canada, 1999)). They observed that (1) prison produced slight increases in recidivism; and (2) "there was some tendency for lower risk offenders to be more negatively affected by the prison sentence." Accordingly, they concluded that:

1. one should not use imprisonment "with the expectation of reducing criminal behaviour";
2. the excessive use of incarceration is costly in the light of its perceived benefits;
3. careful and comprehensive assessments should be carried out to determine who is being adversely affected by prison; and
4. the "primary justification" for imprisonment as a sanction is incapacitation and retribution.

III. CRIMINAL CODE, SECTIONS 718.3, 719, AND 743.1

There are a number of technical issues that relate to where and how terms of imprisonment are served. For the most part, these are determined by the *Criminal Code*.

A. Consecutive Sentences

The ability to impose a consecutive sentence arises from s. 718.3(4):

718.3(4) Where an accused

(a) is sentenced while under sentence for an offence, and a term of imprisonment, whether in default of payment of a fine or otherwise, is imposed,

(b) is convicted of an offence punishable with both fine and imprisonment and both are imposed, or

(c) is convicted of more offences than one, and

(i) more than one fine is imposed,

(ii) terms of imprisonment for the respective offences are imposed, or

(iii) a term of imprisonment is imposed in respect of one offence and a fine is imposed in respect of another offence,

the court that sentences the accused may direct that the terms of imprisonment that are imposed by the court or result from the operation of subsection 734(4) shall be served consecutively.

Otherwise, a sentence commences when imposed (see s. 719(1)).

Some unusual consecutive sentence problems arise in relation to parole eligibility. For a useful tool, see "Multiple Sentences," in *Sentence Calculation: A Handbook for Judges, Lawyers, and Correctional Officials*, 3d ed. (Ottawa: Public Works and Government Services Canada, 2005), the public safety and emergency preparedness publication. One particular problem arises when a prisoner serving a sentence receives an additional consecutive sentence. This triggers the operation of s. 120.1 of the *Corrections and Conditional Release Act*, RSC 1992, c. 22 as amended by SC 1995, c. 42, s. 34. This is discussed under section II.B, Increasing Parole Eligibility, chapter 18, Parole and Early Release.

B. Locus of Confinement

The locus of confinement depends on the length of the sentence either by itself or as an aggregate with other sentences the prisoner must serve. This is also prescribed by s. 743:

743.1(1) Except where otherwise provided, a person who is sentenced to imprisonment for

(a) life,

(b) a term of two years or more, or

(c) two or more terms of less than two years each that are to be served one after the other and that, in the aggregate, amount to two years or more,

shall be sentenced to imprisonment in a penitentiary.

(2) Where a person who is sentenced to imprisonment in a penitentiary is, before the expiration of that sentence, sentenced to imprisonment for a term of less than two years, the person

shall serve that term in a penitentiary, but if the previous sentence of imprisonment in a penitentiary is set aside, that person shall serve that term in accordance with subsection (3).

(3) A person who is sentenced to imprisonment and who is not required to be sentenced as provided in subsection (1) or (2) shall, unless a special prison is prescribed by law, be sentenced to imprisonment in a prison or other place of confinement, other than a penitentiary, within the province in which the person is convicted, in which the sentence of imprisonment may be lawfully executed.

(3.1) Notwithstanding subsection (3), an offender who is required to be supervised by an order made under paragraph 753.1(3)(b) and who is sentenced for another offence during the period of the supervision shall be sentenced to imprisonment in a penitentiary.

(4) Where a person is sentenced to imprisonment in a penitentiary while the person is lawfully imprisoned in a place other than a penitentiary, that person shall, except where otherwise provided, be sent immediately to the penitentiary, and shall serve in the penitentiary the unexpired portion of the term of imprisonment that that person was serving when sentenced to the penitentiary as well as the term of imprisonment for which that person was sentenced to the penitentiary.

(5) Where, at any time, a person who is imprisoned in a prison or place of confinement other than a penitentiary is subject to two or more terms of imprisonment, each of which is for less than two years, that are to be served one after the other, and the aggregate of the unexpired portions of those terms at that time amounts to two years or more, the person shall be transferred to a penitentiary to serve those terms, but if any one or more of such terms is set aside or reduced and the unexpired portions of the remaining term or terms on the day on which that person was transferred under this section amounted to less than two years, that person shall serve that term or terms in accordance with subsection (3).

IV. INTERMITTENT SENTENCES

A court may mitigate the full effect of a custodial sentence by ordering that it be served intermittently—that is, not continuously. This usually, but not always, means on weekends. This is made possible by s. 732 of the *Criminal Code*, which provides:

732(1) Where the court imposes a sentence of imprisonment of ninety days or less on an offender convicted of an offence, whether in default of payment of a fine or otherwise, the court may, having regard to the age and character of the offender, the nature of the offence and the circumstances surrounding its commission, and the availability of appropriate accommodation to ensure compliance with the sentence, order

(a) that the sentence be served intermittently at such times as are specified in the order; and

(b) that the offender comply with the conditions prescribed in a probation order when not in confinement during the period that the sentence is being served and, if the court so orders, on release from prison after completing the intermittent sentence.

(2) An offender who is ordered to serve a sentence of imprisonment intermittently may, on giving notice to the prosecutor, apply to the court that imposed the sentence to allow it to be served on consecutive days.

(3) Where a court imposes a sentence of imprisonment on a person who is subject to an intermittent sentence in respect of another offence, the unexpired portion of the intermittent sentence shall be served on consecutive days unless the court otherwise orders.

The original intermittent sentence provisions were enacted by SC 1972, c. 13, s. 58, along with a set of other new and revised provisions described under the subheading "Absolute and Conditional Discharge, Suspended Sentence, Intermittent Sentence and Probation." These provisions were the result of recommendations in the Ouimet report (Report of the Canadian Committee on Corrections, 1969), which discussed the utility of both weekend and nightly detention and found evidence of beneficial applications of such alternatives in European countries. It recommended that courts "be empowered to impose a sentence of imprisonment to be served intermittently, the total period of imprisonment not to exceed six months." Obviously, Parliament agreed with the Ouimet report, except that it put a 90-day cap on intermittent sentences.

In *R v. Parisian* (1993), 81 CCC (3d) 351 (Man. CA), the offender appealed against a three-month sentence for possessing cannabis resin for the purposes of trafficking. The appellant sought only to serve the sentence intermittently. For the court, Twaddle JA said:

Ordinarily the decision to allow or not to allow a convicted person to serve time intermittently is one to be made by the sentencing judge. This court will only interfere if the decision is made on a wrong principle or is clearly wrong.

In the present case, the offence involved a relatively small quantity of narcotic; the accused was a small player; the sale which the accused intended to make were to persons who frequent a beverage room. Her circumstances are such that a sentence of three months if not served intermittently will cause some hardship because she has two children whom it would be difficult to place for care if she serves her sentence other than intermittently. Additionally, she has the opportunity to take a course of education to upgrade herself if she is free to take it from Monday to Friday. The accused has no prior record.

The learned sentencing judge imposed a sentence which is within the range for this particular offence and this offender, but we think she was wrong to characterize it as one at the lower end of that range. Additionally, she placed undue emphasis on the fact that the accused was unemployed and did not need an intermittent sentence to save her job. The need for the accused to educate herself and make arrangements for her children are equally valid reasons for an intermittent sentence.

In the circumstances, we are of the view that the judge's decision not to allow the sentence to be served intermittently was clearly wrong. Accordingly, we allow the appeal, set aside the sentence of three months imprisonment and substitute one of 90 days to be served intermittently.

Since 1972, the intermittent sentence has become an important element of a fair and rational sentencing scheme that includes both statutorily mandated minimum sentences of imprisonment and judge-made presumptions of incarceration. The most common role for the intermittent sentence is with respect to impaired driving offenders. When Parliament addressed the range of penalties applicable to this kind of offence in 1985 and created new offences with substantially higher maxima when bodily harm or death had occurred, it also tailored the impaired driving simpliciter sentences to integrate them with the availability of intermittent sentences. Previously, the mandated penalty for a third conviction was three months, outside the range of an intermittent sentence. However, the 1985 amendments (SC 1985, c. 19, s. 36) reduced this threshold to 90 days. Obviously, while Parliament was concerned with enhancing the penalties for this category, especially when the consequences are death or bodily harm, it was also concerned with instilling fairness in the system by permitting a judge to consider the appropriateness of an intermittent sentence. The potential scope of this consideration can be appreciated by noting the recent statistics. In 2007, 8,850 convictions were registered for impaired driving, resulting in 4,167 sentences of imprisonment with a median length of 30 days.

The most common use of an intermittent sentence is to respond to a case where a brief period of incarceration is mandated either by the Code or by a presumption of incarceration, but imprisonment for a continuous period will risk the offender's job, schooling, or family. Without an intermittent sentence, some offenders will not be able to maintain their careers, profession, or employment. It is the lowest people on the employment ladder—those with the least marketable skills and the least vocational resources—who will be replaced first. Thus, the working poor offender will likely become even more impoverished, while the middle-class offender will likely keep his or her job. Similarly, a parent from a traditional family has a spouse to care for children during a brief period of confinement. A single parent, if not able to find a willing relative, risks losing a child to the local Children's Aid Society, even over a 14-day sentence. Students struggling to succeed in an increasingly more challenging world risk losing a school term as a consequence of a brief period of incarceration. Again, the more financially able the student is, the easier it is to overcome this obstacle, whether through extra tutoring or re-enrollment. Some may not be able to bounce back.

Still, correctional officials from most provinces regularly express opposition to intermittent sentences because of the administrative and security costs that they generate as prisoners who arrive on their designated days to enter an ordinary jail facility for a few days. Perhaps, the answer lies not in abolishing intermittent sentences but in providing appropriate facilities so that the problems associated with injecting prisoners into a secure jail to mix with the ordinary population would be diminished. Alternatively, perhaps we should be questioning the utility of short jail terms, whether intermittent or not. For now, the utility of intermittent sentences seems clear as do the inequities of abolishing them.

There are some technical problems that need to be considered. See the strange result in *R v. Middleton*, below, arising from an interpretation of s. 732(3) as applied to a series of sentences imposed on an estranged domestic partner who used violence as a tool to respond to separation.

R v. Middleton
[2007] OJ No. 2900 (QL) (CA)

[The offender was convicted of (1) assault causing bodily harm; (2) uttering a threat; and (3) pointing a firearm. He was sentenced to 90 days' imprisonment to be served intermittently for the assault causing bodily harm conviction, with a concurrent 18-month conditional sentence to be followed by 3 years' probation for uttering a threat and pointing a firearm convictions.]

THE COURT:

· · ·

[19] The appellant also argues that the imposition of an 18-month conditional sentence in addition to the intermittent sentence rendered the intermittent sentence unlawful, as the appellant's global sentence would exceed the maximum 90 days prescribed by s. 732 of the *Criminal Code*.

[20] Section 732(3) reads as follows:

> 732(3) Where a court imposes a sentence of imprisonment on a person who is subject to an intermittent sentence in respect of another offence, the unexpired portion of the intermittent sentence shall be served on consecutive days unless the court otherwise orders.

[21] We do not accept that the sentence imposed was "unlawful." However, in our view, s. 732(3) does apply. At the time that the sentencing judge imposed a sentence of imprisonment by means of the conditional sentence for uttering a threat and pointing a firearm, he had already sentenced the appellant to the intermittent sentence for assault causing bodily harm. Section 732(3) has the effect of causing the unexpired portion of the intermittent sentence, which was the full 90 days, to be served on consecutive days.

[22] The sentence, as imposed, was intended to cause the appellant to serve "real jail time" but without loss of employment and consequent support for the child. No one contends that the sentence was unfit or unreasonable although the Crown argues that it is lenient. In our view, although the effect of s. 732(3) was unintended, given the nature of the offences, we would do nothing to disturb its effect.

[23] Accordingly, we would grant leave to appeal the sentence but dismiss the appeal. For the sake of clarity we reiterate that as a consequence of the operation of s. 732(3), the 90-day term of imprisonment is to be served on consecutive days and the balance of the sentence remains unchanged.

NOTE

Can this decision be right? It rests on the view that a conditional sentence is a sentence for imprisonment: see chapter 12, Conditional Sentence of Imprisonment, which deals in detail with conditional sentences. However, it ignores both the rationale for intermittent sentences and the words in s. 732(3), "unless the court otherwise orders." Perhaps this is another example of how a deferential standard of review distorts the appellate process.

V. MAXIMUM SENTENCES

With respect to maximum sentences, recall the discussion of the Supreme Court of Canada decision in *R v. M.(C.A.)* in chapter 2, Judicial Methodology and the Legislative Context. Generally, the maximum sentence is intended for the worst offence committed by the worst offender. Of course, this is an overly simplistic statement, given the infinite ways that offenders from various backgrounds commit offences. But it does indicate the necessarily high threshold for a maximum sentence. In a later chapter, we will look at the indeterminate sentence that flows from a finding that an offender is a dangerous offender pursuant to

s. 753 of the *Criminal Code*. A number of appellate courts have held that a life sentence, as a maximum sentence, should not be imposed on the ground of dangerousness simply to circumvent the dangerous offender procedures. See, for example, *R v. Pontello* (1978), 38 CCC (2d) 262 (Ont. CA), a case of rape. In an earlier rape case, a life sentence was upheld, given the planning, the brutality, and the dangerousness of the offender, who suffered from a personality disorder (see *R v. Hill* (1974), 15 CCC (2d) 145 (Ont. CA)). Since the 1970s, there is a recognition that a dangerous-offender finding will likely result in a longer period of incarceration than a life sentence. In situations where there are patterns of behaviour involving violent sexual offences, there has been a substantial expansion in prosecutorial willingness to pursue dangerous-offender applications: see chapter 15, Preventive Detention and Preventive Supervision.

Recently, there have been examples of courts resorting to maximum sentences, especially life sentences, as a method of responding to perceived gravity as a result of particularly horrendous consequences to victims or an exceptionally egregious record for prior convictions. The following decisions reflect the view that a sentence at the maximum, while available, ought to be uncommon.

R v. Klair
(2004), 186 CCC (3d) 285 (Ont. CA)

SHARPE JA (McCOMBS J concurring): [1] The appellant pleaded guilty to one count of arson causing bodily harm and was sentenced to life imprisonment. He seeks leave to appeal, and if leave is granted, appeals his sentence to this court.

Facts

1. Circumstances of the Offence

[2] In the early afternoon of September 20, 2000, the appellant, at the time seventy years old, was at his son's home babysitting Rajvir Klair, his four-year old grandson. Some of the downstairs tenants were at home although it is not clear whether the appellant was aware of their presence. Shortly after 2 p.m., the appellant started three fires in the bedrooms of his son's house using gasoline as an accelerant. After setting the fires, he walked away from the house. One of the tenants heard smoke alarms and the cries of Rajvir and came upstairs. She could not enter the house to rescue Rajvir because of the intensity of the fire. Rajvir was screaming "monster, monster." After putting her own child in a safe place, the tenant managed to coax Rajvir outside and to douse the flames that covered him.

[3] The appellant returned to the house the next day. He was highly intoxicated. He asked if Rajvir had been saved and, when told that Rajvir was alive, said "Thank God." He stated that he had tried to hang himself with his turban. There were no physical signs of any such attempt, but the appellant was not wearing his turban when he was arrested.

[4] Rajvir suffered horrendous and devastating injuries as a result of the fire. He suffered excruciating pain from second and third degree burns to about sixty percent of his body. He has already undergone approximately twenty operations and further surgery is

expected. Rajvir has almost no use of his right arm and limited movement of his left arm. He lost his left ear, all digits on his left hand, two fingers on his right hand and two toes. He has significant scarring and at the time of sentencing was in poor mental condition.

2. *Circumstances of the Appellant*

[5] The appellant came to Canada from India in 1982. He remains in Canada as a landed immigrant. He worked as a labourer until he retired about ten years ago. He was married in India over forty years ago and has four children. The appellant has no prior criminal record and was an active member in the local Sikh community. He offered letters on the sentencing hearing to the effect that he was well-regarded and respected in his community as a hardworking person of high morals and good character.

[6] The appellant has accepted responsibility for the offence. However, he offered no explanation whatsoever for his conduct. At the sentencing hearing, he denied that he intended to harm his grandson and expressed his remorse.

· · ·

[11] In my view, the trial judge erred by placing undue emphasis upon the consequences of the offence and insufficient attention to the actual circumstances of the offence and the blameworthiness of the appellant. To be more precise, in my view, the trial judge erred by sentencing the appellant to life imprisonment primarily because of the horrific consequences to Rajvir. The appellant intentionally started the fire. However, on the basis of the charge to which he pleaded guilty, and on the facts upon which the Crown relied in the sentencing proceedings, he did not deliberately cause Rajvir to suffer his devastating injuries. Indeed, the defence position that he did not intend to harm Rajvir was not challenged at trial. The appellant pleaded guilty to an indictment alleging that he "unlawfully did intentionally or recklessly cause damage by fire to property ... and did thereby cause bodily harm to Rajvir Klair." He did not plead guilty to attempted murder. The offence to which he pleaded guilty did not include the element of intentional infliction of bodily harm. On the facts admitted by the appellant and relied upon by the Crown, he was plainly guilty of manifest disregard for the safety of the victim, but he was neither charged with, nor did he admit to intentionally causing the horrific harm suffered by Rajvir.

[12] After the trial judge delivered his reasons, and indeed after the oral argument of this appeal, the Supreme Court of Canada released its decision in *R v. Cheddesingh*, [2004] SCJ No. 15 (March 19, 2004). We have received written submissions with respect to this judgment where McLachlin CJC stated, for a unanimous court:

> ... [T]erms such as "stark horror," "worst offence" and "worst offender" add nothing to the analysis and should be avoided. All relevant factors under the *Criminal Code*, RSC 1985, c. C-46, must be considered. A maximum penalty of any kind will by its very nature be imposed only rarely (see A. Manson, *Law of Sentencing* (2001), at p. 106) and is only appropriate if the offence is of sufficient gravity and the offender displays sufficient blameworthiness.

[13] I will return to the facts of *Cheddesingh* below, but I note here that the Supreme Court affirmed the life sentence that had been imposed by the trial judge on the basis of the "stark horror" category.

[14] In the case at bar, the trial judge relied exclusively on the "stark horror" category to justify the life sentence and there was no suggestion that apart from the "stark horror" principle, there was any other basis to justify a life sentence. While the term "stark horror" must now be avoided as unhelpful, the term was used to delineate factors common to a particular type of case for which the maximum life sentence is appropriate. The trial judge based his decision upon those cases and it is still useful to consider them to gauge the gravity of the offence and the blameworthiness of the offender required to justify the maximum sentence of life imprisonment.

[15] While I do not suggest that there is a fixed or inflexible set of factors, cases of this kind that have been found to justify the imposition of the maximum sentence of life imprisonment (formerly the "stark horror" cases) have presented one or more of the following features:

- cruelty, brutality, unusual violence
- terrorizing and torturing victim over a period of time
- intentional, prolonged, repeated violence against victim
- acts needlessly repeated or lack of feeling suggesting sadistic intent to cause terror or even torture
- intentional infliction of pain, fright, panic that is tantamount to torture solely for gratification or other perverse reason
- cruelty and callousness not frequently encountered
- deliberate infliction of brutal, disfiguring, life threatening injuries

[16] It is significant that *Cheddesingh* requires both an offence of "sufficient gravity" and an offender "who displays sufficient blameworthiness." The severe consequences to Rajvir were certainly very grave, but those severe consequences were not accompanied by conduct that rose to a level of blameworthiness sufficient to justify a sentence of life imprisonment. Counsel for the respondent was unable to point us to any case in which a life sentence has been imposed upon a first offender for unintended consequences, even where those consequences were caused recklessly. To do so would, in my view, amount to a significant and unwarranted shift in the law of sentencing and invite life sentences in a significant number of cases involving dire but unintended consequences and where the sentence could not be justified on the basis of the blameworthiness of the accused. As I do not consider the circumstances of the present case to warrant such a change, and as I do not consider it possible to justify a sentence of life imprisonment for this offender for this offence, I would allow the appeal, set aside the sentence of life imprisonment, and in its place substitute a substantial custodial sentence.

[17] The seminal judgment in this area is that of Martin JA in *R v. Horvath* (1982), 2 CCC (3d) 196 (Ont. CA). The accused had subjected his female victim to a prolonged and sadistic attack. He gained access to her apartment on the pretext of wanting to rent it, then bound, gagged, choked, and stabbed her before finally slitting her throat. Martin JA observed that there were two broad categories in which the maximum life sentence was available: first, offences of stark horror, and second, pattern-of-violent-behaviour cases. This must now be read in the light of *Cheddesingh* and the principle that as "sentencing is an inherently individualized process" that cannot be achieved on the basis of solely fixed or pre-determined categories: *R v. M.(C.A.)* [1996 CanLII 230

(SCC), [1996] 1 SCR 500], at p. 567; *R v. Varga* (2001), 159 CCC (3d) 502 (Ont. CA) at p. 527; *R v. McArthur*, [2004] OJ No. 721 (CA).

[18] The appellant has certainly not demonstrated a pattern of violent behaviour. He has no prior convictions of any kind and there is nothing in the record, apart from the offence in question, to indicate that he has any propensity to violence. I will return below to the significance of the absence of psychiatric evidence, but I simply note here that none was presented to indicate that the appellant poses a risk to public safety because of some mental condition or disorder.

[19] To return to *Horvath*, Martin JA wrote that the extremity of the offence itself was sufficient to justify the life sentence. Cautioning that it was not "an exclusive definition" Martin JA stated, at p. 205, that "Mr. Justice Ritchie's graphic phrase 'the stark horror of the crime'" had been used to describe offences "accompanied by unusual features of brutality or cruelty" for which a life sentence could be appropriate. Martin JA added:

> The cruelty and callousness which mark the conduct of the appellant are, fortunately, not frequently encountered, and apart altogether from the psychiatric evidence, clearly indicate a disturbed and dangerous personality.

[20] He concluded, at p. 207, that the offender's "utter lack of feeling for the victim is consistent only with an abnormal personality, and portends peril to others while he remains in his present state."

[21] *Horvath* has been followed in many cases, several of which I review below. The startling feature of these cases attracting the maximum penalty of life imprisonment has been the brutality and cruelty of the actions of the accused. Considered in light of the *Cheddesingh* decision and the dual requirements of an offence of sufficient gravity and an offender of sufficient blameworthiness, the facts of these cases continue to warrant the imposition of a life sentence. In each case, the actions of the accused are exceedingly brutal and cruel, rendering them "sufficiently grave" on their face. Moreover, in each case the accused intended these consequences, thereby becoming "sufficiently blameworthy" for them. In no case do the consequences alone, unaccompanied by brutal or cruel conduct intentionally inflicting the consequences, convert the offence to one for which a life sentence is appropriate.

[22] In *R v. Charlebois* (1987), 22 OAC 235, the accused entered the victim's apartment, grabbed her hair, and repeatedly stabbed her in the face. He slit her throat from ear to ear, cutting her voice box. Her wounds were brutal, disfiguring, and life threatening. Charlebois left the apartment, but returned. As the victim lay helpless, he stabbed her in the back. Charlebois then left the victim to drown in her own blood. The court found that "[i]t would be difficult to devise a scenario which could be worse" and imposed a life sentence.

[23] In *R v. Lieug* (1995), 82 OAC 317 the accused attended at the victim's place of employment with a hammer, a knife, and a bottle of sulphuric acid. He struck the victim several times with the hammer. The victim tried to escape to the bathroom, at which point the victim's employer tried to intervene. Lieug threatened him with the knife and told him that he intended to kill the victim. He then knocked down the bathroom door and spread sulphuric acid across the victim's body, resulting in third degree burns. The

trial judge noted the nature of the assault, its planning, gravity and intensity and noted the absence of remorse and found that the victim would remain in danger if the appellant were ever freed. This court upheld the life sentence.

[24] Another leading decision is *R v. Mesgun* (1997), 36 OR (3d) 739 (CA). Mesgun coaxed his ex-fiancée into his car and asked her to return to the relationship. She refused. He began a savage assault with a knife. For a period of thirty minutes, Mesgun slashed and stabbed the victim in her face, neck, arms, and wrists. He tried to strangle her and gouge out her eyes. When he thought she was dead, he punched her repeatedly in the face. When he realized she was still alive, he attempted to stab her again. The victim opened the car door and fell out. Mesgun drove away, leaving her to die on the street. The trial judge stated, at p. 441: "I am of the view that no case of attempted murder could exceed the brutality and cruelty of this case." This court agreed that Mesgun's intentional, prolonged, and repeated stabbing of the victim, his attempt to gouge out her eyes, his attempt to strangle her lacerated neck, and his abandonment of her on the road to die, all exemplified unusual features of brutality justifying the imposition of life imprisonment.

[25] Finally, in *Cheddesingh* itself the accused broke into two apartments before breaking into the victim's apartment in a senior citizen's residence. He announced his intention to rape the seventy-six-year old female occupant and then entered into a discussion about whether he would follow through. He told her that he had a razor and tried to suffocate her. He then sexually assaulted the victim, digitally penetrating her, performing cunnilingus, and violently raping her. The victim suffered severe lacerations to her vagina, requiring a blood transfusion. She died one month later from cirrhosis associated with vaginal trauma. The trial judge categorized the offence as one of stark horror. He based his finding on Cheddesingh's torturous discussion of whether or not he would rape the victim; the brutal violation of the victim's fundamental rights of privacy and security; the victim's membership in a vulnerable class of persons; the fact that the offences continued over a period of two to three hours; and the fact that the offence debased the victim's life. The life sentence was upheld on appeal by this court ((2002), 60 OR (3d) 721, 168 CCC (3d) 310) and, as I have noted, on appeal to the Supreme Court of Canada.

[26] In my view, the conduct of the appellant in the present case, while entirely deplorable, simply cannot be equated to the type of senseless brutality and cruelty found in *Horvath, Cheddesingh* and the other cases to which I have referred. In each of these cases, the justification for the imposition of the maximum penalty of life imprisonment was that severe and horrific harm had been deliberately inflicted upon the victim. In the present case, the appellant exposed his victim to the risk of similar harm, and for that he must be severely punished. However, I cannot agree that it would be justifiable to sentence him on the same basis as if he had deliberately and callously inflicted the harm.

· · ·

[36] This was a serious crime with disastrous consequences and the objectives of denunciation, deterrence, separating the offender from society and acknowledging the harm done to the victim and to society clearly call for a significant penitentiary sentence. The appellant intentionally set the fires and he exposed his victim to a startling risk of physical harm and death. As noted by the trial judge, the appellant's breach of trust as the victim's grandfather and babysitter is an aggravating factor. However, as

stated by Prof. Manson in the passage from *The Law of Sentencing*, referred to in *Ched-desingh, supra*: "… the imposition of a maximum sentence is, and ought to be, rare. Few situations arise where a lesser term will not adequately protect society and also reflect an appropriate degree of denunciation."

[37] Factors weighing in the appellant's favour are his age and previously unblemished record, his plea of guilty and his acceptance of responsibility for the harm he has caused.

[38] In my view a fit sentence for this offender and this offence is twelve years. The appellant is entitled to credit for two-years of pre-trial custody. At trial, the Crown argued against the usual two for one credit as the appellant had delayed the proceedings while he tried to arrange financial restitution for the loss of his son's home. As the trial judge imposed a life sentence, he did not deal with this submission. I agree with the appellant's submission that in the circumstances of this case, he should not be denied the usual credit for pre-trial custody. Accordingly, the sentence I would impose after taking pre-trial custody into account is eight years.

FELDMAN JA (dissenting):

• • •

[49] Watt J fully considered all of the Code factors. He was also clearly satisfied that the appellant's deliberate conduct, knowing what he was causing to happen to his helpless grandson, was significantly blameworthy conduct that warranted the maximum penalty. Sharpe JA minimizes the blameworthiness of the appellant's conduct on the basis that, in accordance with his plea to the offence under s. 433, he did not intentionally inflict harm on the child. However, Watt J was entitled to view the conduct of the appellant as indicative of the maximum blameworthiness for this offence. While babysitting the four-year old child, the appellant deliberately set the fire with gasoline in three places plus he left the stove on and walked out of the house when the child was burning, with no thought of saving the child. There was no suggestion of intoxication or any other factor that would negate the ordinary inference that a person intends the natural consequences of his actions. His inquiry on his return about whether his grandson had survived, demonstrated that he was aware of what could have happened to the child. Watt J found, as quoted above, that the appellant "deliberately shut his eyes to whether his grandson burned to death, suffocated, or both."

[50] Watt J also considered the fact that there was no expert evidence in this case that the appellant represented a continuing danger, as there has been in many of the stark horror/life sentence cases. He concluded that the circumstances of the offence indicated, without the need for expert testimony, that the appellant has a personality disturbance or other mental disorder.

[51] He distinguished on two bases this court's decision in *R v. Edwards* (2001), 54 OR (3d) 737 at para. 70 (CA) where the court suggested that the absence of expert testimony about the prognosis for successful rehabilitation during a fixed term "told against" the imposition of a life sentence on the basis of stark horror. He noted first, that in that case, Crown counsel on appeal did not press the stark horror argument; second, the court did not say that there must always be expert evidence on the accused's prognosis for ongoing danger if there is only a fixed term sentence, but only that there will

often be such evidence. Watt J commented that expert evidence cannot be a requirement of a finding of stark horror, because an accused cannot be compelled to participate in a psychiatric evaluation, and the opinion of a psychiatrist without such an evaluation may add nothing to the court's assessment.

[52] Based on the circumstances of the crime itself, together with the appellant's failure to give any explanation for his actions, Watt J was satisfied, without expert evidence, that the appellant did have some mental problem that required treatment. Without this treatment, the court could not be assured that he did not represent an ongoing danger to the public or to a segment of it.

[53] My colleague disputes the trial judge's inference of mental disorder. In my view, the trial judge was entitled to draw the inference on the bases that he described. The drawing of inferences is the province of the trial judge: *Housen v. Nikolaisen*, [2002] 2 SCR 235. I also agree with Watt J that in circumstances where the accused elects not to participate in a psychiatric assessment, it would be problematic if the court were precluded from drawing inferences from the circumstances that would allow it to impose the appropriate sentence.

Conclusion

[54] This was a most difficult sentencing decision. The horrific aspects of the crime were not limited to its nature as a deliberate arson. The relationship of the young boy and his grandfather had previously been one of love and trust. The father of the boy was betrayed by his own father. The actions of the appellant were completely unexplained, leaving all involved with continuing unease, as well as despair. The ongoing pain and suffering of the boy is unspeakable. The emotional and financial hardship on the parents is unfathomable. On the other hand, the appellant is an elderly man with no criminal record and a previously good reputation in the community.

[55] The experienced and learned trial judge gave reasons that are lucid and deal with each issue, balancing all of the statutory factors in the context of the relevant case law and the factual circumstances. It is clear that he recognized that the penalty of life imprisonment is to be imposed only rarely. In my view, he made no errors of law or principle and his decision that this was one of those rare cases deserves the deference of this court.

R v. Dennis
[2005] OJ No. 3677 (QL) (CA)

R.A. BLAIR JA: [1] Douglas Edward Dennis is a seventy-year old bank robber and career criminal. He is an addicted gambler and has an extensive criminal record for crimes of dishonesty, gambling-oriented offences, breach of release conditions and, of course, robbery.

[2] In June 2004, he was convicted of the offence of robbery for a fourth time—this time in connection with a bank in Niagara Falls. When he pleaded guilty to that offence, he was sentenced to life imprisonment by Justice D.J. Wallace of the Ontario Court of

Justice. The trial judge imposed the sentence primarily because he was persuaded that a life sentence provided the parole authorities with more flexibility in terms of determining whether Mr. Dennis remained a danger to the public and therefore should or should not be released back into society.

. . .

[5] The crime was committed in the following fashion. Mr. Dennis made an appointment to meet a small loans officer at the bank. When he arrived, he was carrying a bag and a TV remote device. He told the loans officer that he had a bomb in the bag, that there was another bomb located at the door of the bank, and that the device he held in his hand, if activated, would set off the explosives. He handed the bank officials a note with this message on it and saying that the strength of the bombs was sufficient to destroy the building. It also said that he was dying of cancer, had less than a year to live, and had nothing to lose if the bombs were detonated. He demanded that the bank officials open the bank vault.

[6] The demand was not met, as the bank officials in question professed not to know the combination to the vault. Mr. Dennis was therefore left to canvas a series of four tellers at various stations in the bank, as a result of which he obtained the $6,725 mentioned above. He then left the bank, but not before the bank's security camera took what the trial judge referred to as an "excellent" photograph that "[depicted] the offender clearly."

[7] Mr. Dennis did not have a bomb, or bombs, at the bank, but the bank personnel could not have known this and had to take the threat seriously. They were afraid to notify the police until the robber had left and, as directed, gave him time to make good his escape, after which the police were contacted. The area was evacuated and the Niagara Regional Police Service Explosive Disposal Unit was dispatched to the scene. The bag was determined to contain a non-explosive substance (a four-litre plastic jug of plumbing antifreeze wrapped in paper). Mr. Dennis was identified from the surveillance tape and, as mentioned above, subsequently arrested.

[8] The appellant was seventy years of age at the time of his conviction and sentence. He is now seventy-one. He has one family member, a niece, who is supportive of him and who visits him and looks after his finances on the rare occasions when he is "on the street."

[9] In 1976, Mr. Dennis was sentenced to one year in prison for robbery; in 1983, to a total of seven years imprisonment on two counts of robbery; and in 1990, to thirteen years imprisonment for an armed robbery (in conjunction with a charge of unlawful imprisonment) after he held up a bank armed with a gun and took the bank manager hostage. For these, and the other crimes, Mr. Dennis has been sentenced to approximately thirty years in jail over the past forty years of his life. He is a career criminal and likely to re-offend as long as he is physically and mentally capable of doing so.

. . .

[11] While I am not persuaded that the trial judge erred in law by taking into account the particular parole considerations in the fashion he did, it is not necessary to determine that issue for purposes of this appeal. Respectfully—and leaving that issue aside—the trial judge made two errors in principle which, in combination, require us to re-open the question of his sentence, in my view. First, he approached the subject as if his options were to choose between the sentence proposed by the Crown and that

suggested by counsel for Mr. Dennis. Secondly, he gave inadequate consideration to the practical realities arising from the age of the offender in the circumstances of this case. As a result, he failed to recognize that he could have accomplished the very goals he sought to achieve without imposing a sentence of life imprisonment.

[12] The jurisprudence is clear that maximum sentences of any kind are, by their very nature, to be imposed only rarely: see, for example, *R v. Cheddesingh*, [2004] 1 SCR 433 at para. 1; *R v. Klair* (2004), 71 OR (3d) 336 (CA) at para. 12. Here, the trial judge did not find that a life sentence would be otherwise appropriate, apart from his concern to ensure that the parole board had flexibility in determining whether, and when, Mr. Dennis should be released back into society.

[13] Mr. Dennis has a lengthy criminal record, as outlined above, including four prior convictions for robbery. He was sentenced to thirteen years imprisonment for his last robbery offence. Although that crime had been characterized by considerably more violence than the present case, and notwithstanding the submissions of defence counsel at trial, the trial judge was justified in imposing a more lengthy term of imprisonment on this occasion. He was also quite correct in treating the protection of the public as a primary consideration in sentencing. The record fully supports his view that Mr. Dennis is a risk to re-offend—and to re-offend in a violent manner—if he is released. But the goal could have been accomplished for all practical purposes, and in the circumstances of this case, by imposing a fixed term of imprisonment for a period of time between the life sentence sought by the Crown and the ten years suggested by the defence. The trial judge does not seem to have considered this option.

[14] The trial judge could have sentenced Mr. Dennis to a fixed term of fifteen to eighteen years' imprisonment, for example, and exercised his discretion under s. 743.6(1) of the *Criminal Code*—which, in the circumstances, it would have been open for him to do. In that event, Mr. Dennis would not have been eligible for parole for seven and one-half to nine years, and would not have been entitled to statutory parole for ten to twelve years. Given his record, and prior history of release violations, it is unlikely that he would be released before his mandatory statutory release date. At that time, Mr. Dennis, if still alive, would be eighty or eighty-two years of age and subject to whatever conditions the parole board might see fit to require for another five or eight years. It seems to me that the likelihood of Mr. Dennis committing further violent crimes and continuing as a danger to the community at those ages, while not non-existent, is remote at best.

[15] There may be cases where the criminal history and incorrigibility of an offender may justify a maximum sentence in order to deter the offender and protect the public: *R v. Stairs*, [1994] OJ No. 1326 (CA). Here, however, both the paramount factors of specific deterrence and the protection of the public could have been equally well accommodated in reality without the imposition of a life sentence. That being the case, a sentence of life imprisonment ought not to have been ordered, as the trial judge did not find that such a sentence was otherwise warranted.

[16] Having regard to all of the circumstances, I would grant leave to appeal, allow the appeal, setting aside the sentence of life imprisonment and substituting a sentence of 16 years imprisonment with no eligibility for parole before the expiration of seven years of that sentence.

VI. MINIMUM SENTENCES

Minimum sentences have been challenged on Charter grounds. Essentially, the courts have held that the idea of a minimum sentence is not unconstitutional, but a specific example may violate s. 12 of the *Canadian Charter of Rights and Freedoms*, Part I of the *Constitution Act, 1982*, RSC 1985, app. II, no. 44, if it imposes a sentence that is grossly disproportionate to the offence and the circumstances of the offender (see *R v. Smith*, below, and *R v. Goltz*, [1991] 3 SCR 485). However, these cases have adopted a methodology that permits a challenge based either on the facts presented by the offender's case or a "reasonable hypothetical." Note that the offender in *Smith* who successfully challenged a seven-year minimum sentence for importing drugs ultimately received an eight-year sentence given his prior record. The use of the "reasonable hypothetical" approach has produced a dilemma for the courts, as you will see in the dissent of Arbour J in *Morrisey*.

R v. Smith
(1987), 34 CCC (3d) 97 (SCC)

LAMER J:

. . .

In measuring the content of the legislation, the courts are to look to the purpose and effect of the legislation. Dickson J, as he then was, in *R v. Big M Drug Mart Ltd.* (1985), 18 CCC (3d) 385 at p. 414, 18 DLR (4th) 321 at p. 350, [1985] 1 SCR 295, at p. 331, speaking for the majority of this court, stated: "In my view, both purpose and effect are relevant in determining constitutionality; either an unconstitutional purpose or an unconstitutional effect can invalidate legislation." And further, at pp. 415-6 CCC, pp. 351-2 DLR, p. 334 SCR:

> I agree with the respondent that the legislation's purpose is the initial test of constitutional validity and its effects are to be considered when the law under review has passed or, at least, has purportedly passed the purpose test. ...
>
> Thus, if a law with a valid purpose interferes by its impact, with rights or freedoms, a litigant could still argue the effects of the legislation as a means to defeat its applicability and possibly its validity. In short, the effects test will only be necessary to defeat legislation with a valid purpose; effects can never be relied upon to save legislation with an invalid purpose.

Thus, even though the pursuit of a constitutionally invalid purpose will result in the invalidity of the impugned legislation irrespective of its effects, a valid purpose does not end the constitutional inquiry. The means chosen by Parliament to achieve that valid purpose may result in effects which deprive Canadians of their rights guaranteed under the Charter. In such a case it would then be incumbent upon the authorities to demonstrate under s. 1 that the importance of that valid purpose is such that, irrespective of the effect of the legislation, it is a reasonable limit in a free and democratic society.

The undisputed fact that the purpose of s. 5(2) of the *Narcotic Control Act* is constitutionally valid is not a bar to an analysis of s. 5(2) in order to determine if the minimum has the effect of obliging the judge in certain cases to impose a cruel and unusual punishment, and thereby is a prima facie violation of s. 12; and, if it is, to then reconsider under s. 1 that purpose and any other considerations relevant to determining whether the impugned legislation may be salvaged.

The Meaning of Section 12

It is generally accepted in a society such as ours that the State has the power to impose a "treatment or punishment" on an individual where it is necessary to do so to attain some legitimate end and where the requisite procedure has been followed. The Charter limits this power: s. 7 provides that everyone has the right not to be deprived of life, liberty and security of the person except in accordance with the principles of fundamental justice, s. 9 provides that everyone has the right not to be arbitrarily detained or imprisoned, and s. 12 guarantees the right not to be subjected to any cruel and unusual treatment or punishment.

The limitation at issue here is s. 12 of the Charter. In my view, the protection afforded by s. 12 governs the quality of the punishment and is concerned with the effect that the punishment may have on the person on whom it is imposed. I would agree with Laskin CJC in *Miller and Cockriell* [[1977] 2 SCR 680, 70 DLR (3d) 324, 31 CCC (2d) 177], where he defined the phrase "cruel and unusual" as a "compendious expression of a norm." The criterion which must be applied in order to determine whether a punishment is cruel and unusual within the meaning of s. 12 of the Charter is, to use the words of Laskin CJC in *Miller and Cockriell*, supra, at p. 183 CCC, p. 330 DLR, p. 688 SCR, "whether the punishment prescribed is so excessive as to outrage standards of decency." In other words, though the State may impose punishment, the effect of that punishment must not be grossly disproportionate to what would have been appropriate.

In imposing a sentence of imprisonment the judge will assess the circumstances of the case in order to arrive at an appropriate sentence. The test for review under s. 12 of the Charter is one of gross disproportionality, because it is aimed at punishments that are more than merely excessive. We should be careful not to stigmatize every disproportionate or excessive sentence as being a constitutional violation, and should leave to the usual sentencing appeal process the task of reviewing the fitness of a sentence. Section 12 will only be infringed where the sentence is so unfit having regard to the offence and the offender as to be grossly disproportionate.

In assessing whether a sentence is grossly disproportionate, the court must first consider the gravity of the offence, the personal characteristics of the offender and the particular circumstances of the case in order to determine what range of sentences would have been appropriate to punish, rehabilitate or deter this particular offender or to protect the public from this particular offender. The other purposes which may be pursued by the imposition of punishment, in particular the deterrence of other potential offenders, are thus not relevant at this stage of the inquiry. This does not mean that the judge or the legislator can no longer consider general deterrence or other penological purposes that go beyond the particular offender in determining a sentence, but only that the resulting sentence must not be grossly disproportionate to what the offender deserves. If a grossly disproportionate sentence is "prescribed by law," then the purpose which it seeks to attain will fall to be assessed under s. 1. Section 12 ensures that individual offenders receive punishments that are appropriate, or at least not grossly disproportionate, to their particular circumstances, while s. 1 permits this right to be overridden to achieve some important societal objective.

One must also measure the effect of the sentence actually imposed. If it is grossly disproportionate to what would have been appropriate, then it infringes s. 12. The effect of the sentence is often a composite of many factors and is not limited to the quantum or duration of the sentence but includes its nature and the conditions under which it is applied. Sometimes by its length alone or by its very nature will the sentence be grossly disproportionate to the purpose sought. Sometimes it will be the result of the combination of factors which, when considered in isolation, would not in and of themselves amount to gross disproportionality. For example, 20 years for a first offence against property would be grossly disproportionate, but so would three months of imprisonment if the prison authorities decide it should be served in solitary confinement. Finally, I should add that some punishments or treatments will always be grossly disproportionate and will always outrage our standards of decency: for example, the infliction of corporal punishment, such as the lash, irrespective of the number of lashes imposed, or, to give examples of treatment, the lobotomisation of certain dangerous offenders or the castration of sexual offenders.

The numerous criteria proposed pursuant to s. 2(b) of the *Canadian Bill of Rights* and the Eighth Amendment of the American Constitution are, in my opinion, useful as factors to determine whether a violation of s. 12 has occurred. Thus, to refer to tests listed by Professor Tarnopolsky, the determination of whether the punishment is necessary to achieve a valid penal purpose, whether it is founded on recognized sentencing principles, and whether there exist valid alternatives to the punishment imposed, are all guidelines which, without being determinative in themselves, help to assess whether the punishment is grossly disproportionate.

There is a further aspect of proportionality which has been considered on occasion by the American courts: a comparison with punishments imposed for other crimes in the same jurisdiction: see *Solem v. Helm* (1983), 463 US 277 at p. 291. Of course, the simple fact that penalties for similar offences are divergent does not necessarily mean that the greater penalty is grossly disproportionate and thus cruel and unusual. At most, the divergence in penalties is an indication that the greater penalty may be excessive, but it will remain necessary to assess the penalty in accordance with the factors discussed above. The notion that there must be a gradation of punishments according to the malignity of offences may be considered to be a principle of fundamental justice under s. 7, but, given my decision under s. 12, I do not find it necessary to deal with that issue here.

R v. Morrisey
[2000] 2 SCR 90, 148 CCC (3d) 1

GONTHIER J (Iacobucci, Major, Bastarache, and Binnie JJ concurring): ... [1] Is a four-year minimum sentence of imprisonment cruel and unusual punishment for the *is the analysis expanded beyond this particular offender in this section to include all hypotheticals?*

offence of criminal negligence causing death with a firearm? As I set out in these reasons, it is my view that this punishment does not constitute cruel and unusual punishment. The offence of criminal negligence causing death requires proof of wanton and reckless disregard for the lives and safety of other people—a high threshold to pass. This offence does not punish accidents. Nor does it punish the merely unfortunate. It punishes those who use firearms in a manner that represents a marked departure from the standard of care employed by a reasonable person, resulting in death. It is no trivial matter, and Parliament has treated it accordingly.

[2] Considering all of the factors set out in *R v. Smith*, [1987] 1 SCR 1045, and *R v. Goltz*, [1991] 3 SCR 485, a four-year minimum sentence does not constitute a grossly disproportionate sentence, either for this individual offender, or for any reasonable hypothetical offender. Accordingly, I am of the opinion that the minimum sentence does not infringe s. 12 of the *Canadian Charter of Rights and Freedoms*, and the appeal is dismissed on this ground. However, the Court of Appeal failed to take into account the appellant's pre-trial custody, and pursuant to this Court's decision in *R v. Wust*, [2000] 1 SCR 455, 2000 SCC 18, the appellant's sentence should be adjusted to take pre-trial custody into account. This aspect of the trial judge's decision is restored. As a result, I would dismiss the appeal in all respects except for this one aspect of the order.

• • •

ARBOUR J: (dissenting): ... [59] This appeal concerns a challenge, under s. 12 of the *Canadian Charter of Rights and Freedoms*, to the constitutionality of s. 220(a) of the *Criminal Code*, RSC, 1985, c. C-46, which imposes a mandatory minimum sentence of four years upon conviction for criminal negligence causing death with a firearm. I have read Justice Gonthier's reasons and I agree with him that there is no breach of s. 12 of the Charter with regard to the first stage of the constitutional analysis. Indeed, this is consistent with the decisions of both lower courts and the position of the appellant: the mandatory four-year sentence is not so excessive or grossly disproportionate as to constitute cruel and unusual punishment for this offender in the particular circumstances of this case.

[60] However, it is with regard to the second stage of the analysis, where the constitutionality of the sentencing provision is considered in light of reasonable hypotheticals, that I disagree with the reasons of my colleague. Because the offence of criminal negligence causing death with a firearm is so fact-driven, I cannot conclude that the four-year minimum sentence is not grossly disproportionate for "any" reasonable hypothetical offender. My colleague is able to reach this conclusion largely because he has restricted the reasonable hypothetical analysis to "imaginable circumstances which could commonly arise with a degree of generality appropriate to the particular offence" (para. 50). I believe that this approach is inappropriate and, indeed, unworkable for the offence before us, for several reasons.

• • •

[65] Essentially, I believe that it is impossible to canvass, with the requisite richness of factual details, the many varied circumstances in which a charge of manslaughter could arise, even when the factual scenarios are restricted to manslaughter by criminal negligence, and involving the use of a firearm. Furthermore, in my view, real cases, representing situations that have arisen, must be seen as reasonable hypotheticals for

purposes of a s. 12 analysis, no matter how unusual they may appear. If s. 12 had been raised in any one of the reported cases, and the punishment had been found to be grossly disproportionate for that offender, the penalty would have had to be struck down as unconstitutional, no matter how uncommon the circumstances of the case. In the same way, if such a case were to arise in the future—where the Court would not be able to find it a far-fetched projection since it would have already happened—the same result would prevail.

[66] As the law now stands, under the first stage of the s. 12 constitutional analysis, if a minimum penalty is grossly disproportionate in one case, the provision creating that mandatory penalty is struck down as a violation of s. 12. This approach was developed in cases where the offence which attracted the minimum penalty was very different from the offence at issue in the present case. I believe that in order to give effect to Parliament's explicit desire to increase penalties for firearms-related offences, while recognizing the inevitability that a four-year penalty will be grossly excessive for at least some plausible future manslaughter convictions, a different approach is called for in this case. I would therefore uphold the constitutionality of s. 220(a) generally, while declining to apply it in a future case if the minimum penalty is found to be grossly disproportionate for that future offender. Accordingly, I would dismiss the appeal and suggest a more individualized approach to s. 12 challenges to this provision in the future.

. . .

[69] In articulating my concern that the Court cannot possibly canvass all reasonable hypothetical situations in which this minimum sentence could offend s. 12, I do not mean to suggest that all mandatory minimum sentences risk violating s. 12 of the Charter. Lamer J, as he then was, stated in *Smith, supra*, at p. 1077, that a "minimum mandatory term of imprisonment is obviously not in and of itself cruel and unusual." Although mandatory minimum sentences depart from the general principles of sentencing expressed in the Code, in particular the fundamental principle of proportionality (s. 718.1), the constitutional norm requires that they be upheld even though demonstrably unfit, as long as they are not grossly disproportionate to the just punishment that would otherwise be required by the particular circumstances of the offence and of the offender.

[70] When Parliament brought forward the *Firearms Act*, SC 1995, c. 39, it imposed mandatory minimum sentences of four years for several firearms-related offences in addition to criminal negligence causing death with a firearm (s. 220(a)): manslaughter (s. 236(a)); attempted murder (s. 239(a)); discharging a firearm with intent (s. 244); sexual assault with a weapon (s. 272(2)(a)); aggravated sexual assault (s. 273(2)(a)); kidnapping (s. 279(1.1)(a)); hostage-taking (s. 279.1(2)(a)); robbery (s. 344(a)); and extortion (s. 346(1.1)(a)). The mandatory minimum sentences for these crimes formed part of the federal government's overall approach to gun control and reflects Parliament's intent to deter the criminal misuse of firearms: *Reference re Firearms Act (Can.)*, [2000] 1 SCR 783, 2000 SCC 31, at para. 20; see also *R v. Wust*, [2000] 1 SCR 455, 2000 SCC 18, at para. 32. This Court's s. 12 jurisprudence has also stressed the importance of deferring to legislated sentences by affirming a stringent s. 12 test: *R v. Goltz*, [1991] 3 SCR 485, at p. 501, per Gonthier J; *Steele v. Mountain Institution*, [1990] 2 SCR 1385, at p. 1417, per Cory J. And as the Attorney General of Canada brought to

this Court's attention in its written submissions, some of the mandatory four-year minimum sentences enacted by the *Firearms Act* have been challenged on constitutional grounds and upheld.

* * *

[75] To the extent possible, mandatory minimum sentences must be read consistently with the general principles of sentencing expressed, in particular, in ss. 718, 718.1 and 718.2 of the *Criminal Code*: *Wust* (SCC), *supra*, at para. 22. By fixing a minimum sentence, particularly when the minimum is still just a fraction of the maximum penalty applicable to the offence, Parliament has not repudiated completely the principle of proportionality and the requirement, expressed in s. 718.2(b), that a sentence should be similar to sentences imposed on similar offenders for similar offences committed in similar circumstances. Therefore, in my view, the mandatory minimum sentences for firearms-related offences must act as an inflationary floor, setting a new minimum punishment applicable to the so-called "best" offender whose conduct is caught by these provisions. The mandatory minimum must not become the standard sentence imposed on all but the very worst offender who has committed the offence in the very worst circumstances. The latter approach would not only defeat the intention of Parliament in enacting this particular legislation, but also offend against the general principles of sentencing designed to promote a just and fair sentencing regime and thereby advance the purposes of imposing criminal sanctions.

[76] The proper approach to the determination of the constitutional validity of mandatory minimum sentences, under the guidance of the jurisprudence of this Court, is, in my view, to give effect to this inflationary scheme, except when the statutory impossibility of going below the minimum is offensive to s. 12 of the Charter where the mandatory minimum requires the imposition of a sentence that would be not merely unfit, which is constitutionally permissible, but rather one that is grossly disproportionate to what the appropriate punishment should be. The search for the appropriate punishment is not an abstract exercise. It is very much guided by the types of sentences that have been imposed in the past on similarly situated offenders, and because of that, it changes over time, and may come to reflect the inflationary consequences of the proper application of mandatory minimum sentences for particular types of offences. In this respect, I would disagree with Quinn J, who in the firearms manslaughter case of *R v. Scozzafava*, [1997] OJ No. 5804 (QL) (Gen. Div.), at para. 33, observed that the existence of the four-year minimum should not result in a proportional general increase beyond the range of sentences found in pre-1996 cases.

* * *

[82] As I indicated at the outset, I believe that there will unavoidably be a case in which a four-year minimum sentence for this offence will be grossly disproportionate. Since the inflationary effect of the mandatory floor is likely to increase all penalties for this offence, there will arguably be fewer such cases for which four years will be grossly disproportionate and therefore unconstitutional. Nonetheless, in light of the variety of conduct captured by this prohibition, I believe it likely that there will continue to be some. I see little purpose in attempting to tailor a factual scenario that would illustrate this point of gross disproportionality. It could only be done by injecting a high degree

of specificity to the hypothetical, which stretches the use of that jurisprudential technique beyond the purpose for which it was originally designed.

[83] In general terms, I believe that gross disproportionality is likely to manifest itself, for example, in the context of spousal abuse, as suggested by Professor T.L. Quigley, of the University of Saskatchewan, who testified before the Standing Senate Committee on Legal and Constitutional Affairs regarding the mandatory minimum penalties set out in Bill C-68, the *Firearms Act* (*Proceedings of the Standing Senate Committee on Legal and Constitutional Affairs*, Issue No. 60, October 19, 1995, at p. 60:34). Professor Quigley suggested that in the case of an abused woman who finally reacts to her abuser, kills him and is charged with criminal negligence causing death or manslaughter, "[t]here may be compelling reasons why a four-year sentence is grossly disproportionate in those circumstances." Indeed, the recent case of *R v. Ferguson*, [1997] OJ No. 2488 (QL) (Gen. Div.), concerned an accused who intentionally shot her abusive husband, while he was lying on a couch. Charged with murder, the accused was convicted of manslaughter and in the circumstances of the case, sentenced to a two-year-less-a-day conditional sentence. Because the offence occurred prior to the enactment of the *Firearms Act*, the judge ruled that the mandatory minimum sentence for manslaughter with a firearm, provided in s. 236(a), did not apply (at para. 124).

[84] Additionally, the cases of *R v. D.E.C.*, [1995] BCJ No. 1074 (QL) (SC), and *R v. Chivers*, [1988] NWTR 134 (SC), also involved battered women who were convicted of a firearms homicide and received a suspended sentence in conjunction with probation. While battered women's syndrome was not sufficient to act as a complete defence to the charge, it was nonetheless considered a mitigating factor on sentencing.

[85] In other cases involving battered women's syndrome and firearms homicides, courts have imposed relatively short periods of incarceration. For example, in *R v. Pettigrew* (1990), 56 CCC (3d) 390 (BCCA), the accused was convicted of unlawful act manslaughter, after accidentally shooting her husband while he slept, as she attempted to unload a gun. Although the accused was intoxicated at the time, the court recognized that she had a long history of abuse at the hands of her husband and in attempting to unload the gun, she was acting out of concern for her children's and her own safety. She was sentenced to six months' incarceration, followed by 12 months' probation.

[86] Another type of situation in which the four-year mandatory minimum sentence under s. 220(a) could be found to violate s. 12 involves police officers or security guards who are required to carry firearms as a condition of their employment and who, in the course of their duty, negligently kill someone with their firearm. Of course, the law will hold such persons to a high standard of care in the use and handling of their firearms; however, it is nonetheless conceivable that circumstances could arise in which a four-year penitentiary term could constitute cruel and unusual punishment.

[87] For example, a police officer was convicted of criminal negligence causing death when he shot the victim during a confrontation between native protesters and the provincial police in September 1995: *R v. Deane*, [1997] OJ No. 3578 (QL) (Prov.). Fraser Prov. J imposed a conditional sentence of two years less a day, to be served in the community, under the then recently enacted provision permitting this kind of disposition: s. 742.1 of the *Criminal Code*, added SC 1995, c. 22, s. 6. Fraser Prov. J noted

that had the offence occurred in September 1994, a conditional sentence would not have been available to the accused and, similarly, had the offence occurred in September 1996, subsequent to the *Firearms Act* amendments, the accused would have had to face a four-year mandatory minimum, precluding the use of a conditional sentence. Interestingly, Fraser Prov. J queried "whether the legislators considered the fairness of having those accused such as policemen or guards, who have legitimate reasons for possessing a firearm, subject to the same statutory minimum as others who are not required for employment purposes to carry a gun" (para. 21).

[88] Having referred to these disparate scenarios arising from actual cases, I would not want to prejudge the determination of what would be a fit and constitutional sentence in any of these cases. The jurisprudence demonstrates that sentencing principles and practice reject pigeonhole approaches and favour a disposition that is sensitive to all the circumstances of every individual case.

· · ·

[90] These considerations were not acute in previous cases, such as *Smith, supra*, and *Goltz, supra*, since the types of offences considered there contained fewer variables, and gave rise to a lesser spread of sentencing options. Yet McIntyre J in *Smith* wrote a forceful dissent, disagreeing with the use of reasonable hypotheticals in a constitutional challenge of a sentence under s. 12. McIntyre J acknowledged the appropriateness of allowing parties to challenge laws on constitutional grounds where their own rights had not been directly infringed, in order to protect the rights of others who may not be in a position to challenge the legislation and whose rights might be affected, or "chilled," by allowing unconstitutional legislation to remain unchallenged (at pp. 1084-85). However, McIntyre J in *Smith* would not have allowed parties to invoke the rights of hypothetical third parties to support their challenge where the impugned law "does not prohibit any individual from engaging in a constitutionally protected activity" (p. 1085).

VII. MANDATORY MINIMUM SENTENCES AND CONSTITUTIONAL EXEMPTIONS

It has been suggested that the answer to the methodological problem lies in the use of a constitutional exemption—that is, permitting a court to maintain the constitutional validity of a sentencing provision but rule, as a Charter remedy, that it not apply to the particular offender because of an anomalous and "cruel and unusual" effect. For many years, appellate courts have disagreed as to whether this mechanism is available. This issue has now been resolved by the Supreme Court in *R v. Ferguson*, below. The case involved a police officer, originally charged with murder, who was convicted of manslaughter arising from the shooting of a prisoner in custody. Ordinarily, this would trigger the operation of a mandatory minimum sentence of four years. The trial judge concluded that the facts supported the argument that the offender was at the low end of the blameworthiness scale and that a four-year sentence was grossly disproportionate. Hence, it was cruel and unusual and contrary to s. 12. However, since the mandatory minimum sentence had been found to be constitutional in *Morrisey*, the judge applied a constitutional exemption and imposed a conditional sentence on the police officer. The Alberta Court of Appeal reversed and substituted the mandatory four-year term of imprisonment: see *R v. Ferguson* (2006), 207 CCC (3d) 157 (Alta. CA). The majority concluded that the judge had erred by finding the four-year sentence to be cruel and unusual. O'Brien JA dissented and supported the use of a constitutional exemption. The police officer appealed to the Supreme Court, which dismissed the appeal. The reasoning of Chief Justice McLachlin for a unanimous court put to rest the innovative idea that individual circumstances might justify an exemption from an otherwise constitutional sentencing provision.

R v. Ferguson
2008 SCC 6

The judgment of the Court was delivered by

McLACHLIN CJ:

[1] This appeal raises two questions. First, does imposition of the four-year mandatory minimum sentence for manslaughter with a firearm constitute cruel and unusual punishment contrary to s. 12 of the *Canadian Charter of Rights and Freedoms* in the circumstances of this case? Second, can an offender who demonstrates that a mandatory minimum sentence would constitute cruel and unusual punishment in his case obtain a stand-alone constitutional exemption from the application of that minimum sentence?

[2] I conclude that the answer to both questions is no. On the facts of this case, the minimum sentence imposed by s. 236(*a*) of the *Criminal Code*, RSC 1985, c. C-46, is not grossly disproportionate and so does not constitute cruel and unusual punishment in violation of s. 12 of the *Charter*. In any event, a constitutional exemption is not an appropriate remedy for a s. 12 violation. If a minimum sentence is found to be unconstitutional on the facts of a particular case, the law imposing the sentence is inconsistent with the *Charter* and therefore falls under s. 52 of the *Constitution Act, 1982*.

2. Facts and Procedural History

[3] This case arises out of the fatal shooting of Darren Varley by an RCMP officer, in the small town of Pincher Creek in southwestern Alberta, while he was being held in a cell at the RCMP detachment. The RCMP officer who shot Mr. Varley, Michael Esty Ferguson, was charged with second-degree murder but convicted by a jury of the lesser offence of manslaughter. The judge imposed a conditional sentence of two years less a day, notwithstanding the mandatory minimum sentence of four years imposed by s. 236(*a*) of the *Criminal Code* for manslaughter with a firearm ((2004), 39 Alta. LR (4th) 166, 2004 ABQB 928). The majority of the Alberta Court of Appeal overturned that sentence, and held that the mandatory minimum must be imposed ((2006), 65 Alta. LR (4th) 44, 2006 ABCA 261). Constable Ferguson appeals to this Court, contending that a four-year sentence in the circumstances would constitute cruel and unusual punishment contrary to s. 12 of the *Charter*, and that the trial judge was right to grant him a constitutional exemption from the four-year minimum sentence imposed by Parliament.

• • •

IV. Analysis

1. Does Imposition of the Four-Year Minimum Sentence Imposed by Section 236(a) of the Criminal Code Constitute Cruel and Unusual Punishment Contrary to Section 12 of the Charter in the Circumstances of This Case?

[8] Section 236(*a*) imposes a four-year minimum sentence for manslaughter with a firearm:

> 236. Every person who commits manslaughter is guilty of an indictable offence and liable
>
> (*a*) where a firearm is used in the commission of the offence, to imprisonment for life and to a minimum punishment of imprisonment for a term of four years;

[9] Constable Ferguson argues that imposing the minimum sentence in his case violates s. 12 of the *Charter*, which provides a guarantee against cruel and unusual punishment.

> 12. Everyone has the right not to be subjected to any cruel and unusual treatment or punishment.

[10] This Court has held that the four-year mandatory minimum sentence for criminal negligence causing death with a firearm (s. 220(*a*) of the *Criminal Code*) is not unconstitutional: *R v. Morrisey*, [2000] 2 SCR 90, 2000 SCC 39. In so holding, the Court applied the reasonable hypotheticals analysis of cases that might be expected to arise, developed in *R v. Goltz*, [1991] 3 SCR 485. Here we are concerned with the mandatory minimum sentence imposed by s. 236(*a*) for a different offence, manslaughter committed with the use of a firearm.

[11] As Arbour J indicated in her concurring opinion in *Morrisey* (para. 61), there is considerable overlap between unlawful act manslaughter, which is the offence we are dealing with in this case, and criminal negligence causing death, which was the offence before the Court in *Morrisey*. The British Columbia Court of Appeal has taken this fact into account in upholding the constitutionality of s. 236(*a*): *R v. Birchall* (2001), 158 CCC (3d) 340, 2001 BCCA 356. Constable Ferguson's argument at sentencing and in the Court of Appeal appears to have implicitly accepted that, as a matter of precedent, s. 236(*a*) does not violate s. 12 of the *Charter*.

[12] Constable Ferguson relies instead on Arbour J's concurring remarks in *Morrisey* to the effect that, given the wide range of circumstances under which the offences of unlawful act manslaughter and criminal negligence causing death can be committed, it is not possible to conclude on the basis of a reasonable hypotheticals analysis that the mandatory minimum sentence will be constitutional in every possible application. He argues that *Morrisey* should be read as having held that s. 220(*a*) and s. 236(*a*) are constitutional only in most of their applications, and that a constitutional exemption should be granted in those rare cases where applying the sentence would lead to an unconstitutional result.

[13] I have concluded that a constitutional exemption is not an appropriate remedy for a mandatory minimum sentence that results in a sentence that violates s. 12. This does not imply, however, that no remedy is available in the case of a mandatory minimum sentence that brings about an unconstitutional result—for instance, in circum-

stances not previously considered as part of a reasonable hypotheticals analysis. If a mandatory minimum sentence would create an unconstitutional result in a particular case, the minimum sentence must be struck down. It is therefore necessary to consider whether imposition of the mandatory minimum sentence provided for in s. 236(*a*) would result in cruel and unusual punishment on the facts of Constable Ferguson's case.

[14] The test for whether a particular sentence constitutes cruel and unusual punishment is whether the sentence is grossly disproportionate: *R v. Smith*, [1987] 1 SCR 1045. As this Court has repeatedly held, to be considered grossly disproportionate, the sentence must be more than merely excessive. The sentence must be "so excessive as to outrage standards of decency" and disproportionate to the extent that Canadians "would find the punishment abhorrent or intolerable": *R v. Wiles*, [2005] 3 SCR 895, 2005 SCC 84, at para. 4, citing *Smith*, at p. 1072 and *Morrisey*, at para. 26. The question thus becomes: is a four-year sentence of imprisonment grossly disproportionate to the offence of manslaughter as committed by Constable Ferguson?

[15] The appropriateness of a sentence is a function of the purpose and principles of sentencing set out in ss. 718 to 718.2 of the *Criminal Code* as applied to the facts that led to the conviction. It follows that the appropriateness of the minimum sentence of four years that Parliament has prescribed for Constable Ferguson's offence depends on what the jury concluded about Constable Ferguson's conduct.

[16] This poses a difficulty in a case such as this, since, unlike a judge sitting alone, who has a duty to give reasons, the jury gives only its ultimate verdict. The sentencing judge therefore must do his or her best to determine the facts necessary for sentencing from the issues before the jury and from the jury's verdict. This may not require the sentencing judge to arrive at a complete theory of the facts; the sentencing judge is required to make only those factual determinations necessary for deciding the appropriate sentence in the case at hand.

[17] Two principles govern the sentencing judge in this endeavour. First, the sentencing judge "is bound by the express and implied factual implications of the jury's verdict": *R v. Brown*, [1991] 2 SCR 518, p. 523. The sentencing judge "shall accept as proven all facts, express or implied, that are essential to the jury's verdict of guilty" (*Criminal Code*, s. 724(2)(*a*)), and must not accept as fact any evidence consistent only with a verdict rejected by the jury: *Brown*; *R v. Braun* (1995), 95 CCC (3d) 443 (Man. CA).

[18] Second, when the factual implications of the jury's verdict are ambiguous, the sentencing judge should not attempt to follow the logical process of the jury, but should come to his or her own independent determination of the relevant facts: *Brown*; *R v. Fiqia* (1994), 162 AR 117 (CA). In so doing, the sentencing judge "may find any other relevant fact that was disclosed by evidence at the trial to be proven" (s. 724(2)(*b*)). To rely upon an aggravating fact or previous conviction, the sentencing judge must be convinced of the existence of that fact or conviction beyond a reasonable doubt; to rely upon any other relevant fact, the sentencing judge must be persuaded on a balance of probabilities: (ss. 724(3)(*d*) and 724(3)(*e*); see also *R v. Gardiner*, [1982] 2 SCR 368; *R v. Lawrence* (1987), 58 CR (3d) 71 (Ont. HC)). It follows from the purpose of the exercise that the sentencing judge should find only those facts necessary to permit the proper sentence to be imposed in the case at hand. The judge should first ask what the issues on sentencing are, and then find such facts as are necessary to deal with those issues.

[19] Following these principles, the trial judge in this case was required to find facts, consistent with the jury's manslaughter verdict, to the extent that this was necessary to enable him to sentence Constable Ferguson. The sentencing inquiry was shaped by s. 236(*a*)'s prescription of a four-year mandatory minimum sentence. The only issues were whether the sentence should be more than four years, as the Crown contended, and whether the facts of the case were such that a four-year sentence would be grossly disproportionate, as Constable Ferguson contended.

[20] The trial judge correctly turned his mind to the basis on which he had instructed the jury it could reach a verdict of manslaughter. The trial judge had instructed the jury that if it rejected both self-defence and intent for murder (intent to cause death or bodily harm likely to cause death), it must reach a verdict of manslaughter. The trial judge did not leave any other basis for a manslaughter verdict with the jury. Hence the trial judge correctly concluded that on the basis of the jury's verdict, he must find facts consistent with the jury's rejection of both self-defence and intent for murder. On the basis of the jury's rejection of intent for murder, the trial judge properly concluded that the jury had found that when he fired the second shot, Constable Ferguson neither intended to cause death nor bodily harm that he knew was likely to cause death.

[21] However, the trial judge did not stop with these conclusions. He went on to make detailed findings of fact on Constable Ferguson's conduct. It was open to him under s. 724(2)(*b*) of the *Criminal Code* to supplement the jury's findings insofar as this was necessary for sentencing purposes. However, it was not open to him to go beyond what was required to deal with the sentencing issues before him, or to attempt to reconstruct the logical process of the jury: *Brown*; *Fiqia*. Nor was it open to him to find facts inconsistent with the jury's verdict or the evidence; a trial judge must never do this. The trial judge in the case at bar committed both these errors.

[22] First, the trial judge erred in attempting to reconstruct the logical reasoning of the jury. The law holds that the trial judge must not do this, and for good reason. Jurors may arrive at a unanimous verdict for different reasons and on different theories of the case: *R v. Thatcher*, [1987] 1 SCR 652. …

. . .

[24] Second, and more critically, the trial judge went on to develop a theory to support the jury's verdict which was not only speculative, but contrary to the evidence. …

. . .

[28] When the erroneous findings of the trial judge are set aside, no basis remains for concluding that the four-year mandatory minimum sentence prescribed by Parliament constitutes cruel and unusual punishment on the facts of this case. The trial judge recognized as aggravating factors that Constable Ferguson was well trained in the use of firearms and stood in a position of trust with respect to Mr. Varley, and correctly noted that the standard of care was higher than would be expected of a normal citizen. By way of mitigation, the trial judge noted that Constable Ferguson's actions were not planned, that Mr. Varley initiated the altercation in the cell, that Constable Ferguson had little time to consider his response, and that his instincts and training played a role in the shooting. The mitigating factors are insufficient to make a four-year sentence grossly disproportionate. The absence of planning, the apparent fact that Mr. Varley initiated the altercation in the cell, and the fact that Constable Ferguson did not have much time

to consider his response, are more than offset by the position of trust Constable Ferguson held and by the fact that he had been trained to respond appropriately to the common situation of resistance by a detained person. I agree with the Court of Appeal that the mitigating factors do not reduce Constable Ferguson's moral culpability to the extent that the mandatory minimum sentence is grossly disproportionate in his case.

[29] I conclude that there is no basis for concluding that the four-year minimum sentence prescribed by Parliament amounts to cruel and unusual punishment on the facts of this case.

[30] Ordinarily, a s. 12 analysis for a mandatory minimum sentence requires both an analysis of the facts of the accused's case and an analysis of reasonable hypothetical cases: *Goltz*, at pp. 505-6. At his sentencing hearing and in the Court of Appeal, however, Constable Ferguson did not rely on reasonable hypotheticals to contest the constitutionality of s. 236(*a*). He contended simply that s. 236(*a*) was unconstitutional as applied to the facts of his case. The reasonable hypotheticals not having been argued, there was no basis for the sentencing judge or the Court of Appeal to reach a conclusion on whether s. 236(*a*) was unconstitutional on a reasonable hypotheticals analysis. Constable Ferguson offers an alternative argument based on reasonable hypotheticals for the first time in this Court. In my view, Constable Ferguson has not pointed to a hypothetical case where the offender's minimum level of moral culpability for unlawful act manslaughter using a firearm would be less than that in the reasonable hypotheticals considered in *Morrisey*.

. . .

2. *If the Imposition of the Four-Year Mandatory Minimum Sentence Violated Section 12 of the Charter in the Circumstances of this Case, Was the Trial Judge Entitled to Grant a Constitutional Exemption from the Four-Year Minimum and to Impose a Lesser Sentence?*

[33] Having found that the four-year minimum sentence of imprisonment required by s. 236(*a*) does not violate Constable Ferguson's right not to suffer cruel and unusual punishment contrary to s. 12 of the *Charter*, it is not necessary to consider whether a constitutional exemption would have been available had we found a violation of s. 12. As the Court of Appeal recognized, however, there has been considerable debate and disagreement in the lower courts as to whether the remedy of a constitutional exemption is available. The matter having been fully argued, it is appropriate to settle the question of whether a constitutional exemption would have been available to Constable Ferguson, had the minimum sentence violated s. 12 of the *Charter*.

[34] I note at the outset that the issue is not *whether* a remedy lies to prevent the imposition of cruel and unusual punishment contrary to the *Charter*, but *which* remedies are available. The imposition of cruel and unusual punishment contrary to ss. 12 and 1 of the *Charter* cannot be countenanced. A court which has found a violation of a *Charter* right has a duty to provide an effective remedy. The only issue is whether a law imposing such punishment can be permitted to stand subject to constitutional exemptions in particular cases, or whether the only remedy is a declaration that the law is inconsistent with the *Charter* and hence falls under s. 52 of the *Constitution Act, 1982*.

[35] Two remedial provisions govern remedies for *Charter* violations: ss. 24(1) of the *Charter* and s. 52(1) of the *Constitution Act, 1982*. Section 24(1) confers on judges a wide discretion to grant appropriate remedies in response to *Charter* violations:

> 24(1) Anyone whose rights or freedoms, as guaranteed by this Charter, have been in-fringed or denied may apply to a court of competent jurisdiction to obtain such remedy as the court considers appropriate and just in the circumstances.

Section 24(1) has generally been seen—at least until now—as providing a case-by-case remedy for unconstitutional acts of government agents operating under lawful schemes whose constitutionality is not challenged. The other remedy section, s. 52(1) of the *Constitution Act, 1982*, confers no discretion on judges. It simply provides that laws that are inconsistent with the *Charter* are of no force and effect to the extent of the inconsistency:

> 52(1) The Constitution of Canada is the supreme law of Canada, and any law that is inconsistent with the provisions of the Constitution is, to the extent of the inconsistency, of no force or effect.

When a litigant claims that a law violates the *Charter*, and a court rules or "declares" that it does, the effect of s. 52(1) is to render the law null and void. It is common to de-scribe this as the court "striking down" the law. In fact, when a court "strikes down" a law, the law has failed by operation of s. 52 of the *Constitution Act, 1982*.

[36] The usual remedy for a mandatory sentencing provision that imposes cruel and unusual punishment contrary to s. 12 of the *Charter* is a declaration that the law is of no force and effect under s. 52 of the *Constitution Act, 1982*. This was the remedy sought in *Goltz*, *Morrisey*, and *R v. Luxton*, [1990] 2 SCR 711. The mandatory minimum sentence provisions in these cases were held to be constitutional. But it was argued that had the provisions been held to be unconstitutional, the appropriate remedy was the s. 52 remedy of striking down.

[37] In this case, despite the allegation of a constitutional violation, Constable Fer-guson does not request that the law that caused the alleged violation, s. 236(*a*) of the *Criminal Code*, be struck down. Instead, Constable Ferguson argues that if the four-year mandatory sentence is found to violate the *Charter*, a constitutional exemption under s. 24(1) should be granted. The argument for a constitutional exemption proposes that the law remain in force, but that it not be applied in cases where its application re-sults in a *Charter* violation. The judge would thus be free to impose a sentence below the minimum set by law, which would nevertheless continue to stand.

[38] The argument in favour of recognizing constitutional exemptions is simply put. The first prong of the argument is that where a mandatory minimum sentence that is constitutional in most of its applications generates an unconstitutional result in a small number of cases, it is better to grant a constitutional exemption in these cases than to strike down the law as a whole. The s. 52(1) remedy of declaring invalid a law that produces a result inconsistent with the *Charter* is a blunt tool. A law that may be con-stitutional in many of its applications—and indeed ruled constitutional on a reasonable hypothetical analysis—is struck down because in one particular case, or in a few cases, it produces an unconstitutional result. Would it not be better, the argument goes, to allow

the law to stand, while providing an individual remedy in those cases—arguably rare—where its application offends the *Charter*?

[39] The second and complementary prong of the argument asserts that the remedy is available on the wording of the *Charter* and the jurisprudence. Section 24(1), it is argued, grants courts a wide discretion to grant such constitutional remedies as are "appropriate and just." Granting a constitutional exemption and substituting a constitutional sentence removes the law's inconsistency with the *Charter*, making s. 52(1) inapplicable. The cases that have considered the matter, while inconclusive, do not rule constitutional exemptions out as a remedy for unconstitutional sentences flowing from mandatory minimum sentence laws. More generally, granting constitutional exemptions for unconstitutional effects of mandatory minimum sentence laws fits well with the Court's practices of severance, reading in and reading out in order to preserve the law to the maximum extent possible: see *Schachter v. Canada*, [1992] 2 SCR 679.

[40] Attractive as they are, the arguments for constitutional exemptions in a case such as this are, on consideration, outweighed and undermined by counter-considerations. I reach this conclusion on the basis of four considerations: (1) the jurisprudence; (2) the need to avoid intruding on the role of Parliament; (3) the remedial scheme of the *Charter*; and (4) the impact of granting constitutional exemptions in mandatory sentence cases on the values underlying the rule of law.

(1) The Jurisprudence

[41] This Court has not definitively ruled whether constitutional exemptions are available as a remedy for mandatory minimum sentences that produce unconstitutional sentences. In concurring opinions, judges of this Court have expressed both positive and negative evaluations of constitutional exemptions as remedies for unconstitutional minimum sentences.

[42] In his concurring opinion in *Smith*, at pp. 1111-12, Le Dain J considered and rejected the constitutional exemption as a means of upholding minimum sentences that could generate unconstitutional results in some circumstances. He stated that allowing such exemptions would create uncertainty, and the assumed validity or application of the provision could have prejudicial effects in particular cases. On the other hand, Arbour J commented favourably on the possibility of exemptions from mandatory minimum sentence laws in a concurring opinion in *Morrisey*. Arbour J expressed the concern that the mandatory minimum sentences for certain offences would inevitably be declared unconstitutional if judges had no discretion to grant exemptions to avoid unconstitutional results in unusual cases.

[43] Lower courts have taken contradictory positions on the availability of constitutional exemptions from mandatory minimum sentences. The Ontario and New Brunswick courts of appeal have held against the availability of constitutional exemptions from mandatory sentence laws: *R v. Kelly* (1990), 59 CCC (3d) 497 (Ont. CA); *R v. Madeley* (2002),160 OAC 346; *R v. Desjardins* (1996), 182 NBR (2d) 321. By contrast, such exemptions have been granted in Saskatchewan and the Northwest and Yukon Territories and have been recognized in *obiter* in British Columbia: *R v. McGillivary* (1991), 62 CCC (3d) 407 (Sask. CA); *R v. Netser* (1992), 70 CCC (3d) 477 (NWTCA);

R v. Chief (1989), 51 CCC (3d) 265 (YTCA); *R v. Kumar* (1993), 85 CCC (3d) 417 (BCCA). The Quebec Court of Appeal has expressed both positive and negative views on the question in *obiter*: *R v. Lapierre* (1998), 123 CCC (3d) 332; *R v. Chabot* (1992), 77 CCC (3d) 371.

[44] Constitutional exemptions have been recognized and discussed in other contexts. ...

• • •

[47] In summary, the majority of this Court in *Seaboyer* has commented critically on the use of constitutional exemptions as a stand-alone remedy in the case of mandatory laws generally, a view supported by Wilson J in *Osborne* and consistent with the majority's reasoning in *Corbiere*. In *Smith*, Le Dain J rejected their use in the context here at issue, mandatory minimum sentence laws. On the other side of the issue are the remarks of L'Heureux-Dubé and Arbour JJ in their respective concurring opinions in *Rose* and *Morrisey*.

[48] I conclude that while the availability of constitutional exemptions for mandatory minimum sentencing laws has not been conclusively decided, the weight of authority thus far is against them and sounds a cautionary note.

(2) Intrusion on the Role of Parliament

[49] Section 52(1) grants courts the jurisdiction to declare laws of no force and effect only "to the extent of the inconsistency" with the Constitution. It follows that if the constitutional defect of a law can be remedied without striking down the law as a whole, then a court must consider alternatives to striking down. Examples of alternative remedies under s. 52 include severance, reading in and reading down. Constable Ferguson is proposing a constitutional exemption under s. 24(1) as an additional tool for minimizing interference with Parliament's legislative role when a court must grant a remedy for a constitutionally defective provision.

[50] On the other hand, it has long been recognized that in applying alternative remedies such as severance and reading in, courts are at risk of making inappropriate intrusions into the legislative sphere. An alternative to striking down that initially appears to be less intrusive on the legislative role may in fact represent an inappropriate intrusion on the legislature's role. This Court has thus emphasized that in considering alternatives to striking down, courts must carefully consider whether the alternative being considered represents a lesser intrusion on Parliament's legislative role than striking down. Courts must thus be guided by respect for the role of Parliament, as well as respect for the purposes of the *Charter*: *Schachter*; *Vriend v. Alberta*, [1998] 1 SCR 493; *R v. Sharpe*, [2001] 1 SCR 45, 2001 SCC 2. These principles apply with equal force to the proposed alternative remedy of the constitutional exemption. In this case, the effect of granting a constitutional exemption would be to so change the legislation as to create something different in nature from what Parliament intended. It follows that a constitutional exemption should not be granted.

[51] When a court opts for severance or reading in as an alternative to striking down a provision, it does so on the assumption that had Parliament been aware of the provision's constitutional defect, it would likely have passed it with the alterations now being made by the court by means of severance or reading in. For instance, as this Court noted

in *Schachter*, the test for severance "recognizes that the seemingly laudable purpose of retaining the parts of the legislative scheme which do not offend the Constitution rests on an assumption that the legislature would have passed the constitutionally sound part of the scheme without the unsound part" (p. 697). If it is not clear that Parliament would have passed the scheme with the modifications being considered by the court—or if it is probable that Parliament would *not* have passed the scheme with these modifications—then for the court to make these modifications would represent an inappropriate intrusion into the legislative sphere. In such cases, the least intrusive remedy is to strike down the constitutionally defective legislation under s. 52. It is then left up to Parliament to decide what legislative response, if any, is appropriate.

[52] It follows that we must ask whether granting a constitutional exemption for a mandatory minimum sentence would represent a lesser intrusion on Parliament's legislative role than striking it down. In my view, the answer to this question is no, because allowing courts to grant constitutional exemptions for mandatory minimum sentences directly contradicts Parliament's intent in passing mandatory minimum sentence legislation.

[53] A constitutional exemption has the effect of conferring on judges a discretion to reject the mandatory minimum sentence prescribed by Parliament. The mandatory minimum applies, unless the judge concludes that its application constitutes unjustifiable cruel and unusual punishment and that it therefore should not apply.

[54] The intention of Parliament in passing mandatory minimum sentence laws, on the other hand, is to remove judicial discretion to impose a sentence below the stipulated minimum. Parliament must be taken to have specifically chosen to exclude judicial discretion in imposing mandatory minimum sentences, just as it was taken to have done in enacting the rape shield provisions struck down in *Seaboyer*. Parliament made no provision for the exercise of judicial discretion in drafting s. 236(*a*), nor did it authorize any exceptions to the mandatory minimum. There is no provision permitting judges to depart from the mandatory minimum, even in exceptional cases where it would result in grossly disproportionate punishment. Parliament has cast the prescription for the minimum four-year prison sentence here at issue in clear unambiguous terms. Parliament must be taken to have intended what it stated: that all convictions for manslaughter with a firearm would be subject to a mandatory minimum sentence of four years imprisonment. The law mandates a floor below which judges cannot go. To permit judges to go below this floor on a case-by-case basis runs counter to the clear wording of the section and the intent that it evinces.

[55] In granting a constitutional exemption, a judge would be undermining Parliament's purpose in passing the legislation: to remove judicial discretion and to send a clear and unequivocal message to potential offenders that if they commit a certain offence, or commit it in a certain way, they will receive a sentence equal to or exceeding the mandatory minimum specified by Parliament. The discretion that a constitutional exemption would confer on judges would violate the letter of the law and undermine the message that animates it.

[56] It is thus clear that granting a constitutional exemption from a mandatory minimum sentence law that results in an unconstitutional sentence goes directly against Parliament's intention. To allow constitutional exemptions for mandatory minimum

sentences is, in effect, to read in a discretion to a provision where Parliament clearly intended to exclude discretion. If it would be inappropriate to read in such a discretion under s. 52, then necessarily it would be inappropriate to allow judges to grant constitutional exemptions having the same effect under s. 24(1). It cannot be assumed that Parliament would have enacted the mandatory minimum sentencing scheme with the discretion that allowing constitutional exemptions would create. For the Court to introduce such a discretion would thus represent an inappropriate intrusion into the legislative sphere.

[57] I conclude that these considerations are sufficient to exclude constitutional exemptions as an appropriate remedy for unconstitutional mandatory minimum sentences. In the absence of any provision providing for discretion, a court that concludes that a mandatory minimum sentence imposes cruel and unusual punishment in an exceptional case before it is compelled to declare the provision invalid.

(3) The Remedial Scheme of the Charter

[58] As I noted at the outset, remedies for breaches of the *Charter* are governed by s. 24(1) of the *Charter* and s. 52(1) of the *Constitution Act, 1982*.

[59] When a law produces an unconstitutional effect, the usual remedy lies under s. 52(1), which provides that the law is of no force or effect to the extent that it is inconsistent with the *Charter*. A law may be inconsistent with the *Charter* either because of its purpose or its effect: *R v. Big M Drug Mart Ltd.*, [1985]1 SCR 295; *R v. Edwards Books and Art Ltd.*, [1986] 2 SCR 713. Section 52 does not create a personal remedy. A claimant who otherwise has standing can generally seek a declaration of invalidity under s. 52 on the grounds that a law has unconstitutional effects either in his own case or on third parties: *Big M*; see also Peter Sankoff, "Constitutional Exemptions: Myth or Reality?" (1999-2000), 11 *NJCL* 411, at pp. 432-34; Morris Rosenberg and Stéphane Perrault, "Ifs and Buts in Charter Adjudication: The Unruly Emergence of Constitutional Exemptions in Canada" (2002), 16 *SCLR* (2d) 375, at pp. 380-82. The jurisprudence affirming s. 52(1) as the appropriate remedy for laws that produce unconstitutional effects is based on the language chosen by the framers of the *Charter*: see Sankoff, at p. 438.

[60] Section 24(1), by contrast, is generally used as a remedy, not for unconstitutional laws, but for unconstitutional government acts committed under the authority of legal regimes which are accepted as fully constitutional: see *Eldridge v. British Columbia (Attorney General)*, [1997] 3 SCR 624; *Multani v. Commission scolaire Marguerite-Bourgeoys*, [2006] 1 SCR 256, 2006 SCC 6. The acts of government agents acting under such regimes are not the necessary result or "effect" of the law, but of the government agent's applying a discretion conferred by the law in an unconstitutional manner. Section 52(1) is thus not applicable. The appropriate remedy lies under s. 24(1).

[61] It thus becomes apparent that ss. 52(1) and 24(1) serve different remedial purposes. Section 52(1) provides a remedy for *laws* that violate *Charter* rights either in purpose or in effect. Section 24(1), by contrast, provides a remedy for *government acts* that violate *Charter* rights. It provides a personal remedy against unconstitutional government action and so, unlike s. 52(1), can be invoked only by a party alleging a viola-

tion of that party's own constitutional rights: *Big M*; *R v. Edwards*, [1996] 1 SCR 128. Thus this Court has repeatedly affirmed that the validity of laws is determined by s. 52 of the *Constitution Act, 1982*, while the validity of government action falls to be determined under s. 24 of the *Charter*: *Schachter*; *R v. 974649 Ontario Inc.*, [2001] 3 SCR 575, 2001 SCC 81. We are here concerned with a *law* that is alleged to violate a *Charter* right. This suggests that s. 52(1) provides the proper remedy.

[62] It is argued that s. 24(1), while normally applicable to government acts, can also be used to provide a stand-alone remedy for the unconstitutional effects of mandatory minimum sentence laws. The wording of s. 24(1) is generous enough to permit this, it is argued, conferring a discretion on judges to grant "such remedy as the court considers appropriate and just in the circumstances."

[63] The jurisprudence of this Court allows a s. 24(1) remedy in connection with a s. 52(1) declaration of invalidity in unusual cases where additional s. 24(1) relief is necessary to provide the claimant with an effective remedy: *R v. Demers*, [2004] 2 SCR 489, 2004 SCC 46. However, the argument that s. 24(1) can provide a stand-alone remedy for laws with unconstitutional effects depends on reading s. 24(1) in isolation, rather than in conjunction with the scheme of the *Charter* as a whole, as required by principles of statutory and constitutional interpretation. When s. 24(1) is read in context, it becomes apparent that the intent of the framers of the Constitution was that it function primarily as a remedy for unconstitutional government acts.

[64] The highly discretionary language in s. 24(1), "such remedy as the court considers appropriate and just in the circumstances," is appropriate for control of unconstitutional acts. By contrast, s. 52(1) targets the unconstitutionality of laws in a direct non-discretionary way: laws are of no force or effect to the extent that they are unconstitutional.

[65] The presence of s. 52(1) with its mandatory wording suggests an intention of the framers of the *Charter* that unconstitutional laws are deprived of effect to the extent of their inconsistency, not left on the books subject to discretionary case-by-case remedies: see *Osborne, per* Wilson J In cases where the requirements for severance or reading in are met, it may be possible to remedy the inconsistency judicially instead of striking down the impugned legislation as a whole: *Vriend*; *Sharpe*. Where this is not possible—as in the case of an unconstitutional mandatory minimum sentence—the unconstitutional provision must be struck down. The ball is thrown back into Parliament's court, to revise the law, should it choose to do so, so that it no longer produces unconstitutional effects. In either case, the remedy is a s. 52 remedy that renders the unconstitutional provision of no force or effect to the extent of its inconsistency. To the extent that the law is unconstitutional, it is not merely inapplicable for the purposes of the case at hand. It is null and void, and is effectively removed from the statute books.

[66] As pointed out in *Seaboyer*, if the unconstitutional effects of laws are remediable on a case-by-case basis under s. 24(1), in theory all *Charter* violations could be addressed in this manner, leaving no role for s. 52(1). To meet this concern, it is suggested that s. 24(1) should only be used in the case of laws that usually produce constitutional results and only rarely produce an unconstitutional effect. The mandatory minimum sentence provision in s. 236(*a*) is said to be such a law. However one defines the "rare" case, discussed more fully below, the risk is that the role intended for s. 52(1)

would be undermined and that laws that should be struck down—over-inclusive laws that pose a real risk of unconstitutional treatment of Canadians—would remain on the books, contrary to the intention of the framers of the *Charter*.

(4) The Rule of Law

[67] Constable Ferguson's principal argument for constitutional exemptions, as we have seen, is an appeal to flexibility. Yet this flexibility comes at a cost: constitutional exemptions buy flexibility at the cost of undermining the rule of law.

[68] The principles of constitutionalism and the rule of law lie at the root of democratic governance: *Reference re Secession of Quebec*, [1998] 2 SCR 217. It is fundamental to the rule of law that "the law must be accessible and so far as possible intelligible, clear and predictable": Lord Bingham, "The Rule of Law," (2007), 66 *Cambridge LJ* 67, at p. 69. Generality, promulgation, and clarity are among the essential elements of the "morality that makes law possible": Lon L. Fuller, *The Morality of Law*, (2nd ed. 1969), at pp. 33-39.

[69] Constitutional exemptions for mandatory minimum sentence laws raise concerns related to the rule of law and the values that underpin it: certainty, accessibility, intelligibility, clarity and predictability.

[70] As noted in the last section, a constitutional exemption under s. 24(1) is a personal remedy. The remedy proposed by Constable Ferguson is thus distinct from a s. 52 remedy that reads in an exception for a well-defined class of situations—as, for instance, the remedy in *Sharpe*. When a constitutional exemption is granted, the successful claimant receives a personal remedy under s. 24(1), but the law remains on the books, intact. As Wilson J put it in *Osborne*, the legislation remains as enacted "in its pristine over-inclusive form" (p. 77). The mere possibility of such a remedy thus necessarily generates uncertainty: the law is on the books, but in practice, it may not apply. As constitutional exemptions are actually granted, the law in the statute books will in fact increasingly diverge from the law as applied.

[71] Constitutional exemptions from mandatory minimum sentences leave the law uncertain and unpredictable, as Le Dain J pointed out in *Smith*. It is up to judges on a case-by-case basis to decide when to strike down a minimum sentence that is inconsistent with the *Charter*, and when to grant an individual exemption under s. 24(1). But the *Charter* is silent on how a judge should make this decision—the decision, literally, of whether the law stands or falls. In theory, all violations could be remedied under s. 24(1), leaving no role for s. 52(1). The only option would be to introduce a meta-rule as to when a s. 24(1) exemption is available and when a declaration of invalidity should be made under s. 52(1). How such a rule should be fashioned—where the line should be drawn—is far from clear. Constitutional exemptions, it is suggested, should be confined to laws that usually operate constitutionally and only occasionally result in constitutional violations. But how is the judge to decide whether the case before her is rare? The bright line required for constitutional certainty is elusive.

[72] The divergence between the law on the books and the law as applied—and the uncertainty and unpredictability that result—exacts a price paid in the coin of injustice. First, it impairs the right of citizens to know what the law is in advance and govern their conduct accordingly—a fundamental tenet of the rule of law. Second, it risks over-

application of the law; as Le Dain J noted in *Smith*, the assumed validity of the law may prejudice convicted persons when judges must decide whether to apply it in particular cases. Third, it invites duplication of effort. The matter of constitutionality would not be resolved once and for all as under s. 52(1); in every case where a violation is suspected, the accused would be obliged to seek a constitutional exemption. In so doing, it creates an unnecessary barrier to the effective exercise of the convicted offender's constitutional rights, thereby encouraging uneven and unequal application of the law.

[73] A final cost of constitutional exemptions from mandatory minimum sentence laws is to the institutional value of effective law making and the proper roles of Parliament and the courts. Allowing unconstitutional laws to remain on the books deprives Parliament of certainty as to the constitutionality of the law in question and thus of the opportunity to remedy it. Legislatures need clear guidance from the courts as to what is constitutionally permissible and what must be done to remedy legislation that is found to be constitutionally infirm. In granting constitutional exemptions, courts would be altering the state of the law on constitutional grounds without giving clear guidance to Parliament as to what the Constitution requires in the circumstances: Rosenberg and Perrault, at p. 391. Bad law, fixed up on a case-by-case basis by the courts, does not accord with the role and responsibility of Parliament to enact constitutional laws for the people of Canada.

V. Conclusion

[74] I conclude that constitutional exemptions should not be recognized as a remedy for cruel and unusual punishment imposed by a law prescribing a minimum sentence. If a law providing for a mandatory minimum sentence is found to violate the *Charter*, it should be declared inconsistent with the *Charter* and hence of no force and effect under s. 52 of the *Constitution Act, 1982*.

NOTE

Are you satisfied with the reasoning of McLachlin CJC? Does the Charter framework leave no room for an exemption in rare and anomalous circumstances?

While *Ferguson* may signal the end of constitutional exemptions, it is not the end of s. 12 in the context of mandatory minimum sentences. Newly legislated offences will be open to s. 12 scrutiny. Also, with respect to mandatory minimum sentences that have already passed constitutional muster, an accused will still be able to argue that her own personal situation engages s. 12 so long as these circumstances were "not previously considered as part of a reasonable hypotheticals analysis." Of course, the s. 12 test remains: is the sentence "so excessive as to outrage standards of decency" and disproportionate to the extent that Canadians "would find the punishment abhorrent or intolerable"?

VIII. MANDATORY MINIMUM SENTENCES AND PRE-SENTENCE CREDIT

Section 719(3) permits a sentencing judge to give credit for pre-sentence custody. How does this provision interact with a mandated minimum sentence? Imagine a situation where two offenders are accused of robbery, and it is alleged that a firearm was used. Section 344(a) imposes a mandatory sentence of four years. One offender is released on bail, while the other serves 12 months in custody before the trial. Both are convicted. Does fairness not require some credit for the pre-sentence custody? How can the judge give effect to both s. 719(3) and s. 344(a)? See the decision of Rosenberg JA for the Ontario Court of Appeal in *R v. McDonald* (1998), 127 CCC (3d) 57 and compare it with *R v. Lapierre* (1998), 123 CCC (3d) 332 (Que. CA). This issue has now been resolved by the Supreme Court of Canada in *R v. Wust*, below.

R v. Wust
(2000), 143 CCC (3d) 129 (SCC)

ARBOUR J (for the court):

. . .

[18] Mandatory minimum sentences are not the norm in this country, and they depart from the general principles of sentencing expressed in the Code, in the case law, and in the literature on sentencing. In particular, they often detract from what Parliament has expressed as the fundamental principle of sentencing in s. 718.1 of the Code: the principle of proportionality. Several mandatory minimum sentences have been challenged under s. 12 of the Charter, as constituting cruel and unusual punishment: see, for example, *R v. Smith*, [1987] 1 SCR 1045, 34 CCC (3d) 97, 40 DLR (4th) 435, *R v. Goltz*, [1991] 3 SCR 485, 67 CCC (3d) 481, and *Morrisey, supra*.

[19] On some occasions, a mandatory minimum sentence has been struck down under s. 12, on the basis that the minimum prescribed by law was, or could be, on a reasonable hypothetical basis, grossly disproportionate to what the circumstances called for. See for example *Smith*, striking down s. 5(2) of the *Narcotic Control Act*; *R v. Bill* (1998), 13 CR (5th) 125 (BCSC), striking down the four-year minimum sentence for manslaughter with a firearm under s. 236(a) of the Code; *R v. Leimanis*, [1992] BCJ No. 2280 (QL) (Prov. Ct.), in which the s. 88(1)(c) minimum sentence of the BC *Motor Vehicle Act* for driving under a s. 85(a) prohibition was invalidated; and *R v. Pasacreta*, [1995] BCJ No. 2823 (QL) (Prov. Ct.), where the same penalty as in *Leimanis* for driving under a s. 84 prohibition was also struck down.

[20] In other cases, courts have fashioned the remedy of a constitutional exemption from a mandatory minimum sentence, thereby upholding the enactment as valid while exempting the accused from its application: see *R v. Chief* (1989), 51 CCC (3d) 265 (YTCA), and *R v. McGillivary* (1991), 62 CCC (3d) 407 (Sask. CA). Finally, in some of the cases where the courts have upheld a minimum sentence as constitutionally valid, it has been noted that the mandatory minimum sentence was demonstrably unfit or harsh in the case before the court. See, for example, *McDonald*, at p. 85, per Rosenberg JA, and *R v. Hainnu*, [1998] NWTJ No. 101 (QL) (SC) at para. 71.

[21] Even if it can be argued that harsh, unfit sentences may prove to be a powerful deterrent, and therefore still serve a valid purpose, it seems to me that sentences that are unjustly severe are more likely to inspire contempt and resentment than to foster compliance with the law. It is a well-established principle of the criminal justice system that judges must strive to impose a sentence tailored to the individual case: *R v. M.(C.A.)*,

[1996] 1 SCR 500 at para. 92, 105 CCC (3d) 327, per Lamer CJ; *R v. Gladue*, [1999] 1 SCR 688 at para. 93, 133 CCC (3d) 385, 171 DLR (4th) 385, per Cory and Iacobucci JJ.

[22] Consequently, it is important to interpret legislation which deals, directly and indirectly, with mandatory minimum sentences, in a manner that is consistent with general principles of sentencing, and that does not offend the integrity of the criminal justice system. This is entirely possible in this case, and, in my view, such an approach reflects the intention of Parliament that all sentences be administered consistently, except to the limited extent required to give effect to a mandatory minimum.

[23] In accordance with the umbrella principle of statutory interpretation expressed by this Court in *Rizzo & Rizzo Shoes Ltd. (Re)*, [1998] 1 SCR 27 at paras. 20-23, 154 DLR (4th) 193, mandatory minimum sentences must be understood in the full context of the sentencing scheme, including the management of sentences provided for in the *Corrections and Conditional Release Act*, SC 1992, c. 20. Several provisions of the Code, and of other federal statutes, provide for various forms of punishment upon conviction for an offence. Most enactments providing for the possibility of imprisonment do so by establishing a maximum term of imprisonment. In deciding on the appropriate sentence, the court is directed by Part XXIII of the Code to consider various purposes and principles of sentencing, such as denunciation, general and specific deterrence, public safety, rehabilitation, restoration, proportionality, disparity, totality and restraint, and to take into account both aggravating and mitigating factors. The case law provides additional guidelines, often in illustrating what an appropriate range of sentence might be in the circumstances of a particular case. In arriving at a fit sentence, the court must also be alive to some computing rules, for example, the rule that sentences cannot normally be back- or post-dated: s. 719(1) of the Code; see also *R v. Patterson* (1946), 87 CCC 86 (Ont. CA) at p. 87, per Robertson CJ, and *R v. Sloan* (1947), 87 CCC 198 (Ont. CA) at pp. 198-99, per Roach JA, cited with approval by Rosenberg JA, in *McDonald*, at p. 71.

[24] Rarely is the sentencing court concerned with what happens after the sentence is imposed, that is, in the administration of the sentence. Sometimes it is required to do so by addressing, by way of recommendation, or in mandatory terms, a particular form of treatment for the offender. For instance in murder cases, the sentencing court will determine a fixed term of parole ineligibility: s. 745.4 of the Code. However, for the most part, after a sentence of imprisonment is imposed, the *Corrections and Conditional Release Act* comes into play to administer that sentence, with the almost invariable effect of reducing the amount of time actually served in detention. Under this Act, the offender earns statutory remission, that is, time that will be automatically deducted from the sentence imposed. Furthermore, he or she will become eligible for escorted and unescorted temporary absences, work releases, day parole and full parole, and statutory release. In short, it is quite possible, indeed, it is most likely, that the person sentenced will not be incarcerated for the full period of time imposed in the sentence pronounced by the court.

[25] The *Corrections and Conditional Release Act*, in effect, "deems" the time spent lawfully at large by the offender who is released on parole, statutory release or unescorted temporary absence as a continuation of the sentence until its expiration:

s. 128(1). This provision applies to all sentences, even where the term of imprisonment imposed is a statutory mandatory minimum.

[26] The *Firearms Act* addressed the issue of the administration of mandatory minimum sentences, but in a very minimal way by amending one section of Schedule I of the *Corrections and Conditional Release Act*. Schedule I sets out the offences for which the sentencing court has power to delay eligibility for full parole to the lesser of one-half of the sentence or ten years, rather than the standard time for full parole eligibility of the lesser of one-third of the sentence or seven years: s. 120(1) of the *Corrections and Conditional Release Act*, referring to, among other sections, s. 743.6 of the Code. In s. 165, the *Firearms Act* amends Schedule I to include using an imitation firearm in the commission of an offence, as prohibited by s. 85(2) of the Code.

[27] This slight amendment of the *Corrections and Conditional Releases Act* by the *Firearms Act* suggests that while Parliament turned its mind to the administration of sentences when it was introducing the firearms-related minimum sentences, it did not see fit to alter the general administration of sentences in a way that would distinguish the new mandatory minimums from other sentences. It therefore follows that a rigid interpretation of s. 719(3), which suggests that time served before sentence cannot be credited to reduce a minimum sentence because it would offend the requirement that nothing short of the minimum be served, does not accord with the general management of minimum sentences, which are in every other respect "reduced" like all others, even to below the minimum.

[28] In addition, and in contrast to statutory remission or parole, pre-sentence custody is time actually served in detention, and often in harsher circumstances than the punishment will ultimately call for. In *R v. Rezaie* (1996), 112 CCC (3d) 97 (Ont. CA), to which several lower courts have referred in their consideration of pre-sentencing custody, Laskin JA succinctly summarizes the particular features of pre-trial custody that result in its frequent characterization as "dead time" at p. 104:

> ... in two respects, pre-trial custody is even more onerous than post-sentencing custody. First, other than for a sentence of life imprisonment, legislative provisions for parole eligibility and statutory release do not take into account time spent in custody before trial (or before sentencing). Second, local detention centres ordinarily do not provide educational, retraining or rehabilitation programs to an accused in custody waiting trial.

[29] As this quotation from *Rezaie* demonstrates, pre-sentencing custody, pre-trial custody, pre-disposition custody and "dead time" are all used to refer to the time spent by an accused person in detention prior to conviction and sentencing. For the purposes of this decision, I consider all these terms to refer to the same thing; however, I prefer "pre-sentencing custody" as it most accurately captures all the time an offender may have spent in custody prior to the imposition of sentence.

[30] Several years ago, Professor Martin L. Friedland published an important study of pre-sentencing custody in which he referred to Professor Caleb Foote's Comment on the New York Bail Study project, noting that "accused persons ... are confined pending trial under conditions which are more oppressive and restrictive than those applied to convicted and sentenced felons": "Detention Before Trial: A Study of Criminal Cases Tried in the Toronto Magistrates' Courts" (1965), at p. 104. As Rosenberg JA noted in

McDonald at p. 72: "There has been little change in the conditions under which remand prisoners are held in this province in the almost forty years since Professor Friedland did his study." Considering the severe nature of pre-sentencing custody, and that the accused person is in fact deprived of his or her liberty, credit for pre-sentencing custody is arguably less offensive to the concept of a minimum period of incarceration than would be the granting of statutory remission or parole. It is therefore ironic that the applicability of s. 719(3) has encountered such difficulties in the case of minimum sentences, simply because the "interference" with the minimum is at the initial sentence determination stage and thus more readily apparent.

[31] As was pointed out by Rosenberg JA in *McDonald* at p. 73, Parliament enacted the forerunner to s. 719(3) of the *Criminal Code* as part of the *Bail Reform Act*, RSC 1970, c. 2 (2nd Supp.), for the very specific purpose of ensuring that the well-established practice of sentencing judges to give credit for time served while computing a sentence would be available even to reduce a sentence below the minimum fixed by law. During the second reading of what was then Bill C-218, *Amendment of Provisions of the Criminal Code* relating to Arrest and Bail, Justice Minister John Turner described Parliament's intention regarding what is now s. 719(3):

> Generally speaking, the courts in deciding what sentence to impose on a person convicted of an offence take into account the time he has spent in custody awaiting trial. However, under the present *Criminal Code*, a sentence commences only when it is imposed, and the court's hands are tied in those cases where a minimum term of imprisonment must be imposed. In such cases, therefore, the court is bound to impose not less than the minimum sentence even though the convicted person may have been in custody awaiting trial for a period in excess of the minimum sentence. The new version of the bill would permit the court, in a proper case, to take this time into account in imposing sentence. [House of Commons Debates, February 5, 1971, at p. 3118.]

[32] Counsel for the respondent has directed this Court's attention to the remarks of then Justice Minister Allan Rock concerning Bill C-68, an Act respecting firearms and other weapons, during the House of Commons debates and before the Standing Committee on Justice and Legal Affairs. On these occasions, the Justice Minister articulated Parliament's intention that the new mandatory minimum sentences for firearms-related offences act as a strong deterrent to the use of guns in crime. See House of Commons Debates, February 16, 1995, at pp. 9706 et seq.; House of Commons, Standing Committee on Justice and Legal Affairs, Evidence, April 24, 1995, Meeting No. 105, and May 19, 1995, Meeting No. 147. However, when Parliament enacted s. 344(a) as part of the *Firearms Act* in 1995, Parliament did not also modify s. 719(3), to exempt this new minimum sentence from its application, any more than it modified the applicability of the provisions of the *Corrections and Conditional Release Act* to mandatory minimum sentences. For the courts to exempt s. 344(a) from the application of s. 719(3), enacted specifically to apply to mandatory minimum sentences, would therefore defeat the intention of Parliament.

[33] All of the above suggests that if indeed s. 719(3) had to be interpreted such as to prevent credit being given for time served in detention prior to sentencing under a mandatory minimum offence, the result would be offensive both to rationality and to

justice. Fortunately, as was admirably explained by Rosenberg JA in *McDonald*, this result is avoided through the application of sound principles of statutory interpretation.

[34] In his judgment, Rosenberg JA employed several well-established rules of statutory interpretation to conclude as he did, at p. 69, that s. 719(3) provides sentencing judges with a "substantive power to count pre-sentence custody in fixing the length of the sentence." I agree with his analysis. In particular, I approve of his reference to the principle that provisions in penal statutes, when ambiguous, should be interpreted in a manner favourable to the accused (see *R v. McIntosh*, [1995] 1 SCR 686 at para. 29, 95 CCC (3d) 481, per Lamer CJ); to the need to interpret legislation so as to avoid conflict between its internal provisions, to avoid absurd results by searching for internal coherence and consistency in the statute; and finally, where a provision is capable of more than one interpretation, to choose the interpretation which is consistent with the Charter: *Slaight Communications Inc. v. Davidson*, [1989] 1 SCR 1038 at p. 1078, 59 DLR (4th) 416, per Lamer J (as he then was). Without repeating Rosenberg JA's analysis here, I wish to make a few observations.

B. The Distinction Between Punishment and Sentence

[35] Rosenberg JA relied on the distinction between the meaning of the words "punishment" and "sentence," the former being used in s. 344(a) and the latter in s. 719(3). I set out the relevant provisions again, for ease of reference:

> 344. Every person who commits robbery is guilty of an indictable offence and liable
>> (a) where a firearm is used in the commission of the offence, to imprisonment for life and to a minimum punishment of imprisonment for a term of four years ...
>
> 719(3) In determining the sentence to be imposed on a person convicted of an offence, a court may take into account any time spent in custody by the person as a result of the offence.

[36] The distinction between "sentence" and "punishment" was developed by the Canadian Sentencing Reform Commission in its 1987 report, "Sentencing Reform: A Canadian Approach," at pp. 110 et seq. In summary, Rosenberg JA emphasized at pp. 76-78 that "sentencing" is a judicial determination of a legal sanction, in contrast to "punishment" which is the actual infliction of the legal sanction. While this distinction is helpful, I do not think that it is fundamental to sustain the conclusion that s. 719(3) may be applied to s. 344(a). The French version does not employ a similar distinction in the language of the two sections. In French, the expression "la peine" is used interchangeably for "punishment" (s. 344(a)), for "sentencing" (title to s. 718.2) and for "sentence" (i.e., ss. 718.2 and 719). However, the expression "punishment" which is used twice in s. 718.3(1), is referred to in French first as "la peine" and the second time, in the same sentence, as "la punition." What is fundamental is less the words chosen, in the French or English version, but the concepts that they carry. Again, for ease of reference, I set out some of these provisions:

> 344. Quiconque commet un vol qualifié est coupable d'un acte criminel passible:
>> (a) s'il y a usage d'une arme à feu lors de la perpétration de l'infraction, de l'emprisonnement à perpétuité, la peine minimale étant de quatre ans. ...

718.3(1) Lorsqu'une disposition prescrit différents degrés ou genres de peine à l'égard d'une infraction, la punition à infliger est, sous réserve des restrictions contenues dans la disposition, à la discrétion du tribunal qui condamne l'auteur de l'infraction. ...

719(3) Pour fixer la peine à infliger à une personne déclarée coupable d'une infraction, le tribunal peut prendre en compte toute période que la personne a passée sous garde par suite de l'infraction.

[37] Overall, both versions lead to the same conclusion, since the French phrase in s. 719(3), "pour fixer la peine" places the emphasis on the sentencing judge's role of calculating the appropriate sentence, and in doing so, provides the discretion for considering the amount of time already spent in custody by the convicted offender in relation to the offence. Since these sections refer to "la peine," it seems logical to conclude that in determining "la peine minimale" it is acceptable to apply s. 719(3), since "la peine minimale" is merely a subset of "la peine" generally, and has not been excluded expressly from the operation of s. 719(3). No violence is done to the language of the Code when the sections are read together, in French or in English, and are understood to mean, as Parliament intended, that an offender will receive a minimum sentence of four years, to commence when it is imposed, and calculated with credit given for time served.

C. The Effect of Pre-Sentencing Custody on the Legally Detained Accused

[38] I have already commented on the usually harsh nature of pre-sentencing custody and referred to the frequent characterization of this detention as "dead time." Some further comments are required.

[39] Counsel for the respondent urged this Court to consider the apparent fallacy of recognizing pre-sentencing custody as punishment, since it is commonly recognized that Canadian law does not punish innocent citizens. Rosenberg JA in *McDonald*, at p. 77, noted that "accused persons are not denied bail to punish them before their guilt has been determined." He referred to this Court's decision in *R v. Pearson*, [1992] 3 SCR 665 at pp. 687-88, 77 CCC (3d) 124, where Lamer CJ held that the presumption of innocence as guaranteed by s. 11(d) of the Charter has "no application at the bail stage of the criminal process, where the guilt or innocence of the accused is not determined and where punishment is not imposed."

[40] Counsel for the respondent also referred to this passage from Pearson to support the contention that pre-trial custody may not be considered as part of the offender's punishment. With respect, it is important to consider the broader context of Lamer CJ's comments. At that point in the Pearson judgment (at pp. 687-88), Lamer CJ was elaborating on the specific understanding of the s. 11(d) presumption of innocence in the trial context:

Thus the effect of s. 11(d) is to create a procedural and evidentiary rule at trial that the prosecution must prove guilt beyond a reasonable doubt. This procedural and evidentiary rule has no application at the bail stage of the criminal process, where the guilt or innocence of the accused is not determined and where punishment is not imposed. Accordingly, s. 515(6)(d) does not violate s. 11(d).

Looking at this larger context, one cannot conclude that Lamer CJ was proposing that pre-sentencing custody could never be viewed as punishment or that it could not retro-actively be treated as part of the punishment, as provided for by s. 719(3).

[41] To maintain that pre-sentencing custody can never be deemed punishment following conviction because the legal system does not punish innocent people is an exercise in semantics that does not acknowledge the reality of pre-sentencing custody so carefully delineated by Laskin JA, in *Rezaie*, supra, and by Gary Trotter in his text, *The Law of Bail in Canada* (1992), at p. 28:

> Remand prisoners, as they are sometimes called, often spend their time awaiting trial in detention centres or local jails that are ill-suited to lengthy stays. As the Ouimet Report stressed, such institutions may restrict liberty more than many institutions which house the convicted. Due to overcrowding, inmate turnover and the problems of effectively im-plementing programs and recreation activities, serving time in such institutions can be quite onerous.

Therefore, while pre-trial detention is not intended as punishment when it is imposed, it is, in effect, deemed part of the punishment following the offender's conviction, by the operation of s. 719(3). The effect of deeming such detention punishment is not un-like the determination, discussed earlier in these reasons, that time spent lawfully at large while on parole is considered nonetheless a continuation of the offender's sen-tence of incarceration.

[42] If this Court were to conclude that the discretion provided by s. 719(3) to con-sider pre-sentencing custody was not applicable to the mandatory minimum sentence of s. 344(a), it is certain that unjust sentences would result. First, courts would be placed in the difficult situation of delivering unequal treatment to similarly situated offenders: for examples, see *McDonald*, at pp. 80-81. Secondly, because of the gravity of the of-fence and the concern for public safety, many persons charged under s. 344(a), even first time offenders, would often be remanded in custody while awaiting trial. Conse-quently, discrepancies in sentencing between least and worst offenders would increase, since the worst offender, whose sentence exceeded the minimum would benefit from pre-sentencing credit, while the first time offender whose sentence would be set at the minimum, would not receive credit for his or her pre-sentencing detention. An inter-pretation of s. 719(3) and s. 344(a) that would reward the worst offender and penalize the least offender is surely to be avoided.

[43] These examples of the absurd results we could expect from an exclusion of the application of s. 719(3) to mandatory minimum sentences, such as that provided by s. 344(a), are further indication that Parliament intended these two sections to be inter-preted harmoniously and consistently within the overall context of the criminal justice system's sentencing regime.

D. Calculating the Amount of Credit for Pre-Sentence Custody

[44] I see no advantage in detracting from the well-entrenched judicial discretion provided in s. 719(3) by endorsing a mechanical formula for crediting pre-sentencing custody. As we have re-affirmed in this decision, the goal of sentencing is to impose a

just and fit sentence, responsive to the facts of the individual offender and the particular circumstances of the commission of the offence. I adopt the reasoning of Laskin JA in *Rezaie*, at p. 105, where he noted that:

> ... provincial appellate courts have rejected a mathematical formula for crediting pre-trial custody, instead insisting that the amount of time to be credited should be determined on a case by case basis. ... Although a fixed multiplier may be unwise, absent justification, sentencing judges should give some credit for time spent in custody before trial (and before sentencing). [Citations omitted]

[45] In the past, many judges have given more or less two months credit for each month spent in pre-sentencing detention. This is entirely appropriate even though a different ratio could also be applied, for example if the accused has been detained prior to trial in an institution where he or she has had full access to educational, vocational and rehabilitation programs. The often applied ratio of 2:1 reflects not only the harshness of the detention due to the absence of programs, which may be more severe in some cases than in others, but reflects also the fact that none of the remission mechanisms contained in the *Corrections and Conditional Release Act* apply to that period of detention. "Dead time" is "real" time. The credit cannot and need not be determined by a rigid formula and is thus best left to the sentencing judge, who remains in the best position to carefully weigh all the factors which go toward the determination of the appropriate sentence, including the decision to credit the offender for any time spent in pre-sentencing custody.

V. Disposition of the Appeal

[46] I would allow the appeal and set aside the judgment of the Court of Appeal. I would reinstate the sentence imposed on the appellant by Grist J, who granted the appellant one year credit for his seven months of pre-sentencing custody, and sentenced him under s. 344(a) to three and one half years' imprisonment. The concurrent sentence of one year for possession of a restricted weapon would remain unaffected by these reasons.

Appeal allowed.

NOTE

Another aspect of pre-sentence custody is the development of the "enhanced credit" (more than two-for-one) in situations where judges have considered the conditions of confinement to have been especially egregious—for example, during a jail guard strike: see, for example, *R v. Krauchov* (2002), 4 CR (6th) 137 (Ont. CJ); *R v. G.R.*, [2002] OJ No. 4361 (QL) (SC); and *R v. Critton*, [2002] OJ No. 2594 (QL) (SC).

In *R v. Downes* (2006), 79 OR (3d) 321, 205 CCC (3d) 488 (CA), the Ontario Court of Appeal recognized that the concept of credit for pre-sentence custody could apply to cases where there were stringent bail conditions like house arrest. The court eventually gave 5 months' credit for 18 months on bail and offered the following analysis:

... [C]redit for pre-trial bail conditions should be approached in the following manner:

- Time spent on stringent pre-sentence bail conditions, especially house arrest, is a relevant mitigating factor.
- As such, the trial judge must consider the time spent on bail under house arrest in determining the length of sentence.
- The failure of the trial judge to explain why time spent on bail under house arrest has not been taken into account is an error in principle.
- The amount of credit to be given for time spent on bail under house arrest is within the discretion of the trial judge and there is no formula that the judge is required to apply.
- The amount of credit will depend upon a number of factors including, the length of time spent on bail under house arrest; the stringency of the conditions; the impact on the offender's liberty; the ability of the offender to carry on normal relationships, employment and activity.
- Where the offender asks the trial judge to take pre-sentence bail conditions into account, the offender should supply the judge with information as to the impact of the conditions. If there is a dispute as to the impact of the conditions, the onus is on the offender to establish those facts on a balance of probabilities in accordance with s. 724(3) of the *Criminal Code.*

CHAPTER TWELVE

Conditional Sentence of Imprisonment

I. INTRODUCTION

The conditional sentence was created in 1995 (SC 1995, c. 22), coming into force in 1996 with the new Part XXIII of the *Criminal Code*, RSC 1985, c. C-46 (as amended). Its purpose was to reduce the use of imprisonment as a sanction. A conditional sentence is a term of imprisonment that is served in the community. When the court concludes that an appropriate sentence is a jail term of less than two years, it may order that the sentence be served in the community, subject to conditions. Although this is the first such sanction in Canada, most common law jurisdictions have some mechanism that allows offenders to discharge a custodial sentence at home.

The conditional sentence has proven to be the most significant and controversial aspect of the reforms of 1996. There is no doubt, however, that the disposition is well established among sentencing options. While some guidelines have been developed by the courts, controversy has continued about the proper scope of conditional sentences. Are there offences, or classes of offences, for which the conditional sentence should not be an available option? In 2007, Parliament amended the Code to restrict their ambit. We will consider this amendment later. For now, it is sufficient to note that SC 2007, c. 12, s. 1 amended the conditional-sentence regime to exclude any offence that can be characterized as a "serious personal injury offence" under s. 752, a terrorism offence, or a criminal-organization offence. It is the s. 752 reference that will prove to be controversial.

II. BACKGROUND OF THE CONDITIONAL SENTENCE

The idea of suspending dispositions for fixed periods of time can be traced to the Report of the Canadian Committee on Corrections, *Toward Unity: Criminal Justice and Corrections* (1969) ("the Ouimet Report") and the English suspended sentence. Both examples are distinguishable from the traditional Canadian suspended sentence, where the imposition of sentence is suspended but not its execution. In 1984, a bill was tabled that contained proposals for sentencing reform based on *The Criminal Law in Canadian Society* (1982), a statement of government policy concerning the criminal law. The bill included a new option, entitled the "conditional sentence," which was to be defined in the following form:

> Where an offender other than a corporation is convicted of an offence, except an offence for which a minimum punishment is prescribed by law, the court may suspend the imposition of

any other sanction and direct that the offender enter into a recognizance in Form 28 without sureties to keep the peace and be of good behaviour for such period, not exceeding two years, as the court thinks fit.

This proposal would have permitted the suspension of any kind of sentence without conditions, except to avoid further offences. It was essentially the Ouimet model, but it died on the order paper.

The government of Canada issued a green paper on sentencing and corrections in 1990. This led in 1992 to another sentencing reform bill, C-90. Neither the term "conditional sentence" nor any mechanism that might fit that name appeared in these documents. However, that was not the end of the idea. A major criticism of the green paper was the absence of new non-custodial options for sentencing judges. Around the same time as the release of that document came the publication of Morris and Tonry's "Intermediate Sanctions: Between Prison and Parole." Within this category of intermediate sanction would be non-custodial alternatives such as intensive supervision, house arrest, electronic monitoring, day-reporting centres, and community service. The Department of Justice circulated a series of discussion papers that canvassed some of the "intermediate sanction" alternatives. One paper, dated December 9, 1991, returned to the subject of a conditional sentence but defined it as "an alternative to the suspended sentence." In other words, rather than suspending the imposition of a sentence, as has been Canada's approach, the proposal would have suspended the execution of the sentence and amended the consequential breach procedure so that failures to comply would no longer be an offence but rather trigger court intervention. In essence, this would be a revision of the probation scheme. This proposal was ultimately rejected.

The background to s. 742.1 demonstrates a recurring concern with three factors: (1) overuse of imprisonment, (2) greater use of community sentences, and (3) intermediate sanctions. Apart from responding to the overuse of imprisonment, the manner in which the conditional sentence evolved is also important. It was clearly not a revision of probation. The probation provisions and the suspended sentence were continued with only minor amendments. Nor is the conditional sentence a free-standing, discrete sentencing option; it is available in some cases as an alternative mode of serving a sentence of imprisonment.

III. GENERAL PRINCIPLES

After the reform of 1996, trial and appellate courts in the provinces and territories grappled with the proper interpretation of the provisions concerning conditional sentences. Although discrepancies eventually diminished, there remained considerable variations in approach and results, and guidance was clearly needed from the Supreme Court of Canada. As seen in chapter 2, Judicial Methodology and the Legislative Context, that court rarely hears sentencing cases, and its practice in this regard is quite deliberate. In 1999, the Supreme Court heard five cases relating to conditional sentences and judgment was pronounced in all of them on the same day: *R v. Proulx*, [2000] 1 SCR 61; *R v. L.F.W.*, [2000] 1 SCR 132; *R v. R.N.S.*, [2000] 1 SCR 149; *R v. R.A.R.*, [2000] 1 SCR 163; and *R v. Bunn*, [2000] 1 SCR 183. The principal opinion was given by Lamer CJC for a unanimous court in *Proulx*, and it is still the leading statement on the subject. It is also appropriate to look at the other four cases, if only to consider whether the principles in *Proulx* are demonstrably at work in those decisions.

Proulx is lengthy and much of it is reproduced here. The relevant provisions of the Code concerned with conditional sentences are included in the opinion of Lamer CJC, although the amendment of s. 742.1 in 2007, discussed above, must be borne in mind.

R v. Proulx
[2000] 1 SCR 61

LAMER CJC: By passing *An Act to amend the Criminal Code (sentencing) and other Acts in consequence thereof*, SC 1995, c. 22 ("Bill C-41"), Parliament has sent a clear message to all Canadian judges that too many people are being sent to prison. In an attempt to remedy the problem of overincarceration, Parliament has introduced a new form of sentence, the conditional sentence of imprisonment.

As a matter of established practice and sound policy, this Court rarely hears appeals relating to sentences: see *R v. Gardiner*, [1982] 2 SCR 368, at 404; *R v. Chaisson*, [1995] 2 SCR 1118, at 1123; and *R v. M.(C.A.)*, [1996] 1 SCR 500, at para. 33. However, we have decided to hear this case and four related cases because they afford the Court the opportunity to set out for the first time the principles that govern the new and innovative conditional sentencing regime. Given the inevitable length of these reasons, I have summarized the essentials at para. 127.

I. Factual Background

On the morning of November 1, 1995, after a night of partying involving consumption of some alcohol, the respondent decided to drive his friends home even though he knew that his vehicle was not mechanically sound. For a period of 10 to 20 minutes, the respondent, who had only seven weeks of experience as a licensed driver, drove erratically, weaving in and out of traffic, tailgating and trying to pass other vehicles without signalling, despite steady oncoming traffic and slippery roads. As the respondent was trying to pass another vehicle, he drove his car into an oncoming lane of traffic, sideswiped a first car and crashed into a second one. The driver of the second vehicle was seriously injured. The accident also claimed the life of a passenger in the respondent's car. The respondent was in a near-death coma for some time, but ultimately recovered from his injuries. The respondent entered guilty pleas to one count of dangerous driving causing death and one count of dangerous driving causing bodily harm.

• • •

III. Relevant Statutory Provisions

Criminal Code, RSC, 1985, c. C-46

• • •

742.1. Where a person is convicted of an offence, except an offence that is punishable by a minimum term of imprisonment, and the court

(a) imposes a sentence of imprisonment of less than two years, and

(b) is satisfied that serving the sentence in the community would not endanger the safety of the community and would be consistent with the fundamental purpose and principles of sentencing set out in sections 718 to 718.2, the court may, for the purpose of supervising the offender's behaviour in the community, order that the offender serve the sentence in the community, subject to the offender's complying with the conditions of a conditional sentence order made under section 742.3.

· · ·

742.3(1) The court shall prescribe, as conditions of a conditional sentence order, that the offender do all of the following:

(a) keep the peace and be of good behaviour;

(b) appear before the court when required to do so by the court;

(c) report to a supervisor

(i) within two working days, or such longer period as the court directs, after the making of the conditional sentence order, and

(ii) thereafter, when required by the supervisor and in the manner directed by the supervisor;

(d) remain within the jurisdiction of the court unless written permission to go outside that jurisdiction is obtained from the court or the supervisor; and

(e) notify the court or the supervisor in advance of any change of name or address, and promptly notify the court or the supervisor of any change of employment or occupation.

(2) The court may prescribe, as additional conditions of a conditional sentence order, that the offender do one or more of the following:

(a) abstain from

(i) the consumption of alcohol or other intoxicating substances, or

(ii) the consumption of drugs except in accordance with a medical prescription;

(b) abstain from owning, possessing or carrying a weapon;

(c) provide for the support or care of dependants;

(d) perform up to 240 hours of community service over a period not exceeding eighteen months;

(e) attend a treatment program approved by the province; and

(f) comply with such other reasonable conditions as the court considers desirable, subject to any regulations made under subsection 738(2), for securing the good conduct of the offender and for preventing a repetition by the offender of the same offence or the commission of other offences.

· · ·

742.6. ...

(9) Where the court is satisfied, on a balance of probabilities, that the offender has without reasonable excuse, the proof of which lies on the offender, breached a condition of the conditional sentence order, the court may

(a) take no action;

(b) change the optional conditions;

(c) suspend the conditional sentence order and direct

(i) that the offender serve in custody a portion of the unexpired sentence, and

(ii) that the conditional sentence order resume on the offender's release from custody, either with or without changes to the optional conditions; or

(d) terminate the conditional sentence order and direct that the offender be committed to custody until the expiration of the sentence.

. . .

V. Analysis

A. The 1996 Sentencing Reforms (Bill C-41)

In September 1996, Bill C-41 came into effect. It substantially reformed Part XXIII of the *Criminal Code*, and introduced, *inter alia*, an express statement of the purposes and principles of sentencing, provisions for alternative measures for adult offenders and a new type of sanction, the conditional sentence of imprisonment.

As my colleagues Cory and Iacobucci JJ explained in *R v. Gladue*, [1999] 1 SCR 688, at para. 39, "[t]he enactment of the new Part XXIII was a watershed, marking the first codification and significant reform of sentencing principles in the history of Canadian criminal law." They noted two of Parliament's principal objectives in enacting this new legislation: (i) reducing the use of prison as a sanction, and (ii) expanding the use of restorative justice principles in sentencing (at para. 48).

(1) Reducing the Use of Prison as a Sanction

Bill C-41 is in large part a response to the problem of over-incarceration in Canada. It was noted in *Gladue*, at para. 52, that Canada's incarceration rate of approximately 130 inmates per 100,000 population places it second or third highest among industrialized democracies. In their reasons, Cory and Iacobucci JJ reviewed numerous studies that uniformly concluded that incarceration is costly, frequently unduly harsh and "ineffective, not only in relation to its purported rehabilitative goals, but also in relation to its broader public goals" (para. 54). See also Report of the Canadian Committee on Corrections, *Toward Unity: Criminal Justice and Corrections* (1969); *Canadian Sentencing Commission, Sentencing Reform: A Canadian Approach* (1987), at pp. xxiii-xxiv; Standing Committee on Justice and Solicitor General, *Taking Responsibility* (1988), at p. 75. Prison has been characterized by some as a finishing school for criminals and as ill-preparing them for reintegration into society: see generally Canadian Committee on Corrections, *supra*, at p. 314; Correctional Service of Canada, *A Summary of Analysis of Some Major Inquiries on Corrections—1938 to 1977* (1982), at p. iv. At para. 57, Cory and Iacobucci JJ held:

> Thus, it may be seen that although imprisonment is intended to serve the traditional sentencing goals of separation, deterrence, denunciation, and rehabilitation, there is widespread consensus that imprisonment has not been successful in achieving some of these goals. Overincarceration is a long-standing problem that has been many times publicly acknowledged but never addressed in a systematic manner by Parliament. In recent years, compared to other countries, sentences of imprisonment in Canada have increased at an alarming rate. *The 1996 sentencing reforms embodied in Part XXIII, and s. 718.2(e) in particular, must be understood as a reaction to the overuse of prison as a sanction, and must accordingly be given appropriate force as remedial provisions.* [Emphasis in original.]

Parliament has sought to give increased prominence to the principle of restraint in the use of prison as a sanction through the enactment of s. 718.2(a) and (e). Section 718.2(d) provides that "an offender should not be deprived of liberty, if less restrictive sanctions may be appropriate in the circumstances," while s. 718.2(e) provides that "all available sanctions other than imprisonment that are reasonable in the circumstances should be considered for all offenders, with particular attention to the circumstances of aboriginal offenders." Further evidence of Parliament's desire to lower the rate of incarceration comes from other provisions of Bill C-41: s. 718(c) qualifies the sentencing objective of separating offenders from society with the words "where necessary," thereby indicating that caution be exercised in sentencing offenders to prison; s. 734(2) imposes a duty on judges to undertake a means inquiry before imposing a fine, so as to decrease the number of offenders who are incarcerated for defaulting on payment of their fines; and of course, s. 742.1, which introduces the conditional sentence. In *Gladue*, at para. 40, the Court held that "the creation of the conditional sentence suggests, on its face, a desire to lessen the use of incarceration."

(2) Expanding the Use of Restorative Justice Principles in Sentencing

Restorative justice is concerned with the restoration of the parties that are affected by the commission of an offence. Crime generally affects at least three parties: the victim, the community, and the offender. A restorative justice approach seeks to remedy the adverse effects of crime in a manner that addresses the needs of all parties involved. This is accomplished, in part, through the rehabilitation of the offender, reparations to the victim and to the community, and the promotion of a sense of responsibility in the offender and acknowledgment of the harm done to victims and to the community.

Canadian sentencing jurisprudence has traditionally focussed on the aims of denunciation, deterrence, separation, and rehabilitation, with rehabilitation a relative latecomer to the sentencing analysis: see *Gladue*, at para. 42. With the introduction of Bill C-41, however, Parliament has placed new emphasis upon the goals of restorative justice. Section 718 sets out the fundamental purpose of sentencing, as well as the various sentencing objectives that should be vindicated when sanctions are imposed. In *Gladue*, supra, Cory and Iacobucci JJ stated (at para. 43):

> Clearly, s. 718 is, in part, a restatement of the basic sentencing aims, which are listed in paras. (a) through (d). What are new, though, are paras. (e) and (f), which along with para. (d) focus upon the restorative goals of repairing the harms suffered by individual victims and by the community as a whole, promoting a sense of responsibility and an acknowledgment of the harm caused on the part of the offender, and attempting to rehabilitate or heal the offender. The concept of restorative justice which underpins paras. (a), (e), and (f) is briefly discussed below, *but as a general matter restorative justice involves some form of restitution and reintegration into the community. The need for offenders to take responsibility for their actions is central to the sentencing process ... . Restorative sentencing goals do not usually correlate with the use of prison as a sanction. In our view, Parliament's choice to include (e) and (f) alongside the traditional sentencing goals must be understood as evidencing an intention to expand the parameters of the sentencing analysis for all offenders.* [Emphasis added; citation omitted.]

Parliament has mandated that expanded use be made of restorative principles in sentencing as a result of the general failure of incarceration to rehabilitate offenders and reintegrate them into society. By placing a new emphasis on restorative principles, Parliament expects both to reduce the rate of incarceration and improve the effectiveness of sentencing. During the second reading of Bill C-41 on September 20, 1994 (*House of Commons Debates*, vol. IV, 1st Sess., 35th Parl., at p. 5873), Minister of Justice Allan Rock made the following statements:

> A general principle that runs throughout Bill C-41 is that jails should be reserved for those who should be there. Alternatives should be put in place for those who commit offences but who do not need or merit incarceration. ...
>
> Jails and prisons will be there for those who need them, for those who should be punished in that way or separated from society. ... [T]his bill creates an environment which encourages community sanctions and the rehabilitation of offenders together with reparation to victims and promoting in criminals a sense of accountability for what they have done.
>
> It is not simply by being more harsh that we will achieve more effective criminal justice. We must use our scarce resources wisely.

B. The Nature of the Conditional Sentence

The conditional sentence was specifically enacted as a new sanction designed to achieve both of Parliament's objectives. The conditional sentence is a meaningful alternative to incarceration for less serious and non-dangerous offenders. The offenders who meet the criteria of s. 742.1 will serve a sentence under strict surveillance in the community instead of going to prison. These offenders' liberty will be constrained by conditions to be attached to the sentence, as set out in s. 742.3 of the Criminal Code. In case of breach of conditions, the offender will be brought back before a judge, pursuant to s. 742.6. If an offender cannot provide a reasonable excuse for breaching the conditions of his or her sentence, the judge may order him or her to serve the remainder of the sentence in jail, as it was intended by Parliament that there be a real threat of incarceration to increase compliance with the conditions of the sentence.

The conditional sentence incorporates some elements of non-custodial measures and some others of incarceration. Because it is served in the community, it will generally be more effective than incarceration at achieving the restorative objectives of rehabilitation, reparations to the victim and community, and the promotion of a sense of responsibility in the offender. However, *it is also a punitive sanction capable of achieving the objectives of denunciation and deterrence*. It is this punitive aspect that distinguishes the conditional sentence from probation, and it is to this issue that I now turn.

(1) Comparing Conditional Sentences with Probation

There has been some confusion among members of the judiciary and the public alike about the difference between a conditional sentence and a suspended sentence with probation. This confusion is understandable, as the statutory provisions regarding conditions to be attached to conditional sentences (s. 742.3) and probation orders (s. 732.1) are very similar. Notwithstanding these similarities, there is an important distinction between the two. While a suspended sentence with probation is primarily a rehabilita-tive sentencing tool, the evidence suggests that Parliament intended a conditional sen-tence to address both punitive and rehabilitative objectives.

(a) A Comparative Reading of the Provisions

A comparative reading of the provisions governing conditional sentences and probation orders reveals three differences. First, a probation order includes only three compulsory conditions—to keep the peace and be of good behaviour, appear before the court when required, and notify the court or probation officer of any change in employment or ad-dress—whereas there are five such conditions in the case of a conditional sentence. The two additional compulsory conditions of a conditional sentence—to report to a supervi-sor and remain within the jurisdiction unless permission is granted to leave—are listed as optional conditions under a probation order.

The second difference concerns the power of the judge to order the offender to un-dergo treatment. Under a conditional sentence, the sentencing judge can order the of-fender to attend a treatment program, regardless of whether the offender consents. Un-der a probation order, the judge can only impose a treatment order with the consent of the offender (with the exception of drug or alcohol addiction programs since the 1999 amendment to s. 732.1 (SC 1999, c. 32, s. 6)). In practice, however, this difference is not very significant, since it is unlikely that an offender faced with the choice between imprisonment and a suspended sentence with treatment as a condition of probation would refuse to consent to treatment.

The third difference is in the wording of the residual clauses of the provisions gov-erning the imposition of optional conditions. In the case of a conditional sentence, s. 742.3(2)(f) provides that the court may order that the offender comply with such other reasonable conditions as the court considers desirable "for securing the good conduct of the offender and for preventing a repetition by the offender of the same of-fence or the commission of other offences." By contrast, s. 732.1(3)(h) provides that the court may impose such other reasonable conditions of probation "for protecting so-ciety and for facilitating the offender's successful reintegration into the community."

On their face, these three differences do not suggest that a conditional sentence is more punitive than a suspended sentence with probation. Moreover, the penalty for breach of probation is potentially more severe than that for breach of a conditional sen-tence. Pursuant to s. 733.1(1), breach of probation constitutes a new offence, punish-able by up to two years imprisonment, while a breach of condition does not constitute a new offence *per se*. The maximum penalties are also different. In the case of a breach of probation, the offender is subject to the revocation of the probation order and can be sentenced for the original offence (in cases where a suspended sentence was rendered): see s. 732.2(5). By contrast in the case of breaches of conditional sentences, the maxi-mum punishment available is incarceration for the time remaining of the original sen-tence (s. 742.6(9)). Presumably, if a conditional sentence is more onerous than proba-tion, the consequences of breaching a condition should be more onerous as well.

(b) Conditional Sentences Must Be More Punitive Than Probation

Despite the similarities between the provisions and the fact that the penalty for breach of probation is potentially more severe than for breach of a conditional sentence, there are strong indications that Parliament intended the conditional sentence to be more punitive than probation. It is a well accepted principle of statutory interpretation that no legislative provision should be interpreted so as to render it mere surplusage. It would be absurd if Parliament intended conditional sentences to amount merely to probation under a different name. While this argument is clearly not dispositive, it suggests that Parliament intended there to be a meaningful distinction between the two sanctions. I will now consider more specific arguments in support of this position.

The conditional sentence is defined in the Code as a sentence of imprisonment. The heading of s. 742 reads "Conditional Sentence of Imprisonment." Furthermore, s. 742.1(a) requires the court to impose a sentence of imprisonment of less than two years before considering whether the sentence can be served in the community subject to the appropriate conditions. Parliament intended imprisonment, in the form of incarceration, to be more punitive than probation, as it is far more restrictive of the offender's liberty. Since a conditional sentence is, at least notionally, a sentence of imprisonment, it follows that it too should be interpreted as more punitive than probation.

On a related note, with the enactment of s. 742.1, Parliament has mandated that certain non-dangerous offenders who would otherwise have gone to jail for up to two years now serve their sentences in the community. If a conditional sentence is not distinguished from probation, then these offenders will receive what are effectively considerably less onerous probation orders instead of jail terms. Such lenient sentences would not provide sufficient denunciation and deterrence, nor would they be accepted by the public. Section 718 provides that the fundamental purpose of sentencing is "to contribute ... to respect for the law and the maintenance of a just, peaceful and safe society." Inadequate sanctions undermine respect for the law. Accordingly, it is important to distinguish a conditional sentence from probation by way of the use of punitive conditions.

Earlier I drew attention to a subtle difference between the residual clauses in the provisions governing the imposition of optional conditions of probation orders and conditional sentences. While the difference between the two residual clauses is subtle, it is also significant. In order to appreciate this difference, it is necessary to consider the case law and practice that has developed with respect to probation.

Probation has traditionally been viewed as a rehabilitative sentencing tool. Recently, the rehabilitative nature of the probation order was explained by the Saskatchewan Court of Appeal in *R v. Taylor* (1997), 122 CCC (3d) 376. Bayda CJS wrote, at p. 394:

> Apart from the wording of the provision, the innate character of a probation order is such that it seeks to influence the future behaviour of the offender. More specifically, it seeks to secure "the good conduct" of the offender and to deter him from committing the same or other offences. *It does not particularly seek to reflect the seriousness of the offence or the offender's degree of culpability. Nor does it particularly seek to fill the need for denunciation of the offence or the general deterrence of others to commit the same or other offences. Depending upon the specific conditions of the order there may well be a punitive aspect to a probation order but punishment is not the dominant or an inherent purpose. It*

is perhaps not even a secondary purpose but is more in the nature of a consequence of an offender's compliance with one or more of the specific conditions with which he or she may find it hard to comply. [Emphasis added.]

Many appellate courts have struck out conditions of probation that were imposed to punish rather than rehabilitate the offender: see *R v. Ziatas* (1973), 13 CCC (2d) 287 (Ont. CA), at p. 288; *R v. Caja* (1977), 36 CCC (2d) 401 (Ont. CA), at pp. 402-3; *R v. Lavender* (1981), 59 CCC (2d) 551 (BC CA), at pp. 552-53; and *R v. L.* (1986), 50 CR (3d) 398 (Alta. CA), at pp. 399-400. The impugned terms of probation in these cases were imposed pursuant to a residual clause in force at the time whose wording was virtually identical to that presently used in s. 742.3(2)(f).

Despite the virtual identity in the wording of s. 742.3(2)(f) and the old residual clause applicable to probation orders, it would be a mistake to conclude that punitive conditions cannot now be imposed under s. 742.3(2)(f). Parliament amended the residual clause for probation, s. 732.1(3)(h), to read "for protecting society and for *facilitating the offender's successful reintegration into the community*" (emphasis added). It did so to make clear the rehabilitative purpose of probation and to distinguish s. 742.3(2)(f) from s. 732.1(3)(h). The wording used in s. 742.3(2)(f) does not focus principally on the rehabilitation and reintegration of the offender. If s. 742.3(2)(f) were interpreted as precluding punitive conditions, it would frustrate Parliament's intention in distinguishing the two forms of sentence. Parliament would not have distinguished them if it intended both clauses to serve the same purpose.

In light of the foregoing, it is clear that Parliament intended a conditional sentence to be more punitive than a suspended sentence with probation, notwithstanding the similarities between the two sanctions in respect of their rehabilitative purposes. I agree wholeheartedly with Vancise JA, who, dissenting in *R v. McDonald* (1997), 113 CCC (3d) 418 (Sask. CA), stated, at p. 443, that conditional sentences were designed to "permit the accused to avoid imprisonment but not to avoid punishment."

Accordingly, conditional sentences should generally include punitive conditions that are restrictive of the offender's liberty. Conditions such as house arrest or strict curfews should be the norm, not the exception. As the Minister of Justice said during the second reading of Bill C-41 (*House of Commons Debates*, supra, at p. 5873), "[t]his sanction is obviously aimed at offenders who would otherwise be in jail but who could be in the community under *tight* controls" (emphasis added).

There must be a reason for failing to impose punitive conditions when a conditional sentence order is made. Sentencing judges should always be mindful of the fact that conditional sentences are only to be imposed on offenders who would otherwise have been sent to jail. If the judge is of the opinion that punitive conditions are unnecessary, then probation, rather than a conditional sentence, is most likely the appropriate disposition.

The punitive nature of the conditional sentence should also inform the treatment of breaches of conditions. As I have already discussed, the maximum penalty for breach of probation is potentially more severe than that for breach of a conditional sentence. In practice, however, breaches of conditional sentences may be punished more severely than breaches of probation. Without commenting on the constitutionality of these provisions, I note that breaches of conditional sentence need only be proved on a balance of probabilities, pursuant to s. 742.6(9), whereas breaches of probation must be proved beyond a reasonable doubt.

More importantly, where an offender breaches a condition without reasonable excuse, there should be a presumption that the offender serve the remainder of his or her sentence in jail. This constant threat of incarceration will help to ensure that the offender complies with the conditions imposed: see *R v. Brady* (1998), 121 CCC (3d) 504 (Alta. CA); J.V. Roberts, "Conditional Sentencing: Sword of Damocles or Pandora's Box?" (1997), 2 *Can. Crim. L Rev.* 183. It also assists in distinguishing the conditional sentence from probation by making the consequences of a breach of condition more severe.

. . .

C. Application of Section 742.1 of the Criminal Code

. . .

[Section 742.1] lists four criteria that a court must consider before deciding to impose a conditional sentence:

(1) the offender must be convicted of an offence that is not punishable by a minimum term of imprisonment;

(2) the court must impose a term of imprisonment of less than two years;

(3) the safety of the community would not be endangered by the offender serving the sentence in the community; and

(4) a conditional sentence would be consistent with the fundamental purpose and principles of sentencing set out in ss. 718 to 718.2.

In my view, the first three criteria are prerequisites to any conditional sentence. These prerequisites answer the question of whether or not a conditional sentence is possible in the circumstances. Once they are met, the next question is whether a conditional sentence is appropriate. This decision turns upon a consideration of the fundamental purpose and principles of sentencing set out in ss. 718 to 718.2. I will discuss each of these elements in turn.

(1) The Offender Must Be Convicted of an Offence That Is Not Punishable by a Minimum Term of Imprisonment

This prerequisite is straightforward. The offence for which the offender was convicted must not be punishable by a minimum term of imprisonment. Offences with a minimum term of imprisonment are the only statutory exclusions from the conditional sentencing regime.

(2) The Court Must Impose a Term of Imprisonment of Less Than Two Years

Parliament intended that a conditional sentence be considered only for those offenders who would have otherwise received a sentence of imprisonment of less than two years. There is some controversy as to whether this means that the judge must actually impose a term of imprisonment of a *fixed* duration before considering the possibility of a conditional sentence. Far from addressing purely methodological concerns, this question carries implications as to the role of ss. 718 to 718.2 in the determination of the appropriate sentence, the duration of the sentence, its venue and other modalities.

A literal reading of s. 742.1(a) suggests that the decision to impose a conditional sentence should be made in two distinct stages. In the first stage, the judge would have to decide the appropriate sentence according to the general purposes and principles of sentencing (now set out in ss. 718 to 718.2). Having found that a term of imprisonment of less than two years is warranted, the judge would then, in a second stage, decide whether this same term should be served in the community pursuant to s. 742.1. At first sight since Parliament said: "and the court (a) imposes a sentence of imprisonment of less than two years," it seems that the sentencing judge must first impose a term of imprisonment of a fixed duration before contemplating the possibility that this term be served in the community.

This two-step approach was endorsed by the Manitoba Court of Appeal in the present appeal. However, this literal reading of s. 742.1 and the two-step approach it implies introduce a rigidity which is both unworkable and undesirable in practice.

(a) Duration and Venue Cannot Be Separated

This two-step process does not correspond to the reality of sentencing. In practice, the determination of a term of imprisonment is necessarily intertwined with the decision of where the offender will serve the sentence. A judge does not impose a fixed sentence of "x months" in the abstract, without having in mind where that sentence will be served (see *Brady*, supra, at para. 86; *R v. Pierce* (1997), 114 CCC (3d) 23 (Ont. CA), at p. 39; *R v. Ursel* (1997), 96 BCAC 241, at p. 284 (*per* Ryan JA) and pp. 291-92 (*per* Rowles JA)). Furthermore, when a conditional sentence is chosen, its duration will depend on the type of conditions imposed. Therefore, the duration of the sentence should not be determined separately from the determination of its venue.

(b) "Penological Paradox"

There is a contradiction embedded in this rigid two-step process. After having applied ss. 718 to 718.2 in the first stage to conclude that the appropriate sentence is a term of imprisonment of a fixed duration (in all cases less than two years), the judge would then have to decide if serving the same sentence in the community is still consistent with the fundamental purpose and principles of sentencing set out in ss. 718 to 718.2, as required by s. 742.1(b). It is unrealistic to believe that a judge would consider the objectives and principles twice or make a clear distinction in his or her mind between the application of ss. 718 to 718.2 in the first stage and in the second stage. Even if this could be done, it could lead to a "penological paradox," as described by J. Gemmell in "The New Conditional Sentencing Regime" (1997), 39 *Crim. LQ* 334, at p. 337:

> ... the judge must first determine that imprisonment is the only reasonable sanction in the circumstances, then decide whether the offender should nevertheless serve that sentence in the community. The decision to impose a conditional sentence is almost a kind of *reductio ad absurdum* of the original decision that called for imprisonment. [Footnote omitted.]

This second step of the analytical process would effectively compromise the principles of sentencing that led to the imposition of a sentence of imprisonment in the first place. For instance, the principle of proportionality, set out in s. 718.1 as the fundamental principle of sentencing, directs that all sentences must be proportional to the gravity of the offence and the degree of responsibility of the offender. When a judge—in the first stage decides—that a term of imprisonment of "x months" is appropriate, it means that *this* sentence is proportional. If the sentencing judge decides—in the second stage—that *the same term* can be served in the community, it is possible that the sentence is no longer proportional to the gravity of the offence and the responsibility of the offender, since a conditional sentence will generally be more lenient than a jail term of equivalent duration. Thus, such a two-step approach introduces a rigidity in the sentencing process that could lead to an unfit sentence.

(c) A Purposive Interpretation of Section 742.1(a)

These problems can be addressed by a purposive interpretation of s. 742.1. For the reasons discussed above, the requirement that the court "imposes a sentence of imprisonment of less than two years" could not have been intended to impose on judges a rigid two-step process. Rather, it was included to identify the type of offenders who could be entitled to a conditional sentence. At one end of the range, Parliament denied the possibility of a conditional sentence for offenders who should receive a penitentiary term. At the other end, Parliament intended to ensure that offenders who were entitled to a more lenient community measure—such as a suspended sentence with probation—did not receive a conditional sentence, a harsher sanction in this legislative scheme.

Section 742.1(a), when read in conjunction with ss. 718.2(d) and 718.2(e), cautions sentencing judges against "widening the net" of the conditional sentencing regime by imposing conditional sentences on offenders who would otherwise have received a non-custodial disposition (*Gagnon*, supra, at p. 2645; *Mcdonald*, supra, at pp. 437-39). As Rosenberg JA puts it in *Wismayer* ... , at p. 42:

> Parliament's goal of reducing the prison population of nonviolent offenders and increased use of community sanctions will be frustrated if the courts refuse to use the conditional sentence order for offences that normally attract a jail sentence and resort to the conditional sentence only for offences that previously would have attracted non-custodial dispositions.

Erroneously imposing conditional sentences could undermine Parliament's objective of reducing incarceration for less serious offenders.

These concerns are illustrated by the English experience with a similar sentence called a "suspended sentence." As Parker LCJ explained, writing for the Court of Appeal (Criminal Division) in *R v. O'Keefe* (1968), 53 Cr. App. R 91, at pp. 94-95:

> This Court would like to say as emphatically as they can that suspended sentences should not be given when, but for the power to give a suspended sentence, a probation order was the proper order to make. After all, a suspended sentence is a sentence of imprisonment. ...
>
> Therefore, it seems to the Court that before one gets to a suspended sentence at all, a court must go through the process of eliminating other possible courses such as absolute discharge, conditional discharge, probation order, fine, and then say to itself ... this is a

case for imprisonment, and the final question, it being a case for imprisonment: is immediate imprisonment required, or can I give a suspended sentence?

A similar approach should be used by Canadian courts. Hence, a purposive interpretation of s. 742.1(a) does not dictate a rigid two-step approach in which the judge would first have to impose a term of imprisonment of a *fixed* duration and then decide if that fixed term of imprisonment can be served in the community. In my view, the requirement that the court must impose a sentence of imprisonment of less than two years can be fulfilled by a preliminary determination of the appropriate range of available sentences. Thus, the approach I suggest still requires the judge to proceed in two stages. However, the judge need not impose a term of imprisonment of a fixed duration at the first stage of the analysis. Rather, at this stage, the judge simply has to exclude two possibilities: (a) probationary measures; and (b) a penitentiary term. If either of these sentences is appropriate, then a conditional sentence should not be imposed.

In making this preliminary determination, the judge need only consider the fundamental purpose and principles of sentencing set out in ss. 718 to 718.2 to the extent necessary to narrow the range of sentence for the offender. The submissions of the parties, although not binding, may prove helpful in this regard. For example, both parties may agree that the appropriate range of sentence is a term of imprisonment of less than two years.

Once that preliminary determination is made, and assuming the other statutory prerequisites are met, the judge should then proceed to the second stage of the analysis: determining whether a conditional sentence would be consistent with the fundamental purpose and principles of sentencing set out in ss. 718 to 718.2. Unlike the first stage, the principles of sentencing are now considered comprehensively. Further, it is at the second stage that the duration and venue of the sentence should be determined, and, if a conditional sentence, the conditions to be imposed.

This purposive interpretation of s. 742.1(a) avoids the pitfalls of the literal interpretation discussed above, while at all times taking into account the principles and objectives of sentencing. As I stressed in *M.(C.A.)*, supra, at para. 82,

> In the final analysis, the overarching duty of a sentencing judge is to draw upon all the legitimate principles of sentencing to determine a "just and appropriate" sentence which reflects the gravity of the offence committed and the moral blameworthiness of the offender.

(3) The Safety of the Community Would Not Be Endangered by the Offender Serving the Sentence in the Community

This criterion, set out in s. 742.1(b), has generated wide discussion in courts and among authors. I intend to discuss the following issues:

(a) Is safety of the community a prerequisite to any conditional sentence?

(b) Does "safety of the community" refer only to the threat posed by the specific offender?

(c) How should courts evaluate danger to the community?

(d) Is risk of economic prejudice to be considered in assessing danger to the community?

(a) A Prerequisite to Any Conditional Sentence

As a prerequisite to any conditional sentence, the sentencing judge must be satisfied that having the offender serve the sentence in the community would not endanger its safety: see *Brady*, supra, at para. 58; *R v. Maheu*, [1997] RJQ 410, 116 CCC (3d) 361 (CA), at p. 368 CCC; *Gagnon*, supra, at p. 2641; *Pierce*, supra, at p. 39; *Ursel*, supra, at pp. 284-86 (*per* Ryan JA). *If the sentencing judge is not satisfied that the safety of the community can be preserved, a conditional sentence must never be imposed.*

With respect, the Manitoba Court of Appeal in the case before us erred in concluding that safety of the community was the primary consideration in the decision to impose a conditional sentence. As the Alberta Court of Appeal in *Brady*, supra, at para. 58, stated:

> So to suggest that danger is the primary consideration is tendentious. It wrongly implies that absence of danger trumps or has paramountcy over other sentencing principles. Either the offender meets the no-danger threshold, or he does not. If he does, this consideration is spent and the focus must then properly be on the other sentencing principles and objectives.

I agree. It is only once the judge is satisfied that the safety of the community would not be endangered, in the sense explained in paragraphs 66 to 76 below, that he or she can examine whether a conditional sentence "would be consistent with the fundamental purpose and principles of sentencing set out in sections 718 to 718.2." In other words, rather than being an overarching consideration in the process of determining whether a conditional sentence is appropriate, the criterion of safety of the community should be viewed as a condition precedent to the assessment of whether a conditional sentence would be a fit and proper sanction in the circumstances.

(b) "Safety of the Community" Refers to the Threat Posed by the Specific Offender

The issue here is whether "safety of the community" refers only to the threat posed by the specific offender or whether it also extends to the broader risk of undermining respect for the law. The proponents of the broader interpretation argue that, in certain cases where a conditional sentence could be imposed, it would be perceived that wrongdoers are receiving lenient sentences, thereby insufficiently deterring those who may be inclined to engage in similar acts of wrongdoing, and, in turn, endangering the safety of the community.

Leaving aside the fact that a properly crafted conditional sentence can also achieve the objectives of general deterrence and denunciation, I think the debate has been rendered largely academic in light of an amendment to s. 742.1(b) (SC 1997, c. 18, s. 107.1) which clarified that courts must take into consideration the fundamental purpose and principles of sentencing set out in ss. 718 to 718.2 in deciding whether to impose a conditional sentence. This ensures that objectives such as denunciation and deterrence will be dealt with in the decision to impose a conditional sentence. Since these factors will be taken into account later in the analysis, there is no need to include them in the consideration of the safety of the community.

In my view, the focus of the analysis at this point should clearly be on the risk posed by the individual offender while serving his sentence in the community. I would note

that a majority of appellate courts have adopted an interpretation of the criterion referring only to the threat posed by the specific offender: see *Gagnon*, supra, at pp. 2640-41
(*per* Fish JA); *R v. Parker* (1997), 116 CCC (3d) 236 (NS CA), at pp. 247-48; *Ursel*,
supra, at p. 260.1; *R v. Horvath*, [1997] 8 WWR 357 (Sask. CA), at p. 374; *Brady*, supra,
at paras. 60-61; *Wismayer* ... , at p. 44.

(c) How Should Courts Evaluate Danger to the Community?

In my opinion, to assess the danger to the community posed by the offender while serving his or her sentence in the community, two factors must be taken into account: (1)
the risk of the offender re-offending; and (2) the gravity of the damage that could ensue
in the event of re-offence. If the judge finds that there is a real risk of re-offence, incarceration should be imposed. Of course, there is always some risk that an offender may
re-offend. If the judge thinks this risk is minimal, the gravity of the damage that could
follow were the offender to re-offend should also be taken into consideration. In certain
cases, the minimal risk of re-offending will be offset by the possibility of a great prejudice, thereby precluding a conditional sentence.

(I) RISK OF RE-OFFENCE

A variety of factors will be relevant in assessing the risk of re-offence. In *Brady*, supra,
at paras. 117-27, Fraser CJA suggested that consideration be given to whether the offender has previously complied with court orders and, more generally, to whether the
offender has a criminal record that suggests that the offender will not abide by the conditional sentence. Rousseau-Houle JA in *Maheu*, supra, at p. 374 CCC enumerated additional factors which may be of relevance:

> 1) the nature of the offence, 2) the relevant circumstances of the offence, which can put in
> issue prior and subsequent incidents, 3) the degree of participation of the accused, 4) the
> relationship of the accused with the victim, 5) the profile of the accused, that is, his [or
> her] occupation, lifestyle, criminal record, family situation, mental state, 6) his [or her]
> conduct following the commission of the offence, 7) the danger which the interim release
> of the accused represents for the community, notably that part of the community affected
> by the matter. [Translation.]

This list is instructive, but should not be considered exhaustive. The risk that a par-
ticular offender poses to the community must be assessed in each case, on its own facts.
Moreover, the factors outlined above should not be applied mechanically. As Fraser
CJA held in *Brady*, supra, at para. 124:

> Forgetting a court date once ten years ago does not automatically bar an offender from any
> future conditional sentence. Nor does turning up for his trial guarantee an offender a con-
> ditional sentence. The sentencing judge must of course look at all aspects of these previous
> disobediences of courts. That includes frequency, age, maturity, recency, seriousness of
> disobedience and surrounding circumstances.

The risk of re-offence should also be assessed in light of the conditions attached to
the sentence. Where an offender might pose some risk of endangering the safety of the
community, it is possible that this risk can be reduced to a minimal one by the imposition

of appropriate conditions to the sentence: see *Wismayer* ... , at p. 32; *Brady*, supra, at para. 62; *Maheu*, supra, at p. 374 CCC. Indeed, this is contemplated by s. 742.3(2)(f), which allows the court to include as optional conditions "such other reasonable conditions as the court considers desirable ... for securing the good conduct of the offender and for preventing a repetition by the offender of the same offence or the commission of other offences." For example, a judge may wish to impose a conditional sentence with a treatment order on an offender with a drug addiction, notwithstanding the fact that the offender has a lengthy criminal record linked to this addiction, provided the judge is confident that there is a good chance of rehabilitation and that the level of supervision will be sufficient to ensure that the offender complies with the sentence.

This last point concerning the level of supervision in the community must be underscored. As the Alberta Court of Appeal stressed in *Brady*, supra, at para. 135:

> A conditional sentence drafted in the abstract without knowledge of what actual supervision and institutions and programs are available and suitable for this offender is often worse than tokenism: it is a sham.

Hence, the judge must know or be made aware of the supervision available in the community by the supervision officer or by counsel. If the level of supervision available in the community is not sufficient to ensure safety of the community, the judge should impose a sentence of incarceration.

(II) GRAVITY OF THE DAMAGE IN THE EVENT OF RE-OFFENCE

Once the judge finds that the risk of recidivism is minimal, the second factor to consider is the gravity of the potential damage in case of re-offence. Particularly in the case of violent offenders, a small risk of very harmful future crime may well warrant a conclusion that the prerequisite is not met: see *Brady*, supra, at para. 63.

(d) Risk of Economic Harm Can Be Taken into Consideration

The meaning of the phrase "would not endanger the safety of the community" should not be restricted to a consideration of the danger to physical or psychological safety of persons. In my view, this part of s. 742.1(b) cannot be given this narrow meaning. As Finch JA stated in *Ursel*, supra, at p. 264 (dissenting in part but endorsed by the majority on this issue, at p. 287):

> I would not give to this phrase the restricted meaning for which the defence contends. Members of our community have a reasonable expectation of safety not only in respect of their persons, but in respect as well of their property and financial resources. When homes are broken into, motor-vehicles are stolen, employers are defrauded of monies, or financial papers are forged, the safety of the community is, in my view, endangered. We go to considerable lengths to protect and secure ourselves against the losses that may result from these sorts of crimes, and I think most ordinary citizens would regard themselves as threatened or endangered where their property or financial resources are exposed to the risk of loss.

I agree with this reasoning. The phrase "would not endanger the safety of the community" should be construed broadly, and include the risk of any criminal activity. Such a broad interpretation encompasses the risk of economic harm.

(4) Consistent with the Fundamental Purpose and Principles of Sentencing
     Set Out in Sections 718 to 718.2

Once the sentencing judge has found the offender guilty of an offence for which there is no minimum term of imprisonment, has rejected both a probationary sentence and a penitentiary term as inappropriate, and is satisfied that the offender would not endanger the community, the judge must then consider whether a conditional sentence would be consistent with the fundamental purpose and principles of sentencing set out in ss. 718 to 718.2.

A consideration of the principles set out in ss. 718 to 718.2 will determine whether the offender should serve his or her sentence in the community or in jail. The sentencing principles also inform the determination of the duration of these sentences and, if a conditional sentence, the nature of the conditions to be imposed.

• • •

(c) Principles Militating For and Against a Conditional Sentence

First, a consideration of ss. 718.2(d) and 718.2(e) leads me to the conclusion that *serious consideration* should be given to the imposition of a conditional sentence in all cases where the first three statutory prerequisites are satisfied. Sections 718.2(d) and 718.2(e) codify the important principle of restraint in sentencing and were specifically enacted, along with s. 742.1, to help reduce the rate of incarceration in Canada. Accordingly, it would be an error in principle not to consider the possibility of a conditional sentence seriously when the statutory prerequisites are met. Failure to advert to the possibility of a conditional sentence in reasons for sentence where there are reasonable grounds for finding that the first three statutory prerequisites have been met may well constitute reversible error.

I pause here to consider an interpretive difficulty posed by s. 718.2(e). By its terms, s. 718.2(e) requires judges to consider "all available sanctions *other than imprisonment* that are reasonable in the circumstances" (emphasis added). A conditional sentence, however, is defined as a sentence of imprisonment. As a sentence of imprisonment, it cannot be an alternative to imprisonment. It would therefore appear as though s. 718.2(e) has no bearing on the sentencing judge's decision as to whether a conditional sentence or a jail term should be imposed. Indeed, if interpreted in the technical sense ascribed to imprisonment in Part XXIII of the *Criminal Code*, s. 718.2(e) would only be relevant to the judge's preliminary determination as to whether a sentence of imprisonment, as opposed to a probationary measure, should be imposed. Once the sentencing judge rejects a probationary sentence as inappropriate, the legislative force of s. 718.2(e) is arguably spent.

This interpretation seems to fly in the face of Parliament's intention in enacting s. 718.2(e)—reducing the rate of incarceration. As this Court held in *Gladue*, supra, at para. 40:

> The availability of the conditional sentence of imprisonment, in particular, alters the sentencing landscape in a manner which gives an entirely new meaning to the principle that imprisonment should be resorted to only where no other sentencing option is reasonable

in the circumstances. *The creation of the conditional sentence suggests, on its face, a desire to lessen the use of incarceration. The general principle expressed in s. 718.2(c) must be construed and applied in this light.* [Emphasis added.]

Moreover, if this interpretation of s. 718.2(c) were adopted, it could lead to absurd results in relation to aboriginal offenders. The particular circumstances of aboriginal offenders would only be relevant in deciding whether to impose probationary sentences, and not in deciding whether a conditional sentence should be preferred to incarceration. This would greatly diminish the remedial purpose animating Parliament's enactment of this provision, which contemplates the greater use of conditional sentences and other alternatives to incarceration in cases of aboriginal offenders.

The language used in the French version avoids this difficulty. The French version reads as follows:

> 718.2 Le tribunal détermine la peine à infliger compte tenu également des principes suivants.
>
> e) *l'examen de toutes les sanctions substitutives applicables* qui sont justifiées dans les circonstances, plus particulièrement en ce qui concerne les délinquants autochtones. [Emphasis added.]

The use of "*sanctions substitutives*" for "sanctions other than imprisonment" in the French version of this provision means that s. 718.2(e) plays a role not only in the decision as to whether imprisonment or probationary measures should be imposed (preliminary step of the analysis), but also in the decision as to whether to impose a conditional sentence of imprisonment since conditional sentences are clearly "*sanctions substitutives*" to incarceration.

The French version and the English version of s. 718.2(e) are therefore in conflict. In conformity with a long-standing principle of interpretation, to resolve the conflict between the two official versions, we have to look for the meaning common to both: see for instance *Kwiatkowsky v. Minister of Employment and Immigration*, [1982] 2 SCR 856, at pp. 863-64; *Gravel v. City of St-Léonard*, [1978] 1 SCR 660, at p. 669; *Pfizer Co. v. Deputy Minister of National Revenue for Customs and Excise*, [1977] 1 SCR 456, at pp. 464-65; *Tupper v. The Queen*, [1967] SCR 589, at p. 593; *Goodyear Tire and Rubber Co. of Canada v. T. Eaton Co.*, [1956] SCR 610, at p. 614; P.-A. Côté, *Interprétation des lois* (3rd ed. 1999), at pp. 412-15. Accordingly, the word "imprisonment" in s. 718.2(c) should be interpreted as "incarceration" rather than in its technical sense of encompassing both incarceration and a conditional sentence. Read in this light, s. 718.2(e) clearly exerts an influence on the sentencing judge's determination as to whether to impose a conditional sentence as opposed to a jail term.

Both ss. 718.2(d) and 718.2(e) seek to vindicate the important objective of restraint in the use of incarceration. However, neither seeks to do so at all costs. Section 718.2(d) provides that "an offender should not be deprived of liberty if less restrictive sanctions *may be inappropriate in the circumstances*" (emphasis added). Section 718.2(e) provides that "all available sanctions other than imprisonment *that are reasonable in the circumstances* should be considered" (emphasis added). In my view, a determination of when less restrictive sanctions are "appropriate" and alternatives to incarceration "reasonable" in the circumstances requires a consideration of the other principles of sentencing set out in ss. 718 to 718.2.

In determining which principles favour of a conditional sentence and which favour incarceration, it is necessary to consider again the nature and purpose of the conditional sentence. Through an appreciation of Parliament's intention in enacting this new sanction and the mischief it seeks to redress, trial judges will be better able to make appropriate use of this innovative tool.

The conditional sentence, as I have already noted, was introduced in the amendments to Part XXIII of the Code. Two of the main objectives underlying the reform of Part XXIII were to reduce the use of incarceration as a sanction and to give greater prominence to the principles of restorative justice in sentencing—the objectives of rehabilitation, reparation to the victim and the community, and the promotion of a sense of responsibility in the offender.

The conditional sentence facilitates the achievement of both of Parliament's objectives. It affords the sentencing judge the opportunity to craft a sentence with appropriate conditions that can lead to the rehabilitation of the offender, reparations to the community, and the promotion of a sense of responsibility in ways that jail cannot. However, it is also a punitive sanction. Indeed, it is the punitive aspect of a conditional sentence that distinguishes it from probation. As discussed above, it was not Parliament's intention that offenders who would otherwise have gone to jail for up to two years less a day now be given probation or some equivalent thereof.

Thus, a conditional sentence can achieve both punitive and restorative objectives. To the extent that both punitive and restorative objectives can be achieved in a given case, a conditional sentence is likely a better sanction than incarceration. Where the need for punishment is particularly pressing, and there is little opportunity to achieve any restorative objectives, incarceration will likely be the more attractive sanction. However, even where restorative objectives cannot be readily satisfied, a conditional sentence will be preferable to incarceration in cases where a conditional sentence can achieve the objectives of denunciation and deterrence as effectively as incarceration. This follows from the principle of restraint in s. 718.2(d) and (e), which militates in favour of alternatives to incarceration where appropriate in the circumstances.

I turn now to the question of when a conditional sentence may be appropriate having regard to the six sentencing objectives set out in s. 718.

(I) DENUNCIATION

Denunciation is the communication of society's condemnation of the offender's conduct. In *M.(C.A.)*, supra, at para. 81, I wrote:

> In short, a sentence with a denunciatory element represents a symbolic, collective statement that the offender's conduct should be punished for encroaching on our society's basic code of values as enshrined within our substantive criminal law. As Lord Justice Lawton stated in *R v. Sargeant* (1974), 60 Cr. App. R 74, at p. 77: "society, through the courts, must show its abhorrence of particular types of crime, and the only way in which the courts can show this is by the sentence they pass."

Incarceration will usually provide more denunciation than a conditional sentence, as a conditional sentence is generally a more lenient sentence than a jail term of equivalent duration. That said, a conditional sentence can still provide a significant amount of denunciation. This is particularly so when onerous conditions are imposed and the duration of the conditional sentence is extended beyond the duration of the jail sentence that would ordinarily have been imposed in the circumstances. I will discuss each point in turn.

First, the conditions should have a punitive aspect. Indeed, the need for punitive conditions is the reason why a probationary sentence was rejected and a sentence of imprisonment of less than two years imposed. As stated above, conditions such as house arrest should be the norm, not the exception. This means that the offender should be confined to his or her home except when working, attending school, or fulfilling other conditions of his or her sentence, e.g. community service, meeting with the supervisor, or participating in treatment programs. Of course, there will need to be exceptions for medical emergencies, religious observance, and the like.

Second, although a literal reading of s. 742.1 suggests that a conditional sentence must be of equivalent duration to the jail term that would otherwise have been imposed, I have explained earlier why such a literal interpretation of s. 742.1 should be eschewed. Instead, the preferred approach is to have the judge reject a probationary sentence and a penitentiary term as inappropriate in the circumstances, and then consider whether a conditional sentence of less than two years would be consistent with the fundamental purpose and principles of sentencing, provided the statutory prerequisites are met. This approach does not require that there be any equivalence between the duration of the conditional sentence and the jail term that would otherwise have been imposed. The sole requirement is that the duration and conditions of a conditional sentence make for a just and appropriate sentence: see *Brady*, supra, at para. 111; *Ursel*, supra, at pp. 284-86 and 291-92; *Pierce*, supra, at p. 39; J.V. Roberts, "The Hunt for the Paper Tiger: Conditional Sentencing after *Brady*" (1999), 42 *Crim. LQ* 38, at pp. 47-52.

The stigma of a conditional sentence with house arrest should not be underestimated. Living in the community under strict conditions where fellow residents are well aware of the offender's criminal misconduct can provide ample denunciation in many cases. In certain circumstances, the shame of encountering members of the community may make it even more difficult for the offender to serve his or her sentence in the community than in prison.

The amount of denunciation provided by a conditional sentence will be heavily dependent on the circumstances of the offender, the nature of the conditions imposed, and the community in which the sentence is to be served. As a general matter, the more serious the offence and the greater the need for denunciation, the longer and more onerous the conditional sentence should be. However, there may be certain circumstances in which the need for denunciation is so pressing that incarceration will be the only suitable way in which to express society's condemnation of the offender's conduct.

(II) DETERRENCE

Incarceration, which is ordinarily a harsher sanction, may provide more deterrence than a conditional sentence. Judges should be wary, however, of placing too much weight on deterrence when choosing between a conditional sentence and incarceration: see *Wismayer* ... , at p. 36. The empirical evidence suggests that the deterrent effect of incarceration is uncertain: see generally *Sentencing Reform: A Canadian Approach: Report of the Canadian Sentencing Commission* (1987)], at pp. 136-37. Moreover, a conditional sentence can provide significant deterrence if sufficiently punitive conditions are imposed and the public is made aware of the severity of these sentences. There is also the possibility of deterrence through the use of community service orders, including those in which the offender may be obliged to speak to members of the community about the evils of the particular criminal conduct in which he or she engaged, assuming the offender were amenable to such a condition. Nevertheless, there may be circumstances in which the need for deterrence will warrant incarceration. This will depend in part on whether the offence is one in which the effects of incarceration are likely to have a real deterrent effect, as well as on the circumstances of the community in which the offences were committed.

(III) SEPARATION

The objective of separation is not applicable in determining whether a conditional sentence would be consistent with the fundamental purpose and principles of sentencing because it is a prerequisite of a conditional sentence that the offender not pose a danger to the community. Accordingly, it is not necessary to completely separate the offender from society. To the extent that incarceration, which leads to the complete separation of offenders, is warranted in circumstances where the statutory prerequisites are met, it is as a result of the objectives of denunciation and deterrence, not the need for separation as such.

(IV) RESTORATIVE OBJECTIVES

While incarceration may provide for more denunciation and deterrence than a conditional sentence, a conditional sentence is generally better suited to achieving the restorative objectives of rehabilitation, reparations, and promotion of a sense of responsibility in the offender. As this Court held in *Gladue*, supra, at para. 43, "[r]estorative sentencing goals do not usually correlate with the use of prison as a sanction." The importance of these goals is not to be underestimated, as they are primarily responsible for lowering the rate of recidivism. Consequently, when the objectives of rehabilitation, reparation, and promotion of a sense of responsibility may realistically be achieved in the case of a particular offender, a conditional sentence will likely be the appropriate sanction, subject to the denunciation and deterrence considerations outlined above.

I will now consider examples of conditions that seek to vindicate these objectives. There are any number of conditions a judge may impose in order to rehabilitate an offender. Mandatory treatment orders may be imposed, such as psychological counseling and alcohol and drug rehabilitation. It is well known that sentencing an offender to a term of incarceration for an offence related to a drug addiction, without addressing the addiction, will probably not lead to the rehabilitation of the offender. *The Final Report of the Commission of Inquiry into the Non-Medical Use of Drugs* (1973) noted at p. 59 that

These adverse effects of imprisonment are particularly reflected in the treatment of drug offenders. Our investigations suggest that there is considerable circulation of drugs within penal institutions, that offenders are reinforced in their attachment to the drug culture, and that in many cases they are introduced to certain kinds of drug use by prison contacts. Thus imprisonment does not cut off all contact with drugs or the drug subculture, nor does it cut off contact with individual drug users. Actually, it increases exposure to the influence of chronic, harmful drug users.

House arrest may also have a rehabilitative effect to a certain extent insofar as it prevents the offender from engaging in habitual anti-social associations and promotes pro-social behaviors such as attendance at work or educational institutions: see Roberts, "The Hunt for the Paper Tiger: Conditional Sentencing after *Brady*," supra, at p. 65.

The objectives of reparations to the victim and the community, as well as the promotion of a sense of responsibility in offenders and acknowledgment of the harm done to victims and to the community, may also be well served by a conditional sentence. For example, in some cases, restitution orders to compensate the victim may be made a condition. Furthermore, the imposition of a condition of community service can assist the offender in making reparations to the community and in promoting a sense of responsibility. An interesting possibility in this regard would be an order that the offender speak in public about the unfortunate consequences of his or her conduct, assuming the offender were amenable to such a condition. Not only could such an order promote a sense of responsibility and an acknowledgment of the harm done by the offender, it could also further the objective of deterrence, as I discussed above. In my view, the use of community service orders should be encouraged, provided that there are suitable programs available for the offender in the community. By increasing the use of community service orders, offenders will be seen by members of the public as paying back their debt to society. This will assist in contributing to public respect for the law.

(V) SUMMARY

In sum, in determining whether a conditional sentence would be consistent with the fundamental purpose and principles of sentencing, sentencing judges should consider which sentencing objectives figure most prominently in the factual circumstances of the particular case before them. Where a combination of both punitive and restorative objectives may be achieved, a conditional sentence will likely be more appropriate than incarceration. In determining whether restorative objectives can be satisfied in a particular case, the judge should consider the offender's prospects of rehabilitation, including whether the offender has proposed a particular plan of rehabilitation; the availability of appropriate community service and treatment programs, whether the offender has acknowledged his or her wrongdoing and expresses remorse; as well as the victim's wishes as revealed by the victim impact statement (consideration of which is now mandatory pursuant to s. 722 of the Code). This list is not exhaustive.

Where punitive objectives such as denunciation and deterrence are particularly pressing, such as cases in which there are aggravating circumstances, incarceration will generally be the preferable sanction. This may be so notwithstanding the fact that restorative goals might be achieved by a conditional sentence. Conversely, a conditional sentence may provide sufficient denunciation and deterrence, even in cases in which restorative objectives are of diminished importance, depending on the nature of the conditions imposed, the duration of the conditional sentence, and the circumstances of the offender and the community in which the conditional sentence is to be served.

Finally, it bears pointing out that a conditional sentence may be imposed even in circumstances where there are aggravating circumstances relating to the offence or the offender. Aggravating circumstances will obviously increase the need for denunciation and deterrence. However, it would be a mistake to rule out the possibility of a conditional sentence *ab initio* simply because aggravating factors are present. I repeat that each case must be considered individually.

Sentencing judges will frequently be confronted with situations in which some objectives militate in favour of a conditional sentence, whereas others favour incarceration. in those cases, the trial judge will be called upon to weigh the various objectives in fashioning a fit sentence. As La Forest J stated in *R v. Lyons*, [1987] 2 SCR 309, at p. 329, "[i]n a rational system of sentencing, the respective importance of prevention, deterrence, retribution and rehabilitation will vary according to the nature of the crime and the circumstances of the offender." There is no easy test or formula that the judge can apply in weighing these factors. Much will depend on the good judgment and wisdom of sentencing judges, whom Parliament vested with considerable discretion in making these determinations pursuant to s. 718.3.

(d) Appropriate Conditions

In the event that a judge chooses to impose a conditional sentence, there are five compulsory conditions listed in s. 742.3(1) that must be imposed. The judge also has considerable discretion in imposing optional conditions pursuant to s. 742.3(2). There are a number of principles that should guide the judge in exercising this discretion. First, the conditions must ensure the safety of the community. Second, conditions must be tailored to fit the particular circumstances of the offender and the offence. The type of conditions imposed will be a function of the sentencing judge's creativity. However, conditions will prove fruitless if the offender is incapable of abiding by them, and will increase the probability that the offender will be incarcerated as a result of breaching them. Third, punitive conditions such as house arrest should be the norm, not the exception. Fourth, the conditions must be realistically enforceable. This requires a consideration of the available resources in the community in which the sentence is to be served. I agree with Rosenberg JA, who, in "Recent Developments in Sentencing," a paper prepared for the National Judicial Institute's Supreme Court of Nova Scotia Education Seminar in Halifax, February 25-26, 1999, at p. 63, wrote that:

> the courts must be careful not to impose conditions that are purely cosmetic and are incapable of effective enforcement. For example, I would think that any condition that can only be effectively enforced through an intolerable intrusion into the privacy of innocent persons would be problematic. Conditions that impose an unacceptable burden on the supervisor might also be of dubious value. If the conditions that the court imposes are impractical, the justice system will be brought into disrepute.

D. Burden of Proof

It is submitted by the intervener the Attorney General for Ontario that the offender has the burden of proving that a conditional sentence should be imposed pursuant to s. 742.1. According to the Attorney General:

> [W]hen a sentencing court determines that a reformatory sentence of imprisonment is an appropriate sentence for an offender, there is, in effect, a rebuttable presumption that this custodial sentence will prevail unless the offender can convince the sentencing Court to make the sentence of imprisonment "conditional." [Emphasis in original]

The Attorney General for Ontario's position seems to be premised on a rigid two-step approach, which I rejected for the reasons explained earlier. The Attorney General submits that the offender has to establish that: (a) he or she would not endanger the safety of the community by serving a conditional sentence; and (b) the imposition of a conditional sentence would be consistent with the fundamental purpose and principles set out in ss. 718 to 718.2.

I disagree. The wording used in s. 742.1 does not attribute to either party the onus of establishing that the offender should or should not receive a conditional sentence. To inform his or her decision about the appropriate sentence, the judge can take into consideration all the evidence, no matter who adduces it (*Ursel*, supra, at pp. 264-65 and 287).

In matters of sentencing, while each party is expected to establish elements in support of its position as to the appropriate sentence that should be imposed, the ultimate decision as to what constitutes the best disposition is left to the discretion of the sentencing judge. This message is explicit in ss. 718.3(1) and (2):

> 718.3(1) Where an enactment prescribes different degrees or kinds of punishment in respect of an offence, the punishment to be imposed is, subject to the limitations prescribed in the enactment, in the discretion of the court that convicts a person who commits the offence.
>
> (2) Where an enactment prescribes a punishment in respect of an offence, the punishment to be imposed is, subject to the limitations prescribed in the enactment, in the discretion of the court that convicts a person who commits the offence, but no punishment is a minimum punishment unless it is declared to be a minimum punishment.

The sentencing judge can take into account the submissions and evidence presented by counsel (s. 723), but is in no way bound by them in the decision as to the sentence. Having said this, in practice, it will generally be the offender who is best situated to convince the judge that a conditional sentence is indeed appropriate. Therefore, it would be in the offender's best interests to establish those elements militating in favour of a conditional sentence: see *Ursel*, supra, at pp. 264-65; *R v. Fleet* (1997), 120 CCC 457 (Ont. CA), at para. 26. For instance, the offender should inform the judge of his or her remorse, willingness to repair and acknowledgment of responsibility, and propose a plan of rehabilitation. The offender could also convince the judge that he or she would not endanger the safety of the community if appropriate conditions were imposed. It would be to the great benefit of the offender to make submissions in this regard. I would also note the importance of the role of the supervision officer in informing the judge on these issues.

E. Deference Owed to Sentencing Judges

In recent years, this Court has repeatedly stated that the sentence imposed by a trial court is entitled to considerable deference from appellate courts: see *Shropshire*, [[1995] 4 SCR 227; 102 CCC (3d) 193], at paras. 46-50; *M.(C.A.)*, supra, at paras. 89-94; *McDonnell*, supra, at paras. 15-17 (majority); *R v. W.(G.)*, SCC, No. 26705, October 15, 1999, at paras. 18-19. In *M.(C.A.)*, at para. 90, I wrote:

> Put simply, absent an error in principle, failure to consider a relevant factor, or an overemphasis of the appropriate factors, a court of appeal should only intervene to vary a sentence imposed at trial if the sentence is demonstrably unfit. Parliament explicitly vested sentencing judges with a *discretion* to determine the appropriate degree and kind of punishment under the *Criminal Code*. [Emphasis in original.]

Several provisions of Part XXIII confirm that Parliament intended to confer a wide discretion upon the sentencing judge. As a general rule, ss. 718.3(1) and 718.3(2) provide that the degree and kind of punishment to be imposed is left to the discretion of the sentencing judge. Moreover, the opening words of s. 718 specify that the sentencing judge must seek to achieve the fundamental purpose of sentencing "by imposing just sanctions that have *one or more* of the following objectives" (emphasis added). In the context of the conditional sentence, s. 742.1 provides that the judge "may" impose a conditional sentence and enjoys a wide discretion in the drafting of the appropriate conditions, pursuant to s. 742.3(2).

Although an appellate court might entertain a different opinion as to what objectives should be pursued and the best way to do so, that difference will generally not constitute an error of law justifying interference. Further, minor errors in the sequence of application of s. 742.1 may not warrant intervention by appellate courts. Again, I stress that appellate courts should not second-guess sentencing judges unless the sentence imposed is demonstrably unfit.

As explained in *M.(C.A.)*, supra, at para. 91:

> This deferential standard of review has profound functional justifications. As Iacobucci J explained in *Shropshire*, at para. 46, where the sentencing judge has had the benefit of presiding over the trial of the offender, he or she will have had the comparative advantage of having seen and heard the witnesses to the crime. But in the absence of a full trial, where the offender has pleaded guilty to an offence and the sentencing judge has only enjoyed the benefit of oral and written sentencing submissions (as was the case in both *Shropshire* and this instance), the argument in favour of deference remains compelling. A sentencing judge still enjoys a position of advantage over an appellate judge in being able to directly assess the sentencing submissions of both the Crown and the offender. A sentencing judge also possesses the unique qualifications of experience and judgment from having served on the front lines of our criminal justice system. *Perhaps most importantly, the sentencing judge will normally preside near or within the community which has suffered the consequences of the offender's crime. As such, the sentencing judge will have a strong sense of the particular blend of sentencing goals that will be "just and appropriate" for the protection of that community. The determination of a just and appropriate sentence is a delicate art which attempts to balance carefully the societal goals of sentencing against the moral*

blameworthiness of the offender and the circumstances of the offence, while at all times taking into account the needs and current conditions of and in the community. The discretion of a sentencing judge should thus not be interfered with lightly. [Emphasis added.]

This last justification is particularly relevant in the case of conditional sentences. Crafting appropriate conditions requires knowledge of both the needs and resources of the community.

VI. Summary

At this point, a short summary of what has been said in these reasons might be useful:

1. Bill C-41 in general and the conditional sentence in particular were enacted both to reduce reliance on incarceration as a sanction and to increase the use of principles of restorative justice in sentencing.

2. A conditional sentence should be distinguished from probationary measures. Probation is primarily a rehabilitative sentencing tool. By contrast, Parliament intended conditional sentences to include both punitive and rehabilitative aspects. Therefore, conditional sentences should generally include punitive conditions that are restrictive of the offender's liberty. Conditions such as house arrest should be the norm, not the exception.

3. No offences are excluded from the conditional sentencing regime except those with a minimum term of imprisonment, nor should there be presumptions in favour of or against a conditional sentence for specific offences.

4. The requirement in s. 742.1(a) that the judge impose a sentence of imprisonment of less than two years does not require the judge to first impose a sentence of imprisonment of a fixed duration before considering whether that sentence can be served in the community. Although this approach is suggested by the text of s. 742.1(a), it is unrealistic and could lead to unfit sentences in some cases. Instead, a purposive interpretation of s. 742.1(a) should be adopted. In a preliminary determination, the sentencing judge should reject a penitentiary term and probationary measures as inappropriate. Having determined that the appropriate range of sentence is a term of imprisonment of less than two years, the judge should then consider whether it is appropriate for the offender to serve his or her sentence in the community.

5. As a corollary of the purposive interpretation of s. 742.1(a), a conditional sentence need not be of equivalent duration to the sentence of incarceration that would otherwise have been imposed. The sole requirement is that the duration and conditions of a conditional sentence make for a just and appropriate sentence.

6. The requirement in s. 742.1(h) that the judge be satisfied that the safety of the community would not be endangered by the offender serving his or her sentence in the community is a condition precedent to the imposition of a conditional sentence, and not the primary consideration in determining whether a conditional sentence is appropriate. In making this determination, the judge

should consider the risk posed by the specific offender, not the broader risk of whether the imposition of a conditional sentence would endanger the safety of the community by providing insufficient general deterrence or undermining general respect for the law. Two factors should be taken into account: (1) the risk of the offender re-offending; and (2) the gravity of the damage that could ensue in the event of re-offence. A consideration of the risk posed by the offender should include the risk of any criminal activity, and not be limited solely to the risk of physical or psychological harm to individuals.

7. Once the prerequisites of s. 742.1 are satisfied, the judge should give serious consideration to the possibility of a conditional sentence in all cases by examining whether a conditional sentence is consistent with the fundamental purpose and principles of sentencing set out in ss. 718 to 718.2. This follows from Parliament's clear message to the judiciary to reduce the use of incarceration as a sanction.

8. A conditional sentence can provide significant denunciation and deterrence. As a general matter, the more serious the offence, the longer and more onerous the conditional sentence should be. There may be some circumstances, however, where the need for denunciation or deterrence is so pressing that incarceration will be the only suitable way in which to express society's condemnation of the offender's conduct or to deter similar conduct in the future.

9. Generally, a conditional sentence will be better than incarceration at achieving the restorative objectives of rehabilitation, reparations to the victim and the community, and promotion of a sense of responsibility in the offender and acknowledgment of the harm done to the victim and the community.

10. Where a combination of both punitive and restorative objectives may be achieved, a conditional sentence will likely be more appropriate than incarceration. Where objectives such as denunciation and deterrence are particularly pressing, incarceration will generally be the preferable sanction. This may be so notwithstanding the fact that restorative goals might be achieved. However, a conditional sentence may provide sufficient denunciation and deterrence, even in cases in which restorative objectives are of lesser importance, depending on the nature of the conditions imposed, the duration of the sentence, and the circumstances of both the offender and the community in which the conditional sentence is to be served.

11. A conditional sentence may be imposed even where there are aggravating circumstances, although the need for denunciation and deterrence will increase in these circumstances.

12. No party is under a burden of proof to establish that a conditional sentence is either appropriate or inappropriate in the circumstances. The judge should consider all relevant evidence, no matter by whom it is adduced. However, it would be in the offender's best interests to establish elements militating in favour of a conditional sentence.

13. Sentencing judges have a wide discretion in the choice of the appropriate sentence. They are entitled to considerable deference from appellate courts. As

explained in *M.(C.A.)*, supra, at para. 90: "Put simply, absent an error in principle, failure to consider a relevant factor, or an overemphasis of the appropriate factors, a court of appeal should only intervene to vary a sentence imposed at trial if the sentence is demonstrably unfit."

VII. Application to the Case at Hand

In the case at hand, Keyser J considered that a term of imprisonment of 18 months was appropriate and declined to permit the respondent to serve his term in the community. She found that, while the respondent would not endanger the safety of the community by serving a conditional sentence, such a sentence would not be in conformity with the objectives of s. 718. In her view, even if incarceration was not necessary to deter the respondent from similar future conduct or necessary for his rehabilitation, incarceration was necessary to denounce the conduct of the respondent and to deter others from engaging in similar conduct.

While Keyser J seems to have proceeded according to a rigid two-step process, in deviation from the approach I have set out, I am not convinced that an 18-month sentence of incarceration was demonstrably unfit for these offences and this offender. I point out that the offences here were very serious, and that they had resulted in a death and in severe bodily harm. Moreover, dangerous driving and impaired driving may be offences for which harsh sentences plausibly provide general deterrence. These crimes are often committed by otherwise law-abiding persons, with good employment records and families. Arguably, such persons are the ones most likely to be deterred by the threat of severe penalties: see *R v. McVeigh* (1985), 22 CCC (3d) 145 (Ont. CA), at p. 150-51; *R v. Biancofiore* (1997), 119 CCC (3d) 344, at paras. 18-24; *R v. Blakely* (1998), 40 OR (3d) 541 (CA), at pp. 542-43.

I hasten to add that these comments should not be taken as a directive that conditional sentences can never be imposed for offences such as dangerous driving or impaired driving. In fact, were I a trial judge, I might have found that a conditional sentence would have been appropriate in this case. The respondent is still very young, he had no prior record and no convictions since the accident, he seems completely rehabilitated, he wants to go back to school, he has already suffered a lot by causing the death of a friend and was himself in a coma for some time. To make sure that the objectives of denunciation and general deterrence would have been sufficiently addressed, I might have imposed conditions such as house arrest and a community service order requiring the offender to speak to designated groups about the consequences of dangerous driving, as was the case in *Parker*, supra, at p. 239, and *R v. Hollinsky* (1995), 103 CCC (3d) 472 (Ont. CA).

However, trial judges are closer to their community and know better what would be acceptable to their community. Absent evidence that the sentence imposed by the trial judge was demonstrably unfit, the Court of Appeal should not have interfered to substitute its own opinion for that of the sentencing judge. The trial judge did not commit a reversible error in principle and she appropriately considered all the relevant factors. Although the Court of Appeal's decision is entitled to some deference (see the companion appeal *R v. R.A.R.*, 2000 SCC 8, at paras. 20-21), in my opinion it erred in holding that the sentencing judge had given undue weight to the objective of denunciation. I see no ground for the Court of Appeal's intervention.

VIII. Disposition

I would allow the appeal. Accordingly, the 18-month sentence of incarceration imposed by the trial judge should be restored. However, given that the respondent has already served the conditional sentence imposed by the Court of Appeal in its entirety, and that the Crown stated in oral argument that it was not seeking any further punishment, I would stay the service of the sentence of incarceration.

NOTE

Proulx answered a number of questions arising from the creation of the conditional sentence. It will be noted that on the spectrum of sentencing objectives the court plainly asserted that in addition to restorative or rehabilitative objectives a conditional sentence should include a punitive element. But *Proulx* did not make the judge's role easy. The difficulty in applying the principles set out to the hard cases that commonly come to court is illustrated in the companion cases released the same day as *Proulx*. In *R v. Bunn*, [2000] 1 SCR 183, a case of breach-of-trust theft by a lawyer, the Supreme Court upheld the conditional sentence 5 to 3. The fact that the offender was the sole caregiver for a disabled spouse was a significant factor militating against a custodial term. In *R v. L.F.W.*, [2000] 1 SCR 132, the judges split evenly on whether to uphold a conditional sentence for a man who, more than 25 years before, committed offences of indecent assault and gross indecency on a young girl between the ages of 6 and 12. The offender had apparently committed no other offences in the interim, had dealt successfully with an alcohol problem, and had a good work record. In *R v. R.N.S.*, [2000] 1 SCR 149, the judges unanimously agreed that a 9-month sentence of imprisonment should be restored in a case of sexual assault and invitation to sexual touching committed on a stepdaughter who was between the ages of 5 and 8. The case of *R v. R.A.R.*, [2000] 1 SCR 163 involved a sexual assault conviction and two convictions for common assault committed at a workplace by an employer on an employee in her early 20s. L'Heureux-Dubé J and five other judges allowed the appeal, restoring the one-year term of imprisonment. In dissent, Lamer CJC would have maintained the 9-month conditional sentence with house arrest and sex-offender treatment, although he remarked that a lengthier conditional sentence would have been preferable. In the result, conditional sentences were maintained only in *Bunn* and *L.F.W.*, but not without significant dissent. For the three other offenders, a sentence of imprisonment was substituted although stayed, because the conditional sentences had already been served and the Crown was not requesting additional punishments.

Proulx remains the leading statement of the law relating to conditional sentences. But it did not eliminate dispute about when the conditional sentence is an appropriate option or how conditions for such sentences should be structured.

IV. RESTRICTING THE CONDITIONAL SENTENCE

A. Judicial Action

Section 742.1 lists a number of statutory criteria that must be met before a sentencing court may impose a conditional sentence of imprisonment. One of these (s. 742.1(a)) restricts the imposition of a conditional sentence to terms of two years or less. In *Fice*, [2005] 1 SCR 742, the Supreme Court considered whether credit for time served could reduce a penitentiary term to bring the sentence below two years and thus make the offender eligible for a conditional sentence. A majority of the court concluded that the reduction might change the venue of imprisonment from the penitentiary to a provincial jail but it could not result in a conditional sentence. To allow otherwise would disturb the approach to conditional sentences set out in *Proulx*. According to those principles, the judge must first determine whether an appropriate sentence would be a term of less than two years. Only then is the offender eligible for a conditional sentence. If credit for time served could make the offender eligible for a conditional sentence, it would indirectly transform that credit into a mitigating factor. Instead, according to the majority, the credit for time served should be considered as part of the total punishment. The minority took the view that s. 719 allows the court to give credit for time served, and if this credit brings the term below two years a sentencing court is entitled to impose a conditional sentence if the conditions for such a sentence are otherwise met. As between the two positions, the majority claims to be consistent with *Proulx* while the minority claims to be consistent with the Code. In dissent, Fish J concluded:

[75] Where an offender has at the time of sentence already spent time in custody and a court would otherwise have imposed a sentence of more than two years, the deterrent and punitive purposes will in some instances have been satisfied by the time spent in custody.

[76] A further custodial sentence may well frustrate *both* of Parliament's main objectives in reforming Part XXIII of the *Criminal Code*. The first, it will be recalled, was to reduce the use of incarceration as a sanction; the second, to give greater prominence to the principles of restorative justice, including rehabilitation.

[77] A conditional sentence of imprisonment, on the other hand, will in some circumstances promote both of Parliament's objectives without overlooking the need for punishment or denunciation. Where this is the case, I see no reason of principle, policy or precedent to limit the sentencing court to a choice between a probationary sentence that is too lenient and a custodial sentence that is too severe.

[78] Conditional sentences were introduced by Parliament to afford judges greater flexibility in sentencing: Section 742.1 should not be interpreted so as to frustrate this evident purpose.

[79] In my respectful view, nothing in *Proulx* was meant to prevent trial courts from imposing conditional sentences where, on account of the time already served, further institutional detention is not required and a term of imprisonment to be served in the community best responds to the principles and purposes of sentencing set out by Parliament in the *Criminal Code*. At its highest, from the Crown's perspective, *Proulx* is silent on that issue.

While this may seem to be both persuasive and good sentencing policy, it did not find favour with a majority of the Supreme Court, although it seems entirely consistent with both the Code and with *Proulx*. Is there any argument available that would allow the court to re-open this issue? For further discussion of the issues involved, see Roberts, "Pre-Trial Custody, Terms of Imprisonment, and the Conditional Sentence: Crediting 'Dead Time' to Effect 'Regime Change' in Sentencing" (2005), 9 *Can. Crim. LR* 191; Healy, "The Effect of Pre-Sentence Custody in Eligibility for a Conditional Sentence" (2005), 9 *Can. Crim. LR* 261.

B. Legislative Action

A recurring question is whether conditional sentences should not be an option for certain offences or classes of offences. This question arises not only in individual cases but as a general issue of policy. In 2006, the government introduced a bill that would have precluded conditional sentences or excluded from conditional-sentence consideration all indictable offences punishable by imprisonment by 10 years or more. This was amended in Committee and, in 2007, Parliament passed an important amendment that reflects the continuing concern about this broad question but does not have the enormous impact of the original proposal. The purpose of the amendment is to restrict the availability of conditional offences for three categories of offences in which the maximum punishment is more than 10 years. The section now reads as follows:

> 742.1 If a person is convicted of an offence, other than a serious personal injury offence as defined in section 752, a terrorism offence or a criminal organization offence prosecuted by way of indictment for which the maximum term of imprisonment is ten years or more or an offence punishable by a minimum term of imprisonment, and the court imposes a sentence of imprisonment of less than two years and is satisfied that the service of the sentence in the community would not endanger the safety of the community and would be consistent with the fundamental purpose and principles of sentencing set out in sections 718 to 718.2, the court may, for the purpose of supervising the offender's behaviour in the community, order that the offender serve the sentence in the community, subject to the offender's compliance with the conditions imposed under section 742.3.

Of these three classes of offences, the widest is the serious personal injury offence as defined in s. 752. Thus, conditional sentences will no longer be an option in respect of any indictable offence involving the use of violence, endangerment, or the infliction of severe psychological damage, provided that the maximum punishment is 10 years or more. This classification also includes sexual assault as defined in ss. 271, 272, and 273. The amendment does not compel a sentence of imprisonment for the three classes of offences, but that will be its effect in most instances. Recall that prior to imposing a conditional sentence of imprisonment the court must have decided to impose a term of imprisonment. It would be anomalous if a court were to impose a non-custodial sentence—for example, probation—for an offence in the classes covered by the amendment of s. 742.1. It is logically possible, but unlikely in the general run of cases. The amendments also raise some ambiguities relating to the classification of serious personal injury offences. For example, does this include careless storage of a firearm or the negligent creation of holes in ice?

V. HARD CASES

As the paragraph above explains, with the amendment of s. 742.1 by SC 2007, c. 12, s. 1 on May 31, 2007, the applicable scope for conditional sentences has been diminished. Many of the categories of "hard cases" that generated controversies and provocative headlines have been eliminated. By "hard cases," we mean situations where the nature of the offence may suggest that "deterrence and denunciation" should be the primary sentencing concerns, but individual factors point away from custody. Understanding the actual effect of this amendment will require some time, given the potential breadth and vagueness of s. 752. However, it is clear that some catgegories of "hard cases" will continue to present difficult sentencing problems. The following two cases deal with a large-scale public fraud and a marijuana grow-op. When reading these cases, note how the various judges deal with the compendious objective of "deterrence and denunciation," keeping in mind the state of current criminological thinking about general deterrence. Also note the role of personal factors and the extent of disparate judicial authorities, some supporting custody and others supporting conditional sentences.

R v. Coffin
(2006), 210 CCC (3d) 227 (Que. CA) (references omitted)

THE COURT: ... [8] Paul R. Coffin pleaded guilty to fifteen counts of fraud against the Government of Canada in what has come to be known as the "Sponsorship Scandal." The total amount misappropriated through these frauds is $1,556,625.

[9] The trial judge sentenced him to two years less a day to be served in the community pursuant to section 742.1 of the *Criminal Code*.

[10] In addition to the conditions set out in section 742.3 of the *Criminal Code*, the trial judge imposed the following conditions:

> [55] The following optional conditions will also be part of the order:
>
> - Mr. Coffin will surrender his passport to the registrar of this Court and will not retrieve it nor obtain another one before the expiration of the conditional sentence;
> - Mr. Coffin will offer and accept to speak publicly about his downfall and the ethics in the business world;
> - Mr. Coffin will be compelled to a curfew during week days i.e. from Monday inclusive to Friday inclusive. He must be home from 9:00 p.m. to 7:00 a.m. the following day except for health reasons, work or public speeches. The curfew will not apply on Saturdays and Sundays;
> - All billings or invoices issued from Communication Coffin must be under the exclusive signature and responsibility of an independent controller to whom supporting documents will be provided;
>
> · · ·

Agreed Statement of Facts

1. Between April 1997 and May 2002, the accused through the company 2794101 Canada inc. of which he is shareholder, director and directing mind and will, doing business under the name "Coffin Communications," entered with the Government of Canada into 32 contracts, copies of which are filed the present as "Recueil de contrats volumes 1 & 2."

2. The object of these contracts was to afford visibility to the Government of Canada who was to sponsor certain cultural and sports events in exchange for having its logos, flags and signs made visible to the public attending such events.

3. These contracts generally provided that a certain amount of money would be paid to the events. Rather than pay directly to the events, the moneys however would transit through the accused's company and then be paid by the latter to the event organizers. The contracts provided that the accused's company would be entitled to 12 percent of the amount of the sponsorship for administering said sponsorship. After 1999, the amount of the sponsorship and agency commissions transited through the company Media I.D.A. Vision inc. who paid the event organizers the amount of the sponsorship and the accused's company its 12 percent commission.

4. The contracts also provided in addition to the amount of the sponsorship per se, an amount for production costs. These were provided in order to pay for tangible goods (such as banners, flags, caps, T-shirts, trophies, medals, prizes etc. ...) or intangibles such as publicity campaigns and advertisements promoting the sponsor and the event. The contracts provided that the accused's company would be entitled to 17.65 percent of the amount disbursed (evidenced by proof of purchase) if such tangible or intangible production was sub-contracted outside the accused's firm. If the production took place within the accused's firm, then generally only its actual cost would be reimbursed by the sponsor.

5. The accused signed and sent or caused to be sent to the Government of Canada all the invoices filed with the present as "Recueil de factures F-1 à F-228."

6. All such invoices were accepted and paid to the accused by the Government of Canada with 97 checks filed with the present as "Recueil de chèques CH 1 à CH 97." The sum of these payments total $3,234,626.31.

7. Out of these payments,

   • approximately $1,478,975 were paid pursuant to billings for production costs that were not incurred by the accused,
   • $53,500 (representing 50% of the sponsorship plus GST paid in 1998 to Power-streak (count 13)) were returned by the event to and at the request of the accused and his associate,
   • $24,150 were billed as GST to the Government of Canada and never paid by the accused to the ... events.

· · ·

[14] The respondent is 62 years old and has been working in the field of advertising since 1967. In 1991, he started his own agency.

[15] His reputation was excellent and he was involved in his community, twice serving, for example, as president of the Optimist Club of the town in which he resides. The respondent is well-liked by his family members and friends. After the death of his wife, he began a relationship with the woman with whom he now shares his life.

[16] The trial judge went on to note that the respondent claims to have cooperated fully with Crown representatives. He chose to reimburse the losses incurred by the Government of Canada. To this end, he obtained a $306,700 loan secured by hypothec on his home, redeemed the money he had invested in his registered retirement savings plan (RRSP) and borrowed $500,000 from his friends and family. This enabled him to reimburse $1 million in settlement of an action that had been brought against him.

[17] He agreed to give lectures on ethics at universities in Montréal to encourage students to respect the rules of honesty, and he has received an invitation to speak at McGill University.

[18] The trial judge then reviewed the submissions of Crown counsel and counsel for the Defence, with the former recommending a 34-month prison sentence and the latter a sentence to be served in the community.

· · ·

[37] The trial judge was correct in stating that sentencing is an individualized process. This statement is also consistent with Supreme Court decisions.

[38] That being said, the judge is not relieved of the task of considering the application of all of the principles and objectives as set out by Parliament in sections 718, 718.1 and 718.2 of the *Criminal Code*.

[39] The trial judge noted all the mitigating circumstances:

1. the post-offence conduct of the accused;
2. his guilty plea;
3. the restitution of the ill-gotten money;
4. his remorse;
5. his undertaking to give lectures on ethics in business;
6. his unblemished reputation prior to his guilty plea;
7. his age;
8. his public apologies.

[40] With respect, however, the judge failed to assign the proper weight to the following principles and objectives:

40.1. the gravity of the offence, which justifies a proportionate sentence (s. 718.1);
40.2. the objectives of denunciation and deterrence (s. 718(a) and (b));
40.3. the sentences *generally* imposed for this type of crime, according to the principle of harmonization in sentencing (s. 718.2(b)).

Gravity of the Offence and Degree of Responsibility of the Offender

[41] Section 718.1 of the *Criminal Code* provides that the sentence must be proportionate to the gravity of the offence.

[42] The Crown prosecutor faults the trial judge for having omitted any [TRANSLATION] "discussion regarding the objective gravity of the offence, the circumstances in which it was committed and the resulting cynicism of Canadian taxpayers with respect to politics and democratic institutions." In particular, the trial judge failed to mention the following factors relating to the gravity of the offence:

1. the duration of the fraud (5 years and 1 month),
2. the large amount of money stolen ($1,556,625),
3. the privileged position of the accused,
4. the premeditation.

[43] It is generally recognized that the nature and gravity of the offence are fundamental considerations in sentencing. Every sentence must be proportionate to the offence committed, given its nature and the surrounding circumstances.

[44] The Crown prosecutor is correct: this type of fraud risks provoking cynicism in citizens and particularly taxpayers with respect to the public institutions that are the very foundations of democratic life.

[45] Taxes are levied to collect the funds necessary to fulfil the needs of citizens, particularly the most impoverished.

[46] The fallacious argument that "stealing from the government is not really stealing" cannot be used to downplay the significance of this crime. The government of the country has no assets itself; rather, it manages sums common to all of its citizens. Defrauding the government is equivalent to stealing from one's fellow citizens.

[47] The respondent drew up 373 fraudulent invoices, one by one, over a period of more than five years. This cannot be dismissed as a momentary lapse of judgment. We also should not lose sight of the total amount stolen nor of the additional fact that the respondent has made only partial restitution. Finally, even though the respondent's actions do not amount to a breach of trust within the meaning of section 336 *Cr. C*, the fact remains that he illegitimately took advantage of his privileged position to misappropriate public funds for his own personal use.

[48] In short, the crime committed by the respondent is a particularly serious one, and the trial judge should have taken this fact into account.

Denunciation and Deterrence

[49] Denunciation and deterrence are crucial objectives. Their significance was downplayed by the trial judge, even though he did acknowledge it during oral argument and in his judgment.

[50] On this subject, the Crown prosecutor correctly writes the following:

[TRANSLATION] The sentencing objectives of general deterrence and denunciation must be achieved as a function of objective criteria such as the nature of the offence, its gravity, the circumstances in which it was committed, the amount of money involved, the characteristics of the victim or victims, the publicity it received, its social impact, etc.—in short, criteria that will help the public understand that this conduct was highly reprehensible and that it carries with it serious criminal consequences.

[51] In *Proulx*, the Chief Justice described the objective of denunciation in the following terms:

> [102] Denunciation is the communication of society's condemnation of the offender's conduct. In *M.(C.A.)*, *supra*, at para. 81, I wrote:
>
> > In short, a sentence with a denunciatory element represents a symbolic, collective statement that the offender's conduct should be punished for encroaching on our society's basic code of values as enshrined within our substantive criminal law. As Lord Justice Lawton stated in *R v. Sargeant* (1974), 60 Cr. App. R. 74, at p. 77: "society, through the courts, must show its abhorrence of particular types of crime, and the only way in which the courts can show this is by the sentences they pass."

[52] In *R v. Latimer*, the Supreme Court found that denunciation was even more important in certain circumstances, which are also present in this case:

> [86] ... Furthermore, denunciation becomes much more important in the consideration of sentencing in cases where there is a "high degree of planning and premeditation, and where the offence and its consequences are highly publicized, [so that] like-minded individuals may well be deterred by severe sentences": *R v. Mulvahill and Snelgrove* (1993), 21 BCAC 296, at p. 300. This is particularly so where the victim is a vulnerable person with respect to age, disability, or other similar factors.

[53] In *Proulx*, the Supreme Court recognized that a conditional sentence of imprisonment was less severe than incarceration:

> [40] Although a conditional sentence is by statutory definition a sentence of imprisonment, this Court, in *R v. Shropshire*, 1995 CanLII 47 (SCC), [1995] 4 SCR 227, at para. 21, recognized that there "is a very significant difference between being behind bars and functioning within society while on conditional release." See also *Cunningham v. Canada*, 1993 CanLII 139 (SCC), [1993] 2 SCR 143, at p. 150, *per* McLachlin J. These comments are equally applicable to the conditional sentence. Indeed, offenders serving a conditional sentence in the community are only partially deprived of their freedom. Even if their liberty is restricted by the conditions attached to their sentence, they are not confined to an institution and they can continue to attend to their normal employment or educational endeavours. They are not deprived of their private life to the same extent. Nor are they subject to a regimented schedule or an institutional diet.
>
> • • •
>
> [43] I would add that the fact that a conditional sentence cannot be reduced through parole does not in itself lead to the conclusion that as a general matter a conditional sentence is as onerous as or even more onerous than a jail term of equivalent duration. There is no parole simply because the offender is never actually incarcerated and he or she does not need to be reintegrated into society. But even when an offender is released from custody on parole, the original sentence continues in force.

[54] Finally, also in *Proulx*, the Chief Justice recognized that incarceration has a greater denunciatory effect than a conditional sentence and that it is called for in certain cases:

> [102] ... Incarceration will usually provide more denunciation than a conditional sentence, as a conditional sentence is generally a more lenient sentence than a jail term of equivalent duration. That said, a conditional sentence can still provide a significant amount of denunciation. This is particularly so when onerous conditions are imposed and the duration of the conditional sentence is extended beyond the duration of the jail sentence that would ordinarily have been imposed in the circumstances.
>
> ...
>
> [106] The amount of denunciation provided by a conditional sentence will be heavily dependent on the circumstances of the offender, the nature of the conditions imposed, and the community in which the sentence is to be served. As a general matter, the more serious the offence and the greater the need for denunciation, the longer and more onerous the conditional sentence should be. However, there may be certain circumstances in which the need for denunciation is so pressing that incarceration will be the only suitable way in which to express society's condemnation of the offender's conduct.

[55] Once again in *Proulx*, the Chief Justice made similar comments on the principle of deterrence:

> [107] Incarceration, which is ordinarily a harsher sanction, may provide more deterrence than a conditional sentence. Judges should be wary, however, of placing too much weight on deterrence when choosing between a conditional sentence and incarceration: see *Wismayer* ... , at p. 36. The empirical evidence suggests that the deterrent effect of incarceration is uncertain: see generally *Sentencing Reform: A Canadian Approach* ... , at pp. 136-37. Moreover, a conditional sentence can provide significant deterrence if sufficiently punitive conditions are imposed and the public is made aware of the severity of these sentences. There is also the possibility of deterrence through the use of community service orders, including those in which the offender may be obliged to speak to members of the community about the evils of the particular criminal conduct in which he or she engaged, assuming the offender were amenable to such a condition. Nevertheless, there may be circumstances in which the need for deterrence will warrant incarceration. This will depend in part on whether the offence is one in which the effects of incarceration are likely to have a real deterrent effect, as well as on the circumstances of the community in which the offences were committed.

[56] In *R v. Dobis*, Justice MacPherson, after reviewing the case law on matters of fraud, had the following to say on Justice Lamer's remarks:

> [49] It is clear that no category of offence is excluded from the conditional sentence regime: see *Proulx, supra*, at pp. 126-27 SCR, p. 501 CCC. Specifically, a conditional sentence is a possible sentence in a fraud case, even with respect to a large-scale fraud: see *Bunn, supra*.
>
> [50] However, it is also clear that certain offences will usually lead to custodial sentences. ...

[51] This court has said repeatedly that general deterrence is central to the sentencing process in cases involving large-scale frauds with serious consequences for the victims: see McEachern, Bertram, Gray and Holden, *supra*. Importantly, the court has said the same thing since the introduction of the conditional sentencing regime. Conditional sentences have been rejected in large-scale fraud cases such as *Pierce, supra*, and *Ruhland, supra*, and commented on adversely in the leading Ontario case dealing with conditional sentences, *R v. Wismayer* 1997 CanLII 3294 (ONCA), (1997), 33 OR (3d) 225, 115 CCC (3d) 18 (CA).

[57] In short, while a certain deference must be shown before imposing a custodial sentence based on the principle of general deterrence, the fact remains that such a sentence is justified in the present case, which involves large-scale fraud against the government by a person in a particularly privileged position.

Harmonization in Sentencing

[58] Section 719.2(b) [sic] of the *Criminal Code* provides that a sentence should be similar to sentences imposed on offenders for similar offences committed in similar circumstances.

[59] The trial judge was required to examine the precedents to determine what sentence is generally imposed for this type of crime. This preliminary stage does not involve statistical analysis and is not a restriction that binds the judge.

[60] In the present case, the prosecution is correct in its contention that the various Canadian appellate courts have *generally* imposed imprisonment in cases of large-scale premeditated fraud that took place over relatively long periods of time.

[61] In these cases, the courts recognized that a custodial sentence was necessary to achieve the objectives of denunciation and deterrence, even where the offender (1) had no record, (2) enjoyed a good reputation in his or her milieu, (3) had, on some occasions, partially repaid the victims, (4) expressed remorse, (5) was not likely to re-offend.

[62] The list of cases cited by the Crown prosecutor is eloquent in this respect. It would be unnecessarily repetitive to analyze each case in detail. It is sufficient to rely on one case in particular, *R v. Bogart*, a judgment of the Court of Appeal for Ontario, which presents the most similarities to the present case.

[63] The accused Bogart pleaded guilty to defrauding approximately $1 million from the Ontario Health Insurance Plan. The fraud took place over seven years. The trial judge sentenced him to two years less a day to be served in the community and ordered him to pay $791,780.53 in restitution. By the time of the hearing, the accused had already repaid over $200,000.

[64] The Court of Appeal for Ontario (Laskin, Rosenberg and Goudge JJA) recognized that there were remarkable mitigating circumstances:

> [20] The respondent can certainly point to a powerful catalogue of mitigating circumstances. They include:
>
> • The respondent is a cancer survivor who has overcome this disease to become an excellent doctor;

- He serves a sector of the population that few doctors treat:

  — persons who are HIV positive or who have AIDS;

- Perhaps because of his own disease, he has an empathy with his patients that others may not have, and his patients correspondingly depend on him and do not want him incarcerated;

- Although he did not do so immediately, he eventually pleaded guilty to the charge against him;

- At the sentencing hearing, he expressed great remorse and accepted responsibility for what he had done;

- He has served over half of his conditional sentence and has complied with all its terms;

- He is making regular monthly restitution payments and has now repaid approximately 25 per cent of the amount of the restitution order; and

- He has no previous criminal record.

[65] Nevertheless, the Court concluded that a conditional sentence was demonstrably unfit in such circumstances and substituted a custodial sentence of eighteen months:

· · ·

[33] Still, the Supreme Court of Canada has acknowledged that a conditional sentence can meet the need for general deterrence in some cases. See *R v. Proulx*, 2000 SCC 5 (CanLII), [2000] 1 SCR 61, 140 CCC (3d) 449. But where the need for general deterrence is "particularly pressing," incarceration will normally be the preferable option. In *R v. Wismayer* 1997 CanLII 3294 (ONCA), (1997), 33 OR (3d) 225, 115 CCC (3d) 18, one of this court's leading decisions on conditional sentences, Rosenberg JA recognized at p. 243 OR, p. 38 CCC that the need for general deterrence is particularly pressing in the case of a large-scale, well-planned fraud by a person in a position of trust:

> General deterrence, as the principal objective animating the refusal to impose a conditional sentence, should be reserved for those offences that are likely to be affected by a general deterrent effect. Large scale well-planned fraud by persons in positions of trust, such as the accused in *R v. Pierce*, would seem to be one of those offences.
>
> · · ·

[66] This should not be seen to imply that conditional sentences may not be imposed in cases of fraud; indeed, the decisions cited by the respondent illustrate that they may. It should be noted however that, generally speaking, conditional sentences have been granted by appellate courts in response to particular circumstances.

[67] In *R v. Bunn*, a decision of the Supreme Court, the amount of money defrauded was only $86,000.

[68] ... [C]ounsel for the respondent have also cited one decision of the Court of Appeal of Alberta, two of the Court of Appeal for Ontario, four of this Court and one of the Court of Appeal of Saskatchewan, all of which granted conditional sentences in cases of fraud.

[69] Of all the judgments relied upon by the respondent, only *Moulton* involved the misappropriation of public funds (approximately $274,000). In other cases of fraud against the government or one of its agencies, appellate courts have imposed custodial sentences. See *R v. Kerntopf* (5 years), *R v. Dudek* (4 years), *R v. Bouchard* (1 year), *R v. Poirier* (3 years), *R v. Oliynyk* (1 year) and *R v. Bernston* (1 year).

[70] A reading of the Canadian appellate decisions leads to the conclusion that custodial sentences are appropriate "in principle" in cases of large-scale fraud; this does not mean, however, that the sentence may not be served in the community in specific cases. In addition, the other decisions of this Court that the respondent cites may be distinguished from the present case. In *R v. Toman*, the Court noted that, [TRANSLATION] "in the present case, the respondent did not set up a system with the aim of defrauding the public ... ." In *R v. Cantin*, Justice Beauregard took into account the fact that Cantin was in good faith because [TRANSLATION] "he believed that his business practices were shrewd, but not really fraudulent." The same cannot be said of the respondent. In *R v. Alain*, Justice Gendreau concluded that Alain's fraud [TRANSLATION] "cannot be compared to one in which personal benefit is the sole objective and greed the only motive." Finally, in *R v. Verville*, Justice Thibault pointed out that Verville had used a rather unsophisticated method to commit the crime and that, because he had contributed to the ruin of his own business, he was [TRANSLATION] "the first victim of his dishonest actions." Again, we are far from such a situation in the present case. To paraphrase *a contrario* the words of Justice Gendreau, one sees that, in the case of the fraud committed by the respondent, personal benefit was the sole objective and greed the only motive. ...

[71] Applying the words of Chief Justice Lamer in *M.(.A.)* on the standard of intervention of an appellate court sitting in review of a sentence, we find that the trial judgment contains errors of principle in that it "overemphasizes" certain factors and fails to consider other relevant factors.

[72] After affirming that denunciation and general deterrence were the "prime objectives" of the sentence to be imposed (at para. 51), the trial judge focused his analysis almost exclusively on subjective factors relating to the respondent. The following paragraph, which was central to his decision, bears repeating:

> [44] After having considered the applicable principles of sentencing in ss. 718-718.2, the circumstances of the crimes, the post-offence conduct of the accused, his guilty plea to all the charges, his complete restitution of the ill-gotten money to the satisfaction of the Government of Canada, his genuine remorse, his commitment to tell business people how to conduct themselves with reference to his own personal downfall, his unblemished reputation prior to his guilty plea, his age, his public apologies, I unhesitatingly conclude that the range of a fit sentence in this case is under two years.

[73] Except for "the circumstances of the crimes," the other elements accepted and analyzed bear on the respondent's personal situation.

[74] Although the factors noted by the trial judge are generally accurate, even so, certain qualifications are required.

[75] The trial judge refers to the "complete restitution of the ill-gotten money to the satisfaction of the victim." Records of the transaction confirm that the total amount of

money defrauded was $1,556,625. Moreover, these documents also indicate that the respondent owed $33,559 to the Government of Canada, which in turn owed him $105,834. After reimbursement, the loss incurred by the Government is $484,350, before interest.

[76] It is true that these documents indicate that the respondent and his company paid income tax (an unspecified amount) on the sums illegally obtained. It is also true that, in an earlier civil suit, the Government of Canada determined that it was to their advantage to recover $1 million and grant an acquittance. This does not mean that the respondent has made "complete restitution" of the money he misappropriated to his own benefit.

[77] The trial judge also noted the respondent's full cooperation with the Commission of Inquiry and his remorse. While these observations are accurate, it should be added that his cooperation and regrets only came into being after he was summoned before the Commission of Inquiry.

[78] Other than referring to "the circumstances of the crimes," the trial judge made no mention at all of the seriousness of these offences, which have the effect of undermining the confidence of citizens in their public institutions.

[79] Of course, trial judges are not obliged to record all of their reasons in detail. The fact remains, however, that a reading of the judgment in this case reveals an overemphasis on certain factors and a failure to assign the proper weight to objectives that the judge himself had defined as priorities.

[80] These errors of principle justify the intervention of this Court.

[81] But there is more: the sentence is "demonstrably unfit."

[82] The sentence imposed does not fall within any "range" that has been generally defined by Canadian appellate courts in cases involving equally large-scale frauds against public institutions. Of course, these decisions were not binding on the trial judge, but if he believed that the circumstances of the present case justified not applying them, it would have been preferable for him to say so.

[83] It should also be noted that the sentence is much more lenient than what was proposed by counsel for the respondent. ...

. . .

[86] In light of the objectives and principles set out above, and having regard to all the aggravating and mitigating circumstances also noted and in particular the reimbursement of $1 million, a custodial sentence of eighteen months is appropriate and should be imposed on the respondent.

R v. Wallis
2007 BCCA 377 (CanLII)

LEVINE JA (Kirkpatrick JA concurring):

Introduction

[1] The appellant, Keith Gordon Wallis, applies for leave to appeal, and if leave is granted, appeals the sentence of fifteen months in jail and one year probation imposed after he was convicted of unlawful production of marihuana contrary to s. 7(1) of the *Controlled Drugs and Substances Act*. He claims the sentencing judge erred in not imposing a conditional sentence.

Circumstances of the Appellant

[2] The appellant ran a grow operation of 638 plants in his house, powered by stolen electricity. He co-owned the house with his parents. After his conviction, he sold the house, realizing a financial loss because of the damage to the house from the grow operation.

[3] The appellant was 28 years old when he committed the offence, and 32 at the time of sentencing. He had no prior criminal record. He is a high school graduate, and completed a pre-apprenticeship program in auto mechanics at BCIT. The appellant was steadily employed until he quit his job in 2002 to develop and manage the grow operation full time. He has been employed since his arrest for this offence. He paid his parents for the losses they suffered on the sale of the house.

[4] The appellant has the support of his parents and friends. He financially supports and has a close relationship with his twelve-year-old daughter, who lives with her mother and step-father.

Positions of Counsel at Sentencing

[5] At the sentencing hearing, Crown counsel suggested a jail sentence of one year. He took no position on whether the sentence should be served in custody or by a conditional sentence. Defence counsel submitted that a one year conditional sentence was appropriate.

Reasons for Sentence

[6] In lengthy reasons, the sentencing judge reviewed the circumstances of the offence and the offender.

• • •

[9] He then reviewed (at paras. 48 and 49) the mitigating and aggravating factors. The mitigating factors were the appellant's lack of a prior criminal record, his relationship with and support of his child, parents, and friends, and his steady employment. The aggravating factors focused on the circumstances of the offence: the appellant left his secure, well-paid employment to undertake a criminal enterprise; he was motivated solely by greed; the grow operation was large and sophisticated; the appellant stood to

profit greatly from his enterprise; he was the sole operating mind of the enterprise; and he created a serious risk to his neighbours by setting up an electrical by-pass at his house. The sentencing judge noted (at para. 50) that the appellant was not a mere "gardener" or custodian of the enterprise.

[10] The sentencing judge concluded (at para. 59) that considering the appellant's motivation of greed and his deceit of family and friends in setting up and operating the grow operation, he was "not satisfied on a balance of probabilities that the safety of the community would not be endangered if this defendant was allowed to serve his sentence in the community."

[11] The sentencing judge then went on to consider the effect of marihuana grow operations on the community. He considered (at para. 60) as aggravating factors the prevalence of this criminal activity in the community, and its corrupting influence.

[12] In conclusion, the sentencing judge said (at para. 67):

> In my view, the sentence which I impose must satisfy both the need for denunciation of the high degree of moral culpability of the defendant and deterrence of others from engaging in a criminal behaviour which is, as stated earlier, causing harm in so many ways to the members of this community and to the social contract and respect for the rule of law. A conditional sentence would, in the circumstances of this offence and this offender, utterly fail to achieve these objectives.

• • •

[13] The appellant claims that the sentencing judge erred in finding that the appellant was a danger to the community; by placing too little emphasis on the appellant's personal circumstances; by overemphasizing the aggravating factors and placing too little weight on the mitigating factors; by overemphasizing the principles of deterrence and denunciation; and in characterizing the community as uniquely affected by marihuana grow operations and not allowing counsel to make submissions on this issue.

• • •

Danger to the Community

[17] The sentencing judge found the safety of the community would continue to be endangered if the appellant served his sentence in the community, because he was motivated by greed and proceeded in secret in committing the offence.

• • •

[20] In determining whether the appellant was a danger to the community, the sentencing judge gave no weight to the evidence of the personal characteristics of the appellant, concluding that none of those factors was predictive of the appellant's future conduct. Rather, he focused on the appellant's criminal conduct, motivated by greed and carried out in secrecy. Because the criminal conduct was not anticipated by those closest to him before he offended, the sentencing judge found that the facts that he had not previously offended, was steadily employed, had a positive relationship with his family and friends, and expressed remorse for the offence were not predictive of his future conduct.

[21] Motive and manner of carrying out an offence may be relevant factors, but if greed and secrecy were determinative, there would be few offenders who would not be found to be a continuing danger to the community.

[22] The sentencing judge was clearly offended by the appellant's criminal conduct, and for good reason. When otherwise law-abiding citizens turn to criminal enterprise, respect for societal norms, governed by law, is undermined.

[23] The sentencing judge was also concerned about the effect of the offence on the community, implicitly addressing the second factor that Lamer CJC in *Proulx* said must be taken into account in assessing the danger to the community: the gravity of the damage if the appellant re-offended.

[24] In my opinion, however, the sentencing judge underemphasized the appellant's personal characteristics in concluding he was at risk to re-offend, and overemphasized the gravity of the damage in the event of re-offence. In the result, his conclusion that the appellant remained a danger to the community was unreasonable.

Principles and Purposes of Sentencing

[25] The sentencing judge found (at paras. 66-67) that the overriding principles of sentencing in this case were denunciation and general deterrence, supporting his conclusion that "incarceration will be the only suitable way in which to express society's condemnation of the offender's conduct or to deter similar conduct in the future."

[26] The sentencing judge's rejection of a conditional sentence is consistent with what this Court has said on many occasions: the principles of deterrence and denunciation are of prime importance in cases of this kind: see, for example, *R v. Van Santvoord*, 2007 BCCA 23 (decided after this sentencing decision). In *Van Santvoord*, Ryan JA, for the Court, cited *R v. Su*, 2000 BCCA 480 (CanLII), 2000 BCCA 480, and *R v. Vu*, 2003 BCCA 339 (CanLII), 2003 BCCA 339, and said (at para. 38):

> *Su* remains a guideline and has been referred to in many subsequent decisions of this court for the principles that denunciation and deterrence are appropriate sentencing objectives where commercial marihuana operations are involved, for the proposition that a conditional sentence for the owner of the operation is generally unsuitable, and for a guideline range.

[27] See also Ryan JA's more recent comments in *R v. Craig*, 2007 BCCA 234 (CanLII), 2007 BCCA 234 at para. 126, and *R v. Huynh and Ta*, 2007 BCCA 235 (CanLII), 2007 BCCA 235 at para. 46.

[28] The factors the sentencing judge considered in this case, including the motive of greed, the planning and deliberation in setting up the operation, the size and potential profitability of the operation, and the appellant's ownership of the operation, were all factors that led this Court in *Van Santvoord* to set aside a fine of $20,000 and substitute a sentence of one year in jail.

[29] Concern for the effect on the community of grow operations is also reflected in *Van Santvoord* (at para. 42), where Ryan JA for the Court said:

> ... [O]ver the years other cases of marihuana production have demonstrated that its illegal production creates the risk that it will attract other illegal activities and dangerous consequences to the community in which it takes place.

[30] See also *R v. Hill*, 2007 BCCA 309 (CanLII), 2007 BCCA 309 at para. 25 where Smith JA, for the Court, held that it was appropriate for a sentencing judge to take judicial notice of the existence in this province of a significant and lucrative marihuana industry:

> That there is a significant and lucrative illegal marihuana industry in this province and that it has grown in scale and pervasiveness in recent years can hardly have escaped the notice of any informed citizen of the province. These aggravating facts are within the first class mentioned in *R v. Find* 2001 SCC 32 (CanLII), [2001 SCC 32 at para. 48] and the sentencing judge did not err in judicially noticing them. Indeed, this Court has taken judicial notice of the illegal drug trade in previous cases. For example, in *R v. Chang* 2002 BCCA 644 (CanLII), (2002), 179 BCAC 72, 2002 BCCA 644, Esson JA referred, at ¶ 12, to "the serious social problems that have been and are being created by the great level of drug distribution going on in our community and throughout this province"; in *R v. Aitkens* 2004 BCCA 411 (CanLII), (2004), 202 BCAC 167, 2004 BCCA 411, Newbury JA remarked at ¶ 7 that "[d]rug trafficking has become a blight in our society in general"; and in *R v. Van Santvoord*, 2007 BCCA 23 (CanLII), 2007 BCCA 23, Ryan JA said at ¶ 42 that "over the years other cases of marihuana production have demonstrated that its illegal production creates the risk that it will attract other illegal activities and dangerous consequences to the community in which it takes place."

[31] The impact of crime on the community is a factor that local judges are in a position to be aware of and reflect in their sentencing decisions, and is one of the reasons appellate courts show deference to those decisions: see *R v. M.(C.A.)*, 1996 CanLII 230 (SCC), [1996] 1 SCR 500 at paras. 91-92.

[32] This Court has not precluded the imposition of a conditional sentence for production of marihuana where the circumstances of the offence or the offender demonstrate that principles of sentencing other than denunciation and deterrence should be given more consideration. These include rehabilitation and restorative objectives, including reparation for harm done and acknowledgment of responsibility. In every case, consideration of the fundamental principle that "[a] sentence must be proportionate to the gravity of the offence and the degree of responsibility of the offender," as set out in s. 718.2 of the Code, is of major importance, and may lead to the conclusion that a conditional sentence is appropriate in the particular circumstances.

[33] If that were not so, the Court would be violating the basic principles of sentencing set out in the Code, and the guidelines set out by the Supreme Court of Canada in *Proulx*. These are: that incarceration is a last resort for all offenders (Code s. 718.2(d) and (e), *Proulx*, at paras. 100, 127(7)); no offence (except one punishable by a minimum term of imprisonment) is excluded from the conditional sentencing regime, and there is no presumptive sentence for specific offences (*Proulx*, at para. 127(3)); sentencing is an individualized process (*Proulx*, at para. 82); and a conditional sentence can provide significant denunciation and deterrence (*Proulx*, at paras. 102, 107, 127(8)).

[34] Examples of cases where consideration of all of the principles of sentencing led to the conclusion that a conditional sentence was appropriate in the particular circumstances are: *R v. Nguyen*, 2001 BCCA 461 (CanLII), 2001 BCCA 461; *R v. Godwin*, 2005 BCCA 477 (CanLII), 2005 BCCA 477, *R v. Gan*, 2007 BCCA 59 (CanLII), 2007 BCCA 59, and *R v. Kreutziger*, 2005 BCCA 231 (CanLII), 2005 BCCA 231.

[35] In *Nguyen*, this Court substituted a conditional sentence of 12 months for a jail sentence of nine months and one year probation for the mother of two young children, where the father of the children carried on a grow operation in her home. She knew little of the business and did not participate. In *Godwin*, this Court substituted a 12 months conditional sentence for a sentence of 12 months in jail for a 38 year old man diagnosed as a schizophrenic while serving a previous conditional sentence. The evidence was that he committed the marihuana production and related offences during the onset of the mental illness, and by the time of sentencing and the appeal, was managing his illness in the community with significant community support. In *Gan*, this Court substituted a 12 months conditional sentence for three months in jail to be served intermittently, for a 69 year old illiterate immigrant convicted of unlawful production of marihuana, who was unable to work at his former employment in a restaurant because of arthritis.

[36] None of these cases involved the principal operator and owner of a large grow operation, who had quit his regular and well-paid employment to carry out the operation.

[37] In *Kreutziger*, 2005 BCCA 231 (CanLII), 2005 BCCA 231, the Court substituted a conditional sentence of two years less a day for a jail sentence of three years because of "a number of extenuating circumstances which must be considered, the most compelling of which is that it has now been seven years since the date of the offence" (para. 21).

[38] In *R v. Tran*, 2004 BCCA 430 (CanLII), 2004 BCCA 430, the appellant cited *Kreutziger* in support of his argument that because three years had passed since the offence date it would be "counter productive" to send him to jail. The Court rejected that argument, saying (at para. 8):

> … it is not for this Court to convert a sentence of imprisonment to a conditional sentence when there is no error in law or principle in the sentence when it was imposed, merely because of some delay in the proceedings.

[39] For the same reason, I would not accede to the appellant's argument that the time that has elapsed between his arrest and this appeal should result in a different sentence than that imposed by the sentencing judge.

[40] In the circumstances of this offence and this appellant, the sentencing judge properly emphasized the principles of denunciation and deterrence. The sentence of incarceration is proportionate to the gravity of the offence and the responsibility of the offender. The offence is driven by greed, and has obvious deleterious effects on the communities in which it appears to thrive. The appellant, for no reasons that would serve to mitigate the circumstances of the offence, turned his back on lawful society, and embarked on a criminal enterprise that endangered his community. I find no basis to interfere with the sentence imposed.

Conclusion

[41] I would grant leave to appeal, and dismiss the appeal.

THACKRAY JA (dissenting): [42] I have had the opportunity to read and consider the reasons for judgment of my colleague Madam Justice Levine. I cannot agree with her decision that on the facts of this case a jail sentence is appropriate.

· · ·

Pre-Sentence Report

[48] The judge had before him the pre-sentence report referred to by counsel in their submissions. The report is dated 8 April 2005 by which time Mr. Wallis had been on bail for nearly two years. The author of the report interviewed Mr. Wallis, his mother, the mother of his daughter and Mr. Wallis' employer. I will replicate parts of the report:

> By all accounts subject has positive peer associations and spends his leisure time in constructive activities. His last intimate relationship, a 3 year common-law relationship with a single mother, ended approximately one year ago. He is currently single. He works out at the gym at least three times a week, jogs the seawall and enjoys riding his motorcycle. He is very involved in the life of his 10 year old daughter who is a gifted soccer player. Subject attends as many of her practices and games as possible and has week-end access every second week. He now has a very close relationship with her mother ... . [She] confirmed that subject has always been actively involved in co-parenting her and supporting their child, even during periods when their relationship was strained. She now considers him to be a close friend and confidant. She advises that he also has a positive relationship with her husband and her other child. They often participate in shared family activities on alternate Sundays when subject returns their daughter from her access visit.
>
> **EDUCATION, VOCATION, EMPLOYMENT, FINANCES**
>
> Subject graduated from secondary school in 1992 and in 1993 completed a 10 month pre-apprentice automotive mechanics program at BCIT. He did not pursue an apprenticeship in that field, choosing instead a higher paying job in a sawmill in order to better provide for his soon to be born child.
>
> ... After his arrest he worked for a concrete cutting/coring company in Langley for approximately 6 months before moving on to a decking company in the Aldergrove/Abbotsford area. He worked there for approximately 12 months up until he sold his house in August of last year. He then took some personal time before starting his current job.
>
> Subject now works as an iron worker for [...] . He enjoys his work and feels there is the potential for growth on the job. He hopes to develop the skill level required to become a unionized iron worker. Subject's employer, [...] , confirms that subject has worked for him since October 2004 and that he is a valued, hardworking and dedicated employee. [...] is aware of subject's upcoming Court appearance for sentencing in this matter.
>
> Subject's current financial situation is stable. He advises that he is debt free and that he has saved a few thousand dollars for emergencies. In addition to monthly cost of living expenses he pays between $350 and $400 per month in child support. He earns $18.00 per hour.

BEHAVIOUR, EMOTIONAL STATUS

Subject does not have past or current behavioural, emotional, psychological or health issues. He appears to be an average, well-adjusted young man.

SUBSTANCE MISUSE

There is no history of substance misuse.

COURT HISTORY

Present offence.

ATTITUDE AND RECEPTIVENESS TO PREVIOUS AND PROPOSED INTERVENTIONS

Although this is the subject's first criminal conviction, he came to the attention of BC Corrections in August 1992 when he served a 7-day jail sentence re: a motor vehicle infraction through the electric monitoring program. That sentence was completed successfully.

Subject has demonstrated a positive attitude towards community supervision and a willingness to comply with the expectations of any order imposed by the Court.

ATTITUDE AND UNDERSTANDING REGARDING OFFENCE

Subject regrets his behaviour with regards to the present offence. He appears to have rationalized his involvement by conceiving of the operation as a victimless crime and a justifiable, though unconventional, means of earning an income. He now recognized that his thinking was erroneous and that his actions caused many individuals, including his family, to suffer.

[49] The judge noted at paragraph 14 of his reasons that the pre-sentence report "paints a generally positive picture of the defendant, his history and his present circumstances." That understates the positive and supportive nature of the report which was described by *Crown* counsel at the hearing as "more supportive of an accused" than any other he had seen "in recent history." However, apart from noting the author's concern as to the technical suitability of electronic monitoring, the judge made no reference to the report in his reasons for judgment. In this case where the circumstances of the offender had to be of great significance to the sentence, where there was a detailed and positive report and where the position of both counsel was based upon the information supplied in the report, the report deserved a careful analysis.

Supporting Letters

[50] The judge noted that there were eight letters of support. Five of the letters were lost from the Provincial Court file, but copies of three were located in defence counsel's file. The others, including what must be considered an important letter from Mr. Wallis' employer, have not been found. The letter from the employer was referred to in defence counsel's submissions to the judge and the indications are the employer said Mr. Wallis' employment was secure and the employer would accommodate any conditions contained in a conditional sentence order. Nevertheless, the judge said:

[18] Each of the letter-writers, as might be expected, speaks glowingly of the defendant and most of them express their surprise at learning that he had been charged and convicted of this crime. The vast majority of them describe the defendant's criminal activity as entirely out-of-character for the person they believe him to be.

· · ·

And later in his reasons:

[54] The fact that none of the persons who wrote letters of support for the defendant had any suspicion, let alone knowledge, of his criminal behaviour shows how deceitful he was in his dealings with them. I have borne their ignorance of the defendant's true character in mind in assessing the weight I can attach to their letters.

That latter comment is inappropriate, especially with respect to the message sent to the Court by Mr. Wallis' employer. The judge gave no positive weight to the letters. Rather, he turned the letters against Mr. Wallis on the unusual basis that the writers did not know or suspect his criminal activity. It cannot be an acceptable practice to reject the views of people speaking in support of an accused person and instead turn their support letters against the accused.

· · ·

Circumstances of Mr. Wallis

[66] At paragraph 47 the judge set forth mitigating and aggravating factors in Mr. Wallis' case. He then said as follows:

[50] In many of the numerous marijuana grow-operation cases which appear before the courts in this community, the defendant is found to be a mere "gardener" or custodian of the enterprise who is paid a relative pittance for his or her labour. That is not the case here.

[51] Nor is this a case in which an otherwise law-abiding citizen faces severe financial difficulties and succumbs to temptation.

[52] In the present case, the defendant had secure, well-paid employment and was the owner, with his parents, of the house in which the grow-operation was discovered. Instead of being satisfied with his comfortable circumstances, he chose to establish a large, sophisticated and expensive criminal enterprise. It must have taken some considerable time and money to convert the house into a grow-operation and the defendant could have abandoned the enterprise at any time. But such was his *greed* that he pursued its creation without regard for his family members or the public at large.

[53] The defendant submits that his personal circumstances and in particular his relationship with his daughter should be given considerable weight by the court and ought to lead to the imposition of a conditional sentence. This submission, in my respectful opinion, is *breathtaking in its brazen boldness*. Each of the circumstances that counsel for the defendant has outlined existed before the defendant decided to engage in criminal activity. He *callously* put his own desire for illegal gain ahead of concern for his daughter, her mother, his parents and his brother. Now he is asking the court to give both weight and consideration to matters to which he gave neither.

[54] The fact that none of the persons who wrote letters of support for the defendant had any suspicion, let alone knowledge, of his criminal behaviour shows how *deceitful* he

was in his dealings with them. I have borne their ignorance of *the defendant's true character* in mind in assessing the weight I can attach to their letters.

[55] The fact that the defendant set up an electrical by-pass in a house located in a residential area is a serious aggravating factor. Once again, it shows the *callousness* of his actions. In the pursuit of his criminal goal, he completely disregarded the safety of his neighbours.

[56] There is no evidence before me as to when the grow-operation was established but it seems self-evident that the defendant must have intended to make use of it for more than a single harvest. It defies logic to suggest that someone motivated by *greed* would incur the expense and risk involved in setting up such a sophisticated operation in order to enjoy the benefits of only one crop.

[57] One must also assume that the defendant had a plan for the distribution and sale of the marijuana produced by the grow-operation, activities that would have involved him in further criminality.

[58] The foregoing illustrates both the careful and *secret planning* the defendant must have engaged in over some time and the degree of his culpability. These facts must be borne in mind and given appropriate weight in the determination of a fit sentence.

[Emphasis added.]

[67] My colleague noted at paragraph 22 of her reasons that the judge "was clearly offended by the appellant's criminal conduct, and for good reason." I have highlighted words in the above quotations that show just how personally offended the judge was over Mr. Wallis' entry into crime and the fact that he kept his criminal activity secret.

[68] It is not the place of the judiciary to take personal offence and turn that into a factor in sentencing. In my opinion the judge being "clearly offended," as can be seen by the above-noted comments, and his use of the supportive letters, led him into error. Furthermore, the fact that Mr. Wallis left a lawful occupation for a criminal enterprise is but one circumstance in the many that should have been weighed and cannot be used, as it was, to overcome all of the mitigating factors.

Danger to the Community

[69] On the issue of danger to the community the judge continued to emphasize the greed of Mr. Wallis and the secretive manner in which he operated:

[59] Counsel for the defendant submits that the latter no longer poses any danger to re-offend. However, given the secretive manner in which the defendant behaved in the present case and the fact that he was motivated solely by greed, this suggestion must be viewed with some degree of caution, if not scepticism, in my respectful opinion. For my part, I am not satisfied on a balance of probabilities that the safety of the community would not be endangered if this defendant was allowed to serve his sentence in the community.

[70] The judge was concerned that the safety of the community would continue to be endangered if the appellant served his sentence in the community because he was motivated by greed and proceeded in secret in committing the offence. He made no reference to nor explained why he declined to accept the Crown's position that "the safety of the community would not be endangered by the defendant serving his sentence in the community" nor to the Crown's agreement that "a conditional sentence

would be consistent with the principles of sentencing set out in sections 718 to 718.2 of the *Criminal Code*."

[71]   The judge did not discuss the factors that must be taken into account in determining whether the appellant was a danger to the community. He focused almost entirely on Mr. Wallis' criminal conduct which he repeatedly said was motivated by greed and carried out in secrecy. My colleague said it correctly when she noted (at paragraph 21) that "motive and manner of carrying out an offence may be relevant factors, but if greed and secrecy were determinative there would be few offenders who would not be found to be a continuing danger to the community."

[72]   The sentencing judge's strong disapproval of the appellant's conduct, in my opinion, supplanted an analysis of the proper legal principles. He underemphasized the appellant's personal characteristics in concluding he was at risk to re-offend. His opinion that Mr. Wallis posed a significant risk to re-offend did not have any foundation in the evidence, and thus the conclusion that he posed a risk to the community was not open to be found and he erred in principle in so finding.

[73]   This is in keeping with the conclusion reached by Madam Justice Levine who held (at paragraph 24) that the judge's "conclusion that the appellant remained a danger to the community was unreasonable." Thus, as found by both my colleague and myself, the judge erred in his weighing of the evidence. This cannot be compartmentalized and treated as simply an error without a result. It *must* be taken into account by this Court in determining whether the judge had a proper basis for the sentence which he meted out. In that this Court is unanimous that he erred and the error was germane to the sentence, this Court is not bound by his decision as to what was a fit sentence.

· · ·

In keeping with that standard, I have no hesitation in saying that the sentence imposed in the case at bar was not a fit sentence. It is a sentence that is detrimental to all directly affected parties and can only be supported on the basis of general deterrence. In this case that is not enough to justify the destabilization of a segment of society.

· · ·

[76]   The circumstances in *Copeland* were vastly different from those in the case at bar. Mr. Copeland had a significant criminal record and it was held that his previous sentence for another drug offence relating to a grow-operation "obviously had no deterrent effect." Furthermore, if the words of Lowry JA are correct that, since *Su*, custodial sentences have "generally been considered necessary," there are many exceptions to the general rule. The fact that *Su* expressed no more than a general rule was made clear in *R v. Tran*, 2001 BCCA 503 (CanLII), [2001] BCJ No. 1983, 2001 BCCA 503 where Mackenzie JA said:

> [8]   ... The learned trial judge rightly, in my view, rejected the submission that *Su* stands for the proposition that a conditional sentence is never appropriate in cases of marihuana cultivation. The circumstances of the particular offender must be considered.

R v. Proulx

[77] While it is instructive to consider previous cases with similar circumstances, *R v. Proulx*, 2000 SCC 5 (CanLII), [2000] 1 SCR 61 remains the leading authority on the interpretation and application of the statutory framework for conditional sentences. As pointed out by my colleague, it provides that in assessing the danger to the community posed by the offender serving his or her sentence in the community, one of the two matters that must be taken into account is the risk of the offender re-offending. She noted that the Chief Justice discussed the relevant factors in assessing that risk including criminal record; compliance with court orders; the nature of the offence; the relevant circumstances of the offence; the offender's personal circumstances, including occupation, lifestyle, family situation, age, and mental state; and the offender's conduct following the commission of the offence.

[78] The judge had before him evidence on all of those factors, but ignored most of them. In determining specifically whether the appellant was a danger to the community he gave no weight to the evidence of the personal characteristics of the appellant, in effect concluding that because the criminal conduct was not predicted by those closest to Mr. Wallis before he offended, the fact that he had not previously offended, was steadily employed, had a positive relationship with his family and friends and expressed remorse for the offence were found of no consequence.

[79] One of the factors that *Proulx* says is to be taken into account is the offender's conduct since the commission of the offence. Separately, the Chief Justice spoke of "subsequent incidents" as an additional factor in assessing the nature of the offence. In the case at bar the crime was committed in 2002 and early 2003 and the charge was laid on 2 June 2003. Mr. Wallis has been on judicial interim release for over four years. There have been no "subsequent incidents" and, as testified to in the supporting letters and in the pre-sentence report, his conduct has been exemplary over that period of time.

Judicial Delay

[80] There is no suggestion that the excessive time from the laying of the charge until now can be laid at the feet of Mr. Wallis. At the oral hearing of this appeal Crown counsel was asked by the Court to explain the long period of time. He was unable to do so. This is not a case wherein it can be said that the offender created a time zone in which to portray himself as a reformed person. It is a case in which the judicial system has moved slowly and Mr. Wallis has demonstrated throughout his resolve to act honestly.

[81] Mr. Wallis has been under and abided by the conditions of the parole order for over four years. That order provides that he keep the peace and be of good behaviour, report to a bail supervisor when directed, remain within British Columbia, not change his address without permission and deposit his passport with the Court. He has done all of this and surrendered himself into custody at each hearing and when reasons for judgment were delivered by the various courts.

[82] In *R v. Tran*, 2005 BCCA 430 (CanLII), [2005] BCJ No. 1898, 2005 BCCA 430 it was two years from the offence to sentencing. This Court said (at paragraph 8) "it is not for this Court to convert a sentence of imprisonment to a conditional sentence when there is no error in law or principle in the sentence when it was imposed, merely

because of some delay in the proceedings." Mr. Tran had a criminal record and was on probation at the time of the offences; thus *R v. Kreutziger*, 2005 BCCA 231 (CanLII), [2005] BCJ No. 850, 2005 BCCA 231 was distinguished.

[83] In *Kreutziger* the offender was sentenced in 2002 to a three-year term of imprisonment for an offence which occurred in 1998. The total delay between the offence and appeal was seven years. Oppal JA wrote the majority reasons in which he said:

> [21] ... While the sentencing judge correctly addressed the principle of general deterrence, there are a number of extenuating circumstances which must be considered, the most compelling of which is that it has new been seven years since the date of the offence. It must be noted that the delay is no fault of the appellant. His counsel at trial is deceased. In my view, *it would now be counterproductive to sentence the appellant to an unconditional term of imprisonment.*

> [Emphasis added.]

[84] The prison term was set aside and a conditional sentence of two years less a day was imposed. Madam Justice Levine wrote concurring reasons in which she said:

> [25] In my opinion, a sentence of three years incarceration for a first offence of trafficking in a large amount of cocaine could not be said to be unfit *at the time the sentence was pronounced.* ...

> [26] If it were not for the passage of seven years from the date the offence occurred to the resolution of this appeal, I would not interfere with the sentence that was imposed. *In the particular circumstances of this case, however, I agree that it would be counterproductive to send the appellant to prison.*

> [Emphasis added.]

[85] That logic must be applied to the case at bar. No benefit to society can be made out in this case by now putting Mr. Wallis in jail. Indeed, to the contrary, the detriment to his child, her mother and Mr. Wallis' employer and employment are readily obvious. Paraphrasing Madam Justice Levine, it would be counter-productive to send Mr. Wallis to prison.

[86] It must be recognized, in deference to His Honour Judge Lenaghan, that when he delivered his reasons for sentence on 17 June 2005 he could not have predicted two further years would pass before the judicial process would conclude.

Where Imprisonment Would Be "Counter-Productive"

[87] The theme of "counter-productive" imprisonment was applied by this Court in *R v. Godwin*, 2005 BCCA 477 (CanLII), [2005] BCJ No. 2070, 2005 BCCA 477. Mr. Godwin was sentenced to [a] one-year term of imprisonment for marijuana production, mischief and theft of electricity. This Court substituted that sentence with a conditional one even though the trial judge had relied upon *Su* and *Copeland*. The Court said:

> [21] To take the appellant out of the community and away from the Strathcona Mental Health Team with its co-ordinated resources for vocational rehabilitation, for offences best

seen as part of a short period of criminality already significantly punished, seems counter-productive, as both counsel recognized in arriving at the proposed disposition, not only for the appellant, but also for the community. Since being diagnosed [for schizophrenia] the appellant has gained insight into both his chronic condition and his criminal behaviour. He accepts the need for medication and community assistance. Fortunately, in this case, the diagnosis has been made and the required community assistance has been made available, including the necessary medications. Mr. Godwin has been fully compliant. Not all who suffer this terrible illness are so fortunate.

[22] In our view, counsel fashioned, with the appellant's consent, a punishment best suited to satisfy the principles of sentencing for this offender and this offence. This is precisely the type of case where the guideline set down at para.13 in *Su, supra*, should not be applied.

[88] In *R v. Shaw*, 2005 BCCA 380 (CanLII), (2005), 199 CCC (3d) 93, 2005 BCCA 380 this Court recognized the counter-productive result in a case wherein the trial judge had sentenced the offender to two years' imprisonment for the production of marijuana. The Court said:

[14] … The appellant is working and supporting his spouse and two small infant children as well as caring for his ailing father. No useful purpose will be served by maintaining a custodial sentence.

The Court referred to *Su*, but set aside the custodial sentence in favour of a two year less a day conditional sentence.

Rehabilitation

[89] The issue of rehabilitation seems to have been overlooked by the sentencing judge. In *Proulx*, Lamer CJC, after noting that "offenders who meet the criteria of s. 742.1 will serve a sentence under strict surveillance in the community instead of going to prison," said:

[22] The conditional sentence incorporates some elements of non-custodial measures and some other of incarceration. Because it is served in the community, it will generally be more effective than incarceration at achieving the restorative objectives of rehabilitation, reparations to the victim and community, and the promotion of a sense of responsibility in the offender. *However, it is also a punitive sanction capable of achieving the objectives of denunciation and deterrence.*

[Emphasis in original.]

[90] In concentrating on the criminal act and deterrence the judge lost sight of the fact that a conditional sentence is punitive and denunciatory and that rehabilitation is a vital factor in sentencing. The evidence would suggest that rehabilitation has already been achieved and in any event there can be no suggestion that it will be accomplished by now jailing Mr. Wallis. Indeed, I would see it as more likely to have the opposite result.

・・・

[96] If in the circumstances of this case Mr. Wallis is to be given a jail sentence it must be that every offender who is a major player in a marijuana grow operation must,

regardless of his or her circumstances, go to jail. I say that because it is difficult to imagine any set of circumstances more favourable to an offender than in the case of Mr. Wallis. In *R v. Innes*, 2001 BCCA 478 (CanLII), [2001] BCJ No. 1713, 2001 BCCA 478, the sentencing judge referred to *Su* and imposed a jail sentence. This Court dismissed the appeal, but the Court said:

> [8] Counsel for the appellant submitted that in saying this [that in cases where there is a large and sophisticated grow operation the Court must primarily address the issues of deterrence and denunciation] the sentencing judge said, in effect, that a conditional sentence is never available where the offence of production involves a high number of plants in a sophisticated grow operation. I agree with counsel that if this is what the sentencing judge meant, it would be wrong.

[97] My colleague, in paragraphs 32 and 33, acknowledges that the principles of sentencing do not preclude the imposition of a conditional sentence for the production of marijuana. Nevertheless, in spite of all of the positive matters weighing in favour of a conditional sentence, she would have him sent to jail based on the principles of denunciation and deterrence.

[98] I do not in any way suggest that those principles are to be undervalued or that there will be many cases where the principal of a significant grow operation will avoid a jail sentence. However, if in the circumstances of this case a jail sentence is found to be required, it would shut the door to conditional sentences for owners of grow operations regardless of all personal characteristics and regardless of all mitigating circumstances.

[99] This is not what was intended by *Proulx* wherein the Chief Justice said at paragraph 44:

> The particular circumstances of the offender and the offence must be considered in each case.

[100] I am of the opinion that the appropriate sentence for this offender in these circumstances is a conditional sentence of 15 months. For over four years Mr. Wallis has lived a lawful and productive life, returned to lawful employment, expressed regret for his sojourn into crime and lived up to his word. During that time he also restored his parents' financial losses on the house he co-owned with them and in which he carried on the grow operation. All of these actions are reflective of the principles and purposes of sentencing set out in s. 718 of the Code and in *Proulx* and a conditional sentence would fulfill the requirements of both.

[101] I acknowledge the frustration experienced by sentencing judges in trying to discern consistent guidelines from the decisions of this Court and can only make reference again to *Proulx* where Lamer CJC at paragraph 82 emphasized the importance of an individualized approach to sentencing. Sentencing individual offenders for particular crimes requires a consideration of all the facts and circumstances of the particular case. The inevitable result of that process, as Lamer CJC acknowledged, is a variation in sentences imposed for particular crimes.

[102] I would grant leave to appeal, allow the appeal, set aside the sentence imposed by the sentencing judge and substitute a conditional sentence of 15 months.

NOTE

The decisions in *Coffin* and *Wallis* are good examples of the observation that the rejection of conditional sentences in "hard cases" almost always results from a conclusion that the combined effect of "denunciation and deterrence" requires custody—that is, that a conditional sentence of imprisonment is inconsistent with the purposes and principles found in ss. 718 to 718.2 for this reason. This analytical view requires closer scrutiny. First, although there continues to be some debate about the existence of a general deterrent effect, most sentencing scholars agree that any deterrent effect is a product of the certainty of being caught and the combined impact of arrest, prosecution, conviction, and sentence. There seems to be no evidence to suggest that an increase in sentence alone can produce more general deterrence (see Doob and Webster, "Sentence Security and Crime: Accepting the Null Hypothesis," in M. Tonry, ed., *Crime and Justice* (Chicago: University of Chicago Press, 2004). Consequently, there should be no support for the claim that general deterrence can be enhanced by deciding that a sentence of imprisonment should be custodial rather than community-based on strict conditions. And this is essentially what the Supreme Court endorsed in *Proulx*.

As far as denunciation is concerned, in *R v. M.(C.A.)*, a case that antedates the conditional sentence regime, Chief Justice Lamer explained the denunciatory role of sentencing as follows:

> Retribution requires that a judicial sentence properly reflect the moral blameworthiness of that particular offender. The objective of denunciation mandates that a sentence should also communicate society's condemnation of that particular offender's conduct. In short, a sentence with a denunciatory element represents a symbolic, collective statement that the offender's conduct should be punished for encroaching on our society's basic code of values as enshrined within our substantive criminal law. As Lord Justice Lawton stated in *R v. Sargeant* (1974), 60 Cr. App. R 74, at p. 77: "[S]ociety, through the courts, must show its abhorrence of particular types of crime, and the only way in which the courts can show this is by the sentences they pass." The relevance of both retribution and denunciation as goals of sentencing underscores that our criminal justice system is not simply a vast system of negative penalties designed to prevent objectively harmful conduct by increasing the cost the offender must bear in committing an enumerated offence. Our criminal law is also a system of values. A sentence which expresses denunciation is simply the means by which these values are communicated. In short, in addition to attaching negative consequences to undesirable behaviour, judicial sentences should also be imposed in a manner which positively instills the basic set of communal values shared by all Canadians as expressed by the *Criminal Code*.

This recognizes that our criminal law is more than a system of negative sanctions; it is also a "system of values." While disapproval and abhorrence may be the values that need to be expressed in some cases, there are other values that cannot be excluded from the sentencing matrix. These include compassion, mercy, acknowledgment of hardship, maintaining the integrity of family, and encouraging hard work. These values can, in appropriate cases, present expressive needs that diminish what would otherwise be the required denunciatory element of a sentence.

The answer to "hard cases" requires more than simply an attempt to compare sympathetic personal factors with the need to express disapproval of an offence. The focus must be on whether the court, as the official spokesperson for the legal regime, needs to use this occasion to express its disapprobation of this conduct, or are there values that the court ought to be contemplating? Are there other principles or objectives of sentencing that might diminish the comparative significance of denunciation in this case?

The following is a framework that might be useful in dealing with hard cases and the elusive objective of denunciation:

1. *Gravity of the offence does not compel denunciation:* The facts of the offence, or the circumstances of the offender, may mean that a harsh, denunciatory sentence is unnecessary.

2. *Circumstances of offender make denunciatory objective unfair:* Here, the major issue is fairness as a reflection of the values of mercy and compassion. In other words, regardless of the claim for denunciation, is it unfair to make this offender the bearer of that message? The most common claim made is infirmity due to age, illness, or disability and the intrinsic hardship that custody would produce. A similar claim can arise from psychiatric disorders, including substance abuse, where the offender has sought treatment and participated cooperatively in treatment. A good example is the case of *R v. Jacobson*, a charge of producing and possession of marijuana for the purpose of trafficking. In this case, not only would custody have been "devastating" given the "fragile and precarious" mental state of the accused, but there was some reason to suspect that the depression and addiction had some bearing on the offence. This brings into play the "reduced gravity" claim raised above. A similar, albeit less compelling argument, can arise in the case of a youthful first offender. In *R v. Kutsukake*, the Ontario Court of Appeal reduced a 12-month custodial sentence for criminal negligence causing death to an 18-month conditional sentence. Sharpe JA commented that

> the only purpose to be served by requiring the appellant to serve her sentence in an institution would be denunciation of the unlawful conduct. That factor does not, in the circumstances of this case, outweigh the other factors that point to a conditional sentence. Moreover, I am of the view that denunciation of the unlawful conduct can be achieved without the appellant returning to jail. She has seen the inside of a prison and has served 41 days in custody. I am persuaded that an additional sentence to be served in the community under the conditions described below will serve as a sufficient denunciation of her conduct, consistent with the principles established in *Proulx*.

3. *Hardship to third party makes denunciatory objective unfair:* Again the value reflected here is fairness, and one of the best examples is in *R v. Bunn*, one of the companion cases to *Proulx*. There, a conditional sentence was approved in the case of a "breach of trust" theft by a lawyer. The offender was the sole caregiver to a disabled spouse. Custody for him would have produced considerable hardship for her.

4. *Denunciatory message can be expressed without custody:* The classic example is *Hallinsky*, a case that antedates the conditional sentence regime that involved an offender convicted of a driving offence after causing the death of his close friend. The offender be-

gan lecturing to high school students about the human effects on him and other survivors of his conduct. This was approved in *Proulx* and popped up again recently in *Kutsukake*. If the goal is to denounce, and perhaps even to deter others who are similarly situated, conveying the message directly is likely more effective than a judicial pronouncement within the walls of a courtroom. Counsel can be imaginative in attempting to replicate this process. The key is to identify the right audience and an appropriate method of reaching them that will demonstrate the offender's commitment to the message.

VI. SUPERVISION AND BREACH

Of central importance to the effectiveness of conditional sentencing are measures relating to supervision and breach. Indeed, in several jurisdictions sentencing judges have expressed reluctance to impose a conditional sentence unless and until provincial authorities invest greater resources in mechanisms for effective supervision of conditions.

The procedure and principles applicable in cases of alleged breach of conditions have proved problematic, and ss. 742.6 and 742.7 of the Code were amended in an attempt to clarify some of the difficulties (see SC 1999, c. 5 and SC 2004, c. 12). This matter has not been considered by the Supreme Court to date, but many of the relevant questions were addressed in *Whitty*, reproduced below. For further exposition of these issues, though written before the amendments of 1999, see the editorial "Breach of a Conditional Sentence by Allegedly Committing Another Offence" (1998), 3 *Can. Crim. LR* 1. Of course, a breach may occur for reasons other than commission of a new crime.

The general view now accepted is that an allegation of breach, even if allegedly by the commission of a new offence, leads to a renewal or revival of the original sentencing hearing. On this basis, it is preferable that the offender be brought before the original sentencing judge, but this is not obligatory. If the Crown establishes a breach on a balance of probabilities, the offender may seek to establish a reasonable excuse. Section 742.6(4) requires that an allegation of a breach be supported by the supervisor's report and that "where appropriate" this report should have as attachments the "signed statements of witnesses." It is not settled whether these witnesses must have first-hand knowledge of the facts constituting the alleged breach, and this issue is (at the time of writing) before the Supreme Court of Canada on appeal from *McIvor* (2006), 210 CCC (3d) 161 (BCCA).

In the absence of a reasonable excuse, the Crown may seek to vary the original sentencing order in any of the ways set out in s. 742.6(9), but typically by way of an order that the remainder of the term be served in jail. Such an order is not mandatory and the court at the breach hearing may decide to vary the conditions of the sentence instead.

The situation with regard to appeals from decisions at breach hearings is not entirely clear but the cases support several observations. If the Crown fails to prove a breach, there is no appeal because there is no statutory basis for it: see *Cross* (2004), 192 CCC (3d) (NSCA). The offender may appeal against either the finding that there was a breach or the variation of sentence ordered by the court. The premise for this is that the breach hearing is a continuation of the original sentencing.

R v. Whitty
(1999), 135 CCC (3d) 77 (Nfld. CA)

GUSHUE JA (Marshall JA concurring): The principal issue in this appeal is whether
s. 742.6(9) of the *Criminal Code of Canada* violates s. 7, s. 11(d) and/or s. 11(h) of the
Canadian Charter of Rights and Freedoms. The collateral issue raised at the trial level
was whether, if s. 742.6(9) does violate any or all of the above Charter provisions, it is
"saved" by s. 1 of the Charter?

Facts

Following the respondent's conviction of theft (s. 334) and of using a forged document
(s. 368(1)(c)), he was sentenced on September 9, 1996 to nine months' imprisonment
to be served conditionally. Included in the order was the mandatory condition requiring
the respondent "to keep the peace and be of good behaviour."

On March 25, 1997 the respondent was arrested and charged with assault (s. 266)
and two counts of uttering threats (s. 264.1(2)). The trial of these matters was scheduled
for June 5, 1997.

On April 15, 1997 the Crown applied, pursuant to s. 742.6 of the *Criminal Code*, to
have the conditional sentence varied on the ground that the respondent had breached a
term or terms of that sentence. The written allegation from the complainant was attached to a "conditional sentence report," which was filed. The complainant also testified at the hearing, as did the respondent. He denied having committed the offences
with which he was charged while serving the conditional sentence. Counsel for the respondent then applied to have s. 742.6(9) declared to be in contravention of ss. 7, 11(d)
and 11(h) of the Charter.

Following the hearing, in a written judgment, the trial judge concluded that
s. 742.6(9) violates s. 7 of the Charter, (1) by relieving the Crown of the burden of proof
beyond a reasonable doubt in establishing that a breach of the conditional sentence occurred; and (2) by placing an onus on the accused to establish a reasonable excuse, once
the Crown established a breach.

The Crown's s. 742.6 application was consequently dismissed and it is from that
decision that this appeal is taken.

• • •

Crown Argument

(a) Section 11

The Crown points out that s. 11(d) of the Charter protects the right of a person "charged
with an offence" to be presumed innocent. Thus the section is limited to those who have
been charged with a criminal offence. The Crown argues that to attempt to place a
s. 742.6 hearing within this category would require considerable expansion of the
wording. The respondent here was not charged with any new offence.

As to s. 11(h), the Supreme Court of Canada in *R v. Schmidt* (1987), 33 CCC (3d)
193, stated at page 211:

> The right is that of a person charged with an offence not to be tried for the offence again if he or she has already been finally acquitted of the offence.

In the present case, the Crown submits that the s. 742.6 application does not result in the respondent being charged with any offence.

Further, he would not be convicted or acquitted of any offence; nor is it proposed that he be punished or sentenced for any offence. The whole purpose of s. 742.6 is not to impose further punishment, but rather to ensure that the order that a period of imprisonment be served outside of a prison provides deterrence and protection of the public if the conditional sentence is not being complied with. The Crown relies on the case of *R v. Shubley*, [1990] 1 SCR 3, 52 CCC (3d) 481, where McLachlin J stated at p. 23:

> I conclude that the sanctions conferred on the superintendent for prison misconduct do not constitute "true penal consequences," within the Wigglesworth test. Confined as they are to the manner in which the inmate serves his time, and involving neither punitive fines nor a sentence of imprisonment, they appear to be entirely commensurate with the goal of fostering internal prison discipline and are not of the magnitude or consequence that would be expected for redressing wrongs done to society at large. Certainly the discipline meted to the appellant in this case is not such as to attract the application of s. 11(h).

(I would interject here that *R v. Wigglesworth*, [1987] 2 SCR 541, 37 CCC (3d) 385, stated that a matter could fall within s. 11 either because by its very nature it is a criminal proceeding or because a conviction could lead to a true penal consequence. Such would apply to an offence which is criminal in nature, even if such offence might carry only relatively minor consequences, e.g. a minor traffic offence. The headnote in *Wigglesworth* states that s. 11 applies to offences which are of a public nature, intended to promote public order and welfare within a public sphere of activity, as compared to matters which are private, domestic or disciplinary, which, although regulatory, protective or corrective, are primarily intended to maintain discipline, etc. All prosecutions for criminal offences under the *Criminal Code* and for quasi-criminal offences under Provincial legislation are automatically subject to s. 11, since they are the very kind of offences to which it was intended that s. 11 apply. A true penal consequence which would attract the application of s. 11 is imprisonment or a fine imposed for the purpose of redressing the wrong done to society at large, rather than maintaining internal discipline within a limited sphere of activity.)

Madam Justice McLachlin stated also in *Shubley*:

> Forfeiture of remission does not constitute the imposition of a sentence of imprisonment by the superintendent, but merely represents the loss of a privilege dependent on good behaviour ... cancellation of earned remission does not constitute punishment, but is rather the withholding of a reward.

The Crown argues that a decision under s. 742.6, which orders that the remainder of a sentence be served in the penitentiary, is not the further imposition of a period of imprisonment. The respondent is already serving a period of imprisonment. Rather, it is the place of imprisonment which is changed. Nor should it be assumed that incarceration is a greater form of punishment than a conditional sentence. The Crown concludes on this issue that s. 11 of the Charter has no application because the respondent is not charged with an offence. Wilson J, in *Wigglesworth* is quoted [at p. 558]: "[I]t is ... preferable to restrict s. 11 to the most serious offences known to our law, i.e., criminal and penal matters, and to leave other offences subject to the more flexible criteria of fundamental justice in s. 7."

Section 7

The Crown states that while proof beyond a reasonable doubt is an immutable Charter right when a person is charged with a criminal offence, it is not an immutable principle in every context. Thus, before considering the principles of fundamental justice there must first be a deprivation of "life, liberty or security." Such is not the case in a s. 742.6 application because no additional punishment can be imposed. The Crown draws an analogy between sections of the *Parole Act*, RSC 1985, c. P-2, which give the Parole Board the power to change the degree of supervision required, and counsel quotes from *R v. Evans* (1986), 30 CCC (3d) 313 (Ont. CA), where Robins JA stated at page 316: "These sections do not change the sentence imposed on the inmate by the court that convicted him and, consequently, do not impose an additional penalty." In our opinion, they do no more than change the manner or condition under which certain inmates must serve the balance of their sentence.

The Crown's submission is that a judge acting under a s. 742.6 application cannot impose a period of imprisonment. He or she can only vary the place in which it will be served. Thus, the respondent's liberty interests as protected by s. 7 of the Charter are not affected.

The Crown, in support of the proposition that not every deprivation of liberty is a violation of s. 7 and, further, that a standard of proof below a reasonable doubt does not by itself violate the Charter, quotes from *R v. Pearson* (1992), 77 CCC (3d) 124 (SCC), where Lamer CJC stated at page 136:

> This, of course, does not mean that there can be no deprivation of life, liberty or security of the person until guilt is established beyond reasonable doubt by the prosecution at trial [...] certain deprivations of liberty and security of the person may be in accordance with the principles of fundamental justice where there are reasonable grounds for doing so, rather than only after guilt has been established beyond a reasonable doubt. [...] While the presumption is pervasive in the criminal process, its particular requirements will vary according to the context in which it comes to be applied.

Lamer CJC, at page 137, added:

> Each of these cases may be seen as an example of the broad but flexible scope of the presumption of innocence as a principle of fundamental justice under s. 7 of the Charter. The principle does not necessarily require anything in the nature of proof beyond reasonable doubt, because the particular step in the process does not involve a determination of guilt. Precisely what is required depends upon the basic tenets of our legal system as exemplified by specific Charter rights, basic principles of penal policy as viewed in the light of "an analysis of the nature, sources, rationale and essential role of that principle within the judicial process and in our legal system, as it evolves."

The Crown maintains that an allegation that a conditional sentence is not being complied with cannot be equated with a criminal charge, nor indeed is it as serious as e.g., a decision to deny bail. Not only are the potential consequences to, in this case, the respondent markedly different, society must be ensured that those "imprisoned at home" are being deterred and are no more a danger than those who receive periods of "real imprisonment." There is no question that the onus is on the Crown to establish that the conditional sentence order was breached; however, there is no onus on the respondent at this stage and he is not convicted of anything by such a finding. There is no presumption of guilt. Indeed a s. 742.6 hearing commences with a presumption that the respondent has not breached the conditional sentence. Such presumption stands until the Crown establishes (on a balance of probabilities) that a breach occurred. Constitutional standards developed in the context of criminal charges cannot be applied automatically to s. 742.6 hearings.

The Crown concludes that s. 742.6 must be read in its entirety. It allows for a quick response (within 30 days maximum) to allegations of breaches of conditional sentences. While proof beyond a reasonable doubt is not required, the trial judge is granted flexibility unheard of when a criminal charge is involved because that judge can decide to "take no action" even when he or she is persuaded that a conditional sentence has been breached and no reasonable excuse exists.

To place this "onus" (if such it can be termed) on the respondent, particularly after the Crown has established the existence of a breach, is to afford an extra or additional benefit upon the respondent—not a burden.

I do not intend to deal with the submissions made with respect to the possible application of s. 1 of the Charter because, as will be seen, it is unnecessary for the disposition of the appeal.

The Crown concludes that it was open to Parliament to have created an offence section in the *Criminal Code* for breaches of conditional sentencing orders. Such would result in a criminal record for failing to comply and would also allow for additional periods of imprisonment to be imposed. Therefore, on balance, s. 742.6 appears to be a measured response in comparison, particularly when one considers the discretion granted to the judge "to take no action." As to the means being proportional to the objective, when one considers that the alternative is to turn the procedure into a criminal trial, the means utilized in s. 742.6 are deemed by the Crown to be quite proportionate.

In summary, the Crown states that if the purpose of the legislation is to be achieved, use of the reasonable doubt standard would be totally impractical because s. 742.6 hearings would become another and further criminal trial. Apart from the fact that the administrative burden would be a heavy one to bear, conditional sentences could be completed before such a hearing could be held thereby rendering any breach moot.

Respondent's Argument

Counsel for the respondent takes a diametrically opposed position to that taken by the Crown in respect of both s. 7 and 11 of the Charter.

(a) Section 11

In considering the *Wigglesworth* test, the respondent states that s. 742.6 is an offence under the "by nature" test because its purpose is to "regulate conduct within a limited sphere of activity." As to the "true penal consequence" test, the likelihood of imprisonment results in a breach of a conditional sentence order constituting an "offence." The respondent also states that the judicial determination of "guilt" or "innocence" of the breach places s. 742.6 within the context of a criminal offence that warrants s. 11 protection. The purpose of the penalty permitted under s. 742.6 is to redress the wrong done to society at large. Counsel appears to be saying that until a breach of condition occurs (which presumably means that such breach has been established as having occurred), the safety of the public is not in jeopardy, but may be considered to be as a result of such breach. The respondent visualizes a considerable difference between serving the sentence in the community, i.e. at home, and serving the sentence "within the confines of a correctional facility." He concludes from this that this change constitutes a true penal consequence pursuant to *Wigglesworth*. It is also submitted that the finding of a breach of a conditional sentence order is a finding of "guilt" by the court; therefore, the procedures under s. 742.6 constitute the respondent being charged with an offence within the meaning of s. 11 of the Charter.

As to s. 11(d) specifically, it is clear that the respondent starts with the premise that the respondent has been charged with an offence and that the establishing of a breach of his conditional sentence order implies a finding of guilt. A conditional sentence order is analogized as being "remarkably similar" to a probation order, as well as to a suspended sentence. In the former case a breach of probation must be proved beyond a reasonable doubt and counsel argues that the only difference between a suspended sentence and a conditional sentence order is one of semantics in that Parliament has omitted to use the word "offence" for breach of a conditional sentence order.

With respect to s. 11(h) of the Charter the respondent's submission here is that s. 742.6 places him at substantial risk of being tried and punished twice for the same offence. If he was found not to have breached the conditional sentence order, at a further criminal trial he may still have been convicted of the offence which constitutes a breach. Alternatively, if there is a finding that there has been a breach of the order and he is ordered to serve a period of time in custody, but yet is acquitted at trial, he would have been punished for an offence for which he was exonerated. It is the respondent's further argument that if he was found to have breached the conditional sentence order and convicted at trial, he would be sentenced twice for the same offence inasmuch as a concurrent sentence is not available in relation to conditional sentence orders.

(b) Section 7

The respondent submits that a breach of s. 11(d) and/or s. 11(h) of the Charter violates the principle of fundamental justice, thus breaching s. 7 as well. The concept of imprisonment (by which the respondent obviously means imprisonment in a prison or correctional facility) should not be imposed unless the accused person is fully protected by the principles of fundamental justice, i.e. proof beyond a reasonable doubt that the offence was committed. Otherwise, guilt of an accused person would be determined without that person having the benefit of a presumption of innocence.

The respondent also takes issue with the position of the Crown that the conditional sentencing regime cannot logically survive unless the provisions of s. 742.6 are permitted to stand. It is denied that there will be a substantial increase in the burden on the courts in scheduling. Further, even if efficiency and usefulness are affected, they are nevertheless less pressing objectives than that of deprivation of liberty; the "rational connection" to expediency and efficiency cannot override the lack of "rational connection" to protecting the accused person.

Analysis

I am in substantial agreement with the submissions of the Crown generally, and fully subscribe to the statement that the respondent was not charged with any new offence. In order to deal with the actual issue in this matter, it is important to first understand the nature of a conditional sentence order.

· · ·

Section 742.1 appears deceptively simple. It is not simple. It is an alternate sentencing regime. Where an offender is convicted of an offence, the trial judge must first consider whether there should be a term of imprisonment. If the judge is of the opinion that, given the principles of sentencing, the nature of the offence and the antecedents of the offender, there ought to be a fine, or a suspension of sentence, or if there should be imprisonment and that imprisonment should exceed two years, s. 742.1 has no application. If, however, the judge is of the view that there should be a sentence of imprisonment and such sentence should be less than two years, it is then incumbent upon the judge to consider whether that sentence is to be served in prison or whether, having been satisfied that the requirements of s. 742.1(b) have been met, he or she will order the offender to serve the sentence "in the community" (which would normally mean at home), subject to conditions, both mandatory and optional. While the judge obviously must take s. 742.1 into consideration, the decision as to whether or not a conditional sentence is to be imposed is solely within his or her discretion.

Several points are immediately apparent. A conditional sentence is not the same as the suspension of sentence and probation. In the latter, the judge makes a decision that there will be no period of imprisonment on the mandatory undertaking by the offender that, for a period of time of up to three years, he will comply with certain prescribed conditions. If during the probation period the Crown takes the view that a condition of probation has been breached by the offender, the separate criminal charge of breach of probation may be laid and, if established, which would have to be on the basis of proof beyond a reasonable doubt, then the original sentence is also open for reassessment and a possible term of imprisonment. It is apparent that any such breach would be one having true penal consequences, as referred to in *Wigglesworth*.

Contrary to the position put forward by the respondent, such is not the case with a conditional sentence. Section 742.1 clearly states that a conditional sentence is a term of imprisonment—one that is being served in the community rather than behind prison bars. As noted earlier, the trial judge appears also to have been of the view that a conditional sentence is not a sentence of imprisonment because there is no deprivation of the liberty of the offender. This runs counter to what has been already stated by this Court in various cases, including *R v. W.(L.F.)* (1997), 119 CCC (3d) 97, *R v. Oliver* (1997),

147 Nfld. & PEIR 210, *R v. Quilty* (1997), 156 Nfld. & PEIR 320, and *R v. M.(J.)* (1998), 160 Nfld. & PEIR 38. Indeed, these cases state that because s. 742.1 makes reference specifically to the conditional sentence being a term of imprisonment, a curtailment of the offender's liberty in some manner, e.g. house confinement, is an essential and necessary ingredient of a conditional sentence. As pointed out by Green JA in *M.(J.)*, the conditions imposed must, in the circumstances, accomplish a "roughly equivalent deterrent effect." Green JA further added that:

> … a conditional sentence can have the potential of imposing greater restrictions on liberty than would a comparable term of incarceration. As such, it need not be regarded as a more lenient type of punishment in a specific case. It is, rather, a different form of punishment designed to achieve the same sentencing objectives.

Thus, the conditional sentence, when imposed, is one having true penal consequences. A sentencing judge, having been satisfied, at least at that stage, that society or the community will not be endangered if the offender is required to serve the sentence in the community, makes such a disposition and imposes certain terms and conditions which must be complied with by the offender. Apart from the compulsory conditions provided for in s. 742.3, one of which is to keep the peace and be of good behaviour, certain optional conditions may also be added to suit the circumstances.

A summary of what occurs after a breach of any condition is alleged to have occurred is set out at paragraphs 10 and 11 above. A full reading of s. 742.6 shows clearly that the offender's interests are stringently protected and that even if a breach is established, on a balance of probabilities, to have occurred, considerable discretion is afforded the judge in arriving at the remedy. Obviously, the disposition would be governed by the nature of the breach and, particularly, whether the breach leads the judge to revisit the original finding that a conditional sentence for that offender would not endanger the safety of the community and, as well, to revisit whether, in light of what has happened, a conditional sentence would continue to be consistent with general sentencing principles.

As has been stated, the aspect of s. 742.6(9)(a) with which exception is taken, and which the trial judge found to be flawed, is that the Crown need only demonstrate on a balance of probabilities that a breach has occurred.

Both the appellant and the respondent rely on *Wigglesworth* to support their respective positions and those arguments are set out above. As seen, that decision of the Supreme Court of Canada stated that a matter could fall within s. 11 of the Charter either because by its very nature it is a criminal proceeding or because a conviction could lead to a true penal consequence. It has been concluded that because a sentence in the form of a term of imprisonment has been imposed, there has already been a true penal consequence to the respondent. The original proceeding was also by its nature a criminal one. I agree with the Crown, however, that the procedure under s. 742.6 cannot be so categorized. The respondent having already been sentenced to imprisonment, this hearing is one aimed only at determining whether changed circumstances should lead to a variation of the manner in which that imprisonment should be served. It is not a further criminal charge.

The approach taken by the trial judge, however, would have the "de facto" effect of turning the s. 742.6 hearing into a criminal trial—one requiring proof beyond a reasonable doubt of the breach. Yet it is not a criminal trial. The breaching of a conditional sentence order is not a criminal offence, as a breach of a probation order would be. Obviously, the alleged breach could amount to a criminal offence, as would appear to be the case here, but it is just as obvious that a breach could (and undoubtedly usually would) be something less. It is also important to note that even if a criminal offence is alleged to have occurred as a result of the breach, something far less that the commission of such offence, e.g. preliminary acts leading up to the ultimate act, would be sufficient to establish a breach of a condition to keep the peace and be of good behaviour.

It cannot be overlooked as well that the trial judge's approach of requiring proof beyond a reasonable doubt of any breach would likely decimate the conditional sentence regime. The simple and expeditious procedure currently contained in the legislation for dealing with a breach would be replaced by what would be in effect another criminal trial—many of which trials would not be heard until after the original sentence was served.

One could well say that the sentencing process as contemplated by the conditional sentencing legislation is intended to be a continuous process, rather than an "all or nothing" approach. The sentencing court, in agreeing to impose a conditional sentence, makes the best assessment it can on the information available at the sentencing hearing, while attempting to ensure that such sentence will be consistent with general sentencing principles. However, unlike other sentences, it is not a final disposition. If, subsequently, there is a failure to abide by the conditions of the order, the court is then presented with further information on which it may make a more informed decision. Having assessed such information, the court may decide that sentencing principles can only be complied with by the serving of the remainder of the sentence in prison. Thus, that decision is reached based on actual experience, rather than speculation at the original hearing as to the likelihood of the offender complying with conditions. As stated, even if a breach is established, the court does not have to order a jail term. Even with the new information, a conditional sentence may still be consistent with sentencing principles.

In summary, the respondent was not charged with a further offence. All that was being sought by the Crown was "… a change in the form in which (his) sentence is served (which), whether it be favourable or unfavourable to the prisoner, is not, in itself, contrary to any principle of fundamental justice" (per McLachlin J in *Cunningham v. Canada* (1993), 80 CCC (3d) 492 (SCC) at p. 499). In other words, we are dealing with an application to vary a sentence. I see no breach of the respondent's rights under either s. 7 or 11 of the Charter. The guilt or innocence of the respondent was no longer at issue and no further punishment was being sought. There existed therefore no requirement for proof beyond a reasonable doubt of any breach alleged to have been committed. Emphasis must further be placed on the powers granted the judge in s. 742.6(9) to accept a "reasonable excuse" as an answer to a breach, and in subsection (a) of that section to "take no action" in any event. Such powers are not granted a judge in dealing with a criminal offence.

All of the above leads me to the conclusion that the appeal must succeed. The trial judge's order dismissing the Crown's application is set aside and the matter is remitted to Provincial Court for continuation of the hearing under s. 742.6(9) of the *Criminal Code*.

O'NEILL JA (dissenting): I have read in draft the decision of my brother Gushue JA and, with respect, I am unable to agree with his disposition of this matter.

On September 9, 1996 the respondent was sentenced to a term of imprisonment of nine months and the trial judge, under s. 742.1 of the *Criminal Code*, ordered that the sentence be served conditionally. No conditions other than the compulsory conditions under s. 742.3(1) were prescribed.

On March 25, 1997, during the term of the conditional sentence, the respondent was charged with assault and two counts of uttering threats which were alleged to have occurred during the term of the conditional sentence. The charges were laid following a complaint by his estranged wife and her boyfriend. The trial of these matters was scheduled for June 5, 1997, at around the same time that the term of the conditional sentence would end.

On March 31, 1997, a conditional sentence report was filed alleging a breach of condition. Attached to the conditional sentence report was a statement from the complainant setting out details of the alleged offences which were alleged to constitute the breach of condition. The Crown applied to have the respondent's conditional sentence varied. At the hearing, the respondent's wife gave evidence as did the respondent. He denied having committed the offences.

The conditional sentence being served by the respondent would have ended, as already noted, in June 1997, unless, during the term of the conditional sentence, he was sentenced to a term of imprisonment for another offence, in which case the running of the conditional sentence would be suspended during the period of imprisonment for that other offence, unless otherwise ordered by the court under s. 742.4(3) or 742.6(9): see s. 742.7. Section 742.7 contemplates a situation where an offender, during the term of the conditional sentence, is convicted and imprisoned for another offence, whenever committed, which would, of course, include the period that the offender is "at large" under the conditional sentence order.

The respondent applied to the judge hearing the application to have s. 742.6(9) of the *Criminal Code* declared to be in contravention of ss. 7, 11(d) and 11(h) of the *Canadian Charter of Rights and Freedoms* and argued that s. 742.6(9) could not be saved under s. 1 of the Charter.

The judge concluded that s. 742.6(9) violated s. 7 of the Charter: (1) by relieving the Crown of the burden of proof beyond a reasonable doubt in establishing that a breach of the conditional sentence occurred, and (2) by placing an onus on the offender to establish a reasonable excuse once the Crown established the breach. He also concluded that s. 742.6(9) is not saved by s. 1 of the Charter. The Crown's application was dismissed.

The Crown appeals to this Court and seeks the allowing of the appeal, a declaration that the constitutionality of s. 742.6 of the *Criminal Code* be confirmed and an order that the matter be remitted to the Provincial Court for a new hearing.

The Issues on Appeal

The issues argued before the trial judge and on the appeal to this Court were whether the onus on the Crown being that of "on a balance of probabilities," and the onus on the offender with respect to "without reasonable excuse, the proof of which lies on the offender," violate the Charter.

The Imposition of a Conditional Sentence Under Section 742.1 and the
Nature of the Proceeding Under Section 742.6(9)

· · ·

To have decided on a sentence of imprisonment, it must be assumed that the sentencing judge had decided that, consistent with the objectives and principles of sentencing as set out in ss. 718 and 718.2 of the *Criminal Code*, which, of course are applicable to sentencing of any type, a fit sentence is a term of imprisonment. If that sentence is less than two years, and there being no minimum term of imprisonment with respect to that offence, the sentencing judge must then consider whether he is satisfied that the sentence, if served in the community, would not endanger the safety of the community and would still be consistent with the objectives and principles in ss. 718 and 718.2 already referred to. If so satisfied, the sentencing judge may order that the offender serve the sentence in the community subject to the offender's complying with the compulsory conditions set out in s. 742.3(1) and such further optional conditions if any, under s. 742.3(2), as the judge may prescribe. At the same time, the sentencing judge will have been aware of the procedures which may become applicable under ss. 742.4 and 742.6, the former dealing with changes which may be made to the optional conditions following upon a change of circumstances, and the latter setting out the powers of the court following an allegation that there has been a breach of a condition.

It will be helpful to examine the status of the offender who has been ordered to serve his sentence in the community.

There is a body of judicial thought to the effect that the references to "serving the sentence in the community" and "serve the sentence in the community" in s. 742.1 should, in effect, be read as if the words "of imprisonment" appeared after the word "sentence" in each. With due respect to those who hold a contrary view, it is, in my view, an error to construe the status of an offender serving a conditional sentence as one serving a term of imprisonment. Indeed, the sentencing judge, in the imposition of a conditional sentence, has made a very important and far reaching decision in concluding that the offender need not serve the sentence in prison, or "in custody" as that term is used in s. 742.6(9).

Section 742.6 sets out the procedure to be followed and the powers of a court where a breach of a condition of a conditional sentence order is alleged. Section 742.6(9) is as follows:

Powers of court 742.6(9)

Where the court is satisfied, on a balance of probabilities, that the offender has without reasonable excuse, the proof of which lies on the offender, breached a condition of the conditional sentence order, the court may

    (a) take no action;

    (b) change the optional conditions;

    (c) suspend the conditional sentence order and direct

        (i) that the offender serve in custody a portion of the unexpired sentence, and

        (ii) that the conditional sentence order resume on the offender's release from custody, either with or without changes to the optional conditions; or

    (d) terminate the conditional sentence order and direct that the offender be committed to custody until the expiration of the sentence.

Counsel for the Crown argued that the onus on the Crown to establish a breach of condition only on a balance of probabilities was appropriate because, under the legislation, an offender alleged to have committed a breach of the conditional order is not charged with a criminal offence and, therefore, the criminal standard is not required nor is it appropriate. Further, the Crown argued that once the Crown has established, on the balance of probabilities, that a condition had been breached, it was not unreasonable that the onus be on the offender to establish a reasonable excuse for having committed the breach.

In support of its position, the Crown argued that s. 742.6 is designed to allow for a simple and expeditious procedure for dealing with breaches of conditional sentences. It also points to the requirement that since a hearing with respect to any allegation of a breach must be held within thirty days, then, where the conditional sentence is a short one, or where a significant period of the conditional sentence has been completed, the offender would face no penalty since a hearing based on the criminal standard of proof could not reasonably be expected to be conducted within the required time. Crown counsel argued that it is the section's simplicity and flexibility which are its keys.

The Crown argued as well that when a "conditional sentence turns out not to be appropriate," presumably when a breach has occurred, the public should know that there is a quick and expeditious procedure for dealing with it. In that context, the Crown argued that the trial judge's decision here would have a devastating effect on conditional sentence procedures and would endanger the public's acceptance of conditional sentences and the courts' ability to have confidence in ordering them.

In any consideration of s. 742.6, one must look at the very real and broad powers which the court has under s. 742.6(9)(c) and (d) which could involve the actual imprisonment of the offender for a long period of time. This power is all the more far reaching when one considers that the usual remission benefits may not be available to an offender who has been ordered, under s-ss. (c) and (d), to serve any part of the conditional sentence period in custody. Still important, but to a lesser extent, is the power given to the court under s-ss. (b) and (c) to change the optional conditions, which could result in serious restrictions on the offender's liberty such as the equivalent of house arrest or strict curfews. The powers of the court under s. 742.9 become all the more significant here where, as noted earlier, the offender, when placed on the conditional sentence, was only made subject to the compulsory conditions as set out in s. 742.3(1).

The fact that the court may "take no action," as contemplated by s. 742.6(9)(a), does not in any way take away from these broad powers. This option permits the application, in appropriate cases, of the principle of "*de minimis non curat lex*" which has been part of the criminal law in many jurisdictions for years. At the same time, s. 742.6(9)(a) permits a trial judge to conclude that, notwithstanding the breach, which may be a serious one, a court may conclude that a continuation of the conditional sentence as originally set may still be consistent with sentencing principles and can be justified in the particular circumstances.

The Applicability of Section 11 of the Charter

Sections 11(d) and (h) of the Charter are as follows:

> 11. Any person charged with an offence has the right. ...
>
> (d) to be presumed innocent until proven guilty according to law in a fair and public hearing by an independent and impartial tribunal; ...
>
> (h) if finally acquitted of the offence, not to be tried for it again and, if finally found guilty and punished for the offence, not to be tried or punished for it again.

The trial judge did not rule that s. 11 applied nor did he rely on it in reaching his decision. In fact, the trial judge concluded that "it seems doubtful that s. 11 of the Charter has application." However, the issue as to the applicability of s. 11 was argued on the appeal to this Court.

Crown counsel takes the position that Parliament has deliberately chosen not to create an offence for the breaching of a conditional sentence order. In support of this position, it was argued that a s. 742.6 hearing does not involve a decision on the guilt or innocence of an offender, nor can any additional punishment be imposed on the offender following a finding that there was a breach.

This argument has its basis in the position taken by Crown counsel that the offender is actually serving a sentence of imprisonment in the community, and, although the form of imprisonment can be changed, there can be no additional punishment imposed. Indeed, in his argument, Crown counsel, perhaps disingenuously, refers to a person serving a conditional sentence as being "an inmate." (*Black's Law Dictionary*, 6th ed., describes "inmate" as "a person confined to a prison, penitentiary or the like." There are other definitions of "inmate" in *Black's* but none is of any relevance here.)

The following excerpts are from the appellant's factum with respect to ss. 11(d) and (h) of the Charter and succinctly set out its position: ss. 11(d) and (h) of the Charter require that the person is charged with an offence. In this case that essential prerequisite is missing. Parliament has specifically chosen not to create an offence for breaching a conditional sentence order. An "inmate" who has breached a conditional sentence, unlike a person on probation, for instance, has previously been found to have committed an offence for which a period of imprisonment was deemed appropriate. The serving of the sentence in the community does not alter the nature of the sentence. Therefore, s. 742.6 of the Code creates a procedural mechanism for dealing with "inmates" who are serving their sentence in the community. The standard of reasonable doubt has no application. ... A decision under s. 742.6, ordering that the remainder of a sentence be served in a penitentiary, is not the imposition of a period of imprisonment. The Respondent is already serving the period of imprisonment. It is the place of imprisonment which is changed. It should not be assumed that incarceration is a greater form of punishment than a conditional sentence.

In the result, it was Crown counsel's position that s. 11 of the Charter has no application since it provides a right to the criminal standard and onus of proof only when a person is charged with a criminal offence and further, that an order under s. 742.6(9) of the *Criminal Code* cannot result in the imposition of a period of imprisonment.

For the respondent, it was argued that the procedure set out in s. 742.6 of the *Criminal Code* for the revocation of a conditional sentence constitutes, in effect, an offender "being charged with an offence" as that phrase is used in s. 11 of the Charter.

In his argument, counsel for the respondent referred to *R v. Wigglesworth* (1987), 60 CR (3d) 193, 37 CCC (3d) 385 (SCC), where Wilson J, for the majority in the Supreme Court of Canada, set out a two-part test to determine whether a matter constituted an offence pursuant to s. 11. At pp. 209-210 she said: "... a matter could fall within s. 11 either because by its very nature it is a criminal proceeding or because a conviction in respect of the offence may lead to a true penal consequence."

. . .

Although framed differently in the legislation, I have difficulty in seeing that the procedure to deal with alleged breaches of conditions of conditional sentence orders should be any different than the procedures to be applied with respect to breaches of probation, where the orders of probation in respect of same were made as part of a conditional discharge, an intermittent sentence, or a suspended sentence, or where a probation order was made along with a fine or a term of imprisonment. In each of these situations, the breach must be proved beyond a reasonable doubt just as any other criminal offence and there is no onus of any kind on the accused.

In my view, the magnitude of the options open to the court in s. 742.6(9)(c) and (d), is severe enough to warrant the protection granted by s. 11. The options include, not merely a change in the method of serving a sentence—the position argued by the Crown—but the committal of the offender to a corrections facility for all or part of the term remaining in the sentence imposed and the consequences following upon that term of imprisonment. In my view, the powers given to the judge subject the offender to "true penal consequences" and demand that the offender, following an allegation of a breach of condition, be given the full protection of s. 11(d) of the Charter which would require that the Court be satisfied beyond a reasonable doubt that a breach has occurred.

Having concluded that s. 742.6(9) is in breach of s. 11(d) of the Charter, I will not be dealing with whether it is also in breach of s. 11(h) of the Charter.

Does Section 742.6(9) Breach Section 7 of the Charter?

Section 7 of the Charter is as follows:

> 7. Everyone has the right to life, liberty and security of the person and the right not to be deprived thereof except in accordance with the principles of fundamental justice.

Clearly, inherent in the "principles of fundamental justice" is the right to be presumed innocent and only to be convicted of an offence upon proof beyond a reasonable doubt. As argued by counsel for the respondent, s. 7 defines the parameters of fundamental justice—life, liberty and security of the person—and these can only be taken away if the principles of fundamental justice are applied to the procedure which could result in any of these being taken away.

With respect to s. 7 of the Charter, the Crown repeats its position that in a s. 742.6 hearing application, no additional punishment can be imposed, and the duration of the restriction on the offender's liberty is not affected—there is no additional penalty.

Crown counsel takes that argument further and says that an offender subjected to a s. 742.6 hearing faces no risk of imprisonment, since the offender is already serving the period of imprisonment that had been imposed earlier. Crown counsel, however, admits that *Cunningham v. Canada*, [1993] 2 SCR 143, 80 CCC (3d) 492, may be authority for concluding that the power of the court under s. 742.6(9)(c) and (d) to vary the place or form of imprisonment does affect the offender's liberty interests as protected by s. 7 of the Charter.

In *Cunningham*, the appellant had been serving a twelve-year term of imprisonment. Under the *Parole Act* in force at the time of his sentencing, he would be entitled to be released on mandatory supervision after serving approximately two-thirds of the sentence, provided he was of good behaviour. During his term of imprisonment, the *Parole Act* was amended to allow the Commissioner of Corrections, within six months of the "presumptive release date," to refer a case to the National Parole Board, where he has reason to believe that the inmate is likely, prior to the expiration of his sentence, to commit an offence causing death or serious harm, and the Parole Board could, if it saw fit, delay the inmate's release. The appellant was ordered to be detained until his sentence expired, subject to annual review. McLachlin J for the Court, in discussing whether the appellant had suffered a deprivation of liberty which would attract the protection of s. 7 of the Charter, said at p. 148: "In my view, the appellant has shown that he has been deprived of liberty. The argument that because the appellant was sentenced to 12 years' imprisonment there can be no further impeachment of his liberty interest within the 12-year period runs counter to previous pronouncements, and oversimplifies the concept of liberty." This and other courts have recognized that there are different types of liberty interests in the context of correctional law. In *Dumas v. Leclerc Institute*, [1986] 2 SCR 459, at p. 464, Lamer J (as he then was) identified three different deprivations of liberty: (1) The initial deprivation of liberty; (2) a substantial change in conditions amounting to a further deprivation of liberty; and (3) a continuation of the deprivation of liberty.

Later, on p. 150, McLachlin J continued: "… the manner in which he may serve a part of that sentence, the second liberty interest identified by Lamer J in *Dumas*, supra, has been affected. One has more liberty, or a better quality of liberty, when one is serving time on mandatory supervision than when one is serving time in prison."

McLachlin J concluded that the appellant by virtue of the change in the Parole Regulations had "suffered deprivation of liberty." At p. 151, she said: "The change in the manner in which the sentence was served in this case meets this test. There is a significant difference between life inside a prison versus the greater liberty enjoyed on the outside under mandatory supervision. Such a change was recognized as worthy of s. 7 protection in *Gamble* [[1988] 1 SCR 595]."

Although on the particular facts in *Cunningham*, the Court ruled that the appellant had not established that the changes to the *Parole Act* deprived him of his liberty contrary to the principles of fundamental justice, the case does make clear that a change in the way a sentence is to be served can attract s. 7 protection. This Court in *R v. Lambert* [93 CCC (3d) 88 at pp. 94-95] considered the implications of s. 743.6(1) of the *Criminal Code* which permits a judge to order that an accused serve one-half of his sentence before eligibility for parole. There, Crown counsel had argued that the making of an order under s. 741.2 was not part of the punishment or sentence imposed for the offence but was merely the fixing of the parole eligibility period. The Court stated:

> [P]ostponing the eligibility date for full parole, thereby creating a veiled warning and risk of a longer period of incarceration, on any reasonable interpretation is an additional price or disadvantage for a prisoner. It is obviously an extra burden to be endured. Unquestionably, the section 741.2 order adversely affected the appellant. It is true that the four-year "sentence" remains the same, but the order giving rise to a potentially longer period of imprisonment, or at least to an extended span of strict supervision and control, means an escalation of the sanction or punishment for the offence. The variation in the "manner" in which the sentence is to be served clearly entails a more "severe treatment."

Lambert does not raise any Charter question because the order under s. 741.2 being considered was made by the sentencing judge when the sentence was imposed and he was empowered under s. 743.6(1) to make that order as part of the sentence. However, *Lambert* clearly recognizes the principle that the way in which a sentence is being served "might indicate an escalation of the sanction or punishment" and a more "severe treatment."

Here, as already noted, the respondent, on being ordered to serve his sentence conditionally, was only placed on the compulsory conditions set out in s. 742.3(1) of the *Criminal Code*.

• • •

I should add that no probation order was made to follow the period of the conditional sentence imposed on the offender.

Obviously, the trial judge in concluding that the conditional sentence was appropriate saw no need for any further conditions which might in any way fetter or restrict the liberty of the offender. That decision would have been made by the trial judge after a consideration of all the facts which would of course have been proved beyond a reasonable doubt.

Whether a Breach of Condition Hearing Is a Sentencing Hearing

In concluding that s. 742.6(9) breached s. 7 of the Charter, the trial judge said:

> [T]he breach procedure is really a continuation of the original sentencing process and not a separate administrative procedure akin to a parole hearing. Consequently the application of a different burden of proof (balance of probabilities) and the imposition of an obligation on the accused to show reasonable excuse for the breach is not in keeping with the principles of fairness and fundamental justice. This finding is reinforced considering that the consequences to the accused can range from immediate termination of his conditional sentence to the changing of the optional conditions. The optional conditions can involve the addition of community service hours, attendance at treatment programs, or "any other reasonable conditions." It is difficult to conceive of the imposition of any of these consequences as not being an interference with the liberty of the accused. The accused serving a conditional sentence of imprisonment is more than just an extra-mural prisoner, he is outside the walls as a result of a judicial determination that service of his sentence can be achieved in all its aspects both denunciatory and rehabilitative without the necessity of

incarcerating him. It stands to reason therefore that a change to this determination requires more than the application of a purely administrative function. I find therefore that s. 742.6(9) requirements relieving the prosecution of the burden of proof beyond a reasonable doubt and the imposition on the accused of the onus to show reasonable excuse does contravene s. 7 of the Charter.

Section 673 of the *Criminal Code* states that "sentence" includes an order made under s. 742.3. In my view, any change which may be made to a conditional sentence order, by way of: (1) a change in the optional conditions, (2) the suspension of the conditional sentence, which could direct the offender to serve in custody any part of the unexpired sentence, with or without changes to the conditions, or (3) by terminating the conditional sentence order and directing that the offender serve the balance of the sentence in custody, results in a change, and potentially, a very substantial change, in the sentence being served by the offender.

In *R v. Gardiner* (1982), 68 CCC (2d) 477 (SCC), Dickson J, in discussing the principles of sentencing, said at pp. 513-514: "One of the hardest tasks confronting a trial judge is sentencing. The stakes are high for society and for the individual. Sentencing is the critical stage of the criminal justice system, and it is manifest that the judge should not be denied an opportunity to obtain relevant information by the imposition of all the restrictive evidential rules common to a trial. Yet the obtaining and weighing of such evidence should be fair. A substantial liberty interest of the offender is involved and the information obtained should be accurate and reliable."

And later on p. 514:

> To my mind, the facts which justify the sanction are no less important than the facts which justify the conviction; both should be subject to the same burden of proof. Crime and punishment are inextricably linked. "It would appear well established that the sentencing process is merely a phase of the trial process."

And later at p. 515:

> In my view, both the informality of the sentencing procedure as to the admissibility of evidence and the wide discretion given to the trial judge in imposing sentence are factors militating in favour of the retention of the criminal standard of proof beyond a reasonable doubt at sentencing: "[B]ecause the sentencing process poses the ultimate jeopardy to an individual enmeshed in the criminal process, it is just and reasonable that he be granted the protection of the reasonable doubt rule at this vital juncture of the process." The rationale of the argument of the Crown for the acceptance of a lesser standard of proof is administrative efficiency. In my view, however, the administrative efficiency argument is not sufficient to overcome such a basic tenet suffusing our entire criminal justice system as the standard of proof beyond a reasonable doubt. I am by no means convinced that if the standard of proof were lowered, conservation of judicial resources would be enhanced .... There would seem in principle no good reason why the sentencing judge in deciding disputed facts should not observe the same evidentiary standards as we demand of juries.

In my view, the same principles which governed the trial judge in considering the appropriate disposition of the matter following trial, should equally apply if any change is to be made in how the sentence is to be served. The alleged breach giving rise to the application by the Crown, whether that breach, in itself, would constitute a criminal offence, should be proved beyond a reasonable doubt as in any sentencing hearing such as this, in reality, is, albeit an extended one, but nevertheless contemplated by the legislation.

Clearly a sanction, by way of increased punishment, is being sought by the Crown and it follows, in my view, that the facts necessary to ground a change in the sentence must be proved beyond a reasonable doubt just as any facts which may be relied on by the Crown in the original sentencing hearing to support a particular sentence must be proved beyond a reasonable doubt.

Because, to use the words of Dickson J in *Gardiner*, "a substantial liberty interest of the offender is involved … ," then any facts which may be relied on by the Crown to change the manner in which the sentence is being served, should be proved beyond a reasonable doubt.

Can Section 742.6(9) Be Saved by Section 1 of the Charter?

Section 1 of the Charter is as follows:

> 1. The *Canadian Charter of Rights and Freedoms* guarantees the rights and freedoms set out in it subject only to such reasonable limits prescribed by law as can be demonstrably justified in a free and democratic society.

In his decision, the trial judge reviewed the relevant law with respect to whether s. 742.6(9) could be saved by s. 1 of the Charter, including *R v. Laba* (1994), 34 CR (4th) 360, 94 CCC (3d) 385 (SCC), where Sopinka J set out the Oakes test (*R v. Oakes*, [1986] 1 SCR 103, 24 CCC (3d) 321) at p. 390:

> Taking into account the modification suggested by the Chief Justice in his reasons in *Dagenais v. Canadian Broadcasting Corp.* [34 CR (4th) 269 (SCC)], released concurrently herewith … the test can be stated as follows: 1) In order to be sufficiently important to warrant overriding a constitutionally protected right or freedom the impugned provision must relate to concerns which are pressing and substantial in a free and democratic society; 2) The means chosen to achieve the legislative objective must pass a three-part proportionality test which requires that they (a) be rationally connected to the objective, (b) impair the right or freedom in question as little as possible and (c) have deleterious effects which are proportional to both their salubrious effects and the importance of the objective which has been identified as being of "sufficient importance."

The trial judge reviewed the impugned legislation in the light of that test and referred specifically to the second step in the inquiry as set out by Sopinka J at p. 392 of *Laba*:

> The second step in the inquiry into whether an impugned provision is a proportional means of achieving a given end is to determine whether the government has demonstrated that the provision impairs constitutionally protected rights or freedoms as little as possible. This usually involves determining whether alternative means of achieving the objective were available to Parliament.

The trial judge concluded that s. 742.6(9) is not saved by s. 1 of the Charter. He said:

> In drafting s. 742.6(9), Parliament could have chosen to leave the burden of proof as beyond a reasonable doubt and not placed an onus on the accused to show reasonable excuse. In examining the mandatory conditions of a conditional sentence, reporting when required, remaining within the jurisdiction of the court and notifying the court of any change of address, these are clearly all matters which would seem to be easily proven in the event of a breach of any of them. Likewise, the optional conditions seem by and large the sort of allegations that would be easily proven. Consequently it is very difficult to see why there would be any logical reason to lessen the burden of proof or shift the onus to the accused. There is no obvious practical advantage in doing this and no apparent justification for the impairment of the right of the accused to the usual burden of proof in a criminal proceeding. In the case at bar, the situation is especially problematic in that what is alleged is a separate criminal offence that forms the basis for the alleged breach. In this case the accused is clearly at a severe disadvantage on the facts before me in that the Crown need only prove the allegation on a balance of probabilities and in so doing is relying on the largely uncorroborated allegation of a single witness. There is little the accused can do in the face of such a process when the threshold for the prosecution to meet is reduced to this level. The Crown has not demonstrated in this case that Parliament has chosen the alternative which impairs s. 7 as little as is reasonably possible.

I agree with the reasoning of the trial judge and in his conclusion that s. 742.6(9) contravenes s. 7 and is not saved by s. 1 of the Charter.

Conclusion

As to the disposition of the matter by the trial judge, the Crown argued that there was no basis for dismissing the Crown's application since the finding of unconstitutionality related only to the question of onus, and a consideration of the merits of the application, regardless of onus, was and is a separate issue. The Crown argued that the trial judge, having reached a decision on the constitutional issue, should still have considered the Crown's application to determine if a breach had been established and what order if any should issue. I do not deem it necessary to specifically deal with this matter in light of the decision of this Court that the matter be remitted to the Provincial Court for continuation of the hearing.

In my opinion, the trial judge was not in error in concluding that s. 742.6(9) of the *Criminal Code* contravenes s. 7 and is not saved by s. 1 of the *Canadian Charter of Rights and Freedoms*. I would dismiss the appeal.

Appeal allowed.

CONDITIONAL SENTENCING: CRITICAL RESEARCH FINDINGS

Since the creation of the conditional sentence in 1996, a considerable amount of research has been conducted into the penal innovation of allowing an offender to serve a term of imprisonment in the community. National data on the use of conditional sentences of imprisonment are still not available. The following points summarize the principal findings from research to date; additional references are provided at the end of the chapter for readers interested in more detail.

Has the conditional sentence of imprisonment achieved its goal of reducing the number of sentenced admissions to custody?

An analysis of provincial correctional statistics reveals that conditional sentencing has had a significant impact on the rates of admissions to custody, which have declined by 13 percent since the introduction of conditional sentencing. This represents a reduction of approximately 55,000 offenders who otherwise would have been admitted to custody. However, there was also evidence of "net widening": over all jurisdictions included in the analysis, 5,399 offenders who prior to 1996 would have received a non-custodial sanction were sentenced to a conditional sentence, which is a form of custody. Considerable variation emerged between provinces: in some jurisdictions, net widening was quite significant; in other provinces, the opposite occurred. The reduction in the number of sentenced admissions to provincial correctional institutions has, to a large degree, been offset by an increase in the use of remand detention in recent years. Over the past decade the number of adults in remand increased by 83 percent. Nevertheless it is clear that over the decade since the introduction of conditional sentencing, many thousands of offenders have been able to serve their terms of custody in the community rather than a provincial correctional facility.

How many people are serving a conditional sentence on any given day?

The average count of people serving a conditional sentence in 2004-5 (the most recent year for which data are available) was 18,916. The average count of offenders on a conditional sentence increased by fully one-third over the period 2002–2005. Over the period 1997-98 to 2003-4 the conditional sentence population doubled. Conditional sentence offenders still represent a relatively small percentage (5 percent) of the total admissions to the adult correctional population in 2004-5.

What kinds of offences result in the imposition of a conditional sentence?

Approximately one-quarter (28 percent) of conditional sentence admissions in 2005 were for a violent offence. Property offences accounted for 34 percent while other *Criminal Code* violations accounted for 20 percent, 15 percent for drug offences, and the remainder for related federal statute violations. Data from 2003-4 reveal that drug trafficking accounted for 18 percent of all conditional sentences imposed, followed by fraud (11 percent), theft (10 percent), and assault (9 percent). Assaults and break and enter accounted for a further 23 percent (the remaining conditional sentences involved one of a range of relatively minor crimes). In half the conditional sentences imposed in 2003-4 the offender had no prior record. This reflects the tendency for courts to use the conditional sentence for offenders for whom prison is an appropriate sanction, but who are first offenders.

How long are the terms of conditional imprisonment?

Since the decision in *R v. Proulx*, conditional sentences have become longer. In 2005, one-third of all conditional sentences were under 6 months, and another third were between 6 and 12 months. Almost 4 orders in 10 (38 percent) were for periods of 1 year or longer.

What kinds of conditions are imposed on conditional sentence offenders?

The conditional sentence carries a number of statutory conditions applicable to all offenders on whom the sentence is imposed. However, judges have the discretion to impose additional conditions crafted to respond to the specific needs of the individual offender. Data on conditions are quite sketchy at present. A recent analysis of conditional sentences imposed in five jurisdictions in Canada found that "attend counselling" and "abstain from the use of illegal drugs or alcohol" were the optional conditions most often imposed. Residence restrictions and house arrest are also frequently imposed. An analysis of conditional sentences imposed in Nova Scotia and New Brunswick reveal that residence requirement or house arrest was imposed in 60 percent of conditional sentences.

How often do conditional sentence orders result in breach?

The majority of conditional sentence orders terminate without the offender having breached the conditions of the order. In 2005, 22 percent of orders were breached in Nova Scotia and 31 percent in Alberta. The optional—that is, non-statutory—conditions most likely to result in a breach hearing were to make restitution/compensation and peform unpaid community work. Alberta provides breach data broken down by ethnicity. These data reveal that Aboriginal offenders have a higher breach rate than their non-Aboriginal counterparts. In terms of specific offences, the highest breach rates were associated with break-and-enter and robbery. This reflects the fact that offenders convicted of these offences tend to be a higher risk to re-offend.

One of the messages of the judgment in *Proulx* was that conditional sentences should contain a punitive element. It is perhaps not surprising therefore that conditional sentences imposed since *Proulx* was decided have become more onerous, carrying more and more intrusive conditions.

J.V. Roberts, "Serving Time at Home"
from J.V. Roberts, *The Virtual Prison*
(Cambridge: Cambridge University Press, 2004) (edited selection)

What is it like to live under house arrest? This reading summarizes findings from interviews with offenders who are serving a sentence of imprisonment—but at home. All offenders were serving a conditional sentence of imprisonment. The research also explored the experiences and perceptions of people who live with offenders serving these sentences. Their views are important for two reasons: first, because they share many of the restrictions imposed on offenders, and, second, because they play an important role in ensuring that the offender complies with the conditions imposed by the court.

> It is like being with the people that I love, and doing my time with them, but it's not easy. Actually, I think it's tougher than being in jail.

Many people may be surprised to learn that offenders will on occasion choose prison over a community-based sanction. This reaction reflects the perception that prison is always and everywhere more punitive than its alternatives. In addition, research that examines the nature of the impact of conditions such as electronic monitoring and home confinement demonstrates that there are important parallels: many (but by no means all) of the pains of imprisonment can be reproduced in the home. Payne and Gainey (1998) provide a fascinating comparison between the pains of imprisonment and those of life on electronic monitoring. They point out that many of the traditional pains of imprisonment, including loss of personal autonomy [and] deprivation of liberty are endured by people on electronic monitoring. It is interesting to note that several individuals in Canada commented that while community imprisonment was clearly preferable to prison, it was not necessarily easier; living on a conditional sentence created challenges and difficulties not encountered in prison. In one sense prison was the easier sanction, because they simply had to "wait out" the sentence: "I didn't like being behind bars, but being out is harder than being in jail." Another offender described life on a conditional sentence in the following words: "You have to think about what you are doing in the world." It is also significant that some individuals expressed pride at having lived through the absolute house arrest. One said: "It's been a long haul but I'm proud of what I've done." Such statements are seldom heard from people leaving prison, or ending a period on parole.

Daily Life in the Virtual Prison

> I was working in the kitchen while in remand, that was the only thing worthwhile in prison ... the community is the better way to go. It's also a lot harder, it teaches you [to make] a lot of sacrifices.

> The hardest part would be dealing with your friends and family, explaining why you couldn't go out.

Many of the offenders that we interviewed had been sentenced to absolute (i.e., 24-hour) house arrest. The consequences of this condition included the following: preventing offenders from participating in social activities; interfering with family outings and special occasions; creating stigma when other people realised that the offender was serving a sentence. For one offender, the hardest condition was performing community service on top of his job. Nevertheless, he found it a rewarding experience: "When you're working 50 hours a week, it makes for some very long days. But it wasn't just a punishing experience, it was a rewarding experience."

Impact of Conditional Sentence on Children of the Offender

An important consideration in imposing community rather than prison is the presence of a family. There is an additional incentive for courts to avoid incarcerating the offender if he or she has dependents, and many of the offenders who spoke to us about the experience of home confinement had families, often with small children. The most punitive element for these offenders was the impact that the sentence had upon their children, whose interactions with their parents and daily lives were affected for the duration of the sentence. One offender noted that the sentence was "especially hard on the kids to accept what has happened." She added: "It's hard on the kids, because we used to go out, especially in the summer. Every time they ask me I say I can't." Several offenders complained of the restrictions that absolute house arrest introduced upon their children's lives.

A female offender discussed the house arrest condition in the context of other conditions imposed: "the absolute curfew is the hardest thing. I can't go anywhere without telling my PO [probation officer]. Absolute curfew is like house arrest. My daughter wants to go the park, but I can't take her." She added that it put a lot of strain on her when she had to try and explain why they couldn't go to the park: "Sometimes I'd say, 'oh, I'm tired' or 'we just can't do that today.' It's hard because I don't know what to say. [pause] I have to make excuses." However, she added that staying home was easier than going to jail. She would rather stay home and be with her kids, and believed that if she did not have kids she would have been sent to jail.

Effect on Inter-Personal Relationships

One must be wary of generalizations with respect to the effect of home detention on issues such as relationships; close confinement for long periods will have different effects depending upon the personalities of the individuals involved, the nature of the relationship and the home environment. Although it has yet to be formally tested, it may well be that an *intensification* effect exists: home environments characterised by conflict and tension are likely to become worse as a result of the enforced confinement of the offender. Walters (2002) found that offenders on curfew orders in England and Wales reported that the curfew placed a strain on their relationships; it was hard to "walk away from arguments" (p. 32). It is worth noting that these offenders were on curfew orders for a relatively short period of time. The maximum term of the order is six months; fully 70 percent were serving curfew orders of less than four months. Facing a curfew order of two years would be a far more daunting proposition, which would create even more stress upon relationships.

Partners were also affected by the conditional sentence. One offender said:

> [It has] been very hard on my girlfriend. She felt strapped down. She couldn't go nowhere, I couldn't drive her anywhere ... . [I]t was also hard for her because she didn't want to tell her friends that I was on a conditional sentence ... . My girlfriend often tells me how it affects [their relationship]. All we can do is cook some supper if I get groceries on Sunday. All we can do is watch movies if she goes and gets them. I don't have problem with [the other conditions imposed] but the twenty-four hours at home are too much.

On the other hand, home detention in generally positive environments may well enhance human relationships. There is certainly evidence from the Canadian research that this is the case; young adult offenders confined to homes that they shared with loving parents reported that the sentence had been a positive experience. The restrictions on the offenders' movements can help rupture anti-social contacts, and prevent these individuals from being drawn into life patterns that can lead to further offending.

In general, the limited research on the effect of home confinement has found that offenders report that relationships with co-residents improved. Research reported by Dodgson et al. (2001), is an exception. These researchers interviewed offenders on the Home Detention Curfew and found that the experience of being on the program had made no difference to their relationships with others. However, it must be recalled that these offenders were on the program for a relatively short period of time (a maximum of 60 days) which is probably insufficient time to affect these relationships. Moreover, of those who had noticed a change, twice as many said that matters had improved rather than worsened (Dodgson et al., 2001).

Feeling Pressure to Lie to Others About the Sentence

Few members of the public stop to think about the impact of a conditional sentence on the ways that people react to the offender. However, these reactions can amplify the stigma associated with the sentence. Offenders talked about the stigma that they had felt when they had told their co-workers about the court order and its associated restrictions. And some individuals expressed concern about potential "whistle-blowers," people who might call the police if they believed that the offender was violating some condition of his or her order. This is illuminating because it underlines the important reality that surveillance is not the exclusive domain of probation officers. If it were, ensuring compliance would be impossible, as probation officers simply have too many clients to adequately monitor their behaviour. The negative reaction of others appears to create pressure on conditional sentence offenders to passively hide their status, or actively deceive other people.

Offenders sentenced to a conditional sentence and obliged to wear an electronic monitor will often have to explain their status to people with whom they have some relationship. In Canada, few offenders are subject to electronic monitoring, since the equipment is not currently available in most provincial correctional systems. However, the restrictions on their movements mean that most offenders have to confront the question of how much to disclose to other people. Fearful of the consequences, many offenders elected to hide their status, particularly with respect to the workplace. In the case of employers, some offenders said nothing rather than explain the true state of affairs. As one individual noted, "I think I'll get fired if I tell my employer." In some cases, however, it was impossible to hide the fact of the sentence, as there were occasions when they were invited to stay after work and this had compelled them to explain why this was not possible.

Having to explain the court order to other people—particularly to children—was a source of considerable anxiety for many offenders. In the case of relatively young children, some offenders resorted to deception, or simply said (in response to requests to go out) that they "couldn't go out right now." Other offenders explained matters more fully, and explained why:

> My son is fourteen ... . I sat down with him this summer and I told him what I did and what had happened. The main reason I told him is because he's approaching that age. I told him I don't want him to follow in my footsteps.

Positive Lifestyle Changes

In Canada, the optional conditions that a court may impose should reduce the likelihood of the offender re-offending. In pursuit of this objective, courts order offenders to follow treatment, abstain from consuming alcohol and other such conditions. Indeed, there is some evidence that offenders do change their lifestyles when confined to home. A number of offenders reported that their life patterns had changed while on the sanction and that several of these changes, particularly with respect to drugs and alcohol, had persisted afterwards. For some offenders, serving time at home creates an inverted lifestyle. For example, some offenders have jobs which require them to work far from home. One truck driver whose conditional sentence order permitted him to drive his truck across the province noted that work had become pleasurable: while working, he was able to go to roadside restaurants, and move around relatively freely. However, once he was at home, his life became constrained, and he was unable to leave the house, even to visit the local newsagent. For this individual, life at work had become far more attractive than home life.

Research with home confinement offenders reported by Rubin (1990) found that respondents showed a reduction of drug and alcohol use after being on home confinement. This finding contradicts the view that conditional sentence offenders spend much of their time drinking or taking drugs, safe in the knowledge that their behaviour cannot be monitored while home, merely their presence (Harkins, 1990). The explanation for the more abstemious conduct of these offenders appears to be that their alcohol consumption had been associated with spending most evenings in pubs; even when this was once again possible (after the sentence was over), the desire to do so was not as strong.

Loss of Spontaneity

Serving a term of imprisonment at home means that daily life has to be planned far more carefully. Offenders have to consider whether particular acts will constitute a breach of the court order, and they have to contact their sentence supervisors in order to apply for permission to attend particular events. For older offenders, making an application to a younger probation officer was a "humbling" experience, as one such individual remarked. In order to join people for a coffee after one of his group therapy meetings he had to obtain the permission of his probation officer, otherwise he would have been in breach as the order required him to return directly home once the meeting had ended.

Most (but by no means all) offenders seemed concerned about the consequences of breaching the order by returning home late. One individual noted that "I never actually ran out of time [returning home after a court authorised shopping trip] but I was always worried about running out of time." Time pressures were a source of considerable stress for these offenders. This was compared to the leisurely pace of shopping without such a constraint to which members of the public have become accustomed. For the general public, the worst consequence of dawdling while shopping is missing the bus home; for conditional sentence offenders, being late home may result in arrest and, ultimately, committal to custody.

Conclusion

The portrait of community custody that emerges from this research is quite different from the image projected by the news media. Offenders serving their prison sentences at home are subject to numerous constraints that change their life in a dramatic manner. As well, there is little discussion in the media of the impact on innocent third parties, or the role that family members play in helping to "administer" the sentence of the court. One of the strengths of this sanction is that it draws upon the resources of the community—the social networks of the offender—to achieve some of its objectives. This strategy however comes with a cost: the effect of the sentence is amplified through these networks, and other peoples' lives are affected in significant ways. Of course, this is true of imprisonment as well. When an offender is committed to custody, his partner and his family suffer the loss of their loved one, and have to accustom themselves to the inconveniences of visiting hours. The isolation of a prison sentence, however, has a destructive effect upon social relations; this is why such a high percentage of relationships fail to survive a lengthy term of incarceration. A conditional sentence may actually strengthen the links between people.

Families and partners of offenders sentenced to conditional sentence have an onerous task thrust upon them, and, in most jurisdictions, no institutional support or back up. Yet despite all this, there is ample evidence in the research to date that offenders and their families see a positive element to conditional sentence, and not simply because the sanction spares them the experience of prison. Although on occasion home detention caused tension among family members or between partners, there is more evidence to suggest that the increased time at home has a positive effect on relationships. Many (but by no means all) recognize that serving a conditional sentence creates opportunities for them to change their lifestyle, and to preserve social relations that otherwise would be threatened or ruptured by incarceration. In this sense, offenders perceive the sanction as a novel form of custody. Whatever other people may feel about this new form of custody, offenders seem well aware of the potential of the sanction.

PROBLEMS

1. Smith and Jones were married in 1992. In March 2006, Jones told Smith that she had decided to leave the relationship. Although she planned to stay in the matrimonial home temporarily, Jones told Smith that she did not want to continue a sexual relationship. On April 15, 2006, an argument escalated and Smith struck Jones. Jones left the matrimonial home and Smith was charged with common assault. It was a term of release that he not

communicate with Jones. Smith subsequently persisted in his efforts to contact Jones, notwithstanding his undertaking pursuant to s. 515(2) not to communicate with her. On one occasion, he met her on the street, and grabbed her by the shoulders and pushed her. These events were part of an unsolicited and unwanted attempt at reconciliation and resulted in new criminal charges: two charges of breach of an undertaking, plus assault and criminal harassment. Smith pleaded guilty to all charges.

Smith has no previous record. Aside from these offences, he could be considered a person of good character. In the year prior to the end of his marriage, five close relatives had died, including his grandparents, who had raised him. He was under a great deal of stress and had no one close to him to discuss his personal problems. Smith had spent a month in pre-trial custody prior to his sentencing. A psychiatrist called by Smith testified that the period of pre-trial custody had impressed Smith with the seriousness of his conduct and its impact on Jones. The psychiatrist offered the opinion that Smith represented no danger to Jones or anyone else and proposed a treatment plan that, in his view, could be implemented in the community through regular sessions with him but that would not be available, at least through someone with his expertise, inside an institution.

Defence counsel agrees that these offences usually call for a term of imprisonment, but argues for a conditional sentence of 18 months. Crown counsel agrees with the 18 months, but argues that the sentence should be served in custody. How would you sentence Smith?

2. Mary Blanchard is a 30-year-old Aboriginal woman from a small northern Ontario community. She has been living in Thunder Bay for the past 10 years. On January 20, 2005, she was charged with two counts of trafficking, arising from the sale of small quantities of marijuana and cocaine to an undercover officer. On March 10, 2005, she entered guilty pleas to the two charges and the sentencing was adjourned until April 15 to allow for the preparation of a pre-sentence report.

The pre-sentence report indicates that Blanchard has a substantial record for property offences and drug possession. In 2000 and 2002, she was convicted of trafficking in small quantities of cocaine. She received short jail terms (30 and 60 days) for both offences. It is apparent that she has suffered from both alcohol and substance abuse for many years. During this time she has not been gainfully employed for any substantial period. On two occasions she entered a residential drug treatment program but both times left prematurely. She is a talented artist but has produced very little work since leaving her community in 1998.

Blanchard's counsel is seeking a conditional sentence. She has advised the court that a bed is waiting for Blanchard in a residential drug treatment centre. She has also submitted that Blanchard has been reunited with her family, who want her to return home after she has completed the treatment program. Her community, although poor, has organized an after-care schedule that involves a number of community volunteers who will be available to Blanchard on a daily basis to assist her in avoiding a relapse. They have also arranged for her to teach art part time at the local school.

The Crown has argued that trafficking requires a punitive response. Moreover, no hard evidence has been adduced about Blanchard's home community that would support reliance on s. 718.2(e).

Can the judge consider Blanchard's Aboriginal background? Since most trafficking cases lead to incarceration, would a conditional sentence produce unjustifiable disparity? Can a conditional sentence be crafted that would meet the principles articulated in *Proulx* and *Wells*?

3. On January 15, 2007 Dave Rankin pleaded guilty in Windsor, Ontario to theft of $140,000 from his employer. His counsel adduced evidence that Rankin was severely depressed by his spouse's illness and, in compensation, developed a gambling addiction. As a result, he lost his savings and resorted to an ill-conceived theft from his employer, a trust company. The judge sentenced Rankin to 20 months' imprisonment to be served, pursuant to s. 742.1, in the community. Aside from the mandatory conditions, Rankin was ordered to continue with treatment for his gambling addiction and to refrain entirely from gambling or entering a casino or race track.

On April 2, 2007, Rankin was charged with "over 80" after being stopped in a holiday roadside check in London, Ontario. After consulting with his lawyer, he had agreed to a breathalyzer test and blew 130 mg alcohol/100 ml of blood. He appeared in court on April 20 and a trial date was set for August 12, 2007. In the meantime, his conditional sentence supervisor learned about this new charge on April 19 and commenced a breach application under s. 742.6 on the basis that Rankin had "failed to keep the peace and be of good behaviour as evidenced by the commission of a new offence"—namely, "impaired driving/over 80." As a result, a warrant was issued for Rankin's arrest on April 21. On May 2, 2007, he was arrested in Windsor at his home and subsequently released by the officer in charge pursuant to s. 742.6(1)(e) on a promise to appear in court on May 20 to answer the breach allegation.

Assume that Rankin appears in court on May 20 without counsel and asks for time to retain one.

- If he has no counsel, can the matter be adjourned to June 15, even though this is more than 30 days from the date of his arrest?
- Can the court proceed to entertain the breach allegation on June 15, given that it is based on a criminal charge for which he has not been found guilty or pleaded guilty to the new charge?
- What happens to the conditional sentence pending the determination of the breach?
- At the hearing of the breach allegation, can the Crown make its case without *viva voce* evidence by filing the allegation, complete with the supervisor's report and any written statements in support plus proof of notice upon the offender?
- Assume that you ultimately hear the breach allegation on September 5, 2000. Does it matter whether Rankin was convicted or acquitted on the impaired charge?
- If you decide that the breach has been made out, what remedy under s. 742.6(9) is appropriate?
- If you are considering some time in custody short of termination, what effect will this have on the conditional sentence?
- If you are concerned about the duration of the sanction, can you give any credit for the time between the breach allegation and the breach finding?

CHAPTER THIRTEEN

Collateral Sentencing Orders

I. INTRODUCTION

The sentencing process is often largely consumed by questions about which of the sanctions discussed in the previous chapters—for example, imprisonment, monetary penalties, and probation—should be imposed on an offender. However, this is only part of the puzzle. Various provisions in the *Criminal Code*, RSC 1985, c. C-46, as amended, either permit or require the imposition of other orders as part of a sentence, such as driving prohibitions, weapons and firearms prohibitions, orders to provide a DNA sample to the state, and orders to comply with the *Sex Offender Information Registration Act*, SC 2004, c. 10. In each case, care should be taken to ensure that the applicable statutory requirements are met before any of these orders are sought or imposed. It is essential to distinguish between those situations in which an order *may* be imposed at the discretion of the court and those situations where it *must* be imposed. Even in the latter category, as some of the cases below demonstrate, there may be room, albeit narrow, to argue for an exemption.

II. DRIVING PROHIBITIONS

One of the most common and long-standing collateral sentencing orders is the prohibition found in s. 259(1) of the *Criminal Code*, which requires an order prohibiting the offender from operating a motor vehicle if he or she is convicted of impaired operation, driving "over 80"—that is, with a blood alcohol level over 80 mg of alcohol in 100 ml of blood—or refusing to provide a breath sample:

(a) for a first offence, for not more than three years and not less than one year;
(b) for a second offence, for not more than five years and not less than two years;
(c) for each subsequent offence, not less than three years.

While this section is applied primarily in the case of offences committed by persons operating motor vehicles, it also applies to those operating a vessel, aircraft, or railway equipment.

Section 259(2) of the Code permits, at the discretion of the court, a similar prohibition following a conviction under ss. 220 (criminal negligence causing death); 221 (criminal negligence causing bodily harm); 236 (manslaughter); 249 (dangerous operation of a motor vehicle, vessel, aircraft, or railway equipment); 249.1 (flight from a law enforcement officer causing death or bodily harm); 250 (failure to keep watch of a person towed on the water); 251 (unseaworthy vessel and unsafe aircraft); 252 (failure to stop at the scene of an accident); or 255(2) and (3) (impaired driving or driving over 80 causing bodily harm or death), when the offence was committed by means of a motor vehicle, vessel, aircraft, or railway equipment. Under s. 259(2), the length of the prohibition depends on the maximum sentence to which the underlying offence subjects the offender.

Prohibition orders made under s. 259 of the *Criminal Code* apply throughout Canada. In addition to this sanction, provincial and territorial legislation provides for contemporaneous licence suspensions, the length of which varies by jurisdiction. Recently, some provinces have passed legislation establishing alcohol ignition interlock device programs. These devices are affixed to motor vehicles and thwart attempts to operate the ignition if the driver cannot provide a breath sample that is free of alcohol (or within an acceptable limit). Typically, these programs are geared at drivers who have completed prohibitions and suspensions and are considered to be "reinstated" drivers: see, for example, *Highway Traffic Act*, RSO 1990, c. H.8, s. 41.2. Section 259 was recently amended to provide a discretion to the sentencing judge to permit a person subject to a prohibition to drive, after prescribed minimum periods, if he or she registers in an alcohol interlock device program established by a province: see ss. 259(1.1) to (1.4). To date, no province has enacted legislation that will permit someone to drive during the currency of a prohibition or suspension.

It is often said that the harshest penalty faced by those convicted of drunk-driving-related offences is the inconvenience posed by the driving prohibition. If it were not for the prohibition, many of those charged with this offence might well plead guilty. Of course, the inflexible approach of the *Criminal Code* would be very difficult to dislodge from a political perspective. Do you think exceptions to driving prohibitions should be made for people who require their cars to maintain their employment or discharge important family obligations (such as child or elder care)? If so, how could such exceptions be effectively enforced?

III. FIREARMS PROHIBITIONS

The following provisions form part of a comprehensive reform of firearms legislation enacted by SC 1995, c. 39, s. 139, which replaced Part III of the *Criminal Code* in its entirety. It contains a restructured mandatory prohibition (s. 109) and a discretionary prohibition (s. 110). The mandatory prohibition is broader in its application than were its predecessors. Beyond offences involving violence, it now applies to a number of weapons offences and to offences under ss. 6 and 7 of the *Controlled Drugs and Substances Act*, SC 1996, c. 19.

A. Criminal Code, Sections 109 to 110

109(1) Where a person is convicted, or discharged under section 730, of

(a) an indictable offence in the commission of which violence against a person was used, threatened or attempted and for which the person may be sentenced to imprisonment for ten years or more,

(b) an offence under subsection 85(1) (using firearm in commission of offence), subsection 85(2) (using imitation firearm in commission of offence), 95(1) (possession of prohibited or restricted firearm with ammunition), 99(1) (weapons trafficking), 100(1) (possession for purpose of weapons trafficking), 102(1) (making automatic firearm), 103(1) (importing or exporting knowing it is unauthorized) or section 264 (criminal harassment),

(c) an offence relating to the contravention of subsection 5(1) or (2), 6(1) or (2) or 7(1) of the *Controlled Drugs and Substances Act*, or

(d) an offence that involves, or the subject-matter of which is, a firearm, a cross-bow, a prohibited weapon, a restricted weapon, a prohibited device, any ammunition, any prohibited ammunition or an explosive substance and, at the time of the offence, the person was prohibited by any order made under this Act or any other Act of Parliament from possessing any such thing,

the court that sentences the person or directs that the person be discharged, as the case may be, shall, in addition to any other punishment that may be imposed for that offence or any other condition prescribed in the order of discharge, make an order prohibiting the person from possessing any firearm, cross-bow, prohibited weapon, restricted weapon, prohibited device, ammunition, prohibited ammunition and explosive substance during the period specified in the order as determined in accordance with subsection (2) or (3), as the case may be.

(2) An order made under subsection (1) shall, in the case of a first conviction for or discharge from the offence to which the order relates, prohibit the person from possessing

(a) any firearm, other than a prohibited firearm or restricted firearm, and any cross-bow, restricted weapon, ammunition and explosive substance during the period that

(i) begins on the day on which the order is made, and

(ii) ends not earlier than ten years after the person's release from imprisonment after conviction for the offence or, if the person is not then imprisoned or subject to imprisonment, after the person's conviction for or discharge from the offence; and

(b) any prohibited firearm, restricted firearm, prohibited weapon, prohibited device and prohibited ammunition for life.

(3) An order made under subsection (1) shall, in any case other than a case described in subsection (2), prohibit the person from possessing any firearm, cross-bow, restricted weapon, ammunition and explosive substance for life.

(4) In subparagraph (2)(a)(ii), "release from imprisonment" means release from confinement by reason of expiration of sentence, commencement of statutory release or grant of parole.

(5) Sections 113 to 117 apply in respect of every order made under subsection (1).

110(1) Where a person is convicted, or discharged under section 730, of

(a) an offence, other than an offence referred to in any of paragraphs 109(1)(a), (b) and (c), in the commission of which violence against a person was used, threatened or attempted, or

(b) an offence that involves, or the subject-matter of which is, a firearm, a cross-bow, a prohibited weapon, a restricted weapon, a prohibited device, ammunition, prohibited ammunition or an explosive substance and, at the time of the offence, the person was not prohibited by any order made under this Act or any other Act of Parliament from possessing any such thing,

the court that sentences the person or directs that the person be discharged, as the case may be, shall, in addition to any other punishment that may be imposed for that offence or any other condition prescribed in the order of discharge, consider whether it is desirable, in the interests of the safety of the person or of any other person, to make an order prohibiting the person from possessing any firearm, cross-bow, prohibited weapon, restricted weapon, prohibited device, ammunition, prohibited ammunition or explosive substance, or all such things, and where the court decides that it is so desirable, the court shall so order.

(2) An order made under subsection (1) against a person begins on the day on which the order is made and ends not later than ten years after the person's release from imprisonment after conviction for the offence to which the order relates or, if the person is not then imprisoned or subject to imprisonment, after the person's conviction for or discharge from the offence.

(3) Where the court does not make an order under subsection (1), or where the court does make such an order but does not prohibit the possession of everything referred to in that subsection, the court shall include in the record a statement of the court's reasons for not doing so.

(4) In subsection (2), "release from imprisonment" means release from confinement by reason of expiration of sentence, commencement of statutory release or grant of parole.

(5) Sections 113 to 117 apply in respect of every order made under subsection (1).

The following cases address a number of technical and conceptual issues that relate to the imposition of these provisions.

R v. Keays
(1983), 10 CCC (3d) 229 (Ont. CA)

DUBIN JA: This appeal brought by the Crown raises issues with respect to the interpretation of s. 98(1) of the *Criminal Code*, which provides as follows:

> 98(2) Where a person is convicted of an indictable offence in the commission of which violence against a person is used, threatened or attempted and for which the offender may be sentenced to imprisonment for ten years or more or of an offence under section 83, the court shall, in addition to any other punishment that may be imposed for that offence, make an order prohibiting him from having in his possession any firearm or any ammunition or explosive substance for any period of time specified in the order that commences on the day the order is made and expires not earlier than
> > (a) in the case of a first conviction for such an offence, five years, and
> > (b) in any other case, ten years,
> after the time of his release from imprisonment after conviction for the offence.

In this case the accused was convicted of possession of a weapon for a purpose dangerous to the public peace, and the evidence disclosed that during the commission of that offence, an act of violence occurred.

Following his conviction, the Crown introduced into evidence the criminal record of the respondent, which disclosed two prior convictions for robbery while armed. Both those convictions preceded the date of the proclamation of s. 98(1) of the *Criminal Code*.

The learned trial judge held that since the convictions for robbery while armed preceded the effective date of s. 98(1), they were irrelevant and thus treated the conviction for possession of a weapon for a purpose dangerous to the public peace as a first conviction and limited the prohibition period to that of five years.

In this respect we think that he erred. In our view, it is not a case of a first conviction under s. 98(1) if a person convicted for an offence described in s. 98(1) has been previously convicted of such an offence even though such an offence had been committed prior to the proclamation of s. 98(1) into law. To interpret the section in this manner is not giving it a retrospective effect. Retrospectivity does not occur by merely bringing into play facts which have preceded the enactment.

. . .

In responding to the appeal, counsel for the respondent supported the judgment on two alternative grounds. He first argued that s. 98(1) is only applicable if the offence for which the accused had been convicted is an offence for which a person could not be convicted without committing an act of violence. Obviously, a person who is convicted of the offence of possession of a weapon for a purpose dangerous to the public peace could do so without committing an act of violence or threatening violence. However, in this case the evidence clearly disclosed that an act of violence was committed. In our view, once it is shown that a person has been convicted of an indictable offence in the commission of which violence against the person is used, threatened or attempted and for which the offender may be sentenced to imprisonment for 10 years or more, s. 98(1) becomes applicable, notwithstanding that the offence for which the accused has been convicted could have been committed without violence. That matter has been fully resolved by the judgment of this court in *R v. Broome* (1981), 63 CCC (2d) 426, 24 CR (3d) 254, and on that ground also the respondent fails.

However, a further point was made by counsel for the respondent which was not canvassed before the trial judge in light of the ground relied on by him in disposing of this matter. As has been noted, the Crown adduced evidence that the respondent in this case had been previously convicted on two occasions for robbery while armed. If those armed robberies were accompanied by violence, then the order under s. 98(1) must be one for not less than 10 years. But to constitute a second offence under s. 98(1) the person must have been previously convicted of an indictable offence in the commission of which violence against the person was used, threatened or attempted and for which the offender could have been sentenced to imprisonment for 10 years or more. But, by definition, a person could commit robbery while armed without an act of violence. Section 302(d) provides:

> 302. Every one commits robbery who ...
>
> (d) steals from any person while armed with an offence weapon or imitation thereof.

Thus mere proof of a conviction for robbery while armed does not constitute proof that an act of violence was actually committed during the commission of the offence.

Since this matter was not canvassed before the learned trial judge, we think the Crown should be given the opportunity to prove whether, during the course of the commission of the two armed robberies upon which the Crown relies, the accused had committed any acts of violence.

In the result therefore, the appeal will be allowed, the order under appeal set aside and the matter remitted to the trial judge to afford the Crown the opportunity of adducing evidence with respect to the two prior convictions.

Appeal allowed.

R v. Avery
(1986), 30 CCC (3d) 16 (NWTCA)

HARRADENCE JA (dissenting): The respondent Frederick Allen Avery was convicted of an offence under s. 85 of the *Criminal Code*. Following this conviction, a firearms prohibition order was entered against Mr. Avery on June 18, 1985. The order prohibited the respondent from possessing firearms, ammunition or explosive substances for a period of five years.

On August 13, 1985, the respondent was charged with violating the firearms prohibition order, contrary to s. 98(12) of the *Criminal Code*, when in an apparent attempt to comply with the order, Mr. Avery sold a rifle to one Mr. Bourque. The rifle was impounded and the respondent charged.

The trial judge dismissed the charge on the ground that the firearms prohibition order, made pursuant to s. 98(1) of the *Criminal Code*, was defective in that it did not contain the mandatory provision required by s. 98(13) specifying a reasonable period of time within which the respondent could dispose of firearms already in his possession. The Crown appeals.

· · ·

I deal first with the argument that a prosecution under s-s. (12) may be supported where the order fails to comply with s-s. (13). Such an interpretation is to construe the word "shall" as other than imperative.

Further, this construction continues to expose the person against whom the order is made to criminal prosecution, not because of wrongdoing on his part but because he has been denied the benefit of the protection Parliament has mandated he shall have. He has been denied this protection through no fault of his own but because the court failed to give effect to the mandatory provisos of s-s. (13) of the *Criminal Code* of Canada.

· · ·

I am therefore of opinion that if the period required by s-s. (13) is not contained in the order, then the legal mechanism by which s-s. (12) can be brought to bear is not in place and the section is not available to create an offence for breach of the prohibition. This in no way detracts from the validity of the order and the prohibition it contains is in full force and effect. An offence for its breach is created by another section of the *Criminal Code*. I have in mind s. 88 of the *Criminal Code* of Canada. However, a prosecution under that section would enjoy little chance of success if a firearm was in lawful possession prior to the making of the order and a reasonable time for its disposition had not expired at the time the charge was laid. The protection contained in s-s. (13) against the mischief created in the previous enactment would not be contravened.

· · ·

There is one final point to illustrate the important nexus of the reasonable disposal period in s. 98(13) to the *actus reus* in s. 98(12). The prosecution must not only prove the wrongful deed; it is legally incumbent upon the Crown at some point in the proceedings and whether or not by a primary or secondary burden of proof, to show that the crime was committed without a legal excuse. By the addition of s. 98(13), and limited to the facts of *Avery*, Parliament has pre-empted this Crown argument. This proposition is consistent with the genesis of this unique *actus reus*. As Glanville Williams explains (*ibid.*, p. 19):

> A further step must now be taken. *Actus reus* includes, in the terminology here suggested, *not merely the whole objective situation that has to be proved by the prosecution, but also the absence of any ground of justification or excuse*, whether such justification or excuse be stated in any statute creating the crime or implied by the courts in accordance with general principles.

(Emphasis added.)

As the accused could not through his conduct have committed the wrong physical act which Parliament contemplated, dismissal of the charge under s. 98(12) was proper and the appeal will be dismissed.

KERANS JA: This is a Crown appeal from an acquittal on a charge, under s. 98(12) of the *Criminal Code*, of possession of a weapon in violation of an earlier judge's order prohibiting possession as a consequence of a conviction for violent crime.

The fact was not denied that the accused was in possession of a gun in contravention of the terms of a prohibition order made March 20, 1985, and entered June 18, 1985, pursuant to s. 98. The earlier order (which by happenstance had been made by him) was "defective." This was correct in the sense that he had failed to make any order under s. 98(13) nor indeed to address his mind to the issue posed by that subsection, which provides:

> 98(13) An order made pursuant to subsection (1), (2), (6) or (7) shall specify therein a reasonable period of time within which the person against whom the order is made may surrender to a police officer or firearm officer or otherwise lawfully dispose of any firearm or any ammunition or explosive substance lawfully possessed by him prior to the making of the order, and subsection (12) does not apply to him during such period of time.

This provision is not without relevance in this case because the offence occurred within four months after the order and came to light because the accused was trying to sell his gun in an apparent attempt to rid himself of it in rough compliance with the prohibition. The learned trial judge, admirably aware of his own earlier failing, perceived that he had unfairly exposed the accused to this charge.

· · ·

In this case the accused could have, and did not, seek relief from the original error by appeal if not writ. In the fact of his having failed to do so, he must obey the order which he chose to let stand. When he argues now that he should not be convicted for the breach of it because it is bad, he is saying he did not have to obey it. A collateral attack is nothing less than a request for an affirmation of defiance.

The reason for the rule is that the law must encourage respect for due process by itself respecting it. It is a rule of practical necessity. For example, in *R v. Adams* (1978), 45 CCC (2d) 459, 6 CR (3d) 257, [1979] 2 WWR 108 (BCCA), an accused appealed a conviction for escape from lawful custody on the ground that his original detention was illegal. Craig JA observes at p. 469:

> [i]f a trial Judge permitted an accused to go behind a warrant of committal ... the judge would be holding, in effect, that the jailer had no right to detain the accused, yet the jailer would have to detain the accused because the warrant was still subsisting.

Worse, can a jailer refuse to detain because he thinks the committal bad, and wait until he is charged before demonstrating it is bad? The rule is designed to avoid an invitation to anarchy.

The great difficulty with the rule is that it can work a harsh result on an unsophisticated accused who, like the accused before us, fails to appreciate the need to make a direct attack on a bad order. His relative lack of blameworthiness cannot avoid favourable contrast, in cases of this sort, with errors by judicial officers, as often as not compounded by other errors by governmental officials. The accused's situation in such a case obviously stirs sympathy. Very often, I suspect, the Crown does not proceed with charges *ex debito justitiae*. Sometimes, as here, the Crown is less sympathetic than are the courts. Unfortunately, perhaps, the Crown discretion is not directly reviewable. Fortunately, the power to grant a discharge permits Canadian courts in most cases to offer relief where the blameworthiness of the accused is minimal: see *R v. Campbell and Mlynarchuk* (1972), 10 CCC (2d) 26, 21 CRNS 273, [1973] 2 WWR 246.

. . .

I would allow the appeal and declare the accused guilty of a breach of the order which he indubitably breached. In the circumstances, however, I would invoke s. 662.1(1) and grant him an absolute discharge.

Appeal allowed.

NOTE

What about constitutionality? Does the mandatory prohibition offend s. 12 of the Charter? For a number of years there has been a controversy over whether the remedy known as a constitutional exemption applied to mandatory prohibitions. You will see that, in some cases, courts have held that the effect of a sanction that is otherwise valid constitutionally might be so disproportionate in the circumstances of the particular offender that it supports a claim under s. 12 of the *Canadian Charter of Rights and Freedoms*, Part I of the *Constitution Act, 1982*, RSC 1985, app. II, no. 44. As a result, some courts have upheld the statutory provision, but granted an exemption to the offender: see, for example, *R v . Chief* (1989), 51 CCC (3d) 265 (YCA), and *R v. Netser* (1992), 70 CCC (3d) 477 (NWTCA), cases involving claims that the offender was a subsistence hunter. Other courts have held either that the provision is valid and should be applied or that the provision should be struck down, without allowing for an intermediate remedy such as the constitutional exemption: see, for example, *R v. Kelly* (1990), 59 CCC (3d) 497 (Ont. CA), a case involving police officers who were convicted of assault causing bodily harm, arising from an incident when they were off duty. Since this controversy first arose, there have been two important developments. First, the *Criminal Code* has been amended through the addition of s. 113 to accommodate specific exemptions relating to subsistence hunting as well as to other situations that may amount to a "virtual prohibition against employment."

More important, the Supreme Court has been busy. In 2008, it ruled that there should be no constitutional exemptions in response to mandatory penalties: see *R v. Ferguson*, 2008 SCC 6, and the accompanying note in chapter 11.

As well, the Supreme Court looked specifically at the new s. 109 and the impact of s. 12 of the Charter in the context of a marijuana production conviction.

R v. Wiles
2005 SCC 84, [2005] 3 SCR 895

CHARRON J: [1] Does the mandatory weapons prohibition order under s. 109(1)(c) of the *Criminal Code*, RSC 1985, c. C-46, when imposed upon conviction of the offence of production of cannabis, violate the appellant's right "not to be subjected to any cruel and unusual treatment or punishment" guaranteed by s. 12 of the *Canadian Charter of Rights and Freedoms*? If so, is the infringement a reasonable limit prescribed by law as can be demonstrably justified in a free and democratic society under s. 1 of the *Charter*? These are the constitutional questions raised on this appeal.

[2] Mr. Wiles entered a plea of guilty on two charges of unlawfully producing cannabis, contrary to s. 7(1) of the *Controlled Drugs and Substances Act*, SC 1996, c. 19 ("*CDSA*"), the second offence having been committed while he was on release in respect of the first. The marihuana grow operation was discovered on the first occasion when the police responded to a 911 call made accidentally by one of Mr. Wiles' daughters. At this time, the police noted that Mr. Wiles possessed six firearms, all properly stored and licensed. The firearms were left in his possession. At sentencing, the Crown sought the mandatory prohibition orders under s. 109(1)(c) of the *Criminal Code* in addition to the sentence jointly agreed upon by counsel. Under the terms of s. 109, a 10-year minimum prohibition order is mandatory upon first conviction of any one of certain enumerated drug offences (s. 109(2)). Upon subsequent convictions, the prohibition order is for life (s. 109(3)). Mr. Wiles challenged the constitutionality of s. 109(1)(c), alleging that the imposition of the mandatory weapons prohibition orders constitutes "cruel and unusual punishment" in violation of s. 12 of the *Charter*. The relevant legislative and *Charter* provisions are annexed.

[3] The Crown concedes that a weapons prohibition order constitutes a "treatment or punishment" within the meaning of s. 12 of the *Charter*. In my view, this concession is well made. Although the purpose of the prohibition order is primarily preventative, in taking away the privilege to possess weapons, it may have some punitive effect on the offender. The question then is whether the loss of this privilege upon conviction of the offence of production is "cruel and unusual."

[4] This Court has dealt with s. 12 on many occasions and there is no controversy on the test that must be met. Treatment or punishment which is disproportionate or

"merely excessive" is not "cruel and unusual": *R v. Smith*, [1987] 1 SCR 1045, at p. 1072. The treatment or punishment must be "so excessive as to outrage standards of decency": *Smith*, at p. 1072; *R v. Goltz*, [1991] 3 SCR 485, at p. 499; *R v. Luxton*, [1990] 2 SCR 711, at p. 724. The court must be satisfied that "the punishment imposed is *grossly* disproportionate for the offender, such that Canadians would find the punishment abhorrent or intolerable": *R v. Morrisey*, [2000] 2 SCR 90, 2000 SCC 39, at para. 26 (emphasis in original).

[5] The court must first determine whether the treatment or punishment is grossly disproportionate for the individual offender having regard to all contextual factors. Relevant factors may include: the gravity of the offence, the personal characteristics of the offender, the particular circumstances of the case, the actual effect of the treatment or punishment on the individual, relevant penological goals and sentencing principles, the existence of valid alternatives to the treatment or punishment imposed, and a comparison of punishments imposed for other crimes in the same jurisdiction: see *Morrisey*, at paras. 27-28. If the treatment or punishment is grossly disproportionate for the individual offender in light of all relevant contextual factors, the court proceeds to determine whether the infringement can be justified under s. 1 of the *Charter*. If it is not disproportionate for the individual offender, the court must still consider whether the treatment or punishment is disproportionate having regard to reasonable hypotheticals. In *Goltz*, it was made clear that reasonable hypotheticals cannot be "far-fetched or only marginally imaginable" (p. 515). They cannot be "remote or extreme examples" (p. 515). Rather they should consist of examples that "could commonly arise in day-to-day life" (p. 516).

[6] Mr. Wiles presented no evidence as to his need for the firearms found in his possession and made no argument that the prohibition orders had any particular impact upon him. He bases his constitutional argument, rather, on the general effect of the mandatory weapons prohibition, essentially raising two grounds. First, he contends that by virtue of its mandatory nature, s. 109(1)(c) does not permit a distinction between big marihuana grow operators and small ones. To make his point, he raises the hypothetical of a 75-year-old grandmother experimenting with growing a single marihuana plant on the kitchen windowsill who is caught and charged under s. 7(1) of the *CDSA*. This hypothetical offender would be subject to the same minimum weapons prohibition as the large commercial producer. On this point, Mr. Wiles asks this Court to draw on its analysis in *Smith* where the mandatory imposition of a minimum seven-year jail sentence for the offence of importing narcotics was held to be unconstitutional, essentially on the basis of its grossly disproportionate effect on hypothetical offenders. Second, Mr. Wiles submits that s. 109(1)(c) is grossly disproportionate because it does not require any consideration as to whether the underlying offence involved violence or whether the individual offender poses a future risk to public safety.

[7] At the sentencing hearing, Chief Judge Batiot found that the mandatory prohibition infringed s. 12 of the *Charter* because there was not necessarily a nexus between the purpose of the mandatory prohibition—the reduction of the risk of future violence—and the offence of production under s. 7 of the *CDSA* ((2004), 110 CRR (2d) 1, 2003 NSPC 14). With respect to this particular offender, he noted that "but for" s. 109, there would not be any mention of a firearms prohibition, as it would have been "irrelevant," given that the accused's firearms were legally stored, and not used to defend his

grow operation (para. 16). Therefore, the fact that the mandatory prohibition attached to all offences under s. 7(1) without regard to whether the individual accused posed a risk of future violence rendered it "grossly disproportionate" and a violation of the accused's right not to be subjected to cruel and unusual punishment. Similarly, because s. 109 did not provide for discretion not to impose the prohibition in cases, such as the one at hand, where the accused did not present "an actual or potential danger with [a] firearm" (para. 41), the accused's right was not minimally impaired, and the violation could not be upheld as a demonstrably justified limit under s. 1. The sentencing judge therefore read down the section to provide for a discretionary rather than mandatory order and declined to make the prohibition orders.

[8] Bateman JA for the Nova Scotia Court of Appeal, Oland and Hamilton JJA concurring, overturned the sentencing judge's decision, holding that the test for an infringement of s. 12 had not been met ((2004), 220 NSR (2d) 126, 2004 NSCA 3). The Court of Appeal found that there was a connection between the mandatory prohibition and s. 7 offences, based on evidence presented at the hearing as to the frequency with which firearms are used to protect grow-operations against theft, to the point, as noted by the sentencing judge (at para. 17), that in any raid, the police will assume guns are present and will take the necessary precautions for the officers' safety. The Court of Appeal also found that the sentencing judge failed to take into account the ameliorative effects of the exception provided for by s. 113 of the *Criminal Code* in cases where the prohibition would result in a deprivation of livelihood or sustenance. In Bateman JA's opinion, this provision eliminated those cases where the imposition of a mandatory prohibition might be found to be "grossly disproportionate."

[9] I agree with the Court of Appeal. Mr. Wiles has not established that the imposition of the mandatory weapons prohibition orders constitutes cruel and unusual punishment. As noted by the Court of Appeal, the prohibition has a legitimate connection to s. 7 offences. The mandatory prohibition relates to a recognized sentencing goal—the protection of the public, and in particular, the protection of police officers engaged in the enforcement of drug offences. The state interest in reducing the misuse of weapons is valid and important. The sentencing judge gave insufficient weight to the fact that possession and use of firearms is not a right or freedom guaranteed under the *Charter*, but a privilege. It is also a heavily regulated activity, requiring potential gun-owners to obtain a licence before they can legally purchase one. *In Reference re Firearms Act (Can.)*, [2000] 1 SCR 783, 2000 SCC 31, this Court held that requiring the licensing and registration of firearms was a valid exercise of the federal criminal law power. If Parliament can legitimately impose restrictions on the possession of firearms by general legislation that applies to all, it follows that it can prohibit their possession upon conviction of certain criminal offences where it deems it in the public interest to do so. It is sufficient that Mr. Wiles falls within a category of offenders targeted for the risk that they may pose. The sentencing judge's insistence upon specific violence, actual or apprehended, in relation to the particular offence and the individual offender takes too narrow a view of the rationale underlying the mandatory weapons prohibition orders.

[10] Insofar as the individual offender is concerned, there is no evidence as to any effect that the prohibition orders will have on Mr. Wiles, apart from the loss of the firearms already in his possession. Since he was legally in possession of the firearms, the

sentencing judge inferred that he was a recreational hunter and shooter. Even assuming that to be the case, the loss of this privilege would not support the sentencing judge's finding of gross disproportionality. As a twice convicted producer of a controlled substance, Mr. Wiles' loss of the privilege to possess firearms for recreational purposes falls far short of punishment "so excessive as to outrage our standards of decency." In addition, the mandatory provision does not have a grossly disproportionate effect having regard to any reasonable hypothetical. Again here, I agree with the Court of Appeal that the sentencing judge did not properly weigh the ameliorative effect of s. 113 of the *Criminal Code* which permits the court to lift the order for sustenance or employment reasons. As stated by Bateman JA, "[t]his is a key companion provision to s. 109(1)(c) which would eliminate, where appropriate, any unacceptable consequences of a firearms prohibition" (para. 57).

[11] For these reasons, I would dismiss the appeal.

IV. DNA DATABANK ORDERS

In 1998, Parliament enacted the *DNA Identification Act*, a piece of legislation that amended the *Criminal Code* in two important ways. First, it created a specific power for the seizure, with a warrant, for bodily samples for investigative purposes. Second, it provided for the establishment of a DNA databank and provided judges with the power to order that, in certain circumstances, samples be taken from offenders for the purposes of creating a databank of information for investigative purposes.

487.051(1) Subject to section 487.053, if a person is convicted, discharged under section 730 or, in the case of a young person, found guilty under the *Young Offenders Act*, chapter Y-1 of the Revised Statutes of Canada, 1985, or the *Youth Criminal Justice Act* of a designated offence, the court

(a) shall, subject to subsection (2), in the case of a primary designated offence, make an order in Form 5.03 authorizing the taking, from that person, for the purpose of forensic DNA analysis, of any number of samples of one or more bodily substances that is reasonably required for that purpose, by means of the investigative procedures described in subsection 487.06(1); or

(b) may, in the case of a secondary designated offence, make an order in Form 5.04 authorizing the taking of such samples if the court is satisfied that it is in the best interests of the administration of justice to do so.

Exception

(2) The court is not required to make an order under paragraph (1)(a) if it is satisfied that the person or young person has established that, were the order made, the impact on the person's or young person's privacy and security of the person would be grossly disproportionate to the public interest in the protection of society and the proper administration of justice, to be achieved through the early detection, arrest and conviction of offenders.

Criteria

(3) In deciding whether to make an order under paragraph (1)(b), the court shall consider the criminal record of the person or young person, the nature of the offence and the circum-

stances surrounding its commission and the impact such an order would have on the person's or young person's privacy and security of the person and shall give reasons for its decision.

Section 487.052 also provides the authority for a sample for offences committed before the DNA databank provisions came into force.

The purposes and mechanics, as well as the impact of these provisions on individual privacy interests, are discussed in the two cases below.

R v. Hendry
(2001), 161 CCC (3d) 275 (Ont. CA)

[This judgment addresses a number of cases in which judges failed to make orders concerning secondary designated offences (s. 487.051(1)(b)) and retrospective applications (s. 487.052).]

ROSENBERG JA:

. . .

Statutory Provisions

[3] In summary, the legislative scheme provides that after an offender has been found guilty the judge may order that he or she provide samples for forensic DNA analysis. These samples are then sent to the DNA data bank for analysis. The DNA profile is stored in the data bank and is available for comparison with evidence obtained from other investigations. In these appeals, the offenders had committed a secondary designated offence after the scheme came into effect or a designated offence (primary or secondary) before the scheme came into effect. In either case, the judge has a discretion to make the order where it is in the best interests of the administration of justice to do so. That discretion is described in similar terms under s. 487.051(1)(b) (secondary designated offences) and s. 487.052 (designated offences committed before the scheme came into effect).

[4] Section 487.04 defines "primary designated offences" and "secondary designated offences." The former include sexual interference under s. 151. The latter include break and enter (s. 348) and assault (s. 266). The other relevant sections are the following: 487.051(1) Subject to section 487.053, if a person is convicted, discharged under section 730 or, in the case of a young person, found guilty under the *Young Offenders Act*, of a designated offence, the court (a) shall, subject to subsection (2), in the case of a primary designated offence, make an order in Form 5.03 authorizing the taking, from that person, for the purpose of forensic DNA analysis, of any number of samples of one or more bodily substances that is reasonably required for that purpose, by means of the investigative procedures described in subsection 487.06(1); or (b) may, in the case of a secondary designated offence, make an order in Form 5.04 authorizing the taking of such samples if the court is satisfied that it is in the best interests of the administration of justice to do so. (2) The court is not required to make an order under paragraph (1)(a) if it is satisfied that the person or young person has established that, were the order

made, the impact on the person's or young person's privacy and security of the person would be grossly disproportionate to the public interest in the protection of society and the proper administration of justice, to be achieved through the early detection, arrest and conviction of offenders. (3) In deciding whether to make an order under paragraph (1)(b), the court shall consider the criminal record of the person or young person, the nature of the offence and the circumstances surrounding its commission and the impact such an order would have on the person's or young person's privacy and security of the person and shall give reasons for its decision. 487.052(1) Subject to section 487.053, if a person is convicted, discharged under section 730 or, in the case of a young person, found guilty under the *Young Offenders Act*, of a designated offence committed before the coming into force of subsection 5(1) of the *DNA Identification Act*, the court may, on application by the prosecutor, make an order in Form 5.04 authorizing the taking, from that person or young person, for the purpose of forensic DNA analysis, of any number of samples of one or more bodily substances that is reasonably required for that purpose, by means of the investigative procedures described in subsection 487.06(1), if the court is satisfied that it is in the best interests of the administration of justice to do so. (2) In deciding whether to make the order, the court shall consider the criminal record of the person or young person, the nature of the offence and the circumstances surrounding its commission and the impact such an order would have on the person's or young person's privacy and security of the person and shall give reasons for its decision. ... 487.054 The offender or the prosecutor may appeal from a decision of the court made under subsection 487.051(1) or 487.052(1).

· · ·

Burden of Proof

[9] Under s. 487.051(1)(b) and s. 487.052, the trial judge is to make a DNA data bank order if "satisfied" that it is in the best interests of the administration of justice. The section does not place the persuasive burden on either the Crown or defence. Once again some assistance can be obtained from the sentencing regime in resolving the question of the burden of proof. In *R v. Proulx* (2000), 140 CCC (3d) 449 (SCC), at para. 121, Lamer CJC rejected a submission from the Crown that the offender bears the legal burden of proof where the offender is seeking a conditional sentence: In matters of sentencing, while each party is expected to establish elements in support of its position as to the appropriate sentence that should be imposed, the ultimate decision as to what constitutes the best disposition is left to the discretion of the sentencing judge.

[10] He pointed out, however, at para. 122, that the offender will ordinarily bear the tactical burden of coming forward with information to support imposition of a conditional sentence. Having said this, in practice, it will generally be the offender who is best situated to convince the judge that a conditional sentence is indeed appropriate. Therefore, it would be in the offender's best interests to establish those elements militating in favour of a conditional sentence. ...

[11] In my view, similar considerations apply to the making of the DNA data bank order. Strictly speaking, there is no burden on either Crown or defence under s. 487.051(1)(b) or s. 487.052. However, under s. 487.052 the order is made "on appli-

cation by the prosecutor" and as a practical matter it will be the Crown that asks the judge to exercise his or her discretion under s. 487.051(1)(b). Thus, in my view the Crown bears an evidential burden to produce sufficient information to raise the issue. The trial judge must then be satisfied, after weighing and balancing all the relevant considerations, that the order should be made.

• • •

Best Interests of the Administration of Justice

[17] In *R v. Briggs*, Weiler JA dealt with many of the issues that may arise in interpreting s. 487.051(1)(b) and s. 487.052. In particular, she held as follows:

(1) Whether or not there is evidence at the scene of the crime of which the offender was convicted that would likely yield a DNA profile of the perpetrator is not necessarily a relevant consideration.

(2) The phrase "best interests of the administration of justice" does not import as a prerequisite to making the order that there be reasonable and probable grounds to believe a further offence will be committed.

(3) The state interest in obtaining a DNA profile from an offender is not simply law enforcement by making it possible to detect further crimes committed by this offender. Rather, the provisions have much broader purposes including the following:

1. Deter potential repeat offenders;
2. Promote the safety of the community;
3. Detect when a serial offender is at work;
4. Assist in the solving of "cold" crimes;
5. Streamline investigations; and
6. Most importantly, assist the innocent by early exclusion for investigative suspicion or in exonerating those who have been wrongfully convicted.

(4) Provisions in the *Criminal Code* and the *DNA Identification Act* restricting the use that can be made of the DNA profile and protecting against improper use of the information offer significant protection of the offender's privacy.

(5) The procedures for seizures of bodily substances authorized by the provisions are of short duration and involve no, or minimal, discomfort. There is a minimal intrusion with no unacceptable affront to human dignity.

(6) A person convicted of a crime has a lesser expectation of privacy.

(7) The trial judge is entitled to look at the offender's entire record, not just the crimes that may be designated offences.

[18] I would summarize the effect of these holdings as follows. In balancing the offender's right to privacy and security of the person against the state interests in obtaining the offender's DNA profile, the court must consider the following. The legislation offers significant protections against misuse of the DNA profile information, thus minimizing an improper intrusion into the offender's privacy. Having been convicted of a designated offence, the offender already has a reduced expectation of privacy. In the ordinary case of an adult offender the procedures for taking the sample have no, or at

worst, a minimal impact on the security of the person. Thus, in the case of an ordinary adult offender there are important state interests served by the DNA data bank and few reasons based on privacy and security of the person for refusing to make the order.

[19] I do, however, wish to highlight one aspect of the DNA data bank legislative scheme that is of some concern. As Weiler JA points out in *Briggs*, a purpose of the *DNA Identification Act* is to protect the privacy of individuals with respect to personal information. To that end, the legislation includes some safeguards against appropriation of the information collected by the data bank for purposes other than those set out in the Act. The main purpose of the legislation is to provide the mechanism for comparison of DNA profiles gathered in a criminal investigation with the DNA profiles in the data bank. If there is a match, the Commissioner of the RCMP may inform the law enforcement agency of that fact along with any information, other than the DNA profile itself, that is contained in the data bank in relation to that DNA profile. Unauthorized use is an offence under the Act.

[20] Thus, use of the DNA data bank information resembles the use of fingerprint information that law enforcement agencies collect and have collected for many years under the *Identification of Criminals Act*, RSC 1985, c. I-1, with this important difference. So far as I am aware, fingerprint information can only be used for comparison purposes. It does not provide any personal information about the offender. A DNA profile is different. It is capable of providing the most intimate details of the person because it can show the person's genetic makeup. The DNA sample can be analyzed to determine, for example, if the person carries certain genes that make the person more susceptible to disease. It is not beyond the realm of possibility that in the future scientists may claim to be able to isolate genes that make a person more prone to violence. To guard against abuse, it is the policy of the DNA data bank to only use "non-coding" or "junk" DNA, that is, only that part of the DNA that does not predict any medical, physical or mental characteristics. This policy or convention is not, however, written into the legislation.

[21] Further, subject to certain exceptions, as where the offender's conviction is quashed and a final acquittal entered, the DNA bank is permitted to keep the sample, even after the DNA profile has been obtained. There are good forensic reasons for this. As the technology improves it may be possible to obtain additional comparison information from the sample. However, if government policy changes in the future the present limitations on the use of the information and the conventions for analysis may also change. The risk that personal information about medical, physical or mental characteristics may be obtained and used for purposes other than forensic comparison cannot be entirely discounted. The issue does not arise in this case, but such use of the bodily sample might well have implications under the *Canadian Charter of Rights and Freedoms*.

[22] I agree with Weiler JA's analysis in *Briggs* and with the importance of collecting DNA profiles for the salutary purposes she identifies. The courts must nevertheless keep in mind the distinction between routine fingerprinting and DNA profiling. This distinction is highlighted by the fact that under s. 487.051(3) and s. 487.052(2) the court is required to give reasons for making the DNA order. That said, and leaving aside other considerations, I would expect that in most cases the balance would be struck in favour of making the order under s. 487.051(1)(b) or s. 487.052, as the case may be.

[23] There are, of course, other considerations. Under both of these provisions, the court is instructed to take into account the criminal record of the offender, the nature of the offence and the circumstances surrounding its commission. I will consider the latter two factors first. As explained by Weiler JA, the legislation is not focused solely on the possibility that this offender will commit another offence in which DNA profile information may prove useful. Thus, as she said, the fact that the offence of which the accused was convicted is not ordinarily one where DNA evidence might be found is not necessarily relevant. The legislation has already struck a balance by limiting the reach of the DNA data bank orders to persons convicted of serious offences, being those designated as primary or secondary offences. However, the description of some of these offences can also embrace some relatively minor conduct. For example, assaulting a police officer is a secondary designated offence, but this could include merely pushing a police officer who was in the execution of his or her duty. The trivial circumstances of the particular offence may be a factor favouring not making the order.

[24] The court is also directed to consider the offender's record. If the offender has no prior record and the circumstances of the secondary designated offence are relatively minor, the court may be justified in not making the order. However, particularly if the offender has a record that includes offences described as primary designated offences, I would think it exceptional that the order not be made. In general, the more serious the record the less likely the court could exercise its discretion against making the order.

[25] On balance, I would expect that in the vast majority of cases it would be in the best interests of the administration of justice to make the order under s. 487.051(1)(b) and s. 487.052, as the case may be. This follows simply from the nature of the privacy and security of the person interests involved, the important purposes served by the legislation and, in general, the usefulness of DNA evidence in exonerating the innocent and solving crimes in a myriad of situations.

R v. R.C.
2005 SCC 61, [2005] 3 SCR 99

The judgment of McLachlin CJ and Major, Binnie, Deschamps, and Fish JJ was delivered by

FISH J:

[1] R.W.C. stabbed his mother in the foot with a pen that lay on the floor beside his bed—after his mother had dumped dirty laundry on him because he refused to rise, dress and go off to school. For this he was charged with "assault with a weapon" and breach of an undertaking. R.W.C. had no previous convictions of any kind and pleaded guilty to both offences. He was 13 years old at the time.

[2] Assault with a weapon is one of the offences for which the trial court must make an order permitting DNA samples to be taken from anyone found guilty unless the person found guilty establishes that the effect of doing so would be "grossly disproportionate to the public interest," within the meaning of s. 487.051(2) of the *Criminal Code*, RSC 1985, c. C-46.

[3] The issue in this case is whether Gass J, of the Supreme Court of Nova Scotia (Family Division), erred in concluding that the appellant had discharged that burden. This in turn depends on whether Gass J misinterpreted or misapplied the governing statutory provisions. The Nova Scotia Court of Appeal held, on three grounds, that she had. In my respectful view, the Court of Appeal erred with regard to all three grounds.

[4] I would therefore allow the appeal, set aside the judgment of the Court of Appeal and affirm the decision of Gass J.

II

[5] When he committed the offence that concerns us here, R.W.C., as I have already mentioned, was 13 years old and therefore a "young person" within the meaning of the *Youth Criminal Justice Act*, SC 2002, c. 1 ("*YCJA*").

. . .

III

[16] Since 1995, Parliament has enacted two complementary schemes regulating the collection and use of DNA in the criminal justice system: DNA search warrants and the DNA Data Bank.

[17] The constitutionality of DNA search warrants was considered and upheld by this Court in *R v. S.A.B.*, [2003] 2 SCR 678, 2003 SCC 60. At issue here is the second legislative scheme, the Data Bank contemplated by ss. 487.051 to 487.055 of the *Criminal Code* and the *DNA Identification Act*, SC 1998, c. 37 ("*DNA Act*"). The *Criminal Code* provisions allow a court to order the collection of bodily substances from certain convicted offenders for inclusion in the Data Bank. The *DNA Act*, on the other hand, regulates the use of those substances once collected.

[18] When a DNA order is made, a sample of one or more bodily substances—blood, hair or buccal cells—is taken and sent to the National DNA Data Bank of Canada, where it is assigned a bar code and separated from information identifying the offender. The biological sample is processed and a profile created from the non-coding portions of the DNA sequence. This profile is put in a database known as the Convicted Offenders Index. A separate index, the Crime Scene Index, contains DNA profiles from unsolved crime scenes. The two indices are routinely compared and, when a match is found, investigators are alerted to the discovery of a match.

[19] Orders for taking DNA samples are made under either s. 487.051 or s. 487.052 of the *Criminal Code*. Section 487.052 applies to offences committed before the *DNA Act* was in force ... .

. . .

[20] Parliament has thus drawn a sharp distinction between "primary" and "secondary" designated offences, which are defined in s. 487.04 of the *Criminal Code*. Where the offender is convicted of a secondary designated offence, the burden is on the Crown to show that an order would be in the best interests of the administration of justice. Where an offender is convicted of a primary designated offence, however, ss. 487.051(1)(a) and (2), read together, provide that a DNA order must be made unless the judge is satisfied that the offender has established that s. 487.051(2) should apply instead.

[21] Much like the provision at issue in *R v. Araujo*, [2000] 2 SCR 992, s. 487.051(2) can be described as a "constitutional compromise" that seeks to strike an appropriate balance between individual rights and societal interests. In applying this provision, courts must determine whether a DNA order would adversely affect the individual's privacy and security interests in a manner that is grossly disproportionate to the public interest. We are neither invited nor required in this case to decide whether s. 487.051(2) passes constitutional muster.

[22] By its very terms, s. 487.051(2) implies that the public interest in a DNA order lies in the protection of society through the early detection, arrest and conviction of offenders. Section 3 of the *DNA Act*, for example, states that the purpose of the legislation is to assist in the identification of persons alleged to have committed designated offences.

[23] Other objectives include deterring potential repeat offenders, detecting serial offenders, streamlining investigations, solving "cold cases," and protecting the innocent by eliminating suspects and exonerating the wrongly convicted: see *R v. Briggs* (2001), 157 CCC (3d) 38 (Ont. CA) at para. 22, leave to appeal dismissed [2001] 2 SCR xii; *R v. Jordan*, 2002 NSCA 11, at paras. 32-39; and *R v. T. (T.N.)*, 2004 ABCA 238, at para. 2.

[24] These objectives, however laudable, may be seen to conflict with privacy and security interests that warrant judicial protection. Although the public interest is presumed to outweigh privacy interests in the case of primary designated offences, the exception in s. 487.051(2) recognizes that this is a rebuttable presumption.

[25] The making of a DNA order clearly engages two aspects of privacy protected by the *Canadian Charter of Rights and Freedoms*. The first relates to the person, and the second arises in what has been called the "informational context": *S.A.B.*, at para. 40; *R v. Dyment*, [1988] 2 SCR 417, at pp. 428-30.

[26] The physical intrusion caused by the taking of a DNA sample is minimal. In this regard, the comments of Arbour J in *S.A.B.* are apposite:

> With regards to privacy related to the person, the taking of bodily samples under a DNA warrant clearly interferes with bodily integrity. However, under a properly issued DNA warrant, the degree of offence to the physical integrity of the person is relatively modest (*R v. F. (S.)* (2000), 141 CCC (3d) 225 (Ont. CA), at para. 27). A buccal swab is quick and not terribly intrusive. Blood samples are obtained by pricking the surface of the skin—a procedure that is, as conceded by the appellant (at para. 32 of his factum), not particularly invasive in the physical sense. With the exception of pubic hair, the plucking of hairs should not be a particularly serious affront to privacy or dignity.
>
> Importantly, s. 487.07(3) of the legislation requires that the person who is authorized to take samples do so in a manner that respects the offender's privacy and is "reasonable in the circumstances." Thus, as Weiler JA articulated in *R v. Briggs* ... at para. 35, "a person would not ordinarily be required to expose a part of the body that is not ordinarily exposed to view."
>
> • • •
>
> In my view, the statutory framework alleviates any concern that the collection of DNA samples pursuant to a search warrant under ss. 487.04 to 487.09 of the *Criminal Code* constitutes an intolerable affront to the physical integrity of the person. [paras. 44, 45 and 47]

The same is true of samples taken pursuant to an order under s. 487.051(1)(a).

[27] Of more concern, however, is the impact of an order on an individual's informational privacy interests. In *R v. Plant*, [1993] 3 SCR 281, at p. 293, the Court found that s. 8 of the *Charter* protected the "biographical core of personal information which individuals in a free and democratic society would wish to maintain and control from dissemination to the state." An individual's DNA contains the "highest level of personal and private information": *S.A.B.*, at para. 48. Unlike a fingerprint, it is capable of revealing the most intimate details of a person's biological makeup.

[28] Without constraints on the type of information that can be extracted from bodily substances, the potential intrusiveness of a DNA analysis is virtually infinite. Comprehensive safeguards have therefore been put in place to regulate the use of the bodily substances and of the information contained in a profile: see *S.A.B.*, at paras. 49-50; see also *Briggs*, at para. 39.

[29] The court must consider the impact of a DNA order on each of these interests to determine whether privacy and security of the person are affected in a grossly disproportionate manner. This inquiry is highly contextual, taking into account not only that the offence is a primary designated offence, but also the particular circumstances of the offence and the character and profile of the offender.

[30] Some of the factors that may be relevant to this inquiry are set out in s. 487.051(3): the criminal record of the offender, the nature of the offence and the circumstances surrounding its commission, and the impact such an order would have on the offender's privacy and security of the person (*Jordan*, at para. 62).

[31] This is by no means an exhaustive list. The inquiry is necessarily individualized and the trial judge must consider all the circumstances of the case. What is required is that the offender show that the public interest is clearly and substantially outweighed by the individual's privacy and security interests.

[32] The central controversy in this case is whether a youth court judge may, in contemplating a DNA order with respect to a young person, take into account the underlying principles and defining characteristics of criminal justice legislation adopted by Parliament specifically for dealing with young persons.

[33] Section 487.051(1)(a) applies expressly to a "person" or "young person." Accordingly, the question is not whether youth criminal justice legislation supercedes or displaces the DNA order provisions, or governs the making or rejection of DNA orders under their auspices. Rather, the question is whether legislation designed specifically and exclusively for dealing with young persons who commit criminal offences may be considered in applying to them the provisions of the *Criminal Code* that govern the making of DNA orders.

[34] There has been some dispute whether, in answering this question, we should look to the now-repealed *Young Offenders Act*, RSC 1985, c. Y-1 ("*YOA*"), or to the new *YCJA*. The latter came into force April 1, 2003, after R.W.C. had pleaded guilty to the offence. Its transitional provisions stipulate that, where proceedings are commenced under the *YOA*, the *YOA* applies (s. 159 of the *YCJA*), except for sentencing (s. 161). The Crown submits that the appeal in this case is governed by the *YOA*.

[35] In my view, the result in this case does not turn at all on whether the *YOA* or the *YCJA* is held to apply. In all relevant aspects, the two Acts share the same basic

assumptions and governing principles: some are simply spelled out in greater detail in the *YCJA*.

[36] Most significantly, both the *YOA* and the *YCJA* extend to youth justice courts exclusive jurisdiction in respect of offences alleged to have been committed by young persons, and stipulate that, notwithstanding any other Act of Parliament, the young person shall be dealt with according to their terms (s. 14 *YCJA*; s. 5(1) *YOA*). Both Acts incorporate the provisions of the *Criminal Code* with "any modifications that the circumstances require" (s. 140 *YCJA*; similar wording in s. 51 *YOA*). While no specific provision of either Act modifies s. 487.051(1)(a) or (2) of the *Code*, it is clear that Parliament intended their shared principles to be respected whenever young persons are brought within the Canadian system of criminal justice.

[37] In particular, Parliament has taken care to ensure that the consequences of conviction for young persons are imposed in a manner that advances the objectives of youth criminal justice legislation. This legislative policy is apparent in both Acts. To disregard it is to frustrate Parliament's will.

[38] The *YOA*, for example, declared in s. 3(1)(a.1) that "young persons should not in all instances be held accountable in the same manner or suffer the same consequences for their behaviour as adults," recognized in s. 3(1)(c) their "state of dependency and level of development and maturity," and held in s. 3(1)(f) that young persons have "a right to the least possible interference with freedom that is consistent with the protection of society." Likewise, the *YCJA*, states in s. 3 that the criminal justice system for young persons must be separate from that of adults and must "emphasize … enhanced procedural protection to ensure that young persons are treated fairly and that their rights, including their right to privacy, are protected."

[39] A DNA order, while it is not a sentence, is undoubtedly a serious consequence of conviction. This is evident from the comprehensive procedural protections that are woven into the scheme of the DNA Data Bank. The taking and retention of a DNA sample is not a trivial matter and, absent a compelling public interest, would inherently constitute a grave intrusion on the subject's right to personal and informational privacy.

[40] Both the *YOA* and the *YCJA* protect young persons from publication of their identities. Both emphasize rehabilitation rather than punishment. And both require the destruction of youth records after a finite time period.

[41] In creating a separate criminal justice system for young persons, Parliament has recognized the heightened vulnerability and reduced maturity of young persons. In keeping with its international obligations, Parliament has sought as well to extend to young offenders enhanced procedural protections, and to interfere with their personal freedom and privacy as little as possible: see the United Nations *Convention on the Rights of the Child*, Can. T.S. 1992 No. 3, incorporated by reference in the *YCJA*.

[42] In protecting the privacy interests of young persons convicted of criminal offences, Parliament has not seen itself as compromising, much less as sacrificing, the interests of the public. Rather, as Binnie J noted in *F.N. (Re)*, [2000] 1 SCR 880, 2000 SCC 35, protecting the privacy interests of young persons serves rehabilitative objectives and thereby contributes to the long-term protection of society … .

[43] Moreover, Parliament has recognized in enacting youth criminal justice legislation that "most young offenders are one-time offenders only and, the less harm

brought upon them from their experience with the criminal justice system, the less likely they are to commit further criminal acts" (*Re Southam Inc. and The Queen* (1984), 48 OR (2d) 678 (HC), at p. 697, *per* J. Holland J, aff'd. (1986), 53 OR (2d) 663 (CA), leave to appeal refused, [1986] 1 SCR xiv).

[44] It is not surprising, then, that the Court of Appeal for Ontario has held that the balancing of factors under the discretionary prong of s. 487.051(1)(b) must take into account the age of the young person and the principles of youth criminal justice legislation. ...

[45] The same holds true for decisions made pursuant to s. 487.051(1)(a) and (2): In determining whether the young person has established that the public interest in the protection of society and the proper administration of justice is clearly and substantially inferior to his or her privacy and security interests, the sentencing judge must examine both sides of the equation through the lens of the applicable youth criminal justice legislation.

IV

[46] The Nova Scotia Court of Appeal held that it owed no deference to the decision of Gass J in this case because that decision was made pursuant to a mandatory provision of the *Criminal Code*.

[47] With respect, I prefer the view taken on this point by the Court of Appeal for Ontario in *Briggs*, where Weiler JA (Austin and Borins JJA concurring) recognized that "a judge has a discretion to make an order authorizing the taking of a sample of DNA with respect to both primary and secondary offences although that discretion would appear to be more limited with respect to primary offences" (para. 3).

[48] Subsection (1)(a) of s. 487.051 of the *Criminal Code*, which is framed in mandatory terms, cannot be read in isolation from subs. (2). Read together, these provisions make the issuance of a DNA order mandatory only where (1) a person or young person has been convicted of a primary designated offence and (2) the burden cast upon that person or young person by s. 487.051(2) has not been discharged. Put differently, the court is not required to make the order if it is satisfied that the person or young person has established gross disproportionality. Such is the language of discretion.

[49] Accordingly, absent an error in principle, failure to consider a relevant factor, or an overemphasis of the appropriate factors, a court of appeal should only intervene to vary a decision to either make or refuse to make a DNA Data Bank order if the decision was clearly unreasonable: see, in the sentencing context, *R v. M.(C.A.)*, [1996] 1 SCR 500.

V

[50] The Court of Appeal intervened in this instance on three grounds.

[51] First, it found that Gass J had erred in holding that "the principles and purposes of the [*YCJA*] inform or otherwise modify the application of s. 487.051(1)(a) and (2)" (para. 17). In my respectful view, Gass J did not err at all in this regard. In balancing the governing factors under s. 487.051(2) in cases involving young offenders, I have already explained why sentencing judges commit no error in taking into account the principles and objectives of youth criminal justice legislation, such as the *YOA* or the *YCJA*.

[52] Second, the Court of Appeal held that Gass J failed to deal with certain circumstances that ought to have informed the balancing of factors under s. 487.051(2). In dealing with this branch of the matter, it is essential to bear in mind that all of the relevant circumstances were canvassed by counsel and considered by the trial judge cumulatively at the DNA stage. That is to say, the hearing on sentence was incorporated by reference into the DNA hearing that followed immediately afterward. There was no confusion at all regarding the different legal considerations applicable to each of the two distinct decisions—one relating to sentence, the other to the DNA order. But the facts were not in dispute and the predisposition report, relevant at both stages, was not challenged by either side.

[53] Quite properly, Crown counsel thus acknowledged in this Court that, at trial, the submissions on sentencing, the sentencing disposition, the DNA hearing, and the DNA order in this matter all proceeded more or less simultaneously, without objection.

[54] It must be borne in mind as well that the trial judge, when asked by defence counsel whether she required more facts for the purposes of the DNA hearing, replied:

I'm certainly satisfied that the Court has ample facts before it based on the facts that were given prior to the disposition or the sentencing hearing and the information provided in the presentence report and the submissions of counsel.

[55] In this light, I am not prepared to hold that the trial judge failed to consider the facts to which she thus adverted compendiously. Nor am I prepared to fault the appellant's counsel taking the judge at her word.

[56] More specifically, the Court of Appeal reproached Gass J for relying only on the age of the offender, the absence of a criminal record and the nature of the offence in refusing the DNA order. In its view, she had failed to address this additional information in the record:

- at the time of the commission of this assault offence the young person was on an undertaking to keep the peace and be of good behaviour;
- the only evidence of the young offender's remorse came through his father's report on the PSR interview;
- his school attendance has been an ongoing problem and precipitated this assault;
- the young offender's latest academic school report was not good;
- the young offender had a history of using illicit drugs and alcohol, although he maintained such use was in his past;
- the young offender has an anger management problem with a tendency to lose control of his behaviour as evidenced by this offence;
- there is a history of violence in the young offender's family;
- the assault against the mother continued after the stabbing with the pen, until it was stopped by the intervention of the young offender's uncle. [para. 23]

[57] The Court of Appeal's finding that Gass J had failed to consider this "relevant information" cannot be reconciled with the record as we have it. The opposite is in fact true. Gass J mentioned specifically that R.W.C. was bound by an undertaking at the time of the offence. She specifically mentioned as well R.W.C.'s anger management issues

in her reasons on the DNA order, and on at least three separate occasions in her reasons for sentence. She stated that she did not wish to minimize them, but found that they were being addressed appropriately through the conditions she had imposed as part of R.W.C.'s probation order. That conclusion has not been attacked by the Crown.

[58] Likewise, Gass J expressly considered R.W.C.'s history of family violence, both in her reasons on the DNA order and her reasons for sentence. And she mentioned at least twice that the assault was precipitated by a dispute regarding his attendance at school.

[59] The Court of Appeal erred as well in stating that the only evidence of R.W.C.'s remorse came from his father's interview for the predisposition report. As appears from the extract of the probation report reproduced above, R.W.C. had personally expressed his remorse to the probation officer, who also noted R.W.C.'s willingness to accept the consequences imposed upon him for his actions. ...

[60] Again, the Court of Appeal reproached Gass J for failing to mention R.W.C.'s "ongoing problem" with "school attendance" and an academic report that was "not good." These purported omissions by the trial judge should cause no surprise: In her representations on sentence, Crown counsel had expressly adopted the probation officer's assessment that "[o]verall in the home and school, the offender's behaviour appears to be compliant" (emphasis added).

[61] Other omissions imputed to Gass J by the Court of Appeal were either included in the predisposition report, which Gass J said that she had considered, or had been drawn to her attention moments earlier during counsels' submissions, or referred to by Gass J herself in her judgment on sentence.

[62] With respect, I am satisfied for all of these reasons that the Court of Appeal erred in holding that Gass J had failed to consider relevant information in declining to make a DNA order. And I turn now to the third ground upon which the Court of Appeal set aside her decision at trial.

[63] The Court of Appeal held that Gass J had failed to particularize her decision: In its view, she had "apparently concluded that taking a DNA sample from a young offender was, prima facie, an impermissible violation of the young person's privacy and security interests" (para. 16), and had "lacked an evidentiary foundation upon which to base a denial of the presumptively mandatory order" (para. 13).

[64] With respect, I find this reproach as well to be unwarranted.

[65] Gass J instructed herself impeccably in law on several occasions. She noted that the young person had been found guilty of a primary designated offence and that a DNA order could therefore be refused only if the conditions of s. 487.051(2) were met by R.W.C. The Nova Scotia Court of Appeal in *S.A.B.*, she noted, had held that "cases where an order that is properly sought under [s. 487.051(1)(a)] may be refused will be very rare indeed" (para. 5), and that "the young person ... bears the burden of persuading the court that he falls within that exception. That has to be established by evidence on the record" (para. 21).

[66] Gass J went on to deal in very specific terms with the circumstances of this case. She noted that R.W.C. was 13 years of age, had no criminal record, and was involved in a fight with his mother in which he stabbed her with a pen in the foot. Gass J did not conclude that taking a DNA sample from young persons constituted, prima facie, an impermissible violation of their rights, but took care to explain that she saw R.W.C.'s

circumstances as "significantly different than the minimal infringement involved in the taking of a sample from a 35 year old individual with an extensive criminal record or even of the taking of a bodily sample from a 17 year old with an extensive criminal record" (para. 31).

[67] Gass J took into consideration the principles of the *YCJA*, the level of development of an early adolescent, and the young person's circumstances as they were described in the predisposition report. Though counsel for R.W.C. had offered to call the young person to testify on his own behalf, Gass J was satisfied that the court had ample facts before it. I am not prepared to say that she erred in this regard.

[68] In the circumstances, the offence committed by R.W.C. was clearly at the low end of the spectrum of primary designated offences. I should not be understood to be minimizing the gravity of his offence: R.W.C. committed a reprehensible assault on his mother. But it was committed in the course of dispute between a 13-year-old boy and his mother about going to school and as a reflexive response to the humiliation of having his dirty laundry dumped on him in his bed. His need for anger management, evidenced by this unacceptable attack on his mother, was addressed appropriately by Gass J.

[69] R.W.C. was a first-time offender. Gass J weighed the public interest in ordering that a DNA sample be taken from him and retained in the DNA Data Bank against the impact of such an order on his privacy and security interests. She conducted this exercise in light of the principles and objects of youth criminal justice legislation, and found that the impact of the order would be grossly disproportionate.

[70] Her finding was reasonable in the circumstances and should not have been set aside by the Court of Appeal.

VI

[71] For the foregoing reasons, I would allow the appeal and restore the order of the Supreme Court of Nova Scotia (Family Division).

The reasons of LeBel, Abella, and Charron JJ were delivered by

[72] ABELLA J (dissenting): I have had the benefit of reading the reasons of Fish J. With respect, I do not agree with his conclusion that the trial judge appropriately declined to make the DNA data bank order anticipated by s. 487.051(1)(a) of the *Criminal Code*, RSC 1985, c. C-46.

[73] Section 487.051(1)(a) requires that a DNA order be made in the case of a primary designated offence, such as the one in this case, unless the offender has established a grossly disproportionate impact on his or her "privacy and security of the person." The statutory onus is on the offender to rebut the presumption that a DNA order should issue.

[74] The data bank provisions explicitly extend their grasp to young offenders found guilty of a designated offence under either the *Young Offenders Act*, RSC 1985, c. Y-1, or the *Youth Criminal Justice Act*, SC 2002, c. 1. While I agree with Fish J that the principles of the *Young Offenders Act* and the *Youth Criminal Justice Act* are theoretically relevant to this determination, I am unable to see how they can be applied, as they were by the trial judge, so as to neutralize the clear language of the *Code*.

· · ·

Analysis

[84] As Fish J points out (at para. 20), s. 487.051 of the *Code* draws a "sharp distinction" between DNA orders made in respect of those who commit offences designated as primary, such as in this case, and those designated as secondary. ...

• • •

[85] Sections 487.051(1)(a) and (2) provide that when someone is convicted of a primary designated offence, a DNA order must be made unless the judge is satisfied that the offender has established that the impact of the order on his or her privacy and security of the person would be grossly disproportionate to the public's interest in the early detection, arrest and conviction of offenders. Any refusal would, based on the language of the provision, be exceptional.

[86] Three points bear emphasis: the onus is on the offender to satisfy the court that the order should not be made; the threshold for discharging the onus is gross disproportionality; and both adult and young offenders are explicitly made subject to the provisions.

[87] Section 487.051(1)(b) of the Code deals with secondary designated offences. It too makes specific reference to young persons being embraced by the provision's scope. The test, however, is completely different. If the offence is designated as secondary, a DNA order is not presumptively required. A discretion is given to the trial judge, who may make the order if satisfied that it is in the best interests of the administration of justice to do so based on the factors set out in s. 487.051(3): the criminal record, the nature of the offence, the circumstances surrounding its commission, and the impact such an order would have on the person's privacy and security. In other words, the best interests of the administration of justice are determined by balancing these factors.

[88] The test for primary designated offences, on the other hand, makes no reference to these factors and there is significantly less scope for discretion. The test, moreover, is not what is in the best interests of the administration of justice, as it is in the case of secondary offences. Instead, in the case of more serious offences Parliament has already codified the public interest and proper administration of justice as requiring a DNA order to achieve the early detection, arrest, and conviction of offenders. That is the articulated basis for carving out those more serious offences from the scheme, making a DNA data bank order presumptively mandatory and making the hurdle for avoiding the order far more onerous. Only if an offender, youthful or adult, can demonstrate that the impact of such an order on his or her privacy and security is grossly disproportionate to the public interest in the protection of society, can a court refuse to make the order.

[89] And this, in turn, is a question of evidence. Factors such as the offender's age, record and personal circumstances may well be advanced as part of the offender's evidentiary package if they relate to the question of impact on the offender's privacy and security of the person, but, unlike the case of secondary offences, they are not the focus of the inquiry. What is being weighed, instead, is whether the offender has discharged his burden of showing that the impact on his or her privacy and security interests is so overwhelming as to grossly outweigh society's interest in its own protection.

[90] Is this burden different for young offenders? As previously indicated, not only is no distinction drawn in s. 487.051(1) between adult and young offenders, young

persons are specifically included. By expanding the operation of the provision to include young persons without words of limitation, Parliament has signalled its view that DNA data banks orders can or should be made even where the offender is not an adult. In the case of less serious offences, it has formulated a balancing test and, in the case of serious offences, designed a highly stringent one. Both tests apply to both adult and young offenders.

[91] This is not to say that Parliament has failed to recognize the unique privacy and security needs of young persons. On the contrary, there are a number of provisions in both the *DNA Identification Act*, SC 1998, c. 37, and the *Code* that explicitly recognize them. For example, s. 9.1 of the *DNA Identification Act*, provides that "[a]ccess to information in the convicted offenders index" will be "permanently removed without delay" once the young offender's record is destroyed under the *Young Offenders Act*. Similarly, s. 10.1 of the *DNA Identification Act* provides for the destruction of bodily substances collected from a young offender "when the last part of the record in relation to the same offence is … required to be destroyed." Section 487.07(4) of the *Code* provides that a young person against whom a DNA warrant is executed has, in addition to any other rights arising from his or her detention under the warrant, the right to a reasonable opportunity to consult with, and have the warrant executed in the presence of, counsel and a parent, adult relative or other appropriate adult.

[92] That means, as for adult offenders, that a court can only decline to make a DNA data bank order in respect of a primary designated offence where there is evidence that the impact on the young person's privacy and security interests is grossly disproportionate to the public interest in the early detection, arrest and conviction of offenders. The court cannot simply infer a disproportionate impact on the basis that the offender is a young person. Such an approach would effectively turn the presumption on its head.

[93] While young offender legislation contains principles and protections to which all young offenders are always entitled, I have difficulty seeing how those principles and protections assist in any meaningful way in this case. The question is whether there was evidence that the impact of the order on this particular young person's privacy and security was so overwhelming as to be grossly disproportionate to the public's interest in protecting itself from potentially violent offenders. The test is the same for adult and young persons because the crime solving and public protection concerns that motivated Parliament are the same for both—both can be victims of wrongful convictions, both can be wrongfully accused, and both risk re-offending.

[94] Counsel for R.W.C. conceded that no evidence had been adduced with respect to the impact on his client. Rather, he had urged the trial judge to take judicial notice of the probable and likely effect of a DNA data bank order on young people in general. His argument was that because of the offender's age, lack of a criminal record and the domestic nature of the crime, the impact of a DNA order would be grossly disproportionate to R.W.C.

[95] The trial judge concluded that the case of R.W.C. was "so far removed from the usual situations contemplated by the legislative scheme" (para. 40) that the taking of the sample could not reasonably be justified. There was no evidence to support this, or any other conclusion about the impact on R.W.C. of such an order.

[96] The trial judge wisely expressed concern for the possibility that a DNA order could have a disproportionate impact on a young person. This is the kind of reality a judge dealing with young offenders is required to be sensitive to. But it ignores the legislative reality that Parliament has deemed the privacy and security interests of a young person convicted of a primary designated offence to be outweighed by the public interest in the protection of society and the proper administration of justice.

[97] The trial judge's error, with respect, was in basing her conclusion on generic considerations about impact, rather than on evidence of how disproportionate the impact was on this particular young offender. She essentially melted the test for primary offences into the one for secondary offences, turning an order that Parliament directed to be presumptively mandatory, into one that was presumptively inapplicable in the case of young offenders, replacing the requirement for evidence of gross disproportionality with a presumption of gross proportionality.

[98] This was a violent domestic incident involving the use of a weapon. The fact that the weapon was a pen does not diminish the fact that this was an offence designated to be primary and therefore governed by s. 487.051(1)(a). The stabbing was part of an escalating conflict which culminated in R.W.C. striking repeatedly at his mother's head with closed fists. Were it not for the intervention of a relative, the injuries sustained by the mother might have been far more serious.

[99] The trial judge made an express finding of fact that there was the potential for future violence if not addressed by remedial means. The record amply supports this finding. It is this very potential that the DNA data bank order is meant to address in the case of primary designated offences.

[100] The denial of an otherwise mandatory order must have a factual underpinning. I agree with Bateman JA of the Court of Appeal that the youth court judge lacked such a foundation ... ((2004), 222 NSR (2d) 41, 2004 NSCA 30, at paras. 40-41).

[101] For these reasons, I would dismiss the appeal.

[Bastarache J provided separate, dissenting reasons for judgment.]

NOTE

The DNA databank provisions can be technically complicated and require careful attention. They have generated other judicial interpretations. *R v. Rodgers*, 2006 SCC 15, [2006] 1 SCR 554 dealt with the situation of a prisoner still serving a sentence for sexual assault that antedated the provisions. Section 487.055 appears to permit an *ex parte* hearing in this circumstance. The Court of Appeal held that this provision must be interpreted as providing a presumptive hearing upon notice, not an *ex parte* one. A majority of the Supreme Court (Fish, Binnie, and Deschamps JJ dissenting) reversed and agreed with the judge of first instance that an *ex parte* hearing did not violate either s. 7 or s. 8 of the Charter. Fish J, for the dissenters, concluded:

> In the present matter, we have been shown no cause or justification for proceeding *ex parte*, while the reasons for giving notice are both compelling and self-evident. The judge retains discretion, in any event, to order an *ex parte* hearing when there is a reasonable basis for doing so in the particular circumstances of the case.

Will this decision encourage Parliament to use *ex parte* hearings in other situations? What does this decision say about the minimum requirements of fundamental justice?

V. SEX OFFENDER REGISTRIES

In 2005, Parliament enacted the *Sex Offender Information Registration Act* (2004, c. 10). This legislation, which amended the *Criminal Code*, is aimed at monitoring the movement and activities of offenders convicted of committing sexual offences against adults or children. As set out in the principal provisions of this amending legislation, below, orders made under these provisions obligate an offender to report and file information with the police for periods of 10 years, 20 years, or life. These provisions of the *Criminal Code* operate alongside various pieces of provincial legislation that oblige sex offenders to provide information and be accountable to the police: for example, see *Christopher's Law (Sex Offender Registry), 2000* (SO 2000, c. 1).

> 490.012(1) A court shall, on application of the prosecutor, make an order in Form 52 requiring a person to comply with the *Sex Offender Information Registration Act* for the applicable period specified in subsection 490.013(2), (3) or (4) as soon as possible after it imposes a sentence on the person for an offence referred to in paragraph (a), (c), (d) or (e) of the definition "designated offence" in subsection 490.011(1), or renders a verdict of not criminally responsible on account of mental disorder for such an offence.
>
> *Order*
> (2) A court shall, on application of the prosecutor, make an order in Form 52 requiring a person to comply with the *Sex Offender Information Registration Act* for the applicable period specified in subsection 490.013(2), (3) or (4) as soon as possible after it imposes a sentence on the person for an offence referred to in paragraph (b) or (f) of the definition "designated offence" in subsection 490.011(1), if the prosecutor establishes beyond a reasonable doubt that the person committed the offence with the intent to commit an offence referred to in paragraph (a), (c), (d) or (e) of that definition.
>
> *Order*
> (3) A court shall, on application of the prosecutor, make an order in Form 52 requiring a person in respect of whom an order may be made under subsection (1) or (2) to comply with the *Sex Offender Information Registration Act* for the applicable period specified in subsection 490.013(5), as soon as possible after it imposes a sentence on the person for a designated offence or renders a verdict of not criminally responsible on account of mental disorder for such an offence, if the prosecutor establishes that
>> (a) the person was, before or after the coming into force of that Act, previously convicted of, or found not criminally responsible on account of mental disorder for, an offence referred to in paragraph (a), (c), (d) or (e) of the definition "designated offence" in subsection 490.011(1);
>> (b) the person is not, and was not at any time, subject to an obligation under section 490.019; and
>> (c) no order was made under subsection (1) in connection with the previous offence.

Exception

(4) The court is not required to make an order under this section if it is satisfied that the person has established that, if the order were made, the impact on them, including on their privacy or liberty, would be grossly disproportionate to the public interest in protecting society through the effective investigation of crimes of a sexual nature, to be achieved by the registration of information relating to sex offenders under the *Sex Offender Information Registration Act*.

Reasons for decision

(5) The court shall give reasons for its decision.

Date order begins

490.013(1) An order made under section 490.012 begins on the day on which it is made.

Duration of order

(2) An order made under subsection 490.012(1) or (2)

(a) ends 10 years after it was made if the offence in connection with which it was made was prosecuted summarily or is an offence for which the maximum term of imprisonment is two or five years;

(b) ends 20 years after it was made if the offence in connection with which it was made is one for which the maximum term of imprisonment is 10 or 14 years; and

(c) applies to the person for life if the offence in connection with which it was made is one for which the maximum term of imprisonment is life.

Duration of order

(3) An order made under subsection 490.012(1) or (2) applies to a person for life if they are, or were at any time, subject to an obligation under section 490.019.

Duration of order

(4) An order made under subsection 490.012(1) or (2) applies to a person for life if they are, or were at any time, subject to an order made previously under either of those subsections.

Duration of order

(5) An order made under subsection 490.012(3) applies to a person for life.

An important issue that arises in this area concerns the application of s. 490.012(4) and whether the order would be grossly disproportionate in the circumstances. There are numerous decisions that address this issue. The following judgment in *R v. Redhead* considers a number of issues associated with the application of s. 490.012(4).

R v. Redhead
(2006), 206 CCC (3d) 315 (Alta. CA)

THE COURT:

[1] In each of these matters, the Crown appeals the trial judge's refusal to grant an order under s. 490.012 of the *Criminal Code*, RSC 1985, c. C-46 ("*CCC*"), compelling each respondent to register personal information pursuant to the *Sex Offender Information Registry Act*, SC 2004, c. 10 ("*SOIRA*"), and report to the nearest registration centre on an annual basis for 20 years.

Background

R v. Redhead

[2] The respondent Redhead sexually assaulted a 28 year old complainant, who has the mental capacity of a 7 year old, in the early morning hours. When the complainant tried to run away, the respondent caught her, bit her, and forced her to have sexual intercourse with him twice. He was intoxicated at the time of the assault.

[3] The respondent pled guilty to sexual assault, and the trial judge accepted a joint submission for a 30 month custodial sentence. However, the trial judge refused to grant an order under s. 490.012 of the *CCC* ("*SOIRA* order") because the respondent's judgment was clouded by alcohol at the time of the offence, he was not a pedophile, and he was not likely to re-offend.

. . .

R v. McIntyre

[5] The respondent McIntyre picked up the complainant prostitute in his minivan and negotiated a price in exchange for oral sex and sexual intercourse. They drove a short distance and parked, whereupon the respondent held a screwdriver to the complainant's neck, and proceeded to have both oral sex and sexual intercourse with her. He then drove the complainant back to where he had picked her up.

[6] The respondent was convicted of sexual assault with a weapon, and sentenced to four years in custody. The trial judge refused to grant a *SOIRA* order because the victim was not a child and the respondent had no prior related record.

Issues

[7] In *R v. Redhead*, the Crown alleges the trial judge erred in:

1. Applying the wrong standard in deciding whether to grant a *SOIRA* order;
2. Finding the respondent had established the criteria under s. 490.012(4) for refusal of the *SOIRA* order in the absence of any relevant evidence; and
3. Considering irrelevant factors in deciding to refuse the *SOIRA* order, namely: the respondent was intoxicated at the time of the offense, he had no related record, and the complainant was not a child.

[8] In *R v. McIntyre*, the Crown alleges the trial judge erred in:

1. Finding the respondent had established the criteria in s. 490.012(4) for refusal of the *SOIRA* order in the absence of any relevant evidence; and
2. Considering irrelevant factors in deciding to refuse the *SOIRA* order, namely: the respondent was a first offender, and the complainant was not a child.

[9] The respondent McIntyre also raises, for the first time on appeal, the issue of whether granting an order under s. 490.012(1) violates s. 11(i) of the *Canadian Charter of Rights and Freedoms*, Part I of the *Constitution Act, 1982*, being Schedule B to the *Canada Act 1982* (UK), 1982, c. 11 (the "*Charter*"). Although not raised by Redhead, the Court will also consider that issue in relation to his appeal.

. . .

Standard of Review

[12] A *SOIRA* order does not constitute a sentence. Like a DNA order, a *SOIRA* order is a consequence of conviction, and thus the standard of review for sentencing does not apply. However, the standard of review applied to DNA orders is informative given the parallels between DNA orders and *SOIRA* orders: both are consequences of a conviction; both exist to assist the police in investigating future crimes; and both infringe upon the privacy and liberty rights of the offender.

[13] This Court can alter a DNA order decision only where there is an error of principle, failure to consider a relevant factor, an over emphasis of appropriate factors, or a clearly unreasonable decision: *R v. Christie* (2004), 2004 ABCA 287 at para. 16; *R v. Hendry* (2001), 161 CCC (3d) 275 at 284 (Ont. CA). That same standard is applicable to *SOIRA* orders.

Analysis

[14] Upon sentencing an offender convicted of a designated offence within the meaning of s. 490.011(1) of the *CCC*, a court is required by s. 490.012 to make an order compelling the offender to comply with the *SOIRA* for the period specified in ss. 490.013(2), (3) or (4).

[15] A person who is registered under the *SOIRA* is required to provide information concerning his or her identity and whereabouts, and to report to the registration centre closest to his or her main residence on an annual basis for the period specified in the legislation. The *SOIRA* allows the RCMP to maintain a national database of convicted sex offenders, which can only be used by police to assist in the investigation of crimes of a sexual nature.

[16] If the court is satisfied the offender has established that the impact of such an order on his or her privacy or liberty would be grossly disproportionate to the public interest in protecting society through the effective investigation of crimes of a sexual nature, the offender falls within the exception provided under s. 490.012(4).

[17] Each of the offences in these appeals is a designated offence within the meaning of s. 409.011 of the *CCC*. Therefore, an order under s. 490.012(1) is mandatory unless the respondent falls within the s. 490.012(4) exception. In both cases under appeal, the respondents would be required to report annually for 20 years.

[18] The court making an order under s. 490.012 is required to provide reasons: s. 490.012(5).

Ground 1: R v. Redhead

[19] Did the trial judge err in applying the wrong standard in deciding whether to grant an order under s. 490.012?

[20] The test to determine whether the exception in s. 490.012(4) applies is: whether the impact of a *SOIRA* order on the liberty and privacy interests of a convicted sex offender would be grossly disproportionate to the public interest of effectively investigating crimes of a sexual nature. Thus, the court must assess the impact of a *SOIRA* order on the offender, including the impact on his or her privacy and liberty interests and

determine whether that impact is grossly disproportionate to the public interest: *R v. R.E.M.*, [2005] BCJ No. 1191 (SC) and *R v. A.G.N.*, [2005] BCJ No. 2781 (Prov. Ct.).

[21] The trial judge in *R v. Redhead* considered whether the imposition of a *SOIRA* order would be disproportionate to the respondent's privacy interest. In reaching that conclusion, the trial judge relied upon the respondent's lack of a prior record of sexual assault, the influence of alcohol on him, and the lack of evidence that the respondent was a pedophile. However, as discussed below, those factors are not relevant to the impact of the order on the offender.

[22] Moreover, there is no indication that the trial judge considered whether the impact of the registration and reporting requirements on the offender would be grossly disproportionate to the public interest. Thus, the trial judge in *R v. Redhead* erred in applying the incorrect standard in refusing to grant the *SOIRA* order.

[23] This issue was not raised in *R v. McIntyre*.

Ground Two: *R v. Redhead and R v. McIntyre*

Did the Trial Judges Err in Finding the Respondents Had Established the Criteria in Section 490.012(4) for Refusal of the SOIRA Order in the Absence of Any Relevant Evidence?

Impact on Offender

[24] The first part of the test for an exemption under s. 490.012(4) requires the court to assess the impact of a *SOIRA* order on the offender, including the impact on his or her privacy and liberty interests. The Crown maintains that neither respondent presented evidence relating to that impact, and therefore *SOIRA* orders should have been granted in each case.

[25] The New Brunswick Court of Appeal held there is no legal basis for refusing a *SOIRA* order where the offender has not adduced evidence to refute the order: *R v. Hayes* (2005), 288 NBR (2d) 197 (CA); see also *R v. Woodburn*, 2005 ONCJ 30 at para. 14. However, failure to adduce evidence during the *SOIRA* application is not necessarily determinative. The court may consider evidence at trial and in the pre-sentence report: *R v. L.S.*, [2005] BCJ No. 1801 (Prov. Ct.), or take judicial notice of relevant evidence.

[26] Under s. 490.012(4), the offender bears the evidentiary burden of establishing that the impact of a *SOIRA* order on him or her would outweigh the public interest in protecting society by investigating crimes of a sexual nature: *R v. L.S.*, *supra* at para. 16; *R v. Casaway*, 2005 NWTSC 37 at para. 12.

[27] Subsection 490.012(4) does not specify the criteria a court must consider in assessing the impact on an offender. In contrast, comparable provisions relating to the test for imposing a DNA order in s. 487.051(3) of the *CCC* expressly require the court to consider the criminal record of the offender and the circumstances of the offence, as well as the impact such an order would have on the person's privacy and security. The absence of reference to the record and the offence in s. 490.012(4) suggests that Parliament did not intend those factors to be determinative in deciding whether to impose a *SOIRA* order.

[28] The assessment of how reporting obligations might disproportionally impact an offender requires an evidentiary foundation. The focus of that inquiry must be on the offender's present and possible future circumstances, and not on the offence itself.

[29] Different evidence is required to assess the extent to which the offender will require monitoring, which will necessarily include an examination of the nature of the particular circumstances of the offence and record of the offender. But that evidence is irrelevant to the determination of the impact of the registration and reporting on the offender.

[30] Thus, the analysis under s. 490.012(4) is restricted to the impact of a *SOIRA* order on the offender. Nevertheless, that subsection clearly contemplates that factors other than the offender's privacy and liberty interests may be considered, as it requires the court to consider the impact on an offender, including any impact on the offender's privacy and security interests.

[31] Other factors might include unique individual circumstances such as a personal handicap, whereby the offender requires assistance to report: *R v. J.D.M.*, [2005] AJ No. 1258 (Prov. Ct.). Courts have also considered the intangible effects of the legislation, including stigma, even if only in the offender's mind; the undermining of rehabilitation and reintegration in the community; and whether such an order might result in police harassment as opposed to police tracking: *J.D.M.*, *ibid.*; *A.G.N.*, *supra* at para. 21; *R v. Have* (2005), 194 CCC (3d) 151 (Ont. CJ).

[32] Counsel for McIntyre argues the impact of a *SOIRA* order on an offender is self-evident given the onerous obligations imposed on a registrant under such an order. Courts have held the 10 to 20 year reporting requirement has a substantial impact on any offender's liberty, considering it is enforceable by imprisonment: *R v. Worm*, 2005 ABPC 92 at para. 53; *R v. Burke*, 2005 ONCJ 422 at para. 22. But in Casaway, *supra* at para. 19, the Court held that the burden of a 20 year order was lessened by flexibility in location and method of reporting. In *Have*, *supra*, the Court concluded the mandatory reporting obligation was a significant infringement on liberty, and the stigma attached to such an order might undermine treatment, rehabilitation, and re-integration into the community.

[33] However, given the onus on the offender to demonstrate why the impact of such an order would be disproportional to the public interest, it appears there is no presumption of impact in the legislation arising from the length of reporting obligations alone. Patently, the impact on anyone who is subject to the reporting requirements of a *SOIRA* order is considerable. But absent disproportional impact, the legislation mandates that anyone convicted of a prescribed offence is subject to the prescribed reporting period.

[34] This Court has held that the failure of an offender to adduce evidence of the impact of a DNA order on his or her privacy and security mandates the issuance of the order: *R v. Isbister* (2002), 303 AR 22, 2002 ABCA 54. Similarly, an offender has the onus to adduce evidence of the impact of a *SOIRA* order on him or her when seeking an exemption.

[35] In both cases before this Court, the trial judges erred in overlooking the lack of evidence of the impact of a *SOIRA* on the offender.

Public Interest

[36] The purpose of the Sex Offender Registry is stated in s. 2 of the *SOIRA*: "to help police services investigate crimes of a sexual nature." Subsection 2(2) specifies, "in the interest of protecting society through the effective investigation of crimes of a sexual nature, police services must have rapid access to certain information relating to sex offenders." The underlying assumption is that a sex offender will re-offend: *Have*, *supra* at para. 16.

[37] In *Have*, the Court determined the purpose and value of the legislation is related to the investigation of predatory offenders with a propensity to commit similar offences in the future, particularly those involving child abduction, where time is of the essence. Counsel for McIntyre relies on that case, arguing that because McIntyre had no related criminal record and the nature of the offence was less severe, he was a low risk to re-offend and not the type of offender Parliament had intended to register under *SOIRA*.

[38] We do not agree. The language of s. 490.012 does not suggest its application is so limited. Rather, the absence of such limiting language reflects Parliament's recognition of predictable repetitive behaviour of sexual offenders, and the inordinate consequences of sexual offences for victims of any age.

[39] Courts in some jurisdictions have found that where the offender is a low risk to re-offend, his inclusion would dilute the registry and make it less effective, rather than serve the public interest: *A.G.N.*, *supra* at para. 2; *J.D.M.*, *supra* at para. 48. The test in these jurisdictions is: how would registering the offender forward the public interest through the effective investigation of sexual crimes?: *Burke*, *supra* at para. 9.

[40] The Court in *Burke* at para. 57, suggested three factors that reduce the public interest in registering the offender: that the offender knew the victim; the circumstances of the offence; and a lack of criminal history: see also *A.G.N.* at para. 25; *R.E.M.*, *supra* at para. 74; see also *Casaway*, *supra* at para. 12.

[41] Courts have considered the severity of the offence: *Worm*, *supra* at para. 53, and the limited deterrent effect on both the offender and others: *J.D.M.*, *supra* at para. 48. An offender's cooperation in the past, the ease of exposure of misbehavior, an acceptance of responsibility for the incident, and a willingness to undergo treatment, have all been considered as factors in determining whether inclusion on the registry would serve the public interest.

[42] However, had Parliament intended that courts should determine whether there exists a public interest in registering an offender on a case-by-case basis, factoring in all of the individual circumstances surrounding each offender and his or her offence, it could have made that intention clear in the wording of the provision. Instead, Parliament has pronounced that there is a public interest in having those who commit the prescribed offences registered. The language of s. 490.012(4) presumes a "public interest in protecting society through the effective investigation of crimes of a sexual nature, to be achieved by the registration of information relating to sex offenders," but questions whether the impact on the offender would be grossly disproportionate to that public interest. Thus, the focus of the inquiry is not on whether there is a public interest in having the offender registered, but rather on whether the impact on the offender would be grossly disproportionate to the public interest.

Proportionality

[43] Courts agree that the standard for this aspect of the test is very high and the offender must establish more than a mere disproportionate impact: *L.S.*, *supra* at para. 35. Something more is required than the "mere imbalance in the competition between requirements of the *SOIRA* legislation and the privacy and security rights" of the offender: *J.D.M.*, *supra* at para. 53. The term grossly means a "marked and serious imbalance": *J.D.M.*, *ibid.*

[44] If the exception in s. 490.012(4) is so narrow that the *SOIRA* order is effectively mandatory, then the exception becomes meaningless: *Have*, *supra* at para. 17. However, in the absence of evidence of the impact of such an order on the offenders, it is impossible to assess whether such impact would be grossly disproportionate to the public interest.

[45] It follows that both trial judges erred in failing to address the proportionality aspect of the test under s. 490.012(4).

· · ·

Conclusion

[48] Given that both trial judges erred in finding the respondents had established the criteria for refusal of the *SOIRA* orders in the absence of any evidence in that regard, the Crown appeals in both *R v. Redhead* and *R v. McIntyre* are allowed.

[49] Orders in Form 52 are made under s. 490.012(1) of the *CCC*, requiring that each respondent comply with the *SOIRA* for a period of twenty years.

VI. OTHER PROHIBITION ORDERS: CRIMINAL CODE, SECTIONS 161 AND 446(5)

Section 161 of the *Criminal Code* allows a judge to include within the terms of a sentence for various sexual offences an order that prohibits the offender from being in public places, parks, and swimming pools where children under the age of 14 are, or might be, present. A related provision, which authorized the imposition of similar restrictions, s. 179(1)(b), was found to be overly broad and in violation of s. 7 of the *Charter*: see *Regina v. Heywood* (1994), 94 CCC (3d) 481 (SCC). The majority of the Court held that the provision was invalid because it was overly broad in its geographical ambit, it applied for the life of the offender, and there was no mechanism in place for review. When the case was argued before the Supreme Court, s. 161 had already been enacted.

Order of prohibition

161(1) When an offender is convicted, or is discharged on the conditions prescribed in a probation order under section 730, of an offence referred to in subsection (1.1) in respect of a person who is under the age of fourteen years, the court that sentences the offender or directs that the accused be discharged, as the case may be, in addition to any other punishment that may be imposed for that offence or any other condition prescribed in the order of discharge, shall consider making and may make, subject to the conditions or exemptions that the court directs, an order prohibiting the offender from

(a) attending a public park or public swimming area where persons under the age of fourteen years are present or can reasonably be expected to be present, or a daycare centre, schoolground, playground or community centre;

(b) seeking, obtaining or continuing any employment, whether or not the employment is remunerated, or becoming or being a volunteer in a capacity, that involves being in a position of trust or authority towards persons under the age of fourteen years; or

(c) using a computer system within the meaning of subsection 342.1(2) for the purpose of communicating with a person under the age of fourteen years.

Offences

(1.1) The offences for the purpose of subsection (1) are

(a) an offence under section 151, 152, 155 or 159, subsection 160(2) or (3), section 163.1, 170, 171 or 172.1, subsection 173(2) or section 271, 272, 273 or 281;

(b) an offence under section 144 (rape), 145 (attempt to commit rape), 149 (indecent assault on female), 156 (indecent assault on male) or 245 (common assault) or subsection 246(1) (assault with intent) of the *Criminal Code*, chapter C-34 of the Revised Statutes of Canada, 1970, as it read immediately before January 4, 1983; or

(c) an offence under subsection 146(1) (sexual intercourse with a female under 14) or section 153 (sexual intercourse with step-daughter), 155 (buggery or bestiality), 157 (gross indecency), 166 (parent or guardian procuring defilement) or 167 (householder permitting defilement) of the *Criminal Code*, chapter C-34 of the Revised Statutes of Canada, 1970, as it read immediately before January 1, 1988.

Duration of prohibition

(2) The prohibition may be for life or for any shorter duration that the court considers desirable and, in the case of a prohibition that is not for life, the prohibition begins on the later of

(a) the date on which the order is made; and

(b) where the offender is sentenced to a term of imprisonment, the date on which the offender is released from imprisonment for the offence, including release on parole, mandatory supervision or statutory release.

Court may vary order

(3) A court that makes an order of prohibition or, where the court is for any reason unable to act, another court of equivalent jurisdiction in the same province, may, on application of the offender or the prosecutor, require the offender to appear before it at any time and, after hearing the parties, that court may vary the conditions prescribed in the order if, in the opinion of the court, the variation is desirable because of changed circumstances after the conditions were prescribed.

Offence

(4) Every person who is bound by an order of prohibition and who does not comply with the order is guilty of

(a) an indictable offence and is liable to imprisonment for a term not exceeding two years; or

(b) an offence punishable on summary conviction.

There are few cases that interpret this new provision.

Section 446(5) of the Code also provides for a specialized sentencing prohibition. Anyone convicted of cruelty to animals may be prohibited from "owning or having the custody or control of an animal or a bird during any period not exceeding two years."

CHAPTER FOURTEEN

Sentencing for Murder

I. INTRODUCTION

For the purposes of sentencing, murder is treated differently from all other offences under the *Criminal Code*, RSC 1985, c. C-46, as amended. On a conviction for murder (first or second degree), the sentencing judge has no discretion; the offender must be sentenced to life imprisonment. With first-degree murder, the offender must serve 25 years' imprisonment before he or she becomes eligible for parole. There is more flexibility with second-degree murder. The trial judge may set the offender's parole ineligibility between 10 and 25 years. Because of this mandated severity, many murder trials are effectively about whether the offence was murder (with the mandatory sentencing regime) or manslaughter (with a maximum sentence of life imprisonment but no minimum sentence). As discussed later in this chapter, the constitutionality of the sentencing provisions for murder have been challenged because the lack of flexibility can sometimes lead to an injustice. However, the challenges have been unsuccessful.

The sentencing scheme for murder is also unique because of its inclusion of jury input. As set out in ss. 745 and 746 of the *Criminal Code*, on a conviction for second-degree murder, the trial judge must seek a recommendation from the jury on the appropriate length of parole ineligibility. Moreover, after an offender has served 15 years of his or her sentence for either first- or second-degree murder (if the ineligibility period was set at more than 15 years), he or she may bring an application under s. 746 of the Code to have the period of ineligibility shortened or terminated. This provision, known colloquially as the "faint hope clause," has proven very controversial in recent years.

In the next part, we set out the *Criminal Code* provisions that are relevant to sentencing individuals convicted of murder. However, before examining this specialized sentencing regime in more detail, consider the materials under section III, Murder in Canada: Empirical and Constitutional Considerations, which attempt to place these provisions in context.

II. CRIMINAL CODE, SECTIONS 745 TO 745.5

Sentence of Life Imprisonment

745. Subject to section 745.1, the sentence to be pronounced against a person who is to be sentenced to imprisonment for life shall be

(a) in respect of a person who has been convicted of high treason or first degree murder, that he be sentenced to imprisonment for life without eligibility for parole until the person has served twenty-five years of the sentence;

(b) in respect of a person who has been convicted of second degree murder where that person has previously been convicted of culpable homicide that is murder, however described under this Act, that that person be sentenced to imprisonment for life without eligibility for parole until the person has served twenty-five years of the sentence;

(c) in respect of a person who has been convicted of second degree murder, that the person be sentenced to imprisonment for life without eligibility for parole until the person has served at least ten years of the sentence or such greater number of years, not being more than twenty-five years, as has been substituted therefor pursuant to section 745.4; and

(d) in respect of a person who has been convicted of any other offence, that the person be sentenced to imprisonment for life with normal eligibility for parole.

Persons Under Eighteen

745.1 The sentence to be pronounced against a person who was under the age of eighteen at the time of the commission of the offence for which the person is convicted of first degree murder or second degree murder and who is to be sentenced to imprisonment for life shall be that the person be sentenced to imprisonment for life without eligibility for parole until the person has served

(a) such period between five and seven years of the sentence as is specified by the judge presiding at the trial, or if no period is specified by the judge presiding at the trial, five years, in the case of a person who was under the age of sixteen at the time of the commission of the offence;

(b) ten years, in the case of a person convicted of first degree murder who was sixteen or seventeen years of age at the time of the commission of the offence; and

(c) seven years, in the case of a person convicted of second degree murder who was sixteen or seventeen years of age at the time of the commission of the offence.

Recommendation by Jury

745.2 Subject to section 745.3, where a jury finds an accused guilty of second degree murder, the judge presiding at the trial shall, before discharging the jury, put to them the following question:

You have found the accused guilty of second degree murder and the law requires that I now pronounce a sentence of imprisonment for life against the accused. Do you wish to make any recommendation with respect to the number of years that the accused must serve before the accused is eligible for release on parole? You are not required to make any recommendation but if you do, your recommendation will be considered by me when I am determining whether I should substitute for the ten year period, which the law would otherwise require the accused to serve before the accused is eligible to be considered for release on parole, a number of years that is more than ten but not more than twenty-five.

Persons Under Sixteen

745.3 Where a jury finds an accused guilty of first degree murder or second degree murder and the accused was under the age of sixteen at the time of the commission of the offence, the judge presiding at the trial shall, before discharging the jury, put to them the following question:

You have found the accused guilty of first degree murder (or second degree murder) and the law requires that I now pronounce a sentence of imprisonment for life against the accused. Do you wish to make any recommendation with respect to the period of imprisonment that the accused must serve before the accused is eligible for release on parole? You are not required to make any recommendation but if you do, your recommendation will be considered by me when I am determining the period of imprisonment that is between five years and seven years that the law would require the accused to serve before the accused is eligible to be considered for release on parole.

Ineligibility for Parole

745.4 Subject to section 745.5, at the time of the sentencing under section 745 of an offender who is convicted of second degree murder, the judge who presided at the trial of the offender or, if that judge is unable to do so, any judge of the same court may, having regard to the character of the offender, the nature of the offence and the circumstances surrounding its commission, and to the recommendation, if any, made pursuant to section 745.2, by order, substitute for ten years a number of years of imprisonment (being more than ten but not more than twenty-five) without eligibility for parole, as the judge deems fit in the circumstances.

745.5 At the time of the sentencing under section 745.1 of an offender who is convicted of first degree murder or second degree murder and who was under the age of sixteen at the time of the commission of the offence, the judge who presided at the trial of the offender or, if that judge is unable to do so, any judge of the same court, may, having regard to the age and character of the offender, the nature of the offence and the circumstances surrounding its commission, and to the recommendation, if any, made pursuant to section 745.3, by order, decide the period of imprisonment the offender is to serve that is between five years and seven years without eligibility for parole, as the judge deems fit in the circumstances.

From time to time, amendments have been made to these provisions. What determines whether changes apply to a particular accused? What if a more lenient regime is enacted after sentencing is complete? In the case below, the offender is applying for an extension of time to appeal his sentence 15 years after the appeal period expired on the basis that he was 17 years old at the time of the offence and, hence, the new s. 745.1(b) ought to apply retroactively to him.

R v. Giesbrecht (E.H.)
[2007] MJ No. 465 (QL) (Man. CA)

[1] SCOTT CJM: The applicant has applied for an extension of time to appeal his sentence. What makes this relatively commonplace application so different is that it is made more than 15 years after the applicant was sentenced to life imprisonment without eligibility for parole for 25 years following his conviction for first degree murder, and 13 years after his conviction appeal to the Supreme Court of Canada was dismissed.

Within these unique circumstances, the critical event is the change to the law that occurred just prior to the applicant's conviction appeal being heard by this court. At that time, the *Criminal Code* (the *Code*) was changed to provide that persons who committed murder when they were under the age of 18 became eligible for parole after serving five to ten years of their life sentences. At the time the offence was committed, the applicant was 17 years of age.

The Facts

[2] On November 25, 1991, the applicant was found guilty of first degree murder. The sole issue at trial was whether or not he was insane or guilty of first degree murder. The sentence mandated at that time (by the *Code*) for first degree murder was life imprisonment without the possibility of parole for 25 years.

[3] A conviction appeal was taken to this court. On May 15, 1992, after the notice of appeal had been filed but before the appeal was heard, the *Code* was revised and sec. 742.1 (now 745.1) was enacted. Notwithstanding this change in the law, the only issues raised in this court related to the defence of insanity and the severance of counts. The appeal was dismissed on March 10, 1993. Leave to appeal to the Supreme Court was sought and obtained respecting the weight to be given to expert psychiatric evidence. The appeal was heard and dismissed on June 14, 1994.

[4] Throughout, the applicant was represented by experienced criminal defence counsel. While it is clear from the material filed in support of the application that his counsel was aware of the new sec. 742.1 change to the law, this ground of appeal was not raised in any legal forum until the applicant's present application was filed on June 17, 2005.

[5] From the material filed by the applicant, it is apparent that he, too, was aware of the changes to the law but was of the view (for reasons that are not explained) that he could only take advantage of sec. 742.1 if the conviction appeal was successful. He asserts that he was not aware of the possibility of a sentence appeal respecting the issue of parole eligibility until he was advised of such by different defence counsel in the spring of 2004. The applicant states that, "If I had been aware that such an appeal was possible, I would have pursued such an appeal." In other words, his intention to appeal, he says, was present but was thwarted by his lack of knowledge. The applicant confirms that no discussion took place with his first counsel respecting his sentence appeal, though some legal work was done post-conviction with respect to a possible application under sec. 690 of the *Code*. Sec. 690, which concerns an application to the Minister of Justice "for the mercy of the Crown," was repealed in 2002. Legal Aid funding for such an application was eventually denied.

[6] The applicant's trial counsel also swore an affidavit in support of the motion in which he indicated that he does not recall giving the applicant any advice regarding the impact of sec. 742.1 on his case.

• • •

[8] In support of his application, the applicant relies on sec. 44(e) of the federal *Interpretation Act* and sec. 11(i) of the *Charter*, which read as follows:

44. Where an enactment, in this section called the "former enactment," is repealed and another enactment, in this section called the "new enactment," is substituted therefor,

. . .

(e) when any punishment, penalty or forfeiture is reduced or mitigated by the new enactment, the punishment, penalty or forfeiture if imposed or adjudged after the repeal shall be reduced or mitigated accordingly[.]

11. Any person charged with an offence has the right

. . .

(i) if found guilty of the offence and if the punishment for the offence has been varied between the time of commission and the time of sentencing, to the benefit of the lesser punishment.

[9] With respect to sec. 44(e) of the *Interpretation Act*, the applicant places strong reliance on the decision of the Supreme Court of Canada in *R v. Dunn*, [1995] 1 SCR 226, where Major J, for eight of the nine members of the Supreme Court, held (at para. 27):

I conclude that s. 44(e) of the *Interpretation Act* resolves the question raised by this appeal. Where an amendment to a sentencing provision has been passed after conviction and sentence by the trial judge, but before the appeal has been "decided," the offender is entitled to the benefit of the lesser penalty or punishment. The court of appeal, in reviewing a trial decision on sentence, is "adjudging" that sentence, in that it considers it judicially. The respondent's contention that "adjudge" extends only to the options on penalty that may be ordered at trial is too narrow an approach to the interpretation of s. 44(e), and disregards the meaning of the word "adjudge."

[10] Therefore, prisoners who were "in the system" at the time the amendments to the *Code* took place were given the benefit of the new parole eligibility regime. See, for example, *R v. Tourangeau*, (1995), 137 Sask. R 277 (CA).

. . .

The leading Manitoba cases are *R v. Mohammed*, (1989), 61 Man. R. (2d) 192 (CA), and *R v. D.B.R.*, 2005 MBCA 21. As noted by Hamilton JA in *D.B.R.* (at para. 6):

[6] An order to extend time is a discretionary order, with the overriding objective that justice be done in the circumstances. The criteria that are normally considered on such an application are:

1. there was a continuous intention to appeal from a time within the period when the appeal should have been commenced;
2. there is a reasonable explanation for the delay; and
3. there are arguable grounds of appeal.

Hamilton JA went on to describe this last criterion as "a low threshold"; one which "is meant to ensure that the appeal is not frivolous" (at para. 7).

. . .

[17] The applicant places strong reliance on *R v. Olah*, (1997), 100 OAC 1. Ruston, one of the offenders, was convicted of first degree murder. He was 17 years old at the

time of the offence. In March 1992, he was sentenced to life imprisonment without eligibility for parole for 25 years. Section 742.1 of the *Code* came into force two months later. At trial, Ruston attempted to delay his sentencing hearing until the enactment of the new sentencing provisions, but the trial judge eventually became concerned with the delay and Ruston was compelled to proceed to sentencing before the provisions were declared in force. The Ontario Court of Appeal, having regard to both sec. 11(i) of the *Charter* and sec. 44(e) of the *Interpretation Act*, allowed Ruston's sentence appeal and reduced his period of parole ineligibility from 25 years to ten. A significant distinguishing factor, however, between *Olah* and the facts before this court is that Ruston swiftly took advantage of the pending *Code* changes.

[18] Many applications for an extension of time to appeal falter on the issue of the explanation for the delay. See *Roberge* at para. 7, *R v. Keen*, (1996), 29 OR (3d) 93 (CA), *R v. Jordan*, [1989] BCJ No. 1689 (CA) (QL), and *R v. Meidel*, 2000 BCCA 39, 136 BCAC 115.

[19] An analogous and helpful decision is that of the Supreme Court in *R v. Thomas*. The applicant was convicted of second degree murder in 1984. While his appeal was pending, *R v. Vaillancourt*, [1987] 2 SCR 636, had been argued and was under reserve in the Supreme Court. After the applicant's appeal was dismissed, the Supreme Court's reasons were released in *Vaillancourt*. The Supreme Court's ruling in *Vaillancourt* could have affected the outcome of the applicant's case but his notice of application for an extension of time was not filed for another two years, nearly three years beyond the prescribed time. Sopinka J noted (at p. 716):

> In a case in which the applicant alleges that he or she was convicted under a provision which has since been declared invalid, he or she should not be placed in a worse position than any other applicant. On the other hand, since we cannot do perfect justice, the applicant should not artificially be brought into the system.

The application was dismissed because of the lack of an adequate explanation for the delay, and because there was no demonstrated intention to appeal within the prescribed time period.

[20] As earlier noted, an applicant is usually required to demonstrate that an actual intention to appeal was formed during the appeal period and continued through to the time that the extension was sought. An intermittent interest in doing so is not sufficient. See *R v. Cooper*, 2004 BCCA 540, 204 BCAC 279, where the court noted (at para. 16):

> [16] I ... find the delay to be inordinate. While Mr. Cooper did, from time to time, make some effort to contact his lawyer, the efforts were minimal. The most that can be said of his intention was that it surfaced on occasion but not often and not with any vigour. What he had was a sporadic interest in appealing, but not what could be defined as a bona fide intention to appeal.

To the same effect, Glube CJNS in *Trimper* concluded that while the Crown had been continuously considering an appeal, it was not consistently intending to appeal, and the application to extend the time was accordingly denied.

[21] Dissatisfaction with the result without more is not synonymous with an intention to appeal where there has been extensive delay. As Wood JA stated in *R v. Rojas* (1991), 2 BCAC 182 (at para. 18):

> [18] I understand that it is entirely probable the applicant has, since 1984, been dissatisfied with the fact of his conviction and dissatisfied with the sentence which he received. But even for a person as disadvantaged as Mr. Rojas apparently is, and I speak here of his ability to read and write and his intellectual capacity to deal with the nuances and circumstances surrounding the legal process of appeal, I find it inconceivable that he could have allowed the matter to drift for such a length of time, if he truly intended to pursue appeals, without taking definitive action to let someone know that fact.

[22] In *R v. McAvoy*, 2005 BCCA 325, 213 BCAC 218, the British Columbia Court of Appeal concluded that an intention to appeal that was subsequently abandoned may amount to there being no *bona fide* intention to appeal.

[23] A lack of intention to appeal is not inevitably determinative. See *R v. Strattner (H.G.)* (1992), 83 Man. R (2d) 190 (CA), *per* Helper JA (at para. 13):

> [13] Although the lack of an intention to appeal against conviction will not necessarily defeat an application for an extension of time in which to bring such proceedings, it is a factor to be considered in determining the merit of the application.

This is because, as we have seen, the ultimate objective is that justice be done. See as well *R v. Hetsberger* (1979), 47 CCC (2d) 154 (Ont. CA), *R v. Leung*, 2003 ABCA 222, 330 AR 198, and *R v. Ubhi* (1992), 17 BCAC 84. But in these latter cases the circumstances were truly exceptional. In *Hetsberger*, the consequences of the conviction were "out of all proportion to the penalty imposed" (at p. 155). *Leung* and *Hetsberger* both involved deportation concerns. In *Ubhi*, the applicant had a limited capacity to understand the requirements of the appeal process. None of these (or any analogous) exceptional circumstances has been demonstrated in this case.

[24] The Crown concedes that the proposed appeal raises an arguable point and that it has not been seriously prejudiced by the delay.

· · ·

[27] In my opinion, this application should fail. There can be no doubt that the applicant and his counsel were personally aware of the pending legislation prior to the time the appeal against conviction was heard in the Manitoba Court of Appeal in 1993. But, the applicant says, it was not until "some time prior to August 2002 various newspaper articles came to my attention about the mandatory ten-year parole hearing of some offenders." Even then, nothing happened for a further two years (the Crown concedes that any delay from October 2004 until present is not in issue).

[28] The affidavits of the applicant and his former counsel raise as many questions as they answer. Despite the applicant's knowledge of the pending legislation in 1992, there is no suggestion that any thought was given to a sentence appeal for another decade. Instead, other possible legal avenues were explored concerning his continuing incarceration. Why was this? We are left to guess.

[29] Nor am I persuaded that the applicant had a continuous intention to appeal throughout the 11-year period following the affirmation of his conviction by the

Supreme Court of Canada. There were sporadic efforts by the applicant to consider appealing but no demonstrated clear intention to do so. At best, he had an intermittent desire to appeal rather than an ongoing intention to appeal. While the lack of a proper explanation for delay is not automatically fatal (see para. 23), the explanation for the very long delay, such as we have in this case, must be plausible and the circumstances truly exceptional. The applicant's explanation for the delay is wholly inadequate.

[30] As observed by Twaddle JA in *Mohammed*, there is an obligation on an accused, albeit not a heavy one, to establish that it is in the interests of justice that an extension of time be granted. This burden has not been met.

[31] The application for an extension of time to appeal is accordingly dismissed.

III. MURDER IN CANADA: EMPIRICAL AND CONSTITUTIONAL CONSIDERATIONS

In this section, we attempt to situate the murder provisions in a broader context by throwing some light on why murder continues to be treated differently for sentencing purposes. Is it because, as a group, those convicted of murder are indeed more dangerous than other types of offenders? Do they tend to re-offend at a greater rate? Or do we hope that the stiff and relatively inflexible sentencing scheme does a good job of deterring would-be offenders? Or does the retention of the current scheme really boil down to a moral judgment? That is, do we sentence those convicted of murder so harshly because we believe that the intentional killing of another human being deserves harsh punishment? Retribution pure and simple. The resolution of these issues is vital to the questions surrounding the constitutionality of this sentencing scheme.

These important questions are difficult to answer. The Canadian Centre for Justice Statistics keeps track of many features of homicides committed in Canada. In its most recent report, "Homicide in Canada, 2006," Statistics Canada provides the following glimpse into the prevalence of homicide in Canada:

> Following two years of increase, the homicide rate fell in 2006. Police reported 605 homicides, 58 fewer than the previous year ... . Overall, there were 1.85 homicide victims per 100,000 population, a 10% decrease from the previous year ... . In comparison, rates for many other types of violent crimes increased in 2006; attempted murder (+3%), aggravated assault (+5%), assault with a weapon/causing bodily harm (+4%) and kidnapping/forcible confinement (+12%) (Silver 2007).
>
> Since 1961, when national homicide statistics were first collected, there have been two distinct trends. Following a period of stability between 1961 and 1966, the homicide rate more than doubled over the next ten years, reaching a peak of 3.03 homicide victims per 100,000 population in 1975. Since 1975, the rate has gradually declined, with some year-to-year fluctuations. However, the 2006 rate remains higher than rates in the early 1960s.[1]

---

[1]   Geoffrey Li, "Homicide in Canada, 2006" (2007), 27 *Juristat* 1 at 2.

With respect to international comparisons of homicides, Statistics Canada provides the following data for selected countries based on rates per 100,000 population:

Turkey	6.23
United States	5.69
Germany	2.90
Switzerland	2.73
Sweden	2.64
New Zealand	2.37
Finland	2.12
Canada	1.85
Scotland	1.83
Hungary	1.64
England and Wales	1.41
France	1.39
Northern Ireland	1.32
Australia	1.06
Denmark	0.90
Japan	0.64
Hong Kong	0.51
Singapore	0.38

You can see that Canada's rate is about one-third that of the United States, and it is significantly less than that of Germany, Switzerland, and Sweden (63 percent, 67 percent, and 70 percent, respectively). However, Canada's rate is greater than that of England and Wales, France, Northern Ireland, Australia, Denmark, and Japan.

These figures represent rates of homicide in general, including murder, manslaughter, and infanticide. This chapter looks principally at first- and second-degree murder. In 1999, Statistics Canada provided the following information about the breakdown of the global homicide rate:

First degree murder, as a proportion of all homicides, has generally been increasing since 1976, although it has declined from 58% in 1996 to 51% in 1998. Conversely, homicides classified by the police as second degree murder have generally been decreasing, and in 1998, represented a proportion of 39%. Despite annual fluctuations, around 9% of all homicides are classified as manslaughter each year, and the remaining 1% are infanticide.[2]

There are many other aspects of homicide explored in the 2006 Statistics Canada report, including use of firearms, homicide rates in the various provinces, youth homicide rates, gang-related homicides, relationships with victims, victim involvement in illegal activities, and gender of perpetrators. Some findings are of particular interest. For example, after three years of increases, the rate of homicides with firearms decreased by 16 percent in 2006,

---

[2]   See O. Fedorowycz, "Homicide in Canada—1998" (1999), 19 *Juristat Service Bulletin* 3.

dropping to a level not seen for 20 years. Also, the number of youth-caused homicides increased in 2006. Eighty-four youths were involved in 54 homicides. This was the highest number and rate since 1961. Youths used firearms less than adults in causing homicides: 17 percent compared with 22 percent. As far as gender is concerned, 87 percent of persons accused of homicide were male and 73 percent of victims were male.

These statistics provide some interesting insights into the commission of murder offences in Canada, but they do not tell us a great deal about the backgrounds of the offenders who commit these offences. The following study, while somewhat dated, addresses the issue of recidivism of those convicted of homicide.

"Recidivism Among Homicide Offenders"
(1992), 4 Forum on Corrections Research 7

How well do murder and manslaughter offenders perform when they are finally released from federal prisons? This article presents statistics that may shed some light on the question.

Offenders Originally Incarcerated for Murder

A recent study followed murder offenders released on full parole between 1975 and 1990 to determine whether their time spent in the community on parole was successful or not. The length of the follow-up period varied—from up to 15 years for those released in 1975, to only a few months for those released in 1990.

Between 1 January 1975 and 31 March 1990, 658 murder offenders were released on full parole. Some of these offenders were released more than once for a total of 752 full-parole releases. ... [M]ore than three quarters of released murder offenders (77.5%) were not reincarcerated while on parole. Of those who were reincarcerated, 13.3% had their release revoked for a technical violation of their parole conditions and 9.2% for an indictable offence.

Of the 69 indictable offences committed by the released murder offenders, 30.4% (21) were offences against the person, 18.8% (13) were narcotics offences, 17.5% (12) were property offences, 8.7% (6) were robbery and 24.6% (17) were other *Criminal Code* offences.

Five released murder offenders (of a total of 658) were convicted of having committed a second murder while they were on full parole. Three of these were convicted of first-degree murder and two of second-degree murder. All five offenders had originally been convicted of non-capital murder. Besides these, no released murderer has been convicted of attempted murder or any other offence causing death.

Recidivism among murder offenders can be considered another way—murder offender groups can be divided into specific categories. ... [T]he outcome of the full-parole releases, as of 31 July 1990, [can be] compared among those who were convicted of capital murder, non-capital murder, first-degree murder and second-degree murder.

About one in 10 offenders convicted of second-degree murder, none convicted of first-degree murder, about one in three convicted of capital murder and one in four

convicted of non-capital murder had their full parole revoked. Furthermore, 0.6% of second-degree murderers, no first-degree murderers, 2.7% of capital murderers and 3.5% of non-capital murderers committed an offence against another person while on full parole. Comparisons should not be made between these groups based on these data, since the size of some groups (e.g., first-degree murderers) is very small and the follow-up period was very brief.

Offenders Originally Convicted of Manslaughter

Between 1 January 1975 and 31 March 1990, 2,242 offenders originally convicted of manslaughter were released, either on full parole or mandatory supervision. Some of these offenders were released more than once, for a total of 3,172 releases. Of these, 222 (7%) were released at warrant expiry (i.e., at the end of their sentence) and, there-fore, were not released to community supervision.

Of the 93% of manslaughter offenders who were released to community supervi-sion, 47.7% (1,407) were released on full parole and 52.3% (1,543) on mandatory su-pervision. These offenders were followed until 31 July 1990 to determine whether any had been reincarcerated while on release.

Of the full-parole releases, less than one quarter (21.7%) were revoked: 14.6% for a technical violation of the condition of a parole, 6.5% for an indictable offence and 0.5% for a summary offence. About twice the proportion (41.5%) of those released on mandatory supervision were revoked: 30.6% for a technical violation of the conditions of parole, 10% for an indictable offence and 0.9% for a summary offence ... .

Of the 92 (6.5%) full-parole releases of manslaughter offenders that were revoked for an indictable offence, 2.1% were revoked for offences against the person, 0.6% for robbery, 1.7% for property offences, 0.4% for narcotics offences and 1.7% for other *Criminal Code* offences.

Of the releases to mandatory supervision, 10% (154) were revoked for indictable offences: 3.2% were revoked for an offence against the person, 1.2% for robbery, 3.4% for property offences, 0.1% for narcotics offences and 2% for other *Criminal Code* offences.

· · ·

Marital Status

Available data indicate that about half of incarcerated offenders reported their marital status as single. Sentence length appeared to have no bearing on this finding. However, long-term offenders appeared somewhat less likely than other offenders to be involved in common-law relationships.

The breakdown of marital status, in decreasing order of frequency, is:

- single—50.5% of long-term inmates versus 47.5% of short-term inmates;
- common-law—21.5% of long-term inmates versus 28.6% of short-term inmates;
- married—13.5% of long-term inmates versus 11.9% of short-term inmates;

- separated or divorced—11.1% of long-term inmates versus 10.6% of short-term inmates; and
- other (including not specified)—3.4% of long-term inmates versus 1.4% of short-term inmates.

Summary

About one quarter of the total federal-offender population is serving a long-term sentence (i.e. 10 years or more). This is true of both male and female offender populations. Three out of five long-termers are incarcerated and two out of five are on some form of conditional release.

Quebec and the Pacific region have proportionately more long-term offenders, while the Atlantic and Prairie regions have proportionately fewer. Ontario has a more equitable proportion of long-termers.

During the past 10 years, the number of long-term offenders under federal jurisdiction increased by the same proportion as the number of federal offenders in general. During this same period, federal corrections admitted proportionately fewer long-termers, and released proportionately more long-termers, than offenders in general.

The vast majority of long-termers are Caucasian. About half of all long-term offenders are single, while about one in three is married (includes common-law). During the past 10 years, the average age of long-term offenders has increased by almost three years and is now about 38 years. Offenders serving life sentences for first-degree murder as a group, show the most dramatic increase in age.

Long- and short-term offenders have similar histories of federal incarceration, with the majority of both groups having no previous federal incarceration. After a five-year follow-up, only about one in five long-term offenders had been reconvicted of a criminal offence, while none of the 75 released offenders serving life sentences for murder had been subsequently reconvicted of murder.

In the late 1980s and early 1990s, the Supreme Court of Canada was busy shaping the contours of the constitutional requirements of fault. This was largely played out in the context of murder offences. Indeed, it was in *R v. Vaillancourt* (1987), 60 CR (3d) 289 (SCC), a murder case, that the court solidified the subjective fault requirement as a constitutional imperative. A subsequent wave of cases provided the court with an opportuntity to refine its approach. Among these cases were *Arkell* and *Luxton*. Although both cases were concerned with the constitutionality of offence-creating provisions (then s. 213 of the *Criminal Code*), they raised questions relating to the constitutionality of the sentencing provisions for first-degree murder. Given the breadth of the court's approach to these issues, *Arkell* and *Luxton* really address the constitutionality of mandatory sentencing for second-degree murder as well. As the extract by Allan Manson following these cases suggests, these issues appear to have been litigated and decided on an inadequate factual record.

R v. Arkell
(1990), 79 CR (3d) 207 (SCC)

LAMER CJC:

. . .

Analysis

For the reasons I have stated in *R v. Martineau* [(1990), 79 CR (3d) 129 (SCC)], released concurrently, s. 213(a) of the *Criminal Code* is of no force or effect, and the first two constitutional questions should, therefore, be answered accordingly. The third and fourth constitutional questions require an analysis of s. 214(5) of the *Criminal Code*. The main argument of the appellant, as regards his constitutional challenge of the section, is that it is arbitrary and irrational and thereby offends s. 7 of the Charter. In my view, this submission is answered by this court's judgment in *Paré* [(1987), 60 CR (3d) 346 (SCC)]. In that case a unanimous seven-person panel affirmed that s. 214 is a classification section concerned with sentencing and does not create a substantive offence. Wilson J, speaking for the court, put it this way at p. 625:

> It is clear from a reading of these provisions that s. 214 serves a different function from ss. 212 and 213. Sections 212 and 213 create the substantive offence of murder. Section 214 is simply concerned with classifying for sentencing purposes the offences created by ss. 212 and 213. It tells us whether the murder is first degree or second degree. This view of s. 214 was expressly adopted by this court in *R v. Farrant*, [1983] 1 SCR 124 (*per* Dickson J as he then was) at p. 140 and in *Droste v. The Queen*, [1984] 1 SCR 208 (*per* Dickson J as he then was) at p. 218.

Indeed, the appellant concedes that s. 214(5) is a sentencing classification provision.

The argument of the appellant suggests that the sentencing scheme is flawed and in violation of s. 7 of the Charter because it results in the punishment of individuals that is not proportionate to the seriousness of the offences giving rise to the sentences. First, I must note that as a result of this court's decision in *Martineau*, released concurrently, it can no longer be said that s. 214(5) has the potential to classify unintentional killings as first degree murder. A conviction for murder requires proof beyond a reasonable doubt of subjective foresight of death. Therefore, when we reach the stage of classifying murders as either first or second degree, we are dealing with individuals who have committed the most serious crime in our *Criminal Code*, and who have been proven to have done so with the highest level of moral culpability, that of subjective foresight. Section 214(5) represents a decision by Parliament to impose a more serious punishment on those found guilty of murder while committing certain listed offences.

This leads me to a second point, namely, a consideration of the underlying rationale of s. 214(5). Again, I refer to the decision of this court in *Paré*, at pp. 632-33:

> All murders are serious crimes. Some murders, however, are so threatening to the public that Parliament has chosen to impose exceptional penalties on the perpetrators. One such class of murders is that found in s. 214(5), murders done while committing a hijacking, a kidnapping and forcible confinement, a rape, or an indecent assault. ...

The offences listed in s. 214(5) are all offences involving the unlawful domination of people by other people. Thus an organizing principle for s. 214(5) can be found. This principle is that where a murder is committed by someone already abusing his power by illegally dominating another, the murder should be treated as an exceptionally serious crime. Parliament has chosen to treat these murders as murders in the first degree.

I can find no principle of fundamental justice that prevents Parliament, guided by the organizing principle identified by this court in *Paré*, from classifying murders done while committing certain underlying offences as more serious, and thereby attaching more serious penalties to them. In the case of the distinction between first and second degree murder, the difference is a maximum extra 15 years that must be served before one is eligible for parole. This distinction is neither arbitrary nor irrational. The section is based on an organizing principle that treats murders committed while the perpetrator is illegally dominating another person as more serious than other murders. Further, the relationship between the classification and the moral blameworthiness of the offender clearly exists.

Section 214 only comes into play when murder has been proven beyond a reasonable doubt. In light of *Martineau*, this means that the offender has been proven to have had subjective foresight of death. Parliament's decision to treat more seriously murders that have been committed while the offender is exploiting a position of power through illegal domination of the victim accords with the principle that there must be a proportionality between a sentence and the moral blameworthiness of the offender and other considerations such as deterrence and societal condemnation of the acts of the offender. Therefore, I conclude that in so far as s. 214(5) is neither arbitrary nor irrational, it does not infringe upon s. 7 of the Charter. I note that in this appeal there was no argument made as regards s. 12 of the Charter, although that issue was raised in a case heard and disposed of concurrently, *R v. Luxton*.

R v. Luxton
(1990), 79 CR (3d) 193 (SCC)

LAMER CJC:

. . .

For the reasons stated in *R v. Martineau* [(1990), 79 CR (3d) 129 (SCC)], released concurrently, s. 213(a) of the *Criminal Code* infringes ss. 7 and 11(d) of the Charter and cannot be saved by s. 1 of the Charter. Therefore, the first constitutional question is answered in the affirmative and the second question in the negative.

The remaining questions require an examination of the combined effect of s. 214(5)(e) and s. 669 of the Code on the rights guaranteed by ss. 7, 9 and 12 of the Charter, and s. 2(e) of the *Canadian Bill of Rights*. The appellant combines his argument in respect of s. 7 of the Charter and s. 2(e) of the *Canadian Bill of Rights*. He submits that the principles of fundamental justice require that differing degrees of moral blameworthiness in different offences be reflected in differential sentences, and that sentencing be individualized. The appellant cites the following judgments as support

for the view that the combined effect of s. 214(5)(e) and s. 669 offends the principles that a just sentencing system contains a gradation of punishments differentiated according to the malignity of offences and that sentencing be individualized: *Re BC Motor Vehicle Act*, [1982] 2 SCR 486, per Wilson J; *R v. Smith*, [1987] 1 SCR 1045, per Lamer J and per Wilson J; and *R v. Lyons*, [1987] 2 SCR 309, per La Forest J. In my view, assuming that s. 7 incorporates the propositions cited by the appellant as principles of fundamental justice, the combined effect of s. 214(5)(e) and s. 669 is in accordance with them. Section 214(5) of the *Criminal Code* isolates a particular group of murderers, namely, those who have murdered while committing certain offences involving the illegal domination of the victim, and classifies them for sentencing purposes as murderers in the first degree. As a result of s. 669 the murderer is sentenced to life imprisonment without parole eligibility for 25 years. It is of some note that even in cases of first degree murder, s. 672 [now s. 745] of the Code provides that after serving 15 years the offender can apply to the Chief Justice in the province for a reduction in the number of years of imprisonment without eligibility for parole having regard for the character of the applicant, his conduct while serving the sentence, the nature of the offence for which he was convicted and any other matters that are relevant in the circumstances. This indicates that even in the cases of our most serious offenders, Parliament has provided for some sensitivity to the individual circumstances of each case when it comes to sentencing.

I must also reiterate that what we are speaking of here is a classification scheme for the purposes of sentencing. The distinction between first and second degree murder only comes into play when it has first been proven beyond a reasonable doubt that the offender is guilty of murder, that is, that he or she had subjective foresight of death: *R v. Martineau*, handed down this day. There is no doubt that a sentencing scheme must exhibit a proportionality to the seriousness of the offence, or to put it another way, there must be a gradation of punishments according to the malignity of the offences. However, a sentencing scheme also must take into account other factors that are of significance for the societal interest in punishing wrongdoers. In *Lyons*, *supra*, at pp. 328-29, La Forest J considered the dangerous offender designation in the Code and said the following in respect of the relationship between sentencing and its objectives:

> I accordingly agree with the respondent's submission that it cannot be considered a violation of fundamental justice for Parliament to identify those offenders who, in the interests of protecting the public, ought to be sentenced according to considerations which are not entirely reactive or based on a "just deserts" rationale. The imposition of a sentence which "is partly punitive but is mainly imposed for the protection of the public" ... seems to me to accord with the fundamental purpose of the criminal law generally, and of sentencing in particular, namely, the protection of society. In a rational system of sentencing, the respective importance of prevention, deterrence, retribution and rehabilitation will vary according to the nature of the crime and the circumstances of the offender.

In my view the combination of s. 214(5)(e) and s. 669 clearly demonstrates a proportionality between the moral turpitude of the offender and the malignity of the offence, and moreover it is in accord with the other objectives of a system of sentencing identified by La Forest J in *Lyons*. As I have stated, we are dealing with individuals that have

committed murder and have done so with the now constitutionally mandated *mens rea* of subjective foresight of death. Parliament has chosen, once it has been proven that an offender has committed murder, to classify certain of those murders as first degree. Murders that are done while committing offences which involve the illegal domination of the victim by the offender have been classified as first degree murder. Forcible confinement is one of those offences involving illegal domination. The added element of forcible confinement, in the context of the commission of a murder, markedly enhances the moral blameworthiness of an offender. Indeed, forcible confinement is punishable by up to 10 years in prison. The decision of Parliament to elevate murders done while the offender commits forcible confinement to the level of first degree murder is consonant with the principle of proportionality between the blameworthiness of the offender and the punishment. Further, it is consistent with the individualization of sentencing especially since only those who have killed with subjective foresight of death while also committing the offence of forcible confinement are subjected to that punishment. I, therefore, can find no principle of fundamental justice that has been violated by the combination of s. 215(5)(e) and s. 669 of the *Criminal Code*. Equally, for these same reasons I conclude that there is no violation of s. 2(e) of the *Canadian Bill of Rights*.

The appellant also submits in a separate argument that the combination of s. 214(5)(e) and s. 669 contravenes s. 9 of the Charter because of the imposition of a mandatory term of imprisonment by statute for an offence that encompasses a range of moral turpitude. This argument overlaps a great deal with the appellant's s. 7 argument and I would only add the following comments to those I have already made above. The combined effect of the impugned sections do not demonstrate arbitrariness on the part of Parliament. Indeed, as I noted above, Parliament has narrowly defined a class of murderers under an organizing principle of illegal domination and has specifically defined the conditions under which the offender can be found guilty of first degree murder. In order to be found guilty of first degree murder under s. 214(5)(e), the offender must have committed murder with subjective foresight of death and must have committed the murder "while committing or attempting to commit ... forcible confinement." Where the act causing death and the acts constituting the forcible confinement "all form part of one continuous sequence of events forming a single transaction," the death is caused "while committing" an offence for the purpose of s. 214(5); see *Paré, supra*, at p. 632. To commit the underlying offence of forcible confinement, the offender must use "physical restraint, contrary to the wishes of the person restrained, but to which the victim submits unwillingly, thereby depriving the person of his or her liberty to move from one place to another": quote from *R v. Dollan* (1980), 53 CCC (2d) 146 (Ont. HC), as cited with approval in *R v. Gratton* (1985), 18 CCC (3d) 462 (CA) [at p. 473]. It is true that the definition of forcible confinement adopted by the courts allows for varying circumstances in each individual case. But this alone is not a sign of arbitrariness. The offence of forcible confinement as defined falls clearly under the rubric of the organizing principle enunciated by Wilson J in *Paré*, namely, that of the illegal domination of no person by another. The decision of Parliament to attach a minimum 25-year sentence without eligibility for parole in cases of first degree murder, having regard to all these circumstances, cannot be said to be arbitrary within the meaning of s. 9 of the Charter. The incarceration is statutorily authorized, it narrowly defines a class of

offenders with respect to whom the punishment will be invoked and it prescribes quite specifically the conditions under which an offender may be found guilty of first-degree murder. Further, the policy decision of Parliament to classify these murders as first degree murders accords with the broader objectives of a sentencing scheme. The elevation of murder while committing a forcible confinement to first degree reflects a societal denunciation of those offenders who choose to exploit their position of dominance and power to the point of murder.

The appellant's final argument is that the combined effect of s. 215(5)(e) and s. 669 contravenes s. 12 of the Charter. Section 12 of the Charter protects individuals against cruel and unusual punishment. The phrase "cruel and unusual punishment" has been considered by this court in *R v. Smith, supra*. That case held that the criterion to be applied in order to determine whether a punishment is cruel and unusual is whether the punishment is so excessive as to outrage standards of decency. At pp. 1072-73 stated that:

> The test for review under s. 12 of the Charter is one of gross disproportionality, because it is aimed at punishments that are more than merely excessive. We should be careful not to stigmatize every disproportionate or excessive sentence as being a constitutional violation, and should leave to the usual sentencing appeal process the task of reviewing the fitness of a sentence. Section 12 will only be infringed where the sentence is so unfit having regard to the offence and the offender as to be grossly disproportionate.
>
> In assessing whether a sentence is grossly disproportionate, the court must first consider the gravity of the offence, the personal characteristics of the offender and the particular circumstances of the case in order to determine what range of sentences would have been appropriate to punish, rehabilitate or deter this particular offender or to protect the public from this particular offender.

In *Lyons, supra*, La Forest J addressed the meaning of the word "grossly" at pp. 344-45:

> The word "grossly" [as in "grossly disproportionate"], it seems to me, reflects this Court's concern not to hold Parliament to a standard so exacting, at least in the context of s. 12, as to require punishments to be perfectly suited to accommodate the moral nuances of every crime and every offender.

In my view, the combination of s. 214(5)(e) and s. 669 does not constitute cruel and unusual punishment. These sections provide for punishment of the most serious crime in our criminal law, that of first degree murder. This is a crime that carries with it the most serious level of moral blameworthiness, namely, subjective foresight of death. The penalty is severe and deservedly so. The minimum 25 years to be served before eligibility for parole reflects society's condemnation of a person who has exploited a position of power and dominance to the gravest extent possible by murdering the person that he or she is forcibly confining. The punishment is not excessive and clearly does not outrage our standards of decency. In my view, it is within the purview of Parliament, in order to meet the objectives of a rational system of sentencing, to treat our most serious crime with an appropriate degree of certainty and severity. I reiterate that even in the case of first degree murder, Parliament has been sensitive to the particular circumstances of each offender through various provisions allowing for the Royal prerogative

of mercy, the availability of escorted absences from custody for humanitarian and re-habilitative purposes and for early parole: see s. 672, s. 674 [now s. 747] and s. 686 [now s. 751] of the *Criminal Code*. In *Smith, supra*, at p. 1070, I quoted with approval the following statement by Borins DCJ in *R v. Guiller*, Ont. Dist. Ct. [48 CR (3d) 226]:

> It is not for the court to pass on the wisdom of Parliament with respect to the gravity of vari-ous offences and the range of penalties which may be imposed upon those found guilty of committing the offences. Parliament has broad discussion in proscribing conduct as crimin-al and in determining proper punishment. While the final judgment as to whether a punish-ment exceeds constitutional limits set by the Charter is properly a judicial function the court should be reluctant to interfere with the considered views of Parliament and then only in the clearest of cases where the punishment prescribed is so excessive when compared with the punishment prescribed for other offences as to outrage standards of decency.

Therefore, I conclude that in the case at bar the impugned provisions in combination do not represent cruel and unusual punishment within the meaning of s. 12 of the Charter.

A. Manson, "The Easy Acceptance of Long Term Confinement"
(1990), 79 CR (3d) 265 (footnotes omitted)

. . .

The History of Section 742(a)

The creation of two categories of murder, first and second degree, and the current pun-ishments for these offences evolved from the debate over capital punishment which occupied Parliament and the Canadian public for over twenty years. In 1956, a joint committee of the Senate and House of Commons recommended the retention of capital punishment but suggested that the offence of murder be divided into capital and non-capital categories. In 1961, the *Criminal Code* was amended to provide for capital murder which would be punishable by hanging unless the person was under the age of 18 years: *An Act to Amend the Criminal Code* (Capital Murder), SC 1960-61, c. 44, s. 1. Capital murder consisted of a killing that was planned and deliberate, a killing resulting from the direct intervention or counselling by the accused in the course of certain stipu-lated crimes, or the killing of a police officer or prison guard. All other murder was characterized as non-capital and was punishable by life imprisonment. This régime continued in force until 28th December 1967, although as a result of reviews by the Cabinet for the purpose of advising the Governor-General on commutation, the last hangings in Canada took place on 11th December 1962 at the Don Jail in Toronto. In 1967 the Code was again amended, to limit capital murder to those cases where an ac-cused, by his or her own act, caused or assisted in the causing of the death of a police officer or prison officer, or counselled or procured that death: *An Act to Amend the Criminal Code*, SC 1967-68, c. 15, s. 1. This limitation was intended to last for only

five years (s. 4), but was continued for a further five years in 1972: *Criminal Law Amendment (Capital Punishment) Act*, SC 1973-74, c. 38, s. 10. During this semi-moratorium, persons who had been sentenced to death but whose sentences had been commuted could not be released from confinement without the approval of the Governor in Council. Persons who were sentenced to life imprisonment for murder could be released on parole after serving ten years, unless the trial judge increased the period of parole ineligibility. This was the statutory sentencing background against which Parliament resumed the debate on capital punishment in 1976.

The often passionate and partisan Parliamentary discussion in 1976 focussed on the fundamental issue of the legitimacy of capital punishment, and little attention was paid to the elements of the proposed alternatives. In the Standing Committee on Justice and Legal Affairs, a clause-by-clause consideration of the new bill took place. In that committee, statistics were tabled to show the Canadian experience with life imprisonment, as well as the régimes which operated in other jurisdictions where capital punishment had been abolished. The following table indicates the average periods actually served in custody in Canada between 1961 and 1974.

	1961-68	1968-74
Capital Murder (commuted)	12.0	13.2
Non-Capital Murder....................	6.2	7.7

These figures are particularly interesting when put into a comparative context as discussed by the parliamentarians in committee at the time. A United Nations group of experts had only a few years earlier observed that, in countries which employed life imprisonment as an alternative to capital punishment, the most common median length of term served was between 10 and 15 years, and the average custodial term was about 14 years. The Solicitor General offered the committee the following examples of statutory minimum terms of incarceration for comparable offences in various American and European jurisdictions: see the minutes of the standing committee, ante, note 3, p. 72:60:

New York:	15–25 years
California:	7 years
England:..............................	parole review after 4 years
Sweden:	10 years
Denmark:.............................	5 years
Massachusetts:.........................	15 years
Holland:..............................	no statutory minimum

With all the data, both Canadian and comparative, pointing to a period of between 10 and 15 years, why did the proposed legislation include a minimum term for first degree of 25 years? The answer is simple: politics and expedience. Warren Allmand, the Solicitor General, who had been given the responsibility of steering the struggle to abolish capital punishment, had been told by the Canadian Association of Police Chiefs, who supported the death penalty, that only a minimum sentence as severe as 25 years could conceivably be an alternative to the rope: see the minutes of the standing committee, ante, note 3, pp. 72:60-61. In retrospect, Mr. Allmand was probably correct in responding to views of that sort in order to achieve the success of the abolition move-ment. Now, 15 years later, ample time has passed to assess the trade-off in the light of hard evidence about the effects of long term confinement. Instead, what was a political compromise in 1976 is now a constitutional benchmark.

The 25-Year Minimum and Sections 7 and 9 of the Charter

The appellants argued that the principles of fundamental justice, as guaranteed by s. 7 of the Charter, require a scheme of differentiated sentences which respond to varying degrees of moral blameworthiness. Accordingly, so the argument went, a mandatory long term sentence encompassing all kinds of first degree murders denied to individual convicted persons their entitlement to be sentenced according to their particular circum-stances. Without confirming that s. 7 includes constitutional requirements of propor-tionate and individualized sentences, Lamer CJC concludes in *Lauzon* at p. 201 that the longer minimum term mandated for first degree murder by ss. 231(5)(e) and 742 "dem-onstrates a proportionality between the moral turpitude of the offender and the malig-nity of the offence." This conforms, according to Lamer CJC, with the objectives of a rational sentencing system as described in the court's earlier decision in *R v. Lyons*, [1987] 2 SCR 309, per La Forest J at pp. 328-29. He points out that, with respect to convictions pursuant to s. 231(5)(e), the longer mandatory sentence is consistent with an individualized sentencing policy, since it applies only to someone who killed with subjective foresight of death while committing the underlying offence of forcible con-finement, an offence involving the illegal domination of another. For similar reasons, and in accordance with the judgment in *Lyons*, Lamer CJC finds that the sentence does not constitute arbitrary detention in breach of s. 9 of the Charter, since it is statutorily authorized and relates to a narrowly-defined class of offenders for whom specific condi-tions of responsibility are prescribed.

The 25-Year Minimum and Section 12 of the Charter

The manner in which the 25-year minimum term is measured against the s. 12 guaran-tee prohibiting cruel and unusual punishment is especially troubling. The leading case in this regard is *R v. Smith*, [1981] 1 SCR 1045, in which the court confirmed that s. 12 represents a "compendious expression of a norm" (p. 205) which prohibits grossly dis-proportionate punishments. The two judgments in that case offered various tests which might produce a finding of cruel and unusual punishment, including whether the pun-ishment outrages standards of decency. Lamer J at pp. 231-32 discussed eight tests, and McIntyre J at p. 212 synthesized these tests into three categories: (1) whether the pun-ishment outrages the public conscience or degrades human dignity; (2) whether the punishment goes beyond what is necessary to achieve its purpose; and (3) whether the punishment is imposed on a rational basis. In *Luxton*, the test of outraging decency be-comes the single analytical tool used to validate the mandatory long term confinement for first degree murder.

In essence, the judgment in *Luxton* says that it is constitutionally acceptable to im-pose the most severe punishment for the most serious offence. No one would quarrel with the logic of this proposition. While it must be true, it nevertheless misses the point in two significant ways. First, although the reasoning justifies the imposition of a harsher sentence for first degree murder, it ignores the actual length of the term imposed. The same analysis could be applied to justify mandatory terms of 30, 40 or 50 years. Secondly, by truncating the s. 12 analysis into solely a question about societal outrage, the court either ignores the effects of the duration of the sentence or assumes that the community knows the real effects of 25-year minimum terms and accepts them as legitimate aspects of penal policy. The issue of duration and its impact is clearly part of a proper s. 12 analysis, yet no evidence was adduced about the human impact of long term confinement. Although the Supreme Court has reminded us on a number of occasions that legislation might fail to pass Charter muster by reason of either its purpose or its effects, no empirical or expert material was placed before the court to explain the effects of the punishment in question. The argument proceeded entirely on conceptual grounds, with reference primarily to the idea of a hierarchy of punishments. The actual punishment was not assessed in real, human terms.

It is not fair to suggest that Lamer CJC has ignored the question of 25 years of confinement and its relation to the personal circumstances of offenders. He observes at p. 203 that "Parliament has been sensitive to the particular circumstances of each offender through various provisions allowing for the Royal prerogative of mercy, the availability of escorted absences from custody for humanitarian and rehabilitative purposes, and for early parole." In an abstract sense, the possibility of these indulgences exists, but the reality is that they are very rarely used. Last spring, when a 70-year-old woman received a pardon after serving 11 years of a first degree murder term, the newspapers announced that it was the first pardon granted to a person convicted of first degree murder, and that only nine prisoners had received pardons in the past ten years. The Royal prerogative of mercy is available to ameliorate the harshness of sentences, but it is most often used in situations where it has been established that a person was wrongly convicted. The availability of escorted temporary absence passes is another example of the sardonic gap between statutory possibility and practical reality. Passes of this sort for a lifer require the approval of the institution where the prisoner is confined, the approval of the National Parole Board and the deployment of one or two staff persons to act as escorts. The board's own manual advises that this power should be used "very sparingly" in order not to "depreciate" the seriousness of the sentence. Consequently, escorted passes are awarded principally for funerals, visits to sick relatives and other related family events. The reference to early parole must mean the parole ineligibility review pursuant to s. 745 [am. RSC 1985, c. 27 (2nd Supp.), s. 10] of the code, which a prisoner can commence after serving 15 years in custody. This process only provides a new parole eligibility date. The issue of release is then delegated to the parole board for the application of its usual criteria, typically a process which takes a minimum of three years. Again it is important to recognize that the court had no material before it demonstrating how these extraordinary processes really work. Had the court found the mandatory punishment to be illegitimate, these factors, along with issues of legislative objective and real impact, would have been relevant to the s. 1 justificatory analysis.

Conclusion

The rulings in *Luxton* and *Arkell* do not preclude any individual convicted of first degree murder from attempting to challenge the application of the mandatory sentence as it relates to his or her particular circumstances. In *Smith* it was pointed out at pp. 233-34 that the effect of an otherwise acceptable sentence in a particular, personal context might render the punishment grossly disproportionate. The Yukon Court of Appeal, relying on *Smith*, has ruled that a firearms prohibition produced a grossly disproportionate impact on a professional trapper: *R v. Chief* (1990), 74 CR (3d) 57, (YTCA); cf. *R v. Kelly*, Ont. CA, 6th September 1990 (not yet reported). Another example of an individualized inquiry is *Steele v. Mountain Inst.* (1990), 76 CR (3d) 307, affirmed by SCC, 8th November 1990 (not yet reported), in which the continued confinement of a prisoner who had been designated a "criminal sexual psychopath" in 1953 was declared to be cruel and unusual punishment. More pertinent to the issue of murder sentencing, in *R v. Daniels*, Sask. CA 15th July 1990 (not yet reported), Wedge J found that it was cruel and unusual punishment to require native women from Saskatchewan to serve a life sentence for second degree murder in the federal Prison for Women at Kingston, Ontario. In that case the principal argument, also accepted by the court, was that shipping the convicted women out of the province to the Prison for Women resulted in impermissible discrimination contrary to s. 15(1) of the Charter. If one contemplates other circumstances where a sentence may be considered discriminatory in terms of its effect by reason of sex or age, extreme examples may also reach the level of gross disproportionality. Consider the sentencing of a 14-year-old girl tried and convicted as a party in adult court in Newfoundland of first degree murder. After assessing her blameworthiness, her age and the conditions of confinement at the Prison for Women, is it not a grossly disproportionate sentence? Can't a similar argument be made for a 14-year-old boy? While maturity does not lend itself so easily to a reciprocal analysis, it does lead one's mind to cases of disability where the impact of confinement, in personal and access terms, will be dramatically unfair because of the structural and programming limitations of institutions. Equally problematic are cases of special health problems which could produce a severe differential impact on the sentenced person. As time passes and lawyers are confronted with the circumstances of individual cases, other examples of differential impact will appear which arguably approach the standard of gross disproportionality.

The more important question is whether the Supreme Court will decide to reconsider the constitutionality of the mandatory sentence for first degree murder when it is provided with a full, empirical record. Certainly the court has the power to rethink an important issue of this sort, particularly if persuasive material is presented to it. The prospect, however, is doubtful, and one might wonder whether, in the wake of *Luxton* and *Arkell*, a lawyer would have the temerity to bring a new leave application on this issue. However, as discussed above, a s. 12 argument can be based on individual impact, and it may be that, in the context of an individual challenge to the application of the mandatory sentence, the Supreme Court might choose to rehear the general issue.

Given the rate at which the numbers of people serving long terms of incarceration are accumulating in our penitentiaries, it is imperative that some authority, either Parliament or the courts, address their minds to the legitimacy of long term confinement. The 25-year parole ineligibility period was created as a political expedient in the face of compelling data pointing to a lower minimum term. At the time, very little was known about the human effects of long term confinement. Now, over 15 years have passed and no effort seems to have been made to assess this harshest feature of our sentencing régime. It is beginning to dominate the penitentiary environment, and begs for serious reconsideration. While we await a new assessment of this form of long term confinement, lawyers should remember that s. 12 provides an opportunity, albeit a limited one, for justice in the individual case. The judgment in *Luxton* and *Arkell* should not discourage counsel from placing individual cases before the courts, with complete factual records.

For the time being, *Arkell* and *Luxton* effectively preclude further challenges to the legislation that creates the mandatory sentencing scheme for murder. However, as Manson points out, this does not mean that individual litigants must necessarily be deprived of a remedy in exceptional cases.

R v. Latimer
[2001] 1 SCR 3

[In 1997, Robert Latimer was convicted (a second time) of second-degree murder in relation to the death of his 12-year-old daughter, who was a quadriplegic suffering from severe cerebral palsy and who was in constant pain. He argued that his actions were motivated by his concern to free his daughter from her pain. Latimer appealed his conviction to the Saskatchewan Court of Appeal. During the jury deliberations, the jury sent this note to the trial judge:

1. What is the procedure once the verdict has been reached?

2. Sergeant Conlon's testimony he advised R. Latimer to get a lawyer because he would be charged with first degree murder. Why is R. Latimer charged with second degree murder?

3. Is there any possible way we can have input into a recommendation for sentencing?

The third question clearly raised the issue of sentencing. Most of the trial judge's answer was straightforward. It repeated the traditional view that a sentence ought not to concern the jury in its consideration of the verdict. However, he added:

So it may be that later on, once you have reached a verdict, you—we will have some discussions about that, but not at this stage of the game. You must just carry on and answer the question that was put to you, okay?

After returning a verdict of guilty, the jury was asked for its recommendation for a period of parole ineligibility according to s. 745.2 of the *Criminal Code*. Although that section stipulates a period between 10 and 25 years, the jury recommended that Latimer be eligible for parole after serving one year in custody. Notwithstanding the mandatory life sentence, the trial judge sentenced Latimer to a term of imprisonment of one year to be followed by a period of probation of one year less a day. This was essentially a constitutional exemption from the mandatory penalty. The Saskatchewan Court of Appeal allowed a Crown appeal and imposed a sentence of life imprisonment with no eligibility for parole for at least 10 years. In rejecting a constitutional exemption, it relied on its earlier ruling in *Latimer* (1995), 126 DLR (4th) 203 (Sask. CA):

> The real issue for determination on this sentence appeal is whether the appellant should be held answerable for the murder of his daughter. We are asked to treat the conviction as essentially the functional equivalent of manslaughter for the purpose of determining a fit sentence. Although Parliament has not created a separate offence or sentencing regime for murder in such circumstances, we are asked to override the existing requirements by granting a constitutional exemption based on ss. 7 or 12 of the Charter.
>
> This homicide involves a significant degree of premeditation. The appellant contemplated taking Tracy's life before performing the act that caused her death. It was "intentional" in every sense of the word. Although he did so to spare her further pain, this approach ignores many other relevant considerations. As a self-appointed surrogate decision-maker, he was not entitled to take the criminal law into his own hands and terminate her life. Furthermore, society, through the operation of the criminal law is entitled to guard against potential abuses in such situations. Accordingly, statutory penalties are fashioned to meet the broad objectives and purposes of the criminal law.
>
> In the circumstances of this case we reject the appellant's request for a constitutional exemption from the prescribed sentences for second degree murder. It is open to Parliament to modify the existing law by appropriate legislation that establishes sentencing criteria for "mercy" killing. In the meantime, it is not for the court to pass on the wisdom of Parliament with respect to the range of penalties to be imposed on those found guilty of murder. Furthermore, as observed by Lamer CJC in *Luxton, supra*, p. 460, Parliament has been sensitive to the particular circumstances of each offender, even in cases of first degree murder, through various processes allowing for the royal prerogative of mercy, the availability of escorted absences from custody for humanitarian rehabilitation purposes and for early parole.
>
> We dismiss the appellant's application for a constitutional exemption and affirm the sentence imposed by the learned trial judge.

Along with the defence of necessity, whether the mandatory murder punishment ought to have applied to him was one of the issues that ultimately confronted the Supreme Court of Canada. In a unanimous decision, the Supreme Court dismissed the appeal.]

• • •

[10] Tracy underwent numerous surgeries in her short lifetime. In 1990, surgery tried to balance the muscles around her pelvis. In 1992, it was used to reduce the abnormal curvature in her back.

[11] Like the majority of totally involved, quadriparetic children with cerebral palsy, Tracy had developed scoliosis, an abnormal curvature and rotation in the back, necessitating surgery to implant metal rods to support her spine. While it was a successful procedure, further problems developed in Tracy's right hip: it became dislocated and caused her considerable pain.

[12] Tracy was scheduled to undergo further surgery on November 19, 1993. This was to deal with her dislocated hip and, it was hoped, to lessen her constant pain. The procedure involved removing her upper thigh bone, which would leave her lower leg loose without any connecting bone; it would be held in place only by muscle and tissue. The anticipated recovery period for this surgery was one year.

[13] The Latimers were told that this procedure would cause pain, and the doctors involved suggested that further surgery would be required in the future to relieve the pain emanating from various joints in Tracy's body. According to the appellant's wife, Laura Latimer, further surgery was perceived as mutilation. As a result, Robert Latimer formed the view that his daughter's life was not worth living.

[14] In the weeks leading up to Tracy's death, the Latimers looked into the option of placing Tracy in a group home in North Battleford. She had lived there between July and October of 1993, just prior to her death, while her mother was pregnant. The Latimers applied to place Tracy in the home in October, but later concluded they were not interested in permanently placing her in that home at that time.

[15] On October 12, 1993, after learning that the doctors wished to perform this additional surgery, the appellant decided to take his daughter's life. On Sunday, October 24, 1993, while his wife and Tracy's siblings were at church, Robert Latimer carried Tracy to his pickup truck, seated her in the cab, and inserted a hose from the truck's exhaust pipe into the cab. She died from the carbon monoxide.

· · ·

[79] As is reflected in the constitutional questions before the Court, this appeal is restricted to a consideration of the particularized inquiry. In substance, the appellant concedes the general constitutionality of ss. 235 and 745(c) as these sections are applied in combination. Mr. Latimer's challenge to their overall constitutionality was put forward in the alternative but was not pressed forcefully since no substantive argument on point was offered. Furthermore, no reasonable hypothetical situation was presented for the Court's consideration. In short, the appellant's arguments wholly centred on the effect of the sentence in this specific case on this specific offender. Consequently, only the individual remedy sought by the appellant, namely a constitutional exemption, is at issue.

· · ·

[80] The first factor to consider is the gravity of the offence. Recently, Gonthier J, in *Morrisey* [*R v.*, 2000 SCC 39, [2000] 2 SCR 90], provided important guidance for the proper assessment of the gravity of an offence for the purposes of a s. 12 analysis. Specifically, Gonthier J noted, at para. 35, that an assessment of the gravity of the offence requires an understanding of (i) the character of the offender's actions, and (ii) the consequences of those actions.

[81] Certainly, in this case one cannot escape the conclusion that Mr. Latimer's actions resulted in the most serious of all possible consequences, namely, the death of the victim, Tracy Latimer.

[82] In considering the character of Mr. Latimer's actions, we are directed to an assessment of the criminal fault requirement or *mens rea* element of the offence rather than the offender's motive or general state of mind (*Morrisey*, *supra*, at para. 36). We attach a greater degree of criminal responsibility or moral blameworthiness to conduct where the accused knowingly broke the law (*Morrisey*, *supra*, at para. 36; *R v. Martineau*,

[1990] 2 SCR 633, at p. 645). In this case, the *mens rea* requirement for second degree murder is subjective foresight of death: the most serious level of moral blameworthiness (*Luxton, supra*, at p. 724).

[83] Parliament has classified murder offences into first and second degree based on its perception of relative levels of moral blameworthiness. Parliament has also provided for differential treatment between them in sentencing, but only in respect of parole eligibility. As noted by Lamer CJ in *Luxton, supra*, at pp. 720-21:

> I must also reiterate that what we are speaking of here is a classification scheme for the purposes of sentencing. The distinction between first and second degree murder only comes into play when it has first been proven beyond a reasonable doubt that the offender is guilty of murder, that is, that he or she had subjective foresight of death: *R v. Martineau*, handed down this day. *There is no doubt that a sentencing scheme must exhibit a proportionality to the seriousness of the offence, or to put it another way, there must be a gradation of punishments according to the malignity of the offences.* [Emphasis added.]

[84] However, even if the gravity of second degree murder is reduced in comparison to first degree murder, it cannot be denied that second degree murder is an offence accompanied by an extremely high degree of criminal culpability. In this case, therefore, the gravest possible consequences resulted from an act of the most serious and morally blameworthy intentionality. It is against this reality that we must weigh the other contextual factors, including and especially the particular circumstances of the offender and the offence.

[85] Turning to the characteristics of the offender and the particular circumstances of the offence we must consider the existence of any aggravating and mitigating circumstances (*Morrisey, supra*, at para. 38; *Goltz* [*R v.*, [1991] 3 SCR 485], at pp. 512-13). Specifically, any aggravating circumstances must be weighed against any mitigating circumstances. In this regard, it is possible that prior to gauging the sentence's appropriateness in light of an appreciation of the particular circumstances weighed against the gravity of the offence, the mitigating and aggravating circumstances might well cancel out their ultimate impact (*Morrisey, supra*, at para. 40). Indeed, this is what occurs in this case. On the one hand, we must give due consideration to Mr. Latimer's initial attempts to conceal his actions, his lack of remorse, his position of trust, the significant degree of planning and premeditation, and Tracy's extreme vulnerability. On the other hand, we are mindful of Mr. Latimer's good character and standing in the community, his tortured anxiety about Tracy's well-being, and his laudable perseverance as a caring and involved parent. Considered together we cannot find that the personal characteristics and particular circumstances of this case displace the serious gravity of this offence.

[86] Finally, this sentence is consistent with a number of valid penological goals and sentencing principles. Although we would agree that in this case the sentencing principles of rehabilitation, specific deterrence and protection are not triggered for consideration, we are mindful of the important role that the mandatory minimum sentence plays in denouncing murder. Denunciation of unlawful conduct is one of the objectives of sentencing recognized in s. 718 of the *Criminal Code*. As noted by the Court in *R v. M.(C.A.)*, [1996] 1 SCR 500, at para. 81:

> The objective of denunciation mandates that a sentence should communicate society's condemnation of that particular offender's *conduct*. In short, a sentence with a denunciatory element represents a symbolic, collective statement that the offender's conduct should be punished for encroaching on our society's basic code of values as enshrined within our substantive criminal law. [Emphasis in original.]

Furthermore, denunciation becomes much more important in the consideration of sentencing in cases where there is a "high degree of planning and premeditation, and where the offence and its consequences are highly publicized, [so that] like-minded individuals may well be deterred by severe sentences": *R v. Mulvahill and Snelgrove* (1993), 21 BCAC 296, at p. 300. This is particularly so where the victim is a vulnerable person with respect to age, disability, or other similar factors.

[87] In summary, the minimum mandatory sentence is not grossly disproportionate in this case. We cannot find that any aspect of the particular circumstances of the case or the offender diminishes the degree of criminal responsibility borne by Mr. Latimer. In addition, although not free of debate, the sentence is not out of step with valid penological goals or sentencing principles. The legislative classification and treatment of this offender meets the requisite standard of proportionality (*Lyons* [*R. v.*, [1987] 2 SCR 309], at p. 339). Where there is no violation of Mr. Latimer's s. 12 right there is no basis for granting a constitutional exemption.

[88] Having said all this, we wish to point out that this appeal raises a number of issues that are worthy of emphasis. The sentencing provisions for second degree murder include both ss. 235 and 745(c). Applied in combination these provisions result in a sentence that is hybrid in that it provides for both a mandatory life sentence and a minimum term of incarceration. The choice is Parliament's on the use of minimum sentences, though considerable difference of opinion continues on the wisdom of employing minimum sentences from a criminal law policy or penological point of view.

[89] It is also worth referring again to the royal prerogative of mercy that is found in s. 749 of the *Criminal Code*, which provides "[n]othing in this Act in any manner limits or affects Her Majesty's royal prerogative of mercy." As was pointed out by Sopinka J in *R v. Sarson*, [1996] 2 SCR 223, at para. 51, albeit in a different context:

> Where the courts are unable to provide an appropriate remedy in cases that the executive sees as unjust imprisonment, the executive is permitted to dispense "mercy," and order the release of the offender. The royal prerogative of mercy is the only potential remedy for persons who have exhausted their rights of appeal and are unable to show that their sentence fails to accord with the *Charter*.

[90] But the prerogative is a matter for the executive, not the courts. The executive will undoubtedly, if it chooses to consider the matter, examine all of the underlying circumstances surrounding the tragedy of Tracy Latimer that took place on October 24, 1993, some seven years ago. Since that time Mr. Latimer has undergone two trials and two appeals to the Court of Appeal for Saskatchewan and this Court, with attendant publicity and consequential agony for him and his family.

• • •

[91] Mr. Latimer's appeals against conviction and sentence are dismissed. The answers to the constitutional questions are as follows:

> 1. Was the learned trial Justice correct in finding that in this specific case, the mandatory minimum sentence prescribed by ss. 235 and 745(c) of the *Criminal Code* would be cruel and unusual punishment in violation of s. 12 of the *Canadian Charter of Rights and Freedoms*?

No.

This case has spawned an interesting body of literature raising various dimensions of the difficult sentencing issues that it generates: see K. Roach, "Crime and Punishment in the Latimer Case" (2001), 64 *Sask. L Rev.* 469; B. Sneiderman, "Latimer in the Supreme Court: Necessity, Compassionate Homicide, and Mandatory Sentencing" (2001), 64 *Sask. L Rev.* 511; D. Lepofsky, "The Latimer Case: Murder Is Still Murder When the Victim Is a Child with a Disability" (2001), 27 *Queen's LJ* 315; F.C. De Coste, "Conditions of Clemency: Justice from the Offender" (2003), 66 *Sask. L Rev.* 1. Also, for a critique of the earlier decision of the Saskatchewan Court of Appeal ((1995), 41 CR (4th) 1), see T. Quigley, "R v. Latimer: Hard Cases Make Interesting Law" (1995), 41 CR (4th) 89.

Eradicating the mandatory sentencing scheme for murder, whether in general or on a case-by-case basis, is no simple matter. If Parliament were to alter the present law and permit judges to sentence murderers constrained only by the maximum sentence of life imprisonment, the consequences could well be dramatic. It would have the effect of blurring the distinction between manslaughter and murder, for the purposes of sentencing. Still, this might have the effect of inducing more guilty pleas in homicide cases. But the basis on which we currently distinguish liability for murder and manslaughter—that is, the intention of the offender—will be relevant to the length of the sentence that is imposed. Collapsing the categories of homicide in order to achieve a more discretionary sentencing regime may merely result in shifting these sorts of decisions from the "trial phase" to the "sentencing phase" of the proceedings. What will this do to the right to trial by jury in this context? Is a better answer the creation of a new category—for example, "compassionate homicide"?

These issues were considered in the United Kingdom by the Select Committee on Murder and Life Imprisonment. After careful consideration of the evidence and views of many leading experts, the committee rejected a proposal that the mandatory sentence of life imprisonment for murder be changed. See House of Lords, *Report of the Select Committee on Murder and Life Imprisonment* (HL-78-I) (London: HMSO, 1989). One of the most ardent and persistent critics of the life sentence for murder is the British scholar Lord Windlesham. See, in particular, "The Penalty for Murder," in *Responses to Crime* (Oxford: Clarendon Press, 1987); "Life Imprisonment: A Sentence Nobody Can Understand?" in *Responses to Crime—Penal Policy in the Making*, vol. 2 (Oxford: Clarendon Press, 1993); and "Life Sentences: The Defects of Duality," in *Responses to Crime—Legislating with the Tide* (Oxford: Clarendon Press, 1996).

IV. APPLYING THE PROVISIONS

A. Determining Parole Eligibility for Second-Degree Murder

The sentencing provisions for second-degree murder have caused Canadian courts great difficulties. The courts have struggled to reach an appropriate interpretation of the provisions. Until recently, there was some controversy over the general approach to this sentencing function. Courts divided on the issue whether there was a general presumption in favour of imposing the 10-year minimum, leaving the question of dangerousness to the parole board. This view saw increases beyond the minimum only in "unusual circumstances" (see *R v. Gourgon* (1981), 58 CCC (2d) 193 (BCCA) and *R v. Jordan* (1983), 7 CCC (3d) 143 (BCCA)). Others favoured an approach that allowed the sentencing judge to fix the period of parole eligibility at a level that he or she thought was "fit," free from presumptions of restraint (see *R v. Mitchell* (1987), 39 CCC (3d) 141 (NSSCAD) and *R v. Wenarchuk* (1982), 67 CCC (2d) 169 (Sask. CA)). After many years of (sometimes sharp) judicial debate, the Supreme Court of Canada purported to settle the issue in *R v. Shropshire*.

R v. Shropshire
(1995), 43 CR (4th) 269 (SCC)

IACOBUCCI J: This appeal was allowed on June 15, 1995, with reasons to follow. These are those reasons.

At issue in this appeal are the factors and principles that should guide a trial judge in determining whether to extend the period of parole ineligibility on a second degree murder conviction beyond the statutory minimum of 10 years. This appeal also touches on the appropriate standard of appellate review to be exercised when considering a trial judge's decision to postpone the period of parole eligibility. Both of these issues engage the broad theme of when the discretion of a sentencing judge ought to be altered.

I. Background

The respondent, Michael Thomas Shropshire, pleaded guilty to the second degree murder of Timothy Buffam. The offence was committed at the respondent's home in Abbotsford, British Columbia, on May 26, 1992, during a marijuana transaction between the respondent, the deceased, and Lorne Lang, a third person accompanying the deceased. Lang is otherwise known as "Animal." The respondent was acquainted with Buffam and Lang as the trio had had prior narcotics dealings. Without any warning, the respondent shot Buffam three times in the chest as they were about to enter the garage to complete the marijuana deal. The respondent then chased Lang in his vehicle shouting "Hacksaw told me to do it!" Hacksaw is the nickname of another associate.

Two days later, the respondent gave himself up to the police. After a preliminary hearing, the respondent pleaded guilty to second degree murder. He professed remorse for his actions but was unwilling or unable to explain them. No motive for the killing was ever ascertained. The respondent has a prior criminal record including two convictions in Youth Court for robbery, a conviction for impaired driving, and two narcotic offences as an adult.

On June 17, 1993, McKinnon J of the Supreme Court of British Columbia sentenced the respondent to life imprisonment without eligibility for parole for 12 years. This period of non-eligibility for parole is two years more than the minimum (and most common) period of parole ineligibility for second degree murder, namely 10 years. Trial judges are permitted, by virtue of the discretionary power accorded to them by s. 744 of the *Criminal Code*, RSC 1985, c. C-46, to extend the period of parole ineligibility beyond the statutory minimum. The respondent challenged the discretionary s. 744 decision of the trial judge.

On May 4, 1994, a majority of the Court of Appeal for British Columbia allowed the respondent's appeal against sentence, and reduced the period of parole ineligibility to 10 years: (1994) 90 CCC (3d) 234, 45 BCAC 252, 72 WAC 252. Goldie JA dissented and would have dismissed the appeal.

• • •

IV. Issues on Appeal

I would state the issues in the following manner:

1. What are the appropriate factors for a sentencing judge to consider in determining whether a period of parole ineligibility of longer than 10 years should be awarded for an individual convicted of second degree murder?

• • •

V. Analysis

A. What are the appropriate factors for a sentencing judge to consider in determining whether a period of parole ineligibility of longer than 10 years should be awarded for an individual convicted of second degree murder?

The majority of the British Columbia Court of Appeal held that there are only two factors to consider in justifying an enhanced period of parole ineligibility: (1) an assessment of future dangerousness, and (2) denunciation. With respect, I disagree. Although these factors are of relevance in justifying an extension of the period of parole ineligibility, they are by no means determinative or exclusive.

Section 744 of the *Criminal Code* authorizes a trial judge to impose a period of parole ineligibility greater than the minimum 10-year period. This provision, which governs this appeal, reads as follows:

> 744. Subject to section 744.1, at the time of the sentencing under paragraph 742(b) of an offender who is convicted of second degree murder, the judge who presided at the trial of the offender ... may, having regard to the character of the offender, the nature of the offence and the circumstances surrounding its commission ... substitute for ten years a number of years of imprisonment (being more than ten but not more than twenty-five) without eligibility for parole, as the judge deems fit in the circumstances.

The determination under s. 744 is thus a very fact-sensitive process. The factors to be considered in fixing an extended period of parole ineligibility are:

(1) the character of the offender;

(2) the nature of the offence; and

(3) the circumstances surrounding the commission of the offence;

all bearing in mind the discretionary power conferred on the trial judge.

No reference is made to denunciation or assessments of future dangerousness in the statutory language. By elevating "denunciation" and "assessment of future dangerousness" as the only criteria by which extended periods of parole ineligibility can be determined, the majority of the British Columbia Court of Appeal has, in effect, judicially amended the clear statutory language. This is not to say, however, that these two criteria should not be part of the analysis. For example, "denunciation" can fall within the statutory criterion of the "nature of the offence." Similarly, "future dangerousness" can fall within the rubric of the "character of the offender."

On the issue of denunciation, Lambert JA stated that it would not provide a valid basis for ordering a longer period of parole ineligibility unless it is "concluded that the extra denunciation is worth more than $50,000 a year to society" (p. 239). I cannot accept that position. It is entirely inappropriate to require a trial judge to engage in such a cost-benefit budgetary analysis. As submitted by the appellant before this Court:

> The question of how society allocates public resources is for Parliament to determine. By enacting s. 744, Parliament has determined that some of society's resources will be allocated to imprisoning convicted murderers beyond the ten year point. If Parliament determines that the fiscal cost of that incarceration is too high, then they can amend s. 744. It is not the task of individual judges carrying out the sentencing process to engage in that kind of budgetary analysis.

Furthermore, this sort of fiscal analysis would yield undesirable results from a policy perspective.

"Deterrence" is also a relevant criterion in justifying a s. 744 order. Parole eligibility informs the content of the "punishment" meted out to an offender: for example, there is a very significant difference between being behind bars and functioning within society while on conditional release. Consequently, I believe that lengthened periods of parole ineligibility could reasonably be expected to deter some persons from reoffending. Such is also the position of a variety of provincial appellate courts, from which the British Columbia Court of Appeal presently diverges: *R v. Wenarchuk* (1982), 67 CCC (2d) 169 (Sask. CA); *R v. Mitchell* (1987), 39 CCC (3d) 141 (NSCA); *R v. Young* (1993), 78 CCC (3d) 538 (NSCA); *R v. Able* (1993), 65 OAC 37 (CA); *R v. Ly* (1992), 72 CCC (3d) 57 (Man. CA), per Twaddle JA (Scott CJM concurring), at p. 61: "Parliament's purpose in adding a minimum period of parole ineligibility to a life sentence was, in my view, twofold. It was to deter and denounce the crime."

More importantly, the British Columbia Court of Appeal's position is also irreconcilable with the view taken by this Court of the interplay between parole eligibility and deterrence. For example, in *R v. Arkell*, [1990] 2 SCR 695, at p. 704 it was stated:

> ... the distinction between first and second degree murder ... is a maximum extra fifteen years that must be served before one is eligible for parole. ... Parliament's decision to treat more seriously murders that have been committed while the offender is exploiting a

position of power through illegal domination of the victim [i.e. first degree murder] accords with the principle that there must be a proportionality between a sentence and the moral blameworthiness of the offender and other considerations such as deterrence and societal condemnation of the acts of the offender.

The only difference in terms of punishment between first and second degree murder is the duration of parole ineligibility. This clearly indicates that parole ineligibility is part of the "punishment" and thereby forms an important element of sentencing policy. As such, it must be concerned with deterrence, whether general or specific. The jurisprudence of this Court is clear that deterrence is a well-established objective of sentencing policy. In *R v. Lyons*, [1987] 2 SCR 309, La Forest J held at p. 329:

> In a rational system of sentencing, the respective importance of prevention, deterrence, retribution and rehabilitation will vary according to the nature of the crime and the circumstances of the offender. No one would suggest that any of these functional considerations should be excluded from the legitimate purview of legislative or judicial decisions regarding sentencing.

Section 744 must be concerned with all of the factors cited in *Lyons*. In *R v. Luxton*, [1990] 2 SCR 711, the importance of structuring sentences to take into account the individual accused and the particular crime was emphasized. This is also a factor that any order made pursuant to s. 744 ought to take into consideration.

The exercise of a trial judge's discretion under s. 744 should not be more strictly circumscribed than the sentencing itself. The section does not embody any limiting statutory language; rather it is quite the contrary. In its terms, it is very similar to s. 745, which permits an application to be made to reduce the parole ineligibility period after 15 years of incarceration. Section 745 has recently been given judicial scrutiny by this Court in *R v. Swietlinski*, [1994] 3 SCR 481. That case involved an assessment of the relevant considerations for a jury hearing a s. 745 application; Lamer CJ concluded at p. 500:

> It is true that deterrence is one of the functions of the penalty and that it is therefore legitimate for the jury to take this factor into account when hearing an application under s. 745.

There is no reason why the functions of s. 744 should be given a more restrictive interpretation than those of s. 745.

In any event, independent of the effect that parole ineligibility may empirically have on recidivism, Lambert JA's reasoning, in both this case as well as in *R v. Hogben* (1994), 40 BCAC 257, completely precludes the concept of "deterrence" from informing the decision of whether or not to extend the period of parole ineligibility. This in my view constitutes an unduly restrictive interpretation of s. 744 and erroneously contravenes the jurisprudence of this court as well as other appellate courts.

I also find it necessary to deal with Lambert JA's conclusion that a period of parole ineligibility in excess of 10 years will not be justified unless there are "unusual circumstances." This conclusion resonates in the earlier decisions of the British Columbia Court of Appeal in *R v. Brown* (1993), 83 CCC (3d) 394, and *R v. Gourgon* (1981), 58 CCC (2d) 193. In my opinion, this is too high a standard and makes it overly difficult for trial judges to exercise the discretionary power to set extended periods of parole ineligibility. The language of s. 744 does not require "unusual circumstances." As a result, to so require by judicial pronouncement runs contrary to Parliamentary intent.

In my opinion, a more appropriate standard, which would better reflect the intentions of Parliament, can be stated in this manner: as a general rule, the period of parole ineligibility shall be for 10 years, but this can be ousted by a determination of the trial judge that, according to the criteria enumerated in s. 744, the offender should wait a longer period before having his suitability to be released into the general public assessed. To this end, an extension of the period of parole ineligibility would not be "unusual," although it may well be that, in the median number of cases, a period of 10 years might still be awarded.

I am supported in this conclusion by a review of the legislative history, academic commentary, and judicial interpretation of s. 744, and the sentencing scheme for second degree murder.

Section 742(b) of the Code provides that a person sentenced to life imprisonment for second degree murder shall not be eligible for parole "until he has served at least ten years of his sentence or such greater number of years, not being more than twenty-five years, as has been substituted therefor pursuant to section 744." In permitting a sliding scale of parole ineligibility, Parliament intended to recognize that, within the category of second degree murder, there will be a broad range of seriousness reflecting varying degrees of moral culpability. As a result, the period of parole ineligibility for second degree murder will run anywhere between a minimum of 10 years and a maximum of 25, the latter being equal to that prescribed for first degree murder. The mere fact that the median period gravitates towards the 10-year minimum does not, ipso facto, mean that any other period of time is "unusual."

I should pause to repeat that in the instant appeal we are concerned with a period of parole ineligibility for second degree murder of 12 years, this being only two years more than the minimum.

If the objective of s. 744 is to give the trial judge an element of discretion in sentencing to reflect the fact that within second degree murder there is both a range of seriousness and varying degrees of moral culpability, then it is incorrect to start from the proposition that the sentence must be the statutory minimum unless there are unusual circumstances. As discussed *supra*, a preferable approach would be to view the 10-year period as a minimum contingent on what the "judge deems fit in the circumstances," the content of this "fitness" being informed by the criteria listed in s. 744. As held in other Canadian jurisdictions, the power to extend the period of parole ineligibility need not be sparingly used.

For example, in *R v. Wenarchuk*, *supra*, the Saskatchewan Court of Appeal (per Bayda CJS for a five-judge panel) held at p. 173 that:

> [It is no longer appropriate] that the "order (increasing the parole non-eligibility period) should be sparingly made." The order should be made whenever such an order is "fit in the circumstances."

I would equally affirm the following passage from the decision of the Nova Scotia Court of Appeal in *R v. Doyle* (1991), 108 NSR (2d) 1, at p. 5, leave to appeal to this Court refused, [1992] 2 SCR vi, which I find apposite to the present discussion:

The Code does not fix the sentence for second degree murder as life imprisonment with no parole eligibility for ten years. The discretion conferred on the sentencing judge by s. 742(b) and s. 744 is not whether to move from a prima facie period of ten years, but rather what is a fit sentence, applying the proper guidelines. Unusual circumstances are not the prerequisite for moving away from the ten year minimum, although as the cases illustrate, they certainly play a role in the proper exercise of the judicial discretion. ...

It is not the law that unusual circumstances, brutality, torture or a bad record must be demonstrated before the judge may exercise his discretion to move above the ten years minimum. Nor is there any burden on the Crown to demonstrate that the period should be more than the minimum.

On another note, I do not find that permitting trial judges to extend the period of parole ineligibility usurps or impinges upon the function of the parole board. I am cognizant of the fact that, upon the expiry of the period of parole ineligibility, there is no guarantee of release into the public. At that point, it is incumbent upon the parole board to assess the suitability of such release, and in so doing it is guided by the legislative objectives of the parole system: see ss. 101 and 102 of the *Corrections and Conditional Release Act*, SC 1992, c. 20. However, it is clear that the parole board is not the only participant in the parole process. All it is designed to do is, within the parameters defined by the judiciary, decide whether an offender can be released. A key component of those parameters is the determination of when the period of parole eligibility (i.e. when the parole board can commence its administrative review function) starts to run. This is the manner in which the system is geared to function—with complementary yet distinct input from both the judiciary and the parole administrators. It is the role of the sentencing judge to circumscribe, in certain statutorily defined circumstances, the operation of the parole board. The decision of McKinnon J in the case at bar neither skews this balance nor unduly trumps the function of the parole board. As noted by the Saskatchewan Court of Appeal in *Wenarchuk*, *supra*, at pp. 172-73:

> The object of the provision in s. 671 [now s. 744] is not to take away from the Parole Board, or in some way diminish, the Board's function to determine whether the accused is sufficiently rehabilitated (from the standpoint of risk to and the protection of society) to permit his release into society. ... The object, rather, is to give back to the judge some of the discretion he normally has in the matter of sentencing—discretion that the statute took away from him when it provided for a life sentence [for murder]—so that the judge may do justice, not retributive or punitive justice, but justice to reflect the accused's culpability and to better express society's repudiation for the particular crime committed by the particular accused (with that repudiation's attendant beneficial consequences for society, including its protection through individual and general deterrence and, where necessary, segregation from society). ...
>
> An order under s. 671 does not impinge upon the powers of the Board. At most, it has the effect of postponing the Board's exercise of its powers—its full powers.

Applying these legal principles to the particular facts of this case, I do not see any error on the part of the trial judge. He adverted to the fact that the respondent had pleaded guilty and was only 23 years old. He recognized that the Crown was not seeking a period of parole ineligibility beyond the minimum. Nevertheless, in a legitimate exercise of his discretionary power, and after correctly reviewing the factors set out in s. 744, he imposed a 12-year period of parole ineligibility. He referred to the following factors as specifically justifying the 12-year period of parole ineligibility:

(a) the circumstances of the killing were strange in that they provided no real answer to why it took place, and the respondent was unwilling or unable to explain his actions;

(b) the murder was committed during the course of committing another offence, namely a drug transaction; and

(c) the respondent has a record for both narcotic offences and violence.

Factors (b) and (c) clearly fall within the categories ("character," "nature" and "circumstances surrounding") established by s. 744. As to factor (b), I further note that the Manitoba Court of Appeal, in *R v. Ly, supra,* held that the period of parole ineligibility could be increased when the murder is committed in the course of another crime, particularly a crime of violence.

Factor (a), however, presents some difficulty. The respondent raises the question whether the trial judge erred in interpreting the respondent's silence in such a manner as to justify extending the period of parole ineligibility.

In response, I would affirm the analysis of Goldie JA in the court below (at pp. 241-42) and would hold that this silence is readily assimilable within the "circumstances surrounding the offence" criterion. The crux of Goldie JA's comments is that, in the absence of any explanation for a random and seemingly senseless killing, the trial judge was correct in sentencing the respondent in light of his refusal to offer an explanation. It was found that his refusal was deliberate and in and of itself unusual. After all, the respondent, a drug dealer with previous convictions for robbery and armed robbery, shot the victim Buffam in cold blood without provocation of any kind.

It is not for the trial judge to speculate what the respondent might have said to mitigate the severity of the offence. I quite agree with Goldie JA that the right to silence, which is fully operative in the investigative and prosecutorial stages of the criminal process, wanes in importance in the post-conviction phase when sentencing is at issue. However, in so agreeing, I emphasize that the respondent pleaded guilty; I leave for future consideration the question of drawing a negative inference from the silence of the accused when he or she has pleaded not guilty and wishes to appeal the conviction. In the case at bar, the trial judge even went so far as to invite the accused to suggest why he may have committed the offence, but no response was forthcoming. As held by Goldie JA (at p. 242), the respondent "cannot expect to be rewarded for remaining silent in the circumstances." The court and the public clearly have an interest in knowing why a human life was taken by an offender.

Goldie JA's comments and the decision of the trial judge on the "silence" issue are fully consonant with the position taken by the Ontario Court of Appeal. In *R v. Able, supra,* the Court of Appeal increased two co-accused's periods of parole ineligibility. At page 39 it was held:

> No explanation has been forthcoming from either of the appellants with respect to the reason for the killing ... [which] can be best described as a callous, brutal, pointless, execution-style killing of a helpless victim.

I conclude that in certain circumstances, such as those presented in this case, it is proper to take into account the absence of an explanation of attenuating factors.

The respondent suggests that Goldie JA's comments and the decision of the trial judge contravene the pronouncements of this Court in *R v. Gardiner*, [1982] 2 SCR 368. I recognize that, in *Gardiner*, this Court extended certain procedural rights to sentencing proceedings. However, these were limited to the right to counsel, the right to call evidence, the right to cross-examine and the right to address the court. There is no mention made of the creation in its identical form of a substantive right such as the right to silence.

At the sentencing stage, the Crown has already proved beyond a reasonable doubt that the accused has committed the crime for which he or she stood charged or, as in this appeal, the accused has pleaded guilty to the offence; if the accused then seeks to receive the least severe sentence commensurate with his or her conviction (i.e. for second degree murder, life imprisonment with eligibility for parole after 10 years have elapsed) it is incumbent upon the accused to play a somewhat active role in the process. I note that the right to silence is a manifestation of the presumption of innocence: *R v. Broyles*, [1991] 3 SCR 595; *R v. Hebert*, [1990] 2 SCR 151; *R v. Chambers*, [1990] 2 SCR 1293. The presumption of innocence flows to those "charged with an offence" or suspected of having committed one; once an individual has been convicted of an offence he or she is no longer simply "charged."

. . .

VI. Conclusions and Disposition

The trial judge properly considered the relevant factors in exercising the discretionary jurisdiction given to him under s. 744. The Court of Appeal erred in postulating an unduly restrictive and narrow approach to s. 744 and by adopting a standard of appellate review that was tantamount to substituting its opinion for that of the trial judge. Consequently, I would allow the appeal, set aside the decision of the British Columbia Court of Appeal, and restore the trial judge's s. 744 order of a period of parole ineligibility of 12 years.

For commentary on this case, see A. Manson, "The Supreme Court Intervenes in Sentencing" (1995), 43 CR (4th) 306; G. Trotter, "*R v. Shropshire*: Murder, Sentencing and the Supreme Court of Canada" (1995), 43 CR (4th) 288; and J. Norris, "Sentencing for Second-Degree Murder: *R v. Shropshire*" (1996), 1 *Can. Crim. LR* 199.

Despite the authoritative pronouncement in *Shropshire*, the debate about parole eligibility persists. Consider the decision of the British Columbia Court of Appeal in *R v. Mafi* (1999), 142 CCC (3d) 449. After a jury found Mafi guilty of two counts of second-degree murder, the trial judge fixed parole ineligibility at 20 years. By a two-to-one majority, the British Columbia Court of Appeal reduced parole ineligibility to 15 years. The majority (two concurring judgments of McEachern CJBC and Lambert JA) and the minority split over the fundamental approach to sentencing under the murder provisions. The majority judgments rail against the restrictive approach to appellate review of sentencing decisions articulated in *Shropshire*. In the more temperate of the concurring majority judgments, the chief justice of British Columbia suggests that strict adherence to the Supreme Court's approach may "effectively deprive an accused of an effective right of appeal" (at 467). The concern with *Shropshire* is not limited to British Columbia. See also *R v. McKnight* (1999), 135 CCC (3d) 41 (Ont. CA), in which the appellant was convicted of the second-degree murder of his wife and sentenced to life imprisonment without parole eligibility for 17 years. On appeal, the Court of Appeal for Ontario, by a two-to-one majority, reduced the ineligibility period to 14 years. The court (McMurtry CJO dissenting) differed on the appropriate degree of deference required by *Shropshire*.

After *Shropshire*, there has been a marked increase in the number of murder sentencing decisions in which parole ineligibility has been set at more than 10 years: see N. Gorham, "The Effects of Shropshire on Parole Ineligibility for Second Degree Murder" (2002), 1 CR (6th) 324, where, after an empirical inquiry, the author concludes that judges are "much more willing to increase parole ineligibility beyond the 10-year minimum" but that the courts have not attained the objective of a sliding scale.

The following decision looks at such factors as impulsiveness, future danger, the nature of the wounds, and post-offence conduct as they relate to raising parole ineligibility to 20 years.

R v. Trotman
[2007] BCJ No. 718 (QL) (CA)

[1] THACKRAY JA: The appellant, Shem William Trotman, appeals the decision of Madam Justice Satanove, delivered 21 October 2004, that he must serve 20 years in prison before being eligible for release on parole. Mr. Trotman was convicted by a jury of second degree murder which attracts a mandatory life sentence subject to parole eligibility after 10 years. The jury recommended that Mr. Trotman serve 25 years in prison before being eligible to apply for parole.

[2] The judge, in her reasons for judgment, said as follows:

[8] Section 745.4 of the *Code* grants me the discretion to substitute a longer period, not to exceed 25 years, for the 10-year ineligibility period. This discretion may be exercised if, on a consideration of the following factors, I determine that Mr. Trotman should wait a longer period before having an assessment of his suitability to be released into the general public. These factors are:

1. His character;
2. The nature of the offence;
3. The circumstances surrounding its commission;
4. The recommendation, if any, of the jury pursuant to s. 745.2 of the *Criminal Code*.

[3] The judge also cited *R v. Shropshire*, [1995] 4 SCR 227, for the proposition that due regard must be given to future danger to the public posed by Mr. Trotman, the likelihood of his re-offending, denunciation of his actions, and deterrence against similar offences.

[4] With respect to the first of the factors, the judge noted as follows:

> [16] Here, the character of the accused is an aggravating factor. He has a record, which
> includes an assault causing bodily harm committed in 1994, an armed robbery committed
> in 1996, another assault causing bodily harm in 1997, an aggravated assault and assault
> *simpliciter* in 1998, and a break and entry in 2001. Also, significantly, he was on probation
> at the time he committed this heinous crime.

She added, at paragraph 19, that Mr. Trotman "has shown a blatant disregard for law
enforcement in the past. Far short of rehabilitating, the violence of his crimes has been
steadily escalating."

[5] With respect to the nature and circumstances of the offence, the judge described
the crime as a "vicious intentional killing" in which Mr. Trotman inflicted between 34
and 37 knife wounds to the deceased, of which any one of 13 could have caused her
death. She noted that the killing likely took place following sexual intercourse, but, "the
real story as to how the violence escalated to such a degree … will remain a mystery to
this court."

[6] The conviction was appealed to this Court where the appeal was dismissed: *R v.
Trotman*, 2006 BCCA 366. With respect to the injuries, the Court said as follows:

> [25] It is not necessary to describe the evidence of the pathologist in great detail. The
> victim was 24 years old when she died. She was 5 feet, 2 1/2 inches tall and weighed ap-
> proximately 110 pounds. Ms. Lal had been physically beaten and brutally attacked with a
> knife. There were 36 knife injuries. Any of 13 of these injuries, standing alone, was poten-
> tially fatal. There were both stabbing and cutting knife wounds. Blood loss was likely the
> immediate cause of death.

Appellant's counsel agreed that the crime was one of extreme violence and of a sadistic
nature.

[7] Madam Justice Satanove stated:

> [18] The nature and circumstances of the offence are a mixture of aggravating [fac-
> tors] and one mitigating factor, in my view. There is an element of impulsiveness as op-
> posed to planning which can be a mitigating factor, but the nature of the wounds inflicted
> on Ms. Lal, their location and the manner in which they were made suggests an element
> of deliberation. There is also an element of cruelty and vindictiveness which can be in-
> ferred by the nature and circumstances of the killing.

[8] On this appeal counsel for the appellant emphasized the judge's reference to
"the element of impulsiveness," saying that it should be viewed as a mitigating factor.
He submitted that "this is an impulsivity offence with but a small degree of deliberation." The record before this Court does not support that submission. While the judge
referred to impulsiveness as being a mitigating factor, she clearly found that it was offset by the "nature of the wounds," suggesting an "element of deliberation," and the
"cruelty and vindictiveness which can be inferred." This is well supported by the evidence of the pathologist, Dr. Charles Lee, who gave detailed and graphic evidence of the
knife wounds. He testified that the victim was likely pinned or restrained while at least
some of the cuts were inflicted. The following questions and answers then took place:

Q. Can you describe why you come to that conclusion?

A. In particular ... the cuts to the mouth, the fact that they're fairly symmetrical, ... it's less likely that those ... were [in]flicted simply as random slashing attacks. They ... appear a bit more deliberate just because of the fact that they're very symmetrical and ... the location it's not something that's typically injured in a ... random fight. Also, the cuts to the neck. Generally, cuts to the neck require that the person be relatively still simply because the neck is sort of a recessed area that a person generally tends to try and protect them by lowering the jaw and ... cover the neck portion. So that ... would indicate that probably the person was at least in some way restrained.

When discussing the two 3.5 centimetre cuts, one on either side of Ms. Lal's face, Dr. Lee stated:

A. ... it's a cut caused by someone probably just starting off at the edge of the mouth and just cutting laterally, and as he cuts the knife sort of trails off along the ... lateral part of the face, and it was probably done on both sides of the ... face [in] two separate cuts.

In cross-examination Dr. Lee agreed with defence counsel that the injuries suffered by Ms. Lal were the result of "a vicious violent attack ... to say the least."

[9] A review of the circumstances of the crime elicits a further aggravating factor. Mr. Trotman made three 911 calls shortly after exiting the apartment. In the first he said he needed help. In the second he said, "They're trying to kill us" and "The motherfucker's gone. The girl's down. She's not breathing." The use of the 911 call evidence by the jury became one of the grounds of the conviction appeal. This Court noted that there was a "third-party killer scenario" introduced by the 911 calls and that this left it open to the jury to find that "[e]ither the appellant was truthful during the 911 calls when he said that a person other than himself was the killer or he invented those assertions in an attempt to divert suspicion from himself."

[10] On this appeal defence counsel contended that this "post-offence" conduct was not relevant in that it does not go to Mr. Trotman's "level of culpability." I disagree with that submission. It is a factor that was open to the jury to consider in making its recommendation, and to the sentencing judge to take into account in exercising her discretion as to the period of parole ineligibility. The post-offence conduct of Mr. Trotman is a factor in the determination of his character and his level of dangerousness to the public.

[11] The fourth factor, the recommendation of the jury, was that Mr. Trotman serve 25 years in prison before being eligible to apply for parole. Section 745.4 of the *Code* states the judge "may ... substitute for ten years a number of years of imprisonment (being more than ten but not more than twenty-five) without eligibility for parole, *as the judge deems fit in the circumstances*" [emphasis added]. [The emphasized] words, in my opinion, emphasize the high degree of discretion the judge has in setting the period of parole ineligibility. She was obliged to take into account the recommendation of the jury which reflected its opinion that Mr. Trotman bore a high level of culpability and represents a future danger to society.

[12] In addition to the four *Code* section 745.4 factors, the judge noted that denunciation and deterrence were matters to be considered. She said there was no evidence of drugs or alcohol being involved, an indication that she was giving consideration to the principle of specific deterrence.

[13] Nevertheless, the appellant contends that the judge erred in law in imposing a period of ineligibility that was unreasonable and outside the range of sentence for the crime in question. He submitted that the realistic range is between 10 and 20 years and that the circumstances in the case at bar did not justify setting the sentence at the top end of that range.

• • •

[16] In *Shropshire* Iacobucci J, speaking for the Court, stated that an appellate court should interfere with a sentence only if it is convinced the sentence is "unfit"; that is, if it has found the sentence to be "clearly unreasonable." He said "unreasonableness in the sentencing process involves the sentencing order falling outside the 'acceptable range' of orders."

[17] *R v. Bernier*, 2003 BCCA 134, was decided by a five-member bench. Prowse JA, writing for herself and Levine JA, cited the principles from *Shropshire* and stated at paragraph 68 that a sentencing "decision falls outside the 'acceptable range' if 'it is in substantial and marked departure from the sentences customarily imposed for similar offenders committing similar crimes.'" She continued:

> [75] I agree with my colleagues that references to ranges of sentence should not distract the court from giving appropriate weight to the other principles of sentencing set forth in the *Code*, or from adjusting each sentence to the specific circumstances of the offence and the offender. The goal of the Court in each case will be the same—to determine whether the sentence is fit for this offender committing this crime.

Newbury JA added:

> [105] With respect to the matter of ranges, they are general guidelines, not hard and fast categories. They do not preclude lesser or greater sentences, if the circumstances or applicable principles in the particular case warrant. ... I find it useful to regard a range simply as a continuum within which cases may be placed, depending on their facts and their relationship to the principles of sentencing. ... The important point is that there will be cases that are so egregious that they should be placed at the high end or even beyond, just as there will be cases where not even the low end of the range will be an appropriate sentence.

[18] I do not find that any error has been committed by Madam Justice Satanove in her consideration of relevant factors and the sentence imposed. She took into account the appropriate sentencing principles, she was aware of and articulated the aggravating, and indeed mitigating, circumstances and she gave consideration to the jury's recommendation. Further, I do not find that the 20 year period of ineligibility for parole is outside of the acceptable range.

[19] I would dismiss the appeal.

———————

For another murder case dealing with dangerousness and post-offence conduct, see *R v. Crane*, [2007] AJ No. 1377 (QL) (CA), where the court considered a 22-year period of parole ineligibility in a case arising from the forcible confinement, robbery, and murder of a taxi driver. In dismissing the appeal, the court said:

[41] To consider those facts in that manner was not to punish the appellant for post-offence misconduct within the meaning of *R v. Sawchyn* (1981), 60 CCC (2d) 200, [1981] AJ No. 26 (QL) (Alta. CA), leave denied [1981] 2 SCR xi, *R v. Ambrose* (2000), 271 AR 164, [2000] AJ No. 1148 (QL), 2000 ABCA 264, or *R v. F.(D.M.)* (2000), 266 AR 336, [2000] AJ No. 1085 (QL), 2000 ABCA 244. This evidence was relevant to his lack of remorse about the crimes committed here, but it was not used in that way to aggravate parole ineligibility merely for lack of remorse. It was relevant, and effectively used by the trial judge, to decide whether the appellant should be given an earlier or later chance of parole and to decide, more practically, whether a jury some years from now should decide on the facts then known whether parole was a safe alternative to the appellant's continued imprisonment.

[42] Finally, as regards the appellant's argument that there was disparity between the appellant's disposition and that for Baptiste, we are not persuaded that an error in principle, or that a form of unfairness or unfitness, is reflected in the difference. Baptiste is younger, has a less significant criminal record, and did not dominate the actions during the events in the manner that the appellant did, notably by giving instructions and by going to the trunk to stop the victim's noise. Under the terms of s. 718.1 of the *Criminal Code*, a trial judge is to consider "the degree of responsibility of the offender." Even setting aside the evidence of the appellant's efforts to obstruct a witness, the degree of the appellant's responsibility in the crimes here was clearly distinct from that of Baptiste. The trial judge properly exercised his discretion to distinguish them.

Conclusion

[43] The trial judge did not reach an unfit result in the significant increase in parole ineligibility which he imposed. He allowed for the decision as to whether the appellant continued to be a danger to the public to be decided after 15 years by a future jury. On the facts of the offences, the circumstances surrounding the offences and the appellant's character, he could reasonably reach that conclusion. There is no error in principles or factors and the sentence is not unfit. The appeal is dismissed.

B. The Role of the Jury

Another reason why sentencing for murder is unique is the role that is given to the jury upon a conviction for second-degree murder. The jury is permitted to make a "recommendation" on the issue of parole eligibility. Murder is the only offence in the *Criminal Code* that contemplates any formal role for the jury in the sentencing process. This procedure casts the jury in an unusual role. Unlike its task in deciding guilt or innocence, in the sentencing context, the jury need not be unanimous. Indeed, it is possible (although unlikely) that each juror could come to a different conclusion on this issue. More fundamentally, the section only calls for a "recommendation." The reality is that sentencing juries often do not provide unanimous recommendations, leaving the presiding judge with several views on the appropriate period of parole eligibility.

The cases below demonstrate that the courts are ambivalent about how to integrate a jury's recommendation into the ultimate decision. Indeed, the courts cannot even agree on the proper procedure that ought to be employed in eliciting the input of the jury on this issue. Some courts have held that the offender and the Crown may address the jury before it makes its recommendation (see *R v. Atsiqtaq*, [1988] NWTR 315 (SC)). Other courts have held that there is no right to be heard on this issue (see *R v. Nepoose*, infra; *R v. Ok-kuatsiak* (1993), 80 CCC (3d) 251 (Nfld. CA); *R v. Challice* (1994), 20 CRR (2d) 319 (Ont. Ct. (Gen. Div.)); and *R v. Cruz* (1998), 124 CCC (3d) 157 (BCCA)). As we shall see in the next section, the jury has de facto decision-making power on a review of parole eligibility after 15 years.

R v. Nepoose
(1988), 46 CCC (3d) 421 (Alta. CA)

STRATTON JA: The question raised by this appeal is the propriety of the parties adducing evidence and addressing a jury under s. 670 of the *Criminal Code* after a conviction and before the jury respond to the question of whether or not they wish to make a recommendation with respect to ineligibility for parole.

Section 670 reads as follows:

> 670. Where a jury finds an accused guilty of second degree murder, the judge who presides at the trial shall, before discharging the jury, put to them the following question:

> > You have found the accused guilty of second degree murder and the law requires that I now pronounce a sentence of imprisonment for life against him. Do you wish to make any recommendation with respect to the number of years that he must serve before he is eligible for release on parole? You are not required to make any recommendation but if you do, your recommendation will be considered by me when I am determining whether I should substitute for the ten year period, which the law would otherwise require the accused to serve before he is eligible to be considered for release on parole, a number of years that is more than ten but not more than twenty-five.

This appellant was convicted by a jury of second degree murder. Immediately following the delivery of that verdict, the trial judge informed the jury that they had one further task and he then read to them s. 670 of the Code. He then stated that the procedure he contemplated was to have counsel make submissions to the jury as to whether the 10-year period of parole ineligibility should be extended.

Upon calling for submissions from counsel, defence counsel for the trial had this to say:

> Well, the jury has heard the evidence and I think that there is no need for me to make any further submission, I think they understand Mr. Nepoose's family history, his background and the milieu from which he comes. And, I would just simply remind them to or ask them to think about that and make no recommendation at all.

Crown counsel added his own explanation of s. 670 and then presented to the jury a full statement of the appellant's lengthy and serious criminal record including the sentences he received for prior convictions. Ultimately, the jury returned with a recommendation that "the sentence be served a minimum of 20 years before eligibility for parole."

The trial judge pointed out, quite correctly, that he had the responsibility to make the final decision on sentence after considering the factors set out in s. 671, including the jury's recommendation. Counsel then made further brief comments concerning the appellant's age and state of health, whereupon the trial judge ordered that the period of parole ineglibility should be 15 years.

Section 671 of the *Criminal Code* reads as follows:

> 671. At the time of the sentencing under paragraph 669(b) of an offender who is convicted of second degree murder, the judge who presided at the trial of the offender or, if that judge is unable to do so, and judge of the same court may, having regard to the character of the offender, the nature of the offence and the circumstances surrounding its commission, and to the recommendation, if any, made pursuant to section 670, by order, substitute for ten years a number of years of imprisonment (being more than ten but not more than twenty-five), without eligibility for parole, as he deems fit in the circumstances.

The appellant now contends that the trial judge erred in allowing counsel to adduce facts and make submissions to the jury with regard to the period of parole ineligibility. The second ground of appeal was that the 15 years imposed by the trial judge was excessive under all the circumstances.

On the first point, no cases directly on the issue were presented to us for our consideration. A case which touches upon but does not resolve the issue is *R v. Joseph* (1984), 15 CCC (3d) 314 (BCCA). In his judgment in that case, Craig JA of the British Columbia Court of Appeal says at p. 314:

> There was some discussion between counsel and the trial judge with regard to the fact that counsel had not had the opportunity to address the jury regarding any possible recommendation. The trial judge indicated that in the circumstances he was going to deal with the matter on the basis of submissions made to him by counsel. Counsel made some submissions. The judge sentenced Joseph to life imprisonment with a direction that he serve 20 years before being eligible for parole.

and further at p. 316:

> Counsel for Joseph, pointing out that he had not had an opportunity to address the jury, made brief submissions as to why the judge should not give effect to the jury's recommendation. The judge then said that he was going to "accede to the recommendation of the jury" and sentenced Joseph to imprisonment for life, directing that he not be eligible for parole for 20 years.

In reducing the period of ineligibility for parole to 10 years, the British Columbia Court of Appeal neither approved nor disapproved of the procedure followed by the trial judge. It is clear that the Appeal Court simply felt that the period of ineligibility pronounced by the trial judge was inappropriately long. In the result, the *Joseph* case is of little assistance in the present appeal other than to show that the court did not criticize the procedure there adopted.

Defence counsel argued strenuously that the jury's recommendation under s. 670 should be based solely on the evidence leading to the conviction and that the jury should hear no further evidence or argument for the purposes of a s. 670 recommendation.

We agree with that submission which we conclude is supported by the very words and structure of the relevant sections of the Code.

Section 670 is uniquely framed. The precise question required to be put to the jury is set out in quotations and contains within its wording a complete explanation of the jury's responsibility. It is abundantly clear that the jury's decision under s. 670 is not final. No statement whatsoever of the factors to be considered by the jury in making or declining to make such recommendation is set out.

That situation must be contrasted to s. 671, which authorizes the final sentencing decision of the judge and specifies the factors which the judge must have regard to in so doing.

Section 670 may also be compared with s. 672 which allows a jury to be empanelled for the purpose of reviewing, in certain specified circumstances, an earlier decision relating to parole ineligibility. Section 672(2) expressly states what the jury must have regard to in reaching a s. 672 decision. It is significant that a jury's decision under s. 672 is final and not a mere recommendation as in s. 670. A s. 672 jury must have regard to the character of the applicant, his conduct while serving his sentence, the nature of the offence for which he was convicted and such other matters as the judge deems relevant in the circumstances.

If Parliament had intended that a "recommending jury" under s. 670 consider factors other than the material leading to the conviction, I am satisfied it would have so specified as it did for "final" sentencing pronouncements authorized by ss. 671 and 672.

It has been suggested that it is unfair, particularly to an accused, to ask a jury for a recommendation without the benefit of counsel's arguments and the accused's record. The injury which an accused may appear to suffer is really illusory as a s. 670 decision of the jury is not final.

The person empowered to make the final parole ineligibility decision must hear full submissions and must have regard to the specifics set out in s. 671, including the jury's recommendation. With that recommendation before him, the parties may adduce additional evidence and present arguments to the trial judge with respect to the final disposition of the sentencing.

In short, we are of the view that s. 670 is a code of sorts. It is a section which is complete on its own and says with exactitude what is to be presented to the jury on this issue. We conclude that it was the intention of Parliament that a jury, acting under s. 670, should have put to them the exact question set out in the section along with whatever further explanation of the section the trial judge deems necessary. The jury should respond to the question put to it on the basis of only the evidence and arguments of counsel presented prior to and resulting in the conviction and the trial judge's instructions. To allow the jury to hear at that stage of the proceedings the full record of the accused and argument based on that record is, in our view, an error of law. Thus, the recommendation which the trial judge received from the jury was flawed and, although the learned trial judge did not follow that recommendation, we do not know the extent to which it affected his final decision.

In *R v. Walford* (1984), 12 CCC (3d) 257, Nemetz CJBC (Carrothers JA concurring), at p. 259, decided that the approach to be taken by an appellate court in considering an appeal from a period of parole ineligibility set by the trial judge pursuant to s. 671 should be the same as on a normal appeal against sentence, namely, "… to determine what is fit having regard to the facts the trial judge had before him and any relevant new facts before his court which were not before the judge." He continued as follows:

> An appellate court, in my view, has the jurisdiction to vary a sentence whether upwards or downwards despite the trial judge's advantage in seeing and hearing an accused where the appellate court concludes that the sentence imposed was not fit.

We agree with those comments.

In the present case we do not say that the ultimate disposition by the trial judge under s. 671 was not fit, but we do say that we must look at it with special care as that disposition could have been affected by the faulty procedure above mentioned. In the result, we conclude that this court must decide upon a fit parole ineligibility period from a review of the trial record and from the material placed before us at this appeal and in so doing have regard to the factors set out in s. 671 of the Code.

· · ·

In the result, notwithstanding the faulty procedure and the consequent flawed jury recommendation, I agree that the trial judge's determination of 15 years' parole ineligibility was a fit disposition for this appellant under the circumstances of this case.

R v. Ly and Duong
(1992), 72 CCC (3d) 57 (Man. CA)

TWADDLE JA: After a joint trial on a charge of first degree murder, each of the accused was convicted of second degree murder and sentenced to the mandatory term of life imprisonment. Each now appeals from the increased period of parole ineligibility attached to his sentence.

The crime occurred in the course of a rather unsophisticated robbery at the place of Phat Ly's employment. The victim was Phat Ly's employer. Although the robbery was undoubtedly planned and deliberate, the jury by its verdict found that the murder was not.

The circumstances of the victim's death were quite appalling. He had been beaten, tied to furniture by his hands and feet, stabbed by a knife in the neck and face and shot in the head six times. The firearm which was used as most probably a starting pistol which had been bored out to accept bullets and fire them.

When the murder was committed, the offenders were both under the age of 18 years. Neither had a record as a young offender. Events subsequent to the murder, before either was apprehended for this crime, did, however, reuslt in a difference between them.

Phat Ly emigrated to Australia with his mother. He was apprehended there and returned to Canada. He admitted that he had had some involvement with gangs of youths prior to his departure for Australia, but there is nothing to suggest that he was established in a life of crime.

Ky Duong, on the other hand, went to Toronto where he became involved in criminal activity. He was found in each of several residences containing weapons. He was arrested for the crime of break, enter and theft. In August, 1988, some six months after the murder, he became embroiled in a fight between members of rival gangs. A member of the gang which was opposed to Ky Duong was killed in gun-fire. Ky Duong was convicted of manslaughter with respect to that incident and sentenced to serve a term of 6½ years' imprisonment.

With the exception of Ky Duong's criminal activity subsequent to the murder, the jury was well aware of all the circumstances relevant to sentencing when it was asked, pursuant to the Code, whether it wished to make any recommendation with respect to the number of years each accused should serve before he became eligible for release on parole. The jury chose to make a recommendation which was in these terms: "We recommend no more than ten years."

Despite the jury's recommendation, the learned trial judge was of the view that the crime itself merited denunciation by the imposition on each accused of a longer period of parole ineligibility than the minimum. He was also of the view that an even longer period was required in the case of Ky Duong "to reflect the relative role and character of the offenders." He consequently increased the minimum period to 15 years for Phat Ly and to 20 years for Ky Duong. It is from these increased periods of parole ineglibility that the accused appeal.

. . .

The Jury's Recommendation

In conferring a role on the jury in the sentencing process, Parliament must surely have intended to provide the judge with one measure of the public's revulsion at the crime. The judge is not, of course, bound by what the jury recommends, but it is an indication to him of the need for denunciation beyond that inherent in the mandatory sentence.

R v. Joseph (1984), 15 CCC (3d) 314 (BCCA), was a case in which the jury recommended 20 years of parole ineligibility. The trial judge accepted the recommendation, but the British Columbia Court of Appeal reduced the period to 10 years. The Court of Appeal accepted that the circumstances of the offence did not merit additional denunciation.

It is entirely possible that there will be a case in which the opposite is true. A jury may recommend leniency where none is warranted. Ordinarily, however, a trial judge should be slow to disregard a jury's lenient recommendation where there is a mitigating feature such as the youth of the offender.

. . .

In the result, I would allow the sentence appeal of each offender, set aside the period of parole ineligibility imposed on each and substitute, in Phat Ly's case, a period of 12 years and, in Ky Duong's case, a period of 15 years.

LYON JA (dissenting): I have had the advantage of reading the reasons for judgment of my colleague Twaddle JA in these sentence appeals. I must, with respect, disagree with the result he arrives at.

A review of a number of recent decisions on second degree murders committed in furtherance of serious crimes such as robbery and break, enter and theft, indicates sentences for parole ineligibility ranging from the minimum of 10 years to 20 years. However, the majority of the sentences for such murders are in excess of the minimum and tend to range between 14 and 20 years. That there is no uniform consistency in sentencing and that longer periods of ineligibility tend to be given for serious or aggravated murders is the main conclusion one can draw from such a review.

· · ·

Finally, the overriding by the trial judge of the jury's recommendation for minimum eligibility is commented upon by Twaddle JA as another reason for lowering the trial judge's sentences. He states: "Ordinarily, however, a trial judge should be slow to disregard a jury's lenient recommendation where there is a mitigating feature such as the youth of the offender." Again, with respect, I must disagree.

There is nothing sacrosanct about the jury's recommendation. Indeed, as I mention later, the jury's recommendation is made without their receiving any instruction on the general principles of sentencing and, additionally, it is often made without full knowledge of pertinent sentencing information. There is ample authority for the proposition that the trial judge is not bound by the jury's recommendation and that the jury's recommendation is only one of a number of equal factors which the trial judge must consider in passing sentence "as he deems fit in the circumstances" (s. 744, *supra*).

As Bayda CJS said in *Wenarchuk, supra*, at p. 713:

Since the decision in *Gulash* [Sask. CA, March 24, 1976 (unreported)], the terms of s. 218 [re-enacted, 1974-75-76, c. 105, s. 5], as noted, were recast and the section has been replaced by ss. 669 to 674 of the present Code. The appearance, for the first time, in s. 671 of the words "as he deems fit in the circumstances," the provision in s. 672 for judicial review, the removal of the provisions contained in the former s. 218(5)(e), and the current provisions, generally, in ss. 669 to 674 no longer make appropriate the statement that the "order [increasing the parole non-eligibility period] should be sparingly made." The order should be made whenever such an order is "fit in the circumstances." As explained above, it is now no longer a question (if it ever was) of curtailing the powers of the Parole Board. An order under s. 671 does not impinge upon the powers of the Board. At most, it has the effect of *postponing* the Board's exercise of its powers—its full powers.

I also agree with Laycraft CJA (as he then was) when he said in *R v. Modin* (1989), 94 AR 81 at pp. 83-4, 66 Alta. LR (2d) 1, 6 WCB (2d) 406 (CA), in reducing a trial judge's sentence of ineligibility for parole from 20 years (as recommended by the jury) to 15 years:

We must also respectfully disagree with the test for dealing with the jury's recommendation put by the learned trial judge. In our view that recommendation is but one of the several factors which must be taken into account by the trial judge along with all the others. *It is not correct to say that it "should be followed" unless he finds that they are "manifestly in error" or that "there is no good reason why the recommendation not be followed."* The expression of that test *was, in our view, an error in law*. Each factor in s. 671 (now s. 744) must be weighed and none is more important than the other as the process of weighing the factors commences. (My emphasis.)

See also *R v. Ameeriar* (1990), 60 CCC (3d) 431, 10 WCB (2d) 640 (Que. CA). This was a case where the jury was unable to reach unanimity and therefore did not make a recommendation as to parole ineligibility. The trial judge set the period of ineligibility at 15 years. The accused appealed. In dismissing the appeal, Monet JA made the following comments at p. 434:

> The appellant submits that as a general rule the period of ineligibility is limited to 10 years. He then continues that if the jury recommends that a longer period be substituted, the judge would be well advised to take this into consideration and, except for some exceptional reason, to give effect to this recommendation. Conversely, if the jury does not make a recommendation, the judge errs in not applying the general rule and by substituting for the "10-year period," that is, for that period which, within the meaning of the Code, is normally 10 years, a much longer period of time.
>
> *This proposition is unfounded. In my view, the final decision in this matter is for the judge.* (My emphasis.)

See also *R v. Jordan* (1983), 7 CCC (3d) 143 (BCCA), which also appears to indicate that the recommendation of the jury is not the overriding factor in determining parole ineligibility.

Why must the jury's recommendation be only one factor in sentencing? Simply put, because in many, if not most cases, the jury is not in possession of all of the facts; more importantly, it is never instructed in the jurisprudence which surrounds the sentencing function of a judge; and its participation in the process in the limited manner provided by Code, ss. 744 and 745 represents the only occasions when Parliament has permitted jury involvement in what is otherwise a totally judicial function. As Dr. Don Stuart has observed in his work, *Canadian Criminal Law, A Treatise* (1982), at p. 229:

> Sentencing is an onerous task and expertise in this area is elusive. The involvement of the jury in this matter seems anomalous and undesirable. Judges have the advantage of experience.

For many of the reasons given herein, the Law Reform Commission of Canada has recommended that jury involvement in the sentencing process be abolished. See Law Reform Commission of Canada, *Homicide, Working Paper 33*, pp. 79 and 116, and excerpt from the Law Reform Commission of Canada, *The Jury*, Report 16 (1982), appended hereto as Appendix "B."

As patently manifested in the case at bar, the jury's only information concerning the accused and their backgrounds was limited to the evidence adduced at trial through the Crown witnesses who dealt, quite properly, solely with matters relevant to the charge in question. The characters of the accused were not raised nor did the co-accused give evidence. Immediately after rendering their verdicts convicting the two accused, the jury made their parole eligibility recommendation and were then discharged. The following day, the trial judge heard extended representations from Crown and defence counsel, all of which contained, as is customarily the case, background and other information to which the jury was not privy. It was only after considering the totality of evidence, the submissions by counsel on sentence, and then *applying s. 774 and the general principles of sentencing* that the trial judge made his determination.

The jury's recommendation, as previously noted, was made without any knowledge whatsoever of the serious criminal activity of Ky Duong subsequent to the murder for which he was to be sentenced. Nor did they know of Ky Duong's ongoing associations with criminal groups in both Winnipeg and Toronto, matters which had been under police surveillance. Nor did the jury have the additional information which crown and defence counsel later gave the court in speaking to sentence. They did not know Ky Duong was associated with one Bau Diu described by Crown counsel as a dangerous and violent criminal living in Toronto. Nor was the jury apprised of the details of the gangland-type stabbing and shooting which resulted in Ky Duong's plea of guilty to a charge of manslaughter in Toronto.

As the trial judge noted in passing sentence (p. 1540 of the transcript):

> He is presently serving six and a half years manslaughter in Toronto, an offence which occurred after the commission of the crime presently before the court. He also had a conviction for break, enter and theft on May 30th, 1988, this offence also having occurred after the commission of this offence.
>
> Mr. Duong did not make any statements to the police as to his role in the crime.
>
> The evidence of Mr. Tong indicates that Mr. Duong bought the firearm and loaded it with bullets while he was in the car and before setting off to the Dunn-Rite plant.
>
> There is no indication of any remorse by Mr. Duong for his actions in this crime.

This information, save the evidence of Mr. Tong, was unknown to the jury. Taken together with all of the circumstances surrounding the crime itself, it represented, in my opinion, more than adequate justification for the sentence imposed on Ky Duong and for altering the jury's recommendation. The justification for the increased period of parole ineligibility for Phat Ly has earlier been reviewed.

In the result, I would dismiss the appeals against sentence.

The Law Reform Commission of Canada, Appendix "B": *The Jury*
(Ottawa: Supply and Services, 1982), Report 16

The Law Reform Commission of Canada, *The Jury* [Report 16] (Ottawa: Supply and Services, 1982): draft legislation section 26(1) dealing with the judge's instructions to the jury, suggests that:

> As part of his instructions on the law, the judge shall instruct the jury that, in the event of a verdict of guilty, the jury has no prerogative to make any recommendation either as a clemency or as to the severity of the sentence.

This recommendation entails the repeal of the present section 670 of the *Criminal Code*, which provides that where the jury finds an accused guilty of second degree murder, the trial judge shall, before discharging the jury, invite them to make a recommendation regarding eligibility for release on parole. The Report continues on page 70:

The reasons for this departure are several. First, the jury's principal role is to arrive at a verdict of guilt or innocence by weighing the evidence placed before it at trial. It is no part of that role to determine what sentence is appropriate in the event of conviction. To permit the jury to make a recommendation as to clemency or severity of sentence is to confuse the proper role of the jury with the role of the trial judge, whose exclusive responsibility it is to pronounce sentence upon a finding of guilt. Second, the Commission believes that permitting the jury to recommend clemency may compromise the integrity of its verdict. The promise of a collective plea for clemency could well operate as an effective, but unconscionable, inducement to persuade a reluctant juror to vote with the majority. A recommendation for clemency which the trial judge is under no obligation to accept should play no part in a jury's deliberations about guilt or innocence. Third, because the jury will ordinarily be familiar with the facts of the particular case before them, they will not be cognizant of the several different considerations that bear on sentence—the accused's prior criminal record, if any; his reputation in the community; his antecedent and present circumstances.

Do you think we should maintain a role for the jury in second degree murder cases? If you think we should, would you change the process at all to make it more meaningful—that is, by allowing the prosecutor and the offender to make submissions?

V. JUDICIAL REVIEW AFTER 15 YEARS

The judicial review procedure set out in s. 745.6 has received little attention in case law and legal literature. This is because this procedure was enacted in 1976 when the penalty for murder was restructured. It was part of the legislated alternative to hanging, along with the first- and second-degree murder regime, and is commonly known as the "faint hope" clause. Given that a person convicted of first-degree murder must wait 15 years before pursuing an application for judicial review, the first applications were not heard until the late 1980s. The first two cases were *Chartrand* in Quebec and *Vaillancourt* in Ontario, both of whom had originally been sentenced to hang but whose death sentences were commuted as a transitional part of the 1976 legislation. Both men had killed police officers. Consistent with the experience that would unfold over time, the Quebec case succeeded and the Ontario application was rejected. The legislation provides for no right of appeal to the provincial courts of appeal. Accordingly, it was some years before any appellate guidance was provided. The only case in which the Supreme Court has pronounced on these types of hearings is *Swietlinski*, below.

This judicial review procedure is controversial. There are some who argue for its repeal on the basis that by reducing the 25-year minimum incarceration period the procedure undermines the gravity of first-degree murder sentencing. Others have noted the high success rate of applicants in reducing their parole ineligibility periods and suggested that this indicates systemic manipulation. Even if true, this is an ironic view given that the decision maker is a jury from the jurisdiction where the killing took place. Moreover, as you will see from the data below, the success rate is misleading because only a small fraction of eligible prisoners actually apply.

The controversy has not gone unnoticed by politicians. In 1997, a series of amendments to s. 745.6 were passed with the goal of limiting access to its relief. These included the disqualification of multiple murderers, the requirement for pre-vetting by the chief justice of the province, and the requirement for jury unanimity on the issue of granting relief (see s. 745.63(3)). Recent statistics are available (see Public Safety and Emergency Preparedness Portfolio Corrections Statistics Committee, *Corrections and Conditional Release Statistical Overview* (Ottawa: 2006). The statistics show that as of April 9, 2006:

Number of offenders serving life sentences with more than
  15 years parole ineligibility . . . .   1,634 (11.52% of penitentiary prisoners)
Number of prisoners eligible for s. 745 of Application   802
Number of eligible prisoners who have had hearings . . . . . .   154 (19.2% of eligible prisoners)
Number of prisoners who received some reduction . . . .   128 (15.9% of eligible prisoners)

The figure that usually gets quoted is that 83.1 percent of applicants get some relief. While this appears very high, it fails to consider two facts. First, relief can mean anything from immediate eligibility to a reduction to 23 or 24 years of ineligibility from the original 25. More importantly, one has to notice the very low proportion of applications. Only 19.2 percent of eligible prisoners have applied. Accordingly, only 15.9 percent have received reductions.

It is not a given that a s. 745.6 reduction leads immediately to parole upon eligibility. The National Parole Board with its structured processes still performs its statutory decision-making function on the basis of perception of risk. After eligibility, it may take many months before a parole application is ready to be heard and some prisoners in this category have been rejected. As of 2006, 114 prisoners have been released on parole of the 125 who had reached eligibility. It is interesting to note that, of that group, only 16 have been returned to custody, although another 2 have disappeared and are unlawfully at large.

A. Criminal Code, Sections 745.6 to 746

Application for Judicial Review

745.6(1) Subject to subsection (2), a person may apply, in writing, to the appropriate Chief Justice in the province in which their conviction took place for a reduction in the number of years of imprisonment without eligibility for parole if the person

  (a) has been convicted of murder or high treason;

  (b) has been sentenced to life imprisonment for life without parole until more than fifteen years of their sentence has been served; and

  (c) has served at least fifteen years of their sentence.

(2) A person who has been convicted of more than one murder may not make an application under subsection (1), whether or not proceedings were commenced in respect of any of the murders before another murder was committed.

. . .

Judicial Screening

745.61(1) On receipt of an application under subsection 745.6(1), the appropriate Chief Justice shall determine, or shall designate a judge of the superior court of criminal jurisdiction to determine, on the basis of the following written material, whether the applicant has shown, on a balance of probabilities, that there is a reasonable prospect that the application will succeed:

(a) the application;

(b) any report provided by the Correctional Service of Canada or other correctional authorities; and

(c) any other written evidence present to the Chief Justice or judge by the applicant or the Attorney General.

(2) In determining whether the applicant has shown that there is a reasonable prospect that the application will succeed, the Chief Justice or judge shall consider the criteria set out in paragraphs 745.63(1)(a) to (e), with such modifications as the circumstances require.

(3) If the Chief Justice or judge determines that the applicant has not shown that there is a reasonable prospect that the application will succeed, the Chief Justice may

(a) set a time not earlier than two years after the date of the determination, at or after which another applicant may be made by the applicant under subsection 745.6(1); or

(b) decide that the applicant may not make another application under that subsection.

(4) If the Chief Justice or judge determines that the applicant has not shown that there is a reasonable prospect that the application will succeed but does not set a time for another application or decide that such an application may not be made, the applicant may make another application no earlier than two years after the date of the determination.

(5) If the Chief Justice or judge determines that the applicant has shown that there is a reasonable prospect that the application will succeed, the Chief Justice shall designate a judge of the superior court of criminal jurisdiction to empanel a jury to hear the application.

Appeal

745.62(1) The applicant or the Attorney General may appeal to the Court of Appeal from a determination or a decision made under section 745.61 on any question of law or fact or mixed law and fact.

(2) The appeal shall be determined on the basis of the documents presented to the Chief Justice or judge who made the determination or decision, any reasons for the determination or decision and any other document that the Court of Appeal requires.

(3) Sections 673 to 696 apply, with such modifications as the circumstances require.

Hearing of Application

745.63(1) The jury empanelled under subsection 745.61(5) to hear the application shall consider the following criteria and determine whether the applicant's number of years of imprisonment without eligibility for parole ought to be reduced:

(a) the character of the applicant;

(b) the applicant's conduct while serving the sentence;

(c) the nature of the offence for which the applicant was convicted;

(d) any information provided by a victim at the time of the imposition of the sentence or at the time of the hearing under this section; and

(e) any other matters that the judge considers relevant in the circumstances.

(2) In paragraph (1)(d), "victim" has the same meaning as in subsection 722(4).

(3) The jury hearing an application under subsection (1) may determine that the applicant's number of years of imprisonment without eligibility for parole ought to be reduced. The determination to reduce the number of years must be by unanimous vote.

(4) The applicant's number of years of imprisonment without eligibility for parole is not reduced if

(a) the jury hearing an application under subsection (1) determines that the number of years ought not to be reduced;

(b) the jury hearing an application under subsection (1) concludes that it cannot unanimously determine that the number of years ought to be reduced; or

(c) the presiding judge, after the jury has deliberated for a reasonable period, concludes that the jury is unable to unanimously determine that the number of years ought to be reduced.

(5) If the jury determines that the number of years of imprisonment without eligibility for parole ought to be reduced, the jury may, by a vote of not less than two thirds of the members of the jury,

(a) substitute a lesser number of years of imprisonment without eligibility for parole than that then applicable; or

(b) terminate the ineligibility for parole.

(6) If the applicant's number of years of imprisonment without eligibility for parole is not reduced, the jury may

(a) set a time, not earlier than two years after the date of the determination or conclusion under subsection (4), at or after which another application may be made by the applicant under subsection 745.6(1); or

(b) decide that the applicant may not make another application under that subsection.

(7) The decision of the jury under paragraph (6)(a) or (b) must be made by not less than two thirds of its members.

(8) If the jury does not set a date at or after which another application may be made or decide that such an application may not be made, the applicant may make another application no earlier than two years after the date of the determination or conclusion under subsection (4).

Rules

745.64(1) The appropriate Chief Justice in each province or territory may make such rules as are required for the purposes of sections 745.6 to 745.63.

· · ·

Time Spent in Custody

746. In calculating the period of imprisonment served for the purposes of section 745, 745.1, 745.4, 745.5 or 745.6, there shall be included any time spent in custody between

(a) in the case of a sentence of imprisonment for life after July 25, 1976, the day on which that person was arrested and taken into custody in respect of the offence for which he was sentenced to imprisonment for life and the day the sentence was imposed; or

(b) in the case of a sentence of death that has been or is deemed to have been commuted to a sentence of imprisonment for life, the day on which that person was arrested and taken into custody in respect of the offence for which he was sentenced to death and the day the sentence was commuted or deemed to have been commuted to a sentence of imprisonment for life.

This version of the procedure results from a number of revisions. Because the procedure has caught the attention of the public, opportunistic politicians (federal, provincial, and territorial alike) lobbied the government to eradicate, or at least tighten up, the procedure. This lobbying resulted in the following features of the present legislation:

- the preclusion of multiple murderers from applying for relief under the provision (s. 745.6);
- the establishment of a screening process by a judge (s. 745.61); and
- the requirement that the jury be unanimous in its decision to reduce the period of parole ineligibility. Under the previous provisions, the jury was permitted to speak with a two-thirds majority voice on this issue (s. 745.63(3)).[3]

B. Applying the Provisions

The following two decisions, *Vaillancourt* and *Swietlinski*, were decided under the original formulation of the 15-year review.

R v. Vaillancourt
(1988), 66 CR (3d) 66 (Ont. HCJ)

CALLAGHAN ACJHC: The applicant has applied pursuant to s. 672 of the *Criminal Code* ("the Code") for a reduction of the number of years of imprisonment he must serve without eligibility for parole. On 1st October 1973 he was convicted of capital murder and sentenced to hang. This sentence was commuted to a "sentence of imprisonment for life for first degree murder" by operation of s. 25(1) of the *Criminal Law Amendment Act* (No. 2), 1976, proclaimed in force effective 26th July 1976. This enactment provided that the applicant would serve a term of life imprisonment without eligibility for parole until 25 years had been served. It also provided for a review of the ineligibility period pursuant to s. 672 of the Code: see *Criminal Law Amendment Act* (No. 2), 1976. SC 1974-75-76, c. 105, ss. 25(1) and 28(2).

On 27th January 1988 the Honourable Chief Justice of this court promulgated rules of practice ("the rules") for the conduct of applications for review brought pursuant to s. 672. On 15th April 1988 the applicant, by notice of constitutional question, indicated his intention to question the constitutional validity of the interpretation of s. 672(2) of the Code as it is reflected in the rules made by the Honourable Chief Justice, and in particular RR. 6(2), 14 and 16(2).

The applicant submits that the onus of proof in determining the number of years of imprisonment without eligibility for parole under s. 672(2) of the Code must rest with the Attorney General of Ontario and that, to the extent that the aforesaid rules place a

---

[3] This change in the legislation was made retroactive to January 6, 1997, the date that the legislation was amended. Unless an application was already under way by the time the legislation changed, the new requirement of unanimity applied. This has been held to be constitutional (see *R v. Chaudhary* (1999), 139 CCC (3d) 547 (Ont. Sup. Ct.), leave to appeal denied). Note that ss. 745.63(6) and (7) require only a two-thirds majority voice on the number of years that parole ought to be reduced or terminated. Similarly, if a jury refuses to lower or terminate parole ineligibility, the jury may, by a two-thirds majority, stipulate the amount of time that must elapse before another application may be made.

persuasive burden of proof on the applicant, they are *ultra vires* s. 672(5) of the Code. Furthermore, it is submitted that the said rules are contrary to the principles of fundamental justice to the extent that they place an obligation on the applicant to define issues in controversy, adduce evidence and address the jury before the Attorney General of Ontario on the application for review.

. . .

The fundamental issue on this application is the characterization of the review procedures established in s. 672.

The applicant takes the position that the procedure established under s. 672 is part of the sentencing process and involves an assessment of blameworthiness in order to determine the appropriate degree of denunciation which, in the eyes of the representatives of the community, i.e., the jury, needs to be satisfied. The applicant submits that Parliament has, by virtue of s. 672, provided a range of 15 to 25 years within which the jury may assess the degree of blameworthiness that should attach to the applicant's conduct. When blameworthiness is in issue, the applicant submits, it is a fundamental principle of justice that the state must bear the burden of establishing all matters in controversy beyond a reasonable doubt. As s. 672 is silent with respect to the issues of onus and standard of proof, the *Canadian Charter of Rights and Freedoms*, through the guarantees of s. 7 and s. 12, requires that the procedural protections which are attendant upon other proceedings under the Code be applied to a review under s. 672. It is submitted that the rules alter this substantive law and accordingly are *ultra vires* and of no force and effect.

The respondents characterize the review under s. 672 as a process entirely distinct from that of the sentencing process at trial. It is submitted that the review provided under s. 672 is an enlightened review process which seeks to provide hope of earlier release to those serving the longest possible sentences. The respondents take the position that the issue of blameworthiness was fully and finally assessed at trial, conviction and sentence, and that the determination of guilt made at that time is not subject to review under s. 672. Accordingly, the section does not contemplate a reassessment of blameworthiness. Therefore, the onus and burden of persuasion should rest with the applicant, as he is the one moving to set aside a valid judicial order and the impugned rules are not violative of any Charter rights.

. . .

In my view, the language of s. 669(a) is mandatory. From that I infer that Parliament has specified precisely the degree of denunciation consequent upon a conviction for first degree murder. Where a conviction is registered for second degree murder, a jury has the right to make a recommendation with reference to parole eligibility under s. 670 of the Code. In contrast, when the conviction is for first degree murder, no such recommendation is available. The requisite degree of denunciation is established by Parliament in very clear language.

Counsel on behalf of the applicant submitted that the Charter, through ss. 7 and 12, requires that there be a proportional relationship between blameworthiness and punishment, and in this regard referred to the decision in *R v. Smith*, [1987] 1 SCR 1045, where it was held that a punishment is unconstitutional if it is grossly disproportionate to the offence. Counsel for the applicant submitted, therefore, that, in order for the mandatory sentence for first degree murder to be upheld as constitutional, s. 672 of the Code ought to be interpreted as requiring a jury to assess the blameworthiness of the individual offender and offence in order to determine the proportional number of years of ineligibility for parole. With respect, however, I do not agree. In *Smith*, Lamer J, with whom Dickson CJC concurred, expressly stated that a minimum mandatory sentence is not in and of itself cruel and unusual. In my view, the sentence provided in s. 669 of the Code cannot be said to be grossly disproportionate to the offence of first degree murder. A planned and deliberate killing necessarily involves an offence of the most serious order. In such circumstances, a mandatory sentence of life imprisonment without eligibility for parole for 25 years cannot be characterized as being so excessive or grossly disproportionate as to outrage standards of decency.

It was submitted on behalf of the applicant that the jury's role in a review under s. 672 is to reflect the community's condemnation of the offence and repudiation of the offender. On the contrary, that role has already been performed by the trial jury in its finding of guilt and by Parliament in its determination of the mandatory sentence that must be imposed. The issue of blameworthiness was finally assessed at trial, conviction and sentence. The determination of guilt, made at trial beyond a reasonable doubt, concludes all questions of the applicant's blameworthiness in respect of that offence. Accordingly, s. 672 does not, in my view, contemplate a reassessment of blameworthiness. Instead, it strikes a balance between considerations of leniency for the well-behaved convict in the service of his sentence, which may serve to assist in his rehabilitation, and the community interest in repudiation and deterrence of the conduct that led to his incarceration.

The jury under s. 672(2) is undertaking a review process, in the course of which they must consider the applicant's good conduct, and are given specific criteria to be applied in coming to their decision. But that jury does not again determine the degree of denunciation. With reference to the character of the applicant, his conduct while incarcerated and the circumstances of the offence, the jury determines whether or not present circumstances justify leniency and an early consideration of the applicant's case by the parole board. The review contemplated under s. 672 is a process distinct and apart from the sentencing process that took place at the conclusion at the trial. It is to be noted that the jury has no power to increase the penalty imposed at trial, but has the power only to recommend a reduction in that penalty. Accordingly, I must conclude that the review process provided for in s. 672 does not contemplate a proceeding which is part of the sentencing process, nor does blameworthiness fall to be determined again in the course of that review.

• • •

An application under s. 672 of the Code is permissive, and it is the applicant who has the option of determining whether or not to bring the application. There is nothing compelling the applicant to bring the application. In such circumstances, to place a persuasive onus on the applicant is not in my view violative of s. 11 of the Charter. It is the applicant who is seeking to set aside an otherwise valid judicial order. Having discharged the burden of establishing the guilt of the accused at trial beyond a reasonable doubt, the state, in my view, should not again be forced to bear the high cost of the onus of proof in post-conviction review matters. Moreover, it would be highly anomalous for the persuasive burden to revert to the state in the case of a convict such as the applicant, who had years earlier unsuccessfully appealed against the parole ineligibility period determination. The protections afforded by s. 11 of the Charter are simply inapplicable on a review under s. 672.

I am not satisfied that an application under s. 672 of the Code involves a deprivation of liberty within s. 7 of the Charter. The applicant has already been deprived of his liberty by the imposition of sentence. It would *prima facie* be an enhancement of liberty, and not a further deprivation thereof, which is involved in an application for a reduction in the number of years of ineligibility for parole under s. 672. However, even if a deprivation of liberty is at issue in a s. 672 application, such that the principles of fundamental justice must be complied with, the rules impugned in these proceedings do not appear to violate those tenets. As stated by Lamer J in *Re BC Motor Vehicle Act*, [1985] 2 SCR 486 at 513, the phrase "principles of fundamental justice cannot be given an exhaustive content or simple enumeration but will take on concrete meaning as the court addresses alleged violation of s. 7."

R v. Swietlinski
(1995), 92 CCC (3d) 449 (SCC)

LAMER CJC: This case provides an opportunity for this court to consider for the first time the interpretation of s. 745 of the *Criminal Code*, RSC 1985, c. C-46, which authorizes a reduction of the period during which persons convicted of murder are ineligible for parole.

I. Facts

The appellant Roman Swietlinski was convicted of first degree murder. His conviction was upheld by the Ontario Court of Appeal, 5 CR (3d) 324, and by this court, 55 CCC (2d) 481. Since the earlier judgment of this court sets out the facts in detail, I will only give a brief description of the murder. On the night of September 18 to 19, 1976, the appellant met the victim, Mary Frances McKenna, in a bar in Toronto. Apparently, the pair left the bar about midnight on their way to the victim's apartment. The attack which followed was one of unspeakable brutality. The appellant stabbed the victim 132 times using five different knives. The force used was such that some of the knives were broken at the time the police located them.

In the course of the first two years of his sentence the appellant committed various disciplinary offences connected with smuggling and an attempted escape. Apparently, when he was placed in punitive segregation for the latter offence he underwent a complete change of heart and became a "model prisoner." In 1983, he was transferred to a medium security institution and then in 1990, to a minimum security institution. During his confinement in these various penal institutions the appellant became involved in various charitable or religious groups. He participated in work programs in the institutions. Since 1988, he has received several permits for escorted temporary absences. At various times he took part in Alcoholics Anonymous activities. He also participated in some training sessions and requested the assistance of a psychologist.

. . .

III. Judgment of Ontario Court of Justice (General Division)

O'Driscoll J of the Ontario Court (General Division) was designated for empanelling a jury and hearing the case.

At the preliminary hearing provided for in s. 10 of the Ontario Rules of Practice Respecting Reduction in the Number of Years of Imprisonment Without Eligibility for Parole, SOR/88-582, in effect at that time, O'Driscoll J held that statements by members of the victim's family were not admissible as evidence. He based his decision on *R v. Vaillancourt* (1989), 49 CCC (3d) 544, 71 CR (3d) 43, 43 CRR 60 (Ont. CA), in which the Ontario Court of Appeal held that a s. 745 hearing did not form part of the sentencing process. Since s. 735(1.1) of the Code made such statements admissible in order only to facilitate the determination of the sentence, they should be excluded from a s. 745 hearing. Further, O'Driscoll J considered that the statements disclosed no information relevant to the assessment of the factors listed in s. 745(2).

The hearing itself was subsequently held and the jury refused to reduce the period of the appellant's ineligibility for parole. Further, it set November 6, 2001 as the date on which the appellant could again make a similar application. Since that date corresponds to the time when the appellant will have served 25 years of his sentence, the jury's decision amounts to prohibiting the appellant from filing another application under s. 745.

The appellant sought and obtained leave to appeal directly to this court. Section 40 of the *Supreme Court Act*, RSC 1985, c. S-26, authorizes a direct appeal since the Code makes no provision for any other avenue of appeal: *R v. Vaillancourt* (1992), 76 CCC (3d) 384n, [1990] 1 SCR xii, 57 OAC 320n (SCC).

IV. Issues

The appellant raised the following grounds of appeal, most of which relate to the judge's charge to the jury:

1. the judge should not have limited consideration of the appellant's character to his character at the time of the murder: he should also have mentioned the appellant's present character;
2. the judge should not have referred to the three factors mentioned in s. 745(2) as three independent factors, each to be proved on a balance of probabilities;
3. the judge should have reread all of the agreed statement of facts: he should not have omitted the second part, relating to "extenuating circumstances";
4. the judge did not make a fair summation of the psychiatric evidence;
5. in questioning certain witnesses and in his address to the jury, counsel for the Crown introduced inflammatory and highly prejudicial matters.

I feel that the fifth ground provides a sufficient basis for allowing this appeal. Furthermore, the first, second and fourth grounds raise legitimate concerns which only aggravate the inequity resulting from the Crown counsel's inflammatory remarks.

Additionally, since I believe that a new hearing should be ordered, I will deal with the question of the admissibility of statements by the victim's family.

V. Analysis

A. General Observations on Section 745

Section 745 of the Code was adopted in 1976 in connection with the abolition of the death penalty. The compromise arrived at between the supporters and opponents of the death penalty was its replacement by long-term imprisonment without parole. Accordingly, in the case of first degree murder the penalty is life imprisonment with no eligibility for parole for 25 years. In the case of second degree murder, this time period is 10 years, but it may be extended to 25 years by the trial judge on the jury's recommendation. In both cases, however, Parliament provided that after 15 years a jury could be empanelled to reassess the period of ineligibility.

Section 745 put in place a procedure that is original in several respects. However, we need not consider all its aspects in order to deal with the case at bar. What is important is to understand that the procedure is one for reassessing long-term imprisonment imposed by law (in the case of first degree murder) or by a judge (in the case of second degree murder). The purpose of a reassessment procedure, especially when it takes place 15 years after the initial decision, is necessarily to re-examine a decision in light of new information or factors which could not have been known initially. It follows that the primary purpose of a s. 745 hearing is to call attention to changes which have occurred in the applicant's situation and which might justify imposing a less harsh penalty upon the applicant. Accordingly, the jury's decision is not essentially different from the ordinary decision regarding length of a sentence. It is similar to that taken by a judge pursuant to s. 744 of the Code as to the period of ineligibility in cases of second degree murder.

It should also be noted, in the context of an appeal to this court, that s. 745 gives the jury a broad discretionary power. This is quite different from a trial, at which the jury must choose between two options, guilt or innocence, based on very specific rules of law. Moreover, the discretionary nature of the jury's decision is made quite clear by the fact that Parliament did not see fit to grant any right of appeal to the Court of Appeal, although as I mentioned earlier that does not prevent an appeal to this court with leave. Consequently, there is no need to analyze the judge's charge to the jury in the detail that would be appropriate in the case of a trial. This court's function is essentially to determine whether the appellant was given a fair hearing at trial.

The discretionary nature of the decision also compels the jury to adopt a different analytical approach from that used in a trial. At a trial, the jury must decide whether it has been proven beyond all reasonable doubt that the accused committed the crime with which he or she is charged. In such a proceeding, the offence is generally defined by a number of elements which must all be proven for the accused to be convicted. Each element of the offence is thus a necessary condition for a conviction. At a s. 745 hearing, on the other hand, the jury does not determine whether the applicant is guilty: another jury (or, in some cases, a judge) has already performed that task. Its duty rather is to make a discretionary decision as to the minimum length of the sentence that the applicant must serve. The concept of an element of an offence cannot be transposed onto a discretionary decision. When a person makes such a decision he or she does not apply rigid logic, requiring for example that if conditions A, B and C are met, then decision X must be the result. When legislation lists various factors that a decision-maker must take into consideration, a finding reached upon one or all of the factors does not necessarily mandate a conclusion leading to a specific decision. They are instead factors, some of which may work in favour of the applicant and some against him, and which must be assessed and weighed as a whole in arriving at a conclusion. This is quite different from a trial where very strong evidence of one aspect of an offence cannot offset the weakness of evidence of another aspect.

Accordingly, the concepts of burden of proof, proof on a balance of probabilities, or proof beyond a reasonable doubt are of very limited value in a hearing pursuant to s. 745, where the decision lies exclusively in the discretion of the jury. The jury must instead make what it, in its discretion, deems to be the best decision on the evidence: On this point see also *R v. M.(S.H.)* (1989), 50 CCC (3d) 503 at pp. 547-8, [1989] 2 SCR 446, 71 CR (3d) 257 (SCC).

B. Grounds of Appeal

1. Inappropriate Language by Counsel for the Crown

The appellant objected to certain irrelevant and prejudicial language used by counsel for the Crown. Before considering the disputed remarks in detail, it should be recalled that the function of counsel for the Crown in a s. 745 hearing is no different from the function in a criminal trial. Taschereau J described his function as follows in *Boucher v. The Queen* (1954), 110 CCC 263 at p. 267 (SCC) (translation):

> The position held by counsel for the Crown is not that of a lawyer in civil litigation. His functions are quasi-judicial. His duty is not so much to obtain a conviction as to assist the judge and the jury in ensuring that the fullest possible justice is done. His conduct before the court must always be characterized by moderation and impartiality. He will have properly performed his duty and will be beyond all reproach if, eschewing any appeal to passion, and employing a dignified manner suited to his function, he presents the evidence to the jury without going beyond what it discloses.

The first category of unacceptable language had the effect of discrediting the process of reviewing ineligibility established by s. 745. Counsel for the Crown sought, in some measure, to present the procedure as fundamentally inequitable, first, because the victim had no opportunity, as the applicant did, to have her suffering reduced, and secondly, because the 25-year ineligibility period was a bargain compared with the death penalty imposed prior to 1976 and further reducing this period of time would be an additional concession to the accused.

For example, counsel began his opening statement with the following passage:

> Ladies and gentlemen of the jury, in 1976 this country, our government abolished capital punishment. Mr. Swietlinski was convicted of the worst crime known to our criminal justice system. You will hear shortly about the facts of this offence. In 1976, the same year, Mary Frances McKenna, someone that you won't hear very much about in this proceeding—this is an application brought by Mr. Swietlinski—but you won't hear much about a person by the name of Mary Frances McKenna, who was 37 years of age at the time.

He went on to add:

> ... please don't forget the victim in this case, Mary Frances McKenna. She doesn't have a chance to come before a group of people to ask for a second chance.

He concluded his opening statement by reminding the jurors that, "... Mr. Swietlinski, a few years earlier, would have been sentenced to death for this offence ... ." In his final submission to the jury he returned to the same themes:

> Mary Frances McKenna doesn't get a chance to come before a jury and ask to have her parole eligibility reduced. Mary Frances McKenna is gone.
>
> If we wanted revenge, we would have capital punishment. As I say, we don't. We have a compromise. It's a mandatory sentence, life with no eligibility for parole for 25 years, and that's the sentence that our society imposes for the taking of a human life in the manner that Mr. Swietlinski took it. To do otherwise, as Mr. Swietlinski suggested to you about the rules at Millhaven, would be anarchy.

Counsel also sought, in questioning certain witnesses, to draw attention to the fact that the victim could not obtain the second chance the appellant was seeking and to the fact that no assistance programs were available to the victim's family whereas the penitentiary system offered the appellant a vast range of services.

Counsel further sought to discredit the parole process in the following language:

> Normally, issues of parole, parole hearings, are held by, basically, a faceless group of people. They're held in secret, in private, and really all that the Parole Board hears from is the applicant and perhaps his counsel and the kind of people that you're about to hear from, the various corrections people.

Finally, in questioning certain witnesses counsel insinuated that the Beaver Creek Institution, where the appellant had spent the last two years, was too comfortable to be called a prison and that in fact some visitors confused the institution with a neighbouring campground. In his final submission, he suggested that the transfer to this institution was sufficient reward for the appellant's good conduct during his sentence.

The combined effect of these remarks was to imply that the s. 745 hearing was a proceeding unduly favourable to the applicant, even a subversion of Parliament's intent to impose a definite 25-year penalty on first degree murderers. The conclusion that emerged from these observations, and it was not a difficult one to draw, was that the jury should deal more severely with the appellant.

Nevertheless, s. 745 is as much a part of the Code as the provisions providing for no parole for 25 years in cases of first degree murder. The possible reduction of the ineligibility period after 15 years is a choice made by Parliament which the jury must accept. Clearly, the prosecution may not call this choice into question by suggesting to the jury that it is an abnormal procedure, excessively indulgent and contrary to what it argues was Parliament's intent. That amounts to urging the jurors not to make a decision in accordance with the law if they feel that it is bad law. It is clearly unacceptable for a lawyer to make such an observation to the jury: *R v. Morgentaler* (1988), 37 CCC (3d) 449 at pp. 481-3, 44 DLR (4th) 385 at pp. 417-9, [1988] 1 SCR 30 (SCC); *R v. Finta* (1994), 88 CCC (3d) 417, 112 DLR (4th) 513, [1994] 1 SCR 701 (SCC).

In the same way, counsel may not constantly repeat that imprisonment for 25 years is a substitute for the death penalty. That is an invitation to offset the alleged excessive clemency of Parliament by a severity not justified by the wording of s. 745. The jury does not have to decide whether the penalties imposed by Parliament are too severe or not severe enough. It must simply apply the Code. The Code no longer contains the death penalty: on the contrary, s. 745 gives the appellant the right to seek a reduction in his ineligibility period. No one can be permitted to undermine the fairness of the proceeding in which the appellant may obtain such a reduction by constant references to the death penalty.

Additionally, counsel for the Crown sought to draw the jury's attention to other cases of murderers who had used their parole to commit other murders. ...

Similarly, in his opening statement he invited the jury to take into consideration cases of violence other than those of the appellant:

> We read the papers. We open the headlines today and we see concerns about violence in our society, and, in particular, we hear concerns about violence against women. I want you, when you listen to that evidence, to bear in mind that you are here representing the best interests of this community as it pertains not only to Mr. Swietlinski but the broader issues that an application, such as this, brings to bear.

In his final submission he added the following:

> Violence is, unfortunately, increasing in our community. Every time you turn on the news, read the headlines you hear either reports of or people worried about the issue of violence and, in particular, violence against women.
>
> A lot of times people come into contact or read in the paper and hear, read or see on TV something that shocks them, and the facts of this case no doubt shocked you. Well, they have concerns about things going on in our society, and they think to themselves, "Someone should do something about that," and always the someone is someone off in the distance. For the purpose of this case ... you are the they. Consider that when you retire to reach your determination.

It is completely improper to invite the jury to consider isolated cases in which prisoners committed murder after being paroled. Even though the rules applicable in the s. 745 hearing are not as strict as in a criminal trial, the fact remains that the jury must consider only the applicant's case. Although the temptation may sometimes be very strong, the jury must not try the cases of other inmates or determine whether the existing system of parole is doing its job. The appellant should not be punished for the weaknesses of the system.

Furthermore, the other observations I have just referred to may have suggested to the jury that its function was in some way to solve the problem of violence in society. It is true that deterrence is one of the functions of the penalty and that it is, therefore, legitimate for the jury to take this factor into account when hearing an application under s. 745. However, the approach taken by counsel for the Crown was unacceptable. The jury cannot simply be referred to headlines in newspapers, which generally concern themselves with the worst crimes. Such a course could produce a disproportionate reaction in the jury by making it believe it could solve the problem of crime at one stroke and by giving the appellant's case the odour of a general threat. Such a tactic smacks of the in terrorem arguments disapproved by the Quebec Court of Appeal in *R v. Vallieres*, [1970] 4 CCC 69. In my view, it is possible to invite the jury to take the deterrent aspect of the penalty into account, but this should be done in the context of a general submission on the various functions performed by the penalty.

In a trial by jury it is usual for the judge to indicate to the jurors that they must base their decision solely on the evidence and that they should not read the newspapers while the trial is in progress. Sometimes drastic methods such as sequestering the jury or banning publication may be used to keep the jury free from undue influence by the media. That being the case, it is astonishing that counsel for the Crown could have invited the jury to do precisely what any good judge would tell it not to do. It is still more surprising that the trial judge did not react and rectify these remarks.

To sum up, I consider that the remarks of counsel for the Crown seriously compromised the fairness of the hearing. The judge's failure to reprimand him and to tell the jury that such remarks should not be taken into account, only aggravates the lack of fairness. However, the respondent argued that this court should dismiss the appeal because counsel for the appellant did not object to these remarks at trial. I cannot accept that argument. It is true that the absence of an objection is a factor which an appellate court may take into account in deciding whether to dismiss an appeal. In the case at bar, however, the hearing was unfair. The trial judge had a duty to ensure that the hearing was fair: *R v. Potvin* (1989), 47 CCC (3d) 289 at pp. 314-5 (SCC); *R v. L.(D.O.)* (1993), 85 CCC (3d) 289 (SCC), at p. 318. Since he did not do so, this court must intervene, whether counsel for the appellant objected or not.

I would allow the appeal for this reason alone. This conclusion is made all the more necessary when we take into account the court's errors in compartmentalizing the burden of proof and in the review of the evidence, although those errors by themselves are not sufficiently serious to justify a rehearing.

2. Distinction Between Present and Past Character: Burden of Proof

The common error disclosed by the first two grounds of appeal is an excessive compartmentalization of the various factors listed in s. 745(2) that the jury must take into account in arriving at its decision.

The judge's first error was to limit his discussion of the appellant's character to matters prior to or contemporaneous with the murder. He made no reference to the changes in the appellant's character since his imprisonment. As I mentioned, however, the purpose of the s. 745 proceeding is to reassess the penalty imposed on the offender by reference to the way his or her situation has evolved in 15 years. The judge should, therefore, have mentioned both the appellant's past and present character.

The second error results from the following observation by the judge, made at the start of the part of his charge dealing with conduct while serving sentence:

> Ladies and gentlemen, it is for you to say, but it would seem that the evidence establishes for you, on the balance of probabilities, that Roman Swietlinski was a model prisoner after he emerged from the 25 days in "the hole" at Millhaven penitentiary back in 1979 or 1980.

The judge expressed no similar opinion as to the other two factors mentioned in s. 745(2).

It is true that a judge may always give his or her opinion on the facts, so long as he or she makes it clear to the jurors that the final decision is theirs. However, this comment could have led the jury to think that the three factors mentioned in s. 745(2) were separate and that each had to be "establishe[d] ... on the balance of probabilities." As I have shown, this is not a very suitable approach in the case of a discretionary decision. The jury could have thought, in reliance on this comment, that it had to arrive at a decision favourable to the appellant on each of the three criteria.

3. Summary of Psychiatric Evidence

The appellant's psychiatric condition was one of the major questions raised in the court below. The points especially in dispute were the possibility that the appellant suffers from sexual sadism and the possibility of successful psychiatric treatment. Simplifying somewhat, it can be said that Dr. Dickey's testimony was very unfavourable to the appellant while the testimony of Mr. Jean, Drs. Wood-Hill and Quirt was favourable.

The trial judge undertook a lengthy review of the psychiatric evidence. It was probably not necessary to do this in so much detail. The issues were relatively straightforward. The expert testimony was fresh in the minds of the jurors. Moreover, each juror had a copy of the written reports available to him or her. However, when the trial judge considers it necessary or desirable to make such a review, he or she should not unduly devote greater attention to the aspects of the evidence that favour one party, yet this is what the trial judge did here. The judge placed his emphasis on Dr. Dickey's testimony, noting his professional qualifications and repeating certain parts of his testimony word for word. On the other hand, the judge made no mention at all of the testimony of Mr. Jean or Drs. Wood-Hill and Quirt. He simply mentioned short extracts from the written reports of Drs. Wood-Hill and Quirt. Though I am sure it was not intentional, the judge did nevertheless favour the respondent in his summation of the evidence. As an illustration, it can be pointed out that the review of Dr. Dickey's testimony took up 15 pages of the transcript of the charge to the jury while the passage from Dr. Wood-Hill's report extended only for a page and a half.

C. Admissibility of Victim's Statements

As I feel that a rehearing should be ordered, I think it is worth dealing with the question of the admissibility of statements by members of the victim's family. The respondent will undoubtedly seek to introduce such statements at that hearing. Additionally, since there is no right of appeal to the Court of Appeal, the appeal to this court is the only opportunity to introduce uniformity into the rulings of the superior courts on this point.

In *R v. Gardiner*, [1982] 2 SCR 368 (SCC), this court set out the general rules governing evidence at a sentencing hearing. Dickson J (as he then was) noted that the rules which applied to evidence at trial had been made more flexible: now, for example, hearsay evidence can be admitted if it is credible and reliable.

A s. 745 hearing differs from an initial hearing in many respects. However, the purpose of both is to determine the length of sentence. Consequently, evidence should be governed by similar rules. It is well known that the victim's testimony is admissible at a hearing on sentencing: see, e.g., *R v. Landry* (1981), 61 CCC (2d) 317 (NSCA). Since s. 745(2) states that the nature of the offence is one of the criteria the jury must take into account, it is clear that the victim's testimony is relevant and admissible at such a hearing. Since the ordinary rules of evidence have been loosened, this testimony can be presented by means of a written statement. Of course, such a statement should only contain relevant information. Counsel for the Crown clearly cannot use it in an attempt to introduce the type of remarks which I earlier condemned.

I, therefore, consider that the trial judge made an error in refusing to admit statements by members of the victim's family.

VI. *Judgment*

The appellant did not get the fair hearing to which he was entitled. The appeal is, therefore, allowed and a rehearing ordered in accordance with these reasons.

NOTE

Notwithstanding the order for a rehearing by the Supreme Court, the prisoner did not apply again. This shows the rigours of a s. 745.6 application and, perhaps, the impact of being back in the media limelight.

After the 1997 amendments to s. 745.6, aside from making all victim impact evidence statutorily admissible, it also became necessary for the chief justice of the relevant province or her designate to assess a 745.6 application to determine whether it has a reasonable prospect of success. Clearly, the intention of Parliament was to provide some avenue to ensure that a hopeless application does not encumber court resources. How the test plays out is illustrated by the next case.

R v. Fosty
[2002] MJ No. 419 (QL) (QB)

BEARD J: [1] Mr. Fosty has applied under s. 745.6 of the Criminal Code for a reduction in the number of years of imprisonment that he must serve before he is eligible to apply for parole. The first step in this proceeding is a hearing before a judge, referred to as a judicial screening, to determine whether there is a reasonable prospect that the application will succeed. The matter before me is the judicial screening regarding Mr. Fosty's application.

[2] Mr. Fosty was charged with first degree murder and tried together with another accused, Ms. Gruenke. According to the evidence at the trial, Ms. Gruenke was a reflexologist, and the deceased, who was 82 years old, was a client of hers. While the deceased was much older than Ms. Gruenke, their relationship developed into a friendship, and the deceased began buying her gifts and provided her with an allowance. He soon purchased a house and the two began to live together in a platonic relationship.

[3] According to the evidence of a confidant of Ms. Gruenke, the deceased gave Ms. Gruenke an ultimatum to either have sex with him or he would cut off her allowance

and change his will to remove her as a beneficiary. Ms. Gruenke moved out of the house, although they continued to visit and he continued to buy her gifts and give her money. She testified at the trial that she had arranged to meet the deceased on the night of the killing to convince him to leave her alone, and she arranged for her friend, Mr. Fosty, to wait for her outside because she was afraid.

[4] After Mr. Fosty arrived and was waiting outside, Ms. Gruenke and the deceased got into the deceased's car and left, so Mr. Fosty followed them. The deceased stopped the car and, according to Mr. Fosty, Ms. Gruenke got out of the car and the deceased followed her. Mr. Fosty grabbed a nail puller and hit the deceased until he fell to the ground. They then put his body into his car and drove it into the country, where it was left in a snow bank. They returned to the city and planned a false alibi to explain their activities that day.

[5] They were ultimately both convicted of first degree murder and sentenced to the mandatory life in prison with no eligibility to apply for parole before serving twenty-five years in prison.

. . .

[7] Some principles to be considered in an application under s. 745.6 are as follows:

- The purpose of a s. 745.6 proceeding to reduce the period of parole ineligibility is not to reconsider the community's condemnation of the offence or the repudiation of the prisoner. The section strikes a balance between considerations of leniency for the well-behaved convict which may assist in his rehabilitation and the community interest in repudiation and deterrence of the conduct that led to his incarceration. (See *R v. Vaillancourt* (1988), 43 CCC (3d) 238 (Ont. CA).)
- Put another way, the purpose of the procedure is to re-examine the sentence in light of new information or factors which could not have been known initially. It is to call attention to changes that have occurred in the applicant's situation and which might justify imposing a less harsh penalty upon the applicant. (See *R v. Swietlinski* (1994), 92 CCC (3d) 449 (SCC).)
- The role of the jury, whether in determining guilt or in an application under s. 745.6, is to represent the community and its conscience. (See *R v. Nichols* (1992), 71 CCC (3d) 385 (Alta. QB) and *R v. Sherratt* (1991), 63 CCC (3d) 193 (SCC).)
- The burden of proof lies with the applicant/accused to establish that he deserves to be treated with clemency on a balance of probabilities. (See *R v. Swietlinski, supra.*)
- The factors set out in s. 745.63(1)(a) to (e) do not have to be proved individually in the same manner as the elements of an offence relevant to a decision of guilt or innocence. The jury is to make a discretionary decision after considering all of the factors, some of which may work in favour of the applicant and others of which may work against the applicant, and all of which must be assessed and weighed as a whole in arriving at a conclusion. This is different from a trial, where each element of an offence must be proved beyond a reasonable doubt. (See *R v. Swietlinski, supra.*)

- The concepts of burden of proof, proof on a balance of probabilities, or proof beyond a reasonable doubt are of very limited value in a hearing pursuant to s. 745.6, where the decision lies exclusively in the discretion of the jury. The jury must make what, in its discretion, it deems to be the best decision on the evidence. (See *R v. Swietlinski, supra.*)
- Because the purpose of s. 745.6 is to reassess the penalty imposed on the offender by reference to the way his or her situation has evolved in the 15 years following his conviction, the offender's past and present character are both relevant to the decision. (See *R v. Swietlinski, supra.*)
- The test to be met at the screening stage before a judge is relatively low, being that the applicant must show on a balance of probabilities that there is a reasonable prospect of success before a jury. It is the jury, and not the judge, that should decide whether an offender should be given an opportunity to apply for early release in all cases except those where there is no reasonable prospect of success before a jury. For a judge to dismiss any application that is not hopeless is tantamount to usurping the function of the jury. (See *R v. Kent*, [2001] MJ No. 575.)
- A reasonable chance is defined as being in accordance with reason, not absurd, within the limits of reason, not greatly more or less than might be expected. (See *R v. Kent, supra.*)

IV. Analysis

[8] Mr. Fosty has now served 15 years of the life sentence that he received on October 23, 1987, for first degree murder, making him eligible to apply for a reduction in the mandatory minimum 25-year imprisonment to which he was sentenced. The issue to be determined at the screening stage is whether Mr. Fosty has shown, on a balance of probabilities, that there is a reasonable prospect that his application before the jury will succeed. This decision is to be based on a consideration of the criteria set out in s. 745.63(1)(a) to (e) of the Criminal Code. My analysis of those criteria as they relate to Mr. Fosty follows.

(a) The Character of the Applicant

[9] The accused had no criminal record at the time of the offence for which he is now serving a life sentence, and he has been a model prisoner who has caused no discipline problems while serving his sentence.

10] Before his involvement in this matter, he had completed high school and taken some technical training. He had worked with his father, who was and still is a building contractor, and he had developed considerable work skills in the construction trades. He has maintained strong contact with his family and some of his friends, who have visited him in prison. If he is released, he can return to work with his father in the same business.

(b) The Applicant's Conduct While Serving the Sentence

[11] As noted above, Mr. Fosty has caused no problems whatsoever and has had no discipline infractions while serving his sentence. In fact, he has participated in a very positive way in the work and recreational programmes in the prison throughout his time there. Overall, he has received very positive reports from both the professional staff who have done assessments and undertaken his treatment during his incarceration and from the Corrections staff. An example of the high regard in which he is held by the staff includes the following quote from a report prepared several years ago in support of his application for a transfer to a minimum security facility attached to Stony Mountain Institution:

> … Jim has volunteered to help out in all departments when required. I can say without a doubt that he is the most trusted inmate in this institution.
>
> • • •
>
> … I would be more than willing to put my job on the line and say that if given the chance to be set free at the earliest possible moment, he will never commit another crime.

[12] In addition, Mr. Fosty has undergone regular counselling over a lengthy period of time and attended several group programmes to help provide insight into the cause of his offending behaviour and to develop strategies to avoid any re-offending upon his release.

(c) The Nature of the Offence for Which the Applicant Was Convicted

[13] Mr. Fosty was convicted of first degree murder regarding the bludgeoning to death of an elderly man who was then left in his car, which was driven into a snow bank in a ditch in rural Manitoba. Mr. Fosty and his co-accused then fabricated an alibi to cover up their involvement and avoid being caught. As with all first degree murders, the circumstances were terrible and inexcusable.

(d) Any Other Information Provided by the Victim at the Time of the Imposition of the Sentence or at the Time of the Hearing Under This Section

[14] The crown attorney has advised me that neither he nor the police were able to locate any next-of-kin or relatives of the deceased to provide a victim impact statement.

(e) Any Other Matters That the Judge Considers Relevant in the Circumstances

[15] While the crown attorney did not consent to an order being made to permit this matter to proceed to a jury, neither did he strenuously oppose this application. He was candid in acknowledging that "the Applicant could fairly be described as a 'model prisoner' as far as prisoners are capable of being models." As the crown attorney noted, the applicant in *R v. Kent, supra,* had many more strikes against him than does Mr. Fosty. Given that Associate Chief Justice Oliphant found that Mr. Kent had met the threshold test of having a reasonable prospect that his application would succeed before a jury, it would be difficult to find that Mr. Fosty did not meet that test as well.

V. Decision

[16] For the above-noted reasons, I find, on a balance of probabilities, that there is a reasonable prospect that Mr. Fosty's application before a jury would succeed and he would be permitted to apply to the Parole Board for a reduction in his parole ineligibility. I am, therefore, granting his application to make that application to a jury.

Beard J in *Fosty*, above, notes and assesses the "criteria" in s. 745.63(1). By any stretch, these are not criteria. They do not provide elements of a decision-making process. Instead, they are really just factors that the court must consider. The Code does not provide any help in determining the basis upon which a s. 745.6 decision should be made. The following case, *Pitre*, shows some of the evidentiary issues that can arise during a s. 745.6 application.

Pitre v. Attorney General of the Province of British Columbia
[2005] BCJ No. 2536 (QL) (SC)

DAVIES J: [1] This is a ruling made mid-hearing on an application by Mr. Pitre under s. 745.63(1) of the *Criminal Code* for a reduction of the years of his parole ineligibility arising as a consequence of his conviction for first degree murder in 1989.

[2] During cross-examination of the applicant's witness, Mr. Czoka, an experienced corrections officer and administrator with the Corrections Services of Canada, Crown counsel asked questions about the fallibility of corrections assessments. Mr. Czoka responded that, to his knowledge, he had made no errors. Crown counsel followed up with a general question concerning errors occurring in the parole system generally from time to time which Mr. Czoka acknowledged. Mr. Luchenko then referred to recent difficulties at a Vernon halfway house that had been shut down as a consequence of murders committed by parolees previously convicted of murder.

[3] Out of the presence of the jury, I sought to determine the purpose behind the line of questioning and specifically the use of the example of the Vernon halfway house. I was told by the Crown counsel that the evidence was elicited to explore the efficacy of the parole board's classification of offenders and was led in response to Mr. Czoka's evidence about assessment procedures at a minimum risk institution.

[4] I advised Mr. Luchenko I would not permit further questioning in the area pending the hearing of complete submissions the next morning so that the matter could be addressed in the fullness of time with the benefit of appropriate legal research.

[5] I have now heard those submissions and I am satisfied that the questioning in relation to failures in the parole system generally or in specific instances ought not to have occurred and that I must take corrective action.

[6] Before this hearing started the applicant brought an application to challenge potential jurors for cause based upon, amongst other things, possible prejudice against the parole system. My discussions with counsel resulted in that challenge application being abandoned, after counsel for the applicant received my assurance that I would advise the members of the jury panel in the strongest of terms that if any believed that they could not try this case impartially and free of prejudice because of publicity or personal beliefs held about sentences for murder or about parole, they should not sit on this jury.

[7] In *R v. Swietlinski* (1994), 92 CCC (3d) 449, Mr. Justice Lamer, as he then was, speaking for the majority of the Supreme Court of Canada, said at p. 462:

It is completely improper to invite the jury to consider isolated cases in which prisoners committed murder after being paroled. Even though the rules applicable in the s. 745 hearing are not as strict as in a criminal trial, the fact remains that the jury must consider only the applicant's case. Although the temptation may sometimes be very strong, the jury must not try the cases of other inmates or determine whether the existing system of parole is doing its job. The [applicant] should not be punished for the weaknesses of the system.

[8] The line of questioning embarked upon by Crown counsel in his cross-examination of Mr. Czoka is, in my view, precluded by that statement.

[9] I reach that conclusion notwithstanding Mr. Luchenko's submission that the line of cross-examination undertaken by him is relevant in this case to the jury's ability to assess the weight to be given to the evidence of Mr. Czoka as a correctional officer. That submission was based upon the proposition that because the applicant lead evidence which had the purpose of showing that he has performed well within the correctional system, the Crown is allowed to cross-examine upon failures in the system so that the jury can consider the weight to be placed upon the evidence of the correctional officer.

[10] In my view, that is far too narrow an interpretation of the clear warning given by the Supreme Court of Canada in *Swietlinski*. I note that the minority in *Swietlinski* would have allowed the type of questioning which the Crown wishes to continue but that the majority ruled that such questioning was improper. I am bound by the majority decision and I do not see this case as being distinguishable from it.

[11] Questions concerning general failures in the corrections or parole systems should not be allowed. No matter how phrased, such questioning invites improper reasoning and is irrelevant to the jury's task on this hearing which concerns only the application of those factors set forth in s. 745.63 to Mr. Pitre's circumstances.

[12] Mr. Pitre seeks relief as a consequence of the impugned evidence elicited in cross-examination, and I have determined that some of the relief sought should be granted.

[13] Firstly, Mr. Pitre says that no further questioning by counsel for the Crown should be permitted on the issue of whether the parole system makes errors. I agree. To the extent that there is any evidence of failure it is already improperly before the court. To further examine in the area would run afoul of the rulings in *Swietlinski*.

[14] Secondly, Mr. Pitre asks that an immediate warning be given to the jury outlining the extent to which they should disregard the evidence elicited on cross-examination. I agree that such a warning must be given at this time in order to preclude prejudice to a fair hearing. I do not agree necessarily with all of the language suggested by Ms. Sears and I will deliver the warning that I consider to be appropriate and necessary.

[15] Thirdly, Mr. Pitre asks that the applicant be entitled to re-examine Mr. Czoka on the issue of whether most parolees commit offences while on parole. Ms. Sears says such questioning is necessary to correct the prejudicial evidence now before the jury. I do not agree. It seems to me that the remedy sought would result in doing exactly what this hearing must not do, that is "put the parole system on trial." What is at issue here is Mr. Pitre's application, not the success or failure of the system generally.

CHAPTER FIFTEEN

Preventive Detention and Preventive Supervision

I. INTRODUCTION

This chapter addresses the ways in which the sentencing provisions approach the issue of dangerousness. Generally, sentencing that focuses on the detention of offenders on the basis of an assessment of future dangerousness is referred to as "preventive detention." The emphasis is on confinement and control based on a perception of risk or fear of future crimes. In addition to sentencing, the *Criminal Code*, RSC 1985, c. C-46, as amended, addresses perceived dangerousness at a number of points in the criminal process. For instance, at the bail stage, s. 515(10)(b) permits detention before trial when there is a "substantial likelihood" that the accused person will commit further offences while on bail. Sections 810.01, 810.1, and 810.2 of the Code provide for a recognizance with preventive conditions when there are reasonable grounds to believe that an individual will commit a criminal offence. While, technically speaking, these recognizances operate outside the customary charge–trial–conviction criminal justice paradigm, the recognizances provided for in ss. 810.01, 810.1, and 810.2 have been used to achieve post-sentence control over certain individuals. Accordingly, they are considered in this chapter.

As discussed in chapter 2, Judicial Methodology and the Legislative Context, it has long been a principle of Canadian sentencing law that the primary purpose of sentencing is the protection of society. Section 718(c) of the Code identifies the separation of the offenders from society where necessary as an objective of sentencing. Thus, operating within the framework of the various statutory *maxima* established by Parliament, a sentencing judge can impose a sanction with public protection as the primary goal. The discretionary life sentence (for offences like manslaughter and aggravated sexual assault) is sometimes used with preventive detention in mind (see *R v. Pontello* (1977), 38 CCC (2d) 267 (Ont. CA) and *R v. Mesgun* (1997), 121 CCC (3d) 439 (Ont. CA)).

The majority of this chapter focuses on Part XXIV (Dangerous Offenders and Long-Term Offenders) of the *Criminal Code*, which establishes a specialized procedure for sentencing those offenders who are feared to pose a serious risk of reoffending. As set out below, the dangerous offender provisions create a special designation and provide for indeterminate detention for certain offenders. Long-term offenders, who are thought to be a lower risk for recidivism, are dealt with through extended supervision in the community. The revisions in 1997 led to substantial litigation involving questions of retrospective application and integration between the dangerous offender and long-term offender sanctions. This culminated in the important 2003 decision of the Supreme Court of Canada in *R v. Johnson*, [2003] 2 SCR 357, which returned the issue of treatability into the adjudicative matrix.

The last section of this chapter considers recognizances under ss. 810.01, 810.1, and 810.2 of the Code. By and large, Canada has rejected the propriety of further detention following a determinate sentence (that is, post-sentence detention). At one time, certain criminal justice/ mental health personnel attempted to circumvent the inevitable release of dangerous prisoners at warrant expiry by having them committed under mental health legislation (see *Starnaman v. Penetanguishine Mental Health Centre* (1995), 24 OR (3d) 701 (CA)). With the advent of ss. 810.1 and 810.2, this practice may be dying a natural death.

II. DANGEROUS OFFENDERS

A. Background

Canada first enacted preventive detention legislation in 1947, when the habitual offender provisions were enacted (SC 1947, c. 55, s. 18). A "habitual offender" was someone who had previously been convicted at least three times of an indictable offence punishable by more than five years' imprisonment. The following year, Parliament added the designation of "criminal sexual psychopath" to the Code (SC 1948, c. 39, s. 43), defined as anyone who "by a course of misconduct in sexual matters has evidenced a lack of power to control his sexual impulses and who as a result is likely to attack or otherwise inflict injury on any person." Later, in 1961, the "criminal sexual psychopath" label was dropped in favour of the "dangerous sexual offender" (SC 1960-61, c. 43, s. 32).

These early preventive detention provisions attracted a good deal of attention in the influential Report of the Canadian Committee on Corrections, *Toward Unity: Criminal Justice and Corrections* (Ottawa: Queen's Printer, 1969), also known as the Ouimet report. After a study of a group of individuals designated habitual offenders, the report determined that a substantial proportion of this group did not pose a serious threat to the public. The legislation seemed to be catching persistent offenders who, while constituting a serious social nuisance, were not dangerous (at 253). The way it was applied also reflected a disturbing disparity among the provinces. A hugely disproportionate number of individuals were sentenced as habitual offenders in British Columbia, where prosecutorial authorities found these provisions to be a useful tool for getting rid of "undesirables" in the West and stemming the immigration of criminals from eastern Canada (Michael Jackson, "The Sentencing of Dangerous and Habitual Offenders in Canada" (1997), 9 FSR 257). The Ouimet committee recommended substantial amendments to the preventive detention provisions, aimed at ensuring that only those whose background and criminal record created a real apprehension of further violence would be imprisoned indefinitely.

In 1975, the Supreme Court of Canada also expressed concern about the operation of the habitual offender provisions in *Hatchwell v. The Queen*, [1976] 1 SCR 39. Hatchwell was declared to be a habitual offender after being convicted of break and enter and theft of car keys. In reversing his sentence as a habitual offender, Dickson J (as he then was) described a 44-year-old individual with many convictions, the overwhelming majority of which related to property, automobiles in particular. There were no violent offences. As Dickson J said for the majority:

Section 688 [now s. 753] of the Code has two arms. Where an accused has been convicted of an indictable offence, the Court may, upon application, impose a sentence of preventive detention in lieu of any other sentence that might be imposed for the offence for which he was convicted, if (a) the accused is found to be a habitual criminal and (b) the Court is of the opinion that because the accused is a habitual criminal, it is expedient for the protection of the public to sentence him to preventive detention. There can be no doubt the appellant satisfies the habitual criminal criteria (s. 688(2)(a)) in that he, since the age of 18 years, on at least three separate and independent occasions has been convicted of an indictable offence for which he was liable to imprisonment for five years or more and he is leading persistently a criminal life. That leaves, therefore, for determination only the question whether the Crown has established, beyond a reasonable doubt, that because the appellant is a habitual criminal it is expedient for the protection of the public to sentence him to preventive detention.

• • •

Is Hatchwell a menace to society or just a nuisance? Should he be confined to prison for the rest of his life, subject only to annual review of his case by the Parole Board and release from custody only in the absolute discretion of that Board? These are not easy matters of decision for one must balance the legitimate right of society to be protected from criminal depredations and the right of the man to freedom after serving the sentence imposed on him for the substantive offence which he committed. Habitual criminal legislation and preventive detention are primarily designed for the persistent dangerous criminal and not for those with a prolonged record of minor offences against property. The dominant purpose is to protect the public when the past conduct of the criminal demonstrates a propensity for crimes of violence against the person, and there is a real and present danger to life or limb. In those cases the way is clear and the word "menace" seems particularly apt and significant. That is not to say that crimes against property can never be cause for the invocation of preventive detention legislation, for the legislation contains no such exclusion and society is undoubtedly entitled to reasonable protection against crimes involving loss of or damage to property. It would seem to me, however, that when one is dealing with crime of this type, seeking to distinguish between that which is menace and that which is nuisance, there is greater opportunity and indeed necessity to assess carefully the true nature and gravity of the potential threat. For it is manifest that some crimes affecting property are very serious and others are not.

There are no crimes of violence in the record of the appellant. This is not conclusive but it is important. There is no evidence of association with known criminals during periods of freedom from custody. During these sometimes brief periods, the appellant has been gainfully employed. One former employer spoke in laudatory terms of his ability and attitude as a worker and expressed willingness to re-employ him at any time. The appellant is emotionally unstable and immature. The great majority of crimes committed by him appear to proceed from an uncontrolled aberration or fixation about cars. They are not motivated by gain nor by any destructive urge, for in every case, according to the evidence, the property taken was recovered undamaged. The appellant simply drives the stolen vehicles, until such time as he is apprehended. Of late he has shown a preference for large tractor-trailer units. This sort of irrational, senseless conduct is no doubt of annoyance to everyone, incommoding owners and vexing authorities, but it would seem to me that it partakes more of the quality of a nuisance than of a menace. Hatchwell is a bane rather than a danger to society.

• • •

I would allow the appeal, set aside the sentence of preventive detention and remit the case to the Court of Appeal to pass sentence in respect of the substantive offence, after receiving any submissions as to sentence by or on behalf of the appellant.

Major changes to the preventive detention legislation were soon to follow *Hatchwell*. In 1977, the *Criminal Code* was amended to create the current "dangerous offender" regime (SC 1976-77, c. 53, s. 14). A number, but not all, of the changes recommended in the Ouimet report were incorporated into this new legislation. The general structure of the current provisions (set out below) is rooted in these amendments. However, a few major changes, some procedural and others substantive, have since been made to this legislative scheme.

Approximately 20 years after the enactment of the dangerous offender provisions, Parliament was prompted to recalibrate this part of the *Criminal Code* once again. This new interest in preventive detention was the result of a few highly publicized cases involving crimes of catastrophic violence. The most significant was the death of Christopher Stephenson, a 10-year-old boy who was killed by Joseph Fredericks, a sexual offender who had recently been released from prison on mandatory supervision. The inquest into this murder was wide-ranging and transcended the terrible facts of the case. The jury heard evidence that suggested that, had different decisions been taken in Fredericks's situation, both by the prosecutor at the outset of the prosecution and then by the Correctional Service of Canada when Fredericks's mandatory supervision date arrived, the tragedy might have been avoided. The jury also heard evidence that portrayed the existing dangerous offender provisions as being inadequate, unable to deal with "mistakes" at the front end of the system. The jury was presented with the evidence of a justice official from the state of Washington who extolled the virtues of a "sexual predator" statute that had been passed in that jurisdiction. This type of measure, being a hybrid of criminal and mental health legislative power, permits the state, during the currency of a determinate sentence, to apply to have an individual detained indefinitely after a determinate sentence expires. In its sweeping recommendations, the jury recommended that justice officials in Canada develop similar legislation and that a federal–provincial task force be struck to facilitate this recommendation. See Verdict of the Coroner's Jury into the Death of Christopher Stephenson, Brampton, Ontario (January 22, 1993). A few years later, another coroner's jury made similar recommendations, even though the case had nothing to do with the release of dangerous offenders from prison. The case involved a murder committed by a psychiatric patient on temporary leave from a psychiatric hospital. See Verdict of the Coroner's Jury into the Death of Dennis Kerr, Brockville, Ontario (April 12, 1994).

Shortly afterward, the federal government did create a federal/provincial/territorial task force on high-risk offenders (see Report of the Federal/Provincial/Territorial Task Force on High-Risk Violent Offenders, *Strategies for Managing High-Risk Offenders* (January 1995)). The significant proposal that emerged was a recommendation that Parliament pass legislation that would allow an offender to be designated a "long-term" offender, who could be supervised in the community for up to 10 years. The task force also made recommendations to change certain features of the existing dangerous offender provisions. Parliament followed the recommendation to create the new category of "long-term offender" (SC 1997, c. 17, ss. 4-8). In terms of the dangerous offender provisions, Parliament went much further than the task force recommendations and made a few highly significant changes to the process. The enactment of the long-term offender regime led to a significant new interpretation of both regimes by the Supreme Court in *R v. Johnson*, below.

Data from 2006 show that, since 1978, there have been 403 people designated as dangerous offenders. Of that group, 81 percent have been convicted at least once of sexual assault. As of 2006, there were 352 dangerous offenders still on the books: 334 were in custody and 17 on parole. Of this group of 352, 21 percent were of Aboriginal background. (Note that Aboriginal offenders make up 16.6 percent of the penitentiary population, a dramatically inordinate proportion compared with the percentage of Aboriginal Canadians in the country.) In the year 2005-6, there were 22 successful dangerous offender applications.

For more on the history and background of preventive detention in Canada, see Allan Manson, *The Law of Sentencing* (Toronto: Irwin Law, 2000), chapter 10, "Preventive Detention."

B. The Provisions

The provisions of Part XXIV relating to dangerous offenders are set out below. In these provisions, there is occasional reference to "long-term offenders." The provisions respecting the latter are set out separately later in this chapter, although some of the provisions below apply to both types of offenders. It is fair to say that there is a significant degree of procedural integration between the two designations, especially in terms of the specified set of antecedent offences and the requirement of a psychiatric assessment.

C. Criminal Code, Sections 752, 753, 755, 756, 758, and 761

752. In this Part,
"court" means the court by which an offender in relation to whom an application under this Part is made was convicted, or a superior court of criminal jurisdiction;
"serious personal injury offence" means

(a) an indictable offence, other than high treason, treason, first degree murder or second degree murder, involving

(i) the use or attempted use of violence against another person, or

(ii) conduct endangering or likely to endanger the life or safety of another person or inflicting or likely to inflict severe psychological damage upon another person,

and for which the offender may be sentenced to imprisonment for ten years or more, or

(b) an offence or attempt to commit an offence mentioned in section 271 (sexual assault), 272 (sexual assault with a weapon, threats to a third party or causing bodily harm) or 273 (aggravated sexual assault).

752.1(1) Where an offender is convicted of a serious personal injury offence or an offence referred to in paragraph 753.1(2)(a) and, before sentence is imposed on the offender, on application by the prosecution, the court is of the opinion that there are reasonable grounds to believe that the offender might be found to be a dangerous offender under section 753 or a long-term offender under section 753.1, the court may, by order in writing, remand the offender, for a period not exceeding sixty days, to the custody of the person that the court directs and who can perform an assessment, or can have an assessment performed by experts. The assessment is to be used as evidence in an application under section 753 or 753.1.

(2) The person to whom the offender is remanded shall file a report of the assessment with the court not later than fifteen days after the end of the assessment period and make copies of it available to the prosecutor and counsel for the offender.

753(1) The court may, on application made under this Part following the filing of an assessment report under subsection 752.1(2), find the offender to be a dangerous offender if it is satisfied

(a) that the offence for which the offender has been convicted is a serious personal injury offence described in paragraph (a) of the definition of that expression in section 752 and the offender constitutes a threat to the life, safety or physical or mental well-being of other persons on the basis of evidence establishing

(i) a pattern of repetitive behaviour by the offender, of which the offence for which he has been convicted forms a part, showing a failure to restrain his behaviour and a likelihood of his causing death or injury to other persons, or inflicting severe psychological damage on other persons, through failure in the future to restrain his or her behaviour,

(ii) a pattern of persistent aggressive behaviour by the offender, of which the offence for which he or she has been convicted forms a part, showing a substantial degree of indifference on the part of the offender respecting the reasonably foreseeable consequences to other persons of his or her behaviour, or

(iii) any behaviour by the offender, associated with the offence for which he or she has been convicted, that is of such a brutal nature as to compel the conclusion that the offender's behaviour in the future is unlikely to be inhibited by normal standards of behavioural restraint; or

(b) that the offence for which the offender has been convicted is a serious personal injury offence described in paragraph (b) of the definition of that expression in section 752 and the offender, by his or her conduct in any sexual matter including that involved in the commission of the offence for which he or she has been convicted, has shown a failure to control his or her sexual impulses and a likelihood of his causing injury, pain or other evil to other persons through failure in the future to control his or her sexual impulses.

(2) An application under subsection (1) must be made before sentence is imposed on the offender unless

(a) before the imposition of sentence, the prosecution gives notice to the offender of a possible intention to make an application under section 752.1 and an application under subsection (1) not later than six months after that imposition; and

(b) at the time of the application under subsection (1) that is not later than six months after the imposition of sentence, it is shown that relevant evidence that was not reasonably available to the prosecution at the time of the imposition of sentence became available in the interim.

(3) Notwithstanding subsection 752.1(1), an application under that subsection may be made after the imposition of sentence or after an offender begins to serve the sentence in a case to which paragraphs (2)(a) and (b) apply.

(4) If the court finds an offender to be a dangerous offender, it shall impose a sentence of detention in a penitentiary for an indeterminate period.

(4.1) If the application was made after the offender begins to serve the sentence in a case to which paragraphs (2)(a) and (b) apply, the sentence of detention in a penitentiary for an indeterminate period referred to in subsection (4) replaces the sentence that was imposed for the offence for which the offender was convicted.

(5) If the court does not find an offender to be a dangerous offender,

(a) the court may treat the application as an application to find the offender to be a long-term offender, section 753.1 applies to the application and the court may either find that the offender is a long-term offender or hold another hearing for that purpose; or

(b) the court may impose sentence for the offence for which the offender has been convicted.

(6) Any evidence given during the hearing of an application made under subsection (1) by a victim of an offence for which the offender was convicted is deemed also to have been given during any hearing under paragraph (5)(a) held with respect to the offender.

• • •

754(1) Where an application under this Part has been made, the court shall hear and determine the application except that no such application shall be heard unless

(a) the Attorney General of the province in which the offender was tried has, either before or after the making of the application, consented to the application;

(b) at least seven days notice has been given to the offender by the prosecutor, following the making of the application, outlining the basis on which it is intended to found the application; and

(c) a copy of the notice has been filed with the clerk of the court or the magistrate, as the case may be.

(2) An application under this Part shall be heard and determined by the court without a jury.

(3) For the purposes of an application under this Part, where an offender admits any allegations contained in the notice referred to in paragraph (1)(b), no proof of those allegations is required.

(4) The production of a document purporting to contain any nomination or consent that may be made or given by the Attorney General under this Part and purporting to be signed by the Attorney General is, in the absence of any evidence to the contrary, proof of that nomination or consent without proof of the signature or the official character of the person appearing to have signed the document.

• • •

757. Without prejudice to the right of the offender to tender evidence as to his or her character and repute, evidence of character and repute may, if the court thinks fit, be admitted on the question of whether the offender is or is not a dangerous offender or a long-term offender.

758(1) The offender shall be present at the hearing of the application under this Part and if at the time the application is to be heard

(a) he is confined in a prison, the court may order, in writing, the person having the custody of the accused to bring him before the court; or

(b) he is not confined in a prison, the court shall issue a summons or a warrant to compel the accused to attend before the court and the provisions of Part XVI relating to summons and warrant are applicable with such modifications as the circumstances require.

(2) Notwithstanding subsection (1), the court may

(a) cause the offender to be removed and to be kept out of court, where he misconducts himself by interrupting the proceedings so that to continue the proceedings in his presence would not be feasible; or

(b) permit the offender to be out of court during the whole or any part of the hearing on such conditions as the court considers proper.

· · ·

761(1) Subject to subsection (2), where a person is in custody under sentence of detention in a penitentiary for an indeterminate period, the National Parole Board shall, forthwith after the expiration of seven years from the day on which that person was taken into custody and not later than every two years after the previous review, review the condition, history and circumstances of that person for the purpose of determining whether he or she should be granted parole under Part II of the *Corrections and Conditional Release Act* and, if so, on what conditions.

(2) Where a person is in custody under a sentence of detention in a penitentiary for an indeterminate period that was imposed before October 15, 1977, the National Parole Board shall, at least once in every year, review the condition, history and circumstances of that person for the purpose of determining whether he should be granted parole under Part II of the *Corrections and Conditional Release Act* and, if so, on what conditions.

D. Applying the Provisions

Prior to the 1997 amendments to Part XXIV, numerous decisions addressed the content of these provisions. Indeed, in *R v. Lyons* (1987), 61 CR (3d) 1 (SCC), the Supreme Court of Canada rejected a constitutional challenge to the dangerous offender regime in Part XXIV. While it might seem more natural to address questions of constitutionality first, we have decided to delay the discussion of *Lyons* until the next part. Seeing first how the courts have actually applied the dangerous offender provisions provides a context for evaluating how the Supreme Court resolved the constitutional claims.

As the cases below demonstrate, the courts have struggled in applying these criteria, which on their face are quite broad. Employing a correct interpretive approach is vital in this context because, while s. 754 of the Code says that a judge *may* declare someone to be a dangerous offender if the criteria are met, the Court of Appeal for Ontario in *R v. Moore* (1985), 44 CR (3d) 137 (Ont. CA) held that the judge *must* make a dangerous offender designation in these circumstances. While this interpretation is somewhat peculiar, it was made at a time when a second discretion was built into these provisions. Section 753 provided that, upon a declaration that an individual is a dangerous offender, the judge could impose an indeterminate sentence or sentence the offender in the normal manner. The 1997 amendments removed this second discretion, and s. 753(4) now *requires* that the individual be sentenced to an indeterminate period of incarceration once that person has been declared a dangerous offender. With discretion removed at both vital junctures—at the point of applying the criteria and at the point of imposing sentence—it is crucial that the criteria be applied properly.

When considering the following cases, be careful to note two things. First, note the date of the decision. Does it come before 1997 when there was discretion, notwithstanding a dangerous offender finding, to impose an indeterminate sentence? As well, does the case come before the 2003 Supreme Court of Canada decision in *Johnson*? Second, note which branch of s. 753(1) of the Code is being applied. The two branches, which correspond to the bifurcated definition of "serious personal injury offence" in s. 752, call for different tests. Section 753(1)(a) relates to convictions for violent indictable offences punishable by 10 years or more. The question is whether the offender "constitutes a threat to the life, safety or physical or mental well-being of other persons." This is based on the application of the criteria in paragraph (1)(a).

The second, alternative branch for declaring an individual to be a dangerous offender is found in s. 753(1)(b). This follows conviction for certain categories of sexual offences and requires the court to consider (1) whether the offender's conduct in any sexual matter shows a "failure to control his or her sexual impulses," and (2) whether there is a likelihood of "causing injury, pain or other evil to other persons through failure in the future to control his or her sexual impulses."

Apart from the separate tests, is there a significant difference in the level of dangerousness reflected in the two branches of s. 753? Is a more coherent, integrated test called for? Perhaps more important, irrespective of what branch the prosecutor pursues on, what level of risk must be proved before it is appropriate to designate the individual a dangerous offender? Consider this last issue in particular as you read the following cases.

R v. Langevin
(1984), 11 CCC (3d) 336 (Ont. CA)

LACOURCIÈRE JA: This appeal raises broad questions respecting the application of the dangerous offender provisions of Part XXI of the *Criminal Code* and their constitutional validity in the light of the fundamental rights now protected by the *Canadian Charter of Rights and Freedoms*.

On May 12, 1980, the appellant pleaded guilty to the offence of rape, contrary to s. 144 of the Code, before The Honourable Judge F.G. Carter in the County Court Judge's Criminal Court in the County of Huron. After the conviction, the Crown filed an application to have the appellant declared a dangerous offender pursuant to s. 688 of the Code. Following remands for the nomination of a psychiatrist by the appellant and for psychiatric observation, Judge Carter heard the application on September 10, 1980. He found the appellant to be a dangerous offender and, following a remand, sentenced him to an indeterminate period of detention, in lieu of any other sentence that might be imposed for the offence of rape.

• • •

Pattern of Repetitive Behaviour: Section 688(a)(i)

Mr. Gold submitted that, with respect to s. 688(a)(i), the learned trial judge erred in concluding that there existed a "pattern of repetitive behaviour," there being an insufficient number of repeated offences by the appellant as displayed in the reported cases under that paragraph.

In my opinion, this element is not based solely on the number of offences but also on the elements of similarity of the offender's behaviour. The offences committed were remarkably similar. Two young girls were grabbed from behind by the appellant, a stranger, and both were taken to a secluded place and ordered to undress. Both were forced into anal as well as vaginal intercourse. The younger girl was forced to fellate the appellant. Both were threatened to assure their co-operation and were released only after assurances not to tell anyone were extracted from them. In the circumstances, these two offences were properly found to establish a pattern of repetitive behaviour.

As to the failure of the appellant to restrain his behaviour, the learned trial judge concluded as follows:

> Having considered the offender's past behaviour, having heard and analyzed the evidence of the expert witnesses, and the other evidence adduced, I am compelled to conclude that the Crown has established to my satisfaction that there is a likelihood of the offender "causing death or injury to other persons or inflicting severe psychological damage upon other persons, through failure in the future to restrain his behaviour," as required by s. 688(a)(i). Whether such failure to refrain his behaviour stems from an inability to maintain control, or a refusal to maintain control, and whether such loss of control is triggered by aggressiveness or sexual impulse, and whether with or without the aid of alcohol it leads, in considering s. 688(a)(i), to the same result.

I fully agree with this conclusion and with the able and comprehensive analysis of the evidence which supports the finding that the appellant showed a failure to restrain his behaviour as well as the likelihood—not the certainty or probability (see *R v. Carleton* (1981), 69 CCC (2d) 1 at p. 6, 23 CR (3d) 129 at p. 135, [1981] 6 WWR 148; affirmed 6 CCC (3d) 480*n*, 36 CR (3d) 393*n*, [1984] 2 WWR 384*n*)—of causing death, injury or severe psychological damage through failure in the future to restrain his behaviour. In this case there was a strong basis, on the facts and the expert opinions in respect of them, on which the finder of fact could be satisfied beyond a reasonable doubt of the existing likelihood of future conduct.

Although the finding that the appellant is a dangerous offender can be supported on s. 688(a)(i) alone, it is necessary to deal briefly with the other arguments to the effect that the Crown has failed to prove the elements of dangerousness set out in s. 688(a)(iii) and s. 688(b), respectively.

Behaviour of a "Brutal Nature": Section 688(a)(iii)

Mr. Gold submitted that the learned trial judge erred in concluding the Guelph rape satisfied the requirement of behaviour of a "brutal nature" as required by subpara. (iii). The submission is, basically, that any rape by definition contains severe physical and psychological abuse, but that the "brutal nature" requirement of subpara. (iii) requires a greater element of savagery evidenced by sadism, torture or mutilation. The learned trial judge concluded that the appellant's conduct towards the 12-year-old victim was "coarse, savage and cruel" and, accordingly, so "brutal" as to compel the conclusion that the appellant's behaviour in the future was "unlikely to be inhibited by normal standards of behavioural restraint" in the words of the subparagraph. This conclusion was supported by the expert evidence. I am satisfied that the brutal nature of the conduct which must be established before the requirements of the subparagraph are satisfied does not necessarily demand a situation of "stark horror" as exemplified by *R v. Hill* (1974), 15 CCC (2d) 145, and *R v. Pontello* (1977), 38 CCC (2d) 262.

Conduct which is coarse, savage and cruel and which is capable of inflicting severe psychological damage on the victim is sufficiently "brutal" to meet the test.

Failure to Control Sexual Impulses: Section 688(b)

With respect to s. 688(b), it was submitted that there was insufficient evidence of the appellant's failure to control his sexual impulses in the rape of the [D.] girl or in the rape of the [G.] girl and that the appellant's problem, as characterized by Dr. Hill, was related to aggressiveness but not necessarily of a sexual nature. From the nature of the offences and on the evidence of Dr. Fleming and Dr. Arnold, the Crown properly established the likelihood of the appellant causing future injury, pain or other evil through failure in the future to control his sexual impulses. For these reasons, I would not interfere with the finding that the appellant is a dangerous offender.

Apart from *R v. Lyons* and *R v. Johnson*, dealt with in the next section, the Supreme Court of Canada has said relatively little about the dangerous offender provisions. The following case of *R v. Currie* is one of the few times that the court has offered its views on the proper interpretive approach to Part XXIV of the Code. The case concerns the second branch of the test in s. 753(1), which focuses on sexual offences. Currie had a long history of committing sexual offences. In terms of their seriousness, the antecedent offences for the more recent dangerous offender application were far less serious than the past offences. The Court of Appeal for Ontario quashed the trial judge's dangerous offender declaration on the basis that the trial judge should have considered the relative seriousness of the antecedent offences. The Supreme Court of Canada disagreed with this approach and restored the trial judge's decision.

R v. Currie
(1997), 115 CCC (3d) 205 (SCC)

LAMER CJ: This appeal is concerned with the propriety of a dangerous offender designation and the corresponding indeterminate sentence that was imposed by the trial judge after the respondent, Robert Currie, was convicted of sexually assaulting three young girls. At the conclusion of the hearing of this appeal, this Court held, without providing reasons at that time, that neither the designation nor the sentence should be overturned. Our reasons now follow.

I. Facts and Procedural Background

The respondent, Robert Currie, was charged with three counts of sexual assault, for a series of related incidents in which he sexually touched a number of young girls on

November 5, 1988 in a Towers department store in Barrie, Ontario. During the first incident, the respondent approached a group of four girls in the Towers toy section, felt and squeezed the buttocks of three of them, and left the area. During the second, more invasive incident, the respondent followed a group of three sisters near the store's tobacco department. At first, he placed his hand on the eldest girl's breast. Immediately thereafter, he approached the girls from behind and, as the trial judge described, "swept his hand between the legs of two of them in an attempt to touch their genitals." The frightened girls notified store employees and security personnel who eventually apprehended the respondent outside the store and awaited the arrival of the police.

The respondent was convicted of all charges on April 12, 1989 before Tobias J. Prior to sentencing, the Attorney General for Ontario initiated dangerous offender proceedings pursuant to s. 753(b) of the *Criminal Code*, RSC, 1985, c. C-46. Section 753(b) essentially provides that the Crown may apply to have an offender declared a "dangerous offender" and sentenced to an indefinite term of imprisonment if: (a) he has been convicted of a "serious personal injury offence"; and (b) his failure to control his sexual impulses reveals "a likelihood of his causing injury, pain or other evil to other persons" in the future. A "serious personal injury offence" is defined in s. 752 of the *Criminal Code* to include all forms of sexual assault.

These sexual assaults were not isolated incidents. Part of the rationale for seeking to have the respondent declared a dangerous offender was his lengthy history of sexual offences that occurred in the Ottawa, Toronto and Hamilton regions between 1975-1988. As outlined in disturbing detail in the judgments below and in the pleadings filed before this Court, the respondent had been previously convicted of numerous sexual offences, some of which were extremely violent and highly degrading to the victims.

Robert Currie's criminal sexual activity began in and around Ottawa between September and November 1975. In separate incidents, the respondent stalked and sexually attacked four women. All four of the incidents were serious and frightening for the victims, but two were comparatively more severe. On September 30, 1975, the respondent followed a teenage girl into a field. He caught her, undressed her and forced her to perform fellatio and engage in repeated acts of sexual intercourse. When she resisted he pulled her hair and struck her in the face. On November 29, 1975, later on the same night that he had indecently assaulted another victim, the respondent stalked a young woman in Nepean. After approaching her from behind and striking her to the ground, he forced her into the deep snow of a deserted field. He then undressed his victim completely, repeatedly struck her in the face, forced her to perform fellatio, and forced her to submit to multiple acts of anal and vaginal intercourse. He had a hunting knife in his possession during the rape with which he threatened the victim after the attack. She was bleeding heavily when he abandoned her naked in the snow.

As a result of these attacks, on May 20, 1976, the respondent was convicted of indecent assault, rape, and possession of a weapon and sentenced to five years' imprisonment. Since that time, whenever he was at large, his sexually impulsive criminal behaviour continued. In 1979, while on parole in Toronto, the respondent stalked and attacked a woman. When she screamed in response to his attempt to touch her genitals, he jammed his fingers into her mouth, pushed her to the ground and kicked her. He fled the scene, but was immediately apprehended by police and subsequently convicted of indecent assault. In Hamilton in 1981 and 1982, while under intensive police surveillance, the respondent was observed following and stalking a number of women through the city streets. In one case, the girl sensed she was being followed and sought shelter on the porch of a nearby home. In another case, the respondent indecently assaulted a woman he had been following by putting his hand under her clothing between her legs in an effort to touch her genitals. When arrested by police for the latter incident, the respondent stated:

> It was me I did it. I couldn't help myself. I asked for help before but they released me. I needed help but they let me go. I was going to play hockey and I picked this girl up hitchhiking. She was wearing a bathing suit. I got all turned on. It was like she was asking for it. Not this one but the other one. How do you guys do it? I mean when you see these girls wearing bathing suits all day. I need help. I am always stalking women, little kids, and people. I can't stop. ... I can't help myself. ... I'm always thinking about women. ... I didn't mean to harm anybody. I guess I figure it's just a few seconds of being frightened and it's all over and nobody is hurt.

A. *Psychiatric Evidence*

To substantiate its dangerous offender application, the Crown elicited the testimony of a psychiatrist, Dr. Angus McDonald, who participated in a two-month team assessment of the respondent after the commission of the recent Towers department store sexual assaults—the so-called "predicate offences." Dr. McDonald evaluated the respondent as an obsessed and extremely temperamental "sexual deviate" who had a "biological anomaly in the wiring of his brain." As such he was "a very dangerous person to society." In making these findings, Dr. McDonald was influenced by the admission the respondent made to a psychometrist at the Penetanguishene Mental Health Centre in 1989, in which he stated:

> [The] stuff I was doing in '79, I got rid of that. I don't bruise them now but don't get me wrong. They had better give me sex if I want it because I often have a knife and I always have my hands.

By way of conclusion, Dr. McDonald gave the prognosis that the respondent "was not open to treatment any longer and posed a risk to women and female children."

The defence-appointed psychiatrist, Dr. Basil Orchard, acknowledged that the respondent suffered from an impulsive personality disorder and "a polymorphous sexual deviation" that includes "voyeurism, heterosexual pedophilia and hebephilia and impulsive sexual aggressiveness." Given this diagnosis, he admitted that there was a likelihood that the respondent would re-offend. Dr. Orchard did conclude, however, that the respondent was neither schizophrenic nor psychotic and that he had shown change toward less violent behaviour. He prognosticated that if there were future recurrences of the respondent's criminal behaviour, his conduct would tend toward "nuisance-type offences" rather than offences of a violent nature. In sum, he did not "find him particularly dangerous at the present time."

• • •

II. Issues

The fundamental disagreement in the judgments below on the suitability of designating Robert Currie a dangerous offender and imposing an indeterminate sentence raises, in my opinion, the following three issues on appeal to this Court:

(1) Must a trial judge, when evaluating a dangerous offender application under s. 753(b) of the *Criminal Code*, focus on the seriousness of the specific predicate offences that have led to the Crown's dangerous offender application?

(2) Were the dangerous offender designation and the corresponding indeterminate sentence reasonably supported by the evidence?

(3) Were the dangerous offender designation and the corresponding indeterminate sentence premised on any errors of law?

Given our holding at the conclusion of the hearing, it should come as no surprise that the Court resolves each of these issues in favour of the appellant. A thorough explanation is nonetheless warranted and should provide needed guidance for future dangerous offender application hearings.

III. Analysis

It is the stated opinion of this Court that Robert Currie was properly designated a dangerous offender and correctly sentenced to an indeterminate period of incarceration. That opinion is grounded in two basic legal propositions both of which I develop and apply below. Those propositions are: first, given the nature and structure of s. 753(b) of the *Criminal Code*, a presiding trial judge need not focus on the objective seriousness of a predicate offence in order to conclude that a dangerous offender designation is warranted. Second, a finding of dangerousness by a trial judge is a finding of fact, frequently based upon the competing credibility of experts, and as long as it is reasonable, it is a finding which should not be lightly overturned.

A. Must a Trial Judge Focus on the Seriousness of the Predicate Offences?

The Court of Appeal quashed the trial judge's designation of Robert Currie as a dangerous offender principally because it found the trial judge erred by failing to focus on the seriousness of the predicate offences. The respondent has relied upon that finding and insists that, when evaluating the likelihood of danger that an offender presents, the sentencing judge must consider the relative gravity of the predicate offences. Unless there is "some rational relationship between the predicate offences and the sentences," the respondent contends that the offender is being sentenced for his past criminality.

It is true that, when viewed in isolation, the predicate offences appear less serious than much of the respondent's past conduct. Indeed the appellant has admitted that "[t]he predicate offences in this case are properly characterized as offences of a less serious nature than the offender's earlier offences, and thankfully do not approach the gravity of the very violent earlier offences." However, that observation does not necessarily translate into a conclusion that the designation of Robert Currie as a dangerous offender was misplaced. Rather, once an individual has committed an offence specifically defined in the *Criminal Code* as a "serious personal injury offence," he or she has made it possible for the Crown to invoke the *Criminal Code*'s dangerous offender application process. If that process is invoked, it is incumbent upon the trial judge to evaluate the offender's potential danger to the public and this may or may not depend upon the specific nature and objective gravity of the predicate offence.

Section 753(b) of the *Criminal Code* makes this point abundantly clear. ... In short, there are two thresholds that the Crown must surpass in order for the dangerous offender application to be successful. The Crown must first establish that the offender has been convicted of a "serious personal injury offence." Then the focus of the inquiry shifts. The question then becomes whether there is a "likelihood" that the offender will cause "injury, pain or other evil to other persons through [his] failure in the future to control his sexual impulses."

There is no question in this appeal that the predicate sexual assaults committed by the respondent against the young girls in the Towers department store constituted "serious personal injury offences." Section 752(b) of the *Criminal Code* defines "serious personal injury offence" to include "an offence or attempt to commit an offence mentioned in section 271 (sexual assault)." However, the parties fundamentally disagree over the manner in which the trial judge applied the second standard. The respondent alleges that the trial judge erred because he did not take proper notice of the relative gravity of the predicate offences. He submits that an indeterminate sentence is disproportionate to the seriousness of sexual touching.

My problem with this argument is twofold. First, the language of s. 753(b) explicitly states that there is no requirement to focus on the specific nature of the predicate offence. Section 753(b) provides that the prospective dangerousness of the offender is measured by reference to *"his conduct in any sexual matter including that involved in the commission of the offence for which he has been convicted"* (emphasis added). "[A]ny sexual matter" can refer to the predicate offence, but it need not. As long as the offender's past conduct, whatever conduct that might be, demonstrates a present likelihood of inflicting future harm upon others, the designation is justified. Second, the respondent's position is inconsistent with the nature and structure of the dangerous offender statutory scheme created by Parliament. As I indicated above, a crucial element of s. 753(b) is the notion of the "serious personal injury offence." Parliament has said that there are certain types of offences, which are inherently serious, that can trigger a dangerous offender application. As this Court observed in *R v. McCraw*, [1991] 3 SCR 72, at p. 83, sexual assault, whatever form it may take, is one of them. Other offences, presumably less threatening to the personal safety of others, do not trigger s. 753.

As such, I would find it contradictory, as well as callous, to categorize the impugned predicate assaults as "nuisance-type offences." These sexual assaults, while not as violent or grave as some of the respondent's earlier offences, were nevertheless within the category of violent and grave. The predicate offences involved repeated sexual touching of young girls in public and at least two of the victims of the assaults have experienced serious psychological trauma and other side effects. If these sexual assaults were not serious, sexual assault would not be enumerated as a s. 752 offence. Nor would Parliament have ever seen fit to eliminate the distinction between rape and indecent assault—indeed it would have ensured that such a distinction endured.

By definition, therefore, arguments of proportionality do not withstand scrutiny. There may be, as the respondent asserts, an objective difference between the nighttime rape at knife point and the predicate offences, but this distinction is not reflected in s. 752 or 753 of the *Criminal Code*. Indeed the respondent is asking the Court to alter or even reduce the definition of "serious personal injury offence." This alteration would, as the appellant notes, effectively guarantee that an accused who has committed an arguably less serious sexual predicate offence would never be declared a dangerous offender. I cannot imagine that Parliament wanted the courts to wait for an obviously dangerous individual, regardless of the nature of his criminal record and notwithstanding the force of expert opinion as to his potential dangerousness, to commit a particularly violent and grievous offence before he or she can be declared a dangerous offender.

Does it defy reality, as the respondent submits, to treat all "serious personal injury offences" the same in applying s. 753(b)? In my opinion, it does not. This might be problematic if s. 753(b) were a one-stage test. Section 753(b) might not make sense if, for example, it were to provide, without qualification, that a trial judge may designate any person who commits a "serious personal injury offence" as a dangerous offender. But, it is crucial to recognize that the conviction for a "serious personal injury offence" merely triggers the s. 753(b) application process. There remains a second stage to s. 753(b), at which point the trial judge must be satisfied beyond a reasonable doubt of the likelihood of future danger that an offender presents to society before he or she can impose the dangerous offender designation and an indeterminate sentence.

Parliament has thus created a standard of preventive detention that measures an accused's present condition according to past behaviour and patterns of conduct. Under this statutory arrangement, dangerous offenders who have committed "serious personal injury offences" can be properly sentenced without having to wait for them to strike out in a particularly egregious way. For example, suppose a known sexual deviate has been convicted of repeated offences for stalking and sexually assaulting young girls in playgrounds. He operates by offering them candy, touching their private parts, and if the children seem to comply or submit to his criminal advances, by taking them away where he violently sexually assaults them. Now suppose that individual is at large in society and caught by a parent at a playground after having offered a child candy and improperly touching her. In this example, like the present case, the predicate offence is objectively less serious than a violent and invasive rape, but the trial judge need not justify the dangerous offender designation and an indeterminate sentence as a just desert for the isolated act of sexual touching. On the theory of s. 753(b), the offender has committed an inherently "serious personal injury offence." On a dangerous offender application, a trial judge is then entitled to consider his "conduct in any sexual matter" to determine if he presents a future danger to society. Otherwise, we would be saying that an offender's present condition is defined by the precise degree of seriousness of the predicate offences. That is equivalent to assuming that a dangerous individual will always act out, or be caught for that matter, at the upper limits of his dangerous capabilities.

* * *

In my opinion, despite the reference to a "very serious violent crime," *Lyons* does not require that all predicate offences fit that description. As La Forest J indicated at the hearing of this case, when he asserted that Thomas Lyons was arrested and prosecuted for a "very serious violent crime" he was merely referring to the particular facts in *Lyons*. He was not, I would add, stating that predicate offences need to be especially serious and violent to justify a dangerous offender designation. In fact, while specifically aimed at providing the constitutional justification for s. 753 (then s. 688), ... *Lyons* serves to underline the very point of this case—that "serious personal injury offences" are inherently serious and there is thus no need to think that the offender is being punished for his "past criminality." As in *Lyons*, there is nothing in this case that suggests the respondent has been "picked up off the street." Nor is there any more reason here than there was in *Lyons* to suggest that he is being punished for anything other than the predicate offences.

There is, however, another subtle wrinkle to this issue, and I would be remiss if I did not address it. Although the respondent relies upon the judgment of the Ontario Court of Appeal, he has argued that it would be a mistake to conflate their respective positions. On the one hand, the Court of Appeal quashed the dangerous offender designation largely because it found that the trial judge "failed to consider the gravity of the predicate offences in isolation from his previous offences" (p. 451). On the other hand, the respondent submits that the trial judge made the related but opposite error—that he ignored the predicate offences.

This argument is conceptually different, but I find it no more persuasive. For one, the language of s. 753(b) of the *Criminal Code* would seem to suggest that once the offender has been found guilty of a "serious personal injury offence," the trial judge can ignore the nature of the predicate offence. Notwithstanding the unlikelihood of such a scenario, as long as some conduct of the accused "in any sexual matter" demonstrates a likelihood that his sexual urges will cause future "injury, pain or other evil," there is no conceptual need to pay any attention to the predicate offence. Second, and more importantly, there is every indication that the trial judge did not ignore the nature of the predicate offences. In fact, on this very subject he endorsed Dr. McDonald's conclusion that "[a]lthough the predicate offences may appear less serious from an assaultive aspect, they are more blatant, indicating a lessening of control on the part of the respondent." He later concluded that "the violence and the brutality of the respondent's early sexual assaults ... continue to be evidenced in the pattern of his subsequent sexual assaults, including that conduct which resulted in his conviction upon the predicate offences."

As much as our system of criminal justice seeks to sentence the offence, imposing a proper sentence is very much a function of the dual nature of the specific crime and the unique attributes of the offender. Insofar as this duality is concerned, the effectiveness of s. 753(b) should not go unnoticed. The "serious personal injury offence" requirement acts as a gatekeeper to ensure that the sentence is not disproportionate to the offence. At the same time, the manner in which s. 753(b) allows a trial judge to evaluate an offender's present condition ensures that the uniquely dangerous attributes of each offender and his or her patterns of conduct are given due consideration, whatever form they might take.

B. Were the Dangerous Offender Designation and the Corresponding Indeterminate Sentence Reasonably Supported by the Evidence?

On the basis of the language of s. 753(b) of the *Criminal Code* and the principles I have articulated above, I am satisfied that there was enough evidence before Tobias J for him to find that the respondent was a dangerous offender. The respondent's pattern of criminal sexual behaviour and the psychiatric evidence of the Crown-nominated psychiatrist are certainly sufficient proof, if accepted by a trier of fact, to justify such a conclusion.

In this respect, the role of an appellate court is to determine if the dangerous offender designation was reasonable. This standard of reasonableness is similar to the traditional standard employed by appellate courts in their review of verdicts under s. 686(1)(a)(i) of the *Criminal Code*. Reasonableness is the appropriate standard of review in this case because, as much as dangerous offender status is a part of the post-conviction process, the application of general standards of sentence review is not warranted given the broad language of s. 759. Section 759(1) provides:

> 759(1) A person who is sentenced to detention in a penitentiary for an indeterminate period under this Part may appeal to the court of appeal against that sentence on any ground of law or fact or mixed law and fact.

Given this provision, I do not find the "manifestly wrong" or "demonstrably unfit" general sentencing standards developed and applied in cases such as *R v. Shropshire*, [1995] 4 SCR 227, *R v. M.(C.A.)*, [1996] 1 SCR 500, or *R v. McDonnell*, [1997] 1 SCR 948, to be applicable to this situation. However, it is equally true that s. 759 cannot be interpreted as calling for the equivalent of a trial de novo on the dangerous offender application. Some deference to the findings of a trial judge is warranted. After all, credibility should be assessed and findings of fact should be made by the trier of fact. The trier of fact is present when the testimony is being given and has the contemporaneous ability to assess each witness.

. . .

Accordingly, absent an error of law (which I discuss below), the crucial question on appeal is whether the trial judge's findings were reasonable. I can only conclude that they were. For one, there was consensus at the application hearing that Robert Currie is a pedophile and hebephile with a long history of sexual offences, some of which were extremely violent. The Crown-nominated psychiatrist, Dr. McDonald, diagnosed the respondent as an obsessed and temperamental hypersexual individual who was extremely dangerous to women and female children. In Dr. McDonald's view, the respondent inherited a biological anomaly in the wiring of his brain which makes his deviate sexual impulses uncontrollable. While Dr. McDonald accepted that the respondent's predicate assaults were not as serious as some of the assaults he had committed in the past, he found that they were "ominous" and more blatant because they were committed in a very public place. This suggested, in his opinion, a lessening of the respondent's ability to control his deviate impulses and he expected the respondent's offences to increase in severity in the long term.

This evidence alone was sufficient to justify the dangerous offender designation, and I do not accept the respondent's objection that it was a product of overgeneralization.

Experts necessarily bring past experiences to bear on their opinions and, as the appellant submits, Dr. McDonald's opinion was based on an extensive assessment of the respondent. As a result, the trial judge was perfectly entitled to believe Dr. McDonald's diagnosis, and conclude from the respondent's lengthy criminal history that the commission of the predicate offences was part of a pattern of sexual deviation. See *Sullivan* [*R v.* (1987), 37 CCC (3d) 143 Ont. CA)]. However, the trial judge also had the benefit of the testimony of the defence-nominated psychiatrist. Although Dr. Orchard concluded that the predicate offences exhibited a declining danger, he did acknowledge the profound nature of the respondent's sexual problems and also recognized that there was a likelihood that the respondent would re-offend. In fact, Dr. Orchard himself indicated that the respondent exhibited "a lot of tendencies towards violence or dangerous behaviour."

Furthermore, the Crown adduced evidence, which I believe was properly put before the trial judge, of comments the respondent made to a psychometrist in 1989. Robert Currie stated at that time:

> [The] stuff I was doing in '79, I got rid of that. I don't bruise them now but don't get me wrong. They had better give me sex if I want it because I often have a knife and I always have my hands.

This evidence, the reliability and strength of which the trial judge was able to evaluate, and which he was not required to discuss in his reasons to avoid error (*R v. Burns*, [1994] 1 SCR 656, at pp. 662-65, and *R v. Barrett*, [1995] 1 SCR 752, at pp. 752-53), further supports the conclusion that the respondent is dangerous. In fact it is a chilling reminder, from the mouth of the offender himself, of his sexually impulsive and volatile nature.

In my opinion, therefore, it was entirely open to the trial judge to prefer the evidence of Dr. McDonald to that of Dr. Orchard. It was not, however, similarly open to the Court of Appeal to re-evaluate the psychiatric evidence and overturn the dangerous offender designation because of a mere difference of opinion. I cannot overemphasize the point that no appellate court should lightly disturb a finding of dangerousness which is so heavily dependent upon the relative credibility of expert witnesses. In saying this, I have not forgotten the broad language of s. 759. However, having observed both experts and evaluated their reports, Tobias J simply found the opinion of Dr. McDonald to be more credible. It was a reasonable conclusion amply supported by the evidence. It should not have been disturbed by the Court of Appeal.

The reason for this finding is simple. To an outside observer, the predicate assaults can be interpreted in any number of ways. They might, as the Court of Appeal and respondent believe, carry information that suggests that the respondent's condition was improving. By contrast, because they occurred in broad daylight in a crowded public place, they might indicate that the respondent's condition had become more blatant and reflected a lessening of self-control. Further still, the predicate assaults might even be interpreted as part of a pattern that the respondent displayed in his earlier offences. As I noted at the outset of these reasons, on November 29, 1975, on the very day the respondent committed an extremely violent and degrading rape, he had also committed a less violent and less intrusive indecent assault on another victim sometime earlier. It is therefore possible that, even though the predicate offences were less violent than past offences, Robert Currie might have committed more violent and aggressive sexual assaults that very day, had he not been reported by his young victims.

The point is, s. 753(b) entrusts trial judges with evaluating these sorts of patterns, and in this case, the trial judge concluded, in a perfectly reasonable fashion, that the predicate offences exemplified a lessening of self-control. It is plausible to interpret the respondent's pattern of conduct differently, but the *Criminal Code* does not invite either this Court or the Court of Appeal to do so. Unless the trial judge's findings were unreasonable, and absent an error of law, the designation made by the trial judge should stand.

C. Did the Trial Judge Commit an Error of Law?

The respondent alleged, and the Court of Appeal agreed, that the trial judge's conclusions were based upon at least two errors of law. First, Finlayson JA stated that the trial judge misconstrued the burden of proof in dangerous offender proceedings. Second, the Court of Appeal intimated that the trial judge abdicated his sentencing responsibility to the National Parole Board. With respect, I find both of these conclusions unsatisfactory.

(1) Erroneous Burden of Proof

As I stated above, the Court of Appeal's conclusion that the trial judge misconstrued the burden of proof is based upon the following passage in the trial judge's reasons:

> I have not been unmoved by the submissions of counsel for the respondent that the character of his behaviour has changed markedly over a period of 15 years from violent to harmless, with the result that the respondent cannot now be described as dangerous. Nonetheless, these submissions have failed to persuade me that the violence and the brutality of the respondent's early sexual assaults do not continue to be evidenced in the pattern of his subsequent sexual assaults, including that conduct which resulted in his conviction upon the predicate offences.

I cannot accept that this passage reflects an erroneous reversal of the burden of proof. In my opinion, when the passage is read in its entire context, it is obvious that when Tobias J said that the respondent's submission "failed to persuade me" he was really indicating that the respondent's submissions had failed to disturb his findings as regards the respondent's dangerousness. In my opinion, this is clearly confirmed by the passage that immediately followed his impugned comment:

> I am satisfied, therefore, beyond a reasonable doubt, upon a consideration of all of the evidence adduced upon this application, that the predicate offences for which the respondent has been convicted are serious personal injury offences as described in paragraph (b) of the definition of that expression in section 752 of the *Criminal Code*, and that the respondent by his conduct since the year 1975 in those sexual matters herein described, including the predicate offences, has shown a failure to control his sexual impulses, and that there is an existing likelihood of the respondent causing injury, pain or other evil to other persons through failure in the future to control his sexual impulses.
>
> In the result, I declare the respondent a dangerous offender.

The Court cannot forget that s. 753(b) does not require proof beyond a reasonable doubt that the respondent will re-offend. Such a standard would be impossible to meet. Instead, s. 753(b) requires that the court be satisfied beyond a reasonable doubt that there is a "likelihood" that the respondent will inflict harm, and the trial judge took explicit notice of this, citing *R v. Knight* (1975), 27 CCC (2d) 343 (Ont. HC); *R v. Dwyer* (1977), 34 CCC (2d) 293 (Alta. CA); *R v. Carleton* (1981), 69 CCC (2d) 1 (Alta. CA) (aff'd [1983] 2 SCR 58). See also *Langevin*, supra. I am thus unwilling to conclude, on the basis of a few misplaced words, that the trial judge either misunderstood or misapplied the burden of proof on this dangerous offender application.

(2) Abdication of Responsibility

The respondent also contends that in his reasons on sentence, the trial judge effectively surrendered his sentencing responsibilities by deferring to the judgment of the National Parole Board under s. 761(1) of the *Criminal Code*. ... While it is important to recognize that an indeterminate sentence does not automatically follow a dangerous offender designation, I do not interpret Tobias J's reference to the National Parole Board's intermittent power of review as an abdication of responsibility. Instead, I view it as a judicial reminder that, although it may be indeterminate, Robert Currie's sentence need not be permanent.

IV. Conclusion

As the Court indicated at the hearing, the trial judge properly designated the respondent, Robert Currie, a dangerous offender. He was not required to focus on the objective seriousness of the predicate offences and accordingly his decision was wholly reasonable and supported by the evidence. Moreover, absent an error of law, of which there was none, the dangerous offender determination is a finding of fact that is almost always based upon the competing credibility of expert witnesses. As such, it is a decision which should not be lightly disturbed.

For all of these reasons, the appeal is allowed and the Court of Appeal's sentence of time served is set aside. The decision of the trial judge to designate the respondent a dangerous offender and the corresponding decision to impose an indeterminate sentence are restored.

Finally, consider the following excerpt from *R v. Neve*. Lisa Neve was the second woman in Canadian history to be designated a dangerous offender. The prosecutor applied to have her declared a dangerous offender following a conviction for robbery. Consequently, the first branch of s. 753(1) of the Code was engaged. The trial judge found Neve to be a dangerous offender and sentenced her to an indeterminate period of detention. The Court of Appeal for Alberta dismissed Neve's appeal against conviction, but concluded that her designation as a dangerous offender could not stand. The excerpts from the reasons in the Court of Appeal highlight some important contextual considerations relating to the operation of the dangerous offender provisions as a whole. They also address the issue of risk of harm from both qualitative and quantitative perspectives.

R v. Neve
(1999), 137 CCC (3d) 97 (Alta. CA)

FRASER CJA:

• • •

We identify a number of errors in the course of our analysis of these issues. Without in any way minimizing the complexity of these issues or their cumulative effect, Neve's appeal from her designation as a dangerous offender can be summarized this simply. According to Crown records, since 1947 (the year in which predecessor dangerous offender legislation first came into effect in Canada) until July 31, 1997, 219 offenders were designated dangerous offenders in Canada, an average of approximately 4 per year. Other data indicates that between 1978 and 1986, that number increased to an average of 7 per year. In the end, the overarching question to be answered is whether the decision designating Neve a dangerous offender was reasonable. Or to put the matter another way: does Neve, having regard to all relevant circumstances, fall within that very small group of offenders whom Parliament intended be designated as dangerous offenders—and which has led, in all of Canada over a 50-year period, to an average of 4 to 7 criminals a year being detained as dangerous offenders? In our view, for reasons we explain in detail below, the answer to this question is no.

• • •

Before addressing each of these issues in turn, we propose to review the facts relating to the robbery. One cannot overemphasize the importance of context, and hence the facts, not only to the conviction appeal, but also to the dangerous offender appeal. Context weighs heavily at many stages of a dangerous offender proceeding. The dangerous offender legislation requires a court to focus on the person (and all relevant circumstances relating to what that person has done) and not simply on numbers of convictions. Parliament has not chosen to adopt a formulaic "three strikes and you are out" approach to dangerous offender designations in Canada. Instead, before imposing one of the most serious sanctions under Canadian criminal law, a court is required to conduct a contextual analysis, concentrating on the offender and on the qualitative, quantitative and relative dimensions of the crimes the offender has committed.

Understanding the facts relating to this robbery is vital for another reason. Once an offender has been convicted, the findings made at trial stand, both in the sentence proceedings in that case, and in any subsequent criminal proceedings. While this does not preclude a judge's interpreting facts relating to prior offences, including the predicate offence, in light of evidence adduced at a dangerous offender hearing, it does prevent a judge's doing so in a manner which results in contradictory findings to those made at trial. What this means is that although the purpose for which fact findings are used may change, the findings themselves cannot.

A. Background Information and Trial Judgment

When these events occurred, Neve was 18 years old. She had been a prostitute since she was 12. Neve and her friend, Kim, approached the complainant, another prostitute. Neve and Kim believed that the complainant had beaten one of their pregnant friends causing her to miscarry. They asked the complainant if she would like to go for a drink. The complainant agreed. It was about midnight. The complainant climbed into a truck with Neve and Kim. They questioned the complainant about the assault on their friend. She denied any involvement.

Kim drove to a field by a greenhouse just outside northeast Edmonton near a major highway and parked the vehicle. The trial judge found that the complainant was told to take her clothes off. Neve threatened to cut off the complainant's hair. Kim threatened that she would break the complainant's arm if she did not take her clothes off. The complainant refused to do so. Neve and Kim then proceeded to tear the complainant's clothes off, using a knife to cut the clothing so that it could be more easily torn. The complainant, whose evidence was accepted by the trial judge, confirmed that her clothes were being held away from her when the knife was used. In the process, the complainant received what she variously conceded was a "little scratch," a "tiny nick" or a "small cut." The complainant expressly acknowledged that the knife was being used quite carefully to remove her clothing, so as not to hurt her.

· · ·

During examination-in-chief, the complainant testified that Kim struck her about five times in the face. Although the complainant mentioned in cross-examination that Neve also struck her, she could not remember any details whatever, including the effect on her. Even with respect to Kim, the complainant testified that she did not remember having any pain or injury as a result of what Kim did. In fact, the complainant testified:

Q Okay. Now, did you receive any—any injuries as a result of this incident, ma'am?

A Nothing other than just a small cut.

· · ·

Neve and Kim drove away after first circling in the parking lot. The complainant testified that she did not know what was done with her clothes when they were removed from her. She was left without them. It was May and the temperature was then about five degrees Centigrade. She wrapped herself in some fibreglass insulation which she found nearby and made her way to the main highway where, according to her testimony, she was picked up a little bit later by a passing motorist who testified that she was "very, very cold, and she looked somewhat confused."

· · ·

With the complainant's help, the police later apprehended Neve. At the time of her arrest, a knife was found in her jacket pocket. She was informed of her right to counsel, but declined to exercise it. Neve was apparently then under the influence of drugs. At no time was Neve informed of her right to remain silent. Nor was she cautioned about the consequences of choosing to make a statement.

Later, while in a police holding cell, Neve cut her wrists. She was taken to hospital where she was treated. She was then returned to the cell. She told one of the constables that he better not leave because she was going to do the same thing again. A police constable watched over her until 7:30 a.m. While there, he asked Neve some questions about the events which led to her arrest. (It is Neve's answers to these questions which Neve contends were wrongly admitted into evidence at the trial.) The constable asked her the name of the other assailant. Neve replied that it was Kim. Neve then went on to explain the nature of the grievance she had with the complainant. Specifically, the constable testified:

> She—she also told me in reference to the—the alleged assault that she did it to get even because the complainant had beat up one of her—her friends who was pregnant at the time and also that the complainant was yelling—was the type that was yelling and getting out of hand, getting out of control. That was another reason for—for what they did.

Neve later asked to speak to a lawyer. After she had used the phone, she told the constable that instead of calling counsel, she had phoned Kim to advise her to leave the City.

• • •

Not everyone who is a criminal or for that matter a danger to the public is a dangerous offender. In the spectrum of offenders, the dangerous offender legislation is designed to target—and capture—those clustered at or near the extreme end. Were this otherwise, constitutionality might stumble. In other words, the dangerous offender legislation is not intended to be a process of general application but rather of exacting selection.

As an example of the relatively narrow band of offenders to whom this legislation is directed—and has been applied—it is instructive to note that between 1978 and 1986, an average of 7 persons per year were sentenced in Canada as dangerous offenders. On average, each offender committed 12.12 offences, 2.2 of which were non-sexual violent crimes and 3.53 of which were sexual crimes: see *Lyons*, supra, at 348, citing affidavit evidence in the companion case *R v. Milne*, [1987] 2 SCR 512.

During oral argument, we requested confirmation of the number of dangerous offenders in Canada and a brief description of the crimes for which they had been convicted. Apparently, this evidence was readily available. We do not suggest that in future cases, the Crown must call detailed evidence with respect to other dangerous offenders. However, the minimal information we requested, and which the Crown helpfully compiled, is of some assistance: see Supplementary Materials of the Crown Respondent (Dangerous Offender Criminal Records). We concede that this information does not provide the details necessary to permit an assessment of the relative degree of seriousness of the offences committed by those already designated as dangerous offenders (whether vis-à-vis Neve or each other). But by painting as it does a more comprehensive picture of the face of dangerous offenders in Canada, both today and historically, it does provide a backdrop, albeit a very general one, against which a court can undertake its evaluation of whether an offender fits into that scene.

We are not saying that the picture cannot be expanded, whether numerically or in terms of the kinds of offences, or offenders, that might typically attract a dangerous offender designation. Of course, the size of the group may increase. So too may the categories of offences which are considered sufficiently serious to warrant use of this sanction, particularly as society becomes less tolerant of crimes of violence and more aware of the potentially long-lasting and traumatic effects of personal violence on victims. However, what we are saying is that in interpreting the scope of the dangerous offender provisions, one should do so in a manner which preserves their constitutional validity:

Slaight Communications Inc. v. Davidson, [1989] 1 SCR 1038; *Hills v. Canada (Attorney General)*, [1988] 1 SCR 513. Ensuring that the group does not include anyone who falls outside of the intended and actual sweep of the legislation will accomplish this.

· · ·

In all these circumstances, we have concluded that the decision to designate Neve a dangerous offender was not reasonable. It is only by taking the global perspective we have described that it is possible to assess whether Neve, in view of her record, and the circumstances and context of the offences she has committed, belongs in that relatively small group such that the most severe sentence that can be imposed under the Code, short of life imprisonment, is strenuously required: *Lyons*, supra, at 339.

There is no doubt that Neve has a history of offending the law; and we cannot say that Neve will not reoffend. That risk exists and it is a real risk. Indeed, it would be naive to think otherwise. However, the question is not whether there is a possibility or even a probability of Neve's reoffending in the future. While this consideration certainly goes on the scale, the central question which must be addressed at this stage is whether, given her past record and the various factors that we have noted and assessed, Neve falls within the intended small group of dangerous offenders in Canada. In our view, she does not.

Neve is a criminal but the totality of the circumstances here do not warrant a dangerous offender designation at this stage in her life. Neve's life found her moving from one set of extreme circumstances to another: prostitution from a very young age; abuse from her pimp; foster homes; placement centres; and drug and alcohol abuse. When her actual criminal record is parsed out from her thoughts and fantasies, what we have is a young woman with a relatively short criminal record for violence, disposed to telling shocking stories of violence. Considering her within the population of criminals in Canada, it cannot be said at this time that she falls within that "very small group of offenders whose personal characteristics and particular circumstances militate strenuously in favour of preventative incarceration." *Lyons*, supra, at 339.

When all is said and done, the question here is not whether Neve is the most dangerous, or even one of the most dangerous, young women that the psychiatrists who testified have ever seen. Nor is it whether Neve is one of the most dangerous young offenders, male or female. We do not have different classes of offenders in this country where one reviews those in a specific class—young offenders or young women for example—and then chooses the worst in that class to advance into the dangerous offender group. (We are not suggesting by this comment that Neve is the worst or near the worst in any class of offenders in Canada.) Instead, the question is whether, relatively speaking compared to all other offenders in Canada—male and female, young and old, advantaged and disadvantaged—Neve falls into that small group of offenders clustered at or near the extreme end of offenders in this country. For reasons we have explained, Neve is not in that group.

The following case was necessitated by the 1997 amendments to the Code and the introduction of the long-term offender sanction into the Code. Given that those amendments were in effect as of August 1, 1997, there were cases in the system that were based on predicate offences that occurred before that date. How do the principles that generally apply to retroactive application deal with whether the long-term offender option should be on the table for an offence that antedates those provisions? Moreover, how should a judge interpret and apply the dangerous offender test now that the Code contains the long-term offender option? Is there any interrelationship, and, if so, what is it? The Supreme Court addressed these questions in *Johnson*, below.

R v. Johnson
[2003] 2 SCR 357

IACOBUCCI and ARBOUR JJ: This case was heard at the same time as *R v. Edgar*, [2003] 2 SCR 388, 2003 SCC 47, *R v. Smith*, [2003] 2 SCR 392, 2003 SCC 48, *R v. Mitchell*, [2003] 2 SCR 396, 2003 SCC 49, *R v. Kelly*, [2003] 2 SCR 400, 2003 SCC 50, released concurrently herewith. Each case involves an appeal against a sentencing judge's decision to declare an offender dangerous and sentence him to an indeterminate period of detention. In deciding these appeals, the British Columbia Court of Appeal conducted an extensive review of the dangerous offender provisions in light of amendments to Part XXIV of the *Criminal Code*, RSC 1985, c. C-46, which contains the provisions governing dangerous offenders.

The amendments, which took effect August 1, 1997, brought a number of changes to Part XXIV of the *Criminal Code*. For instance, the period before a dangerous offender's first parole hearing was extended from three years under the pre-1997 legislation to seven years under the amended legislation. Another change was the addition of the new category of long-term offender to Part XXIV of the *Code*. While Canada has had legislation providing for the indeterminate incarceration of high risk offenders in one form or another since 1947, the 1997 amendments introduced, for the first time, a mechanism to allow for supervision in the community, for a limited period after the expiry of a determinate sentence, of certain offenders who pose a risk of re-offence. This case requires this Court to consider for the first time the interaction between the dangerous offender provisions and the new long-term offender provisions, both of which govern the sentencing of offenders who pose an ongoing public threat.

This appeal raises two primary issues. The first issue is whether a sentencing judge must, under the current regime, take into account the possibility of a long-term offender designation when considering a dangerous offender application. The second issue is whether the current provisions, particularly the long-term offender provisions which were absent in the pre-1997 legislation, are available in instances in which the predicate offence occurred prior to the 1997 amendments.

· · ·

II. Judicial History

At the sentencing hearing, Tysoe J of the Supreme Court of British Columbia did not consider the availability of the long-term offender provisions, on the basis that the offence for which Mr. Johnson was convicted was committed prior to the 1997 amendments. He held that Mr. Johnson was a dangerous offender as defined by s. 753(1)(b) of the *Criminal Code* and sentenced him to detention in a penitentiary for an indeterminate period: [1998] BCJ No. 3216 (QL).

Ryan JA, for the majority of the British Columbia Court of Appeal ((2001), 158 CCC (3d) 155, 2001 BCCA 456), concluded that the matter ought to have been determined in accordance with the current regime. Under s. 11(i) of the *Canadian Charter of Rights and Freedoms*, any person charged with an offence has the right "if found guilty of the offence and if the punishment for the offence has been varied between the time of commission and the time of sentencing, to the benefit of the lesser punishment." Ryan JA found that under the current regime the long-term offender provisions narrow the scope of the dangerous offender provisions by providing the sentencing judge with the option of sentencing an offender who would previously have been declared dangerous to a lesser punishment. Ryan JA thus concluded that the sentencing judge should have sentenced Mr. Johnson under the current regime, and in so doing should have considered the suitability of the long-term offender provisions.

In reaching this conclusion, Ryan JA considered the dangerous offender provisions prior to the amendments. In her view, implicit in one form or another in each of the criteria under s. 753 is the requirement that the pattern of conduct be substantially or pathologically intractable. If the pattern of conduct is substantially or pathologically intractable, the sentencing judge *must* declare the offender dangerous. The sentencing judge, however, retains the discretion to sentence a dangerous offender to a determinate sentence, but only if a cure for the offender's behaviour is probable within the parameters of the fixed sentence.

Ryan JA then concluded that under the current regime a sentencing judge does not retain the discretion to sentence a dangerous offender to a determinate sentence. However, the sentencing judge must consider the prospects for treatment or cure in order to determine whether the pattern of conduct exhibited by the offender is sufficiently intractable to satisfy the statutory criteria set out in s. 753(1)(a) and (b). If there is a reasonable possibility that a cure will be found within the time-frame of a fixed sentence, or that the offender will be controllable under the long-term offender provisions, the sentencing judge cannot rightly conclude that the offender is a dangerous offender. According to Ryan JA, the primary distinction between the long-term offender provisions and the dangerous offender provisions, under the current regime, is the absence of a requirement under the long-term offender provisions that the pattern of conduct be substantially or pathologically intractable. An offender whose conduct is not pathologically intractable may now qualify for long-term offender status rather than dangerous offender status.

Saunders JA dissented on the basis that she was unable to say with certainty, at the time that the hearing commenced, that the current sentencing regime would result in a lesser punishment than the prior regime. According to Saunders JA, it is possible that an offender who would have been declared dangerous and sentenced to a fixed term under the former regime would be declared a long-term offender and sentenced to a fixed term with a period of probation under the current regime, or that a person who would not have been declared dangerous under the former regime would be declared a long-term offender under the current regime. If the predicate offence was committed prior to the 1997 amendments, the offender should be sentenced under the former regime.

III. Issues

This appeal raises two primary issues: (i) whether, under the current regime, a sentencing judge must take into account the long-term offender provisions prior to declaring an offender dangerous and imposing an indeterminate sentence; and (ii) whether a sentencing judge must take into account the long-term offender provisions in instances in which the predicate offence occurred prior to the enactment of the long-term offender provisions. If the sentencing judge's failure to consider the long-term offender provisions constituted an error of law, a third issue arises as to whether the appeals should be allowed on the basis that the error of law resulted in no substantial wrong or miscarriage of justice.

IV. Analysis

Section 11(i) of the *Charter* guarantees that everyone has the right, "if found guilty of the offence and if the punishment for the offence has been varied between the time of commission and the time of sentencing, to the benefit of the lesser punishment." The question in this appeal is whether the new provisions offer any benefit to the respondent such that his sentencing must be governed retrospectively by the provisions as amended in 1997. In order to answer this question, it is necessary to interpret both the old and the new provisions, to determine which offers the prospect of a lesser punishment to an accused in the position of the respondent who is sentenced under them.

A. Dangerous Offender Applications Under the Current Regime

The Crown submits that an offender who meets the criteria in s. 753(1)(a) or (b) must be declared a dangerous offender and must be given an indeterminate sentence, without regard to whether the offender might also meet the criteria for a long-term offender designation. There are two branches to this argument: first, that under 753(1), courts have no discretion to decline to declare an offender a dangerous offender once the statutory criteria have been satisfied; and second, that s. 753(5)(a) of the *Criminal Code* prevents a sentencing judge from considering the long-term offender provisions on a dangerous offender application until after the court has already found that an offender is not a dangerous offender. We consider each aspect of the argument in turn.

(1) The Sentencing Judge's Discretion

Section 753(1) provides that "[t]he court may, on application made under this Part following the filing of an assessment report under subsection 752.1(2), find the offender to be a dangerous offender" if it is satisfied that the statutory criteria set out in paras. (a) or (b) are met. The Crown submits that the word "may" in s. 753(1) does not create a true discretion, but rather grants a power that is contingent only upon proof of the statutory conditions. On this view, the word "may" in the phrase "[t]he court may ... find the offender to be a dangerous offender" should be treated as imperative; a sentencing judge who finds that the dangerous offender criteria are met *must* make a dangerous offender designation. For the following reasons, it is our opinion that this submission must fail.

The language of s. 753(1) indicates that a sentencing judge retains a discretion whether to declare an offender dangerous who meets the criteria for that designation. As mentioned above, s. 753(1) provides that the court *may* find an offender to be a dangerous offender if it is satisfied that the statutory criteria set out in paras. (a) or (b) are met. On its face, the word "may" denotes a discretion, while the word "shall" is commonly used to denote an obligation: see for example *R v. Potvin*, [1989] 1 SCR 525, at p. 549. Indeed, s. 11 of the *Interpretation Act*, RSC 1985, c. I-21, requires "shall" to be construed as imperative and "may" to be construed as permissive. If Parliament had intended that an offender *must* be designated dangerous if each of the statutory criteria have been satisfied, one would have expected Parliament to have used the word "shall" rather than "may."

That said, cases do exist in which courts have found that the power conferred by "may" is coupled with a duty once all the conditions for the exercise of the power have been met: R. Sullivan, *Sullivan and Driedger on the Construction of Statutes* (4th ed. 2002), at p. 58. See for example, *Brown v. Metropolitan Authority* (1996), 150 NSR (2d) 43, in which the Nova Scotia Court of Appeal ruled that Sackville's Metropolitan Authority was obliged to pay the claimant pursuant to s. 8(1) of the *Community of Sackville Landfill Compensation Act*, SNS 1993, c. 71, despite the fact that the section provided that the Authority *may* pay an amount to a person who is a resident, or an owner or occupier of real or personal property in the municipality on account of damages arising out of the operation of the landfill. But as Sullivan observes, at pp. 59-60:

> In a case like *Brown*, it is wrong to say that "may" means "shall" or "may" is imperative. As Cotton LJ wrote in *Nichols v. Baker*,
>
>> I think that great misconception is caused by saying that in some cases "may" means "must." It can never mean "must," so long as the English language retains its meaning; but it gives a power, and then it may be a question in what cases, where a Judge has a power given him by the word "may," it becomes his duty to exercise it. (*In re Baker; Nichols v. Baker* (1890), 44 Ch. D 262, at 270.)
>
> *The duty, if it arises, is inferred from the purpose and scheme of the Act or from other contextual factors.* [Emphasis added.]

In this case, there is no indication of a duty to find an offender dangerous once the statutory criteria have been met. As we will elaborate, neither the purpose of the dangerous offenders regime, nor the principles of sentencing, nor the principles of statutory interpretation suggest that a sentencing judge must designate an offender dangerous if the statutory criteria in s. 753(1)(a) or (b) have been met. On the contrary, each of these factors indicates that a sentencing judge retains the discretion not to declare an offender dangerous even if the statutory criteria are met. This is particularly true now that it is clear that offenders declared dangerous must be given an indeterminate sentence.

In *R v. Lyons*, [1987] 2 SCR 309, this Court affirmed that the primary purpose of the dangerous offender regime is the protection of the public: see also *Re Moore and The Queen* (1984), 10 CCC (3d) 306 (Ont. HC), cited with approval in *Lyons, supra*, at p. 329. In *Lyons*, La Forest J explained that preventive detention under the dangerous offender regime goes beyond what is justified on a "just deserts" rationale based on the reasoning that in a given case, the nature of the crime and the circumstances of the offender call for the elevation of the goal of protection of the public over the other purposes of sentencing. La Forest J confirmed, at p. 339, that the legislation was designed "to carefully define a very small group of offenders whose personal characteristics and particular circumstances militate strenuously in favour of preventive incarceration."

Indeterminate detention under the dangerous offender regime is warranted only insofar as it actually serves the purpose of protecting the public. As we discuss more thoroughly below, there may be circumstances in which an offender meets the statutory criteria for a dangerous offender designation but the goal of protecting the public can be achieved without indeterminate detention. An interpretation of the dangerous offender provisions that would require a sentencing judge to declare an offender dangerous and sentence him or her to an indeterminate period of detention in each instance in which the statutory criteria for a dangerous offender designation have been satisfied would introduce an unnecessary rigidity into the process and overshoot the public protection purpose of the dangerous offender regime.

Nor is there anything in the purposes of the sentencing regime as a whole, as set out both in the decisions of this Court and in ss. 718 to 718.2 of the *Criminal Code*, which would indicate a duty to find an offender dangerous in each circumstance in which the statutory criteria are met. On the contrary, the underlying objectives of the sentencing regime, of which the dangerous offender provisions form a part, indicate a discretion to impose a just and fit sentence in the circumstances of the individual case.

In *R v. Proulx*, [2000] 1 SCR 61, 2000 SCC 5, Lamer CJ, writing for the Court, emphasized, at para. 82, that "sentencing is an individualized process, in which the trial judge has considerable discretion in fashioning a fit sentence." The rationale flows from the principles of sentencing set out in the *Criminal Code*, including s. 718.1, which states that a sentence "must be proportionate to the gravity of the offence and the degree of responsibility of the offender," and s. 718.2(d), which states that an offender "should not be deprived of liberty, if less restrictive sanctions may be appropriate in the circumstances."

This Court has previously confirmed that dangerous offender proceedings form part of the sentencing process: see for example *R v. Jones*, [1994] 2 SCR 229, at pp. 279-80 and 294-95, and *Lyons*, *supra*, at p. 350. As such, their interpretation must be guided by the fundamental purpose and principles of sentencing contained in ss. 718 to 718.2. The role played by the purpose and principles of sentencing in guiding the interpretation of the dangerous offender provisions is reflected in the comments of La Forest J, in *Lyons*, at p. 329, that preventive detention "simply represents a judgment that the relative importance of the objectives of rehabilitation, deterrence and retribution are greatly attenuated in the circumstances of the individual case, and that of prevention, correspondingly increased."

The proposition that a court is under a duty to declare an offender dangerous in each circumstance in which the statutory criteria are satisfied is in direct conflict with the underlying principle that the sentence must be appropriate in the circumstances of the individual case. A rigid rule that each offender who satisfies the statutory criteria in

s. 753(1) must be declared dangerous and sentenced to an indeterminate period of detention undermines a sentencing judge's capacity to fashion a sentence that fits the individual circumstances of a given case. Thus, rather than suggesting that a sentencing judge is under an obligation to find an offender dangerous once the statutory criteria are met, the principles and purposes underlying the *Criminal Code*'s sentencing provisions actually *favour* a sentencing judge's discretion whether to declare an offender dangerous who has met the statutory criteria in s. 753(1).

The Crown has pointed to a line of lower court judgments, beginning with *R v. Moore* (1985), 16 CCC (3d) 328 (Ont. CA), which say that a sentencing judge must designate an offender dangerous once the statutory criteria for the designation have been satisfied: see also *R v. Boutilier* (1995), 144 NSR (2d) 293 (CA); *R v. Dow* (1999), 120 BCAC 16, 1999 BCCA 177 , decided under the previous legislation; *R v. J.T.H.* (2002), 209 NSR (2d) 302, 2002 NSCA 138; *R v. D.W.M.*, [2001] AJ No. 165 (QL), 2001 ABPC 5, decided under the current regime. There is also a contrary line of cases affirming the court's discretion to decline to make the designation which relies on *Lyons*: see for example *R v. N. (L.)* (1999), 71 Alta. LR (3d) 92, 1999 ABCA 206, decided under the current and previous legislation; *R v. Driver*, [2000] BCJ No. 63 (QL), 2000 BCSC 69, decided under the previous legislation; *R v. O.G.*, [2001] OJ No. 1964 (QL) (CJ); *R v. Tremblay* (2000), 87 Alta. LR (3d) 229, 2000 ABQB 551; and *R v. Roy*, [1999] QJ No. 5648 (QL) (Sup. Ct.), rev'd on a different issue (2002), 167 CCC (3d) 203 (Que. CA), decided under the current regime. Other courts have expressed uncertainty as to which line of cases to follow: see for example *R v. F.W.M.*, [2001] OJ No. 4591 (QL) (SCJ); *R v. Morin* (1998), 173 Sask. R. 101 (QB); *R v. R.C.* (1996), 145 Nfld. & PEIR 271 (Nfld. CA).

However, this Court confirmed in *Lyons*, *supra*, that the phrase "the court may ... find the offender to be a dangerous offender" denotes a discretion. In support of the Court's conclusion that the dangerous offender regime did not violate the prohibition on cruel and unusual punishment, La Forest J stated, at p. 338, that "*the court has the discretion not to designate the offender as dangerous* or to impose an indeterminate sentence, *even in circumstances where all of these criteria are met*" (emphasis added). He reiterated the point at p. 362, stating that a sentencing judge "*does retain a discretion whether or not to impose the designation* or indeterminate sentence, or both" (emphasis added). Insofar as *Moore* and its progeny suggest that sentencing judges must declare an offender dangerous if the statutory criteria have been satisfied, they have been overruled by *Lyons*.

Having determined that the phrase "[t]he court may ... find the offender to be a dangerous offender" denotes a discretion, the next issue that falls to be considered is the legal principles and factors that a sentencing judge must consider in the exercise of that discretion. For the reasons that follow, it is our conclusion that one factor that a sentencing judge must consider is the possibility that the sanctions available pursuant to the long-term offender provisions would be sufficient to achieve the objectives that the dangerous offender provisions seek to advance.

(2) The Exercise of Discretion

Like all discretion exercised in the sentencing context, a judge's discretion whether to declare an offender dangerous must be guided by the relevant principles of sentencing contained in ss. 718 to 718.2 of the *Criminal Code*. As mentioned above, these include the fundamental principle of proportionality contained in s. 718.1 and, most relevant to the central issue in the present appeal, the principle of restraint enunciated in paras. (d) and (e) of s. 718.2, which provide as follows:

> 718.2 A court that imposes a sentence shall also take into consideration the following principles:
>
> . . .
>
> (d) an offender should not be deprived of liberty, if less restrictive sanctions may be appropriate in the circumstances; and
> (e) all available sanctions other than imprisonment that are reasonable in the circumstances should be considered for all offenders, with particular attention to the circumstances of aboriginal offenders.

The joint effect of these principles is that a sentencing judge must consider the possibility that a less restrictive sanction would attain the same sentencing objectives that a more restrictive sanction seeks to attain.

In this case, the sentencing objective in question is public protection: see for example *Lyons, supra*, at p. 329, and *Hatchwell v. The Queen*, [1976] 1 SCR 39, in which Dickson J (as he then was) wrote, at p. 43, that the dominant purpose of preventive detention is "to protect the public when the past conduct of the criminal demonstrates a propensity for crimes of violence against the person, and there is a real and present danger to life or limb." Absent such a danger, there is no basis on which to sentence an offender otherwise than in accordance with the ordinary principles of sentencing. The principles of sentencing thus dictate that a judge ought to impose an indeterminate sentence only in those instances in which there does not exist less restrictive means by which to protect the public adequately from the threat of harm, i.e., where a definite sentence or long-term offender designation are insufficient. The essential question to be determined, then, is whether the sentencing sanctions available pursuant to the long-term offender provisions are sufficient to reduce this threat to an acceptable level, despite the fact that the statutory criteria in s. 753(1) have been met.

In order for the sentencing sanctions available pursuant to the long-term offender provisions to reduce the threat associated with an offender who satisfies the dangerous offender criteria to an acceptable level, it must be possible for the same offender to satisfy both the dangerous offender criteria and the long-term offender criteria. To repeat, the three criteria that must be established on a long-term offender application are: (i) it must be appropriate to impose a sentence of imprisonment of two or more years in respect of the predicate offence; (ii) there must be a substantial risk that the offender will reoffend; and (iii) there must be a reasonable possibility of eventual control of the risk in the community. On a dangerous offender application, the sentencing judge must be satisfied that the offender constitutes a threat to the life, safety or physical or mental well-being of other persons, on the basis of a pattern of repetitive or persistent aggressive behaviour, brutal behaviour, or sexual misconduct described in s. 753(1)(a) and (b).

Almost every offender who satisfies the dangerous offender criteria will satisfy the first two criteria in the long-term offender provisions. In virtually every instance in which an offender is declared dangerous, it would have been appropriate to impose a sentence of imprisonment of two or more years in respect of the predicate offence and there will be a substantial risk that the offender will reoffend. In a certain percentage of those cases there will also be a reasonable possibility of eventual control of the risk in the community. In those instances in which the offender currently constitutes a threat to the life, safety or physical or mental well-being of other persons yet there is a reasonable possibility of eventual control of the risk in the community, an offender will satisfy the criteria in both the dangerous offender *and* long-term offender provisions.

In those instances where both the dangerous and long-term offender provisions are satisfied, it may be that the sentencing sanctions available under the long-term offender provisions are capable of reducing the threat to the life, safety or physical or mental well-being of other persons to an acceptable level. Under s. 753.1(3), long-term offenders are sentenced to a definite term of imprisonment followed by a long-term community supervision order of a maximum of ten years in accordance with the *Corrections and Conditional Release Act*. Supervision conditions under s. 134.1(2) of the Act may include those that are "reasonable and necessary in order to protect society." The very purpose of a long-term supervision order, then, is to protect society from the threat that the offender currently poses—and to do so without resort to the blunt instrument of indeterminate detention. If the public threat can be reduced to an acceptable level through either a determinate period of detention or a determinate period of detention followed by a long-term supervision order, a sentencing judge cannot properly declare an offender dangerous and sentence him or her to an indeterminate period of detention.

The Crown refutes the conclusion that the long-term offender provisions must be considered before a dangerous offender designation is made with reference to *R v. Carleton* (1981), 32 AR 181 (CA), affirmed by this Court in brief oral reasons, [1983] 2 SCR 58. In that case, the Court of Appeal considered whether, prior to the 1997 amendments, prospects of cure or treatment ought to be considered on a dangerous offender application and, if so, at which stage. McGillivray CJA for the majority, held that treatment prospects were irrelevant to the question of whether an offender is a dangerous offender, but that such prospects may be taken into account in determining whether to impose a determinate or indeterminate sentence. The Crown relies on *Carleton* in support of its proposition that it is improper to consider prospective factors, including the possibility of eventual control of the risk in the community, in determining whether an offender is a dangerous offender.

However, there is some question as to whether *Carleton* correctly determined that prospective factors were irrelevant at the designation stage. The Court of Appeal's analysis was based on the assumption that once the statutory criteria were satisfied, the sentencing judge first had to consider whether to declare the offender dangerous, and then had to consider whether to impose an indeterminate sentence. But it is unclear that this two-step approach is the proper one. First, the purpose of the dangerous offender provisions is not to designate offenders as dangerous for the sake of designating offenders dangerous, but to protect the public. No sentencing objective is advanced by declaring an offender dangerous and then imposing a determinate sentence. Moreover, the two-stage approach is inconsistent with the French text, which provides that once the statutory criteria in s. 753 are satisfied, the court "*peut déclarer qu'il s'agit là d'un délinquant dangereux et lui imposer, au lieu de toute autre peine qui pourrait être imposée pour l'infraction dont il vient d'être déclaré coupable, une peine de détention dans un pénitencier pour une période indéterminée.*" This clearly suggests that Parliament intended that a sentencing judge would ask but one question: whether it would be appropriate, in the circumstances of the case, to declare the offender dangerous and thereby impose a period of indeterminate detention.

Carleton thus provides little support for the proposition that a sentencing judge cannot consider treatment prospects at the designation stage. After all, the Court of Appeal was unanimous in *Carleton* that treatment prospects must be considered at some point prior to imposing an indeterminate sentence. If the court had recognized that following a determination that the statutory criteria have been satisfied there is but one question to be asked—whether to declare the offender dangerous and thereupon impose an indeterminate period of detention—it is far from clear that it would subsequently have reached the same conclusion in respect of the relevance of treatment prospects in determining whether to designate an offender dangerous. On the one-stage approach that we have proposed, the Court of Appeal's concurrent findings that the treatment prospects cannot be considered at the designation stage yet must be considered prior to imposing an indeterminate sentence are incompatible.

But even if *Carleton* correctly concluded that under the pre-1997 provisions, prospective factors, including the reasonable possibility of eventual control of the risk in the community, could not properly be considered at the stage of designating an offender dangerous, this is no longer the case under the amended provisions. *Lyons* held, at pp. 337-38, that a sentencing judge's discretion not to impose an indeterminate sentence, even where all of the statutory criteria are met, helped ensure proportionality between the goal of protecting the public on the one hand and the serious effect of indeterminate detention on the accused on the other. Consequently, the discretion helped ensure the dangerous offender provisions' constitutionality. In other words, as we state elsewhere in these reasons, the imposition of an indeterminate sentence is justifiable only insofar as it actually serves the objective of protecting society. Now that it is clear that a sentencing judge has but one discretion to exercise, prospective factors, including the possibility of eventual control of the risk in the community, must be considered at some point leading up to a dangerous offender designation. This is necessary to ensure that an indeterminate sentence is imposed only in those circumstances in which the objective of public protection truly requires indeterminate detention. Consequently, under this analysis, *Carleton*, which was decided prior to the 1997 amendments, has no bearing on the above analysis.

(3) Section 753(5)

The Crown submits that s. 753(5) precludes a sentencing judge from considering the long-term offender provisions until after he or she has already determined that the offender is not a dangerous offender. Section 753(5) provides as follows:

> If the court does not find an offender to be a dangerous offender,
>
>> (a) the court may treat the application as an application to find the offender to be a long-term offender, section 753.1 applies to the application and the court may either find that the offender is a long-term offender or hold another hearing for that purpose; or
>>
>> (b) the court may impose sentence for the offence for which the offender has been convicted.

It is our view that s. 753(5) has no such effect. The sole purpose of s. 753(5) is to ensure that the Crown need not bring one application for a declaration that an offender is a dangerous offender and then, should that first application fail, a separate application seeking a declaration that an offender is a long-term offender. Section 753(5) thus increases the efficiency of the court system and preserves judicial resources by providing for a substantial degree of procedural integration between the two designations. It does not, however, limit the scope of factors that a sentencing judge might properly take into account when determining whether or not to declare an offender dangerous.

Furthermore, s. 759(3)(a) provides that a court of appeal may allow an appeal against a finding that an offender is a dangerous offender and find that the offender is a long-term offender. If a court of appeal has the power to consider the possibility of a long-term offender designation on an appeal, a sentencing judge must have the same power on the initial application. This supports the conclusion that Parliament did not intend the dangerous offender provisions and the long-term offender provisions to be considered in isolation of one another. On a dangerous offender application, a sentencing judge may consider the possibility that a long-term offender designation is appropriate.

(4) Conclusion

For the above reasons, the British Columbia Court of Appeal was correct to conclude that a sentencing judge must take into account the long-term offender provisions prior to declaring an offender dangerous and imposing an indeterminate sentence. If a sentencing judge is satisfied that the sentencing options available under the long-term offender provisions are sufficient to reduce the threat to the life, safety or physical or mental well-being of other persons to an acceptable level, the sentencing judge cannot properly declare an offender dangerous and thereupon impose an indeterminate sentence, even if all of the statutory criteria have been satisfied.

B. Predicate Offences Committed Prior to the 1997 Amendments

As a general matter, persons accused of criminal conduct are to be charged and sentenced under the criminal law provisions in place at the time that the offence allegedly was committed. The *Charter* aside, the four respondents convicted of offences committed prior to the 1997 amendments are properly sentenced under the former regime.

However, s. 11(i) of the *Charter* provides that any person charged with an offence has the right "if found guilty of the offence and if the punishment for the offence has been varied between the time of commission and the time of sentencing, to the benefit of the lesser punishment."

Under the former regime, a dangerous offender application results in one of two sentences: (i) a determinate sentence; or (ii) an indeterminate sentence. In those instances in which an offender would receive a determinate sentence, there is no lesser punishment that the offender might receive under the current regime. If the proper sentence under the former regime is a determinate sentence, the offender must receive a determinate sentence. But in each of the four cases where pre-1997 provisions were in issue, the sentencing judge concluded that the proper sentence was an indeterminate sentence. The question that this appeal raises is whether it is possible that an offender properly sentenced to an indeterminate period of detention under the prior regime would receive a lesser punishment under the current regime.

As the Crown correctly observes, the statutory criteria that must be satisfied under the former s. 753 are precisely the same as the statutory criteria that must be satisfied under the current s. 753(1). The logical inference is that each offender who satisfies the criteria set out in s. 753 must also satisfy the criteria set out in s. 753(1). But it does not thereby follow that every person declared a dangerous offender and sentenced to an indeterminate period of detention under the former regime would continue to be declared a dangerous offender and sentenced to an indeterminate period of detention under the current regime.

As we have discussed, a sentencing judge should declare the offender dangerous and impose an indeterminate period of detention if, and only if, an indeterminate sentence is the least restrictive means by which to reduce the public threat posed by the offender to an acceptable level. The introduction of the long-term offender provisions expands the range of sentencing options available to a sentencing judge who is satisfied that the dangerous offender criteria have been met. Under the current regime, a sentencing judge is no longer faced with the stark choice between an indeterminate sentence and a determinate sentence. Rather, a sentencing judge may consider the additional possibility that a determinate sentence followed by a period of supervision in the community might adequately protect the public. The result is that some offenders who may have been declared dangerous under the former provisions could benefit from the long-term offender designation available under the current provisions.

It thus follows that the Court of Appeal was correct to conclude that the sentencing judges were required to consider the applicability of the long-term offender provisions. If the respondent satisfies the long-term offender criteria and there is a reasonable possibility that the harm could be reduced to an acceptable level under the long-term offender provisions, the proper sentence, under the current regime, is not an indeterminate period of detention, but, rather, a determinate period of detention followed by a long-term supervision order. If this is the case, s. 11(i) of the *Charter* dictates that the respondent is entitled to be sentenced to a period of determinate detention followed by a long-term supervision order.

Importantly, this does not mean that the respondent will, in the end, be sentenced in accordance with the current regime. Under the prior regime, the first parole hearing took place three years after the offender was taken into custody. Under the current regime, an offender sentenced to an indeterminate term is not entitled to a first parole review until the expiration of seven years. If the sentencing judge is not satisfied that the long-term offender criteria have been met, or finds that a determinate sentence followed by a long-term supervision order would not reduce the threat of harm to an acceptable level, the respondent retains the benefit of the early parole hearing.

• • •

V. Disposition

In the result, the appeal is dismissed. We confirm the Court of Appeal's decision to order a new sentencing hearing in accordance with the foregoing principles.

NOTE

After *Johnson*, it is essential for a court dealing with a dangerous offender application that could lead to indeterminate detention to consider whether the facts would support a long-term offender (LTO) offending. Assuming that an LTO option is factually on the table, does the Crown bear any burden—that is, a burden to negate a reasonable possibility of eventual control of risk in the community? The Ontario Court of Appeal in *R v. F.E.D.*, [2007] OJ No. 1278 (QL), dealt with this issue and concluded:

[P]lacing an onus on the Crown to prove beyond a reasonable doubt that there is no reasonable possibility for eventual control of the risk an offender presents in the community in the context of a dangerous offender application would be inconsistent with *Johnson, supra. Johnson* holds that a sentencing judge may exercise the discretion not to declare an offender dangerous where the long-term offender criteria are met. Those criteria include the requirement that the sentencing judge be satisfied that there is a reasonable possibility of eventual control of the risk that an offender presents in the community. If the sentencing judge is uncertain whether that requirement is satisfied, *Johnson* indicates that the sentencing judge should refuse to exercise the discretion not to declare the offender dangerous based on the long-term offender provisions.

• • •

In the context of a dangerous offender application, the issue is whether the sentencing judge should exercise the discretion not to declare an offender dangerous after the sentencing judge has found that the offender satisfies the statutory criteria for that designation. As I have explained, the sentencing judge may exercise that discretion where he or she is satisfied that the public threat can be reduced to an acceptable level through either the long-term offender provisions or a determinate sentence. This is not an issue that requires either party to satisfy a burden of proof; rather, it is an issue for the sentencing judge concerning whether to exercise his or her discretion based on the whole of the evidence adduced. Moreover, given the requirement that an assessment report under s. 752.1(2) of the *Criminal Code* be filed as a pre-condition to making either a dangerous offender designation or a long-term offender designation, I see little risk that the sentencing judge will be left without evidence addressing the issue.

In the context of a stand-alone long-term offender application, the language of the statute appears to suggest a burden on the Crown to prove affirmatively that there is a reasonable prospect of eventual control of the offender in the community: e.g. see *R v. Currie*, [1997] 2

SCR 260 and *R v. Guilford* (1999), 44 WCB (2d) 523 (Ont. SCJ). However, in my view, the requirement in s. 753.1 that there be a reasonable possibility of eventual control of the risk the offender presents in the community is of a different character than the first two criteria in that section and I do not agree that it is necessary to approach this criterion as imposing a burden of proof.

The first two criteria in s. 753.1 are similar to the criteria in the dangerous offender provisions. They speak to the level of risk the offender is likely to pose in the future having regard to the offender's past conduct. They also establish the justification for subjecting an offender to a special sentencing regime based on the need for public protection. Accordingly, these are matters that the Crown should properly bear the onus of proving on the standard of proof beyond a reasonable doubt.

By way of contrast, the third criterion in s. 753.1 is not a justification for subjecting an offender to the long-term offender sentencing regime. Rather, it appears to be aimed solely at addressing whether the offender qualifies for a long-term offender designation as opposed to the more onerous dangerous offender designation. Importantly, as with the dangerous offender provisions, the long-term offender provisions give a sentencing judge a residual discretion to forego the more onerous designation where a lesser sanction would be sufficient to protect the public from the risk the offender presents.

Finally, I note that, in addition to *Proulx, supra*, there are other cases that have held that a requirement that a court be "satisfied" of a particular matter does not necessarily connote a standard of proof beyond a reasonable doubt. See, e.g. *R v. M.(S.H.)* (1989), 50 CCC (3d) 503 (SCC), in which McLachlin J noted that the concept of a standard of proof is "typically concerned with establishing whether something took place" and is "less helpful" when one is engaged in balancing various factors and considerations. See also *R v. A.O; R v. J.M.*, [2007] OJ No. 800 (CA).

Viewed in the context of the foregoing factors, I see no necessity or rationale for viewing the third criterion in s. 753.1 as imposing a burden of proof.

Do you agree? Is it appropriate to say that there is no burden of proof? Or is the Court of Appeal saying that the offender must satisfy the judge of the possibility of eventual control of risk in the community and, if there is doubt, then the offender should be declared a dangerous offender? Does this seem fair? And if so, to what standard must the judge be satisfied?

E. Constitutional Considerations

Not long after the *Canadian Charter of Rights and Freedoms*, Part I of the *Constitution Act, 1982*, RSC 1985, app. II, no. 44, came into force, challenges were made to the dangerous offender provisions. None of them was successful. The leading case on this point is the decision of the Supreme Court of Canada in *R v. Lyons*, infra. The arguments made in *Lyons* represent the typical complaints about preventive criminal justice measures: (1) Is it fair to punish someone for a crime he or she has not yet committed, instead of imposing punishment only for past wrongful acts? (2) Is indeterminate detention not a "cruel and unusual" sort of punishment? and (3) Given that social science tells us that our ability to predict dangerousness is quite weak, is it not arbitrary to detain someone indefinitely on this basis?

As you read through *Lyons*, consider whether the court's responses to these arguments are adequate. Should other, more compelling arguments have been advanced in this case?

R v. Lyons
[1987] 2 SCR 309, 61 CR (3d) 1 (SCC)

LA FOREST J: [1] The broad issues raised in this appeal are whether the dangerous offenders provisions of the *Criminal Code*, RSC 1970, c. C-34, Part XXI, ss. 687 to 695, contravene the rights guaranteed by the *Canadian Charter of Rights and Freedoms* to "liberty" and "not to be deprived thereof except in accordance with the principles of fundamental justice" (s. 7), "not to be arbitrarily detained or imprisoned" (s. 9), "to the benefit of trial by jury" (s. 11), and "not to be subjected to any cruel and unusual treatment or punishment" (s. 12), and if so whether they can be justified under s. 1 of the Charter as being "such reasonable limits prescribed by law as can be demonstrably justified in a free and democratic society."

Facts and Procedural History

[2] On 23rd September 1983 the appellant, Thomas Patrick Lyons, was arraigned on an information containing four charges: unlawfully breaking and entering a dwelling-house contrary to s. 306(1)(b) of the *Criminal Code*; unlawfully using a weapon or imitation thereof in committing a sexual assault, contrary to s. 246.2(a) of the *Code*; unlawfully using a firearm while committing an indictable offence, contrary to s. 83(1)(a) of the *Code*; and unlawfully stealing property of a total value exceeding $200, contrary to s. 294(a) of the *Code*. These offences were alleged to have been committed approximately one month after the appellant's sixteenth birthday.

[3] The appellant elected trial by a judge without a jury on all four charges and waived his right to a preliminary inquiry. He subsequently entered pleas of guilty to all counts in the indictment. O'Hearn Co. Ct. J of the County Court Judge's Criminal Court for District 1, Nova Scotia, requested a pre-sentence report and adjourned the matter of sentence.

[4] Just before the sentence hearing on 4th November 1983, defence counsel was informed, for the first time, that the Crown might bring a dangerous offender application under Part XXI of the *Code*. At the commencement of the hearing, the Crown requested and was granted an adjournment to permit it to consider bringing such an application. The application was subsequently made. On 8th November 1983 consent to the application was obtained from the Deputy Attorney General of Nova Scotia, as required by s. 689(a)(a) of the *Code*.

[5] At the commencement of the hearing of the application on 14th December 1983, an agreed-upon statement of facts was read into the record. Evidence, including expert psychiatric testimony, was tendered on behalf of both the Crown and the appellant.

[6] Though O'Hearn Co. Ct. J had at the outset warned the Crown attorney that he would have an "uphill fight" owing to the age of the appellant, the judge in the end found, on the basis of medical and other evidence presented to him, that it had been established beyond a reasonable doubt that the appellant qualified as a dangerous offender

under the provisions of the *Code*. In his view, it had been shown that the appellant had a "sociopathic personality" and had so little conscience that it did not govern his actions. He concluded that it could be said with "a high degree of confidence" that it was "very likely" that the appellant would constitute a danger to the psychological or physical health and lives of others owing to "his in-built, perhaps congenital indifference to the consequences to others, his lack of affect, his lack of feeling for others." He belonged, the judge stated, to a class of people who, though mentally able to understand the law and to conform their conduct to its dictates, are so irresponsive to the law that they must be dealt with by extraordinary measures.

[7] O'Hearn Co. Ct. J also considered and rejected the appellant's contentions that Part XXI of the *Code* was constitutionally invalid as offending against the guarantees embodied in ss. 7, 9 and 12 of the Charter, and proceeded to sentence the appellant to an indeterminate period of detention in a penitentiary.

[8] The appellant's appeal to the Nova Scotia Supreme Court, Appeal Division, was unanimously dismissed for reasons given by Macdonald JA. On 31st January leave to appeal to this Court was granted.

[9] The following constitutional questions were stated by the court on 26th March 1985:

> 1. Whether the provisions of Part XXI of the *Criminal Code of Canada*, dealing with an application for finding and sentencing, an individual as a dangerous offender, in whole or in part, infringe or deny the rights guaranteed by sections 7, 9, 11, and/or 12 of the *Canadian Charter of Rights and Freedoms*?
>
> 2. If so, then are the provisions of Part XXI of the *Criminal Code*, in whole or in part, justified on the basis of s. 1 of the *Canadian Charter of Rights and Freedoms* and therefore not inconsistent with the *Constitution Act, 1982*?

[10] The appellant also argued that his rights under s. 7 of the Charter were violated by the Crown's failure to give him notice, before his election of a mode of trial and the entry of his plea, that it intended to bring, or contemplated bringing, a "dangerous offender" application under Part XXI of the *Code*. ...

History and Analysis of Part XXI

[12] Part XXI of the *Criminal Code* establishes a scheme for the designation of certain offenders as "dangerous offenders" and for sentencing such persons to a penitentiary for an indeterminate period. It is the product of frequently-amended legislation that has existed in Canada, in one form or another, since 1947. It has its genesis in the *Prevention of Crime Act, 1908* (8 Edw. 7, c. 59), ss. 10 to 16, under which a person convicted of a crime was subject to a "further sentence" of not less than five or more than ten years as preventive detention if he or she was found to be an habitual criminal. During the debates in Parliament on that Act, its author, Lord Gladstone, "made it clear that it was intended to deal not with the generality of 'habituals' but only with that more limited body of 'professional criminals' or 'persistent dangerous criminals' engaged in the more serious forms of crime": Fox, *The Modern English Prison* (1934), London, at p. 168.

• • •

[16] The present legislation, enacted in 1977, clearly pursues the historical purpose of protecting the public, but is now carefully tailored so as to be confined in its application to those habitual criminals who are dangerous to others. In brief, Part XXI provides that, where a person has been found guilty of a "serious personal injury offence," the court may, upon application, find the offender to be a dangerous offender and may thereupon impose a sentence of indeterminate detention in lieu of any other sentence that the offender might have received for the offence.

. . .

[17] To trigger the operation of this procedure, it is necessary by virtue of the opening words of subs. (a) and subs. (b) that the accused have been found guilty of a "serious personal injury offence" .... . Two of the crimes of which the appellant was convicted fall within this definition.

[18] In addition to having been convicted of a serious personal injury offence, s. 688(a) and (b) provides that for the offender to qualify as a dangerous offender it must also be established that he constitutes a threat to the life, safety or well-being of others on the basis of evidence of the dangerous and intractably persistent or brutal behaviour described in paras. (i) to (ii), or that the offender has shown an inability to control his sexual impulses and a likelihood that he will thereby cause injury, pain or other evil to other persons. The findings of the courts below that behaviour described in s. 688 existed was not contested here.

[19] Owing to the nature of the findings that must be made, provision is made for psychological, psychiatric and criminological evidence (s. 690) as well as character evidence (s. 694). Indeed, the evidence of at least two psychiatrists is obligatory. As well, the judge is empowered to make directions and to remand the offender for the purposes of observation (s. 691).

[20] Because of the serious implications of the procedure for the accused, a number of safeguards have been provided. Thus the consent of the provincial Attorney General is required and the offender must, following the application, be given at least seven days' notice of the basis on which it is made (s. 689). The offender is allowed to nominate one of the psychiatric witnesses (s. 690(2)) and failure to do so obliges the court to nominate one on his or her behalf (s. 690(3)). The offender also has a right to be present at the hearing (s. 693), and to appeal against sentence (s. 694(1)). As well, the Solicitor General of Canada is to be furnished with copies of the psychological, psychiatric and criminological evidence and of the observations of the court (s. 695). Finally, and importantly, provision is made for review of the sentence at the expiration of three years from its imposition and every two years thereafter (s. 695.1).

. . .

[22] As already mentioned the case raises issues concerning ss. 7, 9, 11 and 12 of the Charter. Indeed, several s. 7 issues are raised, the most fundamental of which, and hence the one with which I propose to begin, being whether the imposition of preventive detention for an indeterminate period offends against the principles of fundamental justice. The remaining s. 7 issues focus not on the punishment itself, but on the fairness of the process by which the deprivation of liberty is occasioned. I therefore propose to discuss the issues raised by the appellant under the following headings:

1. Does Part XXI violate s. 7 of the Charter? Specifically, does it offend against principles of fundamental justice to impose preventive detention as punishment for committing a crime?
2. Does Part XXI violate s. 12 of the Charter?
3. Does Part XXI violate s. 9 of the Charter?
4. Does Part XXI violate s. 7 of the Charter in other respects? Are the procedures by which the deprivation of liberty is occasioned, the standard of proof required under Part XXI, or the use of psychiatric evidence in a Part XXI application fundamentally unfair to offenders sought to be designated as dangerous? (An aspect of the foregoing inquiry concerns the more discrete question whether s. 17(f) of the Charter requires that a Part XXI application be heard by a jury.)
5. Were the appellant's rights under s. 7 violated by the Crown's failure to give the appellant notice before his election and plea?

A. Does Part XXI by Imposing Indeterminate Detention Offend Against Fundamental Justice Under Section 7 of the Charter?

[23] In *Ref re Section 94(2) of the Motor Vehicle Act*, [1985] 2 SCR 486, this court held that the phrase "principles of fundamental justice" sets out the parameters of the right not to be deprived of life, liberty and security of the person. These principles were stated to inhere in the basic tenets and principles not only of the judicial system but also of the other components of our legal system (at p. 512, per Lamer J). Hence, to determine whether Part XXI violates the principles of fundamental justice by the deprivation of liberty suffered by the offender, it is necessary to examine Part XXI in light of the basic principles of penal policy that have animated legislative and judicial practice in Canada and other common law jurisdictions.

[24] The appellant submits that Part XXI results in a deprivation of liberty that is not in accordance with the principles of fundamental justice, in that it permits an individual to be sentenced for crimes which he or she has not committed or for crimes for which he or she has already been punished. If this statement correctly described what in fact occurs under Part XXI, it would indeed constitute a violation of s. 7. The reality, however, is quite different. What s. 688 does is to permit a judge to impose a sentence of indeterminate detention on an individual for having committed an offence, which sentence is "*in lieu of* any other sentence that might be imposed *for the offence for which the offender has been convicted*" (emphasis added). The individual is clearly being sentenced for the "serious personal injury offence" he or she has been found guilty of committing, albeit in a different way than would ordinarily be done. It must be remembered that the appellant was not picked up off the street because of his past criminality (for which he has already been punished), or because of fears or suspicions about his criminal proclivities, and then subjected to a procedure in order to determine whether society would be better off if he were incarcerated indefinitely. Rather he was arrested and prosecuted for a very serious violent crime and subjected to a procedure aimed at determining the appropriate penalty that should be inflicted upon him in the circumstances.

[25] Thus the appellant's contention that he is being punished for what he might do rather than for what he has done, or, in more traditional terms, that he is being found

guilty in the absence of a finding of the requisite *actus reus*, must be rejected. The punishment, as I noted, flows from the actual commission of a specific crime, the requisite elements of which have been proved to exist beyond a reasonable doubt.

[26] Nor do I find it objectionable that the offender's designation as dangerous or the subsequent indeterminate sentence is based, in part, on a conclusion that the past violent, antisocial behaviour of the offender will likely continue in the future. Such considerations play a role in a very significant number of sentences. I accordingly agree with the respondent's submission that it cannot be considered a violation of fundamental justice for Parliament to identify those offenders who, in the interests of protecting the public, ought to be sentenced according to considerations which are not entirely reactive or based on a "just deserts" rationale. The imposition of a sentence which "is partly punitive but is mainly imposed for the protection of the public" (*Re Moore and R* (1984), 54 OR (2d) 3 (HC)) seems to me to accord with the fundamental purpose of the criminal law generally, and of sentencing in particular, namely, the protection of society. In a rational system of sentencing, the respective importance of prevention, deterrence, retribution and rehabilitation will vary according to the nature of the crime and the circumstances of the offender. No one would suggest that any of these functional considerations should be excluded from the legitimate purview of legislative or judicial decisions regarding sentencing.

[27] It is thus important to recognize the precise nature of the penological objectives embodied in Part XXI. It is clear that the indeterminate detention is intended to serve both punitive and preventive purposes. Both are legitimate aims of the criminal sanction. Indeed, when society incarcerates a robber for, say, ten years, it is clear that its goal is both to punish the person and to prevent the recurrence of such conduct during that period. Preventive detention in the context of Part XXI, however, simply represents a judgment that the relative importance of the objectives of rehabilitation, deterrence and retribution are greatly attenuated in the circumstances of the individual case, and that of prevention correspondingly increased. Part XXI merely enables the court to accommodate its sentence to the common sense reality that the *present* condition of the offender is such that he or she is not inhibited by normal standards of behavioural restraint, so that *future* violent acts can quite confidently be expected of that person. In such circumstances it would be folly not to tailor the sentence accordingly.

[28] It is noteworthy that numerous examples exist, both in Canada and abroad, of ways in which the need to protect the public from the risk of convicted persons reoffending has been taken into consideration by the judiciary and legislature alike.

[29] The case law criteria for imposing a life sentence closely parallel those embodied in Part XXI. Indeed, life sentences and Part XXI sentences are primarily imposed for the same purposes and on the same type of offender. In *R v. Hill* (1974), 15 CCC (2d) 145 (Ont. CA), Jessup JA stated, at pp. 147-48:

> When an accused has been convicted of a serious crime in itself calling for a substantial sentence and when he suffers from some mental or personality disorder rendering him a danger to the community but not subjecting him to confinement in a mental institution and when it is uncertain when, if ever, the accused will be cured of his affliction, in my opinion the appropriate sentence is one of life. Such a sentence in such circumstances amounts to

an indefinite sentence under which the Parole Board can release him to the community when it is satisfied, upon adequate psychiatric examination, it is in the interests of the accused and of the community for him to return to society. The policy expressed in my opinion is that of the Criminal Division of the English court of Appeal: *cf.* Thomas, *Principles of Sentencing*, at pp. 272-9.

· · ·

[30] It is true that the *Hill* principle, which amounts to judge-made dangerous offender law, has clearly been limited by subsequent decisions. However, the basis of the retrenchment has not been a rejection of the principle of indeterminate detention for dangerous offenders. Rather, it has been the concern that the *Hill* principle not be used to circumvent the provisions of Part XXI with its attendant safeguards for the offender. As Martin JA, for the Ontario Court of Appeal, observed in *R v. Crosby* (1982), 1 CCC (3d) 233 at 240:

> The Crown, in our view, properly invoked the dangerous offender legislation in this case. This court has said on more than one occasion that rather than sentence a person who has been convicted of a serious offence and who is a continuing danger to life imprisonment, the prosecution should proceed under the dangerous offender provisions, where the offender has greater protection.

· · ·

[36] From what I have said already, I do not think that it could seriously be argued that the penological objectives embodied in Part XXI themselves violate s. 7 of the Charter. However, it is clear that the present Charter inquiry is concerned also, if not primarily, with the *effects* of the legislation. This requires investigating the "treatment meted out," i.e., what is actually done to the offender and how that is accomplished. Whether this "treatment" violates constitutional precepts seems to me to be an issue more aptly discussed under ss. 9 and 12 of the Charter, because these provisions focus on specific manifestations of the principles of fundamental justice. For convenience, I shall begin with s. 12.

B. Does Part XXI Constitute Cruel and Unusual Punishment Under Section 12 of the Charter?

[37] The appellant contends that Part XXI violates s. 12 of the Charter in that it imposes a punishment that is unusually severe and serves no valid penological purpose more effectively than a less severe punishment (e.g. a determinate sentence).

[38] This issue was addressed in *Re Moore and R*, supra and *R v. Langevin* (1984), 39 CR (3d) 333 (Ont. CA). In *Re Moore*, Ewaschuk J appears to have been influenced by the fact that this court had, in *Ex parte Matticks*, [1973] SCR vi, 15 CCC (2d) 213 [Que.], upheld the previous habitual offender legislation under s. 2(b) of the *Canadian Bill of Rights*, RSC 1970, App. III, which provides that no law of Canada shall be construed or applied so as to "impose or authorize the imposition of cruel and unusual treatment or punishment." If that more Draconian legislation was valid, he reasoned, so must the present legislation be valid. The reasons given by Ewaschuk J for sustaining the legislation may be summarized thus: the legislation would be acceptable to a large segment of the population; the specificity of the statutory requirements ensured their

application on a rational basis; the protection of society is an important social purpose; the legislation is not an affront to public standards of decency given the procedural safeguards built into the process; and finally, the legislation is tailored so as not to be disproportionate to the crime and the offender's potential to harm others. Although all punishment is in some degree degrading to human dignity, he concluded, Part XXI is not impermissibly, or cruelly and unusually, degrading to human dignity.

[39] While I agree with much of this reasoning, it is unnecessary to examine it in any detail. For since that decision, this court, in *Smith v. R*, 25th June 1987, [now reported (sub nom. *R v. Smith*) [1987] 1 SCR 1045], has had the opportunity to review the scope and meaning of s. 12, and it is against the backdrop of that case that this issue must be decided. *Smith* dealt with whether s. 5(2) of the *Narcotic Control Act*, RSC 1970, c. N-1, in providing for a mandatory minimum sentence of seven years on all persons found guilty of importing a narcotic, offended the right of individuals not to be subjected to cruel and unusual treatment or punishment. A majority of this court held that s. 5(2) did violate s. 12 and was not sustainable under s. 1 of the Charter.

[40] Lamer J, speaking for the majority, set out the parameters of the right not to be subjected to cruel and unusual treatment or punishment in the following terms:

> In my view, the protection afforded by s. 12 governs the quality of the punishment and is concerned with the effect that the punishment may have on the person on whom it is imposed. I would agree with Laskin CJC in *Miller*, ... where he defined the phrase "cruel and unusual" as a "compendious expression of a norm." The criterion which must be applied in order to determine whether a punishment is cruel and unusual within the meaning of s. 12 of the Charter is, to use the words of Laskin CJC in *Miller* at p. 688, "whether the punishment prescribed is so excessive as to outrage standards of decency." In other words, though the state may impose punishment, the effect of that punishment must not be grossly disproportionate to what would have been appropriate.
>
> In imposing a sentence of imprisonment, the judge will assess the circumstances of the case in order to arrive at an appropriate sentence. The test for review under s. 12 of the Charter is one of gross disproportionality, because it is aimed at punishments that are more than merely excessive. We should be careful not to stigmatize every disproportionate or excessive sentence as being a constitutional violation, and should leave to the usual sentencing appeal process the task of reviewing the fitness of a sentence. Section 12 will be infringed only where the sentence is so unfit having regard to the offence and the offender as to be grossly disproportionate.
>
> In assessing whether a sentence is grossly disproportionate, the court must first consider the gravity of the offence, the personal characteristics of the offender and the particular circumstances of the case in order to determine what range of sentences would have been appropriate to punish, rehabilitate or deter this particular offender or to protect the public from this particular offender. The other purposes which may be pursued by the imposition of punishment, in particular the deterrence of other potential offenders, are thus not relevant at this stage of the inquiry. This does not mean that the judge or the legislator can no longer consider general deterrence or other penological purposes that go beyond the particular offender in determining a sentence, but only that the resulting sentence must not be grossly disproportionate to what the offender deserves. If a grossly disproportionate

sentence is "prescribed by law," then the purpose which it seeks to attain will fall to be assessed under s. 1. Section 12 ensures that individual offenders receive punishments that are appropriate, or at least not grossly disproportionate, to their particular circumstances, while s. 1 permits this right to be overridden to achieve some important societal objective.

One must measure the effect of the sentence actually imposed. If it is grossly disproportionate to what would have been appropriate, then it infringes s. 12. The effect of the sentence is often a composite of many factors and is not limited to the quantum or duration of the sentence but includes its nature and the conditions under which it is applied. Sometimes by its length alone or by its very nature will the sentence be grossly disproportionate to the purpose sought. Sometimes it will be the result of the combination of factors which, when considered in isolation, would not in and of themselves amount to gross disproportionality. For example, 20 years for a first offence against property would be grossly disproportionate, but so would three months of imprisonment, if the prison authorities decide it should be served in solitary confinement. ...

The numerous criteria proposed pursuant to s. 2(b) of the *Canadian Bill of Rights* and the Eighth Amendment of the American Constitution are, in my opinion, useful as factors to determine whether a violation of s. 12 has occurred. Thus, to refer to the tests listed by Professor Tarnopolsky, the determination of whether the punishment is necessary to achieve a valid penal purpose, whether it is founded on recognized sentencing principles, and whether there exist valid alternatives to the punishment imposed, are all guidelines which, without being determinative in themselves, help to assess whether the punishment is grossly disproportionate.

[41] It is clear from the foregoing that s. 12 is concerned with the relation between the effects of, and reasons for, punishment. At the initial stage of the inquiry into proportionality, those effects are to be balanced against the particular circumstances of the offence, the characteristics of the offender and the particular purposes sought to be accomplished in sentencing that person in the manner challenged. If, in light of these considerations, the punishment is found to be grossly disproportionate, a remedy must be afforded the offender in the absence of social objectives that transcend the circumstances of the particular case and are capable of justifying the punishment under s. 1 of the Charter.

[42] Let us first consider the substantive ways in which the present legislation itself seeks to accommodate the conflicting interests, on the one hand, of society in seeking to protect itself from dangerous criminals and, on the other, of the offender in not being subjected to punishment grossly disproportionate to the offence and the circumstances of the individual case. It seems to me that the legislative criteria embodied in s. 688 for designating offenders as dangerous and for sentencing such persons tend, although not conclusively, to sustain the legislation as not constituting a violation of s. 12. I say "not conclusively" for, as will be seen, it is only when s. 688 is read in the context of the scheme as a whole that the legislation can be upheld.

[43] First, the legislation applies only to persons convicted of a "serious personal injury offence" as defined in s. 687. These offences all relate to conduct tending to cause severe physical danger or severe psychological injury to other persons. Significantly, the maximum penalty for all these offences must be at least ten years' imprison-

ment. Secondly, it must be established to the satisfaction of the court that the offence for which the person has been convicted is not an isolated occurrence, but part of a pattern of behaviour which has involved violence, aggressive or brutal conduct, or a failure to control sexual impulses. Thirdly, it must be established that the pattern of conduct is very likely to continue and to result in the kind of suffering against which the section seeks to protect, namely, conduct endangering the life, safety or physical well-being of others or, in the case of sexual offences, conduct causing injury, pain or other evil to other persons. Also explicit in one form or another in each subsection of s. 687 is the requirement that the court must be satisfied that the pattern of conduct is substantially or pathologically intractable. Finally, the court has the discretion not to designate the offender as dangerous or to impose an indeterminate sentence, even in circumstances where all of these criteria are met.

[44] It seems to me that, having concluded that the legislative objectives embodied in Part XXI are not only of substantial importance to society's well-being but, at least in theory, sufficiently important to warrant limiting certain rights and freedoms, one must equally conclude that the legislative classification of the target group of offenders meets the highest standard of rationality (and I use the word not as a term of art) and proportionality that society could reasonably expect of Parliament. Not only has a diligent attempt been made to carefully define a very small group of offenders whose personal characteristics and particular circumstances militate strenuously in favour of preventive incarceration, but it would be difficult to imagine a better-tailored set of criteria that could effectively accomplish the purposes sought to be attained.

[45] However, the legislative classification of offenders as dangerous is only one aspect of the "means analysis" under s. 12. It is equally important to consider the constitutional validity, under s. 12, of the actual "treatment meted out." There can be no doubt that detention per se, and preventive detention in particular, is not cruel and unusual in the case of dangerous offenders, for the group to whom the legislation applies has been functionally defined so as to ensure that persons within the group evince the very characteristics that render such detention necessary.

[46] It is argued, however, that it is not the detention itself but its *indeterminate quality* that harbours the potential for cruel and unusual punishment. And it is difficult to deny that the effects of an indeterminate sentence on a dangerous offender must be profoundly devastating. It has, for instance, been argued before the court that the imposition of an indeterminate sentence, because of its uncertainty, saps the will of an offender, removing any incentive to rehabilitate himself or herself. However, this is equally true of a "determinate" life sentence such as is provided for by s. 306(1)(b). Indeed, in view of the provisions regarding parole, it is possible, at least theoretically, that a dangerous offender could be released consequent on his first review, three years after the detention was imposed and well in advance of the seven or so years an offender serving a life sentence must serve before his or her first such review. This is, however, rather unrealistic. Evidence before the court indicated that between 1980 and 1986 only six dangerous offenders were granted day parole, two of whom had served 10 to 15 years, three 15 to 20 years, and one more than 20 years.

[47] In truth, there is a significant difference between the effect of a Part XXI sentence and other, more typical sentences. When a person is imprisoned for an absolute

and determinate period, there is at least the certainty that the incarceration will end at the termination of that period. The convicted person, during the term of sentence, can remain in a passive state, secure in the knowledge that he or she will be released thereafter. For the offender undergoing an indeterminate sentence, however, the sole hope of release is parole. The ordinary convict, it is true, can also choose to actively affect the length of his or her sentence by attempting to conform his or her behaviour to meet the expectations of the parole board. But, whatever the legal nature of the interest in the availability of parole may be in general, it seems to me that, as a *factual* matter, the availability of parole is not as important a factor in deciding whether a determinate sentence is cruel and unusual as it is in assessing the constitutionality of a Part XXI sentence.

[48] This is so because in the context of a determinate sentencing scheme the availability of parole represents an additional super-added protection of the liberty interests of the offender. In the present context, however, it is, subsequent to the actual imposition of the sentence itself, the sole protection of the dangerous offender's liberty interests. Indeed, from the point of view of the dangerous offender, his or her detention is never complete until it is factually complete. In this sense, each opportunity for parole will appear to the dangerous offender as the sole mechanism for terminating his or her detention, for rendering it certain. Moreover, it is clear that an enlightened inquiry under s. 12 must concern itself first and foremost with the way in which the effects of punishment are likely to be experienced. Seen in this light, therefore, the parole process assumes the utmost significance, for it is that process alone that is capable of truly accommodating and tailoring the sentence to fit the circumstances of the individual offender.

[49] In my opinion, if the sentence imposed under Part XXI was indeterminate, simpliciter, it would be certain, at least occasionally, to result in sentences grossly disproportionate to what individual offenders deserved. However, I believe that the parole process saves the legislation from being successfully challenged under s. 12, for it ensures that incarceration is imposed for only as long as the circumstances of the individual case require.

[50] When an indeterminate sentence is imposed, Part XXI provides for periodic review, for the purposes of determining whether parole should be granted, of the "*condition, history and circumstances of that person*," after the first three years of detention and every two years thereafter. Section 695.1 provides as follows:

> 695.1(1) Subject to subsection (2), where a person is in custody under a sentence of detention in a penitentiary for an indeterminate period, the National Parole Board shall, forthwith after the expiration of three years from the day on which that person was taken into custody and not later than every two years thereafter, review the condition, history and circumstances of that person for the purpose of determining whether he should be granted parole under the *Parole Act* and, if so, on what conditions.
>
> (2) Where a person is in custody under a sentence of detention in a penitentiary for an indeterminate period that was imposed before the *Criminal Law Amendment Act, 1977* came into force, the National Parole Board shall, at least once in every year, review the condition, history and circumstances of that person for the purpose of determining whether he should be granted parole under the *Parole Act* and, if so, on what conditions.

The criteria in light of which an application for parole is considered are specified in s. 10(1)(a) of the *Parole Act*, RSC 1970, c. P-2:

10(1) the Board may

(a) grant parole to an inmate, subject to any terms or conditions it considers desirable, if the Board considers that

(i) in the case of a grant of parole other than day parole, the inmate has derived the maximum benefit from imprisonment.

(ii) the reform and rehabilitation of the inmate will be aided by the grant of parole, and

the release of the inmate on parole would not constitute an undue risk to society;

[51] While the criteria embodied in s. 10(1)(a) do not purport to replicate the factual findings required to sentence the offender to an indeterminate term of imprisonment, they do afford a measure of tailoring adequate to save the legislation from violating s. 12. It must be remembered that the offender is being sentenced indeterminately because *at the time of sentencing* he was found to have a certain propensity. The sentence is imposed "in lieu of any other sentence" that might have been imposed and, like any other such sentence, must be served according to its tenor. *The offender is not being sentenced to a term of imprisonment until he is no longer a dangerous offender.* Indeed, s. 695.1 provides that the circumstances of the offender be reviewed for the purpose of determining whether *parole* should be granted and, if so, on what conditions; it does not provide that the label of dangerous offender be removed or altered. Finally, the very words of s. 695.1 of the *Code* and s. 10(1)(a) of the *Parole Act* establish an ongoing process for rendering the sentence meted out to a dangerous offender one that accords with his or her specific circumstances.

[52] It may be argued that the legislation could be better tailored. For example, it might have been argued that the review process should focus solely on whether the offender continued to possess the characteristics that defined him or her as a proper subject of indeterminate detention. Indeed, one might say that to ask, as the Parole Board does, whether the individual has been reformed or rehabilitated is to pose a question that ex hypothesis cannot be answered affirmatively, for it was implicit in the designation of the offender as dangerous that he or she was not amenable to rehabilitation by usual means. However, this argument must be rejected for a number of reasons.

[53] To begin with, the criteria actually used serve to emphasize the point made earlier in this judgment that sentencing, even under Part XXI, embodies a complex of penological objectives. I do not think it can be argued, as a matter either of logic or of common sense, that, by virtue of a decision to sentence an offender according to considerations based *primarily* on prevention, other equally valid, subsisting penal goals cease to be relevant. To reiterate, protecting society from the dangerous offender never wholly supplants the other legitimate objectives embodied in a Part XXI sentence.

[54] Seen in this light, it would be preposterous to require of dangerous offenders only that they demonstrate to the parole board that they have ceased to be "dangerous" (in terms identical to those used in Part XXI), for this would require of them a lesser showing than is required of other convicts. It seems to me that, had s. 695.1 provided

for a "dangerous offender review," rather than a parole review, but borrowed the identical criteria employed in the *Parole Act*, it would perhaps be more readily apparent that the review provided for does indeed accomplish the requisite tailoring sufficient to sustain the legislative scheme as a whole. Section 10(1)(a)(iii) requires the board to consider whether the release of the inmate would constitute an "undue risk" to society; if the accused continues to be dangerous, then by definition this criterion remains unsatisfied. Section 10(1)(a) also requires that the board be satisfied that the inmate has derived the maximum benefit from incarceration and that the inmate's reform and rehabilitation would be aided by release.

[55] These criteria seem to me to be no less pertinent reflections of society's concerns in releasing dangerous offenders than they are in releasing other offenders. The fact that dangerous offenders may be less likely to satisfy these requirements is primarily a function of their dangerousness, not of the punishment imposed. Of course, the imposition of an indeterminate sentence may, like all sentences, sap the will of the offender to rehabilitate himself or herself. However, I would have thought the incentive to reform is far greater, at least theoretically, in the case of a dangerous offender. In this regard, I note that the availability of parole has been seen to validate mandatory life sentences in the context of similarly-motivated legislation in the United States: see *Solem v. Helm*, [100 S Ct. 3001 (1983)], per Powell J, for the majority.

[56] Furthermore, I am not sure that to inquire into the presence or absence of less restrictive means is wholly compatible with the insistence of this court in *Smith*, supra, that s. 12 redress only punishment that is *grossly disproportionate* to the circumstances of any given case. The word "grossly," it seems to me, reflects this court's concern not to hold Parliament to a standard so exacting at least in the context of s. 12, as to require punishments to be perfectly suited to accommodate the moral nuances of every crime and every offender.

[57] I would therefore conclude that Part XXI does not violate s. 12 of the Charter.

. . .

C. Does Part XXI Violate Section 9 of the Charter by Authorizing Arbitrary Detention or Imprisonment?

[59] Counsel for the appellant contended that Part XXI violates the right of persons not to be arbitrarily detained or imprisoned, contrary to s. 9 of the Charter. He suggested that Part XXI results in arbitrary detention in the following respects: the test of "likelihood" under Part XXI is unconstitutionally vague; the labelling of persons as dangerous offenders is arbitrary, since it is based on inherently unreliable psychiatric evidence; and there are no guidelines with respect to the invocation of Part XXI such that the prosecutor has unfettered discretion as to when to make a dangerous offender application.

[60] This court has not yet pronounced on the scope of s. 9 and the meaning of the words "arbitrarily detained or imprisoned," and I do not think this would be an appropriate case to do so. The issue was not strenuously argued by the parties or examined in depth in the courts below. More to the point, however, is that, in my view, even assuming that s. 9 were given the broadest possible interpretation, the appellant's submissions in this regard must fail.

[61] There has been considerable controversy in the lower courts as to whether the ambit of protection afforded by s. 9 extends to imprisonment or detention specifically authorized under existing law or whether s. 9 is ipso facto satisfied when imprisonment is imposed in accordance with legislative requirements: see the cases canvassed in *R v. Konechny*, 38 CR (3d) 69 (BCCA), per Lambert JA, dissenting, at pp. 70-71. However, assuming that the right to attack a sentence under s. 9 is not foreclosed by the fact that it is legislatively prescribed, and that the statutory procedures have been judicially complied with (see *Re Mitchell and R* (1983), 42 OR (2d) 481 (sub nom. *Mitchell v. Ont. (AG)*), 6 CCC (3d) 193 (HC), per Linden J at p. 293), it seems to me that in no sense of the word can the imprisonment resulting from the successful invocation of Part XXI be considered "arbitrary." Indeed, when one fleshes out the specific submissions of the appellant in this regard they appear to be merely attempts to recast issues considered elsewhere in this judgment. For example, although the first two submissions made under this heading are directed to the alleged lack of proportionality or adequacy, in constitutional terms, of the legislative means to the objectives sought to be attained, they are not independently addressed to the arbitrary nature of the imprisonment. To the extent that these arguments reflect the appellant's concern that the procedure for the designation of offenders as dangerous is, in general terms, impermissibly unfair, I will address these arguments later under s. 7, where they properly belong. Similarly, to the extent that they belie a fear that punishment is being imposed without due concern for the circumstances of the particular offender, I have already addressed these arguments under s. 12.

[62] However, even giving the word "arbitrary" its broadest signification, it is readily apparent that, not only is the incarceration statutorily authorized, but that the legislation narrowly defines a class of offenders with respect to whom it may properly be invoked, and prescribes quite specifically the conditions under which an offender may be designated as dangerous. If these criteria are themselves unconstitutional, it is because they otherwise fail adequately to safeguard the liberty of the individual, not because they are arbitrary. Indeed, as Ewaschuk J observed in *Re Moore*, supra, at p. 314, "the legislative criteria for finding a person a dangerous offender is [sic] perhaps the most detailed and demanding in the *Criminal Code*." Moreover, implicit in my discussion of the s. 12 issue is the common sense conclusion that the criteria in Part XXI are anything but arbitrary in relation to the objectives sought to be attained; they are clearly designed to segregate a small group of highly dangerous criminals posing threats to the physical or mental well-being of their victims.

[63] As I see it, then, the sole issue left for consideration under s. 9 is whether the lack of uniformity in the treatment of dangerous persons that arises by virtue of the prosecutorial discretion to make an application under Part XXI constitutes unconstitutional arbitrariness. The appellant is not suggesting that prosecutors, in his case or generally, have exercised their discretion arbitrarily in this regard. Indeed, the affidavit evidence filed by the Crown in the companion case of *Milne v. R* [now reported post, p. 55 (sub nom. *R v. Milne*), [1987] 2 SCR 512] indicates that from 1978 to 1986 an average of only seven persons per year were sentenced under Part XXI. On average, each offender committed 12.12 offences, 2.2 of which were violent and 3.53 of which were sexual in nature. This suggests that the legislation has in general not been abused. I have no doubt

that, if and when it is alleged that a prosecutor in a particular case was motivated by improper or arbitrary reasons in making a Part XXI application, a s. 24 remedy would lie. However, I do not think there is any warrant for presuming that the executive will act unconstitutionally or for improper purposes.

[64] More important, however, is the fact that prosecutors always have a discretion in prosecuting criminals to the full extent of the law, an aspect of which involves making sentencing submissions. In this respect, I am in complete agreement with Crown counsel's submission that "... it is the absence of discretion which would, in many cases, render arbitrary the law's application." As he notes, "the absence of any discretion with respect to Part XXI would necessarily require the Crown to always proceed under Part XXI if there was the barest *prima facie* and the Court, upon making a finding that the offender is a dangerous offender, would always be required to impose an indeterminate sentence."

[65] The foregoing also dispenses with the argument, not pursued here, that the judge ought not to have discretion with respect to whether he or she sentences an offender found to be dangerous to an indeterminate sentence. As Ewaschuk J stated in *Re Moore*, supra, at p. 310, the offender cannot be heard to complain of a discretion that can operate only to the offender's benefit. Indeed, it is apparent that one feature of s. 5(2) of the *Narcotic Control Act* that disturbed this court in *Smith*, supra, was the very fact that the imposition of sentence followed automatically upon conviction.

[66] The remaining argument is that the prosecutorial discretion results in a geographical lack of uniformity and that this constitutes impermissible arbitrariness. However, the appellant is not arguing, as the accused did in *Morgentaler v. R*, SCC, 28th January 1988 (not yet reported), that this lack of uniformity is mandated by the terms of the legislation (which may or may not be a meritorious argument). Rather, this argument appears to recast the prosecutorial discretion argument. Moreover, variation among provinces in this regard may be inevitable, and indeed desirable, in a country where a federal statute is administered by local authorities. In any event, it may be observed parenthetically that, while the affidavit evidence suggests that dangerous offender applications are made more frequently in British Columbia (25 per cent of all such applications), and, perhaps surprisingly, never in Quebec, Newfoundland, Manitoba or Prince Edward Island, no attempt has been made to explain the significance of this data, for example, by relating it to the relevant population of offenders potentially coming within the provisions of Part XXI.

[67] Having dealt with the broader issues, I now turn to the more specifically procedural issues raised by the appellant.

D. Are the Part XXI Procedures by Which This Deprivation of Liberty Is Occasioned and Reviewed Fundamentally Unfair?

(i) Does Section 11(f) of the Charter Require a Jury Hearing of a Part XXI Application?

[68] Section 689(2) of the *Code* provides that an application under Part XXI shall be heard and determined by the court without a jury. The appellant submits that the

procedure for designating an offender as dangerous is unfair and contrary to ss. 7 and 11(f) of the Charter, in particular, by denying the offender the right to the benefit of a jury's determination of dangerousness. I shall deal with the s. 11(f) issue first.

[69] Section 11(f) of the Charter provides that:

> 11. Any person charged with an offence has the right ...
>
> (f) ... to the benefit of trial by jury where the maximum punishment for the offence is imprisonment for five years or a more severe punishment.

[70] The key issue, for s. 11 purposes, is whether the Crown application to declare the offender a dangerous offender is equivalent to "charging" the offender with "an offence," for it is obvious that such offenders are liable to detention for periods much longer than five years.

· · ·

[74] There would seem to be no warrant for reconsidering the conclusion of this court that the "labelling" procedure does not constitute the charge of an offence. Nor do I think that a different conclusion can be justified for the purposes of s. 11 of the Charter. As I observed in *Schmidt v. R* (sub nom. *Can. v. Schmidt*), [1987] 1 SCR 500, the phrase "any person charged with an offence" in the opening words of the section must be given a constant meaning that harmonizes with the various paragraphs of the section. It seems clear to me that for the purposes of s. 11 it would be quite inappropriate to conclude that a convicted person is charged with an offence when confronted with a Part XXI application. How can it be said that the right to the presumption of innocence until proven *guilty* (s. 11(d)) and the right to bail (s. 11(e)), for example, could have any application in the context of the unique post-conviction proceeding mandated by Part XXI?

(ii) Does Section 7 of the Charter Require a Jury Hearing and Do the Part XXI Hearing and Review Procedures Otherwise Meet the Standard of Fairness Under That Section?

[75] The conclusion that the appellant is not entitled to the benefit of trial by jury under s. 11(f) does not, however, conclusively decide the question whether he is entitled to a determination by a jury of the question of his dangerousness, or, more generally, whether the procedural incidents of the proceeding are constitutionally adequate to safeguard his liberty.

· · ·

[84] The cases to which I have referred dealt primarily with the use of hearsay evidence in such proceedings and with the question whether dangerousness could constitutionally be proved simply on a preponderance of evidence rather than beyond a reasonable doubt. Quite apart from the specific conclusions of the American courts respecting these matters, I would adopt the functional reasons given by those courts for viewing the "labelling" hearing to be the kind of hearing that attracts a high level of procedural protection for the offender. I find their approach to be more attuned to the distinctive nature of such inquiries, and more congruent with the reality of the very profound consequences that the labelling procedure harbours for the offender. Nevertheless,

I would conclude that it is not required, as a constitutional matter, that the determination of dangerousness be made by a jury.

[85] It is clear that, at a minimum, the requirements of fundamental justice embrace the requirements of procedural fairness: see, e.g., the comments to this effect of Wilson J in *Singh v. Can. (Min. of Employment & Immigration); Thandi v. Can. (Min. of Employment & Immigration); Mann v. Can. (Min. of Employment & Immigration)*, [1985] 1 SCR 177. It is also clear that the requirements of fundamental justice are not immutable; rather, they vary according to the context in which they are invoked. Thus certain procedural protections might be constitutionally mandated in one context but not in another. Suffice it to say, however, that a jury determination is not mandated in the present context. The offender has already been found guilty of an offence in a trial at which he had the option of invoking his right to a jury. Moreover, the procedure to which he was subjected subsequent to the finding of guilt does not impact on his liberty to the same extent as that initial determination. Indeed, this is made clear by the same considerations that led this court, in [*Brusch v. The Queen* (1953), 105 CCC 340 (SCC)], to classify the proceedings as part of the sentencing process. While the legal classification of the proceeding as part of the sentencing process does not necessarily decide the question of the scope of the procedural protection to be afforded the offender, the functional, factual considerations animating that conclusion must be taken into account.

[86] Finally, it is not insignificant that, unlike the situation in [*US v. Maroney*, 335 F2d 302 (1966)], the judge at such a hearing does retain a discretion whether or not to impose the designation or indeterminate sentence, or both.

[87] It is noteworthy, too, that Part XXI provides considerable procedural protection to the offender. Section 689(1)(a) requires that the consent of the Attorney General be obtained either before or after the application is made. Section 689(1)(b) requires that "at least seven days notice be given to the offender by the prosecution, following the making of the application, outlining the basis on which it is intended to found the application." Moreover, the offender has the right to attend, present evidence and cross-examine witnesses, in addition to a right of appeal in the broadest terms on questions of fact, law or mixed fact and law.

[88] It seems to me that s. 7 of the Charter entitles the appellant to a fair hearing; it does not entitle him to the most favourable procedures that could possibly be imagined. I do not think it can be argued that the procedure at a Part XXI application is unfair insofar as it denies to an offender the right to a jury's determination of his or her dangerousness.

· · ·

(iii) Is the Standard of Proof Required Under Part XXI, or the Use of Psychiatric Evidence in a Part XXI Application, Fundamentally Unfair?

[91] The appellant submits that Part XXI is fundamentally unfair in two other respects. He contends, first, that s. 688, in requiring proof that the offender constitutes a *threat* to the life, safety or physical or mental well-being of other persons, or that there is a *likelihood* of the offender causing injury, pain or other evil to other persons through a failure in the future to control his or her sexual impulses, is fundamentally unfair, in that the standard of proof required of the Crown is lower than that traditionally required

in the criminal law process. Secondly, he argues that s. 690, by requiring that psychiatric evidence be tendered on an application under Part XXI, is fundamentally unfair to the extent that such evidence is an unreliable predictor of future conduct.

[92] I do not believe that either of these submissions is valid. First, it is important to recognize exactly what is and what is not required to be proved on such an application. Subsection (a) and (b) of s. 688 both require proof that the offender represents a *threat* of some sort to society. It is nowhere required that it be proved that the offender *will* act in a certain way. Indeed, inherent in the notion of dangerousness is the risk, not the certainty, of harm.

[93] The appellant asserts that a "likelihood" is ipso facto not susceptible of proof beyond a reasonable doubt. He cites in support the following statement of Isabel Grant, in her article "Dangerous Offenders" (1985), 9 *Dalhousie LJ* 347, at p. 360:

> How does one prove beyond a reasonable doubt that at some time in *some* setting, an individual is *likely* to endanger *some* person[?] Surely if we add "beyond a reasonable doubt" to a "future likelihood" the sum total can be no greater than a balance of probabilities, a standard we would never accept in a criminal trial.

However, as Holmes has reminded us, the life of the law has not been logic: it has been experience. The criminal law must operate in a world governed by practical considerations rather than abstract logic and, as a matter of practicality, the most that can be established in a future context is a likelihood of certain events occurring. To doubt this conclusion is, in actuality, to doubt the validity of the legislative objectives embodied in Part XXI, for to require certainty in such matters would be tantamount to rendering the entire process ineffective.

[94] Moreover, I am not convinced, even as a matter of logic, that the appellant's submission is sound. It seems to me that a "likelihood" of specified future conduct occurring is the finding of fact required to be established; it is not, at one and the same time, the means of proving that fact. Logically, it seems clear to me that an individual can be found to constitute a *threat* to society without insisting that this require the court to assert an ability to predict the future. I do not find it illogical for a court to assert that it is satisfied beyond a reasonable doubt that the test of dangerousness has been met, that there exists a *certain* potential for harm. That this is really only an apparent paradox is aptly captured by Morden J in *R v. Knight* (1975), 27 CCC (2d) 343 at 356 (Ont. HC):

> I wish to make it clear that when I refer to the requisite standard of proof respecting likelihood I am not imposing on myself an obligation to find it proven beyond a reasonable doubt that certain events will happen in the future—this, in the nature of things would be impossible in practically every case—but I do refer to the quality and strength of the evidence of past and present facts together with the expert opinion thereon, as an existing basis for finding present likelihood of future conduct.

[95] Having said the foregoing, it seems to me that when the appellant asserts that proof of a likelihood beyond a reasonable doubt still amounts merely to proof of a likelihood, it becomes apparent that what he is challenging is not the standard of proof but the fact that certain persons found to be "dangerous" will in fact not have been dangerous. This is the problem of "false positives," which I will address below.

[96] I believe that the foregoing discussion also disposes of the contention that it is fundamentally unfair to the offender to require proof of dangerousness to be based in part on psychiatric evidence. Counsel for the appellant cited both academic and judicial authority recognizing the inability of psychiatrists, or anyone else, for that matter, to predict accurately future events. This is hardly a revelation. Indeed, the psychiatrists who testified at the hearing in the present case expressly disavowed any such claim.

[97] It seems to me that the answer to this argument can be briefly stated. The test for admissibility is relevance, not infallibility. Judges at Part XXI hearings do not assume that psychiatrists can accurately predict the future; however, psychiatric evidence is clearly relevant to the issue whether a person is likely to behave in a certain way, and indeed is probably relatively superior in this regard to the evidence of other clinicians and lay persons; see Menzies, Webster and Sepejak, "The Dimensions of Dangerousness" (1985), 9 *L & Human Behaviour* No. 1.

. . .

[99] Finally, the unreliability of psychiatric evidence also raises the problem of "false positives" (a statistical term representing the erroneous overprediction of future violence), discussed by Tobriner J for the majority of the California Supreme Court in *People v. Murtishaw*, 175 Cal. Rptr. 738 at 742-43:

> Numerous studies have demonstrated the inaccuracy of attempts to forecast future violent behaviour. Two commentators summarized the results as follows: "Whatever may be said for the reliability and validity of psychiatric judgments in general, there is literally no evidence that psychiatrists reliably and accurately can predict dangerous behaviour. To the contrary, such predictions are wrong more often than they are right." (Ennis & Litwack, *Psychiatry and the Presumption of Expertise: Flipping Coins in the Courtroom* (1974), 62 Cal. L Rev. 693, 737.) Professor Dershowitz in 1969 pointed to the skewed results characteristic of psychiatric forecasts: "it seems that psychiatrists are particularly prone to one type of error—over-predictions … [F]or every correct psychiatric prediction of violence, there are numerous erroneous predictions." (Dershowitz, *The Psychiatrist's Power in Civil Commitment: A Knife That Cuts Both Ways* (Feb. 1969), Psych. Today, at p. 47.) Cocozza and Steadman in 1976 reviewed the various studies and reported that "Whether one examined the legal, behavioural science, or psychiatric literature on predictions of dangerousness, one constantly encounters conclusions similar to the one reached by Dershowitz that psychiatrists are generally inaccurate predictors." (Cocozza & Steadman, *op. cit.*, supra, 29 Rutgers L Rev. at p. 1085.) In 1978 Professor Monahan undertook a further review of studies of violence prediction and noted that the percentage of false positives (erroneous predictions that a subject would engage in violent behaviour) never fell below 54 percent and went as high as 99.7 percent. (Monahan, *The Prediction and Control of Violent Behavior* (1978), pp. 179-196, in Hearings Before the House Subcom. on Domestic and International Scientific Planning, 95th Cong., 2d Sess., pp. 175-252.)

[100] This problem does not appear to undermine the utility and fairness of the scheme so much as to fortify the conclusion that the procedural protections accorded the offender, especially on review, ought to be very rigorous. In its *Report of the Committee on Mentally Abnormal Offenders*, the Butler Commission recognized the difficulties in assessing dangerousness but nevertheless recommended that the British Parliament

enact dangerous offender legislation with reviewable indeterminate sentences. It stated, at p. 60:

> [T]he fact that we cannot quantify the probability of future dangerous behaviour with actuarial precision is often allowed to obscure the fact that we can point with some confidence to categories of people who are more likely than others of the same sex and age-group to act in this way. Some kinds of sexual offence seem to be very repetitive. ... Men with several convictions of violence are considerably more likely than their peers to be convicted of violence in the future. Again, it is sometimes argued that even if there are good grounds—clinical or actuarial—for assigning the individual to a high risk group, he might be one of the minority in that group who in the event will not behave in accordance with probability. But this dilemma is inescapably involved in every decision which is based on probabilities. All that can be done is to weigh the unpleasantness of the consequences for the individual against the harm which he may do to others. If the harm is likely to be slight the decision should be in his favour: if great and highly probable—for example, if a sexual offence is accompanied by serious violence—the best we can do is to make sure that the precautions are as humane as possible.

Similarly, Floud and Young reject the notion that in enacting dangerous offender legislation Parliament unfairly sacrifices innocent persons in favour of the public good (at pp. 48-49):

> This argument is misconceived. Errors of prediction do not represent determinable individuals. It is not that we have difficulty in identifying the subjects of predicted error with the methods available to us; it is that they are in principle indeterminable. There are no hidden individuals identifiable in principle, but not in practice, who certainly would or would not reoffend. In this sense there are no innocent or guilty subjects of predictive judgment. ... The question is not "how many innocent persons are to sacrifice their liberty for the extra protection that special sentences for dangerous offenders will provide?" But "what is the moral choice between the alternative risks: the risk of harm to potential victims or the risk of unnecessarily detaining offenders judged to be dangerous?" *The essential nature of the problem of preventing wilful harm is misrepresented by talk of balancing individual and social costs. The problem is to make a just redistribution of risk in circumstances that do not permit of its being reduced.* There is a risk of harm to innocent persons at the hands of an offender who is judged likely to inflict it intentionally or recklessly—in any case culpably—in defiance or disregard of the usual constraints. His being in the wrong by virtue of the risk he represents is what entitles us to consider imposing on him the risk of unnecessary measures to save the risk of harm to innocent victims. [Emphasis added.]

I agree with this reasoning. Accordingly, the appellant's submissions on this point fail.

NOTE

As mentioned above, the recent amendments to the dangerous offender provisions altered the regime in the following ways: (1) s. 753(4) removes the discretion to impose a fixed sentence on a prisoner declared to be a dangerous offender; (2) s. 752.1 no longer requires the assessment of two psychiatrists, substituting the requirement of just one report;

(3) s. 753(2) allows a dangerous offender application to be made six months after the original imposition of sentence if new information arises; and (4) s. 761(1) delays the first parole review of dangerous offenders from three years to seven years. All of these changes were opposed by the Canadian Bar Association (see Canadian Bar Association (National Criminal Justice Section), *Submission on Bill C-55: Criminal Code Amendments High Risk Offenders* (February 1997)). Indeed, the Federal/Provincial/Territorial Task Force on High-Risk Violent Offenders issued the following caution (above, at 13):

> At their meeting in March, 1994, Ministers [responsible for justice] agreed not to amend Part XXIV of the *Criminal Code*, but rather to make better use of it. The Task Force reiterates its position that a major departure from the Dangerous Offender structure along the lines, for example, of the draft legislation developed in 1993, would run afoul of the Supreme Court of Canada's judgement in *R v. Lyons*. The Court stressed the importance of a well-tailored measure that will target specific high-risk offenders with a form of punishment that flows from the commission of a specific crime. A measure that would allow a Dangerous Offender application later in sentence, without clear evidence of a new offence, could conflict with the Charter protections against double punishment and arbitrary detention.
>
> The Task Force does recommend a few changes to the Dangerous Offender rules in the area of assessment, as described below. These changes should strengthen, rather than weaken, the current system.

Note that the task force did recommend that the law be changed such that, when an offender is declared to be a dangerous offender, an indeterminate sentence is mandatory (supra, at 21).

Do you think the dangerous offender provisions as they exist today would survive a constitutional challenge like the one in *Lyons*? Have the numerous protections in the legislation relied on in the reasons of La Forest J been altered to such a degree that the legislation is now constitutionally infirm? Consider whether *Lyons* is still the authentic baseline or standard for determining the constitutionality of this type of legislation. Does the treatment in 2003 of the 1997 amendments by the Supreme Court in *Johnson* also insulate them from renewed constitutional scrutiny?

III. LONG-TERM OFFENDERS

A. Background

As discussed in the introduction to this chapter, the long-term offender provisions were enacted in 1997. They were created on the recommendation of the Federal/Provincial/Territorial Task Force on High-Risk Violent Offenders. The provisions were designed to catch the type of offender who, while not worthy of the dangerous offender designation, still requires some form of preventive detention. Like the dangerous offender amendments, this measure arose from the government's (and the task force's) concern with "sexual predators." Remember that probation can be attached only to a sentence of imprisonment that is no longer than two years. The answer to this limitation was the creation of the long-term offender designation, which permits up to 10 years of supervision to be added onto a penitentiary sentence if the offender meets the "substantial risk" to reoffend standard in

s. 753.1. Thus, the long-term offender designation is a middle ground between an indeterminate sentence and an ordinary fixed-term sanction.

B. The Provisions

753.1(1) The court may, on application made under this Part following the filing of an assessment report under subsection 752.1(2), find an offender to be a long-term offender if it is satisfied that
> (a) it would be appropriate to impose a sentence of imprisonment of two years or more for the offence for which the offender has been convicted;
> (b) there is a substantial risk that the offender will reoffend; and
> (c) there is a reasonable possibility of eventual control of the risk in the community.

(2) The court shall be satisfied that there is a substantial risk that the offender will reoffend if
> (a) the offender has been convicted of an offence under section 151 (sexual interference), 152 (invitation to sexual touching) or 153 (sexual exploitation), subsection 173(2) (exposure) or section 271 (sexual assault), 272 (sexual assault with a weapon) or 273 (aggravated sexual assault), or has engaged in serious conduct of a sexual nature in the commission of another offence of which the offender has been convicted; and
> (b) the offender
>> (i) has shown a pattern of repetitive behaviour, of which the offence for which he or she has been convicted forms a part, that shows a likelihood of the offender's causing death or injury to other persons or inflicting severe psychological damage on other persons, or
>> (ii) by conduct in any sexual matter including that involved in the commission of the offence for which the offender has been convicted, has shown a likelihood of causing injury, pain or other evil to other persons in the future through similar offences.

(3) Subject to subsections (3.1), (4) and (5), if the court finds an offender to be a long-term offender, it shall
> (a) impose a sentence for the offence for which the offender has been convicted, which sentence must be a minimum punishment of imprisonment for a term of two years; and
> (b) order the offender to be supervised in the community, for a period not exceeding ten years, in accordance with section 753.2 and the *Corrections and Conditional Release Act.*

. . .

(4) The court shall not make an order under paragraph (3)(b) if the offender has been sentenced to life imprisonment.

(5) If the offender commits another offence while required to be supervised by an order made under paragraph(3)(b), and is thereby found to be a long-term offender, the periods of supervision to which the offender is subject at any particular time must not total more than ten years.

(6) If the court does not find an offender to be a long-term offender, the court shall impose sentence for the offence for which the offender has been convicted.

753.2(1) Subject to subsection (2), an offender who is required to be supervised by an order made under paragraph 753.1(3)(b) shall be supervised in accordance with the *Corrections and Conditional Release Act* when the offender has finished serving

(a) the sentence for the offence for which the offender has been convicted; and

(b) all other sentences for offences for which the offender is convicted and for which sentence of a term of imprisonment is imposed on the offender, either before or after the conviction for the offence referred to in paragraph (a).

(2) A sentence imposed on an offender referred to in subsection (1), other than a sentence that requires imprisonment of the offender, is to be served concurrently with the long-term supervision ordered under paragraph 753.1(3)(b).

(3) An offender who is required to be supervised, a member of the National Parole Board, or, on approval of that Board, the parole supervisor, as that expression is defined in subsection 134.2(2) of the *Corrections and Conditional Release Act*, of the offender, may apply to a superior court of criminal jurisdiction for an order reducing the period of long-term supervision or terminating it on the ground that the offender no long presents a substantial risk of reoffending and thereby being a danger to the community. The onus of providing that ground is on the applicant.

(4) The applicant must give notice of an application under subsection (3) to the Attorney General at the time the application is made.

753.3(1) An offender who is required to be supervised by an order made under paragraph 753.1(3)(b) and who, without reasonable excuse, fails or refuses to comply with that order is guilty of an indictable offence and liable to imprisonment for a term not exceeding ten years.

Note the sanctions for breach of long-term supervision that apply after the original sentence and the carceral warrant has expired. First, under s. 753.3(1), failure or refusal to comply without reasonable excuse is a new indictable offence subject to imprisonment. Second, under s. 135.1 of the *Corrections and Conditional Release Act*, the offender on long-term supervision can be suspended or returned to custody, or committed to a community-based residential facility or a mental health facility for up to 90 days.

C. Applying the Provisions

Judicial experience with the new provisions has been limited. Consider the interpretive issue addressed by the British Columbia Court of Appeal in *R v. McLeod* (1999), 136 CCC (3d) 492. That case involved a man who had not been convicted of sexual offences, but was charged with aggravated assault; use of a weapon during an assault; possession of a weapon for a purpose dangerous to the public peace; and uttering a threat to cause death or bodily harm. McLeod pleaded guilty to one count of assault causing bodily harm and one count of possession of a weapon for a purpose dangerous to the public peace. Subsequently, at his sentencing, he was found to be a long-term offender and was sentenced to two years' imprisonment to be followed by seven years' supervision. In the Court of Appeal, it was argued that only the sexual offences set out in s. 753.1(2)(a) can trigger a long-term offender designation. The Court concluded:

It is evident when reading the Report in conjunction with Part XXIV of the *Code*, that the recommendations of the Task Force with respect to the long-term offender proposals were, for the most part, adopted in Bill C-55, *An Act to amend the Criminal Code* (high risk offenders), the *Corrections and Conditional Release Act*, the *Criminal Records Act*, the *Prisons and Reforma-*

tories Act and the *Department of the Solicitor General Act*, SC 1997, c. 17. The provisions with which we are here concerned came into force on August 1, 1997. Thus, while paedophiles and other sexual predators may well have been the primary targets of the new long-term offender provisions, I can find nothing in the background or legislative history confining their application to sexual offenders.

. . .

On the basis of my conclusion that the long-term offender provisions of the *Code* are not restricted in their application to those convicted of the sexual offences set out in s. 753.1(2)(a) of the *Code*, I would dismiss the first ground of appeal.

Does this view of an antecedent offence unduly expand the legitimate reach of the long-term offender provisions? The same issue was addressed more recently by the Saskatchewan Court of Appeal in *Weasel*:

R v. Weasel
(2003), 181 CCC (3d) 358 (Sask. CA) (footnotes omitted)

CAMERON JA: [1] This appeal raises a question of law central to its disposition: Does section 753.1 of the *Criminal Code*, which makes special provision for sentencing long-term offenders, apply only to offenders who are convicted of a sex offence, or does it extend to others, including offenders who are convicted of a violent offence such as assault causing bodily harm?

[2] The appellant, Everett Riel Weasel, was convicted of assault causing bodily harm contrary to section 267(b) of the *Criminal Code*. He had been convicted of this and other offences many times in the past, so the prosecutor asked the trial judge to order an assessment, as permitted by section 752.1(1), for the purpose of determining whether the appellant should be sentenced as a long-term offender under section 753.1. The trial judge acted on the request (with the concurrence of counsel for the appellant) and upon receipt of the assessment found the appellant to be a long-term offender. He then sentenced him to a term of imprisonment of three years, to be followed by a period of community supervision of eight years.

. . .

[6] Subsection (2) lies at the heart of the issue. Anyone familiar with the conventional cast of statutes will appreciate the unconventional terminology of this subsection: "The court shall be satisfied that there is a substantial risk that the offender will reoffend if" the requisites of paragraphs (a) and (b) exist. This terminology is tactless and grating, having regard for judicial independence, but that is not the point. The point is that it lacks clarity. Is the subsection intended to define the term "substantial risk," as it appears in subsection (1)? Or is it intended, instead, to create a presumption of "substantial risk" in those circumstances in which the requisites of paragraphs (a) and (b) exist, leaving the presence or absence of such risk in other circumstances to be assessed without the aid of the presumption?

[7] Depending on what was intended, the drafter might have used conventional language such as this: "A substantial risk that the offender will reoffend means ..."; or

"A substantial risk that the offender will reoffend shall be presumed or deemed to exist if …"; or "Without limiting the generality of paragraph 753.1(1)(b), a substantial risk that the offender will reoffend exists if … ." This would better have identified the intent. As it is, the intent is obscure and the effect uncertain.

[8] If subsection (2) serves in effect to define the term "substantial risk," then section 753.1 would appear to be limited to an offender who has been convicted of a sex offence of the type referred to in the subsection. If, instead, subsection (2) serves in effect to raise a presumption of "substantial risk" in the circumstances described in paragraphs (a) and (b) thereof, then section 753.1 may extend to an offender who has been convicted of an offence of another type and who proves, on independent assessment without the aid of the presumption, to pose a "substantial risk" to re-offend.

[9] The legislative history of section 753.1 is ambiguous but contains an indication the section was intended to apply only to sex offenders. So does some academic comment on the subject. But such case law as exists either holds or suggests otherwise. A better understanding of the issue may be gained through a brief recounting of these.

(i) The Legislative History of Section 753.1

[10] The government placed these long-term offender provisions before Parliament in 1996, and Parliament enacted them in 1997. The government placed them before Parliament as part of a package of amendments contained in Bill C-55. The Bill was introduced for the two-fold purpose of amending the existing dangerous offender provisions (found in section 753 of the *Criminal Code*) and of creating the long-term offender provisions (found in section 753.1).

[11] The Bill drew upon a task force report for its content: The Report of Federal/ Provincial/Territorial Task Force on High Risk Offenders, *Strategies for Managing High-Risk [Violent] Offenders* (Victoria: The Task Force, 1995). The Report spoke of the need for more effective measures for dealing with some categories of offender, stressing sex offenders, who may not qualify as dangerous offenders but may still pose a considerable risk of harm to others by reason of chronic behaviours. Speaking to a proposed new category of offender—the long-term offender—the Report states:

> A sentencing option providing for long term supervision would be aimed at cases where an established offence cycle with observable cues is present, and where a long term relapse prevention approach might be indicted. The success of [a long term supervision] scheme based on the relapse prevention model rests on several key factors.
>
> a. The measure should be focused on particular classes of offender. The inclination to make long-term supervision widely available should be resisted as costly, unwarranted in most cases, and as contributing to "net widening." The target group, and thus the expectations of the scheme, should be well defined;
> b. The criteria should selectively target those offenders who have a high likelihood of committing further *violent* or *sexual* crimes but who would not likely be found to be a Dangerous Offender; [p. 19] [emphasis added].

[12] On introduction of Bill C-55, the Department of Justice and the Solicitor General of Canada issued a document entitled "Protecting Canadians and their families—Measures to Deal with High-Risk Violent Offenders" (August 1996). It stated in part:

> The government has announced new measures to deal with high-risk offenders. The following initiatives will toughen the sentencing and correctional regime for those who pose a high risk of committing another violent crime:
>
> - a new "Long-Term Offender" designation that targets sex-offenders and adds a period of long-term supervision of up to 10 years following release from prison;
>
> • • •
>
> Under the proposed changes, a new sentencing category, to be called Long-Term Offenders, will be added to the *Criminal Code*. It will target sex offenders who are less violent and brutal than those designated as Dangerous Offenders but are found to pose a considerable risk of reoffending.
>
> • • •
>
> The Long-Term Offender procedure will apply to persons convicted of sexual assault, sexual interference, invitation to sexual touching, sexual exploitation, exposure, aggravated sexual assault, and sexual assault with a weapon or causing bodily harm. It could also be applied to a person who committed another offence that had a sexual component—for example, somebody who committed a break and enter with a clear intention of sexually assaulting the occupant.

[13] Later, when Bill C-55 was before the Standing Committee on Justice and Legal Affairs, the Minister of Justice commented upon it, saying this:

> The second element in Bill C-55 has to do with the creation of the category of long-term offender. ...
>
> Naturally and properly, the test for the dangerous offender category is high and exacting. The reality is that 90% of successful dangerous offender applications involve sex offenders. Repeat sex offenders are the most troublesome, high-risk category in the criminal law. The creation of the long-term offender category is intended to provide another mechanism for dealing with this risk. ...
>
> As proposed, the offences that can give rise to a long-term offender designation are all sex crimes and involve patterns of reoffending.

[14] So the Minister of Justice and the Solicitor General seem to have thought the long-term offender provisions were confined to sex crimes and sex offenders, though it might be recalled the Task Force Report had suggested that such provisions "should be focussed on particular classes of offender" and should "target those offenders who have a likelihood of committing further violent or sexual crimes but who would not likely be found to be a Dangerous Offender."

(ii) The Academic Commentary

[15] Some early academic comment also suggests section 753.1 is limited to sex offenders. In a 1998 article touching the issue—Isabel Grant, "Legislating Public Safety: The Business of Risk" (1998) 3 Can. Crim. L. Rev. 177—it is said that:

> The long term offender provisions provide a front end mechanism, at the time of sentencing, for dealing with repeat sex offenders. [p. 228]

Another article—Yukimi Henry, "Psychiatric Gating: Questioning the Civil Committal of Convicted Sex Offenders" (2001), 59 U. T. Fac. L. Rev. 229—states that:

> As part of the 1997 amendments, a new sentencing option was created to deal with sex offenders: the long-term offender designation. ... These new provisions attempt to capture those sexual offenders who do not meet the criteria for the dangerous offender designation, but who are still perceived as a significant public safety risk that cannot adequately be dealt with under existing supervisory provisions. [p. 234]

[16] And in Ruby, *Sentencing*, 5th ed. (Toronto: Butterworths, 1999) at p. 156, subsection 753.1(2) is said to define the term "substantial risk" appearing in subsection 753.1(1):

> "Substantial risk" is defined in section 753.2 as a variety of *Criminal Code* sexual offences or sexual behaviour revealing a likelihood the offender will [inflict serious personal injury on another in the future].

(iii) The Case Law

[17] The leading case on the subject is *R v. McLeod* (1999), 136 CCC (3d) 492 (BCCA). In this case, the British Columbia Court of Appeal concluded that section 753.1 is not restricted in its operation to offenders who have been convicted of a sex offence referred to in paragraph 753.1(2)(a). Madam Justice Prowse spoke to the issue on behalf of the Court, saying:

> [26] In my view, the meaning of 753.1 is straightforward, whether read separately or in the larger context of Part XXIV of the Code. It provides that a court may find an offender to be a long-term offender if the three conditions set out in s-ss. 753.1(1)(a) to (c) are met. ... Subsection 753.1(2)(a) simply provides that the court must find ("shall be satisfied") that there is a substantial risk the offender will reoffend if the conditions set out in that subsection are met. ... Thus, if an offender is convicted of one of the sexual offences delineated in s. 753.1(2)(a), the court must find that there is a substantial risk that the offender will reoffend; that is, that the second condition in s. 753.1(b) has been met. ...
>
> [27] I do not agree with the submission on behalf of Mr. McLeod that the effect of s. 753.1(2)(a) is to restrict the scope of s.753.1(1) to apply only to offenders who are convicted of one or more of the sexual offences listed in s. 753.1(2)(a). If Parliament had intended to limit the designation of long-term offender to those convicted of sexual offences, it could have done so by simply adding that as a fourth condition to be satisfied under s. 753.1(1). Counsel for Mr. McLeod is, in effect, asking us to read a fourth condition into that subsection which does not otherwise exist. [pp. 502-503]

[18] In effect, then, the Court concluded that subsection 753.1(2) does not serve to define the term "substantial risk," appearing in subsection (1), but serves instead to create a conclusive presumption of "substantial risk" in the circumstances to which paragraphs (a) and (b) of subsection (2) are addressed.

[19] This conclusion attracted some academic disagreement, as it did in Manson, *The Law of Sentencing* (Toronto: Irwin Law, 2001), at p. 340:

> Underlying this conclusion is the assumption that the purpose behind enacting the long-term offender provisions was to increase public protection by ensuring supervision in the community upon release. By refusing to treat section 753.1(2) as a definition of substantial risk to reoffend in this context [as per Ruby, *Sentencing*, 5th ed.], the court suggests that protection from other non-sexual forms of violence can also be achieved through the new provisions. However, the only criteria are the three general factors set out in section 753.1(1), none of which make any reference to violence. Could a recidivist burglar who gets a penitentiary sentence be included in the ten-year supervision net? The better answer is to treat section 753.1(2) as defining the risk element of substantial risk to reoffend. This would ensure that the new disposition is used for the kind of sexual crimes the Minister of Justice spoke about when the enacting legislation was introduced, and not to extend to a wide range of offences, both violent and non-violent.

[20] What all of this comes down to, as it did in *R v. McLeod*, is what Parliament had in mind in enacting section 753.1 in the terms it did. This entails interpreting the section along the lines adopted by the Supreme Court of Canada in *Rizzo and Rizzo Shoes Ltd. (Re)*, [1998] 1 SCR 27.

(b) The Resolution of the Issue: Interpreting Section 713.1

[21] In *Re Rizzo & Rizzo Shoes Ltd.*, the Supreme Court of Canada adopted the so-called "modern approach" to statutory interpretation:

> Today there is only one principle or approach, namely, the words of an Act are to be read in their entire context and in their grammatical and ordinary sense harmoniously with the scheme of the Act, the object of the Act, and the intention of Parliament.

The context includes the legislative history of an enactment, though the Court observed that this is of limited assistance, given the frailties of Hansard evidence pertaining to the intent of Parliament.

[22] The principle embodied in the modern approach to statutory construction is accompanied by another when it comes to interpreting penal enactments, namely the subsidiary principle of strict construction: If the attempt to interpret a penal enactment in accordance with the modern approach leaves a reasonable doubt as to the meaning or scope of the text of the enactment, then the meaning most favourable to the accused is to be adopted as long as it is compatible with the intention and goal of Parliament: *R v. Hasselwander*, [1993] 2 SCR 398, per Cory J at pp. 412-413.

[23] What Parliament had in mind, then, in enacting section 753.1, is to be determined in the context of the whole of the enactment in which the section appears, namely Part XXIV of the *Criminal Code*, including the scheme of the enactment and its purpose.

The tendency is to do otherwise—to take an isolated view of the language of the section, treating the section as though it stood alone in providing for the sentencing of long-term offenders. This is not true of the approach taken by the British Columbia Court of Appeal in *R v. McLeod*. The Court went beyond the section itself and considered its scope in the broader context of the provisions dealing with both dangerous offenders and long-term offenders. In our judgment this is essential, for the long-term offender provisions are woven into Part XXIV and form part of an integrated whole larger than the section itself.

[24] Section 753.1 forms part of an integrated sentencing scheme established by Part XXIV and entitled DANGEROUS OFFENDERS AND LONG-TERM OFFENDERS. The purpose of Part XXIV lies in enhancing the effectiveness of conventional sentencing in relation to the two classes of offender for which it makes provision. To that end, it allows for *preventive detention or control* beyond the reach of conventional sentencing. For Dangerous Offenders, it allows for an indeterminate period of detention (section 753). For Long-term Offenders, it allows for a fixed period of detention of at least two years, followed by a fixed period of control by means of community supervision of up to ten years (section 753.1).

[25] These are offenders who, to begin with, have been convicted of "a serious personal injury offence" or "an offence referred to in paragraph 753.1(2)(a)" and who, after that, are found to be a threat of one nature or another to the safety or well-being of others by reason of their historical behaviour and risk of re-offending.

[26] The term "serious personal injury offence" is defined in section 752 to mean:

(a) an indictable offence, other than high treason, treason, first degree murder or second degree murder, involving

(i) the use or attempted use of violence against another person, or

(ii) conduct endangering or likely to endanger the life or safety of another person or inflicting or likely to inflict severe psychological damage upon another person,

and for which the offender may be sentenced to imprisonment for ten years or more, or

(b) an offence or attempt to commit an offence mentioned in section 271 (sexual assault), 272 (sexual assault with a weapon, threats to a third party or causing bodily harm) or 273 (aggravated sexual assault).

[27] The phrase "an offence referred to in paragraph 753.1(2)(a)" embraces an offence under section 151 (sexual interference), 152 (invitation to sexual touching), and 153 (sexual exploitation); one under subsection 173(2) (exposure); and one under section 271 (sexual assault), 272 (sexual assault with a weapon), and 273 (aggravated sexual assault).

[28] These, then, are the two classes of offender and offence with which the scheme is concerned.

[29] The scheme is designed to operate step by step toward achieving its sentencing objectives. Certain conditions or requirements must be fulfilled at each step before advancing to the next. The first step, initiated by the prosecution following conviction but before sentencing, is to gain access to the scheme's sentencing options by means of an application to obtain an assessment of the offender under section 752.1. This is an

entry-like provision, and it applies to all such applications, irrespective of whether the application be aimed at having the offender sentenced as a dangerous offender, or as a dangerous or long-term offender, or as long-term offender only. Section 752.1, the only one of its kind in the scheme, reads thus:

Dangerous Offenders and Long-Term Offenders

752.1(1) Application for remand for assessment—Where an offender is convicted of a serious personal injury offence or an offence referred to in paragraph 753.1(2)(a) and, before sentence is imposed on the offender, on application by the prosecution, the court is of the opinion that there are reasonable grounds to believe that the offender might be found to be a dangerous offender under section 753 or a long-term offender under section 753.1, the court may, by order in writing, remand the offender, for a period not exceeding sixty days, to the custody of the person that the court directs and who can perform an assessment, or can have an assessment performed by experts. The assessment is to be used as evidence in an application under section 753 or 753.1.

(2) Report—The person to whom the offender is remanded shall file a report of the assessment with the court not later than fifteen days after the end of the assessment period and make copies of it available to the prosecutor and counsel for the offender.

[30] As a pre-condition to the operation of this section, the offender must have been convicted of "a serious personal injury offence or an offence referred to in paragraph 753.1(2)(a)." Otherwise, there is no access to the sentencing options of the scheme. If the condition is fulfilled, and if the requirements of the section are met, the court may requisition an assessment. Assuming it does so, the first step is complete.

[31] Upon receipt of the assessment, the scheme contemplates the taking of the next step: Determining if the offender constitutes a dangerous offender under section 753 or a long-term offender under section 753.1, depending on the circumstances, including the aim of the application and the opinion of the court at the first step.

[32] If the offender is determined to be a dangerous or long-term offender, the next step entails sentencing the offender as provided for either by section 753 or by 753.1.

[33] These sections bear close examination for the purpose of determining what Parliament had in mind in enacting section 753.1 in the terms it did.

• • •

[36] None of the steps envisioned by either section 753 or 753.1 can, of course, be taken without the first step having been taken under section 752. And the first step can only have been taken, according to the *pre-condition* appearing in subsection 752(1), "where [the] offender has been convicted of a serious personal injury offence or an offence referred to in paragraph 753.1(2)(a)." This pre-condition to the operation of section 752—and by extension to the operation of sections 753 and 753.1—might be read to different effect.

[37] It might be read as establishing discrete pre-conditions, one reserved exclusively for gaining access to the dangerous offender provisions of section 753 (conviction for "a serious personal injury offence") and the other reserved exclusively for gaining access to the long-term offender provisions of section 753.1 (conviction for "an offence referred to in paragraph 753.1(2)(a)"). Were it to be read thus, the effect would

be to confine the scope of section 753.1 to offenders who have been convicted of a sex offence of the type listed in paragraph 753.1(2)(a), thus excluding offenders who have been convicted of "a serious personal injury offence."

[38] It might also be read as establishing a pre-condition having alternative elements, namely a conviction for "a serious personal injury offence" or "an offence referred to in paragraph 753.1(2)(a)," with either serving to engage section 752.1 and, if the requirements thereof be met, to then engage section 753 or 753.1, whichever is appropriate in the circumstances. Reading the pre-condition to this effect would widen the scope of section 753.1 to include offenders who have been convicted of "a serious personal injury offence."

[39] Of the two readings, the second is more grammatically appealing and more suited to an integrated scheme. Even so, these are rather weak indications of Parliamentary intent. There are stronger ones, found first in the text of these provisions and then in the purpose of the enactment. Let us consider them in turn.

(i) The Text of These Provisions

[40 There are two textual indications suggesting the long-term offender provisions were not meant to apply only to an offender who has been convicted of a sex offence listed in paragraph 753.1(2)(a). One of these is found in subsection 753(5), the other in subsection 753.1(1).

[41] Subsection 753(5) covers the situation where, on a dangerous offender application, the court is not satisfied the offender qualifies as a dangerous offender. Should that happen, the court is empowered to resort to section 753.1, find the offender to be a long-term offender, and sentence the offender accordingly. The effect is this: If an offender has been convicted of "a serious personal injury offence"—assault causing bodily harm let us say—but is not found to be a dangerous offender under section 753, then that person may be found [to] be a long-term offender under section 753.1. This would not be possible were the latter confined to the sex offences listed in paragraph 753.1(2)(a). Madam Justice Prowse took note of this in *R v. McLeod*, at p. 504, saying there was nothing in the text to suggest "the court can only go on to determine whether the offender meets the long-term offender criteria if the predicate offences are sexual offences." We agree.

[42] Turning, then, to subsection 753.1(1), it may be noted that it covers the situation where, following the filing of an assessment report under section 752.1, the court is called upon to determine if the offender is a long-term offender. The court is empowered by subsection 753.1(1) to find "an offender" (meaning the offender to whom the assessment relates) to be a long-term offender if the requirements of paragraphs 753.1(1) (a), (b), and (c) be met. The first of these is that it would be appropriate in the view of the court to impose a sentence of imprisonment of two years or more "for *the offence* for which the offender has been convicted." The words in emphasis appear to be a general reference to an offence of the type underlying Part XXIV, namely a "serious personal injury offence" or "an offence referred to in paragraph 753.1(2)(a)." On what premise, it might be asked, would one construe the words *the offence* to exclude the first but include the second?

[43] Had the intention been to exclude the first, which is to say had Parliament intended to exclude offenders convicted of "a serious personal injury offence" from the purview of the long-term offender provisions, that intention could readily have been achieved by casting paragraph (a) in terms referring not merely to "the offence for which the offender has been convicted" but to "the offence, referred to in paragraph 753.1(2)(a), for which the offender has been convicted," or to "the offence for which the offender has been convicted, being an offence referred to [in] paragraph 753.1(2)(a)." That paragraph (a) is not cast in some such terms is reminiscent of the point made by Madam Justice Prowse, in *R v. McLeod*:

> If Parliament had intended to limit the designation of long-term offender to those convicted of sexual offences, it could have done so by simply adding that as a fourth condition to be satisfied under s. 753.1(1). Counsel ... is, in effect, asking us to read a fourth condition into that subsection which does not otherwise exist. [pp. 502, 503]

[44] These two textual considerations suggest that section 753.1 was not meant to apply only to sex offenders. And that brings us to the purpose of the enactment, which is to say the purpose of Part XXIV, and to the object of section 753.1.

(ii) The Purpose of the Enactment

[45] As noted earlier, the purpose of Part XXIV lies in enhancing the effectiveness of conventional sentencing in relation to the two categories of offender for which it makes provision. To that end, it allows for preventive detention or control beyond the reach of conventional sentencing. This is an idea which is grounded less in punishment for injury already inflicted, as in conventional sentencing, and more in prevention of future injury when the risk of re-offence is substantial. The concern is to better protect members of society from the threat of harm at the hands of offenders who have committed serious crimes against the person and who, because of their demonstrated propensities, are at considerable risk of doing so again. So generally speaking, Part XXIV targets those offenders who, having been convicted of a personal injury offence of a violent or sexual nature, pose a sufficient risk of re-offending as to call for either an indeterminate period of preventive detention or else a fixed term of detention, followed by a fixed period of community supervision.

[46] Were the object of section 753.1 to be seen as allowing for a term of detention followed by a period of community supervision in relation to sex offenders only, it would be difficult to fit the object of the section to the purpose of the enactment. The object would then seem to fall short of the purpose.

[47] And why, it might be asked, would Parliament have intended these preventive detention or control measures, insofar as they extend to long-term offenders, to apply only to offenders who have been convicted of a sex offence of the kind referred to in paragraph 753.1(2)(a)?

[48] No doubt Parliament was intent on including such offenders—given the comparatively high incidence of repetition associated with such offences—and it was intent on doing so expressly. It was intent on doing so expressly for the reason, among others perhaps, that the sex offences referred to in paragraph 753.1(2)(a) do not necessarily

come within the definition of a "serious personal injury offence." Those referred to by reference to sections 271 (sexual assault), 272 (sexual assault with a weapon) and 273 (aggravated sexual assault) fall within the definition. But those referred to by reference to section 153 (sexual exploitation) and subsection 173(2) (sexual exposure) do not. They do not fall within the definition because they are not punishable by imprisonment of ten years or more. Nor do those referred to by reference to section 151 (sexual interference) and 152 (invitation to sexual touching) necessarily fall within the definition, for the use of violence is not necessarily associated with their commission. Nevertheless, Parliament was intent on including persons convicted of such offences.

[49] What this suggests is that the section was intended primarily, though not necessarily exhaustively, as an inclusive provision, given the frequency with which sex offenders re-offend and the limited extent to which sex offences fall within the definition of "serious personal injury offence."

[50] But why would Parliament have wanted to exclude offenders convicted of a "serious personal injury offence"—an offence such as aggravated assault, assault with a weapon, or assault causing bodily harm? Potentially, these offenders are also at substantial risk to re-offend and to inflict serious harm on others. That being so, and since the long-term offender provisions are essentially sentencing provisions aimed at preventive control beyond the reach of conventional sentencing, it is difficult to think of any reason why Parliament should have wanted to exclude such offenders from the scope of section 753.1.

[51] Indeed, excluding them appears senseless. Were section 753.1 to exclude them, then an offender who is convicted of sexual assault, for example, and answers to the description of a long-term offender, could be sentenced to terms of preventive detention and control, but an offender who is convicted of assault causing bodily harm, or aggravated assault, or assault with a weapon, could not, even though this offender may answer to that description as well. This seems at odds not only with the thrust and central purpose of Part XXIV but with common sense. As Madam Justice Prowse observed on behalf of the British Columbia Court of Appeal in *R v. McLeod*:

> While the sexual offender may be a higher profile offender in the community than the spouse-beater, I can find nothing in s. 753.1, read alone, or in the context of Part XXIV, which suggests that the long-term offender designation was not intended to protect the public from the latter by providing for his or her ongoing supervision in the community upon release from custody. [p. 504]

[52] This consideration of the purpose of Part XXIV, combined with these textual considerations of its provisions, lead us to conclude that section 753.1 was not intended to be restricted to an offender who has been convicted of an offence referred to in paragraph 753.1(2)(a), but was intended to extend to an offender who has been convicted of a serious personal injury offence as defined by section 752.

[53] This conclusion is buttressed by the recent decision of the Supreme Court of Canada in *R v. Smith* (2003), 230 DLR (4th) 333, which came down after the case before us was heard. In *R v. Smith*, the accused had been convicted of: (i) uttering a threat of death or bodily harm, contrary to section 264.1(a) of the *Criminal Code* and (ii) assault causing bodily harm, contrary to section 267(1)(b) of the *Code*. Neither featured

any sexual conduct in its commission. At trial, the prosecution applied to have the accused sentenced as a dangerous offender. It did so in reliance on the second of these convictions—a conviction in relation to "a serious personal injury offence" within the definition of this phrase. The trial judge heard the application, declared the accused to be [a] dangerous offender, and sentenced him to an indeterminate period of detention.

[54] On appeal to the Supreme Court of Canada, the Court ordered a new hearing on the authority of its contemporaneous decision in *R v. Johnson* (2003), 230 DLR (4th) 296. It did so on the premise the sentencing judge was required to consider the possibility of declaring the accused a long-term offender before declaring him a dangerous offender:

> [2] ... If an offender satisfies the criteria set out in the long-term offender provisions and the sentencing judge is satisfied that a determinate sentence followed by a long-term supervision order would reduce the threat to the life, safety or physical or mental well-being of other persons to an acceptable level, the sentencing judge cannot properly declare the offender dangerous and thereupon impose an indeterminate sentence.
>
> [3] In this case, the record discloses insufficient evidence to conclude that there is no reasonable possibility that the [accused] would have been declared a long-term offender if the sentencing judge had concluded that the long-term offender provisions were available. Having concluded that the long-term offender provisions are not available to a person who satisfies the dangerous offender criteria, the sentencing judge did not conduct a full inquiry into the suitability of a long-term offender designation. [Smith at p. 336]

[55] Obviously, the Court would not have ordered a re-hearing in this instance if the long-term offender provisions applied only to an offender convicted of a sex offence of the type referred to in paragraph 753.1(2)(a). In this instance the offender had been convicted of a serious personal injury offence that had nothing to do with sex.

(c) Conclusion

[56] Based on the foregoing, we are of the opinion section 753.1 extends to an offender convicted of either a serious personal injury offence, as defined in section 752, or an offence referred to in paragraph 753.1(2)(a). That being so, subsection (2) is ... not to be seen as defining the term "substantial risk" appearing in subsection 753.1. Rather, it is to be seen as creating a conclusive presumption of "substantial risk" in those circumstances to which paragraphs (a) and (b) of the subsection are addressed, leaving the issue of such risk in other circumstances to be determined without the aid of the presumption.

IV. PREVENTIVE RECOGNIZANCES

A. Background

Dangerous offender and long-term offender applications follow the conviction of an individual. Thus, a condition precedent to the operation of those provisions is a conviction for a "serious personal injury offence." We now turn our attention to preventive measures that may be employed in the absence of a trial and conviction.

Building on the use of common law peace bonds and the statutory peace bonds in s. 810 of the *Criminal Code*, in 1993 (SC 1993, c. 45, s. 11) and 1997 (for s. 810.2, see SC 1997, c. 17, s. 9; for s. 810.01, see SC 1997, c. 23, s. 19) Parliament created three new post-sentence preventive vehicles. The impetus for enacting these provisions came, at least in part, from a desire to address concerns about perceived dangerousness once a sentence has been completed. These provisions may be used to impose post-sentence supervision on individuals who are perceived to be dangerous.

While there are differences among the three provisions, they are similar in structure. Section 810.01 is triggered by fear that someone will commit a criminal organization offence. Section 810.1 can be triggered when someone fears on reasonable grounds that a sexual offence against a child will be committed. Section 810.2 addresses fear of a serious personal injury offence. All three of these mechanisms require applications to a court and may result in a recognizance lasting up to 12 months that includes specific conditions. Sections 810.01 and 810.2 require the consent of the provincial attorney general before an information may be received by a provincial court judge. Sections 810.01 and 810.1 require fear that a particular person or persons may be victimized; there is no such requirement in s. 810.2. A breach of any of these recognizances is a hybrid offence, which is punishable by up to two years' imprisonment when prosecuted by indictment.

B. The Provisions

Fear of certain offences

810.01(1) A person who fears on reasonable grounds that another person will commit an offence under section 423.1, a criminal organization offence or a terrorism offence may, with the consent of the Attorney General, lay an information before a provincial court judge.

(2) A provincial court judge who receives an information under subsection (1) may cause the parties to appear before a provincial court judge.

(3) The provincial court judge before whom the parties appear may, if satisfied by the evidence adduced that the informant has reasonable grounds for the fear, order that the defendant enter into a recognizance to keep the peace and be of good behaviour for any period that does not exceed twelve months and to comply with any other reasonable conditions prescribed in the recognizance, including the conditions set out in subsection (5), that the provincial court judge considers desirable for preventing the commission of an offence referred to in subsection (1).

(4) The provincial court judge may commit the defendant to prison for a term not exceeding twelve months if the defendant fails or refuses to enter into the recognizance.

(5) Before making an order under subsection (3), the provincial court judge shall consider whether it is desirable, in the interests of the safety of the defendant or of any other person, to include as a condition of the recognizance that the defendant be prohibited from possessing any firearm, cross-bow, prohibited weapon, restricted weapon, prohibited device, ammunition, prohibited ammunition or explosive substance, or all of these things, for any period specified in the recognizance, and where the provincial court judge decides that it is so desirable, the provincial court judge shall add such a condition to the recognizance.

• • •

(6) A provincial court judge may, on application of the informant, the Attorney General or the defendant, vary the conditions fixed in the recognizance.

• • •

Where fear of sexual offence

810.1(1) Any person who fears on reasonable grounds that another person will commit an offence under section 151, 152, 155 or 159, subsection 160(2) or (3), section 163.1, 170, 171 or 172.1, subsection 173(2) or section 271, 272 or 273, in respect of one or more persons who are under the age of fourteen years, may lay an information before a provincial court judge, whether or not the person or persons in respect of whom it is feared that the offence will be committed are named.

(2) A provincial court judge who receives an information under subsection (1) may cause the parties to appear before a provincial court judge.

(3) The provincial court judge before whom the parties appear may, if satisfied by the evidence adduced that the informant has reasonable grounds for the fear, order the defendant to enter into a recognizance and, for a period fixed by the provincial court judge of not more than twelve months, comply with the conditions fixed by the provincial court judge, including a condition prohibiting the defendant from

(a) engaging in any activity that involves contact with persons under the age of fourteen years, including using a computer system within the meaning of subsection 342.1(2) for the purpose of communicating with a person under the age of fourteen years; and

(b) attending a public park or public swimming area where persons under the age of fourteen years are present or can reasonably be expected to be present, or a daycare centre, schoolground, playground or community centre.

(3.1) The provincial court judge may commit the defendant to prison for a term not exceeding twelve months if the defendant fails or refuses to enter into the recognizance.

. . .

Where fear of serious personal injury offence

810.2(1) Any person who fears on reasonable grounds that another person will commit a serious personal injury offence, as that expression is defined in section 752, may, with the consent of the Attorney General, lay an information before a provincial court judge, whether or not the person or persons in respect of whom it is feared that the offence will be committed are named.

(2) A provincial court judge who receives an information under subsection (1) may cause the parties to appear before a provincial court judge.

(3) The provincial court judge before whom the parties appear may, if satisfied by the evidence adduced that the informant has reasonable grounds for the fear, order that the defendant enter into a recognizance to keep the peace and be of good behaviour for any period that does not exceed twelve months and to comply with any other reasonable conditions prescribed in the recognizance, including the conditions set out in subsections (5) and (6), that the provincial court judge considers desirable for securing the good conduct of the defendant.

(4) The provincial court judge may commit the defendant to prison for a term not exceeding twelve months if the defendant fails or refuses to enter into the recognizance.

(5) Before making an order under subsection (3), the provincial court judge shall consider whether it is desirable, in the interests of the safety of the defendant or of any other person, to include as a condition of the recognizance that the defendant be prohibited from possessing any firearm, cross-bow, prohibited weapon, restricted weapon, prohibited device, ammunition, prohibited ammunition or explosive substance, or all such things, for any period specified in the recognizance, and where the provincial court judge decides that it is so desirable, the provincial court judge shall add such a condition to the recognizance.

(5.1) Where the provincial court judge adds a condition described in subsection (5) to a recognizance order, the provincial court judge shall specify in the order the manner and method by which

(a) the things referred to in that subsection that are in the possession of the defendant shall be surrendered, disposed of, detained, stored or dealt with; and

(b) the authorizations, licences and registration certificates held by the defendant shall be surrendered.

(5.2) Where the provincial court judge does not add a condition described in subsection (5) to a recognizance order, the provincial court judge shall include in the record a statement of the reasons for not adding the condition.

(6) Before making an order under subsection (3), the provincial court judge shall consider whether it is desirable to include as a condition of the recognizance that the defendant report to the correctional authority of a province or to an appropriate police authority, and where the provincial court judge decides that it is desirable for the defendant to so report, the provincial court judge may add the appropriate condition to the recognizance.

C. The Constitutionality of the Provisions

As noted above, the three types of preventive recognizances differ in some respects, but they are similar in a number of crucial ways. The following decision of the Court of Appeal for Ontario in *Budreo* addresses the constitutionality of s. 810.1 (sexual offences) of the Code. It also confronts a number of interpretive issues that are easily applicable to the other recognizances in ss. 810.01 (criminal organizations or terrorism) and 810.2 (serious personal injury offences).

R v. Budreo
(2000), 46 OR (3d) 481 (CA)

LASKIN JA:

Introduction

[1] Section 810.1 of the *Criminal Code*, RSC 1985, c. C-46, enacted by Parliament in 1993, permits the court to impose a recognizance on any person likely to commit any one of a number of listed sexual offences against a child under 14 years of age and to prohibit that person for up to one year from engaging in activities or attending places—a public park, public swimming area, daycare centre, schoolground or playground—where children under 14 are likely to be present. ... A recognizance may be imposed though the person has not committed an offence and has no previous criminal record. If an informant fears on reasonable grounds that the person will commit one of the listed offences and a provincial court judge, after a hearing, is satisfied that the informant has reasonable grounds for the fear, then the person may be ordered to enter into a recognizance. The issue on this appeal is the constitutionality of s. 810.1.

[2] The appellant Wray Budreo is a paedophile. He has a long record of sexual offences against young boys. In November 1994, he was released from prison after serv-

ing a sentence for three convictions for sexual assault. The Crown immediately sought a recognizance under s. 810.1. The appellant brought an application to prohibit the provincial court judge, His Honour Judge Kelly, from holding the s. 810.1 hearing and for a declaration that s. 810.1 was unconstitutional because it violated ss. 7, 9, 11 and 15 of the *Canadian Charter of Rights and Freedoms*.

[3] In a lengthy and well-reasoned decision, Then J concluded that s. 810.1 was constitutional except in two respects. First, he declared "community centre," one of the places a person could be prohibited from attending under s. 810.1(3), to be inoperative because it was overly broad contrary to s. 7 of the Charter and could not be justified under s. 1. Second, he found that s. 810.1(2), which required the provincial court judge to cause the parties to appear before the court, infringed ss. 7 and 9 of the Charter and could not be justified under s. 1. To remedy this violation, however, Then J read down the word "shall" in s. 810.1(2) to read "may."

[4] The appellant Budreo appealed and was supported in his appeal by the intervenor, the Canadian Civil Liberties Association. In oral argument the appellant narrowed the focus of his appeal to three main issues. First, he submitted that s. 810.1 violated s. 7 of the Charter. In his submission, s. 810.1 deprived him of his liberty contrary to the principles of fundamental justice in three ways: s. 810.1 creates a status offence; it is impermissibly broad; and it is impermissibly vague. Second, he submitted that Then J erred in reading down "shall" to "may" in s. 810.1(2) and that he should instead have declared the subsection inoperative. Third, he submitted that Then J erred in holding that a person subject to a s. 810.1 proceeding can be compelled to court by an arrest warrant under s. 507(4) of the Code and can be detained pending the hearing under s. 515. As part of this third submission the appellant asked us to reconsider this court's decision in *R v. Allen* (1985), 18 CCC (3d) 155, 8 OAC 16 (CA) in the light of the Charter.

[5] I would dismiss the appellant's appeal. Because I agree substantially with the reasons of Then J, I will limit my own reasons to summarizing the main points on which I rely, focusing on the specific arguments that were made before us.

Background Facts

[6] The appellant is 55 years old. He has been diagnosed as a paedophile. He has an extensive criminal record dating back to 1961, which includes many convictions for indecent assault and sexual assault committed against young boys. These convictions, in the main, have resulted from the "physical touching" of boys between five and 17 years of age. Of the appellant's 36 convictions, 26 have been for the physical touching of young males.

[7] On November 18, 1994, the appellant was released from the Kingston Penitentiary, after having served a six-year sentence for three counts of sexual assault. These sexual assault convictions concerned three incidents in which the appellant convinced the victims—young boys—to lay down in a park and then fondled their bare stomachs, and in two cases their genitals. In sentencing the appellant, Webber DCJ wrote, "Clearly, Mr. Budreo is a person who has a paedophiliac problem which has existed for many, many years and it appears that there is very little that has been done for him and there is very little that he has done for himself, except on a spasmodic and irregular basis."

[8]　On his release, at the request of the Correctional Service of Canada, the appellant submitted to a psychiatric assessment under the *Mental Health Act*, RSO 1990, c. M.7 to determine whether he was certifiable. The psychiatrist with the Correctional Service who did the assessment declined to certify the appellant. The psychiatrist concluded that the appellant did not pose a sufficient risk of serious harm to himself or to members of the public, that he had made considerable gains toward rehabilitating himself, and that he was "well motivated." Doctors at the Clarke Institute of Psychiatry also concluded that the appellant did not pose a danger to himself or others and, thus, should not be admitted under the *Mental Health Act*.

[9]　Since his release, the appellant has followed a treatment plan devised for him. The treatment plan consists of continued psychiatric counselling directed by a doctor at the Clarke Institute and monthly injections of the anti-androgen drug Luperon.

[10]　Nonetheless, the appellant's release from prison sparked considerable publicity, most of it negative. The appellant had gone first to Peterborough and then to Toronto. He was under continuous police surveillance in both cities and press releases were issued to tell the public of his whereabouts.

[11]　Within three days of his release, the Crown began proceedings under s. 810.1 of the *Criminal Code*. The Crown acknowledges that it sought a recognizance under s. 810.1, not because the appellant had done anything improper or illegal since his release from prison, but because of his criminal record and his diagnosis as a paedophile.

[12]　On November 20, 1994, Detective Wendy Leaver of the Metropolitan Toronto Police Service asked the appellant to agree to enter into recognizance under s. 810.1. The appellant was apparently unwilling to do so. The s. 810.1 application was then scheduled for November 22, 1994 and the appellant was told to obtain counsel.

[13]　Detective Leaver swore an information under s. 810.1 in which she said she feared, on reasonable grounds, that the appellant would commit any one of a number of specified sexual offences against children under the age of 14. She said that her fear was based on the appellant's psychiatric reports between 1963 and 1993, his criminal record, numerous hospital and parole board reports and a conversation with the appellant's treating psychiatrist at the Clarke Institute, who considered the appellant a high-risk paedophile if he did not take Luperon.

[14]　Detective Leaver attended before Judge Kelly on November 22, 1994. The appellant came to court voluntarily. Nonetheless, Detective Leaver asked the appellant to leave the courtroom, and once he had done so, arrested him under s. 507(4) of the *Criminal Code*.

[15]　The appellant was then in custody. The Crown therefore proceeded with a show cause hearing before Judge Kelly to determine whether the appellant would be released on bail pending the s. 810.1 application. The appellant had met with a lawyer the evening before, but that lawyer had not been retained to conduct the show cause hearing. The lawyer did ask that the hearing be adjourned 48 hours and that, in the interim, the appellant be released from custody. The Crown opposed the adjournment. Judge Kelly refused the adjournment request, saying that he would grant it only if the appellant remained in custody. The lawyer then withdrew. The appellant, unrepresented, agreed to the conditions of his release on bail sought by the Crown.

[16] These conditions included that he not engage in any activity involving contact with persons under the age of 14 unless in the presence of and under the supervision of Reverend Hugh Kirkegaard and another adult; that he not be at or be within 50 metres of a public park, swimming area, daycare, school ground, playground, community centre or any other place where persons under 14 can reasonably be expected to be found, except in the presence of and under the supervision of Reverend Kirkegaard and another adult; that he continue to take Luperon (or Provera) at least once a month; and that he continue counselling or treatment at the Clarke Institute. The s. 810.1 hearing was adjourned to November 28, 1994.

[17] On November 28, 1994, Judge Kelly varied the appellant's bail conditions. At the same time, the appellant brought an application for prerogative relief to prevent Judge Kelly from proceeding with the s. 810.1 hearing and for a declaration that ss. 810.1 and 507(4) of the Code violated ss. 7, 9, 11 and 15 of the Charter. Pending the resolution of the constitutional issues, the s. 810.1 hearing has been adjourned.

[18] However, on December 13, 1994, the appellant's bail conditions were further varied by Hoilett J. Under the amended conditions, the appellant continues to be prohibited from activities involving contact with persons under 14 years of age unless in the presence of an adult who does not have a criminal record, he continues to be restricted in his movement in parks and community centres, and he continues to be required to take counselling. The material in the record shows that the appellant was continuing his counselling at the Clarke Institute and was continuing to take Luperon.

[19] Fresh evidence filed on appeal showed that the appellant brought a further application to vary the conditions of his bail, which was opposed by the Crown. In a decision dated October 1, 1998, Keenan J refused the application. In his reasons, he noted that the appellant's bail conditions were virtually identical to the recognizance conditions under s. 810.1; that but for a single breach of the condition not to consume alcohol, the appellant had complied with all the conditions of his bail for four years; that he had co-operated with a Circle of Support and Accountability organized by volunteers of the Mennonite faith; and that, indeed, Detective Leaver had participated in the Circle to supervise the appellant and assist in his treatment. Nonetheless, Keenan J could find "no basis for varying the recognizance of bail." I turn now to the constitutional issues in this appeal.

Discussion

First Issue: Does Section 810.1 Violate Section 7 of the Charter?

. . .

[22] To make out a violation of s. 7 the appellant must show first that s. 810.1 deprives him of his right to life, liberty or security of the person; and second, that this deprivation is contrary to the principles of fundamental justice.

[23] The Crown acknowledges that the appellant meets the first branch of the s. 7 test. Section 810.1 deprives the appellant of his liberty. The conditions in s. 810.1 prevent the appellant from going to many places that other Canadians can freely go to and thus prevent the appellant from participating fully in a community's activities. Although not as serious an intrusion on his freedom as detention or imprisonment, these

conditions in s. 810.1 still restrict the appellant's "liberty" under s. 7 of the Charter. Whether these restrictions on the appellant's liberty are in accordance with the principles of fundamental justice is at the heart of this appeal. The appellant argues that s. 810.1 contravenes the principles of fundamental justice for three reasons: it creates an offence based on status; it is overbroad; and it is void for vagueness.

(i) Does Section 810.1 Create a Status Offence?

[24] The appellant submits that s. 810.1 creates an offence based on a person's status alone, that is based on a person's medical diagnosis or even on a person's past criminal record but without any current offending conduct. The appellant argues that s. 810.1 is punitive, that it punishes a person though that person may have done nothing wrong. An offence based on status alone, according to the appellant, is contrary to the principles of fundamental justice.

[25] Accepting that a status offence contravenes fundamental justice, there are two answers to the appellant's submission. The main answer is that s. 810.1 does not create an offence. It is a preventive provision, not a punitive provision. It aims not to punish past wrongdoing but to prevent future harm to young children, to prevent them from being victimized by sexual abusers. The second answer is that s. 810.1 is not about a person's status. It is about assessing the present risk of a person committing a sexual offence against young children.

[26] Whether s. 810.1 is punitive or preventive permeated the argument of this appeal. Indeed, characterizing s. 810.1 as punitive is central to the appellant's position. If s. 810.1 is punitive, if it creates an offence, then the appellant fairly argues that it contains inadequate constitutional safeguards. Then J, however, held that s. 810.1 was a preventive measure aimed at the protection of children, and I agree with him.

[27] The criminal justice system has two broad objectives: punish wrongdoers and prevent future harm. A law aimed at the prevention of crime is just as valid an exercise of the federal criminal law power under s. 91(27) of the *Constitution Act, 1867*, as a law aimed at punishing crime. Thus, the appellant has not argued, nor could he, that Parliament cannot validly pass a law to prevent future harm to children.

[28] What the appellant does argue is that the law Parliament did pass, s. 810.1, is more punitive than preventive, and thus creates an offence, based solely on a person's status. Some aspects of s. 810.1 are punitive or coercive: the availability of an arrest warrant; detention pending a hearing unless the defendant is released on bail; and jail on the defendant's refusal to enter into a recognizance. These coercive aspects, however, are necessary to preserve the integrity of the s. 810.1 proceedings. By themselves, they do not turn s. 810.1 into a punitive provision. Nor does the stigma that undoubtedly accompanies a s. 810.1 proceeding make the proceeding punitive. That stigma will attach whether the section is preventive or punitive.

[29] To characterize s. 810.1 as punitive, as creating an offence, the appellant would have to show that its purpose is "to mete out criminal punishment" or that it has a "true penal consequence." A true penal consequence, according to the Supreme Court of Canada in *R v. Wigglesworth*, [1987] 2 SCR 541 at p. 561, 52 CCC (3d) 385 is "imprison-

ment or a fine which by its magnitude would appear to be imposed for the purpose of redressing the wrong done to society at large."

[30] By these standards, s. 810.1 does not create an offence. Its purpose is not to punish crime but to prevent crime from happening. Its sanctions are not punitive, nor are they intended to redress a wrong; they are activity and geographic restrictions on a person's liberty intended to protect a vulnerable group in our society from future harm.

[31] As Then J observed, s. 810.1 is analogous to s. 810, the peace bond provision of the *Criminal Code*. Typically, s. 810 is used to protect an identified victim, a person already harmed, from further harm where evidence points to the likelihood of danger to the victim from continuing contact with another person. Courts have consistently held that s. 810 is a preventive measure, that it does not create an offence or mete out a criminal punishment. The appellant did not suggest otherwise. Nor indeed did the appellant suggest that s. 810 was unconstitutional. Instead, he sought to distinguish s. 810 by arguing that it is meant to address breaches of the peace between citizens, and thus it amounts to a private remedy to ensure that named individuals remain law abiding.

[32] I see nothing "private" in s. 810. It authorizes a recognizance order in the same way as does s. 810.1. Both are concerned with preventing victimization. The main differences between s. 810 and s. 810.1 are the group of likely victims and the breadth of restrictions that may be imposed. A recognizance order under s. 810 aims to prevent harm to named individuals and the restrictions are tailored to prevent contact between those persons and the likely perpetrator. A recognizance order under s. 810.1 aims to prevent harm to a large group of children, identified only by their age, and the restrictions must necessarily be more extensive to prevent contact between this large group of children and the likely perpetrator. Section 810.1 is therefore broader than s. 810. But the two sections are similar enough that if s. 810 does not create an offence, it is hard to see how s. 810.1 does either.

[33] Moreover, I do not regard s. 810.1 as authorizing court-ordered restrictions on a person's liberty because of that person's status. Section 810.1 looks not to a person's status but to a person's present risk of future dangerousness. That risk will have to be assessed by looking at all relevant factors in a person's life, factors that are not immutable but will change over time.

[34] Thus, I conclude that s. 810.1 does not create a status offence. It is a preventive measure. Indeed, if the preventive aspect of the federal criminal law power is going to be used anywhere, I cannot think of a more important use than the protection of young children from likely sexual predators. However, although s. 810.1 is properly characterized as a preventive measure, to be constitutionally valid, it must be neither overbroad nor vague.

(ii) Is Section 810.1 Overbroad?

[35] The appellant submits that s. 810.1 is overbroad contrary to ss. 7 and 9 of the Charter. Because I do not think that s. 9 adds anything to the appellant's position, I will focus only on s. 7.

[36] That a law not be overbroad is now accepted as a principle of fundamental justice: [*R v. Heywood* (1994), 94 CCC (3d) 481 (SCC)]. "Overbreadth" looks at the means a legislature has chosen to achieve a legitimate objective. The means chosen must be sufficiently tailored or narrowly targeted to meet their objective. If the means chosen are too broad or too wide, if the law goes further than necessary to accomplish its purpose, the law becomes arbitrary or disproportionate. A person's rights will be limited without good reason. The principles of fundamental justice will be violated.

[37] I accept the legitimacy, and indeed the importance, of Parliament's objective in passing s. 810.1 of the *Criminal Code*. Children are among the most vulnerable groups in our society. The sexual abuse of young children is a serious societal problem, a statement that needs no elaboration. A sizeable percentage of the sexual offences against children—according to the record, approximately 30 per cent—occurs in public places, the very places specified in s. 810.1. The expert evidence shows that recidivism rates for sexual abusers of children are high and that keeping high-risk offenders away from children is a sound preventive strategy. Parliament thus cannot be faulted for its objective in enacting s. 810.1. The state should not be obliged to wait until children are victimized before it acts. The societal interest in protecting children from sexual abuse supports Parliament's use of the preventive part of its criminal law power.

[38] Even accepting the legitimacy of Parliament's purpose, the appellant submits that the means it has chosen in s. 810.1 to achieve that purpose are too broad. The appellant focuses on four aspects of s. 810.1: the extent of the restrictions on his liberty, the imposition of these restrictions without a requirement of any previous offending conduct, the pre-hearing arrest and detention provisions to which he was subjected, and the extent of the procedural protections he was afforded. I will deal with each of these. Overall, however, I am not persuaded that s. 810.1 is overbroad. Parliament might have chosen other means to achieve its objective but the means that it did choose are reasonable and in accordance with the principles of fundamental justice.

1. Extent of Restrictions Does Not Make Section 810.1 Overbroad

[39] If a recognizance is ordered, a defendant may be restricted from participating in any activities or from attending a public park or public swimming area where children under 14 may reasonably be expected to gather or a daycare centre, schoolground or playground. In my view, these restrictions, although limiting a defendant's liberty, are not overbroad. I say that for three reasons. First, the restrictions stop short of detention or imprisonment. I think it fair to conclude that detention or imprisonment under a provision that does not charge an offence would be an unacceptable restriction on a defendant's liberty and would be contrary to the principles of fundamental justice. But as Then J observed, the restrictions contemplated by s. 810.1 permit a defendant to lead a reasonably normal life.

[40] Second, these restrictions on a defendant's liberty are proportional to the important societal interest in s. 810.1, the protection of young children. As McLachlin J observed in *R v. Seaboyer*, [1991] 2 SCR 577 at p. 603, 66 CCC (3d) 321, "the principles of fundamental justice reflect a spectrum of interests, from the rights of the accused to broader societal concerns. Section 7 must be construed having regard to those interests. ..." The defendant's right to liberty is not the only s. 7 interest at stake in s. 810.1.

The societal interest in protecting young children from harm must also be taken into account. Section 810.1 attempts to balance these two interests: the interest of likely child sexual abusers in going where they please, including places where young children gather, and the interest of the state in ensuring that young children can go safely and securely to places typically associated with children's activities. In my view, s. 810.1 strikes a reasonable compromise between these two interests. It provides a measured intrusion into a defendant's liberty consistent with protecting young children from harm.

[41] Third, accepting Then J's deletion of community centres, the restrictions contemplated by s. 810.1 are narrowly targeted to meet Parliament's objective. The only places a defendant may be prohibited from going are where children under age 14 are or can reasonably be expected to be present; and the only activities a defendant may be prohibited from engaging in are those involving contact with children under 14. By limiting the scope of s. 810.1 in this way, I do not accept the submission of the provincial Crown that s. 810.1(3) authorizes the court to impose broader restrictions on a defendant's liberty than activities, areas or places where children are likely to be found. Section 810.1(3) provides that a judge may "order the defendant to enter into a recognizance and comply with the conditions fixed by the provincial court judge, including" the specified conditions. The specified conditions following the word "including" are examples of the kinds of conditions that can be imposed. The context of s. 810.1 and its overall purpose suggest that the word "including" is used to limit the scope of the general term "conditions" to those conditions similar to the specified examples. On this interpretation, a judge could prohibit a defendant from going to a recreation hall where young children were likely to be present but could not, for example, require a defendant to take the drug Luperon, however desirable that may be. This interpretation, in my view, not only appropriately reflects the context and purpose of s. 810.1, it also accords with Charter values. A broader interpretation, permitting the judge to order a defendant to take a course of treatment or to take a particular drug, under a provision that does not create an offence would raise serious Charter concerns. Under the narrower interpretation I have adopted, the restrictions contemplated by s. 810.1 are not overbroad.

2. Lack of a Requirement of a Previous Criminal Record Does Not Make Section 810.1 Overbroad

[42] A recognizance order may be imposed on a defendant who has no previous criminal record, who has committed no overt sexual act, who has seemingly done nothing wrong. All that is required is for the presiding judge to be satisfied the informant has reasonable grounds for the fear that the defendant will commit a sexual offence against a child under 14. The appellant submits that without a triggering requirement of some previous offending conduct, s. 810.1 is overbroad because it applies to too many people. I do not accept this submission.

[43] What s. 810.1 is trying to measure is a defendant's present likelihood of future dangerousness or present risk of committing a sexual offence against children in the future. Predicting future dangerousness is not an exact science. However, the impossibility of making exact predictions does not render s. 810.1 overbroad and contrary to our principles of fundamental justice. La Forest J addressed this point in dealing with the dangerous offender legislation in *R v. Lyons*, [1987] 2 SCR 309 at pp. 364-65, 37 CCC (3d) 1:

However, as Holmes has reminded us, the life of the law has not been logic: it has been experience. The criminal law must operate in a world governed by practical considerations rather than abstract logic and, as a matter of practicality, the most that can be established in a future context is a likelihood of certain events occurring. ...

It seems to me that a "likelihood" of specified future conduct occurring is the finding of fact required to be established; it is not, at one and the same time, the means of proving that fact. Logically, it seems clear to me that an individual can be found to constitute a threat to society without insisting that this require the court to assert an ability to predict the future.

So too did Lamer CJC in dealing with the bail system in *R v. Morales*, [1992] 3 SCR 711 at p. 739, 77 CCC (3d) 91:

The bail system has always made an effort to assess the likelihood of future dangerousness while recognizing that exact predictions of future dangerousness are impossible. The Report of the Canadian Committee on Corrections (Ouimet Report (1969)), one of the studies which led to the current bail system, recognized the impossibility of precise predictions at p. 110:

It has been argued that there is no accurate way of predicting the accused's behaviour pending trial. Even if a measure of predictability could be achieved, any factfinding process for determining this issue would be so time-consuming as to nullify the purpose of bail.

We think the issues involved are no more difficult than others which courts are constantly called upon to resolve in other areas of the law. Some reasonable assessment of the probability of the accused's behaviour pending trial is not impossible. If the prosecution does not make out a reasonable cause for denial of bail, it follows that it should be granted.

The bail system does not aim to make exact predictions about future dangerousness because such predictions are impossible to make. However, *Lyons* demonstrates that it is sufficient to establish a likelihood of dangerousness, and that the impossibility of making exact predictions does not preclude a bail system which aims to deny bail to those who likely will be dangerous.

[44] A previous criminal record for sexual assault against children will no doubt be relevant to predicting future dangerousness in many cases. But insisting on a previous record before a recognizance can be ordered would undermine the preventive purpose of s. 810.1. It would require a child to be victimized before the Crown could act, even if the Crown had highly reliable evidence of dangerousness. If some previous offending conduct were required before a recognizance could be ordered, then the Crown could not protect children from child sexual abusers known to medical authorities but not yet charged or from sexual abusers who could not be charged because the victim was too traumatized to testify or because the victim could not be found. Instead of requiring some previous offending conduct, s. 810.1 invites the presiding judge to consider all the relevant evidence on whether a defendant will commit a sexual offence against

children. I agree with Then J's summary of the kinds of evidence likely to be led before the presiding judge (at p. 365):

> For instance, evidence may be led that the defendant has made a threat or sexual proposition to a specific child or a group of children. More common, no doubt, will be cases where evidence will be led at the hearing concerning the individual's general proclivity to abuse children sexually. This could be based on a relevant criminal record and past behaviour around children. Evidence of a diagnosed medical mental disorder that predisposes the defendant to be sexually attracted to children might weigh in favour of ordering a recognizance, just as evidence of continuing successful treatment will be in the defendant's favour. On the very wording of the section, no one factor can be determinative.

[45] This passage reflects a sensible approach to a proceeding under s. 810.1. Requiring a criminal record or some other offending conduct as a condition of a recognizance order under s. 810.1 is at odds with the preventive purpose of the section. I conclude that s. 810.1 is not overbroad because it fails to require any offending conduct before a recognizance can be ordered.

3. The Pre-Hearing Provisions for Arrest and Bail Do Not Make Section 810.1 Overbroad

[46] The provisions for pre-trial arrest and bail—which, as I will discuss later in these reasons, apply to a proceeding under s. 810.1—carry with them the possibility of a sanction more severe—custody or detention—than any sanction that may be imposed as a result of a hearing under s. 810.1. That possibility, however, does not make the section overbroad. Pre-trial arrest or even pre-hearing detention may be necessary to secure the defendant's attendance at the hearing or to prevent harm to children pending a hearing because of a defendant's unwillingness to comply with reasonable terms of release. In short, as I have already said, pre-trial arrest and detention may be needed in some cases to ensure the integrity and viability of the s. 810.1 proceedings themselves.

4. Procedural Safeguards Are Sufficient to Not Make Section 810.1 Overbroad

[47] The procedural safeguards in s. 810.1 are adequate. Anyone subjected to a s. 810.1 application receives notice of the hearing. The hearing must meet the procedural fairness requirements of a summary conviction trial. No order can be made until after the hearing is completed. The presiding provincial court judge has discretion to limit the restrictions imposed. Any order made is not a lifelong injunction; it can last no longer than a year and may be renewed only after an entirely new hearing. A person subjected to a s. 810.1 order may appeal the order and may, at any time, seek to vary the conditions.

[48] I therefore conclude that s. 810.1 is not overbroad. Instead, it strikes a reasonable balance between the liberty interest of the defendant and the state's interest in protecting young children from harm. A defendant's liberty interest may be restricted only after a hearing complying with the requirements of natural justice and only to the extent needed to avoid unreasonably jeopardizing the safety and security of young children.

(iii) Is Section 810.1 Void for Vagueness?

[49] Like the overbreadth principle, the void for vagueness principle is also concerned with whether the legislature has used precise enough means to achieve its objective. But whereas overbreadth is concerned with whether the legislation is targeted sufficiently narrowly, vagueness is concerned with whether the legislation is defined with sufficient clarity. The rationale for the void for vagueness principle is that, unless a law sufficiently delineates the area of risk of unlawful conduct, citizens will not have the fair notice of the law to which they are entitled, and police officers and others will have too much discretion in deciding how and when to enforce the law. Thus, a law must provide "an intelligible standard according to which the judiciary must do its work" and "an adequate basis for legal debate, that is for reaching a conclusion as to its meaning by reasoned analysis applying legal criteria." Otherwise, the law will be impermissibly vague contrary to the principles of fundamental justice.

[50] The appellant submits that s. 810.1 does not sufficiently delineate an area of risk of unlawful conduct, and thus does not provide fair substantive notice to a citizen, because it allows for restrictions on liberty on an informant's fear on reasonable grounds. The appellant argues that the word "fear" should be contrasted with the word "belief," which is used in *Criminal Code* provisions authorizing an arrest or a search. "Fear," according to the appellant, can be irrational or emotional and is invariably subjective, while "belief" can be assessed objectively.

[51] I do not accept the appellant's argument. The word "fear" or "fears" should not be considered in isolation but together with the modifying words in s. 810.1(1) "on reasonable grounds." Fear alone connotes a state of belief or an apprehension that a future event, thought to be undesirable, may or will occur. But "on reasonable grounds" lends objectivity to the apprehension. In other words, the phrase "fears on reasonable grounds" in s. 810.1(1) connotes a reasonably based sense of apprehension about a future event, or as Then J put it, it "equates to a belief, objectively established, that the individual will commit an offence" (at p. 381).

[52] Moreover, although an informant's fear triggers an application under s. 810.1, under s-s. (3) a recognizance order can only be made if the presiding judge is satisfied by "evidence" that the fear is reasonably based. Section 810.1(3) therefore requires the judge to come to his or her own conclusion about the likelihood that the defendant will commit one of the offences listed in s-s. (1). Although the "evidence" the judge relies on might include hearsay, a recognizance could only be ordered on evidence that is credible and trustworthy.

[53] Despite the need for the informant's state of belief to be objectively assessed and for the presiding judge to come to an independent conclusion, I acknowledge some imprecision in the phrase "fears on reasonable grounds." But some imprecision is to be expected because s. 810.1 requires a prediction about future dangerousness. So too does s. 810, which uses the same phrase. The phrase is not so imprecise that it fails to delineate an area of risk or fails to provide an adequate basis for legal debate. Moreover, it is surrounded by requirements in s. 810.1—the information, the summons, the hearing itself—that give the defendant fair notice of the conduct sought to be prevented; and if a recognizance is ordered, the defendant will have fair notice of the conditions imposed

and, thus, will know how to comply. The threshold for declaring a law void for vagueness is appropriately high. Section 810.1 does not pass this threshold. I would not give effect to this ground of appeal.

Second Issue: Did Then J Err in Reading Down "Shall" to "May" in Section 810.1(2) of the Code?

[54] Section 810.1(2) provided that "a provincial court judge who receives an information under s-s. (1) shall cause the parties to appear before the provincial court judge." Then J held that, in the context of a preventive provision like s. 810.1, making the issuance of process on a defendant mandatory violated ss. 7 and 9 of the Charter and could not be justified under s. 1. In his view, "an automatic issuance of process, with the potential arrest of the defendant, is excessive and unwarranted." It provides "no control on obviously unfounded informations under which a person may be summonsed or arrested" (at pp. 399-401). Thus, it subjects the ordinary citizen to capricious or unjustifiable detention. In Then J's view, and relying on the Supreme Court's decision in *Baron v. Canada*, [1993] 1 SCR 416, 78 CCC (3d) 510, "a residual discretion is a constitutional requirement." The Crown does not take issue with Then J's holding that "shall" in s. 810.1(2) is unconstitutional.

[55] The appellant, however, takes issue with Then J's remedy. Having found that a discretion was a constitutional requirement, Then J applied s. 52 of the *Constitution Act, 1982*, and read down "shall" to "may." The appellant submits that he should simply have declared the subsection inoperative.

[56] The Supreme Court refused to read down "shall" to "may" in *Baron* itself, and in *R v. Swain*, [1991] 1 SCR 933, 63 CCC (3d) 481. Then J distinguished *Baron* on the grounds that the Attorney General in that case had not asked for the remedy of reading down and that, unlike the provision challenged in *Baron*, s. 810.1(2) was not central to the legislative regime in s. 810.1. I think it fair to say, however, that when legislation expressly excludes a judicial discretion, courts have been reluctant to read one in as a constitutional remedy. Nonetheless, in my view, Then J was correct to read down "shall" to "may" in this case.

[57] In deciding on the appropriate remedy under s. 52 for a Charter breach, "the court must apply the measures which will best vindicate the values expressed in the Charter while refraining from intrusion into the legislative sphere beyond what is necessary." Before reading down or reading in, the court must ask "whether it is safe to assume that the legislature would have enacted the legislation in its altered form." Here, "may" in s. 810.1(2) appropriately vindicates Charter values. Giving the presiding judge a discretion whether to summons or arrest a defendant once an information is sworn is an important constitutional safeguard. Thus, the remedy of reading in "may," although explicitly altering the legislation, will "preserve statutory objectives within clear constitutional contours."

[58] Recent legislation shows that we can safely assume Parliament would have enacted s. 810.1(2) with the word "may." In 1997 Parliament added two new provisions to the *Criminal Code* similar to s. 810.1, and in each new provision used the word "may" instead of "shall." Section 810.01 authorizes a recognizance order against a

person likely to commit "a criminal organization offence," and s. 810.2 authorizes a recognizance order against a person likely to commit "a serious personal injury offence." Sections 810.01 and 810.2 are worded similarly to s. 810.1 with necessary modifications for their context. Sections 810.01(2) and s. 810.2(2) are identical to s. 810.1(2) except that in place of "shall cause the parties to appear before the provincial court judge," in the two new provisions Parliament has used "may cause the parties to appear before the provincial court judge." Because Parliament itself has enacted s. 810.01 and s. 810.2 to conform to Then J's decision, we can safely assume that reading down "shall" to "may" does not unnecessarily intrude into the legislative domain. I would not give effect to this ground of appeal.

Third Issue: Do Sections 507(4) and 515 of the Criminal Code Apply to a Proceeding Under Section 810.1?

[59] In *R v. Allen*, this court held that what is now s. 507(4) of the Code, allowing for the issuance of a warrant for the arrest of the accused, applies to s. 810 of the Code. Section 507(4) provides:

> 507(4) Where a justice considers that a case is made out for compelling an accused to attend before him to answer to a charge of an offence, he shall issue a summons to the accused unless the allegations of the informant or the evidence of any witness or witnesses taken in accordance with subsection (3) discloses reasonable grounds to believe that it is necessary in the public interest to issue a warrant for the arrest of the accused.

[60] In *Allen*, the accused argued that s. 507(4) applied to "a charge of an offence" and thus could not apply to a proceeding under s. 810, which did not create an offence. Goodman JA, writing for the court, rejected this argument. Section 507(4) is in Part XVI of the Code; s. 810 is in Part XXVII dealing with summary convictions. Section 795 of the Code, which is also in Part XXVII, states that the provisions of Part XVI "with respect to compelling the appearance of an accused before a justice ... in so far as they are not inconsistent with the Part, apply, with such modifications as the circumstances require, to proceedings under this Part." In Goodman JA's view, s. 795 made s. 507(4) applicable to a proceeding under s. 810 even though s. 810 "does not create an offence" (at p. 158).

[61] Section 515, the provision permitting bail pending trial, also is in Part XVI of the Code; and s. 810.1 is in Part XXVII of the Code. Therefore, applying *Allen*, both ss. 507(4) and 515 apply to proceedings under s. 810.1.

[62] The appellant asked us to reconsider *Allen* on its own terms or in the light of the Charter. In my view, *Allen* was correctly decided. Applying provisions relating to a charge against an accused (ss. 507(4) and 515) to a proceeding commenced by the laying of an information (s. 810.1) is a modification contemplated by s. 795 of the Code. I am supported in this conclusion by the decision of the Saskatchewan Court of Appeal in *R v. Wakelin* (1992), 71 CCC (3d) 115, 97 Sask. R 275 (CA), which reached a similar result.

[63] *Allen*, however, was decided without reference to the Charter. The appellant submits that applying ss. 507(4) and 515 to a s. 810.1 proceeding violates s. 7 of the Charter. The argument has two branches: both permitting pre-hearing arrest and detention because of a fear of future misconduct and permitting a more severe sanction

pending the hearing than could be ordered at the conclusion of the s. 810.1 hearing violates the principles of fundamental justice. I disagree.

[64] First, the presiding judge has a discretion whether to issue a warrant for the arrest of a defendant or to detain a defendant pending a hearing. If a defendant is released pending a hearing, the judge has discretion concerning the bail conditions to be imposed. The existence of this judicial discretion is, as I have already said, an important constitutional safeguard and procedural protection for the defendant. The presiding judge has ample authority to balance the interests of the defendant and the interests of the public pending a s. 810.1 hearing and to ensure that the hearing is held promptly. Second, and repeating what I said earlier, provision for pre-hearing arrest and detention is needed to preserve the integrity of the s. 810.1 proceedings. The court may need the power of arrest and detention to ensure the attendance of a defendant at the hearing or to protect children from the possibility of serious harm pending the hearing.

[65] Moreover, s. 810.1 is not rendered unconstitutional because, in a particular case, an arrest warrant may have been improvidently issued or inappropriate bail conditions may have been imposed pending the hearing. Support for this view may be found in the decision of this court in *R v. Finlay* (1985), 52 OR (2d) 632, 23 CCC (3d) 48 (CA), where it was argued that the provisions of former s. 178.13 of the *Criminal Code*, which gave a judge the power to issue a wiretap authorization, were unconstitutional because the broadly-worded provision did not comply with minimum constitutional standards for search and seizure. Martin JA held that, properly interpreted, the provision complied with the Charter (at p. 70 CCC). The requirement that the authorization be granted only where to do so was in "the best interests of the administration of justice" imported the requirement that the judge be satisfied the granting of the authorization would further or advance the objectives of justice, and, therefore, imported a requirement to balance the state's interest in law enforcement and the individual's interest in privacy. These requirements, in turn, called on the judge to apply minimum constitutional standards under s. 8 of the Charter.

[66] The same analysis applies to the arrest and release procedure imported into s. 810.1. Under s. 507(4), the justice is to compel the defendant's attendance by means of a summons only, unless the allegations of the informant or the evidence "discloses reasonable grounds to believe that it is necessary in the public interest to issue a warrant for the arrest of the accused." Because a hearing under s. 810.1 can only result in the defendant being required to enter into a recognizance, the circumstances in which it would be "necessary in the public interest" to issue an arrest warrant will be limited to cases where that process is necessary to preserve the integrity of the s. 810.1 proceedings. The justice will require the informant to make out a case that the defendant will not otherwise attend court or that the defendant poses an imminent risk to the safety of children, which s. 810.1 is designed to protect.

[67] If the justice does issue an arrest warrant, s. 515 of the *Criminal Code* directs the justice to release the defendant on a simple undertaking without conditions, unless the prosecutor shows cause why some more intrusive order—such as a recognizance with conditions—is required. The discretion under s. 515 must be exercised judicially and bearing in mind the limited conditions that can be imposed following a successful s. 810.1 application.

[68] Finally, although s. 515 provides that the justice may order the detention of the defendant pending the s. 810.1 hearing, that discretion is circumscribed by the provisions of s. 515(10), which authorize detention only where necessary to ensure the defendant's attendance at court, for the protection or safety of the public or "any other just cause," including the maintenance of confidence in the administration of justice. Again, in the light of the limited consequences of a successful s. 810.1 application, only in unusual circumstances will the justice be entitled to order the detention of the defendant pending the hearing. Indeed, it will be a rare case where it would enhance confidence in the administration of justice to detain a defendant who is not alleged to have committed any crime and who can only be required to enter into a recognizance at the conclusion of the proceedings.

[69] So interpreted, these various provisions of the Code strike the appropriate balance between the public interest in the protection of children and the liberty interest of the defendant.

[70] For these reasons, I view ss. 507(4) and 515 in their application to s. 810.1 as being in accordance with the principles of fundamental justice. Therefore, I would not give effect to this ground of appeal.

The reasoning of the lower court decision (by Then J) in *Budreo* was applied in *R v. Baker*, [1999] BCJ No. 681 (QL) (SC), to reject a constitutional challenge to s. 810.2 (serious personal injury offence). This provision is somewhat wider than s. 810.1 because it is not necessary that a specified victim be named in the information or the subsequent recognizance. This reasoning was also applied in the notorious case of Karla Homolka (Teale), below, which received enormous media attention due to the grisly killings that led to her incarceration. Although a s. 810.2 order was originally made, it was set aside on appeal.

Teale v. Noble
(2005) RJQ 181, 36 CR (6th) 258 (SC) (footnotes omitted)

BRUNTON JSC:

[1] For her role in the homicides of Kristen French and Leslie Mahaffy, Karla Teale was sentenced to 12 years of imprisonment. On the eve of her release, after having served her entire sentence, the Attorney General of Quebec gave his consent to Mr. Brian Noble, a peace officer, to lay an information seeking an order under s. 810.2 Cr. C. which targeted Ms. Teale.

[2] Section 810.2 Cr. C. permits a judge to order that a defendant enter into a recognizance for a maximum period of 12 months to keep the peace and be of good behaviour. In general terms, other reasonable conditions can also be included.

[3] The order will only issue if the informant establishes on a balance of probabilities that he or she has reasonable grounds to fear that the defendant will commit a serious personal injury offence as that expression is defined in section 752 Cr. C.

· · ·

[4] After an evidentiary hearing was held, an Order directed against Ms. Teale was issued on June 3, 2005. She has appealed that decision.

[5] In general terms, she raises four grounds of appeal:

- s. 810.2 Cr. C. is unconstitutional;
- the hearing judge erred in refusing a postponement in order to permit Ms. Teale to present a written motion for a stay of proceedings based upon abuse of process;
- Mr. Noble failed to produce sufficient evidence to warrant the issuing of an order. The hearing judge's finding that sufficient evidence had been produced was unreasonable;
- alternatively, if sufficient evidence existed, certain of the conditions imposed in the Order were null as going beyond those contemplated by s. 810.2 Cr. C.

. . .

[20] One need only look to the type of evidence which was presented in the *Budreo* case at first instance on the constitutional question.

> The evidence the parties submitted took the form of affidavits from experts in the field of sexual offences or criminology, cross-examination of those affiants and the submission of scholarly works. In addition to the affidavit evidence, a large amount of documentary evidence was filed in the form of articles and studies to assist the court in dealing with the larger constitutional questions.

[21] It is clear that that material provided great assistance both in first instance and before the Court of Appeal of Ontario. In the absence of that type of proof in the present case, I hold that it would be improper to entertain the constitutional challenge for the first time at the appellate level. The challenge raises complex issues which should be addressed only if a proper factual foundation is set. It has not been in this case.

[22] If I am in error in refusing to entertain the challenge, I would nonetheless hold that based upon the record before me, s. 810.2 Cr. C. is constitutional. No cogent reason has been advanced why the decision in *Budreo* should not be followed.

. . .

[25] Many of Ms. Teale's arguments suggest that s. 810.2 Cr. C. is overbroad and too vague. I respectfully disagree. I adopt the same factors identified in *Budreo* in response to this argument.

- unlike the appellant, I do not believe that s. 810.2 Cr. C. provides the hearing judge with an unfettered discretion to impose any type of condition in the order;
- the impossibility of making exact predictions of future dangerousness does not render s. 810.2 Cr. C. overbroad. Both the dangerous offender legislation and the bail system rely on predictions of future dangerousness;
- the procedural safeguards in s. 810.2 are adequate;
- the recourse to hearsay evidence is not objectionable. Ultimately, the order can only issue on evidence that is judged credible and trustworthy;
- the need for the informant to establish a "fear" of future dangerousness does not render s. 810.2 void for vagueness.

[26] As pointed out by Then J, the need to establish the fear on reasonable grounds

... equates to a belief, objectively established, that the individual will commit an offence.

[27] Finally, Ms. Teale's reliance on s. 11(g) and 11(h) of the Charter is misplaced. Those sections have no application as they are available only to persons charged with an offence. The recourse to s. 810.2 Cr. C. did not result in Ms. Teale being charged with an offence.

[28] The constitutional challenge is dismissed.

• • •

D. The Sufficiency of the Evidence

[42] In order to succeed, the informant had to establish on a balance of probabilities that he had reasonable grounds to fear that Ms. Teale would commit a personal injury offence. It was not enough to invoke Ms. Teale's participation in the sordid homicides of Ms. French and Ms. Mahaffy. Since s. 810.2 Cr. C. proceedings look to the future, the fear relates to the present portrait which is offered of the defendant by the informant.

[43] Nor is it sufficient to equate the fear with a *risk* that the defendant will commit a personal injury offence sometime in the future. There is a temporal component to s. 810.2 Cr. C. proceedings. The fear must reflect a risk of *serious and imminent* danger. This is reflected both in the construction of the section and its subsequent interpretation by the courts.

[44] The section itself imposes a twelve month limit on the duration of the recognizance order. If the section called only for the proof of a fear of specified action sometime in the future, why place a twelve month limit on the court's response? This time limit, combined with the fact that the fear that is to be established is that the defendant will commit a personal injury offence imports a component of imminency.

Judges should take care before exercising their preventive jurisdiction. Both ss. 810 and 810.1 speak of a reasonably grounded fear that the defendant "will" commit an offence. To my mind, as a matter of legislative construction, this takes the appropriate threshold a notch above a simple demonstration that the defendant is more likely than not to commit an offence. *A reasonably grounded fear of a serious and imminent danger must be proved on a balance of probabilities.* (emphasis added)

• • •

[46] The hearing judge held that the informant had established on a balance of probabilities reasonable grounds for his fears of a real and imminent danger that Ms. Teale would commit a personal injury offence. As will be seen, I hold that the proof presented did not establish, on a balance of probabilities, a fear of imminent danger.

[47] The proof presented before the hearing judge consisted generally of the following material. All psychological reports dealing with Ms. Teale over the years were produced. None of the authors of these reports were called as witnesses.

[48] Mr. Noble testified. He directed the hearing judge to various excerpts of the documentary evidence which in his mind objectively established the reasonable grounds for his fear that Ms. Teale would commit a serious personal injury offence.

[49] Ms. Teale responded by producing the Galligan report which had been commissioned to examine the circumstances of the plea bargain involving the appellant and whether it would be appropriate to charge her with sexual assault as regards a victim referred to as Jane Doe. The other significant element of proof produced by Ms. Teale was the testimony of Dr. Louis Morissette. Dr. Morissette, a psychiatrist, had been engaged by counsel for Ms. Teale. He had met her for a period of three and one half hours, days before the hearing. His report was produced as exhibit I-8. Ms. Teale chose not to testify.

[50] After stating that he had considered all the evidence, the hearing judge found that the informant had reasonable grounds to fear that Ms. Teale would commit a personal injury offence. He relied principally upon two elements of proof. Those elements consisted of a report prepared by Madam France Aubut, a psychologist (exhibit R-1, tab 6). The second element referred to the fact that in the recent past, Ms. Teale had been corresponding with an inmate she had met who was serving a sentence for the homicide of his former girlfriend.

[51] As for Dr. Morissette's testimony and report, the hearing judge summarily accorded these elements of proof less weight as they were based upon hearsay in his estimation.

[52] Exercising an appellate jurisdiction, my powers are limited as regards the hearing judge's appreciation of the evidence.

> Appellate courts may not interfere with the findings of fact made and the factual inferences drawn by the trial judge, unless they are clearly wrong, unsupported by the evidence or otherwise unreasonable. The imputed error must, moreover, be plainly identified. And it must be shown to have affected the result. "Palpable and overriding error" is a resonant and compendious expression of this well established norm.

[53] The experienced hearing judge was confronted with a difficult and complex case. He was also confronted with the pressures of time as the appellant's release date loomed on the horizon. Bearing these factors in mind together with my limited powers on appeal, I respectfully find that the hearing judge erred in holding that the informant had met his evidentiary burden. The errors consist of a combination of the following factors:

- the summary dismissal of Dr. Morissette's evidence;
- the lack of explanation of why numerous elements in the proof favourable to the appellant could have no bearing on the ultimate decision which had to be made;
- the lack of a contextual analysis of the two elements which the hearing judge relied upon to render his decision;
- the unreasonable conclusion based upon all the evidence that the appellant represented a "real and imminent" danger to commit a personal injury offence.

...

[56] While it is true that the trier of fact, in assessing the weight to be given to an expert's testimony examines what portion of the factors which lead to the expert's opinion have been proven, the situation in the present case was unique. Almost all of the proof presented was generated from assessments of Ms. Teale, which in turn were based upon

information which she had provided. If the fact that Ms. Teale did not testify affected the weight given to Dr. Morissette's opinion, why did it not affect the weight given to the reports produced by all the interveners in the file, including Madam Aubut?

[57] It is not an answer to reply that Madam Aubut's report was not challenged by Ms. Teale in the parole process and thus it gained extra value. By the time Madam Aubut produced her report, it was clear to all parties that Ms. Teale had chosen to serve her entire sentence. She thus had no interest in challenging any of the reports submitted to the Parole Board or its subsequent decisions.

[58] Furthermore, the testimony of Dr. Morissette was a challenge to Madam Aubut's report or, at the very least, an attempt to put Madam Aubut's report in context. By summarily putting aside the Morissette evidence, the hearing judge's analysis of the Aubut report was flawed.

ii. Lack of Reference to Elements Favourable to the Appellant

[59] I recognize that the hearing judge did not have to refer to every item of evidence in his judgment. However, this was a complex case which called for the analysis of the development, or lack thereof, of Ms. Teale over a period of twelve years. The proof presented was not exclusively negative from Ms. Teale's point of view. Indeed, it could be said that there was a steady stream of opinion over the years contained in the evidence which, if accepted, clearly would show that the informant had not met his burden.

[60] No specific reference was made to any of this proof. The only indirect reference was contained in the following catch-all phrase:

> ... après analyse attentive de toute la preuve, tant orale que documentaire, alors, la réponse à cette question, suite à une analyse complète de la preuve, est oui. La crainte raisonnable est démontrée par prépondérance de preuve.

[61] As mentioned above, the complexity of the case and the presence of many elements of proof favourable to Ms. Teale called for a more in-depth analysis than that detailed in the phrase quoted above.

iii. Contextual Analysis of the Factors Retained

[62] As I have already stated, the hearing judge based his decision primarily on the contents of a report prepared by Madam France Aubut (exhibit R-1, tab 6) and the fact that Ms. Teale had corresponded in the recent past with one Gerbet, an inmate convicted for the homicide of his former girlfriend.

[63] Madam Aubut's November 17, 2004 report consisted of a psychological evaluation pursuant to Ms. Teale having followed a treatment program destined to those who had committed sexual offences. Ms. Teale's participation in the program began in July 2003. The purpose of the program was for the participant to identify these factors which led her to commit the sexual offence(s) and to identify methods to neutralize those same factors in the future.

· · ·

[74] Madam Aubut concluded that the appellant offered an adequate collaboration during the course of the program. However, she refused on more than one occasion to

delve into certain subjects because it was too disagreeable. Madam Aubut gave the example of Ms. Teale refusing to profoundly describe her thoughts, behaviour and emotions when she was committing the offences. For Madam Aubut, this attitude was dangerous—on the one hand it reflected an attitude which Ms. Teale herself identified as one of her risk factors, and on the other, was the complete opposite of the type of behaviour she identified in her prevention plan, i.e. not being secretive and seeking aid from her support group.

[75] Madam Aubut concluded, in part, on this note:

> *Il nous est apparu que Madame Teale est portée à utiliser de façon sélective ses stratégies d'adaptation aux facteurs de risque qu'elle a identifiés. Il faut donc se questionner sur le fait qu'elle pourrait également généraliser, i.e. appliquer ses acquis, de façon sélective lorsqu'elle se retrouvera à l'extérieur des murs. Cette éventualité l'exposerait de nouveau à des situations à risque susceptibles de la projeter dans une progression de son cycle comportemental criminel. Conséquemment, nous considérons que l'impact du programme sur la diminution du risque qu'elle représente est de portée limitée jusqu'à présent.*

[76] For the hearing judge, this conclusion was capital.

> *Il faut se méfier, dans les cas de crimes graves, d'une personne qui n'a pas le courage ou, à tout le moins, la volonté d'aller au fond des choses. C'est un signe évident, selon la Cour, que cette personne, dans la peur de souffrir ou de sombrer, fait passer l'équilibre de sa propre personne devant la protection de ses concitoyens. Elle se trouve, en effet, à bloquer à l'avance un résultat positif de la thérapie dans une sphère importante, c'est-à-dire le fait de ne pas récidiver. Or, nous sommes ici précisément pour éviter une récidive dans l'infliction de sévices graves à la personne.*

[77] Turning to the second specific factor upon which the hearing judge based his decision, the proof revealed that Ms. Teale began a relationship with a male inmate in January 2002. She was surprised exchanging a kiss with him in the institution's library.

[78] Searches revealed that the two had exchanged undergarments and were engaged in correspondence. A photo of the male inmate was found in Ms. Teale's possession. Although both were advised to stop the correspondence, it continued.

[79] The male inmate, Gerbet, was serving time for having killed his former girlfriend.

[80] The hearing judge noted that during the 1993 sentence representations, much was made of the fact that Ms. Teale was a victim of battered woman's syndrome and this explained her participation in the sordid events which led to the homicides of the victims.

[81] Subsequent reports highlighted the fact that the single greatest risk for Ms. Teale to re-offend would arise if she found herself in an abusive relationship. Her relationship with Gerbet, which continued notwithstanding that she had been warned, did not bode well for the future.

[82] I have stated earlier that the hearing judge erred in not considering the two factors he relied upon, together or individually, in the context of all the proof which was presented. At best these factors established that there was a risk that Ms. Teale would

re-offend. They did not establish that there was a real and imminent danger that she would re-offend as is required by s. 810.2 Cr. C.

[83] In commenting on Madam Aubut's report, Dr. Morissette acknowledged that the results of Ms. Teale's participation in the program were not perfect. He added however that one cannot expect perfection in this type of endeavour. If the final assessment notes that the participant did not accomplish her assigned work projects, missed sessions or was not serious in her approach, then one begins to develop warning signs that she is a bad risk. This was not the case for Ms. Teale.

. . .

[85] As for the evidence concerning the correspondence between Ms. Teale and Gerbet, the following points should be noted to fully understand the context of this factor.

[86] First, the nature of the contents of the correspondence was never entered into evidence although it appears that certain letters were seized as early as 2002. Second, no intervener in the correctional system thought the contents of the correspondence so grave for Ms. Teale's personal development as to impose a ban on the exchanges.

[87] Third, no proof was made of Gerbet's character. The parties agreed that he was serving a sentence for having killed his ex-girlfriend. While this is extremely grave, the personality and inherent dangerousness of such an offender is not constant. Was the crime he committed an aberration in an otherwise unblemished past or was he a chronic abuser of women, prone to violent acts? Perhaps it was the latter, but in the absence of evidence, a Court cannot base a decision on speculation or educated guesses.

[88] Fourth, it appears the parties agreed that Gerbet was to be the subject of an eventual deportation order when he would become eligible for parole as he was not a Canadian citizen. This fact would eliminate Ms. Teale being able to interact with him except by way of correspondence. If the various experts who examined her over the years agreed that her entering another abusive relationship would greatly increase the risk of her re-offending, none suggested that this risk could be triggered at a distance. None of these points appear to have been considered by the hearing judge.

iv. The Totality of the Evidence

[89] No one denies that Ms. Teale's involvement in the horrifying homicides of Ms. French and Ms. Mahaffy and her sister Tammy displayed unspeakable depravity. However, the recurring themes in the assessments of her actions on the weight of the evidence is that (1) her participation in the crimes was due principally to the abuse she suffered at the hands of her husband; (2) she has made progress over the years of her incarceration; (3) she will need psychological support for the better part of her life; (4) the possibility that she will re-offend exists; and (5) the possibility does not translate into an imminent risk of re-offending.

[90] At the sentencing hearing, experienced and respected Crown counsel had this to say:

> The Crown's assessment, based on a review of such psychiatric evidence, is that absent the influence and association of someone whose behaviour bears the characteristics of

what truly may be one of this province's and the country's most feared individuals, she is unlikely to re-offend.

[91] The Crown added:

In light of the specific psychiatric evaluation of this accused, it is apparent that continued treatment will be required. I would venture that that is a lifetime proposition.

[92] The Honourable Mr. Justice F.J. Kovacs, in sentencing Ms. Teale, made reference to three psychological assessments. Dr. A.I. Malcolm, a psychiatrist, stated in a May 28, 1993 report that Ms. Teale was "not a dangerous person ... but she will require much assistance." Dr. H.J. Arnot, a psychiatrist, in a May 30, 1993 report stated:

... I do not see her as being a danger now or ever again to society, particularly as long as she is not in contact with her estranged husband, Paul Bernardo or someone like him. In my opinion, Karla requires lengthy psychiatric care. ...

[93] Dr. J.A. Long, a clinical psychologist, in a report dated June 3, 1993 stated:

... she is not a danger to herself nor to anyone else and therefore may be placed in a low-security institution.

[94] The documentary evidence produced before the hearing judge follows Ms. Teale through the years of her incarceration.

. . .

[110] Numerous decisions of the National Parole Board were produced before the hearing judge. In all cases, Ms. Teale's supervised or early release was denied. Two points should be made about these reports. First, Ms. Teale had made the decision to serve her entire sentence. Thus, both she and the Parole Board were aware that no decision of the Parole Board would be subject to review.

[111] Second, the Parole Board appeared to be cognizant of the fact that Ms. Teale's supervised or early release would be extremely difficult to manage due to the negative public opinion directed to her case. The combination of these two factors, at the very least, would not have incited the Parole Board to take the decision, which it might have considered bold, to gradually re-integrate Ms. Teale into society.

[112] I have already had occasion to discuss at length Madam Aubut's report of November 17, 2004. There remains the testimony of Dr. Morissette.

[113] Dr. Morissette's status as an expert was not contested. This is not surprising. Dr. Morissette had been associated with the Philippe Pinel Institute since 1982. This institute houses both those individuals accused of crimes whose mental health is at issue and those found non-criminally responsible. His work included providing evaluation reports on the dangerousness of inmates passing before the Parole Board.

[114] Since 1998, the Institute has been mandated to produce reports on those individuals facing dangerous offender proceedings or long-term offender proceedings.

[115] As I have mentioned earlier in this judgment, Dr. Morissette had the occasion to meet Ms. Teale for a total of three and one-half hours prior to producing his May 26, 2005 report. This short period of time of consultation calls for a certain amount of caution when assessing his conclusions. Having said this, Dr. Morissette's opinions do reflect

those of the majority of the professionals who had occasion to assess Ms. Teale over the years.

[116] His conclusions can be summarized in the following general terms:

- There was no indication of a psychotic personality based upon the results of the H.A.R.E. test. Ms. Teale's results placed her at the extreme low end of the scale and well below the average of federal inmates.
- She scored low on the SVR (Sexual Violence Risk) test.
- The majority of inmates who represent a risk to re-offend have a record of disciplinary offences during their incarceration. Ms. Teale's record was unblemished.
- The results of Ms. Teale's therapy with Madam Aubut were to be expected. It is clear that while Ms. Teale had made progress, she would require on-going professional aid.
- There were no clinical, historical or current mental problems which could lead one to conclude that Ms. Teale was more at risk to re-offend than the average federal inmate.

[117] Dr. Morissette ends his report with this conclusion:

Pour toutes ces raisons, nous croyons que Mme Teale devrait être considérée comme étant à très faible risque de récidive en terme de violence contre les personnes, de violence sexuelle, d'activités criminelles, etc. Sur une échelle de 0 à 10 (0 étant une absolue certitude qu'elle ne commettrait jamais à nouveau de délit et 10 étant une absolue certitude qu'elle commettra à nouveau des délits violents), nous la placerions entre 1 et 3.

[118] I am of the opinion that this statement aptly summarizes the conclusion which should be reached when all the proof I have described is analyzed. The weight of the psychological assessments of Ms. Teale and her progress support this conclusion.

[119] The possibility that Ms. Teale might re-offend one day cannot be completely eliminated. However, her development over the last twelve years demonstrates, on a balance of probabilities, that this is unlikely to occur. She does not represent a real and imminent danger to commit a personal injury offence as is required by s. 810.2 Cr. C.

The appeal should be granted.

CHAPTER SIXTEEN

Aboriginal Offenders

I. INTRODUCTIONS

The materials in this chapter only scratch the surface of a very complex issue—the suitability of invoking Anglo-Canadian criminal justice structures and precepts to deal with Aboriginal offenders. Certainly, one must question how fairly our criminal justice system has responded to Aboriginal offenders. Empirically, there is no doubt that Aboriginal persons are overrepresented in our penal structures. The history of Canada's relationship with its First Nations and the acknowledged constitutional status of Aboriginal rights create an obligation to explore the reasons for overrepresentation, to question the record of systemic unfairness, and to find new ways of applying criminal justice.

The incongruity of applying the standard methodology of sentencing to Aboriginal offenders has been apparent for many years. The case of *R v. Fireman*, infra, is almost 30 years old. Similar examples can be found in many cases involving accused persons from remote communities (see *R v. Naqitarvik* (1986), 26 CCC (3d) 193 (NWT CA) and *R v. Curley, Nagmalik, and Issigaitok*, [1984] NWTR 281 (CA).

R v. Fireman
[1971] 3 OR 380 (CA)

BROOKE JA: This is an appeal by Gabriel Fireman from the sentence of 10 years' imprisonment in the penitentiary imposed upon him by Wright J, on November 19, 1969, upon the appellant's plea of guilty on his arraignment on a charge of manslaughter.

The facts are not in dispute. The appellant and his victim were cousins who lived on friendly terms in their settlement on the shores of Attawapiskat River which is on the west shore of James Bay and distant some 470 miles north-east from the Town of Sioux Lookout and 250 miles north from the Town of Moosonee. On July 30, 1969, a large shipment of liquor was delivered to the settlement at the order of two relatives of the deceased and the appellant. These two shipments were the first that size to have been received by the people of the settlement for private use, and the trial Judge was told that the 12 persons who consumed this liquor, began as the shipments were unloaded and ended some 12 hours later, when Eli Fireman was shot to death by the appellant. Both men were deeply intoxicated. There was no real reason for the shooting. All that can be said is that after a night long of drinking, petty differences spawned arguments which culminated in a fight that ended with the fatal shot being fired. For what little significance it may be, the appellant is not said to have been a cause of the fight, nor directly involved in it.

The settlement is remote. It cannot be reached by road and is visited only twice each year by ship. Recently, mail delivery by aircraft was instituted. However, uncertain weather renders this service doubtful most of the year. The only real communication between the settlement and the rest of the country is through intermittent radio-telephone communication, the control of which is not in the hands of the Indian people at the settlement. The people at the settlement are members of the Cree nation and are called the Swamp Cree. Their dialect is not widely known even amongst the people of their nation. Very few of the people of the settlement speak any English, and it is only in recent years that the children have been taken to the nearest schools which are at the railhead at Moosonee, and there they have been given the opportunity of studying English. It is clear these people have no real familiarity with our way of life.

The police visit the area rarely as there have been very few calls for their services. Heretofore, the people of the settlement have enjoyed an excellent reputation for the 30 years that the settlement's existence has been known, for there have been no previous instances of major crimes there. The affairs of the people are governed by a chief and band council who exert strong control, and who, according to the police witnesses, are respected and obeyed in the community.

The settlement, then, is a truly remote place, cut off from the rest of the country, inhabited by people who have really little contact with our way of life; although, the evidence is that some of our material things are finding their way there now.

The principal occupation of the men of the settlement is trapping. With the approach of winter the population of the settlement dwindles from 500 to 200 persons as the men (in some cases, families) go to the traplines in the wilderness, where they remain for up to six months, returning in the spring with their catch of furs which are disposed of by sale to the Hudson's Bay post at the settlement. A good trapper can net $2,500 for his furs.

At the time of his conviction Gabriel Fireman was 25 years old. He was a good trapper quite capable of carrying on his business which included scheduling arrangements with an aircraft to fly him and his skidoo in and out from the traplines along with his cargo of furs, and he was able to manage the sale of his furs. On the other hand, the appellant is almost completely without an education, having finished the equivalent of our grade five when he was 22 years old. But this is not unusual in his community. In addition, the appellant failed grade seven three times because he did not have enough English to comprehend the basic things which were a part of that course. Perhaps because of the differences in the cultures, the appellant's IQ tests were found to be below the average for our whole society, but they were average for his own community. Some indication of the basic differences may be gained from the fact that he lived in a community where time is told only by seasons, that his sentence of 10 years is something that he is not likely to fully understand for he is unfamiliar with the calendar measurement of time in terms of days, weeks, months or years.

When it was discovered that the appellant had killed his cousin, the people of the settlement, including the families of the appellant and the deceased, were shocked and they rejected the appellant. It is plain from the evidence of the police officers, that under the direction of the chief and the band council, what evidence there was of the event was gathered up and retained for the police and Gabriel Fireman was detained by the people and turned over to the police upon their arrival. He remained ostracized by the community and it was only after he had taken communion at their church that his family would look upon him. It is said that following the process of the preliminary inquiry the community was prepared to accept him.

After considering the appellant's background, some aspects of the values of the people of the settlement, including their apparent different value of death, the learned trial Judge rejected the contention that lesser punishment would suffice and, placing the emphasis on the deterrent aspect of the sentence, imposed the term of 10 years on the appellant.

The appellant's contention is that the learned trial Judge failed to give due consideration to the effect of such a sentence upon the appellant, having regard to his background and the probabilities of his rehabilitation, and that the principle of deterrence to the whole community would have been satisfied by a much shorter term.

In my opinion, one can only proceed to consider the fitness of the sentence meted out to this man upon a proper appreciation of his cultural background and of his character, as it is only then that the full effect of the sentence upon him will be clear. When one considers these things, it is my opinion that even a short term of imprisonment in the penitentiary is substantial punishment to him. In the appellant's case, despite the best efforts of those who must be responsible for his care, the effect of his removal from his environment and his imprisonment would no doubt dull every sense by which he has lived in the north.

He can speak no English. It is not the language that he will use in his daily life upon his return to his home. There is no necessity for his knowing English there. There is little likelihood that he will learn English in the institution when one considers the restrictions on his ability to learn. With the difficulty in communication it is improbable that useful instruction would be available to him and, of some importance, how frustrating his existence when all those around him do not speak his language nor he theirs. I would think his imprisonment would produce a loneliness that would be greater than that in isolation.

On the other hand, does his sentence of 10 years take into consideration the desirability of his rehabilitation? From what I have said, in my view, it follows that it does not. To borrow words from the Canadian Committee on Corrections, I think it is probable that such a term will greatly reduce the chance of this man assuming a normal tolerable role on returning to his society and may well result in the creation of a social cripple.

His sentence as a deterrent to others raises important considerations. Normally, the trial of an accused man takes place in the area where the crime is said to have been committed. Members of the community may witness the trial and some indeed participate in it, and so through witnessing the trial and by word of mouth of those who have been there, what happened is known throughout the community. In this case, while the appellant was arrested at the settlement, his trial took place a very great distance away by reasons of the provisions of the territorial divisions of this Province.

There is no indication in the record that any person from his community participated in or was present at his trial, and it seems unlikely that this was so for the record discloses that there was difficulty in obtaining interpreters who knew the dialect of the Swamp Cree. What knowledge would his community have of the reasons of the learned trial Judge in sentencing the appellant or, for that matter, of this Court in dealing with his appeal? To ask the question is to answer it.

To the appellant and to the people of the settlement the deterrent value of the disposition of this case lies in the fact that the appellant's conduct which the people of the settlement condemned, was condemned by the rest of our society. The people of the settlement participated in and witnessed the arrest of the appellant and they know that he has been segregated from them by proceedings in a distant place. To the rest of the community the deterrent lies in the fact that this unsophisticated man of previous good character was sent to prison for his crime and surely, it is not dependent on the magnitude of the sentence for its value. I do not think it adds greatly to the deterrent value of what has taken place that such a severe sentence be imposed. What is important in these circumstances is that to the whole community justice appears to have been done and that there will be respect for the law. This is best accomplished in the case of this first offender if he is returned to his society before time makes him a stranger and impairs his ability to live there with some dignity.

With the greatest deference to the learned trial Judge, for the above reasons in my view the sentence is too severe and the appeal must be allowed. The determination of the appropriate quantum of sentence is not easy. The crime for which the appellant was convicted is a very serious one and, yet, the appellant has not by his previous conduct indicated that he is a dangerous person from whom society must be protected. Frankly, I think it is doubtful that prison is the answer, but that is our way. However, regard can properly be had to the institutions in our system and their flexibility for some guidance in determining and arriving at a proper conclusion. In this case, as the dominant consideration is the reformation and rehabilitation of this man and of course the respect of the community for our system, I think the appropriate sentence would have been two years less one day.

However, having regard to the time that has transpired since the appellant's conviction and sentencing, there would be little benefit to him in the change required by such a sentence and accordingly the appeal is allowed and the sentence will be reduced to one of two years.

NOTE

The problems faced by Aboriginal offenders and the need to explore different sentencing approaches are not restricted to residents of remote communities. Later in this chapter, we examine sentencing circles, which attempt to shift the procedural and substantive paradigm. In *R v. Morin* (1996), 42 CR (4th) 339 (Sask. CA), a Métis with a long record of prior convictions pleaded guilty to a robbery in Saskatoon. With the support of the local Métis community, the judge agreed to conduct a sentencing circle. Although a sentence in the range of four years would have been the usual result, after hearing the recommendations of the circle, the judge sentenced the offender to 18 months' incarceration to be followed by 18 months' intensive probation. The Crown appealed. The majority of the five-member panel of the Saskatchewan Court of Appeal allowed the appeal principally on the ground that there was no basis to give pre-eminence to rehabilitation. However, the court observed (at 375):

From the perspective of consequences we appear to have two systems of justice. Sentencing circles have a role to play in breaking down that apparent anomaly.

II. AN OVERVIEW OF OVERREPRESENTATION

In the past three decades, a number of studies and commissions of inquiry have document-ed the inordinate overrepresentation of Aboriginal people in Canadian jails. These studies were documented and supported by the research and conclusions of the Royal Commission on Aboriginal Peoples.

Royal Commission on Aboriginal Peoples, *Bridging the Cultural Divide:*
A Report on Aboriginal People and Criminal Justice in Canada
(Ottawa: Supply and Services Canada, 1996) (footnotes omitted)

From our reading of these reports and from what we learned through our research and our hearings, we drew two principal conclusions. The first is that there is a remarkable consensus on some fundamental issues and, in particular, how the Canadian justice system has failed Aboriginal people; the second conclusion is that notwithstanding the hundreds of recommendations from commissions and task forces, the reality for Ab-original people in 1996 is that the justice system is still failing them.

• • •

The justice inquiries that preceded our work documented extensively how this fail-ure has affected the lives of Aboriginal men, women and young people. The clearest evidence appears in the form of the over-representation of Aboriginal people in the criminal justice system. This was first documented in 1967 by the Canadian Corrections Association report, *Indians and the Law*, and in 1974 by the Law Reform Commission of Canada in *The Native Offender and the Law*. Reports and inquiries since then have not only confirmed the fact of over-representation but, most alarmingly, have demon-strated that the problem is getting worse, not better.

• • •

The [Canadian Bar] Association cautioned that "absent radical change, the problem will intensify." The surest evidence that there has been no radical change, and the most damning indictment, is found in the commissions of inquiry appointed since the publi-cation of *Locking Up Natives in Canada*. The Aboriginal Justice Inquiry of Manitoba reported that whereas Aboriginal people accounted for 33 per cent of the population at Stony Mountain Federal Penitentiary in 1984, by 1989 the figure had risen to 46 per cent. In 1983 Aboriginal people accounted for 37 per cent of the population of the prov-incial Headingly Correctional Institution; by 1989 they accounted for 41 per cent. By 1989 Aboriginal women accounted for 67 per cent of the prison population at the Por-tage Correctional Institution for Women, and in institutions for young people, the pro-portion of Aboriginal people was 61 per cent. All together, Aboriginal people made up 56 per cent of the population of correctional institutions (both federal and provincial) in Manitoba in 1989. Aboriginal people account for just under 12 per cent of Manitoba's total population and "thus, Aboriginal people, depending on their age and sex, are pres-ent in the jails up to five times more than their presence in the general population."

The figures received by the Task Force on the Criminal Justice System and its Impact on the Indian and Métis People of Alberta also confirmed that Aboriginal over-representation is getting worse in the province of Alberta. Indeed, because Alberta has the second highest rate of imprisonment per person charged in the whole country, over-representation has even harsher effects than elsewhere. Aboriginal men now make up 30 per cent of the male population in provincial jails and Aboriginal women 45 per cent of the female jail population. The most alarming conclusion of the task force is that for Aboriginal young offenders, "over-representation in the criminal justice system is even more dramatic" than it is for adults, and future population projections indicate that the situation will get much worse.

> Projections indicate that by the year 2011, Aboriginal offenders will account for 38.5 per cent of all admissions to federal and provincial correctional centres in Alberta, compared to 29.5 per cent of all such offenders in 1989. ... In some age categories, for example, the 12-18 years of age group, Aboriginal offenders are projected to account for 40 per cent of the admission of population to correctional facilities by the year 2011.

The fact that in some provinces the coercive intrusion of criminal laws into the lives of Aboriginal people and Aboriginal communities is increasing, not receding, is reflected in the most recent figures from Saskatchewan. John Hylton, a human justice and public policy adviser who has kept a close watch on the situation in Saskatchewan, has broken down total and Aboriginal admissions to provincial correctional centres for the years 1976-77 and compared them to the figures for 1992-93. The breakdown reveals several startling findings:

1. Between 1976-77 and 1992-93, the number of admissions to Saskatchewan correctional centres increased from 4,712 to 6,889, a 46 per cent increase, during a time when the provincial population remained virtually unchanged. The rate of increase was 40.7 per cent for male admissions and 111 per cent for female admissions.
2. During the same period, the number of Aboriginals admitted to Saskatchewan correctional centres increased from 3,082 to 4,757, an increase of 54 per cent. Male Aboriginal admissions increased by 48 per cent, while female Aboriginal admissions increased by 107 per cent.
3. In terms of overall rates of admission, Aboriginals were 65.4 per cent in 1976-77 and 69.1 per cent in 1992-93.
4. Increases in Aboriginal admissions accounted for 77 per cent of the increase in total admissions between 1976-77 and 1992-93.

> These data indicate clearly that the problem of disproportionate representation of the Aboriginal people in Saskatchewan's justice system is growing worse, not better. ... Predictions that were prepared in the early 1980s and that were rejected by some as too extreme, have in some instances proven to be conservative, particularly in the case of female Aboriginal admissions.

Aboriginal over-representation in the country's prisons, while presenting the face of injustice in its most repressive form, is only part of the picture. The Aboriginal Justice Inquiry of Manitoba commissioned a great deal of research on the other parts of a system that from beginning to end treats Aboriginal people differently. The Inquiry reported that

> Aboriginal over-representation is the end point of a series of decisions made by those with decision-making power in the justice system. An examination of each of these decisions suggests that the way that decisions are made within the justice system discriminates against Aboriginal people at virtually every point. ...

> - More than half of the inmates of Manitoba's jails are Aboriginal
> - Aboriginal accused are more likely to be denied bail
> - Aboriginal people spend more time in pre-trial detention than do non-Aboriginal people
> - Aboriginal accused are more likely to be charged with multiple offences than are non-Aboriginal accused
> - Lawyers spend less time with their Aboriginal clients than with non-Aboriginal clients
> - Aboriginal offenders are more than twice as likely as non-Aboriginal people to be incarcerated

> The over-representation of Aboriginal people occurs at virtually every step of the judicial process, from the charging of individuals to their sentencing.

In a society that places a high value on equality before the law, documenting the appalling figures of over-representation might seem to be enough, without any further analysis, to place resolution of this problem at the very top of the national human rights agenda. However, as compelling as the figures are, we believe that it is equally important to understand what lies behind these extraordinary figures, which are a primary index of the individual and social devastation that the criminal justice system has come to represent for Aboriginal people. Understanding the root causes is critical to understanding what it will take by way of a national commitment to bring about real change.

Systemic Discrimination and Aboriginal Crime Rates

Over-representation of the magnitude just described suggests either that Aboriginal peoples are committing disproportionately more crimes or that they are the victims of systemic discrimination. Recent justice studies and reports provide strong confirmatory evidence that both phenomena operate in combination.

The Royal Commission on the Donald Marshall, Jr., Prosecution concluded that

> Donald Marshall, Jr.'s status as a Native contributed to the miscarriage of justice that has plagued him since 1971. We believe that certain persons within the system would have been more rigorous in their duties, more careful, or more conscious of fairness if Marshall had been white.

A research study prepared for that commission, The Mi'Kmaq and Criminal Justice in Nova Scotia, by Scott Clark, found that

> Systemic factors in Nova Scotia's criminal justice system lead to adverse effects for Aboriginal people because they live in or come from Aboriginal communities. Policing that

has been designed specifically for Aboriginal communities is relatively ineffective. Justice processing, including legal representation in courts … [is] often at considerable distance from Native people both physically and conceptually. By the same token, a lack of understanding by many justice system personnel of Mi'Kmaq social and economic conditions and aspirations leads to differential and often inappropriate treatment. Probation and parole services apply criteria that have built-in biases against Natives by failing to allow for their unique social and economic conditions. Indigenous processes are officially bypassed, if not consciously weakened.

The Cawsey report in Alberta also concluded that "systemic discrimination exists in the criminal justice system." The report dealt specifically with the assertion of the police that discrimination on the basis of race did not exist in Alberta.

In their briefs, policing services in Alberta generally express the same response: we do not treat or police people differently on the basis of race, or: race is not a fact in policing functions. On the surface, this may seem satisfactory. However, it does not address systemic discrimination. Systemic discrimination involves the concept that the application of uniform standards, common rules, and treatment of people who are not the same constitutes a form of discrimination. It means that in treating unlike people alike, adverse consequences, hardship or injustice may result. …

It is clear the operational policies applied uniformly to Aboriginal people sometimes have unjust or unduly harsh results. The reasons may be geographical, economic, or cultural. However, it must be acknowledged that the application of uniform policies can have a discriminatory effect.

Before describing some of the ways systemic discrimination contributes to over-representation of Aboriginal people in the criminal justice system, it is important to review the available evidence on the incidence and nature of Aboriginal crime. This is because there is a significant interrelationship between systemic discrimination and crime rates that has powerful implications for the appropriate directions for change.

The available evidence confirms that crime rates are higher in Aboriginal communities than non-Aboriginal communities. Based on 1985 figures, the task force report of the Indian Policing Policy Review concluded that

- crime rates for on-reserve Indians are significantly higher than for off-reserve Indians and than the overall national crime rate; [and that] …
- the rate of on-reserve violent crimes per 1,000 is six times the national average, for property crimes the rate is two times the national average, and for other criminal code offences the rate is four times the national average.

In urban areas, where more than 40 per cent of Aboriginal people live, the available data suggest that Aboriginal people commit more crime and disorder offences than similar groups of non-Aboriginal people but proportionately fewer violent offences than Indians living on-reserve.

The Aboriginal Justice Inquiry of Manitoba (AJI), using 1989-1990 crime rate figures for areas of Manitoba policed by the RCMP, found that the crime rate on Indian reserves was 1.5 times the rate in non-reserve areas. The AJI also found, based on its study of provincial court data, that on the reserves surveyed, 35 per cent of crime fell into a group of four offences: common assault, break and enter, theft under $1,000, and public mischief. Aboriginal persons were charged with fewer property offences and more offences against the person and provincial statute violations than non-Aboriginal persons.

An extensive study conducted for the Grand Council of the Crees in 1991, based on information obtained from police daily reports, current files, youth and adult court files and community interviews, found a significantly higher crime rate in nine Cree communities compared to both the Quebec and the overall Canadian rate. The assault rate in the Cree communities was more than five times the Quebec average and more than three times the national average. There were, however, significant differences among the Cree communities and, as the study itself noted, there was some difficulty in interpreting these findings, owing to a lack of information about the nature and seriousness of the assaults and their degree of comparability. The Cree research also found that much of the interpersonal violence was directed against family members, often in alcohol abuse situations. The high levels of interpersonal violence, particularly family violence, and the close relationship to alcohol abuse, parallels the findings of other studies.

Having concluded that there was a higher rate of crime among Aboriginal people (but one that varied considerably from community to community), the AJI also concluded that systemic discrimination contributed greatly to this. This was also the conclusion drawn by the Cawsey task force in Alberta. Both reports identified over-policing as one of the sources of systemic discrimination. Tim Quigley has described the phenomenon of over-policing and its impact on higher Aboriginal crime rates.

> Police use race as an indicator for patrols, for arrests, detentions. ... For instance, police in cities tend to patrol bars and streets where Aboriginal people congregate, rather than the private clubs frequented by white business people. ... This does not necessarily indicate that the police are invariably racist (although some are) since there is some empirical basis for the police view that proportionately more Aboriginal people are involved in criminality. But to operate patrols or to allocate police on ... [this] basis ... can become a self-fulfilling prophecy: patrols in areas frequented by the groups that they believe are involved in crimes will undoubtedly discover some criminality; when more police are assigned to detachments where there is a high Aboriginal population, their added presence will most assuredly detect more criminal activity.
>
> Consider, for instance, the provincial offence of being intoxicated in a public place. The police rarely arrest whites for being intoxicated in public. No wonder there is resentment on the part of Aboriginal people arrested simply for being intoxicated. This situation very often results in an Aboriginal person being charged with obstruction, resisting arrest or assaulting a peace officer. An almost inevitable consequence is incarceration. ... Yet the whole sequence of events is, at least to some extent, a product of policing criteria that include race as a factor and selective enforcement of the law.

The Aboriginal Justice Inquiry of Manitoba also addressed the systemic effect of police perceptions of Aboriginal people.

> Differences in crime statistics between Aboriginal and non-Aboriginal people result, at least in part, from the manner in which the behaviour of Aboriginal people becomes

categorized and stigmatized. This may happen because, to a certain extent, police tend to view the world in terms of "respectable" people and "criminal" types. Criminal types are thought to exhibit certain characteristics which provide cues to the officer to initiate action. Thus, the police may tend to stop a higher proportion of people who are visibly different from the dominant society, including Aboriginal people, for minor offences, simply because they believe that such people may tend to commit more serious crimes. Members of groups that are perceived to be a danger to the public order are given much less latitude in their behaviour before the police take action. An example might be a group of Aboriginal youth who gather in a park. Because it is believed that their presence may be a precursor to more deviant action, they are subjected to controlling activities by the police.

Over-policing is not unique to Canadian police forces. A similar point is made in a New Zealand report dealing with the effect on crime control strategies of police perceptions of the high rate of Maori crime.

Individual police, both as officers and as members of society, are aware of the high rate of Maori offending. ... Individual police officers, subject to those perceptions, become susceptible to beliefs that Maori men are more likely to be criminal, or that certain types of conduct are more likely to be associated with them. Such beliefs unavoidably, if often unconsciously, affect the exercise of discretionary powers. These individual perceptions and stereotypes are reinforced by the intrinsic attitudes of the police institution which is constantly aware of the wider society's concerns and values. Thus, for example, a social perception of increasing gang or street crime, apparently disproportionately committed by Maori offenders, will lead to an increased allocation of police resources to those areas of activity. Such a concentration leads to a greater number of arrests of mainly Maori people who in turn will maintain the perception of Maori criminality. The likelihood that this perception will bias future use of discretionary powers by the police is thereby increased as well. It is a cyclic process of "deviancy amplification" in which stereotypes and perceptions help stimulate policies in a self-fulfilling weave of unfairness.

Significantly, several of the studies we reviewed concluded that some Aboriginal communities experience the extremes of both over-policing and under-policing. Jean-Paul Brodeur, in his study for the Grand Council of the Crees, provided this review of the research:

In a joint study for the Government of Canada, the Government of Saskatchewan and the Indian Nations, authors Prefontaine, Opekokew and Tyler found that Native communities complained of an excessively rigorous enforcement of the law in relation to minor or petty offences. In his study on RCMP policing of Aboriginals, Loree also concluded that when compared to non-Aboriginal communities, Aboriginal communities received proportionately greater law enforcement attention and proportionately less peace-keeping and other services. The situation is best described by Depew when he states that:

Despite some similarities in Native and non-Native offender profiles, the prevalence of minor and alcohol-related offences provides the basis for Native overrepresentation in the correctional system which in many areas of the country is disturbingly high. ...

Native people also appear to be subject to the extremes of over-policing and under-policing which can lead to disproportionate levels of Native arrests and charges, and under-utilization of policing services, respectively.

Under-policing is an issue identified by Pauktuutit, the Inuit Women's Association of Canada, in its report, *Inuit Women and Justice*, as one of special concern in some smaller Inuit communities where there are no community-based police services. In an appendix documenting the concerns of Inuit women in Labrador, the report demonstrates forcefully how this places women and children at particular risk.

The RCMP has a responsibility to protect and serve our community. Women and elders are major consumers of police services. In order to serve all parts of the communities, the police have to know our communities, they must be a part of our communities. They must also understand what the life of a woman who has been beaten can be like in the community along the Labrador coast where there are no police, or where the police are not very supportive. Without this knowledge and understanding, the RCMP will not be able to respond to the needs of the victims of violence. Until we have the necessary resources in our communities to provide for protection to women on a permanent basis (for example, police based in the community) and to provide a safe place where women can receive counselling, support and protection, many women will not leave and can't leave the violent home. ...

While we recognize that the realities of violence in the family translate into the need for added resources, it is not acceptable, on the one hand, to tell us that this is a funding problem and that there is not enough money provided by the province to provide adequate policing. Yet on the other hand, the federal government provides enough funds to hire two police officers for Labrador and eight in Newfoundland to respond to cigarette smuggling. The communities of Postville, Rigolet, and Makkovik, like other communities on the coast, require police based in the community. Women in these communities are in a dangerous position.

Brodeur points out that simultaneous under- and over-policing prevail not only in Canadian Aboriginal communities but also have characterized the style of policing in Australian Aboriginal settlements and in inner-city areas in England where there are significant black populations. We were struck by the relevance of the following statement, based on the findings of Lord Scarman, who conducted a public inquiry into the riots in Brixton, a predominately black suburb of London.

The true nature of police–black relations in the inner-cities of Britain can only be understood in terms of this simultaneous over-policing and under-policing. There is too much policing against the community and not enough policing that answers the needs of the community.

Brodeur concludes that

[i]n a Canadian context, Aboriginals are submitted to over-policing for minor or petty offences—e.g., drinking violations—and suffer from under-policing with regard to being protected from more serious offences, such as violent assaults against persons (particularly within the family).

The Root Causes of Over-Representation and Aboriginal Crime

Although over-policing and other forms of systemic discrimination undoubtedly play their part in higher crime rates, the evidence available to us leads us to conclude that for many Aboriginal communities, crime and social disorder play more havoc in personal and community well-being than they do in the lives of non-Aboriginal people and communities. Like the figures on over-representation, the statistics on higher crime rates demand further answers to hard questions directed to the root causes. Misunderstanding the roots of the problem can lead only to solutions that provide, at best, temporary alleviation and, at worst, aggravation of the pain reflected in the faces of Aboriginal victims of crimes—in many cases women and children—and in the faces of the Aboriginal men and women who receive their "just" deserts in the form of a prison sentence.

We are not the first commission to grapple with the question of explaining and understanding the causes of Aboriginal over-representation and high crime rates. As the Aboriginal Justice Inquiry of Manitoba observed, an entire sub-specialty of criminology is devoted to determining the causes of crime, and a great deal of academic attention has been directed to the specific issue of Aboriginal over-representation. From our review and analysis of the research, we have identified three primary explanatory theories; although they have significant points of overlap, they point in different directions regarding what must be changed to stem and turn the tide.

One powerfully persistent explanation for the problems facing Aboriginal people in the justice system is cultural difference between Aboriginal people and other Canadians. This was invoked most recently by Chief Justice McEachern in his judgement in the *Gitksan and Wet'suwet'en* case, where the following explanation is offered for Indian disadvantage:

> For reasons which can only be answered by anthropology, if at all, the Indians of the colony, while accepting many of the advantages of the European civilization, did not prosper proportionately with the white community as expected. ... No-one can speak with much certainty or confidence about what really went wrong in the relations between the Indians and the colonists. ... In my view the Indians' lack of cultural preparation for the new regime was indeed the probable cause of the debilitating dependence from which few Indians in North America have not yet escaped.
>
> Being of a culture where everyone looked after himself or perished, the Indians knew how to survive (in most years) but they were not as industrious in the new economic climate as was thought to be necessary by the new-comers in the Colony. In addition, the Indians were a gravely weakened people by reason of foreign diseases which took a fearful toll, and by the ravages of alcohol. They became a conquered people, not by force of arms, for that was not necessary, but by an invading culture and a relentless energy with which they would not, or could not, compete.

A cultural explanatory model has provided the basis for a number of initiatives, referred to generically as the "indigenization" of the criminal justice system. The intent of these initiatives is to close the culture gap by adding to the existing system elements that make it more culturally appropriate for Aboriginal people. Thus, on the assumption that one of the important cultural problems facing Aboriginal people is understanding the language and formal processes of Canadian law, the introduction of Aboriginal court workers is designed to provide a cultural bridge within the existing process. Using the same cultural model, we have seen in different parts of Canada the appointment of Aboriginal police officers, probation officers and justices of the peace. We describe some of these developments in more detail in the next chapter.

There is no doubt that cultural conflict explains much of the alienation that Aboriginal people experience in the justice system, and we return to some of the fundamental cultural differences between Aboriginal and non-Aboriginal understandings of justice later in this report. The difficulty, however, with this explanation and the uses to which it has been put is that it is often based on an underlying assumption that the problem lies with the limitations of Aboriginal culture to adapt to non-Aboriginal legal culture—an assumption of inferiority reflected in the passage from Chief Justice McEachern's judgement just quoted.

Associate Chief Judge Murray Sinclair, one of the commissioners of the Aboriginal Justice Inquiry of Manitoba, recently addressed the limitations of this approach. After reviewing some of the principal conclusions of the Manitoba inquiry—including findings that Aboriginal people are less likely than non-Aboriginal people to plea bargain or to benefit from a negotiated plea, that they are more likely than non-Aboriginal people to plead guilty, even when they are not or do not believe themselves to be guilty, and that they are more likely to leave the legal process without understanding, and therefore without respecting, what has occurred to them or why—he makes the following comments:

> Many times I have heard people ask: "What is it about Aboriginal people that causes them to behave like that?" Such a question suggests the problem lies within the Aboriginal person or with his or her community. That, almost inevitably, leads one to conclude that the answer lies in trying to change the Aboriginal person or his or her community. As a result, almost all our efforts at reform have centred on informing or educating Aboriginal people about the justice system, on finding ways to get them to "connect" with the system or on finding ways to make it easier for them to find their way through it.
>
> Establishing and funding more and better Aboriginal court worker or Aboriginal paralegal programs, printing more and better Aboriginally focused information kits, making more and better audio and video tapes in Aboriginal languages about how courts and laws work, establishing Aboriginal law student programs, hiring more Aboriginal court staff with the ability to speak Aboriginal languages and recruiting or appointing more Aboriginal judges, all find their justification in such thinking.
>
> Attempts, at reforming the system itself in ways that address other, more significant, issues have not been undertaken. The main reason, I believe, is because the non-Aboriginal people who control the system have not seen the problem as lying within "the system." It is time to question whether at least some of the problem lies in the way we do business within the justice system. Perhaps the question should be restated as "what is wrong with our justice system that Aboriginal people find it so alienating?"

We agree with Judge Sinclair that asking the question in this way allows us to address the fundamental differences that Aboriginal people bring to the meaning of justice as a concept and a process.

As Judge Sinclair argues, theories of culture conflict have been applied in the past in a way that locates the source of the problem within Aboriginal culture. There is, however, a further limitation on the exclusively cultural explanation of over-representation in the criminal justice system that takes us deeper into an understanding of Aboriginal crime. This limitation is that an exclusively cultural explanation obscures structural problems grounded in the economic and social inequalities experienced by Aboriginal people. As described by Carole La Prairie,

> What the early task forces and studies failed to recognize or did not want to address, was that the disproportionate representation of Native people as offenders in the system, was not tied exclusively to culture conflict but was grounded primarily in socio-economic marginality and deprivation. ...
>
> Access to justice by way of indigenization has both strengths and weaknesses. It provides employment to a number of Aboriginal people and it may help to demystify the criminal justice process so that Aboriginal people feel less alienated and fearful. What indigenization fails to do, however, is to address in any fundamental way the criminal justice problems which result from the socio-economic marginality. The real danger of an exclusively indigenized approach is that the problems may appear to be "solved," little more will be attempted, partly because indigenization is a very visible activity.

Cast as a structural problem of social and economic marginality, the argument is that Aboriginal people are disproportionately impoverished and belong to a social underclass, and that their over-representation in the criminal justice system is a particular example of the established correlation between social and economic deprivation and criminality.

We observed in our special report on suicide that Aboriginal people are at the bottom of almost every available index of socio-economic well-being, whether they measure educational levels, employment opportunities, housing conditions, per capita incomes or any of the other conditions that give non-Aboriginal Canadians one of the highest standards of living in the world. There is no doubt in our minds that economic and social deprivation is a major underlying cause of disproportionately high rates of criminality among Aboriginal people.

We are also persuaded that some of the debilitating conditions facing Aboriginal communities daily are aggravated by the distinctive nature of Aboriginal societies. Thus, as Carole La Prairie points out in her study for the James Bay Cree, there is evidential support for a correlation between over-crowded housing conditions and interpersonal conflict and violence, which often takes place between close family members residing together. In the case of the James Bay Cree, traditional concepts of order and the cultural values placed on the way people relate to each other in a social context reflect the legacy of nomadic-hunting settlement patterns. People not only have their distinctive roles but have their distinctive places in relationship to each other. Over-crowded housing where these distinctions cannot be reflected or respected can and does exacerbate an already problematic sedentary existence in contemporary Cree communities. Thus, current housing conditions, not only in Cree but other Aboriginal people, contribute to tensions in kinship relationships that may in turn be linked to problems of interpersonal conflict, violence and crime.

Socio-economic deprivation not only has explanatory power in relation to high rates of Aboriginal crime, but it also contributes directly to the systemic discrimination that swells the ranks of Aboriginal people in prison. The most obvious and well documented example of this is the imprisonment of Aboriginal people for non-payment of fines. In a 1974 report entitled *The Native Offender and the Law*, the Law Reform Commission concluded that a large number of Aboriginal offenders were sent to jail for non-payment of fines. The advent of fine option programs, under which a person can pay off a fine through community work, has not significantly changed the fact that Aboriginal people go to prison for being poor. In Saskatchewan, in 1992-93, Aboriginal people made up almost 75 per cent of those jailed for fine default. The Cawsey report, after observing that the Canadian Sentencing Commission recommended a reduction in the use of imprisonment for fine default, concluded that there was little evidence of that recommendation, made in 1987, being implemented in Alberta. The report stated:

> A number of speakers at our community meeting spoke with disdain about a practice associated with the problem of fine default. They stated that some judges keep a "black book" on offenders. Apparently, these notations are used in determining whether an accused will be granted time to pay for fines levied. By means of the "black book" system, a judge keeps a tally on those who have failed to meet the time limits on previous occasions. When appearing in court again, accused persons do not get time to pay if their names have been entered in the "black book" previously.

> • • •

But imprisonment for fine default is only the most obvious example of systemic discrimination built upon socio-economic deprivation. As the Aboriginal Justice Inquiry of Manitoba found, Aboriginal people are more likely to be denied bail and therefore subject to pre-trial detention. While there is certainly no evidence to suggest that judges deliberately discriminate against Aboriginal people, the factors taken into account in determining whether to subject a person to pre-trial detention relate to whether the person is employed, has a fixed address, is involved in educational programs, or has strong links with the community; as a result, social and economic disadvantage can influence the decision in a particular direction, and that direction is toward the doors of remand centres.

Pre-trial detention, once imposed, has a number of effects. It creates additional pressure to plead guilty in order to get the matter over with, it limits the accused's ability to marshal resources, whether financial or community, to put before the court a community-based sentencing plan, and it therefore increases the likelihood of a sentence of imprisonment.

The way apparently neutral and legally relevant criteria applied at various stages of the criminal justice process compound or snowball to produce systemic discrimination against Aboriginal people is described well by Quigley.

> There are also some other factors that might bear on the disproportionate rate of imprisonment and that are more directly related to the sentencing process. Some of these are presently seen as legally relevant criteria—prior criminal record, employment status, educational level, etc. ... Prior criminal record as a factor can have an undue influence on the imprisonment rate for Aboriginal people due to the snowball effect of some of the factors

listed above. If there are more young Aboriginal people, if they are disproportionately unemployed, idle and alienated, and if they are overly scrutinized by the police, it should not be surprising that frequently breaches of the law are detected and punished. Add to that the greater likelihood of being denied bail (which increases the chance of being jailed if convicted), the greater likelihood of fine default and the diminished likelihood of receiving probation, and there is a greater probability of imprisonment being imposed. Some of the same factors increase the chances of the same person re-offending and being detected once again. After that, every succeeding conviction is much more apt to be punished by imprisonment, thus creating a snowball effect: jail becomes virtually the only option, regardless of the seriousness of the offence.

Socio-economic factors such as employment status, level of education, family situation, etc. appear on the surface as neutral criteria. They are considered as such by the legal system. Yet they can conceal an extremely strong bias in the sentencing process. Convicted persons with steady employment and stability in their lives, or at least prospects of the same, are much less likely to be sent to jail for offences that are borderline imprisonment offences. The unemployed, transients, the poorly educated are all better candidates for imprisonment. Given the social, political and economic aspects of our society place Aboriginal people disproportionately within the ranks of the latter; our society literally sentences more of them to jail. This is systemic discrimination.

The Aboriginal Justice Inquiry of Manitoba came to the same conclusion. The commissioners wrote:

> Historically, the justice system has discriminated against Aboriginal people by providing legal sanction for their oppression. This oppression of previous generations forced Aboriginal people into their current state of social and economic distress. Now, a seemingly neutral justice system discriminates against current generations of Aboriginal people by applying laws which have an adverse impact on people of lower socio-economic status. This is no less racial discrimination; it is merely "laundered" racial discrimination. It is untenable to say that discrimination which builds upon the effects of racial discrimination is not racial discrimination itself. Past injustices cannot be ignored or built upon.

There is no doubt in our minds that economic and social deprivation is a significant contributor to the high incidence of Aboriginal crime and over-representation in the justice system. We believe, however, that a further level of understanding is required beyond acknowledgement of the role played by poverty and debilitating social conditions in the creation and perpetuation of Aboriginal crime. We are persuaded that this further understanding comes from integrating the cultural and socio-economic explanations for over-representation with a broader historical and political analysis. We have concluded that over-representation is linked directly to the particular and distinctive historical and political processes that have made Aboriginal people poor beyond poverty.

Our analysis and conclusions parallel those set out in our special report on suicide. In that report we identified some of the risk factors that explain, in part, the high rate of Aboriginal suicide. As we have just demonstrated with respect to the high rate of Aboriginal crime, these factors include culture stress and socio-economic deprivation. We concluded, however, that

Aboriginal people experience [these] risk factors ... with greater frequency and intensity than do Canadians generally. The reasons are rooted in the relations between Aboriginal peoples and the rest of Canadian society—relations that were shaped in the colonial era and have never been thoroughly reshaped since that time.

The relationship of colonialism provides an overarching conceptual and historical link in understanding much of what has happened to Aboriginal peoples. Its relationship to issues of criminal justice was identified clearly by the Canadian Bar Association in its 1988 report, *Locking Up Natives in Canada.*

What links these views of native criminality as caused by poverty or alcohol is the historical process which Native people have experienced in Canada, along with indigenous people in other parts of the world, the process of colonization. In the Canadian context that process, with the advance first of the agricultural and then the industrial frontier, has left Native people in most parts of the country dispossessed of all but the remnants of what was once their homelands; that process, superintended by missionaries and Indian agents armed with the power of the law, took such extreme forms as criminalizing central Indian institutions such as the Potlatch and Sundance, and systematically undermined the foundations of many Native communities. The Native people of Canada have, over the course of the last two centuries, been moved to the margins of their own territories and of our "just" society.

This process of dispossession and marginalization has carried with it enormous costs of which crime and alcoholism are but two items on a long list. ... The relationship between these indices of disorganization and deprivation and Canada's historical relationship with Native people has been the subject of intense scrutiny in the last decade. In the mid-1970s the MacKenzie Valley Pipeline Inquiry focused national attention on the implications for the Native people of the North on a rapid escalation of a large scale industrial development. Mr. Justice Berger (as he then was), in assessing the causes for the alarming rise in the incidence of alcoholism, crime, violence and welfare dependence in the North, had this to say:

I am persuaded that the incidence of these disorders is closely bound up with the rapid expansion of the industrial system and with its persistent intrusion into every part of the Native people's lives. The process affects the complex links between Native people and their past, their culturally preferred economic life, and their individual, familial and political respect. We should not be surprised to learn that the economic forces that have broken these vital links, and that are unresponsive to the distress of those who have been hurt, should lead to serious disorders. Crimes of violence can, to some extent, be seen as expressions of frustrations, confusion and indignation, but we can go beyond that interpretation to the obvious connection between crimes of violence and the change the South has, in recent years, brought to the Native people of the North. With that obvious connection, we can affirm one simple proposition: the more the industrial frontier displaces the homeland in the North, the worse the incidence of crime and violence will be.

Important implications flow from this analysis. The idea that new programs, more planning and an increase in social service personnel will solve these problems misconstrues their real nature and cause. The high rates of social and personal breakdown in the North are, in good measure, the responses of individual families who have suffered the loss of meaning in their lives and control over their destiny.

The principal recommendations which come from the MacKenzie Valley Pipeline Inquiry were that the Native people of the North must have their right to control that destiny—their right to self-determination—recognized and that there must be a settlement of Native claims in which that right is entrenched as a lodestar. Only then could Native people chart a future responding to their values and priorities rather than living under the shadow of ours.

III. THE 1996 AMENDMENTS AND SUPREME COURT GUIDANCE

As seen in chapter 2, Judicial Methodology and the Legislative Context, the 1996 amendments added to the *Criminal Code*, RSC 1985, c. C-46, as amended, a statement of purpose and objectives for sentencing and some of the major substantive principles. Along with proportionality (s. 718.1), the Code also mandates respect for the principle of restraint in ss. 718(c), 718.2(d), and 718.2(e). The last provision makes specific reference to Aboriginal offenders:

> 718.2. A court that imposes a sentence shall also take into consideration the following principles: ...
>
>   (e) all available sanctions other than imprisonment that are reasonable in the circumstances should be considered for all offenders, *with particular attention to the circumstances of aboriginal offenders.*

In *R v. Gladue*, below, the Supreme Court addressed the intended purpose and application of this provision.

R v. Gladue
[1999] 1 SCR 688, 23 CR (5th) 197

[The offender, a 19-year-old woman of Aboriginal background, had pleaded guilty to manslaughter as a result of the stabbing death of her common law husband. At her sentencing hearing, the judge stated that s. 718.2(e) could have no application because both parties lived in an urban environment and not in an Aboriginal community. She was sentenced to three years' imprisonment. On appeal, the B.C. Court of Appeal held that whether or not she lived in an Aboriginal community could not restrict the application of s. 718.2(e), but the majority (Rowles JA dissenting) still dismissed the sentence appeal. In the Supreme Court of Canada, Cory and Iacobucci JJ, writing for a unanimous court, provided important guidance on the role of s. 718.2(e).]

CORY and IACOBUCCI JJ (Lamer CJC and L'Heureux-Dubé, Gonthier, Bastarache, Binnie JJ concurring):

· · ·

[49] Further guidance as to the scope and content of Parliament's remedial purpose in enacting s. 718.2(e) may be derived from the social context surrounding the enactment of the provision. On this point, it is worth noting that, although there is quite a wide divergence between the positions of the appellant and the respondent as to how s. 718.2(e) should be applied in practice, there is general agreement between them, and indeed between the parties and all interveners, regarding the mischief in response to which s. 718.2(e) was enacted.

[50] The parties and interveners agree that the purpose of s. 718.2(e) is to respond to the problem of overincarceration in Canada, and to respond, in particular, to the more acute problem of the disproportionate incarceration of aboriginal peoples. They also agree that one of the roles of s. 718.2(e), and of various other provisions in Part XXIII, is to encourage sentencing judges to apply principles of restorative justice alongside or in the place of other, more traditional sentencing principles when making sentencing determinations. As the respondent states in its factum before this Court, s. 718.2(e) "provides the necessary flexibility and authority for sentencing judges to resort to the restorative model of justice in sentencing aboriginal offenders and to reduce the imposition of jail sentences where to do so would not sacrifice the traditional goals of sentencing."

[51] The fact that the parties and interveners are in general agreement among themselves regarding the purpose of s. 718.2(e) is not determinative of the issue as a matter of statutory construction. However, as we have suggested, on the above points of agreement the parties and interveners are correct. A review of the problem of overincarceration in Canada, and of its peculiarly devastating impact upon Canada's aboriginal peoples, provides additional insight into the purpose and proper application of this new provision.

...

[57] Thus, it may be seen that although imprisonment is intended to serve the traditional sentencing goals of separation, deterrence, denunciation, and rehabilitation, there is widespread consensus that imprisonment has not been successful in achieving some of these goals. Overincarceration is a long-standing problem that has been many times publicly acknowledged but never addressed in a systematic manner by Parliament. In recent years, compared to other countries, sentences of imprisonment in Canada have increased at an alarming rate. The 1996 sentencing reforms embodied in Part XXIII, and s. 718.2(e) in particular, must be understood as a reaction to the overuse of prison as a sanction, and must accordingly be given appropriate force as remedial provisions.

(2) The Overrepresentation of Aboriginal Canadians in Penal Institutions

[58] If overreliance upon incarceration is a problem with the general population, it is of much greater concern in the sentencing of aboriginal Canadians. In the mid-1980s, aboriginal people were about 2 percent of the population of Canada, yet they made up 10 percent of the penitentiary population. In Manitoba and Saskatchewan, aboriginal people constituted something between 6 and 7 percent of the population, yet in Manitoba they represented 46 percent of the provincial admissions and in Saskatchewan 60 percent: see M. Jackson, "Locking Up Natives in Canada" (1988-89), 23 *UBC L Rev.* 215 (article originally prepared as a report of the Canadian Bar Association Committee

on Imprisonment and Release in June 1988), at pp. 215-16. The situation has not improved in recent years. By 1997, aboriginal peoples constituted closer to 3 percent of the population of Canada and amounted to 12 percent of all federal inmates: Solicitor General of Canada, Consolidated Report, *Towards a Just, Peaceful and Safe Society: The Corrections and Conditional Release Act—Five Years Later* (1998), at pp. 142-55. The situation continues to be particularly worrisome in Manitoba, where in 1995-96 they made up 55 percent of admissions to provincial correctional facilities, and in Saskatchewan, where they made up 72 percent of admissions. A similar, albeit less drastic situation prevails in Alberta and British Columbia: Canadian Centre for Justice Statistics, *Adult Correctional Services in Canada, 1995-96* (1997), at p. 30.

[59] This serious problem of aboriginal overrepresentation in Canadian prisons is well documented. Like the general problem of overincarceration itself, the excessive incarceration of aboriginal peoples has received the attention of a large number of commissions and inquiries: see, by way of example only, Canadian Corrections Association, *Indians and the Law* (1967); Law Reform Commission of Canada, *The Native Offender and the Law* (1974), prepared by D. A. Schmeiser; Public Inquiry into the Administration of Justice and Aboriginal People, *Report of the Aboriginal Justice Inquiry of Manitoba*, vol. 1, *The Justice System and Aboriginal People* (1991); Royal Commission on Aboriginal Peoples, *Bridging the Cultural Divide* (1996).

. . .

[61] Not surprisingly, the excessive imprisonment of aboriginal people is only the tip of the iceberg insofar as the estrangement of the aboriginal peoples from the Canadian criminal justice system is concerned. Aboriginal people are overrepresented in virtually all aspects of the system. As this Court recently noted in *R v. Williams*, [1998] 1 SCR 1128, at para. 58, there is widespread bias against aboriginal people within Canada, and "[t]here is evidence that this widespread racism has translated into systemic discrimination in the criminal justice system."

[62] Statements regarding the extent and severity of this problem are disturbingly common. In *Bridging the Cultural Divide, supra*, at p. 309, the Royal Commission on Aboriginal Peoples listed as its first "Major Findings and Conclusions" the following striking yet representative statement:

> The Canadian criminal justice system has failed the Aboriginal peoples of Canada—First Nations, Inuit and Métis people, on-reserve and off-reserve, urban and rural—in all territorial and governmental jurisdictions. The principal reason for this crushing failure is the fundamentally different world views of Aboriginal and non-Aboriginal people with respect to such elemental issues as the substantive content of justice and the process of achieving justice.

[63] To the same effect, the Aboriginal Justice Inquiry of Manitoba described the justice system in Manitoba as having failed aboriginal people on a "massive scale," referring particularly to the substantially different cultural values and experiences of aboriginal people: *The Justice System and Aboriginal People, supra*, at pp. 1 and 86.

[64] These findings cry out for recognition of the magnitude and gravity of the problem, and for responses to alleviate it. The figures are stark and reflect what may fairly be termed a crisis in the Canadian criminal justice system. The drastic overrepre-

sentation of aboriginal peoples within both the Canadian prison population and the criminal justice system reveals a sad and pressing social problem. It is reasonable to assume that Parliament, in singling out aboriginal offenders for distinct sentencing treatment in s. 718.2(e), intended to attempt to redress this social problem to some degree. The provision may properly be seen as Parliament's direction to members of the judiciary to inquire into the causes of the problem and to endeavour to remedy it, to the extent that a remedy is possible through the sentencing process.

[65] It is clear that sentencing innovation by itself cannot remove the causes of aboriginal offending and the greater problem of aboriginal alienation from the criminal justice system. The unbalanced ratio of imprisonment for aboriginal offenders flows from a number of sources, including poverty, substance abuse, lack of education, and the lack of employment opportunities for aboriginal people. It arises also from bias against aboriginal people and from an unfortunate institutional approach that is more inclined to refuse bail and to impose more and longer prison terms for aboriginal offenders. There are many aspects of this sad situation which cannot be addressed in these reasons. What can and must be addressed, though, is the limited role that sentencing judges will play in remedying injustice against aboriginal peoples in Canada. Sentencing judges are among those decision-makers who have the power to influence the treatment of aboriginal offenders in the justice system. They determine most directly whether an aboriginal offender will go to jail, or whether other sentencing options may be employed which will play perhaps a stronger role in restoring a sense of balance to the offender, victim, and community, and in preventing future crime.

E. A Framework of Analysis for the Sentencing Judge

(1) What Are the "Circumstances of Aboriginal Offenders"?

[66] How are sentencing judges to play their remedial role? The words of s. 718.2(e) instruct the sentencing judge to pay particular attention to the circumstances of aboriginal offenders, with the implication that those circumstances are significantly different from those of non-aboriginal offenders. The background considerations regarding the distinct situation of aboriginal peoples in Canada encompass a wide range of unique circumstances, including, most particularly:

(A) The unique systemic or background factors which may have played a part in bringing the particular aboriginal offender before the courts; and

(B) The types of sentencing procedures and sanctions which may be appropriate in the circumstances for the offender because of his or her particular aboriginal heritage or connection.

(a) Systemic and Background Factors

[67] The background factors which figure prominently in the causation of crime by aboriginal offenders are by now well known. Years of dislocation and economic development have translated, for many aboriginal peoples, into low incomes, high unemployment, lack of opportunities and options, lack or irrelevance of education, substance abuse, loneliness, and community fragmentation. These and other factors contribute to

a higher incidence of crime and incarceration. A disturbing account of these factors is set out by Professor Tim Quigley, "Some Issues in Sentencing of Aboriginal Offenders," in *Continuing Poundmaker and Riel's Quest* (1994), at pp. 269-300. Quigley ably describes the process whereby these various factors produce an overincarceration of aboriginal offenders, noting (at pp. 275-76) that "[t]he unemployed, transients, the poorly educated are all better candidates for imprisonment. When the social, political and economic aspects of our society place Aboriginal people disproportionately within the ranks of the latter, our society literally sentences more of them to jail."

[68] It is true that systemic and background factors explain in part the incidence of crime and recidivism for non-aboriginal offenders as well. However, it must be recognized that the circumstances of aboriginal offenders differ from those of the majority because many aboriginal people are victims of systemic and direct discrimination, many suffer the legacy of dislocation, and many are substantially affected by poor social and economic conditions. Moreover, as has been emphasized repeatedly in studies and commission reports, aboriginal offenders are, as a result of these unique systemic and background factors, more adversely affected by incarceration and less likely to be "rehabilitated" thereby, because the internment milieu is often culturally inappropriate and regrettably discrimination towards them is so often rampant in penal institutions.

[69] In this case, of course, we are dealing with factors that must be considered by a judge sentencing an aboriginal offender. While background and systemic factors will also be of importance for a judge in sentencing a non-aboriginal offender, the judge who is called upon to sentence an aboriginal offender must give attention to the unique background and systemic factors which may have played a part in bringing the particular offender before the courts. In cases where such factors have played a significant role, it is incumbent upon the sentencing judge to consider these factors in evaluating whether imprisonment would actually serve to deter, or to denounce crime in a sense that would be meaningful to the community of which the offender is a member. In many instances, more restorative sentencing principles will gain primary relevance precisely because the prevention of crime as well as individual and social healing cannot occur through other means.

(b) Appropriate Sentencing Procedures and Sanctions

[70] Closely related to the background and systemic factors which have contributed to an excessive aboriginal incarceration rate are the different conceptions of appropriate sentencing procedures and sanctions held by aboriginal people. A significant problem experienced by aboriginal people who come into contact with the criminal justice system is that the traditional sentencing ideals of deterrence, separation, and denunciation are often far removed from the understanding of sentencing held by these offenders and their community. The aims of restorative justice as now expressed in paras. (d), (e), and (f) of s. 718 of the *Criminal Code* apply to all offenders, and not only aboriginal offenders. However, most traditional aboriginal conceptions of sentencing place a primary emphasis upon the ideals of restorative justice. This tradition is extremely important to the analysis under s. 718.2(e).

[71] The concept and principles of a restorative approach will necessarily have to be developed over time in the jurisprudence, as different issues and different conceptions

of sentencing are addressed in their appropriate context. In general terms, restorative justice may be described as an approach to remedying crime in which it is understood that all things are interrelated and that crime disrupts the harmony which existed prior to its occurrence, or at least which it is felt should exist. The appropriateness of a particular sanction is largely determined by the needs of the victims, and the community, as well as the offender. The focus is on the human beings closely affected by the crime. See generally, e.g., *Bridging the Cultural Divide*, *supra*, at pp. 12-25; *The Justice System and Aboriginal People*, *supra*, at pp. 17-46; Kwochka, *supra*; M. Jackson, "In Search of the Pathways to Justice: Alternative Dispute Resolution in Aboriginal Communities," [1992] *UBC L Rev.* (Special Edition) 147.

[72] The existing overemphasis on incarceration in Canada may be partly due to the perception that a restorative approach is a more lenient approach to crime and that imprisonment constitutes the ultimate punishment. Yet in our view a sentence focused on restorative justice is not necessarily a "lighter" punishment. Some proponents of restorative justice argue that when it is combined with probationary conditions it may in some circumstances impose a greater burden on the offender than a custodial sentence. See Kwochka, *supra*, who writes at p. 165:

> At this point there is some divergence among proponents of restorative justice. Some seek to abandon the punishment paradigm by focusing on the differing goals of a restorative system. Others, while cognizant of the differing goals, argue for a restorative system in terms of a punishment model. They argue that non-custodial sentences can have an equivalent punishment value when produced and administered by a restorative system and that the healing process can be more intense than incarceration. Restorative justice necessarily involves some form of restitution and reintegration into the community. Central to the process is the need for offenders to take responsibility for their actions. By comparison, incarceration obviates the need to accept responsibility. Facing victim and community is for some more frightening than the possibility of a term of imprisonment and yields a more beneficial result in that the offender may become a healed and functional member of the community rather than a bitter offender returning after a term of imprisonment.

[73] In describing in general terms some of the basic tenets of traditional aboriginal sentencing approaches, we do not wish to imply that all aboriginal offenders, victims, and communities share an identical understanding of appropriate sentences for particular offences and offenders. Aboriginal communities stretch from coast to coast and from the border with the United States to the far north. Their customs and traditions and their concept of sentencing vary widely. What is important to recognize is that, for many if not most aboriginal offenders, the current concepts of sentencing are inappropriate because they have frequently not responded to the needs, experiences, and perspectives of aboriginal people or aboriginal communities.

[74] It is unnecessary to engage here in an extensive discussion of the relatively recent evolution of innovative sentencing practices, such as healing and sentencing circles, and aboriginal community council projects, which are available to aboriginal offenders. What is important to note is that the different conceptions of sentencing held by many aboriginal people share a common underlying principle: that is, the importance of community-based sanctions. Sentencing judges should not conclude that the

absence of alternatives specific to an aboriginal community eliminates their ability to impose a sanction that takes into account principles of restorative justice and the needs of the parties involved. Rather, the point is that one of the unique circumstances of aboriginal offenders is that community-based sanctions coincide with the aboriginal concept of sentencing and the needs of aboriginal people and communities. It is often the case that neither aboriginal offenders nor their communities are well served by incarcerating offenders, particularly for less serious or non-violent offences. Where these sanctions are reasonable in the circumstances, they should be implemented. In all instances, it is appropriate to attempt to craft the sentencing process and the sanctions imposed in accordance with the aboriginal perspective.

(2) The Search for a Fit Sentence

[75] The role of the judge who sentences an aboriginal offender is, as for every offender, to determine a fit sentence taking into account all the circumstances of the offence, the offender, the victims, and the community. Nothing in Part XXIII of the *Criminal Code* alters this fundamental duty as a general matter. However, the effect of s. 718.2(e), viewed in the context of Part XXIII as a whole, is to alter the method of analysis which sentencing judges must use in determining a fit sentence for aboriginal offenders. Section 718.2(e) requires that sentencing determinations take into account the unique circumstances of aboriginal peoples.

[76] In *R v. M.(C.A.)*, [1996] 1 SCR 500, at p. 567, Lamer CJ restated the long-standing principle of Canadian sentencing law that the appropriateness of a sentence will depend on the particular circumstances of the offence, the offender, and the community in which the offence took place. Disparity of sentences for similar crimes is a natural consequence of this individualized focus. As he stated:

> It has been repeatedly stressed that there is no such thing as a uniform sentence for a particular crime. ... Sentencing is an inherently individualized process, and the search for a single appropriate sentence for a similar offender and a similar crime will frequently be a fruitless exercise of academic abstraction. As well, sentences for a particular offence should be expected to vary to some degree across various communities and regions of this country, as the "just and appropriate" mix of accepted sentencing goals will depend on the needs and current conditions of and in the particular community where the crime occurred.

[77] The comments of Lamer CJ are particularly apt in the context of aboriginal offenders. As explained herein, the circumstances of aboriginal offenders are markedly different from those of other offenders, being characterized by unique systemic and background factors. Further, an aboriginal offender's community will frequently understand the nature of a just sanction in a manner significantly different from that of many non-aboriginal communities. In appropriate cases, some of the traditional sentencing objectives will be correspondingly less relevant in determining a sentence that is reasonable in the circumstances, and the goals of restorative justice will quite properly be given greater weight. Through its reform of the purpose of sentencing in s. 718, and through its specific directive to judges who sentence aboriginal offenders, Parliament has, more than ever before, empowered sentencing judges to craft sentences in a manner which is meaningful to aboriginal peoples.

[78] In describing the effect of s. 718.2(e) in this way, we do not mean to suggest that, as a general practice, aboriginal offenders must always be sentenced in a manner which gives greatest weight to the principles of restorative justice, and less weight to goals such as deterrence, denunciation, and separation. It is unreasonable to assume that aboriginal peoples themselves do not believe in the importance of these latter goals, and even if they do not, that such goals must not predominate in appropriate cases. Clearly there are some serious offences and some offenders for which and for whom separation, denunciation, and deterrence are fundamentally relevant.

[79] Yet, even where an offence is considered serious, the length of the term of imprisonment must be considered. In some circumstances the length of the sentence of an aboriginal offender may be less and in others the same as that of any other offender. Generally, the more violent and serious the offence the more likely it is as a practical reality that the terms of imprisonment for aboriginals and non-aboriginals will be close to each other or the same, even taking into account their different concepts of sentencing.

[80] As with all sentencing decisions, the sentencing of aboriginal offenders must proceed on an individual (or a case-by-case) basis: For *this* offence, committed by *this* offender, harming *this* victim, in *this* community, what is the appropriate sanction under the *Criminal Code*? What understanding of criminal sanctions is held by the community? What is the nature of the relationship between the offender and his or her community? What combination of systemic or background factors contributed to this particular offender coming before the courts for this particular offence? How has the offender who is being sentenced been affected by, for example, substance abuse in the community, or poverty, or overt racism, or family or community breakdown? Would imprisonment effectively serve to deter or denounce crime in a sense that would be significant to the offender and community, or are crime prevention and other goals better achieved through healing? What sentencing options present themselves in these circumstances?

[81] The analysis for sentencing aboriginal offenders, as for all offenders, must be holistic and designed to achieve a fit sentence in the circumstances. There is no single test that a judge can apply in order to determine the sentence. The sentencing judge is required to take into account all of the surrounding circumstances regarding the offence, the offender, the victims, and the community, including the unique circumstances of the offender as an aboriginal person. Sentencing must proceed with sensitivity to and understanding of the difficulties aboriginal people have faced with both the criminal justice system and society at large. When evaluating these circumstances in light of the aims and principles of sentencing as set out in Part XXIII of the *Criminal Code* and in the jurisprudence, the judge must strive to arrive at a sentence which is just and appropriate in the circumstances. By means of s. 718.2(e), sentencing judges have been provided with a degree of flexibility and discretion to consider in appropriate circumstances alternative sentences to incarceration which are appropriate for the aboriginal offender and community and yet comply with the mandated principles and purpose of sentencing. In this way, effect may be given to the aboriginal emphasis upon healing and restoration of both the victim and the offender.

(3) The Duty of the Sentencing Judge

[82] The foregoing discussion of guidelines for the sentencing judge has spoken of that which a judge must do when sentencing an aboriginal offender. This element of duty is a critical component of s. 718.2(e). The provision expressly provides that a court that imposes a sentence *should* consider all available sanctions other than imprisonment that are reasonable in the circumstances, and *should* pay particular attention to the circumstances of aboriginal offenders. There is no discretion as to whether to consider the unique situation of the aboriginal offender; the only discretion concerns the determination of a just and appropriate sentence.

[83] How then is the consideration of s. 718.2(e) to proceed in the daily functioning of the courts? The manner in which the sentencing judge will carry out his or her statutory duty may vary from case to case. In all instances it will be necessary for the judge to take judicial notice of the systemic or background factors and the approach to sentencing which is relevant to aboriginal offenders. However, for each particular offence and offender it may be that some evidence will be required in order to assist the sentencing judge in arriving at a fit sentence. Where a particular offender does not wish such evidence to be adduced, the right to have particular attention paid to his or her circumstances as an aboriginal offender may be waived. Where there is no such waiver, it will be extremely helpful to the sentencing judge for counsel on both sides to adduce relevant evidence. Indeed, it is to be expected that counsel will fulfil their role and assist the sentencing judge in this way.

[84] However, even where counsel do not adduce this evidence, where for example the offender is unrepresented, it is incumbent upon the sentencing judge to attempt to acquire information regarding the circumstances of the offender as an aboriginal person. Whether the offender resides in a rural area, on a reserve or in an urban centre the sentencing judge must be made aware of alternatives to incarceration that exist whether inside or outside the aboriginal community of the particular offender. The alternatives existing in metropolitan areas must, as a matter of course, also be explored. Clearly the presence of an aboriginal offender will require special attention in pre-sentence reports. Beyond the use of the pre-sentence report, the sentencing judge may and should in appropriate circumstances and where practicable request that witnesses be called who may testify as to reasonable alternatives.

[85] Similarly, where a sentencing judge at the trial level has not engaged in the duty imposed by s. 718.2(e) as fully as required, it is incumbent upon a court of appeal in considering an appeal against sentence on this basis to consider any fresh evidence which is relevant and admissible on sentencing. In the same vein, it should be noted that, although s. 718.2(e) does not impose a statutory duty upon the sentencing judge to provide reasons, it will be much easier for a reviewing court to determine whether and how attention was paid to the circumstances of the offender as an aboriginal person if at least brief reasons are given.

(4) The Issue of "Reverse Discrimination"

[86] Something must also be said as to the manner in which s. 718.2(e) should not be interpreted. The appellant and the respondent diverged significantly in their inter-

pretation of the appropriate role to be played by s. 718.2(e). While the respondent saw the provision largely as a restatement of existing sentencing principles, the appellant advanced the position that s. 718.2(e) functions as an affirmative action provision justified under s. 15(2) of the Charter. The respondent cautioned that, in his view, the appellant's understanding of the provision would result in "reverse discrimination" so as to favour aboriginal offenders over other offenders.

[87] There is no constitutional challenge to s. 718.2(e) in these proceedings, and accordingly we do not address specifically the applicability of s. 15 of the Charter. We would note, though, that the aim of s. 718.2(e) is to reduce the tragic overrepresentation of aboriginal people in prisons. It seeks to ameliorate the present situation and to deal with the particular offence and offender and community. The fact that a court is called upon to take into consideration the unique circumstances surrounding these different parties is not unfair to non-aboriginal people. Rather, the fundamental purpose of s. 718.2(e) is to treat aboriginal offenders fairly by taking into account their difference.

[88] But s. 718.2(e) should not be taken as requiring an automatic reduction of a sentence, or a remission of a warranted period of incarceration, simply because the offender is aboriginal. To the extent that the appellant's submission on affirmative action means that s. 718.2(e) requires an automatic reduction in sentence for an aboriginal offender, we reject that view. The provision is a direction to sentencing judges to consider certain unique circumstances pertaining to aboriginal offenders as a part of the task of weighing the multitude of factors which must be taken into account in striving to impose a fit sentence. It cannot be forgotten that s. 718.2(e) must be considered in the context of that section read as a whole and in the context of s. 718, s. 718.1, and the overall scheme of Part XXIII. It is one of the statutorily mandated considerations that a sentencing judge must take into account. It may not always mean a lower sentence for an aboriginal offender. The sentence imposed will depend upon all the factors which must be taken into account in each individual case. The weight to be given to these various factors will vary in each case. At the same time, it must in every case be recalled that the direction to consider these unique circumstances flows from the staggering injustice currently experienced by aboriginal peoples with the criminal justice system. The provision reflects the reality that many aboriginal people are alienated from this system which frequently does not reflect their needs or their understanding of an appropriate sentence.

(5) Who Comes Within the Purview of Section 718.2(e)?

[89] The question of whether s. 718.2(e) applies to all aboriginal persons, or only to certain classes thereof, is raised by this appeal. The following passage of the reasons of the judge at trial appears to reflect some ambiguity as to the applicability of the provision to aboriginal people who do not live in rural areas or on a reserve:

> The factor that is mentioned in the *Criminal Code* is that particular attention to the circumstances of aboriginal offenders should be considered. In this case both the deceased and the accused were aboriginals, but they are not living within the aboriginal community as such. They are living off a reserve and the offence occurred in an urban setting. They [sic] do not appear to have been any special circumstances because of their aboriginal status and so I am not giving any special consideration to their background in passing this sentence.

It could be understood from that passage that, in this case, there were no special circumstances to warrant the application of s. 718.2(e), and the fact that the context of the offence was not in a rural setting or on a reserve was only one of those missing circumstances. However, this passage was interpreted by the majority of the Court of Appeal as implying that, "as a matter of principle, s. 718.2(e) can have no application to aboriginals 'not living within the aboriginal community'" (p. 137). This understanding of the provision was unanimously rejected by the members of the Court of Appeal. With respect to the trial judge, who was given little assistance from counsel on this issue, we agree with the Court of Appeal that such a restrictive interpretation of the provision would be inappropriate.

[90] The class of aboriginal people who come within the purview of the specific reference to the circumstances of aboriginal offenders in s. 718.2(e) must be, at least, all who come within the scope of s. 25 of the Charter and s. 35 of the *Constitution Act, 1982*. The numbers involved are significant. National census figures from 1996 show that an estimated 799,010 people were identified as aboriginal in 1996. Of this number, 529,040 were Indians (registered or non-registered), 204,115 Métis and 40,220 Inuit.

[91] Section 718.2(e) applies to all aboriginal offenders wherever they reside, whether on- or off-reserve, in a large city or a rural area. Indeed it has been observed that many aboriginals living in urban areas are closely attached to their culture. See the Royal Commission on Aboriginal Peoples, *Report of the Royal Commission on Aboriginal Peoples*, vol. 4, *Perspectives and Realities* (1996), at p. 521:

> Throughout the Commission's hearings, Aboriginal people stressed the fundamental importance of retaining and enhancing their cultural identity while living in urban areas. Aboriginal identity lies at the heart of Aboriginal peoples' existence; maintaining that identity is an essential and self-validating pursuit for aboriginal people in cities.

And at p. 525:

> Cultural identity for urban Aboriginal people is also tied to a land base or ancestral territory. For many, the two concepts are inseparable. ... Identification with an ancestral place is important to urban people because of the associated ritual, ceremony and traditions, as well as the people who remain there, the sense of belonging, the bond to an ancestral community, and the accessibility of family, community and elders.

[92] Section 718.2(e) requires the sentencing judge to explore reasonable alternatives to incarceration in the case of all aboriginal offenders. Obviously, if an aboriginal community has a program or tradition of alternative sanctions, and support and supervision are available to the offender, it may be easier to find and impose an alternative sentence. However, even if community support is not available, every effort should be made in appropriate circumstances to find a sensitive and helpful alternative. For all purposes, the term "community" must be defined broadly so as to include any network of support and interaction that might be available in an urban centre. At the same time, the residence of the aboriginal offender in an urban centre that lacks any network of support does not relieve the sentencing judge of the obligation to try to find an alternative to imprisonment.

VI. Summary

[93] Let us see if a general summary can be made of what has been discussed in these reasons.

1. Part XXIII of the Criminal Code codifies the fundamental purpose and principles of sentencing and the factors that should be considered by a judge in striving to determine a sentence that is fit for the offender and the offence.

2. Section 718.2(e) mandatorily requires sentencing judges to consider all available sanctions other than imprisonment and to pay particular attention to the circumstances of aboriginal offenders.

3. Section 718.2(e) is not simply a codification of existing jurisprudence. It is remedial in nature. Its purpose is to ameliorate the serious problem of overrepresentation of aboriginal people in prisons, And to encourage sentencing judges to have recourse to a restorative approach to sentencing. There is a judicial duty to give the provision's remedial purpose real force.

4. Section 718.2(e) must be read and considered in the context of the rest of the factors referred to in that section and in light of all of Part XXIII. All principles and factors set out in Part XXIII must be taken into consideration in determining the fit sentence. Attention should be paid to the fact that Part XXIII, through ss. 718, 718.2(e), and 742.1, among other provisions, has placed a new emphasis upon decreasing the use of incarceration.

5. Sentencing is an individual process and in each case the consideration must continue to be what is a fit sentence for this accused for this offence in this community. However, the effect of s. 718.2(e) is to alter the method of analysis which sentencing judges must use in determining a fit sentence for aboriginal offenders.

6. Section 718.2(e) directs sentencing judges to undertake the sentencing of aboriginal offenders individually, but also differently, because the circumstances of aboriginal people are unique. In sentencing an aboriginal offender, the judge must consider:

    (A) The unique systemic or background factors which may have played a part in bringing the particular aboriginal offender before the courts; and

    (B) The types of sentencing procedures and sanctions which may be appropriate in the circumstances for the offender because of his or her particular aboriginal heritage or connection.

7. In order to undertake these considerations the trial judge will require information pertaining to the accused. Judges may take judicial notice of the broad systemic and background factors affecting aboriginal people, and of the priority given in aboriginal cultures to a restorative approach to sentencing. In the usual course of events, additional case-specific information will come from counsel and from a pre-sentence report which takes into account the factors set out in #6, which in turn may come from representations of the relevant aboriginal

community which will usually be that of the offender. The offender may waive the gathering of that information.

8. If there is no alternative to incarceration the length of the term must be carefully considered.

9. Section 718.2(e) is not to be taken as a means of automatically reducing the prison sentence of aboriginal offenders; nor should it be assumed that an offender is receiving a more lenient sentence simply because incarceration is not imposed.

10. The absence of alternative sentencing programs specific to an aboriginal community does not eliminate the ability of a sentencing judge to impose a sanction that takes into account principles of restorative justice and the needs of the parties involved.

11. Section 718.2(e) applies to all aboriginal persons wherever they reside, whether on- or off-reserve, in a large city or a rural area. In defining the relevant aboriginal community for the purpose of achieving an effective sentence, the term "community" must be defined broadly so as to include any network of support and interaction that might be available, including in an urban centre. At the same time, the residence of the aboriginal offender in an urban centre that lacks any network of support does not relieve the sentencing judge of the obligation to try to find an alternative to imprisonment.

12. Based on the foregoing, the jail term for an aboriginal offender may in some circumstances be less than the term imposed on a non-aboriginal offender for the same offence.

13. It is unreasonable to assume that aboriginal peoples do not believe in the importance of traditional sentencing goals such as deterrence, denunciation, and separation, where warranted. In this context, generally, the more serious and violent the crime, the more likely it will be as a practical matter that the terms of imprisonment will be the same for similar offences and offenders, whether the offender is aboriginal or non-aboriginal.

NOTE

The Supreme Court dismissed Ms. Gladue's appeal against the three-year sentence primarily because, by the time the decision was released, she was already in the community on day parole.

IV. CHALLENGING THE TRADITIONAL PARADIGM: THE USE OF SENTENCING CIRCLES

The traditional adversarial manner in which sentencing hearings are conducted has attracted some criticism. As a result, even before the decision in *Gladue*, much attention had been paid to alternative sentencing processes and options that are more consistent with Aboriginal traditions and experience. The importance of exploring alternatives was recognized by the Law Reform Commission of Canada in 1992.

Law Reform Commission of Canada, Report #34,
Aboriginal Peoples and Criminal Justice
(Ottawa: Supply and Services Canada, 1991) (footnotes omitted)

One prevalent focus within the literature on solutions to the problem of over-representation has been on what are called "alternatives to incarceration." While even the most recent of analyses continue to support the creative use of well-designed and adequately funded alternatives to incarceration or community sanctions, we recognize that many experiments with these alternatives in recent years have been severely criticized.

Theoretically, several alternatives to imprisonment exist at the sentencing stage, such as conditional discharges, suspended sentences, community service orders, compensation, restitution and fine option programs. In addition, options such as diversion, victim–offender reconciliation programs and mediation are also alternatives to imprisonment in the sense that they do not entail resort to the ordinary process of trial and sentencing. Our Commission has long supported these alternatives, but they are underused.

Recommendation

13(1) Alternatives to imprisonment should be used whenever possible. The *Criminal Code* provisions creating such alternatives should ensure that those alternatives are given first consideration at sentencing. A judge imprisoning an Aboriginal person for an offence amenable to the use of alternative dispositions should be required to set forth the reasons for using imprisonment rather than a non-custodial option.

The case for the use of creative Aboriginal methods of dispute resolution is cogently argued and described by Jackson in our commissioned study entitled *In Search of the Pathways to Justice*. In our view, special alternative programs for Aboriginal persons are important for several reasons. First, they possess the potential to reduce the number of Aboriginal persons in prisons. Further, they could with very little adjustment incorporate customary law, thus increasing their acceptability to the affected population. Finally, they are organized around the concept of community-involvement and thus can promote social peace and a sense of community control. Alternative programs are consistent with Aboriginal values in that they seek reconciliation between an offender and the community as a whole, and pursue the goal of restoring harmony.

NOTE

In the context of criminal proceedings involving Aboriginal offenders, some judges have complained that the free flow of information is hampered by the bipolar nature of adversarial proceedings. This has led to the development of the "sentencing circle," whereby the usual trappings of our criminal courts are cast aside. Instead, the judge, counsel, the offender, and significant members of his or her community form a circle and engage in a discussion about the appropriate disposition for the offender. The link between the sentencing circle and First Nations culture was discussed in *R v. Morin* (1995), 101 CCC (3d) 124 (Sask. CA), in which Bayda CJS (in dissent) made the following observations:

> In addressing the sentencing circle question it behooves one to be mindful of the origin of the sentencing circle and its underlying philosophy. The sentencing circle has its genesis in the healing circle which from time immemorial has been a part of the culture of many First Nations of Canada and of the indigenous people of other countries. The healing circle originated and developed amongst the First Nations people at a time when they lived in small relatively isolated communities. ... When a member of the community committed a wrongful act against another member, the community resorted to a healing circle to resolve the problems created by the wrongful act. The circle was premised on two fundamental notions: first, the wrongful act was a breach of the relationship between the wrongdoer and the victim and a breach of the relationship between the wrongdoer and the community; and second, the well-being of the community and consequently the protection of its members and the society generally depended not upon retribution or punishment of the wrongdoer, but upon "healing" the breaches of the two relationships. The emphasis was primarily, if not entirely, upon a restorative or healing approach as distinct from a retributive or punitive approach.

In addition to locating the origin of the sentencing circle, this passage underscores the intimate link between the use of the sentencing circle and the restorative or rehabilitative approach to sentencing in the Aboriginal context. Although the sentencing circle is dealt with here—in a discussion of procedural and evidentiary sentencing matters—there is also a large "substantive" component to this issue.

The use of the sentencing circle has received wide acceptance in a number of provinces. However, there is some disagreement about when it is appropriate to construct a sentencing circle. Indeed, as McEachern CJYT held in *R v. Johnson* (1994), 91 CCC (3d) 21 (YCA), the availability of this procedure, along with its precise contours, ought to be the subject of rules of court, pursuant to s. 482(2) of the *Criminal Code*. This would allow all the parties to know what is expected of them.

R v. Moses was the seminal decision in the expansion of sentencing circles beyond a few northern communities. This case explains the purposes of sentencing circles and the process as it was practised in the town of Mayo in the Yukon in 1992. While reading the case, consider how the process fits within the usual sentencing hearing process and whether it could be adapted in conditions other than small remote communities. Also, ask yourself what we learn about the usual sentencing process by examining the sentencing circle process.

R v. Moses
(1992), 71 CCC (3d) 347 (YTC) (footnotes omitted)

STUART TERR. CT. J: The reasons for this sentence will take us on an unusual journey. Unusual, because the process was as influential in moulding the final decision as any substantive factors. Consequently, this judgment examines the process as well as the traditional stuffings of sentences, mitigating and aggravating circumstances.

• • •

In this case, by changing the process, the primary issues changed, and consequently, the decision was substantially different from what might have been decided had the usual process been followed.

The justice system rules and procedures provide a comfortable barrier for justice professionals from fully confronting the futility, destruction, and injustice left behind in the wake of circuit courts. For those who dared in this case to step outside this comfortable barrier, I hope these reasons capture their input and courage.

1. Process

(A) Overview

Rising crime rates, especially for violent offences, alarming recidivist rates and escalating costs in monetary and human terms have forced societies the world over to search for alternatives to their malfunctioning justice systems. In the western world much of the energy expended in this search has focused on sentencing. While the underlying problems of crime and the gross inadequacies of the justice system stem from much broader, deeper ills within society, significant immediate improvement within the court process can be achieved by changing the sentencing process.

Currently, the search for improving sentencing champions a greater role for victims of crime, reconciliation, restraint in the use of incarceration and a broadening of sentencing alternatives that calls upon less government expenditure and more community participation. As many studies expose the imprudence of excessive reliance upon punishment as the central objective in sentencing, rehabilitation and reconciliation are properly accorded greater emphasis. All these changes call upon communities to become more actively involved and to assume more responsibility for resolving conflict. To engage meaningful community participation, the sentence decision-making process must be altered to share power with the community, and where appropriate, communities must be empowered to resolve many conflicts now processed through criminal courts.

An important step towards constructive community involvement must involve significant changes to the sentencing process before, during and after sentencing.

• • •

(C) Sentencing Hearing

In any decision-making process, power, control, the over-all atmosphere and dynamics are significantly influenced by the physical setting, and especially by the places accorded to participants. Those who wish to create a particular atmosphere, or especially to manipulate a decision-making process to their advantage, have from time immemorial astutely controlled the physical setting of the decision-making forum. Among the great predator groups in the animal kingdom, often the place secured by each member in the site they rest or hunt, significantly influences their ability to control group decisions. In the criminal justice process (arguably one of contemporary society's great predators), the physical arrangement in a court-room profoundly affects who participates and how they participate. The organization of the court-room influences the content, scope and importance of information provided to the court. The rules governing the court hearing reinforce the allocation of power and influence fostered by the physical setting.

The combined effect of the rules and the court-room arrangements entrench the adversarial nature of the process. The judge, defence and Crown counsel, fortified by their prominent places in the court-room and by the rules, own and control the process and no one in a court-room can have any doubt about that.

For centuries, the basic organization of the court has not changed. Nothing has been done to encourage meaningful participation by the accused, the victim, or by the community; remarkable, considering how the location of a meeting, the design of the room, furniture arrangements, and the seating of participants are so meticulously considered in most decision-making processes to ensure the setting reinforce the objective of the process. If the objective of the sentencing process is now to enhance sentencing options, to afford greater concern to the impact on victims, to shift focus from punishment to rehabilitation, and to meaningfully engage communities in sharing responsibility for sentencing decisions, it may be advantageous for the justice system to examine how court procedures and the physical arrangements within court-rooms militate against these new objectives. It was in this case.

(D) Advantages of Circle

In this case, a change in the physical arrangement of the court-room produced a major change in the process.

(1) Physical Setting

For court, a circle to seat 30 people was arranged as tightly as numbers allowed. When all seats were occupied, additional seating was provided in an outer circle for persons arriving after the "hearing" had commenced.

Defence sat beside the accused and his family. The Crown sat immediately across the circle from defence counsel to the right of the judge. Officials and members from the First Nation, the RCMP officers, the probation officer and others were left to find their own "comfortable" place within the circle.

(2) Dynamics of the Circle

By arranging the court in a circle without desks or tables, with all participants facing each other, with equal access and equal exposure to each other, the dynamics of the decision-making process were profoundly changed.

Everyone around the circle introduced themselves. Everyone remained seated when speaking. After opening remarks from the judge and counsel, the formal process dissolved into an informal but intense discussion of what might best protect the community and extract Philip from the grip of alcohol and crime.

The tone was tempered by the close proximity of all participants. For the most part, participants referred to each other by name, not by title. While disagreements and arguments were provoked by most topics, posturing, pontification, and the well-worn platitudes, commonly characteristic of court-room speeches by counsel and judges, were gratefully absent.

The circle setting dramatically changed the roles of all participants, as well as the focus, tone, content and scope of discussions. The following observations denote the more obvious benefits generated by the circle setting.

(i) Challenges Monopoly of Professionals

The foreboding court-room setting discourages meaningful participation beyond lawyers and judges.

The judge presiding on high, robed to emphasize his authoritative dominance, armed with the power to control the process, is rarely challenged. Lawyers, by their deference, and by standing when addressing the judge, reinforce to the community the judge's pivotal importance. All of this combines to encourage the community to believe judges uniquely and exclusively possess the wisdom and resources to develop a just and viable result. They are so grievously wrong.

Counsel, due to the rules, and their prominent place in the court, control the input of information. Their ease with the rules, their facility with the peculiar legal language, exudes a confidence and skill that lay people commonly perceive as a prerequisite to participate.

The community relegated to the back of the room, is separated from counsel and the judge either by an actual bar or by placing their seats at a distinct distance behind counsel tables. The interplay between lawyers and the judge creates the perception of a ritualistic play. The set, as well as the performance, discourages anyone else from participating.

The circle significantly breaks down the dominance that traditional court-rooms accord lawyers and judges. In a circle, the ability to contribute, the importance and credibility of any input is not defined by seating arrangements. The audience is changed. All persons within the circle must be addressed. Equally, anyone in the circle may ask a direct question to anyone. Questions about the community and the accused force discussions into a level of detail usually avoided in the court-room by sweeping assumptions and boiler-plate platitudes. In the court-room, reliance upon technical legal language imbues the process with the air of resolutely addressing difficult issues. In fact, behind the facade of legalese, many crucial considerations are either ignored or superficially considered. The circle denies the comfort of evading difficult issues through the use of obtuse, complex technical language.

(ii) Encourages Lay Participation

The circle setting drew everyone into the discussion. Unlike the court-room, where the setting facilitates participation only by counsel and the judge, the circle prompted a natural rhythm of discussion.

The physical proximity of all participants, the ability to see the face of the person speaking, the conversational tone, the absence of incomprehensible rituals, and the intermingling of professionals and lay members of the community during breaks, all a consequence of the circle, broke down many barriers to participation.

The highly defined roles imposed upon professionals by the formal justice process creates barriers to communication. The circle drew out the person buried behind their role, and encouraged a more personal and less professional contribution. The circle, in revealing the person behind the professional facade fostered a greater sense of equality between lay and professional participants in the circle. This sense of equality and the discovery of significant common concerns and objectives is essential to sustain an effective partnership between the community and the justice system.

(iii) Enhances Information

The justice system rarely acquires adequate information to competently target the sentencing process on the underlying causes of criminal behaviour. Too often courts are forced to precariously rely upon bare-bones information, usually based on second or third-hand sources. Consequently, sentencing guided by very incomplete information places too much reliance upon mythological understandings about deterrence and punishment, and upon stereotypical categories used to describe the crime and the offender.

The rituals and specialized language of the sentencing process produce an aura of competence. Rising crime rates (especially rising recidivism) despite staggering increases in expenditures, debunk this illusory aura. Sentencing could be vastly improved by enhancing the quantity and quality of information.

The paucity and stagnancy of sentencing information severely handicaps any endeavour to purposefully employ sentencing remedies. Very little is known in sentencing about offenders, victims, the crucial underlying factors causing the criminal behaviour, or about the larger context of the home and community, and almost nothing is known about how the court process affects the conflict or upon the persons involved. Acting on a woefully incomplete understanding of either the larger circumstances or of the specific life circumstances of those directly affected by crime, the court rarely appreciates whether the sentence resolves or exacerbates the fundamental problems promoting crime.

Of course, all judges and counsel know these circumstances exist, but the court-room setting, and emphasis on getting through the docket, of processing cases as any good bureaucracy might process licence applications, encourages wilful blindness about many relevant circumstances in sentencing. The sentencing process, in searching for an effective sentence to fit the specific needs in each case, is analogous to a "fast forwarded" game of Pin the Tail on the Donkey.

Community involvement through the circle generates not only new information, but information not normally available to the court. Through the circle, participants can respond to concerns, fill in gaps, and ensure each new sentencing option is measured against a broader, more detailed base of information. In the circle, the flow of information is alive, flexible and more readily capable of assessing and responding to new ideas.

Despite psychiatric and alcohol assessments, and an extensive and exceptionally researched pre-sentence report, the circle in this case provided additional relevant and particularly valuable information to probe and assess each new creative option.

Documents, files, reports, and assessments help introduce the offender to the court, but often present a lifeless portrayal which can be easily misconstrued. The circle, by enabling Philip to speak for himself, and by enabling others who have known him all his life to share their knowledge, substantially improved the court's perception.

Court-room procedures and rules often preclude or discourage many sources from contributing crucial information. The circle removes or reduces many of the impediments blocking the flow of essential information into court.

(iv) Creative Search for New Options

Public censure often focuses on the differences in sentences meted out for the same crime. There should be more, not fewer differences in sentences. If the reasons for the differences stems from personal attitudes of judges, the inadequacy of information, an inability to appreciate the remedial impact of various sentencing options, an absence of commonly accepted objectives, or ignorance of the impact of crime on victims, then public concern is warranted. The reasons for the differences, not simply the differences themselves, determine whether the differences are laudable or condemnable.

In a multicultural society, where gross inequities in opportunities, social resources, and social conditions abound, just sentencing cannot be monolithic or measured against any standard national "typical sentence." If the predominate objectives in sentencing are protection of the community, rehabilitation of the offender, minimizing adverse impacts on victims, and particularly greater community involvement, then even greater differences in sentencing for the same crime should be expected and welcomed. In at least two significant ways, the circle will accentuate differences in sentences for the same crime. The circle, by enhancing community participation, generates a richer range of sentencing options. Secondly, the circle by improving the quality and quantity of information provides the ability to refine and focus the use of sentencing options to meet the particular needs in each case.

In this case the circle promoted among all participants a desire to find an appropriate sentence that best served all of the above objectives. Their creative search produced a sentence markedly different from customary sentences for such crimes, and radically departed from the pattern of sentences previously imposed upon Philip for similar offences. The circle forged a collective desire for something different, something unlike the sentences imposed in the past 10 years, something everyone could support, something they believed would work. Fuelled by the expanded and responsive flow of information, the circle participants worked towards a consensus, towards a unique response to a problem that had plagued the community for 10 years and had stolen 10 years of productive life from Philip.

I was surprised by the result, but the new information and the option provided by the community rendered the final sentence obvious and compelling. The combination of new information and an array of new sentencing options can dramatically change

sentencing dispositions from those based on information normally available and dependant upon the limited range of conventional sentencing remedies.

• • •

(vi) Encouraging the Offender's Participation

Philip Moses, as is typical of most offenders, had not significantly participated in any
of the previous seven sentencing hearings which had instrumentally shaped his life.
Most offenders, during formal court proceedings, sit with head bowed, sometimes in
fear, more often in anger as incomprehensible discussions ramble on about their life,
crimes, and about how communities must be protected from such hardened criminals.

Circuit lawyers, usually different each time, carry the primary responsibility to
speak on behalf of offenders such as Philip. Their knowledge of the offender is derived
from a few brief interviews, police reports, criminal records and sometimes from pre-
sentence reports.

However well intentioned they might be, circuit counsel can never know Philip as
well as his family or others within his community. Nor can any counsel fully reflect the
offender's pain, suffering, or desperate search for help. Equally, the anger, resentment
and hostility of many offenders is rarely expressed, as competent counsel manage to
ensure a properly contrite, dutiful face masks any burning feelings which may, if revealed, provoke a harsher sentence. Consequently, the court sentences in blissful ignorance, missing the opportunity to constructively appreciate perceptions and feelings that
may perpetually frustrate rehabilitative plans.

In the circle, the police, mother, brother, Chief of the First Nation, the probation officer,
and other community members expressed constructive concern about Philip. They repeatedly spoke of the need to "reintegrate" Philip with his family and his First Nation.

This was the first time Philip heard anyone from his community, or from his First
Nation offer support. He could no longer believe that the police and the community
were solely interested in removing him from their midst.

These comments within the circle drew Philip into the discussion. His eloquence,
passion, and pain riveted everyone's attention. His contribution moved the search for
an effective sentence past several concerns shared around the circle. No, he did not
convince everyone, nor did he ultimately secure what he sought, but his passion and
candour significantly contributed to constructing the sentence.

(vii) Involving Victims in Sentencing

Many offenders perceive only the state as the aggrieved party. They fail to appreciate the
very human pain and suffering they cause. Absent an appreciation of the victim's suffering, offenders fail to understand their sentence except as the intrusion of an insensitive,
oppressive state bent on punishment. An offender's remorse is more likely to be prompted by a desire to seek mercy from the state or by a recognition that they have been "bad."
Only when an offender's pain caused by the oppression of the criminal justice system
is confronted by the pain that victims experience from crime, can most offenders gain
a proper perspective of their behaviour. Without this perspective, the motivation to
successfully pursue rehabilitation lacks an important and often essential ingredient.

Much work remains to find an appropriate means of including the victim, or in the very least, including the impact on the victim in the sentencing process. The circle affords an important opportunity to explore the potential of productively incorporating the impact upon victims in sentencing.

• • •

(xii) Merging Values: First Nation and Western Governments

Because aboriginal people use the same language, engage in similar play and work, western society assumes similar underlying values govern and motivate their conduct. Particularly within the justice system, this widely spread erroneous assumption has had a disastrous impact on aboriginal people and their communities.

Much of the systemic discrimination against aboriginal people within the justice system stems from a failure to recognize the fundamental differences between aboriginal and western cultures. Aboriginal culture does not place as high a premium on individual responsibility or approach conflict in the direct confrontational manner championed by our adversarial process. Aboriginal people see value in avoiding confrontation and in refraining from speaking publicly against each other. In dealing with conflict, emphasis is placed on reconciliation, the restoration of harmony and the removal of underlying pressures generating conflict.

After extensive exposure to the justice system, it has been assumed too readily that aboriginal people have adjusted to our adversarial process with its obsession on individual rights and individual responsibility, another tragically wrong assumption. Similarly, we have erroneously assumed by inviting their involvement in our system they will be willing and eager participants. If we generally seek their partnership in resolving crime, a process that fairly accommodates both value systems must emerge.

The circle has the potential to accord greater recognition to aboriginal values, and to create a less confrontational, less adversarial means of processing conflict. Yet the circle retains the primary principles and protections inherent to the justice system. The circle contributes the basis for developing a genuine partnership between aboriginal communities and the justice system by according the flexibility for both sets of values to influence the decision-making process in sentencing.

(3) Safeguards: Protecting Individual Rights in Merging the Community and Justice System in the Circle

Courage, patience, and tolerance must accompany all participants in the search for a productive partnership between communities and the justice system. The search need not be foolhardy. Many safeguards can be adapted to protect individual rights while opening the process to community involvement. In this experiment with the circle, the following safeguards were used to cushion any adverse impact on individual rights. Within the justice system, a critical assessment must be made about what is truly inviolable and what has by convention been presumed to be. Many conventions have survived long past the justification for their original creation.

(i) Open Court

The court-room remained the same, only the furniture was rearranged. The door was open, the public retained free access to the room.

The long-standing reasons for open court may not be as persuasive in some sentencing hearings where privacy may be essential to precipitate frank exchanges which reveal extremely sensitive family or personal information. Normally, such information, vital to competently employing any sentencing option, is rarely available as participants are understandably reluctant to share intimate circumstances of their life in an open public court-room, especially in small communities where anonymity is impossible.

In most cases there will be no need to limit access. However, where clear advantages flow from a closed session, the longstanding reasons for open court must be dusted off and re-examined in light of the advantages derived from acquiring extremely sensitive and personal information from offenders, victims or their families and friends.

(ii) Transcripts

The court reporter remained a part of the circle.

In some cases, there are good reasons to question why a transcript embracing all circle discussions is necessary. Some aspects of the discussion may be best excluded from the transcript, or where the circle is closed to the public, the transcript retained in a confidential manner, available only if required by a court of appeal.

To establish appropriate guidelines in assessing the competing values of an open versus a closed process on a case-by-case basis, some of the ancient icons of criminal procedures need an airing and reassessment.

The tradition of a circle—"what comes out in a circle, stays in a circle"—runs counter to the justice tradition requiring both an open court and transcripts. A more flexible set of rules for exceptions must be fashioned to establish a balance in emerging First Nation, community, and justice system values in the circle.

(iii) Upper Limits to Sentence

The circle is designed to explore and develop viable sentencing options drawing upon, whenever possible, community-based resources. The circle is not designed to extract reasons to increase the severity of punishment. Accordingly, at the outset of the circle process, Crown and defence counsel were called upon to make their customary sentencing submissions. Based on these submissions, I indicated the upper-limit sentence for the offence.

By stating at the outset an upper limit to the sentence based on conventional sentencing principles and remedies, the offender enters the circle without fearing a harsher jail sentence provoked by candour or anger within the circle. This constitutes an important basis to encourage offenders to participate.

The upper limit also provides a basis for the circle to appreciate what will happen in the absence of community alternatives. The utility of the upper-limit sentence can be measured against any new information shared in the circle. Any community-based alternative developed by the circle may be substituted for part or all of this sentence.

(iv) Opportunity for Offender To Speak

The *Criminal Code*, s. 668, ensures the offender has an opportunity to speak in his own words before a sentence is imposed. This opportunity is generally offered after all submissions have been made, and the court has all but formally concluded what the sentence will be. It is generally a perfunctory step in the process, rarely used and generally of little effect.

Defence counsel bears the primary and often exclusive responsibility to represent the offender's interest. How far we have come from the time when lawyers were banned and offenders left to make their own submissions. Somewhere on this journey from exclusive reliance upon the offender to essentially exclusive reliance upon defence counsel, we passed a more fitting balance in the participatory roles of counsel and offender. It may be too cute to suggest courts currently sentence defence counsel, not offenders, but the thought does highlight how much sentencing depends upon the work, competence, knowledge, and eloquence of defence counsel.

The inequities in proceeding without counsel are staggering. Similarly, the involvement of communities creates its own inequities within the circle. In a very unequal world, no justice system can create equality, or for that matter render perfect justice. The circle improves the offender's ability to participate, and thereby reduces the obvious inequities in a process that minimizes participation by the very person who is the primary focus of the process. More thought, or innovation must be invested to extract the best from the existing justice process and from the circle to create a viable balance between individual rights and community involvement.

(v) Crown and Defence Counsel

The traditional and essential functions of Crown and defence counsel are not excluded by the circle.

The Crown at the outset placed before the circle the interests of the state in sentencing the offender. The Crown's participation through questions and by engaging in the discussions retains the circle's awareness of the larger interests of the state. Aware of community-provided alternatives, having acquired first-hand knowledge of a broad spectrum of community concerns and armed with detailed information about the offender, the Crown at the end of the circle discussions can more competently assess how the interests of the state, and the interests of the community are best addressed in sentencing.

Especially on circuit, the Crown is forced to make assumptions about what sentences protect the community. Through the circle, these assumptions are examined by members of the very community Crown submissions are designed to protect.

Defence counsel, knowing that at worst the offender faces a conventional sentence presaged at the outset of the hearing, can constructively use the circle to develop a sentencing plan to advance the immediate and long-term interests of his client. Community support generated by the circle, as it did in this case, creates viable alternatives to jail.

(vi) Disputed Facts

Any disputed fact must be proven in the customary manner. Proof of a disputed fact can be carried out in the circle by the examination of witnesses under oath. Alternatively, during a break in the circle discussions, court can be resumed and all the traditional trappings of the court-room engaged to resolve a disputed fact.

The circle moves along a different road to consensus than the adversarial character of the formal court-room hearings. The process in a circle can either resolve disputes in a less adversarial manner, or render the disputed fact irrelevant or unimportant by evolving a sentencing disposition principally relevant upon community-based alternatives. However, the formal court process provides a "safeguard" to be called upon by either counsel at any time a matter in the circle necessitates formal proof.

NOTE

Although much of the development of sentencing circles has occurred in the Yukon and northern Saskatchewan, credit for their modern introduction as a way of responding to the circumstances of Aboriginal offenders should be given to Judge C.C. Barnett, formerly of the BC Provincial Court, who sat for many years in Williams Lake and the Queen Charlotte Islands.

In different communities, sentencing circles have evolved in different forms, but always with the common feature of broad-based community participation. A brief account of their development in Saskatchewan was given by Fafard Prov. Ct. J in *R v. Joseyounen*, [1995] 6 WWR 438:

> The first sentencing circle to be held in Saskatchewan took place in Sandy Bay in July of 1992. I was the presiding judge. Since then many sentencing circles have been held in Northern Saskatchewan (I estimate that I have dealt with over 60 cases in that manner myself), and out of this experience by me and my colleagues on the Provincial Court in the north, there have emerged seven criteria that we apply in deciding if a case for sentencing should go to a circle. These criteria are not carved in stone, but they provide guidelines sufficiently simple for the lay public to understand, and also capable of application so that our decisions are not being made arbitrarily.
>
> It is imperative that the public, aboriginal and others, be able to know and understand what is happening in the development of sentencing circles: the credibility of the administration of justice depends on it.

Fafard J's criteria are:

1. The accused must agree to be referred to the sentencing circle.
2. The accused must have deep roots in the community in which the circle is held and from which the participants are drawn.
3. There are elders or respected non-political community leaders willing to participate.
4. The victim is willing to participate and has been subjected to no coercion or pressure in so agreeing.

5. The court should try to determine beforehand, as best it can, if the victim is subject to battered spouse syndrome. If she is, then she should have counselling made available to her and be accompanied by a support team in the circle.
6. Disputed facts have been resolved in advance.
7. The case is one in which a court would be willing to take a calculated risk and depart from the usual range of sentencing.

These criteria were applied by the majority of the Saskatchean Court of Appeal in *R v. Morin* (1995), 101 CCC (3d) 124 (Sask. CA) to reject the appropriateness of a sentencing circle following a conviction for robbery by an Aboriginal offender who lived in Saskatoon. On the facts, there was some doubt about the offender's sincerity in seeking help from the local Aboriginal community.

In the Yukon, the use of circles has evolved since the decision in *Moses*, above. In *R v. Gingell* (1996), 50 CR (4th) 32 (YTC), Lilles J described the process that has been developed by Kwanlin Dun, the Aboriginal community near Whitehorse. Other alternative forms of sentencing procedure are also in use. See, for example, the decision in *R v. P. (J.A.)* (1991), 6 CR (4th) 126 (YTC), for a description of sentencing in Teslin, a community in the southern Yukon, where the clan leaders sit with the sentencing judge to offer advice on an appropriate sentence.

One of the most successful examples of a circle approach has been used in the community of Hollow Water in Manitoba. Its sentencing circle is described by Ross Gordon Green.

R.G. Green, *Justice in Aboriginal Communities: Sentencing Alternatives*
(Saskatoon: Purich Publishing, 1998) (footnotes omitted)

Hollow Water is located 190 kilometres (118 miles) northeast of Winnipeg on the east shore of Lake Winnipeg. It covers 1620 hectares (4,000 acres) of land within the Canadian Precambrian Shield. The band's native language is Ojibway. As of 1994, the on-reserve population was 490 and off-reserve was 512. This band is a signatory to Treaty 5, signed in 1875. Hollow Water is bordered by the Métis communities of Aghaming, Manigotogan, and Seymourville. The total resident population of Hollow Water and the surrounding communities is 1200. Resources at Hollow Water include a K–12 school, a convenience store, a gas bar, a community hall, a band office, and a water treatment plant. No regular court sittings are held at Hollow Water. Provincial Court for this community is held 100 kilometres (62 miles) to the south in Pine Falls. However, since December of 1993, the Provincial Court of Manitoba has convened at Hollow Water to conduct sentencing circles that have dealt with offenders charged with sexual assault.

Hollow Water represents a unique example of a community-driven approach to dispute resolution and the healing and treatment of both offenders and victims. Rupert Ross described its development:

> In 1984, a group of social service providers got together, concerned about the future of their young people. As they looked into the issues of youth substance abuse, vandalism, truancy and suicide, their focus shifted to the home life of those children and to the substance abuse

and family violence that often prevailed. Upon closer examination of those issues, the focus changed again, for inter-generational sexual abuse was identified as the root problem. Other dysfunctional behaviour came to be seen primarily as symptomatic. By 1987, they began to tackle sexual abuse head on, creating what they have called their Community Holistic Circle Healing Program [CHCH]. They presently estimate that 75 percent of the population of Hollow Water are victims of sexual abuse, and 35 percent are "victimizers."

CHCH co-ordinator Berma Bushie cited frustration with the prevailing criminal justice and child welfare systems as factors contributing to CHCH's development:

> We also studied the *Child Welfare Act*, the legal system and how it was dealing with these [child sexual abuse] cases, and we were horrified to find out that our children were further victimized. ... Child Welfare's practice at the time, and probably still is, is when a child disclosed [he or she was] ... removed from the family and, in a lot of situations, a child was removed from the community. And then there's absolutely no help offered to the offender. Everything was turned over to the legal system and charges laid, court would take place, and that's it. And the child would be expected to testify against the offender in criminal court, and to us that's not protecting our children. So based on the laws that continue to govern us, we feel that we have to ensure protection for our children. We have to have a say in what happens to them.

As of February 6, 1995, the assessment team comprised seven sexual abuse workers, the local child and family service supervisor, a support worker, a councillor from the band, two Native Alcohol (NADAP) workers, a public health nurse, a local band constable, an RCMP officer from Pine Falls, a person from the Roman Catholic church, two people from provincial Child and Family Services, and the local school principal. The procedure followed by CHCH's assessment team is complex and includes provision of support and treatment for victims and victimizers and their respective families.

After initial disclosure of sexual abuse by a child, a thirteen-step process is followed by the assessment team. These steps are: (1) effecting disclosure, (2) protecting the child/victim, (3) confronting the victimizer, (4) assisting the victimizer's spouse, (5) assisting the family or families directly affected and the community, (6) calling together the assessment team, (7) getting the victimizer to admit and accept responsibility, (8) preparing the victimizer, (9) preparing the victim, (10) preparing all family or families, (11) organizing a special gathering, (12) implementing the healing contract, and (13) conducting the cleansing ceremony.

The assessment team is divided into support teams for the victim, victimizer, and family. After ensuring the safety of the victim, the accused is confronted by a member of the assessment team, who encourages the accused to take responsibility for his or her actions and to participate in CHCH. Berma Bushie explained:

> We feel as a community it's our job to go and confront the offender and not to rely on the RCMP, because they haven't been very successful in getting people to take responsibility for what they've done. When people see the RCMP, they just clam up, won't speak, and so we feel as a community we have a better ... track record of getting people to take responsibility for what they've done. ... Nine times out of ten, the offender takes responsibility, and we inform the offender of the plan in place. We inform [him] of the community ap-

proach. We also inform him about the treatment expectations, the circles that ... he's going to have to go through. We also tell the offender that he has to go plead guilty in court.

When criminal charges follow a disclosure, the CHCH approach promotes acceptance of responsibility by the offender through entry of an early guilty plea in court. This practice stands in sharp contrast to the presumption of innocence enjoyed by accused persons in Canadian law and their right to remain silent. In fairness, though, the goal of team members is to help both child complainants and adult accused. After entry of a guilty plea, members of the assessment team then ask the court to adjourn sentencing for at least four months to allow treatment with the offender to begin. Berma Bushie indicated that this period of time was requested so that the assessment team could be assured that the offender was committed to healing.

Offenders are expected to participate in four circles. In the first circle, the offender discloses details of his offence to the CHCH assessment team. In the second circle, the victim tells the offender how the abuse has affected his or her life. In the third circle, the offender describes his actions to his family. Finally, in the fourth circle, the offender faces his community in a sentencing circle. Prior to the introduction of circle sentencing at Hollow Water in December 1993, the assessment team prepared and presented recommendations on sentence to the court sitting in Pine Falls. This procedure was outlined in *R v. S.(H.M.)*.

CHCH has actively opposed offender incarceration and has argued that jail cannot break the generational cycle of violence. Assessment team member Marcel Hardesty supported this analysis. He explained that he had asked a sexual offender, recently returned from jail, whether he would commit the offence again. The offender had responded that he would be sure not to get caught if he did it again. Hardesty questioned the lesson being taught by jail and suggested incarceration only reduces the chances of other victims and abusers coming forward.

CHCH focusses on restoring harmony between victims and offenders and the community-at-large through traditional holistic practices. In this process, a conjunctive relationship has developed between CHCH and the criminal justice system both prior to and after sentencing. A protocol between the Manitoba Department of Justice and CHCH was negotiated in 1991 in which the department recognized CHCH's program as an option for the treatment and supervision of sexual assault offenders and agreed to consider a non-custodial sentence if that was the recommendation of the assessment team. This protocol was negotiated by CHCH to give the assessment team input into sentencing and to avoid repeatedly educating Crown attorneys about the CHCH approach.

The first sentencing circle at Hollow Water occurred December 9, 1993. It involved serious sexual assaults perpetrated by two parents on their children. The assessment team foresaw dire consequences for the offenders if this case went through the conventional system. According to assessment team member Lorne Hagel, Judge Murray Sinclair of the Provincial Court of Manitoba had advised the team that, given the offences and circumstances involved, eight to ten years' incarceration would be a realistic sentence. Judge Sinclair advised me that the initial Crown position on sentence was five to six years' incarceration, while even defence counsel conceded that two-and-a-half to four years might be appropriate for one offender, with less jail time for the other. The

CHCH assessment team made representations to the Provincial Court requesting formation of a sentencing circle and explaining the evolution of community participation in that community. The submission characterized circle sentencing as an extension of the community's role in holding offenders accountable for their actions and heating the pain they inflicted on their victims:

> Up until now the sentencing hearing has been the point at which all of the parties of the legal system (Crown, defence, judge) and the community have come together. Major differences of opinion as to how to proceed have often existed. As we see it, the legal system usually arrives with an outside agenda of punishment and deterrence of the "guilty" victimizer, and safety and protection of the victim and community; the community on the other hand, arrives with an agenda of accountability of the victimizer to the community, and restoration of balance to all parties of the victimization.
>
> As we see it, the differences in the agendas are seriously deterring the healing process of the community. We believe that the restoration of balance is more likely to occur if sentencing itself is more consistent in process and in content with the healing work of the community. Sentencing needs to become more of a step in the healing process, rather than a diversion from it. ... The sentencing circle promotes the above rationale. ... As we see it, the sentencing circle plays two primary purposes (1) it promotes the community healing process by providing a forum for the community to address the parties at the time of sentencing, and (2) it allows the court to hear directly from the people most directly affected by the pain of the victimization. In the past the Crown and defence, as well as ourselves, have attempted to portray this information. We believe that it is now time for the court to hear from the victim, the family of the victim, the victimizer, the family of the victimizer and the community-at-large.

This first sentencing circle commenced at seven o'clock in the morning with a sunrise and pipe ceremony and ended at nine o'clock that night. Winnipeg Free Press reporter Kevin Rollason described the atmosphere and process followed at this circle:

> While the smell of sweet grass filled the air, two circles were formed in the centre of the hall for the sentencing of a man and woman charged with incest. The inner circle of about 40 people held the key participants—including both offenders and victims—while the outer circle consisted of about 200 other relatives, friends and community members. ... Just before court was called to order, a man holding a tray of burning sweet grass and buffalo grass went around the inner circle, allowing each participant to "wash" the smoke over their hair, faces and clothes. Passing an eagle feather from hand to hand, each person spoke in order around the circles. The discussion went around a total of four times. During the first circle, people spoke about why they were there. During the second, participants were able to speak to the victims. The third and fourth circles were designed to be separate—one centering on the effects of the crime and the other on "restoring balance" to the offenders. However, when the proceedings threatened to extend well into the night, the last two circles had to be melded into one.

At the conclusion of the circle, all participants, with the exception of a cousin of one of the victims but including the Crown prosecutor, agreed jail would be counterproductive for these offenders. Judge Sinclair indicated to me that these offenders had progressed from a state of total denial to one of total acceptance and responsibility for their actions. In addition, the two had actively worked in convincing one hundred other sexual abusers from Hollow Water to come forward and admit their actions publicly. At the circle's conclusion, Judge Sinclair imposed a three-year suspended sentence on each offender with probation containing a condition that each offender follow the directions of the CHCH assessment team.

Despite the many disclosures of abuse heard at the initial Hollow Water sentencing circle, few subsequent sentencing circles were conducted and there was no increase in sexual assault charges laid against Hollow Water residents. This suggests that many incidents of abuse were being dealt with locally outside the conventional justice system or were not being dealt with at all. An article on Hollow Water published on April 8, 1995, in *The Globe and Mail* stated that, since 1986, only five offenders had been jailed instead of entering the CHCH program and forty-eight offenders had enrolled in the treatment program.

The limited number of offenders sentenced through sentencing circles or incarcerated outside the CHCH program suggest that many offenders in the program were not being charged. This highlights the interesting and often complex relationship between local dispute-resolution processes and the broader justice system. At one level, the community of Hollow Water was working conjunctively with the formal justice system, through the involvement of CHCH members in court assessments and circle sentencing. At another level, the community was apparently operating separately from the formal system, assuming complete control of dispute resolution. The reality across the criminal justice system in Canada is that the number of cases processed through the formal system represents only a small proportion of ongoing criminal activity. What may be different at Hollow Water is the availability of local resources to address the behaviour of offenders, while at the same time protecting victims within that community.

As part of their local system of social control, and in an effort to hold offenders responsible for their actions and encourage their active participation in treatment, a community review was held on the six-month anniversary of each sentencing circle. Berma Bushie explained:

> One of the things that the community does is, after sentencing, we tell the offenders "for the next three years, you are on probation and every six months we are bringing the case back to the community, for the community to review how you are doing in treatment. ..." [The community review] is one of the ways, besides probation, ... used to make sure that people are following the [sentencing circle's] recommendation.

The review process encourages community assistance in holding offenders accountable for their victimization and promotes active participation in their treatment. As Bushie explained:

> We found that after the first sentencing circle back in December 1993 ... that in the treatment area ... there was a regression on the part of the offenders. They were getting back into their denial process. They were getting back to creating negative support for their case and stuff like that. ... [W]e felt that ... [our assessment] team was not strong enough to stop the regression and to get the people [offenders] back on track with their healing. And

because the community came out to speak and give recommendations to the court for their sentencing [circle] ... we felt as a team ... we needed to go back to the community to report ... what was happening. ... And as a team we felt that, before we thought about going through [the process of charging the offenders with breach of probation and bringing this case back to court, ... we felt that we ... should go back through the community. First, give all the details ... and have the community help us decide where this case should go. ... And they [the community members in attendance at the review] felt that these people should be given a chance, and that, again, they repeated their support for these people. They repeated their expectations of the kinds of treatments they wanted the offenders to take, and the work that they wanted them to do. And we said, "Okay, we'll do that and six months down the line, we'll come back and we'll report to you and see how these people are doing.

A community sentencing review held at Hollow Water on February 22, 1995 for three sexual offenders who had been sentenced through a sentencing circle was attended by approximately thirty community members including one of the victims. The victim in attendance had been victimized by two of the offenders. She was apparently sitting in a circle with her abusers for the first time, although she did not speak. The other victim had moved to Winnipeg. The assessment team members assigned to each victim and offender were present and reported to the circle.

This review followed a similar format to the sentencing circles. During successive rounds of the circle, participants in the review learned of the treatment and progress of all victims and offenders and, in turn, addressed the three offenders and one victim in attendance. Participants also developed recommendations for continued offender treatment and victim support. Comments by participants made it clear there was strong community pressure on the offenders to continue treatment. Several women, while acknowledging the progress made by each offender, openly challenged the offenders not to regress in their treatment and to assist the assessment team by naming their other victims. Berma Bushie commented to the offenders that jail "would have been the easy way out for you." She thanked them for taking responsibility for their actions and for facing their community in the circle.

NOTE

Although sentencing circles provide a more appropriate forum for the sentencing of Aboriginal offenders, they raise a number of questions. Must the offender have pleaded guilty, or is it sufficient that he or she accepts guilt in the circle? Can circles be used for all cases? Can they be modified for use in non-Aboriginal communities? Have they produced constructive results without diminishing the interests of the victim? With respect to the efficacy of sentencing circles, see Julian Roberts and Carole La Prairie, "Sentencing Circles: Some Unanswered Questions" (1996-97), 39 *Crim. LQ* 69.

Given the understandable divisions and loyalties that exist within communities, some observers have questioned whether a sentencing circle can transcend power imbalances inherent in certain offences. This important issue is addressed by Green.

R.G. Green, *Justice in Aboriginal Communities: Sentencing Alternatives*
(Saskatoon: Purich Publishing, 1998) (footnotes omitted)

Justice Co-ordinator Mary Crnkovich described an example of such a power imbalance within an Inuit sentencing circle in northern Quebec. This circle had been formed to consider the sentence of an offender who had assaulted his wife:

> Aside from the fact that the sentence was based on a proposal presented by the accused, the victim could hardly, in her position, oppose such a proposal or complain that it was not working. Again to suggest that her attendance [for counselling] would keep the accused honest, demonstrates, in the author's view, the judge's misunderstanding of the life circumstances of this woman as a victim of violence. How could this woman speak out against her husband? How could she speak out against the mayor [and] ... others in her community [who attended the sentencing circle]? Did the judge really believe she would speak out based on the history of this case to date? The victim's actions or lack thereof during the circle, demonstrated the degree of fear and deference paid to her spouse.

Rupert Ross has suggested that it might be inappropriate to conduct a sentencing circle without previously identifying and addressing power imbalances between offenders and victims. This appears not to have been done in the Inuit circle described above. Such an approach was, however, practised at Hollow Water in cases of serious child sexual abuse. At Hollow Water, each offender and victim was assigned a separate support team, and the two were not brought together until such time as they could face each other on an equal footing. When a sentencing circle was held, the victim was encouraged, but not required, to attend. If the victim chose to attend the circle, he or she was accompanied by a specific worker for support.

• • •

Although reconciliation between parties to an offence is possible during a sentencing circle, offences involving long-standing power imbalances will continue to necessitate vigilance by judges in ensuring, to the extent possible, protection of the victims. Unfortunately, such protection may be short-lived in isolated communities, where the routine departure of the court party after adjournment makes community-based support for such victims essential. Cases of domestic violence underscore the importance of ongoing resources and support at the local level for both victims and offenders. It is unrealistic to expect that a few hours in a sentencing circle will permanently alter historic patterns of offending and imbalances of power. Clearly, sentencing circles can be catalysts to start significant changes in behaviour on the part of offenders. Any chance of achieving this goal, however, depends on the availability and success of locally accessible resources, including support, treatment, and counselling for victims and offenders, and, in cases involving abuse, close supervision of offenders and protection of victims.

The appropriateness of community participation at sentencing may also bring into question the treatment of the victim by the local community as a whole. Caution respecting power imbalances between offenders and victims, in the context of a request for a community-based sentencing hearing, was expressed by the Ontario Court of Justice (General Division) in *R v. A.F.* The victim had been outcast from her community as a result of her complaint and the resulting criminal proceeding. She had moved to Southern Ontario following her disclosure.

More recently, we have seen an evolution of the use of sentencing circles in Aboriginal communities across Canada. There have even been some experimental efforts to construct sentencing circles in urban and non-Aboriginal settings. Of course, these efforts always raise questions about how to appreciate and implement the concept of "community," so integral to the sentencing-circle idea. Still, sentencing circles are most common in Saskatchewan and the Yukon.

The following two Saskatchewan cases involve serious offences—manslaughter and perjury during a murder trial. The decision in *R v. Kahpeaysewat* provides an example of how a properly constructed circle can generate a context that encourages a truly restorative and reparative sentence from both the perspective of the community and the offender. The decision of the Saskatchewan Court of Appeal in *R v. Desnomie* is an example of an appellate court disapproving of the use of the sentencing circle and the sentence that it produced.

R v. Kahpeaysewat
[2006] SJ No. 587 (QL)

HUCULAK PROV. CT. J.: [1] The accused plead guilty to manslaughter on September 26, 2005. In May 2006, a sentencing circle was held. Present were Valerie Kahpeaysewat, her cousin Bernadette Bear, sister Andrea Kahpeaysewat, Gloria Muswa, Elder Ernie Poundmaker, George Laliberte, Wayne Bitternose, Cst. Ernie Loutitt, probation officer Nancy Marrick, Valerie's daughter and daughter-in-law.

Circumstances of the Offence

[2] The circumstances were read in at the circle by the Crown, as follows:

[3] The accused had an on–off relationship with the victim, who she met in 2001. The offence took place on the 22nd day of July, 2004. At the time of the incident, the victim, Frank Nadary, had been drinking with Valerie and other individuals at the apartment of her brother, Leon Kahpeaysewat. The incident began as a result of the victim being asked to leave on several occasions and he refused. Indicating that he would sit quietly and leave Valerie alone, as a result he was permitted to stay. After some time of drinking and playing cards, Valerie stated she was attempting to get some sleep and asked Mr. Nadary to leave and he refused. He then attempted to engage in intimate physical contact despite her demands to be left alone. Mr. Nadary continued with this course of advances until the accused left the room where she had been trying to sleep and moved towards the entrance to the apartment. She then opened the main door to the apartment and repeatedly told the victim to leave the premises. The victim responded by attempting to smother the accused by wrapping his arms around her. He grabbed Valerie by the back of the neck, pulling her hair. Valerie was able to escape his grasp and began to throw various objects in his direction to deter him. When the victim con-

tinued to pursue Valerie, she grabbed a knife that was sitting on the kitchen counter. She swung at Mr. Nadary three times, with the second strike inflicting a mortal wound on the victim. Upon realizing the injury that had been sustained by the victim, Valerie called an ambulance.

[4] In her statement to the police she stated: "We were all drinking and I was trying to sleep. He wouldn't let me sleep, he just kept bugging me and bugging me. And my daughter was sleeping, trying to sleep on the couch and me on the floor with my grandson. And him, he was laying on the other side to my grandson there. But he kept bugging me and I told him, I'm trying to sleep, leave me alone. Leave me alone.' And I got to the point where I got pretty frustrated and angry with him, told him to get out, you know, and he wouldn't listen anyways. How many times I told him to leave, get out, leave me alone,' he just wouldn't listen.

[5] So I got pretty angry and told him to get out and I went and opened the door for him to get out. I tried to push him out, he wouldn't go, he kept trying to get out of the situation, like, come on, Val,' you know, don't be like that, come on Val,' stuff like that, come on babe.' And then I was like—it was like I couldn't breathe, like, you know.

[6] So that's when I grabbed that knife, I think from a sink, I'm not sure. I tried first, I threw cups at him and I kept missing him, I was trying to get him to get out and he wouldn't leave. He kept moving around so I wouldn't hit him with the cups. That's when I grabbed the knife. I was looking, first thing I seen like, I would take it and throw it at him, but those were the cups. And then all of a sudden I had this knife and I was missing him with that, and I didn't know I connected because it was fast. I was trying to scare him out of there but I didn't realize I'd connected and it became a major big thing."

[7] Valerie admitted responsibility for the death of the victim at the earliest possible opportunity and plead guilty to a charge of manslaughter. She expressed remorse for her actions.

[8] Valerie never had the intention of killing the victim. Rather Valerie stated she grabbed the knife in an attempt to keep the victim away from her and force him out of the premises. Despite the fact that Valerie was swinging the knife at Mr. Nadary, he continued to attempt to grab her. Valerie had intended to scare Mr. Nadary and the motion that the knife was swung was toward his arms.

[9] She then described how she went to get help to call an ambulance for Frank. And it was Valerie who contacted other people within the building to make the calls to the police and to get an ambulance.

[10] The officer went back on a couple of occasions to talk about how Frank had been bothering Valerie and in a later statement she said: "Frank wouldn't let me sleep, he kept trying to get me to go lay beside him."

[11] She also described that when they went to the kitchen she went to the door first and told him to get out, and opened the door. And that's when he was putting his arms, or trying to put his arms around her and she told him to go home, but he wouldn't go.

[12] She described her thinking at the time: "I was pretty frustrated. It's kind of hard to describe when you're frustrated and angry at the same time. Like you're having a panic attack or something. Like for me it was like that smothering feeling, anger plus it's kind of hard to breathe for me, you know, when I'm trying to get him away and I can't, it's pretty frustrating."

[13] The police officer asked her how he was bugging her. And she said, "He wanted me to lay beside him and like he was—well he was always perverted, I guess. I called him a pervert because of the way he wanted sex all the time, got sick of him too that way, constantly bugging me in that way. So he wanted me to sleep beside him, he wouldn't sleep and I kept saying, leave me alone I'm trying to sleep,' and he'd be swearing and I'd be swearing at him, leave me alone,' getting angrier and angrier."

[14] Frank was saying things like, "Don't get mad," and trying to kiss up to her and saying "Don't be like this, I love you. Things like that."

[15] A couple of other things that I wanted to make reference to is the autopsy report which showed that Mr. Nadary had a wound, a stab wound, and the stab would have penetrated the heart and so it actually penetrated to a depth of approximately 10 centimeters, and it penetrated both the left and right ventricles of the heart, and that stab wound to the heart was what caused Frank's death. And as well, there was a superficial lacerated wound on Frank's back, on the lower right thorax region which hadn't penetrated the skin.

[16] And I believe that occurs in Valerie's statement—I'll just find the part where there was more than one attempt to strike Frank with the knife. And I believe it was the second blow that was described as the one that killed him.

[17] "She said, I swung at him three times, the second one I connected, the other ones I didn't. But I didn't mean to connect, I just tried to scare him, tried to get him out of the house, the apartment. But he wouldn't leave." She said, "After he went down and my son was coming out of the bedroom, he heard all the commotion, I guess, cause I kept shouting to Frank to get out, get out. I was pretty pissed off more than anything. So my son came out of the bedroom, 'what's going on?' you know, something like that. And my son was trying to give me shit for what had happened."

[18] Frank Nadray's blood alcohol was measured as part of the autopsy and the amount of alcohol in his urine was measured as 249 milligrams of alcohol in 100 milliliters of blood, but the amount of alcohol in his blood was at 191; an elevated reading. Two had a half hours after the police arrived Valerie consented to provide a sample of her breath and it measured 150 milligrams of alcohol in 100 milliliters of blood.

The Accused's Background

[19] The accused is 44 years of age and is an Aboriginal female. Her family life has been very unstable throughout the years. She has seven children and two grandchildren. Her youngest children were apprehended by Social Services and one of her daughters was murdered in 1995. The accused has been in two spousal relationships, which were both very abusive.

[20] The accused's endured a difficult childhood and her home life was marked by violence and abuse. She and her siblings were placed in various foster homes at a young age. From age ten onwards, the accused has been placed in four different foster homes. She lost her mother who was violently killed in 1995. She was sexually, physically and emotionally abused throughout her life and recalls experiencing racism as a child. She was sexually abused by her foster brother, and her grandmother emotionally abused her. She has experienced some psychological problems and has attempted suicide on

two occasions. Her four past relationships involved physical violence. The deceased had been convicted of unlawful confinement and assault on the accused.

[21] The accused has little work experience and is just short of a Grade 11 education. She is currently on social assistance, but has previously worked as a housekeeper. She has attended life skills programming on two occasions and was formerly enrolled in a computer course at Career Campus, which she did not complete. The accused completed the Pathways to Employment Program in 2005. She plans to enroll in the Adult Basic Education Program through the Saskatchewan Indian Institute of Technology.

[22] The accused has been a user of alcohol and drugs for several years. She began drinking at the age of fourteen, and her primary problem relates to her use of alcohol. She had her children taken away by Social Services because of her substance abuse issues. The accused has attended two weeks at a twenty-eight day inpatient treatment program and has completed a six-week residential treatment program. Despite this treatment, her alcohol use increased when she entered into a common-law relationship with the victim. The accused's tumultuous relationship with the victim was marked by heavy bouts of drinking. She claims that she has been sober for approximately one year. Nevertheless, an addictions assessment completed in 2005 suggests that the accused has a high probability of being substance dependant."

[23] Presently the accused is involved in a relationship, but she does not live with her partner. She has indicated that her partner uses drugs and alcohol. The accused remains in contact with two of her siblings and with some of her children and grandchildren.

[24] According to the defence lawyer's sentencing submissions, the accused has made great strides in the past two years, although more needs to be done to address the issues of alcohol, her victimization (sexual, physical and emotional), and the loss of her young child and her mother. She has mental health concerns that continue to need addressing in terms of counselling and therapy.

[25] The accused has been involved in Tamara's House (which provides resources for sexually abused girls). She is living on her own and is working toward a better relationship with her children. She has a twelve-year-old son who she is wishing to have returned to her. She has grandchildren she sees frequently. She attends Sweats and meets with Elders. She has not seen a therapist but does not object to counselling. The accused is in need of long-term and in-depth counselling. She met with Addictions Services, one on one, with Ruth White. Val was withdrawn in the circle, having difficulty expressing her feelings publically, and having difficulty expressing remorse.

[26] The accused has been residing in the community on an undertaking, and has been electronically monitored since October, 2004. With the exception of one violation involving the use of alcohol (pills), the accused has complied with the terms of the undertaking. She has attended required programming and has reported weekly to the probation office. In addition, the accused has been attending individual counseling at Saskatoon Health Region, Community Addiction Services. She has become involved in cultural traditions, such as Sweats and Healing Circles. The PSR reports that the accused is a medium risk to re-offend, which is based on her substance abuse issues, her negative peer association, family and personal relationship issues, transience and lack of vocational skills.

[27] Dr. Menzie's report dated April 6, 2006, sets out her history, including the circumstances of the offence, and her relationship with Frank Nadary. In his opinion, Valerie Kahpeaysewat is a battered woman.

· · ·

[28] The following are Dr. Menzie's conclusions and recommendations.

Conclusions and Recommendations

This 44 year old woman, by her own account, is the product of alcoholic parents and a deprived, unsettled and abusive childhood. Although she said she was not physically or sexually abused while at home, evidently, she was sexually assaulted during her first foster home placement around the age of 10 or 11. She left school when she was 17 with Grade 9 and since then has done little in terms of gainful employment. She has been involved in a number of relationships and has seven surviving children. She has no significant psychiatric history and apparently did not begin to abuse alcohol until 1995.

Kahpeaysewat reported that in 1995, her mother died and about six months later, her 3½ year old daughter was killed by a babysitter. These deaths led to alcohol abuse until 2004, when evidently she stopped drinking.

Kahpeaysewat had been involved with the victim for about three years and throughout the relationship was afraid of him because he was intimidating, controlling and violent. The victim's violent behaviour towards Kahpeaysewat is confirmed by the material I reviewed including police reports. Accordingly, I am of the opinion that she was a battered woman. In addition, she reported symptoms consistent with post-traumatic stress disorder, precipitated by the victim's behaviour during the relationship. These aspects suggest that at the time of the homicide, Kahpeaysewat was suffering from significant features of battered woman syndrome. Likely she was vulnerable to developing this syndrome as a result of abuse in childhood, previous abusive intimate relationships and the significant impact of the deaths of her mother and daughter which both occurred within months of each other.

This syndrome, *inter alia*, results in chronic fear and helplessness, both of which make it difficult to end the relationship. In this case, Kahpeaysewat had been threatened by the victim who had recently been convicted of assaulting her. It appears that at the time of the homicide, Kahpeaysewat did not intend to kill the victim. However, she was afraid of him at the time.

It would be reasonable to include the fact that Kahpeaysewat suffered a degree of battered woman syndrome at the homicide as a mitigating factor in terms of the sentence. It would also be helpful to include alcohol rehabilitation and psychotherapy/counseling to help her deal with the deaths of her mother and daughter as well as the aftermath of her relationship with the victim and his death.

[29] The accused in this case was charged with assault with a weapon in 1991 on her ex-spouse, Mr. Fox. He had abused her throughout their relationship. According to her lawyer, at the time of this offence Val was pregnant with her daughter. Mr. Fox had her by the hair and was hitting her, so she gouged him with a small screwdriver. She plead guilty right away.

Frank Nadray's Background

[30] This information was provided by the Crown at the sentencing circle. He was born June 8, 1967 in Fort Smith in the Northwest Territories. He died July 22, 2004 in Saskatoon, so he was only 37 years old at the time of death. One of the last entries in the police records before his death show that Frank was 5 feet 11 inches tall, 151 pounds. So that and the autopsy photos show me that Mr. Nadary was a tall and a slim man.

[31] About five months before he died Mr. Nadary had a conversation with his probation officer, a man by the name of Brian Jones, and he told Mr. Jones that he came from a very dysfunctional family. That he had suffered physical and sexual abuse during his childhood, that he was exposed to solvents as a child. His father died when he was five years of age and by about the age of 12 he was placed in group homes.

[32] He first came into conflict with the law at a relatively young age. He was first sentenced at the age of 17 and by the age of 18 his offending had the effect of severing him from his home community, both because he went to jail and because he believed that his home community had banned him from being there.

[33] Information from George Laliberte led George to believe that Frank had a firm belief that he was not entitled to go home, that he had been banned from his community. It seems that even 15 years later when Frank was in Saskatoon and got to know George, that he still spoke longingly and lovingly of his home and of his mother, who continued to reside there, and it appears that it was a pain in his life that never went away, that he couldn't go home, or he believed he couldn't go home.

[34] His removal from his home in Fort Smith in the Northwest Territories also had the effect of thrusting Mr. Nadary into an English-speaking environment; for the first 18 years of his life he spoke Dene. And until his death his facility in the English language was limited, somewhat limited, despite the fact that he lived in predominantly English-speaking communities after that. And when I spoke with George, one of the messages I got was that some of Frank's frustration and his anger and his loneliness appeared to relate to his dislocation from his home community.

[35] It was in July of 2000 that Frank took up residence in Saskatchewan and January 21st of 2000 is the first record that the Saskatoon Police Service have of a report in which Frank and Valerie are indexed as parties, as both being involved. It was a complaint from Valerie that she wanted Frank removed from her residence. And at that time she identified Frank as being a renter or a roommate in her residence.

[36] But it appears that in the year 2001 the relationship became closer and at least at times it was an intimate spousal relationship. The Crown stated in the circle that "I think there will be agreement that it was not a healthy relationship at all times and for either of the parties who were involved in it."

[37] For the circle, efforts had been made to locate friends or family for Frank, but despite efforts, only two individuals were located. Two individuals in the circle also knew Frank Nadray; George Laliberte and Wayne Bitternose attended. Both provided information to the circle.

[38] According to George Laliberte, he had met Frank Nadray 4 years ago at the Correctional Centre. He pointed to a number of problems Frank had. He described Frank Nadray as a man who loved Valerie. He had a big heart. Mr. Laliberte's view was

the two shouldn't have had a relationship and predicted something like this would happen. According to George Laliberte, it could have gone either way. According to George Laliberte, Frank needed help and George offered it to him but it did not happen.

[39] Wayne Bitternose met Frank Nadray at the Regional Psychiatric Centre in 1996 and considered him a good friend. He never saw Frank's violent side. He described Frank as loving Val. He heard the two couldn't stay away from each other. He saw Frank as a lost person. His view was that the violence went both ways, with Val being violent towards Frank. He expressed his anger toward Val for Frank's death. He saw him as a nice man who didn't deserve to be killed. Efforts had been made to locate friends or family for Frank, but despite efforts only two individuals were located.

Sentencing Considerations

[40] Sentencing is a complex process of balancing numerous factors and the principles of sentencing. The process is subjective. The sentencing judge must consider the appropriate sentencing principles to achieve a sentence that balances rehabilitation against the need to denounce and deter. It is an inherently individualized process. The search for parity is often a fruitless exercise of academic abstraction. The challenge in sentencing is harmonizing the traditional emphasis on sentencing with the remedial requirements.

Sentencing for Manslaughter

[41] The accused plead guilty to manslaughter contrary to section 236 of the *Criminal Code*. There is a wide range of circumstances in which the crime of manslaughter many be committed; therefore, there are various sentencing options available. As a result, all sentencing objectives must be addressed and consideration must be given to the type of offender that committed the crime, along with the particular circumstances of the offence. Although it is important to achieve parity among sentences, sentencing must be individualized.

[42] The sentence can be and is tailored to meet the degree of moral fault of the offender. *R v. Creighton* (1993), 83 CCC (3d) 346 p. 374 (McLachlin J). There is no minimum sentence for manslaughter. Manslaughter can occur in a wide variety of ways; therefore the penalties are flexible.

[43] Manslaughter encompasses a wide range of different factual scenarios. It is necessary that an unlawful act has caused death, but otherwise circumstances range from near accident to near murder. As evidenced by the many cases that have been referred to by counsel, for both the Crown and the defence, there is a vast range of sentences for the crime of manslaughter depending on the particular circumstances of a case. The various sentencing principles, which the law provides in regard to a sentence for manslaughter may call for a very substantial period of incarceration in the range of 12 to 15 years at the one extreme and on the other end, to a conditional sentence as is now provided for in section 742.1 of the *Criminal Code*.

• • •

[46] The Crown's position is that the appropriate sentence is 5 years, over the time in remand and bail supervision. The defence's position is for a conditional sentence.

• • •

Aboriginal Offender: Gladue Factors

[54] Section 718.2(e) requires a sentencing judge to determine whether the aboriginal offender should be incarcerated. The sentencing judge must examine the unique systemic background circumstances common to all aboriginal offenders and then consider the particular circumstances which result in the offender committing the offence for which he is before the court. Armed with that information he or she must determine whether the goals of restorative justice should be given more weight than the traditional objects of sentencing, such as denunciation and deterrence, in deciding whether the aboriginal offender should be incarcerated

• • •

[56] The *Gladue* factors comprehended the root socio-economic circumstances which play a part in bringing an offender into contact with the criminal justice system (*R v. Laliberte*, [2000] 4 WWR 491, at para. 69) … .

• • •

[58] Each situation must be examined in light of *Gladue*. At the same time, judges are required to take into account all the principles and objectives of sentencing, including denunciation, deterrence and parity. In the *John* decision ([2004] SJ No. 61), it was established that in cases involving aboriginal offenders, s. 718.2(e) requires the court to determine whether the offender should be imprisoned. The court stated that consideration must be given to the systemic background and the surrounding circumstances of the offence, offender, victim and community. It then must be determined whether restorative justice should be emphasized.

[59] In this case, these socio-economic factors figure significantly into sentencing considerations, since Valerie Kahpeaysewat's tragic upbringing, the murder of her child, racism, victimization, abuse, addictions, family dislocation, poverty, fragmentation, lack of education and employment, family dysfunction, and her shattered life all contributed in a major way to her criminal record.

[60] On July 14, 2006, the newspaper had an article with the heading "Sask. Leads in Spousal Homicide." Saskatchewan spouses are twice as likely to die from domestic violence compared to elsewhere in Canada. From 1995 to 2004, the average homicide rate in Saskatchewan was 8.4 victims to one million spouses, according to the report *Family Violence in Canada: A Statistical Profile*, 2006. I have read this report from the Canadian Centre for Justice Statistics—Statistics Canada. Women were more likely than men to report being targets of ten or more violent spousal episodes (Mihorean, 2005). Most spousal violence incidents are committed by males. The difference is very significant statistically. Between 1995 and 2004, two-thirds (65%) of spousal homicides involved a history of domestic violence (p. 55). Females accused of spousal homicide were more likely than male accused to have experienced a history of family violence.

[61] Domestic violence in the aboriginal community is a serious issue. The factors contributing to this are complex. What sentence the accused receives will not change this. The *Gladue* factors play a prominent role in creating the conditions where violence is turned inward toward family, friends and self. The tragedy is that without significant resources and a change in the socio-economic conditions, little will change.

The Circle

[62] Since 1992, judges in the Provincial Court of Saskatchewan have utilized sentencing circles. The circle provided an opportunity to engage in a restorative process. In this case, the offender publically accounted for her criminal conduct and took responsibility for her actions. Information was provided that provided greater insight into the dynamic of the offence. Participants were given an opportunity to provide input into sentencing options. This was a difficult and emotional process for the participants.

[63] In the circle, Cst. Ernie Louttit referred to the numerous occasions that the police were involved in the life of the accused and the victim. He noted twelve occasions. His view was the death could have gone either way; that this result was predictable. This is a chilling statement. The prosecutor provided me with a summary of police occurrence reports involving the accused and Mr. Nadary, starting in January 2001 and ending in January 2004. On a number of occasions the accused was the complainant, in particular, reporting breaches of Mr. Nadary's no contact order of probation.

[64] In August, 2001, Mr. Nadary was charged with break and enter, assault and unlawful confinement. Valerie was the victim. He was convicted and received a suspended sentence and probation of eighteen months. In March, 2002, Frank Nadary was convicted of breach of probation concerning the no contact with Valerie condition. He received a three-month conditional sentence. On March 14, 2003, the accused made a complaint that Frank assaulted her. The charge did not proceed as she was unsure whether she wanted to proceed. In August, 2003, Frank Nadary was charged with assault causing bodily harm on Valerie, among other charges. He was convicted of common assault and sentenced to six months jail, followed by two years probation.

[65] There were numerous breach charges against Frank Nadary. Many were in relation to the non-contact order with the accused and abstention of alcohol condition. In January, 2004, the accused complained to police that Frank Nadary is writing her from jail. No action was taken as the police were unable to locate the existing probation order. Frank Nadary would have still been on probation from February, 2004.

[66] In the circle, the accused's aunt, cousin and sister participated. Her daughters were present for part of the circle. They all described her dysfunctional childhood and her difficult, fractured life. Sadly, all of the victim's relatives had been victims of domestic violence. They described Frank Nadary's possessiveness and obsession with the victim. They described how he would follow her. The accused's family were prepared to assist and support her.

Case Law

[67] Both Crown and defence provided numerous cases to support their position. Many of the Crown's cases can be distinguished as they relate to pre-*Criminal Code* amendments, and many refer to "home invasion" types of circumstances. Many of these cases were summarized in *R v. Machiskinic*, Sask. QB 2004, which I will not repeat here.

[68] From my perspective, the most relevant cases are those in relation to domestic violence. There are some Saskatchewan cases I believe are relevant to consider: *R v. Machiskinic, supra, R v. W.L.Q.* (2005) [2005] SJ No. 13, and *R v. J.S.* (1998), [1998]

SJ No. 247. In *R v. Machiskinic*, *supra*, the accused stabbed her common-law husband during a drunken altercation. Here it was held that a conditional sentence was not consistent with the fundamental principles of sentencing and would endanger the safety of the community. She had a lengthy record (14 convictions, including 1 assault). She was given credit of six months of remand time, and one year for the eighteen months' bail. This case referred to institutional sentences of imprisonment and conditional sentences at pp. 3, 9 and 10.

[69] Her case can be distinguished on her lengthy record and history of assaults on her spouse. Further, the judge was not satisfied that serving the sentence in the community would not endanger the safety of the community and concluded that a sentence of three and a half to four years was appropriate, reduced by the bail conditions and remand time, to two and a half years.

[70] In *R v. W.L.Q.* (2005), a similar set of circumstances exist with the stabbing of a common-law spouse. Alcohol was a factor. It can be distinguished in that she failed to attend alcohol and drug rehabilitation programs which were imposed as a condition. She had twelve prior convictions, including assault causing bodily harm. She posed a high risk to re-offend. The judge found four years to be the appropriate sentence, minus credit of six months for three months' remand and three-quarter's time credit for electronic monitoring. Her sentence was three years. The judge also found she posed a danger to the community and a sentence of less than two years was inappropriate. She had threatened to kill the victim on the night of the offence.

[71] In *R v. J.S.* (1998) (Sask. Prov. Ct.), the stabbing was of the offender's mother. Alcohol was a factor. This was not a spousal situation. She was sentenced to two years but was also given credit for six months on remand. She was directed to serve at the healing lodge to address the root causes of her destructive behaviour. The defence did not argue for a conditional sentence but rather on having her sentenced to two years with a recommendation to transfer to the Okemaw Ohci Healing Lodge for Women to focus on treatment and healing. Alcohol was a major problem. She had previously breached conditions.

Appropriate Sentence

[72] I have considered the principles and objectives of sentencing. I have taken into account all the aggravating factors, such as her prior record, her son and daughter were in the apartment at the time of the offence, her consumption of alcohol, and the victim was a spouse. She is not a youthful offender. She used a weapon. The mitigating factors are her history of physical, sexual and emotional abuse, post-traumatic stress disorder, her participation in the circle, the *Gladue* factors, her suffering a form of battered spouse syndrome, she was victimized by Frank Nadary and the fact she was remorseful. I find that Valerie Kahpeaysewat's stabbing of Frank Nadary was a derivative crime borne of the unresolved effects of past conditions of abuse, indignities and profound grief. I have concluded that a community-based sentence is the appropriate sentence for this offender. In my opinion, a sentence of two years less a day served in the community in the form of a conditional sentence, followed by probation, is the appropriate sentence for this particular offender, for this offence and this community. I find that a penitentiary term is not appropriate, nor is probation alone.

[73] In determining the appropriate range and in finding that a community-based sentence is appropriate, I have considered the circumstances required by *Gladue*, the decisions of the Saskatchewan and other courts.

[74] This offender, by serving her sentence in the community, would not endanger the safety of the community. This individual does not pose a risk to society while serving in the community. I have taken into account her risk of re-offending and the gravity of the damage that could issue in the event of re-offending. I have considered whether she is likely to abide by the order, the nature of the offence, the circumstances of the offence, her degree of participation, her profile, including lifestyle, occupation, criminal record, conduct following the offence, and the danger the offender represents to the community offended by the offence.

[75] I have referred to the offender's personal circumstances and Dr. Menzie's report. I referred to comments made in the circle. She is remorseful and took responsibility for the offence. She has been on judicial interim release since October 2004 under electronic monitoring, with numerous conditions. She breached once by taking pills. She has been working toward dealing with issues such as addictions. There is a significant likelihood she will abide by the court order. There is little risk to the community in the effect of a re-offence.

[76] Having decided that the three pre-requisites for a conditional sentence have been satisfied, I must determine whether the imposition of a conditional sentence of imprisonment is consistent with the principles of sentencing set out in ss. 718 to 718.2. If a conditional sentence can facilitate both a punitive and a restorative objective and both objectives can be achieved in a given case, a conditional sentence is likely the better sanction than imprisonment.

[77] The primary question here is whether the principles of denunciation and deterrence can be satisfied by the imposition of a community-based sentence. In my opinion, the principles of deterrence and denunciation can be satisfied by the imposition of strict conditions in a conditional sentence of imprisonment. ...

[78] Incarceration will usually provide more denunciation than a conditional sentence of imprisonment, but a conditional sentence which deprives or restricts an offender's liberty can effectively satisfy those principles. The Supreme Court of Canada made it clear in *Proulx* that severe restrictions on the offender's liberty are to be the norm and not the exception.

[79] The court can effectively denounce the offender's conduct by imposing sufficiently stringent conditions such as house arrest, which will make it clear to members of the community that the offender's conduct carries severe consequences. The sanction will be visible, restrictive, enforceable, and capable of attracting a severe sanction for failing to comply with the conditions.

[80] As Chief Justice Lamer noted in *Proulx*, judges should be wary of placing too much weight on deterrence. The public nature of the sentence in this community is a constant reminder of the offender's conduct and the consequences of such conduct, and in my opinion is a more effective deterrent than a prison sentence served in some distant community. Sanctions other than imprisonment may be at least as onerous as a prison sentence. A person who serves the sentence in the community still carries a societal stigma

of being a convicted offender serving a criminal sentence. Deterrence, to the extent that it is effective, can be satisfied by the imposition of a community based sentence.

[81] After a full consideration of the seriousness of the offence, all the principles of sentencing, including rehabilitation and the principles of restorative justice, as well as the principles of deterrence and denunciation, I find that a sentence of two years less one day to be served in the community is a fit and appropriate sentence for this individual. I have taken into account the time she has been on bail supervision.

· · ·

[83] The accused will comply with the following conditions for the full term of the conditional sentence:

(a) the accused shall reside at her residence and shall be confined to her residence for the first six months of the conditional sentence, leaving only at such times as the probation officer or the supervisor monitoring the conditional sentencing order shall permit, attend treatment, or perform other authorized activities, subject to medical emergencies. Thereafter, the accused shall be confined to her residence between the hours of 6:00 p.m. and 7:00 a.m. for the next six months, and for the remaining part between the hours of 7:00 p.m. and 7:00 a.m.

(b) the accused must personally present herself to any peace officer or the probation officer or supervisor monitoring the conditions of this order, and shall follow the lawful instructions of the probation officer/supervisor as they pertain to treatment.

(c) the accused shall perform 240 hours of community service over a period of two years less one day. The type of community service shall be determined, assigned and coordinated by the supervisor.

(d) the accused shall abstain from the purchase, possession or consumption of alcohol and non-prescription (illicit) drugs, and must not enter any premises where the primary function is the sale or consumption of alcohol. She shall submit to alcohol and/or drug testing as arranged and directed by the probation officer;

(e) the accused shall take such treatment and counselling as ordered by the Chief Probation Officer, including addictions, personal, grief, etc.

[84] Her sentence will be followed by two years' probation with the standard terms, reporting, continued addictions treatment and personal counselling. There will be a DNA order and a ten-year weapons prohibition order. The sentence should not be considered lenient, nor should it be read to mean the life of Frank Nadary had no value. The tragedy reminds us of the need to intervene early in cases of domestic violence and provide support and resources to the victim, as well as the perpetrator. The socio-economic and environmental back-drop to domestic violence must also be addressed which is beyond the scope of this court.

R v. Desnomie
(2005), 275 Sask. R 167 (CA)

GERWING JA (orally: Cameron and Vancise JJA concurring): [1] The Crown appeals a sentence of 18 months conditional, including six months of electronic monitoring, and $100 surcharge on a charge that the respondent, in a trial on second degree murder charge gave evidence which was contrary to the evidence she gave at the preliminary on the same matter, contrary to s. 136(1) of the *Criminal Code*.

[2] The second degree murder preliminary and trial related to the death of a child, Antonio Kakakaway. The accused in that trial was the grandmother of the deceased and his primary caregiver. The accused Kakakaway called an ambulance for the child, suggesting that he had fallen from his crib. He died in hospital two days later. Medical experts reported that the injury was produced by greater force than a fall and testimony was led to this effect. Further, the child's body had numerous bruises, scrapes and lacerations which varied in age.

[3] The respondent contacted police and offered information, as a former friend of the accused Kakakaway, including that the latter had told her she was guilty. She also told the investigating officers and subsequently the preliminary inquiry that on a second occasion the accused, Kakakaway, had told her she was tired and stressed out and that the child had been crying all day. She said she hit him and he fell to the floor unconscious.

[4] The accused Kakakaway was committed for trial on second degree murder. During the course of that trial, the respondent denied the second conversation and testified that she had lied at the preliminary inquiry about the admission that the accused Kakakaway had struck the victim.

[5] It is critical to note that the trial judge was satisfied that Antonio Kakakaway was the victim of a homicide, dying from "blunt force injury consistent with a blow from an adult person." The trial judge correctly instructed himself that the respondent's credibility as a witness was damaged by her admission that she had lied at the preliminary inquiry. The trial judge, in the circumstances, and because the accused Kakakaway did not have exclusive access to the victim over the time period when the injury could have occurred, acquitted her. It is clear that if the respondent had testified as she did at the preliminary inquiry her testimony would have been relevant and could have affected the outcome of the trial.

[6] The trial judge in this matter, for reasons which are not clear, convoked a sentencing circle which she said was for information purposes. Given the nature of this offence, it is highly doubtful a sentencing circle should have been called, but in any event, it is of no utility, having been attended almost exclusively by members of the respondent's family. At the sentencing circle, she admitted she lied at the trial. She said she knew Antonio had been injured by Kakakaway and that her testimony at the preliminary was the truth.

[7] The conditional sentence in no way reflects the gravity of the situation. To repeat, the respondent gave false testimony in the course of a trial for second degree murder of a child. The investigation of who caused a homicide is one of the most significant that a court can undertake and one that must be carried out with openness and with the greatest attention to seeking the truth in order to preserve society's respect for

the judicial system. It is fundamental in any judicial proceeding that witnesses treat the process with respect and tell the truth, and that if they do not, the court deal with them appropriately to show not only other witnesses, who may potentially do the same, but society that it takes extremely seriously the process of ascertaining the truth. This can no where be more important, both for the system itself and for the respect society gives to the system as a means of resolving disputes in society, than in the case of a homicide. The courts must treat this process with utmost seriousness, not only for the parties involved in each case, but because society must be confident that these questions can be fully dealt with in an appropriate manner by the court system. Structure in society depends on this.

. . .

[10] Cases in other jurisdictions indicate that it is frequent for persons convicted of lying under oath in murder trials to be sentenced to federal custody. See for example, *R v. Gushue* [(1976), 32 CCC (2d) 189 (Ont. CA)] and *R v. Glauser* [(1981), 25 CR (3d) 287 (Alta. CA)].

[11] In this case, the Crown asked at the trial for two years less a day and in this Court says that it feels bound to ask for no more than that.

[12] In the circumstances of this case, the sentence imposed took no account of the above principles with respect to determining the gravity of the offence with respect to which the false evidence was given. It in no way is adequate for specific or general deterrence and undercuts the respect of society for the process of the Court and the Court's guardianship of that process.

[13] In the circumstances, the sentence is increased to two years less a day. In imposing this sentence, we are not to be taken to suggest that federal incarceration would not be appropriate. Were it not for the concession by the Crown and the way this matter unfolded before the trial judge, it is probable that a substantial term of federal incarceration would be appropriate.

[14] The Crown noted that months served on the conditional sentence have imposed minimal inconvenience on the respondent. In light of this and in light of the lenient sentence being imposed because of the Crown concession, no credit is allowed for any time served under the conditional sentence. That is, there will be a sentence imposed of two years less a day to run from today's date. The Crown appeal is allowed to this extent.

QUESTIONS

1. What is the source of the Court of Appeal's concern that this was an inappropriate case for a sentencing circle? Was it the composition of the circle or the nature and severity of the offence?

2. What does this decision say about deference and the use of sentencing circles?

V. CONDITIONAL SENTENCES AND ABORIGINAL OFFENDERS

In chapter 12, Conditional Sentence of Imprisonment, we discussed in detail the new sanction of a conditional sentence that was the subject of the Supreme Court's attention in *R v.
Proulx*. Although a number of conditional-sentence cases were argued at the same time as
Proulx, one judgment that was not released until later was *R v. Wells*, below. It dealt with
the application of the conditional sentence regime to an Aboriginal offender.

R v. Wells
2000 SCC 10, 1 SCR 207, 30 CR (5th) 254

[The offender was convicted of sexual assault involving an 18-year-old victim who was
either asleep or unconsious by reason of intoxication. He was sentenced to 20 months'
incarceration. Prior to the Supreme Court decision in *Gladue* dealing with s. 718.2(e),
his sentence appeal was heard and dismissed. Fresh evidence was filed indicating his
involvment with the Aboriginal community and his efforts to deal with his alcohol abuse
problem by attending an Aboriginal treatment centre. On appeal to the Supreme Court,
the relationship between s. 718.2(e) and conditional sentences was a central issue.]

IACOBUCCI J for the court:

. . .

[36] In *Gladue*, *supra*, the Court concluded that, as a general principle, s. 718.2(e)
indicates that a custodial sentence is the penal sanction of last resort for all offenders,
to be used only where no other sanction is appropriate. As to the words "with particular
attention to the circumstances of aboriginal offenders," the Court reasoned that sentencing judges should pay particular attention to the fact that the circumstances of aboriginal offenders are unique in comparison with those of non-aboriginal offenders. Section
718.2(e) has a remedial purpose for all offenders, focusing as it does on the concept of
restorative justice, a sentencing approach which seeks to restore the harmony that existed prior to the accused's actions. Again, the appropriateness of the sentence will take
into account the needs of the victims, the offender, and the community as a whole.

[37] While the objective of restorative justice, by virtue of s. 718.2(e), applies to all
offenders, the requirement to pay "particular attention to the circumstances of aboriginal offenders" recognizes that most traditional aboriginal conceptions of sentencing
hold restorative justice to be the primary objective. In addition, s. 718.2(e) has a particular remedial purpose for aboriginal peoples, as it was intended to address the serious
problem of overincarceration of aboriginal offenders in Canadian penal institutions. In
singling out aboriginal offenders for distinct sentencing treatment in s. 718.2(e), it is
reasonable to assume that Parliament intended to address this social problem, to the
extent that a remedy was possible through sentencing procedures.

[38] In order to provide guidance to sentencing judges as to the manner in which
the remedial purpose of s. 718.2(e) could be given effect, the reasons in *Gladue* set out
a framework of analysis for the sentencing judge. In considering the circumstances of
aboriginal offenders, the sentencing judge must take into account, at the very least, both

the unique systemic or background factors that are mitigating in nature in that they may have played a part in the aboriginal offender's conduct, and the types of sentencing procedures and sanctions which may be appropriate in the circumstances for the offender because of his or her particular aboriginal heritage or connection (*Gladue*, at para. 66). In particular, given that most traditional aboriginal approaches place a primary emphasis on the goal of restorative justice, the alternative of community-based sanctions must be explored.

[39] In the search for a fit sentence, therefore, the role of the sentencing judge is to conduct the sentencing process and impose sanctions taking into account the perspective of the aboriginal offender's community. As was noted in *Gladue*, it is often the case that imposing a custodial sentence on an aboriginal offender does not advance the remedial purpose of s. 718.2(e), neither for the offender nor for his community. This is particularly true for less serious or non-violent offences, where the goal of restorative justice will no doubt be given greater weight than principles of denunciation or deterrence.

[40] However, the scope of s. 718.2(e), as it applies to all offenders, restricts the adoption of alternatives to incarceration to those sanctions that are "reasonable in the circumstances." Again, as was expressly stated in *Gladue*, the Court in no way intended to suggest that as a general rule, the greatest weight is to be given to principles of restorative justice, and less weight accorded to goals such as denunciation and deterrence. Indeed, such a general rule would contradict the individual or case-by-case nature of the sentencing process, which proceeds on the basis of inquiring whether, given the particular facts of the offence, the offender, the victim and the community, the sentence is fit in the circumstances.

···

(1) Significance of the Goal of Restorative Justice in Sentencing Aboriginal Offenders Convicted of Serious Crimes

[43] The appellant submits that in according greater weight to the goals of denunciation and deterrence based on the nature of his offence, the sentencing judge did not take into account, as required by s. 718.2(e), the paramount significance of restorative justice within aboriginal communities. The appellant also submits that on the same basis, the Court of Appeal was in error when it held that it would be unreasonable to conclude that a fit sentence for a non-aboriginal offender would not also be a fit sentence for an aboriginal offender. It is important to note, however, that consistent with the reasoning in Gladue, *supra*, the Court of Appeal was referring to "serious crimes," rather than offences in general, as follows (at p. 140):

> For *serious* crimes, it would not be reasonable to conclude that a fit sentence for a non-aboriginal person would not also be fit for an aboriginal person, and this point was made by Esson JA speaking for the majority in the British Columbia Court of Appeal decision of *R v. Gladue* (1997), 119 CCC (3d) 481 at p. 506, who stated, "To put it another way, the particular circumstances could not reasonably support a conclusion that the sentence, if a fit one for a non-aboriginal person, would not also be fit for an aboriginal person." [Emphasis added.]

[44] Let me emphasize that s. 718.2(e) requires a different *methodology* for assessing a fit sentence for an aboriginal offender; it does not mandate, necessarily, a different *result*. Section 718.2(e) does not alter the fundamental duty of the sentencing judge to impose a sentence that is fit for the offence and the offender. Furthermore, in *Gladue*, as mentioned the Court stressed that the application of s. 718.2(e) does not mean that aboriginal offenders must always be sentenced in a manner which gives greatest weight to the principles of restorative justice and less weight to goals such as deterrence, denunciation, and separation (at para. 78). As a result, it will generally be the case, *as a practical matter*, that particularly violent and serious offences will result in imprisonment for aboriginal offenders as often as for non-aboriginal offenders (*Gladue*, at para. 33). Accordingly, I conclude that it was open to the trial judge to give primacy to the principles of denunciation and deterrence in this case on the basis that the crime involved was a serious one.

[45] Whether a crime is indeed serious in the given circumstances is, in my opinion, a factual matter that can only be determined on a case-by-case basis. I am not suggesting that there are categories of offences which presumptively exclude the possibility of a non-custodial sentence. Indeed, Lamer CJ specifically rejected such an approach in relation to the conditional sentencing regime (*Proulx, supra*, at para. 79). ...

[48] I cannot conclude that the trial judge misconstrued the seriousness of the crime. In addition, the judge's use of the words "near major" or "major" instead of "serious" does not constitute a reversible error. I find no error in principle, no overemphasis of the appropriate factors, nor a failure to consider a relevant factor, and, accordingly, defer to the trial judge's assessment of the particular circumstances of the offence and offender (*M. (C.A.)* [[1996] 1 SCR 500]. Therefore, the trial judge made a reasonable determination as to the availability of a conditional sentence.

[49] I would like to add at this point that the reasons in *Gladue, supra*, do not foreclose the possibility that, in the appropriate circumstances, a sentencing judge may accord the greatest weight to the concept of restorative justice, notwithstanding that an aboriginal offender has committed a serious crime. As was concluded in *Gladue*, at para. 81, the remedial purpose of s. 718.2(e) directs the sentencing judge not only to take into account the unique circumstances of aboriginal offenders, but also to appreciate relevant cultural differences in terms of the objectives of the sentencing process:

• • •

[50] The generalization drawn in *Gladue* to the effect that the more violent and serious the offence, the more likely as a practical matter for similar terms of imprisonment to be imposed on aboriginal and non-aboriginal offenders, was not meant to be a principle of universal application. In each case, the sentencing judge must look to the circumstances of the aboriginal offender. In some cases, it may be that these circumstances include evidence of the community's decision to address criminal activity associated with social problems, such as sexual assault, in a manner that emphasizes the goal of restorative justice, notwithstanding the serious nature of the offences in question.

[51] As Lamer CJ noted in *M. (C.A.), supra*, at para. 92, sentencing requires an individualized focus, not only of the offender, but also of the victim and community as well:

> It has been repeatedly stressed that there is no such thing as a uniform sentence for a particular crime. ... Sentencing is an inherently individualized process, and the search for a single appropriate sentence for a similar offender and a similar crime will frequently be a fruitless exercise of academic abstraction. As well, sentences for a particular offence should be expected to vary to some degree across various communities and regions in this country, *as the "just and appropriate" mix of accepted sentencing goals will depend on the needs and current conditions of and in the particular community where the crime occurred.* [Emphasis added.]

[52] In this respect, I note that the appellant introduced evidence of the availability of an aboriginal-specific alcohol and drug abuse treatment program. There was, however, an indication that this program would be inappropriate for the appellant as a sexual offender. In addition, there was no evidence of the existence of, or the appellant's participation in, an anti-sexual-assault program.

(2) Extent of the Sentencing Judge's Obligation to Inquire into the Circumstances of an Aboriginal Offender

[53] As noted in Gladue, *supra*, at para. 83, it will be necessary in every case for the sentencing judge to take judicial notice of systemic or background factors that have contributed to the difficulties faced by aboriginal people in both the criminal justice system, and throughout society at large. In addition, the judge is obliged to inquire into the unique circumstances of aboriginal offenders.

[54] At times, it may be necessary to introduce evidence of this nature. It is to be expected in our adversarial system of criminal law that counsel for both the prosecution and the accused will adduce this evidence, but even where counsel do not provide the necessary information, s. 718.2(e) places an affirmative obligation upon the sentencing judge to inquire into the relevant circumstances. In most cases, the requirement of special attention to the circumstances of aboriginal offenders can be satisfied by the information contained in pre-sentence reports. Where this information is insufficient, s. 718.2(e) authorizes the sentencing judge on his or her own initiative to request that witnesses be called to testify as to reasonable alternatives to a custodial sentence.

[55] Having said that, it was never the Court's intention, in setting out the appropriate methodology for this assessment, to transform the role of the sentencing judge into that of a board of inquiry. It must be remembered that in the reasons in *Gladue*, this affirmative obligation to make inquiries beyond the information contained in the pre-sentence report was limited to "appropriate circumstances," and where such inquiries were "practicable" (at para. 84). The application of s. 718.2(e) requires a practical inquiry, not an impractical one. As with any other factual finding made by a court of first instance, the sentencing judge's assessment of whether further inquiries are either appropriate or practicable is accorded deference at the appellate level.

[The appeal was dismissed.]

For a discussion of *Wells*, *Proulx*, and *Gladue* in the context of an Aboriginal offender convicted of trafficking, see *R v. Laliberte* (2000), 31 CR (5th) 1 (Sask. CA).

VI. SECTION 718.2(e) AND ACADEMIC CONTROVERSY

Once the decision in *Gladue* started to percolate through the justice system, it raised a number of practical questions. These related to the issue of how a judge could obtain the information needed to make the inquiries that the Supreme Court said were required. On their own initiative, a group of judges in Toronto worked with Aboriginal Legal Services (ALS) to devise a process that has become known as "the *Gladue* court," in which experienced judges deal with Aboriginal offenders, obtaining relevant information in report form after relevant inquires by ALS court workers: see the discussion in Megan Stephens, "Lessons from the Front Lines of Canada's Restorative Justice Experiment: The Experience of Sentencing Judges" (2007), 33 *Queen's LJ* 19-78.

Another interesting development arose from a criminological perspective. There is no question that our jails and penitentiaries contain an overrepresentation of Aboriginal prisoners. The Supreme Court in *Gladue* emphasized that this fact was a principal motivation behind the enactment of s. 718.2(e). However, the fact of overrepresentation raises a series of questions:

- What is the source(s) of this situation?
- Can it be remedied by the sentencing process?
- Is s. 718.2(e) an appropriate mechanism to address this situation?

In 2001, two well-respected criminologists, P. Stenning and J. Roberts, published their controversial "Empty Promises" article in the *Saskatchewan Law Review*. They examined admissions data from British Columbia and Ontario and concluded, *inter alia*, that this evidence does not support the conclusion that Aboriginal offenders suffer discrimination at the hands of sentencing courts. In other words, it is wrong to look to the sentencing process to explain overrepresentation. This article met with a great deal of opposition and criticism. To its credit, the *Saskatchewan Law Review* enlisted a number of scholarly commentators to join in a "colloquy" based on "Empty Promises," which included an opportunity for a rejoinder by Roberts and Stenning.

The following series of excerpts are from the original piece, the published colloquy, and the rejoinder. Before you read them, think about the three questions listed above and try to answer them. After you have read the material, go back to the questions. Do you still have the same views as you did before reading the excerpts.

P. Stenning and J. Roberts, "Empty Promises: Parliament, The Supreme Court, and the Sentencing of Aboriginal Offenders"
(2001) 64 *Sask. L Rev.* 137 (footnotes omitted)

I. Introduction

For well over twenty years, the problem of the over-representation of Aboriginal people in Canada's prisons has preoccupied many people, including correctional authorities, members of the judiciary, justice policy-makers, and criminal justice scholars. Most recently, debate has focused on a specific provision of the *Criminal Code* concerning the sentencing of Aboriginal offenders. The provision was enacted as part of more general sentencing reform legislation in 1996, and has subsequently been the subject of two lengthy and unanimous Supreme Court of Canada decisions: *R. v. Gladue*, and *R. v. Wells*.

In this article, we consider the history and current judicial interpretations and applications of this provision in light of the available research concerning the nature, extent, and causes of the Aboriginal "over-representation" problem. Specifically, we consider the extent to which the provision and its subsequent judicial interpretations and applications were informed by knowledge about the causes of Aboriginal incarceration. Finally, we propose an alternate model for considering the plight of socially disadvantaged offenders, including many Aboriginal offenders, in sentencing decisions.

II. The Legislation

Bill C-41 received Royal Assent on July 13, 1995, and was proclaimed in force in September 1996. For the first time, Parliament set out the purposes and principles of sentencing and codified jurisprudence regarding the objectives of sentencing. One of these principles is that of restraint with respect to the use of imprisonment. But, by adding s. 718.2(e) to the *Criminal Code*, the legislation went beyond general support for restraint and identified Aboriginal offenders as a group in need of special attention:

> 718.2 A court that imposes a sentence shall also take into consideration the following principles: …
>
> (*e*) all available sanctions other than imprisonment that are reasonable in the circumstances should be considered for all offenders, *with particular attention to the circumstances of [A]boriginal offenders.*

How did these last nine words regarding Aboriginal offenders (which we henceforth refer to as the Aboriginal sentencing provision) come about?

III. Origins of the Aboriginal Sentencing Provision

In 1992, the first of two recent sentencing reform Bills was introduced in Parliament. Bill C-90, the precursor to Bill C-41, included a clause similar to what has now become paragraph 718.2(e) of the *Criminal Code*. David Daubney—who chaired the House of Commons Standing Committee on Justice and Solicitor General when it prepared its influential 1988 report on sentencing and imprisonment, and who subsequently became the head of the Sentencing Reform Team at the Department of Justice, which piloted the sentencing reform legislation through Parliament—has written that the last nine words of the paragraph were specifically designed to reflect an acknowledgement of the "disproportionate involvement of [A]boriginal Canadians with our justice system."

Bill C-90 did not proceed beyond second reading in the House of Commons, partly because the government allowed almost a full year to elapse between the first and second readings of the Bill, but mainly because a general election was called shortly after second reading. The second reading debate centred primarily around the Bill's provisions for alternative measures and, although there was some considerable discussion about the situation and needs of Aboriginal offenders, there was no discussion specifically on the Aboriginal sentencing provision as such. But the inclusion of those nine words in the successor Bill C-41, which became law in 1996, was to change the Aboriginal sentencing landscape.

There was, however, almost no substantive debate in Parliament about the Aboriginal sentencing provision during the passage of Bill C-41 either. The provision raised suspicions among some opposition MPs that it concealed a broader government agenda favouring a separate Aboriginal justice system. One opposition member, speaking during the Second Reading debate on Bill C-41, stated:

> Finally, again with respect to the purpose and principles of sentencing, it is deplorable that the bill tries to sneak through the back door the concept of a parallel system of justice for Aboriginals. It is so well hidden that it is almost necessary to read Clause 718.2(e) twice to discover this enormity hidden under nine sneaky words. ...

Despite such initial reservations expressed by some members, the nine words to which the member referred attracted very little discussion during the subsequent debates of this Bill in the House of Commons, in its Justice and Legal Affairs Committee, or in the Senate. During his appearance before the House of Commons Standing Committee on Justice and Legal Affairs, Justice Minister Allan Rock explained the inclusion of the Aboriginal sentencing provision in the following terms:

> The reason we referred specifically there to aboriginal persons is that they are sadly over-represented in the prison populations of Canada. I think it was the Manitoba justice inquiry that found that although aboriginal persons make up only 12% of the population of Manitoba, they comprise over 50% of the prison inmates. Nationally aboriginal persons represent about 2% of Canada's population, but they represent 10.6% of persons in prison. Obviously there's a problem here.

Given the controversy that the Aboriginal sentencing provision has subsequently generated, there is substantial irony in the fact that the main reason for the paucity of parliamentary debate about paragraph 718.2(e) (and, for that matter, many other very significant provisions of Bill C-41) was that the debate on the Bill was completely dominated by controversy over some words in another provision of the proposed s. 718.2. The original proposed paragraph 718.2(a)(i) required judges to take into account "evidence that the offence was motivated by bias, prejudice or hate based on race, national or ethnic origin, language, colour, religion, sex, age, mental or physical disability, or sexual orientation."

Opposition members forcefully argued that singling out particular bases for such bias, prejudice, or hate to receive particular attention from sentencing judges was itself unacceptably discriminatory. One member, for instance, argued that if he were attacked and injured simply because he was a member of a particular political party against which the attacker was prejudiced, such prejudice should not be considered any less relevant in sentencing the offender than prejudice based on racial origin or sexual orientation. To do otherwise, he argued, would amount to unacceptable discrimination against some victims of hate crimes and in favour of others. As a concession to these persistent criticisms of paragraph 718.2(a)(i), the government eventually agreed to add the words "or any other similar factor" to the end of the paragraph.

Interestingly, the requirement in paragraph 718.2(e) for judges to give particular attention to the circumstances of Aboriginal offenders generated almost no similar discussion in the parliamentary debates of Bill C-41. The result was that when the courts came to consider how the Aboriginal sentencing provision should be interpreted and applied, they had little parliamentary guidance on which to draw. There was, however, quite a bit of information about Aboriginal over-representation and sentencing available from other sources by the time Bill C-41 was drafted and debated in 1994 and 1995, and it is to this knowledge that we turn next.

IV. Other-Representation and Aboriginal Sentencing: The State of Knowledge In 1994

The main idea embodied in paragraph 718.2(e)—that courts should exercise restraint and consider all reasonable alternatives before imposing a sentence of incarceration—has a long history in North America. In 1962, in its Model Penal Code, the American Law Institute proposed that courts should deal with offenders without imposing sentences of imprisonment unless certain specified conditions were met. In Canada, this recommendation was endorsed by the Ouimet Committee in its 1969 report and has subsequently been advocated, with variations, in numerous commission and law reform reports.

It was not until the late 1980s, however, that serious consideration was given to legislatively specifying Aboriginal offenders as being in need of particular attention in this regard. In June 1988, the Canadian Bar Association published a report in which it analyzed the "grossly disproportionate" involvement of Native people in Canada's justice and corrections systems, and set out recommendations to address and reduce this "stark and appalling" problem.

Two months later, the House of Commons Standing Committee on Justice and Solicitor General published its report on its review of sentencing and corrections, the "Daubney Report." The Committee devoted a separate chapter of its report to issues concerning Native offenders, commenting that "[o]ne reason why Native inmates are disproportionately represented in the prison population is that too many of them are being *unnecessarily* sentenced to terms of imprisonment."

On its face, the Aboriginal sentencing provision in paragraph 718.2(e) appears to reflect somewhat similar assumptions: (a) that the problem of over-representation of Aboriginal people in Canadian correctional institutions is at least partly a product of inappropriate sentencing of Aboriginal offenders, and (b) that modifying the sentencing methodology for Aboriginal offenders would contribute in some significant way to alleviating this problem. A number of major public inquiries and other governmental and non-governmental research studies into the situation of Aboriginal people and the criminal justice system—which had been conducted by 1994, the time of the Second Reading debate of Bill C-41, and presumably should have influenced the drafting of the legislation and the debate—raised serious doubts about the corrections of both of these assumptions. The major findings of these various inquiry and research activities may be summarized as follows:

- Data were available to demonstrate considerable regional variation in the "over-representation" of Aboriginal people in Canadian penal institutions, and clearly indicated that, in some regions (*e.g.* Quebec), Aboriginal people were not "over-represented."

- Data were insufficient to definitely identify the principal causes of Aboriginal over-incarceration in those regions in which they were over-incarcerated. However, there was a clear recognition, both in the reports of official inquiries and in the extant research literature, that sentencing practices likely played a minimal role, if any at all, in causing Aboriginal over-incarceration.

- There was a clear recognition, both in the reports of official inquiries and in the extant research literature, that factors other than sentencing practices (*e.g.* greater Aboriginal rates of offending, greater susceptibility to criminal justice processing, differential policing), and particularly factors outside the criminal justice system (poverty, unemployment, higher proportion of youths, alcohol abuse etc.), were probably the key factors leading to Aboriginal over-incarceration.

- There was some evidence that, to the extent that sentencing judges were discriminating between Aboriginal and non-Aboriginal offenders, they were more likely to discriminate *in favour of* rather than *against* Aboriginal offenders (*i.e.* more likely to give non-carceral sentences and, if carceral sentences were given, more likely to order shorter terms of incarceration). In particular, there was no evidence that sentencing judges were frequently or routinely discriminating *against* Aboriginal offenders.

- There was evidence that other groups in society, especially Blacks, were as much or more "over-represented" in Canadian penal institutions in some regions of the country as Aboriginal people were in other regions; that the over-representation of these other groups was just as related to social disadvantage as was the case for Aboriginal offenders, and that most of these factors were the same or similar for both groups. Furthermore, while Aboriginal offenders constitute a unique minority, most offenders in Canada's prisons have backgrounds that include substance abuse and other kinds of social disadvantage.

The self-styled Aboriginal Justice Inquiry in Manitoba (referred specifically to by the Minister of Justice in explaining why the Aboriginal sentencing provision was included in Bill C-41) stopped short of suggesting that discriminatory sentencing practices were responsible for Aboriginal over-representation in the correctional system. Rather, the Inquiry argued, "[a]s a direct result of Aboriginal people being over-represented in *enter-*

ing our court system, Aboriginal people are over-incarcerated, as well." It nevertheless recommended that "[t]he Manitoba Court of Appeal encourage more creativity in sentencing by trial court judges so that the use of incarceration is diminished and the use of sentencing alternatives is increased, *particularly for Aboriginal peoples*."

In addition, the Inquiry argued that "[c]ultural factors should not be seen as extraordinary considerations for the court. Rather, they should be considered in the normal course of sentencing each and every Aboriginal defendant," and recommended that "[t]he *Criminal Code* be amended to provide that cultural factors be taken into account in sentencing, and that in the meantime judges be encouraged to take this approach." The striking similarity of the language of the Aboriginal sentencing provision in Bills C-90 and C-41 to the language of the Manitoba Inquiry's recommendations suggests that the inclusion of this provision was probably inspired by the latter. The Justice Minister's specific reference to the Manitoba Inquiry when introducing the provision to the House of Commons is also noteworthy in this respect.

• • •

We can summarize the main arguments in this article as follows:

- While the over-representation of Aboriginal people in Canadian prisons is an undeniable, important, and pressing problem, there is little evidence that the problem has arisen as a result of discriminatory sentencing *per se*. However, there is strong evidence that the over-representation of Aboriginal offenders varies significantly from one region of the country to another and that in some regions they are not over-represented in prisons at all.

- This being the case, adopting a "different methodology" for sentencing Aboriginal offenders generally is unlikely to significantly affect the problem of Aboriginal over-representation and will likely result in unjustifiable inequities for offenders, victims, and communities.

- The Supreme Court's interpretation and directions for the application of paragraph 718.2(e) rely on a general "pan-Indian" view of Aboriginal culture and circumstances as "unique." This is not consistent with the known diversity within Aboriginal communities, nor with what is known about differences and similarities between Aboriginal and non-Aboriginal people, including offenders and victims, with respect to both their circumstances and their views about justice. The wording of the Aboriginal sentencing provision in paragraph 718.2(e) does not compel such an approach.

- A superior way of paying "particular attention to the circumstances of Aboriginal offenders" would be to establish a statutory mitigating factor that would recognize the role of social or economic deprivation in precipitating the crime for which the offender is being sentenced. Such a "social/cultural disadvantage" plea, however, should be equally available to any offender whose circumstances may justify it, regardless of his or her racial or cultural origins.

- The plea for consideration would need to establish some discernible element of causality. Simply claiming membership in some disadvantaged group or population would be insufficient, just as, for example, asserting a lack of employment is, by itself, insufficient to justify mitigation of punishment in a case of domestic violence.

• Aboriginal offenders in many parts of the country would, in practice, be more likely to benefit from consideration of such a factor in sentencing than offenders from many other racial or cultural groups because a larger proportion of the Aboriginal than the non-Aboriginal population is more likely to have experienced such social disadvantage. In other parts of the country, however, this is also likely to be true for offenders from some other racial, ethnic, cultural, or immigrant groups.

The responsibility for the current confusion with respect to the sentencing of Aboriginal offenders lies as much with Parliament as with the Supreme Court. Parliament enacted the last nine words of paragraph 718.2(e) with almost no serious debate about what they might accomplish or how they might accomplish it. There was no attention given either to the available publicly funded research knowledge about the problem they were apparently addressing or to the likelihood that sentencing practices can contribute in any significant way to a solution.

The result, regrettably, is a provision that will be extremely difficult to implement without unacceptable and unfair discrimination and disparity, and that will be unlikely to make any substantial and positive contribution to the serious, and in some respects growing, problem of Aboriginal incarceration. Faced with the unavoidable task of trying to make some sense of such a provision, the confusion surrounding the Supreme Court's decisions in *Gladue* and *Wells*, and the fact that it felt it had to write a second lengthy decision to explain the first, is understandable, if not entirely excusable.

Susan Haslip recently recommended that Parliament should legislate affirmative sentencing discrimination in favour of Aboriginal offenders and offenders from some other unspecified "minority groups," and invoke the "notwithstanding clause" in s. 33 of the *Charter* to insulate it from constitutional challenge. In light of the currently available research knowledge about the problems of Aboriginal and non-Aboriginal incarceration and the sentencing of Aboriginal and non-Aboriginal offenders, we believe that such an approach could not possibly be justified and would inevitably result in constitutionally sanctioned inequity and injustice for many offenders, victims, and communities.

In our view, those last nine words in paragraph 718.2(e), and the Supreme Court's efforts to interpret and apply them to the sentencing of Aboriginal offenders, can rightly be seen as offering little more than an empty promise to Aboriginal people and a bitter pill for sentencing judges who struggle to do the right thing, but become daily more aware of their powerlessness in the face of a situation far beyond their control. It would have been better if those last nine words had never been included in paragraph 718.2(e); then, the unrealistic expectation that they would help alleviate the current excessive entanglement of Aboriginal people in the criminal justice system would not have arisen. Alternatively, had Parliament added some more inclusive words to the paragraph (such as "or other similarly disadvantaged offenders") as it did in the case of paragraph 718.2(a)(i), at least concerns about unacceptably discriminatory sentencing might have been allayed somewhat while still legislatively acknowledging the plight of Aboriginal people.

Could the Supreme Court have interpreted and applied the Aboriginal sentencing provision in paragraph 718.2(e) in a more reasonable and defensible way than it did in

Gladue and *Wells*? We doubt it. In *Gladue*, the Supreme Court was careful to state that paragraph 718.2(e) was not intended to create an automatic "Aboriginal discount," as complained by some newspaper editorials, but rather to "alter the method of analysis which sentencing judges must use in determining a fit sentence for [A]boriginal offenders." But there is no avoiding the conclusion that the alternative methodology, as the Supreme Court has outlined it in its decisions in *Gladue* and *Wells*, will, if judges take it seriously, result in a different pattern of sentencing outcomes for Aboriginal offenders. And, since the language of the judgment is overwhelmingly uni-directional *vis-à-vis* the greater use of alternatives to incarceration and shorter terms of custody where incarceration is inevitable, the result will be that some Aboriginal offenders will receive community-based sanctions where comparable, equally disadvantaged, non-Aboriginal offenders would be sentenced to prison. Despite all of the Court's rationalizations to the contrary, it is hard to see how this could be regarded as equitable or consistent with the value of parity in sentencing.

As well, some Aboriginal offenders who still receive sentences of incarceration will serve shorter terms of custody than similarly disadvantaged non-Aboriginal offenders convicted of similar crimes. This makes no sense from the perspective of sound sentencing policy and carries no benefit for the interests of Aboriginal communities across Canada. Furthermore, given that so many offences by Aboriginal offenders involve Aboriginal victims, many of those being women, it also raises the disconcerting possibility that the criminal justice system will come to be perceived as discriminatory against Aboriginal victims generally and Aboriginal women in particular. At the end of the day, however, it violates a cardinal principle of sentencing-equity that is relevant to all kinds of offenders, victims, and communities, and this violation is simply not fair.

J. Rudin and K. Roach, "Broken Promises: A Response to Stenning and Roberts' 'Empty Promises'"
(2002) *Sask. L Rev.* 3 (footnotes omitted)

A. *Formal as Opposed to Substantive Equality*

Although they rely heavily on the principle of parity and the danger of "unacceptable and unfair discrimination and disparity" in sentencing, Stenning and Roberts unfortunately do not define what they mean by discriminatory sentencing and their understanding of equality. They allude to equality concerns in discussing the enactment of Bill C-41, and allude to the political controversy about including crimes committed because of bias on the basis of sexual orientation. They seem to display some sympathy to proposals made by Bloc Quebeçois Member of Parliament Pierrette Venne. Venne moved unsuccessfully in Parliament for the reference to Aboriginal offenders in s. 718.2(e) to be removed and for the list of hate based crimes to be made non-exclusive. They also suggest that the enactment of s. 718.2(e) under the affirmative action provision of s. 15(2) of the *Charter* would result "in constitutionality sanctioned inequity," suggesting opposition to the idea that affirmative action is consistent with equality. They also argue that s. 718.2(e) results in horizontal inequality by singling out Aboriginal offenders, while many other offenders, including some racial minorities, suffer from similar adverse social conditions. Piecing together a coherent approach to equality from these observations is somewhat speculative, but it seems likely that if Stenning and Roberts had developed their view of discrimination more fully, they would have been required to embrace notions of formal equality.

Formal equality is based on the idea that discrimination occurs when similarly situated people are treated differently. In itself this is a somewhat empty concept of equality, because so much depends on determining the grounds of who is similarly situated. The concept of formal equality at its best is based on the idea that all individuals are equal and similarly situated. On a formal equality model, discriminatory sentencing would occur if a similarly situated Aboriginal offender received a harsher sentence than a similarly situated non-Aboriginal offender. The reason for such a disparate sentence would have to be some form of intentional or conscious discrimination against the Aboriginal offender that would be triggered by the judge's awareness that the offender was Aboriginal.

In the United States, the concept of formal equality has been used to oppose affirmative action programs on the footing that they draw distinctions on the basis of race, gender or disability; these distinctions should never be drawn between formally equal human beings. Stenning and Roberts' article echoes another element of the conservative American critiques of affirmative action: singling any group out for special treatment causes horizontal inequities because of the inevitably over and under inclusive nature of using membership in a group as a criteria for allocating benefits. In other words, the critics argue: why should a white man who has overcome economic hardships be denied a benefit that may be given to an advantaged African-American woman? Using sentencing as a form of affirmative action to improve the conditions of previously disadvantaged groups would be suspect under the regime of formal equality. It would always be suspect to draw distinctions on the basis of group membership, and it would be especially inequitable to single out Aboriginal offenders over other offenders who may have experienced similarly adverse social conditions. A formal equality approach, or something quite close to it, underlies Stenning and Roberts' arguments: s. 718.2(e) was intended to remedy discriminatory sentencing, and available evidence suggests that Aboriginal people do not suffer from discriminatory sentencing. It also helps to explain their argument that s. 718.2(e) is an unfair form of affirmative action because, like all group based programs, it is inevitably over and under inclusive by including some Aboriginal persons who have not suffered adverse social conditions, while excluding some non-Aboriginal persons who have suffered adverse social conditions.

The idea of formal equality has been quite thoroughly discredited in Canadian law. In its first landmark case involving the interpretation of equality rights under s. 15 of the *Charter*, a unanimous Supreme Court denounced formal equality: they felt that formalistic equality was reflective of a past age when the Court ignored gender or other forms of discrimination on the formalistic footing that laws drew distinctions on the basis of pregnancy or Indian status as opposed to gender. Building on jurisprudence under the *Human Rights Code*, the Court stressed that discrimination could occur from similar treatment, even in the absence of an intent to discriminate. The Supreme Court has reaffirmed its commitment to substantive equality, which finds discrimination not only in formal discrimination, but also in failures to take account of the disadvantaged positions of groups in Canadian society. For the same reason, the Court also accepts distinctions that are designed to ameliorate the positions of disadvantaged groups as consistent with equality. The Supreme Court has also accepted considerable over and [under] inclusiveness in ameliorative programs by, for example, upholding as ameliorative a casino project that benefited bands but not other Aboriginal people. The recognition of the disadvantaged position of Aboriginal people in the criminal justice system in both s. 718.2(e) and *Gladue* is supported by a substantive equality approach. Distinctions that proponents of formal equality would denounce as reverse discrimination and dangerously based on race can, under substantive equality, be justified on the basis that they attempt to ameliorate the position of the disadvantaged.

An acceptance of Stenning and Roberts' vision of formal equality or parity would roll back equality thinking to the 1970s. The danger, however, is that this vision of formal equality is making something of a comeback as doubts are expressed in many quarters about group-based remedies and affirmative action. It also has a strong residual appeal in the criminal law: the formal equality idea that each individual should receive identical treatment is strong whether it is linked to the due process idea of rights protection or the just deserts idea of parity in punishment. Nevertheless, we believe the formal equality vision should be rejected in favour of more modern visions of equality that accept the possibility of unintentional effects-based discrimination and reject the idea that group-based measures designed to assist the disadvantaged are a form of reverse discrimination.

• • •

Where we part company with our colleagues, however, is when they suggest that sentencing should not be part of the solution to Aboriginal over-representation or that s. 718.2(e) runs unacceptable risks of discrimination and disparity. Rather, we agree with the Supreme Court when they went to the state in *Gladue*:

> What can and must be addressed, though, is the limited role that sentencing judges will play in remedying injustice against aboriginal peoples in Canada. Sentencing judges are among those decision-makers who have the power to influence the treatment of aboriginal offenders in the justice system. They determine most directly whether an aboriginal offender will go to jail, or whether other sentencing options may be employed which will play perhaps a stronger role in restoring a sense of balance to the offender, victim, and community, and in preventing future crime.

When we use sentencing as an instrument to respond to other social problems it is inequitable, and perhaps discriminatory, to argue that sentencing cannot be used as one of many instruments to reduce Aboriginal over-representation in prison. Reducing Aboriginal over-representation in prison is, in our view, as important as attempting to reduce crime through sentencing.

We also disagree with Stenning and Roberts when they suggest that Aboriginal over-representation is merely a localized regional phenomenon, and that the causes behind this over-representation are the same as those faced by all other socially disadvantaged groups. The data presented in this paper demonstrates that Aboriginal people are disproportionately imprisoned throughout Canada, with the possible exception of Quebec, but are now also most likely over-represented in that province. The data that Stenning and Roberts rely on to support their conclusion that Aboriginal offenders receive shorter sentences than non-Aboriginal offenders do not, in our view, support the confident conclusions reached. Even if such conclusions could be supported, they would not undermine the reality of Aboriginal over-representation in prison or the need to reduce it. Indeed, they would only suggest that the drastic problem of Aboriginal over-representation in prison could easily and quickly become much worse should the discretionary decisions of sentencing judges change or be curtailed.

We also have argued that relating Aboriginal over-representation to social disadvantage misstates and over-simplifies a complex problem by ignoring the unique legacy of colonialism faced by Aboriginal people. It also risks assimilating Aboriginal people to just another disadvantaged minority. In our view, as well as in the view of the Royal Commission on Aboriginal Peoples, social disadvantage alone is an inadequate explanation of Aboriginal over-representation. To say such is not to embrace the "pan Indian" approach that Stenning and Roberts criticize: it only recognizes that all Aboriginal people in Canada have been touched by the legacy of colonialism and that steps taken to alleviate that unjust legacy should apply, albeit in different ways, to all Aboriginal people in Canada, whether they live in cities or on reserves, and whether they have status under the *Indian Act* or not.

We also disagree with Stenning and Roberts' implicit assumptions that sentencing options should be constrained by formal equality or parity, and desert principles that focus on desert as a determinant rather than a limit on punishment. Formal equality that treats all offenders the same, or does not allow for group-based amelioration of the disadvantaged, is only a recipe for continued inequality and colonialism. Similarly, an insistence on parity in punishment places formal regularity in patterns of punishment before the need for restraint and reductions in the use of imprisonment. The neglect of where punishment scales will be anchored runs the risk of accepting Canada's high rate of imprisonment, and the often inarticulate and questionable starting points for incarceration used by Canadian judges. Even on the basis of the desert principles recognized in Canadian law, there is no support for crude offence-based measures of parity and there is room for arguing that community sanctions for Aboriginal offenders can be a meaningful and proportionate response to many crimes. Finally, desert is not the only goal in Canadian sentencing. Sentencing is used as an instrument to address other social problems in Canada. We do not understand why Parliament and the Supreme Court are being criticized for adding the pressing problem of Aboriginal over-representation to that list. Section 718.2(e) simply recognizes the possibility that sentencing decisions can be used to alleviate Aboriginal over-representation in prison as well as the excessive incarceration of all offenders in Canada.

Those truly interested in restraint in imprisonment should welcome s. 718.2(e) and *Gladue* as a valuable start to reducing the use of imprisonment in Canada. To criticize s. 718.2(e) and *Gladue* as discriminatory is to play into the hands of those opposed to recognition of the special position of Aboriginal people in Canadian society, and to a law and order mentality that sees imprisonment as the routine and necessary response to crime.

At some point in the future, it tragically may be necessary to criticize s. 718.2(e) and *Gladue* as ineffectual in reducing Aboriginal over-representation in prison. To dismiss them as empty promises in these early days, however, is to risk making failure a self-fulfilling prophecy. It also risks inhibiting the use of community sanctions to keep Aboriginal people out of jail and providing an excuse for those who do not want to address Aboriginal over-representation in prison. To argue for the repeal of the reference to Aboriginal people in s. 718.2(e) sets up Aboriginal people and Canadian society for yet another broken promise. There have been too many broken promises already.

Jean-Paul Brodeur, "On the Sentencing of Aboriginal Offenders: A Reaction to Stenning and Roberts"
(2002) *Sask. L Rev.* 45 (footnotes omitted)

I have two minor reservations with regard to the facts as they are given by the authors. First, it seems to me that the authors do not always follow the same standards of proof that they impose upon their opponents. While repeatedly claiming that the views they criticize are not based on sufficient data, they qualify their own assertions with words such as "likely" and "probably." The clause "some evidence" is pervasive throughout the paper. Second, the data in tables 1 and 2, which play a crucial part in showing that the sentencing courts are actually more lenient towards Aboriginal offenders than towards non-Aboriginal offenders, respectively originate from British Columbia and from Ontario, whereas Aboriginal over-representation is starkest in the prairie provinces (the same objection applies to my own use of the Quebec data). In addition to these minor reservations, I want to make a general point: "revisionist" papers that criticize the allegation of racial or ethnic discrimination in explaining the over-representation of minorities in the criminal justice system are paradoxically both compelling and unconvincing. Two quotes from the work of Robert Reiner on police discrimination epitomize the predicament of research in this respect. Reiner wrote in 1989 that despite methodological caveats, "the quantity and quality of [the] evidence [on police racial discrimination] is such as to render any doubts about discrimination fanciful." He also wrote in 1992 that it was "inconceivable that this [statistical] approach could ever conclusively establish racial discrimination." Therein lies the paradox. On the one hand, the sum of evidence on over-representation is so overwhelming that it seemingly does not allow for explanations other than discrimination. On the other hand, most statistical attempts to demonstrate the presence of discrimination are inconclusive when all variables are duly accounted for. Revisionist literature on discrimination is therefore compelling when it undermines the statistical evidence given to bolster the case of sentencing discrimination. However, it never quite succeeds in convincing us that there is no fire under all that smoke.

· · ·

This list of factors cited in *Gladue* is said to be "almost identical to the facts listed as leading to 'systemic discrimination' in the criminal justice system against Blacks by the Marshall Inquiry in Nova Scotia in 1989." Consequently, if the nature of social deprivation is substantially the same for various categories of marginalized offenders, taking a social deprivation factor into account only in the sentencing of the Aboriginal offenders is inconsistent with s. 718.2(b) of the *Code*, which states that "a sentence should be similar to sentences imposed on similar offenders for similar offences committed in similar circumstances."

In a thought-provoking paper, Anthony Doob demonstrated how vague the meaning of the adjective "similar" was in this last paragraph by contrasting examples where offences, offenders, circumstances, and sentences could formally be viewed as similar, but were actually quite different when put in context. Within the limits of this rejoinder, it is impossible to examine in detail how similar the systemic deprivation factors cited by the authors truly are when viewed in the context of an Aboriginal reservation and of a Black ghetto. To suggest the point quickly: "high unemployment" has a different meaning in the context of an Aboriginal reservation where there are simply no job opportunities and in an urban context where the White majority exclude Blacks from segments of the labour-market; "substance abuse" is not the same when it refers to young men smoking crack cocaine and to kids committing suicide by sniffing gasoline; "loneliness" is not experienced in a similar way in bush reservations and urban ghettoes.

It is possible to continue with *every one* of the systemic factors quoted above: a surface similarity would be shown to conceal a substantial difference when context is taken into account. Hence my criticism of the authors: they use concepts such as similarity, uniqueness, and diversity on the level of abstraction suiting the purpose of their demonstration. Occasionally they stress differences and miss common features. For instance, there is admittedly much diversity in the way Aboriginal peoples experience their situation within Canada, but this diversity does not dissolve the notion of being an Aboriginal to the extent that there would be as much difference between a Cree and a Mohawk as between a Cree and a Black. On the other hand, there is a commonality between Aboriginal peoples in places as different as Greenland, Australia, South America, and Canada: that of having been overwhelmed by foreigners who allowed them a precarious survival.

In line with these remarks, the authors dispose perfunctorily of the historical argument for remedying past oppression through an Aboriginal deprivation factor in sentencing. There are indeed other minorities who have a long history of being discriminated against: the Blacks in Africville in Nova Scotia or the Chinese immigrants who built this country's railways. However, there is no Canadian minority other than the Aboriginal people who can claim to have been this country's first inhabitants. Similarly, no minority has a history of being oppressed that goes as far back.

Do these remarks imply that we should atone, and that the Aboriginal people should uniquely benefit from a mitigating deprivation factor on the basis of their harrowing history of past oppression? The philosopher Kant's maxim can be applied to answer this question by assessing the ethical character of behaviour: a form of behaviour is ethical to the extent that it can be universalized with benefit to mankind. According to this criteria, universally sentencing minorities on the basis of a historical deprivation factor would bring chaos to justice as there are few countries where one or several minorities could not claim to benefit from such a factor, for example: all Aboriginal peoples; historical peoples who have been scattered between various countries such as Jews, Palestinians, Armenians, and Kurds; and former slaves in the US and the Caribbean. The list would be endless.

Would the establishment of a general statutory mitigating factor that would "recognize the role of social or economic deprivation in *precipitating* the crime for which the offender is being sentenced" be a better solution? The authors do not present a detailed argument for this solution and my comments on it shall be brief. First, in view of my remarks on the logical contradiction involved in the "collective individualization" of sentences, it seems that "individualizing" sentences on the encompassing basis of social class only compounds difficulties. Second, how will it be possible to determine, with any degree of precision or consistency, the sentencing quantum of this discount with respect to the principles of proportionality and parity? Lastly, the statutory social deprivation factor proposed by the authors is based upon what is now called the "root-cause" theory of crime (that broad and deep-seated social and economic factors "precipitate" crime). In view of the fact that the steep decline in US crime rates does not seem to be caused by any major social or economic change in that country, the root-cause theory of crime has drawn increased criticism.

Alan Cairns, "Seeing and Not Seeing: Explaining Mis-Recognition in the Criminal Justice System"
(2002) *Sask. L Rev.* 53 (footnotes omitted)

The phrase "with particular attention to the circumstances of [A]boriginal offenders," and its incorporation in legislation proclaimed in 1996, emerged in what might appropriately be called a culturally-conducive intellectual climate. From the defeat of the 1969 White Paper to the enactment of the 1996 amendment to the *Criminal Code*, the philosophy of differential recognition of Aboriginal people has flourished. It has done so to such an extent that the 1969 White Paper, with its assimilationist objectives, and which at the time was consonant with, and indeed reflected, progressive thinking, is now routinely referred to as the "infamous" White Paper.

That evolution, from the Trudeau vision to the contrary constitutional vision of the Royal Commission on Aboriginal Peoples (RCAP), requires no more than a brief listing for our purposes: it includes various supportive judicial decisions, commencing with *Calder v. British Columbia (Attorney General)*; s. 35(1) of the 1982 *Constitution Act*, which recognized and affirmed "the existing aboriginal and treaty rights of the aboriginal peoples of Canada," and s. 25 of the *Charter* which protected Aboriginal, treaty, or other rights or freedoms of Aboriginal peoples from abrogation or derogation by the *Charter*, and significantly enhanced the constitutional recognition and status of Aboriginal peoples; between 1983 and 1987, four constitutional conferences were explicitly devoted to Aboriginal issues, with the leaders of the major Aboriginal organizations sitting around the table with First Ministers; and the diffusion of the idea that Aboriginal peoples were made up of individual nations—between sixty and eight, according to the RCAP, somewhat less for other authors, but many more if we include the several hundred Indian bands which have officially added "nation" to their title, which triggered an emerging multinational definition of Canada.

The Charlottetown Accord of 1992, and the 1992 establishment of the Royal Commission on Aboriginal Peoples and its ongoing activities until it reported in 1996, framed the period when the discussions in Parliament that led to Bill C-41 were underway. The establishment of the RCAP followed the Oka crisis of 1990, and the role of Elijah Harper in defeating the Meech Lake Accord. In these years, the relationship of

Aboriginal peoples, especially Indian, to the Canadian state had a prominence and urgency not previously seen in the twentieth century. That Royal Commission was to be the equivalent for Aboriginal peoples of what the Bi and Bi Commission had been for French Canadians. Its mandate was generous, its public hearings were lengthy, and its research was probably the most extensive ever undertaken anywhere on the relations between indigenous peoples and settler majorities. The overall message of the Royal Commission from its mandate to its massive *Report* was clear: that the existing condition of Aboriginal peoples in Canadian society was unacceptable, assimilation was neither an attainable nor a desirable goal, and that some version of positive differential treatment in terms of rights and institutional accommodation had to be worked out. The Royal Commission redefined Canada as a multinational federation to be held together by treaties. In sum, the Royal Commission was an instrument of Aboriginal nationalism, and its *Report* was a massive plea for a positive recognition of difference as a justification for wardship. Further, it did not shy away from asserting the illegitimacy of "conventional [Canadian] democracy" with its settler institutions of representation, and hence of the foreign nature of the laws which they passed.

Although the 1992 Charlottetown Accord was rejected in a national referendum, its Aboriginal components clearly indicated the momentum behind the drive for a special status for Aboriginal peoples, by then commonly called nations, in the Canadian constitutional order. Although the bargaining process from which the Accord emerged is not known in detail, it is self-evident that the inclusion of the major Aboriginal organizations (Native Women's Association of Canada excepted) in the closed sessions in which the details were hammered out, is the basic explanation for the remarkably positive package of Aboriginal proposals in the Accord. Elsewhere, I have summarized the Accord's constitutional philosophy as follows:

> Virtually every major institution of the Canadian state would in future have a distinctive Aboriginal input or presence—Senate, House of Commons, Supreme Court (tentatively), first ministers' conferences, and amending formula. The Charter, a crucial symbol of citizenship to many Canadians, would have a greatly weakened application to Aboriginal peoples; further, depending on the jurisdiction of Aboriginal governments, their peoples would have an attenuated relationship to either or both of the two traditional orders of Canadian government, federal and provincial.

From one perspective, the preceding is simply background context for the Aboriginal sentencing provision, with negligible explanatory power. From another, it represents the "geist," the spirit of the times which influenced policy makers in this and other policy areas. That spirit lies behind the instruction in s. 718.2(e) to a court imposing a sentence to pay "particular attention to the circumstances of [A]boriginal offenders," when it examines "all available sanctions other than imprisonment that are reasonable in the circumstances ... for all offenders." Stenning and Roberts are explicit that in some settings the over-representation of Blacks exceeds that of Aboriginals, and that the over-representation of Blacks and some "other groups" was "just as related to social disadvantage as was the case for Aboriginal offenders." However, other groups do not emerge from the general category "all offenders" with a legislative mandate to be accorded special attention in sentencing practices. While Black prison admissions in

Ontario from 1986 to 1993 were proportionally nearly twice the rate of Aboriginal admissions, and while other offenders might have experienced equal or greater social disadvantage, they lacked the visibility and sympathetic recognition that s. 718.2(e) accorded to Aboriginal offenders. Section 718.2(e) generates a search for, and often presupposes an Aboriginal uniqueness in the category of offenders that is difficult to sustain. For example, Stenning and Roberts assert that the Court's attempt in *Gladue* to identify "systemic and background factors" for Aboriginal offenders that are "*unique, and different from those of non-[A]boriginal offenders*" generated a list of factors, none of which "is unique to Aboriginal offenders, either in kind or degree," and in any case is not applicable to all Aboriginal offenders. The competition between a socially disadvantaged Aboriginal offender and an equally disadvantaged Black offender for sympathetic judicial attention is not fought on a level playing field.

Over-representation of members of a defined social category is more likely to elicit special and positive attention when they occupy a prominent place on the public agenda and can make claims for special contemporary treatment as a form of redress for historical maltreatment. Black Canadians and all the other socially disadvantaged offenders who face criminal charges in courtrooms lack the positive, supportive spillover that Aboriginal, especially Indian, people possess. This gives the latter a special capacity to make claims on the moral conscience of Canadians, a capacity buttressed by their positive constitutional recognition in s. 35 of the 1982 *Constitution Act*.

Whether singling out Aboriginal offenders from other equally, or even more seriously, disadvantaged offenders is morally justified, is a separate question. Elsewhere, I have argued that "citizens plus" is an appropriate label to describe the civic relationship of Aboriginal peoples to the Canadian state. That they have a special place in the constitutional order is a constitutional fact, not a matter for debate. The manifestation of that special place, that "*citizens plus*" status in the sentencing provisions of the *Criminal Code*, however, is morally problematic. It offends too deeply the parity and fairness assumptions of one of the most symbolic instruments that regulates citizen–state relations; the *Criminal Code*.

. . .

We are not prisoners of the spirit of the times, nor of the various frameworks—legislative, institutional and constitutional—that we have inherited. They do, however, offer a "natural" way of perceiving and understanding whatever little world that we seek to explain.

The genesis of nine little words—"with particular attention to the circumstances of [A]boriginal offenders"—is found not simply in over-representation data, but in the moral and intellectual history of the last half-century. The visibility of Aboriginal peoples, indeed the very category "Aboriginal peoples," their positive constitutional recognition, the emergence of a cohort of law professors committed to the enhancement of Aboriginal status, the diffusion of the "nation" label, the emergence of Nunavut, and a major royal commission (the list could be greatly lengthened) are developments which would have astonished our predecessors of fifty years ago. To us, they are part of the air we breathe. They help explain why Aboriginal offenders are much more likely to be singled out for special judicial attention in sentencing provisions of the *Criminal Code* than other equally and similarly or even more profoundly disadvantaged offenders.

The others do not have the positive momentum of recent history behind them. The Aboriginal sentencing provision reflects the transformation of Canadian constitutional culture in recent decades.

This constitutional culture has to be adapted to our constitutional arrangements. The tendency to think of Aboriginal over-representation in pan-Canadian terms is influenced by the constitutional assignment of both s. 91(24) "Indians, and Lands reserved for the Indians" and s. 91(27) "Criminal Law" to Ottawa. Consequently, both the *Indian Act* and the *Criminal Code* are federal, country-wide laws. The populations and activities they regulate have a coast-to-coast dimension. Changes in the laws are debated in the Canadian Parliament and apply to Canada as a whole. This setting is not an inducement to focus on the different realities between Nova Scotia and Saskatchewan.

As Stenning and Roberts illustrate, the provincialized/territorialized view of Aboriginal over-representation which would automatically occur if we had thirteen *Criminal Codes* and thirteen *Indian Acts*, is not impossible under present arrangements but its emergence is less natural and accordingly less likely.

What demands our attention (Aboriginal over-representation)—and what is likely to escape it (the variation in Aboriginal prison, representation between Nova Scotia and Saskatchewan, for example, and the over-representation in some settings of non-Aboriginal groups)—is not solely dictated by the data, but by the climate of opinion which influences what we see, and the constitutional arrangements which channel our vision. Mis-recognition of huge interprovincial/territorial variations in Aboriginal prison representation is explained in part by the jurisdictional allocations of legislative power in the 1860s.

M. Carter, "Of Fairness and Faulkner"
(2002) *Sask. L Rev.* 63 (footnotes omitted)

III. *Equality with a Vengeance*

A. *In Application to Section 718(2)(e)*

"Equality with a vengeance" posits that if everyone cannot receive a benefit, then no one should. Assuming, for present purposes, that a non-custodial sentence is a "benefit," equality with a vengeance analysis applies to s. 718(2)(e) in such a way as to argue that Aboriginal status alone should not result in people receiving the benefit of doing *less* jail time than non-Aboriginal people in the same circumstances. The authors imply that their ultimate goal is to have all offenders receive the high level of consideration for a non-custodial disposition that Aboriginal people may receive, but they argue that in the short term, equality demands that Aboriginal people receive no more than the mean.

This is the only explanation for the authors' indication that s. 718(2)(e) should have been challenged under s. 15 of the *Charter* in *R v. Gladue* and *R v. Wells*. Those cases did not involve non-Aboriginal people demanding as much consideration for non-custodial sentences as Aboriginal people would receive. On the contrary, a successful equality challenge of s. 718(2)(e) in cases like these would result in Aboriginal people doing more jail time in the name of equality.

B. *Non-Custodial Sentences Are Not Conventional "Benefits"*

"Equality with a vengeance" arguments respond to the unequal distributions of benefits. As problematic as these arguments are in any context, they are misapplied to sentencing law. This is because non-custodial sentences cannot be considered "benefits" in any conventional sense. At best, they are limited relaxations of one of the least explicable and most violent processes of our legal system. That fact needs to play some significant role in any discussion aimed at making people do more jail time than the law might otherwise be interpreted to allow. Since no consensus exists in relation to why we punish people then, to some considerable extent, criminal punishment represents the abandonment of people's fortunes to irrational intuitions. Therefore, this places the decision to spare some people a degree of punishment within an entirely different order of state activity than anything else that might be defined as a benefit.

A judge's decision to allow a non-custodial sentence represents the creation of only a small rent in the fabric of punitive discipline that the criminal justice system otherwise weaves. These judicial decisions must be distinguished from things like the provision of positive economic benefits to some classes of individuals, but not others, which are more commonly the focus of an equality analysis. Given our lack of certainty concerning the purpose of the penal enterprise and our commitment as academics to reasoned analysis, equality arguments in this area should attempt to pull more people out of the fabric of harshest punishment rather than demand that a few should be returned.

This points to a less vengeful equality perspective that seeks to preserve whatever benefits s. 718(2)(e) provides. Such a perspective suggests that, although the best situation might be for everyone to receive a benefit, it is nonetheless preferable that some people receive it rather than no one. The wording of s. 718(2)(e) itself assists in this effort to retain the non-punitive benefits that the section may afford. Clearly, Aboriginal people are *not* the only ones who should receive this benefit. Notwithstanding the way in which the wording of the section accommodates some of Stenning and Roberts' concerns about the exclusive targeting of this benefit, their insistence upon the legal insignificance of history compels them to demand the removal of the specific reference to the circumstances of Aboriginal people.

The next part of this discussion will demonstrate that Stenning and Roberts' ahistoricism is fatal to their claim that s. 718(2)(e) will result in "unacceptably discriminatory sentencing." History is critical to discrimination analysis in Canadian law.

• • •

VI. *Causal Connection*

Professors Stenning and Roberts submit:

> Offenders should be able to point to a causal chain that relates their Aboriginal status ... to the offence. To suggest that such factors must automatically be considered if the offender happens to be Aboriginal but not otherwise, as the Supreme Court interprets paragraph 718(2)(e) to require,—is inherently unfair.

Such causal connection tests respond to the gap that always exists in inductive reasoning between evidence for a cause and certainty that such cause has been identified. In other areas of the law, our courts have decided that the interests of justice compel them to accept something in the nature of a rebutable presumption that certain forms of status are markers for certain claims to consideration. In *Moge v. Moge*, for example, the Supreme Court of Canada resisted demands that spousal support claims by women who have been in long-term, "traditional" marriages be established in accordance with a strict causal connection test.

Anyone with the briefest experience working in Canada's western and northern criminal courts must make the inductive assumption that there is some strong but very complex relationship between the historic and contemporary life experiences of Aboriginal people and their disproportionate involvement with the criminal justice system. Therefore, very little will be compromised when sentencing courts use the Aboriginal status of people convicted of offences as a reason to make special efforts to consider non-custodial sentences in these cases. Rather than placing the onus of making the precise connections that the authors call for upon individual Aboriginal people, the weight of evidence of disproportionate involvement with the justice system should very often be allowed to speak for itself. Indeed, it might be expected that erring on the side of the evidence in this way would appeal to academics with the empirical sensibilities of Professors Stenning and Roberts.

VII. Conclusion

We are not relieved of our obligation to try to respond to the impact of our history on the present by the fact that our efforts to do so may be imperfect, complex, and resistant of categorization in relation to simplistic notions of juridical fairness and formal equality. Extraordinary circumstances require extraordinary measures and, perhaps, some concessions to the crude way that law and legal analysis otherwise compel us to carve up the social world. Whatever s. 718(2)(e)'s contribution may be to the solutions that we are seeking, it can only be a small one, but it is a start.

J.V. Roberts and P. Stenning, "The Sentencing of Aboriginal Offenders in Canada: A Rejoinder"
(2002) *Sask. L Rev.* 7 (footnotes omitted)

The important point which we feel needs to be reiterated at the outset of our consideration of the issue of "over-incarceration" or "over-representation" is that the mere fact of statistically disproportionate representation of Aboriginal people in Canada's criminal justice and correctional systems cannot simply be assumed to be evidence of "over-incarceration" in this latter sense of unjustified disproportionate representation. All too often this critical distinction gets lost in debates about Aboriginal "over-incarceration" or "over-representation."

This distinction was critical to the argument we made in our original article: (a) paragraph 718.2(e) of the *Code*, and the Supreme Court's interpretation of it in *Gladue* and *Wells*, seemed to be founded, implicitly if not explicitly, on the assumption of Aboriginal "over-incarceration" in the sense of unjustified disproportionate representation, both in absolute terms and by comparison with non-Aboriginal offenders, which has been, to a significant degree, a product of inappropriate sentencing practices; (b) the research evidence on this issue which was available in 1994 (when the Aboriginal sentencing provision was discussed in Parliament) and thereafter, as well as the findings of various commissions of inquiry that had considered the issue, did not support such assumptions; and (c) these research and other findings were not adequately considered either by Parliament in deciding to enact the Aboriginal sentencing provision or by the Supreme Court in its decision interpreting the provision in *Gladue* and *Wells*.

With this in mind, let us now turn to one claim about "over-representation" which has been incorrectly attributed to us by some of our critics (specifically, Rudin and Roach, and Daubney). This is the claim that the over-representation of Aboriginal people in Canada's judicial and correctional systems is not a "national" problem. Another version of this claim is that such over-representation is "restricted to a handful of provinces in western Canada" or is merely a localized regional phenomenon. We have never made such claims. What we have said, and what we will stand by, is that the extent of over-representation of Aboriginal people within our criminal justice system has varied significantly between different regions of the country, such that it is most serious in the Prairie provinces, less acute in Ontario and the Maritime provinces, and has been apparently non-existent in Quebec.

This observation is both indisputable and is not seriously disputed by any of our critics. It has been confirmed by Statistics Canada in a recent publication: "Consistent Aboriginal over-representation has been the focus of much concern. ... However, ... there is considerable variation across the country with respect to the presence of Aboriginal people in the general adult and adult inmate populations." The data presented by Rudin and Roach also confirm this finding. The increase in the proportion of Aboriginal offenders in Quebec prisons from 1% to 2%, which they report as having occurred by 1999-2000, may well be an anomaly; as recently as 1998, Aboriginal offenders still represented only 1% of admissions to Quebec correctional facilities.

The importance of this variation in Aboriginal "over-representation" is that it raises serious questions about some of the hypotheses which have commonly been advanced to "explain" such Aboriginal over-representation, and which seemed to have so greatly influenced those who advocated for the Aboriginal sentencing provision, as well as the Supreme Court in interpreting and applying it. Most important of these is the claim that "colonialism" is the primary root cause of such modern-day over-representation. This is important for two reasons: in the first place, it underpins the Supreme Court's claim that the modern circumstances of Aboriginal offenders are "unique"; and secondly, it provides a justification for the Supreme Court's instruction to judges that, in applying the Aboriginal sentencing provision, they must consider (via judicial notice) the historical disadvantages faced by Aboriginal people in general, in determining an appropriate sentence for the individual Aboriginal offender before them. As we noted in our original article, the wording of paragraph 718.2(e) does not, on its face, necessarily dictate either of these interpretations of it.

. . .

VII. Paragraph 718.2(e) as Symbolic Legislation

Many of our critics have argued that the Aboriginal sentencing provision is justified even if the problem it was apparently intended to address ("over-incarceration" of Aboriginal people) is not in any significant way related to, or caused by, sentencing practices. While different versions of this argument have been presented, a common thread seems to be that Parliament and the Supreme Court are justified in mandating such instructions to sentencing judges as a means of symbolically "signalling" to them society's concern over the problem of Aboriginal "over-incarceration" and society's (and the government's) intention to "do something about it."

As Carter so revealingly expresses it: "people of reason, and academics in particular, should be expected to rally behind" the Aboriginal sentencing provision regardless of the fact that it violates on its face the principle of equality before the law and that there is precious little evidence that it will address the problem of Aboriginal over-incarceration in any significant or effective way, because we may have to start somewhere in making the system operate less punitively in general. We should support paragraph 718.2(e) as "a beachhead in the struggle to subdue the most violent and irrational product of our legal system" (incarceration). Carter states this despite his assertion that "[n]o one who is concerned about Canada's tendency to over-incarcerate its citizens believes that Aboriginal people are the only ones who should be spared some degree of this most punitive measure." Aboriginal people, however, should be placed "at the front of the list for consideration" for "outstanding historical and social reasons."

We reject such arguments for three reasons. First, these arguments offend principles of justice and equality before the law which are fundamental to the legitimacy of our criminal justice system—a legitimacy which it is vital to maintain if that system is to continue to command public confidence and support.

Carter has suggested that if the Aboriginal sentencing provision were challenged as offending the equality requirements of s. 15 of the *Charter*, the courts would likely either reject the claim entirely, or support the provision under the affirmative action exemption under ss. 15(2). While we would not be surprised if the Supreme Court were to adopt such a position, we do not believe that it would be morally justified in doing so. Specifically, in our view, the current available knowledge of the nature and extent of Aboriginal over-representation in Canada's prisons, and the use (and questionable relevance) of the historical disadvantages which Aboriginals have collectively experienced, for understanding and effectively responding to such modern-day over-representation, do not provide solid grounds for such an exclusive exemption for Aboriginal offenders within sentencing principles, especially when the over-representation of other groups in society is taken into account.

Rudin and Roach assert that paragraph 718.2(e) does not exclude claims from other disadvantaged groups. We agree, and have never suggested otherwise. However, there is no escaping the fact that those nine words in paragraph 718.2(e), and the interpretation which the Supreme Court has given them, allow Aboriginal offenders to claim some *special* consideration above and beyond that available to other visible minority offenders, mentally disordered offenders, elderly offenders, and indigent (but not indigenous) offenders, who may in fact be equally deserving of such consideration. We think that Cairns said it best in his commentary: "The manifestation of that special place, that 'citizens plus' status, in the sentencing provisions of the *Criminal Code* ... is morally problematic. It offends too deeply the parity and fairness assumptions of one of the most symbolic instruments that regulates citizen–state relations; the *Criminal Code*." To this we would simply add that fairness and parity are not just reasonable assumptions, but are now codified sentencing principles, to which all judges must adhere.

Secondly, we wonder where such an approach to sentencing policy might end. If sentencing judges are to address the problem of over-incarceration despite the fact that it apparently has almost nothing to do with sentencing, what other social problems would we have sentencing judges address? Many, if not most, non-Aboriginal offenders probably earn more than most Aboriginal people, and this situation is almost certainly, at least partly, caused by discriminatory employment practices. Imposing heavier fine on non-Aboriginal offenders would contribute toward the diminution of the wealth differential between the two groups, but would make poor sentencing policy.

In this connection, Rudin and Roach's analogy with deterrence is thoroughly wide of the mark. They note that deterrence aims to address the problem of impaired driving. Since impaired driving is not *caused* by sentencing, Rudin and Roach argue that this should not preclude sentencing judges from attempting to address other social problems such as the over-incarceration of Aboriginal people. Similarly, income inequality is not caused by sentencing, but we do not consider sentencing judges to be the most appropriate people to address that social problem. The analogy between deterrence and such social problems fails because deterrence is a codified objective of sentencing, while addressing other social problems such as the disproportionate custodial representation of specific minorities, or correcting income inequalities, is not. Furthermore, impaired driving is a criminal offence, for which judges are required by law to sentence those who are convicted. However distressing Aboriginal over-representation is, it is not comparable to a criminal offence.

Supposing it were the case (it may in fact be the case) that police or the Crown discriminates against Aboriginal persons in terms of arrest and bail decision-making. Should judges reduce the use of custody for *all* Aboriginal offenders because *some* Aboriginals are arrested or denied bail in circumstances in which a comparable non-Aboriginal is released? Such a proposal would make a mockery of justice, and no correct-thinking member of the judiciary would condone such a practice. Yet that is where Rudin and Roach's logic leads us. Addressing any such "front end" discrimination is properly and primarily the responsibility of those responsible for policing and prosecutorial policy, not the judiciary.

Finally, we reject the symbolic justification for the Aboriginal sentencing provision, as we did in our original article, because it undesirably diverts attention from the real root causes of disproportionate representation of Aboriginal people in our prison system (which do not include sentencing practices to any significant extent), and from the kinds of remedies which might actually and effectively respond to this problem. In doing so, it (and in particular the Supreme Court's interpretation of it) quite unfairly suggests that sentencing judges have played some significant role in generating this problem in the first place.

X. *Conclusion*

At the end of the day, we still believe that the Aboriginal sentencing provision, as interpreted by the Supreme Court, promises Aboriginal communities more than it can deliver and represents an inappropriate, unjustified and ineffective legislative response to a pressing social problem. The provision strikes us [as] an ephemeral response to a deeper problem, yet it changes a sentencing structure designed to outlast specific problems and to reflect core values that do not change because of shifting criminal justice statistics (in this case, the over-representation statistics).

We do, however, still believe that if parliamentarians and the various parties in the *Gladue* and *Wells* litigations had paid closer attention to the available research on the nature and causes of the problem of disproportionate Aboriginal incarceration, more appropriate and effective responses to it, rather than the Aboriginal sentencing provision, might have been identified and adopted. In our original article, we suggested, as a preferable alternative to the Aboriginal sentencing provision, a more general "social disadvantage" mitigating factor which would be equally available to all eligible offenders, regardless of race, ethnicity or any other categorical classification.

We have no problem recognizing and conceding the potential difficulties with such a proposal, as noted by Brodeur in his response to our article. Nevertheless we continue to have some optimism that with careful consideration, it could constitute a progressive reform, and may be of greater benefit to the sentencing process in general, and Aboriginal offenders in particular, than some of our critics would concede. First, it would result in a general reduction in the use of custody for offenders who successfully raise the issue at sentencing. Second, Aboriginal offenders in particular would be the beneficiaries, for, as we all agree, their claim for mitigation is particularly compelling. Third, by avoiding a conflict with consensual, codified principles of sentencing such as equity, the proposal may well find greater support among members of the judiciary. Finally, these progressive reforms would be accomplished without the negative commentary from news media, members of the public, the occasional academic, and even some Aboriginal people themselves.

Perhaps the most important argument which we have tried to make, both in our original article and in this rejoinder is that good public policy on this important issue is more likely to emerge if public, academic and judicial debate about it is informed by the available research and knowledge on the subject, with due recognition given to the outstanding gaps in this knowledge.

VII. RECENT RESEARCH AND DATA

The high rates of Aboriginal admissions to custody continues to be a troubling issue. It has been documented repeatedly by commissions of inquiry, all levels of government, and academics. Yet answers to the questions about what factors have produced this situation and what are the best strategies for remedying it prove elusive.

A. Provincial

The following tables (from J.V. Roberts and R. Melchers, "The Incarceration of Aboriginal Offenders: An Analysis of Trends, 1978-2001" (2003), 45 *Canadian Journal of Criminology and Criminal Justice* 211-42; Statistics Canada, *Adult Correctional Services in Canada, 2003-4* (Ottawa: Statistics Canada, 2005)) provide an idea of the intractability of the problem. Despite the efforts of governments and courts to reduce the disproportionate rate of Aboriginal admissions to federal and provincial custody, matters have actually deteriorated. According to the 2001 Census, Aboriginal Canadians represent approximately 3 percent of the general population in Canada. At the federal level, Aboriginal Canadians represented almost one-fifth (18 percent) of admissions to federal facilities in 2003-4, the most recent year for which data are available.

Table 1 shows that in 2004, the most recent year for which data are available, Aboriginal Canadians accounted for an even higher percentage of provincial admissions (21 percent) than in 1978, when national statistics, including the ethnicity of the individual offender, were first published. In 1978, only 16 percent of admissions to custody were Aboriginal. In addition, despite the Aboriginal reference in section 718.2(e) and the decision in *Gladue*, there has been no amelioration of the problem.

Table 2 reveals that, consistent with the distribution of First Nations peoples across the country, the problem of over-representation is very marked in some jurisdictions and absent in others. Thus in Saskatchewan fully four-fifths of admissions to custody were Aboriginal. The Yukon and Manitoba also recorded very high rates of Aboriginal admissions, while in the East of the country Aboriginals account for a much smaller percentage of admissions to provincial correctional institutions.

B. Federal

The Corrections Service of Canada publishes an annual report entitled "Statistical Overview" that provide some interesting data. The 2006 report contained the table represented as Table 16.3.

The upper part of table 16.3 shows that, since *Gladue*, there has been a marginal increase in the number of Aboriginal penitentiary prisoners, an increase of 6.5 percent over five years. You will recall that after the Supreme Court issued its decision in *Gladue*, the Court was criticized in the media for promoting a two-tier sentencing system. One aspect of the Supreme Court ruling was the view that, as the severity of offences increases, so does the likelihood that sentences for Aboriginal and non-Aboriginal offenders would be similar. The Court remarked that this would be especially true for crimes of violence. The data showing a small increase in the Aboriginal penitentiary population suggests that sentencing judges are following the Supreme Court's guidance, although one can glean only so much from penitentiary counts.

The lower part of table 16.3 shows a similar increase (7.8 percent) in the number of Aboriginal people supervised on federal parole or statutory release. This increase is interesting. For a number of years, there has been concern that Aboriginal prisoners are granted parole at a lower rate than non-Aboriginals. Over the past decade, there has been an increase in the general parole-granting rate from about 31.7 percent in 1996-97, reaching a high of

Table 16.1   Admissions to Provincial and Territorial Custody, Canada, 1978-79 to 2003-4

	Number of non-Aboriginal admissions to custody (percent change)	Number of Aboriginal admissions to custody (percent change)	Aboriginal admissions as percentage of all admissions
1978-79	76,526	14,576	16
1979-80	78,143 (+2)	13,789 (−5)	15
1980-81	88,334 (+13)	14,380 (+4)	14
1981-82	95,590 (+8)	16,868 (+17)	15
1982-83	111,598 (+17)	19,693 (+17)	15
1983-84	110,286 (−1)	19,462 (<1)	15
1984-85	102,730 (7)	21,041 (+1)	17
1985-86	99,019 (−4)	20,280 (−4)	17
1986-87	96,503 (−3)	19,766 (−3)	17
1987-88	96,147 (<1)	21,227 (+7)	18
1988-89	93,770 (−2)	21,995 (+4)	19
1989-90	94, 394 (<1)	20,720 (−6)	18
1990-91	93,541 (<1)	21,293 (+3)	19
1991-92	57,829 (−38)	17,998 (−15)	17
1992-93	61,777 (+7)	18,106 (+1)	17
1993-94	98,754 (+60)	21,035 (+16)	17
1994-95	97,968 (−1)	19,970 (−5)	16
1995-96	95,663 (−2)	18,899 (−5)	16
1996-97	90,700 (−5)	17,297 (−8)	16
1997-98	83,754 (−8)	14,874 (−14)	15
1998-99	77,322 (−8)	15,723 (+6)	17
1999-00	69,309 (−10)	15,560 (−1)	18
2000-01	65,579 (−5)	15,349 (−1)	19
2002-03	66,884 (+2)	17,779 (+16)	21
2003-04	64,099 (−4)	17,039 (−4)	21
% Change 1978-79 to 2003-04	−15	+17	

Source: Adapted from J.V. Roberts and R. Melchers, "The Incarceration of Aboriginal Offenders: An Analysis of Trends, 1978-2001" (2003), 45 *Canadian Journal of Criminology and Criminal Justice* 211-42.

Table 16.2 Provincial Variation in Aboriginal Admissions to Custody, 1978-79 and 2003-4*

	Percent of Aboriginal admissions to custody, 1978-79	Percent of Aboriginal admissions to custody, 2003-4
Saskatchewan.....................	61	80
Yukon...........................	51	73
Manitoba	50	68
Alberta..........................	26	39
British Columbia	15	20
Ontario..........................	9	9
Nova Scotia	—	7
Newfoundland and Labrador..........	3	—
Quebec..........................	1	2
Prince Edward Island...............	3	2
Provincial/territorial total............	16	19

* Excludes Nunavut; New Brunswick and Northwest Territories data are unavailable.

Source: Adapted from Statistics Canada, *Adult Correctional Services in Canada, 2003-4* (Ottawa: Statistics Canada, 2005).

40.5 percent in 2003-4, and then back to 34.8 percent in 2005-6. During the same period, the rate for non-Aboriginal prisoners has fluctuated between 40 and 46 percent, but since 1999 has averaged approximately 45 percent each year. The small increase in parole granting may account for some of the increase in the number of Aboriginal offenders supervised in the community as shown in table 16.3. However, the gross number of Aboriginal offenders also includes those on statutory release.

At the end of the day, the overrepresentation problem continues to be substantial and the gap in parole granting between Aboriginal and non-Aboriginal offenders continues to exist. The explanations for both are complex.

Table 16.3   The Number of Aboriginal Offenders Under Federal Jurisdiction Is Increasing

Aboriginal Offenders		Year				
		2001-2	2002-3	2004-5	2004-5	2005-6
Incarcerated						
Atlantic Region	Men	79	90	86	83	75
	Women	5	5	6	3	9
Quebec Region	Men	194	212	202	184	201
	Women	5	6	5	3	3
Ontario Region	Men	297	304	289	290	296
	Women	6	14	11	11	12
Prairie Region	Men	1,175	1,212	1,202	1,213	1,268
	Women	71	64	66	69	85
Pacific Region	Men	384	391	414	426	405
	Women	11	15	20	14	19
National Total	Men	2,129	2,209	2,193	2,196	2,245
	Women	98	104	108	100	128
	Total	2,227	2,313	2,301	2,296	2,373
Community						
Atlantic Region	Men	28	24	27	31	33
	Women	3	2	1	5	8
Quebec Region	Men	59	57	84	67	82
	Women	0	0	2	2	3
Ontario Region	Men	103	104	117	112	109
	Women	11	10	10	10	9
Prairie Region	Men	578	551	573	598	605
	Women	58	54	48	57	66
Pacific Region	Men	184	184	208	186	212
	Women	6	6	10	17	14
National Total	Men	952	920	1,009	994	1,041
	Women	78	72	71	91	100
	Total	1,030	992	1,080	1,085	1,141
Total Incarcerated & Community		3,257	3,305	3,381	3,381	3,514

Source: Correctional Service of Canada.

CHAPTER SEVENTEEN

Appeals

I. INTRODUCTION

In sentencing, as in all other matters, there is no right of appeal unless it is specifically provided by statute. The *Criminal Code* makes provision in Part XXI for appeals against sentence in indictable cases and in Part XXVII for appeals in summary conviction matters.

The first part of this chapter reviews basic principles relating to appeals against sentence as set out in the Code and in the jurisprudence of the Supreme Court of Canada. This review is somewhat skeletal, not least because as "a matter of established practice and sound policy" (*Proulx*, [2000] 1 SCR 61, para. 2) the Supreme Court infrequently hears appeals in sentencing matters. Thus the first part presents a formal sketch of the framework for sentencing appeals. The second part examines some practical considerations that arise in these matters.

The function of appellate courts is to correct error and provide guidance for lower courts. As in other matters, however, this general proposition allows for different perspectives. A judge or a court that takes a wide view of error or the need for guidance will intervene more frequently to disturb in some way the judgment of the lower court. Proponents of this view believe that the ultimate function of the appellate court is to ensure that justice is done in the case and thus the threshold of appellate intervention is flexible. Another judge or court might take a narrower view of the role of appellate intervention. From this perspective deference to the conclusion of the trial court is an important principle of restraint that justifies appellate intervention only where that conclusion is conspicuously anomalous.

These two perspectives are caricatures to some extent. They do not describe categories that can be easily contrasted— for example, as between liberal activism and conservative restraint. The jurisprudence is replete with examples that run in both directions and indeed with examples that seem to run in both directions at once. An important theme that runs through this chapter is the threshold for appellate intervention in sentencing matters and the extent to which appellate courts should substitute a different order for that imposed at first instance.

On a sentencing appeal there is only one question at issue: was the sentence fit? If it is not fit, it calls for correction.

II. GENERAL PRINCIPLES

A. Role of Appellate Courts

Typically, at the beginning of a considered judgment in a sentencing matter, it is common-place to find a paragraph such as this:

> An appellate court should not interfere with a sentence unless it is demonstrably unfit, or there
> has been an error in principle, a failure to consider a relevant factor, consideration of improper
> factors, or an overemphasis of the appropriate factors: *R v. M. (C.A.)* [1996] 1 SCR 500 at para.
> 90; *R v. McDonnell* [1997] 1 SCR 948 at para. 46. A sentence will be demonstrably unfit if it
> is clearly unreasonable, or is a substantial and marked departure from the sentences customar-
> ily imposed for similar offenders committing similar crimes: *R v. Shropshire*, [1995] 4 SCR
> 227 at para. 46; *R v. M. (C.A.)*, *supra* at para. 92. An error in principle, a failure to consider a
> relevant factor, consideration of improper factors, or an overemphasis of appropriate factors
> are grounds that give rise to appellate review for reasons of inconsistency.

As will be seen below, there are other grounds that will attract appellate review, but a passage such as this restates basic points about the substantive reasons for appellate inter-vention with the terms of a sentence. The appellate court should be reluctant to intervene and the appellant, correspondingly, must persuade the court that there is a good reason to intervene. In *McDonnell*, below, Sopinka J reviewed the approach to follow. Consider closely what the Supreme Court said about this deferential standard of appellate review.

R v. McDonnell
[1997] 1 SCR 948

SOPINKA J: ...

[15] Two recent cases, *R v. Shropshire*, [1995] 4 SCR 227, and *R v. M. (C.A.)*, [1996] 1 SCR 500, set out the applicable standard of review of sentencing decisions. Iacobucci J, writing for the Court, stated in *Shropshire* at paras. 45-50:

Section 687(1) reads as follows:

> 687(1) Where an appeal is taken against sentence, the court of appeal shall, unless
> the sentence is one fixed by law, consider the *fitness* of the sentence appealed against,
> and may on such evidence, if any, as it thinks fit to require or to receive,
>
>   (*a*) vary the sentence within the limits prescribed by law for the offence of
> which the accused was convicted; or
>   (*b*) dismiss the appeal.

The question, then, is whether a consideration of the "fitness" of a sentence incorpo-rates the very interventionist appellate review propounded by Lambert JA. With respect, I find that it does not. An appellate court should not be given free reign to modify a sen-tencing order simply because it feels that a different order ought to have been made. The formulation of a sentencing order is a profoundly subjective process; the trial judge has the advantage of having seen and heard all of the witnesses whereas the appellate court can only base itself upon a written record. A variation in the sentence should only be made if the court of appeal is convinced it is not fit. That is to say, that it has found the sentence to be clearly unreasonable.

I would adopt the approach taken by the Nova Scotia Court of Appeal in the cases of *R v. Pepin* (1990), 98 NSR (2d) 238, and *R v. Muise* (1994), 94 CCC (3d) 119. In *Pepin*, at p. 251, it was held that:

> ... in considering whether a sentence should be altered, the test is not whether we would have imposed a different sentence; we must determine if the sentencing judge applied wrong principles or (if) the sentence is clearly or manifestly excessive.

Further, in *Muise* it was held at pp. 123-24 that:

> In considering the fitness of a sentence imposed by a trial judge, this court has consistently held that it will not interfere unless the sentence imposed is clearly excessive or inadequate. ...
>
> • • •
>
> The law on sentence appeals is not complex. If a sentence imposed is not clearly excessive or inadequate it is a fit sentence assuming the trial judge applied the correct principles and considered all relevant facts. ... My view is premised on the reality that sentencing is not an exact science; it is anything but. It is the exercise of judgment taking into consideration relevant legal principles, the circumstances of the offence and the offender. The most that can be expected of a sentencing judge is to arrive at a sentence that is within an acceptable range. In my opinion, that is the true basis upon which Courts of Appeal review sentences when the only issue is whether the sentence is inadequate or excessive.
>
> • • •
>
> Unreasonableness in the sentencing process involves the sentencing order falling outside the "acceptable range" of orders; this clearly does not arise in the present appeal. An error of law involves a situation such as that found in *R v. Chaisson*, [1995] 2 SCR 1118, in which a sentencing judge, while calculating the total time period of incarceration for the purposes of a "half-time" parole ineligibility order under s. 741.2 of the *Code*, erroneously included two offences in the calculations notwithstanding the fact that these specific offences were not listed in the schedule of offences to which the s. 741.2 orders apply. [Emphasis in original.]

[16] The deferential approach set out in *Shropshire* was confirmed and refined in *M. (C.A.)*. In that case, Lamer CJ, on behalf of the Court, stated at paras. 90-92:

> Put simply, absent an error in principle, failure to consider a relevant factor, or an overemphasis of the appropriate factors, a court of appeal should only intervene to vary a sentence imposed at trial if the sentence is demonstrably unfit. Parliament explicitly vested sentencing judges with a *discretion* to determine the appropriate degree and kind of punishment under the *Criminal Code*. As s. 717(1) reads:
>
> > 717(1) Where an enactment prescribes different degrees or kinds of punishment in respect of an offence, the punishment to be imposed is, subject to the limitations prescribed in the enactment, in the *discretion* of the court that convicts the person who commits the offence.

This deferential standard of review has profound functional justifications. As Iacobucci J explained in *Shropshire*, at para. 46, where the sentencing judge has had the benefit of presiding over the trial of the offender, he or she will have had the comparative advantage of having seen and heard the witnesses to the crime. But in the absence of a full trial, where the offender has pleaded guilty to an offence and the sentencing judge has only enjoyed the benefit of oral and written sentencing submissions (as was the case in both *Shropshire* and this instance), the argument in favour of deference remains compelling. A sentencing judge still enjoys a position of advantage over an appellate judge in being able to directly assess the sentencing submissions of both the Crown and the offender. A sentencing judge also possesses the unique qualifications of experience and judgment from having served on the front lines of our criminal justice system. Perhaps most importantly, the sentencing judge will normally preside near or within the community which has suffered the consequences of the offender's crime. As such, the sentencing judge will have a strong sense of the particular blend of sentencing goals that will be "just and appropriate" for the protection of that community. The determination of a just and appropriate sentence is a delicate art which attempts to balance carefully the societal goals of sentencing against the moral blameworthiness of the offender and the circumstances of the offence, while at all times taking into account the needs and current conditions of and in the community. The discretion of a sentencing judge should thus not be interfered with lightly.

Appellate courts, of course, serve an important function in reviewing and minimizing the disparity of sentences imposed by sentencing judges for similar offenders and similar offences committed throughout Canada. ... But in exercising this role, courts of appeal must still exercise a margin of deference before intervening in the specialized discretion that Parliament has explicitly vested in sentencing judges. It has been repeatedly stressed that there is no such thing as a uniform sentence for a particular crime. ... Sentencing is an inherently individualized process, and the search for a single appropriate sentence for a similar offender and a similar crime will frequently be a fruitless exercise of academic abstraction. As well, sentences for a particular offence should be expected to vary to some degree across various communities and regions in this country, as the "just and appropriate" mix of accepted sentencing goals will depend on the needs and current conditions of and in the particular community where the crime occurred. For these reasons, consistent with the general standard of review we articulated in *Shropshire*, I believe that a court of appeal should only intervene to minimize the disparity of sentences where the sentence imposed by the trial judge is in substantial and marked departure from the sentences customarily imposed for similar offenders committing similar crimes. [Emphasis in original.]

[17] I have included extensive references to these cases because in my view they are highly significant to the case at bar. *M. (C.A.)* set out that, in the absence of an error of principle, failure to consider a relevant factor, or overemphasis of the appropriate factors, a sentence should only be overturned if the sentence is demonstrably unfit. The respondent submitted that the sentencing judge in the present case failed to consider relevant factors and that the sentence was demonstrably unfit. Moreover, both the respondent and the Court of Appeal appear to have treated the failure of the sentencing judge to characterize the offence as a major sexual assault as an error in principle. I will discuss these contentions in turn.

...

[46] In my opinion, the decision to order concurrent or consecutive sentences should be treated with the same deference owed by appellate courts to sentencing judges concerning the length of sentences ordered. The rationale for deference with respect to the length of sentence, clearly stated in both *Shropshire* and *M. (C.A.)*, applies equally to the decision to order concurrent or consecutive sentences. In both setting duration and the type of sentence, the sentencing judge exercises his or her discretion based on his or her first-hand knowledge of the case; it is not for an appellate court to intervene absent an error in principle, unless the sentencing judge ignored factors or imposed a sentence which, considered in its entirety, is demonstrably unfit. The Court of Appeal in the present case failed to raise a legitimate reason to alter the order of concurrent sentences made by the sentencing judge; the court simply disagreed with the result of the sentencing judge's exercise of discretion, which is insufficient to interfere.

Since *Shropshire*, *M.(C.A.)*, and *McDonnell*, the restrictive and deferential approach approved by the Supreme Court remains settled law. As suggested above, this trilogy of cases is routinely cited by appellate courts. Despite this consistency in the law, it must be recalled that the line between the margin for deference and the margin of reversible error is not always consistently drawn.

Layered over, under, and all around this policy of deference are the challenging and Byzantine principles relating to standards of appellate review, which apply in theory with the same vigour and coherence in sentencing appeals as in any other area. These principles, distilled to their essential elements, are as follows. Appellate intervention is justified if the court finds palpable and overriding error on a question of fact, but on a question of law the standard is correctness. On a question of mixed fact and law, it depends: correctness if there is some extricable question that is chiefly a question of law and palpable and overriding error if it is chiefly a question of fact. In short, appellate intervention is justified either to set the instant case right due to a serious error of fact or to set the law right for the instant case and future cases due to an error of law—or both.

B. Jurisdiction

With respect to indictable offences, the rights of appeal for the accused and the Crown are set out in ss. 675 and 676, respectively. In those sections, the Code refers specifically to a "sentence." In addition to orders relating to the more conspicuous sentencing options, s. 673 defines a "sentence" to include various other orders and dispositions. Rights of appeal against sentence in summary conviction matters are provided in s. 813 and, although there is no analogue to s. 673 in Part XXVII, that definition is applicable *mutatis mutandis*. Where an indictable offence is tried with a summary conviction offence, an appeal against sentence on the latter may be taken under Part XXI.

Summary conviction appeals may be taken as of right to the "appeal court," which is defined by the Code as the superior court of the province or territory. In indictable matters, all appeals against sentence require leave of the Court of Appeal or a judge of that court. In several jurisdictions it is standard practice for the leave application and the appeal to be heard together. In others, the application is presented to a single judge who decides whether the case should be heard by a panel of the court.

The Supreme Court of Canada may hear sentencing appeals on a question of law or on a question of general importance. Although it has said in *Gardiner* and *Proulx* that it will rarely hear such cases, the language of s. 40(1) of the *Supreme Court Act* gives the Court a broad discretion to consider sentencing appeals.

Appellate review is essential to ensure the fitness of sentences, but an appellate court cannot interfere with a sentence unless it is properly seized of an appeal against sentence. On an appeal against conviction, for example, the court cannot open a question about the fitness of sentence. See *W. (G.)*, [1999] 3 SCR 597. It remains to be seen whether this principle applies with equal force in cases where the accused represents herself before the appellate court. To take an extreme example, suppose that the accused acts for herself on appeal against conviction, but it is transparently clear to the appellate court that the sentence was not only wrong in principle but also illegal. Would it not be appropriate for the court to suggest that the appellant be granted an extension of time in which to consider filing an appeal against sentence?

C. Powers

The most important power affecting the conduct of sentencing appeals is the discretion to admit fresh evidence, which is found in ss. 683 and 687. As a general rule on appeals of any kind, fresh evidence refers to relevant information that was not available to be produced at first instance through the exercise of due diligence. The admissibility of such evidence is governed by the principles stated by the Supreme Court in *Palmer*, [1980] 1 SCR 759. The same principles apply in sentencing appeals.

R v. Lévesque
[2000] 2 SCR 487

GONTHIER J:

I. Issue

[1] This appeal concerns the rule that applies to the admission of fresh evidence on appeal from a sentence. In *Palmer v. The Queen*, [1980] 1 SCR 759, this Court set out the principles governing the admission of fresh evidence on appeal from a verdict. In the case at bar, it must be determined whether the criteria that apply are the same for both types of appeal, and whether the majority of the Court of Appeal erred by admitting in evidence the two expert reports tendered by the respondent, despite the objections of the appellant.

II. Facts

[2] On June 22, 1996, the respondent and his two accomplices went to the home of the Fortier family intending to make off with large amounts of money that he believed were kept in a safe. While these three individuals were in the shed located behind the house, they were surprised by David Fortier, aged thirteen. After grabbing him and tying him up, the respondent questioned him about the location of the safe and the people who were in the house. He put a shotgun cartridge in his mouth, which he then taped shut, and threatened him several times, both verbally and with his gun. The respondent then left the shed, taking David, with his gun pointed at the boy's head, and escorted him towards the house. The two accomplices followed. Once the respondent was inside the house, he attacked Bertrand Fortier, David's father, as he sat watching television with his wife. A fight broke out and a shot was fired in the fray. While this was going on, the two accomplices fled and one of the Fortier boys called the police. Mr. Fortier ultimately wrestled the respondent to the ground and the police arrived shortly afterward.

[3] On December 18, 1996, the respondent pleaded guilty to fifteen counts arising from the events of June 22, 1996. In appealing his sentence, the respondent is seeking to have three new reports admitted in evidence. The first, dated April 3, 1997, is entitled [TRANSLATION] "Psychological/psychiatric assessment report." This report was prepared by Marc Daigle, a psychologist, for Correctional Service Canada. The second report was written by Louis Morissette, a psychiatrist, at the respondent's request. It is dated March 17, 1998. The appellant objects to the admission of these two reports in evidence, but consents to the admission of the third report, which is by Jacques Bigras, a psychologist. That report is dated March 31, 1998, and was prepared for Correctional Service Canada at the end of a course taken by the respondent during his incarceration.

III. Relevant Legislation

[4] The relevant provisions of the *Criminal Code*, RSC, 1985, c. C-46, are as follows:

683(1) For the purposes of an appeal under this Part, the court of appeal may, where it considers it in the interests of justice,

(a) order the production of any writing, exhibit or other thing connected with the proceedings;

(b) order any witness who would have been a compellable witness at the trial, whether or not he was called at the trial,

(i) to attend and be examined before the court of appeal, or,

(ii) to be examined in the manner provided by rules of court before a judge of the court of appeal, or before any officer of the court of appeal or justice of the peace or other person appointed by the court of appeal for the purpose;

(c) admit, as evidence, an examination that is taken under subparagraph (b)(ii);

(d) receive the evidence, if tendered, of any witness, including the appellant, who is a competent but not compellable witness;

687(1) Where an appeal is taken against sentence, the court of appeal shall, unless the sentence is one fixed by law, consider the fitness of the sentence appealed against, and may on such evidence, if any, as it thinks fit to require or to receive,

(a) vary the sentence within the limits prescribed by law for the offence of which the accused was convicted; or

(b) dismiss the appeal.

IV. Proceedings

A. Court of Québec, Criminal and Penal Division, No. 505-01-008036-960, February 19, 1997

[5] On December 18, 1996, the respondent pleaded guilty to charges of kidnapping, confinement, assault with a weapon, uttering threats, disguise with intent, pointing a firearm, possession of an unregistered restricted weapon, robbery, breaking and entering a dwelling-house, and conspiracy to commit robbery. After the guilty pleas were entered, Judge Yves Lagacé ordered that a pre-sentence report be prepared pursuant to s. 721 of the *Criminal Code*. On February 19, 1997, after hearing submissions from both counsel and the testimony of Bernard Fortier, the accused's brother, the probation officer Philippe David, and the respondent himself, Judge Yves Lagacé sentenced the respondent to several terms of imprisonment to be served concurrently. The longest sentence was imprisonment for a term of ten years and six months on the kidnapping charge.

B. Quebec Court of Appeal, [1998] QJ No. 2680 (QL)

[6] On appeal, the respondent filed two motions seeking leave to adduce fresh evidence, in the form of the reports by Marc Daigle, a psychologist, and Louis Morissette, a psychiatrist. On April 6, 1998, a panel of three judges of the Court of Appeal (Beauregard, Gendreau and Baudouin JJA) referred that request to the panel that would determine the application to appeal the sentence.

[7] These motions were heard by Deschamps, Chamberland and Nuss JJA on July 8, 1998. They unanimously allowed the application for leave to appeal, since in their view the trial judge had erred by comparing this case with cases involving hostage-taking for ransom in determining the appropriate sentence. That finding is not in issue in this appeal. The majority of the Court of Appeal also allowed the motions to adduce fresh evidence, Chamberland JA. dissenting.

1. DESCHAMPS JA (NUSS JA concurring)

[8] After stating that the principles laid down in *Palmer, supra*, are to be applied more flexibly in criminal cases than in civil cases, and that the provisions governing the admission of fresh evidence on appeal are different, depending on whether the Court is ruling in respect of a verdict (s. 683 of the *Criminal Code*) or a sentence (s. 687 of the *Criminal Code*), Deschamps JA said that a liberal approach must be taken on an appeal from a sentence when the admissibility of fresh evidence is in dispute. At para. 12, she concluded: [TRANSLATION] "while the two sections [ss. 683 and 687 of the *Criminal*

Code] do not establish different rules, it is my view that at the very least the wording of s. 687 prescribes a flexible and liberal approach."

[9] Deschamps JA was of the opinion that the report prepared by the psychologist, Marc Daigle, met the requirements for admissibility. She noted that the appellant did not ask to have this assessment done and that the report was written less than two months after the probation officer's report, which was submitted to the trial judge. In addition, the report could not have been tendered at trial, since the psychological assessment takes place after sentencing. She says at para. 15:

[TRANSLATION] While it is true that the appellant could have requested a separate expert opinion following receipt of the pre-sentence report, I cannot criticize him for failing to do so since, first, the appellant could not have foreseen that Mr. Daigle would have had an opinion diametrically opposed to that of Mr. David and, second, that would amount to encouraging competing expert opinions in cases where accused persons are dissatisfied with pre-sentence reports.

Ultimately, Deschamps JA felt that it was in the interests of justice to admit the psychologist's report by Mr. Daigle in evidence, since [TRANSLATION] "it explains the appellant's past in greater detail and shows his personality from a perspective that was not evident in the trial record. Whereas the pre-sentence report refers to a significant probability of reoffending, the psychologist's report by Mr. Daigle states the opposite" (para. 16).

[10] According to Deschamps JA, the admissibility of the report prepared by the psychiatrist, Dr. Morissette, was more debatable. She commented that the report was prepared at the respondent's request and that thirteen months had intervened between sentencing and the preparation of the report. She also stated that the portion of the report in which Dr. Morissette responded to the probation officer's report did not carry much weight. Nonetheless, she determined that the report was admissible, since it shed additional light on Mr. Daigle's report.

[11] In view of the error committed by the trial judge and in light of the fresh evidence, Deschamps JA substituted a sentence of five and a half years for the sentence of ten and a half years imposed by Judge Lagacé.

2. CHAMBERLAND JA (dissenting)

[12] In the view of Chamberland JA, the reports by Mr. Daigle and Dr. Morissette should not be admitted in evidence. It was his opinion that the respondent, by exercising minimal diligence, could have sought other opinions for the purpose of countering the probation officer's opinion concerning his personality and submitted them to the trial judge. At para. 31 he stated:

[TRANSLATION] I appreciate that the provisions governing fresh evidence differ depending whether the Court is being asked to rule as to guilt (section 683 Cr. C.) or the sentence (section 687 Cr. C.) but not, in my view, to the point that the Court must, unless there are completely exceptional circumstances (which are not found in the case at bar) or unless, of course, the other party consents, admit evidence that was readily available at trial (*R v.*

Stolar, [1988] 1 SCR 480; *Palmer and Palmer v. R.*, [1980] 1 SCR 759). In short, it is my view that the present adversarial debate concerning the appellant's personality should have been conducted at trial rather than on appeal.

[13] In view of the error committed by the trial judge in sentencing, Chamberland JA would have substituted a sentence of imprisonment for eight years and six months for the sentence imposed by Judge Lagacé. He allowed the motion to submit fresh evidence for the sole purpose of admitting in evidence the report by Jacques Bigras, the psychologist.

V. Analysis

A. The Criteria Laid Down in Palmer

[14] In *Palmer*, *supra*, this Court considered the discretion of a court of appeal to admit fresh evidence pursuant to s. 610 of the *Criminal Code*, the predecessor of s. 683. After emphasizing that, in accordance with the wording of s. 610, the overriding consideration must be "the interests of justice," McIntyre J set out the applicable principles, at p. 775:

> (1) The evidence should generally not be admitted if, by due diligence, it could have been adduced at trial provided that this general principle will not be applied as strictly in a criminal case as in civil cases: see *McMartin v. The Queen*.
>
> (2) The evidence must be relevant in the sense that it bears upon a decisive or potentially decisive issue in the trial.
>
> (3) The evidence must be credible in the sense that it is reasonably capable of belief, and
>
> (4) It must be such that if believed it could reasonably, when taken with the other evidence adduced at trial, be expected to have affected the result.

In *R v. M. (P.S.)* (1992), 77 CCC (3d) 402 (Ont. CA), at p. 410, Doherty JA wrote the following concerning these principles:

> The last three criteria are conditions precedent to the admission of evidence on appeal. Indeed, the second and third form part of the broader qualitative analysis required by the fourth consideration. The first criterion, due diligence, is not a condition precedent to the admissibility of "fresh" evidence in criminal appeals, but is a factor to be considered in deciding whether the interests of justice warrant the admission of the evidence: *McMartin v. The Queen*, [[1964] SCR 484], at pp. 148-50; *R v. Palmer*, *supra*, at p. 205.

In my view this is a good description of the way in which ... the principles set out in *Palmer* interact.

[15] This court was recently asked to apply these criteria in *R v. Warsing*, [1998] 3 SCR 579. In that case, the British Columbia Court of Appeal determined that the accused had not satisfied the due diligence criterion and refused to admit fresh evidence. At para. 51, Major J, for the majority, pointed out that due diligence is only one factor and its absence, particularly in criminal cases, should be assessed in light of other circumstances. In other words, failure to meet the due diligence criterion should not be

used to deny admission of fresh evidence on appeal if that evidence is compelling and it is in the interests of justice to admit it.

B. Criteria Applicable to Appeals Against Sentence

[16] Relying on the different wording of ss. 683 and 687 of the *Criminal Code* and the fact that the words used in s. 687, in her view, convey [TRANSLATION] "a much more discretionary connotation" (para. 10), Deschamps JA expressed the view that the rules set out in *Palmer* are to be applied more flexibly in an appeal from a sentence. With respect, I do not share that view. Although the rules concerning sources and types of evidence are more flexible in respect of sentence, the criteria for admitting fresh evidence on appeal are the same, regardless of whether the appeal relates to a verdict or a sentence.

[17] For purposes of comparison, I will reproduce again the relevant passages of ss. 683 and 687 of the *Criminal Code*:

683(1) For the purposes of an appeal under this Part, the court of appeal may, *where it considers it in the interests of justice*, ...

687(1) Where an appeal is taken against sentence, the court of appeal shall, unless the sentence is one fixed by law, consider the fitness of the sentence appealed against, and may on such evidence, if any, *as it thinks fit to require or to receive*, ... [Emphasis added.]

At first glance, it seems to me that the applicable criterion is not different: see *R v. Hogan* (1979), 50 CCC (2d) 439 (NSCA), at p. 449; and *R v. Edwards* (1996), 105 CCC (3d) 21 (Ont. CA), at p. 27. If a court of appeal thinks *fit* to admit fresh evidence, it will do so because it is *in the interests of justice* to admit it. Furthermore, I do not see how the discretion conferred on courts of appeal by s. 687 could be broader than the discretion conferred by s. 683 since, if such were the case, courts of appeal could exercise their discretion in a manner contrary to the interests of justice. However, it is assumed that the legislator did not intend statutes to apply in a way contrary to justice: P.-A. Côté, *The Interpretation of Legislation in Canada* (2nd ed. 1991), at p. 373. Like McIntyre J in *Palmer*, *supra*, at p. 775, I believe that the overriding consideration must be the interests of justice, regardless of whether the appeal is from a verdict or a sentence.

[18] In any case, it is my belief that the criteria stated by this Court in *Palmer* already call for a relaxed and flexible application and could hardly be relaxed any further. In accordance with the last three criteria, a court of appeal may admit only evidence that is relevant and credible, and could reasonably, when taken with the other evidence adduced at trial, be expected to have affected the result. If these criteria were made more flexible, it would be open to a court of appeal to accept evidence that was not relevant or credible, and that could not reasonably, when taken with the other evidence adduced at trial, be expected to have affected the result to which they led at trial. In my view, it would serve no purpose and be contrary to the interests of justice to introduce this kind of flexibility.

[19] Failure to satisfy the first criterion, due diligence, is not always fatal. As Major J said in *Warsing*, *supra*, at para. 51:

It is desirable that due diligence remain only one factor and its absence, particularly in criminal cases, should be assessed in light of other circumstances. If the evidence is compelling and the interests of justice require that it be admitted then the failure to meet the test should yield to permit its admission.

This passage clearly shows that the due diligence criterion must be applied flexibly. In my view, it is not necessary to make it more flexible in the context of appeals from sentence. While due diligence is not a necessary prerequisite for the admission of fresh evidence on appeal, it is an important factor that must be taken into account in determining whether it is in the interests of justice to admit or exclude fresh evidence. As Doherty JA said in *M. (P.S.)*, *supra*, at p. 411:

> While the failure to exercise due diligence is not determinative, it cannot be ignored in deciding whether to admit "fresh" evidence. The interests of justice referred to in s. 683 of the *Criminal Code* encompass not only an accused's interest in having his or her guilt determined upon all of the available evidence, but also the integrity of the criminal process. Finality and order are essential to that integrity. The criminal justice system is arranged so that the trial will provide the opportunity to the parties to present their respective cases and the appeal will provide the opportunity to challenge the correctness of what happened at the trial. Section 683(1)(d) of the *Code* recognizes that the appellate function can be expanded in exceptional cases, but it cannot be that the appellate process should be used routinely to augment the trial record. Were it otherwise, the finality of the trial process would be lost and cases would be retried on appeal whenever more evidence was secured by a party prior to the hearing of the appeal. For this reason, the exceptional nature of the admission of "fresh" evidence on appeal has been stressed: *McMartin v. The Queen*, *supra*, at p. 148.
>
> The due diligence criterion is designed to preserve the integrity of the process and it must be accorded due weight in assessing the admissibility of "fresh" evidence on appeal.

In my view, these considerations are equally relevant in the context of an appeal from sentence. Accordingly, due diligence in producing fresh evidence is a factor that must be taken into account in an appeal from sentence, on the same basis as the other three criteria set out in *Palmer*.

[20] While the admission of fresh evidence in an appeal from a sentence cannot lead to a new trial, unlike admission of fresh evidence in an appeal from a verdict (see the wording of ss. 687 and 683 of the *Criminal Code*), I do not believe that this difference justifies the application of different tests. The integrity of the criminal process and the role of appeal courts could be jeopardized by the routine admission of fresh evidence on appeal, since this would create a two-tier sentencing system. That kind of system would be incompatible with the high standard of review applicable to appeals from sentences and the underlying "profound functional justifications": see *R v. M. (C.A.)*, [1996] 1 SCR 500, at para. 91. Despite the fresh evidence, the sentencing judge, unlike the appeal judge, has the benefit of being able to directly assess the other evidence, the testimony and the submissions of the parties, as well as being familiar with the needs and current conditions of and in the community where the crime was committed: see *M. (C.A.)*, *supra*, at para. 91. Furthermore, appeal courts are not the appropriate forum in which to determine questions of fact, and they should do so only when the fresh evidence presents certain characteristics such as would justify expanding their traditional

role. This Court has already identified those characteristics, in *Palmer*. In my view, whether the appeal relates to a verdict or a sentence, the criteria laid down by this Court in *Palmer* are the criteria that are to be applied where a court of appeal is determining whether to admit fresh evidence.

[21] In addition to citing the different wording of ss. 683 and 687 of the *Criminal Code*, Deschamps JA refers to cases decided in other provinces. A number of courts of appeal have considered the issue of admission of fresh evidence on an appeal from a sentence: see *R v. Lockwood* (1971), 5 CCC (2d) 438 (Ont. CA); *Hogan, supra*; *R v. Irwin* (1979), 48 CCC (2d) 423 (Alta. CA); *R v. Langille*, (1987), 77 NSR (2d) 224 (CA); *R v. Archibald* (1992), 15 BCAC 301; *R v. Lemay* (1998), 127 CCC 528 (3d) (Que. CA); *R v. Gauthier*, [1996] QJ No. 952 (QL) (CA); *R v. McDow* (1996), 147 NSR (2d) 343 (CA); *Edwards, supra*; *R v. Riley* (1996), 107 CCC (3d) 278 (NSCA); and *R v. Mesgun* (1997), 121 CCC (3d) 439 (Ont. CA). Some courts of appeal have maintained that the criteria to be applied are the same, whether the appeal relates to a verdict or a sentence: see *Hogan, supra*, at p. 449, and *Edwards, supra*, at p. 27. Others have stated that the rules relating to the admission of fresh evidence were applied more flexibly or informally in the context of an appeal from a sentence: see *Hogan, supra*, at p. 453; *Langille, supra*; *Edwards, supra*, at p. 28; and *Riley, supra*, at p. 283. However, a careful review of the jurisprudence reveals that, far from applying different criteria, courts of appeal have invariably applied the criteria set out in *Palmer*, whether expressly or by implication (for examples of the application of the due diligence criterion, see *Lockwood, Hogan, Irwin, Langille, Edwards* and *Mesgun*; for examples of the application of the relevance criterion, see *Edwards* and *Lemay*; and for an example of the application of the criteria relating to credibility and effect on the result, see *Langille*). In addition, as I have already explained, it is neither desirable nor really possible to relax the rule laid down in *Palmer*, in view of its inherent flexibility and the requirements associated with the interests of justice.

[22] I therefore find that the criteria set out in *Palmer* are applicable to applications to tender fresh evidence in an appeal from a sentence. Before applying these criteria to the two reports in the case at bar, I believe it is worthwhile to briefly discuss the concepts of admissibility and probative value in the context of the admission of fresh evidence on appeal, as well as certain specific characteristics of the sentencing process.

· · ·

[28] To summarize, the probative value of fresh evidence must be considered in order to determine whether it is admissible on appeal. To facilitate determination of the probative value of fresh evidence, it is desirable that it be tested by the party challenging it. For this purpose, that party should make a formal motion to the court of appeal and explain how it wishes to test the fresh evidence. Failure by a party to test fresh evidence does not relieve a court of appeal from applying the criteria established in *Palmer*.

[29] The application of those criteria in the context of an appeal from a sentence will inevitably be influenced by the specific characteristics of the sentencing process, even though the criteria for the admission of fresh evidence remain fundamentally the same. I will now briefly consider some of these specific characteristics and their interaction with the *Palmer* criteria.

D. Application of the Criteria in the Context of an Appeal Against Sentence

[30] As pointed out by Macdonald JA in *Langille, supra*, the strict rules of a trial do not apply to a sentencing hearing. For example, hearsay evidence may be accepted at the sentencing stage *where found to be credible and trustworthy*: see *R v. Gardiner*, [1982] 2 SCR 368, at p. 414. This relaxation of the rules is explained by the fact that the judge must determine the appropriate sentence for the accused, and to do so must have as much information as possible about him. In my view, the *Palmer* criteria do not compromise the more flexible nature of the rules relating to the sources and types of evidence on which judges may base their sentences. The criteria concerning the admission of fresh evidence on appeal do not relate to the sources and types of evidence and do not demand that the strict rules of a trial apply to fresh evidence proffered on an appeal from a sentence. To be admissible, the fresh evidence need only be relevant and credible and, when taken with the other evidence adduced at trial, be expected to have affected the result. The purpose of the due diligence criterion is to protect the interests and the administration of justice and to preserve the role of appeal courts: see: *M. (P.S.), supra.*

[31] Another specific characteristic of the sentencing process that should be emphasized is the importance of opinion evidence. At the sentencing stage, judges must often consider reports prepared by probation officers, correctional service officers, psychologists or psychiatrists reporting their opinions concerning the personality of the accused, and his or her chances of rehabilitation and risk of reoffending. As I have already noted, the probative value to be assigned to an expert opinion is directly related to the amount and quality of admissible evidence on which it relies: *Lavallee* [[1990] 1 SCR 852], at p. 897. Accordingly, before admitting new opinion evidence on appeal, it may be necessary to determine the basis of that opinion (for example, the version of events relied on by the expert, the documents he or she consulted, and so forth) and to establish whether the facts on which the opinion is based have been proven and are credible.

[32] Quite often, fresh evidence submitted to an appeal court in the context of an appeal from a sentence relates to events subsequent to the sentence, or consists of information from the penitentiary administration relating to an accused's progress in terms of adjustment and rehabilitation: see, for example, *Archibald, Lemay, Gauthier, McDow, Riley* and *Mesgun*. It is frequently the case that the Crown consents to the introduction of this fresh evidence, since the facts reported are seldom controversial: see *Edwards, supra*, at p. 28; *Gauthier, supra*, at para. 14; *McDow, supra*, at para. 18; *Mesgun, supra*, at para. 8; and C. Ruby, *Sentencing* (5th ed. 1999), at p. 607. In the case at bar, the appellant consented to the production of the report by Jacques Bigras, the psychologist. It is important to bear in mind that whether or not consent is given, the production of fresh evidence on appeal is possible only with the leave of the court of appeal: *Hogan, supra*, at p. 448. Evidence relating to events subsequent to the sentence or an accused's rehabilitation process normally meet the due diligence criterion, since by their very nature they were not available at the time of sentencing. However, in order to be found to be admissible, the evidence must also satisfy the other criteria, particularly the criterion relating to the likelihood that the result would be affected. The court of appeal may properly take into account the fact that the Crown has consented or that admission is

uncontested particularly when assessing the relevance, credibility and probative value of fresh evidence.

[33] Having completed my review of the concepts of admissibility and probative value and of the specific characteristics of the sentencing process, I now turn to the application of the *Palmer* criteria to the two reports in question in the instant case.

E. Application to the Case at Bar

[34] In this case, the majority of the Court of Appeal found (at para. 16) that the report by the psychologist, Mr. Daigle, was admissible because it explained the respondent's past in greater detail and showed his personality from a perspective that was not evident in the trial record. The report by the psychiatrist, Dr. Morissette, was admitted in evidence because it shed additional light on Mr. Daigle's report (para. 17). In my opinion, these grounds are inadequate to justify the admission of those two reports, since they could justify the admission of a very broad range of additional evidence on appeal. Furthermore, the admission of any evidence on appeal which merely adds certain details to or clarifies the evidence adduced at trial would be contrary to the *Palmer* criteria and the limited role of appellate courts in respect of sentencing.

[35] In my view, neither of these two reports should have been admitted in evidence. It is worthwhile to reproduce the applicable criteria again, that is, the criteria set out in *Palmer*:

(1) The evidence should generally not be admitted if, by due diligence, it could have been adduced at trial provided that this general principle will not be applied as strictly in a criminal case as in civil cases.

(2) The evidence must be relevant in the sense that it bears upon a decisive or potentially decisive issue relating to the sentence.

(3) The evidence must be credible in the sense that it is reasonably capable of belief.

(4) The evidence must be such that if believed it could reasonably, when taken with the other evidence adduced at trial, be expected to have affected the result.

1. Report by the Psychologist, Mr. Daigle

[36] The report by Mr. Daigle, a psychologist, is relevant in that it expresses opinions regarding the respondent's personality, dangerousness and risk of reoffending. In addition, this report is reasonably capable of belief, particularly in that it was prepared independently and not at the request of the respondent. In addition, it can be concluded that this report satisfies the due diligence criterion. Although Mr. Daigle relied on facts prior to sentencing and the respondent could have sought the opinion of another psychologist concerning his personality and dangerousness, this particular report was not available at the time of sentencing and the respondent could not have obtained it before sentencing. This report was prepared for classification purposes for Correctional Service Canada, while the respondent was at the Regional Reception Centre in Québec.

[37] Despite the foregoing, I find that Mr. Daigle's report should not have been admitted in evidence by the Court of Appeal, since its probative value is not such that if it had been presented to the trial judge it might have affected the result. I note, first, that

Mr. Daigle did not look into the proceedings at trial, did not read the testimony and did not consult the court documents (p. 1 of the report). While he did not prepare his report at the respondent's request, he relied only on his version of the facts. That version portrays the respondent as a victim who did not wish to commit the robbery and was allegedly acting in response to threats by his accomplices (pp. 1-2 of the report). This account makes no mention of the violence and the threats against the child. In addition, according to the report, Bertrand Fortier attacked the respondent rather than the reverse (p. 2 of the report). As well, the respondent told Mr. Daigle that he wanted to commit the robbery in order to win back his former girlfriend (p. 7 of the report).

[38] The version of the facts set out in Mr. Daigle's report differs in quite a few respects from the version given by the respondent under oath at trial. I will point out only the most obvious contradictions: the respondent stated during his testimony that he wanted to commit the robbery to repay a drug debt; that he planned the crime with one of his accomplices; and that he grabbed Bertrand Fortier while he was sitting in the living room.

[39] It is true that the version of the facts set out in Mr. Daigle's report is not wholly inconsistent with the respondent's testimony at trial. In that testimony, the respondent also sought to portray himself as a victim by claiming that he did not want to commit the robbery; that he would have run away if the opportunity had presented itself; and that he was only following the orders of his accomplices when he tied up the Fortier boy, put a cartridge in his mouth and took him hostage. However, the respondent's testimony is confused and full of contradictions, and is also inconsistent with the account given by the Fortier family. The trial judge clearly rejected the respondent's version of the facts. He found that the crime was planned (pp. 4-6 of the reasons) and that the respondent scratched the face of the Fortier boy with his weapon (p. 6 of the reasons) and threatened to kill him several times (p. 4 of the reasons). He also stated, at p. 7 of his reasons:

> [TRANSLATION] Your submissions at the beginning of the sentencing submissions dealt a lot with how you were in fact a victim, I was talking about bad luck just now, we choose our friends, we choose our girlfriends. When something goes wrong, you can't always blame other people.
>
> It is quite clear from an exchange between the trial judge and counsel for the respondent just before sentencing that the judge did not assign much weight to the defence theory that the respondent was a victim in this case.

[40] Mr. Daigle therefore relied on a version of the facts that was not accepted by the trial judge, or on facts that were not established in evidence. Since the probative value of an expert opinion depends on the *amount* and *quality* of admissible evidence on which it relies (*Lavallee, supra*, at p. 897), I find that little probative value can be assigned to the psychologist's report prepared by Mr. Daigle. Having regard to that low probative value and the fact that the trial judge, on passing sentence, stressed the seriousness of the offences committed by the respondent rather than his personality, I am of the view that Mr. Daigle's report would not have affected the result if it had been introduced at trial with the other evidence. Accordingly, the Court of Appeal should not have admitted it in evidence, since it does not meet the *Palmer* criteria.

2. Report by the Psychiatrist, Dr. Morissette

[41] The report prepared by Dr. Morissette, a psychiatrist, does not meet the due diligence criterion. It is dated March 17, 1998, that is, more than a year after sentencing. Unlike the report by the psychologist, Mr. Daigle, Dr. Morissette's opinion was solicited by the respondent. I agree with Chamberland JA that the respondent, by exercising minimal diligence, could have sought this opinion before sentence was passed and submitted Dr. Morissette's report to the trial judge for the purpose of countering the probation officer's opinion concerning his personality (see *Mesgun*, *supra*, at para. 8).

[42] Nonetheless, failure to meet the due diligence criterion is not always fatal: *Warsing*, *supra*, at para. 51. It is therefore necessary to consider the other three criteria set out in *Palmer* in order to determine whether their strength is such that failure to satisfy the due diligence requirement is overborne: *R v. McAnespie*, [1993] 4 SCR 501, at pp. 502-3.

[43] Like the psychologist's report prepared by Mr. Daigle, the psychiatrist's report written by Dr. Morissette is relevant, since it communicates an opinion concerning the respondent's personality, danger to others and risk of reoffending. Furthermore, there is nothing to indicate that it is not reasonably capable of belief, even though it was prepared at the respondent's request. However, its probative value is low. Like the psychologist, Mr. Daigle, Dr. Morissette based his opinion on a version of the facts that was not established or adopted at trial. Although he reviewed the report prepared by the probation officer, he does not seem to have read the testimony or consulted the trial transcript. His description of the events of June 22, 1996, is very brief and does not reflect the seriousness of the offences committed or the violence employed. Furthermore, the respondent gave Dr. Morissette an explanation that was completely different from the explanation he gave under oath in respect of his participation in the events. At p. 15 of the report we read:

> [TRANSLATION] Mr. Lévesque now explains that at the time of his arrest and when he arrived at the penitentiary, he did not to want to say that he had committed a robbery for a woman … , he did not want to say that he was so dependent on a woman that he would commit a robbery … . He felt that it would look "better" if he explained the reason for his robbery in terms of a drug debt. He is now telling us that he never had a drug debt, that he never cheated a drug dealer. According to his explanation, the only purpose of the robbery was financial gain in order to impress Francine, since Mr. Lévesque felt that if he had more money she might come back to him.

In addition, none of the details of the respondent's love life referred to by Dr. Morissette were established in evidence at trial. Thus, for the reasons I stated concerning the psychologist's report by Mr. Daigle, I find that the psychiatrist's report by Dr. Morissette is of little probative value and would not have affected the result if it had been adduced at trial with the other evidence.

[44] In my view, as in *McAnespie*, *supra*, at pp. 502-3, "the strength of the other factors is *not* such that failure to satisfy the due diligence requirement in this case is overborne by the other factors" (emphasis in original). Accordingly, the report by the psychiatrist, Dr. Morissette, should not have been admitted in evidence on appeal.

VI. Disposition

[45] For the foregoing reasons, I would allow the appeal, set aside the judgment of the Court of Appeal of Quebec and, for the reasons stated by Chamberland JA, substitute a sentence of imprisonment for eight years and six months for the sentence imposed by the trial judge.

The following are the reasons delivered by

[46] ARBOUR J (dissenting): I have had the benefit of the reasons of my colleague, Justice Gonthier, on this appeal. With respect, on the very particular facts of this case, I believe that the majority of the Court of Appeal was entitled to admit the reports prepared respectively by Marc Daigle and Dr. Louis Morissette. Here, the trial judge fundamentally mischaracterized the principal crime, of which the respondent had been convicted, in determining the just and appropriate sentence, with the result that the Court of Appeal was, for all intents and purposes, required to sentence afresh. In these specific circumstances, it was for the Court of Appeal to equip itself, pursuant to its broad statutory discretion under s. 683(1) of the *Criminal Code*, RSC, 1985, c. C-46, with whatever evidence it deemed fit and necessary to decide the question of sentence. Accordingly, I would dismiss the appeal.

[47] I am in general agreement with the statement of the law governing the admission of fresh evidence in appeals against sentence, provided by my colleague at paras. 16-22 of his opinion. However, in view of the fundamental error committed by the trial judge, I do not believe that the principles articulated by Gonthier J are germane to the disposition of this appeal. I must also emphatically disagree with Gonthier J that *R v. Lavallee*, [1990] 1 SCR 852 (*per* Wilson J), applies as stringently as he suggests in the sentencing context.

[48] The Court of Appeal was unanimous that the trial judge erred in concluding that kidnapping for ransom was the dominant offence committed by the respondent. There is no challenge before us to the unanimous conclusion of the Court of Appeal that robbery was the central, predominant offence, the hostage-taking being merely [TRANSLATION] "ancillary to the main criminal operation carried out by the [respondent] and his cohorts" ([1998] QJ No. 2680 (QL), at para. 35).

[49] The trial judge's initial error in identifying kidnapping as the [TRANSLATION] "central matter alleged" against the respondent, which he described as [TRANSLATION] "one of the most serious crimes in the *Criminal Code* … right after murder" (see CQ, No. 505-01-008036-960, February 19, 1997, at p. 2), tainted his entire analysis, and produced a sentence that did not accurately reflect the circumstances of the offence. The Court of Appeal's task was thus not simply to assess the fitness of the sentence imposed at first instance, and, to this end, to determine the admissibility of the reports tendered by the respondent as fresh evidence on appeal. Instead, having set aside the sentence, the Court of Appeal was required to intervene essentially for the purpose of sentencing the respondent anew. In these circumstances, I believe that the Court of Appeal was entitled to consider what it deemed to be evidence relevant to the exercise of determining a just and appropriate sentence. Like a sentencing judge, a court of appeal, in circumstances such as these, must

ha[ve] wide latitude as to the sources and types of evidence upon which to base [its] sentence. [It] must have the fullest possible information concerning the background of the accused if [it] is to fit the sentence to the offender rather than to the crime.

(*R v. Gardiner*, [1982] 2 SCR 368, *per* Dickson J (as he then was), at p. 414.)

[50] This "wide latitude" reflects the legal environment of a sentencing hearing—described in *R v. M. (C.A.)*, [1996] 1 SCR 500, at para. 92, as an "inherently individualized process"—wherein the sentencing judge's task is to develop a composite picture or understanding of the offender, including his past and present circumstances as well as his prospects for rehabilitation and the danger that he will re-offend, with a view to crafting a just and appropriate sentence. In this environment, as was recognized in *Gardiner, supra*, at p. 414:

> ... it is manifest that the judge should not be denied an opportunity to obtain relevant information by the imposition of all the restrictive evidential rules common to a trial. ...
>
> It is commonplace that the strict rules which govern at trial do not apply at a sentencing hearing and it would be undesirable to have the formalities and technicalities characteristic of the normal adversary proceeding prevail. The hearsay rule does not govern the sentencing hearing. Hearsay evidence may be accepted where found to be credible and trustworthy.

[51] The holding in *Lavallee, supra*, that the weight properly attributable to expert opinion is a direct function of the amount and quality of admissible evidence on which it is based, is a product of the general rule governing the inadmissibility of hearsay evidence at trial, where considerations of probative value are critical to the presumption of innocence and the fundamental fairness of the trial process. The sentencing environment is entirely different and permits, indeed encourages, recourse to evidentiary materials that would not be appropriate in the determination of guilt or innocence. Hearsay evidence is admissible in sentencing proceedings (see s. 723(5) of the *Code*). For example, probation officers' reports, produced pursuant to s. 721 of the *Code*, will inevitably contain opinions and hearsay of the type that would not be admissible at trial. Similarly, victim impact statements, prepared in accordance with s. 722(2) of the *Code*, must be considered by the sentencing judge, and may be given whatever weight the sentencing judge sees fit, regardless of the fact that they often contain non-expert opinions and hearsay information that would have no probative value, even if relevant, in the trial proper. Finally, s. 724(1) of the *Code* explicitly provides that "[i]n determining a sentence, a court may accept as proved any information disclosed at the trial or at the sentencing proceedings. ..."

[52] In my opinion, the nature of the sentencing process, and of the statutory rules that govern it, contemplate that the sentencing court should have the benefit of "the fullest possible information concerning the background of the [offender]," from the widest array of sources. It is therefore inappropriate to tie the probative value of evidence tendered under these rules to the probative value of evidence proffered at trial, and thus, more specifically, to assess the weight of an expert opinion on the basis of the quantity and quality of non-hearsay evidence introduced to support that opinion. Indeed, such a requirement would largely rob the permissive use of hearsay, recognized

and endorsed by this Court in *Gardiner*, *supra*, of all its utility. A sentencing court must be entitled to receive and rely on any credible and trustworthy evidence which assists it in obtaining as complete an understanding of the offender as possible. The extent to which evidence presented on sentencing conflicts with the facts upon which the conviction was founded is a matter for the sentencing court to take into consideration, but is not, as such, a matter for exclusion of the evidence in question. A sentencing court is entitled to discount any part of an expert opinion that may be based on a misapprehension of the circumstances of the offence as found by the trial judge, while making use of any insight that the opinion may properly provide into the personality of the accused, his personal and emotional life, as well as his dangerousness and risk of recidivism.

[53] In the case at bar, while I accept that the Daigle and Morissette reports each contain an account of the events surrounding the offences committed by the respondent that differ from facts accepted by the trial judge, I cannot agree that they are of little probative value.

[54] In my opinion, it was open to the Court of Appeal to find both reports sufficiently credible and trustworthy to assist in the development of a fuller picture of the respondent, based as they were on the experts' face-to-face psychological assessment and evaluation of the former. As such, I believe that the Court of Appeal was entitled to consider and rely on all or part of the opinions offered therein in sentencing the respondent. Even though the Daigle and Morissette reports were tendered as fresh evidence on appeal, they were not tendered simply to demonstrate that the sentence imposed by the trial judge was unfit, in light of the subsequent opinions offered by these experts. As indicated above, the sentence imposed by the trial judge was unfit because of his misunderstanding of the central offence of which the respondent was convicted. Having set aside that sentence, the Court of Appeal was free to admit any evidence that it deemed to be of assistance in discharging its sentencing function.

[55] For these reasons, I believe that the Court of Appeal's decision to admit the reports by Marc Daigle and Dr. Morissette was correct and should be upheld. I would therefore dismiss the appeal.

R v. Angelillo
2006 SCC 55, [2006] 2 SCR 728

CHARRON J:

1. Introduction

[1] During sentencing, is it appropriate for the court to consider evidence of facts tending to establish the commission of another offence in respect of which the offender has been charged but not convicted? If such evidence is admissible in principle, is it in the interests of justice in the instant case to allow the Crown to introduce this fresh evidence on appeal?

[2] After pleading guilty to a charge of theft, Gennaro Angelillo was sentenced to a term of imprisonment of two years less a day to be served in the community, subject to

his complying with certain conditions that are not in issue in this appeal. At the time of sentencing, Crown counsel was unaware that Mr. Angelillo was under police investigation once again for incidents that had occurred after his guilty plea and that later led to new charges. Relying on that evidence, the Crown introduced three motions in the Quebec Court of Appeal in which it sought leave to introduce fresh evidence, leave to appeal the sentence and a stay of sentence. The Court of Appeal dismissed the motion to introduce fresh evidence, because in its view [TRANSLATION] "[t]his evidence is not relevant" and because "[t]o accept what the prosecution is proposing would mean accepting that the respondent can be punished more severely for committing an offence of which he might be found not guilty" ([2004] QJ No. 11670 (QL), at paras. 6 and 14). The court also dismissed the other two motions. The Crown has appealed to this Court.

[3] As was the case in the Court of Appeal, the main issue in this appeal relates to the admissibility of the fresh evidence. The rules governing admissibility are the same in this Court, and they are well known. The Court of Appeal had to determine pursuant to s. 687(1) of the *Criminal Code*, RSC 1985, c. C-46 ("*Cr. C.*"), whether it was appropriate to require or receive additional evidence. According to the rules laid down in *Palmer v. The Queen*, [1980] 1 SCR 759, and applied in *R v. Lévesque*, [2000] 2 SCR 487, 2000 SCC 47, an appellate court should not generally admit evidence if, by due diligence, it could have been adduced at trial—although this general principle is not to be applied as strictly in a criminal case as in civil cases—and should only admit evidence that is relevant and credible and that could reasonably be expected to have affected the result had it been adduced at trial together with the other evidence.

[4] The Crown submits that the Court of Appeal erred in holding that evidence of facts tending to establish the commission of another offence is irrelevant to the determination of the appropriate sentence, regardless of the purpose being pursued, unless the offence in question resulted in a conviction. The Crown wishes to produce this fresh evidence not to prove that the other offence was committed, but for the sole purpose of establishing Mr. Angelillo's character—a distinction that was accepted by the Ontario Court of Appeal in *R v. Edwards* (2001), 155 CCC (3d) 473, but rejected by the Court of Appeal in the case at bar. In light of the sentencing submissions, and more particularly of the pre-sentence report, according to which Mr. Angelillo [TRANSLATION] "has done some soul-searching, which seems to be sincere, about his inappropriate behaviour" and his "time in court [has] had a major deterrent effect," the Crown contends that the fresh evidence easily meets the requirement of relevance.

[5] Although I have concluded that the fresh evidence is relevant and I recognize that, in principle, evidence of facts tending to establish the commission of another offence of which the offender has not been convicted can in certain cases be admitted to enable the court to determine a just and appropriate sentence, I would, for the reasons that follow, dismiss the appeal. Since the fresh evidence constitutes the basis for outstanding charges against Mr. Angelillo for which he has not yet stood trial, it can be admitted only in the context of the procedure provided for in s. 725(1)(b) or (b.1) *Cr. C.* The conditions for that procedure include a requirement that the offender's consent be obtained. Furthermore, I feel that the Crown has not shown due diligence. Accordingly, the Court of Appeal's decision not to admit the fresh evidence is affirmed and the appeal is dismissed.

2. Facts and Judgments Below

2.1 Court of Québec

[6] On January 13, 2003, Mr. Angelillo pleaded guilty in the Court of Québec to a charge of theft over $5,000, contrary to s. 334(a) *Cr. C.* More than 37 times over a period of about a month and a half, Mr. Angelillo, who was employed as a security guard, failed to make deposits his employer had instructed him to make and instead took the money for his own use, thus misappropriating more than $425,000. He used a large part of that amount to pay debts he had incurred to persons associated with organized crime, who were threatening him and his family. The police also seized $150,000 during a search of his home.

[7] For reasons that are not apparent from the record, the sentencing hearing was not completed until April 21, 2004, more than 15 months after the guilty plea. At that time, Judge Corte sentenced Mr. Angelillo to a term of imprisonment of two years less a day to be served in the community followed by two years' probation, and ordered him to pay $268,430 as restitution under s. 738 *Cr. C.* In imposing this sentence, the court accepted the submissions of the defence rather than those of Crown counsel, who had asked for an unconditional three-year term of imprisonment.

[8] Judge Corte noted that the offender had no criminal record, had pleaded guilty at the start of the proceedings and had expressed remorse, and that the pre-sentence report was favourable to him. She also noted that Mr. Angelillo had three jobs at the time and was the sole source of support for his wife and for his three children, who were respectively 15 months, four years and seven years old. Referring to the pre-sentence report dated May 15, 2003, the judge added that the offender [TRANSLATION] "has done some sincere soul-searching about his inappropriate behaviour [and] has undertaken a rehabilitation process ... and also counselling," and that "his time in court has had a major deterrent effect on him." The report also stated that Mr. Angelillo was not dangerous and that his risk of re-offending was low. Judge Corte noted that there was a special circumstance in Mr. Angelillo's case, namely that he had stolen because his life and the lives of his family were being threatened by creditors who had ties to organized crime. There was physical evidence confirming that Mr. Angelillo had been threatened, and this fact was not disputed by the Crown. Judge Corte therefore concluded that, in this instance, the penological objectives of deterrence and denunciation could be achieved by imposing a conditional sentence with certain conditions restricting Mr. Angelillo's freedom.

2.2 Fresh Evidence

[9] Following that decision, the Crown introduced motions in the Court of Appeal for leave to appeal, for a stay of sentence and for leave to introduce fresh evidence. Through the last of these motions, the Crown intended to file evidence showing: (1) that, on August 20, 2003, Mr. Angelillo was arrested at an Insta-Chèque counter while attempting to cash a forged certified cheque from the National Bank of Canada made payable to him in the amount of $12,000; and (2) that, on January 21, 2004, during a search of Mr. Angelillo's home, police officers found a National Bank stamp with

the words [TRANSLATION] "certified cheque" on it and a starter kit containing a set of non-personalized cheques, which came from a National Bank branch where Mr. Angelillo worked as a cleaner. These allegations were the basis for the new charges against Mr. Angelillo.

[10] The Crown argues that this evidence was not available at trial and that it acted diligently to produce all the relevant evidence before Judge Corte. In support of this argument, the Crown has submitted an affidavit from the prosecutor responsible for the case at trial. The affidavit states that, in early June 2003, after the detective sergeant responsible for the case had committed an indiscretion by telling Mr. Angelillo the sentence the Crown intended to seek, Crown counsel told the detective sergeant that her presence at the sentencing hearing would no longer be required and that from then on counsel would be in contact only with the detective sergeant's supervisor. Before the hearing, counsel checked the *plumitif*, in which there was nothing about Mr. Angelillo, but did not contact either the detective sergeant or her supervisor. On April 21, 2004, shortly after Judge Corte handed down her sentence, the detective sergeant ran into counsel at the courthouse by chance and told her the facts that the Crown is now seeking to introduce as fresh evidence. According to the affidavit of the police officer responsible for the new investigation, the detective sergeant had been aware of this investigation since January 19, 2004.

2.3 Court of Appeal

[11] The Quebec Court of Appeal (Beauregard, Mailhot and Doyon JJA) dismissed the three motions filed by the Crown because, in the court's view, the evidence was not relevant. The court began by stating that, because of the presumption of innocence, the fact that Mr. Angelillo had been charged proved nothing. It added that, in the present case, what the Crown wished to prove was not that he had been charged with another crime, but that the charge was substantiated. The court rejected the Crown's submission that the fresh evidence was admissible as character evidence under the principles stated by Rosenberg JA in *Edwards*. In the court's view, it is contrary to the presumption of innocence to consider, in sentencing an accused, facts that could constitute the basis for a separate criminal charge that has not resulted in conviction (para. 11). The court concluded that taking into account evidence of facts tending to establish that an accused has committed another offence of which he or she has not been convicted amounts to punishing the accused more severely for having committed an act in respect of which he or she might ultimately be found not guilty (para. 14).

3. Analysis

3.1 Admissibility of Fresh Evidence

[12] As mentioned above, an appellate court considering a motion to admit fresh evidence must decide, under s. 687(1) *Cr. C.*, whether it thinks fit to require or receive additional evidence. What must guide the court of appeal in assessing the admissibility of fresh evidence is therefore a concern to serve the interests of justice.

[13] In *Lévesque*, at para. 35, this Court adapted to an appeal against sentence the four criteria set out in *Palmer* for determining whether it is in the interests of justice to admit fresh evidence on an appeal from a verdict:

(1) The evidence should generally not be admitted if, by due diligence, it could have been adduced at trial provided that this general principle will not be applied as strictly in a criminal case as in civil cases.

(2) The evidence must be relevant in the sense that it bears upon a decisive or potentially decisive issue relating to the sentence.

(3) The evidence must be credible in the sense that it is reasonably capable of belief.

(4) The evidence must be such that if believed it could reasonably, when taken with the other evidence adduced at trial, be expected to have affected the result.

[14] In *Lévesque*, the Court recognized that the strict rules of a trial do not apply to a sentencing hearing, because in order to determine the appropriate sentence the judge must have as much information as possible about the accused (para. 30). The Court held that the *Palmer* criteria do not compromise this more flexible application of the rules and noted that those criteria are just as important where the appeal relates to the sentence. It will be helpful for the purposes of the case at bar to recall why this is true:

> The integrity of the criminal process and the role of appeal courts could be jeopardized by the routine admission of fresh evidence on appeal, since this would create a two-tier sentencing system. That kind of system would be incompatible with the high standard of review applicable to appeals from sentences and the underlying "profound functional justifications": see *R v. M. (C.A.)*, [1996] 1 SCR 500, at para. 91. Despite the fresh evidence, the sentencing judge, unlike the appeal judge, has the benefit of being able to directly assess the other evidence, the testimony and the submissions of the parties, as well as being familiar with the needs and current conditions of and in the community where the crime was committed: see *M. (C.A.)*, *supra*, at para. 91. Furthermore, appeal courts are not the appropriate forum in which to determine questions of fact, and they should do so only when the fresh evidence presents certain characteristics such as would justify expanding their traditional role. This Court has already identified those characteristics, in *Palmer*. In my view, whether the appeal relates to a verdict or a sentence, the criteria laid down by this Court in *Palmer* are the criteria that are to be applied where a court of appeal is determining whether to admit fresh evidence. [para. 20]

[15] In accordance with the last three of the *Palmer* criteria, an appellate court can therefore admit evidence only if it is relevant and credible and if it could reasonably be expected to have affected the result had it been adduced at trial together with the other evidence. With respect to the first criterion, this Court has stated a number of times that failure to meet the due diligence criterion should not be used to refuse to admit fresh evidence on appeal if the evidence is compelling and if it is in the interests of justice to admit it (*Lévesque*, at para. 15; *R v. Warsing*, [1998] 3 SCR 579, at para. 51). The fact remains that this criterion is an important one whose specific purpose is to protect the interests and the administration of justice and to preserve the role of the appellate court (*Lévesque*, at para. 30, citing *R v. M. (P.S.)* (1992), 77 CCC (3d) 402 (Ont. CA), at p. 410).

[16] In the present case, I am of the view that the Crown did not act with due diligence and that, in the interests of the administration of justice, the failure to do so is determinative. The conflict between Crown counsel and the detective sergeant may explain why the evidence that the Crown now seeks to introduce by motion was not adduced during the sentencing hearing, but this circumstance does not constitute evidence of due diligence. The record shows unequivocally that the Crown could have submitted the evidence in question to the trial judge were it not for that breakdown in communication. It cannot be in the interests of the administration of justice to condone such a lack of co-ordination and co-operation between the Crown and the police.

[17] Since I consider the lack of due diligence to be determinative in the case at bar, it is not necessary to make a final determination as to the decisiveness of the fresh evidence or to decide whether that evidence—which Mr. Angelillo contests vigorously—is sufficiently credible. However, I feel that it may be helpful to make a few general comments regarding the relevance of evidence of acts that have resulted neither in charges nor in convictions, since the Court of Appeal seems to have rejected out of hand the reasoning of Rosenberg JA of the Ontario Court of Appeal in *Edwards*. The court stated in particular that it did not see the distinction Rosenberg JA had drawn in saying that evidence of such acts cannot be adduced for the purpose of obtaining a disproportionate sentence against the offender for the offence in question or of punishing the offender for an offence of which he or she has not been convicted, but that such evidence can be adduced to shed light on the offender's background and character. In my view, Rosenberg JA was correct in drawing that distinction, and it is an important one. I will therefore begin by discussing certain general principles relating to the admissibility of extrinsic evidence for sentencing purposes before commenting on the relevance of the evidence the Crown wished to adduce in the case at bar.

Fish J delivered a concurring opinion in which he agreed with the foregoing.

A recurring concern in sentence appeals is the extent to which an appeal may be taken and a decision rendered on the basis of a change in circumstances since the sentence was originally imposed. This concern is not a free-standing ground of appeal, but arises as an incident in the course of a sentencing appeal that is otherwise properly framed. It almost always arises on appeals by the offender. For example, suppose an offender has been given a lengthy suspended sentence for a sequence of property offences. A significant feature of the case is that the offender committed the offences to support his drug addiction. Since the sentence was imposed the offender has successfully followed a rigorous program of rehabilitation. A plausible argument can be made that the profile of the offender, and particularly the risk of reoffending, should be viewed differently. This does not raise a question of evidence that could have been produced at first instance, but it is new evidence about the offender. Section 687 of the Code allows the appellate court to receive any evidence that it considers appropriate. But if it admits and considers evidence of developments since the sentence was originally imposed, the court is, in effect, considering a case that is different from the case before the sentencing judge. Should the appellate court be entitled to take this information into account?

D. Orders

If a court allows an appeal from sentence it is entitled to make any order that could have been made by the sentencing judge. Indeed, it must make an order that it considers a fit sentence in the matter because there is no power for an appellate court to remit a case to the sentencing judge for reconsideration. (See, for example, *Pelletier* (1989), 52 CCC (3d) 340 (Que. CA).) Because the function of the appellate court is to ensure a fit sentence, and because the court is empowered to receive any evidence it considers appropriate, the absence of a power to remit might be considered a factor that weighs in favour of a more interventionist approach.

The Supreme Court affirmed in *Hill*, [1977] 1 SCR 827 that when an appellate court varies a sentence it can reduce or increase it.

III. PRACTICAL CONSIDERATIONS

Sentence appeals in indictable cases require leave, but they do not in summary conviction matters. In either case, as we have seen previously, appellate courts will not intervene to review or vary a sentence unless there is a good reason to do so. That, at any rate, is the prevailing statement of principle, but there are many instances that might seem to contradict it.

In all instances, the underlying theme of sentence appeals is a claim that the sentence is unfit and should be varied. While this is a claim in any sentence appeal, there are also many instances in which the reason advanced for reviewing a sentence is somewhat more formal. For example, if a judge fails to provide an opportunity for submissions to be made on sentence, this may be considered a defect that calls the fitness of the sentence into question and may justify not only appellate review but modification of the sentence. Similarly, if the reasons for sentence are deficient, an appellate court might well find in this a sufficient basis to review the sentence and modify it.

Appellate intervention typically occurs in two situations. Either the court at first instance has imposed a sentence that is out of line in some material aspect with other cases of a similar nature or there is some particular aspect of the individual case that calls for attention in the sentence. These two situations are not mutually inconsistent and might arise in a single case. In the first case, the emphasis is placed on the general norm, while, in the second, it is focused on the particular features of the individual case.

It is inevitable that appellate judges will have varying views of what is a case for deference and what is a case for intervention. Where one might see a question of principle, another might see none. Where one might see a case of manifest unfitness in a sentence, another might see a difference of opinion that does not merit interference. There are discrepancies in sentence appeals as surely as there are discrepancies at first instance. This is a necessary corollary of a system that insists, rightly, on individualized sentencing.

In the following case the Court of Appeal for Quebec altered the sentence imposed. At the time that sentence was pronounced, penitentiary time was the norm for importing heroin and cocaine in large quantities and the range was typically around 10 years. The accused pleaded guilty, and substantial submissions, well supported by evidence, were made on the sentencing hearing. The trial judge clearly went out of her way to temper the length of the sentence, based on favourable and sympathetic facts, and she reached a conclusion of 8 years for each offender after giving credit for time served. Both the Crown and the offenders appealed. The latter succeeded. Consider carefully the basis on which the Court of Appeal intervened and the significance of the result.

Fortin v. The Queen
2005 QCCA 735 (CanLII) (footnotes omitted)

[This is an unofficial translation posted by CanLII.]

[2] Annie Fortin was born on January 28, 1979 and is 26 years old. Sébastien Renaud was born on August 9, 1977 and is 28 years old.

[3] On May 6, 2002, on their way back from Costa Rica, they were arrested at Toronto's Pearson Airport. They were hiding 4,170 grams of heroin (70% pure) and 1,468 grams of cocaine (56% pure) in their luggage.

[4] In the spring of 2002, Annie Fortin was going through a difficult time. She was depressed and in debt. At one point she became close to Sébastien Renaud's sister, Noémie, who introduced her to a certain Rosie. Rosie asked Ms. Fortin if she would be interested in taking a trip to Costa Rica to bring drugs back to Canada.

[5] Ms. Fortin was interested in the proposal. Rosie insisted that she find herself a travelling companion, however. Ms. Fortin therefore approached two friends, who refused, before speaking to Sébastien Renaud, who agreed.

[6] At that time, the plan involved going to Costa Rica and bringing back a few pairs of shoes filled with ecstasy. In payment, they each would receive $3000, their trip to and accommodation in Costa Rica would be paid for, and they would be given $250 in pocket money.

[7] There was never any question of heroin or cocaine; they did know, however, that bringing back ecstasy constitutes an illegal transaction.

[8] The trial judge found that they had [TRANSLATION] "agreed to import a small quantity of ecstasy" and that [TRANSLATION] "it was only once they were in Costa Rica that they agreed to import a larger quantity of drugs. ... [T]hey agreed to bring back to Canada what they knew at that time to be a significant quantity of an illegal substance."

[9] The appellants met with Rosie several times in preparation for the trip. When she told them that the departure date was set and the tickets had been purchased, they hesitated. Annie Fortin felt threatened; Rosie told her that she would have to reimburse the cost of the plane tickets if she and her friend reneged. She was afraid. Sébastien Renaud was also worried, and when he voiced his concerns to Rosie, she answered that she knew where his mother and sister lived.

[10] The trial judge was satisfied on a balance of probabilities of the existence of threats from Rosie, but she added that these threats *do not constitute* [TRANSLATION] "the event that triggered their agreement to commit the crime."

[11] The appellants left on April 29, 2002.

[12] In Costa Rica, two men were waiting for them. The appellants say that they were Colombian. The men took their luggage, brought them to San Jose, and then gave

them the bags that they were to bring back to Canada. It was clear to the appellants that they did not contain shoes. When they expressed their concerns to the two men about this change in plans, they were told not to ask questions.

[13] The trial judge was satisfied on a balance of probabilities of the existence of threats from the two men in Costa Rica.

[14] The appellants felt caught in a trap.

[15] Apprehensive, they telephoned Rosie, who told them not to worry and to do what they were told.

[16] They considered leaving the bags there, but quickly rejected this option, convinced that members of the organization were waiting for them in Canada.

[17] They did not seriously consider going to the police in Costa Rica, fearing they were corrupt.

[18] They left Costa Rica on May 6, 2002.

[19] At no time did they consider turning themselves in to authorities once they arrived on Canadian soil.

[20] They both claim they were relieved that their adventure was over when customs officials stopped them and found the narcotics in their bags.

[21] They did not know exactly what their luggage contained, but they were aware that it was not ecstasy. The trial judge found that [TRANSLATION] "they realized they had imported cocaine when they were arrested at the airport" and that they [TRANSLATION] "learned only several weeks after their arrest" that the bags also contained heroin.

[22] Three experts—a psychologist, a psychiatrist and a criminologist—testified. They all agreed that the risk of re-offending was nil or practically nil in the case of both appellants.

[23] The appellants are remorseful and regret what happened. Both reaffirm their intention to lead productive lives.

[24] The nearly three-year period between the offences and the sentencing confirms that they are on the right path. Sébastien Renaud is working. Annie Fortin has gone back to university after having worked and is studying anthropology and psychology.

[25] Both have partners with whom they share their lives and make plans for the future.

[26] Both receive very strong support from their families.

. . .

[27] The appellants raise five grounds of appeal:

- the trial judge erred in her interpretation and application of the principles to be considered, specifically with respect to the objective of social deterrence;
- the trial judge erred in not according exceptional treatment to this case, which can only be considered exceptional;
- the trial judge erred in applying what she perceived to be a kind of "sentence threshold" established in the case law, even though she had raised several factors that favour greater clemency;
- in applying this "sentence threshold," the trial judge erred in treating the weak, vulnerable, gullible and naïve couriers, who had been recruited despite themselves, as severely as the traffickers, who have made crime a way of life;

• the sentences are clearly unreasonable having regard to all the circumstances of the case and all the more so in light of the trial judge's finding that the appellants deserved to be treated with clemency.

· · ·

[28] In *R v. Proulx*, 2005 SCC 5 (CanLII), [2000] 1 SCR 61, the Supreme Court of Canada affirmed the broad discretionary power of a trial judge in sentencing matters. Chief Justice Lamer notes, at para. 123, that sentences imposed by trial judges are entitled to considerable deference from appellate courts, and that "absent an error in principle, failure to consider a relevant factor, or an overemphasis of the appropriate factors, a court of appeal should only intervene to vary a sentence imposed at trial if the sentence is demonstrably unfit" (at para. 123).

[29] How does this apply to the present case?

[30] The trial judge's analysis is complete and detailed. All the objectives, principles and factors relevant to sentencing are dealt with exhaustively.

[31] The case law from Quebec and elsewhere in Canada is replete with decisions reaffirming that denunciation and deterrence are the primary factors to consider in cases involving the importation of heroin and cocaine, although sentencing is not so rigid an exercise as to require reliance on only those two factors in all cases.

[32] Heroin is the most harmful drug on the market, while cocaine is a close second.

[33] These drugs are produced in other countries, hence the importance of attaching a harsh penalty to their importation into Canada.

[34] Consumption of these drugs is a social evil and a tragedy for all victims, both direct and indirect.

[35] The severity of punishment in such cases is justified by the hope that it will make it more difficult for criminal organizations to recruit drug couriers and that it will discourage people who are tempted by something that they see as nothing more than a simple adventure.

[36] In *R v. Smith*, 1987 CanLII 64 (SCC), [1987] 1 SCR 1045, Justice Lamer (as he then was) wrote the following, at 1053:

Those who import and market hard drugs for lucre are responsible for the gradual but inexorable degeneration of many of their fellow human beings as a result of their becoming drug addicts. The direct cause of the hardship cast upon their victims and their families, these importers must also be made to bear their fair share of the guilt for the innumerable serious crimes of all sorts committed by addicts in order to feed their demand for drugs. Such persons, with few exceptions (as an example, the guilt of addicts who import not only to meet but also to finance their needs is not necessarily the same in degree as that of cold-blooded non-users), should, upon conviction, in my respectful view, be sentenced to and actually serve long periods of penal servitude.

[37] In our view, these comments are as relevant today as they were twenty years ago.

[38] Despite the seriousness of the crime, the case law does recognize those "few exceptions" where long periods of imprisonment are not appropriate. In *Smith, supra,* Justice Lamer provides one example. There are others in the case law; see, for instance,

R v. Marshall, [1988] BCJ No. 2367, where the British Columbia Court of Appeal reduced the sentence imposed on a writer with no criminal record to 5 years for importing 4 ounces of heroin into Canada. See also *R v. Borges*, [2000] JQ No. 4732, where this Court reduced the 30-month prison sentence of a 21-year-old man with no criminal record to a suspended sentence of two years less one day for importing 1,214 grams of cocaine.

[39] In our view, the situation of the appellants warrants exceptional treatment. Indeed, the trial judge implicitly recognized this fact when she wrote the following at paragraph 97: [TRANSLATION] "the particular circumstances of the accused, taken as a whole, favour the leniency of the Court" and when she stated that she accepted that the appellants believed that they were importing ecstasy (and not heroin or cocaine) [TRANSLATION] "in terms of their premeditation and their state of mind." Her error consists of not having translated this clemency into a lenient sentence. In fact, in light of the circumstances as a whole, the punishment is harsh. As such, it is "demonstrably unfit" and warrants our intervention.

[40] At trial, the Crown sought a 15-year prison sentence, and its position has not changed on appeal. For its part, the defence suggested a suspended sentence of 2 years less one day. On appeal, however, in light of the trial judge's findings of fact, it seeks a sentence of 4 or 5 years in prison.

[41] In our view, the objectives, principles and factors relevant to sentencing, in the very particular circumstances of the present case, justify imposing a sentence of 5 years of imprisonment.

[42] A number of factors weigh against imposing a lighter sentence:

- the appellants have been convicted of a serious crime, which attracts a maximum sentence of life in prison;
- the drugs imported (heroin and cocaine) are the most harmful on the market;
- the quantity of drugs imported is significant;
- the appellants do not use drugs; they consciously agreed to smuggle the drugs for lucre and as a way to fulfil their wish to travel;
- although they initially believed they would be smuggling ecstasy, they were aware that this was an illegal transaction;
- after realizing that they were being asked to smuggle something other than ecstasy and in a larger quantity than originally planned, they nevertheless decided to continue the transaction and to try to import the drug into Canada instead of turning themselves in to Canadian customs officials. It should also be noted that they do not seem to have made any real effort to find out the exact nature of the drug they had been asked to smuggle;
- contrary to what the appellants submit, they were not drawn in "despite themselves"; both are intelligent young people who knew what they were doing when they told Rosie that they were interested in the proposed trip to Costa Rica. The threats they received do not entirely excuse their actions since, as the trial judge found, they were not [TRANSLATION] "the event that triggered the commission of the crime."

[43] At the same time, certain factors make this case an exceptional one and, as the trial judge determined, justify a more lenient sentence than what is usually imposed in this type of case:

- the psychological and economic vulnerability of the appellants when they were recruited;
- their age and complete lack of criminal record;
- the practically non-existent risk of re-offending in the case of both appellants;
- the strong support they both receive from family and friends;
- the mitigating circumstances surrounding the perpetration of the crime, notably:
  - the threats they received in Montréal and Costa Rica when they wanted to back out of the agreement;
  - the fact that they were recruited to smuggle a small amount of ecstasy;
  - the fact that at all times, even once they arrived in Canada, they were unaware of the type of drug they were carrying;
- their immediate collaboration with authorities as soon as customs officials became suspicious;
- their sincere remorse and regret;
- the fact that they are, for all intents and purposes, rehabilitated.

[44] In our opinion, it is important to emphasize the psychological vulnerability of the appellants when they were recruited. The psychiatrist Morissette wrote that the decisions Ms. Fortin made in the spring of 2002 can be explained not by any lack of intellectual capacity but rather by [TRANSLATION] "her emotional and interpersonal naiveté, a certain developmental immaturity, a selective vulnerability ... ." He added that Rosie [TRANSLATION] "deceived Ms. Fortin, but Ms. Fortin was also easily manipulated for the purpose of getting the plan underway."

[45] The psychologist Gadoua is in full agreement. He writes that Ms. Fortin's motives for accepting Rosie's offer [TRANSLATION] "express confusion and lack of judgment: aware of threats and manipulation, she became paralyzed and passive, her judgment and behaviour altered. She no longer had the capacity to stop the process ... ." A little later, he adds that [TRANSLATION] "[she] hesitated for a good period of time, during which she became confused. She was especially sensitive to threats and manipulation, which stirred up remnants of trauma that were still within her" and finally, "without realizing it, she adopted survival modes linked to her still unresolved internal confusion and distress (victim of a criminal act) in order to avoid even further personal disintegration."

[46] The psychiatrist Morissette wrote that the decision made by Mr. Renaud during the same period is [TRANSLATION] "the result of a decision made too quickly, the result of the attraction of easy money and finally, the result of a (relative) sense of responsibility in that he did not want to involve his mother in his problems."

[47] The psychologist Gadoua wrote that Mr. Renaud's motivation for accepting the proposed job was [TRANSLATION] "staying physically and psychologically safe since he was a child and adolescent when he was a victim of physical abuse giving rise to sequelae related to post-traumatic stress syndrome." He added that the threats he received

made it so that [TRANSLATION] "he was unable to exercise his practical judgment dis-passionately" and spoke of [TRANSLATION] "internal distress significantly [impairing] his social functioning as well as his judgment."

[48] The psychiatrist Morissette wrote the following regarding the two appellants:

> [TRANSLATION] In a certain way, the two protagonists were "perfect" recruits, as they were generally inexperienced and completely lacking in criminal experience. In addition, they each (for their own reasons) had trouble trusting or opening up to others and, despite their youth, had over a number of years developed very good social functioning (resourcefulness, financial autonomy, etc.).

[49] In summary, in view of their respective weaknesses, the appellants fed off each other's fears.

[50] After a careful consideration of all the factors, we find that a 5-year prison sentence is just in the circumstances.

[51] In the case of the appellant Renaud, it is appropriate to take into account and give double credit for the time served in interim detention (4 months) and to subtract 8 months from the sentence.

[52] FOR THESE REASONS, THE COURT:

[53] *ALLOWS* the appeal;

[54] *OVERTURNS* the sentence for the sole purpose of *substituting* for the sentences previously imposed the following:

- In the case of the appellant Annie Fortin, a sentence of 5 years' imprisonment;
- In the case of the appellant Sébastien Renaud, a sentence of 4 years and 4 months' imprisonment.

The other elements of the sentence remain unchanged.

QUESTION

How would you explain this decision in view of the principles of appellate review examined in the first part of this chapter?

CHAPTER EIGHTEEN

Parole and Early Release

I. INTRODUCTION

This chapter provides an overview of parole and early release in Canada. From a procedural perspective, these issues can be technical and complex. Rather than addressing the many issues in detail, we sketch the framework of early release and set out some aspects of the substantive discussions about its legitimacy and efficacy. We deal only with the federal context and the National Parole Board (NPB). Provinces have their own correctional statutes that govern temporary absences. In Ontario, Quebec, and British Columbia, there are provincial parole boards as well. For the most part, the elements are similar and sometimes identical. As well, some of these provinces have raised the question of disbanding their provincial boards in favour of the NPB. When concerned about a non-federal prisoner, particularly one from British Columbia, Ontario, or Quebec, one should consult the relevant provincial or territorial legislation

For a discussion of the history of parole in Canada, see Cole and Manson, *Release from Imprisonment: The Law of Sentencing, Parole, and Judicial Review* (Toronto: Carswell, 1990), 159-89. The major events in the history of federal early release are as follows:

1899 The enactment of the *Ticket of Leave Act*, providing for licences to be granted to prisoners by the governor general, on the advice of the minister of justice, which permitted the prisoner to be at large subject to recommitment for breaching a term of the licence or committing a new offence.

1959 The establishment of the NPB, which, pursuant to the terms of the *Parole Act*, was empowered to grant, suspend, and revoke parole.

1970 The provision of "mandatory supervision," which required federal prisoners who were released by reason of remission to be supervised subject to recommitment for breaching a condition or committing a new offence; this applied only to penitentiary prisoners.

1986 The passage of the detention provisions, which empowered the NPB to detain a prisoner until the warrant expiry date if there were grounds to believe that an offence involving death or serious harm would be committed if he or she was released.

1992 The passage of the *Corrections and Conditional Release Act*, SC 1992, c. 20 (CCRA), which replaced both the *Penitentiary Act* and the *Parole Act*; among other important provisions, it replaced the remission-based release on mandatory supervision with statutory release after two-thirds of a sentence is served.

The CCRA includes a general statement of purpose and applicable principles:

100. The purpose of conditional release is to contribute to the maintenance of a just, peaceful and safe society by means of decisions on the timing and conditions of release that will best facilitate the rehabilitation of offenders and their reintegration into the community as law-abiding citizens.

101. The principles that shall guide the Board and the provincial parole boards in achieving the purpose of conditional release are

(a) that the protection of society be the paramount consideration in the determination of any case;

(b) that parole boards take into consideration all available information that is relevant to a case, including the stated reasons and recommendations of the sentencing judge, any other information from the trial or the sentencing hearing, information and assessments provided by correctional authorities, and information obtained from victims and the offender;

(c) that parole boards enhance their effectiveness and openness through the timely exchange of relevant information with other components of the criminal justice system and through communication of their policies and programs to offenders, victims and the general public;

(d) that parole boards make the least restrictive determination consistent with the protection of society;

(e) that parole boards adopt and be guided by appropriate policies and that their members be provided with the training necessary to implement those policies; and

(f) that offenders be provided with relevant information, reasons for decisions and access to the review of decisions in order to ensure a fair and understandable conditional release process.

102. The Board or a provincial parole board may grant parole to an offender if, in its opinion,

(a) the offender will not, by reoffending, present an undue risk to society before the expiration according to law of the sentence the offender is serving; and

(b) the release of the offender will contribute to the protection of society by facilitating the reintegration of the offender into society as a law-abiding citizen.

II. THE ELEMENTS OF PAROLE

The following discussion provides a clear picture of how the system works generally, but does not include a technical analysis of the relevant procedures. Although parole litigation has not been extensive, there is a small body of case law that should be consulted to obtain a more detailed account of these elements.

In order to help you understand this technical aspect of penal law, we have prepared a short glossary of some of the basic terms that apply to the different kinds of releases, and the various consequential processes that can occur. We have listed them in sequential, not alphabetical, order.

Full parole This is defined by s. 99 simply as the "authority granted to an offender to be at large during the offender's sentence." Parole and its applicable conditions continues until warrant expiry unless it is suspended, cancelled, terminated, or revoked.

Day parole Section 99 defines this as the authority granted by the NPB to an offender "to be at large during the offender's sentence in order to prepare the offender for full parole or statutory release, the conditions of which require the offender to return to a penitentiary, a community-based residential facility or a provincial correctional facility each night, unless otherwise authorized in writing."

Temporary absence There are two types: escorted (ETA) and unescorted (UTA). For prisoners serving a life sentence for murder and dangerous offenders, the jurisdiction over UTAs is vested in the NPB. For most other prisoners, UTAs can be granted by the institution head (see CCRA, s. 116(2)). Again, with the exception of murderers, ETAs are granted by the institutional head for limited periods (usually less than 5 days, but up to 15 days, with the approval of the commissioner), or for an unlimited period for medical reasons (see CCRA, s. 17). Assuming that the prisoner does not present an undue risk, the statutory reasons for an ETA include "medical, administrative, community service, family contact, personal development for rehabilitative purposes, or compassionate reasons, including parental responsibilities." A common reason for an ETA, besides a medical reason, is to attend a family funeral.

Statutory release This is the point, usually after serving two-thirds of a sentence, that a prisoner is entitled to be released pursuant to s. 127, unless the prisoner is subject to detention, discussed below.

Detention Prisoners who have committed offences within stipulated categories (see Schedules I and II, which list sexual offences, offences of violence, and serious drug offences) can be referred to the Board to consider whether they should be detained instead of released on statutory release. Either the CSC or the Commissioner can refer a case to the Board if there are reasonable grounds to believe that the offender, before the expiration of sentence, is likely to commit an offence causing death or serious harm, a sexual offence involving a child, or a serious drug offence. The Board can then conduct a hearing to decide whether it should deny release because of any of these likelihoods. The detention process is governed by ss. 129-32.

Suspension The parole or statutory release of an offender is subject to suspension under s. 135(1) by decision of a member of the NPB or a designate when that person is satisfied that the offender has breached a condition or that it is "necessary and reasonable to suspend the parole or statutory release in order to prevent a breach of any condition thereof or to protect society." The suspension decision is accompanied by a warrant of apprehension and the recommitment to custody of the offender. Unless the suspension is cancelled, the Board must conduct a post-suspension hearing.

Revocation   At a post-suspension hearing, if the Board is satisfied that the offender does not present an "undue risk," the suspension is cancelled and the offender can continue in the community subject to conditions. However, if the Board is not satisfied, then it ends the parole of statutory release by revocation or termination. A revocation means that the prisoner is returned to custody to serve the unexpired portion of the sentence. The prisoner can apply again for parole subject to the eligibility provisions but is not entitled to statutory release until two-thirds of the unexpired portion of the sentence has been served.

Termination   This option is available at a post-suspension hearing if the Board concludes that there is undue risk, but that the risk is "due to circumstances beyond the offender's control": see ss. 135(5)(b) and (7). Upon termination, the prisoner is returned to custody and can apply again for parole. However, the original statutory release date, based on two-thirds of the original sentence, is maintained.

A. Eligibility

The law in effect on the date of sentencing determines the prisoner's eligibility for all forms of statutory release. For murder, this has usually been stipulated in the *Criminal Code*. For all other offences, eligibility has been established by the parole legislation in force at the time of the offence. Currently, the CCRA establishes the day parole eligibility date (DPED) and the full parole eligibility date (PED) as follows:

119(1) Subject to section 746.1 of the *Criminal Code*, subsection 140.3(2) of the *National Defence Act* and subsection 15(2) of the *Crimes Against Humanity and War Crimes Act*, the portion of a sentence that must be served before an offender may be released on day parole is

(a) one year, where the offender was, before October 15, 1977, sentenced to preventive detention;

(b) where the offender is an offender, other than an offender referred to in paragraph (b.1), who was sentenced to detention in a penitentiary for an indeterminate period, the longer of

(i) the period required to be served by the offender to reach the offender's full parole eligibility date, determined in accordance with section 761 of the *Criminal Code*, less three years, and

(ii) the period required to be served by the offender to reach the offender's full parole eligibility date, determined in accordance with subsection 120.2(2), less three years;

(b.1) where the offender was sentenced to detention in a penitentiary for an indeterminate period as of the date on which this paragraph comes into force, the longer of

(i) three years, and

(ii) the period required to be served by the offender to reach the offender's full parole eligibility date, determined in accordance with subsection 120.2(2), less three years;

(c) where the offender is serving a sentence of two years or more, other than a sentence referred to in paragraph (a) or (b), the greater of

(i) the portion ending six months before the date on which full parole may be granted, and

(ii) six months; or

(d) one half of the portion of the sentence that must be served before full parole may be granted, where the offender is serving a sentence of less than two years.

• • •

120(1) Subject to sections 746.1 and 761 of the *Criminal Code* and to any order made under section 743.6 of that Act, to subsection 140.3(2) of the *National Defence Act* and to any order made under section 140.4 of that Act, and to subsection 15(2) of the *Crimes Against Humanity and War Crimes Act*, an offender is not eligible for full parole until the day on which the offender has served a period of ineligibility of the lesser of one third of the sentence and seven years.

Life sentence

(2) Subject to any order made under section 743.6 of the *Criminal Code* or section 140.4 of the *National Defence Act*, an offender who is serving a life sentence, imposed otherwise than as a minimum punishment, is not eligible for full parole until the day on which the offender has served a period of ineligibility of seven years less any time spent in custody between the day on which the offender was arrested and taken into custody, in respect of the offence for which the sentence was imposed, and the day on which the sentence was imposed.

Essentially, this scheme provides for full parole eligibility after serving one-third of a sentence and day parole eligibility six months before that date. Before 1992, the day parole eligibility date was one-sixth of the sentence. The prolongation to six months before full parole eligibility diminished the use of long periods of successive day paroles. The NPB also has authority over UTAs for lifers and prisoners serving a sentence for a schedule I or II offence (see ss. 116(1) and 107(1)(e)). Generally, eligibility for a UTA occurs at one-half of the parole eligibility period (see s. 115(1)(c)). No maximum security prisoners can qualify for a UTA (see s. 115(3)).

A person sentenced to imprisonment for life as a maximum sentence (that is, for an offence other than murder) is eligible for parole after serving seven years. For all life sentences, credit toward eligiblity begins when the prisoner is arrested for the offence, and includes any days in custody after that time. For all other offences, credit toward parole eligibility accumulates only after the sentence is imposed.

B. Increasing Parole Eligibility

Amendments to the *Criminal Code* in 1992 permit a trial judge, in certain circumstances, to increase the period of parole ineligibility up to one-half of the sentence. The *Criminal Code* now provides

743.6(1) Notwithstanding subsection 120(1) of the *Corrections and Conditional Release Act*, where an offender receives, on or after November 1, 1992, a sentence of imprisonment of two years or more, including a sentence of imprisonment for life imposed otherwise than as a minimum punishment, on conviction for an offence set out in Schedule I or II to that Act that was prosecuted by way of indictment, the court may, if satisfied, having regard to the circumstances of the commission of the offence and the character and circumstances of the offender, that the expression of society's denunciation of the offence or the objective of specific or general deterrence so requires, order that the portion of the sentence that must be served before the offender may be released on full parole is one half of the sentence or ten years, whichever is less.

· · ·

(2) For greater certainty, the paramount principles which are to guide the court under this section are denunciation and specific or general deterrence, with rehabilitation of the offender, in all cases, being subordinate to these paramount principles.

More recently, Parliament added ss. 743.6(1.1) and (1.2) to include organized crime and terrorism offences within this regime.

After a variety of approaches by appellate courts, the Supreme Court addressed this issue in *R v. Zinck* and discussed the relevant factors that a judge should consider before making an order under s. 743.6 of the Code (formerly s. 741.2).

R v. Zinck
2003 SCC 6, [2003] 1 SCR 41

I. Introduction

LeBEL J: [1] On November 20, 1996, the appellant Thomas Zinck shot and killed his 19-year-old neighbour, Stéphane Caissie. He was charged with second degree murder. He pleaded guilty to manslaughter. The trial judge sentenced him to a 12-year term of imprisonment and ordered that his parole eligibility be delayed for six years under s. 743.6 of the *Criminal Code*, RSC 1985, c. C-46. The appellant challenged this part of his sentence in the New Brunswick Court of Appeal and now in this Court, where it is the sole issue remaining on appeal. In his view, the order to delay parole eligibility was made without evidence of the exceptional circumstances which would justify it, without sufficient reasons being given by the trial judge, and after a hearing conducted in breach of procedural fairness. None of these grounds has been established. For the reasons which follow, I would dismiss this appeal.

II. Background

[2] At the time of his trial, Zinck was 56 years old. He had a long history of run-ins with the law. His extensive criminal record speaks for itself. It goes back some 30 years. It includes a conviction for robbery, for which he received a 10-year jail sentence, together with a string of thefts and other property crimes. A number of alcohol and gun offences, as well as breaches of parole or probation, are also listed in this record.

[3] The victim was a neighbour of the accused. Based on the evidence, it seems that they got along well. At the time, Zinck drank heavily. He was also fond of firearms and kept a number of them in his house. Before the shooting, three successive break-ins had occurred at the Caissie house. It appears that Zinck took it on himself to watch for burglars. This plan led to Caissie's tragic death. On the day of the shooting, Zinck had been drinking heavily. It seems that he thought he had noticed burglars. So he went to Caissie's house, where the victim was in bed. Zinck was carrying a loaded gun. He started banging on the door. Stéphane Caissie went to the door to check what was going on. He opened the door. The gun went off. Caissie was killed instantly.

[4] Zinck was never able to explain what happened. As the trial judge found, he was heavily intoxicated at the time of the shooting, he was fascinated with guns especially when he was drunk, and he had said, shortly after the shooting, that he had "got one" (a burglar). As mentioned above, he was charged with murder, but agreed to plead guilty to the reduced and included offence of manslaughter.

[5] On November 17, 1997, following the guilty plea, Godin J adjourned the sentencing hearing to December 22. Zinck had legal representation throughout. During the hearing, Crown counsel reviewed the circumstances of the crime and the record of the accused. He asked the court to consider a 15-year term of imprisonment as a fit punishment for the offence. Then, close to the end of his submissions, the Crown prosecutor raised the issue of delayed parole and of the application of s. 743.6 of the *Code*. He asked the trial judge to consider applying this provision and delaying parole. His argument on the issue was very brief. Counsel stated only that he was asking for delayed parole because Zinck had violated parole before.

[6] After a break of a few hours, defence counsel made representations on behalf of his client. His argument addressed the issues pertaining to what should be the appropriate punishment. Despite the application for delayed parole made by the Crown, the lawyer who was then acting for the appellant never mentioned the issue during his argument.

· · ·

[8] The judge noted that the Crown had applied for delayed parole. He agreed that the case was a proper one for the application of s. 743.6. His specific reasons on the question remained faithful to the virtue of conciseness:

> In addition, having regards to Section 743.6 of the *Criminal Code*, I am satisfied, having regards to the circumstances of the commission of the offence and the character and the circumstances of the offender, that the expression of society's denunciation of the offence requires an order that the portion of the sentence that must be served before the offender may be released on full parole is at least one-half of the sentence.

· · ·

V. Analysis

A. The Issue

[14] This appeal is concerned solely with the question of delayed parole under s. 743.6 of the *Criminal Code* (formerly s. 741.2). The fitness of the 12-year jail term was not questioned in our Court. No issues of inadequate representation by trial counsel

in connection with the Crown's application for delayed parole eligibility were raised in the Court of Appeal or in our Court.

[15] The appeal raises closely connected procedural and substantive issues. First, Zinck challenges the procedural fairness of the process which led to the order delaying his eligibility for parole. He submits that the prosecution should give notice in advance of its intention to apply for delayed parole, in order to allow the accused to respond effectively to such an application. Following both parties' submissions, the reasons of the trial judge should address the issue with clarity and precision. Second, the appellant raises the argument that a proper interpretation of s. 743.6 requires that it be applied only in limited cases, upon evidence of extraordinary or exceptional circumstances.

[16] The respondent, supported by the intervener, the Attorney General of Ontario, advances a more flexible application of delayed parole. In their opinion, the law does not require prior notice, written or otherwise. Evidence of exceptional circumstances is not required, although the respondent acknowledges that this kind of order represents an exception to normal sentencing practices and should be treated as such. Delayed parole eligibility may be justified if the Crown merely satisfies the judge that the order is necessary in order to express society's denunciation of the offence or to meet societal objectives of specific or general deterrence.

· · ·

B. The Nature of Orders for Delayed Parole

[18] The delayed parole scheme under s. 743.6 reflects a relatively recent change in legislative policy on sentencing. It is true that a related provision, which is now found in s. 745.4, had provided for a number of years that a sentencing judge must fix the period of parole ineligibility of an accused convicted of second degree murder. This exception aside, the principles of sentencing drew a clear distinction between the functions of courts, which determined the proper punishment for an offence, and the role of agencies which ran the jails and oversaw the execution of sentences. Eligibility for parole fell within the mandate of the National Parole Board. Considerations relating to parole eligibility normally remained irrelevant to the determination of the fitness of the sentence: *R v. M. (C.A.)*, [1996] 1 SCR 500, at para. 62, *per* Lamer CJ. While some courts may have increased the length of a jail term to manipulate the term of parole ineligibility, such a practice is quite improper. (See H. Dumont, *Pénologie: Le droit canadien relatif aux peines et aux sentences* (1993), at p. 151; see also A. Manson, "Judges and Parole Eligibility: Section 741.2" (1995), 37 CR (4th) 381.)

[19] Determining the date and conditions of parole eligibility is usually the prerogative of an administrative body, the Parole Board, in the discharge of its supervisory functions over the execution of sentences. Over time, however, the focus of legislation has shifted. The *Corrections and Conditional Release Act* (the "Act") now puts more emphasis than before on the protection of the public and less on pure rehabilitation objectives and concerns. (See, for example, ss. 4, 102 and 126 of the Act; also, Dumont, *supra*, at p. 299.) Nevertheless, the decision-making process under the Act remains much different from the judicial determination of a fit sentence. It is largely based on the ongoing observation and assessment of the personality and behaviour of the offender

during his or her incarceration, which focuses on dangerousness and the offender's ability to re-enter the community (Dumont, *supra*, at p. 333). Such a process may extend over several years and lead to decisions that are highly attentive to context and based, at least in part, on what actually happened during the incarceration of the offender.

[20] At the end of this process of observation and review, full parole may be granted. The granting of full parole does not amount to a reduction of the jail sentence. The offender is still serving his or her sentence until the end of the term. Our Court has defined such a decision as an alteration of the conditions under which the sentence is being served (*Cunningham v. Canada*, [1993] 2 SCR 143, at pp. 150-51, *per* McLachlin J (as she then was); *M. (C.A.)*, *supra*, at para. 61). At the same time, under s. 128 of the Act, the offender on full parole is entitled to remain at large and is not obliged to live within the four walls of the correctional institution. Although the sentence is not over and measures of supervision remain in place, full parole grants an offender a very substantial degree of personal freedom. As mentioned above, this process generally used to fall outside the functions of the sentencing courts, which did not have to concern themselves about parole eligibility, its conditions and its supervision.

[21] In respect of second degree murder, s. 745.4 created a first exception to this principle when it brought initial access to parole within the province of the sentencing judge (*R v. Shropshire*, [1995] 4 SCR 227). This power was granted in the case of one class of crimes, where delaying parole beyond the statutory minimum of 10 years had become the sole discretion the judge could exercise at the time of sentencing.

[22] The adoption of s. 743.6 altered more significantly the nature and scope of sentencing decisions in Canadian criminal law. Section 743.6 applies to a wide spectrum of offences. Some of them carry minimum sentences. In many cases, punishment may range from conditional discharge to life imprisonment. The sentencing judge already had to exercise a broad discretion in determining the appropriate punishment for the specific crime committed by a particular offender. Now, whenever s. 743.6 applies, judges may have to factor in parole ineligibility as an additional variable.

[23] It is now well established that the power to delay parole eligibility is part of the sentencing process. Deferred access to parole has now become a part of the punishment, in the case of criminal offences falling within the scope of s. 743.6. Indeed, as this Court held in *R v. Chaisson*, [1995] 2 SCR 1118, at para. 11 (*per* La Forest J): "The inclusion of s. 741.2 of the *Code* should ... be understood to indicate an intention on the part of Parliament explicitly to allow a trial judge to *reduce* the discretion of the Parole Board in certain circumstances, by requiring an accused to serve one half of his or her term of imprisonment before being able to seek parole. The point is that under s. 741.2 the determination of conditional release eligibility has now become a factor in *sentencing*, and not simply a matter exclusively in the hands of the Parole Board" (emphasis in original); see also *Goulet* [(1995), 97 CCC (3d) 61], at p. 65, *per* Griffiths JA.

[24] Delaying parole can be a significant component of a sentence. It may almost entirely extinguish any hope of early freedom from the confines of a penal institution with its attendant rights or advantages. In this manner, it brings a new element of truth, but also of harshness, to sentencing. The time served in a penitentiary will be closer to the sentence imposed, although, under the Act, the sentence is not over. Given its potential impact, it would have been preferable to be clear about when and why this new

sentencing tool is to be used. Regrettably, the drafting of s. 743.6 left many substantive and procedural questions unanswered. As Fish JA of the Quebec Court of Appeal pointed out in one of the earliest cases on the interpretation of this provision, which was decided, like the *Goulet* case, before the enactment of s. 743.6(2), its conceptual basis remains "elusive." It concerns offences in respect of which the sentencing judge must first apply the normal principles of sentencing to the facts in order to determine a fit punishment for the crime. Then, the court must use the same principles all over again, in respect of the same facts—although now with a priority to deterrence and denunciation pursuant to s. 743.6(2)—in order to decide whether parole should be delayed (*R v. Dankyi* (1993), 86 CCC (3d) 368, at p. 376). The nature of the analytical process required in order to apply this provision remains far from clear. This degree of uncertainty goes a long way towards explaining the problems courts have encountered in their search for a workable and consistent interpretation of s. 743.6, as well as the development of apparently conflicting jurisprudential currents in provincial appellate courts. It remains to be seen whether this conflict amounts to more than a question of semantics, given that Canadian courts have tried to ascertain what the provision really means and how it should work. I will now turn to this problem.

C. The Interpretation of Section 743.6

• • •

[26] Many judgments have referred in some way to delayed parole as an exceptional measure. Until now, our Court has had no opportunity to consider this issue, which was not raised in *Chaisson*. In *Shropshire*, we reviewed the criteria and procedures governing delayed parole eligibility, but only in the context of a second degree murder, under what is now s. 745.4. Our Court held in that case that the prosecution need not demonstrate unusual circumstances, and that the law did not require that the power to delay parole be used sparingly (*Shropshire*, at para. 31, *per* Iacobucci J). As mentioned above, the provision at issue in *Shropshire* applied to a particular crime. The problems of the exercise of judicial discretion, the interplay of the sentencing factors, and their respective importance, arise in a different manner under s. 743.6. A method of interpretation and application, coordinating the application of this provision with the classical principles of sentencing and defining its sphere of application, remains to be developed.

[27] The theme of the exceptional character of the measure has been much stressed in an important strand of Canadian appellate jurisprudence. Many judgments express the view that the order to delay parole should be considered an exceptional one. ...

[28] Other appellate decisions adopted what appears to be a significantly different and broader approach to the interpretation and application of s. 743.6. According to these decisions, a sentencing judge does not have to look for unusual circumstances before ordering delayed parole. The judge has been granted discretionary power to be used in the appropriate circumstances, where consideration of the relevant sentencing factors justifies its exercise. The Alberta Court of Appeal summarized the gist of this jurisprudential approach in the following manner:

> This court has previously had occasion to consider the scope of s. 743.6 in *R v. Matwiy* ...
> (1996), ... 105 CCC (3d) 251 (CA). This court did not impose on trial judges a requirement

that they satisfy themselves that the circumstances were "extraordinary" or "unusual" or "particularly aggravating" so as to permit such an order to be made. The point made by Mr. Justice Iacobucci in *R v. Shropshire, supra*, with respect to what is now s. 745.4 applies with equal force to this section. There is nothing in s. 743.6 which indicates that it is a condition precedent to its exercise that either the circumstances of the offence or the offender be in this "unusual" category, let alone so unusual, in order for a trial judge to impose an order under this section. To judicially impose such a threshold requirement would fetter and undermine the general discretion which Parliament has given to trial judges. What the section does require, and this was confirmed by this court in *Matwiy*, is that the trial judge be convinced that denunciation or specific or general deterrence will not be properly met without a s. 743.6 order, taking into account all relevant circumstances. ...

VI. The Function of Section 743.6

[29] The extent of this jurisprudential conflict has been overplayed. It does not reflect a basic disagreement between courts in Canada as to the nature of this provision and its place in the sentencing process. On the contrary, both views address the same difficulty and adopt ultimately consistent solutions to the integration of delayed parole into the process of sentencing. Under both approaches, the same method must be used. That method accepts that delayed parole is a decision that remains out of the ordinary and must be used in a manner that is fair to the offender. Both jurisprudential approaches to the application of s. 743.6 appear to require that the sentencing judge use a two-step intellectual process when deciding whether to delay parole. The addition of this section has not abolished the first duty of the sentencing judge. He or she must first determine what would be the appropriate punishment for the crime. The issue of parole eligibility is not considered at this stage. Courts consider all relevant factors and weigh them, in the circumstances of the case and taking into account the character of the offender. On the basis of this analysis, the judge determines the duration of the jail sentence, if imprisonment is required by law or appears necessary.

[30] At this point, the analysis may shift to the exercise of the power to delay parole. The position of s. 743.6 in the *Criminal Code* signals that it should not be applied in a routine manner. The power should not be exercised in a mechanical or automatic way, nor invoked in connection with every jail term imposed for an offence covered by s. 743.6. The judge must once again apply the sentencing factors. In this part of the process, however, the addition of s. 743.6(2) requires that, in the course of this second balancing, priority be given to the factors of general and specific deterrence, and of denunciation. The other factors remain relevant, but, to the extent of any conflict, subordinated to those identified by Parliament. It is worth noting that Parliament has not given priority to these specific factors in the application of s. 745.4.

[31] At this stage, having given priority to the factors of deterrence and denunciation as required by law, and having duly considered all the criteria and principles relevant to sentencing, based on the evidence at the sentencing hearing and at trial, the court must arrive at its conclusion as to whether this additional punishment is required. The prosecution has the burden of demonstrating that it is. The judge must satisfy himself or herself that the order is needed to reflect the objectives of sentencing, with awareness

of the special weight ascribed by Parliament to the social imperatives of denunciation and deterrence. Nevertheless, at the end of this intellectual process, the sentencing decision must remain alive to the nature and position of delayed parole in criminal law as a special, additional form of punishment. Hence it should not be ordered without necessity, in a routine way. This idea is acknowledged by Griffiths JA of the Ontario Court of Appeal in *Goulet* (p. 65). It is this aspect of s. 743.6 that explains the development of the jurisprudential current emphasizing its exceptional nature. The other stream of jurisprudence, which shies away from using the vocabulary of an "exceptional measure," does not seem, in practice, to have applied s. 743.6 in a different manner. None of these judgments has suggested that a delayed parole order should be considered an ordinary measure, to be applied in the normal course; they agree that it should be invoked only on the basis of demonstrated need.

[32] The application of s. 743.6 will probably never be an easy task for judges. Sentencing remains a heavy responsibility for trial and appellate judges throughout Canada. The exercise of the power to delay parole adds to the difficulties of this task. With a proper understanding of the nature of the measure, it is to be hoped that its application will be less problematic.

[33] As mentioned above, courts must perform a double weighing exercise. First, they must evaluate the facts of the case, in light of the factors set out in s. 718 of the *Code*, in order to impose an appropriate sentence. Then, they must review the same facts primarily in the perspective of the requirements of deterrence and denunciation, which are given priority at this stage, under s. 743.6(2). The decision to delay parole remains out of the ordinary, but may and should be taken if, after the proper weighing of all factors, it appears to be required in order to impose a form of punishment which is completely appropriate in the circumstances of the case. This decision may be made, for example, if, after due consideration of all the relevant facts, principles and factors at the first stage, it appears at the second stage that the length of the jail term would not satisfy the imperatives of denunciation and deterrence. This two-stage process, however, does not require a special and distinct hearing. It should be viewed as one sentencing process, where issues of procedural fairness will have to be carefully considered.

VII. *Procedural Issues and Fairness*

[34] Acknowledging that delayed parole should not be a routine part of every sentencing decision under s. 743.6 does not imply that there should be a special and distinct hearing on the issue, where evidence of unusual or extraordinary circumstances must be introduced. Section 743.6 does not require the creation of such an additional procedure. A two-step intellectual process does not turn the sentencing hearing into two separate procedures. It should be enough that the issue be raised in a fair and timely manner so as to allow the offender to respond effectively. A breach of this basic obligation would justify quashing the order, as courts have done on occasion. (See *Corneau v. La Reine*, [2001] RJQ 2509 (CA), at p. 2515.) Beyond this, the sentencing hearing should not be overburdened with formalistic and unnecessary procedural requirements.

[35] The need for fairness does not impose any obligation to give written notice to the offender before the hearing that delayed parole will be applied for. Such an obligation would often be impractical, especially since sentencing hearings frequently take

place immediately after the conviction or guilty plea. In addition, the *Criminal Code* does not expressly require written notice any more than did s. 745.4, which was considered in *Shropshire, supra.*

[36] The obligation to assure fairness in the process is of critical importance, but it may be discharged in different and equally valid ways. When possible, the Crown may give notice in writing or verbally before the hearing. The application may be made at the sentencing hearing itself. The issue may also be raised by the judge in the course of the hearing. Whenever and however the question is brought up, the offender must be informed clearly that he is at risk in this respect. The offender must be allowed to make submissions and to introduce additional evidence, if needed, in response to the request for delayed parole. Courts should be generous if adjournments are requested for this purpose. Fairness must be preserved, but in a flexible manner, taking into account the specifics of each case, without pointless procedural constraints.

[37] At the end of the process, the offender is entitled to reasons. The judgment must state with sufficient clarity the reasons why the delayed parole order is made. It must remain consistent with the principles set out in *R v. Sheppard*, [2002] 1 SCR 869, 2002 SCC 26. The reasons need not be elaborate. The basis of the decision must be at least ascertainable from the record; precision and clarity remain advisable in the drafting of such judgments. Deficiencies in reasons may sometimes require quashing an order for the sake of the perceived fairness and the transparency of the criminal process.

VIII. Application of Principles

[38] A review of the judgment and proceedings in this case confirms that none of the grounds of appeal have been established. The trial judge did not err in his application of s. 743.6. The order was justified on the basis of the record and was made after a hearing that did not breach the rules of procedural fairness.

[39] I concede that the part of the reasons dealing expressly with the issue of delayed parole is somewhat imprecise. A more detailed analysis should have been attempted. The reasons, though, must be viewed as a whole and read in connection with the evidence and the submissions made at the hearing. Although not extensive, the reasons permit an appellate court to ascertain and review the basis of the order made by the trial judge. Thus, they do not breach the *Sheppard* standard. Godin J carefully reviewed all relevant facts, particularly the gratuitousness of the crime and the need to protect the public. They confirm his conclusion that the objectives of deterrence and denunciation could not be satisfied without delaying parole eligibility.

[40] Procedural fairness was observed. In its submissions, the Crown asked for delayed parole. The accused, through his counsel, could have made his own submissions or presented evidence to oppose the Crown's request. He could have requested an adjournment, if the Crown's move took him by surprise. None of this was attempted. It was never suggested that this was a case of inadequate representation. The accused was given a sufficient opportunity to respond to the Crown's request. He failed to use it. He cannot fault the judge for this.

[41] The Court of Appeal took the appropriate approach to the review of a sentencing decision. In the absence of an error of principle, a breach of the principles of procedural fairness or a clearly erroneous and material finding of fact, it decided that it should

not intervene. Its decision was well founded. It can be upheld under both the narrow and the broad interpretations of s. 743.6, which can be reconciled, as indicated above.

IX. Disposition

[42] For these reasons, I would dismiss the appeal.

PROBLEM

In 1999, Smith is convicted of manslaughter. The victim was viciously beaten to death while Smith was severely intoxicated. Smith has a previous record for manslaughter in 1985, for which he was sentenced to 10 years' imprisonment. Since his release from that sentence, he was convicted on two occasions of assault causing bodily harm. Smith has been in custody for 2 years pending the trial. The Crown has submitted that the only appropriate sentence is a life sentence. The trial judge has questioned the applicable parole eligibility rule. First, if sentenced to life, when would Smith be eligible for parole? Second, can the judge use s. 743.6 to delay parole? See *R v. Shorting* (1995), 102 CCC (3d) 385 (Man. CA).

C. Parole by Exception

Although it rarely occurs, it is possible for some prisoners to be considered for parole before their eligibility date. This has become known as parole by exception.

121(1) Subject to section 102 and notwithstanding section 119 or 120 or any order made under section 741.2 of the *Criminal Code*, parole may be granted at any time to an offender

(a) who is terminally ill;

(b) whose physical or mental health is likely to suffer serious damage if the offender continues to be held in confinement;

(c) for whom continued confinement would constitute an excessive hardship that was not reasonably foreseeable at the time the offender was sentenced; or

(d) who is the subject of an order to be surrendered under the *Extradition Act* or the *Fugitive Offenders Act* and to be detained until surrendered.

(2) Subsection (1) does not apply to any offender who is

(a) serving a sentence of life imprisonment imposed as a minimum punishment or commuted from a sentence of death; or

(b) serving, in a penitentiary, a sentence of detention for an indeterminate period.

This provision does not apply to prisoners serving life sentences or indeterminate sentences. In May 2000, a subcommittee of the House of Commons Standing Committee on Justice and Human Rights released a review of the CCRA five years after its enactment ("the five-year review"). With respect to parole by exception, the subcommittee recommended that "offenders serving life sentences or indeterminate sentences who are terminally ill and who present, in the opinion of the NPB, no undue risk" should also be eligible for extraordinary consideration. However, any such decisions must be approved by the chair of the NPB (see Sub-committee on Corrections and Conditional Release Act of the

Standing Committee on Justice and Human Rights, *A Work in Progress: The Corrections and Conditional Release Act* (Ottawa: Public Works Canada, 2000), 39-40. This recommendation has not been adopted.

D. Accelerated Parole

This mechanism, intended to fast-track non-violent offenders, was first introduced in 1992 with the CCRA. Section 125 of the CCRA and its related regulations provide that cases of first-time penitentiary prisoners who are not serving a sentence for murder, a life sentence, or an offence from the list that would qualify for detention, shall be sent to the NPB prior to day parole eligibility. For this category of offender, eligibility for day parole is earlier and is determined by s. 119.1:

> 119.1 The portion of the sentence of an offender who is eligible for accelerated parole review under sections 125 and 126 that must be served before the offender may be released on day parole is six months, or one sixth of the sentence, whichever is longer.

The file is then reviewed without a hearing by the NPB. If the NPB is "satisfied that there are no reasonable grounds to believe that the offender, if released, is likely to commit an offence involving violence before the expiration of the offender's sentence," it orders that the offender be released on day parole (see ss. 126(2) and 126.1). A successful day parole usually leads to full parole. If the board does not order release, the prisoner must get reasons and is subsequently entitled to a hearing on reaching full parole eligibility.

This mechanism received substantial consideration by the House of Commons subcommittee, which conducted the five-year review of the CCRA.

Sub-committee on Corrections and Conditional Release Act of the Standing Committee on Justice and Human Rights, *A Work in Progress: The Corrections and Conditional Release Act*
(Ottawa: Public Works Canada, 2000), 33-35

> 4.24 The Sub-committee repeatedly heard at its hearings that the conditional release programs most successful in reducing recidivism were those that relied on discretionary decisions by either the Correctional Service or the National Parole Board. In its brief, the Canadian Resource Centre for Victims of Crime stated:
>
> > It is interesting to note that the conditional releases with the highest success rates are those that rely on the judgments of professionals and are based on proper risk assessments that focus on public safety, where the lowest success rates are for those releases by law, including statutory release and accelerated parole review.
>
> 4.25 While the Sub-committee notes the lower success rate among offenders released under accelerated parole review for day and full parole, it does not believe that accelerated parole review should be eliminated. In fact, it believes that two amendments should suffice to make accelerated parole review correspond to the Sub-committee's position on conditional release: tightening the eligibility criteria; and changing the

risk of recidivism criterion to be taken into account by the National Parole Board in reviewing cases.

4.26 The Sub-committee considers it crucial to recognize a significant difference between the accelerated parole review procedure and statutory release. Unlike statutory release as it currently stands, accelerated parole review ensures that all eligible offenders' cases are carefully reviewed by the Correctional Service of Canada and the National Parole Board. Moreover, under the Act, if after reviewing a case the Board has reason to believe that the offender will commit a violent offence listed in Schedule I of the Act before the expiry of the warrant of committal, the Board is required to deny release under the accelerated parole review procedure.

4.27 Unlike the current conditions governing statutory release, accelerated parole review is not a right, but is a simplified case review procedure reserved for offenders considered non-violent who are serving a first federal term of incarceration.

4.28 Under section 125 of the Act, an offender eligible for accelerated parole review is:

- sentenced to a federal penitentiary for the first time;
- not serving a sentence for murder or aiding and abetting murder;
- not serving a life sentence;
- not convicted of an offence listed in Schedule I of the Act;
- not convicted of a criminal organization offence; and
- not subject to a court order making them ineligible for parole before serving at least half of their sentence (this condition includes offences listed in Schedule II of the Act).

4.29 Unlike other offenders, those who meet all these conditions are automatically streamed into a simplified review procedure for possible day or full parole, with no requirement for a hearing before the National Parole Board. They may also benefit from day parole, not six months before their full parole eligibility dates as is the case for offenders ineligible for accelerated parole review, but after serving six months or one-sixth of their sentences, whichever is longer. In reviewing these cases, the Board must also use the criterion of violent recidivism, not general recidivism, as is the case for offenders ineligible for accelerated parole review.

4.30 Although the Sub-committee considers it important to retain accelerated parole review, so first time federal offenders considered non-violent need not be subjected to the negative influence of some repeat offenders, it also considers two amendments to the accelerated parole review procedure essential. The Sub-committee believes offenders incarcerated for Schedule I or Schedule II offences should not be eligible. As well, the recidivism criterion taken into account by the National Parole Board in reviewing these cases should specify general recidivism, not violent recidivism. It is the Sub-committee's view that the Parole Board should grant parole only if it is convinced there are no reasonable grounds to believe that any offence will be committed before the expiry of the warrant of committal.

Recommendation 13

The Sub-committee recommends that the *Corrections and Conditional Release Act* be amended to ensure that the accelerated parole review procedure is not available to offenders incarcerated for offences listed in Schedule II to the Act, regardless of whether there has been a judicial determination of parole eligibility.

Recommendation 14

The Sub-committee also recommends that the *Corrections and Conditional Release Act* be amended to ensure that the National Parole Board, in reviewing the cases of offenders eligible for accelerated parole review and determining whether they should be released on day parole or full parole, takes into account the general recidivism criterion.

The scope of applicability, particularly regarding those excluded from the accelerated parole regime, is set out in detail in s. 125(1):

125(1) This section and section 126 apply to an offender sentenced, committed or transferred to penitentiary for the first time, otherwise than pursuant to an agreement entered into under paragraph 16(1)(b), other than an offender

(a) serving a sentence for one of the following offences, namely,

(i) murder,

(ii) an offence set out in Schedule I or a conspiracy to commit such an offence,

(ii.1) an offence under section 83.02 (providing or collecting property for certain activities), 83.03 (providing, making available, etc. property or services for terrorist purposes), 83.04 (using or possessing property for terrorist purposes), 83.18 (participation in activity of terrorist group), 83.19 (facilitating terrorist activity), 83.2 (to carry out activity for terrorist group), 83.21 (instructing to carry out activity for terrorist group), 83.22 (instructing to carry out terrorist activity) or 83.23 (harbouring or concealing) of the *Criminal Code* or a conspiracy to commit such an offence,

(iii) an offence under section 463 of the *Criminal Code* that was prosecuted by indictment in relation to an offence set out in Schedule I, other than the offence set out in paragraph (1)(q) of that Schedule,

(iv) an offence set out in Schedule II in respect of which an order has been made under section 743.6 of the *Criminal Code*,

(v) an offence contrary to section 130 of the *National Defence Act* where the offence is murder, an offence set out in Schedule I or an offence set out in Schedule II in respect of which an order has been made under section 140.4 of the *National Defence Act*, or

(vi) a criminal organization offence within the meaning of section 2 of the *Criminal Code*, including an offence under subsection 82(2);

(a.1) convicted of an offence under section 240 of the *Criminal Code*;

(b) serving a life sentence imposed otherwise than as a minimum punishment; or

(c) whose day parole has been revoked.

(1.1) For greater certainty, this section and section 126

(a) apply to an offender referred to in subsection (1) who, after being sentenced, committed or transferred to penitentiary for the first time, is sentenced in respect of an offence, other than an offence referred to in paragraph (1)(a), that was committed before the offender was sentenced, committed or transferred to penitentiary for the first time; and

(b) do not apply to an offender referred to in subsection (1) who, after being sentenced, committed or transferred to penitentiary for the first time, commits an offence under an Act of Parliament for which the offender receives an additional sentence.

The issue of eligibility for accelerated parole and the legitimacy of some of the exclusions have been the subject of considerable litigation, which has also shed light on the general functioning of the parole process.

De Luca v. Canada (Attorney General)
2003 FCT 261 (2003), FTR 8 (TD), [2003] FCJ No. 353 (QL)

MARTINEAU J: [1] This is an application for judicial review of the decision by the Correctional Service of Canada (the "Service") that the applicant is not eligible for accelerated parole review under the *Corrections and Conditional Release Act*, SC 1992, c. 20 (the "Act"), accompanied by an application for mandamus ordering the Service to review his case for the purpose of referral to the National Parole Board (the "Board").

[2] The decision issued by the Service on July 25, 2002, reads as follows:

[TRANSLATION] Having examined your file and more particularly the transcript of the Court's notes in case number (500-73-0015270015), we note that the Court pointed to certain factors that are related to criminal organization offences as described in the following place(s):

Page 7, 3rd paragraph "[TRANSLATION] the evidence that this is a highly structured criminal organization; the fact that the network had some international ramifications, in particular in ... even in Colombia; Michel De Luca enjoyed the confidence of the organization and played a role as an intermediary; and the duration of the accused's involvement, which was for close to one year."

These factors meet the tests under section 2 of the *Criminal Code* and thus exclude you from accelerated parole review under section 125(1)(a)(vi) of the *Corrections and Conditional Release Act*.

Your dates of eligibility have been calculated in accordance with section 119(1)(c) for day parole and section 120(1) for full parole.

. . .

[4] Since the Service refers in its decision to the exception under paragraph 125(1(a)(vi) of the Act, the definitions of "criminal organization offence" and "criminal organization" in section 2, as well as section 467.1, subparagraph 718.2(a)(vi) and subsection 743.6(1.1) of the *Criminal Code*, RSC 1985, c. C-46 (the "Code"), as these read before the amendments made by the Act to amend the *Criminal Code*, SC 2001, c. 32, are also relevant:

"Criminal organization offence" means

(a) an offence under section 467.1 or an indictable offence under this or any other Act of Parliament committed for the benefit of, at the direction of or in association with a criminal organization for which the maximum punishment is imprisonment for five years or more, or

(b) a conspiracy or an attempt to commit, being an accessory after the fact in relation to, or any counselling in relation to, an offence referred to in paragraph (a);
"criminal organization" means any group, association or other body consisting of five or more persons, whether formally or informally organized,

(a) having as one of its primary activities the commission of an indictable offence under this or any other Act of Parliament for which the maximum punishment is imprisonment for five years or more, and

(b) any or all of the members of which engage in or have, within the preceding five years, engaged in the commission of a series of such offences;

. . .

[5] In the present case, the Court must determine whether the Service erred in law or otherwise refused to carry out its legal duty by determining that the applicant was not eligible for accelerated parole review and by refusing to review his case under subsection 125(2) of the Act for the purpose of referral to the Board under section 126 of the Act.

[6] First, it should be noted that this is not a case in which, in the exercise of its discretion, the Court should refuse to hear an application for judicial review or to exercise the powers conferred on it by sections 18 and 18.1 of the *Federal Court Act*, RSC 1985, c. F-7. Although I need not rule on this point, even if under subsection (4)(g), sections 90 *et seq.* of the Act and sections 74 *et seq.* of the *Corrections and Conditional Release Regulations*, SOR/92-620, the applicant could have disputed the Service's decision by way of a grievance, I am of the view that his failure to file such a grievance is not fatal in this instance. Indeed, the point at issue is the correct interpretation of the scope of subparagraph 125(1)(a)(vi) of the Act, which refers to a "criminal organization offence" within the meaning of section 2 of the Code. However, the administrative interpretation reported in the Bulletin of April 22, 1999 (Applicant's Record, at pages 161-62), on which the Service implicitly relies in its reasoning, is disputed by the applicant, who considers it a usurpation of authority. This case is therefore clearly distinguished from the decisions cited by the respondent in support of its preliminary objection (*Giesbrecht v. Canada* (1998), 148 FTR 81 (FCTD); *Condo v. Canada (Attorney General)*, [2003] FCJ No. 91 (QL); *Anderson v. Canada (Armed Forces) (CA)*, [1997] 1 FC 273 (FCA); and *Bordage v. Archambault Institution*, (2000), 204 FTR 133, [2002] FCJ No. 710 (FCA)). That objection is consequently overruled.

[7] The applicant, for whom this is a first conviction and first penitentiary sentence, was convicted by Judge Elizabeth Corte of the Court of Quebec (Criminal and Penal Division) (the "court") of the offence under section 465 of the Code, as a result of his participation in a conspiracy to import a substance listed in Schedule I of the *Controlled Drugs and Substances Act*, SC 1996, c. 19, in this instance cocaine (exhibit A-1 of the affidavit of Michel De Luca). For this offence, the applicant was sentenced to six years imprisonment, which was set at four years from the date of sentencing, May 27, 2002, taking into account the period of his pre-trial detention.

[8]　According to the record, the applicant was never prosecuted for the commission of the offence referred to in section 467.1 of the Code, nor was he convicted by the court of a "criminal organization offence" within the meaning of section 2 of the Code. That being the case, it should be noted here that the offence under section 467.1 of the Code requires evidence beyond a reasonable doubt of membership by the accused in a criminal organization and of the nature of the alleged offence.

· · ·

[9]　Let us note at this point that the applicant acknowledged his guilt on the conspiracy offence; however, he has never made any admission whatsoever as to the perpetration of a criminal organization offence. A person convicted of a criminal act always has the benefit of a reasonable doubt about the issues pertaining to the sentence that will be given to him. Consequently, the prosecution had to prove beyond a reasonable doubt all the aggravating circumstances that it cited and that were not covered by the applicant's confession (*R v. Gardiner*, [1982] 2 SCR 368, at p. 414).

[10]　In the case at bar, the respondent concedes that the applicant was not charged or convicted of any of the offences specifically mentioned in subsection 125(1) of the Act. However, he submits that the applicant is ineligible for accelerated parole review because of the general implication of subparagraph 125(1)(a)(vi) of the Act, for during sentencing the court accepted as an aggravating factor the fact that the applicant had played an "[TRANSLATION] intermediary role" and had "[TRANSLATION] the confidence ... of the other members of the organization" involved in the conspiracy, characterizing the latter as a "[TRANSLATION] highly structured criminal organization" (sentence, transcript, respondent's record, at pages 56 and 58). The respondent submits that it can reasonably be inferred that the specific offence for which the applicant was convicted, the conspiracy, was therefore "for the benefit of, at the direction of or in association with a criminal organization," and that the Service's decision not to consider the applicant eligible for accelerated parole review has a valid basis in fact and in law.

[11]　I am unable to adopt the argument of the respondent, since the Service bases itself on an administrative interpretation of the scope of subparagraph 125(1)(a)(vi) of the Act that is erroneous and contrary to the Act. I also find that its decision is patently unreasonable.

[12]　Absent a conviction by the court on any of the offences expressly indicated in subsection 125(1) of the Act, and with the exception of the cases expressly provided for in the Act or the Code (for example, where an order was made by the court under subsection 743.6(1.1) of the Code), it is clear that sections 125 and 126 of the Act apply automatically to offenders sentenced or transferred for the first time to the penitentiary. This is the applicant's situation. The fact that in determining the appropriate sentence for the commission of the offence for which the applicant was convicted the court could take into account the aggravating factor indicated in subparagraph 718.2(a)(iv) of the Code does not alter the primary nature of the offence for which the applicant was convicted and is serving his sentence. This was and remains a conspiracy offence that is not expressly covered by subsection 125(1) of the Act.

[13]　The exceptions under subsection 125(1) of the Act must be strictly construed; for the exception under subparagraph 125(1)(a)(vi) of the Act to apply, the court must necessarily, in my opinion, have specifically convicted the offender of a "criminal organ-

ization offence," and that is not the case in this instance. Furthermore, although the court, when handing down the sentence, referred in connection with aggravating circumstances to a "highly structured criminal organization," I note that it never expressly mentioned that the record had established beyond a reasonable doubt that the conspiracy offence of which it had convicted the applicant had been committed "for the benefit of, at the direction of or in association with a criminal organization" or that "the highly structured criminal organization" that was at issue in the sentencing actually constituted a "criminal organization" within the meaning of section 2 of the Code.

[14] On the other hand, I stop at this point to note that under subsection 125(3) of the Act, when the Service reviews the case of an offender, it must ascertain for which offence(s) the offender was convicted; however, that does not authorize the Service to substitute itself for the court. The Service has no jurisdiction to determine whether, according to the evidence in the record, the offender may have committed a "criminal organization offence" within the meaning of section 2 of the Code. The interpretation of subparagraph 125(1)(a)(vi) of the Act proposed by the respondent is not only incompatible with the strict construction given to the other exceptions under subsections 125(1) and (1.1) of the Act, which require a prior conviction on each of these offences, but it runs directly counter to the presumption of innocence recognized in section 6 of the Code and subsection 11(d) of the *Canadian Charter of Rights and Freedoms*, Part I of the *Constitution Act, 1982*, constituting Schedule B of the *Canada Act 1982* (UK) 1982, c. 11. But the withdrawal of the accelerated review status has direct consequences on the freedom of the individual who is incarcerated. Consequently, the Service can deprive an offender of eligibility for the day parole provided in sections 119 and 119.1 of the Act only in compliance with the principles of fundamental justice and any provision of the Act that is applicable in that case.

[15] In this regard, the scheme of the Code clearly suggests that *actes de gangstérisme* (or *infractions d'organisation criminelle* ["criminal organization offences"] as they are now designated [in the French version of the Code]) may give rise to distinct convictions provided of course that distinct charges have been brought before the court, which is not the case in this instance. Where there are distinct convictions, the sentences imposed by the court shall or may be served consecutively. Moreover, I note that Parliament seems to have specifically considered the question of the impact of a conviction for a criminal organization offence on the offender's eligibility for parole. For example, under subsection 743.6(1.1) of the Code, notwithstanding section 120 of the Act, where an offender receives a sentence of imprisonment of two years or more on conviction for a criminal organization offence, the court may order that the portion of the sentence that must be served before the offender may be released on full parole is one half of the sentence or ten years, whichever is less. I conclude therefore that there would have to be some provision that is otherwise more specific than the present provisions of the Act to allow the Service to exclude from accelerated parole review, on its own initiative and *a posteriori*, an offender who has not first been convicted of a "criminal organization offence" under the Act in a fair and public hearing by an independent and impartial court.

[16] I am well aware that criminal organizations are a menace to society and public order. Nevertheless, I do not think it is the job of this Court to correct any statutory deficiency that may result from the fact that, prior to the 2001 amendments to the Code, it

seemed impossible for the prosecution to obtain a conviction related to a "criminal organization offence" other than for the specific offence under the old section 467.1 of the Code. In this regard, I note that the new sections 467.11, 467.12 and 467.13 of the Code cover a much more varied set of situations and that a criminal act committed for the benefit of, at the direction of or in association with a criminal organization is expressed covered by section 467.12 of the Code, which now makes it a specific offence.

[17] In the case that concerns us, I conclude from the evidence in the record that under sections 119.1 and 126.1 of the Act, the applicant is eligible for accelerated parole review, and that under subsection 125(2) of the Act, the Service is required to review the applicant's case for the purpose of its referral to the Board for a determination under section 126 of the Act. The applicant is therefore entitled to the relief he seeks in his application for judicial review.

Compare the approach in *De Luca* with that in the following case.

Bedi v. Canada (Attorney General)
[2004] FCJ No. 2096 (QL), 264 FTR 30 (TD)

BLAIS J: [1] This is an application for judicial review of a decision not to direct day parole of Mahesh Bedi (applicant). The applicant submits that the initial decision, the review by the two-member panel of the National Parole Board (NPB), and the affirmation on appeal by the National Parole Board's Appeal Division (Appeal Division) all erred in law and based their decisions on erroneous findings of fact.

Relevant Facts

[2] The applicant was convicted on August 13, 2003 in the Ontario Court of Justice on the charges of: possession [for] the purpose of trafficking, possession of cocaine, four charges of possession of a loaded prohibited weapon, two charges of possession of a firearm with serial number defaced, possession of stolen property, four counts of possession of a firearm and possession of the proceeds of crime. He was sentenced to four and a half years in a federal penitentiary.

[3] On December 24, 2003, the Peel Parole Office completed an assessment for decision which recommended that the NPB direct accelerated day and full parole (the issue of full parole was not addressed by the NPB at that time).

[4] On February 13, 2004, based on the written submissions, a one member panel of the NPB refused to direct day parole, a decision which was subsequently upheld by an oral hearing before the NPB which took place on April 29, 2004.

[5] On June 28, 2004, the applicant appealed this decision to the National Parole Board's Appeal Division. On August 3, 2004, the Appeal Division dismissed the appeal.

Issues

[6]:

1. What is the applicable standard of review?
2. Did the NPB and the Appeal Division apply the proper test in deciding not to direct day parole?

Analysis

What Is the Applicable Standard of Review?

· · ·

I find that the above analysis properly covers the most current jurisprudence on the subject matter, and correctly arrives at the conclusion that the applicable standard of review for questions of fact is that of manifestly or patently unreasonable, and for questions of law, that of reasonableness.

Did the NPB and the Appeal Division Apply the Proper Test in Deciding Not to Direct Day Parole?

[9] At hand, we have the decision of the NPB not to direct day parole, as well as the decision of the Appeal Division confirming the order not to direct day parole. In such a circumstance, the role of this Court is to analyse the decision of the NPB and determine its lawfulness

· · ·

[10] The applicant submits that the NPB committed a reviewable error in substituting the applicable standard of "likely to commit" with that of the "potential to commit." Having carefully read the decision of the NPB as well as that of the Appeal Division, I find that the proper test of "likely to commit" was applied.

[11] In regards to the decision by the two-member panel of the NPB, the section marked "accelerated review decision" clearly reads:

> The Board is satisfied that there are reasonable grounds to believe that, if released, you are likely to commit an offence involving violence before the expiration of your sentence and therefore, directs that you will not be released. (Page 2 of the NPB Accelerated Parole Review Decision Sheet) [my emphasis]

[12] Then again, at the conclusion of the reasons for decision, the Board member states that:

> In summary, the interplay between crime, drugs and dangerous weapons, combined with a lack of programming to address criminal values, attitudes and faulty decision-making skills, leads the Board to conclude that there are reasonable grounds to believe that you are likely to commit an offence involving violence prior to the expiration of your sentence. Therefore, day parole is not directed. (Page 3 and 4 of the NPB Accelerated Parole Review Decision Sheet)

· · ·

[15] Therefore, the legislation requires the NPB to take into account indications of potential violence. I find that it is precisely that which was done, when the NPB mentioned that even though the applicant was a first time offender, his offences included numerous convictions for weapons offences, the applicant participated heavily in the cocaine dealing business, and he had criminal values and associations, all of which demonstrated a potential to commit an offence involving violence.

. . .

[19] As for the determination of the NPB not to direct day parole, seeing as to how the appropriate test was applied, this becomes simply an analysis of the facts presented to the NPB. Being an expert in this field, the Board is in the best situation to analyse the facts presented to it, as well as the credibility of the applicant during the oral hearings.

> First, this is a matter of judicial review and the reviewing Court, and this Court on appeal from the reviewing Court, cannot simply substitute its views of the facts and the law for those of the Tribunal and render what it considers the right conclusion. We must proceed on the record as we have it, confining ourselves to the criteria for judicial review, and remembering at all times that a denial of natural justice cannot readily be cured on such review. While we must ensure that the Tribunal conducts itself in a lawful way, it is for the Tribunal to render a decision on the facts once those facts are properly litigated before it. (*Canada (A.G.) v. McKenna*, [1999] 1 FC 401 at paragraph 6)

. . .

[24] As such, I find that the "likely to commit violence" test was lawfully applied and that the ultimate decision of the NPB, based on the facts, is not unreasonable. The intervention of this Court is therefore not warranted.

NOTE

Another accelerated parole issue that has implications for future cases is the question of retrospective application of the exclusions in s. 125(1) to offences committed prior to its enactment. Essentially, this is a question about the applicability of the Supreme Court decision in *R v. Gamble*, [1988] 2 SCR 595 in which Wilson J stated, "[I]t is fundamental to any legal system which recognizes the rule of law that an accused must be tried and punished under the law in force at the time the offenses were committed." There have been inconsistent judicial rulings on this issue: see *Abel v. Edmonton Institution for Women*, [2000] AJ No. 1296 (QL), [2001] 5 WWR 341 (QB); compare *R v. Caruana* (2002), 48 CR (5th) 285 (Ont. SC).

E. Statutory Release

Until 1992, all prisoners in Canada were entitled to earn remission at the rate of 15 days per month. If completely earned and not forfeited for disciplinary offences, this could amount to remission credits totalling approximately one-third of the prisoner's sentence. At the point when the days actually served in custody and the number of earned remission credits equalled the total sentence, the prisoner was entitled to be released. For provincial prisoners, this meant an unconditional release, but federal prisoners were released on mandatory supervision. Provincial prisoners can still earn remission (see s. 6 of the *Prisons and Reformatories Act*, RSC 1985, c. P-20). However, in 1992, the CCRA abolished remission for federal prisoners and replaced it with "statutory release," which occurs after two-thirds of a sentence has been served.

127(1) Notwithstanding the *Prisons and Reformatories Act*, an offender sentenced, committed or transferred to penitentiary is entitled to be released on the date determined in accordance with this section and to remain at large, subject to this Act, until the expiration of the sentence according to law.

(2) Subject to subsections (4) and (5), the statutory release date of an offender sentenced to imprisonment for one or more offences committed before the day on which this section comes into force shall be determined by crediting against the sentence

(a) any remission, statutory or earned, standing to the offender's credit on that day; and

(b) the maximum remission that could have been earned on the balance of the sentence pursuant to the *Penitentiary Act* or the *Prisons and Reformatories Act*, as those Acts read immediately before that day.

(3) Subject to subsection (4), the statutory release date of an offender sentenced to imprisonment for one or more offences committed on or after the day on which this section comes into force is the day on which the offender completes two thirds of the sentence.

(4) The statutory release date of an offender sentenced to imprisonment for one or more offences committed before the day on which this section comes into force and for one or more offences committed on or after the day on which this section comes into force is the later of

(a) the day determined by crediting against the sentence the aggregate of

(i) any remission, statutory or earned, standing to the offender's credit on that day, and

(ii) the maximum remission that could have been earned on the balance of the sentence pursuant to the *Penitentiary Act* or the *Prisons and Reformatories Act*, as those Acts read immediately before that day, and

(b) the day on which the offender completes two thirds of the sentence.

(5) subject to subsections 130(7) and 138(2), the statutory release date of an offender who is on parole or who is subject to mandatory supervision under the *Parole Act* on the day on which this section comes into force, and whose parole or release subject to mandatory supervision is revoked on or after that day, is the day on which the offender completes two thirds of the unexpired portion of the sentence after being recommitted to custody pursuant to subsection 138(1).

(6) An offender who is entitled to be released on statutory release may choose to remain in custody for all or any portion of the sentence the offender is serving.

(7) an offender sentenced, committed or transferred (otherwise than pursuant to an agreement entered into under subsection 16(1) to penitentiary on or after August 1, 1970 who is released on statutory release is subject to supervision in accordance with this Act, but no other offender released under this section is subject to supervision.

Prisoners on statutory release are subject to compulsory conditions that are prescribed by regulation and any other conditions that the NPB "considers reasonable and necessary in order to protect society and to facilitate the offender's successful reintegration into society" (see s. 133(3)). Like prisoners on parole, the prisoner on statutory release can be returned to custody if the statutory release is suspended, terminated, cancelled, or revoked.

F. Detention

Probably the most significant change to the function of the NPB was the introduction of the detention provisions that permit the denial of release on statutory release. The history of this enactment goes back to the early 1980s, when the NPB was criticized following a few high-profile offences that were committed by offenders who had been released on mandatory supervision. Although these releases were the result of the statutory process and not the result of the NPB's discretion, the media and the public do not always appreciate these distinctions. In response, the strategy of "gating" was devised. Because the *Parole Act* authorized the suspension and revocation of an offender on parole or mandatory supervision "to protect society," it was reasoned that a prisoner could be immediately suspended and recommitted to confinement based on a *prediction* of his or her post-release conduct. This metaphor of "gating" conveyed both a return to custody from the prison gate and also the negating of the expected release.

In late 1982, nine prisoners who were about to be released were immediately suspended at the penitentiary gates. A series of *habeas corpus* applications were commenced across the country, arguing that the NPB had no authority to deny anyone their release on mandatory supervision. When two of these cases reached the Supreme Court of Canada, a unanimous court agreed that the *Parole Act* only authorized suspension and revocation based on post-release conduct (see *R v. Moore* (1983), 33 CR (3d) 97 (SCC)).

Shortly after the Supreme Court decision, new legislation was introduced that would amend the *Parole Act* by using a predictive test similar to that found in the dangerous offender provisions of the *Criminal Code*. In 1985, the bill passed the House of Commons, but was rejected by the Senate. In the summer of 1986, Prime Minister Mulroney recalled Parliament and passed the amendment to the *Parole Act*. The extraordinary move of recalling Parliament during the summer had been taken in the past only to declare war or legislate an end to public sector strikes. On this occasion, the argument made was that there were 50 dangerous prisoners in custody who, without this legislation, would be released into the community. (Notwithstanding the apparent identification of 50 prisoners within the entire system as the reason for immediate legislative action, since 1986 the detention rate rose to a high of 484 prisoners in 1995-96. The rate has since dropped to 233 prisoners detained in 1998-99.)

In *R v. Cunningham*, below, the Supreme Court confirmed the constitutional validity of the detention provisions. *Cunningham* also marks the beginning of the "balancing" methodology of Charter analysis whereby the Supreme Court has asserted that the definition of rights encompassed by s. 7 of the *Canadian Charter of Rights and Freedoms*, Part I of the *Constitution Act, 1982*, RSC 1985, app. II, no. 44, required balancing the rights of the individual with larger societal rights. (Up to this point, many observers had assumed that any balancing would occur within the strictures of s. 1.)

R v. Cunningham
(1990), 80 CCC (3d) 492 (SCC)

[In 1981, the prisoner had been sentenced to 12 years' imprisonment for manslaughter. He expected to be released on mandatory supervision on April 8, 1989. He had maintained good behaviour in prison. In 1988, his parole officer recommended him for parole and requested a community assessment because the appellant had indicated that he would be returning to his home community, not far from the scene of the crime. Subsequently, he was referred by the commissioner to the NPB for a detention hearing.]

McLACHLIN J:

. . .

His community, alerted to his release by the community assessment, evinced concern at his early release given the violence of the crime. Further assessments made in the six months preceding the early release date suggested that he remained homicidal when drunk. There was said to be a 50% chance of his returning to alcohol, and a 50% chance that if drunk he would commit an act of violence. There was also evidence that he was somewhat unstable and had not accepted his responsibility for the crime. While this evidence was brought forward in the six months preceding the anticipated release date, similar observations may be found in the prison records for preceding years. Following a detention hearing, the appellant was ordered to be detained until his sentence expired on February 13, 1993, subject to annual reviews. The appellant brought an action to the Supreme Court of Ontario for a writ of *habeas corpus*.

. . .

My conclusion is that while the appellant's liberty may be said to have been adversely affected by the changes to the *Parole Act*, the deprivation was not contrary to the principles of fundamental justice.

The first question is whether the appellant has suffered a deprivation of liberty which attracts the protection of s. 7 of the Charter. This raises two subsidiary questions: (1) has the appellant shown that he has been deprived of liberty?; (2) if so, is the deprivation sufficiently serious to attract Charter protection?

In my view, the appellant has shown that he has been deprived of liberty. The argument that because the appellant was sentenced to twelve years' imprisonment there can be no further impeachment of his liberty interest within the twelve-year period runs counter to previous pronouncements, and oversimplifies the concept of liberty. This and other courts have recognized that there are different types of liberty interests in the context of correctional law. In *Dumas v. LeClerc Institute*, [1986] 2 SCR 459, at p. 464, Lamer J (as he then was) identified three different deprivations of liberty: (1) the initial deprivation of liberty; (2) a substantial change in conditions amounting to a further deprivation of liberty; and (3) a continuation of the deprivation of liberty. In *R v. Gamble*, [1988] 2 SCR 595, at p. 645, this Court held by a majority, per Wilson J (Lamer and L'Heureux-Dubé JJ concurring) that the liberty interest involved in not continuing the period of parole ineligibility may be protected by s. 7 of the Charter:

... the continuation of the 25-year period of parole ineligibility deprives the appellant of an important residual liberty interest which is cognizable under s. 7 and which may be appropriately remedied by way of habeas corpus if found to be unlawful.

American authority is to the same effect. In *Greenholtz v. Inmates of Nebraska Penal and Correctional Complex*, 442 US 1 (1979), at pp. 9-10, the Supreme Court of the United States per Burger CJ held that an expectation of liberty created by a parole statute created a liberty interest in parole release that is protected by the Due Process Clause of the Fourteenth Amendment. This finding was affirmed in *Board of Pardons v. Allen*, 482 US 369 (1987). Notwithstanding a vigourous dissent by O'Connor J (Rehnquist CJ and Scalia J concurring) in that case, relying on *Board of Regents of State Colleges v. Roth*, 408 US 564 (1972), this remains the law in the United States.

I do not find it useful to ask whether the liberty interest was "vested" or "not vested." The only questions which arise under the Charter are whether a protected liberty interest is limited, and if so, whether that limitation accords with the principles of fundamental justice. To qualify an interest as "vested" or "not vested" does not really advance the debate, except in the sense that a vested interest might be seen as being more important or worthy of protection than one which is not vested. In that event, I think it better to speak directly of the importance of the interest, rather than introducing the property law concept of vesting. At the same time, it is important to recognize that liberty interests may cover a spectrum from the less important to the fundamental. A restriction affecting the form in which a sentence is served, the issue here, may be less serious than would be an *ex post facto* increase in the sentence.

In the case at bar, the appellant was sentenced to twelve years and was required under his warrant of committal, both before and after the amendment of the *Parole Act*, to serve that sentence in its entirety. Thus the duration of the restriction of his liberty interest has not been affected. As Lamer J held for the Court in *Dumas*, supra, at p. 464, "In the context of parole, the continued detention of an inmate will only become unlawful if he has acquired the status of a parolee." The appellant had never acquired parolee status, and his sentence, contrary to his counsel's submissions, has not been increased.

However the manner in which he may serve a part of that sentence, the second liberty interest identified by Lamer J in *Dumas*, supra, has been affected. One has "more" liberty, or a better quality of liberty, when one is serving time on mandatory supervision than when one is serving time in prison. The appellant had a high expectation, contingent on his good behaviour, that he would be released on mandatory supervision on April 8, 1989, had the *Parole Act* not been amended; indeed, he would automatically have been released on mandatory supervision given his good behaviour. The effect of the 1986 amendment of the *Parole Act* was to reduce that expectation of liberty, in the sense that it curtailed the probability of his release on mandatory supervision. This resulted from the new power of the Commissioner to refer exceptional cases to the Parole Board based on events and information in the six months immediately preceding the presumptive release date. As the British Columbia Court of Appeal put it in *Re Ross and Warden of Kent Institution* (1987), 34 CCC (3d) 452 (BC CA), at p. 454: "The effect of the 1986 amendments ... is to alter the right of an inmate to serve a portion of his sentence on mandatory supervision by qualifying that right."

I conclude that the appellant has suffered deprivation of liberty. The next question is whether the deprivation is sufficiently serious to warrant Charter protection. The Charter does not protect against insignificant or "trivial" limitations of rights: *R v. Edwards Books and Art Ltd.*, [1986] 2 SCR 713, at p. 759 (per Dickson CJ); *R v. Jones*, [1986] 2 SCR 284, at p. 314; *Lavigne v. Ontario Public Service Employees Union*, [1991] 2 SCR 211, at p. 259; *Andrews v. Law Society of British Columbia*, [1989] 1 SCR 143, at pp. 168-69. It follows that qualification of a prisoner's expectation of liberty does not necessarily bring the matter within the purview of s. 7 of the Charter. The qualification must be significant enough to warrant constitutional protection. To require that all changes to the manner in which a sentence is served be in accordance with the principles of fundamental justice would trivialize the protections under the Charter. To quote Lamer J in *Dumas*, supra, at p. 464, there must be a "substantial change in conditions amounting to a further deprivation of liberty."

The change in the manner in which the sentence was served in this case meets this test. There is a significant difference between life inside a prison versus the greater liberty enjoyed on the outside under mandatory supervision. Such a change was recognized as worthy of s. 7 protection in *Gamble, supra*.

Having concluded that the appellant has been deprived of a liberty interest protected by s. 7 of the Charter, we must determine whether this is contrary to the principles of fundamental justice under s. 7 of the Charter. In my view, while the amendment of the *Parole Act* to eliminate automatic release on mandatory supervision restricted the appellant's liberty interest, it did not violate the principles of fundamental justice. The principles of fundamental justice are concerned not only with the interest of the person who claims his liberty has been limited, but with the protection of society. Fundamental justice requires that a fair balance be struck between these interests, both substantively and procedurally (see *Re BC Motor Vehicle Act*, [1985] 2 SCR 486, at pp. 502-3, per Lamer J; *Singh v. Minister of Employment and Immigration*, [1985] 1 SCR 177, at p. 212, per Wilson J; *Pearlman v. Manitoba Law Society Judicial Committee*, [1991] 2 SCR 869, at p. 882, per Iacobucci J). In my view the balance struck in this case conforms to this requirement.

The first question is whether, from a substantive point of view, the change in the law strikes the right balance between the accused's interests and the interests of society. The interest of society in being protected against the violence that may be perpetrated as a consequence of the early release of inmates whose sentence has not been fully served needs no elaboration. On the other side of the balance lies the prisoner's interest in an early conditional release.

The balance is struck by qualifying the prisoner's expectation regarding the form in which the sentence would be served. The expectation of mandatory release is modified by the amendment permitting a discretion to prevent early release where society's interests are endangered. A change in the form in which a sentence is served, whether it be favourable or unfavourable to the prisoner, is not, in itself, contrary to any principle of fundamental justice.

Indeed, our system of justice has always permitted correctional authorities to make appropriate changes in how a sentence is served, whether the changes relate to place, conditions, training facilities, or treatment. Many changes in the conditions under which sentences are served occur on an administrative basis in response to the prison-er's immediate needs or behaviour. Other changes are more general. From time to time, for example, new approaches in correctional law are introduced by legislation or regu-lation. These initiatives change the manner in which some of the prisoners in the system serve their sentences.

The next question is whether the nature of this particular change in the rules as to the form in which the sentence would be served violates the Charter. In my view, it does not. The change is directly related to the public interest in protecting society from per-sons who may commit serious harm if released on mandatory supervision. Only if the Commissioner is satisfied on the facts before him that this may be the case can he refer the matter to the Parole Board for a hearing. And only if the Board is satisfied that there is a significant danger of recidivism can it order the prisoner's continued incarceration. Thus the prisoner's liberty interest is limited only to the extent that this is shown to be necessary for the protection of the public. It is difficult to dispute that it is just to afford a limited discretion for the review of parole applicants who may commit an offence causing serious harm or death. Substantively, the balance is fairly struck.

Nor does the procedure established under the Act and Regulations violate the princi-ples of fundamental justice. The change was made by law. The new procedure provides for a hearing to consider whether the expectation of release on mandatory supervision was warranted. The prisoner is entitled to representation throughout. The material on which the matter may be referred for hearing is limited. Under s. 21.3(3) of the *Parole Act*, the reference together with the relevant information is to be submitted no later than six months before the presumptive release date. The only exception to this general rule is provided where either the behaviour of the inmate or information obtained within the six months warrants a review. There are also provisions for new hearings to review the detention in the future. These requirements provide safeguards against arbitrary, capri-cious orders and ensure that curtailment of release on mandatory supervision occurs only when it is required to protect the public and then only after the interests of the prisoner in obtaining the release have been fully and fairly canvassed.

· · ·

I conclude that the appellant has not established that the changes to the *Parole Act* deprived him of his liberty contrary to the principles of fundamental justice. No viola-tion of s. 7 having been made out, it is unnecessary to consider the arguments under s. 1 of the Charter.

I turn to the final issue: whether the Commissioner's referral of the appellant's case to the Parole Board was illegal and contrary to the law. Under s. 21.3(3), the Commis-sioner may refer an inmate's case to the Board no later than six months preceding his "presumptive release" on mandatory supervision. An exception to this general rule is permitted where, due to the inmate's behaviour or information received within the six month period, the Commissioner has reason to believe that the inmate is likely, prior to the expiration of his sentence, to commit an offence causing death or serious harm. The Commissioner must have formed the belief on the basis of "information obtained within those six months" (s. 21.3(3)(a)(ii)).

The Commissioner referred the appellant's case as a "Commissioner's Referral based upon new information," offering the opinion that "without treatment intervention there are reasonable grounds to believe that this inmate is likely to commit an offence causing death or serious harm prior to warrant expiry date." The Commissioner's memorandum included two psychiatric reports, a letter from the Crown prosecutor and an updated RCMP report. All this information was received within the six months before the presumptive release date. It is argued that the information relied on by the Commissioner, while nominally arising within the six-month period before the appellant's prospective date for release on mandatory supervision, in fact is no more than an update of information which was on the appellant's file before that period. It is true that references to the appellant's volatility, drinking problems, lack of acceptance of guilt and tendency to violence when drunk may be found in the files prior to the six-month period. But that should not, in my view, prevent the Commissioner from relying on new and revised reports to the same effect when they come to his attention within the six-month period before the prospective release date. Indeed, it would be an unusual case where information coming forward in the six-month pre-release period did not find its echoes and antecedents in the previous prison record, given the long-standing nature of the problems typically involved in these cases.

I would agree with the motions judge that an objective test is appropriate. The issue put before this Court was whether the information could be said to be "new" in the substantive sense, rather than merely the temporal sense. The motions judge, having considered all the material, concluded on an objective test that it had not been established that the Commissioner had acted illegally in the sense of not forming his opinion on the basis of information obtained within six months. My review of the record does not persuade me that he was wrong.

In my view, the Commissioner did not violate the Act by referring the appellant's case to the National Parole Board for reconsideration of his eligibility for release on mandatory supervision.

NOTE

Since the decision in *Cunningham*, the scope of the detention provisions has been expanded. The list of offences that can lead to detention now includes serious drug offences and sexual offences involving children. For the extensive lists, see schedules I and II to the Act and s. 129(9).

The significant elements of the current detention provisions are set out below. Note that they encompass two stages: referral by the Correctional Service or commissioner and the detention hearing before the NPB. The standard for detention is whether the NPB is satisfied that the offender is likely to commit an offence causing death or serious harm, a sexual offence involving a child, or a serious drug offence if released.

Corrections and Conditional Release Act
SC 1992, c. 20, as amended by SC 1995, c. 42, ss. 129-132

129(1) Before the statutory release date of an offender who is serving a sentence of two years or more that includes a sentence imposed for an offence set out in Schedule

I or II or an offence set out in Schedule I or II that is punishable under section 130 of the *National Defence Act*, the Commissioner shall cause the offender's case to be reviewed by the Service.

(2) After the review of the case of an offender pursuant to subsection (1), and not later than six months before the statutory release date, the Service shall refer the case to the Board together with all the information that, in its opinion, is relevant to it, where the Service is of the opinion

(a) in the case of an offender serving a sentence that includes a sentence for an offence set out in Schedule I, that

(i) the commission of the offence caused the death of or serious harm to another person and there are reasonable grounds to believe that the offender is likely to commit an offence causing death or serious harm to another person before the expiration of the offender's sentence according to law, or

(ii) the offence was a sexual offence involving a child and there are reasonable grounds to believe that the offender is likely to commit a sexual offence involving a child before the expiration of the offender's sentence according to law; or

(b) in the case of an offender serving a sentence that includes a sentence for an offence set out in Schedule II, that there are reasonable grounds to believe that the offender is likely to commit a serious drug offence before the expiration of the offender's sentence according to law.

(3) Where the Commissioner believes on reasonable grounds that an offender who is serving a sentence of two years or more is likely, before the expiration of the sentence according to law, to commit an offence causing death or serious harm to another person, a sexual offence involving a child or a serious drug offence, the Commissioner shall refer the case to the Chairperson of the Board together with all the information in the possession of the Service that, in the Commissioner's opinion, is relevant to the case, as soon as is practicable after forming that belief, but the referral may not be made later than six months before the offender's statutory release date unless

(a) the Commissioner formed that belief on the basis of behaviour of the offender during the six months preceding the statutory release date or on the basis of information obtained during those six months; or

(b) as a result of any recalculation of the sentence under this Act, the statutory release date of the offender has passed or less than six months remain before that date.

(3.1) Where paragraph (3)(b) applies and the statutory release date has passed, the Commissioner shall, within two working days after the recalculation under that paragraph, make a determination whether a referral is to be made to the Chairperson of the Board pursuant to subsection (3) and, where appropriate, shall make a referral, and the offender is not entitled to be released on statutory release pending the determination.

(4) At the request of the Board, the Service shall take all reasonable steps to provide the Board with any additional information that is relevant to a case referred pursuant to subsection (2) or (3).

· · ·

[Sections 129(5), (6), and (7), dealing with applicable procedures when the commissioner makes a referral to the NPB after the six months before statutory release, have been omitted.]

(8) The Commissioner may delegate to the correctional authorities of a province the powers of the Service and of the Commissioner under this section in relation to offenders who are serving their sentences in a correctional facility in that province.

(9) In this section and sections 130 and 132, "serious drug offence" means an offence set out in Schedule II; "sexual offence involving a child" means

(a) an offence under any of the following provisions of the *Criminal Code* that was prosecuted by way of indictment, namely,

(i) section 151 (sexual interference),

(ii) section 152 (invitation to sexual touching),

(iii) section 153 (sexual exploitation),

(iv) subsection 160(3) (bestiality in presence of child or inciting child to commit bestiality),

(v) section 170 (parent or guardian procuring sexual activity by child),

(vi) section 171 (householder permitting sexual activity by child),

(vii) section 172 (corrupting children),

(viii) subsection 212(2) (living off the avails of prostitution by a child), and

(ix) subsection 212(4) (obtaining sexual services of a child),

(b) an offence under any of the following provisions of the *Criminal Code* involving a person under the age of eighteen years that was prosecuted by way of indictment, namely,

(i) section 155 (incest),

(ii) section 159 (anal intercourse),

(iii) subsections 160(1) and (2) (bestiality and compelling bestiality),

(iv) section 271 (sexual assault),

(v) section 272 (sexual assault with a weapon, threats to a third party or causing bodily harm), and

(vi) section 273 (aggravated sexual assault),

(c) an offence under any of the following provisions of the *Criminal Code*, chapter C-34 of the Revised Statutes of Canada, 1970, as they read immediately before January 1, 1988, that was prosecuted by way of indictment, namely,

(i) section 146 (sexual intercourse with a female under 14),

(ii) section 151 (seduction of a female between 16 and 18), and

(iii) section 167 (householder permitting defilement),

(d) an offence involving a person under the age of eighteen years under any of the following provisions of the *Criminal Code*, chapter C-34 of the Revised Statutes of Canada, 1970, as they read immediately before January 1, 1988, that was prosecuted by way of indictment, namely,

(i) section 153 (sexual intercourse with step-daughter),

(ii) section 155 (buggery or bestiality),

(iii) section 157 (gross indecency), and

(iv) section 166 (parent or guardian procuring defilement), or

(e) an offence involving a person under the age of eighteen years under any of
the following provisions of the *Criminal Code*, chapter C-34 of the Revised Statutes
of Canada, 1970, as they read immediately before January 4, 1983, that was prosecuted by way of indictment, namely,

    (i) section 144 (rape),

    (ii) section 145 (attempt to commit rape),

    (iii) section 149 (indecent assault on female), and

    (iv) section 156 (indecent assault on male).

(10) In determining whether an offender is likely to commit an offence causing
death or serious harm to another person, a sexual offence involving a child or a serious
drug offence, it is not necessary to determine whether the offender is likely to commit
any particular offence.

130(1) Where the case of an offender is referred to the Board by the Service pursuant to subsection 129(2) or referred to the Chairperson of the Board by the Commissioner pursuant to subsection 129(3) or (3.1), the Board shall, subject to subsections
129(5), (6) and (7), at the times and in the manner prescribed by the regulations,

(a) inform the offender of the referral and review, and

(b) review the case, and the Board shall cause all such inquiries to be conducted
in connection with the review as it considers necessary.

(2) An offender referred to in subsection (1) is not entitled to be released on statutory release before the Board renders its decision under this section in relation to the
offender.

(3) On completion of the review of the case of an offender referred to in subsection
(1), the Board may order that the offender not be released from imprisonment before
the expiration of the offender's sentence according to law, except as provided by subsection (5), where the Board is satisfied

(a) in the case of an offender serving a sentence that includes a sentence for an
offence set out in Schedule I, or for an offence set out in Schedule I that is punishable
under section 130 of the *National Defence Act*, that the offender is likely, if released,
to commit an offence causing the death of or serious harm to another person or a
sexual offence involving a child before the expiration of the offender's sentence according to law,

(b) in the case of an offender serving a sentence that includes a sentence for an
offence set out in Schedule II, or for an offence set out in Schedule II that is punishable under section 130 of the *National Defence Act*, that the offender is likely, if released, to commit a serious drug offence before the expiration of the offender's sentence according to law,

(c) in the case of an offender whose case was referred to the Chairperson of the
Board pursuant to subsection 129(3) or (3.1), that the offender is likely, if released,
to commit an offence causing the death of or serious harm to another person, a sexual offence involving a child or a serious drug offence before the expiration of the
offender's sentence according to law.

···

(4) Where the Board is not satisfied as provided in subsection (3) but is satisfied
that

(a) at the time the case was referred to it, the offender was serving a sentence that included a sentence for an offence set out in Schedule I or II, or for an offence set out in Schedule I or II that is punishable under section 130 of the *National Defence Act*, and

(b) in the case of an offence set out in Schedule I or an offence set out in Schedule I that is punishable under section 130 of the *National Defence Act*, the commission of the offence caused the death of, or serious harm to, another person or the offence was a sexual offence involving a child, it may order that if the statutory release is later revoked, the offender is not entitled to be released again on statutory release before the expiration of the offender's sentence according to law.

• • •

[Section 131, dealing with the mandatory annual reviews of prisoners who have been detained under s. 130(3), has been omitted.]

132(1) For the purposes of the review and determination of the case of an offender pursuant to section 129, 130 or 131, the Service, the Commissioner or the Board, as the case may be, shall take into consideration any factor that is relevant in determining the likelihood of the commission of an offence causing the death of or serious harm to another person before the expiration of the offender's sentence according to law, including

(a) a pattern of persistent violent behaviour established on the basis of any evidence, in particular,

(i) the number of offences committed by the offender causing physical or psychological harm,

(ii) the seriousness of the offence for which the sentence is being served,

(iii) reliable information demonstrating that the offender has had difficulties controlling violent or sexual impulses to the point of endangering the safety of any other person,

(iv) the use of a weapon in the commission of any offence by the offender,

(v) explicit threats of violence made by the offender,

(vi) behaviour of a brutal nature associated with the commission of any offence by the offender, and

(vii) a substantial degree of indifference on the part of the offender as to the consequences to other persons of the offender's behaviour;

(b) medical, psychiatric or psychological evidence of such likelihood owing to a physical or mental illness or disorder of the offender;

(c) reliable information compelling the conclusion that the offender is planning to commit an offence causing the death of or serious harm to another person before the expiration of the offender's sentence according to law; and

(d) the availability of supervision programs that would offer adequate protection to the public from the risk the offender might otherwise present until the expiration of the offender's sentence according to law.

(1.1) For the purposes of the review and determination of the case of an offender pursuant to section 129, 130 or 131, the Service, the Commissioner or the Board, as the case may be, shall take into consideration any factor that is relevant in determining the likelihood of the commission of a sexual offence involving a child before the expiration of the offender's sentence according to law, including

(a) a pattern of persistent sexual behaviour involving children established on the basis of any evidence, in particular,

(i) the number of sexual offences involving a child committed by the offender,

(ii) the seriousness of the offence for which the sentence is being served,

(iii) reliable information demonstrating that the offender has had difficulties controlling sexual impulses involving children,

(iv) behaviour of a sexual nature associated with the commission of any offence by the offender, and

(v) a substantial degree of indifference on the part of the offender as to the consequences to other persons of the offender's behaviour;

(b) reliable information about the offender's sexual preferences indicating that the offender is likely to commit a sexual offence involving a child before the expiration of the offender's sentence according to law;

(c) medical, psychiatric or psychological evidence of the likelihood of the offender committing such an offence owing to a physical or mental illness or disorder of the offender;

(d) reliable information compelling the conclusion that the offender is planning to commit such an offence; and

(e) the availability of supervision programs that would offer adequate protection to the public from the risk the offender might otherwise present until the expiration of the offender's sentence according to law.

(2) For the purposes of the review and determination of the case of an offender pursuant to section 129, 130 or 131, the Service, the Commissioner or the Board, as the case may be, shall take into consideration any factor that is relevant in determining the likelihood of the commission of a serious drug offence before the expiration of the offender's sentence according to law, including

(a) a pattern of persistent involvement in drug-related crime established on the basis of any evidence, in particular,

(i) the number of drug-related offences committed by the offender,

(ii) the seriousness of the offence for which the sentence is being served,

(iii) the type and quantity of drugs involved in any offence committed by the offender,

(iv) reliable information demonstrating that the offender remains involved in drug-related activities, and

(v) a substantial degree of indifference on the part of the offender as to the consequences to other persons of the offender's behaviour;

(b) medical, psychiatric or psychological evidence of such likelihood owing to a physical or mental illness or disorder of the offender;

(c) reliable information compelling the conclusion that the offender is planning to commit a serious drug offence before the expiration of the offender's sentence according to law; and

(d) the availability of supervision programs that would offer adequate protection to the public from the risk the offender might otherwise present until the expiration of the offender's sentence according to law.

G. Suspension and Revocation

Suspension and revocation are the major enforcement instruments of conditional release supervision. They permit designated officers to suspend a release and return an offender to custody if satisfied that it is "necessary and reasonable ... in order to prevent a breach of condition or to protect society." Once the offender has been returned to custody, the case is reviewed and the suspension can be cancelled or the case can be referred to the NPB to determine whether the release should be terminated or revoked. Both result in return to confinement under s. 138(1), but there are some differences in consequences that arise from the fact that termination is usually a result of "circumstances beyond the offender's control" (see s. 135(5)(b)). For example, after a revocation, there is no obligation to conduct a parole review for one year, even if the prisoner is eligible (see s. 138(5)). Also, what are known as "one-shot statutory releases" are not affected by termination, but are triggered by revocation (see ss. 130(4), 130(6), and 138(6)).

Corrections and Conditional Release Act
SC 1992, c. 20, as amended by SC 1995, c. 42, ss. 135-138

135(1) A member of the Board or a person, designated by name or by position, by the Chairperson of the Board or by the Commissioner, when an offender breaches a condition of parole or statutory release or when the member or person is satisfied that it is necessary and reasonable to suspend the parole or statutory release in order to prevent a breach of any condition thereof or to protect society, may, by warrant,

(a) suspend the parole or statutory release;

(b) authorize the apprehension of the offender; and

(c) authorize the recommitment of the offender to custody until the suspension is cancelled, the parole or statutory release is terminated or revoked or the sentence of the offender has expired according to law.

(2) A person designated pursuant to subsection (1) may, by warrant, order the transfer to penitentiary of an offender who is recommitted to custody pursuant to subsection (1) in a place other than a penitentiary.

(3) The person who signs a warrant pursuant to subsection (1) or any other person designated pursuant to that subsection shall, forthwith after the recommitment of the offender, review the offender's case and

(a) where the offender is serving a sentence of less than two years, cancel the suspension or refer the case to the Board together with an assessment of the case, within fourteen days after the recommitment or such shorter period as the Board directs; or

(b) in any other case, within thirty days after the recommitment or such shorter period as the Board directs, cancel the suspension or refer the case to the Board together with an assessment of the case stating the conditions, if any, under which the offender could in that person's opinion reasonably be returned to parole or statutory release.

(4) The Board shall, on the referral to it of the case of an offender serving a sentence of less than two years, review the case and, within the period prescribed by the regulations, either cancel the suspension or terminate or revoke the parole.

(5) The Board shall, on the referral to it of the case of an offender serving a sentence of two years or more, review the case and, within the period prescribed by the regulations, unless the Board grants an adjournment at the offender's request,

(a) cancel the suspension, where the Board is satisfied that, in view of the offender's behaviour since release, the offender will not, by reoffending before the expiration of the offender's sentence according to law, present an undue risk to society;

(b) where the Board is not satisfied as provided in paragraph (a), terminate the parole or statutory release of the offender if it was suspended by reason of circumstances beyond the offender's control or revoke it in any other case; or

(c) where the offender is no longer eligible for the parole or entitled to be released on statutory release, terminate or revoke it.

(6) If in the Board's opinion it is necessary and reasonable to do so in order to protect society or to facilitate the reintegration of the offender into society, the Board, when it cancels a suspension of the parole or statutory release of an offender, may

(a) reprimand the offender in order to warn the offender of the Board's dissatisfaction with the offender's behaviour since release;

(b) alter the conditions of the parole or statutory release; and

(c) order the cancellation not to take effect until the expiration of a specified period not exceeding thirty days after the date of the Board's decision, where the offender violated the conditions of parole or statutory release on the occasion of the suspension and on at least one previous occasion that led to a suspension of parole or statutory release during the offender's sentence.

(6.1) Where a person referred to in subsection (3) or the Board cancels a suspension under this section, the person or the Board, as the case may be, shall forward a notification of the cancellation of the suspension or an electronically transmitted copy of the notification to the person in charge of the facility in which the offender is being held.

(7) Independently of subsections (1) to (6), where the Board is satisfied that the continued parole or statutory release of an offender would constitute an undue risk to society by reason of the offender reoffending before the expiration of the sentence according to law, the Board may, at any time,

(a) where the offender is no longer eligible for the parole or entitled to be released on statutory release, terminate or revoke the parole or statutory release; or

(b) where the offender is still eligible for the parole or entitled to be released on statutory release,

(i) terminate the parole or statutory release, where the undue risk to society is due to circumstances beyond the offender's control, or

(ii) revoke the parole or statutory release, where the undue risk to society is due to circumstances within the offender's control.

(8) The Board may exercise its power under subsection (7) notwithstanding any new sentence to which the offender becomes subject after being released on parole or statutory release, whether or not the new sentence is in respect of an offence committed before or after the offender's release on parole or statutory release.

(9) Where the Board exercises its power under subsection (7), it shall review its decision at times prescribed by the regulations, at which times it shall either confirm or cancel its decision.

(9.1) Where an offender whose parole or statutory release has not been terminated or revoked is incarcerated as a result of an additional sentence for an offence under an Act of Parliament, the parole or statutory release, as the case may be, is revoked on the day on which the offender is incarcerated as a result of the additional sentence.

(9.2) Subsection (9.1) does not apply where the additional sentence is to be served concurrently with, and is in respect of an offence committed before the commencement of, the sentence to which the parole or statutory release applies.

(9.3) Where an offender who is released on parole receives an additional sentence described in subsection (9.2) and the day determined in accordance with section 119, 120 or 120.2, as the case may be, on which the offender is eligible for parole is later than the day on which the offender received the additional sentence, the parole becomes inoperative and the offender shall be reincarcerated.

(9.4) Unless the lieutenant governor in council of a province in which there is a provincial parole board makes a declaration under subsection 113(1) that subsection (9.1) applies in respect of offenders under the jurisdiction of that provincial parole board, subsection (9.1) does not apply in respect of such offenders, other than an offender who

(a) is serving a sentence in a provincial correctional facility pursuant to an agreement entered into under paragraph 16(1)(a); or

(b) as a result of receiving an additional sentence referred to in subsection (9.1), is required, pursuant to section 743.1 of the *Criminal Code*, to serve the sentence in a penitentiary.

(9.5) Where an offender to whom subsection (9.1) does not apply who is on parole that has not been revoked or terminated receives an additional sentence, for an offence under an Act of Parliament, that is to be served consecutively with the sentence the offender was serving when the additional sentence was imposed, the parole becomes inoperative and the offender shall be reincarcerated until the day on which the offender has served, from the day on which the additional sentence was imposed, the period of ineligibility in relation to the additional sentence and, on that day, the parole is resumed, subject to the provisions of this Act, unless, before that day, the parole has been revoked or terminated.

(10) For the purposes of this Part, an offender who is in custody by virtue of this section continues to serve the offender's sentence.

(11) For the purposes of this Act, where a suspension of parole or statutory release is cancelled, the offender is deemed, during the period beginning on the day of the issuance of the suspension and ending on the day of the cancellation of the suspension, to have been serving the sentence to which the parole or statutory release applies.

. . .

[Section 135.1, dealing with suspension and revocation in relation to long-term offenders, has been omitted.]

136. When the parole or statutory release of an offender is terminated or revoked or where it becomes inoperative pursuant to subsection 135(9.3) or (9.5), a member of the Board or a person designated, by name or by position, by the Chairperson of the Board or by the Commissioner may, by warrant, authorize the apprehension and recommitment to custody of the offender pursuant to section 137.

137(1) A warrant of apprehension issued under section 11.1, 18, 118, 135, 135.1 or 136 or by a provincial parole board, or an electronically transmitted copy of such a warrant, shall be executed by any peace officer to whom it is given in any place in Canada as if it had been originally issued or subsequently endorsed by a justice or other lawful authority having jurisdiction in that place.

(2) A peace officer who believes on reasonable grounds that a warrant is in force under this Part or under the authority of a provincial parole board for the apprehension of a person may arrest the person without warrant and remand the person in custody.

(3) Where a person has been arrested pursuant to subsection (2), the warrant of apprehension, or an electronically transmitted copy thereof, shall be executed within forty-eight hours after the arrest is made, failing which the person shall be released.

138(1) Where the parole or statutory release of an offender is terminated or revoked, the offender shall be recommitted to custody and shall serve the portion of the sentence that remained unexpired on the day on which the parole or statutory release was terminated or revoked.

(2) An offender whose parole or statutory release has been terminated is

(a) eligible for parole in accordance with section 120, 120.1, 120.2 or 120.3, as the case may be; and

(b) entitled to be released on statutory release in accordance with section 127.

(3) An offender whose parole or statutory release has been terminated is not liable to forfeit

(a) any remission with which the offender was credited pursuant to the *Prisons and Reformatories Act*; or

(b) any credits under the *Transfer of Offenders Act*.

(4) An offender whose parole or statutory release has been revoked is eligible for parole in accordance with section 120, 120.1, 120.2 or 120.3, as the case may be.

(5) Notwithstanding sections 122 and 123, the Board is not required to conduct a review for the purpose of parole of the case of an offender referred to in subsection (4) within one year after the date on which the offender's parole or statutory release is revoked.

(6) Subject to subsections 130(4) and (6), an offender whose parole or statutory release has been revoked is entitled to be released on statutory release in accordance with section 127.

NOTE

There are two cautions about these sanctions and the applicable processes. First, the procedures and requirements that govern suspension, cancellation, termination, and revocation are technical and detailed; a careful search of case law should be conducted to find any judicial decisions that may impose specific interpretations on the statutory provisions. Second, amendments to the CCRA have returned to the era of automatic consequences for the commission of an offence while on conditional release. Section 135(9.1) provides for revocation when a person on parole or statutory release is incarcerated for an additional sentence. There is only limited scope to be exempted from this provision. Section 135(9.2) creates an exception when the additional sentence is a concurrent one that arises from an offence committed before the release. Many practising lawyers seem to be unaware of this amendment. Certainly, it is up to the judge in these circumstances whether to make the new sentence concurrent, but counsel need to know the CCRA implications before making their submissions. On what bases do you think one could argue that a new offence should be concurrent?

As an example of the technicalities of the suspension and revocation process, and the need for access to judicial scrutiny, see the following decision of the BC Court of Appeal.

Chiu v. Canada (National Parole Board)
[2007] BCJ No. 577 (QL) (CA)

Introduction

CHIASSON JA: [1] This is an application for an extension of the time to appeal and, if granted, an appeal from a refusal to grant relief in the nature of *habeas corpus* because the appellant was denied his right to procedural fairness and natural justice under s. 7 of the *Canadian Charter of Rights and Freedoms*, Part I of the *Constitution Act, 1982*, being Schedule B to the *Canada Act 1982* (UK), 1982, c. 11.

[2] The case concerns the rights of a parolee related to a hearing determining whether parole should be revoked.

[3] For the reasons that follow I would extend the time to appeal, allow the appeal and order that the appellant be released on full parole subject to the conditions that had been imposed on him.

Background

[4] The appellant had been convicted for offences related to the importation into Canada of large amounts of heroin and was on full parole on condition that he not have contact with anyone with a criminal record or anyone whom he suspected of having a criminal record, "[s]pecifically those involved in drug dealing or trafficking."

[5] In February 2005, Correctional Service of Canada received information that the appellant had breached the condition by associating with individuals involved in criminal activities and a warrant was issued for his arrest. The appellant admitted to his parole officer that he had associated with such individuals. Subsequently, he denied having done so. The appellant's parole was suspended and he was returned to custody.

[6] The appellant was informed that the RCMP had linked him to an investigation involving a large quantity of ecstasy and equipment for making drugs. His parole officer reviewed the appellant's case and referred it to the Parole Board with a recommendation that his parole be revoked because the appellant was likely to commit a serious drug offence.

[7] On April 11, 2005, the appellant was given a copy of the documents that the Board would be considering on a review of his case and on May 5, 2005, he was told that his post-suspension hearing was scheduled for June 2, 2005.

[8] On May 31, 2005, the parole officer received a report from the RCMP containing a synopsis of evidence concerning the appellant that was to be sent to Crown counsel for charge approval. The synopsis, which was 45 pages in length, was provided to the Board on June 1, 2005, which immediately provided it to the appellant. Relying on s. 141 of the *Corrections and Conditional Release Act*, SC 1992, c. 20 ("*CCRA*"), on June 1, 2005, counsel for the appellant wrote to the Board asking for an adjournment of the June 2, 2005 hearing because the synopsis had not been provided until the afternoon of June 1, 2005. No alternative date for the hearing was proposed.

[9] On June 2, 2005, the appellant delivered a written Postponement Report that stated: "lack of 14 days notice at fault of system. Hearing date as soon as possible following notice period under law, section 141 CCRA." Crossed out were the words: "Mr. Chiu is fully aware that this request places hearing past the 90 day review requirement."

[10] On June 2, 2005, the Board adjourned the hearing to June 8, 2005. Counsel for the appellant was so advised that day by a telephone message and replied on Friday, June 3, 2005, stating that the date did not allow for 14 days notice of the RCMP synopsis and that she expected the hearing to be set after June 15, 2005. The Board confirmed the June 8 date by a telephone message to counsel on Monday, June 6, 2005. The written record of the message also stated the Board's position that the Board "*had* to vote on [the appellant's] case prior to his 90 days" (emphasis in original).

[11] On June 7, 2005, counsel wrote again to the Board stating that the appellant was not prepared "to waive his right to 15 days notice of information to be assessed at his parole suspension hearing." Counsel also stated that she was not available on June 8.

[12] Later on June 7, 2005 a further telephone message was left for counsel dealing with the provision of the RCMP material and noting that the appellant could waive the 90 day requirement and that if the appellant were not to postpone or attend the hearing, a decision would be made "to meet our 90 days deadline."

[13] The appellant attended the hearing on June 8, 2005. The discussion that took place at that time will be addressed in some detail later in these reasons. The appellant was advised that the Board would consider its options. On June 13, 2005, the appellant received a copy of the Board's June 10, 2005 decision confirming the revocation of his parole.

[14] The Board stated that it concluded the appellant's "risk to reoffend is undue" because he had violated a condition of his parole that he not associate with people involved in criminal activity. The Board also said:

The police report containing the information described above was received by the Board on June 1st, the day prior to your first scheduled hearing ... on June 2nd. You would not waive your right to have 15 days to consider this new information. As a consequence, the hearing did not take place on that day and a second hearing was scheduled on June 8th. This was the only other opportunity the Board had to meet with you prior to the expiration of the 90 day period within which the Board must render a decision on the matter of your suspension. This period ends June 21st. The fifteen day period you and your assistant have insisted the Board observe ends on June 22nd. At the hearing today, you indicated that on the advice of your lawyer acting as your assistant, you would not proceed with the hearing. You could not give another date prior to June 21st on which you and your assistant would be prepared to participate in a hearing. Nor would you sign a form agreeing to a postponement of your hearing beyond the 90 day period within which a decision must be made.

In the interests of fairness the Board will convene a post revocation hearing at the earliest practicable opportunity to review this decision to revoke your full parole. At that time you and your assistant can respond to the information contained in the police report and address any of the other issues relating to your behaviour in the community that led to your suspension.

[15] On June 23, 2005, the appellant appealed the Board's decision to the Board's appeal division.

[16] On July 7, 2005, the "post-revocation hearing" was held. The appellant attended, but refused to discuss the RCMP synopsis and on July 13, 2005 the Board confirmed the revocation of the appellant's parole.

[17] The appeal division dismissed the appellant's appeal stating: "[a]lthough you had a right to an in-person hearing, your failure to proceed with the scheduled hearing or to agree to a postponement resulted in your impliedly having waived your right to be heard."

[18] The appellant's application in the Supreme Court for relief in the nature of *habeas corpus* was dismissed on May 1, 2006.

[19] The time for initiating this appeal expired on May 31, 2006. On July 9, 2006, the appellant filed an application to extend the time to appeal and a notice of appeal.

• • •

Positions of the Parties

[25] The appellant raises two points in issue:

The Learned Chambers Judge erred in law by failing to uphold the Appellant's rights to disclosure pursuant to s. 141(1) of the *Corrections and Conditional Release Act*, procedural fairness and natural justice, and s. 7 of the *Canadian Charter of Rights and Freedoms*.

The Learned Chambers Judge erred in law by failing to uphold the Appellant's statutory right to an oral hearing and/or the presence of an assistant at the hearing pursuant to s. 140(1), (7) and (8) of the *Corrections and Conditional Release Act*, procedural fairness and natural justice, and s. 7 of the *Canadian Charter of Rights and Freedoms*.

[26] The respondents state their position as follows:

Subsection 141(2) of the *CCRA* [not s. 141(1)] applies to the disclosure of the RCMP report to the Appellant by the Board. The Chambers Judge committed no error in law or principle in concluding that the disclosure of the RCMP report was consistent with s. 141(2) and the Board's duty to act fairly and without any violation of the Appellant's *Charter* rights.

Subsection 140(1)(d) of the *CCRA* provides that the Board shall conduct a review of the case of an offender by way of a post-suspension hearing in the presence of the offender *unless* the offender refuses to attend the hearing. The Chambers Judge committed no error in law or principle in concluding that as the Appellant refused to attend the rescheduled hearing, the Board made its decision on the file material in compliance with s. 140(1)(d), acted fairly and did not violate the Appellant's *Charter* rights.

The issue of the right of an assistant at a hearing was not raised before the Chambers Judge and therefore is not discussed in the Reasons. The Board acted fairly with regard to the presence of the Appellant's assistant at a hearing with the Appellant by notifying the assistant that if she could not appear on the already rescheduled hearing date within the Board's statutory time frame to make a decision, then the Appellant could elect to postpone the hearing to a date past the statutory time frame to allow for the assistant to attend and for the Board to retain jurisdiction to make the decision. [Emphasis in original.]

[27] The respondents also contend that even if there was a breach of procedural fairness, this Court should not intervene because the appellant was not prejudiced thereby.

Discussion

[28] As noted, I agree with the judge's conclusion concerning the disclosure of information and would dismiss that ground of appeal. The question of the absence of representation was not pressed at the hearing of the appeal, but, in any event, on the basis of my conclusions I do not find it necessary to address the issue.

[29] I consider whether the appellant's right to a hearing was violated.

[30] The following exchanges took place at the June 8, 2005 hearing (CF is a hearing officer, analogous to a court clerk; RC is the appellant; PS is a Board member; and TK is a parole officer.)

CF: ... I received confirmation that the necessary reports for hearing today were shared with you. Are you ready to proceed with the hearing?
RC: Yes.

...

PS: Mr. Chiu are you wanting to go ahead with the hearing today[?]
RC: No, I talked to my lawyer.

...

PS: ... Ms. Turko [the appellant's lawyer] ... has advised you not to go ahead with the hearing today.
RC: Yes.

PS: ... We are in a bit of a bind ... you are entitled to 15 days to consider the report, but unfortunately what happens is that 15 days takes you to the end of another time limit which we have to observe and that's 90 days after the time we receive the report—we have to make a decision within that period of time.

RC: Yes.

PS: Otherwise we lose jurisdiction and you know we have no say in the matter at that point ... have you talked to Ms. Turko about a specific time when you might be available for a hearing?

RC: Well, she is supposed to come in this weekend and go over the report with me.

PS: OK, so the two of you have not set a ...

RC: No, we—the last time I saw her was on Thursday.

• • •

PS: Alright, so what you're saying today is that you don't want to go ahead with the hearing on the advice of your assistant. Mr. McDougall [a peer counsellor who was present] isn't your assistant today right, he's just ...

RC: Here to help me.

PS: ... offering support. Alright well that's fair enough. So you don't want to talk about these outstanding charges with us ... .

• • •

PS: Alright. OK. So, Mr. Chiu is saying that he doesn't want to go ahead with the hearing today so that's his option.

CP: OK.

PS: and what we will do is we'll I guess consider our options and ... you will be advised what the decision is when we've made it I guess.

• • •

TK: My only question is do you need to ... a postponement?

PS: he's not willing to postpone it I understand, is that right?

RC: well, if whatever it is that needs to be signed if Donna [Turko] says it's ok to sign it I will sign it.

• • •

PS: ... this particular letter doesn't say that you are not willing to postpone. I have heard that is the position that she is encouraging you to take so if you're meeting with her on the weekend then I guess maybe that issue can be discussed.

RC: OK.

[31] June 8, 2005 was a Wednesday. The decision was dated Friday, June 10, 2005.

[32] I make a number of observations concerning this discussion.

[33] The Board member was wrong, stating that the appellant was entitled to 15 days to review the report (the RCMP synopsis) for the reasons previously stated. He also incorrectly said that the 90 day period would have expired before the expiration of 15 days after the appellant received the report.

[34] Section 135(5) of the *CCRA* states that the Board must review and decide the case within a period prescribed in the regulations to the legislation. Section 163(3) of the *Corrections and Conditional Release Regulations*, SOR/92-620 requires the Board

to render its decision within 90 days after the matter has been referred to it by the appellant's parole officer. This was done on March 23, 2005. The 90 day period expired on June 21, 2005. The report was provided to the appellant on June 1, 2005.

[35] The Board member was not correct in his assertion that the 90 day period would have expired before the 15 day period. In its reasons, the Board stated that the 15 day period would have expired on June 22, 2005, which also was wrong.

[36] In its reasons, the Board stated that June 8, 2005 was the only opportunity the Board had to meet with the appellant before the expiration of the 90 day period. This suggestion was not conveyed to the appellant before the decision was rendered and it is not supported by any evidence. The transcript of the June 8, 2005 discussion suggests that the Board contemplated a hearing on another date before the expiration of the time limit ("... have you talked to Ms. Turko about a specific time when you might be available for a hearing?").

[37] The Board's appeal division and the judge concluded that the appellant waived his right to an oral hearing. In my view, he did not do so.

[38] In an affidavit filed to support his appeal to the Board's appeal division, the appellant stated that he did not waive his right to a hearing. He said the same thing in his affidavit filed in the court below. In his Postponement Report, he crossed out a statement acknowledging that his request for time to review the report would take the matter beyond the 90 day period.

[39] The transcript of the June 8, 2005 hearing does not support a waiver by the appellant of his right to an oral hearing. On a fair reading of the transcript, the appellant sought an adjournment so that he could obtain the advice of his counsel whether to postpone the 90 day period and the Board acceded to his request ("... if you're meeting with her on the weekend then I guess maybe that issue [whether to postpone the 90 day time limit] can be discussed").

[40] The respondents argue and the judge held that the appellant refused to attend the hearing because he stated he did not want to participate in it before obtaining the advice of his lawyer. At no time was it made clear to the appellant that his position was considered to be a waiver of his right to a hearing and that the Board would proceed to decide the matter in his absence if he were not to participate.

[41] At the outset of the proceeding, the hearing officer did state that the Board members had two options: "to cancel the suspension or revoke full parole" and during the discussion the Board member said that the Board would consider its options, but the hearing ended with the clear understanding that the appellant would consult with his lawyer on the weekend and that part of that consultation would be consideration of whether to waive the 90 day time limit.

[42] In my view, the appellant did not waive his right to a hearing and the Board proceeded contrary to the statutory provision entitling the appellant to a hearing.

[43] The appellant seeks relief in the nature of *habeas corpus*. Having failed to hold a hearing in accordance with the legislation, the Board lost jurisdiction to revoke the appellant's parole. There is no lawful basis for his detention.

· · ·

[47] There was no statutory authority for the July hearing, a fact recognized by the Board's appeal division. By the time of that hearing, the appellant had an appeal pend-

ing before the Board. He also was under the cloud of the RCMP's investigation. We do not know why he declined to comment on the report, but he was entitled to take that position at that time. It does not support a conclusion that his request for time to study the report and, as stated at the hearing, to obtain the advice of his lawyer about the report, was not genuine or that he was not prejudiced by the failure to provide to him his right to a hearing.

[48] I have concluded that the appeal should be allowed.

[49] Granting relief in the nature of *habeas corpus* in this case leaves in place the conditions of the appellant's parole. (See: *Dumas v. Leclerc Inst. of Laval*, [1986] 2 SCR 459, citing *R v. Miller*, [1985] 2 SCR 613 at paras. 10-12—a grant of relief in the nature of *habeas corpus* need not afford to the subject full liberty, but may keep in place the existing constraints on the subject's liberty.)

Conclusion

[50] I would grant the application for an extension of time, allow the appeal and grant the requested relief in the nature of *habeas corpus* directed to the Warden of Ferndale Institution and the National Parole Board, ordering that the appellant be re-released on parole on the conditions imposed initially on him.

III. THE PAROLE DEBATE

Over the years, the legitimacy, efficacy, and fairness of parole have been the subject of substantial debate in Canada. Aside from questions about whether parole decisions are made fairly or arbitrarily, there are some important intrinsic issues about a system of discretionary conditional release. The "truth in sentencing" advocates argue that parole distorts the judicially imposed sentence and that every day before warrant expiry should be served. Alternatively, a number of critics of parole have argued that release should not be a matter of discretion but should be determined by a stipulated fraction of the sentence subject to "good behaviour" during imprisonment. Many American jurisdictions, especially those with sentencing commissions, have adopted this approach, requiring service of a substantial portion of the sentence prior to release.

There are important questions to ask about the relationship between sentencing and parole. The truth-in-sentencing advocates tend to ignore the simple fact that the two mechanisms can be legally and legitimately distinct. At the same time, there can be an integration of objectives. One sometimes sees reasons for denying parole framed in terms that reflect concern about undermining the sentence in the light of seriousness of the offence. Given that eligibility is a function of the sentence and is determined by Parliament, is this a legitimate concern? Integrating objectives relates to matters like protection of the community, rehabilitation of the offender, and assisting with reintegration. It is not about giving the NPB power to assess proportionality and other sentencing principles.

In Canada, in its 1987 report, the Canadian Sentencing Commission supported the abolition of parole. However, the commission was content to retain remission-based release. Recently, the argument has been raised that the reverse should occur: abolish statutory release and permit only discretionary-based release decisions. While reading the following excerpt from the Sentencing Commission, which antedates the CCRA and makes reference to the old *Parole Act* provisions, consider the basic question: should a discretionary release model be retained? In this context, ask yourself whether the new phenomenon of mandatory minimum sentences provides another argument in favour of retention. That is, if mandatory sentences are required, does parole provide a necessary vehicle to respond to offences of lesser gravity within the specific category.

Canadian Sentencing Commission, *Sentencing Reform: A Canadian Approach*
(Ottawa: Supply and Services Canada, 1987) (footnotes omitted)

The purpose underlying the newly-created system of discretionary parole release was based on a rehabilitation-oriented model of justice. It is within this framework that the release criteria to guide the parole board in the exercise of its discretion were formulated.

· · ·

Although parole was based on a model of rehabilitation, this model has never been implemented in Canada. According to this model, prison serves as a kind of maximum-security hospital and parole provides the necessary period for convalescence. Since treatment and recovery periods are difficult to quantify in advance, a true rehabilitation model can only be realized in the context of a system of indeterminate sentencing. Canada never adopted a system of indeterminate sentencing and hence, in adopting parole, only adopted part of the rehabilitation model. In the US, however, indeterminate sentencing and discretionary parole release together formed the package required for a real attempt at a rehabilitative model. It is disenchantment with this rehabilitation model that has led a number of US states, over the past 15 years, to abolish discretionary parole release as well as to create sentencing commissions to move toward a system of determinate sentencing. Some states that have abolished discretionary parole release have retained a parole board to release and supervise those inmates serving life sentences. In addition, parole boards have been retained to fulfill the discretionary release function for those inmates sentenced prior to the abolition of parole. Given the adoption of the Commission's recommendations, similar provisions must be made for Canada's Parole Board. So far 11 states have abolished discretionary parole release: Alaska, Arizona, California, Colorado, Connecticut, Illinois, Indiana, Maine, Minnesota, New Mexico and North Carolina. The problems created by adopting only one element of the rehabilitation model are illustrated in the above criteria for parole release. Under our current system of determinate sentencing, it is difficult to understand how one would determine whether an offender has derived "maximum benefit from imprisonment." We have seen in the historical chapter that one of the most frequently recurring themes in official reports on incarceration was that imprisonment had a debilitating rather than a rehabilitative effect on prisoners. Hence, some would argue it is hard to imagine any benefits accruing to someone who spends a number of years in a penitentiary. In addition, since it is impossible to predict accurately who will re-offend (or when, or why), the issues of risk to society and reform of the inmate are tenuous grounds upon which to release, suspend or revoke inmates on full parole.

2.1.3 Effects of Parole on the Meaning of the Sentence

a) Time Served in Custody

Terms of imprisonment in this country are substantially affected by parole release. While the relative merits of parole remain controversial, some characteristics and consequences of the system are clear enough. First, approximately one-third of eligible prisoners are granted release on full parole at some point in their sentences. The majority of all prisoners who are released on full parole were granted full parole upon their first application. Paroled prisoners serve an average of 40% of their sentence inside prison before obtaining release. Over three-quarters of those released on full parole serve less than half of their sentences in prison. (These statistics are all drawn from the 1981 *Solicitor General's Study of Conditional Release.*) Tables (data from 1977 to 1981) provided by the Statistical Liaison Office of the National Parole Board corroborate the view that parole intervention in time actually served in prison is substantial. The following trends emerge:

- 95% of offenders convicted of offences against the person (excluding murder, attempted murder and manslaughter) who received sentences of over 10 years serve less than 10 years in prison;

- 70% of offenders convicted of attempted murder, second-degree murder and manslaughter who received sentences of over ten years served less than ten years in prison. This figure would actually be higher if it did not also encompass cases of second degree murder. Those convicted of second degree murder serve a mandatory period of at least 10 years before becoming eligible for parole. Hence, they automatically increase the percentage of offenders who serve ten years or more in prison.

- 98% of offenders convicted of drug offences and who received sentences of over 10 years served less than 10 years in prison.

These statistics make it clear that there is a substantial difference between the sentence a judge hands down and the length of time an offender actually serves in prison. Moreover, there is a great deal of variation in the parole release rates across different parts of the country. In 1978, for example, there was a 26% difference between the regions demonstrating the highest and lowest rates of parole (Solicitor General of Canada, 1986). These variations—as well as the indeterminate nature of parole—may lead offenders and public alike to perceive parole as inequitable.

b) Sentence Equalization

Another consequence of parole is that known as "sentence equalization": offenders serving longer sentences are more likely to get released on parole than are offenders sentenced to shorter terms. This leads to the result—paradoxical to some quarters such as the public—that the more serious offences (e.g., manslaughter and attempted murder) have higher parole release rates than less serious offences such as theft and fraud. This pattern is noted in a recent report (Hann and Harman, 1986) for the Ministry of the Solicitor General. These authors found that for the period of 1975/76 through 1981/82 parole release rates for manslaughter were between 51% and 64%. These percentages are approximately ten percentage points in excess of a less serious offence (robbery) and 20 to 30 percentage points above the release rates for break and enter.

···

To summarize, it is clear that offenders convicted of more serious offences (such as manslaughter) serve a significantly smaller proportion of their sentences in custody than offenders convicted of much less serious crimes (such as fraud). As well, an offender convicted of a serious armed robbery may serve the same time in custody as a purse-snatcher. One consequence of this, as Mandel (1975) has pointed out, is to scramble the rankings of seriousness derived from the existing maximum penalty structure. Proportionality is lost in the shuffle from the sentence handed down by the judge to the early release of the offender on parole.

Another manifestation of the equalization effect can be seen in statistics of time served by parolees versus mandatory supervision releases. Thus, while inmates eventually released on parole were assigned, on average, much longer sentences than inmates released on mandatory supervision, the two groups ended up spending approximately the same amount of time in prison. This was noted by the *Solicitor General's Study of Conditional Release* (1981), and is also apparent from more recent data provided by the National Parole Board (1984).

The following statistics for manslaughter and robbery cases for the period 1982-83 illustrate the point. If one compares average sentence lengths of parole releases to mandatory supervision releases the difference is striking: those convicted of manslaughter and later released on parole were sentenced on average to 84 months. Those convicted on manslaughter and released on mandatory supervision were sentenced, on average, to 57 months. However, in terms of time served in prison the two groups are quite similar: 38 months for parolees, 41 months for those released on mandatory supervision.

The 1981 study of Conditional Release concluded: "Both sentence mitigation and sentence equalization, then, clearly appear to be effects of parole, despite the very firm National Parole Board position that they are not objectives" (p. 39). This effect seems undesirable for two reasons. First, because it violates the principle of proportionality, offering in effect a greater discount in time served to those convicted of more serious offences. This militates against equity and justice. Second, because it illustrates how the current system requires parole authorities to encroach upon the sentencing authority of the courts. This Commission is of the opinion that sentence equalization is a negative consequence of parole, and, thus, concurs with the position taken by the Goldenberg Committee (1974) in its report on parole in Canada.

2.1.4 Consideration of Parole and Remission by Sentencing Judges

The already murky waters of sentencing are clouded still further by judges considering, at time of sentencing, release on parole and remission. (Remission will be dealt with in greater detail in the next section). This consideration may take many forms. For example, it is possible that at least some judges are aware of the unstated yet clearly manifested policy to release higher proportions of serious offenders (for reasons of sentence mitigation and equalization) on full parole. If they are, judges may be increasing the lengths of sentences for certain offenders in anticipation of early release on full parole. Whether they follow this particular strategy or not, what evidence is there that judges are affected by the possibility of parole and remission? In the Commission's survey of sentencing judges (Research #6), only 35% of respondents stated that they never took parole into account at sentencing. Hogarth (1971) reported that two-thirds of judges in his sample admitted they sometimes adjusted their sentences in light of the possibility of parole being granted. To quote the *Solicitor General's Study of Conditional Release*: "In more candid moments, some judges will admit in effect to tripling the sentence in order to provide for a fixed period of 'denunciatory' imprisonment (prior to full parole eligibility), for a remission period, and for a 'parole' or 'rehabilitation' period" (p. 111).

The question of whether judges should consider parole and remission has generated an inconsistent response. The case law does not provide for a uniform approach to this question. There appears to be support in some provinces for the position that this is a valid consideration for judges in the determination of the sentence (see Campbell and Cole, 1986; Ruby 1980). Clearly, inconsistent application of a rule concerning the consideration of parole and remission can lead to unwarranted disparities in sentencing. Ruby (1980) sums it up: "Regardless of the merits of the discussion it would certainly be desirable that some measure of uniformity on this issue be attained, as a prisoner serving a lengthy term in Ontario will quite rightfully have a sense of grievance with regard to the consideration given there to his parole possibilities as compared to that of his fellows in other provinces" (p. 327).

2.1.5 Concerns: Lack of Equity, Clarity and Predictability

It is difficult to discuss concerns regarding equity and predictability as separate issues since by and large, if a process lacks one, it lacks all three. So, for example, problems of equity arise when full parole release is seen to lack clarity and predictability. Concerns with the operation of these principles in the current system of discretionary release have been raised in earlier chapters but some points bear repetition here.

Critics of parole have long argued that the criteria for parole release are too vague and broad to provide any real guidance to the decision-maker. One regrettable consequence is that parole decisions—both regarding release and revocation—are often seen to be arbitrary by inmates.

Previous government reports have alluded to negative reactions to parole on the part of offenders. The Sub-committee on the Penitentiary System in Canada (1977) noted that "inmates are under the impression that the Parole Board does not, in all circumstances, treat them fairly. The records contain many examples of inmates whose parole has been revoked because they arrived a few minutes late and who were also charged with being unlawfully at large" (p. 151). This same report also stated the following (in reference to the need for a mechanism other than revocation): "It is, therefore, extremely disconcerting to hear of inmates having their paroles suspended and revoked for essentially trivial reasons" (p. 151).

One of the recommendations (#64) of the 1977 Sub-Committee on the Penitentiary System in Canada acknowledged these perceptions:

> The appearance of arbitrariness in parole, especially in parole revocation without notice
> or reasons, is an unsettling factor in penitentiary life. There is also much resentment of the

fact that mandatory supervision places discharges under conditions similar to parole for a period of time equal to that of their earned and statutory remission.

The parole system should be reviewed with a view to lessening these arbitrary aspects.

Similar findings emerged from surveys of offenders conducted by this Commission. In one (Ekstedt, 1985), those who had experience with parole expressed reservations about the fairness of decisions. That the system is perceived to be arbitrary by those most critically affected by it lends a very real support to the concerns repeated in the literature. In addition to the perceived unfairness of a process grounded in wide discretion is the dilemma that some judges do and others do not consider the likelihood of full parole release in setting the length of a term of imprisonment. The practice of the Parole Board of effectively equalizing sentence lengths through parole release is further seen to undermine the sentence of the court.

There is no clear understanding on the part of offenders, criminal justice professionals, judges or the public as to the laws and practices surrounding discretionary parole release. The laws are complex, the practices vary and the result is that there is no shared understanding of what a sentence of imprisonment actually means. It is, in fact, not possible to predict with any accuracy the actual time in custody that most inmates will serve. Due to the wide discretion given to release authorities and the individualized nature of the release criteria, no convicted offender receiving a lengthy term of imprisonment can know how much time he or she faces in custody after hearing the sentence of the court.

Although general support was expressed for some form of early release, a recurring concern in submissions received by the Commission was the accountability of the releasing authority in the exercise of its discretion. Support was expressed for greater clarity in release criteria, guidelines for the releasing authority to ensure uniformity of approach and the need for some body to review early release decisions. Many groups and individuals stressed the need for better communication between judges who impose the sentence and the parole board and correctional authorities who ultimately administer it. The overall picture of a process fragmented by different approaches to sentencing emerged from the submissions.

The concerns expressed above primarily address the problems of discretionary parole release within the context of the existing sentencing structure. The concerns become even more pronounced when full parole release is considered within the context of the commission's proposals regarding principles of sentencing and its integrated set of recommendations. Proportionality and discretionary release on full parole are not natural allies. The reason for this is obvious—proportionality can only be drawn between two determinate quantities. The judge imposes a fixed term of imprisonment. This sentence is stated in open court and is subject to review by a higher court. The parole release date, of course, remains undetermined at the time of sentencing. In fact, in some cases the release decision is made on the basis of evidence that may not be revealed to the accused. The decision of the board is therefore not subject to public scrutiny or judicial review.

. . .

5. List of Recommendations

10.1 The Commission recommends the abolition of full parole, except in the case of sentences of life imprisonment.

10.2 The Commission recommends that earned remission be retained by way of credits awarded for good behaviour which may reduce by up to one-quarter the custodial portion of the sentence imposed by the judge.

10.3 The Commission recommends that all offenders be released without conditions unless the judge, upon imposing a sentence of incarceration, specifies that the offender should be released on conditions.

10.4 The Commission recommends that a judge may indicate certain conditions but the releasing authority shall retain the power to specify the exact nature of those conditions, modify or delete them or add other conditions.

10.5 The Commission recommends that the nature of the conditions be limited to explicit criteria with a provision that if the judge or the releasing authority wishes to prescribe an "additional" condition, they must provide reasons why such a condition is desirable and enter the reasons on the record.

10.6 The Commission recommends that where an offender, while on remission-based release, commits a further offence or breaches a condition of release, he or she shall be charged with an offence of violating a condition of release, subject to a maximum penalty of one year.

10.7 The Commission recommends that voluntary assistance programs be developed and made available to all inmates prior to and upon release from custody to assist them in their re-integration into the community.

10.8 The Commission recommends that a Sentence Administration Board be given the power to withhold remission release according to the criteria specified in the recently enacted legislation: *An Act to Amend the Parole Act and the Penitentiary Act.*

10.9 The Commission recommends that all inmates be eligible to participate in a day release program after serving two-thirds of their sentence, with the exception of those who meet the requirements for withholding remission release.

10.10 The Commission recommends that the granting of special leave according to explicit criteria remain at the discretion of the prison administration. Inmates shall be eligible for special leave passes immediately upon being placed in custody.

10.11 The Commission recommends that parole by exception be abolished and that cases where the inmate is terminally ill or where the inmate's physical or mental health is likely to suffer serious damage if he or she continues to be held in confinement shall be dealt with by way of the Royal Prerogative of Mercy.

10.12 The Commission recommends that the Sentence Administration Board should conduct the necessary review and forward submissions regarding clemency to the Solicitor General.

10.13 The Commission recommends that the Canadian immigration law should provide necessary authority for the deportation of convicted offenders in specified circumstances.

10.14 The Commission recommends that where a judge imposes a custodial sanction, he or she may recommend the nature of the custody imposed.

10.15 The Commission further recommends that federal and provincial governments provide the necessary resources and financial support for the establishment and maintenance of open custody facilities.

10.16 The Commission recommends that the mandatory life imprisonment sentence be retained for first and second degree murder and high treason.

10.17 The Commission recommends that inmates serving sentences for first degree murder or high treason be eligible for release on conditions after serving a minimum of 15 years up to a maximum of 25 years in custody. The court would set the date of eligibility for release within that limit.

10.18 The Commission recommends that inmates serving a life sentence for second degree murder be eligible for release on conditions after serving a minimum of ten years, and a maximum of 15 years in custody. The court would set the date of eligibility for release within that limit.

10.19 The Commission recommends that at the eligibility date, the inmate have the burden of demonstrating his or her readiness for release on conditions for the remainder of the life sentence.

10.20 The Commission recommends that the ineligibility period set by the court be subject to appeal.

F.E. Gibson, "The Renewal of Parole"
(1990), 32 *Canadian Journal of Criminology* 487

The past several years have been a time of intense public scrutiny and challenge for the National Parole Board. Growing public concern about crime and violence crystallized to some extent around national headlines about violent crimes committed by parolees, or by offenders on temporary absence or under mandatory supervision. Two major coroner's inquests, several inquiries and studies, and, of course, the Report of the Canadian Sentencing Commission (1987) raised fundamental questions about the purpose of parole and its relationship to other agencies of criminal justice and the community.

The past decade has also seen the National Parole Board under pressure to make the changes necessary to keep up with the evolution of Canadian jurisprudence. Not only has the common law concept of the "duty to act fairly" evolved and thereby exerted pressure on the decision making of the Board; but 1982 also saw the introduction of the *Canadian Charter of Rights and Freedoms* which will continue to shape the parole decision making process in Canada.

While draft amendments to the *Parole Act* (1988) and *Taking Responsibility*, the Report of the Standing Committee on Justice and Solicitor General (1988) strongly endorsed the concept of parole, they also contemplated major reform. Similarly, recent public opinion surveys indicate strong support for parole but equally strong demands for reform. The Board can expect continuing public scrutiny, continuing demands from community and victims groups to demonstrate its commitment and contribution to public protection, and continued demands from the courts and organizations representing offenders to demonstrate that its decision making is fair and consistent. These concerns, the increased public scrutiny and demands for accountability, have led to a very healthy process of reflection and renewal. The Board has clarified its purpose and the principles which must guide its decision making process.

Legal Mandate

The *Parole Act* gives the Board exclusive jurisdiction and absolute discretion to grant, deny, terminate, or revoke day parole and full parole for inmates in federal, territorial, and provincial prisons, except for cases under the jurisdiction of provincial parole boards. Ontario, Quebec, and British Columbia have parole boards with, generally speaking, jurisdiction over inmates serving a definite sentence of less than two years in their own provincial institutions.

Almost all offenders, except those serving life or indeterminate sentences, accumulate remission credits and are released to serve in the community the portion of the remission time left to their credit, subject to mandatory supervision. The adoption by Parliament of Bill C-67 in July 1986, authorized the Board to delay, until warrant expiry, the release of certain offenders considered to present an immediate and serious risk to commit a violent act causing death or serious harm. The Board may also prescribe conditions, including residence in an approved facility, on certain offenders with violence in their records who are being released.

Purpose of Parole

Within this framework, the Board undertook a fundamental review of its purpose, its mission. This review resulted in a reaffirmation of the Board's paramount commitment to public protection through facilitating the offender's safe reintegration into the community and promoting timely opportunities for rehabilitation.

The Board's mission statement provides that:

> The National Parole Board, as part of the Criminal Justice System, makes independent, quality conditional release decisions and clemency recommendations. The Board, by facilitating the timely reintegration of offenders as law-abiding citizens, contributes to the protection of society.

The mission sets out the business of the National Parole Board. It also rejects certain models or visions of parole.

The Parole Board is not in the business of punishing offenders or "resentencing." While Boards in some jurisdictions have this as an explicit part of their mandate, the National Parole Board plays a role in administering the sentence of the court in a manner that respects the sentence and contributes to public protection. Parole cannot be granted until the denunciatory portion of an offender's sentence—as determined in regulation as the parole eligibility date—has been served. After that point, structured, gradual release into the community with conditions necessary to manage risk and appropriate to the needs of the offender is possible only because the offender has time remaining under sentence. Similarly, the Board may revoke parole on the basis of a violation of the conditions of parole because the offender is still under sentence.

The National Parole Board is not a mechanism for controlling prison or penitentiary population. Again, one can find releasing bodies in other jurisdictions with an explicit mandate to reduce the number of prisoners to manageable levels. Parole in Canada explicitly rejects this approach. The *Parole Act* does not allow it. The National Parole Board's commitment to public protection does not allow it.

The commitment to public protection demands that parole decisions first be based on a careful assessment of risk, using the best available tools and information. But this does not mean that the Board simply acts as a filter for the correctional system, allowing only the best risks back into the community. Over 90% of all offenders currently incarcerated will re-enter the community—with or without parole. Criminologists and corrections practitioners have long recognized the potentially debilitating effects of incarceration and the difficulty many offenders have in making the transition from prison or penitentiary to the community. This is a critical stage for offenders. Gradual release with quality supervision and community-based support and programs, as provided through day or full parole, gives offenders a far greater chance of success than does "cold turkey" release on warrant expiry or even mandatory supervision, where conditions are legally restricted. Because release on mandatory supervision is generally not based on risk, it provides no incentive for offenders to participate in programs.

Some offenders are very clearly "bad risks" for release into the community and, until treatment and programs within the institution have substantially reduced the risk they pose, they should not be given parole. Some offenders are clearly "good risks" and can reintegrate into the community with only minimal control. But most offenders fall somewhere between. The Parole Board must then assess the risk each offender poses, satisfy itself that the risk can be managed, set the conditions necessary to manage the risk, and provide appropriate reassessment of the offender's progress within the institution or in the community. The National Parole Board is responsible for ensuring that the timing, conditions, and plans for release adequately address risk, the needs of the offender, and the capacity of the community to address those needs.

To reiterate, corrections and parole have a dual mandate: administer the sentence of the court; and use the time during which they are responsible for the offender to promote rehabilitation, facilitate the offender's safe reintegration into the community, and break the cycle of recidivism. The National Parole Board plays a crucial role in making or refusing release decisions in the interests of public safety.

Respect for and Sensitivity to Individuals

Over the past decade, the National Parole Board, like other administrative decision making bodies, has tried to keep pace with the rapid evolution in case law and, particularly, the implications of the Charter. As part of its process of renewal, the Board made a commitment to the principles of fairness, consistency, and respect for and sensitivity to individuals in its decision making process.

Its first "core value," articulated as part of the mission exercise, is intended to guide the Board in all of its activities:

> We recognize and respect the inherent dignity of individuals and the equal and inalienable rights of all members of society.

This core value goes beyond respect of the rights of offenders. In the past, many within the Board characterized the offender as "the client." The renewed understanding of our purpose has helped to change that focus. The community is our client and this demands that we be respectful of and sensitive to the impact of our decisions on all of those with an interest in our work, including victims and victims organizations, and the diverse communities we serve. Strengthened partnership and communication with victims and the community also contribute to quality decisions.

This value is reflected, as well, in the Board's increasing reliance on hearings. The hearing is a method to assess the offender in a non-adversarial way. Offenders are notified in advance of the information the Board will use in making its decision and are given the opportunity to respond. They are entitled to assistants to help them present their case to the Board and are informed, in writing, of the board's decision and reasons. Offenders also have access to a formal appeal process. The Board has committed itself to meeting the expanding natural justice requirements and strengthening procedural safeguards. Enabling offenders to be informed participants in the decision making process contributes to quality decisions. As well, the board is actively involved with CSC in finding the best way to obtain quality information from victims, and to provide to victims, as individuals, information that respects their interests and needs.

Implementing the Mission

The Board has always taken some measure of pride, or at least comfort, in the fact that the "success rate" of offenders on day and full parole is significantly greater than of those released on mandatory supervision. Unfortunately, little is heard by the public about our success stories, the many parolees who became successful contributors to their community and who sometimes turn their efforts to helping other offenders make the transition.

But the events of the past several years have reminded all of us in the corrections enterprise that our success rates do not and can never justify complacency. We have always known that our failures can have tragic human consequences. However rare statistically, these failures quite rightly receive intense media and public attention. This scrutiny serves to remind us that we will be and should be judged on the quality of each individual decision and the effectiveness of the implementation of each decision, that we must recognize and learn from our mistakes, that we must work constantly to improve the quality of corrections and parole.

In 1989, the National Parole Board committed itself to a strategy for implementing its mission. This strategy was based on three related themes: professionalism, openness, and accountability.

The Board has become more *professional*. On March 1, 1988, the Board implemented decision policies to structure the review process and guide the consideration for parole. These policies ensure that all Board decisions are based on common criteria, respect natural justice requirements, and focus on risk to society as the primary criterion for conditional release. In 1989, based upon the results of the board's monitoring of the policies and the experience of applying them, the decision policies were reviewed, and a number of revisions were made to refine and improve them.

Over the past two years, the Board has integrated its decision policies into its day to day operations. These policies have contributed to improved consistency and to the national character of the Board. As well, hearing assistants will be available to support members and remove some of the administrative burden associated with requirements, such as the taping of hearings and the procedural safeguards that are essential features of the duty to act fairly.

Board members received, and will continue to receive, extensive training on the application of the decision policies, on approaches to risk assessment, on the needs of victims, and on the special needs and circumstances of female offenders and aboriginal offenders. The Board is currently examining what kinds of multicultural training may be necessary. We are intensifying our work in these ares.

Openness means, in part, working closely with our partners in criminal justice. We are, for example, strengthening our relationships with our partners, the Courts, the prosecution, the police, and corrections agencies, particularly the Correctional Service of Canada. The missions of the Correctional Service of Canada and the National Parole Board both recognize that rehabilitation and reintegration promote the protection of society. There is a strong sense of partnership between CSC and NPB, as both agencies share the challenge of meeting their objectives within the current social and fiscal environment. The policies of the Board demand that offenders participate in programs prior to release on parole. The Correctional Service of Canada is responsible for the delivery of these programs and whatever other treatment may be necessary. While CSC produces or compiles most of the information by which an inmate's readiness for release can be assessed, it is the Board that makes the determination. The Board is responsible for the decision, and the CSC is responsible for the supervision of all inmates on conditional release. Both agencies are currently reviewing the case preparation and decision process in order to identify and eliminate overlap and duplication. This exercise has the potential not only to reduce costs and administrative burden, but also to contribute to correctional effectiveness, and quality decision making.

Of particular importance for the future is the relationship of sentencing and parole. Clearly, the question of whether parole serves to change or make uncertain rather than simply administer sentences has been at the base of many of the calls for both sentencing and parole reform. Questions have been raised, for example, about the appropriateness of current eligibility dates, about whether sentencing judges take parole into account in setting sentences, and about whether parole boards consider the reasons for sentence when deliberating about parole. Perhaps most important, greater communication and mutual understanding are necessary between sentencing judges and parole boards. They must work together to develop a framework which respects the unique mandates of each, but which ensures that sentencing and parole complement one another in their common pursuit of a just and safe society.

Openness also means strengthening our relationships with all elements of the community we serve, particularly victims and victims organizations. In 1989, at the First Canadian Organization for Victims of Crime Conference, the NPB released a handbook entitled *Victims: questions and answers on parole*, designed to answer those questions victims ask in the aftermath of their trauma. In the last two years, the Board has had increased interactions with victims. Victims and their organizations are demanding more information from various components of the criminal justice system throughout the various phases of criminal investigation, trial, sentence, and sentence administration. The publication of the handbook is recognition of the legitimate interest of victims to be informed of the NPB's policies and programs. The Board is continuing to work with victims and victims organizations to clarify and refine relationships and ensure the effective participation of victims and the community in the Board's policy development.

But most important, openness means openness to public scrutiny—to ensure that the Board is accountable. For example the report of the Standing Committee, *Taking Responsibility*, proposed that board hearings be open to the public. There is also a growing interest on the part of victims, police, media representatives and others to attend hearings, to understand the Board, how it operates and the reasons for its decisions. The Board has therefore undertaken a broad study of the hearing process. Its objectives are to ensure national consistency in the parole process; to eliminate any unnecessary expenditures; and to provide a framework to respond to the objectives of openness and accountability, recognizing the diversity of the offender population and the diverse communities to which they will return.

The Board has become more *accountable*. We have strengthened our capacity to monitor and review decisions. We can and must do more. We must continue to put in place the structures and processes necessary to demonstrate that each decision was made on the basis of sound information and was directed to protecting society, contributing to crime prevention by reducing recidivism, and respecting the needs of the community and the rights of the offender. Our business is decision making. It is against each individual decision that we should and will be measured. All that we do must be directed to improving the quality of those decisions.

The Board has come to understand more clearly and fully its role in contributing to a just, peaceful, and safe society. Its mission makes it part of the solution. Its commitment to openness, professionalism, and accountability will ensure that renewal continues in partnership with the community.

NOTE

The comments of the Sentencing Commission are now 20 years old. The CCRA has abolished remission-based release and replaced it with statutory release. Nonetheless, do the concerns expressed by the Commission still have resonance?

Table 18.1   Federal Releases from Institutions

Release type	2002-3	2003-4	2004-5	2005-6	2006-7
Day parole	2097	2178	2173	2343	2245
Full Parole					
Full parole from					
day parole.	1190	1207	1180	1204	1239
Direct full parole.	201	235	209	236	168
Total full parole	1391	1442	1389	1440	1407
Statutory release.	5080	5106	5092	5216	5250
Warrant expiry					
WED.	219	230	221	227	231
WED (to long-term					
supervision)	11	14	21	30	33
Total WED	230	244	242	257	264

Source: CSC and NPB.

Before answering, you might want to examine the following data. First, table 18.1 is a composite of tables from the NPB Performance Monitoring Report, 2006-07, published in July 2007 (tables 35 and 37). The table gives a sense of the gross numbers of prisoners released by the various routes during the five years from 2002 to 2007.

In table 18.1, there are two subcategories of prisoners who fall under full parole. The larger group includes those who were on day parole when they were granted full parole; the smaller group refers to those granted full parole directly from a federal institution. There are also two subcategories of prisoners who must serve their entire sentence: those who have been detained under s. 130(3) and long-term offenders designated by the sentencing judge under s. 753.1 of the *Criminal Code*. These prisoners are grouped under the heading warrant expiry (WED).

The following recent data from the 2006 CSC Statistical Overview shows the relationship between release on both parole and statutory release and success or reincarceration.

To put table 18.2 into context, the data indicates that the federal full-parole granting has been "relatively stable" over the past decade, averaging about 43.3 percent, with a high of 45.7 percent in 2004-5. This does not mean that more than 40 percent of prisoners received full parole. The percentage refers to the number of applications made annually. During the period 1996 to 2006, 21.7 percent of prisoners were not reviewed for parole, but chose instead to wait until statutory release. Of those who were reviewed but denied, 56 percent succeeded in obtaining parole later in their sentence. Also, note that the reported granting rates include those who were eligible for, and received, accelerated parole. This skews the data such that the real granting rate for non-accelerated cases is much lower.

Table 18.2   Outcome Rates for All Federal Full Parole with Determinate Sentence

Outcome	2002-3		2003-4		2004-5		2005-6		2006-7	
	#	%	#	%	#	%	#	%	#	%
Successful Completions.......	1,164	72.6	1,047	73.0	1,050	72.8	984	70.7	924	70.5
Revoked for breach of conditions	275	17.2	261	18.2	254	17.6	264	19.0	259	29.8
Revocation with offence										
Non-violent offences	141	8.8	110	7.7	117	8.1	127	9.1	120	9.2
Violent offences	23	1.4	17	1.2	21	1.5	17	1.2	7	0.5
Total revocation with offence..............	164	10.2	127	8.9	138	9.6	144	10.3	127	9.7
Total completions...........	1,603	100.0	1,435	100.0	1,442	100.0	1,392	100.0	1,310	100.0

Source: National Parole Board Performance Monitoring Report, 2006-7.

Table 18.2 shows another interesting fact. In 2006-7, the number of full parole completions decreased by 5.9 percent, or 82 offenders. Since 2002-3, the number of full parole completions has decreased by 18.3 percent, or 293 offenders per year. This is significant because the number of parole releases went up and down marginally during the same period (see table 18.1). Table 18.2 confirms that the number of revocations for breach of conditions, not for new offences, has increased dramatically over the past five years.

Compare the reconviction rates between parole releases and statutory releases. Remember, the parole releases result from a review and favourable exercise of discretion. Statutory releases occur by operation of law at two-thirds of the sentence, subject, of course, to the possibility of a detention hearing.

CHAPTER NINETEEN

Prisoners and the Review of Penitentiary and Parole Decision Making

I. INTRODUCTION

This chapter examines two interrelated issues: the prisoner as a rights-bearing person and the evolution of remedies available to prisoners in the courts. In this post-Charter era, the question whether prisoners are rights-bearing individuals might seem moot and self-evident. However, one must remember the relevant history. At common law, the convicted offender suffered "civil death." This included the disabilities that flowed from the status of felon, which included outlawry, corruption of the blood, and attainder. Certainly, the felon was disenfranchised. This particular disability survives to this day in many jurisdictions. Second, there is the issue of judicial remedies. It is trite to say that a right without a remedy is hardly a real right. For many years, Canadian courts seemed to follow their American counterparts in adopting a hands-off approach to prison and parole issues. This meant that most legal grievances remained beyond the scope of judicial scrutiny. Even the historic remedy of *habeas corpus* acquired some peculiar characteristics, which, until very recently, created impediments to its development and use. (For a detailed account of prisoners' efforts to obtain remedies, see the chapter entitled "The Prisoner Before the Courts" in Cole and Manson, *The Law of Parole, Sentencing, and Judicial Review* (Toronto: Carswell, 1990), 39-108.)

II. THE PRISONER AS A RIGHTS-BEARING PERSON

Before the Charter, Canadian courts looked at the issue of civil liberties as it applied to prisoners and reasoned that prisoners were entitled to the exercise of the same civil liberties as other citizens except for those that are removed by statute or those necessarily unavailable as a function of incarceration (see the decision of Dickson J in *Solosky v. The Queen*, [1980] 1 SCR 821, where he said that "a person confined to prison retains all of his civil rights, other than those expressly or impliedly taken from him by law"). This is now replicated by statute as one of the principles that guide the Corrections Service of Canada. Section 4(e) of the *Corrections and Conditional Release Act*, SC 1992, c. 20 provides:

(e) that offenders retain the rights and privileges of all members of society, except those rights and privileges that are necessarily removed or restricted as a consequence of the sentence.

With the entrenchment of the Charter in 1982, it was clear that the rights and freedoms it guaranteed applied to all persons. Early Charter decisions explicitly accepted that the rights to life, liberty, and the security of the person applied to people in prison. Accordingly, statutory provisions that affect the exercise of civil liberties could now be challenged. However, the concept of rights-bearing engages a larger scope of questions than simply whether the guarantees of s. 7 apply to that person. The equality guarantees in s. 15 apply to stipulated groups of people and to analogous groups. Are prisoners an analogous group? We will return to this question soon. More to the point is the applicability of s. 1, which permits the state to show that a law that limits guaranteed rights or freedoms can be "demonstrably justified in a free and democratic society." Is this a tool that can be used to deny prisoners full access to civil liberties and constitutional rights, which are the natural incidents of being recognized at law as rights-bearing people?

Certainly, one of the central signs of full membership in a democratic community is the right to vote in the election of members of the various legislatures and governments. However, disenfranchisement has been a common historical consequence for those in prison and, in some jurisdictions, even upon release. In Canada, prior to the Charter, this was the response to those in jail. However, s. 3 of the Charter provides:

> 3. Every citizen of Canada has the right to vote in an election of members of the House of Commons or of a legislative assembly and to be qualified for membership therein.

The opening phrase, "[e]very citizen," seems to answer the question. Indeed, some appellate courts agreed and struck down prohibitions against voting in provincial elections by prisoners. The federal legislation was all embracing in its efforts to deny all prisoners the right to vote in federal elections and the Supreme Court of Canada found this prohibition to be overbroad and struck it down in 1993: see the first *Sauvé* case, [1993] 2 SCR 438. However, Parliament responded by enacting a new prohibition that applied only to prisoners serving sentences of two years or more, which would exclude all penitentiary prisoners from the vote. This remained on the books for a decade before new litigation reached the Supreme Court of Canada, which, in a 5:4 decision, once and for all ensured the enfranchisement of all Canadian prisoners.

Sauvé v. Canada (Chief Electoral Officer)
2002 SCC 68, [2002] 3 SCR 519

The judgment of McLachlin CJ and Iacobucci, Binnie, Arbour and LeBel JJ was delivered by

THE CHIEF JUSTICE: [1] The right of every citizen to vote, guaranteed by s. 3 of the *Canadian Charter of Rights and Freedoms*, lies at the heart of Canadian democracy. The law at stake in this appeal denies the right to vote to a certain class of people—those serving sentences of two years or more in a correctional institution. The question is whether the government has established that this denial of the right to vote is allowed under s. 1 of the *Charter* as a "reasonable limi[t] ... demonstrably justified in a free and democratic society." I conclude that it is not. The right to vote, which lies at the heart of Canadian democracy, can only be trammeled for good reason. Here, the reasons offered do not suffice.

I. Statutory Provisions

[2] The predecessor to s. 51(e) of the *Canada Elections Act*, RSC 1985, c. E-2, prohibited all prison inmates from voting in federal elections, regardless of the length of their sentences. This section was held unconstitutional as an unjustified denial of the right to vote guaranteed by s. 3 of the *Charter*: *Sauvé v. Canada (Attorney General)*, [1993] 2 SCR 438. Parliament responded to this litigation by replacing this section with a new s. 51(e) (SC 1993, c. 19, s. 23), which denies the right to vote to all inmates serving sentences of two years or more. Section 51(e), which is now continued in substantially the same form at s. 4(c) of the Act (SC 2000, c. 9), and the relevant *Charter* provisions are set out below.

Canada Elections Act, RSC 1985, c. E-2

51. The following persons are not qualified to vote at an election and shall not vote at an election: ...

(e) Every person who is imprisoned in a correctional institution serving a sentence of two years or more;

Canadian Charter of Rights and Freedoms

1. The *Canadian Charter of Rights and Freedoms* guarantees the rights and freedoms set out in it subject only to such reasonable limits prescribed by law as can be demonstrably justified in a free and democratic society. ...

3. Every citizen of Canada has the right to vote in an election of members of the House of Commons or of a legislative assembly and to be qualified for membership therein. ...

15(1) Every individual is equal before and under the law and has the right to the equal protection and equal benefit of the law without discrimination and, in particular, without discrimination based on race, national or ethnic origin, colour, religion, sex, age or mental or physical disability.

II. Judgments

A. Federal Court, Trial Division, [1996] 1 FC 857

[3] The trial judge, Wetston J, held that s. 51(e) of the *Canada Elections Act* violated the *Charter* guarantee of the right to vote without being demonstrably justified, and was therefore void. Although he found that the government's objectives were pressing and substantial, he concluded that the denial of voting rights to all inmates serving a sentence of two years or longer was overbroad and failed the minimal impairment test. In addition, he found at p. 913 that denying the right to vote "hinder[ed] the rehabilitation of offenders and their successful reintegration into the community." The negative consequences of the challenged provision were thus disproportionate to any benefits it might produce.

B. *Federal Court of Appeal, [2000] 2 FC 117*

[4] The majority of the Federal Court of Appeal, per Linden JA, reversed the trial judge and upheld the denial of voting rights, holding that Parliament's role in maintaining and enhancing the integrity of the electoral process and in exercising the criminal law power both warranted deference. The denial of the right to vote at issue fell within a reasonable range of alternatives open to Parliament to achieve its objectives and was not overbroad or disproportionate. Desjardins JA, applying the "stringent formulation of the *Oakes* test," emphasized the absence of evidence of benefits flowing from the denial and would have dismissed the appeal.

III. Issues

[5] 1. Does s. 51(e) of the *Canada Elections Act* infringe the guarantee of the right of all citizens to vote under s. 3 of the *Charter* and if so, is the infringement justified under s. 1 of the *Charter*?

2. Does s. 51(e) of the *Canada Elections Act* infringe the equality guarantee of s. 15(1) of the *Charter* and if so, is the infringement justified under s. 1 of the *Charter*?

IV. Analysis

[6] The respondents concede that the voting restriction at issue violates s. 3 of the *Charter*. The restriction is thus invalid unless demonstrably justified under s. 1. I shall therefore proceed directly to the s. 1 analysis.

A. *The Approach to Section 1 Justification*

[7] To justify the infringement of a *Charter* right, the government must show that the infringement achieves a constitutionally valid purpose or objective, and that the chosen means are reasonable and demonstrably justified: *R v. Oakes*, [1986] 1 SCR 103. This two-part inquiry—the legitimacy of the objective and the proportionality of the means—ensures that a reviewing court examine rigorously all aspects of justification. Throughout the justification process, the government bears the burden of proving a valid objective and showing that the rights violation is warranted—that is, that it is rationally connected, causes minimal impairment, and is proportionate to the benefit achieved.

[8] My colleague Justice Gonthier proposes a deferential approach to infringement and justification. He argues that there is no reason to accord special importance to the right to vote, and that we should thus defer to Parliament's choice among a range of reasonable alternatives. He further argues that in justifying limits on the right to vote under s. 1, we owe deference to Parliament because we are dealing with "philosophical, political and social considerations," because of the abstract and symbolic nature of the government's stated goals, and because the law at issue represents a step in a dialogue between Parliament and the courts.

[9] I must, with respect, demur. The right to vote is fundamental to our democracy and the rule of law and cannot be lightly set aside. Limits on it require not deference, but careful examination. This is not a matter of substituting the Court's philosophical

preference for that of the legislature, but of ensuring that the legislature's proffered justification is supported by logic and common sense.

[10] The *Charter* distinguishes between two separate issues: whether a right has been infringed, and whether the limitation is justified. The complainant bears the burden of showing the infringement of a right (the first step), at which point the burden shifts to the government to justify the limit as a reasonable limit under s. 1 (the second step). These are distinct processes with different burdens. Insulating a rights restriction from scrutiny by labeling it a matter of social philosophy, as the government attempts to do, reverses the constitutionally imposed burden of justification. It removes the infringement from our radar screen, instead of enabling us to zero in on it to decide whether it is demonstrably justified as required by the *Charter*.

[11] At the first stage, which involves defining the right, we must follow this Court's consistent view that rights shall be defined broadly and liberally: *Hunter v. Southam Inc.*, [1984] 2 SCR 145, at p. 156; *R v. Big M Drug Mart Ltd.*, [1985] 1 SCR 295, at p. 344; *Eldridge v. British Columbia (Attorney General)*, [1997] 3 SCR 624, at para. 53. A broad and purposive interpretation of the right is particularly critical in the case of the right to vote. The framers of the *Charter* signaled the special importance of this right not only by its broad, untrammeled language, but by exempting it from legislative override under s. 33's notwithstanding clause. I conclude that s. 3 must be construed as it reads, and its ambit should not be limited by countervailing collective concerns, as the government appears to argue. These concerns are for the government to raise under s. 1 in justifying the limits it has imposed on the right.

[12] At the s. 1 stage, the government argues that denying the right to vote to penitentiary inmates is a matter of social and political philosophy, requiring deference. Again, I cannot agree. This Court has repeatedly held that the "general claim that the infringement of a right is justified under s. 1" does not warrant deference to Parliament: *M. v. H.*, [1999] 2 SCR 3, at para. 78, per Iacobucci J. Section 1 does not create a presumption of constitutionality for limits on rights; rather, it requires the state to justify such limitations.

[13] The core democratic rights of Canadians do not fall within a "range of acceptable alternatives" among which Parliament may pick and choose at its discretion. Deference may be appropriate on a decision involving competing social and political policies. It is not appropriate, however, on a decision to limit fundamental rights. This case is not merely a competition between competing social philosophies. It represents a conflict between the right of citizens to vote—one of the most fundamental rights guaranteed by the *Charter*—and Parliament's denial of that right. Public debate on an issue does not transform it into a matter of "social philosophy," shielding it from full judicial scrutiny. It is for the courts, unaffected by the shifting winds of public opinion and electoral interests, to safeguard the right to vote guaranteed by s. 3 of the *Charter*.

[14] *Charter* rights are not a matter of privilege or merit, but a function of membership in the Canadian polity that cannot lightly be cast aside. This is manifestly true of the right to vote, the cornerstone of democracy, exempt from the incursion permitted on other rights through s. 33 override. Thus, courts considering denials of voting rights have applied a stringent justification standard: *Sauvé v. Canada (Attorney General)* (1992), 7 OR (3d) 481 (CA) ("*Sauvé No. 1*"), and *Belczowski v. Canada*, [1992] 2 FC 440 (CA).

[15] The *Charter* charges courts with upholding and maintaining an inclusive, participatory democratic framework within which citizens can explore and pursue different conceptions of the good. While a posture of judicial deference to legislative decisions about social policy may be appropriate in some cases, the legislation at issue does not fall into this category. To the contrary, it is precisely when legislative choices threaten to undermine the foundations of the participatory democracy guaranteed by the *Charter* that courts must be vigilant in fulfilling their constitutional duty to protect the integrity of this system.

[16] Nor can I concur in the argument that the philosophically based or symbolic nature of the government's objectives in itself commands deference. To the contrary, this Court has held that broad, symbolic objectives are problematic, as I discuss below: see *UFCW, Local 1518 v. KMart Canada Ltd.*, [1999] 2 SCR 1083, at para. 59, *per* Cory J; *Thomson Newspapers Co. v. Canada (Attorney General)*, [1998] 1 SCR 877, at para. 87, *per* Bastarache J; *RJR-MacDonald Inc. v. Canada (Attorney General)*, [1995] 3 SCR 199, at paras. 143-44, *per* McLachlin J (as she then was). Parliament cannot use lofty objectives to shield legislation from *Charter* scrutiny. Section 1 requires valid objectives *and* proportionality.

[17] Finally, the fact that the challenged denial of the right to vote followed judicial rejection of an even more comprehensive denial, does not mean that the Court should defer to Parliament as part of a "dialogue." Parliament must ensure that whatever law it passes, at whatever stage of the process, conforms to the Constitution. The healthy and important promotion of a dialogue between the legislature and the courts should not be debased to a rule of "if at first you don't succeed, try, try again."

[18] While deference to the legislature is not appropriate in this case, legislative justification does not require empirical proof in a scientific sense. While some matters can be proved with empirical or mathematical precision, others, involving philosophical, political and social considerations, cannot. In this case, it is enough that the justification be convincing, in the sense that it is sufficient to satisfy the reasonable person looking at all the evidence and relevant considerations, that the state is justified in infringing the right at stake to the degree it has: see *RJR-MacDonald, supra*, at para. 154, *per* McLachlin J; *R v. Butler*, [1992] 1 SCR 452, at pp. 502-3, *per* Sopinka J. What is required is "rational, reasoned defensibility": *RJR-MacDonald*, at para. 127. Common sense and inferential reasoning may supplement the evidence: *R v. Sharpe*, [2001] 1 SCR 45, 2001 SCC 2, at para. 78, *per* McLachlin CJ. However, one must be wary of stereotypes cloaked as common sense, and of substituting deference for the reasoned demonstration required by s. 1.

[19] Keeping in mind these basic principles of *Charter* review, I approach the familiar stages of the *Oakes* test. I conclude that the government's stated objectives of promoting civic responsibility and respect for the law and imposing appropriate punishment, while problematically vague, are capable in principle of justifying limitations on *Charter* rights. However, the government fails to establish proportionality, principally for want of a rational connection between denying the vote to penitentiary inmates and its stated goals.

B. *The Government's Objectives*

[20] The objectives' analysis entails a two-step inquiry. First, we must ask what the objectives are of denying penitentiary inmates the right to vote. This involves interpretation and construction, and calls for a contextual approach: *Thomson Newspapers, supra*, at para. 87. Second, we must evaluate whether the objectives as found are capable of justifying limitations on *Charter* rights. The objectives must not be "trivial," and they must not be "discordant with the principles integral to a free and democratic society": *Oakes, supra*, at p. 138. To borrow from the language of German constitutional law, there must be a constitutionally valid reason for infringing a right: see D. Grimm, "Human Rights and Judicial Review in Germany," in D.M. Beatty, ed., *Human Rights and Judicial Review: A Comparative Perspective* (1994), 267, at p. 275. Because s. 1 serves first and foremost to protect rights, the range of constitutionally valid objectives is not unlimited. For example, the protection of competing rights might be a valid objective. However, a simple majoritarian political preference for abolishing a right altogether would not be a constitutionally valid objective.

[21] Section 51(e) denying penitentiary inmates the right to vote was not directed at a specific problem or concern. Prisoners have long voted, here and abroad, in a variety of situations without apparent adverse effects to the political process, the prison population, or society as a whole. In the absence of a specific problem, the government asserts two broad objectives as the reason for this denial of the right to vote: (1) to enhance civic responsibility and respect for the rule of law; and (2) to provide additional punishment, or "enhanc[e] the general purposes of the criminal sanction." The record leaves in doubt how much these goals actually motivated Parliament; the Parliamentary debates offer more fulmination than illumination. However, on the basis of "some glimmer of light," the trial judge at p. 878 concluded that they could be advanced as objectives of the denial. I am content to proceed on this basis.

[22] This leaves the question of whether the objectives of enhancing respect for law and appropriate punishment are constitutionally valid and sufficiently significant to warrant a rights violation. Vague and symbolic objectives such as these almost guarantee a positive answer to this question. Who can argue that respect for the law is not pressing? Who can argue that proper sentences are not important? Who can argue that either of these goals, taken at face value, contradicts democratic principles? However, precisely because they leave so little room for argument, vague and symbolic objectives make the justification analysis more difficult. Their terms carry many meanings, yet tell us little about why the limitation on the right is necessary, and what it is expected to achieve in concrete terms. The broader and more abstract the objective, the more susceptible it is to different meanings in different contexts, and hence to distortion and manipulation. One articulation of the objective might inflate the importance of the objective; another might make the legislative measure appear more narrowly tailored. The Court is left to sort the matter out.

[23] At the end of the day, people should not be left guessing about why their *Charter* rights have been infringed. Demonstrable justification requires that the objective clearly reveal the harm that the government hopes to remedy, and that this objective remain constant throughout the justification process. As this Court has stated, the objective

"must be accurately and precisely defined so as to provide a clear framework for evaluating its importance, and to assess the precision with which the means have been crafted to fulfil that objective": *per* Cory J in *UFCW, Local 1518, supra*, at para. 59; see also *Thomson Newspapers, supra*, at para. 96; *RJR-MacDonald, supra*, at para. 144. A court faced with vague objectives may well conclude, as did Arbour JA (as she then was) in *Sauvé No. 1, supra*, at p. 487, that "the highly symbolic and abstract nature of th[e] objective ... detracts from its importance as a justification for the violation of a constitutionally protected right." If Parliament can infringe a crucial right such as the right to vote simply by offering symbolic and abstract reasons, judicial review either becomes vacuously constrained or reduces to a contest of "our symbols are better than your symbols." Neither outcome is compatible with the vigorous justification analysis required by the *Charter*.

[24] The rhetorical nature of the government objectives advanced in this case renders them suspect. The first objective, enhancing civic responsibility and respect for the law, could be asserted of virtually every criminal law and many non-criminal measures. Respect for law is undeniably important. But the simple statement of this value lacks the context necessary to assist us in determining whether the infringement at issue is demonstrably justifiable in a free and democratic society. To establish justification, one needs to know what problem the government is targeting, and why it is so pressing and important that it warrants limiting a *Charter* right. Without this, it is difficult if not impossible to weigh whether the infringement of the right is justifiable or proportionate.

[25] The second objective—to impose additional punishment on people serving penitentiary sentences—is less vague than the first. Still, problems with vagueness remain. The record does not disclose precisely why Parliament felt that more punishment was required for this particular class of prisoner, or what additional objectives Parliament hoped to achieve by this punishment that were not accomplished by the sentences already imposed. This makes it difficult to assess whether the objective is important enough to justify an additional rights infringement.

[26] Quite simply, the government has failed to identify particular problems that require denying the right to vote, making it hard to say that the denial is directed at a pressing and substantial purpose. Nevertheless, despite the abstract nature of the government's objectives and the rather thin basis upon which they rest, prudence suggests that we proceed to the proportionality analysis, rather than dismissing the government's objectives outright. The proportionality inquiry allows us to determine whether the government's asserted objectives are in fact capable of justifying its denial of the right to vote. At that stage, as we shall see, the difficulties inherent in the government's stated objectives become manifest.

C. Proportionality

[27] At this stage the government must show that the denial of the right to vote will promote the asserted objectives (the rational connection test); that the denial does not go further than reasonably necessary to achieve its objectives (the minimal impairment test); and that the overall benefits of the measure outweigh its negative impact (the proportionate effect test). As will be seen, the vagueness of the government's justifica-

tory goals coupled with the centrality of the right to vote to Canadian democracy, the rule of law, and legitimate sentencing, make the government's task difficult indeed.

1. Rational Connection

[28] Will denying the right to vote to penitentiary inmates enhance respect for the law and impose legitimate punishment? The government must show that this is likely, either by evidence or in reason and logic: *RJR-MacDonald*, *supra*, at para. 153.

[29] The government advances three theories to demonstrate rational connection between its limitation and the objective of enhancing respect for law. First, it submits that depriving penitentiary inmates of the vote sends an "educative message" about the importance of respect for the law to inmates and to the citizenry at large. Second, it asserts that allowing penitentiary inmates to vote "demeans" the political system. Finally, it takes the position that disenfranchisement is a legitimate form of punishment, regardless of the specific nature of the offence or the circumstances of the individual offender. In my respectful view, none of these claims succeed.

[30] The first asserted connector with enhancing respect for the law is the "educative message" or "moral statement" theory. The problem here, quite simply, is that denying penitentiary inmates the right to vote is bad pedagogy. It misrepresents the nature of our rights and obligations under the law, and it communicates a message more likely to harm than to help respect for the law.

[31] Denying penitentiary inmates the right to vote misrepresents the nature of our rights and obligations under the law and consequently undermines them. In a democracy such as ours, the power of lawmakers flows from the voting citizens, and lawmakers act as the citizens' proxies. This delegation from voters to legislators gives the law its legitimacy or force. Correlatively, the obligation to obey the law flows from the fact that the law is made by and on behalf of the citizens. In sum, the legitimacy of the law and the obligation to obey the law flow directly from the right of every citizen to vote. As a practical matter, we require all within our country's boundaries to obey its laws, whether or not they vote. But this does not negate the vital symbolic, theoretical and practical connection between having a voice in making the law and being obliged to obey it. This connection, inherited from social contract theory and enshrined in the *Charter*, stands at the heart of our system of constitutional democracy.

[32] The government gets this connection exactly backwards when it attempts to argue that depriving people of a voice in government teaches them to obey the law. The "educative message" that the government purports to send by disenfranchising inmates is both anti-democratic and internally self-contradictory. Denying a citizen the right to vote denies the basis of democratic legitimacy. It says that delegates elected by the citizens can then bar those very citizens, or a portion of them, from participating in future elections. But if we accept that governmental power in a democracy flows from the citizens, it is difficult to see how that power can legitimately be used to disenfranchise the very citizens from whom the government's power flows.

[33] Reflecting this truth, the history of democracy is the history of progressive enfranchisement. The universal franchise has become, at this point in time, an essential part of democracy. From the notion that only a few meritorious people could vote (expressed

in terms like class, property and gender), there gradually evolved the modern precept that all citizens are entitled to vote as members of a self-governing citizenry. Canada's steady march to universal suffrage culminated in 1982, with our adoption of a consti-tutional guarantee of the right of all citizens to vote in s. 3 of the *Charter*. As Arbour JA observed in *Sauvé No. 1*, *supra*, at p. 487:

> ... [T]he slow movement toward universal suffrage in Western democracies took an irre-versible step forward in Canada in 1982 by the enactment of s. 3 of the *Charter*. I doubt that anyone could now be deprived of the vote on the basis, not merely symbolic but ac-tually demonstrated, that he or she was not decent or responsible. By the time the *Charter* was enacted, exclusions from the franchise were so few in this country that it is fair to as-sume that we had abandoned the notion that the electorate should be restricted to a "decent and responsible citizenry," previously defined by attributes such as ownership of land or gender, in favour of a pluralistic electorate which could well include domestic enemies of the state.
>
> Under s. 3 of the *Charter*, the final vestiges of the old policy of selective voting have fallen, including the exclusion of persons with a "mental disease" and federally appointed judges: see *Canadian Disability Rights Council v. Canada*, [1988] 3 FC 622 (TD); and *Muldoon v. Canada*, [1988] 3 FC 628 (TD). The disenfranchisement of inmates takes us backwards in time and retrenches our democratic entitlements.

[34] The right of all citizens to vote, regardless of virtue or mental ability or other distinguishing features, underpins the legitimacy of Canadian democracy and Parlia-ment's claim to power. A government that restricts the franchise to a select portion of citizens is a government that weakens its ability to function as the legitimate representa-tive of the excluded citizens, jeopardizes its claim to representative democracy, and erodes the basis of its right to convict and punish law-breakers.

[35] More broadly, denying citizens the right to vote runs counter to our constitu-tional commitment to the inherent worth and dignity of every individual. As the South African Constitutional Court said in *August v. Electoral Commission*, 1999 (3) SALR 1, at para. 17, "[t]he vote of each and every citizen is a badge of dignity and of person-hood. Quite literally, it says that everybody counts." The fact that the disenfranchise-ment law at issue applies to a discrete group of persons should make us more, not less, wary of its potential to violate the principles of equal rights and equal membership em-bodied in and protected by the *Charter*.

[36] In recognition of the seminal importance of the right to vote in the constellation of rights, the framers of the *Charter* accorded it special protections. Unlike other rights, the right of every citizen to vote cannot be suspended under the "notwithstanding clause." As Arbour JA said in *Sauvé No. 1*, *supra*, at p. 486:

> It is indeed significant that s. 3 of the *Charter* is immune from the notwithstanding clause contained in s. 33, which permits Parliament and the legislatures to enact legislation which would otherwise violate the *Charter*. It confirms that the right to vote must be protected against those who have the capacity, and often the interest, to limit the franchise. Unpopu-lar minorities may seek redress against an infringement of their rights in the courts. But like everybody else, they can only seek redress against a dismissal of their political point of view at the polls.

[37] The government's vague appeal to "civic responsibility" is unhelpful, as is the attempt to lump inmate disenfranchisement together with legitimate voting regulations in support of the government's position. The analogy between youth voting restrictions and inmate disenfranchisement breaks down because the type of judgment Parliament is making in the two scenarios is very different. In the first case, Parliament is making a decision based on the experiential situation of all citizens when they are young. It is not saying that the excluded class is unworthy to vote, but regulating a modality of the universal franchise. In the second case, the government is making a decision that some people, whatever their abilities, are not morally worthy to vote—that they do not "deserve" to be considered members of the community and hence may be deprived of the most basic of their constitutional rights. But this is not the lawmakers' decision to make. The *Charter* makes this decision for us by guaranteeing the right of "every citizen" to vote and by expressly placing prisoners under the protective umbrella of the *Charter* through constitutional limits on punishment. The *Charter* emphatically says that prisoners are protected citizens, and short of a constitutional amendment, lawmakers cannot change this.

[38] The theoretical and constitutional links between the right to vote and respect for the rule of law are reflected in the practical realities of the prison population and the need to bolster, rather than to undermine, the feeling of connection between prisoners and society as a whole. The government argues that disenfranchisement will "educate" and rehabilitate inmates. However, disenfranchisement is more likely to become a self-fulfilling prophecy than a spur to reintegration. Depriving at-risk individuals of their sense of collective identity and membership in the community is unlikely to instill a sense of responsibility and community identity, while the right to participate in voting helps teach democratic values and social responsibility (testimony of Professor Jackson, appellants' record at pp. 2001-2). As J.S. Mill wrote:

> To take an active interest in politics is, in modern times, the first thing which elevates the mind to large interests and contemplations; the first step out of the narrow bounds of individual and family selfishness, the first opening in the contracted round of daily occupations ... . The possession and the exercise of political, and among others of electoral, rights, is one of the chief instruments both of moral and of intellectual training for the popular mind ... .

(J.S. Mill, "Thoughts on Parliamentary Reform" (1859), in J.M. Robson, ed., *Essays on Politics and Society*, vol. XIX, 1977, 311, at pp. 322-23)

To deny prisoners the right to vote is to lose an important means of teaching them democratic values and social responsibility.

[39] Even if these difficulties could be overcome, it is not apparent that denying penitentiary inmates the right to vote actually sends the intended message to prisoners, or to the rest of society. People may be sentenced to imprisonment for two years or more for a wide variety of crimes, ranging from motor vehicle and regulatory offences to the most serious cases of murder. The variety of offences and offenders covered by the prohibition suggests that the educative message is, at best, a mixed and diffuse one.

[40] It is a message sullied, moreover, by negative and unacceptable messages likely to undermine civic responsibility and respect for the rule of law. Denying citizen law-breakers the right to vote sends the message that those who commit serious

breaches are no longer valued as members of the community, but instead are temporary outcasts from our system of rights and democracy. More profoundly, it sends the unacceptable message that democratic values are less important than punitive measures ostensibly designed to promote order. If modern democratic history has one lesson to teach it is this: enforced conformity to the law should not come at the cost of our core democratic values.

[41] I conclude that denying penitentiary inmates the right to vote is more likely to send messages that undermine respect for the law and democracy than messages that enhance those values. The government's novel political theory that would permit elected representatives to disenfranchise a segment of the population finds no place in a democracy built upon principles of inclusiveness, equality, and citizen participation. That not all self-proclaimed democracies adhere to this conclusion says little about what the Canadian vision of democracy embodied in the *Charter* permits. Punitive disenfranchisement of inmates does not send the "educative message" that the government claims; to the contrary, it undermines this message and is incompatible with the basic tenets of participatory democracy contained in and guaranteed by the *Charter*.

[42] The government also argues that denying penitentiary inmates the vote will enhance respect for law because allowing people who flaunt the law to vote demeans the political system. The same untenable premises we have been discussing resurface here—that voting is a privilege the government can suspend and that the commission of a serious crime signals that the offender has chosen to "opt out" of community membership. But beyond this, the argument that only those who respect the law should participate in the political process is a variant on the age-old unworthiness rationale for denying the vote.

[43] The idea that certain classes of people are not morally fit or morally worthy to vote and to participate in the law-making process is ancient and obsolete. Edward III pronounced that citizens who committed serious crimes suffered "civil death," by which a convicted felon was deemed to forfeit all civil rights. Until recently, large classes of people, prisoners among them, were excluded from the franchise. The assumption that they were not fit or "worthy" of voting—whether by reason of class, race, gender or conduct—played a large role in this exclusion. We should reject the retrograde notion that "worthiness" qualifications for voters may be logically viewed as enhancing the political process and respect for the rule of law. As Arbour JA stated in *Sauvé No. 1, supra,* at p. 487, since the adoption of s. 3 of the *Charter*, it is doubtful "that anyone could now be deprived of the vote on the basis ... that he or she was not decent or responsible."

[44] Denial of the right to vote on the basis of attributed moral unworthiness is inconsistent with the respect for the dignity of every person that lies at the heart of Canadian democracy and the *Charter*: compare *August, supra*. It also runs counter to the plain words of s. 3, its exclusion from the s. 33 override, and the idea that laws command obedience because they are made by those whose conduct they govern. For all these reasons, it must, at this stage of our history, be rejected.

[45] This brings us to the government's final argument for rational connection—that disenfranchisement is a legitimate weapon in the state's punitive arsenal against the individual lawbreaker. Again, the argument cannot succeed. The first reason is that using

the denial of rights as punishment is suspect. The second reason is that denying the right to vote does not comply with the requirements for legitimate punishment established by our jurisprudence.

[46] The argument, stripped of rhetoric, proposes that it is open to Parliament to add a new tool to its arsenal of punitive implements—denial of constitutional rights. I find this notion problematic. I do not doubt that Parliament may limit constitutional rights in the name of punishment, provided that it can justify the limitation. But it is another thing to say that a particular class of people for a particular period of time will completely lose a particular constitutional right. This is tantamount to saying that the affected class is outside the full protection of the *Charter*. It is doubtful that such an unmodulated deprivation, particularly of a right as basic as the right to vote, is capable of justification under s. 1. Could Parliament justifiably pass a law removing the right of all penitentiary prisoners to be protected from cruel and unusual punishment? I think not. What of freedom of expression or religion? Why, one asks, is the right to vote different? The government offers no credible theory about why it should be allowed to deny this fundamental democratic right as a form of state punishment.

[47] The social compact requires the citizen to obey the laws created by the democratic process. But it does not follow that failure to do so nullifies the citizen's continued membership in the self-governing polity. Indeed, the remedy of imprisonment for a term rather than permanent exile implies our acceptance of continued membership in the social order. Certain rights are justifiably limited for penal reasons, including aspects of the rights to liberty, security of the person, mobility, and security against search and seizure. But whether a right is justifiably limited cannot be determined by observing that an offender has, by his or her actions, withdrawn from the social compact. Indeed, the right of the state to punish and the obligation of the criminal to accept punishment are tied to society's acceptance of the criminal as a person with rights and responsibilities. Other *Charter* provisions make this clear. Thus s. 11 protects convicted offenders from unfair trials, and s. 12 from "cruel and unusual treatment or punishment."

[48] The second flaw in the argument that s. 51(e) furthers legitimate punishment is that it does not meet the dual requirements that punishment must not be arbitrary and must serve a valid criminal law purpose. Absence of arbitrariness requires that punishment be tailored to the acts and circumstances of the individual offender: *R v. Smith*, [1987] 1 SCR 1045, at p. 1073. In the immortal words of Gilbert and Sullivan, the punishment should fit the crime. Section 51(e) *qua* punishment bears little relation to the offender's particular crime. It makes no attempt to differentiate among inmates serving sentences of two years and those serving sentences of twenty. It is true that those serving shorter sentences will be deprived of the right to vote for a shorter time. Yet the correlation of the denial with the crime remains weak. It is not only the violent felon who is told he is an unworthy outcast; a person imprisoned for a non-violent or negligent act, or an Aboriginal person suffering from social displacement receives the same message. They are not targeted, but they are caught all the same. For them the message is doubly invidious—not that they are cast out for their apparently voluntary rejection of society's norms, but that they are cast out arbitrarily, in ways that bear no necessary relation to their actual situation or attitude towards state authority.

[49] Punishment must also fulfill a legitimate penal purpose: see *Smith, supra,* at p. 1068. These include deterrence, rehabilitation, retribution, and denunciation: *R v. M. (C.A.),* [1996] 1 SCR 500, at para. 82. Neither the record nor common sense supports the claim that disenfranchisement deters crime or rehabilitates criminals. On the contrary, as Mill recognized long ago, participation in the political process offers a valuable means of teaching democratic values and civic responsibility.

[50] This leaves retribution and denunciation. Parliament may denounce unlawful conduct. But it must do so in a way that closely reflects the *moral culpability* of the offender and his or her circumstances. As Lamer CJ indicated in *M. (C.A.), supra,* at para. 80:

> Retribution in a criminal context, by contrast [to vengeance], represents an objective, reasoned and measured determination of an appropriate punishment which properly reflects the *moral culpability* of the offender, having regard to the intentional risk-taking of the offender, the consequential harm caused by the offender, and the normative character of the offender's conduct. [Emphasis in original.]

Denunciation as a symbolic expression of community values must be individually tailored in order to fulfill the legitimate penal purpose of condemning a *particular* offender's conduct (see *M. (C.A.), supra,* at para. 81) and to send an appropriate "educative message" about the importance of law-abiding behavior.

[51] Section 51(e) imposes blanket punishment on all penitentiary inmates regardless of the particular crimes they committed, the harm they caused, or the normative character of their conduct. It is not individually tailored to the particular offender's act. It does not, in short, meet the requirements of denunciatory, retributive punishment. It follows that it is not rationally connected to the goal of imposing legitimate punishment.

[52] When the facade of rhetoric is stripped away, little is left of the government's claim about punishment other than that criminals are people who have broken society's norms and may therefore be denounced and punished as the government sees fit, even to the point of removing fundamental constitutional rights. Yet, the right to punish and to denounce, however important, is constitutionally constrained. It cannot be used to write entire rights out of the Constitution, it cannot be arbitrary, and it must serve the constitutionally recognized goals of sentencing. On all counts, the case that s. 51(e) furthers lawful punishment objectives fails.

[53] I conclude that the government has failed to establish a rational connection between s. 51(e)'s denial of the right to vote and the objectives of enhancing respect for the law and ensuring appropriate punishment.

2. Minimal Impairment

[54] If the denial of a right is not rationally connected to the government's objectives, it makes little sense to go on to ask whether the law goes further than is necessary to achieve the objective. I simply observe that if it were established that denying the right to vote sends an educative message that society will not tolerate serious crime, the class denied the vote—all those serving sentences of two years or more—is too broad, catching many whose crimes are relatively minor and who cannot be said to have broken

their ties to society. Similarly, if it were established that this denial somehow furthers legitimate sentencing goals, it is plain that the marker of a sentence of two years or more catches many people who, on the government's own theory, should not be caught.

[55] The question at this stage of the analysis is not *how* many citizens are affected, but whether the *right* is minimally impaired. Even one person whose *Charter* rights are unjustifiably limited is entitled to seek redress under the *Charter*. It follows that this legislation cannot be saved by the mere fact that it is less restrictive than a blanket exclusion of all inmates from the franchise. First, it is difficult to substantiate the proposition that a two-year term is a reasonable means of identifying those who have committed "serious," as opposed to "minor," offences. If serious and minor offences are defined by the duration of incarceration, then this is a tautology. If the two-year period is meant to serve as a proxy for something else, then the government must give content to the notion of "serious" vs. "minor" offences, and it must demonstrate the correlation between this distinction and the entitlement to vote. It is no answer to the overbreadth critique to say that the measure is saved because a limited class of people is affected: the question is *why* individuals in this class are singled out to have their rights restricted, and *how* their rights are limited. The perceived "seriousness" of the crime is only one of many factors in determining the length of a convicted offender's sentence and the time served. The only real answer the government provides to the question "why two years?" is because it affects a smaller class than would a blanket disenfranchisement.

[56] Nor is it any answer to say that the infringement will end when the imprisonment ends. The denial of the right to vote during the period of imprisonment affects penitentiary inmates consistently, to an absolute degree, and in arbitrary ways that bear no necessary relation to their actual situation or attitude towards state authority. Section 51(e) thus denies a prisoner's rights in precisely the same fashion as its unconstitutional predecessor.

3. Proportionate Effect

[57] If a connection could be shown between the denial of the right to vote and the government's objectives, the negative effects of denying citizens the right to vote would greatly outweigh the tenuous benefits that might ensue.

[58] Denial of the right to vote to penitentiary inmates undermines the legitimacy of government, the effectiveness of government, and the rule of law. It curtails the personal rights of the citizen to political expression and participation in the political life of his or her country. It countermands the message that everyone is equally worthy and entitled to respect under the law—that everybody counts: see *August, supra*. It is more likely to erode respect for the rule of law than to enhance it, and more likely to undermine sentencing goals of deterrence and rehabilitation than to further them.

[59] The government's plea of no demonstrated harm to penitentiary inmates rings hollow when what is at stake is the denial of the fundamental right of every citizen to vote. When basic political rights are denied, proof of additional harm is not required. But were proof needed, it is available. Denying prisoners the right to vote imposes negative costs on prisoners and on the penal system. It removes a route to social development and rehabilitation acknowledged since the time of Mill, and it undermines correctional

law and policy directed towards rehabilitation and integration (testimony of Professor Jackson, appellants' record at pp. 2001-2). As the trial judge clearly perceived at p. 913, s. 51(e) "serves to further alienate prisoners from the community to which they must return, and in which their families live."

[60] The negative effects of s. 51(e) upon prisoners have a disproportionate impact on Canada's already disadvantaged Aboriginal population, whose overrepresentation in prisons reflects "a crisis in the Canadian criminal justice system": *R v. Gladue*, [1999] 1 SCR 688, at para. 64, *per* Cory and Iacobucci JJ. To the extent that the disproportionate number of Aboriginal people in penitentiaries reflects factors such as higher rates of poverty and institutionalized alienation from mainstream society, penitentiary imprisonment may not be a fair or appropriate marker of the degree of individual culpability. Added to this is the cost of silencing the voices of incarcerated Aboriginal people; with due respect, the fact that 1,837 Aboriginal people are disenfranchised by this law, while close to 600,000 are not directly affected, does not justify restricting the rights of those 1,837 individuals for reasons not demonstrably justified under the *Charter*: see Court of Appeal decision at para. 169. Aboriginal people in prison have unique perspectives and needs. Yet, s. 51(e) denies them a voice at the ballot box and, by proxy, in Parliament. That these costs are confined to the term of imprisonment does not diminish their reality. The silenced messages cannot be retrieved, and the prospect of someday participating in the political system is cold comfort to those whose rights are denied in the present.

[61] In the final analysis, even if there were merit in the Court of Appeal's view that the trial judge relied too heavily on the absence of concrete evidence of benefit, it is difficult to avoid the trial judge's conclusion, at p. 916, that "the salutary effects upon which the defendants rely are tenuous in the face of the denial of the democratic right to vote, and are insufficient to meet the civil standard of proof."

[62] I conclude that s. 51(e)'s disenfranchisement of prisoners sentenced to two years or more cannot be justified under s. 1 of the *Charter*. I leave for another day whether some political activities, like standing for office, could be justifiably denied to prisoners under s. 1. It may be that practical problems might serve to justify some limitations on the exercise of derivative democratic rights. Democratic participation is not only a matter of theory but also of practice, and legislatures retain the power to limit the modalities of its exercise where this can be justified. Suffice it to say that the wholesale disenfranchisement of all penitentiary inmates, even with a two-year minimum sentence requirement, is not demonstrably justified in our free and democratic society.

D. *The Guarantee of Equality Under Section 15(1) of the Charter*

[63] Having found that s. 51(e) unjustifiably infringes s. 3 of the *Charter*, it is unnecessary to consider the alternative argument that it infringes the equality guarantee of s. 15(1).

V. *Conclusion*

[64] I would allow the appeal, with costs to the appellants. Section 51(e) infringes s. 3 of the *Charter*, and the infringement is not justified under s. 1. It follows that

s. 51(e) is inconsistent with the *Charter* and is of no force or effect by operation of s. 52 of the *Constitution Act, 1982.* I would answer the constitutional questions as follows:

1. Does s. 51(e) of the *Canada Elections Act*, RSC 1985, c. E-2, infringe the right to vote in an election of members of the House of Commons, as guaranteed by s. 3 of the Canadian Charter of Rights and Freedoms?
   Yes.
2. If the answer to Question 1 is yes, is the infringement a reasonable limit, prescribed by law, which can be demonstrably justified in a free and democratic society, pursuant to s. 1 of the *Canadian Charter of Rights and Freedoms?*
   No.

It is unnecessary to answer the constitutional questions regarding s. 15(1) of the *Charter.*

The reasons of L'Heureux-Dubé, Gonthier, Major and Bastarache JJ were delivered by

GONTHIER J (dissenting):

I. Introduction

A. Specific Issue Before This Court

[65] Is Parliament able to temporarily suspend the exercise of the right to vote for criminals incarcerated for the commission of serious crimes for the duration of their incarceration? This is the question raised by this appeal. The answer will depend on whether s. 51(e) of the *Canada Elections Act*, RSC 1985, c. E-2 (the "Act"), which prohibits "[e]very person who is imprisoned in a correctional institution serving a sentence of two years or more" from voting, is in breach of ss. 3 or 15 of the *Canadian Charter of Rights and Freedoms* in a manner not justifiable under s. 1.

[66] The trial judge was of the view that s. 51(e) of the Act did not satisfy the test mandated by s. 1 of the *Charter.* I am in respectful disagreement with the reasons of my colleague, Chief Justice McLachlin, which support the disposition reached by the trial judge. I generally agree with the reasoning of the majority of the Federal Court of Appeal below that this provision is constitutionally sound. In my view, s. 51(e) of the Act is not an infringement of s. 15 of the *Charter*, and while having been conceded to be an infringement of the s. 3 *Charter* right, it is capable of being justified under s. 1 of the *Charter* as a reasonable limitation thereupon.

B. The More Fundamental Issue Arising from the Context of the Case at Bar

[67] My disagreement with the reasons of the Chief Justice, however, is also at a more fundamental level. This case rests on philosophical, political and social considerations which are not capable of "scientific proof." It involves justifications for and against the limitation of the right to vote which are based upon axiomatic arguments of principle or value statements. I am of the view that when faced with such justifications,

this Court ought to turn to the text of s. 1 of the *Charter* and to the basic principles which undergird both s. 1 and the relationship that provision has with the rights and freedoms protected within the *Charter*. Particularly, s. 1 of the *Charter* requires that this Court look to the fact that there may be different social or political philosophies upon which justifications for or against the limitations of rights may be based. In such a context, where this Court is presented with competing social or political philosophies relating to the right to vote, it is not by merely approving or preferring one that the other is necessarily disproved or shown not to survive *Charter* scrutiny. If the social or political philosophy advanced by Parliament reasonably justifies a limitation of the right in the context of a free and democratic society, then it ought to be upheld as constitutional. I conclude that this is so in the case at bar.

II. Legislative Provision in Question

[68] I am of the view that by enacting s. 51(e) of the Act, Parliament has chosen to assert and enhance the importance and value of the right to vote by temporarily disenfranchising serious criminal offenders for the duration of their incarceration. This point is worth underlining. The Chief Justice and I are in agreement that the right to vote is profoundly important, and ought not to be demeaned. Our differences lie principally in the fact that she subscribes to a philosophy whereby the temporary disenfranchising of criminals does injury to the rule of law, democracy and the right to vote, while I prefer deference to Parliament's reasonable view that it strengthens these same features of Canadian society.

[69] The reasons of the Chief Justice refer to the historical evolution of the franchise in Canada. This evolution has generally involved the weeding out of discriminatory exclusions. It is undeniable and, obviously, to be applauded, that, over time, Canada has been evolving towards the universalization of the franchise in such a manner. The provision in question in the case at bar, however, is strikingly and qualitatively different from these past discriminatory exclusions. It is a temporary suspension from voting based exclusively on the serious criminal *activity* of the offender. It is the length of the sentence, reflecting the nature of the offence and the criminal activity committed, that results in the temporary disenfranchisement during incarceration. Thus, far from being repugnant and discriminatory, based on some irrelevant personal characteristic, such as gender, race, or religion, s. 51(e) of the Act distinguishes persons based on the perpetrating of *acts* that are condemned by the *Criminal Code*, RSC 1985, c. C-46. Parliament has recognized this distinction as being different from other exclusions by its continued assertion that being convicted of a serious criminal offence is a ground for temporary disenfranchisement.

· · ·

[71] A further dimension of this qualitative difference is that serious criminal offenders are excluded from the vote for the reason that they are the *subjects of punishment*. The disenfranchisement only lasts as long as the period of incarceration. Thus, disenfranchisement, as a dimension of punishment, is attached to and mirrors the fact of incarceration. This fact makes the Canadian experience significantly different from the situation in some American states which disenfranchise ex-offenders for life, a situ-

ation addressed by many American academics: see, for example, L.H. Tribe, "The Disenfranchisement of Ex-Felons: Citizenship, Criminality, and 'The Purity of the Ballot Box'" (1989), 102 *Harv. L. Rev.* 1300.

[72] It is important to look at prisoner disenfranchisement from the perspective of each serious criminal offender rather than perceive it as a form of targeted group treatment. Disenfranchised prisoners can be characterized loosely as a group, but what is important to realize is that each of these prisoners has been convicted of a serious criminal offence and is therefore serving a personalized sentence which is proportionate to the act or acts committed. Punishment is guided by the goals of denunciation, deterrence, rehabilitation and retribution and is intended to be morally educative for incarcerated serious criminal offenders. Each prisoner's sentence is a temporary measure aimed at meeting these goals, while also being aimed at the long-term objective of reintegration into the community.

[73] The reasons of the Chief Justice express the view that the temporary disenfranchisement of serious criminal offenders necessarily undermines their inherent "worth" or "dignity." I disagree. In fact, it could be said that the notion of punishment is predicated on the dignity of the individual: it recognizes serious criminals as rational, autonomous individuals who have made choices. When these citizens exercise their freedom in a criminal manner, society imposes a concomitant responsibility for that choice. As Professor J. Hampton, one of the Crown's experts, writes in an article cited by Linden JA below, "Punishment, Feminism, and Political Identity: A Case Study in the Expressive Meaning of the Law" (1998), 11 *Can. JL & Jur.* 23, at p. 43:

> By telling people "you can have your right to vote suspended if, through your actions, you show contempt for the values that make our society possible," *this law links the exercise of freedom with responsibility for its effects*. Indeed, *not* to construct a punishment that sends this message is … to indirectly undermine the values of a democratic society. [Underlining added; italics in original.]

[74] If there is any negative connotation associated with this temporary disenfranchisement, it arises from the fact that a criminal act was perpetrated, an act for which the criminal offender is consequently being punished. This is not stereotyping. Criminal acts are rightly condemned by society. Serious criminals being punished and temporarily disenfranchised are not in any way of less "worth" or "dignity" because social condemnation is of the criminal acts and its purpose is not to diminish the individual prisoner as a person.

[75] The argument that the temporary disenfranchisement of serious criminal offenders undermines the inherent "worth" or "dignity" of prisoners presents a potentially problematic line of reasoning. Is it possible to "punish" serious criminals without undermining their "worth"? It must be so. This is inherently recognized in the *Charter* itself insofar that s. 12 only renders unconstitutional punishment that is "cruel and unusual." The *Criminal Code* and its provisions are declaratory of values, values on which Canadian society rests: see *R v. Keegstra*, [1990] 3 SCR 697, at pp. 769 and 787. Protecting and enhancing these values through the imposition of punishment for criminal activity is not an affront to dignity. On the contrary, the temporary disenfranchisement of serious criminal offenders reiterates society's commitment to the basic moral values which

underpin the *Criminal Code*; in this way it is morally educative for both prisoners and society as a whole.

[76] The punishment of serious criminal offenders is also aimed at protecting society and the "dignity" and "worth" of those members of society who have been or may become the victims of crime. Punishment is intended to act as a general deterrent to potential criminals and as a specific deterrent vis-à-vis incarcerated persons. *Charter* analysis is meant to consider the *Charter* rights of other members of society: see *R v. Sharpe*, [2001] 1 SCR 45, 2001 SCC 2, at para. 187; *Keegstra, supra*, at p. 756. Serious criminal activity is clearly often an affront to numerous *Charter* values.

[Justice Gonthier went on to consider the application of s. 1]

· · ·

[91] Justifying, therefore, is not a matter of one value clearly prevailing over the other, but is rather a matter of developing the significance of the values being dealt with and asking whether Parliament, in its attempt to reconcile competing interests, has achieved a rational and reasonable balance. Proportionality, in the context of *Charter* analysis, does not mean a perfect solution, as any balance arising from competing interests will involve preferring one value over the other to some extent.

[92] As emerges from the submissions before this Court, there seem generally to be two options available for dealing with the issue at hand. The first, that chosen by the Chief Justice, is to prefer an inclusive approach to democratic participation for serious criminal offenders incarcerated for two years or more. This view locates democratic participation as a central dimension of rehabilitation, insofar as the incarcerated offenders remain citizens with the fullest exercise of their democratic rights. By the same token, the unrestricted franchise enhances democratic legitimacy of government, and confirms or enhances the citizenship or standing of prisoners in society. To do otherwise, it is suggested, undermines the "dignity" or "worth" of prisoners. The alternative view, adopted by Parliament, considers that the temporary suspension of the prisoner's right to vote, in fact, enhances the general purposes of the criminal sanction, including rehabilitation. It does so by underlining the importance of civic responsibility and the rule of law. This approach sees the temporary removal of the vote as a deterrent to offending or re-offending and the return of the vote as an inducement to reject further criminal conduct. In withdrawing for a time one expression of political participation concurrently with personal freedom, the significance of both are enhanced. Rather than undermine the dignity or worth of prisoners, the removal of their vote takes seriously the notion that they are free actors and attaches consequences to actions that violate certain core values as expressed in the *Criminal Code*.

[93] Both of these approaches, however, entail accepting logically prior political or social philosophies about the nature and content of the right to vote. The former approach, that accepted by the reasons of the Chief Justice, entails accepting a philosophy that preventing criminals from voting does damage to both society and the individual, and undermines prisoners' inherent worth and dignity. The latter approach also entails accepting a philosophy, that not permitting serious incarcerated criminals to vote is a social rejection of serious crime which reflects a moral line which safeguards the social contract and the rule of law and bolsters the importance of the nexus between in-

dividuals and the community. Both of these social or political philosophies, however, are *aimed at the same goal*: that of supporting the fundamental importance of the right to vote itself. Further, both of these social or political philosophies are supported by the practices of the various Canadian provinces, the practices of other liberal democracies, and academic writings. Finally, neither position can be proven empirically—rather, the selection of one over the other is largely a matter of philosophical preference. What is *key* to my approach is that the acceptance of one or the other of these social or political philosophies dictates much of the constitutional analysis which ensues, since the reasonableness of any limitation upon the right to vote and the appropriateness of particular penal theories and their relation to the right to vote will logically be related to whether or not the justification for that limitation is based upon an "acceptable" social or political philosophy.

[94] The reasons of the Chief Justice hold, at para. 18, that the challenge of the government is to present a justification that is "convincing, in the sense that it is sufficient to satisfy the reasonable person looking at all the evidence and relevant considerations, that the state is justified in infringing the right at stake to the degree it has." I agree with this test, subject only to a recognition that as the context of the case at bar involves evaluating competing social or political philosophies, the analysis runs the risk of lapsing into the realm of *ipse dixit*. In the realm of competing social or political philosophies, *reasonableness* is the predominant s. 1 justification consideration.

[95] The reasons of the Chief Justice apply something seemingly more onerous than the "justification" standard referred to just above. She describes the right to vote as a "core democratic right" and suggests that its exemption from the s. 33 override somehow raises the bar for the government in attempting to justify its restriction (paras. 13 and 14). This altering of the justification standard is problematic in that it seems to be based upon the view that there is only one plausible social or political philosophy upon which to ground a justification for or against the limitation of the right. This approach, however, is incorrect on a basic reading of s. 1 of the *Charter*, which clearly does not constrain Parliament or authorize this Court to prioritize one reasonable social or political philosophy over reasonable others, but only empowers this Court to strike down those limitations which are not reasonable and which cannot be justified in a free and democratic society.

[96] The analysis cannot be skirted by qualifying the right to vote as a core democratic right. It does not follow from the fact that Parliament is denied the authority to remove or qualify the right to vote in its sole discretion under s. 33 that limitations on that right may not be justified under s. 1, or that a more onerous s. 1 analysis must necessarily apply. Constitutional writers and commentators point out that s. 33 was a political compromise, meant to bring together provinces opposed to the entrenchment of constitutional rights, with those in favour: P. Macklem et al., *Canadian Constitutional Law* (2nd ed. 1997), at pp. 597 and 646. Indeed Macklem et al. write at p. 597: "Added to the Charter at the last moment, this controversial provision captured the final political compromise among the provinces and federal government that facilitated the adoption of the Charter." There is little evidence of the intention behind excluding democratic rights (along with mobility rights, language rights, and enforcement provisions) from the ambit of s. 33, nor has this Court ever seriously considered the significance of such

exclusion. The Chief Justice's conclusion at para. 11 that "[t]he framers of the *Charter* signaled the special importance of this right ... by exempting it from legislative override ..." requires examination before it can be used as support for nearly insulating the right to vote from s. 1 limitations. In fact, s. 33 and s. 1 are clearly different in their purpose, and the *Charter* clearly distinguishes their application to the right to vote. It does not behoove the Court to read s. 33 into s. 3 by finding in s. 3, when divorced from s. 1, the statement of a political philosophy which preempts another political philosophy which is reasonable and justified under the latter section. The *Charter* was not intended to monopolize the ideological space.

[97] There is a flaw in an analysis which suggests that because one social or political philosophy can be justified, it necessarily means that another social or political philosophy is not justified: in other words, where two social or political philosophies exist, it is not by approving one that you disprove the other. Differences in social or political philosophy, which result in different justifications for limitations upon rights, are perhaps inevitable in a pluralist society. That having been said, it is only those limitations which are not reasonable or demonstrably justified in a free and democratic society which are unconstitutional. Therefore, the most significant analysis in this case is the examination of the social or political philosophy underpinning the justification advanced by the Crown. This is because it will indicate whether the limitation of the right to vote is reasonable and is based upon a justification which is capable of being demonstrated in a free and democratic society. If the choice made by Parliament is such, then it ought to be respected. The range of choices made by different legislatures in different jurisdictions, which I will review below, supports the view that there are many resolutions to the particular issue at bar which are reasonable; it demonstrates that there are many possible rational balances.

[98] The role of this Court, when faced with competing social or political philosophies and justifications dependent on them, is therefore to define the *parameters* within which the acceptable reconciliation of competing values lies. The decision before this Court is therefore not whether or not Parliament has made a proper policy decision, but whether or not the policy position chosen is an acceptable choice amongst those permitted under the *Charter*. ...

. . .

D. *Symbolic Arguments and Evidentiary Problems*

[99] A subject that is related to and follows from the above discussion concerning the evaluation of competing social or political philosophies is the role of symbolic arguments in *Charter* adjudication. In the context of the *Charter* analysis, it is important not to downplay the importance of symbolic or abstract arguments. Symbolic or abstract arguments cannot be dismissed outright by virtue of their symbolism: many of the great principles, the values upon which society rests, could be said to be symbolic. In fact, one of the more important dimensions of s. 3 of the *Charter* is clearly its symbolism: the affirmation of political equality reflected in all citizens being guaranteed the right to vote, subject only to reasonable limits prescribed by law that can be demonstrably justified in a free and democratic society. The case at bar concerns debates about

symbolism, as the arguments involved relate to abstract concepts such as democracy, rights, punishment, the rule of law and civic responsibility. To choose a narrow reading of rights over the objectives advanced by Parliament is to choose one set of symbols over another.

[100] In her reasons, the Chief Justice claims at para. 16 that Parliament is relying on "lofty objectives," and suggests at para. 23 that the presence of "symbolic and abstract" objectives is problematic. However, the reasons of the Chief Justice have the very same objective—to protect the value of the right to vote and the rule of law—and rely on equally vague concepts. Breaking down the meaning and value of the right to vote, one is unavoidably led to abstract and symbolic concepts such as the rule of law, the legitimacy of law and government, and the meaning of democracy. The Chief Justice discusses these concepts at length, along with theories of individual motivation. For instance, relying on the philosopher J.S. Mill, she suggests at para. 38 that "[t]o deny prisoners the right to vote is to lose an important means of teaching them democratic values and social responsibility." This type of statement is as symbolic, abstract and philosophical as the government's claim that denying serious incarcerated criminals the right to vote will strengthen democratic values and social responsibility.

[101] Most of the evidence in this case is that of expert opinions on the matters of political theory, moral philosophy, philosophy of law, criminology, correctional policy, and penal theory. I would suggest distinguishing between two kinds of expert evidence in this case. First, there is very limited social scientific evidence, e.g. in the field of criminology, that seeks to establish the practical or empirical consequences of maintaining or lifting the ban on prisoner voting. Second, there is copious expert testimony in the nature of legal and political philosophy. I do not think that the Court need necessarily defer to this second type of expertise, or take into account the "skill" and "reputation" of the experts in weighing this evidence (as the trial judge purported to do at [1996] 1 FC 857, at pp. 865-66). First, most if not all of the philosophers or theorists on which these experts rely never in fact even addressed the specific issue of prisoner enfranchisement or disenfranchisement. Second, legal theory expert testimony in this context essentially purports to justify axiomatic principles. Therefore, these arguments are either persuasive or not. In this context, it is appropriate for courts to look not only to such theoretical arguments but also beyond, to factors such as the extent of public debate on an issue, the practices of other liberal democracies and, most especially, to the reasoned view of our democratically elected Parliament.

[102] The evidence in this case, offered by both the appellants and the Crown, is abstract and symbolic and does not lend itself to being easily demonstrated. For example, it was submitted before this Court that the Crown ought to have to demonstrate actual benefits or actual effectiveness of the provision which Parliament has chosen. On the facts, this is a nearly impossible task. The same demand, however, if made with regard to the effectiveness of the *Criminal Code* in general or in its specific provisions, would raise similar challenges: can it be shown that the *Criminal Code* is generally effective? It is as if to say that because there are still criminals, we ought to do away with the *Criminal Code*, because the existence of crime itself points towards an effectiveness problem. Symbolic or abstract arguments must be examined seriously for what they are, because that is effectively all that is before this Court. Further, one must not deny

that the choices between and the interpretation of these symbolic or abstract arguments are clearly connected to significant concrete effects.

[103] A key justification before this Court, to be analysed in depth below, is that serious crime reflects contempt for the rule of law and a rejection of the basis for the operation of a free and democratic society. This, if it is symbolic or abstract, reflects a core value of the community, a value that is reflected throughout the *Criminal Code* and in the provision before us today. As will be argued below, this value is based on a reasonable social or political philosophy. Temporarily removing the vote from serious criminal offenders while they are incarcerated is both symbolic and concrete in effect. Returning it on being released from prison is the same.

・・・

[157] I support the analysis of the courts below: reason, logic and common sense, as well as extensive expert evidence support a conclusion that there is a rational connection between disenfranchising offenders incarcerated for serious crimes and the objectives of promoting civic responsibility and the rule of law and the enhancement of the general objectives of the penal sanction. The rational connection between the disenfranchisement and the first objective is explained above, in my discussion of dignity and the fact that removing the right to vote from serious incarcerated criminals does no injury to, but rather recognizes their dignity (see paras. 68-76). It is also explained above in the section entitled "A Rational and Reasonable Social or Political Philosophy Underpins the Crown's Justification for the Limitation of the Section 3 Right" (see especially paras. 114-121), and below in my discussion of the salutary effects of the measure (see especially paras. 180-183). In the latter section, I discuss the legislation's expression of societal values and its signalling effect. The Chief Justice prefers a different line of reasoning. Citing Mill as her authority, she states that "denying penitentiary inmates the right to vote is more likely to send messages that undermine respect for the law and democracy than messages that enhance those values" (para. 41). However, apart from one philosopher, she provides no support for this contention; she simply replaces one reasonable position with another, dismissing the government's position as "unhelpful" (para. 37 of the Chief Justice's reasons).

・・・

[163] I am of the view that no less intrusive measure would be equally effective. Since Parliament has drawn a line which identifies which incarcerated offenders have committed serious enough crimes to warrant being deprived of the vote, any alternative line will not be of equal effectiveness. Equal effectiveness is a dimension of the analysis that should not be underemphasized, as it relates directly to Parliament's ability to pursue its legitimate objectives effectively. Any other line insisted upon amounts to *second-guessing* Parliament as to what amounts to "serious" crime.

[164] The trial judge below stressed that the legislative process did undertake a rigorous evaluation of the line chosen regarding "serious" crime. He noted that the legislative history of s. 51(e) of the Act involved a report from the Lortie Commission. Notably, the Lortie Commission, despite the conclusion of a Research Study commissioned under it which recommended that all prisoners get the right to vote, concluded that prisoners who had been convicted of an offence punishable by a maximum of life imprisonment and who had been sentenced to a prison term of 10 years or more should be disqualified

from voting for the duration of their incarceration. A Special Committee on Electoral Reform, which reviewed the Lortie Commission's Report, recommended, however, that a two-year cutoff was appropriate since this would catch "serious offenders." Wetston J stated, at p. 877:

> The Special Committee spent a great deal of time trying to determine whether a two-year limit for the disqualification was appropriate, or whether a cutoff of five years, or seven years, or ten years (as recommended by the Lortie Commission) was more justifiable. Eventually, the Special Committee recommended a two-year cutoff since, in their view, serious offenders may be considered to be those individuals who have been sentenced to a term of two years or more in a correctional institution. Generally, that means a federal penitentiary, but not exclusively.

...

173] I agree with the Crown that the impugned provision is not arbitrary: it is related directly to particular categories of conduct. I also note that the two-year cutoff line also reflects practical considerations: it reflects a distinguishing between offenders incarcerated in federal rather than provincial institutions (s. 743.1 of the *Criminal Code*); persons sentenced to a term of imprisonment of two years or more are not eligible to serve their sentence in open custody (s. 742.1 of the *Criminal Code*); and persons subject to a sentence of imprisonment of two years or more are subject to having a court delay parole until one half of the sentence is served (s. 743.6 of the *Criminal Code*).

[174] In my view, it is particularly inappropriate, in the case at bar, to find the justification of the limitation of the right to be unconvincing at this phase of the *Oakes* test. First, as was noted above, there is a need for deference to Parliament in its drawing of a line, especially since this Court gave the impression that it was up to Parliament to do exactly that after the first *Sauvé* case was heard in 1993. Second, also as developed above, the analysis of social and political philosophies and the accommodation of values in the context of the *Charter* must be sensitive to the fact that there may be many possible reasonable and rational balances. Developing this point, it is important to note that, given the theoretical nature of the arguments raised by both parties in the case at bar, they do not gain proportionally in strength as the bar is moved higher. Symbolic and theoretical justifications such as employed in this case do not get stronger as the line changes. The fundamental premises underlying the line chosen would be the same if the cutoff was 10 years, or even 25 years. See, for example, *Driskell* [*v. Manitoba (Attorney General)*, [1999] 11 WWR 615], in which similar analytical problems to those in the case at bar arose and resulted in a line of five years being held unconstitutional. Line drawing, amongst a range of acceptable alternatives, is for Parliament. This view is compounded by the point developed above that it is plain that any alternate line would not be equally effective, in that the line drawn reflects Parliament's identification of what amounts to serious criminal activity. The Federal Court of Appeal was correct to find the provision in question minimally impairing.

...

[185] The reasons of the Chief Justice suggest that to be temporarily disenfranchised while incarcerated is to be severed from the body politic and silenced as an unworthy outsider. Above, I explained how temporary disenfranchisement does not un-

dermine the "worth" or "dignity" of any offender but is instead focussed at criminal offences. I also have discussed how temporary disenfranchisement is to be seen as a dimension of punishment that is tailored towards rehabilitation and reintegration: it is therefore ultimately focussed upon inclusion rather than exclusion. One other point which I would like to make briefly is to note that, while being temporarily disenfranchised is clearly a significant measure, which is part of the reason why it carries such great symbolic weight, it does not amount to the complete extinguishment of all means of political expression or participation. There are many other avenues by which serious criminals who are incarcerated for two or more years may still exercise political expression: they can write to and lobby elected representative, publish their ideas or policy proposals, or in other ways make their views known.

NOTE

Suavé is a rich and fascinating decision. It has become a landmark decision in the international struggle for prisoner enfranchisement. The European Human Rights Court referred to it at length in its decision that resulted in striking down a comprehensive voting prohibition in United Kingdom legislation: see *Hirst v. United Kingdom (No. 2)*, no. 74025/01, EHCR 2005, at paras. 35-37. In Canada, it has also become one of the leading decisions dealing with the application of s. 1 of the Charter, and the scope of justificatory evidence relevant to a s. 1 analysis.

On the equality front, the case represents an important stage in the analysis of whether prisoners are an analogous group that should be recognized under s. 15(1) of the Charter. Of course, this is not an easy question. It requires a careful application of equality jurisprudence and theory, coupled with a historical understanding of the characteristics of "prisonerhood" in Canada. This kind of analysis goes beyond looking at the rigours and exigencies of prison conditions. It should focus on the centrality of individual dignity such that it becomes important to examine factors like denials of access to justice and the treatment of women and Aboriginal peoples. Prior to *Suavé (No. 2)*, there were a number of cases in which this argument was made, although perhaps not with adequate supporting evidence. In each decision, the argument was rejected. This was the obstacle facing those participants in *Sauvé (No. 2)* who argued this point. Certainly, the minority decision of Gonthier J looked at this question and reached a similar result. However, it is significant to revisit what the Chief Justice, for the majority, said on this issue (at para. 63):

Having found that s. 51(e) unjustifiably infringes s. 3 of the *Charter*, it is unnecessary to consider the alternative argument that it infringes the equality guarantee of s. 15(1). [Emphasis added.]

Clearly, this says that there was no need to consider the s. 15 arguments. But it implies that the question of whether prisoners constitute an analagous ground under s. 15(1) is still open. If this is an acceptable reading, it means that the precedential value of earlier case law has been swept away, leaving the matter to be re-argued in any court.

III. RELIEF IN THE NATURE OF CERTIORARI

A. Jurisdiction

The supervisory jurisdiction over federal decision makers was moved to the Federal Court when it was established in 1972. At the time, it was anticipated that the new s. 28 remedy in the *Federal Court Act* might apply to prisoners. This provision included a broad "review and set aside" power that applied to any decision required by law to be made on a judicial or quasi-judicial basis. However, any expectation that this would provide a remedy for prisoners was dashed in *Martineau and al. v. Matsqui Institution Inmate Disciplinary Board*, [1978] 1 SCR 118, where the majority held that neither the commissioner's directives nor the incipient duty to act fairly placed penitentiary discipline decisions in this category of decisions required "by law" to be made on a judicial or quasi-judicial basis. In dissent, Laskin CJ was critical of the majority's conception of "law," and described it as "too nihilistic" for him to accept. Shortly afterward, the issue returned to the Supreme Court as a *certiorari* application under s. 18 of the *Federal Court Act* in what has been commonly called *Martineau (No. 2)*. In the interim, the Supreme Court had firmly rejected the traditional classification approach to judicial review and adopted the general duty to act fairly as the standard for procedural obligation owed by public and statutory decision makers (see *Re Nicholson and Haldimand-Norfolk Regional Board of Police Commissioners*, [1979] 1 SCR 311).

In *Martineau*, the defendant had been charged with the serious disciplinary offences of having two persons in a cell and committing an indecent act. He was convicted of an apparently included offence that was recorded as "being in an indecent position." He was convicted and sentenced to 15 days' dissociation. At his hearing, he was absent when some of the evidence against him was heard. The commissioner's directive dealing with disciplinary hearing procedures expressly stated that no finding should be made against an inmate for a serious or flagrant offence unless he or she has appeared at the hearing so that the evidence can be given in his or her presence. Martineau sought *certiorari* in the Federal Court—Trial Division. The Correctional Service disputed the court's jurisdiction to grant such relief. Although the court of first instance agreed that it had jurisdiction, on appeal to the Federal Court of Appeal, the arguments against remedial jurisdiction prevailed. Jackett CJ was content that disgruntled prisoners could satisfy their grievances by writing to their member of parliament. On appeal to the Supreme Court, shortly after its acceptance of the duty to act fairly, the argument in favour of a remedy received a more welcome reception. The court allowed the prisoner's appeal unanimously. For the majority, Pigeon J accepted that *certiorari* was available to challenge disciplinary decisions on procedural grounds, but that its use should be restricted to "cases of serious injustice." The opinion of Dickson J has, in subsequent years, been accepted as more accurately explaining the proper scope of *certiorari* as an evolving remedy.

Martineau v. Matsqui Institution Disciplinary Board
(1979), 50 CCC (2d) 1 (SCC)

DICKSON J:

• • •

The appeal raises in general terms the question of the supervisory role, if any, of the Federal Court, Trial Division, in respect of disciplinary boards within Canadian penitentiaries. It also calls for consideration of three related issues of importance in Canadian administrative law.

First, it compels resolution of the continuing debate concerning the review jurisdiction of the Trial Division and Court of Appeal under, respectively, ss. 18 and 28 of the *Federal Court Act*, RSC 1970, c. 10 (2nd Supp.), an issue left open by this Court in earlier judgments. If the Court of Appeal lacks jurisdiction under s. 28 to entertain an application to review and set aside, then the question which must be asked, and to which this case must give the answer, is whether the impugned decision or order can be challenged by application for *certiorari* under s. 18 of the Act.

Second, the case calls for closer analysis of the duty to act fairly—the English "fairness doctrine"—than has hitherto been necessary.

Third, the appeal raises the question of the potential breadth of the common law remedy of *certiorari* in Canada.

• • •

It has been argued that s. 18 purports to transfer jurisdiction from provincial Courts to the Trial Division of the Federal Court and clothes the latter with exclusive jurisdiction to grant relief by way of *certiorari* against federal boards, commissions or other tribunals, but that s. 28 removes that jurisdiction from the Trial Division in respect of *certiorari*, despite the express words of s. 18. In other words, the terms of s. 28 completely exclude what s. 18 apparently granted. If that view be correct, and s. 18 is indeed sterile and without independent life, then a narrow reading of s. 28 will virtually deny Canadians recourse against federal tribunals. It is not disputed that the Inmate Disciplinary Board of Matsqui Institution is a federal board, commission or other tribunal.

• • •

Thus, *Howarth, supra*, distinguishes between ss. 18 and 28 review jurisdiction in the Federal Court, the new remedy under s. 28 not being exhaustive of Federal Court jurisdiction to review federal Government action. The consequence, as Mr. Justice Pigeon puts it, is that under the *Federal Court Act* "a distinction is made between two classes of orders of federal boards."

• • •

Restrictive reading of s. 28 of the *Federal Court Act* need not, of necessity, lead to a reduction in the ambit for judicial review of federal Government action. Section 18 is available. Section 28 has caused difficulties, not only because of the language in which it is cast but, equally, because it tended to crystallize the law of judicial review at a time when significant changes were occurring in other countries with respect to the scope and grounds for review. Sections 18 and 28 of the *Federal Court Act* were obviously intended to concentrate judicial review of federal tribunals in a single federal

Court. As I read the Act, Parliament envisaged an extended scope for review. I am therefore averse to giving the Act a reading which would defeat that intention and posit a diminished scope for relief from the actions of federal tribunals. I simply cannot accept the view that Parliament intended to remove the old common law remedies, including *certiorari*, from the provincial superior Courts, and vest them in the Trial Division of the Federal Court, only to have those remedies rendered barren through the interaction of ss. 18 and 28 of the Act. I would apply the principle laid down by Brett LJ in *R v. Local Government Board* (1882), 10 QBD 309 at p. 321, that the jurisdiction of a Court ought to be exercised widely when dealing with matters perhaps not strictly judicial, but in which the rights or interests of citizens are affected.

VI

The dominant characteristic of recent developments in English administrative law has been expansion of judicial review jurisdiction to supervise administrative action by public authorities. *Certiorari* evolved as a flexible remedy, affording access to judicial supervision in new and changing situations. In 1689 Chief Justice Holt could say, in *Re Cardiffe Bridge* (1689), 1 Salk. 146, 91 ER 135 "wherever any new jurisdiction is erected, be it by private or public Act of Parliament, they are subject to the inspections of this Court by writ of error, or by *certiorari* and *mandamus*." And in *Groenwelt v. Burwell et al.* (1694), 1 LD Raym. 454 at pp. 467-9, 91 ER 1202, Holt CJ, held again, in the context of the censors of the College of Physicians of London, that

> it is plain, that the censors have judicial power ... where a man has power to inflict imprisonment upon another for punishment of his offence, there he hath judicial authority ... for it is a consequence of all jurisdictions, to have their proceedings returned here by *certiorari*, to be examined here. ... Where any Court is erected by statute, a *certiorari* lies to it. ...

Nor has perception of *certiorari* as an adaptable remedy been in any way modified. The amplitude of the writ has been affirmed time and again: see, for example, the judgment of Lord Parker LJ in *R v. Criminal Injuries Compensation Board, Ex. p. Lain*, [1967] 2 QB 864 at p. 882:

> The position as I see it is that the exact limits of the ancient remedy by way of *certiorari* have never been and ought not to be specifically defined. They have varied from time to time being extended to meet changing conditions. At one time the writ only went to an inferior court. Later its ambit was extended to statutory tribunals determining a *lis inter partes*. Later again it extended to cases where there was no *lis* in the strict sense of the word but where immediate or subsequent rights of a citizen were affected. The only constant limits throughout were that it was performing a public duty.

Roskill LJ, in *Re Liverpool Taxi Owners' Ass'n*, [1972] 2 All ER 589 at p. 596 expressed the thought in these words:

> The long legal history of the former prerogative writs and of their modern counterparts, the orders of prohibition, *mandamus* and *certiorari* shows that their application has always been flexible as the need for their use in differing social conditions down the centuries had changed.

The principles of natural justice and fairness have matured in recent years. And the writ of *certiorari*, in like measure, has developed apace. The speeches in *Ridge v. Baldwin et al.*, [1964] AC 40, show the evolutionary state of administrative law.

Does *certiorari* lie to the Inmate Disciplinary Board? The usual starting point in a discussion of this nature is the "Electricity Commissioners" formula, found at p. 205 of *R v. Electricity Com'rs, Ex p. London Electricity Joint Committee Co. (1920), Ltd., et al.*, [1924] 1 KB 171 (CA), where Atkin LJ had this to say:

> Wherever any body of persons having legal authority to determine questions affecting the rights of subjects, and having the duty to act judicially, act in excess of their legal authority they are subject to the controlling jurisdiction of the King's Bench Division exercised in these writs.

Difficulty has arisen from the statement of Atkin LJ in part from the fact that his words have been treated as if they had been engraved in stone, and in part because it is not clear what Atkin LJ meant. How far, if at all, did he mean to limit the use of orders for *certiorari* and prohibition by the phrase "and having the duty to act judicially"? What did he mean by "judicially" in the context? It will be recalled that in the *Electricity Com'rs* case itself *certiorari* and prohibition issued to a group of administrators who were acting far more as part of the legislative than of the judicial process.

Rights of Subjects

The term "rights of subjects" has given concern, often being treated by Courts as the *sine qua non* of jurisdiction to permit review. There has been an unfortunate tendency to treat "rights" in the narrow sense of rights to which correlative legal duties attach. In this sense, "rights" are frequently contrasted with "privileges," in the mistaken belief that only the former can ground judicial review of the decision-maker's actions. *Lain, supra*, is invaluable on this branch of Lord Atkin's test. There the absence of any legal right on the part of the claimants to *ex gratia* payments from the criminal injuries compensation board would seem to pose an insuperable obstacle, but Ashworth J disposed of this impediment without trouble and in broadest language (p. 892):

> For my part I doubt whether Atkin LJ was propounding an all-embracing definition of the circumstances in which relief by way of *certiorari* would lie. In my judgment the words in question read in the context of what precedes and follows them, would be of no less value if they were altered by omitting "the rights of" so as to become "affecting subjects."

Lord Denning aptly summarized the state of the law on this aspect in *Schmidt v. Secretary of State for Home Affairs*, [1969] 2 Ch. 149 (CA). There, the Master of the Rolls stated [p. 170]:

> The speeches in *Ridge v. Baldwin* ... show that an administrative body may, in a proper case, be bound to give a person who is affected by their decision an opportunity of making representations. It all depends on whether he has some right or interest, or, I would add, some legitimate expectation, of which it would not be fair to deprive him without hearing what he has to say.

· · ·

When concerned with individual cases and aggrieved persons, there is the tendency to forget that one is dealing with public law remedies, which, when granted by the Courts, not only set aright individual injustice, but also ensure that public bodies exercising powers affecting citizens heed the jurisdiction granted them. *Certiorari* stems from the assumption by the Courts of supervisory powers over certain tribunals in order to assure the proper functioning of the machinery of Government. To give a narrow or technical interpretation to "rights" in an individual sense is to misconceive the broader purpose of judicial review of administrative action. One should, I suggest, begin with the premise that any public body exercising power over subjects may be amenable to judicial supervision, the individual interest involved being but one factor to be considered in resolving the broad policy question of the nature of review appropriate for the particular administrative body.

Duty to Act Judicially

Prior to the decision in *Ridge v. Baldwin, supra*, it was generally accepted that *certiorari* would only be granted when the nature of the process by which the decision was arrived at was a judicial process or a process analogous to the judicial process: *Nakkuda Ali v. Jayaratne*, [1951] AC 66, [1950] 2 WWR 927 (PC). This notion of a "super-added duty to act judicially," as a separate and independent precondition to the availability of natural justice, and inferentially, to recourse to *certiorari*, was unequivocally rejected by Lord Reid in *Ridge, supra* (p. 75):

> If Lord Hewart meant that it is never enough that a body simply has a duty to determine what the rights of an individual should be, but that there must always be something more to impose on it a duty to act judicially before it can be found to observe the principles of natural justice, then that appears to me impossible to reconcile with the earlier authorities.

In the *Electricity Commissioners* case itself, *supra*, Lord Reid observed, the judicial element was inferred from the nature of the power.

Perhaps the best expression of the significance of the decision in *Ridge v. Baldwin, supra*, is found in the reasons of Lord Widgery CJ in *R v. London Borough of Hillingdon, Ex p. Royco Homes Ltd.*, [1974] 2 All ER 643 at p. 649 (QBD), wherein he considered the availability of *certiorari* to review the grant of a planning permission by a local authority:

> Accordingly it may be that previous efforts to use *certiorari* in this field have been deterred by Atkin LJ's reference to it being necessary for the body affected to have the duty to act judicially. If that is so, that reason for reticence on the part of applicants was, I think, put an end to in the House of Lords in *Ridge v. Baldwin* ... in the course of his speech Lord Reid made reference to that oft-quoted dictum of Atkin LJ and pointed out that the additional requirement of the body being under a duty to act judicially was not supported by authority. Accordingly it seems to me now that that obstacle, if obstacle it were, has been cleared away and I can see no reason for this court holding otherwise than that there is power in appropriate cases for the use of the prerogative orders to control the activity of a local planning authority.

A flexible attitude toward the potential application of *certiorari* was furthered in another recent English case, this one in the Court of Appeal, in *R v. Barnsley Metropolitan Borough Council, Ex p. Hook*, [1976] 3 All ER 452.

In a *habeas corpus* case, *Re H.K. (An Infant)*, [1967] 2 QB 617, Lord Parker was of the opinion that the immigration officers who refused to admit a boy into the United Kingdom were acting in an administrative and not in a judicial or quasi-judicial capacity: nevertheless, he held they must act honestly and fairly, otherwise their decision could be questioned by *certiorari*. And in the *Liverpool Taxi Owners* case, *supra*, Roskill LJ spoke of the power of the Courts to intervene in a suitable case when the function was administrative and not judicial or quasi-judicial (p. 596):

> The power of the court to intervene is not limited, as once was thought, to those cases where the function in question is judicial or quasi-judicial. The modern cases show that this court will intervene more widely than in the past. Even where the function is said to be administrative, the court will not hesitate to intervene in a suitable case if it is necessary in order to secure fairness.

Then there is the well-known passage in the speech of Lord Morris of Borth-y-Gest in *Furnell v. Whangarei High Schools Board*, [1973] AC 660 at p. 679 (PC), speaking for a Privy Council majority of three: "[n]atural justice is but fairness writ large and juridically. It has been described as 'fair play in action.' Nor is it a leaven to be associated only with judicial or quasi-judicial occasions." In the same case, the penultimate paragraph from the speech of Viscount Dilhorne and Lord Reid, dissenting, reads (p. 691):

> It is not in this case necessary to decide whether the function of the subcommittee is to be described as judicial, quasi-judicial or administrative. I am inclined to think that it is at least quasi-judicial, but if it be administrative, it was the duty of the sub-committee before they condemned or criticised Mr. Furnell "to give him a fair opportunity of commenting or contradicting what is said against him." That they did not do.

Professor John Evans, writing in 23 *McGill LJ* 132 at pp. 134-5 (1977), has noted:

> Recent English decisions have severed the availability of *certiorari* and prohibition from the requirement that the body must act "judicially" in the sense that it is bound by the rules of natural justice. It may be concluded, therefore, that there is nothing in the judgment of Pigeon J [in *Howarth*] to prevent the Trial Division from quashing decisions of a "purely administrative" nature or from developing procedural requirements derived from the "duty to act fairly."

In the view of another commentator, Professor Jones 21 *McGill LJ* 434 at p. 438 (1975):

> Certainly in England and in most other parts of the Commonwealth, the requirement for judicial review that the exercise of a statutory power must not only affect the rights of a subject, but also be subject to a superadded duty to act judicially, is now thoroughly discredited. In other words, the ratio of *Nakkuda Ali v. Jayaratne* in the Privy Council—and hence, one would have thought, of *Calgary Power v. Copithorne* in the Supreme Court of Canada—is no longer good law.

The authorities to which I have referred indicate that the application of a duty of fairness with procedural content does not depend upon proof of a judicial or quasi-judicial function. Even though the function is analytically administrative, Courts may intervene in a suitable case.

In the case at bar, the Disciplinary Board was not under either an express or implied duty to follow a judicial type of procedure, but the board was obliged to find facts affecting a subject and to exercise a form of discretion in pronouncing judgment and penalty. Moreover, the board's decision had the effect of depriving an individual of his liberty by committing him to a "prison within a prison." In these circumstances, elementary justice requires some procedural protection. The rule of law must run within penitentiary walls.

In my opinion, *certiorari* avails as a remedy wherever a public body has power to decide any matter affecting the rights, interests, property, privileges, or liberties of any person.

VIII

Fairness

The approach taken to the "fairness" doctrine by the Court in *Re Nicholson and Haldimand-Norfolk Regional Board of Com'rs of Police* (1978), 88 DLR (3d) 671, [1979] 1 SCR 311, 23 NR 410, notably its differentiation from traditional natural justice, permits one to dispense with classification as a precondition to the availability of *certiorari*. Conceptually, there is much to be said against such a differentiation between traditional natural justice and procedural fairness, but if one is forced to cast judicial review in traditional classification terms, as is the case under the *Federal Court Act*, here can be no doubt that procedural fairness extends well beyond the realm of the judicial and quasi-judicial, as commonly understood.

Once one moves from the strictures of s. 28 of the *Federal Court Act*, the judgment in *Nicholson, supra,* permits departure from the rigidity of classification of functions for the purposes of procedural safeguards. In finding that a duty of fairness rested upon the Police Commissioners in a dismissal case, Chief Justice Laskin, speaking for a majority of the Court, employed the English fairness cases to import that duty. While the cases were there used to establish minimal protection for the constable under the *Judicial Review Procedure Act, 1971* (Ont.), c. 48, the same cases have been employed in England to extend the reach of *certiorari* to decisions not strictly judicial or quasi-judicial. After referring to the emergence of a notion of fairness "involving something less than the procedural protection of traditional natural justice," the Chief Justice had this to say (p. 681 DLR, p. 325 SCR):

> What rightly lies behind this emergence is the realization that the classification of statutory functions as judicial, quasi-judicial or administrative is often very difficult, to say the least; and to endow some with procedural protection while denying others any at all would work injustice when the results of statutory decisions raise the same serious consequences for those adversely affected, regardless of the classification of the function in question: see, generally, Mullan, "Fairness: The New Natural Justice," 25 *Univ. of Tor. LJ* 281 (1975).

The Chief Justice also quoted a passage from Lord Denning's judgment in *Selvarajan v. Race Relations Board*, [1976] 1 All ER 12 (CA), in which the Master of the Rolls summed up his earlier decisions and formulated the "fundamental rule" (p. 19):

> that, if a person may be subjected to pains or penalties, or be exposed to prosecution or proceedings, or deprived of remedies or redress, or in some such way adversely affected by the investigation and report, then he should be told the case made against him and be afforded a fair opportunity of answering it.

Of particular interest in the passage is the absence of reference to "rights." The imprecise "rights/privileges" dichotomy is utterly ignored.

IX

One matter remains—the so-called "disciplinary exception." There are authorities (see *R v. Army Council, Ex p. Ravenscroft*, [1917] 2 KB 504; *Dawkins v. Lord Rokeby* (1871), 8 QB 255; *Re Armstrong and Whitehead* (1973), 11 CCC (2d) 327, [1973] 2 OR 495) which hold that review by way of *certiorari* does not go to a body such as the armed services, police, or firemen, with its own form of private discipline and its own rules. Relying on this analogy, it is contended that disciplinary powers are beyond judicial control and that this extends to prison discipline. I do not agree.

In *Fraser v. Mudge et al.*, [1975] 3 All ER 78 (CA), it was held that the *English Prison Act, 1952*, requiring the Home Secretary to give an inmate charged with an offence a proper opportunity of presenting his case, did not entitle the inmate to legal representation at the hearing, but Lord Denning MR observed that those who heard the case had the duty to act fairly. Judicial review was not precluded.

There is the more recent case of *R v. Board of Visitors of Hull Prison, Ex. p. St. Germain et al.*, [1979] 1 All ER 701. The central issue in that case was whether *certiorari* would go to quash a disciplinary decision of a board of visitors, the duties of which embraced inquiry into charges against inmates. The Divisional Court found that disciplinary procedures within the prison were judicial, but invoked the "disciplinary exception," and held that the actions of the board of visitors were not amenable to the review by way of *certiorari*. A unanimous Court of Appeal disagreed, however, holding that adjudication by boards of visitors in prisons were, indeed, amenable to *certiorari*. The Court rejected the submission that prisoners have no legally enforceable rights. Megaw LJ concluded that the observance of procedural fairness in prisons is properly a subject for review. Shaw LJ held that despite deprivation of his general liberty a prisoner remains invested with residuary rights appertaining to the nature and conduct of his incarceration. Waller LJ accepted the proposition of Lord Reid in *Ridge v. Baldwin et al.*, [1964] AC 40, that deprivation of rights or privileges are equally important and applied that proposition to the context of prison discipline.

. . .

The Supreme Court of the United States in *Wolff v. McDonnell* (1978), 418 US 539, was called upon to consider what "due process," assured by the Fourteenth Amendment of the *American Constitution*, required in a prison setting. The Court, speaking through Mr. Justice White, held that where the prisoner was in peril of losing good time, or be-

ing placed in solitary confinement, he was entitled to written notice of the charge and a statement of fact findings and to call witnesses and present documentary evidence where it would not be unduly hazardous to institutional safety or correctional jails. However, there was no constitutional right to confront and cross-examine witnesses or to counsel.

It seems clear that although the Courts will not readily interfere in the exercise of disciplinary powers, whether within the armed services, the police force or the penitentiary, there is no rule of law which necessarily exempts the exercise of such disciplinary powers from review by *certiorari*.

The authorities, in my view, support the following conclusions:

1. *Certiorari* is available as a general remedy for supervision of the machinery of Government decision-making. The order may go to any public body with power to decide any matter affecting the rights, interests, property, privileges, or liberty of any person. The basis for the broad reach of this remedy is the general duty of fairness resting on all public decision-makers.

2. A purely ministerial decision, on broad grounds of public policy, will typically afford the individual no procedural protection, and any attack upon such a decision will have to be founded upon abuse of discretion. Similarly, public bodies exercising legislative functions may not be amenable to judicial supervision. On the other hand, a function that approaches the judicial end of the spectrum will entail substantial procedural safeguards. Between the judicial decisions and those which are discretionary and policy-oriented will be found a myriad decision-making processes with a flexible gradation of procedural fairness through the administrative spectrum. That is what emerges from the decision of this Court in *Nicholson, supra*. In these cases, an applicant may obtain *certiorari* to enforce a breach of the duty of procedural fairness.

3. Section 28 of the *Federal Court Act*, that statutory right of review compels continuance of the classification process in the Federal Court of Appeal, with clear outer limits imposed on the notion of "judicial or quasi-judicial." No such limitation is imported in the language of s. 18, which simply refers to *certiorari*, and is therefore capable of expansion consistent with the movement of the common law away from rigidity in respect of the prerogative writs. The fact that a decision-maker does not have a duty to act judicially, with observance of formal procedure which that characterization entails, does not mean that there may not be a duty to act fairly which involves importing something less than the full panoply of conventional natural justice rules. In general, Courts ought not to seek to distinguish between the two concepts, for the drawing of a distinction between a duty to act fairly, and a duty to act in accordance with the rules of natural justice, yields an unwieldy conceptual framework. The *Federal Court Act*, however, compels classification for review of federal decision-makers.

4. An inmate disciplinary board is not a Court. It is a tribunal which has to decide rights after hearing evidence. Even though the board is not obliged, in discharging what is essentially an administrative task, to conduct a judicial proceeding, observing the procedural and evidential rules of a Court of law, it is, none the

less, subject to a duty of fairness and a person aggrieved through breach of that duty is entitled to seek relief from the Federal Court, Trial Division, on an application for *certiorari*.

5. It should be emphasized that it is not every breach of prison rules of procedure which will bring intervention by the Courts. The very nature of a prison institution requires officers to make "on the spot" disciplinary decisions and the power of judicial review must be exercised with restraint. Interference will not be justified in the case of trivial or merely technical incidents. The question is not whether there has been a breach of the prison rules, but whether there has been a breach of the duty to act fairly in all the circumstances. The rules are of some importance in determining this latter question, as an indication of the views of prison authorities as to the degree of procedural protection to be extended to inmates.

6. A widening of the ambit of *certiorari* beyond that of a s. 28 application will, undoubtedly, at times, present a problem in determining whether to commence proceedings in the Court of Appeal or in the Trial Division. However, the quandary of two possible forums is not less regrettable than complete lack of access to the Federal Court.

7. It is wrong, in my view, to regard natural justice and fairness as distinct and separate standards and to seek to define the procedural content of each. In *Nicholson, supra*, the Chief Justice spoke of a "notion of fairness involving something less than the procedural protection of the traditional natural justice." Fairness involves compliance with only some of the principles of natural justice. Professor de Smith, *Judicial Review of Administrative Action* (1973), 3rd ed. p. 208, expressed lucidly the concept of a duty to act fairly:

In general it means a duty to observe the rudiments of natural justice for a limited purpose in the exercise of functions that are not analytically judicial but administrative.

The content of the principles of natural justice and fairness in application to the individual cases will vary according to the circumstances of each case, as recognized by Tucker LJ, in *Russell v. Duke of Norfolk et al.*, [1949] 1 All ER 109 at p. 118.

8. In the final analysis, the simple question to be answered is this: Did the tribunal on the facts of the particular case act fairly toward the person claiming to be aggrieved? It seems to me that this is the underlying question which the Courts have sought to answer in all the cases dealing with natural justice and with fairness.

XI

I would allow the appeal, set aside the judgment of the Federal Court of Appeal, and restore the judgment of Mr. Justice Mahoney of the Federal Court, Trial Division. There should be no costs in this Court nor in the Federal Court of Appeal.

Appeal allowed.

B. The Standard of Review

Although it was important to ensure that penitentiary and parole decisions were amenable to judicial review and subject to the duty to act fairly, the issue of the applicable standard of review still remained. This has been an important issue in administrative law generally. Canadian courts started to articulate an approach of deference, but also recognized that not all decision makers and not all decisions warranted the same degree of deference. Cases like *Pushpanathan*, [1998] 1 SCR 982, and *Baker*, [1999] 2 SCR 817, have advanced this analysis substantially. But see the recent important decision of the Supreme Court of Canada in *Dunsmuir v. New Brunswick*, [2008] SCJ No. 9 (QL), in which the majority concluded that there should be only two standards of review in administrative law: correctness and reasonableness. Correctness involves no deference. Reasonableness is a qualitative inquiry with regard to matters such as justification, transparency, and intelligibility. As well, reasonableness involves asking whether the decision falls within a set of acceptable outcomes on the facts and law.

The following penitentiary case demonstrates how these issues apply to that specific context. The prisoner was serving a 12-year sentence for robbery and other related offences. He was originally confined at Kingston Penitentiary, but was transferred to Warkworth Institution, a medium-security penitentiary, in 1995. He was involuntarily transferred back to Kingston Penitentiary in 1996 on the basis of information received that he "may be contemplating or planning to escape." Subsequently, he became concerned that his institutional files contained erroneous information, including an indication that he had assaulted another prisoner when he was, in fact, the victim of the assault, and various references to escapes or planned escapes. He pursued a grievance, attempting to have the erroneous information removed. It moved through all levels up to the commissioner, but the prisoner received no relief except an assurance that his objections would be recorded in his file. Representing himself, he brought a judicial review application challenging the various decisions that had been made about his file and his complaint.

Tehrankari v. Correctional Service of Canada
[2000] FCJ No. 495 (QL)

LEMIEUX J: The central questions in this judicial review application, pursuant to section 18.1 of the *Federal Court Act*, by Allen Tehrankari (the "applicant"), an inmate in Kingston Penitentiary, a maximum security prison operated by the Correctional Service of Canada ("CSC" or "Service"), is the scope of the obligation contained in section 24 of the *Corrections and Conditional Release Act*, 40-41 Elizabeth II, c. 20, assented to on June 18, 1992 (the "Act"), as it relates to the CSC and in what circumstances can this Court intervene when a request for correction is refused. Section 24 of the Act reads:

> 24(1) The Service shall take all reasonable steps to ensure that any information about an offender that it uses is as accurate, up to date and complete as possible.
>
> (2) Where an offender who has been given access to information by the Service pursuant to subsection 23(2) believes that there is an error or omission therein,
>
> (a) the offender may request the Service to correct that information; and

(b) where the request is refused, the Service shall attach to the information a notation indicating that the offender has requested a correction and setting out the correction requested. ...

24(1) Le Service est tenu de veiller, dans la mesure du possible, à ce que les renseignements qu'il utilise concernant les délinquants soient à jour, exacts et complets.

(2) Le délinquant qui croit que les renseignements auxquels il a eu accès en vertu du paragraphe 23(2) sont erronés ou incomplets peut demander que le Service en effectue la correction; lorsque la demande est refusée, le Service doit faire mention des corrections qui ont été demandées mais non effectuées.

The decision sought to be reviewed was made by the Commissioner of the CSC on July 23, 1998 at the final grievance level prescribed by section 90 of the Act and sections 74 to 80 of the *Corrections and Conditional Release Regulations*, SOR/92-620.

• • •

The applicant could not, in this judicial review proceeding, challenge decisions which relate back to 1995 and 1996 and, in particular, decisions involving involuntary transfer, the raising of his security level and administrative segregation which could have been challenged at the appropriate time where he would have been entitled, subject to some exceptions, to the information which CSC was relying on to make those decisions (see sections 28 to 45 of the Act). The applicant cannot, through a review from the Commissioner's decision in this matter, make a collateral attack on past decisions which he had an opportunity to challenge directly at the appropriate time subject to the time limits prescribed under section 18 of the *Federal Court Act*.

However, at the hearing, the applicant refocussed the issue properly on the interpretation of section 24 of the Act and counsel for the respondent joined issue on this point. In the circumstances, I will proceed on a limited basis and limit any remedies to the application of the section.

(2) The Prison Context

Any remedy flowing from this proceeding must take into account the prison context is a special one. For example, in *Cardinal v. Director of Kent Institution*, [1985] 2 SCR 643, Le Dain J pointed out the minimal or essential requirements of procedural fairness in the circumstances must be "fully compatible with the concern that the process of prison administration, because of its special nature and exigencies, should not be unduly burdened or obstructed by the imposition of unreasonable or inappropriate procedural requirements. There is nothing to suggest that the requirement of notice and hearing by the Director, where he does not intend to act in accordance with a recommendation by the Segregation Review Board for the release of an inmate from segregation, would impose an undue burden on prison administration or create a risk to security" (see page 660). My colleague Nadon J in *Cartier v. Canada (Attorney General)*, [1998] 165 FTR 209 (FCTD) expressed the same caution about the special prison context when interpreting the scope of subsection 27(3) of the Act which provides for certain information not to be disclosed where the Commissioner has reasonable grounds to believe that disclosure of the information would jeopardize the safety of any person or the security of the penitentiary.

(3) Standard of Review

A word needs to be said about the standard of review applicable in this case keeping in mind the type of decision made and the decision-maker (see *Baker v. Canada (Minister of Citizenship and Immigration)*, [1999] 2 SCR 817). In *Baker, supra,* L'Heureux-Dubé J pointed out it was held in *Pushpanathan v. Canada (Minister of Citizenship and Immigration)*, [1998] 1 SCR 982, a decision which related to the determination of a question of law in that case (the interpretation of the exclusion provisions in section 2 of the *Immigration Act* as they relate to the definition of Convention refugee) made by the Immigration and Refugee Board, was subject to a standard of review of correctness but on other questions, the standard of review varied.

In *Baker, supra,* the Supreme Court of Canada enumerated the four factors to be examined to assess the standard of review on these questions.

The first factor to be examined is the presence or absence of a privative clause in the Act. There is no privative clause contained in the Act insulating the decisions of the Commissioner taken in the grievance process.

The second factor is the expertise of the decision-maker. The decision-maker here is the Commissioner of the Correctional Service or his or her delegate. There can be no doubt, that in matters related to prison administration, the Commissioner has expertise relative to the Courts which leads to substantial deference in decisions taken by the Commissioner in matters of internal prison management.

The third factor is the purpose of the provision, in particular, and the Act as a whole. Parliament in sections 3 and 4 of the Act, has said what the purpose of the Federal Correctional Service is and what are the applicable principles which shall guide it in achieving that purpose. Section 3 provides:

> 3. The purpose of the federal correction system is to contribute to the maintenance of the just, peaceful and safe society
>
> (a) carrying out sentences imposed by the Courts through the safe and humane custody and the supervision of offenders and
>
> (b) assisting the rehabilitation of offenders and their reintegration into the community as law-abiding citizens through the provision of programs in penitentiaries and in the community. ...

> 3. Le système correctionnel vise à contribuer au maintien d'une société juste, vivant en paix et en sécurité, d'une part, en assurant l'exécution des peines par des mesures de garde et de surveillance sécuritaires et humaines, et d'autre part, en aidant au moyen de programmes appropriés dans les pénitenciers ou dans la collectivité, à la réadaptation des délinquants et à leur réinsertion sociale à titre de citoyens respectueux des lois.

In terms of the principles that guide the Service, section 4 provides:

> 4. The principles that shall guide the Service in achieving the purpose referred to in section 3 are
>
> (a) that the protection of society be the paramount consideration in the corrections process;
>
> (b) that the sentence be carried out having regard to all relevant available information, ... and information obtained from victims and offenders;

(c) that the Service enhance its effectiveness and openness through the timely exchange of relevant information with other components of the criminal justice system, and through communication about its correctional policies and programs to offenders, victims and the public; ...

(e) that offenders retain the rights and privileges of all members of society, except those rights and privileges that are necessarily removed or restricted as a consequence of the sentence; ...

(g) that correctional decisions be made in a forthright and fair manner, with access by the offender to an effective grievance procedure; ...

4. Le Service est guidé, dans l'exécution de ce mandat, par les principes qui suivent:

a) la protection de la société est le critère prépondérant lors de l'application du processus correctionnel;

b) l'exécution de la peine tient compte de toute information pertinente dont le Service dispose, ... des renseignements obtenus au cours du procès ou dans la détermination de la peine ou fournis par les victimes et les ...

c) il accroît son efficacité et sa transparence par l'échange, au moment opportun, de renseignements utiles avec les autres éléments du système de justice pénale ainsi que par la communication de ses directives d'orientation générale et programmes correctionnels tant aux délinquants et aux victimes qu'au grand public; ...

e) le délinquant continue à jouir des droits et privilèges reconnus à tout citoyen, sauf de ceux dont la suppression ou restriction est une conséquence nécessaire de la peine qui lui est infligée; ...

g) ses décisions doivent être claires et équitables, les délinquants ayant accès à des mécanismes efficaces de règlement de griefs ... .

The particular provision involved is section 24 which mandates the Service to take all reasonable steps to ensure that any information about an offender that it uses is as accurate, up-to-date and complete as possible conditioned by a provision which says that where an offender believes there is an error or omission in the information, the offender may request the Service to correct that information and, if the request is refused, the Service must attach to the information a notation indicating the offender has requested a correction and setting out the correction requested.

As I view it, section 24 of the Act is part of an offender's "rights package" established by Parliament in 1992 when the Act was passed to modernize previous legislation, i.e. the *Penitentiaries Act* and the *Parole Act*, a modernization which was compelled by decisions of the Supreme Court of Canada and lower courts on prisoners' rights.

The signal given by Parliament in section 24, in the form of a statutory duty imposed on the Service, is that the "information banks" reflected in various reports maintained about offenders should contain the best information possible: exact, correct information without relevant omissions and data not burdened by past stereotyping or archaisms related to the offender. In Parliament's view, the quality of the information prescribed by section 24 leads to better decisions about an offender's incarceration and, in this manner, leads to the achievement of the purposes of the Act. Section 24 of the Act, however, is not concerned with the inferences or assessments drawn by the Service from file information. Section 24 cannot be used to second guess decisions by the CSC provided the information base on which those conclusions are drawn comply with this provision. Section 24 deals with primary facts; this point will be expanded on later.

The precise decision which section 24 gives rise to is the decision by the Service whether or not to rectify the record of an offender who believes the information about him/her is inaccurate. Such a decision, limited to primary facts, does not involve considerable choices by the CSC and turns on the application of proper legal principles and involves the rights and interests of an offender.

The fourth factor is the nature of the problem in question especially whether it relates to the determination of law or facts. The decision whether to correct the record involves an appreciation of the facts in an offender's files but must be based on a correct interpretation of what the law requires.

To conclude on this point, I would apply a correctness standard if the question involved is the proper interpretation of section 24 of the Act; however, I would apply the standard of reasonableness simpliciter if the question involved is either the application of proper legal principles to the facts or whether the refusal decision to correct information on the offender's file was proper. The patently unreasonable standard applies to pure findings of fact. ... (Subsection 18.2(4) of the *Federal Court Act*, RSC 1985, c. F-7.)

I find the applicant has made out his case on the balance of probabilities; the information he complained of in his files did not meet the standards required by section 24.

(3) On What Basis Can the Refusal to Correct Be Reviewed?

Paragraph 24(2)(b) provides "where the request is refused, the Service shall attach to the information a notation ... ." Do these words preclude this Court reviewing the CSC's decision not to correct because the only remedy provided by the Act in such a case is a notation to be attached to the offender's file?

Properly construed, these words enable the CSC to correct or refuse to correct the information—because there is this choice, the CSC exercises a discretion when making the decision to correct or not. (See *Baker v. Canada (MCI)*, *supra*, at paragraph 52.) If so, such a discretion is reviewable on proper principles governing the review of discretionary decisions such as bad faith, improper purpose, irrelevant consideration and error of law. (See *Maple Lodge Farms Ltd. v. Government of Canada*, [1982] 2 SCR 2 at pp. 7-8.)

F. Conclusion

Under section 24 of the Act, the CSC must take reasonable steps to ensure that any information in an offender's files is as accurate, up-to-date and complete. For reasons given, I have found the specific information in the applicant's files which the applicant complained of do not comply with the standards of the section. The applicant requested correction but the CSC refused the request.

I find the Commissioner, in exercising his discretion to refuse to correct the information requested, committed a number of reviewable errors.

First, he did not properly interpret the scope of the CSC's obligations in terms of the accuracy, completeness and up-to-date nature of the information. This misinterpretation led him to conclude some of the information on file was valid or justified. Second, he failed to appreciate the nature and limits of the discretion inherent in a decision to refuse to correct information. Parliament simply did not intend inaccurate information remain on file counterbalanced only by an offender's correction request noted on file. The CSC, in the circumstances, was obligated to consider why a correction was not appropriate. Third, whatever appreciation the Commissioner had on the scope of the discretion to refuse a correction, such refusal had to be based on proper considerations which were lacking in this case. To refuse to correct misinformation on the grounds the Service exercised its option to increase the applicant's security level or to justify inaction to correct on the basis the information was still relevant for administrative purposes amount to, in my view, improper considerations.

I conclude the applicant succeeds in this judicial review application. The question remains as to the appropriate remedy.

I am sensitive to the fact the information the applicant sought to have corrected in his files is dated in 1997 and that the CSC has a continuous process of reevaluating offenders. Indeed, a file correction relating to one item the applicant complained of here was made in the applicant's OSLRD file (see page 85 of the applicant's record) but this information does not seem to have been reflected in other files (see applicant's record, page 86).

I am also sensitive to what was said by Le Dain J in *Cardinal, supra*, regarding imposing burdens on the CSC. As I see it, the case management officer is the point person with the offender. The application record reveals the CMO interfaces on a daily basis with an offender.

In the circumstances, the CMO is required to review the offender's current files and determine whether they should be corrected in accordance with these reasons. What should be reviewed is limited to those matters in the applicant's original complaint. The applicant is to be advised of the results of the CMO's review and proposed action.

G. Disposition

For all these reasons, this judicial review is allowed, the decision of the Commissioner is set aside, and the matter remitted for reconsideration on the basis of these reasons.

NOTE

The issue of expertise is an important one that should not be answered too quickly. Is Lemieux J suggesting that all internal prison decision makers are experts regardless of the nature of the decision? Is he overemphasizing the prison context in a way that would tilt the balance in favour of administrative decision making? What about parole decisions? Because parole board members deal with release issues on a daily basis, does that make them experts, especially when the central issue is now one of assessing risk? We accept that the clinical predictions of forensic psychiatrists can be wrong as often as they are right, so why should we give more deference to the National Parole Board?

The standard of review analysis in *Tehrankari* has been followed consistently. *Brown v. Canada (Attorney General)*, [2006] FCJ No. 571 (QL), is an example of its application in a case dealing with information issues and the grievance process. The case highlights the importance in prison and parole decision making of maintaining an accurate record, a difficult task for the kept when the keeper also controls the information. Here, McTavish J dealt with a case in which the prisoner was charged criminally with assault, but these charges were subsequently withdrawn when they could not be validated. The prisoner consistently denied being involved. However, information relating to the allegations of assault remained on his institutional "preventative security" and "offender management system" files, although he had repeatedly tried to have it removed. McTavish J granted judicial review to remove the remarks indicating that he had committed an assault on another prisoner. With respect to future parole decisions, she noted:

> Finally, with respect to Mr. Brown's concerns regarding the potential future use that the National Parole Board may make of the information on his file, it must be observed that, in acknowledging that the allegation of assault could not be verified and should thus not have been considered in assessing Mr. Brown's Offender Security Level, the Correctional Service of Canada has implicitly recognized that the allegations made by JB are not reliable.
>
> Moreover, there is a duty on the National Parole Board to act fairly, and to base its decisions on reliable information: *Canada v. Zarzour*, 153 CCC (3d) 284, at para. 27. In the event that at some point in the future, Mr. Brown forms the view that the Parole Board has made improper use of the information currently on his file in denying him parole, it would be open to him to seek judicial review of any negative decision that he might receive.

IV. HABEAS CORPUS

A. Jurisdiction and Scope of Review

At least since the *Magna Carta*, forms of *habeas corpus* have been available to enforce liberty and free illegally detained prisoners. Blackstone described *habeas corpus* as applicable to "all manner of illegal confinement." By virtue of this remedy, superior courts became the repository of the liberty rights of all prisoners. Yet, in the mid-20th century in Canada, it started to lose its vigour as a remedy to protect liberty.

In parole cases, where the loss of parole was clearly a loss of liberty, *habeas corpus* was available, but only in a limited number of situations. First, the issue had to engage an arguable jurisdictional defect or illegality such that success meant release from custody. Second, the illegality had to be apparent without going behind the warrant (see *Mitchell v. The Queen*, [1976] 2 SCR 570). In *Mitchell*, the majority held that a court could not go behind a warrant of suspension or revocation to find a jurisdictional defect or illegality. This was a case where a parolee attempted to argue that his committal breached the due process guarantee of the *Canadian Bill of Rights* because he was given no reasons for his suspension and no opportunity to respond to any allegations against him before he was revoked and recommitted to custody. An earlier decision had held that the usual practice of seeking *certiorari* in aid of *habeas corpus* to enable a court to examine affidavit material was no longer available because *certiorari* jurisdiction had been transferred to the Federal Court. Accordingly, it was argued in *Mitchell*, one could not obtain *certiorari*-in-aid from a superior court. In dissent, Laskin CJ pointed out the distinction between *certiorari* to quash and *certiorari* to bring up the record that had been missed by some of his colleagues. Although the *Mitchell* decision was a blow to *habeas corpus*, it came just before the Supreme Court adopted the duty to act fairly. How could a parolee ever raise a fairness argument if he or she could not use an affidavit or transcript to go behind a warrant of committal?

Looking at penitentiary issues, a narrow conception of the scope of *certiorari* (and prohibition, its temporal flip-side) was used to deny remedies to prisoners. In retrospect, actions for declaratory relief were likely available to prisoners, but these were not attempted. The probable reason was cost and delay. *McCann v. The Queen*, [1976] 1 FC 570 (TD), a successful action for a declaration under the *Canadian Bill of Rights* that long-term confinement in segregation at the BC penitentiary constituted cruel and unusual punishment, demonstrates both the potential role and the enormous amount of time and money involved in such actions.

Another issue that arose related to involuntary transfers to a higher security institution. If made unfairly or without jurisdiction, the decision would seem to be open to challenge, but the question was how? Was *habeas corpus* an available vehicle for this purpose, or was it necessary to seek *certiorari* in the Federal Court? Certainly, *habeas corpus* was a less expensive and more expeditious remedy. Aside from the issue of extrinsic material, it was also argued that an involuntary transfer was not the proper subject matter of *habeas corpus* because it would not result in complete liberty, but merely a transfer back to the original place of confinement.

These issues came together in a trilogy of cases decided by the Supreme Court in the mid-1980s: *Cardinal v. Kent Institution*, [1985] 2 SCR 643; *Morin v. National Special Handling Unit Review Committee*, [1985] 2 SCR 662; and *R v. Miller*, [1985] 2 SCR 613. The lead decision on the role of *habeas corpus* was the *Miller* case, which dealt with an inmate's transfer from Matsqui Institution in British Columbia to the special handling unit, located then at Millhaven Institution in Ontario. Although initially denied *habeas corpus* relief, the Ontario Court of Appeal reversed and supported a modern approach to the remedy. The Crown appealed to the Supreme Court.

R v. Miller
[1985] 2 SCR 613

LE DAIN J: ... [3] According to the respondent's affidavit in support of his application for *habeas corpus* with *certiorari* in aid, he was an inmate in Matsqui penitentiary on June 2, 1981, when a "disturbance" occurred in the dining area where he was employed. He claimed that he was not in the dining area at the time and that he was not responsible in any way for the disturbance. He was, nevertheless, placed in administrative segregation in Matsqui on June 5th and in segregation in Kent Institution and Millhaven, to which he was subsequently transferred, on July 11th and July 23rd respectively. On July 29, 1981, he was placed in the special handling unit at Millhaven.

[4] Confinement in a special handling unit is reserved for particularly dangerous inmates, as indicated by s. 5 of Commissioner's Directive 274 of December 1, 1980, which defines "Special Handling Unit" as follows:

> "Special Handling Unit" (SHU) is a facility established to deal exclusively with inmates who, in addition to requiring maximum security, have been identified as being particularly dangerous.

According to the directive, a special handling unit programme of confinement consists of four phases, the first of which is a period of assessment in administrative segregation. According to the respondent's affidavit, which describes the nature of the confinement in the various phases in considerable detail, in the first phase consisting of administrative segregation the inmate is cut off from all association with other inmates and is confined to his cell for all but one hour of the day. In subsequent phases of the programme limited association with other inmates and somewhat longer periods outside the cell are permitted, but speaking generally, it may be said that confinement in a special handling unit is a significantly more restrictive form of detention than the normal one in a penitentiary, involving the loss or denial of several privileges or amenities enjoyed by the general inmate population.

[5] According to the respondent's affidavit, he was advised by letter about two weeks after he was placed in the special handling unit that he had been put there because of his involvement in the disturbance at Matsqui and specifically because he had broken windows in the kitchen and had manufactured an explosive device. The respondent states that he was never given an opportunity to confront the evidence, if any, of his involvement in the incident at Matsqui on which the decision to confine him in the special handling unit was based. He was never charged with a disciplinary offence arising out of that incident nor was any criminal charge laid against him. He was not given a psychological examination, and there was nothing in his background or in the nature of the offences of which he was convicted to suggest that he was a particularly dangerous inmate. In October, 1981, he attended a hearing of the National Special Handling Unit Review Committee, but he was not informed of the evidence against him nor given any opportunity to meet it. He was told that he could only secure his release from the special handling unit into normal association with the general population of the penitentiary by good behaviour. In the respondent's submission there was no basis nor justification whatever for placing him in the special handling unit.

[6] In his application for *habeas corpus* with *certiorari* in aid the respondent contended that confinement in the special handling unit at Millhaven is not authorized by statute or regulation and is therefore unlawful, and further or alternatively, that his confinement in the special handling unit was carried out in a manner that denied him procedural fairness. The respondent conceded that he was lawfully required to be detained in a penitentiary. His mandatory supervision release date was July 3, 1983, and we were informed at the hearing of the appeal that he had been released.

· · ·

[9] The question whether a provincial superior court has jurisdiction to issue *certiorari* in aid of *habeas corpus* to review the validity of a detention imposed by federal authority arises, as has been indicated, because of the terms of s. 18 of the *Federal Court Act*, which confers on the Trial Division of the Federal Court of Canada an exclusive original jurisdiction to issue *certiorari* against any federal board, commission or other tribunal.

· · ·

[13] On the question of jurisdiction to issue *certiorari* in aid of *habeas corpus* I am in respectful agreement with the conclusion of Laskin CJ in *Mitchell*, essentially for the reasons given by him, which I understand to be the importance of making the *habeas corpus* jurisdiction of the provincial superior courts an effective one and the distinction

between *certiorari* to quash and *certiorari* in aid, regarded as a procedural or evidentiary device to make *habeas corpus* more effective. With reference to this distinction Laskin CJ said at pp. 246-7 CCC, p. 83 DLR, p. 578 SCR:

> It is quite clear to me that there is a marked difference between *certiorari*, used to quash a conviction or an order by its own strength, and *certiorari* in aid of *habeas corpus* to make the latter remedy more effective by requiring production of the record of proceedings for that purpose.

[14] One must approach this issue, I think, from the same point of departure as was adopted by Laskin CJ that the provisions of the *Federal Court Act* indicate a clear intention on the part of Parliament to leave the jurisdiction by way of *habeas corpus* to review the validity of a detention imposed by federal authority with the provincial superior courts. While s. 18 of the *Federal Court Act* confers an exclusive and very general review jurisdiction over federal authorities by the prerogative and extraordinary remedies, to which specific reference is made, it deliberately omits reference to *habeas corpus*. That this was not an oversight but a well-considered decision is indicated by s. 17(5) of the Act, which expressly confers exclusive jurisdiction on the Federal Court with respect to an application for *habeas corpus* by a member of the Canadian Forces serving outside Canada. I agree with Laskin CJ that because of its importance as a safeguard of the liberty of the subject *habeas corpus* jurisdiction can only be affected by express words. One may think of reasons why it was thought advisable to leave the *habeas corpus* jurisdiction with respect to federal authorities with the provincial superior courts, including the importance of the local accessibility of this remedy. The important thing, as I see it, is that the decision to create this exception to the exclusive review jurisdiction of the Federal Court, with whatever problems arising from concurrent or overlapping jurisdiction it might cause, is really determinative of the question of jurisdiction to issue *certiorari* in aid. There can be no doubt that *certiorari* in aid is important, if not essential, to the effectiveness of *habeas corpus*. This was emphasized by both Anderson JA, with whom the other members of the British Columbia Court of Appeal agreed on this issue in *Cardinal* and *Oswald*, and by Cory JA in the case at bar. In many cases it may not be possible for a court to determine whether there has been an absence or excess of jurisdiction if the record of the tribunal which imposed or authorized the detention is not brought before it. The importance of *habeas corpus* itself, and by implication the importance of maintaining it as a fully effective remedy is, as Laskin CJ observed, given particular emphasis by its inclusion as a guaranteed right in s. 2(c)(iii) of the *Canadian Bill of Rights*. To this recognition may now be added the constitutional guarantee of the right to *habeas corpus* in s. 10(c) of the *Canadian Charter of Rights and Freedoms*. Because of the clear intention to leave the *habeas corpus* jurisdiction over federal authorities with the provincial superior courts and the importance of *certiorari* in aid to the effectiveness of *habeas corpus*, it cannot, in my opinion, have been intended that the reference to *certiorari* in s. 18 of the *Federal Court Act* should have the effect of undermining or weakening the *habeas corpus* jurisdiction of the provincial superior courts by the exclusion or denial of *certiorari* in aid. Certainly such a construction is to be avoided if at all possible. It can be avoided by application of the distinction emphasized by Laskin CJ between *certiorari* as an independent and separate mode of review

having as its object to quash the decision of an inferior tribunal and *certiorari* as an ancillary procedure used to serve an essentially evidentiary purpose. A very full discussion of this distinction, with reference to many of the decisions in which it has been noted and applied, is to be found in Cromwell, "*Habeas Corpus* and Correctional Law," 3 *Queen's LJ* 295 at pp. 320-3 (1977). Applying the distinction to the reference to *certiorari* in s. 18 of the *Federal Court Act*, it is reasonable to conclude, because of the association in that section of *certiorari* with the other prerogative and extraordinary remedies, that the reference is to the independent remedy of *certiorari* to quash. It is unlikely that Parliament intended to confer an exclusive jurisdiction to issue *certiorari* in aid when it had clearly withheld the jurisdiction to issue *habeas corpus*. For these reasons I conclude that a provincial superior court has jurisdiction to issue *certiorari* in aid of *habeas corpus* to review the validity of a detention authorized or imposed by a federal board, commission or other tribunal as defined by s. 2 of the *Federal Court Act*, and that accordingly the Ontario Court of Appeal did not err in concluding as it did on this issue.

III

[15] In view of this conclusion on the question of jurisdiction to issue *certiorari* in aid of *habeas corpus* it may not be strictly necessary to deal with the question which was treated as an alternative issue by the British Columbia Court of Appeal in *Cardinal* and *Oswald* and by the Ontario Court of Appeal in the case at bar—whether on *habeas corpus* without *certiorari* in aid a court may consider affidavit or other extrinsic evidence to determine whether there has been an absence or excess of jurisdiction. It is well established that affidavit evidence is admissible on *certiorari* to show jurisdictional error. Both Courts of Appeal were led, however, by their analysis of this question to reach a conclusion on it at variance with that of Ritchie J in *Mitchell*, without much explicit consideration of the jurisprudence of this Court on which the opinion of Ritchie J purported to be based. Moreover, this question may well be an issue in the *Morin* appeal. For these reasons it is probably desirable that it be dealt with here in order to remove the uncertainty which now necessarily exists concerning it.

• • •

[17] In *Re Shumiatcher*, [1962] SCR 38, the relevant issue was whether the court could look at certain solemn declarations which the applicant for *habeas corpus* was charged with having induced a person to make, knowing them to be false, and thereby being a party, by virtue of s. 22(1) of the *Criminal Code*, to the offence defined by s. 114 (now s. 122). The application for *habeas corpus* challenged the validity of the committal for trial on the ground that the person making the solemn declarations was not a person permitted, authorized or required by law to make them, within the meaning of s. 114. The solemn declarations made reference to a statement of claim. Judson J framed the issue as follows, at p. 45:

> This brings me to the question of what use may be made of this material on a motion for *habeas corpus* before a Judge of this Court.
> The Crown's submission is that I am limited to looking at the warrant of committal and that I cannot look at these declarations and the statement of claim any more than I can look at the evidence—seven or eight volumes of it—given on the preliminary hearing.

[18] After quoting from the judgments of this Court in *Re Trepanier* (1885), 12 SCR 111; *Ex parte Macdonald* (1896), 27 SCR 683, and *Goldhar v. The Queen*, [1960] SCR 431, with reference to *habeas corpus* against a warrant of committal after conviction, and observing that this Court did not have jurisdiction to issue *certiorari* in aid of *habeas corpus*, Judson J concluded on this issue as follows, at p. 47:

> In my opinion the jurisdiction of this Court is similarly limited in an inquiry into a committal for trial. In the absence of power to issue a writ of *certiorari* in aid of *habeas corpus*, a Judge of this Court has no power to look at the evidence at the preliminary hearing or to receive affidavit evidence relating to it.
>
> My jurisdiction is limited to a consideration of the warrant of committal and the other material that I have referred to—the recognizances and the order of Judge Hogarth. I cannot look at evidence, whether a transcript of the evidence at the preliminary hearing or evidence sought to be introduced by way of affidavit identifying a portion of such evidence.
>
> I am founding my reasons on this branch of the case entirely on that principle and I am expressing no opinion on the point on which I heard full argument—whether there does exist, by virtue of provincial legislation, permission to take a declaration of this kind.

[19] In *Goldhar*, the issues raised on the application for *habeas corpus* were the regularity on its face of a calendar of sentences as a certificate of the appellant's conviction and the applicable maximum penalty, having regard to a change that had taken place in the law. Fauteux J (as he then was), with whom Taschereau, Abbott and Judson JJ concurred, expressed the rationale for the exclusion of extrinsic evidence on an application for *habeas corpus* as follows, at p. 439:

> The question, which counsel for the appellant admittedly sought to be determined by way of *habeas corpus* proceedings, is stated in the reasons for judgment of other members of the Court. In my view, it is one which would require the consideration of the evidence at trial and which, in this particular case, extends beyond the scope of matters to be inquired under a similar process. To hold otherwise would be tantamount to convert the writ of *habeas corpus* into a writ of error or an appeal and to confer, upon every one having authority to issue the writ of *habeas corpus*, an appellate jurisdiction over the orders and judgments of even the highest Courts. It is well settled that the functions of such a writ do not extend beyond an inquiry into the jurisdiction of the Court by which process the subject is held in custody and into the validity of the process upon its face.
>
> I agree with the view that the appellant has been convicted and sentenced by a Court of competent jurisdiction, that the calendar is a certificate regular on its face that the appellant has been so convicted and sentenced and that, with the material before him, Martland J rightly dismissed the application for a writ of *habeas corpus*.

[20] The above passage, in my respectful opinion, reflects the true distinction or criterion respecting the consideration of extrinsic evidence on an application for *habeas corpus*—the distinction between issues going to the merits and issues going to jurisdiction. The issues in both *Shumiatcher* and *Goldhar* were clearly issues going to the merits. The same is true of *Re Trepanier*, where the applicant alleged that the convicting magistrate erred on the facts in convicting him. He sought a writ of *habeas corpus* with

certiorari in aid to bring up the record of the proceedings to ascertain whether there was sufficient evidence to convict. This was clearly an attempt to employ *habeas corpus* to review the merits of a conviction. Ritchie CJ said at p. 113:

> The jurisdiction of the magistrate being unquestionable over the subject-matter of complaint and the person of the prisoner, and there being no ground for alleging that the magistrate acted irregularly or beyond his jurisdiction, and the conviction and warrant being admitted to be regular, the only objection being that the magistrate erred on the facts and that the evidence did not justify the conclusion as to the guilt of the prisoner arrived at by the magistrate, I have not the slightest hesitation in saying that we cannot go behind the conviction and inquire into the merits of the case by the use of the writ of *habeas corpus*.

[21] In the subsequent case of *Re Sproule* (1886), 12 SCR 140, the issues were jurisdictional but the Court held that extrinsic evidence could not be considered on *habeas corpus* to contradict the record of a superior court that is regular on its face. The conviction and sentence by the court of *oyer* and *terminer* and general jail delivery had been confirmed by the Supreme Court of British Columbia and Ritchie CJ spoke in terms of the conclusive character of the record of a superior court as follows at p. 191:

> I venture to propound without fear of successful contradiction, that by the law of England and of this Dominion, where the principles of the common law prevail, that if the record of a superior court contains the recital of facts requisite to confer jurisdiction, which the records in this case did, it is conclusive and cannot be contradicted by extrinsic evidence; and if the superior courts have jurisdiction over the subject-matter and the person, as the court of *oyer* and *terminer* and general gaol delivery and the Supreme Court of British Columbia had in this case, the records of their judgments and sentences are final and conclusive, unerring verity, and the law will not, in such a case, allow the record to be contradicted.

[A]nd he emphasized the distinction in this respect between the records of inferior courts and those of superior courts as follows at p. 193:

> And I venture humbly, and with all respect, to suggest that the difficulty in this case has arisen from a misapprehension of what can, and what cannot, be done under a writ of *habeas corpus*, but more especially from not duly appreciating the distinction between the validity and force of records of courts of inferior, and of courts of superior, jurisdiction, but treating records of superior and inferior courts as being of the same force and effect.

[22] *Re Sproule* was applied by this Court in *Ex parte Macdonald, supra*, and *Re Henderson*, [1930] SCR 45, where there were jurisdictional issues involved, in support of the more general or unqualified proposition that the court was limited on *habeas corpus* to an examination of the warrant of committal in determining whether there had been an absence or excess of jurisdiction.

[23] Thus the true basis of this Court's jurisprudence with respect to the admission or consideration of extrinsic evidence on an application for *habeas corpus* consists of two principles: the principle that extrinsic evidence must not be permitted to convert an application for *habeas corpus* into an appeal on the merits, and the principle that the record of a superior court is conclusive as to the facts on which the court's jurisdiction depends and cannot be contradicted by extrinsic evidence. It has been suggested that

the court was particularly concerned about the first principle when it was exercising an original jurisdiction in respect of *habeas corpus*, and that this may have led to the broad and unqualified expression of the rule respecting the consideration of extrinsic evidence on *habeas corpus* that is to be found in some of its decisions: see Sharpe, *The Law of Habeas Corpus* (1976), p. 51, note 2. With respect to the second principle, I agree with the suggestion in Sharpe, "*Habeas Corpus* in Canada," 2 *Dal. LJ* 241 at p. 261 (1975), that it should apply only to the records of superior courts or courts of general common law jurisdiction. In *Mitchell v. The Queen* (1975), 24 CCC (2d) 241, 61 DLR (3d) 77, [1976] 2 SCR 570, neither of these principles was applicable. As I have indicated, the grounds of attack were clearly jurisdictional, and the record, dependent as it was on the proceedings and decisions of an inferior tribunal, was not of the character entitled to be treated as conclusive of the facts of jurisdiction. In my respectful opinion, the view expressed in *Mitchell* that the affidavit evidence could not be considered went beyond the true basis of the court's jurisprudence on this question. In fact, two members of the majority in the result (Martland and de Grandpré JJ), as well as the minority (Laskin CJ, Spence and Dickson JJ), did consider the affidavit evidence in deciding whether there had been an absence or excess of jurisdiction in ordering the detention.

[24] As the British Columbia and Ontario Courts of Appeal pointed out in *Cardinal* and *Oswald* and in the case at bar, it may only be possible to establish jurisdictional error on *habeas corpus* by affidavit evidence, even where the record is brought up by *certiorari* in aid. This is particularly true of a violation of natural justice or a denial of procedural fairness. This is a compelling reason, in my opinion, for confining the rule against consideration of extrinsic evidence on an application for *habeas corpus* within its proper boundaries.

[25] Support for a broader approach to the admission or consideration of extrinsic evidence on *habeas corpus* to determine issues of jurisdiction may be found in the decision of the House of Lords in *Schtraks v. Government of Israel et al.*, [1964] AC 556, which was relied on by the Courts of Appeal in *Cardinal* and *Oswald* and the case at bar. There it was held that fresh evidence was admissible on an application for *habeas corpus* to show that the magistrate lacked jurisdiction to make the committal order in an extradition case because the offence was of a political character. Lord Hodson appears to have held in effect that the rule concerning the admission of affidavit evidence on *habeas corpus* is the same as it is on *certiorari*, as suggested by the following passage at pp. 605-6:

> Proceeding by *habeas corpus* is analogous to that by *certiorari* to remove a conviction, see Short and Mellor's *Crown Practice* (1908), p. 319. Affidavits are not admissible to controvert facts found by the judgment of a court of competent jurisdiction, though they may be received to show some extrinsic collateral matter essential to jurisdiction or to show total want or excess of jurisdiction.

[26] I am therefore of the opinion that, subject to the limitation arising from the conclusive character of the records of courts of superior or general common law jurisdiction, a court may on an application for *habeas corpus* without *certiorari* in aid consider affidavit or other extrinsic evidence to determine whether there has been an absence or excess of jurisdiction.

IV

[27] I turn to the question whether *habeas corpus* will lie to determine the validity of the confinement of an inmate of a penitentiary in a special handling unit and to obtain his release from such confinement, if it is found to be unlawful, into normal association with the general population of the penitentiary.

[28] This issue turns on the view that one takes of the proper role of *habeas corpus* and the extent to which it should be adapted to the reality of the various forms of confinement or detention within penal institutions. An important policy consideration, in the context of the exclusive review jurisdiction of the Federal Court, is the extent to which the use of *habeas corpus* to determine the validity of a particular form of detention amounts to an indirect assumption of the Federal Court's review jurisdiction with respect to the administrative decisions of federal correctional authorities.

[29] Those who oppose the resort to *habeas corpus* to challenge the validity of a particular form of confinement or detention in a penal institution contend that it fails to meet two essential conditions of the traditional availability of this remedy: (a) that there be a deprivation of liberty, and (b) that what is sought is the complete liberty of the applicant and not merely his or her transfer to another form of detention or restraint of liberty. This view of the traditional role of *habeas corpus* is reflected in the decisions in *Ex parte Rogers* (1843), 7 Jur. 992, and *R v. Governor of Wandsworth Prison, Ex parte Silverman* (1952), 96 Sol. J 853. In *Rogers* a prisoner applied for *habeas corpus* to obtain his release from a part of a prison "where the confinement was stricter and the food more scanty" to the place in the prison where he had been confined before the transfer. In dismissing the application Denman CJ, with whom Williams, Coleridge and Wightman JJ concurred, said:

> It is quite clear that we cannot entertain this application. The object of the writ of *habeas corpus* is, generally, to restore a person to his liberty, not to pronounce a judgment as to the room or part of a prison in which a prisoner ought to be confined.

In *Silverman*, a prisoner in preventive detention complained that he was not receiving the special treatment which the applicable statute required to be provided, and he sought by an application for *habeas corpus* to be transferred to a place where such treatment was provided. In dismissing the application for *habeas corpus* Hilberry J is reported to have held that if a writ of *habeas corpus* were issued,

> the only question would be whether the applicant should be released or not; and the prison governor's return would state that he was being detained under a sentence of preventive detention, which would be a perfectly good answer.

[30] These cases were relied on by Hugessen ACJ, as he then was, in *Berrouard v. The Queen*, an unreported judgment of November 30, 1981, and related unreported decisions (referred to by the Quebec Court of Appeal in *Morin*) in dismissing applications for *habeas corpus* to challenge the validity of confinement in what appears from the expressions used to have been a special handling unit. I quote from an English version of what he said, as reported in *Re Morin and Yeomans et al.* (1982), 1 CCC (3d) 438 at p. 441:

[TRANSLATION] These six motions for *habeas corpus* each raise the same point of law. In each case, the applicant alleges that he is at present serving a sentence and that he has been unjustifiably transferred into a special detention unit, or a special segregation unit.

An essential pre-condition to the granting of the remedy of *habeas corpus* is the privation of the subject's liberty: *Massella v. Langlais* (1955), 112 CCC 1, [1975] 4 DLR 346, [1955] SCR 263. Similarly, in a motion for *habeas corpus*, the principal object of this remedy is the obtaining of liberty for the subject: *R v. Governor of Wandsworth Prison; Ex p. Silverman* (1952), 96 Sol. Jo. 853 (Queen's Bench Div. Ct., Hilberry, Streatfeild and McNair JJ); *Ex parte Rodgers* (1843), 7 Jur. 992 (Court of Queen's Bench, Denman CJ, Williams, Coleridge and Wightman JJ). I have read with much interest the judgment of my colleague Chief Justice McEachern, of the Supreme Court of British Columbia, in *Cardinal* and *Oswald v. Attorney-General*, an unreported judgment delivered on December 30, 1980. With all respect which I have for my colleague, I am not in agreement with his position that the writ of *habeas corpus* can be used to modify the conditions of detention since, even if the writ is granted, the prisoner's detention will continue after the final judgment is delivered. This is also our case.

It accordingly follows that I am in agreement with the decision of my colleague Mr. Justice Jean-Paul Bergeron in the *Morin v. Yeomans* case, an unreported judgment delivered on November 18, 1981.

[31] In *Morin*, which, as I have said, was a case of *habeas corpus* without *certiorari* in aid, Bergeron J referred to the conclusion of McEachern CJSC in *Cardinal* and *Oswald* that *habeas corpus* would lie to determine the validity of a particular form of detention in a penitentiary and said he could not agree with it. He held that judicial review of the administrative decisions of the federal correctional authorities fell within the exclusive jurisdiction of the Federal Court by way of *certiorari*. In his view, the conditions of detention of a person who was otherwise lawfully imprisoned under a valid warrant of committal could not give rise to *habeas corpus*. In dismissing the appeal from the judgment of Bergeron J, the Quebec Court of Appeal noted that the appellant had taken proceedings by way of *certiorari* in the Federal Court to challenge the validity of his confinement in the special handling unit and that there would therefore be the danger of conflicting judgments if it were held that the Superior Court had jurisdiction to issue *habeas corpus* to determine the same issue. The Court of Appeal concluded that proceedings to challenge administrative action within federal penitentiaries was within the exclusive jurisdiction of the Federal Court. Thus it would appear that the Superior Court and the Court of Appeal in *Morin* were influenced in the view which they took of the proper application of *habeas corpus* by the implications of a concurrent or overlapping review jurisdiction with respect to the administrative decisions of the federal correctional authorities.

[32] The British Columbia courts in *Cardinal* and *Oswald* and the Ontario Court of Appeal in the case at bar applied the notion of a "prison within a prison" in holding that *habeas corpus* would lie to determine the validity of confinement in administrative segregation or a special handling unit, and if such confinement be found unlawful, to order the release of the inmate into the general population of the penitentiary. The concept of a "prison within a prison" is referred to by Sharpe, *The Law of Habeas Corpus*,

p. 149, where he speaks in favour of such an application of *habeas corpus*, and by Dickson J, as he then was, in *Martineau [v. Matsqui Institution Disciplinary Board (No. 2)*, [1980] 1 SCR 602], where, with reference to the decision of the disciplinary board which sentenced the inmate for a disciplinary offence to 15 days in the penitentiary's special corrections unit, he said at p. 622:

> Moreover, the board's decision had the effect of depriving an individual of his liberty by committing him to a "prison within a prison." In these circumstances, elementary justice requires some procedural protection. The rule of law must run within penitentiary walls.

This statement reflects the perception that a prisoner is not without some rights or residual liberty (see also *Solosky v. The Queen*, [1980] 1 SCR 821 at p. 839) and that there may be significant degrees of deprivation of liberty within a penal institution. The same perception is reflected in the reasons for judgment of McEachern CJSC and Anderson JA in *Cardinal* and *Oswald* and Cory JA in the case at bar on this issue. In effect, a prisoner has the right not to be deprived unlawfully of the relative or residual liberty permitted to the general inmate population of an institution. Any significant deprivation of that liberty, such as that effected by confinement in a special handling unit, meets the first of the traditional requirements for *habeas corpus*, that it must be directed against a deprivation of liberty.

[33] Moreover, the principle that *habeas corpus* will lie only to secure the complete liberty of the subject is not invariably reflected in its application. There are applications of *habeas corpus* in Canadian case-law which illustrate its use to release a person from a particular form of detention although the person will lawfully remain under some other restraint of liberty. Examples are the use of *habeas corpus* to recover the custody of children (*Stevenson v. Florant*, [1927] AC 211; aff'g [1925] SCR 532; *Dugal v. Lefebvre*, [1934] SCR 501); to release a person on parole where the parole has been unlawfully revoked (*Re Cadeddu and The Queen* (1982), 4 CCC (3d) 97; *Swan v. Attorney General of British Columbia* (1983), 35 CR (3d) 135); and to transfer an inmate from an institution in which he has been unlawfully confined to another institution (*Re Bell and Director of Springhill Medium Security Institution et al.* (1977), 34 CCC (2d) 303; *R v. Frejd* (1910), 18 CCC 10, 22 OLR 566). In all of these cases the effect of *habeas corpus* is to release a person from an unlawful detention, which is the object of the remedy. The use of *habeas corpus* to release a prisoner from an unlawful form of detention within a penitentiary into normal association with the general inmate population of the penitentiary is consistent with these applications of the remedy.

[34] An enlarged approach to the concept of custody for purposes of *habeas corpus* is reflected in American case-law. Formerly American courts took the view that *habeas corpus* would only lie where a favourable judgment would result in immediate release from all forms of detention: *McNally v. Hill* (1934), 293 US 131. Since then the concept of custody has been greatly expanded to permit a wider use of *habeas corpus* for the protection of prisoners' rights. In *Jones v. Cunningham* (1963), 371 US 236, where *habeas corpus* was held to be available to an applicant who was not in physical custody but on parole, the Court said at p. 243 that *habeas corpus* is "not now and never has been a static, narrow, formalistic remedy; its scope has grown to achieve its grand purpose—the protection of individuals against erosion of their right to be free from wrong-

ful restraints upon their liberty." In *Peyton v. Rowe* (1968), 391 US 54, *habeas corpus* was allowed to challenge the validity of a sentence yet to be served. In *Johnson v. Avery* (1969), 393 US 483, *habeas corpus* was allowed to challenge the validity of a condition of confinement in the form of a prison regulation which limited the access of illiterate inmates to the courts by forbidding their fellow prisoners from serving as jailhouse lawyers. It was held that the unlawful regulations made the custody unlawful. In *Wilwording v. Swenson* (1971), 404 US 249, the United States Supreme Court reversed the Missouri courts which had held that *habeas corpus* would not lie where the object was not to secure the release of the petitioners from the penitentiary altogether but to challenge their living conditions and disciplinary measures. The Supreme Court affirmed the approach it had adopted in *Johnson v. Avery*. It should be noted, however, that in *Preiser v. Rodriguez* (1973), 411 US 475, Stewart J, speaking for the majority, expressed himself in terms which might suggest that the question was regarded as still being open. He said at p. 499: "This is not to say that *habeas corpus* may not also be available to challenge such prison conditions. See *Johnson v. Avery*, 393 US 483 (1969); *Wilwording v. Swenson, supra,* at 251. When a prisoner is put under additional and unconstitutional restraints during his lawful custody, it is arguable that *habeas corpus* will lie to remove the restraints making the custody illegal. See Note, Developments in the Law—*Habeas Corpus*, 83 *Harv. L Rev.* 1038, 1084 (1970)." The note to which Stewart J referred approved the approach adopted in the leading case of *Coffin v. Reichard* (1944), 143 F2d 443 (6th Cir.), where it was said at p. 445: "A prisoner is entitled to the writ of *habeas corpus* when, though lawfully in custody, he is deprived of some right to which he is lawfully entitled even in his confinement, the deprivation of which serves to make his imprisonment more burdensome than the law allows or curtails his liberty to a greater extent than the law permits." After referring to *Coffin* the note states at pp. 1085-6:

> No other circuit purports to follow *Coffin*. Most courts instead believe that *habeas* jurisdiction is lacking when the petitioner is not asking for the invalidation of a custody imposed by sentence, on the theory that the petitioner is not seeking a present or future release. But this fails to recognize that the lawfulness of a custody depends, not merely upon the legal basis for some kind of custody, but upon the lawfulness of the specific type and manner of confinement in question. Where the specific detention abridges federally protected interests—by placing petitioner in the wrong prison, denying him treatment, imposing cruel and unusual punishment, impeding his access to the courts, and so on—it is an unlawful detention and *habeas* lies to release the petitioner therefrom. It is immaterial that the petitioner might then be placed in a different, lawful custody or that his being sentenced to a term of confinement might itself be lawful. The custody requirement, and the corresponding insistence on discharge from custody, do not prevent *habeas corpus* from being an appropriate remedy for the review of unlawful prison administration.

Since that note was written the point of view expressed in it has been adopted by federal courts of appeal. See, for example, the following cases recognizing the availability of *habeas corpus* to challenge the validity of various forms of segregated confinement in a prison on the ground of a violation of due process: *McCollum v. Miller* (1982), 695 F2d 1044 (7th Cir.); *Krist v. Ricketts* (1974), 504 F2d 887 (5th Cir.); *Bryant v. Harris*

(1972), 465 F2d 365 (7th Cir.); *Dawson v. Smith* (1983), 719 F2d 896 (7th Cir.), and *Streeter v. Hopper* (1980), 618 F2d 1178 (5th Cir.).

[35] After giving consideration to the two approaches to this issue, I am of the opinion that the better view is that *habeas corpus* should lie to determine the validity of a particular form of confinement in a penitentiary notwithstanding that the same issue may be determined upon *certiorari* in the Federal Court. The proper scope of the availability of *habeas corpus* must be considered first on its own merits, apart from possible problems arising from concurrent or overlapping jurisdiction. The general importance of this remedy as the traditional means of challenging deprivations of liberty is such that its proper development and adaptation to the modern realities of confinement in a prison setting should not be compromised by concerns about conflicting jurisdiction. As I have said in connection with the question of jurisdiction to issue *certiorari* in aid of *habeas corpus*, these concerns have their origin in the legislative judgment to leave the *habeas corpus* jurisdiction against federal authorities with the provincial superior courts. There cannot be one definition of the reach of *habeas corpus* in relation to federal authorities and a different one for other authorities. Confinement in a special handling unit, or in administrative segregation as in *Cardinal* and *Oswald* is a form of detention that is distinct and separate from that imposed on the general inmate population. It involves a significant reduction in the residual liberty of the inmate. It is in fact a new detention of the inmate, purporting to rest on its own foundation of legal authority. It is that particular form of detention or deprivation of liberty which is the object of the challenge by *habeas corpus*. It is release from that form of detention that is sought. For the reasons indicated above, I can see no sound reason in principle, having to do with the nature and role of *habeas corpus*, why *habeas corpus* should not be available for that purpose. I do not say that *habeas corpus* should lie to challenge any and all conditions of confinement in a penitentiary or prison, including the loss of any privilege enjoyed by the general inmate population. But it should lie in my opinion to challenge the validity of a distinct form of confinement or detention in which the actual physical constraint or deprivation of liberty, as distinct from the mere loss of certain privileges, is more restrictive or severe than the normal one in an institution.

B. Refining the Scope of Habeas Corpus: Steele v. Mountain Institution

Steele v. Mountain Institution, [1990] 2 SCR 1385, a unanimous judgment written by Cory J, confirmed *habeas corpus* relief for a prisoner who had been imprisoned for almost 37 years as a "criminal sexual psychopath," a predecessor to the modern dangerous offender designation. Steele was 18 years old when he was given that designation after his conviction for attempted rape. His counsel argued that, in the absence of any indicia of dangerousness, it was cruel and unusual punishment in violation of s. 12 of the *Canadian Charter of Rights and Freedoms*, Part I of the *Constitution Act, 1982*, RSC 1985, app. II, no. 44, to continue his confinement. Over the years, Steele had been released on parole, but parole privileges had been revoked for breach of conditions. Instead of returning to the National Parole Board, he brought his case to court.

Steele v. Mountain Institution
[1990] 2 SCR 1385

CORY J: Theodore Steele, the respondent, has attained the age of 55. For almost 37 of those years he has been detained in an institution. In my view the issue raised on this appeal is whether the Parole Board erred in refusing to release him on parole with the result that his continuing imprisonment constitutes cruel and unusual punishment.

The period of incarceration has been long indeed. When the respondent entered prison, Mr. St. Laurent was Prime Minister and General Eisenhower was President. He remained incarcerated through the Cuban missile crisis, the assassination of President Kennedy, the Vietnam War, the FLQ crisis, the Watergate scandal, the Iran/Iraq War, the easing of tension between the Soviet Union and the United States, and the enactment of the *Canadian Charter of Rights and Freedoms*. An era has passed.

. . .

It will be remembered that it was determined by Paris J, and upheld by the Court of Appeal, that although the indeterminate continuing detention of a dangerous offender had been held in *Lyons, supra*, to be constitutional, nevertheless, in certain rare cases such as this one, the continuing detention of an offender would constitute cruel and unusual punishment in violation of s. 12 of the Charter. If this position is correct it would mean that while the parole review process would work effectively in the vast majority of cases, there would be the occasional case in which even the most responsible and careful application of the parole review process could not prevent a continuing detention from becoming cruel and unusual punishment.

I must, with respect, differ from that conclusion. It seems to me to fly in the face of the decision of this Court in *Lyons, supra*, where this Court observed at p. 363 that "the fairness of certain procedural aspects of a parole hearing may well be the subject of constitutional challenge, at least when the review is of the continued incarceration of a dangerous offender." In my view the unlawful incarceration of Steele was caused, not by any structural flaw in the dangerous offender provisions, but rather by errors committed by the National Parole Board. These errors are apparent upon a review of the record of Steele's treatment by the Board over the long years of his detention.

In 1948, provisions for the indeterminate sentencing of "criminal sexual psychopaths" were enacted. The same group of amendments to the Code provided for a review of the condition, history and circumstances of the offender's detention once every three years by the Minister of Justice. In 1958, the National Parole Board was created by the *Parole Act*, SC 1958, c. 38. At this time the authority for conducting the review of the sentences of criminal sexual psychopaths was transferred to the Parole Board. Section 8(a) of the *Parole Act* established the following criteria for granting parole:

8. The Board may

(a) grant parole to an inmate if the Board considers that the inmate has derived the maximum benefit from imprisonment and that the reform and rehabilitation of the inmate will be aided by the grant of parole;

These criteria remained in effect until 1968 when they were replaced by the provisions of s. 16(1) cited above. These provisions require the Board to grant parole where: (i) the inmate has derived the maximum benefit from imprisonment; (ii) the inmate's reform and rehabilitation will be aided by the grant of parole; and (iii) the inmate's release would not constitute an undue risk to society.

In reviewing the indeterminate sentences of dangerous offenders, it is fundamentally important that the Board consider these criteria. As La Forest J stated in *Lyons* at pp. 340-41:

> ... in the context of a determinate sentencing scheme the availability of parole represents an additional, superadded protection of the liberty interests of the offender. In the present context, however, it is, subsequent to the actual imposition of the sentence itself, the sole protection of the dangerous offender's liberty interests. ...
>
> Seen in this light, therefore, the parole process assumes the utmost significance for it is that process alone that is capable of truly accommodating and tailoring the sentence to fit the circumstances of the individual offender.

It is only by a careful consideration and application of these criteria that the indeterminate sentence can be made to fit the circumstances of the individual offender. Doing this will ensure that the dangerous offender sentencing provisions do not violate s. 12 of the Charter. If it is clear on the face of the record that the Board has misapplied or disregarded those criteria over a period of years with the result that an offender remains incarcerated far beyond the time he or she should have been properly paroled, then the Board's decision to keep the offender incarcerated may well violate s. 12. In my opinion, this is such a case.

First, Steele's imprisonment had long ago reached the point at which he had derived "the maximum benefit from imprisonment." During his incarceration governments have changed, wars have begun and ended and a generation has grown to maturity. He has been in prison longer than the vast majority of the most cruel and callous murderers. Indeed, it is uncertain whether imprisonment provided Steele with any benefit at all. During the first 20 years of his detention there were no facilities in British Columbia that could provide the psychiatric treatment Steele needed. By the time it was available, Steele was a middle-aged institutionalized offender who, not surprisingly, viewed the treatment program as a means of gaining his release rather than as an opportunity for rehabilitation.

Throughout the period of his imprisonment, numerous observers expressly stated not only that Steele had received the maximum benefit from imprisonment, but also that continued detention would cause him to deteriorate. As early as 1960, Dr. P. Middleton warned that any treatment facilities available in the penitentiary would not offset "the pernicious effects of association" with other inmates. Others who made this same point include: Dr. D.C. MacDonald, Deputy Warden W.H. Collins and Field Representative P.D. Redecopp in 1964; Dr. J.C. Bryce in 1968; Mr. Lee Pulos in 1970; Field Parole Officer William F. Foster and Mr. Pulos, again, in 1972; Dr. Milton H. Miller and Dr. A. Saad in 1974; and Dr. W.J. Ross in 1981. Even Dr. Noone, who testified for the Crown in this application, acknowledged the detrimental effects of indeterminate sentencing for dangerous offenders. While some observers expressed the opinion that Steele should not be released, not one of them appears to have argued that continued incarceration had been or would be beneficial for Steele.

The second criterion has also long been satisfied. Steele has deteriorated in the prison environment. Many, indeed the great majority of those psychiatrists and psychologists who assessed him, expressed the opinion that his rehabilitation could only be facilitated and attained by his gradual, supervised release into the community. It appears that the Parole Board acknowledged this in its decisions to grant Steele limited freedom between 1968 and 1970 and between 1980 and 1987. During both of these periods the Board permitted Steele to undertake a programme of escorted passes that resulted in brief stays in a half-way house environment. These periods of relative freedom were terminated when Steele infringed his parole conditions by drinking alcohol and breaking curfew. Unfortunately, despite assessments by observers suggesting that these parole violations were merely adjustment problems, the Board seems to have presumed that Steele was incapable of benefitting from an association with the community outside the prison.

There remains then the third and most important criterion, namely whether the offender constitutes an undue risk to society. If an inmate's release continues to constitute an undue risk to the public, then his or her detention can be justifiably maintained for a lifetime. There can be no doubt that in the ordinary course of events the assessment as to whether or not an inmate's release would pose an undue risk to the community is best left in the discretion of the experts who participate in the Parole Board review decisions. However, in light of the inordinate length of Steele's period of incarceration, it is appropriate to consider whether the Board erred in its evaluation that Steele did in fact constitute a danger to the community.

Of the psychiatrists and psychologists who interviewed Steele and whose reports were provided to the Parole Board, sixteen expressed a recommendation as to whether or not he should be paroled. Thirteen of the sixteen recommended that he should be released on some form of supervised parole. Two stated that he should not be released. One psychologist changed his mind over the course of several years from a position which cautioned against parole to one of arguing in favour of parole. Those recommending release were: Dr. MacDonald in 1956 and 1964; Dr. Middleton in 1960; Dr. Bryce in 1968; Dr. Lipinski in 1970 and 1972; Dr. Bulmer in 1970; Mr. Pulos in 1970 and 1972; Mr. P. DesLauriers in 1972; Dr. Robert Halliday in 1973; Dr. Miller, Dr. Saad, Mr. F.M. Van Fleet and Mr. K.S. Oey in 1974; and Dr. Tyhurst in 1979 and 1985. Those counselling against release were: Dr. Eaves in 1979 and 1980; and Dr. Noone in 1985 and 1988. Dr. W.J. Ross considered that Steele was not "a good risk" when he first assessed him in 1978; however, by 1981 he was recommending that Steele be released on gradual parole.

On the application, Paris J heard testimony from three psychiatric experts. Of those, Dr. Marcus and Dr. Koopman testified that Steele was not dangerous and should be released. Dr. Noone stated that Steele remained an untreated sexual psychopath who should not be released. After carefully reviewing the evidence in extensive detail, Paris J concluded that Steele's release would not endanger the public.

Upon the evidence presented to this Court, the careful reasons and conclusion of Paris J on this issue are in my view preferable to those of the Parole Board which as will be demonstrated did not properly exercise its jurisdiction.

It is difficult to find any evidence of acts committed by Steele during the past two decades that would suggest that he remained an undue risk to society. His parole violations resulted not from a tendency to repeatedly engage in violent or sexually deviant behaviour, but from the difficulties he had in abiding by parole curfew restrictions and abstaining from drinking alcohol. The nature of these problems was described by Dr. Marcus in these words:

He finds it very hard to adhere to inflexible rules such as those that are imposed when he is on parole. ... His personality style is always to stretch the clock. ... It is a similar attitude which has led Mr. Steele into situations where he has been in breach of parole conditions relating to meeting curfews. Here again Mr. Steele holds the view that he is now 53 years old and after a lifetime in prison he should not be held to requirements which treat him in a somewhat childlike [manner]. It is precisely this attitude which has made him a bad parole prospect in terms of meeting all the expectations and rules imposed by his Parole Officer. Yet, in my opinion, what must be kept firmly in mind in the context of assessing the degree of risk of harm to others that Mr. Steele poses at the present time, is that Mr. Steele in the course of these recent infractions did not repeat the pattern either of his original offence nor of his re-offending while on parole in 1962.

The problems inherent in requiring chronic alcoholics to meet rigid drinking restrictions have been well documented in the *Report of the Inquiry into Habitual Criminals in Canada*, vol. 1 (1984), where Judge Leggett wrote at p. 83:

Many of the habitual criminals are alcoholic. This disease has been a significant factor in the "revolving-door syndrome" of these individuals. When released on parole, a condition to abstain from alcohol is frequently included as a condition to such release. While some of the habitual criminals have been able to abide by this condition and successfully complete parole, many others have not. Those who have failed to abide by such conditions have found themselves, sooner or later, re-incarcerated as a result of the revocation of their parole.

Steele may have a problem with alcohol and in dealing with rigid discipline. But those factors in themselves cannot justify his continued detention. If breaches of a domestic curfew and the consumption of alcohol were the sole criteria for liberty then a significant proportion of our society should be incarcerated for an indefinite period. That is not to say that breaches of the conditions of parole should not be seriously considered. However, all the circumstances of the breach and any explanations as to the reasons for its occurrence should also be taken into account.

The statutory criteria should be applied to the individual inmate and considered in light of all the relevant circumstances. One of those circumstances will be length of the term served. The passage of several decades in prison may not in itself justify parole. However, it may well serve as an indication that the inmate is no longer dangerous. Surely with the passage of very long periods of time sexual appetite might reasonably be expected to decline to an extent that it may at least be controlled, if not extinguished. As well, a lengthy incarceration with the concomitant institutionalizing effect upon the inmate may serve to explain and perhaps to some extent excuse certain breaches of discipline.

In my view the evidence presented demonstrates that the National Parole Board has erred in its application of the criteria set out in s. 16(1)(a) of the *Parole Act*. The Board appears to have based its decision to deny parole upon relatively minor and apparently explicable breaches of discipline committed by Steele, rather than focussing upon the crucial issue of whether granting him parole would constitute an undue risk to society. As a result of these errors, the parole review process has failed to ensure that Steele's sentence has been tailored to fit his circumstances. The inordinate length of his incarceration has long since become grossly disproportionate to the circumstances of this case.

It will only be on rare and unique occasions that a court will find a sentence so grossly disproportionate that it violates the provisions of s. 12 of the Charter. The test for determining whether a sentence is disproportionately long is very properly stringent and demanding. A lesser test would tend to trivialize the Charter.

As well, it should not be forgotten that there is in place a method whereby appellate courts can review sentences to ensure that they are appropriate. In *R v. Smith*, [1987] 1 SCR 1045, Lamer J set out the strict test for reviewing a sentence under s. 12 of the Charter. At page 1072 he wrote:

> The test for review under s. 12 of the Charter is one of gross disproportionality, because it is aimed at punishments that are more than merely excessive. We should be careful not to stigmatize every disproportionate or excessive sentence as being a constitutional violation, and should leave to the usual sentencing appeal process the task of reviewing the fitness of a sentence. Section 12 will only be infringed where the sentence is so unfit having regard to the offence and the offender as to be grossly disproportionate.

The history of the offence and the offender which I have set out makes it apparent that the sentence is now "so unfit having regard to the offence and the offender as to be grossly disproportionate." This is one of those rare cases where the sentence continuing Steele's detention after 37 years in prison violates s. 12 of the Charter.

It is necessary to make a further comment. As I have made clear above, the continuing detention of a dangerous offender sentenced pursuant to the constitutionally valid provisions of the *Criminal Code* will only violate s. 12 of the Charter when the National Parole Board errs in the execution of its vital duties of tailoring the indeterminate sentence to the circumstances of the offender. This tailoring is performed by applying the criteria set out in s. 16(1) of the *Parole Act*. Since any error that may be committed occurs in the parole review process itself, an application challenging the decision should be made by means of judicial review from the National Parole Board decision, not by means of an application for *habeas corpus*. It would be wrong to sanction the establishment of a costly and unwieldly parallel system for challenging a Parole Board decision. As well, it is important that the release of a long term inmate should be supervised by those who are experts in this field. I agree with the comments of Locke JA:

> In the case of persons subject to an indeterminate sentence who have spent many years in prison, it is highly desirable that their release, if and when it occurs, should be conditional, should be subject to supervision by those experienced in the parole or probation fields, and should be accompanied by the sort of assistance which will increase their likelihood of adjusting to the change in environment and, if possible, becoming self-sufficient and useful members of society. Under the present statutory and administrative arrangements, it seems that this can be achieved only in association with release by the parole board, in the exercise of its discretion under s. 761 of the *Criminal Code*.

However, in view of Steele's age and the length of his detention, it would be unfair to require him to commence new proceedings by way of judicial review from the National Parole Board decision. In these highly unusual circumstances, I would confirm Steele's release on the basis of the application for *habeas corpus*. I further agree with the position taken by the Court of Appeal that since his release cannot be regulated through normal parole procedures, it is appropriate, in the interest of public safety, to maintain the conditions placed by the Court of Appeal upon his release.

NOTE

In total, 13 judges examined Steele's case and all agreed that he was entitled to be released as a result of a breach of s. 12 of the Charter. This serves as an important example of the potential use of *habeas corpus* to bring forward a Charter claim. Moreover, one must note the characterization of a liberty interest as provided in *R v. Miller*, above, where Le Dain J held that *habeas corpus* was avialable to challenge "a significant reduction in the residual liberty of the inmate," which can, in some circumstances, relate to the conditions of confinement. Along with cases like *R v. Gamble*, [1988] 2 SCR 595, which dealt with s. 7 and parole ineligibility for first-degree murder after a conviction under the wrong law, there appeared to be a renaissance in the use of *habeas corpus* as an accessible and effectual remedy.

However, the final paragraph in the judgment of Cory J in *Steele* blunted this progress. His admonition about establishing a "costly and unwieldy parallel system for challenging a Parole Board decision" was made in the context of a lifetime indeterminate sentence. This was a case where it was legitimate to ask whether there was any need to supervise Steele in the community. This is the key to Cory J's comments. Clearly, a court does not have supervisory resources. However, given that the relief is sought under s. 24(1) of the Charter, the court is empowered to do what is "appropriate and just." In *Steele*, that meant imposing conditions on his release. Although there may be some preventive detention cases that raise a procedural fairness argument that might better be dealt with by way of judicial review that returns the matter to the National Parole Board, cases that engage fundamental questions about the legality of confinement, like *Steele*, should not be barred from access to *habeas corpus*.

Regrettably, some superior courts were persuaded that the final paragraph in *Steele* meant that no parole issue should be dealt with by way of *habeas corpus* and that all issues should be raised by judicial review in the Federal Court. This elevated Cory J's comment in *Steele* from a caution raised in the context of indeterminate sentences to a complete denial of *habeas corpus* relief in a much larger class of cases. Moreover, deference to Federal Court jurisdiction quickly moved from just parole cases to other penitentiary issues, primarily transfers to higher security. While this raised questions of consistency with the role of *habeas corpus* as explained in *Miller*, it was not long before Courts of Appeal started to reach the same conclusion based on a fuzzy notion that jurisdiction was discretionary and could be declined. By 2004, the doors of *habeas corpus*, that "great and efficacious writ" were almost completely closed to penitentiary prisoners who wanted to challenge the legality of deprivations of their residual liberty. The Supreme Court of Canada unanimously opened the doors by rejecting any discretionary jurisdiction and recognizing the prisoner's right to select her remedy regardless of concurrent jurisdiction in the Federal Court. When you read the case below, note how Justices Lebel and Fish deal with the issue of burden of proof on a *habeas corpus* application. This part of the judgment represents the first time in Canada that this issue has been authoritatively considered.

May v. Ferndale Institution
2005 SCC 82, [2005] 3 SCR 809

The judgment of McLachlin CJ and Binnie, LeBel, Deschamps, Fish, and Abella JJ was delivered by

LeBEL and FISH JJ:

I. Introduction

[1] These cases involve the overlap and potential conflict of jurisdiction between provincial superior courts and the Federal Court. At stake is the right of federal prisoners to challenge the legality of their detention by way of *habeas corpus* in provincial superior courts. The question to be resolved in these cases is whether the Supreme Court of British Columbia should have declined *habeas corpus* jurisdiction in favour of Federal Court jurisdiction on judicial review. If the court properly exercised its jurisdiction, we will also have to assess whether the appellants have been unlawfully deprived of their liberty.

[2] In our view, the Supreme Court of British Columbia has properly exercised its *habeas corpus* jurisdiction. This is not one of the limited circumstances pursuant to which a superior court should decline to exercise its jurisdiction: first, these cases do not involve a statute that confers jurisdiction on a court of appeal to correct the errors of a lower court and release the applicant if need be; and second, Parliament has not put in place a complete, comprehensive and expert procedure for review of an administrative decision.

[3] Moreover, we believe that the appellants have been unlawfully deprived of their liberty. The respondents did not comply with their statutory duty to provide all the information or a summary of the information considered in making the transfer decisions. The appeal should therefore be allowed.

II. Facts and Judicial History

[4] Each of the appellants are prisoners serving life sentences for murder and/or manslaughter. Terry Lee May was convicted of first-degree murder for killing one adolescent boy so that he could sexually assault another without interference. David Edward Owen was convicted of second-degree murder for beating his ex-wife to death. Maurice Yvon Roy was convicted of second-degree murder for killing his common law wife. Gareth Wayne Robinson was convicted on two counts of manslaughter after he stabbed his girlfriend, and then, three years later, struck his wife on the head with a hammer. Segen Uther Speer-Senner was convicted of second-degree murder in circumstances unspecified in the record before us. After varying periods of incarceration, the appellants became residents of Ferndale Institution, a minimum security federal penitentiary located in British Columbia.

[5] Between November 2000 and February 2001, all five appellants were involuntarily transferred from Ferndale Institution to medium-security institutions. Mr. May, Mr. Roy, Mr. Robinson and Mr. Speer-Senner were transferred to Mission Institution

and Mr. Owen, to Matsqui Institution. It is not in issue that a transfer from a minimum- to a medium-security institution involves a significant deprivation of liberty for inmates. Consequently, the appellants filed grievances and also applied for *habeas corpus* relief with *certiorari* in aid directing the responsible correction officials to transfer them back to Ferndale Institution. Their applications were not joined, but the arguments before the British Columbia Court of Appeal were adopted by all five appellants.

[6] The transfers were the result of a direction from the Correctional Service of Canada ("CSC") to review the security classifications of all inmates serving life sentences in minimum-security institutions who had not completed their violent offender programming in the aftermath of a sensational crime committed by a former inmate in another province. CSC used computer applications to assist the classification review process. Mr. Roy, Mr. Robinson, Mr. Speer-Senner and Mr. Owen were advised that their transfers were based on a computerized reclassification scale which yielded a medium-security rating. Mr. May was told that his security rating had been adjusted because the security classification tool could not rate him as minimum-security because he had not completed violent offender programming. There were no allegations of fault or misconduct.

[7] The appellants attacked the decision-making process leading to their transfers. They submitted that a change in general policy, embodied in a direction to review the security classification of offenders serving a life sentence at Ferndale Institution using certain classification tools, was the sole factor prompting their transfers. They said that the transfers were arbitrary, made without any "fresh" misconduct on their parts, and made without considering the merits of each case. The appellants also claimed that their right to procedural fairness was breached by the failure to disclose the scoring matrix for one of the classification tools, leaving them unable to challenge the usefulness of that tool in the decision-making process.

[8] The Supreme Court of British Columbia dismissed the *habeas corpus* application: [2001] BCJ No. 1939 (QL), 2001 BCSC 1335. Bauman J first considered whether a provincial superior court had jurisdiction to review a federal prisoner's involuntary transfer on an application for *habeas corpus* (with *certiorari* in aid) and, in the affirmative, whether it should decline to exercise it. The issue arose because the Federal Court is granted exclusive jurisdiction in respect of *certiorari* proceedings involving the decisions of federal tribunals by its constituent statute.

[9] Bauman J found that he had jurisdiction to hear the application. He relied on *R v. Miller*, [1985] 2 SCR 613, which held that provincial superior courts have retained concurrent jurisdiction with the Federal Court to issue *certiorari* in aid of *habeas corpus* to review the validity of a detention authorized or imposed by a federal board, commission or other tribunal as defined by s. 2 of the *Federal Court Act*, RSC 1985, c. F-7 (formerly RSC 1970 (2nd Supp.), c. 10) ("*FCA*").

[10] Bauman J then dealt with the substantive issues, which he agreed to examine under his *habeas corpus* jurisdiction. He found against the appellants. He held that they had not made out their allegations of failure to disclose relevant information, the computer matrix not being available, and that the transfers had not been arbitrary. In his opinion, although the transfers had been prompted by a general instruction issued to CSC, the decisions had been made after an individualized assessment of all relevant

factors. He concluded that they had not been made in the absence or in excess of juris-diction. The applications for *habeas corpus* and *certiorari* in aid were then dismissed.

[11] The British Columbia Court of Appeal dismissed the appeal: (2003), 188 BCAC 23, 2003 BCCA 536. On the jurisdiction issue, the Court of Appeal had asked for and received written submissions from counsel on the issue raised in *Spindler v. Millhaven Institution* (2003), 15 CR (6th) 183 (Ont. CA).

[12] In *Spindler*, prisoners had been placed in a maximum-security prison as a re-sult of a new policy applicable to convicted murderers. They raised arguments which were similar to the submissions of the appellants in the present appeals. The Ontario Court of Appeal had held that, where a remedy is available in the Federal Court on the exercise of a statutory power granted under a federal statute to a federally appointed individual or tribunal, the provincial superior court should decline to hear an applica-tion for *habeas corpus* if no reasonable explanation for the failure to pursue judicial re-view in the Federal Court was offered by the petitioner. In doing so, the Ontario Court of Appeal agreed with the British Columbia Court of Appeal's decision in *Hickey v. Kent Institution*, [2003] BCJ No. 61 (QL), 2003 BCCA 23.

[13] Ryan JA felt that those comments were particularly apt in the case at bar. Al-though the issues raised in these cases were not identical to those raised in *Spindler*, they all involved policies and procedures adopted by the Commissioner of Corrections in determining the security classifications of the appellants. In her view, these cases should have been heard by the "specialized" Federal Court. The appellants had offered no reasonable explanation for failing to pursue judicial review in the Federal Court, so Ryan JA was of the opinion that Bauman J ought to have declined to hear the applica-tions in these cases, though it is implicit from her reasons that he had jurisdiction to do so. Nevertheless, Ryan JA decided to examine the substantive issue, but she found no error in Bauman J's conclusion that there were no procedural flaws which would entitle the appellants to an order for *habeas corpus*.

[14] Since the Supreme Court of British Columbia heard the application, the record indicates that the situation of most of the appellants has changed. On June 30, 2002, Mr. May was transferred from medium- to minimum-security confinement at Ferndale Institution. On February 6, 2003, Mr. Speer-Senner was also transferred back to Fern-dale Institution. On January 30, 2005, Mr. Owen was released on full parole. The record is silent with respect to the updated situation of Mr. Roy; however, at the hearing, Ms. Pollack, one of the counsel for the appellants, informed us that only Mr. Robinson is still incarcerated in a medium-security institution.

III. Issues and Position of the Parties

[15] These cases revolve around two core issues. First, whether the Supreme Court of British Columbia should have declined *habeas corpus* jurisdiction and, second, whether the appellants have been unlawfully deprived of their liberty.

[16] The appellants argue that the jurisdiction of provincial superior courts to grant *habeas corpus* is not affected by the fact that the unlawful detention results from a breach of relevant statutory and regulatory rules and of principles of natural justice by a federal authority. The applicant is entitled to choose the forum in which to challenge

unlawful restrictions of liberty in the prison context. In addition, the appellants contend that the decisions to transfer them from a minimum-security institution to medium-security institutions were arbitrary and unfair.

[17] On the other hand, the respondents submit that the Court of Appeal did not err in holding that the lower court should have declined *habeas corpus* jurisdiction in the instant case. *Habeas corpus* jurisdiction should be assessed purposively, in view of the comprehensive statutory schemes that provide effective comparable remedies. In any event, the respondents contend that the transfer decisions were lawfully made.

IV. Analysis

A. Did the Superior Court of British Columbia Properly Exercise Its Habeas Corpus Jurisdiction?

[18] Should the Supreme Court of British Columbia have declined *habeas corpus* jurisdiction in favour of Federal Court jurisdiction on judicial review? This issue is particularly important in the context of recent jurisprudential and legal developments and to ensure that the rule of law applies inside Canadian prisons. The continuing relevance of *habeas corpus* is also at stake in a changing social and legal environment. In the case of prisons, access to relief in the nature of *habeas corpus* is critical in order to ensure that prisoners' rights are respected. Accordingly, we will review and discuss five subjects: (1) the nature of *habeas corpus*; (2) the *Miller*, *Cardinal* and *Morin* trilogy (*R v. Miller*, [1985] 2 SCR 613; *Cardinal v. Director of Kent Institution*, [1985] 2 SCR 643; *Morin v. National Special Handling Review Committee*, [1985] 2 SCR 662) and the concurrent jurisdiction of the superior courts and of the Federal Court; (3) the rise of a limited discretion of superior courts to decline to exercise their *habeas corpus* jurisdiction; (4) the expansion of the limited discretion to decline *habeas corpus* jurisdiction in the prison context by provincial courts of appeal; and (5) the need for and protection of federal prisoners' access to *habeas corpus*.

(1) The Nature of Habeas Corpus

[19] The writ of *habeas corpus* is also known as the "Great Writ of Liberty." As early as 1215, the *Magna Carta* entrenched the principle that "[n]o free man shall be seized or imprisoned except by the lawful judgement of his equals or by the law of the land." In the 14th century, the writ of *habeas corpus* was used to compel the production of a prisoner and the cause of his or her detention: W.F. Duker, *A Constitutional History of Habeas Corpus* (1980), at p. 25.

[20] From the 17th to the 20th century, the writ was codified in various *habeas corpus* acts in order to bring clarity and uniformity to its principles and application. The first codification is found in the *Habeas Corpus Act*, 1679 (Engl.), 31 Cha. 2, c. 2. Essentially, the Act ensured that prisoners entitled to relief "would not be thwarted by procedural inadequacy": R.J. Sharpe, *The Law of Habeas Corpus* (2nd ed. 1989), at p. 19.

[21] According to Black J of the United States Supreme Court, *habeas corpus* is "not now and never has been a static, narrow, formalistic remedy; its scope has grown to achieve its grand purpose—the protection of individuals against erosion of their right

to be free from wrongful restraints upon their liberty": *Jones v. Cunningham*, 371 US 236 (1962), at p. 243. In his book, Sharpe, at p. 23, describes the traditional form of review available on *habeas corpus* as follows:

> The writ is directed to the gaoler or person having custody or control of the applicant. *It requires that person to return to the court, on the day specified, the body of the applicant and the cause of his detention.* The process focuses upon the cause returned. If the return discloses a lawful cause, the prisoner is remanded; *if the cause returned is insufficient or unlawful, the prisoner is released.* The matter directly at issue is simply the excuse or reason given by the party who is exercising restraint over the applicant. [Emphasis added.]

[22] *Habeas corpus* is a crucial remedy in the pursuit of two fundamental rights protected by the *Canadian Charter of Rights and Freedoms*: (1) the right to liberty of the person and the right not to be deprived thereof except in accordance with the principles of fundamental justice (s. 7 of the *Charter*); and (2) the right not to be arbitrarily detained or imprisoned (s. 9 of the *Charter*). Accordingly, the *Charter* guarantees the right to *habeas corpus*:

> 10. Everyone has the right on arrest or detention ...
>
> (c) to have the validity of the detention determined by way of *habeas corpus* and to be released if the detention is not lawful.

[23] However, the right to seek relief in the nature of *habeas corpus* has not always been given to prisoners challenging internal disciplinary decisions. At common law, for a long time, a person convicted of a felony and sentenced to prison was regarded as being devoid of rights. Convicts lost all civil and proprietary rights. The law regarded them as dead. On that basis, courts had traditionally refused to review the internal decision-making process of prison officials: M. Jackson, *Justice Behind the Walls: Human Rights in Canadian Prisons* (2002), at pp. 47-50. By the end of the 19th century, although the concept of civil death had largely disappeared, the prisoner continued to be viewed in law as a person without rights: M. Jackson, *Prisoners of Isolation: Solitary Confinement in Canada* (1983), at p. 82.

[24] It was this view that provided the original rationale for Canadian courts' refusal to review the internal decisions of prison officials. The "effect of this hands-off approach was to immunize the prison from public scrutiny through the judicial process and to place prison officials in a position of virtual invulnerability and absolute power over the persons committed to their institutions": Jackson, *Prisoners of Isolation*, at p. 82.

[25] Shortly after certain serious incidents in federal penitentiaries occurred in the 1970s and reviews of their management took place, this Court abandoned the "hands-off" doctrine and extended judicial review to the decision-making process of prison officials by which prisoners were deprived of their residual liberty. In *Martineau v. Matsqui Institution Disciplinary Board*, [1980] 1 SCR 602, Dickson J (as he then was) laid the cornerstone for the modern theory and practice of judicial review of correctional decisions:

> In the case at bar, the disciplinary board was not under either an express or implied duty to follow a judicial type of procedure, but the board was obliged to find facts affecting a

subject and to exercise a form of discretion in pronouncing judgment and penalty. Moreover, the board's decision had the effect of depriving an individual of his liberty by committing him to a *"prison within a prison."* In these circumstances, elementary justice requires some procedural protection. *The rule of law must run within penitentiary walls.*
[Emphasis added; p. 622]

[26] Dickson J made it clear that *"certiorari* avails as a remedy wherever a *public
body* has power to decide any matter affecting the rights, interest, property, privileges,
or *liberties* of *any person,"* including prisoners (pp. 622-23). However, he did not specifically examine whether provincial superior courts have jurisdiction to issue *certiorari* in aid of *habeas corpus* to review the validity of a detention imposed by federal
authority. The question would certainly arise in the present case because s. 18 of the
FCA confers on the Federal Court exclusive jurisdiction to issue *certiorari* against any
"federal board, commission or other tribunal." A few years later, a trilogy of cases dealt
with this important issue.

(2) The Miller, Cardinal and Morin Trilogy and the Concurrent Jurisdiction of the Superior Courts and the Federal Court

[27] In 1985, in the trilogy of *Miller*, *Cardinal*, and *Morin*, the Court expanded the
scope of *habeas corpus* by making the writ available to free inmates from restrictive
forms of custody within an institution, without releasing the inmate. *Habeas corpus*
could thus free inmates from a "prison within a prison." Each case involved challenges
by prisoners of their confinement in administrative segregation and their transfer to a
special handling unit. This unit was reserved for particularly dangerous inmates and
was characterized by more restrictive confinement.

[28] In *Miller*, Le Dain J., writing for the Court, recognized that confinement in a
special handling unit or in administrative segregation is a form of detention that is distinct and separate from that imposed on the general inmate population because it involves a significant reduction in the residual liberty of the inmate. In his view, *habeas
corpus* should lie "to challenge the validity of a distinct form of confinement or detention in which the actual physical constraint or deprivation of liberty, as distinct from
the mere loss of certain privileges, is more restrictive or severe than the normal one in
an institution" (p. 641).

[29] The issue remained, however, whether the remedy should be sought in a provincial superior court or the Federal Court. Le Dain J pointed out that Parliament had
made a conscious decision not to include *habeas corpus* in the list of prerogative remedies over which the Federal Court has exclusive jurisdiction. *Habeas corpus* jurisdiction, as an essential safeguard of the liberty interest, could only be affected by express
words, which were not present in s. 18(1) of the *FCA* (pp. 624-25). Therefore, *habeas
corpus* remained within the long standing inherent jurisdiction conferred to provincial
superior court judges appointed under s. 96 of the *Constitution Act, 1867*. To remove
that jurisdiction from the provincial superior courts would require clear and direct statutory language such as that used in s. 18(2) of the *FCA* referring to members of the Canadian Forces stationed overseas.

[30] Le Dain J specifically addressed the issue, which arises in these cases, of whether jurisdiction for judicial review of federal boards by the Federal Court under s. 18 of the *FCA* trumped the provincial superior courts' *habeas corpus* jurisdiction. He concluded, without any ambiguity, "that a *provincial superior court has jurisdiction* to issue *certiorari in aid* of *habeas corpus* to review the validity of a detention authorized or imposed by a *federal board, commission or other tribunal* as defined by s. 2 of the Federal Court Act" (p. 626 (emphasis added)).

[31] Throughout his analysis, Le Dain J carefully examined which forum was the most appropriate to review the legality of federal prisoners' detention, with reference to s. 18 of the *FCA*, the importance of local accessibility of the *habeas corpus* remedy, and the problems arising out of concurrent jurisdiction. Dealing with the issue of concurrent jurisdiction, he stated:

> After giving consideration to the two approaches to this issue, I am of the opinion that the better view is that *habeas corpus* should lie to determine the validity of a particular form of confinement in a penitentiary notwithstanding that the same issue may be determined upon *certiorari* in the Federal Court. The proper scope of the availability of *habeas corpus* must be considered first on its own merits, apart from possible problems arising from concurrent or overlapping jurisdiction. *The general importance of this remedy as the traditional means of challenging deprivations of liberty is such that its proper development and adaptation to the modern realities of confinement in a prison setting should not be compromised by concerns about conflicting jurisdiction.* [Emphasis added; pp. 640-41]

[32] The same reasoning was also applied by this Court in *Cardinal* and *Morin*, the companion cases to *Miller*. In our view, the trilogy supports two distinct propositions. First and foremost, provincial superior courts have jurisdiction to issue *certiorari* in aid of *habeas corpus* in respect of detention in federal penitentiaries in order to protect residual liberty interests. This principle is crucial in these cases. In the prison context, the applicant is thus entitled to choose the forum in which to challenge an allegedly unlawful restriction of liberty. Under *Miller*, if the applicant chooses *habeas corpus*, his or her claim should be dealt with on its merits, without regard to other potential remedies in the Federal Court. The second proposition, which does not arise in these cases, is that *habeas corpus* will lie to determine the validity of the confinement of an inmate in administrative segregation, and if such confinement is found unlawful, to order his or her release into the general inmate population of the institution.

(3) The Emergence of a Limited Discretion to Decline Jurisdiction

[33] As we have seen, the starting point is that a prisoner is free to choose whether to challenge an unlawful restriction of liberty by way of *habeas corpus* in a provincial superior court or by way of judicial review in the Federal Court. Historically, the writ of *habeas corpus* has never been a discretionary remedy. It is issued as of right, where the applicant successfully challenges the legality of the detention:

> *In principle, habeas corpus is not a discretionary remedy: it issues ex debito justitiae on proper grounds being shown.* It is, however, a writ of right rather than a writ of course, and

there is a long-established practice of having a preliminary proceeding to determine whether there is sufficient merit in the application to warrant bringing in the other parties.

This means, simply, that it is not a writ which can be had for the asking upon payment of a court fee, but one which will only be issued where it is made to appear that there are proper grounds. While the court has no discretion to refuse relief, it is still for the court to decide whether proper grounds have been made out to support the application. *The rule that the writ issues ex debito justitiae means simply that the court may only properly refuse relief on the grounds that there is no legal basis for the application and that habeas corpus should never be refused on discretionary ground such as inconvenience.* [Emphasis added.]

(Sharpe, at p. 58)

[34] Thus, as a matter of general principle, *habeas corpus* jurisdiction should not be declined merely because of the existence of an alternative remedy. Whether the other remedy is still available or whether the applicant has foregone the right to use it, its existence should not preclude or affect the right to apply for *habeas corpus* to the Superior Court of the province: Sharpe, at p. 59.

[35] However, given that alternative remedies to *habeas corpus* are often available and in consideration of the development of various forms of judicial review and of rights of appeal in the law of civil and criminal procedure, questions have arisen as to the proper scope of the traditional writ of *habeas corpus* and about the existence of a discretion of superior courts to decline jurisdiction. Courts have sometimes refused to grant relief in the form of *habeas corpus* because an appeal or another statutory route to a court was thought to be more appropriate. The obvious policy reason behind this exception is the need to restrict the growth of collateral methods of attacking convictions or other deprivations of liberty: Sharpe, at pp. 59-60. So far, these situations have primarily arisen in two different contexts.

[36] Strictly speaking, in the criminal context, *habeas corpus* cannot be used to challenge the legality of a conviction. The remedy of *habeas corpus* is not a substitute for the exercise by prisoners of their right of appeal: see *In re Trepanier* (1885), 12 SCR 111; *Re Sproule* (1886), 12 SCR 140, at p. 204; *Goldhar v. The Queen*, [1960] SCR 431, at p. 439; *Morrison v. The Queen*, [1966] SCR 356; *Karchesky v. The Queen*, [1967] SCR 547, at p. 551; *Korponay v. Kulik*, [1980] 2 SCR 265.

[37] Our Court reaffirmed this in *R v. Gamble*, [1988] 2 SCR 595. In *Gamble*, the Court considered *inter alia* whether a superior court judge should have declined to exercise his *habeas corpus* jurisdiction. The appellant had been denied parole eligibility because of a pre-*Charter* law, the continued application of which was alleged to violate the *Charter*.

[38] Wilson J, writing for the majority, found that while superior courts do have the discretion not to exercise their *habeas corpus* jurisdiction, this discretion should "be exercised with due regard to the constitutionally mandated need to provide prompt and effective enforcement of *Charter* rights" (p. 634). Considering the argument that *habeas corpus* jurisdiction should not be asserted because a parallel mechanism already exists in the Federal Court, she held that the assertion of *Charter* rights by way of *habeas corpus* does not create a parallel system and that those who argued that jurisdiction should be

declined on this basis did "no credit to that existing system by attempting to place procedural roadblocks in the way of someone like the appellant who is seeking to vindicate one of the citizens' most fundamental rights in the traditional and appropriate forum" (p. 635). However, referring to the criminal process, she ultimately confirmed that:

> Under section 24(1) of the Charter courts should not allow habeas corpus applications to be used to circumvent the appropriate appeal process, but neither should they bind themselves by overly rigid rules about the availability of habeas corpus which may have the effect of denying applicants access to courts to obtain Charter relief. [Emphasis added; p. 642.]

[39] A second limitation to the scope of *habeas corpus* has gradually developed in the field of immigration law. It is now well established that courts have a limited discretion to refuse to entertain applications for prerogative relief in immigration matters: *Pringle v. Fraser*, [1972] SCR 821; *Peiroo v. Canada (Minister of Employment and Immigration)* (1989), 69 OR (2d) 253 (CA) (leave to appeal denied, [1989] 2 SCR x). In the words of Catzman JA in *Peiroo*:

> Parliament has established in the [*Immigration Act*], particularly in the recent amendments which specifically address the disposition of claims of persons in the position of the appellant, a *comprehensive scheme* to regulate the determination of such claims and to provide for review and appeal in the Federal Court of Canada of decisions and orders made under the Act, the ambit of which review and appeal *is as broad as or broader than* the traditional scope of review by way of *habeas corpus* with *certiorari* in aid. In the absence of any showing that the available review and appeal process established by Parliament is *inappropriate or less advantageous* than the *habeas corpus* jurisdiction of the Supreme Court of Ontario, it is my view that this court should, in the exercise of its discretion, decline to grant relief upon the application for *habeas corpus* in the present case, which clearly falls within the purview of that *statutory review and appeal process*. [Emphasis added; pp. 261-62]

[40] In *Reza v. Canada*, [1994] 2 SCR 394, the trial judge refused to hear a constitutional challenge to the *Immigration Act* brought in provincial superior court. The Court confirmed once again that the trial judge "properly exercised his discretion on the basis that Parliament had created a *comprehensive scheme of review of immigration matters* and the Federal Court was an effective and appropriate forum" (p. 405). Thus, it can be seen from these cases that, in matters of immigration law, because Parliament has put in place a complete, comprehensive and expert statutory scheme which provides for a review at least as broad as that available by way of *habeas corpus* and no less advantageous, *habeas corpus* is precluded.

[41] From the two recognized exceptions to the availability of *habeas corpus*—criminal appeals and the "*Peiroo* exception," adopted in *Reza*—we turn now to the decision of this Court in *Steele v. Mountain Institution*, [1990] 2 SCR 1385. *Steele* has on occasion been thought, mistakenly in our view, to have established a rule of general application barring access to *habeas corpus* whenever an alternative remedy is available. In light of the unusual circumstances of that case, we think it important to consider more closely its true significance.

[42] The issue here is not whether the result in *Steele* was justified in the circumstances—we believe that it was—but whether *Steele* created a fresh and independent
exception to the availability of *habeas corpus*. In our view, it did not. *Steele* was the
product of a convergent set of unusual facts and can only be understood in that light.
Without any discussion of the principles governing access to *habeas corpus*, the Court
in *Steele* granted that remedy while questioning its availability. No judicial barrier to
the venerable right to *habeas corpus*, now constitutionalized in Canada, can be made
to rest on so fragile a jurisprudential foundation.

[43] Nor should this Court's decision in *Idziak v. Canada (Minister of Justice)*,
[1992] 3 SCR 631, be thought to have decided otherwise: the Court did not in that case
elevate the result in *Steele* into a principled rule barring access to *habeas corpus* in
matters not caught by the two recognized exceptions set out above. The decisive issue
in *Idziak* was whether Parliament had created with respect to extradition a comprehensive statutory scheme similar to the scheme created by Parliament for immigration
matters. The Court held that it had not. Accordingly, there was no reason for provincial
superior courts to decline to exercise their *habeas corpus* jurisdiction where the impugned detention resulted from proceedings in extradition.

[44] To sum up therefore, the jurisprudence of this Court establishes that prisoners
may choose to challenge the legality of a decision affecting their residual liberty either
in a provincial superior court by way of *habeas corpus* or in the Federal Court by way
of judicial review. As a matter of principle, a provincial superior court should exercise
its jurisdiction when it is requested to do so. *Habeas corpus* jurisdiction should not be
declined merely because another alternative remedy exists and would appear as or more
convenient in the eyes of the court. The option belongs to the applicant. Only in limited
circumstances will it be appropriate for a provincial superior court to decline to exercise
its *habeas corpus* jurisdiction. For instance, in criminal law, where a statute confers
jurisdiction on a court of appeal to correct the errors of a lower court and release the
applicant if need be, *habeas corpus* will not be available (i.e. *Gamble*). Jurisdiction
should also be declined where there is in place a complete, comprehensive and expert
procedure for review of an administrative decision (i.e. *Pringle* and *Peiroo*).

(4) The Expansion of the Limited Discretion to Decline Habeas Corpus
      Jurisdiction in the Prison Context by Provincial Courts of Appeal

[45] The British Columbia Court of Appeal, in these cases and in *Hickey*, and the
Ontario Court of Appeal in *Spindler*, each discussed earlier, have recently restricted
access to relief in the form of *habeas corpus* in the provincial superior courts. The respondents rely heavily on this line of decisions to support the position that superior
courts should generally decline jurisdiction in favour of statutory judicial review when
it is available. If such an approach were to be accepted by our Court, the *habeas corpus*
jurisdiction of superior courts might be significantly curtailed. It might evolve into a
discretionary residual jurisdiction, available only when everything else has failed. Such
a result would be inconsistent with this Court's jurisprudence. Given their importance
in the courts below, we will now review and comment on *Hickey* and *Spindler*.

[46] In *Hickey*, an inmate who was serving a life sentence was ordered to be transferred to a special handling unit. The inmate opposed the transfer by way of *habeas corpus* instead of using the internal grievance procedures or applying by way of judicial review to the Federal Court. Ryan JA, for the British Columbia Court of Appeal, ultimately held that the trial judge had jurisdiction. However, referring to *Steele*, she further stated:

> It is trite that the court has a discretion to refuse to entertain an application for *habeas corpus* if there exists a viable alternative to the writ. *In the context of prison law the fact that there is in place a complete, comprehensive and expert procedure for review of a decision affecting the prisoner's confinement is a factor which militates against hearing a petition for habeas corpus.* But there will be exceptions. ...
>
> In the case at bar the appellant provided the Supreme Court with no explanation as to why he had not pursued either the grievance procedures or judicial review to the Federal Court. Without any information setting out why these procedures were inadequate to deal with Mr. Hickey's situation, the Chambers judge ought not to have heard the application for *habeas corpus*. [Emphasis added; paras. 50 and 53]

(See also the companion case to *Hickey*, *Bernard v. Kent Institution*, [2003] BCJ No. 62 (QL), 2003 BCCA 24, at paras. 6-7.)

[47] In *Spindler*, the inmates were serving life sentences for murder and were incarcerated in a maximum-security penitentiary. They applied for *habeas corpus* claiming that their detention was illegal and seeking an order directing that they be moved to "a penitentiary of a lower security level." The motions judge stated that he had jurisdiction to consider the *habeas corpus* application but declined to do so holding that the Federal Court was the more appropriate forum. Doherty JA dismissed the appeal. Relying on *Steele* and agreeing with *Hickey*, he said:

> As I read Steele, supra, except in exceptional circumstances, a provincial superior court should decline to exercise its habeas corpus jurisdiction where the application is in essence, a challenge to the exercise of a statutory power granted under a federal statute to a federally appointed individual or tribunal. Those challenges are specifically assigned to the Federal Court under the *Federal Court Act* RSC 1985 c. F-7 s. 18, s. 28. By directing such challenges to the Federal Court, Parliament has recognized that individuals or tribunals exercising statutory powers under federal authority must exercise those powers across the country. It is important that judicial interpretations as to the nature and scope of those powers be as uniform and consistent as possible. *By giving the Federal Court jurisdiction over these challenges, Parliament has provided the means by which uniformity and consistency can be achieved while at the same time, facilitating the development of an expertise over these matters in the Federal Court.* [Emphasis added; para. 19]

[48] Finally, in the case at bar, Ryan JA, for the British Columbia Court of Appeal, relied on *Hickey* and *Spindler* to support her conclusion that the Chambers judge ought to have refused to hear the application for *habeas corpus*. She further explained:

> In my view the observations of Doherty JA, with regard to the importance of pursuing remedies in the Federal Court are particularly apt in the case at bar. While the issues raised in the cases at bar may not be identical to those raised in *Spindler*, *supra*, all, like *Spindler*,

involve policy and procedure adopted by the Commissioner in determining the security classifications of the appellants. *In my view these cases ought to have been heard by that specialized court.*

The appellants have offered no reasonable explanation for failing to pursue judicial review in the Federal Court. In my view, the Chambers judge in this case ought to have refused to hear the applications in this case. [Emphasis added; paras. 21-22]

[49] The position adopted by the British Columbia Court of Appeal and the Ontario Court of Appeal can be summarized as follows. First, the court has a discretion to refuse to entertain an application for *habeas corpus* if there exists a viable alternative to the writ. Second, in the context of prison law, the existence of a complete, comprehensive and expert procedure for review of a decision affecting the prisoner's confinement is a factor which militates against hearing a petition for *habeas corpus*. Third, by giving the Federal Court jurisdiction over these challenges, Parliament has provided the means by which uniformity and consistency can be achieved while at the same time facilitating the development of an expertise over these matters in the Federal Court. Fourth, except in exceptional circumstances, a provincial superior court should decline to exercise its *habeas corpus* jurisdiction where the application is, in essence, a challenge to the exercise of a statutory power granted under a federal statute to a federally appointed tribunal. And fifth, the applicant has to provide a reasonable explanation as to why he or she has not pursued either the grievance procedures or judicial review to the Federal Court.

[50] Given the historical importance of *habeas corpus* in the protection of various liberty interests, jurisprudential developments limiting *habeas corpus* jurisdiction should be carefully evaluated and should not be allowed to expand unchecked. The exceptions to *habeas corpus* jurisdiction and the circumstances under which a superior court may decline jurisdiction should be well defined and limited. In our view, the propositions articulated by the Court of Appeal in these cases, as in *Hickey* and *Spindler*, unduly limit the scope and availability of *habeas corpus* review and are incompatible with this Court's jurisprudence. With respect, we are unable to reconcile this narrow view of superior court jurisdiction with the broad approach adopted by the *Miller* trilogy and confirmed in subsequent cases. In principle, the governing rule is that provincial superior courts should exercise their jurisdiction. However, in accordance with this Court's decisions, provincial superior courts should decline *habeas corpus* jurisdiction only where (1) a statute such as the *Criminal Code*, RSC 1985, c. C-46, confers jurisdiction on a court of appeal to correct the errors of a lower court and release the applicant if need be or (2) the legislator has put in place complete, comprehensive and expert procedure for review of an administrative decision.

(5) Confirming Federal Prisoners' Access to Habeas Corpus

[51] The British Columbia Court of Appeal erred in barring access to *habeas corpus* in these cases. Neither of the two recognized exceptions to the general rule that the superior courts should exercise *habeas corpus* jurisdiction are applicable here. The first exception has no application in these cases because they do not involve a criminal conviction, but rather administrative decisions in the prison context. The second exception does not apply since, for the reasons explained below, Parliament has not enacted a

complete, comprehensive and expert procedure for review of a decision affecting the confinement of prisoners. Moreover, as will be shown below, a purposive approach to the issues that arise here also clearly favours a concurrency of jurisdiction.

[52] The respondents argue that the same reasoning that applies to immigration cases should apply to prison law. In their view, Parliament has created a comprehensive statutory scheme, in the *Corrections and Conditional Release Act*, SC 1992, c. 20 ("*CCRA*"), and its regulations, for the resolution of inmate grievances, including those relating to decisions to transfer, segregate or otherwise restrict liberty.

[53] The respondents contend that the scheme dovetails with Parliament's intention that review of such matters generally occurs in the Federal Court. The scheme is specifically tailored to individuals who are incarcerated and provides internal grievances or appeals for decisions that have an impact upon the liberty of inmates. Many of the decisions made by correction officers require the application of policy developed in the specialized circumstances of the federal prison system. According to the respondents, the Federal Court has acquired considerable expertise in reviewing the decisions of grievance boards.

[54] We must therefore examine the legal and regulatory framework of inmate classification in the federal penitentiary system in order to determine whether Parliament has put in place a complete statutory code for the administration and review of inmates' grievances. The starting point is the administrative decision by which inmates are classified for security purposes. By virtue of s. 30(1) of the *CCRA*, CSC "shall assign a security classification of maximum, medium or minimum to each inmate." Security classifications are made pursuant to the statutory factors provided for in ss. 17 and 18 of the *Corrections and Conditional Release Regulations*, SOR/92-620 ("*Regulations*").

[55] As a matter of principle, CSC must use the "least restrictive measures consistent with the protection of the public, staff members and offenders": s. 4(d) of the *CCRA*. Where a person is to be confined in a penitentiary, CSC must provide the "least restrictive environment for that person" taking into account specific criteria: s. 28 of the *CCRA*. Section 30(2) of the *CCRA* further provides that CSC "shall give each inmate reasons, in writing, for assigning a particular security classification or for changing that classification." Of course, correctional decisions, including security classifications, must "be made in a forthright and fair manner, with access by the offender to an effective grievance procedure": s. 4(g) of the *CCRA*.

[56] Inmates who are dissatisfied with transfer decisions can grieve the decisions through the correction system. Sections 90 and 91 of the *CCRA* establish the general framework for the inmate grievance procedure. The *CCRA* requires that inmates have access to a fair and expeditious grievance procedure, to be prescribed by regulation and Commissioner's Directives: ss. 96(u), 97 and 98. The nuts and bolts of the procedure are found in ss. 74 to 82 of the *Regulations*. The process allows inmates to pursue any complaint up the successive administrative rungs of CSC so that supervisors are reviewing the actions of their subordinates. Pursuant to s. 74(1) of the *Regulations*, when an inmate is unhappy with an action or a decision of a staff member, the inmate may submit a complaint to the staff member's supervisor. Written complaints by offenders are to be resolved informally if at all possible. If complaints are not resolved to the satisfaction of the inmate, he or she has access to the grievance procedure.

[57] The grievance procedure has essentially three levels. At the first level, if the inmate is dissatisfied with the resolution of a complaint by the staff member's supervisor, the inmate can grieve to the Warden of the institution: s. 75(a) of the *Regulations*. At the second level, if the inmate is dissatisfied with the Warden's decision, or if the Warden is the origin of the complaint, the inmate may bring a grievance to the Regional Head: s. 75(b) and 80(1) of the *Regulations*. At the third level, if the inmate is dissatisfied with the Regional Head's response, the inmate may grieve directly to the Commissioner of Corrections: s. 80(2) of the *Regulations*. The Commissioner has delegated his or her authority as the final decision-maker with respect to grievances to the Assistant Commissioner: ss. 18 and 19 of the *Commissioner's Directive 081*, "Offender Complaints and Grievances," 2002-03-04 ("*CD 081*"). Ultimately, by virtue of ss. 2 and 18 of the *FCA*, the inmate may challenge the fairness and *Charter* compliance of the decision at the third level by way of judicial review before the Federal Court.

[58] As mentioned earlier, the law requires that inmates have access to an effective, fair and expeditious grievance procedure. As a result, the inmate is entitled to written reasons at all levels of the grievance procedure: ss. 74(3), 74(5), 77(3), 79(3) and 80(3) of the *Regulations*. Naturally, the inmate is required to participate in the resolution process and *CD 081* requires that confidentiality of complaints and grievances be preserved "to the greatest possible extent" (ss. 6(c) and 6(e)). The *Regulations* also prescribe that decisions on complaints and grievances must be issued "as soon as practicable": ss. 74(3), 74(5), 77(3), 79(3) and 80(3); see also ss. 6(d), 7 and 8 of *CD 081* for a more precise timetable. Finally, the institution must show that corrective action is taken when a grievance is upheld: s. 10 of *CD 081*.

[59] The question before us is whether the grievance procedure is a complete, comprehensive and expert procedure for review of an inmate's security classification. In *Pringle*, Laskin J (as he then was), writing for the Court, held:

> *I am satisfied that in the context of the overall scheme for the administration of immigration policy the words in s. 22 ("sole and exclusive jurisdiction to hear and determine all questions of fact or law, including questions of jurisdiction") are adequate not only to endow the Board with the stated authority but to exclude any other court or tribunal from entertaining any type of proceedings*, be they by way of *certiorari* or otherwise, in relation to the matters so confided exclusively to the Board. [Emphasis added; p. 826]

[60] The decisive issue for Laskin J therefore was the intention of the legislature to grant exclusive jurisdiction to the Board. However, there is no such language in the *CCRA* or in the *Regulations*. In fact, it is clear that it was not the intention of the Governor-in-Council, the regulator, to grant paramountcy to the grievance procedure over the superior courts' *habeas corpus* jurisdiction. Section 81(1) of the *Regulations* provides:

> 81(1) Where an offender decides to pursue a *legal remedy* for the offender's complaint or grievance in addition to the complaint and grievance procedure referred to in these Regulations, *the review of the complaint or grievance pursuant to these Regulations shall be deferred until a decision on the alternate remedy is rendered* or the offender decides to abandon the alternate remedy.

[61] Section 81(1) makes it clear that the regulator contemplated the possibility that an inmate may choose to pursue a legal remedy, such as an application for *habeas corpus*, in addition to filing an administrative grievance under the *Regulations*. The legal remedy supersedes the grievance procedure. The regulator did not intend to bar federal prisoners' access to *habeas corpus*. But there is more.

[62] In our view, the grievance procedure can and should be distinguished from the immigration context for several other reasons. The scheme of review which militated against the exercise of *habeas corpus* jurisdiction in *Pringle* and *Peiroo* is substantially different than the grievance procedure provided in the *CCRA*. The *Immigration Act* in force at the time of *Peiroo* provided for an appeal from decisions of immigration authorities to an independent administrative tribunal, the Immigration Appeal Division, vested with all the powers of a superior court of record including jurisdiction to issue summons, administer oaths and enforce its orders: s. 71.4(2). It was a process wherein the impartiality of the adjudicator was statutorily assured, the grounds for review were articulated, and the process for review was clearly laid out: ss. 63, 64 and 71.4-78. A detailed procedure was also provided for the manner in which applications and appeals were to be brought before the Federal Court: ss. 83.1-85.2.

[63] In contrast, the internal grievance process set out in the *CCRA* prescribes the review of decisions made by *prison authorities by other prison authorities*. Thus, in a case where the legality of a Commissioner's policy is contested, it cannot be reasonably expected that the decision-maker, who is subordinate to the Commissioner, could fairly and impartially decide the issue. It is also noteworthy that there are no remedies set out in the *CCRA* and its regulations and no articulated grounds upon which grievances may be reviewed. Lastly, the decisions with respect to grievances are not legally enforceable. In *Peiroo*, the Ontario Court of Appeal emphasized that Parliament had put in place a complete, comprehensive and expert statutory scheme that provided for a review at least as broad as *habeas corpus* and no less advantageous. That is clearly not the case in this appeal.

[64] Therefore, in view of the structural weaknesses of the grievance procedure, there is no justification for importing the line of reasoning adopted in the immigration law context. In the prison context, Parliament has not yet enacted a comprehensive scheme of review and appeal similar to the immigration scheme. The same conclusion was previously reached in *Idziak* with regard to extradition (pp. 652-53).

[65] As we have seen, these cases do not fall within the recognized exceptions where a provincial superior court should decline to exercise its *habeas corpus* jurisdiction. The respondents submit that this Court should assess the *habeas corpus* jurisdiction of the superior courts purposively by acknowledging that the statutory scheme provides for effective and comparable remedies. A purposive approach, however, also requires that we look at the entire context. In our view, the following five factors militate in favour of concurrent jurisdiction and provide additional support for the position that a provincial superior court should hear *habeas corpus* applications from federal prisoners: (1) the choice of remedies and forum; (2) the expertise of provincial superior courts; (3) the timeliness of the remedy; (4) local access to the remedy; and (5) the nature of the remedy and the burden of proof.

[66] First, in the prison context, the applicant may choose either to seek relief in the provincial superior courts or in the Federal Court. In *Idziak*, this Court noted that the applicants in the *Miller*, *Cardinal* and *Morin* trilogy each had a choice of whether to seek a remedy in the provincial superior courts or in Federal Court. The applicants' decision to resort to the provincial superior courts for their remedy was accepted (pp. 651-52).

[67] Furthermore and as noted previously, this Court recognized in *Miller* that the availability of *habeas corpus* "must be considered first on its own merits, apart from possible problems arising from concurrent or overlapping jurisdiction. The general importance of this remedy as the traditional means of challenging deprivations of liberty is such that its proper development and adaptation to the modern realities of confinement in a prison setting should not be compromised by concerns about conflicting jurisdiction" (p. 641).

[68] Second, the greater expertise of the Federal Court in correctional matters is not conclusively established. The Federal Court has considerable familiarity in federal administrative law and procedure and deservedly enjoys a strong reputation in these parts of the law as in other federal matters. On the other hand, prison law revolves around the application of *Charter* principles in respect of which provincial superior courts are equally well versed. Moreover, prison law and life in the penal institution remain closely connected with the administration of criminal justice, in which the superior courts play a critical role on a daily basis. In this context, we find no strong grounds for the adoption of a policy of deference in favour of judicial review in the Federal Court.

[69] Third, a hearing on a *habeas corpus* application in the Supreme Court of British Columbia can be obtained more rapidly than a hearing on a judicial review application in the Federal Court. Rule 4 of the *Criminal Rules of the Supreme Court of British Columbia*, SI/97-140, provides for a hearing of a *habeas corpus* application on six days notice. In contrast, the request for hearing a judicial review application in the Federal Court is filed at day 160 following the impugned decision, if all time limits have run completely: s. 18.1(2) of the *FCA* and Rules 301-314 of the Federal Court Rules, 1998, SOR/98-106. This is a matter of great significance for prisoners unlawfully deprived of their liberty. It is also relevant if counsel is acting *pro bono* or on limited legal aid funding or if the prisoner is representing himself. The importance of the interests at stake militates in favour of a quick resolution of the issues.

[70] Fourth, relief in the form of *habeas corpus* is locally accessible to prisoners in provincial superior courts. Access to justice is closely linked to timeliness of relief. Moreover, it would be unfair if federal prisoners did not have the same access to *habeas corpus* as do provincial prisoners. Section 10(c) of the *Charter* does not support such a distinction. In *Gamble*, Wilson J recognized the importance of access by federal prisoners to the superior courts of the province where they are incarcerated:

> This Court has previously recognized *"the importance of the local accessibility of this remedy"* of *habeas corpus* because of the traditional role of the court as "a safeguard of the liberty of the subject": *R v. Miller*, [1985] 2 SCR 613, at pp. 624-25. *Relief in the form of habeas corpus should not be withheld for reasons of mere convenience.* [Emphasis added; p. 635]

[71] Finally, a writ of *habeas corpus* is issued as of right where the applicant shows that there is cause to doubt the legality of his detention: Sharpe, at p. 58. In contrast, on judicial review, the Federal Court can deny relief on discretionary grounds: D.J. Mullan, *Administrative Law* (2001), at p. 481. Also, on *habeas corpus*, so long as the prisoner has raised a legitimate ground upon which to question the legality of the deprivation of liberty, the onus is on the respondent to justify the lawfulness of the detention: Sharpe, at pp. 86-88. However, on judicial review, the onus is on the applicant to demonstrate that the "federal board, commission or other tribunal" has made an error: s. 18.1(4) of the *FCA*.

[72] Our review of the relevant factors favours the concurrent jurisdiction approach. This approach properly recognizes the importance of affording prisoners a meaningful and significant access to justice in order to protect their liberty rights, a *Charter* value. Timely judicial oversight, in which provincial superior courts must play a concurrent if not predominant role, is still necessary to safeguard the human rights and civil liberties of prisoners, and to ensure that the rule of law applies within penitentiary walls.

B. Have the Appellants Been Unlawfully Deprived of Their Liberty?

[73] Having concluded that the British Columbia Court of Appeal erred in finding that the Chambers judge should have declined to exercise his *habeas corpus* jurisdiction, we must now consider whether the Chambers judge erred in denying the appellants' *habeas corpus* application on its merit.

[74] A successful application for *habeas corpus* requires two elements: (1) a deprivation of liberty and (2) that the deprivation be unlawful. The onus of making out a deprivation of liberty rests on the applicant. The onus of establishing the lawfulness of that deprivation rests on the detaining authority.

[75] With respect to the first element of *habeas corpus*, the appellants claim that transfer to a more restrictive institutional setting deprives them of their residual liberty. With respect to the second element of *habeas corpus*, the appellants contend that the deprivation of their residual liberty was unlawful because it was arbitrary and violated CSC's statutory duty to disclose entrenched in s. 27(1) of the *CCRA*.

(1) Deprivation of Liberty

[76] The decision to transfer an inmate to a more restrictive institutional setting constitutes a deprivation of his or her residual liberty: *Miller*, at p. 637; *Dumas v. Leclerc Institute*, [1986] 2 SCR 459, at p. 464. As a result, there is no question that the appellants have discharged their burden of making out a deprivation of liberty. We must therefore go on to consider whether that deprivation was lawful.

(2) Lawfulness of the Deprivation of Liberty

[77] A deprivation of liberty will only be lawful where it is within the jurisdiction of the decision-maker. Absent express provision to the contrary, administrative decisions must be made in accordance with the *Charter*. Administrative decisions that violate the *Charter* are null and void for lack of jurisdiction: *Slaight Communications Inc. v. Davidson*, [1989] 1 SCR 1038, at p. 1078. Section 7 of the *Charter* provides that an

individual's liberty cannot be impinged upon except in accordance with the principles of fundamental justice. Administrative decisions must also be made in accordance with the common law duty of procedural fairness and requisite statutory duties. Transfer decisions engaging inmates' liberty interest must therefore respect those requirements.

[78] The appellants raise two arguments with respect to the lawfulness of the deprivation in these cases. First, they argue that the transfer decisions were arbitrary because they were solely based on a change in policy, in the absence of any "fresh" misconduct on their part. Second, they submit that the respondents did not comply with their duty of disclosure by withholding a relevant scoring matrix. We will consider each argument in turn.

[LeBel and Fish JJ then proceeded to examine the re-classification and transfer decisions, and whether the processes under the new policy complied with the duty to act fairly. The significant issue was the failure of the CSC to disclose the scoring matrix used to weight the various factors used in the Security Re-classification Scale to produce a score. This score led to the transfer of the prisoners to higher security.]

[110] In our view, the information provided by the respondents to the courts below as to the nature and role of the matrix was misleading. At the hearing before this Court, counsel for the respondents indicated that, at the time of the reclassifications, the scoring matrix was not available because it was the practice not to produce it. Counsel explained that it was thought to be a duplication of information already disclosed.

[111] The new evidence clearly provides information on the numerical values to be assigned to each factor and to the manner in which a final score is generated by the computerized tool. Given that the appellants had repeatedly requested this information—and not solely the factors used to establish their security classification—it is disingenuous to suggest that the information was believed to be duplicative. This behaviour is highly objectionable. The Chambers judge was falsely led to believe that the scoring matrix was not available when, in fact, it was.

[112] The new evidence confirmed that the scoring matrix existed. The duty to disclose information used in making transfer decisions is substantial. Therefore, if the scores generated by the computerized tool played a role in the transfer decisions, its scoring matrix should have been disclosed. In fact, it does appear that the scores generated by the computerized tool played an important role. As a result, the transfer decisions were unlawful.

[113] An analysis of SOP directives reveals that inmates were presumptively reclassified through the use of the SRS. SOP 700-14 states that security reclassification shall be determined primarily by using the SRS (paras. 1-18). The SRS classification is only subject to variation in limited situations. Discretion is provided when the score in within 5 per cent of the sanctioned cut-off values: SRSFS, at pp. 9-10. In other cases, no discretion is allowed. The SRS classification may not be modified unless an override security classification is relied upon.

[114] The procedure applicable to the override classification confirms the presumptive nature of the SRS rather than invalidating it. SOP 700-14 makes it clear that the

override is not normally relied upon and requires a detailed justification for bypassing the SRS score:

> Normally, there will be no overrides above or below the rating produced by the Custody Rating Scale or the Security Reclassification Scale. Where the caseworker believes that it is necessary to override or underride the results of the Custody Rating Scale or the Security Reclassification Scale, he/she shall include a detailed justification in the *Assessment for Decision* in conformity with section 18 of the *Corrections and Conditional Release Regulations*, by setting out the analysis under the three headings of institutional adjustment, escape risk and risk to public safety. [para. 23]

[115] The override must also be approved by a supervisor or, in some cases, by the Assistant Commissioner, Correctional Operations and Programs (para. 25). It is noteworthy that the override function was not used in the instant cases. This suggests that the computer application ultimately fixed the security classification of each appellant.

[116] Based on the evidence, we cannot accept the respondents' argument that the SRS was only a preliminary assessment tool. Although it is true that an individual assessment of each inmate's security classification is made subsequently to the SRS assessment, in our view, the SRS presumptively classifies inmates and constitutes an important aspect of the classification process.

[117] Considering the nature of the scoring matrix and its role in the SRS, its non-disclosure constituted a major breach of the duty to disclose inherent in the requirement of procedural fairness. The appellants were deprived of information essential to understanding the computerized system which generated their scores. The appellants were not given the formula used to weigh the factors or the documents used for scoring questions and answers. The appellants knew what the factors were, but did not know how values were assigned to them or how those values factored into the generation of the final score.

[118] How can there be a meaningful response to a reclassification decision without information explaining how the security rating is determined? As a matter of logic and common sense, the scoring tabulation and methodology associated with the SRS classification score should have been made available. The importance of making that information available stems from the fact that inmates may want to rebut the evidence relied upon for the calculation of the SRS score and security classification. This information may be critical in circumstances where a security classification depends on the weight attributed to one specific factor.

[119] Hence, given the importance of the information contained in the scoring matrix, the presumptive validity of the score and its potential effect on the determination of security classification, it should have been disclosed. The respondents had a duty to do so under s. 27(1) of the *CCRA*.

[120] In conclusion, the respondents failed to disclose all the relevant information or a summary of the information used in making the transfer decisions despite several requests by the appellants. The respondents concealed crucial information. In doing so, they violated their statutory duty. The transfer decisions were made improperly and, therefore, they are null and void for want of jurisdiction. It follows that the appellants were unlawfully deprived of their liberty.

V. Conclusion

[121] For the foregoing reasons, the appeal should be allowed. The applications for *habeas corpus* and the motion to adduce new evidence are granted. The transfer decisions are declared null and void for want of jurisdiction. The appellant still incarcerated in a medium-security institution pursuant to the impugned decision is thus to be returned to minimum-security institutions.

[While the Court was unanimous on the *habeas corpus* issue, it split on the breach-of-fairness question and the appellants' entitlement to a remedy. For the dissenters (Major, Bastarache, and Charron JJ), Justice Charron wrote:]

[122] I have considered the reasons of LeBel and Fish JJ and agree that the Supreme Court of British Columbia has properly exercised its *habeas corpus* jurisdiction in this matter. I also agree with their analysis on the limited circumstances in which a superior court should decline to exercise its jurisdiction in *habeas corpus* matters. However, I do not agree with their conclusion that the appellants have been unlawfully deprived of their liberty and therefore I would not interfere with the Chambers judge's dismissal of their applications for *habeas corpus*.

. . .

[125] On the procedural fairness issue, my colleagues aptly reject the appellants' contention that *Stinchcombe* disclosure requirements apply (*R v. Stinchcombe*, [1991] 3 SCR 326). They describe the applicable statutory duty of disclosure in this administrative context. I agree with this analysis. I also agree in the circumstances of these cases that the "scoring matrix," utilized to compute the SRS score, should have been disclosed to the appellants. However, I respectfully disagree with my colleagues' conclusion that the failure to provide this information constituted a breach of statutory duty rendering the transfer decisions null and void for want of jurisdiction. It is not every instance of non-disclosure that deprives the decision-maker of its jurisdiction. As I will explain, in these cases, each appellant was provided with sufficient information to know the case he had to meet. Hence, procedural fairness was achieved. On the motion to introduce the scoring matrix as fresh evidence, I conclude that the evidence would have had no impact on the dismissal of the *habeas corpus* applications. Hence, I would dismiss the motion and the appeal.

[Analysis omitted]

NOTE

There is a curious aspect to this reversal by the Supreme Court of what had quickly become a national trend to encourage, or at least condone, decisions by Superior Court judges not to hear *habeas corpus* applications brought by penitentiary prisoners. In *May v. Ferndale*, the underlying decision of the BC Court of Appeal favouring a deferral to the Federal Court relied heavily on the judgment of the Ontario Court of Appeal in *Spindler v. Warden of Millhaven Institution*. If you look at the ruling in *Spindler*, you will see that Justice Charron, while a member of the Ontario Court of Appeal, concurred in that decision. To her credit, she brought an open mind to the issue when both she and it reached Ottawa.

C. The Timing of Habeas Corpus

Another Supreme Court of Canada decision brought a pragmatic examination of the issue of timing. Historically, it had been accepted that one could not use *habeas corpus* to challenge a form of confinement until that confinement had begun—that is, the remedy was not available until the alleged illegal custody had in fact started. This made some practical sense because the jailer's return to a *habeas corpus* application was usually the warrant of committal, and this generally accompanied the prisoner. But, beyond this practical point, is there any reason to deny *habeas corpus* in a situation where the allegedly illegal custody is certain and imminent?

Idziak v. Minister of Justice, [1992] 3 SCR 631, 17 CR (4th) 161, was an extradition case. The minister's decision to surrender Idziak was challenged on s. 7 Charter grounds. Counsel for the government of Canada, on behalf of the requesting state, argued that *habeas corpus* could not be used to attack the warrant of committal because it had not yet been executed. The Supreme Court held that there would be no point in forcing a person to wait until after he or she had been extradited and subjected to the impugned confinement before he or she could bring *habeas corpus* to challenge it. As long as the future confinement was not speculative, *habeas corpus* was an appropriate remedy to seek. The existence of the warrant that would result in a loss of residual liberty was sufficient.

The ruling in *Idziak* became important in a totally unrelated context. After the Arbour Inquiry into the Prison for Women, the Correctional Service followed its plan to close the Prison for Women (P4W) in favour of smaller, regional facilities. Unfortunately, the Edmonton institution was opened prematurely, and incidents, such as walkaways and a homicide, resulted. Consequently, the commissioner announced the policy that no maximum-security women prisoners would be transferred to the new facilities. But where would they go? In the Prairies and the Maritimes, any women already in the new facilities who were classified as maximum security were transferred to nearby men's institutions, and housed there in separate units. A handful of women prisoners were kept at the P4W, pending its closure. In the spring of 1997, it was announced that the P4W was finally being closed and the remaining women would be moved to a range at Kingston Penitentiary, a male maximum-security institution, which had been painted pink and was being prepared for them. Although the actual date of the transfer was kept secret for security reasons, every prisoner was given written notice that the transfer would take place within the next few weeks. The prisoners, with the support of the Canadian Association of Elizabeth Fry Societies, commenced a *habeas corpus* application challenging the legality of their transfer to a male institution. The challenge raised a number of s. 15 Charter arguments and was supported by volumes of social science and expert opinion about the distinct nature of women's confinement and the confinement of Aboriginal women, in particular. On the first appearance in court, counsel for the prisoners argued that an order should issue prohibiting the imminent transfer until the legailty of the confinement issue had been resolved. The Correctional Service argued that the *habeas corpus* application was premature until the prisoners had been transferred and any legal questions should be raised by judicial review in the Federal Court. The presiding judge rejected this position and ordered that the prisoners not be transferred until the s. 15 challenge had been resolved. (Clearly, if the transfer had gone ahead, P4W would have immediately ceased to exist as a penitentiary, and it would have been impossible to return the prisoners to that form of confinement.) The presiding judge also decided that the case raised difficult factual issues and that it should proceed as a trial and not as an application. The Correctional Service appealed this interlocutory ruling to the Ontario Court of Appeal. The appeal was heard on December 12, 1997, a few weeks before the trial was set to begin. The right to seek *habeas corpus* prior to the transfer was confirmed in a brief oral judgment.

Beaudry et al. v. Commissioner of Corrections, Warden of Prison for Women and Warden of Kingston Penitentiary
[1997] OJ No. 5082 (QL) (CA)

BROOKE, ROBINS, and MOLDAVER JJA: Applying the rationale of the decisions of the Supreme Court of Canada in *Miller v. The Queen, Gamble v. The Queen*, and *Idziak v. Canada (Minister of Justice)*, we are of the opinion that the judge below did not err in holding that the applicants, that is the respondents in this appeal, are entitled to seek relief by way of *habeas corpus* even though they are not yet in the Regional Treatment Centre.

We make no decision as to the remedies, if any, that may be available to the applicants and leave such issues to the trial of this matter which we are advised is scheduled to proceed on January 5, 1998.

The appeal is dismissed.

NOTE

A few days after the Court of Appeal decision, above, the matter ended without trial in a consent judgment that provided that the prisoners would not be sent to Kingston Penitentiary. In 2000, the P4W was finally closed.

V. PAROLE DECISIONS AND THE CHARTER

As demonstrated in *Cunningham*, chapter 18, and in *Steele*, above, parole decisions implicate a prisoner's liberty interest and can raise issues under ss. 7, 9, and 12 of the Charter. However, in such cases the question will be for the court to scrutinize whether the National Parole Board has respected or violated the prisoner's Charter rights. A different question is whether the National Parole Board is empowered to scrutinize whether another state agency had respected a prisoner's Charter rights. In other words, can a prisoner argue that material placed in front of the National Parole Board not be considered because it was obtained in violation of the prisoner's rights?

The majority and minority decisions in *Mooring*, below, reflect two very different perspectives on the decision-making role of the National Parole Board. It is also significant to note that the Supreme Court did not comment on the propriety of using *habeas corpus* to raise this issue.

Mooring v. Canada (National Parole Board)
[1996] 1 SCR 75, 104 CCC (3d) 97

[Mooring was on mandatory supervision when he was arrested and charged with various offences arising from the police seizure of a stolen gun and what could have been housebreaking equipment from his van. These charges were stayed, apparently because Crown counsel believed that the search of the applicant's van violated the Charter and that evidence concerning the search would not be admissible at trial. However, the National Parole Board revoked Mooring's mandatory supervision, relying upon this evidence. Mooring's *habeas corpus* application was dismissed. The judge held that the Parole Board was entitled to take into account evidence that may have been obtained in violation of the Charter. This was reversed on appeal to the BC Court of Appeal. The majority held that the Parole Board was a court of competent jurisdiction within the meaning of s. 24 of the Charter, with the ability to exclude evidence where such evidence was obtained by a Charter violation. The board appealed to the Supreme Court.]

SOPINKA J (L'Heureux-Dubé, Gonthier, Cory, and Iacobucci JJ concurring): ... [9] This appeal concerns the National Parole Board's decision to revoke the respondent's parole based in part on evidence gathered in a manner that may have violated the respondent's constitutional rights. Specifically, the court must determine whether or not the board is a "court of competent jurisdiction" for the purpose of making an order excluding evidence under s. 24(2) of the *Canadian Charter of Rights and Freedoms*. If the board is not a court of competent jurisdiction, the court must determine what practice the board should follow when faced with information that has been gathered in a manner that would be excluded by a court of competent jurisdiction.

· · ·

A. Is the National Parole Board a "Court of Competent Jurisdiction"?

[21] In my view, the National Parole Board is not a court of competent jurisdiction within the meaning of s. 24 of the *Charter*. I have arrived at this conclusion based on a review of previous decisions of this court, as well as on an examination of the basic structure and function of the Parole Board.

[22] Previous decisions of this court have considered the definition of the phrase "court of competent jurisdiction" in s. 24 of the *Charter*. In *Mills v. The Queen*, [1986] 1 SCR 863, for example, the court was faced with the issue of whether or not a preliminary inquiry judge was a court of competent jurisdiction within the meaning of s. 24. Although Lamer J (as he then was) disagreed with the majority on the final disposition of that case, a majority of the court accepted Lamer J's definition of a "court of competent jurisdiction" (at p. 890):

A court of competent jurisdiction in an extant case is a court that has jurisdiction over the person, the subject-matter and has, under the criminal or penal law, jurisdiction to grant the remedy.

Subsequent decisions of this court have reaffirmed the three-tiered test of *Mills*: see, for example, *Cuddy Chicks Ltd. v. Ontario (Labour Relations Board)* (1991), 81 DLR (4th) 121, [1991] 2 SCR 5, 50 Admin. LR 44, and *Tetreault-Gadoury v. Canada (Employment and Immigration Commission)* (1991), 81 DLR (4th) 358, [1991] 2 SCR 22, 50 Admin. LR 1. In each case it was held that a court or tribunal will only be a "court of competent jurisdiction" where the body in question has jurisdiction over the parties, the subject-matter, and the remedy sought by the complainant.

[23] Most recently, this court applied the three-tiered test of *Mills* in *Weber v. Ontario Hydro*, [1995] 2 SCR 929. Writing for a majority of the court, McLachlin J made the following observations (at pp. 962-63):

It is thus Parliament or the legislature that determines if a court is a court of competent jurisdiction; as McIntyre J puts it [in *Mills*], the jurisdiction of the various courts of Canada is fixed by Parliament and the legislatures, not by judges. Nor is there magic in labels; it is not the name of the tribunal that determines the matter, but its powers. (It may be noted that the French version of s. 24(1) uses *tribunal* rather than *cour*.) The practical import of fitting *Charter* remedies into the existing system of tribunals, as McIntyre J notes, is that litigants have "direct" access to *Charter* remedies in the tribunal charged with deciding their case.

It follows from *Mills* that statutory tribunals created by Parliament or the legislatures may be courts of competent jurisdiction to grant *Charter* remedies, provided they have jurisdiction over the parties and the subject-matter of the dispute and *are empowered to make the orders sought*. [Emphasis added.]

Clearly then, decisions of this court have established that jurisdiction over the parties, the subject-matter and the remedy are necessary conditions for a statutory tribunal to be considered a court of competent jurisdiction within the meaning of s. 24.

[24] Even assuming that the Parole Board has jurisdiction over the parties and the subject-matter, I am satisfied, on the basis of (i) the structure and function of the board, and (ii) the language of the board's constituting statute, that it is not empowered to make the order sought.

[25] The Parole Board acts in neither a judicial nor a quasi-judicial manner: *Mitchell v. The Queen*, [1976] 2 SCR 570, at p. 593. The elements of a parole hearing are described by David Cole and Allan Manson in *Release from Imprisonment* (Toronto: Carswell, 1990). The authors point out that several elements of the hearing distinguish Parole Board proceedings from those which take place before a traditional court. For example, counsel appearing before the Parole Board serve an extremely limited function. According to Cole and Manson (at p. 428):

Although counsel is present as an advocate, since the hearing is inquisitorial there is no one against whom counsel can act as an adversary. Indeed, counsel should recall throughout that as far as the Board is concerned, the only occasion on which he may speak, as outlined in the Regulation, is at the end of the hearing when he is given an opportunity to address the Board on behalf of the client.

In addition, the traditional rules of proof and evidence do not apply in post-suspension proceedings before the board. As Cole and Manson point out (at p. 431):

> While the Board will consider legal defences or mitigating circumstances where a new charge has been laid, in the post-suspension hearing context Board members do not regard themselves as constrained by the formal rules of the criminal law respecting the admissibility of evidence, the presumption of innocence, or the necessity for proof beyond a reasonable doubt.

Other differences between parole hearings and more traditional court proceedings include (1) the board lacks the power to issue subpoenas, (2) "evidence" is not presented under oath, and (3) the panel presiding over the hearing may have no legal training.

[26] In the decision currently under review, the appeal division of the board described its function in the following terms:

> The function of the Board at a post-suspension review is quite distinct from that of the courts. The Board must decide whether the risk to society of [the respondent's] continued conditional release is undue. In making that determination, the Board will review all information available to it, including any information indicating a return to criminal activity in the community. This applies whether or not the charges in court have been withdrawn, stayed or dismissed.

Clearly then, the Parole Board does not hear and assess evidence, but instead acts on information. The Parole Board acts in an inquisitorial capacity without contending parties—the state's interests are not represented by counsel, and the parolee is not faced with a formal "case to meet." From a practical perspective, neither the board itself nor the proceedings in which it engages have been designed to engage in the balancing of factors that s. 24(2) demands.

[27] In the risk assessment function of the board, the factors which predominate are those which concern the protection of society. The protection of the accused to ensure a fair trial and maintain the repute of the administration of justice which weighs so heavily in the application of s. 24(2) is overborne by the overriding societal interest. In assessing the risk to society, the emphasis is on ensuring that all reliable information is considered provided it has not been obtained improperly. As stated by Dickson J, as he then was, in *R v. Gardiner*, [1982] 2 SCR 368, in relation to sentencing proceedings:

> One of the hardest tasks confronting a trial judge is sentencing. The stakes are high for society and for the individual. Sentencing is the critical stage of the criminal justice system, and it is manifest that the judge should not be denied an opportunity to obtain relevant information by the imposition of all the restrictive evidentiary rules common to a trial. Yet the obtaining and weighing of such evidence should be fair. A substantial liberty interest of the offender is involved and the information obtained should be accurate and reliable.

[28] These principles apply *a fortiori* to proceedings before the Parole Board in which the subject has already been tried, convicted and sentenced. As stated by the Supreme Court of the United States in *Morrissey v. Brewer*, 408 US 471 (1972), at p. 489:

We emphasize there is no thought to equate this second stage of parole revocation to a criminal prosecution in any sense. It is a narrow inquiry; the process should be flexible enough to consider evidence including letters, affidavits, and other material that would not be admissible in an adversary criminal trial.

[29] Like the basic structure and function of the Parole Board, the language of the board's enabling statute makes it clear that the board lacks the ability or jurisdiction to exclude relevant evidence. The language of the *Corrections and Conditional Release Act* confers on the board a broad inclusionary mandate. Not only is it not bound to apply the traditional rules of evidence, but it is required to take into account "all available information that is relevant to a case." No mention is made of any power to apply exclusionary rules of evidence. Indeed, such a provision would conflict with its duty to consider "*all* available information that is relevant."

[30] I conclude from the foregoing that the board does not have jurisdiction over the remedy sought. It is not, therefore, a court of competent jurisdiction within the meaning of s. 24 of the *Charter*.

[31] I am supported in this conclusion by the decisions of the US circuit courts. The US Supreme Court has not specifically dealt with the applicability of the exclusionary rule to parole proceedings, although the logical extension of the statement in *Morrissey* to which I refer above would suggest that the rule does not apply. The issue has been dealt with by 10 of the federal circuit courts. Except for the Fourth Circuit, all have held the rule inapplicable. In the Fourth Circuit, which is the exception, the Court of Appeals refused to apply the exclusionary rule in state probation proceedings: see *Grimsley v. Dodson*, 696 F2d 303 (1982). One circuit, the Second Circuit, admits of an exception in the case of warrantless searches.

[32] In *United States v. Winsett*, 518 F2d 51 (9th Cir. 1975), it was held that a board's mandate to consider "all reliable evidence" was inconsistent with allowing the board to exclude relevant evidence. The statement in *Pratt v. United States Parole Commission*, 717 F Supp. 382 (EDNC 1989), is typical of the reasoning in these cases (at p. 387):

> ... this parole revocation proceeding is a far cry from a full blown criminal prosecution. Constitutional protections vindicated by the exclusionary rule do not apply with full force in the minimum due process environment of the parole revocation hearing. Societal costs thought worthy of paying for the operation [of] the rule have already been exacted. Nothing is served by exacting that full measure of costs a second time. The very special needs of supervision ... would be sacrificed if parole authorities were prohibited from weighing the full extent of petitioner's conduct by reason of the exclusionary rule. The parole revocation decision must meet the preponderance of proof standard ... after those tenets of minimum due process have been followed. Nowhere does the beyond-a-reasonable-doubt burden apply. The right to a trial by jury does not apply. The parolee does not even enjoy the right to a judicial decision maker. Neither, in my view, does a parolee have the right to insist on strict adherence to fourth amendment standards. And, for the reasons set out above, in my view the exclusionary rule does not apply either.

See also *United States ex rel. Sperling v. Fitzpatrick*, 426 F2d 1161 (2d Cir. 1970), and *United States v. Bazzano*, 712 F2d 826 (3d Cir. 1983). In each case, the courts have held that policy considerations favour denying parole or probation boards the authority to exclude relevant information. In my view, many of these policy considerations are equally relevant in the Canadian context. As a result, I conclude that the Parole Board is not a court of competent jurisdiction for the purposes of excluding relevant evidence under s. 24(2) of the *Charter*.

B. Procedures Where Evidence Is Gathered Improperly

[33] Having found that the National Parole Board is *not* a court of competent jurisdiction within the meaning of s. 24 of the *Charter*, it remains to be determined what procedures the board must follow when faced with evidence that has been gathered in a manner violating the rights of the parolee.

[34] The law is well settled that statutory tribunals such as the Parole Board are bound by a duty of fairness in deciding upon the rights or privileges of individuals. For example, in *Cardinal v. Director of Kent Institution*, [1985] 2 SCR 643, it was held that a prison director was required to act fairly in determining whether or not to segregate a prisoner from the rest of the prison population. Writing for a unanimous court, Le Dain J held (at p. 653) that:

> This Court has affirmed that there is, as a general common law principle, a duty of procedural fairness lying on every public authority making an administrative decision which is not of a legislative nature and which affects the rights, privileges or interests of an individual: *Re Nicholson and Haldimand-Norfolk Regional Board of Com'rs of Police*, [1979] 1 SCR 311; *Martineau v. Matsqui Institution Disciplinary Board (No. 2)*, [1980] 1 SCR 602; *A-G Can. v. Inuit Tapirisat of Canada et al.*, [1980] 2 SCR 735.

Clearly, the Parole Board's decision to revoke a parolee's conditional release has a profound effect on the rights of the parolee. The board's decision will conclusively determine whether the applicant is released into the community or retained in the confines of a prison or penitentiary. As a result, in making that decision to grant or revoke parole, the board is required to act fairly.

[35] The duty of the Parole Board to act fairly can also be found in the board's constituting statute, the *Corrections and Conditional Release Act*. For example, s. 4(g) of that Act provides that all correctional decisions must be "made in a forthright and fair manner, with access by the offender to an effective grievance procedure." Similarly, s. 101(f) of the Act provides that the Parole Board must pursue a "fair and understandable conditional release process." Finally, s. 147(1)(a) of the Act provides that an appeal of the board's decision lies in all cases where the board "failed to observe a principle of fundamental justice." Clearly, these provisions impose upon the board a duty to act in accordance with the principles of fairness.

[36] What is the content of the board's "duty to act fairly"? The content of the duty of fairness varies according to the structure and the function of the board or tribunal in question. In the parole context, the Parole Board must ensure that the information upon which it acts is reliable and persuasive. To take an extreme example, information extracted by torture could not be considered reliable by the board. It would be manifestly unfair for the board to act on this kind of information. As a result, the board would be

under a duty to exclude such information, whether or not the information was relevant to the decision. Wherever information or "evidence" is presented to the board, the board must make a determination concerning the source of that information, and decide whether or not it would be fair to allow the information to affect the board's decision.

[37] In determining whether or not it would be fair to consider a particular piece of information, the board will often be guided by decisions of the courts regarding the exclusion of relevant evidence. For instance, where incriminating statements are obtained from the offender, the law of confessions based on an admixture of reliability and fairness will be pertinent although not binding. The board may, in appropriate circumstances, conclude that reliance on a coerced confession is unfair. Decisions concerning s. 24(2) of the *Charter* will also be relevant to the board's final decision. However, cases decided under s. 24(2) should not be determinative of the board's decision to exclude relevant information based on the principles of fairness. Obviously, different considerations will often apply in the parole context. For example, s. 101(a) of the *Corrections and Conditional Release Act* requires "that the protection of society be the paramount consideration in the determination of any case." This will accordingly be a guiding principle where the board is required to rule on the admissibility of a particular piece of information. The board's expertise and experience concerning the protection of society will aid the board in arriving at a decision. Should the board fail to abide by the principles of fairness in making those decisions, an appeal lies to the appeal division under s. 147(1)(a) of the *Corrections and Conditional Release Act*. The board's decision is also subject to judicial review.

[38] As a statutory tribunal, the board is also subject to the dictates of s. 7 of the *Charter*. In this regard, it must comply with the principles of fundamental justice in respect to the conduct of its proceedings. This does not mean that it must possess or exercise a power to exclude evidence that has been obtained in a manner that contravenes the *Charter*. If this were so, it would tend to make the inclusion of s. 24(2) of the *Charter* superfluous. While the principles of fundamental justice are not limited to procedural justice, it does not follow that a tribunal that applies the rules of fairness and natural justice does not comply with s. 7. If the myriad of statutory tribunals that have traditionally been obliged to accord nothing more than procedural fairness were obliged to comply with the full gamut of principles of fundamental justice, the administrative landscape in the country would undergo a fundamental change. The statement in *Reference re: Section 94(2) of the Motor Vehicle Act*, [1985] 2 SCR 486, to the effect that the principles of fundamental justice involve more than natural justice meant that the court was empowered in appropriate circumstances to invalidate substantive law and was not limited to judicial review of the procedural practices of a statutory body.

[39] It is a basic tenet of our legal system that the rules of natural justice and procedural fairness are adjusted by reference to the context in which they are administered. This is one of the basic tenets of our legal system to which Lamer J (as he then was) referred in *Reference re: Section 94(2) of the Motor Vehicle Act* as the source of the principles of fundamental justice. In my opinion, adherence by the board to the practice and procedures outlined above constitutes full compliance with the principles of fundamental justice and, therefore, with s. 7 of the *Charter*.

C. Disposition

[40] I would allow this appeal on the ground that the National Parole Board is not a court of competent jurisdiction. I would accordingly set aside the judgment of the British Columbia Court of Appeal. Ordinarily, I would remit the respondent's case to the Parole Board, to be dealt with in accordance with these reasons. However, since the respondent's sentence has already expired, the Parole Board is *functus officio*.

MAJOR J (McLachlin J concurring, dissenting):

I. Introduction

... [42] I have read the reasons of my colleague Justice Sopinka which set out the facts and statutory provisions relevant to this appeal. With respect, I do not agree with his conclusion that the National Parole Board lacks the jurisdiction under s. 24(2) to exclude evidence which has been obtained in a manner that infringes *Charter* rights. Nor do I agree that more than a decade after the introduction of the *Charter*, the application of the common law doctrine of procedural fairness by the Parole Board is sufficient to protect the constitutional rights of parolees.

[43] In my view, the National Parole Board is a "court of competent jurisdiction" within the meaning of s. 24 of the *Charter*. I have reached this conclusion based on an examination of the previous decisions of this court, the statutory provisions which govern the Parole Board and the application of basic *Charter* principles.

[44] As a "court of competent jurisdiction" for the purposes of granting an exclusionary remedy under s. 24(2), the National Parole Board can determine whether to exclude from its consideration information which was obtained in contravention of *Charter* rights where the admission of such evidence would bring the administration of justice into disrepute. As a result, in a parole determination or revocation hearing, the parolee has a direct opportunity to raise a breach of *Charter* rights and to seek an effective remedy.

[45] The National Parole Board has the jurisdiction and the responsibility to consider whether a breach of *Charter* rights has occurred according to the legal tests established in the jurisprudence of this court for determining violations of these rights.

[46] The National Parole Board must then determine, under s. 24(2), whether the admission of the evidence in a parole granting or revocation hearing would bring the administration of justice into disrepute. In the context of the National Parole Board, the administration of justice means the administration of the parole process.

[47] Although the National Parole Board has the jurisdiction to exclude evidence, it also has a mandate to admit a broad range of evidence in keeping with its paramount goal of protecting the public from recidivist offenders. In light of its legislated mandate, it will be an unusual case where the National Parole Board will exclude evidence under the s. 24(2) test of bringing the administration of the parole process into disrepute.

• • •

[52] I agree with this description of *Charter* rights and the role of s. 24 in guaranteeing that *Charter* rights are actually enforced. If the *Charter* is to remain a "vibrant and

vigorous instrument for the protection of the rights and freedoms of Canadians" there must be an effective remedy where there has been a violation.

[53] Following *Mills*, a trilogy of cases determined that where the enabling statute grants the power to determine questions of law, an administrative tribunal has the power and responsibility not to apply provisions of that enabling statute which are incompatible with the *Charter*: *Douglas/Kwantlen Faculty Assn. v. Douglas College*, [1990] 3 SCR 570; *Cuddy Chicks Ltd. v. Ontario (Labour Relations Board*, [1991] 2 SCR 5; *Tetreault-Gadoury v. Canada (Employment and Immigration Commission)*, [1991] 2 SCR 22. In these cases the court affirmed the correctness of the three-pronged test enunciated by Lamer J in *Mills* for determining a "court of competent jurisdiction": jurisdiction over the parties, the subject-matter and the remedy sought by the complainant. It was not necessary, however, to determine whether the tribunals in question were courts of competent jurisdiction under s. 24 of the *Charter*. The power and responsibility not to apply statutory provisions which are unconstitutional was found to flow from s. 52(1) of the *Constitution Act, 1982*, which declares every law which is inconsistent with the *Charter* to be of no effect.

[54] Of particular relevance to this appeal are the comments of La Forest J, who wrote the majority judgment in each of the trilogy of cases, about the advantages of having constitutional issues determined by an administrative tribunal. This question is discussed in detail in *Douglas/Kwantlen Faculty Assn. v. Douglas College*. At pp. 603-4, La Forest J notes that the primary advantage of having tribunals determine constitutional questions is to ensure that a citizen can rely on *Charter* guarantees when the tribunal is in a position to determine the rights of that citizen:

> ... [I]f there are disadvantages to allowing arbitrators or other administrative tribunals to determine constitutional issues arising in the course of exercising their mandates, there are clear advantages as well. *First and foremost, of course, is that the Constitution must be respected. The citizen, when appearing before decision-making bodies set up to determine his or her rights and duties, should be entitled to assert the rights and freedoms guaranteed by the Constitution.* [Emphasis added.]

[55] In *R v. Seaboyer*, [1991] 2 SCR 577, McLachlin J noted that it is this right of a Canadian citizen to rely on *Charter* guarantees when there is a final determination of "rights and duties" which helps to explain why the arbitrator in *Douglas College* was held to be able to determine constitutional questions but the preliminary inquiry judge in *Mills* was not:

> The position of a judge or magistrate on a preliminary inquiry is readily distinguished from the position of the arbitrator in *Douglas College*. The legislation governing the arbitrator in that case conferred on him wide powers to decide both questions of fact and law and to finally resolve the dispute between the parties. That task could not be achieved without deciding the *Charter* issue. As La Forest J put it in *Douglas College*, at p. 604: "The citizen, when appearing before decision-making bodies set up to determine his or her rights and duties, should be entitled to assert the rights and freedoms guaranteed by the Constitution." The contrary is true for a judge on a preliminary inquiry, whose only task is to determine whether prosecution in other proceedings is warranted. The rights of

the accused need not and should not be resolved at this initial stage. The lack of power in a preliminary inquiry judge to decide constitutional questions does not prevent an accused from asserting his or her *Charter* rights; it merely defers the process until the accused is before the decision-making body charged with the task of fully determining the accused's "rights and duties"—the trial court.

Thus, the decisions in the trilogy of cases are consistent with the principle enunciated by Lamer J in *Mills* that where there is a *Charter* right there must also be a *Charter* remedy.

[56] In *Douglas College*, La Forest J also noted a number of other advantages which flow from allowing tribunals to determine constitutional questions. By raising *Charter* issues before the tribunal, the *Charter* issue can be dealt with in the context in which it arises without necessitating duplicate, expensive and time-consuming application to a court. A specialized tribunal in reaching its decision sifts the facts and compiles a record for the benefit of a reviewing court. Also the expertise and specialized competence of the tribunal can be of invaluable assistance in constitutional interpretation in order to ensure the primacy of the Constitution.

[57] In the recent case of *Weber v. Ontario Hydro*, [1995] 2 SCR 929, this court addressed the question of whether an administrative tribunal could be a court of competent jurisdiction for the purposes of granting a remedy under s. 24 of the *Charter*. The issue in that case was whether a labour arbitrator had the jurisdiction to award damages under s. 24 of the *Charter* for surveillance by the employer which allegedly breached the rights guaranteed by ss. 7 and 8. The majority held that a labour tribunal is a court of competent jurisdiction for the purpose of granting damages pursuant to s. 24.

[58] In holding that a labour tribunal is a court of competent jurisdiction, McLachlin J for the majority applied the three-pronged test for the definition of a court of competent jurisdiction established in *Mills* and relied on the advantages of having tribunals decide constitutional issues which are set out in *Douglas College*. McLachlin J noted that the question of whether a tribunal is a court of competent jurisdiction is answered by examining the enabling statute since it is Parliament and not judges who establish jurisdiction. She also held that there is no magic in labels and that the fact that a body is labelled a "tribunal" rather than a "court" is not determinative. At pp. 962-63, she concluded:

> It is thus Parliament or the legislature that determines if a court is a court of competent jurisdiction; as McIntyre J puts it, the jurisdiction of the various courts of Canada is fixed by Parliament and the legislatures, not by judges. Nor is there magic in labels; it is not the name of the tribunal that determines the matter, but its powers. (It may be noted that the French version of s. 24(1) uses *tribunal* rather than *cour*.) The practical import of fitting *Charter* remedies into the existing system of tribunals, as McIntyre J notes, is that litigants have "direct" access to *Charter* remedies in the tribunal charged with deciding their case.

> It follows from *Mills* that statutory tribunals created by Parliament or the legislatures may be courts of competent jurisdiction to grant *Charter* remedies, provided they have jurisdiction over the parties and the subject-matter of the dispute and are empowered to make the orders sought.

[59] It is also important to note that the majority of the court in *Weber* rejected the argument that only a court of law in the traditional sense with legally trained judges should be regarded as a court of competent jurisdiction. Iacobucci J, in dissent, summarized the view which was not accepted at p. 942:

> In short, the choice of the word "court" in s. 24(1) reflects an intention to confer the ability to decide questions of remedies for *Charter* violations on those institutions which are conceptually "courts." It is the characteristics of a "court": the rules of procedure and evidence, the independence and legal training of its judges, the possibility of hearing from a third party intervener such as an Attorney General or an *amicus curiae*, which make it the most suitable forum to hear a s. 24(1) application.

[60] In my opinion, the recent decision of this court in *Weber* is correct and is consistent with earlier case law. While the trilogy of tribunal cases did not decide the issue of whether tribunals are courts of competent jurisdiction for the purposes of s. 24, it did decide that where a tribunal has the power to consider questions of law, it can and must also make determinations about the constitutional validity of the provisions of its enabling statute. In those cases this court clearly rejected the view that the lack of legal training on the part of tribunal members precludes them from making constitutional determinations. As La Forest J noted in *Cuddy Chicks*, at pp. 16-17:

> It must be emphasized that the process of *Charter* decision-making is not confined to abstract ruminations on constitutional theory. In the case of *Charter* matters which arise in a particular regulatory context, the ability of the decision-maker to analyze competing policy concerns is critical. Therefore, while board members need not have formal legal training, it remains that they have a very meaningful role to play in the resolution of constitutional issues. The informed view of the board, as manifested in a sensitivity to relevant facts and an ability to compile a cogent record, is also of invaluable assistance.

[61] The considerations which animated this court's decisions in the trilogy of tribunal cases apply with equal force when considering whether a tribunal has the jurisdiction to grant *Charter* remedies under s. 24. Of primary importance is the ability of the citizen to rely upon and assert *Charter* rights in a direct manner in the normal procedural context in which the issue arises.

[62] It is also axiomatic to the earlier case law that in order to protect the vibrancy and vigour of *Charter* protections, the citizen must have access to a meaningful remedy for *Charter* violations where there is to be a final determination of his or her rights and duties.

[63] Given that administrative tribunals, such as the Parole Board in this case, have jurisdiction to impose punitive sanctions, it would be an unusual result if they lacked the ability to grant individuals *Charter* remedies, not at large but within the parameters of their legislated jurisdiction.

[64] There is no reason in principle why any of the practical advantages enunciated by La Forest J in the trilogy should apply with any less force to a tribunal granting a remedy under s. 24 than to a tribunal declining to enforce a constitutionally invalid statutory provision. If anything, tailoring a specific *Charter* remedy for a specific applicant before a tribunal is more suited to a tribunal's special role in determining rights on a

case-by-case basis in the tribunal's area of expertise. It has less serious ramifications than determining that a statutory provision will not be applied on *Charter* grounds.

• • •

[70] Sopinka J concludes that even assuming the Parole Board has jurisdiction over the parties and the subject-matter he is satisfied that the board is not empowered to make the order sought. By relying on factors such as the lack of an adversarial process, the lack of formal rules of evidence and the lack of legal training of Parole Board members he finds that the Parole Board is not a court of competent jurisdiction. My colleague resurrects the requirement that a "court of competent jurisdiction" must be a traditional court. The majority of the court in *Weber* rejected this view. Moreover, the factors relied on by Sopinka J have never been accepted as reasons for limiting a tribunal's power to determine constitutional issues.

[71] The *Weber* case is consistent with the prior case law of this court which holds that the test for a "court of competent jurisdiction" is to be determined by an examination of the statute to see whether the tribunal in question has been granted jurisdiction over the parties, the subject-matter and the remedy sought. It is therefore necessary to turn to an examination of the statute which governs the National Parole Board to determine whether it meets this tripartite test.

[72] It is indisputable that the National Parole Board has jurisdiction over the party and the subject-matter. The party is an offender eligible for parole and the subject-matter is the granting or revocation of parole. Section 107(1) of the *Corrections and Conditional Release Act* grants the Parole Board the exclusive jurisdiction and absolute discretion to finally determine whether parole should be granted or revoked:

> 107(1) Subject to this Act, the *Prisons and Reformatories Act*, the *Transfer of Offenders Act* and the *Criminal Code*, the Board has exclusive jurisdiction and absolute discretion
>
> (a) to grant parole to an offender;
>
> (b) to terminate or to revoke the parole or statutory release of an offender, whether or not the offender is in custody under a warrant of apprehension issued as a result of the suspension of the parole or statutory release;
>
> (c) to cancel a decision to grant parole to an offender, or to cancel the suspension, termination or revocation of the parole or statutory release of an offender.

[73] The more difficult question on this appeal is whether the National Parole Board has been granted jurisdiction over the remedy sought. Some care should be taken to appropriately define the remedy sought by the respondent in this case.

[74] As Lambert JA pointed out in the reasons for the majority in the British Columbia Court of Appeal ((1994), 93 CCC (3d) 415), the test would not lead anywhere if the remedy was considered to be applying the *Charter* in order to exclude evidence at a parole hearing: that remains the question and not the answer. The majority of this court in *Weber* rejected the view that enabling legislation must expressly confer the jurisdiction to grant a *Charter* remedy before this stage of the test is met. Such an approach would require that any adjudicative bodies pre-existing the *Charter* would be barred from applying it unless their constituting statutes were amended. This view is clearly untenable and inconsistent with the result in *Mills*. Provincial courts are a ready

example of bodies entitled to grant *Charter* remedies without their constituting statutes being amended.

[75] On the other hand, I would respectfully reject the definition of remedy chosen by Lambert JA, who held (at p. 437) that "the remedy is the granting of parole." This approach defines the remedy at too great a level of abstraction and seems to mix the remedy and subject-matter. I accept the argument of the appellants that to define the remedy in this manner is tantamount to saying that every tribunal which can make an order of some nature has *Charter* jurisdiction.

[76] In my view, the correct approach lies between these two extremes. The remedy to be considered under the third stage of the *Mills* test is the specific remedy which the applicant seeks *under the Charter* for the breach of a *Charter* right. However, the question to be determined is not whether the legislation grants the jurisdiction to direct this remedy *under the Charter* but rather simply whether it grants the jurisdiction to grant this sort of remedy.

[77] For example, in *Mills* the remedy sought under the *Charter* was a stay of proceedings in order to remedy pre-trial delay. A preliminary inquiry judge is not a court of competent jurisdiction because he does not have the power under the *Criminal Code* to grant a stay of proceedings. On other hand, a trial judge has the jurisdiction to grant this sort of remedy and thus is a court of competent jurisdiction although there is no specific legislative authorization in the *Criminal Code* to grant *Charter* remedies. Likewise in *Weber*, a labour arbitration board was found to be a court of competent jurisdiction to award damages under s. 24(1) because an award of damages lies within the sphere of remedies that this kind of board is authorized to grant. A specific legislative jurisdiction to grant *Charter* damages was not required.

[78] In this case the respondent seeks to have evidence excluded under s. 24(2) of the *Charter*. The remedy sought is the exclusion of evidence. Therefore, the final stage in the application of the *Mills* test is whether the legislation which governs the National Parole Board either expressly or implicitly grants the jurisdiction to exclude evidence. In my view, it does.

[79] In deciding what information to consider in parole determination deliberations, the National Parole Board must strike a balance between the inclusion and the exclusion of information. Thus, although the board has the jurisdiction to exclude evidence on a limited number of grounds, it also has a broad inclusionary mandate. The board's statutory obligation to include a broader range of information than would be considered under the traditional rules of evidence is fully in keeping with its role of public protection and as a watchguard against recidivism by parolees.

[80] Section 101 provides that the National Parole Board should take into consideration all available information that is relevant to the case:

> 101. The principles that shall guide the Board and the provincial parole boards in achieving the purpose of conditional release are ...
>
> (b) that parole boards take into consideration all available information that is relevant to a case, including the stated reasons and recommendations of the sentencing judge, any other information from the trial or the sentencing hearing, information and assessments provided by correctional authorities, and information obtained from victims and the offender.

[81] In argument, the appellants emphasized the fact the statute uses the term "information" which is broader than the term "evidence" and my colleague relies on the fact that the board is not bound by formal rules of evidence. Neither of these considerations resolves the issue of whether the board is entitled to exclude evidence. Evidence is simply a subset of the term "information" and there may be exclusion beyond that provided for in formal evidentiary rules.

[82] In my opinion, the statute expressly contemplates a power to exclude information from its consideration since it restricts the board to a consideration of *relevant* information. In *Seaboyer*, at p. 609, McLachlin J held that it is a principle of fundamental justice that a finder of fact consider only what is relevant and, with limited exceptions, all that is relevant. She also noted that this relevancy principle underlies the formal rules of evidence:

> It is fundamental to our system of justice that the rules of evidence should permit the judge and jury to get at the truth and properly determine the issues. This goal is reflected in the basic tenet of relevance which underlies all our rules of evidence: see *Morris v. The Queen*, [1983] 2 SCR 190, and *R v. Corbett*, [1988] 1 SCR 670. In general, nothing is to be received which is not logically probative of some matter requiring to be proved and everything which is probative should be received, unless its exclusion can be justified on some other ground.

[83] The governing statute also requires that the board exclude evidence which it deems to be unreliable or inaccurate. Section 147(1)(d) of the *Corrections and Conditional Release Act* provides for an appeal of the board's decision to the appeal division on the ground that the board "based its decision on erroneous or incomplete information."

[84] As noted by Sopinka J the duty to not consider information which is unreliable or unpersuasive also arises from the common law doctrine of procedural fairness which applies to a statutory tribunal such as the Parole Board: see *Cardinal v. Director of Kent Institution*, [1985] 2 SCR 643, at 653. In *R v. Gardiner*, [1982] 2 SCR 368, at p. 414, Dickson J, as he then was, stated in relation to sentencing proceedings which, like parole hearings, involve a relaxation of formal evidentiary rules: "A substantial liberty interest of the offender is involved and the information obtained should be accurate and reliable."

[85] The governing statute contemplates that the board must exclude from its consideration any information which is irrelevant or which is unreliable. Thus, although it is not bound by formal evidentiary rules, the board is bound to observe the two guiding principles which inform the traditional rules of evidence: relevance and reliability. The statutory requirement that the board must exclude from its consideration information which is irrelevant or unreliable establishes that the board has jurisdiction to exclude evidence. Therefore, the board has jurisdiction over the remedy sought by the respondent in this case, and the third stage of the *Mills* test is met. ...

[86] The fact that the National Parole Board meets the three requirements of the *Mills* test is sufficient to establish that the board is a court of competent jurisdiction to grant a remedy under s. 24 of the *Charter*. It is worth noting that the governing statute also contemplates that the board must apply the *Charter*. Section 147(1) provides:

necessarily a gap in the Federal Court Rules for "… the direct and proper way to contest an originating notice of motion which the respondent thinks to be without merit is to appear and argue at the hearing of the motion itself" (page 52). While the Court of Appeal did not have to decide whether an originating notice of motion could be struck out, Mr. Justice Strayer commented: "This is not to say that there is no jurisdiction in this court either inherent or through rule 5 by analogy to other rules, to dismiss in summary manner a notice of motion which is so clearly improper as to be bereft of any possibility of success. (See e.g. *Cynamid Agricultural de Puerto Rico Inc. v. Commissioner of Patents* (1983), 74 CPR (2d) 133 (FCTD); and the discussion in *Vancouver Island Peace Society et al. v. Canada (Minister of National Defence) et al.*, [1994] 1 FC 102; 64 FTR 127, at 120-121 FC (TD)). Such cases must be very exceptional and cannot include cases such as the present where there is simply a debatable issue as to the adequacy of the allegations in the notice of motion." (pages 54 and 55)

In *Canadian Pasta Manufacturers' Association v. Aurora Importing & Distributing Ltd.*, an unreported 23 April 1997 decision in proceeding A-252-97, the Federal Court of Appeal struck out a judicial review proceeding with the words "we are all of opinion that this application for judicial review could not possibly succeed."

The test for striking out, from *David Bull Laboratories*, that an originating notice of motion must be "… so clearly improper as to be bereft of any possibility of success" is, if possible, an even more stringent test than is to be applied in striking out an action under Rule 419. To make a regular thing of interlocutory motions to strike out judicial review proceedings would be a waste of time and resources. But alternately, it would be an equally irresponsible waste of time and resources, paid for in a large part by the taxpayer, to allow a futile judicial review proceeding, which will not lead to any practical result, to proceed beyond a motion to strike out.

Here the Applicant submits he ought to be allowed to have parallel proceedings, an appeal under the *Corrections and Conditional Release Act* and this judicial review, primarily because the latter may be more convenient and expedient. But convenience and expedience are not the test. Nor is the test whether one forum is better than the other. I must ask myself whether a forum consisting of the Appeal Division of the Board, constituted under *Corrections and Conditional Release Act*, is an adequate forum: see *Canadian Pacific Ltd. v. Matsqui Indian Band* (1995), 26 Admin. LR (2d) 1 at 29 (SCC).

There is a recent case very much on point, a decision of Mr. Justice McKeown, in *Fehr v. The National Parole Board*, (1995) 93 FTR 161 and specifically his consideration of proceeding T-769-94, beginning at page 171 of the Fehr decision. In that instance Ms. Fehr, a penitentiary inmate whose day parole had been revoked on the ground that while free on parole she was an undue risk to society, had not exhausted all appeal procedures under the *Corrections and Conditional Release Act*, namely by first appealing to the Appeal Division of the Board.

Mr. Justice McKeown recognizes that the existence of an alternate statutory appeal remedy does not automatically preclude an application to the Court for *certiorari*, for it is at the discretion of the Court whether to hear such a case and here he refers to *Harelkin v. University of Regina*, [1979] 2 SCR 561. He concludes that the Applicant ought to have pursued an appeal to the Appeal Division of the Board before coming to the Court as the legislation setting up that appeal provided an adequate alternate remedy to *certiorari*. In the *Fehr* case the Applicant sought a review of the Parole Board's decision, together with *certiorari*, the same remedy sought in the present instance by Mr. Mackie.

Mr. Justice McKeown did qualify his reasoning to some degree by pointing out that, while the appeal route is to avoid a multiplicity of proceedings, an applicant still might have judicial review when the statutory remedy is not broad enough to cover all of the issues which are properly for appeal: "The purpose of having an appeal route is to avoid a multiplicity of proceedings before the court. As such, where an appeal route exists, it should, in general, be pursued to the extent that it may be, before seeking judicial review. I wish to make clear, however, that a decision may only be appealed to the extent provided for in the legislation. Judicial review may still be available for issues which may not be properly appealed" (page 171).

In the present instance the jurisdiction of the Appeal Board is broad. It is set out clearly in section 147(1) of the Act: "(1) An offender may appeal a decision of the Board to the Appeal Division on the ground that the Board, in making its decision, (a) failed to observe a principle of fundamental justice; (b) made an error of law; (c) breached or failed to apply a policy adopted pursuant to subsection 151(2); (d) based its decision on erroneous or incomplete information; or (e) acted without jurisdiction or beyond its jurisdiction, or failed to exercise its jurisdiction."

Mr. Mackie's grounds for appeal, set out in the motion for judicial review, may be summarized as an error on the part of the Board in law and in jurisdiction by applying legislation retrospectively and failing to observe the principles of natural justice and procedural fairness, all clearly within the Appeal Board's mandate.

The merits of the Applicant's case, which may well be substantial, are not at issue. Rather it is the adequacy of the Applicant's alternate remedy. Assessment of this alternate remedy is not a matter of working in a factual vacuum, which is sometimes the case in an interlocutory proceeding, for the issues and facts are clear. Mr. Mackie has a remedy by way of an appeal to the Appeal Division of the National Parole Board. The grounds of the appeal are clearly set out in his Originating Notice of Motion. The faults alleged on the part of the Board which initially heard his case are clearly within the statutory scope of the Appeal Board.

There is no prejudice to require the Applicant to complete the appeal, which he has begun, before the Appeal Board under the *Corrections and Conditional Release Act*, as a precondition to coming to this Court. He presently has a completely adequate remedy before the Appeal Board. It is an appeal to a specialized and expert Board. If that remedy is not as quick as might be the situation in the Federal Court, the likely difference in time to a hearing is marginal. I am reinforced in this view by the fact that not only has the Applicant this alternate remedy, but also he has in fact commenced that parallel remedial process. Mr. Mackie's situation is similar to that of the applicant in the *Fehr* decision, an application for *certiorari* and review in which there was an adequate alternative remedy of appeal to the same Appeal Board. This being the situation the present judicial review proceeding is futile. It is plain and obvious that it could not possibly succeed: it is so clearly improper to have and indeed to have subsequently commenced a parallel alternative remedy that this judicial review application is bereft of any chance of success. It is therefore struck out.

147(1) An offender may appeal a decision of the Board to the Appeal Division on the ground that the Board, in making its decision,

    (a) failed to observe a principle of fundamental justice;

    (b) made an error of law;

    (c) breached or failed to apply a policy adopted pursuant to subsection 151(2).

[87] The legislation requires that the Parole Board has to observe the principles of fundamental justice in making its decision. This echoes the wording of s. 7 of the *Charter*, which guarantees the right not to be deprived of liberty except in accordance with the principles of fundamental justice.

[88] It is appropriate that the Parole Board, which can substantially interfere with a liberty interest by granting, denying or revoking parole, should be required to apply the principles of fundamental justice. The principles of fundamental justice require more than the common law doctrine of procedural fairness relied on by Sopinka J.

[89] The legislation also permits review for errors of law, which implicitly recognizes that the board can determine issues of law. The capacity of a statutory tribunal to decide questions of law has been held by this court in the trilogy of tribunal cases to be determinative of whether a tribunal can decide *Charter* issues which arise in the exercise of its statutory mandate.

[90] Finally, an appeal is allowed for failure to apply policies adopted under s. 151(2). The policy adopted under s. 151(2) in relation to appeals sets out the mandate of the appeal division in terms which require it to ensure compliance with the *Charter*:

> The Appeal Division reviews decisions of the Board, upon the appeal of a decision by the offender pursuant to s. 147(1) of the *Corrections and Conditional Release Act. The Appeal Division, through its review process, and decision-making authority, and the issuance of Appeal Division Reports, contributes to the quality of conditional release decisions by ensuring that decisions and decision-making processes are fair and equitable and comply with* the legislation, *the Charter of Rights and Freedoms,* the Board's policies and procedures, and principles of the National Parole Board Mission Statement. [Emphasis added.]

[91] The application of the *Mills* test leads to the conclusion that the board is a court of competent jurisdiction for the purposes of granting a remedy under s. 24(2) and an examination of the governing statute demonstrates a legislative intention that *Charter* principles apply to the determination of the liberty interests of parolees. It remains only to consider policy issues. ...

[92] As discussed earlier, the policy considerations raised by Sopinka J (that the board does not use an adversarial process, that formal rules of evidence do not apply and that not all board members have legal training) have been rejected by this court as inadequate reasons for preventing a statutory tribunal from determining constitutional issues. On the other hand, the advantages of having a tribunal decide such issues, set out by La Forest J in *Douglas College*, apply in support of recognizing the Parole Board as a court of competent jurisdiction.

[93] Recognition of the Parole Board as a court of competent jurisdiction would enable the *Charter* issue to be dealt with in the context in which it arises without, as previously noted, necessitating an expensive and time-consuming application to a

court. The Parole Board's determination would find facts and compile a record for the benefit of a reviewing court. The expertise and specialized competence of the tribunal could be of invaluable assistance in constitutional interpretation particularly on the question of when the admission of unconstitutionally obtained evidence in the parole determination process might bring the administration of justice into disrepute.

[94] However, the overriding policy consideration which militates in favour of finding that the Parole Board is a court of competent jurisdiction is the fact that the Parole Board has the exclusive jurisdiction to finally determine the liberty interests of a parolee. I agree with Lambert JA who concluded that if the Parole Board is not a court of competent jurisdiction then the parolee is deprived of *Charter* protection with respect to unconstitutionally obtained evidence, at p. 440:

> Counsel for the National Parole Board has firmly maintained that the National Parole Board is not a court of competent jurisdiction under s. 24 of the Charter. If he is right, then when the National Parole Board refuses to consider whether to grant the Charter remedy of exclusion of evidence that is relevant and admissible, because it was obtained in the course of a Charter breach, then that refusal cannot be a jurisdictional error or an error in law. Accordingly, on that approach there can be no remedy whatever for a breach of a prisoner's Charter rights leading to a loss of statutory release. The reason is that if the National Parole Board is not a court of competent jurisdiction neither the Supreme Court of British Columbia nor the Federal Court, Trial Division, can say that there was an error in jurisdiction or an error in law in the National Parole Board failing to consider a question that it is not empowered to consider.
>
> That result, on the basis of the reasoning of counsel for the National Parole Board, would put the prisoner beyond the protection of the Charter in relation to evidence improperly obtained.

[95] In my view, it is wholly inconsistent with the principles of *Charter* interpretation enunciated by this court on numerous occasions for a *Charter* right to exist without a citizen having access to a *Charter* remedy.

[96] If the *Charter* is to be a robust and vigorous instrument for the protection of the rights of all Canadians and if *Charter* guarantees are to be meaningful and respected there must be access to a *Charter* remedy where rights have been violated. The broad and liberal interpretation of the *Charter* espoused by this court requires at a minimum respect for what Lamer J in *Mills* (at p. 894) termed "the basic proposition that there should always be a court of competent jurisdiction to award such relief as is just and appropriate in the circumstances." Access to a remedy should not be denied to a citizen simply because he is already under detention by the state. The *Charter*'s benefits apply to everyone, including prisoners: see *Weatherall v. Canada (Attorney-General)*, [1993] 2 SCR 872.

[97] The proposition that there must be a *Charter* remedy where rights have been violated applies with particular force to a tribunal which has the power to finally determine issues which substantially affect the liberty of an individual. The role of the National Parole Board cannot be compared to that of a preliminary inquiry judge whose only role is to determine whether there is a sufficiency of evidence to proceed to trial. Nor can it be compared to that of a statutory tribunal whose mandate is limited to the

granting of civil remedies such as damages. It is much more directly analogous to that of a trial court judge, who, subject to appeal for errors of law or jurisdiction, can finally determine the liberty interest of an individual.

[98] Sopinka J seeks to minimize the impact of finding that the National Parole Board cannot grant a *Charter* remedy by noting that the parolee still enjoys the protection of the common law guarantee of procedural fairness. With respect, it cannot be assumed that the common law doctrine of procedural fairness is co-extensive with the guarantee of the "principles of fundamental justice" in the *Charter* which is echoed in the *Corrections and Conditional Release Act*.

[99] Procedural fairness is simply one aspect of the doctrine of natural justice which is applied at common law to administrative tribunals. This court has consistently refused to restrict the substantive guarantee of fundamental justice in s. 7 to the procedural realm. In *Reference re: Section 94(2) of the Motor Vehicle Act*, [1985] 2 SCR 486, this court was unanimous in finding that " 'fundamental justice,' as the term is used in the *Charter*, involves more than natural justice (which is largely procedural) and includes as well a substantive element": *per* McIntyre J at pp. 521-22. As Lamer J writing for the majority elaborated at pp. 501-3:

> ... I am of the view that it would be wrong to interpret the term "fundamental justice" as being synonymous with natural justice as the Attorney-General of British Columbia and others have suggested. To do so would strip the protected interests of much, if not most, of their content and leave the "right" to life, liberty and security of the person in a sorely emaciated state. Such a result would be inconsistent with the broad, affirmative language in which those rights are expressed and equally inconsistent with the approach adopted by this Court toward the interpretation of *Charter* rights in *Law Society of Upper Canada v. Skapinker*, [1984] 1 SCR 357, *per* Estey J and *Hunter v. Southam Inc.*, *supra*. ...
>
> [T]he principles of fundamental justice are to be found in the basic tenets of our legal system. They do not lie in the realm of general public policy but in the inherent domain of the judiciary as guardian of the justice system. Such an approach to the interpretation of "principles of fundamental justice" is consistent with the wording and structure of s. 7, the context of the section, i.e., ss. 8 to 14, and the character and larger objects of the *Charter* itself. It provides meaningful content for the s. 7 guarantee all the while avoiding adjudication of policy matters.
>
> Thus, it seems to me that to replace "fundamental justice" with the term "natural justice" misses the mark entirely.

[100] In the context of the admission of evidence, procedural fairness looks only to the use of evidence in the proceedings (i.e., issues of reliability and relevancy), whereas the principles of fundamental justice require an examination of whether constitutional guarantees were respected in the manner in which the evidence was obtained.

[101] Moreover, the mere fact that protections found in the common law may be substantially co-extensive with *Charter* protections is not sufficient justification for denying a citizen the opportunity to obtain a just and appropriate remedy for a *Charter* breach.

[102] The *Charter* provides significant protections to Canadians and governs every aspect of the interaction between the state and the individual in Canada. The view that

a citizen must be content with the protections offered by the common law in spite of *Charter* guarantees is a reactionary approach to constitutional rights which has not been endorsed by this court.

[103] Our constitutional jurisprudence has developed on the basis that the *Charter* should be given a broad and purposive interpretation. It is consistent with this view that a generous approach be taken to granting *Charter* remedies. Generally speaking, it is preferable to find tribunals capable of granting constitutional remedies where those lie within their statutory mandate. In the event that a tribunal errs in this regard, a court can correct the error. As La Forest J points out, statutory tribunals "can expect no curial deference with respect to constitutional decisions": *Cuddy Chicks*, at p. 17.

• • •

[105] I therefore conclude that the majority of the British Columbia Court of Appeal was correct to hold that the National Parole Board is a court of competent jurisdiction for the purposes raised on this appeal and would dismiss the appeal.

• • •

IV. Remedy

[117] I am in agreement with both parties that Lambert JA, on behalf of the court below, misconceived the nature of *certiorari* in aid of *habeas corpus* believing it to be necessary to quash the decision of the National Parole Board. Only the Federal Court has jurisdiction to grant *certiorari* as a remedy with respect to a decision of the National Parole Board. *Certiorari* in aid of *habeas corpus* is the means by which a reviewing court may obtain the evidentiary record for the purpose of determining an application for *habeas corpus*: see *Re Cardinal and Oswald and the Queen* (1982), 67 CCC (2d) 252 (BCCA), at pp. 269-270, rev'd on other grounds [1985] 2 SCR 643 (*sub nom. Cardinal v. Director of Kent Institution*).

[118] This appeal arose from an application for *habeas corpus*. Once it is determined that the respondent was unlawfully detained owing to the failure of the National Parole to exercise its jurisdiction to determine the constitutional issue raised by the respondent, the respondent is entitled to request the court to grant a writ of *habeas corpus* to relieve him from unlawful detention. However, the court retains the discretion at common law not to issue a writ of *habeas corpus* but rather to direct that the constitutional challenge be remitted back to the tribunals for a determination on the merits: *R v. Pearson*, [1992] 3 SCR 665, at p. 701 *per* Lamer CJ. In my view, in most instances the appropriate remedy would be an order remitting the matter back to the National Parole Board for a further hearing.

V. Disposition

[119] In the particular circumstances of this case in which the respondent's sentence has already expired, I agree with Sopinka J that the National Parole Board is *functus officio*. I would therefore uphold that portion of the order of the British Columbia Court of Appeal which granted the writ of *habeas corpus*.

NOTE

Lamer CJ and La Forest J concurred with the decision of Sopinka J in two short opinions. The concurring decision of Lamer CJ is interesting. Essentially, he observed that the crucial distinction is whether the tribunal is empowered to accept and exclude evidence. This has substantial implications for the original decision in *Mills*, because a justice at a preliminary inquiry has clear authority to exclude evidence. Accordingly, Lamer CJ concluded that the decision in *Mooring* effectively reversed *Mills* such that a justice at a preliminary inquiry should be considered a "court of competent jurisdiction" for s. 24 Charter purposes.

Before considering whether you agree with the views expressed by Sopinka or Major JJ, can you articulate an argument for denying the state's use of illegally obtained evidence in a criminal trial, but permiting the same evidence to be used to recommit the person if he or she happens to be a parolee?

VI. JUDICIAL REVIEW AND THE PAROLE BOARD'S APPEAL DIVISION

Administrative law has always recognized that statutory review mechanisms that provide a parallel avenue of review should preclude the usual judicial review jurisdiction until that avenue has been exhausted. This is not simply a mechanical exhaustion of remedies issue but a question whether there is an alternative remedy. A statutory avenue should be pursued as long as it provides the individual with a comparable opportunity for review. Section 147 of the *Corrections and Conditional Release Act*, SC 1992, c. 20, established the "Appeal Division."

Section 147(1) provides that an offender can appeal a decision on the ground that the board

(a) failed to observe a principle of fundamental justice;

(b) made an error of law;

(c) breached or failed to apply a policy adopted pursuant to s. 151(2);

(d) based its decision on erroneous or incomplete information; or

(e) acted without jurisdiction or beyond its jurisdiction, or failed to exercise its jurisdiction.

Pursuant to s. 147(4), the Appeal Division of the National Parole Board (NPB) can affirm the original decision, affirm but order a new review, or "reverse, cancel or vary the decision." However, s. 147(5) provides:

The Appeal Division shall not render a decision under subsection (4) that results in the immediate release of an offender from imprisonment unless it is satisfied that

(a) the decision appealed from cannot reasonably be supported in law, under the applicable policies of the Board, or on the basis of the information available to the Board on its review of the case; and

(b a delay in releasing the offender would be unfair.

Does s. 147 sufficiently empower the Appeal Division to qualify it as an alternative remedy? Can the Appeal Division entertain claims under the Charter? Do the restrictions in s. 147(5), above, diminish the effectiveness of the Appeal Division as a potential alternative remedy compared to the Federal Court? Or are they the same discretionary factors that a court would consider in determining, after an error had been found, whether a remedy should be granted? In this context, it is important to note that the subject matter is liberty—an issue high on the list of interests potentially at stake.

The trend in Federal Court decisions, as illustrated by *Mackie*, below, favours the requirement that the offender appeal to the Federal Court of Appeal before seeking judicial review.

Re Mackie and Warden of Drumheller Institution
[1997] FCJ No. 1000 (QL) (TD)

HARGRAVE PROTHONOTARY (Reasons for Order): The Respondents' motion is to strike out the Originating Notice of Motion on the grounds that the Applicant, a prison inmate with a statutory release date of 18 July 1997, but ordered detained by the National Parole Board (the "Board") pursuant to section 130 of the *Corrections and Conditional Release Act*, SC 1992, c. 20, has an adequate alternative remedy and thus cannot succeed on his judicial review application in this Court. Indeed, the Applicant has availed himself of the alternate remedy by filing an appeal of the Board's decision with the Appeal Division of the Board under section 147(1) of the Act, but believes he can obtain a quicker remedy from this Court. It is interesting that the Applicant began his appeal to the Appeal Division of the Board on 30 May 1997, two weeks after beginning this judicial review application.

Delay is, according to the Applicant, a main reason for proceeding in the Federal Court: had the Board not detained the Applicant, he would be on parole as of 18 July 1997. However, the Applicant's material indicates that the Appeal Division of the Board will not take up his case until perhaps October 1997, or a little later. I would point out, assuming the application were to proceed in this Court with a fairly minimal extension within which the Respondents might file their affidavits and with the Applicant filing his material without any waiting time, the Applicant might be in a position to apply for a hearing date in the latter half of August. In the normal course of events the Applicant would have to wait between one and three months for a one day hearing date and from two to four months for a date for a two day judicial review hearing. At best the Applicant might obtain a short judicial review hearing by the end of September, as opposed to perhaps sometime in October before the Appeal Division of the Board.

The time difference in which the remedies might be obtained is only one factor in determining whether this proceeding ought to be allowed to go forward. However, to begin, there is the issue of whether the Respondent can strike out the Originating Notice of Motion.

In *David Bull Laboratories (Canada) Inc. v. Pharmacia Inc.* (1995), 176 NR 48 the Federal Court of Appeal considered, without deciding the point, whether an originating notice of motion might be struck out under Rule 419. Rule 419 is limited to actions. The Court of Appeal touched on Rule 5, the gap rule, but pointed out that there was not

NOTE

After having his application struck out, Mr. Mackie went to the Appeal Division, which gave him no relief. He commenced a new judicial review application in respect of the Appeal Division decision. Campbell J in *Mackie v. Canada*, [1987] FCJ No. 1731 (QL), 157 FTR 97 (TD) granted judicial review and concluded:

> I find that each of these two opinions are highly prejudicial to Mr. Mackie and, therefore, should have been disclosed pursuant to s. 141(1) to allow him an opportunity to respond. This was not done. In my opinion, the failure of the Appeal Division to find that this nondisclosure constitutes a breach of s. 141(1) is a reviewable error in law.
>
> While the Appeal Division's decision is under review in this application, in my opinion, merely setting it aside and referring the matter back to the Appeal Division for redetermination will not satisfy the need to do justice to Mr. Mackie. Mr. Mackie is entitled to a new hearing on the merits before different decision makers. From the following quote in the Appeal Division's decision, it appears that the Appeal Division feels constrained to achieve this result:
>
> > Mr. Mackie, the role of the Appeal Division is to ensure that the law and Board policy are adhered to, that the Rules of Natural Justice have been respected and that the Board's decision has been based on adequate information. It is not our role to review the available information and to simply substitute our discretion for that of a Regional Board which dutifully exercised its discretion in a manner consistent with the law and Board policy.
>
> Accordingly, to achieve the just result required, I set aside the Appeal Division's decision and refer this matter back to the panel that made it with the direction that, pursuant to s. 147(4)(c) of the Act, it order a new review of the case before a differently constituted panel of the Board, such review to be conducted forthwith.

As far as the practice of requiring resort to the Appeal Division of the NPB, it seems to have become entrenched: see *Lafontaine v. Canada (Attorney General)*, [2001] FCJ No. 779 (QL).